The Life and Times
of Pancho Villa

Friedrich Katz

STANFORD UNIVERSITY PRESS
Stanford, California ≈ 1998

Stanford University Press
Stanford, California

©1998 by the Board of Trustees of the
Leland Stanford Junior University

Printed in the United States of America

CIP data are at the end of the book

To Jana, Jackie, and Leo

Acknowledgments

In the course of the many years during which I have worked on this book, I have had the generous help of many institutions, as well as of friends, colleagues, students, and members of my family. These acknowledgments are therefore unusually long.

I am deeply grateful to the institutions that helped to finance this undertaking: the University of Chicago, the John Simon Guggenheim Foundation, the Social Sciences Research Council, and the American Philosophical Society.

I would also like to thank the many archives and libraries in many parts of the world that have helped me so enormously in my research. In Mexico City, I thank the Archivo General de la Nación, the Instituto Mora, the Hemeroteca Nacional, the Archivo de la Secretaría de Relaciones Exteriores, the Archivo de la Secretaría de la Defensa Nacional, the Archivo de la Secretaría de la Reforma Agraria, the Archivo Porfirio Díaz at the Universidad Iberoamericana, the Archivo de la Universidad Nacional Autónoma de Mexico, the Archivo del Instituto Nacional de la Revolución Mexicana, the Biblioteca Nacional, the Biblioteca del Instituto Nacional de Antropología e Historia, and the Colegio de Mexico.

In addition, I wish to thank the owners of private archives in Mexico City who allowed me to consult their holdings. These include the Archivo Calles-Torreblanca, and especially its director, Norma Mereles de Ogarrio, the archives of Roque González Garza, Martín Luis Guzmán, and Martínez del Río, the family of Elías Torres for allowing me to see his papers, and the Centro de Estudios de Historia de México (CONDUMEX).

In Chihuahua, I thank the Archivo de Ciudad Guerrero, Archivo Municipal de Ciudad Juárez, the Centro de Investigaciónes y Documentación del Estado de Chihuhua (CIDECH), and Dr. Rubén Osorio, for allowing me to consult his private archive.

In Durango, I thank the Archivo del Estado de Durango and the Archivo de San Juan del Río. In Nuevo León, I thank Mario Cerruti for informing me of the whereabouts of the private archives of Juan F. Brittingham, and Juan Ignacio Barragán, the owner of the archive, who allowed me to consult its holdings.

An equally large number of archives and libraries in the United States have been of great help to me. These include the University of Chicago Library, the Newberry Library at Chicago, the Bancroft Library at the University of California at Berkeley, the special collection room at Claremont College in Pomona, the Huntington Library in Los Angeles, the Sterling Library of Yale University, the special collections section of the Library of the University of Illinois at Carbondale, the Lilly Library of Indiana University at Bloomington, the Widener and Houghton Libraries of Harvard University, the University of New Mexico at Albuquerque, which allowed me to consult the microfilms of the Papers of Senator Albert Bacon Fall, the Historical Museum at Columbus, the Deming Courthouse, which sent me transcripts of proceedings against the Villistas captured at Columbus, the New York Public Library, the Nettie Lee Benson Library at the University of Texas at Austin, the special collections department at the Library of the University of Texas at El Paso, the Museum of the Daughters of the American Revolution in San Antonio, and the National Archives and Library of Congress in Washington, D.C.

In Germany, I thank the Foreign Office Archives in Bonn, the German Central Archives in Potsdam, and the German Central Archive in Merseburg. In France, I thank the Archives Nationales and the Archives du Ministère des Affaires Étrangères in Paris. In Great Britain, I thank the Public Record Office, the British Science Museum, and the private archive that contains the papers of the Tlahualilo Company. In Spain, I thank the Archives of the Foreign Ministry, and in Austria, the Haus Hof und Staats Archiv in Vienna.

Over the many years during which I have worked on this book, a remarkable number of friends, colleagues, and students have helped me along, many by putting new sources at my disposal, others through stimulating discussions about some of my ideas as well as theirs, and still others by reading parts or all of the manuscript and making extremely valuable suggestions.

I thank Eugenia Meyer, who for so many years has helped me in every respect: the Programa de Historia Oral that she headed has carried out extremely important and valuable interviews with surviving Villistas in the 1970s. She has thus established a major source for the history of Villismo, and for this alone I am extremely grateful to her. In addition, she has shown me innumerable marks of friendship by helping me to gain access to the archives of the Defense Ministry in Mexico, by putting new sources at my disposal, by discussing some of the most important ideas of the book with me, and by her constant encouragement.

I also thank Alicia Olivera de Bonfil and Laura Espejel for allowing me to consult their important interviews with former revolutionaries. I also want to thank Villa's granddaughter, Guadalupe Villa, who provided me with some very valuable information.

A number of friends and colleagues have shown great generosity in putting their personal archives at my disposal. Ruben Osorio allowed me to see the numerous materials that he had collected, both from written and oral sources, on the history of Villismo and of Chihuahua. Russell Chace of York University, who has done research on Chihuahua for many years, allowed me to copy whatever materials in his archives I found of interest. Ana Alonso and Daniel Nugent of the University of Arizona and Maria Teresa Koreck of the University of Michigan were equally generous with their research. Their insights into the history of Chihuahua, both in unpublished manuscripts and in their oral communications, were of enormous help to me. The same is true of Mark Wasserman, thanks to his remarkable work on Chihuahua. Hans Werner Tobler of the Eidgenössische Technische Hochschule in Zurich provided me with interesting and important materials from his research in the papers of U.S. military intelligence in the National Archives in Washington, D.C. I also thank John Hart of the University of Houston for the materials on U.S. economic interests in Mexico that he put at my disposal.

I have profited much from Richard Estrada's work on the Orozco revolution in Chihuahua, and I am extremely grateful to him and to Manuel González for allowing me to consult the partly unpublished memoirs of José María Jaurrieta. I thank William Meyers for helping me to gain access to the papers of Elías Torres. My repeated discussions with Alicia Hernandez about the Mexican Revolution, and especially its military aspects, have been of great help to me, and she also put highly interesting materials at my disposal. I am greatly indebted to the Chihuahuan historians Carlos González, Victor Orozco, and Jesús Vargas Valdés, all of whom put both their profound knowledge of Chihuahua and important sources at my disposal.

I want to express my gratitude to Marta Rocha Islas, who allowed me to consult her notes on the archive of Governor Ignacio Enríquez. I thank William French for the materials on Parral that he showed me. I am grateful to Rosa Maria Meyer who helped me gain access to the archives of the Martínez del Río family, and I thank that family for allowing me to consult this very important family archive.

I would like to express my gratitude to Michael Desch for drawing my attention to U.S. war plans in connection with Mexico, and to Enrique de la Plasencia for his valuable indications converning important data in the Amaro papers about the assasination of Villa.

I was lucky enough to have first-class research assistants, who greatly helped me in going through the very extensive sources that I needed to consult to complete this book. I thank Richard Estrada, Angeles Garciadiego, William Meyers, Antonio Ruiz, Marta Rocha, Marco Antonio Martínez, Miguel Vallebueno, and Gonzalo Zeballos.

I thank Christopher Boyer and James Kalven for helping me to eliminate the linguistic results of having been brought up in languages other than English for many years.

I have profited much from the many discussions I have had on the nature of the Mexican Revolution, and on Mexican history in general, with the late Guillermo Bonfil, with Adolfo Gilly, Alan Knight, Enrique Semo, and John Coatsworth.

I thank Susan Lundy, Linnea Cameron, and Tonja Hopkins, who wrote and rewrote the chapters in this book and were thus forced to participate in the adventurous life of Pancho Villa.

I thank Maria Teresa Franco, who first drew my attention to a letter of Villa's, written after his imprisonment, that is sharply critical of Madero. I thank David Walker, who put his enormous collection of data on the revolution in Durango at my disposal. Juan Mora was of great help to me in providing data on the revolution in Nuevo León. Josefina Moguel helped me in my work in the Condumex archives. I thank the two heads of the archive of Foreign Relations, José Maria Muria and Jorge Alvarez, for their great help when I worked in the archives of the Secretaria de Relaciones Exteriores de Mexico. Alvaro Matute first drew my attention to and showed me some important materials from the papers of General Amado Aguirre. I would like to thank Fernando Perez Correa for allowing me to consult important files from the archives of the long term governor of Coahuila, Miguel Cárdenas.

I constantly had to confront my ideas with challenges from my extremely bright students, first at the University of Texas and then at the University of Chicago. I have learned much from these exchanges, and I hope that they were able to profit from them too.

I owe a special debt of thanks to those of my colleagues who read part or the whole of the book to my great benefit. Colin Lucas, Guillermo de la Peña, and Daniel Nugent read the first part of this book. John Coatsworth, John Womack, Javier Garciadiego, and Claudio Lomnitz read the whole of the book, and my debt to them is enormous. Finally, I wish to thank the members of my family who suffered thorough the many years during which I wrote this book. There has been not one vacation during the past fifteen years of our life that my wife, Jana, did not share with Pancho Villa. My son Leo read some parts of the manuscript, and my daughter Jackie read the whole of it and gave me unstinting and constant encouragement. It is to all of them that I dedicate this book.

As this book was going to press, I heard of the tragic death of Daniel Nugent, one of the most remarkable and talented historians of Mexico I have ever known. His advice, his help, and his friendship were of enormous importance to me, and I would like this book to be considered a tribute to his memory.

F.K.

Contents

10 pages of photographs follow page 486

Preface

Alongside Moctezuma and Benito Juárez, Pancho Villa is probably the best-known Mexican personality throughout the world. Villa legends pervade not only Mexico but the United States as well and have even reached beyond. They exist not only in the popular mind, in popular tradition, and in popular ballads but in movies made both in Mexico and in Hollywood. There are legends of Villa the Robin Hood, Villa the Napoleon of Mexico, Villa the ruthless killer, Villa the womanizer, and Villa as the only foreigner who has attacked the mainland of the United States since the war of 1812 and gotten away with it. Whether correct or incorrect, exaggerated or true to life, these legends have resulted in Pancho Villa the leader obscuring his movement, and the myths obscuring the leader. So much attention has focused on Villa himself that the characteristics of his movement that in many respects make it unique in Latin America, and in some ways among twentieth-century revolutions, have either been forgotten or neglected. Villa's División del Norte was probably the largest revolutionary army that Latin America ever produced. The revolution he led was the only social revolution ever to occur along the border of the United States. It was also one of the few genuine revolutions produced by what might best be described as a frontier region on the American continent.

Perhaps even more exceptional, this was one of the few revolutionary movements with which a U.S. administration in the twentieth century attempted, not only to come to terms, but even to forge an alliance. Equally remarkable, the Villa movement was part of one of the few twentieth-century revolutions that still enjoy enormous legitimacy in its own people's eyes. In Russia, Leningrad has been renamed St. Petersburg, and in China, students questioned Mao's revolution on

Tiananmen Square, but no one in Mexico is thinking of renaming the streets that bear the names of Villa or of other revolutionary heroes. In fact, not only the official government party but one of the main opposition parties and a newly emerged guerrilla movement in Chiapas all claim to be the legitimate heirs of the revolutionaries of 1910–20, among whom Villa's movement constituted a decisive force.

Finally, both Villa and the leader of the strongest popular movement in southern Mexico, Emiliano Zapata, differed in significant ways from the revolutionary leaders that emerged elsewhere in the twentieth century. In contrast to such men as Lenin, Mao Tse-tung, Ho Chi Minh, or Fidel Castro, all of whom were highly educated intellectuals who led well-organized political movements, both Villa and Zapata came from the lower classes of society, had little education, and organized no political parties. It is on these characteristics of the Villa movement and on the personality of its leader that this book focuses. It seeks to examine the social composition of the movement, about which there is as much debate as about the personality of its leader. While for some it was a genuine peasant movement, others saw it as a revolution dominated by the riffraff of the frontier: cattle rustlers, bandits, marginals, men without roots or ideology. The latter interpretation has been greatly strengthened by the personality of a few of its leaders who managed to pass from history into legend, such as Rodolfo Fierro, "the killer," and Tomás Urbina, "the bandit." Were these men in fact characteristic of the leadership of Villa's movement? There are as yet no studies of the vast array of secondary leaders who flocked to Villa's movement, of the social composition of his army, or of the social basis of his support.

One of the most important criteria for assessing a revolutionary leader, or any political figure for that matter, is what he or she did while in power. Villa controlled Chihuahua for two years, but little has been done to study either the program he developed for the state or the changes he actually implemented.

I faced two major difficulties in writing this book. The first, far less important than the second, is the fact that Villa, unlike the other major revolutionary figures in Mexico such as Zapata, Carranza, and Obregón, left no archive, and the state archives of Chihuahua were destroyed by fire in 1940. What greatly helped me to compensate for this was that when I was completing this book, other archival sources that had long been inaccessible to researchers became available. They included the files of Mexico's Secretaría de la Defensa Nacional, the records of the Sección de Terrenos Nacionales in the archives of the Secretaría de la Reforma Agraria, the files of U.S. military intelligence and the FBI, and the papers of a number of Villa's collaborators.

The most serious difficulty I had to deal with was to extract the historical truth from the multifaceted layers of legend and myth surrounding Villa. What made this task especially difficult was that, on the one hand, Villa was enamored of his own myths and did his best to embroider them. On the other hand, not one but a whole series of myths surround Villa and his movement: the myths expressed in popular ballads, the myth of the victors, who for many years shaped a hostile official historiography about him, and the Hollywood myths, often very contradictory in nature, to name but a few. These myths colored many of the thousands of articles and memoirs written about Villa. For this reason I have tried as much as possible to rely on contemporary documents, which are far less tainted and affected by the myths.

This book comprises four major parts, ordered chronologically but representing four major phases both in Villa's life and in the history of Mexico. The first part deals with Villa's early life as an outlaw and his emergence as a secondary leader of the Mexican Revolution until early 1913. It also assesses the special conditions that transformed Chihuahua into a leading center of revolution and assesses the unique role that Chihuahua played in both 1910–11 and 1912 in the broader history of the Mexican Revolution.

The second part deals with the period when Villa emerged as a national leader and Chihuahua once more became a central area of the Mexican Revolution. It begins with Villa's dramatic rise to national prominence in 1913 and ends with his disastrous military defeats at the end of 1915. Part 2 assesses the nature of his revolutionary movement in comparison to the other major movements that emerged at the same time in Mexico. It also attempts to assess the impact of Villismo as an ideology and a social movement, and its impact on the state of Chihuahua, Mexico as a whole, and, last but not least, the United States. This is the period in Villa's life that has been studied most intensely and has given rise to the greatest controversies surrounding his personality and his movement.

The third part of the book deals with the years 1915 to 1920: the nature of Villa's guerrilla warfare in that period, his attack on Columbus, New Mexico, and its paradoxical results, his reemergence as a national force in 1916–17, and his subsequent decline.

The last part describes Villa's surrender, his life as a hacendado, his assassination and its aftermath, and the evolution of the Villa legend. Finally, an assessment is made of what conclusions can be reached about Villa's personality and the character and impact of his movement. The concluding chapter also tries to show where, in the opinion of this author, unanswered questions, persistent discrepancies, and legitimate grounds for continuing debate remain.

This book is by no means the first to have been written about Villa. Outstanding works such as Martín Luis Guzmán's *Memorias de Pancho Villa* already exist (see Bibliography). These works, though, tend to focus on the man rather than on his movement, and many of the sources I was able to utilize were unavailable to their authors.

This book pretends neither to give a final answer to the many problems that Villa and his movement have raised nor to resolve the controversies that they have aroused. There is little doubt that new documents relating to and new interpretations of both Villa and his movement will emerge. In addition, as has been the case with Danton, Robespierre, and other major revolutionary figures (and Villa, whatever one may think of him, was a major revolutionary figure), each generation will look at Villa from a different perspective, so that discussions on this subject will continue for a long time to come. What I hope to have achieved is to help clarify the parameters of that debate

The Life and Times
of Pancho Villa

Prologue

It was a scene he would have loved. Despite the cold, blustery weather that November day in 1976, throngs of people lined the street in the old city of Parral in the state of Chihuahua. They had heard the news that Pancho Villa's remains, which were buried in Parral, would, as the result of a decree passed by the Mexican president, be transferred to the Monument of the Revolution in Mexico City. This constituted a belated recognition by a Mexican government of his revolutionary merits. As Villa's casket, flanked by members of his family, came into view, masses of people began clapping and cheering. Many burst into the old rallying cry of "Viva Villa!"[1]

What would have impressed Villa was the fact that practically none of these enthusiastic spectators had ever known him, since more than 50 years had elapsed since his death, and even the parents of many who now stood on the streets of Parral to watch him go to join the remains of his enemies in the mausoleum of revolutionary heroes in Mexico City had never seen, heard, or met him. It was a measure of the influence he still exercised in his adopted state that so many years after his death, thousands came out to cheer him. Another expression of the emotions his memory aroused was the fact that thousands of others are said to have refused to come out, that many sent harsh letters of protest to the newspapers, and some avidly read Rodrigo Alonso Cortés's 1972 book *Francisco Villa, el quinto jinete del apocalipsis* (Pancho Villa, the Fifth Rider of the Apocalypse), which depicts Villa as a monster, and similar works.[2]

Villa might have expected this mixture of love and hate, of respect and contempt in Mexico. He would have been more surprised to find the same mixture manifesting itself north of the border, in a country for which, in the later years of his life, he had nourished an ever-increasing hatred: the United States. In November 1979, a statue of him was brought to Tucson, Arizona. It aroused emotions that were at least as strong as in Mexico and was greeted with a similar mixture of love and hate, of respect and contempt.[3]

These competing reactions reflect the contradictions of the man himself and the contradictions within the many legends about him.

The Early Life of Pancho Villa: The Legends

Villa's early life remains shrouded in mystery. This is partly because in contrast to the other main figures of the Mexican Revolution, he had for many years been an outlaw, roaming through vast areas of northern Mexico.

That fact alone is a major obstacle to anyone wishing to unravel the story of his early life. The task is made even more difficult by the many legends, forged by both friends and foes, through which researchers have to hew their way.

There are three basic versions of Villa's early life, which I shall call the white legend, the black legend, and the epic legend. The first, based largely on Villa's own reminiscences, portrays him as a victim of the social and economic system of Porfirian Mexico: a man the authorities prevented from living a quiet, law-abiding life, although he attempted to do so. The black legend portrays him as an evil murderer, with no redeeming qualities. The epic legend, largely based on popular ballads and traditions that seem to have emerged mainly in the course of the revolution, portrays Villa as a far more important personality in prerevolutionary Chihuahua than do either his own account or the black legend. What all three legends have in common is that they are based, not on contemporary documents, but rather on reminiscences, popular ballads, rumors, memoirs, and hearsay. What they also have in common is that none of the three legends, black, white, or epic, is entirely consistent within itself.

The white legend is primarily based on an autobiography that Villa dictated to one of his secretaries, Manuel Bauche Alcalde, at the height of his power in 1914. These memoirs came into the possession of one of Mexico's greatest novelists, Martín Luis Guzmán, who after some rewriting and editing published part of them as the first part of a 1984 book entitled *Memorias de Pancho Villa* (Memoirs of Pancho Villa).[4] In this book, I have relied on Villa's original memoirs, which the family of Martín Luis Guzmán generously allowed me to consult.

One of the few aspects of Villa's life about which all agree is that he was born in 1878, on the Rancho de la Coyotada, part of one of the largest haciendas in the state of Durango, owned by the López Negrete family. His parents, Agustín Arango and Micaela Arambula, were sharecroppers on the hacienda. The child who would later be known as Francisco Villa was baptized Doroteo Arango. (Different opinions exist about his real name.) His father died at an early age, and his mother had to support her five children.

Beyond this point, the white, black, and epic legends begin to diverge.

The White Legend

"The tragedy of my life begins on September 22, 1894, when I was sixteen years old," Villa recounts in his memoirs. He was working as a sharecropper on the Hacienda de Gogojito. After his father died, he had become head of his family, consisting of his mother, his brothers Antonio and Hipólito, and two sisters, Marianita, aged 15, and Martina, who was 12.

When he returned home from work that day in 1894, he found Don Agustín López Negrete, "the Master, the owner of the lives and honor of us the poor people," standing in front of his mother, who was telling him: "Go away from my house! Why do you want to take my daughter?"

When he heard these words, the young Doroteo Arango became so furious that he ran to the house of his cousin Romualdo Franco, took the latter's gun, and shot López Negrete in the foot.

López Negrete began loudly calling for help. Five of his retainers appeared, armed with rifles, and set out to shoot Doroteo. "Don't kill this boy," López Negrete told them, however. "Take me home."

Young Arango realized that although the hacendado had prevented him from being killed, he might very well have him arrested, so he quickly mounted his horse and fled:

My conscience told me that I had done the right thing. The master, with five armed men, with all the power at his disposal, had tried to impose a forced contribution of our honor. The sweat of his serfs, the work of his serfs, our constant and tiring labor in order to enrich him, the master, was not sufficient for him. He also needed our women, his serfs; his despotism led to the profanation of our home.

Seeing that I was still free, I got on my horse and headed for the Sierra de la Silla, opposite Gogojito.[5]

From that moment on, Doroteo led the life of an outlaw in the mountains of Durango, relentlessly pursued by the authorities. He tells of how he managed again and again, with almost uncanny skill, to foil or defeat his pursuers as a boy of 16 or 17.

A few months after fleeing into the mountains, he was caught by three men, who jailed him in San Juan del Río. Arango was convinced that he would soon be shot. "At 10:00 the next day, they took me out of the room where they had locked me up, in order [for me] to grind a barrel of Nixtamal [dough from which tortillas are made]."[6] Hitting the guard nearest him with the pestle of the metate, Arango escaped into the Los Remedios mountains, located near the prison.

A few months later, in October 1895, he was caught again when seven men found him asleep and ordered him to surrender. This time Arango managed to foil his captors even more dramatically. He suggested to his captors that they roast some ears of corn before taking him to prison in town. They were hungry, there were seven of them, and they saw no reason to fear the boy they had captured, so they agreed.

What these men did not know was that the boy had a gun hidden under his blanket and a horse grazing nearby. When two of them went to cut corn stalks, and two others had gone to cut wood, Arango got out his gun, opened fire on his three remaining guards, ran to his horse, and once more managed to escape.[7]

He tells proudly of how only a few months later he defeated another party of men sent out to capture him, leading them into an ambush and killing three *rurales*.[8]

Arango came to feel that the life he had been leading was too dangerous and decided to take new measures both to elude his pursuers and to ease his life as an outlaw. He first decided to change his name. Since his father, Agustín Arango, had been the illegitimate son of Jesús Villa, he now began calling himself Francisco Villa. He became convinced that surviving alone was too difficult and so decided to join two outlaws who were roaming in the vicinity, Ignacio Parra and Refugio Alvarado. Before they accepted him into their company, the two men told him:

"Look, young man, if you want to go with us, you have to do everything that we tell you. We know how to kill and rob. We tell you this so that you should not be afraid." These crude words, clear and precise like the blow of a hammer, did not intimidate me. . . . men who pompously call themselves honest also kill and rob. In the name of the law that they apply for the benefit and protection of the few in order to threaten and sacrifice the many, the high authorities of the people rob and kill with the greatest impunity.[9]

A new and far more agreeable life now began for the newly named Francisco Villa. Instead of being a hunted fugitive, barely managing to survive, he became a successful outlaw, reaping the rewards of banditry. Only one week after joining Parra and Alvarado, his share of the loot came to over 3,000 pesos. This was more than ten times the yearly wage of an agricultural worker in Chihuahua at the time. But it was only the beginning. A short time later, the band robbed a wealthy miner of 150,000 pesos, and Villa left the gang for a time with 50,000 pesos in his pocket. It was a fortune by the standards of the time, but within eleven months, Villa had used it all, mainly by giving it away. In his memoirs, Villa proudly states, "I gave it to the poor." His mother received 5,000 pesos, and 4,000 were given to other members of his family. To an old man named Antonio Retana, who had a large family, could not see well, and was extremely poor, Villa gave the means to establish a tailor shop and hired an employee to run it. "After eight or ten months I had returned to the poor the money that the rich had taken from them."[10]

Having spent all his money, Villa returned to the gang and resumed his life as an outlaw. He soon fell out with his partners, however, over the wanton killing by one of them of an old man who had refused to sell him bread. Thereafter, he continued to wander through the mountains of Durango, committing a few robberies, finding new partners, and having repeated shoot-outs with the authorities. Finally, he had had enough of life as an outlaw. "One day, I said to Luis Orozco, 'Hombre, we can't live like this. Let's go to Chihuahua and look for work.' One month later we went to Parral."[11]

There, Villa labored in a variety of occupations, but was again and again forced to give everything up and flee when the authorities discovered his identity. First he worked as a miner, but he had to give this up after bruising his feet. He then worked for a mason, making bricks. When his identity was discovered, he fled, began stealing cattle, and attempted to sell them on the Chihuahua meat market. When this proved unprofitable, because the interests controlling the meat business would not give him access to the slaughterhouse, he became a miner again. This did not last long, and again because of persecution by the authorities, Villa had to resume life as an outlaw.

In spite of constant persecution, he bought a house in the town of Chihuahua and decided to settle there. It was there, sometime in 1910, that he met Abraham González,

the noble martyr for democracy . . . who invited me to fight for the revolution for the rights of the people that had been trampled upon by tyranny. . . . There I understood for the first time that all the suffering, all the hatred, all the rebellions that had accumulated in my soul during so many years of fighting had given me such a strength of conviction and such a clear will that I could offer all this to my country . . . to free her from the snakes that were devouring her entrails.[12]

Villa describes himself as a victim of both the despotism of the hacendados and the arbitrariness of the Porfirian authorities. A man with a sense of honor and dignity could take no other course than the one he took when he attacked the hacendado who had sought to outrage his sister. Every attempt he made at giving up life as an outlaw was thwarted by ruthless officials linked either to the government of Durango or to the Creel-Terrazas clan, which dominated Chihuahua.

The picture he paints of himself is not altogether flattering. He mainly, although not always, took from the rich, and sometimes, although less frequently, gave to the poor. He quotes his mother as telling him, "My dear son, where did you get so much money? These men are leading you to perdition. You are committing crimes, and it will be on my conscience if I fail to make you understand."[13]

By his own description, he was not an entirely unwilling outlaw. Shortly after he joined Ignacio Parra, the gang leader gave him 3,000 pesos to outfit himself and buy a horse. Instead, Villa preferred to keep the money and steal the horse of a passerby.[14] He could have attempted to give up life as an outlaw earlier and with greater ease had he used the 50,000 pesos he obtained from one of his first robberies to settle down and begin a different life.

Another aspect of his early life that Villa emphasizes is his prowess as a fighting man. As a boy of 16 or 17, he outwitted pursuers sent to catch him four times, killing a number of men in the process. He saw his fight against the authorities as linked in some way to the revolution, but he made no claim to have in any way participated in the many uprisings, protests, and political mobilizations that occurred in Chihuahua before the revolution.

What Villa did insist on is that although he had killed many men, he was not a coldblooded murderer. His victims had either died when Villa had to defend himself or were men who had betrayed him.

The Black Legend

Very different kinds of stories circulated about Villa in Chihuahua. Some of them were picked up in 1914 by U.S. intelligence agents, who attempted to sketch a biographical profile of Villa. One report sent by John Biddle, a colonel on the U.S. general staff, to the chief of the War College Division gave a far more bloodthirsty picture of Villa than the one provided in his autobiography:

One story has it that the sheriff of the county eloped with Villa's sister and fled to the mountains. Villa pursued him with some ardent men, caught the couple, forced the man to go through a marriage ceremony, made him dig his own grave, and Villa shot him and rolled his body to the grave. One account is that he was incarcerated when fourteen years of age for cattle stealing and a few months after his release was again confined for homicide at Guanavací[,] Chihuahua.[15]

In another report forwarded to U.S. military intelligence, Dr. Carlos Husk, a physician who worked in Mexico for the American Smelting and Refining Company, and who knew Villa well, wrote: "In his bandit days, his notoriety was so widespread that nearly every crime committed and unaccounted for in northern Mexico was charged to him, and while there is no doubt that he participated in many, it was physically impossible for him to have accomplished everything in that line that his enemies accused him of, and he, of course, says that he never committed murder in cold blood, only killing those who were seeking him for the same purpose."[16]

The most systematic and comprehensive version of the black legend was written by Celia Herrera, a member of a family who developed a kind of blood feud with Villa, and many of whose members Villa killed.[17]

Herrera depicts a vicious killer and murderer without any redeeming qualities. Villa became an outlaw, according to her, not because he had avenged the honor of his sister but because he had murdered another boy, a friend of his, with whom he had had an altercation. This was the prelude to a spate of killings that increased in scope, intensity, and gruesomeness from year to year. In 1900, Villa killed Claro Reza, a former companion, a butcher who owed him money and refused to pay up.

In 1902, he joined a gang of criminals headed by an outlaw named José Beltrán. They attacked the house of a man named Inocencio Chávez and pistol-whipped his wife when she refused to tell them where he had hidden his money. In 1904, they attempted to murder a cattleman named Amaya and plunder his house. When they were prevented from carrying out their planned robbery by the arrival of a policeman, they became so furious that they murdered two of Amaya's cowboys when they encountered them on the street. In 1908, the gang entered the house of Alejandro Muñoz in the town of San Isidro. They requested a large sum of money from him, and when he did not give it to them, they tortured him, cutting off parts of his feet. Then they knifed him to death. On October 13, 1910, they attacked the hacienda of Talamantes, where they found only the owner's youngest daughter, Josefa Sota. When she refused to hand over her money, they buried her alive.

According to this account, Abraham González never asked Villa to participate in the revolution. In fact, he got involved only by coincidence: he was visiting a girlfriend at a small ranch when a federal force, believing that some revolutionaries were hidden there, attacked it. Thinking that they were pursuing him, Villa shot back and fled. He then decided to join Pascual Orozco, together with his gang. Orozco at first refused, since he considered Villa nothing more than a bandit. While negotiations were going on, federal troops attacked Orozco, Villa joined in responding to the attack, and Orozco reluctantly accepted the bandit into his army. He was to regret this decision, since Villa later stole the pay destined for the revolutionary troops.

Needless to say, according to Herrera, Villa never attempted to settle down and lead a more peaceful and law-abiding life in Chihuahua.

The Epic Legend

What the white and the black legends have in common is that they do not attribute any great political or social importance to Villa prior to the outbreak of the Mexican Revolution. The epic legend, by contrast, states that in his years as an outlaw, Villa became the idol of Chihuahua's peasantry and the scourge of the Terrazas. No one has better described the epic legend than the U.S. correspondent John Reed:

An immense body of popular legend grew up among the peons around his name. There are many traditional songs and ballads, celebrating his exploits—you can hear the shepherds singing them around their fires at night, repeating verses handed down by their fathers or composing others extemporaneously. For instance, they tell the story of how Villa, fired by the story of the misery of the peons at the hacienda of Los Alamos, gathered a small army and descended upon the big house, which he looted and distributed the spoils among the poor people. He drove off thousands of cattle from the Terrazas range and ran them across the border. He would suddenly descend upon a prosperous mine and seize the bullion. When he needed corn he captured a granary belonging to some rich man. He recruited almost openly in the villages, far removed from the well traveled roads and railways, organizing the outlaws of the mountains.[18]

The epic legend not only painted Villa as a more influential man than he had described himself in his memoirs but as a more generous one as well. One version of this legend reached all the way to U.S. President Woodrow Wilson. In a conversation with the British ambassador, Wilson described Villa as "a sort of Robin Hood [who] had spent an eventful life in robbing the rich in order to give to the poor. He had even at one time kept a butcher's shop for the purpose of distributing to the poor the proceeds of his innumerable cattle raids."[19]

It is extremely difficult to separate truth from legend, to determine the veracity of these contradictory accounts, because so few documents exist for this early period of Villa's life. None of Villa's accounts of his own life, the accusations of his enemies, and the ballads that form the basis of the epic legend are corroborated by contemporary documents. Villa's autobiography is based exclusively on his memoirs, while Celia Herrera quotes only one document dealing with Villa's life prior to the outbreak of the revolution—a report by a local *jefe político* stating that in 1907, Villa and some companions had stolen 22 head of cattle and mules.[20]

Extricating fact from fiction and separating truth from legend with regard to Villa's early life requires not only examination of all contemporary documents, including a critical evaluation of both Villa's memoirs and those of his contemporaries, but an understanding of the milieu in which he lived prior to the revolution, that of Mexico's northern frontier, and above all the state of Chihuahua. It was in many respects a region with a history far different from that of the rest of Mexico, a place where heroism and bloodthirstiness had come together in an inextricable and violent mix.

PART ONE

From Outlaw to Revolutionary

CHAPTER ONE

From the Frontier to the Border

There is enormous animosity against the hacienda for which I have no explanation, and which would have seemed incredible to me, if I did not feel it every moment. Many of the servants whom we considered loyal have greatly disappointed us; they have been captivated by the promises made by the revolutionaries that the lands would be divided among them, and right now all they think about is the realization of such a beautiful dream. Many of them have received great benefits from the hacienda and they are the ones who demand land with the greatest eagerness, not because we have caused them any harm, but because of their desire for their own profit.

—The administrator of the hacienda
of Santa Catalina to its owner[1]

On the eve of the Spanish Conquest, what is today the state of Chihuahua had been part neither of the Aztec empire nor of the complex civilization known as Mesoamerica, which included the inhabitants of central and southern Mexico. In contrast to Mesoamerica, Chihuahua had no large cities, no dense population living on intensive agriculture, and no highly stratified social groups. Instead, it was thinly populated by groups of hunters, gatherers, and some agriculturists, loosely organized into different tribes. The Aztecs had shown no interest in conquering this nomadic population, to which they collectively referred in the most derisive way as *chichimecas*, the sons of dogs.

The Aztecs' lack of interest is not surprising. The vast state of Chihuahua consists mostly of deserts and inhospitable mountain ranges. Large parts of central Chihuahua are taken up by the sand dunes of Samalayuca, while the even more arid Bolsón de Mapimí is located in the southeastern part of the state. The huge Sierra Madre, in western Chihuahua, are mostly just as inhospitable. Agriculture could be practiced only in limited regions, irrigated by rivers and lakes, mainly in the northwestern part of the state and to a lesser degree in eastern Chihuahua near the Conchos River. Some of the most important resources of Chihuahua were of no interest to the Aztecs. There were no cattle to graze on the fertile pastureland in the central part of the state, and the Aztecs lacked the technology to extract its rich mineral ores. They had no use either for its huge timber resources.

Initially, the Spaniards, too, showed little interest in the region. Their attitude changed at the end of the sixteenth and the beginning of the seventeenth centuries, when large silver mines were discovered near the present cities of Chihuahua and Parral. Spanish settlements were soon established, and haciendas sprang up around them to supply the miners with food and to profit from the mining boom. Since it was difficult to attract laborers or immigrants from central Mexico or from Spain to this vast, undeveloped, and dangerous region, the Spaniards attempted to enslave the local population, most of whom were Tarahumara, whose way of life was predominantly nomadic. When Indian slavery proved to be both unsuccessful (many slaves fled into the Sierra Madre) and illegal (the Spanish Crown soon banned Indian slavery), new methods of influencing the Indians were attempted.

The Jesuits and Franciscans tried to settle them in missions. Although temporarily subdued, the Tarahumara staged a number of uprisings, however, and the majority of them finally faded into the Sierra Madre, where the Spaniards had great difficulty in locating them, and where they resumed their nomadic way of life.[2]

Until the middle of the eighteenth century, the population of Chihuahua gradually expanded as more mines were developed, new haciendas were set up, and migrants decided to settle there. That expansion abruptly halted in the mid eighteenth century, when Apache raiders began to make their presence felt in Chihuahua. Until then, the Apaches had lived far to the north of Chihuahua, but in the eighteenth century, they were pushed southward by the far more powerful Comanches, and they began raiding Spanish settlements. The few hundred soldiers that Spain had stationed on the frontier were unable to put up an effective resistance, and many of Spain's hacendados as well as its miners fled southward or into a few large towns.[3]

Faced with the possible loss of this potentially rich province, the Spanish crown decided to set up a series of fortified settlements inhabited by armed peasant freeholders. Extraordinary benefits were given to migrants from Spain and from central Mexico, as well as to local Indians, who were willing to settle in these military colonies. They were granted large amounts of land and exempted from paying taxes for ten years. Indian military colonists, in contrast to the Indian peasants of central Mexico, who were considered wards of the crown, were given full rights of Spanish citizenship.[4]

By the end of the eighteenth century, these colonists began to be a fighting force able effectively to resist the Apache raiders. When the crown held out not only a stick in the shape of these military colonies but a carrot as well, offering to supply all Apaches who settled near Spanish towns with food, clothing, and alcohol, many of the nomadic raiders settled down. Although it was never completely pacified, the region was more peaceful than ever before. For the first time, the peasant freeholders were able to fully enjoy the fruits of their land and labor, for which they gave credit to the Spanish crown. As a result, when the Mexican war of independence broke out in 1810, not only did the military colonists along New Spain's northern frontier not join the revolutionaries in central and southern Mexico, but many of them decided to fight on the side of Spain.[5]

A century later, in 1910, after the Mexican government had again pacified the frontier, the descendants of these military colonists took a completely different attitude and fought in the forefront of the Mexican Revolution. The reason for that change in attitude can be found in the development of Chihuahua in the nineteenth century.

The peace the Spanish crown brought to the frontier did not survive Spanish colonial rule. By 1830, the Apaches were raiding again. Weak Mexican governments, generally toppled after one or two years by military coups or by rival political factions, had neither the means nor the will to fight the Apaches. The payments in food and in kind that had kept them peaceful were canceled just as the Apaches began to sense the military weakness of the new Mexican government. The Mexican army was far more adept at staging coups in Mexico City than at fighting Apache raiders. Attacks on haciendas increased to such a degree that by the mid nineteenth century, most hacendados had abandoned their estates. By contrast, the military colonists stayed and fought, since they had nowhere else to go.[6]

Describing this period, the inhabitants of the old military colony of Namiquipa proudly wrote in a petition they drafted at the end of the nineteenth century, "all neighboring haciendas had been abandoned because of the constant danger of aggression by the barbarians between 1832 and 1860 and only Namiquipa remained to fight the barbarians and to constitute a lonely bastion of civilization in this remote region."[7] This was true not only of Namiquipa but of many other military colonies and free villages in large parts of Chihuahua. In these years, they created what was in many respects a unique kind of society in Mexico, limited to northern Chihuahua and a few other regions that were prey to Apache attacks. It was a society that embodied a unique combination of savagery and democracy. Savagery was characteristic of both sides in the conflict. The Apaches frequently killed and tortured their prisoners, including women and children, and the Mexican authorities offered bounties for Apache scalps, also including those of women and children. The savagery at times extended to Tarahumara Indians, who did not raid Mexican settlements but frequently lost their lands and their properties to white and mestizo settlers.[8]

On the other hand, this Chihuahuan society of free *rancheros* perhaps most closely corresponded to the kind of U.S. frontier society painted in vivid colors by Frederick Jackson Turner. His hypothesis, which captured the minds of generations of Americans, was that the U.S. frontier created a unique kind of self-reliant, autonomous, independent farmer. These farmers, according to Turner, were unencumbered by the class differences and power structures of the eastern United States. The state was weak, the traditional wealthy families did not go west, and so a kind of egalitarian, self-reliant society was created in the west of the United States, which largely shaped the mentality of that country.

In recent years, this hypothesis has aroused much controversy in U.S. historiography.[9] Some historians argue that land speculators, wealthy landowners, and bankers were very much present in the settlement of what is generally considered the U.S. frontier—as was the state in the shape of the U.S. Army. In much of

Chihuahua and some other parts of northern Mexico, the contrary was the case in the period from about 1830 to the 1860s. The state, which in the shape of Spanish colonial authorities, the army, wealthy landowners, and the Catholic church had been present at the genesis of the northern Mexican frontier in the sixteenth, seventeenth, and eighteenth centuries, had largely disappeared in northwestern Chihuahua by the 1830s. Many of the missions that the Jesuits had established vanished toward the end of the colonial period after the order was expelled from New Spain in 1767; the remaining missions were largely abandoned when Spanish rule ended in Mexico in 1821. Wealthy miners and hacendados fled as the Apaches advanced, and bankers and land speculators saw no value in lands that were constantly prey to nomadic attacks. The Mexican federal government and the federal army were far too weak and riven by internal dissension to have any significant presence in Chihuahua and northern Mexico, so the free rancheros were left to their own devices. The society they developed was poor but largely egalitarian. Chihuahuans were self-reliant and self-confident, with a fierce sense of pride in being able to maintain themselves in the face of such adversity. From the 1860s onward, that society would once again be transformed by the return of both the state and the hacendados to Chihuahua. The man who did most to engineer that return was one of the state's most important, flamboyant, and memorable figures, Luis Terrazas.

The Rise of Luis Terrazas

In the 1860s, after Mexico defeated the French invaders and put an end to Maximilian's empire, a more stable administration was established. Fearing that Chihuahua would be annexed by the United States if it was not brought firmly under Mexican control, the central government did everything in its power to fight the Apaches. New military colonies were established; settlers were given land if they were ready to fight against the Indian raiders; and, above all, the hacendados were induced to return. The man who was largely responsible for this new policy was Luis Terrazas.

The son of a well-to-do butcher, Terrazas did not come from one of Chihuahua's ruling families, although he soon married into one of them. He joined the Liberal party in Chihuahua, became one of its leaders, and, in the course of the civil wars between Liberals and Conservatives, became Liberal governor of the state in 1859. Being more adept than his predecessors at fighting off the Apache raiders, he quickly became popular.[10]

Terrazas's organizational talents were not the sole reason for his success. His chief innovation was to divert tax revenues earmarked for the federal government in Mexico City to setting up militias to fight the Indians. While this approach was unpopular in Mexico's capital, it gained Terrazas prestige and support among many segments of Chihuahua's population, including its military colonists, who regarded the central authorities as useless exploiters and parasites.

Terrazas did not devote all of his energies to fighting the Apaches. He also used the governorship to acquire some of the largest haciendas in the state. He acquired his largest estate by expropriating the property of another hacendado,

Pablo Martínez del Río, who had the misfortune to choose the wrong side in the war between the French and Mexico. He obtained other estates by buying them cheap from hacendados who had abandoned them and saw no way of settling them again. Since he was governor of the state, Terrazas controlled the militia and was able to attract many laborers who had fled the countryside to work on his estates, because he was able to offer them a greater degree of protection than other hacendados. There is no evidence that when he began forming his empire in the 1860s, Terrazas expropriated any of the lands of the peasant freeholders in the military colonies. There were sufficient abandoned estate lands to meet his ambitions, and he needed the fighting power of the military colonists. While Terrazas was governor of the state, his cousin Joaquín Terrazas commanded militia units composed of peasant freeholders who were far more effective in fighting the Apaches than the few federal troops stationed in Chihuahua. The activities of this cousin reflected to the credit of Terrazas, and he gained a large measure of popularity in his native state.

In 1876, the situations of Terrazas and of Mexico profoundly changed when General Porfirio Díaz, one of the heroes of Mexico's struggle for independence against Napoleon III, carried out a successful military coup and assumed power in Mexico. It was the beginning of the longest dictatorship in the history of Mexico. With the exception of four years from 1880 to 1884 when an ally of Díaz's, Manuel González, assumed the country's presidency, Díaz would rule Mexico until 1911, when he was overthrown by a popular uprising. In many respects, the Díaz regime met the fondest hopes of Mexico's wealthiest men, such as Luis Terrazas.

In economic terms, Mexico underwent unprecedented economic growth. Newly constructed railroads linked Mexico to the United States, as well as to port cities in Mexico. The result was a tremendous increase in foreign investment in Mexico, as well as spectacular economic growth. Between 1884 and 1900, about $1,200,000,000 worth of foreign investment flooded into the country, and the gross national product rose at an annual rate of 8 percent. Mexico now enjoyed an unprecedented era of political stability. Uprisings by members of the elite and the military, which had been the hallmark of Mexico's history since independence, practically ceased. This was owing not only to the power of the state, whose revenues increased significantly thanks to economic growth and foreign investment, but also to the fact that members of the elite became intermediaries for foreign investors and thus had a major stake in maintaining the political stability that was a precondition for foreign investment. The increasing power of the state and the existence of railroads that greatly increased the mobility of government military forces allowed the regime to crush popular and middle-class uprisings wherever they occurred. Possibilities of political instability were drastically reduced by falsified elections, which led to a rubber-stamp congress that Díaz completely controlled. The result of political growth and economic stability was that Mexico's upper class were now able to accumulate enormous wealth. They did so not only by becoming intermediaries for foreign investors but also because they were able, thanks to the communication revolution that had taken place in Mexico, to export large amounts of goods both to the United States and to Europe. Díaz's policies of keeping down popular protest, muzzling the opposition press, preventing the formation of labor unions, and not allowing strikes greatly contributed to this enrichment. So did another of Porfirio Díaz's policies: large-scale expropriation of land that belonged to village communities.

Unlike other members of Mexico's ruling class, Luis Terrazas by no means found Díaz's assumption of power an unmitigated blessing. In 1876, his political acumen had failed him, and instead of siding with Díaz, he had supported his rival, President Sebastián Lerdo de Tejada. As a result supporters of Terrazas were ousted from the governorship of Chihuahua, which was now occupied by a powerful rival of Terrazas's, Angel Trias. Terrazas thus suffered a setback, but it was by no means a decisive defeat. Díaz's policy was not to kill or exterminate members of the elite who had opposed him, but to remove them from power, allowing them to enrich themselves by all means at their disposal in the hope that they would thus be dissuaded from engaging in costly and destabilizing uprisings. Thanks to the newly built railroads, Terrazas was able to export huge numbers of cattle to the United States. His family also controlled the largest bank in Chihuahua, the Banco Minero, and played a major role as an intermediary or even as a partner for foreign entrepreneurs who invested in Chihuahua. Terrazas profited, too, from another aspect of Porfirian "modernization," the confiscation on a vast scale of lands belonging to communal villages or to small landowners, which would play a decisive role in both Terrazas's and Díaz's downfall in 1911.

The fact that he had become one of the richest men in Mexico did not, however, satisfy Terrazas. He wanted to regain political power in his native state. In 1879, he briefly succeeded in doing so. In that year, Terrazas's rival Angel Trias suffered a sharp decline in popularity when he raised taxes in order to fight the Apaches but had little success to show for it. The people of rural western Chihuahua staged a revolt and forced Trias to resign in favor of Terrazas, and as a consequence the latter once more became governor of Chihuahua. Díaz, who was on the verge of handing power over to his temporary successor Manuel González, was not willing to intervene, and González had no problem with tolerating Terrazas's assumption of power. In 1884, when Díaz once again became president of Mexico, Terrazas once more lost control of his native state, and it would take eighteen years, until 1903, for him to regain it. In the meantime, though, he would become the wealthiest man in Mexico.

Two developments greatly contributed to Terrazas's accumulation of new wealth but would have devastating consequences for Chihuahua's peasant freeholders. In 1885, U.S. troops captured the last major Apache leader, Geronimo, and Apache raids into Mexico practically ceased. And in the same year, Chihuahua was linked by railroads both to central Mexico and to the United States.

All this resulted in an enormous economic boom. Chihuahua's miners and cattle ranchers were able to sell their products across the border in the United States, and U.S. investors discovered that returns on investments could be very large in Chihuahua. Land prices rose, and the situation of Chihuahua's peasant freeholders underwent a dramatic change.

The Seeds of Revolution:
The Offensive Against Chihuahua's Free Villages

For years the military colonists who had fought against Apache raiders had been considered the heroes of Chihuahua. Their deeds were sung in *corridos* (popular ballads). They had marched in triumph through the streets of Ciudad Chihuahua, and governor after governor had praised them for their exploits. The free villagers of Chihuahua saw themselves as "defenders of civilization against the barbarians."[11] Ironically, however, the destruction of their enemies, the Apaches, also heralded their own elimination as a social class. After the capture of Geronimo, the rulers of Mexico and Chihuahua no longer had any need for the fighting skill and spirit of the military colonists. What they now wanted was their land, the value of which had increased enormously as a result of railway construction, foreign investment, and the economic boom.

In contrast to what had happened a century earlier, when peace between the Spaniards and Apaches gave Chihuahua's free villagers the possibility of enjoying their lands and rights and had converted them into grateful adherents of the Spanish colonial government, a very different situation arose once peace was established in late-nineteenth-century Chihuahua.

In the years between 1884 and 1910, the state's free villagers lost most of their lands and their traditional rights and suffered an attack upon their sense of dignity, which was based on their economic independence and freedom from outside interference. These tendencies affected not only the former military colonists but all of Chihuahua's peasant freeholders. The composition of this population was by no means homogeneous. It embraced at least five groups.

At the top—in a certain sense, the aristocracy of Chihuahua's free villagers—were the inhabitants of the first five military colonies that Viceroy Teodoro de Croix had set up in 1776. These were Namiquipa, Cruces, Casas Grandes, Janos, and Galeana. These colonies had received a huge amount of land: 112,359 hectares each.[12]

The second group consisted of colonies, such as San Andrés and Cuchillo Parado, that had been founded later, either by the Spanish colonial administration or by the Mexican government, and whose recipients had received far less land than the original five colonies. While the lands of these communities were in part individually owned and sections could be sold either to inhabitants of these villages and towns or to outsiders who wanted to settle there, much of the land was communal and was either utilized jointly—this was the case with pastureland—or rented out to individual community members.

The third group of free villagers consisted of Indians, mainly Tarahumara. They had obtained their lands from two different sources. Some had received it from the colonial authorities on the same terms under which Indian villages had been allowed to keep their common land in central and southern Mexico. The lands belonged to the community, could not be sold, and were far smaller in extent than those of the military colonies. A second group of Indians had originally possessed no lands of their own but had been settled on missions that officially belonged to the Jesuit order. After the expulsion of the Jesuits by the Spanish crown in 1767, some of them were given the same status as those Indian villages dependent upon the crown. Many of them soon lost their land, because the Jesuits were not there to protect their holdings. The expulsion of some Indians from the former Jesuit properties was followed in the nineteenth century by a more massive process whereby mestizos and whites, who came either from other parts of Chihuahua, from other parts of Mexico, or, after 1848, from territories annexed by the United States, took over much land that had originally belonged to the Indians. Many Indians were forced onto marginal land or into remote mountain regions of the Sierra Madre. Nevertheless, a substantial number of Indian villages still managed to retain land of their own.

The fourth group comprised communities inhabited mainly by squatters who lived either on public land or on abandoned haciendas—at times with the tacit approval of the estate owners, who could thus count on more men to defend their properties from Apache raids.

Finally, there were groups of landless villagers who grazed their cattle on unclaimed public lands.[13]

The expropriation and subjugation of Chihuahua's free villagers did not proceed smoothly and without major obstacles. Not only were these northern villagers armed, but they had a long fighting tradition. After all, the Apaches, whom they had fought for more than a century, were considered by some observers to be the best guerrilla fighters in the world.

The resentment and shock that the attacks by the federal government, the state government, and the hacendados on their lands and their rights produced among Chihuahua's peasant freeholders were all the greater since, unlike the situation that existed in central and southern Mexico, these attacks were to a large degree unexpected.

In southern and central Mexico, conflicts over land between hacendados and free villages had a long tradition, going back all the way to the colonial period, and perhaps even to precolonial times. While such conflicts were not absent in the north, they tended until the 1880s to be overshadowed by the common interest of landowners and free villagers in fending off Apache attacks. Land values were low as long as the Indian wars raged, and this had also tended to reduce conflicts between the villagers and the hacendados. In the 1860s, under the governorship of Terrazas and at the initiative of President Benito Juárez, lands were granted to new military colonists and to veterans of the war against the French.[14]

In the 1880s, however, the attitudes of both the central government and of the state administration of Chihuahua toward these military colonists underwent a change. The first indication of this was a new government policy with respect to public lands, where traditionally anyone had been able to graze cattle or collect wood.

A large part of the state consisted of such unclaimed land belonging to the central government, which had two different options for disposing of it. The first was to do what the U.S. government had done after the Civil War and proclaim a homestead act to open the land to farmers and small ranchers, which would have contributed, as it did in the United States,[15] to the easing of social tensions and the creation of a kind of safety valve for landless peasants from central Mexico. Such a policy would not have created a predominant class of small landowners in Chihuahua, since the government-owned lands were largely inappropriate for small-scale agriculture, but it would have helped to stabilize the social situation in the state.

The Mexican government instead opted for a very different policy, which was to play a major role in the outbreak of the Mexican Revolution 25 years later. Instead of being opened up or even sold to small settlers, the land was given away or sold in huge chunks. As payment for their work, surveying companies were allowed to keep a third of the public lands they surveyed. The other two-thirds were sold by the government to hacendados or foreign entrepreneurs, with the vague understanding that in return they would bring in colonists from Europe.

The surveying companies began their work on a large scale in 1884. Chihuahua's free villagers rapidly felt the effects of their activity. With the approval of the federal government, the surveying companies launched their first attack on the five original and largest military colonies, each of which had been adjudicated 112,359 hectares by the Spanish colonial authorities. The surveying companies refused to recognize these properties and attempted (not always successfully) to limit the collective holdings of these five military colonies to 28,080 hectares each. Other communities were affected in more indirect ways by the activities of the surveying companies. Grazing lands that had been part of the public domain, and had thus been accessible to all inhabitants, were suddenly closed off. Wild cattle and game, which could be hunted by everyone at will as long as the land where they roamed was public property, were now closed to Chihuahua's free villagers. They also lost the right to exploit the woodlands and other resources they had freely enjoyed.[16]

The activities of the surveying companies in the years between 1884 and 1892 weakened but did not destroy the economic basis of Chihuahua's free peasantry.[17] Chihuahua's landowners knew the fighting capacities of their erstwhile allies and were afraid of provoking them. A series of measures taken by both the federal and the state governments had already aroused the anger of many of Chihuahua's villagers. They had lost much of the independence and freedom that they had enjoyed throughout most of the nineteenth century. A law passed in 1884 stated that *jefes políticos* (i.e., district administrators) would not be elected anymore, but would be appointed by the state authorities. At the same time, their power over the villages was greatly strengthened. In many cases, villagers were not allowed to take cases to the courts without getting prior approval of the new jefes políticos.[18]

In 1891, the state government struck another blow at the traditional autonomy of the inhabitants of Chihuahua. A decree was passed whereby district capitals would not elect their own mayors; henceforth, these officials too would be appointed by the state governor. While these measures had generated dissatisfaction among many of Chihuahua's free villagers, they had, with a few exceptions, not led to any violent reactions. In the first years after they were implemented, some villagers found compensation for the losses they had suffered. Many went to work in newly opened mines or in railway construction. Others utilized the newly built railroads to find work across the border in the United States. Between 1890 and 1893, however, a series of violent uprisings shook Chihuahua, shattering the Porfirian peace in the state.

The First Revolts in the Chihuahuan Countryside

Several factors contributed to transforming the deep dissatisfaction of Chihuahua's villagers into violent upheavals. Beginning in 1891, many mines in the state closed or sharply reduced the number of their employees, either because of a cyclical economic crisis or because of new tariffs imposed by the United States. At the same time, owing to bad harvests, food prices rose.[19]

Chihuahua's hacendados had been cautious about pressing their claims to village lands. One of the state's wealthiest hacendados, Enrique Muller, for example, had not yet used coercion to force the inhabitants of Namiquipa from some of their lands he now claimed as his own.[20] Some outsiders, however, showed less restraint. These outsiders included the brothers Limantour, one of whom, José Yves Limantour, was by then one of the most powerful men in the Díaz administration. Their father, José Yves Limantour Sr., a financial genius regarded by many of his contemporaries as a genial crook, had migrated from France to California in the 1840s and established close personal ties to the Mexican governor of that province, Micheltorena. He acquired large amounts of land, both in what was to become the U.S. part of California and in Baja California, which remained part of Mexico. In the 1850s, he claimed to own most of the San Francisco Bay area, as well as large parts of present-day Los Angeles. U.S. courts discounted his claims, stating that his certificates of ownership were faked.[21]

The Mexican authorities, on the other hand, recognized his claims to lands in Mexico, and the value of his properties there was greatly enhanced when he bought large amounts of former church property from the Mexican state in the 1850s and 1860s. After his death, his sons struck a deal with the Mexican government. They exchanged their father's lands, which were spread out over diverse parts of Mexico, for one huge chunk of public land in the mountain region of western Chihuahua. The Limantour brothers did not respect the rights of the villagers living there. According to their lawyers, "they could not occupy these lands because they had to fight the natives who occupy the major part of the towns and villages which are part of this property."[22]

The uprisings on the Limantour properties were part of a more general wave of revolts that erupted in the mountain region of western Chihuahua between 1889 and 1893. They were brought about, not only by the dissatisfaction of the villagers, but also because the latter were firmly convinced that they enjoyed the support of their traditional patron and ally, Luis Terrazas, and thus felt that they had a genuine chance of succeeding.

In spite of his removal from political power in 1884, Terrazas had not done at all badly in the years that followed. His economic empire had grown by leaps and bounds. Demand for Mexican cattle had increased rapidly in the United States, and as the main cattle exporter in Chihuahua, Terrazas profited from the boom. At the same time, he secured a concession for the establishment of the Banco Minero, which was to become the largest bank in the state.

Not satisfied with mere economic success, Terrazas began plotting to regain control of his native state. Economic considerations may have played an important role in his decision, since as foreign capital began streaming into Chihuahua, the political elite that dominated the state had a unique opportunity to profit by acting as intermediaries. However, regaining political power was no easy undertaking. In order to prevent Terrazas from accumulating too much power, Díaz had named a rival, Lauro Carrillo, as governor of the state. Carrillo's term of office expired in 1891, when new elections were due, but he had announced his candidacy for another term.

Terrazas knew the rules of the political game as it was played in Porfirian Mexico. Votes counted for very little and could not force a governor from power. If he wanted to defeat his rival, Terrazas had to convince Porfirio Díaz that Carrillo was incapable of maintaining peace in Chihuahua. Terrazas's hopes for a political turnabout were strengthened in March 1891, when Carrillo's protector, Carlos Pacheco, an influential minister in the Díaz government, was ousted from his post in the cabinet and died a few weeks later. The possibility that Díaz might drop Carrillo thus increased, and Terrazas became even more intent on proving that Carrillo was incapable of keeping order in Chihuahua. To that end, he surreptitiously encouraged rebellions, and when they erupted, he urged the rebels to hold out against the efforts to suppress them.[23]

Carrillo was by no means ignorant of Terrazas's plans. On the one hand, he realized what was at stake and was intent on securing a peaceful settlement with the rebellious villagers. On the other, although willing to make some concessions, he could not afford to be labeled a weakling by either Díaz or the state's upper classes. The dilemma he faced was clearly expressed by the way Carrillo dealt with a series of peasant uprisings in Chihuahua. He did not carry out the kind of search-and-destroy operations so characteristic of the Díaz administration's war against the rebellious Yaqui Indians in neighboring Sonora. Most prisoners were not shot, the civilian population was not decimated or imprisoned, and rebellious villages were not razed. Carrillo offered most rebels an amnesty if they would lay down their arms, but generally did not accede to their demands. In some exceptional cases, however, he proved flexible. In Temosachic, for example, he removed the mayor, against whom the villagers had rebelled.[24]

On the whole, Carrillo's tactics paid off. His willingness to grant amnesty persuaded many villagers who had fled into the mountains in order to engage in guerrilla warfare, and who felt isolated because other villagers had not joined their rebellion, to accept the government's offer. By avoiding attacks on the civilian population and not carrying out mass reprisals, Carrillo prevented the kind of escalation of violence and counterviolence so characteristic of many guerrilla struggles.

There was, however, one exception to this generally peaceful denouement. It occurred in the small village of Tomóchi in the western mountains of Chihuahua. The Tomóchi revolt led to the fall of Carrillo, after the villagers inflicted on the Porfirian army the greatest defeat it suffered prior to the outbreak of the Mexican Revolution of 1910–11. In many ways, the Tomóchi revolt prepared Chihuahua's countryfolk for the revolutionary upheaval that was to occur twenty years later.

The Revolt That Shook Chihuahua

Tomóchi was not a well known and prestigious military colony like Namiquipa, Cruces, or Janos. It was an obscure village of scarcely 200 inhabitants in a small valley in the western mountain district of Guerrero. The economic and social grievances of its inhabitants were no different from those that had led other villages to revolt. A regional strongman, Joaquín Chávez, had named a relative of his, Juan Ignacio Chávez, an outsider, as mayor of Tomóchi. The resentment the villagers felt at this imposition was further strengthened by Mayor Chávez's behavior. He grazed his cattle on the villagers' land without paying rent or asking permission. He forced the villagers to work either for him or for the Limantours at very low wages, and when a few young men went to work at a nearby mine, where they were better paid, he threatened them with the *leva*—that is, conscription into the army, which many considered akin to slavery or deportation. When the villagers continued to protest, Joaquín Chávez inflicted a profound humiliation upon them. He rerouted the annual silver transport, the *conducta*, which regularly passed through Tomóchi on its way from the mine of Pinos Altos to the capital of Chihuahua. This was an insult, for it implied that the villagers were thieves and outlaws who could not be relied upon to respect property rights.[25]

When the villagers reacted to this insult by staging a noisy demonstration in front of the mayor's office, the latter sent an alarming report to his superior, claiming that the villagers were rebelling against the federal government and were intent on capturing the silver transport. He requested federal troops to quell them. There is not the slightest evidence that the villagers ever attacked the silver transport or ever intended to do so, but it was a cunning tactic on the mayor's part. It is unlikely that the government would have sent federal troops to quell a dispute between the mayor and the inhabitants of a small village. In all probability, the mayor would have been discredited for provoking such unrest. Once the government became convinced that foreign mines and foreign capital were threatened, however, the situation changed completely. Díaz approved the governor's decision to send troops to Tomóchi as rapidly as possible so that Mexico's reputation abroad would not suffer.[26] A detachment of 50 soldiers arrived in Tomóchi, a skirmish occurred, there were some casualties, and most of the village's men withdrew into the mountains. Governor Carrillo sent a triumphant message to Díaz stating that the rebellion had been quelled, and that while some of the participants had disappeared into the countryside, many were surrendering. Díaz congratulated the governor on his success.[27] The governor was mistaken. This small village was to prove one of the greatest challenges that the Díaz regime would face during its long tenure in office.

Up to this point, the behavior of the villagers of Tomóchi had been similar to that of other rebellious communities, but from the moment they left Tomóchi, the villagers were guided by other considerations and reacted in different ways from most villagers in Chihuahua. Their rebellion was inspired, not only by social and economic considerations, but by religious factors and convictions as well.

In the course of the nineteenth century, the influence of the Catholic church seems to have been eroding in the mountain region of western Chihuahua. In the colonial period, Jesuit and Franciscan missionaries had been active in this part of New Spain. In fact, a missionary had settled for many years in Tomóchi itself and converted the Tarahumara Indians who originally lived there. When they intermarried with Spaniards, the roots of Catholicism seemed firm and unshakable. The expulsion of the Jesuits by the colonial authorities and the weakening of the church in independent Mexico eroded the church's position. In many villages such as Tomóchi, there were no resident priests. After the Jesuits' expulsion, clergy only came to Tomóchi on rare occasions to say mass and officiate at deaths, marriages, and burials. The weakening of Catholicism was reflected in conversions to Protestantism and the appearance of autonomous religions. In San Isidro, for example, some of the most prominent families, such as the Orozcos, were receptive to the teachings of missionaries from the United States and converted to Protestantism.[28]

In Tomóchi, a kind of dissident offshoot of Catholicism with popular roots had developed by the time of the rebellion. Most villagers were adherents of a cult that had developed around an 18-year-old girl in Sonora, Teresita, known as the Saint of Cabora (the village where she lived).[29] Teresita had visions of Christ, preached a humanistic creed, and was said to perform miracles and cures. She did not at that time call for rebellion or social revolt. The interpretation given to her teachings by the inhabitants of Tomóchi owed more to their leader and spokesman, Cruz Chávez, than to the Saint of Cabora. Chávez (no relation of either the regional strongman or the mayor), who was 34 years old in 1891, was a born leader. As one witness who knew him put it, "he was a handsome and friendly man . . . when he gave orders though, his capacity to dominate came out very clearly. His eyes became like a lances, and no one could resist them, so that he could frequently gain obedience just by looking at someone."[30] It was Chávez who declared in the name of most of the villagers that after their conflict with the mayor, they would recognize no other authority than the law of God, and it was he who persuaded his supporters that Teresita legitimized their resistance to authority. In order to confirm this view and to renew their faith, once they left Tomóchi, the villagers decided to make a pilgrimage to Cabora in order to meet Teresita.

It was a hazardous journey. Troops from Chihuahua pursued them, and other troops mobilized by the governor of the neighboring state of Sonora tried to intercept them. In one battle, the men of Tomóchi defeated one contingent of Sonoran troops sent to intercept them, eluded another, and finally arrived in Cabora only to find that Teresita was not there. Their religious faith was nevertheless reinforced when Cruz Chávez celebrated a rousing mass in the chapel of the Saint of Cabora. The men of Tomóchi now returned to their village along the same arduous route by which they had come, crossing the western Sierra Madre and again eluding both Sonoran and Chihuahuan troops. The trip further strengthened their desire to resist the federal government. Paradoxically, the fact that they had not met the Saint of Cabora may have reinforced this resolve. Had they met Teresita, another interpretation of her teachings might have emerged, but since this was not the case, Cruz Chávez's views prevailed.

The fact that they had either defeated or eluded the troops sent out to pursue them must have strengthened their conviction that God and the Saint of Cabora were on their side and would protect them. Their hopes seemed to have come true for several months after their return to Tomóchi. The government, which had withdrawn its garrison from their village, left them alone. Governor Carrillo, who had suffered a considerable loss of prestige and power because of his inability to resolve the dispute with Tomóchi, sent an emissary to the village and attempted to make a deal. He offered them amnesty and guaranteed their lives if they would lay down their arms and recognize the legitimacy of the municipal and regional authorities. The villagers refused. Their hatred of their former mayor was too strong to allow them to accept his return. Cruz Chávez had convinced them not only that God was on their side but that they were invincible. In addition, Luis Terrazas, who hoped that a continuing conflict with Tomóchi would weaken his rival, Carrillo, may have secretly encouraged them to resist.[31]

Terrazas's hopes and expectations proved to be justified. Porfirio Díaz, fearing a further exacerbation of the conflict in Chihuahua, removed Governor Carillo (as a consolation he was nominated to a seat in the senate) and replaced him with a compromise candidate, acceptable to both rival factions, Miguel Ahumada. The new governor now decided to stamp out the rebellion in Tomóchi once and for all. In his eyes, Tomóchi had become a festering sore. Rebels from other villages had begun to congregate there, and its example inspired other villagers.

The governor believed that subduing a village with fewer than 100 fighting men should not be too difficult. The federal commander sent to Tomóchi for this purpose, General José María Rangel, who led both a battalion of the regular army and auxiliary forces, was so confident of the superior power of his soldiers that he did not even wait for additional troops who were on their way to the village to join him before launching a frontal attack on the village. Rangel's forces suffered not just a defeat but a nearly complete rout. The men of Tomóchi, many of them veterans of the Apache wars, killed most of Rangel's officers and then decimated his retreating troops. Their inferiority in numbers was more than made up for by their superior morale and equipment. They were armed with Winchester repeating rifles in contrast to the one-shot rifles of the federal troops. Rangel was defeated, the commander of federal troops in Chihuahua reported, "because of his contempt for his enemy and the betrayal of many persons within this city and in Chihuahua who hold important positions."[32]

In addition, at a decisive moment in the battle, the auxiliary forces from Chihuahua refused to support the federal troops. Having fought the Apaches alongside Cruz Chávez and men from Tomóchi in the peasants' militias that Joaquín Terrazas had commanded, both the commander of the auxiliaries, Santana Pérez, and many of their number were unwilling to fight their former comrades, and some of them may have turned their guns on the federal soldiers.[33]

Rangel's defeat strengthened the conviction of the men of Tomóchi that God and the Saint of Cabora were indeed protecting them. The experiences of the next expedition that the government sent out to subdue them must have further reinforced this belief. After his defeat, Rangel was relieved of his command, and a personal friend of Porfirio Díaz's, General Felipe Cruz, was sent at the head of a cavalry detachment to subdue Tomóchi. Cruz never even reached the village. After marching for two days and drinking countless bottles of liquor, Cruz finally attained such a drunken stupor that he mistook a cornfield for the inhabitants of Tomóchi. Like Don Quijote attacking the windmills, Cruz at the head of his troops charged into the field, cutting down the corn with his sword. He then returned to Chihuahua and wrote in a glowing report to his superiors in Mexico City that he had finally subdued Tomóchi.[34]

The ridicule the government suffered when this episode became known in Chihuahua was among the motives that impelled both Díaz and Governor Ahumada to destroy Tomóchi once and for all. Opposition to Díaz was growing in many parts of Mexico. Local rebellions had erupted in the states of Mexico, Yucatán, and Guerrero, and Díaz feared that Tomóchi might become the rallying point for a national revolution.[35] This time 1,200 men, many of them veterans of the Yaqui campaign in neighboring Sonora, were sent from both Chihuahua and Sonora to subdue Tomóchi. For the villagers, who soon learned of this enormous expedition, there was only one rational way to survive: to retreat into the mountains and wage guerrilla warfare. But Cruz Chávez, convinced that God was on his side, decided to wait it out in the village itself. The troops were coming in two separate contingents from two sides, half of them from Sonora led by a veteran Indian fighter, Lorenzo Torres, the other half from Chihuahua under the command of General Rangel, who at all costs wanted to avenge the defeat he had suffered previously. Cruz Chávez rejected any suggestion that it might be better to attack the two troop contingents separately rather than to face the overwhelming reality of a united federal force. God and the Saint of Cabora were on their side, he reiterated, and they would triumph. They nearly did. The federal troops were gripped by a kind of superstitious terror. Heriberto Frías, one of Mexico's great writers, who took part in the expedition as a soldier, vividly describes the feelings of the federal troops: "all agreed that without any exaggeration, every rebel was worth ten federal soldiers."[36]

Soon after arriving in Tomóchi, the troops were met by 30 women dressed in black, slowly advancing toward them. Before the federal commander could make up his mind how to react to this unexpected demonstration, the "women," once they were close enough to the government troops, suddenly discarded their black shawls and turned out to be men, who immediately opened fire with their Winchester repeating rifles. This surprise attack seemed to confirm the superstitious fears of the soldiers, and the men of Tomóchi nearly provoked a federal rout. With the greatest difficulty, the officers forced their men to return to battle. In spite of the fact that the federal army had a cannon and fourteen times as many fighting men as the villagers, the battle lasted for nearly two weeks, with the government troops suffering hundreds of casualties. When only a handful of villagers were left alive, General Rangel sent an emissary to them promising to respect their lives if they surrendered. They refused. He then sent another emissary with an offer that they could retreat into the mountains, and that his troops would not interfere if they left Tomóchi of their own free will. Chávez again rejected the offer. Government troops finally stormed Chávez's house, the last bastion where the survivors still held out. Seven men, among them Cruz Chávez himself, were finally captured, offered cigarettes by their captors, and then shot in cold blood. "The conclusion of the Tomóchi campaign," the commander of federal forces in Chihuahua wrote Díaz, "was a horror story."[37]

It was a victory that bore all the hallmarks of a defeat. The government tried to obscure this fact by calling the destruction of an obscure village of fewer than 100 men by over 1,200 government soldiers "a heroic triumph." Strict censorship was imposed by the government on news about Tomóchi, but Heriberto Frías, from his vantage point as a participant, wrote a novel under an assumed name in which the campaign was depicted. In the mountains of Chihuahua, countless corridos recounted the villagers' fight. "How courageous are the Tomóchis, who knew how to die in the face of a rain of bullets in defense of their home and their land" was typical of the many ballads Tomóchi inspired.[38] The story of Tomóchi became known all over Mexico. It had a profound effect on the country's peasants, and above all on the inhabitants of the mountain ranges of western Chihuahua. The conviction that one of them was worth ten federal soldiers would sustain them twenty years later, when in the first months of the revolution, they faced Díaz's federal army almost alone.

There were more immediate consequences of the uprisings. There is little doubt that on March 30, 1893, when Celso Anaya and Simon Amaya began an uprising in Santo Tomás that called for the overthrow of Porfirio Díaz, they were inspired by the resistance of Tomóchi. Their movement was crushed by government troops, but some of the survivors were able to find refuge in the United States. From there they mobilized new groups of sympathizers, and a few months later, they crossed back into Mexico again and occupied the border town of Palomas, where they issued a manifesto against the Díaz government that called for an uprising and concluded, "Long live Tomóchi!" Events in Tomóchi seem also to have influenced the men who in 1893 occupied the town of El Mulato. They were led by "Hermana María," who described herself as a saint and called on the peasants to recognize her as such. Government troops crushed the movement before it could garner further support.[39]

While sporadic local uprisings took place throughout the mountain ranges of western Chihuahua in the 1880s and early 1890s, the generalized revolt that the government feared never materialized. To a great degree, this was because the villagers remained largely isolated from the rest of Chihuahuan society in their violent opposition to both the state government and the Díaz administration. Wealthy patrons and traditional caudillos, above all, Luis Terrazas, who had given them support in the early stages of their revolt, withdrew it once they had achieved their main aim of toppling the Carrillo administration in Chihuahua. The new social classes that were developing at a rapid pace in the state after 1884, the middle classes and the industrial working class, had no desire to revolt against the government. The middle classes not only profited from the establishment of peace and the ensuing economic boom, they also benefited from the political structures that Díaz had set up in Chihuahua. Nationally, the Díaz government had grown more and more dictatorial, but paradoxically, in Chihuahua, a kind of genuine two-party system emerged as a result of Díaz's policies. Both Terrazas and his rivals sought the support of the newly emerging middle classes, and they were ready to make substantial concessions to secure it. Chihuahua's economic boom, increasing demands for labor by newly opened mines, industrial enterprises, and railway construction, sent wages soaring. As a result, the industrial workers saw no reason to revolt against the government, not even when the recession of 1892–94 plunged many of them into misery.

In 1903, a profound political change took place in Chihuahua. In that year, Porfirio Díaz, realizing how powerful erstwhile rivals such as Terrazas had become, decided to co-opt them into his regime. He realized that the fears that he had entertained at the beginning of his regime, that these regional strongmen might rise against him, no longer had any basis. These caudillos had become highly dependent on foreign investment, and any kind of uprising and the resulting instability would have put an end to that great source of income. In 1903, with the approval of Díaz, Luis Terrazas once again became governor of Chihuahua.

The Final Offensive Against Chihuahua's Free Villagers

For many of Chihuahua's free villagers and erstwhile military colonists, especially in western Chihuahua, June 3, 1903, was a day of hope and perhaps even of rejoicing. On that day, Luis Terrazas, their patron and protector of many years, the man under whose leadership they had fought the Apaches and for whom they had staged an uprising in 1879, reassumed the governorship of Chihuahua. Many villagers believed that now that he was in power again, after 20 years, he would do what he had done before: maintain their traditional rights and act as a shield against the increasing encroachment of the federal government upon them. What they did not see was that the conditions for the alliance between them and Terrazas that had existed a quarter of a century before had now disappeared.

In earlier times, Terrazas had needed the free villagers' help to ward off Apache attacks, to counteract the influence of the federal government, and to defend himself against rival power brokers in Chihuahua. By 1903, the Apaches were gone, the federal government had become Terrazas's closest ally, and Chihuahua's elite was linked to the Terrazas clan by a multiplicity of economic, family, and political ties. Terrazas had in fact turned against his erstwhile allies among the free villagers long before he became governor of Chihuahua again. Surveying companies controlled by the Terrazas clan participated in the expropriation of public lands.[40] Terrazas frequently abolished a traditional right granted to neighboring communities to graze their cattle on his estates. In addition, after having encouraged the villagers of Tomóchi to resist, he abandoned them to their fate. These facts were not known to many villagers in the western mountains of Chihuahua. His surveying company seemed to have concentrated its activities on regions outside of western Chihuahua, the restrictions he imposed on the grazing rights of villagers did not affect all villagers in the state, and his involvement in Tomóchi had largely remained a secret.

The hopes that Chihuahua's free villagers pinned on Terrazas were clearly expressed by a flood of petitions and calls for redress that they addressed to him. Terrazas was willing to accede to a number of these demands. When Heliodoro Arias Olea wrote him in the name of the inhabitants of Bachiniva protesting against the abuses of the local caciques, Comaduran and Baray, Terrazas ordered new and free elections, in which Arias Olea was elected mayor.[41] Terrazas also acceded to the demands of 150 Tarahumara Indians from the village of Nonoava, who complained to him that for 40 years the owners of a neighboring hacienda, the Ochoa family, had been occupying their lands. Terrazas felt that the Indians' claims were justified and called on the Ochoas to return the disputed lands.[42]

Terrazas's attitude was partly based on political expediency. Comaduran had

been a political foe, and by removing him from power, Terrazas not only eliminated a potential enemy but also gained the support of the inhabitants of Bachiniva. Perhaps this was not the only reason for Terrazas's actions and attitude.
To a certain degree, he may have wanted to abide by the rules of the game he
had played for so long. In his many years as caudillo of Chihuahua, Terrazas had
repeatedly called on the villagers for help, thus accumulating innumerable obligations, which the peasant freeholders were now cashing in on. But Terrazas had
not become governor in order to redeem village rights. There was one convenient
way of escaping his obligations without relinquishing power: this was to resign
from office and have another family member, unburdened by Terrazas's political
debts, assume control of Chihuahua.

Apart from his advanced age, this may have been one of the reasons why Terrazas, after serving as governor from 1903 to 1904, named his son-in-law Enrique
Creel as interim governor and allowed him to rule Chihuahua. In the eyes of the
Terrazas family clan, the slate had now been wiped clean. Once the head of the
family had relinquished his office, they felt no obligation whatsoever to his former allies. Creel, who had never been a traditional caudillo, had no links to Chihuahua's free villagers. As a convinced social Darwinist, he despised them, and
he now turned against them with a ruthlessness unmatched in the state's history.
Within seven years, Creel's policies would provoke one of the most far-reaching
rural uprisings in Mexico's history. In the short run, though, he achieved an astonishing degree of success.

Creel's attack on Chihuahua's free villagers was partly based on the fact that
now that he and the family clan were in control of their native state, they wanted
to make the most out of the enormous opportunities that the links between political and economic power presented. There were also more concrete motives for
the governor's policies. After 1904, two railway companies, the Mexican Northwestern and the Kansas Orient and Pacific Railroad, were making plans and proceeding to build new lines to western Chihuahua. As a result, land prices rose
again, creating a new incentive for land expropriation.[43]

The legal underpinnings for Creel's offensive were provided by two laws that
the state legislature passed at the behest of the governor. The first was a law of
1904 that replaced the elected heads of municipalities with officials appointed by
the state government. The motivations for this decree are easy to understand.
Elected mayors had frequently been the first line of defense of villages and communities against land expropriations and other abuses by the state government.
These elected officials repeatedly protested measures against their communities
and at times even refused to implement them. By appointing his own men, often
outsiders, to rule over local communities, Creel eliminated this obstacle to his
policies.[44] In addition, state control of municipal government was necessary if
Creel wanted to implement the second law that the legislature passed at his behest in 1905: a new land law.

Although the reform laws of 1857 had sufficed in most of Mexico to create the
legal basis for large-scale expropriations of village lands and for the economic destruction of village communities, they nevertheless contained some restrictions
that Creel wanted to eliminate. They established the federal government as the
supreme arbiter in a large number of land questions. Creel's new law replaced the

federal authorities with the state government—that is, with the Creel administration. According to the reform laws, the lands of village communities were to be
sold in individual lots to members of the communities. Creel's land law opened
the sale of community holdings to outsiders. The older laws had protected some
municipal lands from expropriation; Creel's new law eliminated all of these restrictions.[45] This law had a catastrophic impact on the free villagers of Chihuahua. Earlier expropriations had already transformed many of them from freeholders who were relatively well-to-do or had sufficient land to become prosperous farmers into poor peasants practicing subsistence agriculture and eking out
a living on relatively small plots of land. The new law made many of them landless laborers, forced to look for work outside their villages in order to survive.
This may have been one of the reasons why Creel adopted it, since in boom times
there was a labor shortage in Chihuahua.

Creel's measures provoked great resentment among Chihuahua's free villagers
but did not immediately lead to armed resistance. The villagers at first sought
peaceful means of redress. They sent innumerable petitions and letters of protest
to the Secretaría de Fomento (ministry of development) in Mexico City and to
Porfirio Díaz himself. These documents were invariably sent to the same section
of the Secretaría, which in practically all cases gave a similar answer, which
amounted to a kind of ping-pong game with the villagers. When the villagers
protested the abuses of local authorities, they were told to address their complaints to the governor. When they stated that it was at the initiative of the governor or at least with his support that the local authorities were proceeding
against them, they were told to call on the courts. When they replied that the
judges were corrupt and biased appointees of the governor, they were again told
they had no other recourse than to appeal either to these same courts or to the
governor himself. The Secretaría did this even in cases where its own officials
stated in internal memoranda that the grievances of the villagers were justified.
This conviction was never expressed to the petitioners themselves. As a result, a
vicious circle was created from which there was no way out for the villagers except
full-scale capitulation or revolution.[46]

Creel developed what might be called a cumulative strategy in order to deal
with Chihuahua's free villages. Both he and his allies concentrated their first efforts against small communities and against Tarahumara Indians, who constituted the poorest, least educated, and thus most vulnerable elements of Chihuahuan society. Not only were they the poorest of Chihuahua's free villagers,
most were illiterate, and many could not speak Spanish. In May 1904, fifteen inhabitants of the village of Temeychic sent an urgent letter to the federal government protesting that Alberto Terrazas, the son of Luis Terrazas, and Felipe Terrazas, another relative, were selling land that belonged to them. They wrote that
they had tried to deliver a protest resolution to the surveyor who was measuring
their land, but that the latter had not accepted it. The ministry did not even find
the case worth looking at and decided that it was not competent to deal with it.[47]

This attitude was characteristic of the Secretaría's policies toward Chihuahua's
free villagers until 1908. In the name of 300 Tarahumara Indians, José Vega sent a
bitterly worded petition to the federal government in June 1905. A company
headed by a Senor Sandoval, which the villagers called "a company of hangmen,"

had forced the Indians to work without pay and then expelled them by force from their land.[48] The Secretaría's answer was short and brutal. It stated that their land had already been ceded to Sandoval in 1884. If they wanted to, the ministry wrote, the Indians could certainly buy it back from him. When the villagers again insisted on their rights to this land and demanded its division among them, the ministry told them to address their complaint to the governor, who, as was to be expected, refused to heed their claims.

A spokesman for the Indian peasants of Monterde y Arremoyo, Feliciano Ochoa, protested against the sale of lands that the village had possessed since "time immemorial." Ochoa's complaint arrived at the same time that the ministry received a letter from Governor Creel stating that a Mr. Rufus Bragg of the Monterde land company wanted to buy this land, and that the protesting Indians did not really object to the sale of their properties. "Their protests," Creel wrote, "were inspired by speculators who hoped in this way to drive up the price of the land." The ministry fully supported Creel's position, called the sale legal, and only included a vague declaration that the "legitimate rights" of the Indians should not be violated. The federal government, however, was not ready to take any action to protect these "legitimate rights." The Indians were told once again to recur to the governor, who was one of their main opponents.[49]

The success of the Creel government in expropriating the holdings of the Indian villages without encountering much active resistance led the hacendados and the authorities to adopt measures that gave a different dimension to the land problem in Chihuahua. The authorities no longer confined their attacks to Indians in remote regions, but began to stage a frontal attack on what might be called the core of Chihuahuan rural society: some of the most important former military colonies in the state.

Unwritten agreements, which had frequently existed for centuries, were renounced or broken. At the same time, there were attacks on legal guarantees that did have a basis in written law. The attacks on unwritten agreements consisted mainly in abolishing the rights of free communities to graze their cattle on hacienda land. As long as cattle exports were nonexistent, the open range was plentiful, and the fighting strength of free villages was needed to ward off the Apaches, the hacendados had no objection to allowing the cattle of free villages to graze on their large estates. Once cattle exports became of great importance to the economy of the haciendas, however, the hacendados frequently abolished these traditional rights and kept the inhabitants of neighboring free villages from grazing their cattle on the large estates. Sometimes this was done by installing barbed wire around the haciendas, sometimes in even more drastic form by confiscating cattle that found their way onto hacienda land. These measures by the hacendados were all the harder for the free villagers to bear since their access to public lands had also been undermined by the activities of the surveying companies. The second part of the offensive against the free villagers consisted in a direct attack on their ownership of their lands.

With the same stubbornness and endurance with which they had fought the Apaches, the military colonists resorted to every possible legal means to resist the attacks on their lands and their autonomy. They sent protests to the governor, to the Secretaría de Fomento in Mexico City, and to Porfirio Díaz. At times they even hired expensive lawyers and litigated in the courts. They wrote letters of protests to the newspapers and demonstrated in the city of Chihuahua. When all this proved of no avail, they finally revolted and contributed decisively to toppling both the state and the federal governments.

One of the first villages attacked by Creel was the old and prestigious military colony of San Andrés. To many inhabitants of Chihuahua, San Andrés, located on the margins of the western mountains, epitomized the military colony. Reading the memoirs of Joaquín Terrazas, Chihuahua's greatest Indian fighter, is like reading the history of San Andrés.[50] There was scarcely an Indian campaign in which its riflemen, reputed to be the best shots in Chihuahua, did not participate. Nevertheless, a few years after the defeat of the Apaches, Joaquín Terrazas's relatives decided to accomplish what the Apaches could never do: the economic destruction of a substantial part of San Andrés's free villager. In 1904, in the name of 120 Indian inhabitants of San Andrés, their spokesman, Macario Nieto, wrote to the state government of Chihuahua and asked that the municipal lands that belonged to the Indian inhabitants of the village be divided among them. The interim governor, Cortazar, agreed and promised that each of the village's Indians would receive three hectares of land. It was a decision that would give the Indians a measure of security and assure their most urgent needs. Within a few months, however, the governor reversed his decision and sent a message to San Andrés stating that surveyors had found that there was not sufficient land to carry out the planned distribution.[51]

This argument was contested by Nieto, who stated that in reality the municipal authorities wanted "the lands that are ours to be taken over by the rich."[52] In Nieto's eyes, the villagers' main enemy was their own mayor, Lucas Murga, whose family owned the neighboring hacienda of San Juan Guadalupe. Not only had the mayor appropriated many of the common lands for himself, but in order to prevent the villagers from suing, he had stolen their property titles and refused to return them. Protests by the Indians of San Andrés to the state governor were of no avail. An appeal to the federal government drew the standard reply that it was a matter for the governor to decide.

The villagers nevertheless felt that they had another iron in the fire. Nearly two centuries before, in 1735, the owners of the neighboring hacienda of San Juan Guadalupe, under constant siege by the Apaches, had called on the inhabitants of San Andrés to help them in the defense of the hacienda. The villagers had done so, the Apaches were repelled, and the grateful hacendado deeded them a large tract of land. The villagers occupied the land but were not in possession of the deed to it. It is not clear whether they lost the deed, or whether the hacendado, whether on purpose or not, had neglected to give it to them. In 1904, when an official came to survey the lands of San Andrés, the inhabitants asked him to respect the property they had received from the hacienda. Since they could produce no deed or title to the land, the surveyor refused to heed their request. Naively, the villagers then asked the Murga family, which had acquired the hacienda of San Juan Guadalupe, to give them a copy of the deed. It is not surprising that the hacienda's owners refused to consider this request.

Nieto then wrote to the Secretaría de Fomento in Mexico City asking for a copy of their property title from the National Archives. The federal government was as unhelpful in this matter as it had been with respect to the communal lands of the village. It refused either to ask the National Archives for a deed or to suggest to the peasants in what other archives (for instance, the Notarial Archives in Chihuahua) they might find the deed. The correspondence between the village spokesman and the federal government dragged on for three years, between 1904 and 1907. It produced no results for the villagers, with one exception: Nieto himself was given some land. Obviously, the government had hoped to bribe him, but Nieto refused to be bought off. In 1907, the villagers presented their last petition to the federal government. As time passed, they finally gave up any hope of redress from Mexico City. Three years later, the riflemen of San Andrés were among the first to join the forces of a revolutionary leader operating near San Andrés, Francisco (Pancho) Villa.

Buoyed by the success of his campaigns against the free villagers, Creel now felt strong enough to deal with one of the most stubborn and recalcitrant military colonies in the state: Namiquipa. For many years the inhabitants of this old, prestigious military colony had been able to hold on to their lands in spite of massive claims on their property made by one of Chihuahua's wealthiest hacendados, Enrique Muller, a partner of Luis Terrazas's. Muller had gotten hold of bogus titles to properties in Namiquipa as well as in Galeana in 1865 but had enormous difficulty in forcing the inhabitants to give up their properties. Despite the demands of Muller and his heirs, the villagers had still managed to hold on to some of their lands, but with Creel at the helm of Chihuahua, they faced final defeat. Applying his own municipal land law of 1905, Creel now proceeded to sell large chunks of their remaining municipal property. In a letter to Porfirio Díaz, 120 inhabitants of Namiquipa wrote in July 1908 that "the government of the state has shown its contempt for us by stealing our lands, our pastures, and our woods, which we need in order to practice agriculture and livestock raising."[53]

Once again, as they had done so frequently in earlier times, the inhabitants of Namiquipa told of the long, heroic history of their village. Every piece of their land had been paid for with the blood of their ancestors: "All neighboring haciendas had been abandoned because of the constant danger of aggression by the barbarians between 1832 and 1860 and only Namiquipa remained to fight the barbarians and to constitute a lonely bastion of civilization in this remote region." They insisted that the merits of their ancestors consisted, not only in fighting the Apaches, but in the support they had given to the Liberals, and especially Luis Terrazas, in campaigns against the Conservatives and the French. Their letter to Díaz was a call for help, a call on the president to respect the promise he had given them in 1889 to safeguard their lands. It concluded by stating, "if you do not grant us your protection, we would have to leave our homes and emigrate in order to be able to survive."

What comes out clearly from this petition is that the villagers were victims, not only of Creel's land law, but of his reorganization of the state government as well. Previous petitions by the village had been signed by its municipal authorities. Creel had dismissed their elected officials and appointed his own men to municipal offices, so that the villagers could no longer count on the help of the mayor and the village administration.

The villagers first attempted to resist these attacks on their properties by writing protests to newspapers and staging nonviolent demonstrations. A spokesman for the inhabitants of Namiquipa, Delfino Ochoa from Bocoyna, and a number of other local leaders wrote letters describing the attacks against them and calling for redress to the opposition newspaper editor Silvestre Terrazas, whose *El Correo de Chihuahua* published all of them. Fifty inhabitants of Namiquipa staged a protest demonstration in Chihuahua. All to no avail.[54]

What is remarkable about the free villagers' resistance in the years between 1905 and 1908 is not its emergence but rather its limited scope in comparison to the wave of uprisings that had swept Chihuahua in the years 1891 to 1895. This contrast is all the more striking in that attacks on the autonomy and the land of the free villagers were greater and far more brutal after 1905 than they had been before. In the 1890s, only a few villages lost their municipal autonomy. Creel's laws, however, affected every village in the state. Nevertheless, the immediate reaction of the villagers to the harsh measures taken against them by Creel was far more restrained than their violent reaction to the relatively mild measures implemented in the 1890s.

This was partly because of the very different economic situations in the state in the two periods. Whereas the years between 1891 and 1895 had been years of recession and bad harvests, there was a great economic boom between 1905 and 1907. Demand for labor outstripped supply, and wages were rising. Expropriated villagers could find work in neighboring mines, in the cotton fields of the Laguna in neighboring Coahuila, or at even better-paid jobs across the border in the United States.

In 1891–95, Chihuahua's oligarchy was divided, and one of its main representatives, Luis Terrazas, the traditional patron of the villagers of western Chihuahua, was surreptitiously supporting their rebellion. Between 1905 and 1907, the villagers faced a united oligarchy, and their traditional patrons had turned against them. Perhaps an even more important explanation for the relative passivity of Chihuahua's villagers was the fact that Creel's political and economic measures succeeded in undermining village solidarity; they deepened cleavages within the communities. By replacing elected officials with his own appointees, Creel utilized existing divisions within villages for his own ends. His municipal land law of 1905, from which not only hacendados but wealthier villagers allied to his administration profited, further exacerbated these divisions. San Andrés was by no means the only village where a polarization took place between the poorest and the richer inhabitants, with the latter controlling the municipality and profiting from the expropriation of the poorest members of the community. In a similar way, Creel was able to divide what had once been the united community of Cuchillo Parado, the lands of which were threatened by a close associate of Luis Terrazas's, Carlos Muñoz.[55]

In 1903, when the villagers created an Association of Inhabitants of Cuchillo Parado in order to ward off Muñoz's attack on their land, they elected two men as their leaders and representatives, Toribio Ortega and Ezequiel Montes. Ortega was in many ways predestined to become a leader of his village. He belonged to one of the 31 families that had originally received land from Benito Juárez in 1865. His natural intelligence and leadership qualities were enhanced by his relatively higher degree of education and knowledge of the world beyond the village border. In 1884, Ortega had left his home to become an apprentice in a department store in the city of Chihuahua. Two years later, he returned to Cuchillo Parado and set up his own store. His store soon went bankrupt, perhaps because a hacendado expropriated the villagers' lands, causing them to lose buying power.[56] Ortega migrated to the United States, worked there for one year as a laborer, saved some money, and returned to Cuchillo Parado to buy some land and establish himself as a relatively well situated landowner, already recognized as a leader by many of the villagers.

His authority was soon challenged by an outsider who settled in the village: Ezequiel Montes. According to a village chronicler, he was "a gypsy without a fatherland."[57] He arrived in the village in 1890 as a liquor salesman "who played boring popular songs on an old harp in order to entertain the laborers who came to buy his liquor." He soon settled in the village, and since he was a man of "uncommon intelligence and refined hypocrisy" as well as an excellent speaker who ably "nurtured people's passions," he soon became an influential leader in Cuchillo Parado. In 1903, he was elected together with Toribio Ortega to head the Association of Inhabitants of Cuchillo Parado, whose primary aim was to ward off the hacendado Muñoz's attempt to take over the village lands. The unity between the two men disappeared when Creel co-opted Montes, appointing him mayor of Cuchillo Parado. Montes became a typical cacique, employed his newfound power and official support against the villagers, and began expropriating their lands.[58]

While Creel was a master at manipulating village divisions for his own ends, he rarely created them. Rather, he utilized existing cleavages. Unlike the Indian communities of central and southern Mexico, the military colonies of Chihuahua had never been egalitarian in character. Until the promulgation of the reform laws of the 1850s, the *ejidos* (public lands) of the core areas of Mexico were common property and could be neither sold nor bought, but land was more freely marketed in the north, although some restrictions existed and some communal land could not be sold. As a result, social differences in the northern communities were far greater than among the free peasantry in the rest of Mexico. This was clearly the case in Namiquipa. In 1892, when the villagers asked that Porfirio Díaz divide among them the lands that until then had belonged to the community, they did not ask for an egalitarian division. Different families controlled different amounts of land, which they wanted Díaz to adjudicate to them, and each family contributed a sum proportional to the land it occupied in order to pay the fees of the lawyer who finally secured Díaz's approval of their claims in 1893.[59] This division between rich and poor, however, was only one of the many cleavages that characterized the village.

Soon after the end of the Apache wars, new immigrants began settling in the village. In 1889, 32 of 195 families were recent immigrants. Their number had swelled to 111 by 1900. The divisions among the villagers had become so deep that by that time, the mayor did not know how to deal with them and went to the federal government for advice. Once the municipal lands had been divided, the mayor asked, should these newcomers also receive land? The mayor had pinpointed a problem that existed in his village, but his calls for advice from either the federal or the state government were more than naive. Neither gave him any advice, since neither had the slightest intention of ever dividing the lands of Namiquipa among its inhabitants.[60]

The Hesitations of the Federal Government

In the eyes of the state authorities, the mayor of Namiquipa's letter only emphasized the illegitimacy of many of the villagers' claims and revealed the scope offered by these divisions for an attack on traditional village structures and rights. In 1908, the attitudes of the state and federal governments toward Chihuahua's free villagers began to diverge. As dissatisfaction with the Díaz administration began to increase in much of Mexico, some officials of the federal government began to worry about a possible uprising in Chihuahua. They had not forgotten how effective the 100 or so men of Tomóchi had been when they had kept more than 1,000 federal troops at bay. The federal authorities on the one hand and Creel on the other envisaged two very different strategies to contain mounting rural discontent in Chihuahua. The federal government showed a readiness to make limited concessions to the free villagers: further expropriations of village lands should cease, and the status quo should be observed. Creel, on the other hand, felt that any concessions to the villagers would only encourage them to become more recalcitrant and rebellious. He advocated a policy of absolute inflexibility.

These different approaches were clearly expressed when the first serious clash between state and federal governments occurred with respect to the land question in 1908. At issue was the complaint of one of the oldest military colonies in Chihuahua, the village of Janos in the Galeana district in Chihuahua.

In August 1908, the villagers of Janos sent their spokesman and leader, Porfirio Talamantes, to Mexico City to lodge a protest with the federal government against the policies of Governor Creel. The villagers had asked that the community lands be divided among them. Instead, Creel's appointee, the mayor, was selling off most of the land to outsiders and wealthy villagers. In a bitterly worded protest, Talamantes called on the federal government for redress. He insisted that the division of communal lands was a federal and not a state responsibility and demanded that the Mexico City administration see to it that the village inhabitants and not outsiders should benefit from the division of communal lands. "We shall never receive land under the present circumstances," he concluded, "because outsiders and even foreigners will always get preference. We simply ask for the application of the federal laws of June 25, 1856. The owners of the colony of Fernández Lcal [Americans who had bought land in Chihuahua], located two leagues from Janos, are enjoying a comfortable life in the United States, while we, who suffered from the invasion of barbarians, whom our fathers fought, cannot keep our land."[61]

The Secretaría de Fomento, the branch of the federal government in charge of public lands, was at first inclined to dismiss the whole matter. It had consulted with Creel, who had written the Mexico City officials that Talamantes was a "disturber of the public order" who had been punished for his misdeeds. These "misdeeds" amounted to sending a petition to the governor accusing the mayor of Janos of being "a coward . . . a man capable of petty vengeance . . . who forced someone to confess either through inquisitorial means or by making false promises." As a result, Talamantes had been fined 30 pesos for "lack of respect for the authorities." In addition, Creel wrote, Talamantes did not represent the inhabitants of Janos, who approved of the division of their municipal lands.[62] The Secretaría accordingly sent a short note to Talamantes telling him that it would not consider his demands, since he did not speak for the inhabitants of his village, and since all of them welcomed the land distribution that Creel was carrying out.

A few days later, the Secretaría received a letter of protest signed by over 100 inhabitants of Janos. They wrote that Creel's statement—that their lands were being divided among them and that they fully agreed with that division—was a lie. There was no land division; the mayor was simply taking the best village lands for himself. They protested against the expropriation of their lands, insisted that Talamantes was their genuine representative, and told the federal government that the state law being applied to their village was illegal and that only the federal government had the authority to dispose of their communal property.[63]

This time the federal government did act. It asked Creel for a copy of the state's land law, stating that the federal authorities had never known of its existence (a somewhat strange argument, since more than four years had passed since the law had been signed and adopted by the Chihuahuan legislature, and countless protests against its application had been sent to Mexico City). After studying the law, the Secretaría came to a conclusion that, in the Porfirian setting, was nothing short of revolutionary. Undersecretary Andrés Aldasoro wrote Creel in March 1909 that his municipal land law of 1905 was "unconstitutional, since the transformation of all properties belonging to civilian communities is a federal matter."[64]

All property titles based on the 1905 law were illegal, Aldasoro said, and the application of that law to Janos was highly irregular. Creel was asked to take measures to correct the irregularities his government had created. A month later, the Secretaría sent an engineer named López Moctezuma to Janos to examine the situation in the village. The inhabitants of Janos were told of this decision, although Aldasoro's message to Creel that his land law was unconstitutional was kept a secret. Talamantes and his villagers were jubilant, feeling that they had finally won a victory in their long and arduous struggle.

Labeling Creel's law unconstitutional and sending a federal official to reverse his decision was a slap in the face to one of the most powerful men in Mexico. There is no clear explanation why the Secretaría de Fomento acted as it did. It had waited more than four years before even examining the law. It is doubtful that Aldasoro's boss, Olegario Molina, the minister, was motivated by an objection in principle to land expropriations. Molina, the most powerful cacique of the southeastern state of Yucatán, was himself one of the great expropriators of village lands in his native region. Were the attacks on Creel simply an expression of the constant struggle of rival cliques for power in Mexico? Was the administration of President Díaz genuinely concerned that attacks on villages in Chihuahua could lead to another Tomóchi? Díaz seems to have been involved in some way in the matter, for in his reply to Aldasoro's letter, Creel referred to the indications of the "Señor Presidente."

Creel's Counteroffensive

Creel's response was at first moderate and even humble and obsequious in tone. He stated that he was preoccupied by Aldasoro's letter, was consulting his lawyers, and would do whatever was necessary to change and adapt the law to the Mexican constitution. At the end of his reply, however, beneath its obsequiousness, there was a clear-cut threat. He stated that all property titles in Chihuahua were based on the same principles as the 1905 law. "Revoking that law," he wrote, "was a grave matter," and he spoke of the possibility of "serious disorders" and "great harm," since approximately 10,000 people had benefited from this law.[65]

Couched in diplomatic and deferential language, Creel had formulated a warning that the federal government understood all too well. A short time after he received Creel's reply, Aldasoro caved in. In a private letter to Creel, Aldasoro thanked him for his "goodwill," stated that he was going on a trip to Europe, and offered to bring Creel anything he asked for from any country he visited.[66] Although Creel had only promised to examine whatever legal possibilities existed for changing his law, the Secretaría never challenged him again. López Moctezuma, the official who was to have gone to Janos to hear the villagers' grievances, first went to see Creel and asked the governor whether he should proceed with his visit to the village. Creel told him, López Moctezuma reported to the Secretaría, "that he did not find it convenient that I should go to the village, since once the villagers whom Mr. Talamantes is representing see that the government is giving them some help, and that as a result of their petition this ministry is sending an official, this would be sufficient to increase their demands, which could finally lead to unrest in the village, which for thousands of motives should be prevented."[67] The Secretaría did not even notify the villagers that López Moctezuma's visit, on which they had based so many hopes, had been canceled.

Both Creel and the mayor now felt that they should show the villagers of Janos once and for all who was master of Chihuahua and how high the costs of protest were. In a letter dated nearly a year later, in May 1910, the villagers wrote that the mayor, "an official without a human heart, unjust and cruel with everyone who opposes him, a man who is the subject of terrible accusations, and who in spite of this still leads our now ruined village," was cutting off their water supplies and charging for use of pasture and wood that for a century the villagers had always been able to obtain free of charge. "In this year of 1910," they concluded, "when our independence will be a hundred years old, in our village we are treated far worse than when the viceroys ruled over our land."[68]

Now that the federal government had capitulated to his demands, Creel felt encouraged to proceed even more harshly against every rebellious village.

In 1908, when the federal government had begun to question Creel's conduct in Janos, it had expressed similar doubts about his policies in Namiquipa. Federal authorities had not, as they had done before, played the usual ping-pong game with the protests of the villagers of Namiquipa against the confiscation of their lands, and told them to submit their claims either to the judicial authorities or to the governor. The Secretaría de Fomento had on the contrary written Creel and asked him for an explanation of events in Namiquipa. When the governor sent no reply, the Secretaría became insistent and time and time again reminded him that it wanted his opinion.[69]

Creel's hesitation in dealing with the case of Namiquipa was no coincidence. Not only was this community one of the oldest and most prestigious military colonies in Chihuahua, with documented claims going back to the Spanish colonial period. It was also one of the few instances in Chihuahua, if not the only one, where Porfirio Díaz had ratified a village's claims in 1893. Nevertheless, after Aldasoro's surrender, Creel felt the time had also come to put an end to Namiquipa's demands, and he sent a 14-page memorandum to the federal government listing "offenses" that the inhabitants of Namiquipa had committed over many years by refusing to hand over most of their lands to Enrique Muller. He considered it "monstrous" that villagers could lay claim to so much land. He dealt with the thorny problem of Díaz's recognition of the villagers' claim by denying that such a recognition had taken place. The Secretaría had written him that it had sent back all documents from Namiquipa to the state government, and Creel stated that he could not find any record of the 1893 decision in the Chihuahuan archives. Even if such records had existed, he doubted whether the present inhabitants of the village could lay claim to being the descendants of the original military colonists.

The main thrust of Creel's argument was that while lawyers might still examine the legality of the village's claims, the federal government should do everything in its power to discourage the villagers from further pressing their claims. "The government should do nothing," he wrote, "which might inspire the inhabitants of Namiquipa to continue with their complaints and the protests that they have so frequently sent to the government in the hope of confirming their claim to the sixty-four *sitios* that they demand."[70]

The last documents to be found in the files for Namiquipa and Janos are letters from the Secretaría written in January 1911, when most of Chihuahua was in the throes of revolution and Madero's army was on the verge of decisive victory, saying that new land surveys should be done both in Janos and Namiquipa.[71] It was a belated and now useless acknowledgment by the federal government that there might have been some justification for the villagers' claims. In the meantime, both villages had evolved into hotbeds of rebellion, and Talamantes had become one of the local revolutionary leaders.

Creel's Last Victory

In theory, the federal government had not capitulated to Creel. It had not given up its attitude that Creel's law was unconstitutional, that village lands should be divided among the villagers rather than sold, and that the ultimate authority in making decisions about village lands rested with the federal government rather than with the state authorities. In practice, however, it kept its reservations about Creel's land law a secret, and those most affected by it, the inhabitants of the free villages, were never told that the federal government even mildly disapproved of the way they were being treated by Creel and his administration. With the federal government effectively off his back, Creel's relentless attacks on the free villagers of Chihuahua became even more virulent, especially where his own personal interests were concerned. Creel never showed any compunction about problems such as possible conflicts of interests. Two old Chihuahuan military colonies located in the northeastern part of the state, San Carlos and San Antonio, had for nearly a century pastured their livestock on lands that Creel, who owned the huge nearby hacienda of Los Orientales, claimed as his own. In 1908, without any warning, Creel's hacienda administrators told the villagers that they would no longer be allowed to graze their cattle on the pastures they had used for so long.

More than 100 peasants from San Carlos and San Antonio then sent a bitter letter of protest to the federal government.[72] Like other former military colonists in Chihuahua, they insisted that they had earned the right to their land with their blood. San Carlos had received its lands from the state government in 1829, and San Antonio in 1852. Their one obligation in return had been to fight the Apaches, and this they had done with zeal and energy. They recounted the dangerous lives their ancestors had led, facing the possibility of Indian attacks almost daily. In 1872 and in 1879, they had each time captured more than 100 "barbarians," whom they had handed over to armed government forces who had come to fight the Apaches. The villagers not only asked for redress and for protection from Creel's hacienda officials, they also requested the government to give them title to their lands.

Creel's reaction was swift. The mayor appointed by Creel wrote to the jefe político, who was also a Creel appointee, who in turn informed the federal authorities that no villager had ever protested lack of access to their pastureland. At the same time, Creel sent surveyors to the villages to apply his law of 1905 and to sell the villagers' lands.

Unlike other military colonists, the inhabitants of San Carlos and San Antonio decided they would work within the system. They sent a delegation of three men to Mexico City, who hired an expensive lawyer, General Manuel F. Loera, who had close connections to Olegario Molina, the head of the Secretaría de Fomento. Unlike other lawyers, who took money from villagers and then did nothing for them, Loera was ready to work for the sums paid to him. He sent a personal appeal to Molina, presented the villagers' petition to the Secretaría,[73] and sent a surveyor to both villages so as to be able to propose a concrete plan of action to the government. The surveyor went to San Carlos and San Antonio, drafted a plan for the division of the village lands in accordance with the colonists' wishes, and also suggested that vacant lands in the neighborhood of San Antonio should be distributed to 228 landless families who were living in the vicinity.[74]

Having just capitulated to Creel over Janos and Namiquipa, the Secretaría was not about the renew the struggle with one of Mexico's most powerful men over the fate of two obscure villages. Officials wrote Loera that his surveyor's plan could not be accepted, that he had no authority to send anyone to Chihuahua, and that the villagers would have to clear things with the governor.[75] Neither Loera nor the villagers were ever told that the federal authorities considered Creel's measures illegal. Only in August 1910 was a short note written to the governor stating that in the opinion of Porfirio Díaz, village lands should be divided rather than sold.[76] The governor did not bother to reply. With the same vindictiveness he had shown in the case of Janos, Creel took his revenge on the protesting villagers of San Antonio and San Carlos.

The surveyor Creel sent to carry out the expropriation of most of the villages' lands was accompanied, a report sent to Porfirio Díaz noted, "by workers whose task it was to place barbed wire along a line established by the surveyor." In addition, Creel replaced the mayor of San Carlos, who had sided with the villagers.[77]

In spite of all these efforts, Creel's men encountered such strong resistance that they could not implement their plan; seeing that the courts would not help them, the villagers armed themselves and told the invaders to go back to where they came from. Prudently, Creel decided to tolerate this attitude.

Creel now proceeded against the villagers at another level. For years, their cattle had been grazing on his lands and his on theirs. Overnight, he took away their grazing rights, and when the villagers continued to send some of their cattle onto his lands, a report to Porfirio Díaz noted, Creel "imprisoned the leader of these disobedient peasants, took away their cattle without paying them a cent for them, and only freed their leader after keeping him in jail for one month and after a long sermon, in which he told him that one of the reasons he would prevail was that he had 100 times more land than they had. . . . This man became the leader of the revolution in these two villages in 1910."[78]

Creel's persecution of Chihuahua's free villagers was not owing to cupidity alone. It was closely linked to the concept of order and progress that Creel shared with the small oligarchy of *científicos* whose influence was decisive in Porfirian Mexico. In his eyes, "progress" meant improving education, introducing the newest technology (i.e., electricity, street cars, etc.), granting paid vacations to civilian employees to improve their efficiency, and other such positivist reforms. It also meant the elimination of what Creel considered to be inefficient and antimodern groups—for example, the free villagers. In his opinion, only large estates and middle-sized ranches were effective and efficient producers. This explains his unusual display of emotion in his letter to the federal government concerning the demands of the inhabitants of Namiquipa, which he called "monstrous." Inefficient villagers, he obviously felt, had no right to such large resources.[79]

Creel and the Chihuahuan Middle Class

While the majority of free villagers had undergone a relentless series of attacks since 1884, significant segments of other social groups in Chihuahua, outside of the ruling oligarchy, had long benefited from the changes in the state during the Porfirian era. This was true for a large number of what, for want of a better term, might be called the middle class. It comprised such heterogeneous groups as small shopkeepers, small ranchers whose properties were larger than those of subsistence-oriented peasants, artisans, miners, teachers, and better-off employees of domestic and foreign corporations. As the economy developed, their numbers rose and so probably did their incomes. In three of the main districts in Chihuahua, 75 percent of small industrial establishments and artisan shops were founded between 1898 and 1907.[80] In Ciudad Chihuahua, 87 percent of such establishments began business between 1898 and 1906.[81] The number of industrial workers (including miners) rose from 13,566 in 1895 to 24,333 in 1910, while the number of employees rose from 501 in 1895 to 4,399 in 1910.

The middle classes certainly benefited from the "modernization" that occurred in many parts of Chihuahua, a process in which Enrique Creel played an important role. Its manifestations were apparent all over Chihuahua: telegraph lines were built and electric lighting established in the state's major cities. New, modern construction could be seen in the capital city of Chihuahua, and the state's most distinguished educational institution, the Literary and Scientific Institute, took on new pupils and expanded its curriculum. In Chihuahua, primary education developed at a more rapid pace than elsewhere in Mexico. By the end of the Porfirian era, the literacy rate had jumped from 19 to 28 percent.[82]

In Chihuahua's villages, part of the middle class shared the profits from the expropriation of former military colonists with the oligarchy. They too were able to acquire lands that impoverished peasants were forced to sell. Nevertheless, even during the economic boom, a strong opposition developed among a not-insignificant sector of Chihuahua's middle classes. Some of the most embittered opponents of the regime were men who might be designated village notables, who, thanks to either greater wealth, greater literacy, or simply personal prestige, had been elected by their communities to direct their affairs. Once Creel abolished municipal autonomy, they were replaced by men the governor himself appointed.

One such village headman who became a relentless foe of the Creel administration, which he finally helped to overthrow, was Heliodoro Arias Olea of the town of Bachiniva. Sometime before Terrazas and Creel assumed the governorship of Chihuahua, Arias Olea had been displaced from his position as mayor by a neighboring hacendado, Luis J. Comaduran. When Terrazas became governor, Arias Olea sent a letter of protest to the state administration in the name of the villagers of Bachiniva, describing how the mayor, together with a close ally, Pedro Baray, exercised power over "the life and death" of the village's inhabitants. The petition accused Comaduran and Baray of having assumed control of irrigation installations in Bachiniva. When a neighboring hacienda claimed some village lands known as Rancho Viejo, the mayor told the villagers that he would protect their rights. In order to do so, he asked for and received from the community's inhabitants all deeds and documents that constituted proof of Bachiniva's possession of these lands. But soon the documents in Comaduran's care disappeared, the neighboring hacienda received control of Rancho Viejo, and the mayor obtained a large bribe. In addition, the villagers accused the municipal authorities of keeping all village revenues for themselves, so that no money remained to pay for a school.[83] Opponents of Comaduran and Baray were intimidated, and at times murdered, either by servants from Comaduran's Hacienda del Carmen or by four "bandits" who lived in the village.

Since Heliodoro Arias Olea had supported Terrazas during his fight for supremacy in Chihuahua, Terrazas allowed new elections to take place in 1904, and Arias Olea once more became mayor of Bachiniva. His administration did not, however, last long. Creel felt no sense of obligation to Terrazas's former ally, and he reversed the electoral results and again gave power to Comaduran and Baray. Arias Olea thus once again led the villagers' opposition to the government, and he did so in a way that particularly angered Governor Creel. Arias Olea was an amateur poet, and at a public meeting, he recited a poem directed against both Porfirio Díaz and Enrique Creel. After praising Mexico's national heroes— Hidalgo, Morelos, and Juárez—he wrote:

> The basic constitution for which you gave your blood and for which you died
>   has been torn to shreds like a flower battered by a hurricane.
> There are no individual guarantees anymore. Not even fragments of justice
>   remain.
> It is being sold in the courts as the holy sacraments were sold in the church.
> The rulers commit thousands of arbitrary acts; your laws are myths to them.
> They make and unmake villages and cities, and they have become kings.
> In Chihuahua, the result is even worse. Without recurring to the farce of elec-
>   tions, Enrique Creel, thanks to his millions, has assumed the governorship.
> As soon as he began to control our destinies, his evil tendencies began.[84]

It did not take long for Creel to hear about the poem. Heliodoro Arias Olea was arrested and sentenced to spend one year in Mexico's most terrible prison, the subterranean dungeons of San Juan de Ulúa off the port city of Veracruz. His spirit unbroken, Arias Olea wrote another poem castigating Governor Creel and the Porfirian government while in prison.[85]

The prison guards listened to the poem, and the next day, they took Arias Olea to a special cell, saying that he was mad and that they would cure him. For weeks, he was subjected to diverse kinds of torture. For many hours, he was put into a small room where the guards had installed four smoking ovens, so that the smoke nearly suffocated him. He was then sent to another room, prevented from sleeping for days, and cement was poured onto the floor. Electrodes were put onto the toilet seat, so that he suffered an electric shock when sitting down. Attempts were made to poison his food. The room in which he slept was converted into a toilet, with prisoners putting their excrement into it, so that the stench became unbearable. And still Heliodoro Arias Olea remained unbroken. When he was finally released, his sentence having expired, he told a commission of five officers who had come to take him from prison, "I may be near death, but I am not a worm." He so impressed them that they gave him a standing ovation. A huge crowd welcomed him back when he arrived in his hometown of Bachiniva. On that same day, Creel expressed to a friend the hope that Arias Olea had become a broken man; "Is he finally regretting his libelous remarks?" he asked him. Three years later, Arias Olea answered the question by becoming one of the leaders of the revolution in Bachiniva.[86]

Some of the most bitter opponents of the government belonged to a social group generally not prone to revolutionary sympathies: shopkeepers. The scion of one of Mexico's wealthiest hacendado families, Pablo Martínez del Río, went so far as to characterize the revolution as a movement of independent peasants led by shopkeepers.[87] This was an exaggeration, but there is little doubt that many Mexican shopkeepers had reasons for hostility to the government. Village shopkeepers such as Toribio Ortega in Cuchillo Parado were frequently ruined when their clients lost their land and with it their buying power. Other merchants could not prosper because hacienda peons and even industrial workers were frequently paid in scrip redeemable only at the company stores. Merchants who established themselves in large cities had difficulty competing with foreign shopkeepers, who in many cases were exempt from paying taxes.

Teachers made up another "middle-class" group, but one that benefited from Creel's reforms and his expansion of the school system in the state. Yet they produced some of the revolution's most able leaders. One reason is that teachers deeply resented the lack of freedom that the Creel administration imposed on the state.

Prior to the assumption of power by Terrazas and Creel, many local notables had benefited from some aspects of the political system Díaz had established in Chihuahua. As a result of his having removed Terrazas from power and turned it over to a rival clique, the situation of these notables had significantly improved. Both sides, Terrazas and his rivals, had vied for the political support of these notables and were willing to make concessions in order to secure it. Once Creel became governor and abolished municipal elections, however, local notables lost practically all bargaining power. Creel's control of the judicial system made it very difficult for anyone not connected to his administration to win a court case or for lawyers who were not part of a clique called "el Universal" to operate with any degree of success.[88]

Apart from their economic and political grievances, two ideological tendencies seem to have fueled the opposition of the middle classes to both the Creel administration at the local level and the Díaz administration at the national one. The first was a nostalgia for democratic institutions that had in fact existed during the heyday of the frontier in Chihuahua. The other was economic nationalism. In a report to the State Department in 1910, the U.S. consul in Chihuahua estimated "anti American feeling general over state particularly cities and along railways."[89] There were many ostensible reasons for this anti-American attitude: the huge economic influence of U.S. enterprises in Chihuahua; the privileges enjoyed by foreigners; and the discrimination to which Mexicans were subjected when looking for work in American-owned enterprises and when crossing the border into the United States. Anti-Americanism was especially widespread in the Galeana district, where Mormon colonists had settled and incurred antagonism because of their religion and their way of life.[90] Anti-American nationalism did not, however, express itself in manifestations of xenophobia as it did during the Boxer Rebellion in China. Mexicans who crossed the border tended to admire both the greater economic wealth of the United States and its democratic institutions.

The opposition of large segments of Chihuahua's middle classes to the Terrazas and Creel administration of the state was paralleled by a similar opposition of the industrial working class in Chihuahua, whose numbers had tripled between 1895 and 1910. More than any social group in Chihuahua, they responded favorably to the radical propaganda of the Partido Liberal Mexicano (PLM), and the one type of organization they were allowed to form (unions were not permitted), mutual aid societies, soon became radicalized. Among these industrial workers, two groups would play a particularly important role during the Mexican revolution: the miners, who constituted about a third of the industrial working force in Chihuahua, and the state's railwaymen. While these two groups shared the grievances of all industrial workers with regard to the Terrazas and Creel regime—resentment of its repressive policies with regard to unions and indignation at the higher wages paid to foreign workers, with a corresponding surge in nationalism—both miners and railwaymen had special grievances of their own. What the miners resented was the fact that so many of them were dismissed by their employers during the economic crisis of 1907 and 1908. Railwaymen were less affected by unemployment, but all the more by the privileges given to U.S. railroad employees, who frequently did not even speak Spanish, but were preferred to their Mexican counterparts, not only receiving higher wages but also having greater access to higher status in the railway system.

Chihuahua's Radical Opposition

Until 1907, political opposition in Chihuahua expressed itself in two very different ways. The first was unsuccessful revolutionary activities centered around the only existing, although illegal, opposition political formation in the state, the PLM.[91] The other was a far more diffuse manifestation of political opposition centered around the newspaper *El Correo de Chihuahua*.

The PLM was founded in 1901 by a group of intellectuals disillusioned by Porfirio Díaz's close relationships to the Mexican clergy and his gradual abandonment of the original anticlerical policies of the Mexican liberal movement. The party soon became far more radical than the Juárez liberals had ever been. Under the leadership of two brothers, Ricardo and Enrique Flores Magón, it advocated prohibiting the reelection of the president and limiting presidential terms to four years. It called for radical limits to the influence of foreigners by obligating those who invested in Mexico to become Mexican citizens. It advocated granting industrial workers an eight-hour day and raising their daily wage to eight pesos. It also called for far-reaching land reform and the breakup of the largest estates. The PLM's newspaper, *Regeneración*, was soon suppressed by the government. The Flores Magón brothers fled to the United States, where they continued publishing their newspaper and smuggling it into Mexico. By 1905–6, the party was calling for the revolutionary overthrow of the Díaz regime and planned a series of revolutionary uprisings. In Chihuahua, it had a strong influence among industrial workers and the middle class, but far less impact on the rural population. Indeed, Chihuahua became one of the main targets of the PLM's revolutionary strategy.

The Flores Magóns drew up plans for simultaneous attacks from Mexico and the United States on the border city of Ciudad Juárez in Chihuahua by Mexican sympathizers of the liberal movement living in the United States and by supporters in Mexico. Concrete plans for such an uprising were soon elaborated, and Ricardo Flores Magón went to the border to coordinate them. The liberal leaders did not know that Enrique Creel had set up a whole network of American and Mexican informers, who had penetrated their ranks and knew exactly what they intended to do.[92] A large number of the Mexican conspirators were arrested on Creel's order in Chihuahua, while U.S. police pursued and later prosecuted the Flores Magón brothers on charges of violating U.S. neutrality laws. Later plans for an attack by Flores Magón sympathizers on the town of Casas Grandes in Chihuahua were also betrayed to the authorities by informers in the Magonist ranks sent there by Creel. The plot was unsuccessful, and its leader, Juan Sarabia, fell into government hands.

The imprisonment of its leaders did not prevent the PLM from continuing to have great influence in Chihuahua. In spite of government restrictions, control of the mails, and so on, *Regeneración* continued to circulate throughout Chihuahua and was bolstered by financial contributions from people whose commitment not only angered but puzzled Enrique Creel. "Had they had to pay a 25 centavos tax to the government . . . they would have cried to high heaven, but many of them have deprived their children of bread in order to send five pesos to the Flores Magón," he commented bitterly. "This social and political phenomenon is worth studying for the effect that it has produced on certain classes of society."[93]

In spite of their support among industrial workers and parts of the middle classes in Chihuahua, the Magonistas failed to unleash a revolution. There were some obvious reasons for the liberal failure: the infiltration of their movement by government agents and the persecution they suffered on both sides of the border by both Mexican and U.S. authorities. Yet infiltration and persecution do not provide a sufficient explanation. In part their calls for revolution came at the wrong time; 1905 was still a year of economic boom, and for many industrial workers, as well as for many dissatisfied members of the middle classes, economic opportunities diminished the negative impact of Creel's political and economic measures.

A perhaps even more important explanation for the failure of the liberals' tactics was their belief in spontaneous upheavals. While *Regeneración* did carry out political agitation, the liberals did not wait for the kind of general popular political awakening and politicization that tends to precede any genuine revolution. The political party they founded, based on intellectual leaders, newspapers, and secret clubs, was more in tune with European than Mexican traditions. The industrial workers constituted a new class in Mexican history and had no difficulties in accepting these new forms of organization. But large segments of the middle classes, and above all the peasantry, were used to a different kind of political organization, with roots in the nineteenth century. It was based on leadership by a charismatic local caudillo rather than by intellectuals. Moreover, revolutions are generally preceded by strong divisions at the top, which by 1905 had not yet come about in Mexico. When all of these conditions were finally met in 1910, revolution broke out; but it was not led by the intellectuals of the PLM. Rather, it was led by a caudillo in the old tradition of nineteenth-century Mexico. His coming was prepared by what could be called the moderate wing of the Chihuahuan opposition.

Chihuahua's Moderate Opposition

The views of the more moderate members of Chihuahua's middle-class opposition were expressed by Silvestre Terrazas in his newspaper *El Correo de Chi-*

huahua. Terrazas, who by 1908 had found many points of agreement with the liberals, came from what might be called the opposite end of the political spectrum from the PLM.[94] The Magonistas had begun their political careers with anticlericalism as their main issue; Silvestre Terrazas began his, at the age of 21, in 1891, as secretary to José de Jesús Ortíz, the bishop of Chihuahua. The bishop soon gained such confidence in Terrazas that he named him editor of the newspaper of the archdiocese of Chihuahua, the *Revista Católica.* Not long after Díaz came to power, a reconciliation between his administration and the church had taken place. As a result, church publications and leaders rarely criticized Díaz or his most important appointees (a situation that began to change in the final years of the Díaz administration). Church leaders nevertheless had a number of points of disagreement with the regime, which they openly expressed, and which seemed to have shaped many of Silvestre Terrazas's attitudes. While the church did not oppose foreign investment in principle, it was highly critical of U.S. penetration into Mexico.[95]

Under Silvestre Terrazas's direction, the *Revista Católica* attacked both U.S. Protestant missionaries and the Mormons, who were making considerable inroads in Chihuahua. It opposed the liberalism inherent in U.S. society and extended its opposition to what it felt were U.S. monopolies controlling much of Mexico's economy. At the same time, some segments of the church had become mildly critical of some agrarian structures in the country. While the church generally supported the existence of large estates in Mexico, its support was far more restrained than in the early nineteenth century, when the church had been one of the largest landowners in the country. Having lost most of its landed property and its special link to hacendados (which in the early nineteenth century had consisted, as in colonial times, in being the main creditor of many landowners), the church was more critical of some aspects of Mexico's agrarian structure. It strongly opposed debt peonage and the sale of alcoholic beverages by landowners to peasants at company stores, and demanded that in accordance with the teachings of the Bible, peasants not be forced to work on Sundays. These ideas continued to influence Silvestre Terrazas. In 1899, he founded *El Correo de Chihuahua,* which absorbed the *Revista Católica* and at first did not greatly deviate from the political opinions of its predecessor. Until 1905, it supported both Porfirio Díaz and Luis Terrazas and only rarely criticized Enrique Creel.

In 1906, there was a radical change in the attitude of Silvestre Terrazas and his newspaper. It began with a "technical" question, the meaning of which went far beyond technicalities. In 1903, before ending his term as governor of Chihuahua, Miguel Ahumada had resigned his office in order to become governor of the state of Jalisco. New elections had then been called, and Luis Terrazas had become governor for a four-year period, which the legislature had established until 1907. Silvestre Terrazas raised the question in his newspaper of whether Luis Terrazas's term should not expire one year earlier—that is, at the same time that Ahumada's term was to end. This was a technicality, but its consequences, had it been accepted, would have been anything but technical. Creel, whom Luis Terrazas had designated as interim governor, would then have been in office illegally. The implied opposition that these questions reflected was transformed into outright opposition when *El Correo* opposed Creel's election to the governorship in 1907 on legal grounds. Mexican and Chihuahuan law stated that only a native-born citizen of Mexico whose parents had also been Mexican citizens could become governor of a state. Since Creel's father, Reuben W. Creel, had been not only a U.S. citizen but U.S. consul in Chihuahua, Silvestre Terrazas asserted that Creel lacked the necessary legal qualifications for the office.

At the same time that Silvestre Terrazas was attacking the rule of both Luis Terrazas and Enrique Creel on legal grounds, he was expressing his support for popular opposition movements not only in Chihuahua but outside the state as well. In 1906, *El Correo* sharply protested the massacre of striking miners by Mexican government forces at Cananea in neighboring Sonora. It protested even more against the presence of an armed force of American volunteers that had come to Cananea to help quell the strike.

Silvestre Terrazas was equally vehement in his support of striking railway mechanics in Chihuahua, who were demanding equal rights, equal pay, and equal working conditions with American railway employees. By 1907 and 1908, *El Correo* had become a forum where every kind of grievance against the state government was aired. Silvestre Terrazas printed letters by villagers from Namiquipa and Cruces protesting the expropriation of their lands. Residents of towns such as Ciudad Juárez, Jiménez, and Namiquipa wrote the newspaper decrying the abuses committed by jefes políticos and mayors.

It is not clear what caused this evolution in Silvestre Terrazas's attitude. Was it owing to a personal change of heart or did it reflect a new policy of the Catholic church, to which Silvestre Terrazas had been so intimately linked, and which would never condemn him? While the majority of clerics continued to support the regime of Porfirio Díaz, which had lifted so many of the restrictions imposed on the church by Juárez and his liberals, its attitude toward Enrique Creel seems to have been more negative. The church hierarchy may have felt that Creel was doing too little to oppose the penetration of American Protestant missionaries in Chihuahua, who in fact were increasingly successful in gaining adherents. Creel did nothing to prevent their propaganda and in fact surreptitiously contributed money to Protestant churches.[96]

As a result of his opposition to the state's political regime, both Silvestre Terrazas and his newspaper now became the objects of increasing repression and persecution.

In April 1907, at the height of his campaign against Creel, Silvestre Terrazas was imprisoned for the first time. More imprisonments would follow in 1909 and 1910. The ostensible reason for his incarceration in 1907 was a libel suit brought by a mayor whom *El Correo* had accused of illegally carrying out searches. Silvestre Terrazas remained in prison for two weeks, after which a judge granted him a writ of *amparo* (restraining order) and he was released.

Economic pressure was also exercised. Creel's Banco Minero withdrew advertising from *El Correo*, as did other enterprises linked to Creel and Luis Terrazas. When a particularly galling issue came out, the governor stationed men around the offices of *El Correo* to buy up all available copies of the paper and thus prevent it from gaining any kind of circulation.[97]

What is striking about this repression is not so much that it took place at all—

this was to be expected in a dictatorship like that of Porfirio Díaz—but its relatively mild character. In a twentieth-century Latin American dictatorship, Silvestre Terrazas would probably have been killed or at least tortured, his house and his office would have gone up in flames, his staff would have been arrested, his family might have disappeared. Silvestre Terrazas's relatively benign treatment did not constitute a complete exception in Mexico. Díaz could be ruthless and savage with opponents from the lower classes of society (around the time Silvestre Terrazas was arrested, dozens of striking workers in the mines of Cananea and the textile mill of Río Blanco had been massacred), but Díaz was more cautious in his treatment of the middle classes. Opposition journalists were imprisoned and at times tortured, but rarely were they killed. Filomeno Mata, perhaps Díaz's most famous opponent among newspapermen, was imprisoned 34 times. This also means that he left prison 33 times, something that would have been unlikely in a latter-day Latin American military dictatorship. Some governors were more ruthless than Díaz, but Creel followed the Mexican dictator's cautious policies. This may have been because Creel himself was not a bloodthirsty man but perhaps also owing to fears that persecuting Silvestre Terrazas too much might antagonize groups within the Catholic church.

Unlike the Magonistas, Silvestre Terrazas never called for a revolution to overthrow the regime, although in 1910 he was quite sympathetic to the Madero revolution. Nevertheless, his paper, because it was legal and had a large and steadily increasing circulation in Chihuahua, played a greater role in galvanizing opposition to the regime than did the Flores Magón and *Regeneración*. In fact, in 1910, Luis Terrazas to a large degree attributed the paternity of the revolution to the agitation of his distant cousin.[98]

The Crisis of 1908–1910

The transformation of dissatisfaction with the existing regime into revolutionary fervor was linked to three distinct phenomena: the large-scale destruction of the economic basis of the free villages by Creel and Terrazas; the great depression of 1908, which seems to have affected Chihuahua more than most of the rest of Mexico; and a political crisis at both the national and regional levels. To these developments within Mexico must be added an evolution of the situation north of the border.

The economic crisis of 1908–10 was the most serious that Porfirian Mexico ever suffered. It affected the whole of the country but was felt most keenly in the northern states, the economies of which were most closely linked to that of the United States. Decreasing prices of silver and copper and recession and financial panic in the United States led to the widespread closing of mines in northern Mexico. One of the largest U.S. mining companies doing business in Mexico, the American Smelting and Refining Company (ASARCO), shut down its mines at Santa Eulalia and Santa Bárbara in Chihuahua, throwing more than 1,000 people out of work. Most mines in the largest mining center in the state, Hidalgo de Parral, also shut down. The economic empire of William C. Greene, an American tycoon who owned a large number of mines, most of them in

Sonora, and had set up vast lumberyards in western Chihuahua, collapsed, greatly increasing the number of unemployed, especially in western Chihuahua.[99]

Many villagers who worked part-time in the mines or in the lumberyards were affected. Previously when enterprises had closed in Chihuahua, unemployed workers had been able to find work elsewhere. They could go to the neighboring states of Sonora and Coahuila or cross the border into the United States. Now, however, Sonora and Coahuila were hit by the same crisis that affected Chihuahua, and Mexican workers were being laid off by the thousands in the southwestern United States. The United States proclaimed a ban on Mexican immigration, and more than 2,000 Mexicans were given railway tickets by their companies to El Paso, where they crossed into Chihuahua, swelling the ranks of the unemployed.

As a last resort, some of the unemployed returned to their native villages to live off the produce of the family fields as long as the crisis lasted. But many discovered that their families had lost their fields because of Creel's land law. And those who still owned land were affected by droughts in both 1908 and 1909.

Not only the unemployed but even workers who managed to hold on to their jobs were profoundly shaken by the crisis. Their wages were drastically cut at a time when food prices were rising because of bad harvests. "The economic situation has been particularly bad," the German consul in Chihuahua reported in 1909, "because of increases in the cost of necessary food and beans. Most food prices have doubled, and beans have gone from 6 to 15 pesos per hectoliter. The purchasing power of the public has been seriously reduced. . . . The population's consumption has been reduced to the most essential foods. The earnings of the workers have been reduced still further, and wages have dropped to between $0.75 and 1 peso a day."[100] This meant that price increases of between 200 and 300 percent were accompanied by wage cuts.

The middle classes of the state were particularly affected by the crisis. Many small enterprises went bankrupt. They had lost many of their clients, whose buying power had run out once they became unemployed, and when merchants attempted to obtain loans to weather the storm, they found that funds were either unavailable or the cost was prohibitive. "Even though the banks have been somewhat more liberal in their loans," the German consul wrote in 1909, "the cost of money has remained quite high and has made business difficult. Even first-rate companies have been unable to obtain funds at less than 10 percent while the interest rates of the banks have been 12 percent per annum, and the rates of the private money lenders have ranged from 18 to 24 percent."[101] The banks restricted most of their credit to companies owned by the oligarchy, and at a time of crisis, they called in their outstanding loans, foreclosing on small owners unable to repay. In other parts of Mexico, regional strongmen, worried by the possible social consequences of the crisis, attempted to secure federal help to alleviate its results or even helped the unemployed themselves. In neighboring Coahuila, one of the state's richest men, Evaristo Madero, called on Porfirio Díaz to set aside funds to help the starving and the poor.[102] His grandson, Francisco Madero, used part of the income from his estates to feed the hungry, regardless of whether they worked on his haciendas or not.[103]

Enrique Creel showed no such concern. In November 1908, he wrote to Díaz saying that because of early frosts, "the harvest of beans has been completely lost, while that of corn has been reduced by half. As a result, the price of basic foodstuffs is very high and causes great harm to the poorest segments of society. . . . The low price of silver is causing great harm to mining in the state and different companies have closed their mines, so that lack of employment is being felt in many mining districts and business is slackening. . . . In general, economic prospects for the next few years are not good."

Unlike Evaristo Madero, Creel did not even mention relief for the needy in his letter. Instead, he concluded, "I am from now on taking prudent and necessary steps to prevent deficit in public spending. With this aim I am reducing the budgets of all municipalities of the state to the most necessary expenses in proportion to probable income."[104] This was the only practical consequence that Creel was willing to draw from the crisis. Moreover, balancing the budget meant not only decreasing expenditures but increasing revenues—that is, taxes. Since the largest foreign companies and the business enterprises belonging to the oligarchy were practically tax-exempt, Creel increased the taxes paid by the lower and middle classes. This occurred precisely at the height of the recession, when they were least able to pay.

The past administration's "tax increases and other acts," the last Porifirian governor of Chihuahua, Miguel Ahumada, wrote to Porfirio Díaz in 1911, "created such a climate of resentment and lack of confidence that if the minister of foreign affairs [Creel] were to come here, his life would be in jeopardy."[105]

As a result of the crisis of 1908 and the policies of Creel and Terrazas, an unprecedented unity among groups that had never collaborated before was created in Chihuahua in opposition to both the state and the federal governments. For the first time, cooperation began to emerge among the urban middle classes, industrial workers, and free villagers.

That unity was reinforced by a bizarre event that contributed to undercutting Creel's legitimacy in the eyes of many of Chihuahua's inhabitants. This was the robbery at the Banco Minero. Perhaps if it had occurred when Chihuahua's economy was booming, when prosperity seemed to be on the rise, it would not have provoked the repercussions it did.

The Robbery of the Banco Minero

The case remains, in many respects, an unsolved mystery.

On March 1, 1908, 300,000 pesos were stolen from the Banco Minero, which was jointly owned by Enrique Creel and his brother Juan. The break-in damaged not only the governor's fortune but his prestige as well. The building where the bank was located also housed his residence. Enormous police activity followed the robbery. Dozens of suspects were arrested, frequently without warrants, and held incommunicado. American detectives were brought in to help the police. Within three weeks, this intensive activity by law enforcement agencies seemed to have paid off. A woman confessed to knowing who the robbers were and stated that she had been paid $5,000 to hide their identity. Five suspects, among them bank employees, were arrested, and one of them soon confessed.[106] While the money was not recovered, the administration's prestige was vindicated by the rapid success of the police.

Within a few days of this "success," Silvestre Terrazas and his newspaper stepped into the fray, the government's case started to crumble, and the governor personally came under a cloud of suspicion. On March 21, *El Correo de Chihuahua* wrote that on the day the robbery occurred, one of the accused had been seen on the Chuviscar Bridge by a number of persons including the jefe político of Chihuahua. At the same time, a number of other witnesses had seen one of the other alleged burglars watching a bullfight. As suspicions against the authorities increased, the case became a political issue. *El Correo's* circulation increased dramatically, and the newspaper was frequently sold out soon after it was printed. Hitherto apolitical organizations, such as the Workers' Mutual Aid Societies, which had been founded with the consent of the governor in order to provide insurance to workers in times of need, began collecting money for the accused. The government's case seemed to break down entirely when Silvestre Terrazas received an anonymous letter signed "CAG" in which the writer claimed to be the real perpetrator of the burglary and as proof of his statement enclosed 100 quartered 1,000-peso bills. The government's case was further discredited when rumors surfaced that the accused had been threatened, tortured, and subjected to simulated executions. These rumors were confirmed after the victory of the revolution, when the arrested men told harrowing tales of having been stood before open graves with an execution squad leveling their rifles at them in an effort to force them to confess. After eight months, the prisoners were finally released. Their sufferings had aroused a wave of sympathy. The wife of one of the prisoners, who had also been arrested, had gone mad, and the wife of another had given birth prematurely in jail.

For a short time, the government seemed to have recovered some of its lost prestige when three new suspects were arrested and confessed to the crime. One of them stated that he had written the anonymous letter to Silvestre Terrazas. It was again Silvestre Terrazas who a few days later dealt a crippling blow to the government. He published correspondence between the accused and their lawyer stating that Creel had promised them privileged conditions in prison as well as money if they would confess to the robbery. The prisoners did not deny their part in the robbery but now demanded that Creel keep his word. Silvestre Terrazas probably knew of, but never published, a letter that the accused subsequently sent to Porfirio Díaz stating that the robbery had in fact taken place at the initiative of Enrique's brother, Juan Creel, who had invited them to his home four weeks before the incident and promised them a large sum of money if they would break into the bank. While the letter was never published before the revolution, rumors to the same effect—namely, that Juan Creel, possibly with the complicity of the governor, had organized the robbery of his own bank—began to surface, further discrediting the administration.

What many people in Chihuahua believed was most clearly voiced by Abraham González, the revolutionary governor of Chihuahua in 1910–11, in a conversation with an American friend. "It seems that after Enrique [Creel] left for Washington, Juan [Creel] got to playing the stock market and lost 200,000 pesos belonging to the bank. To cover the theft, he had a man come down from El Paso and burn the hole into the vault. Then he arrested the two bank clerks. Incidentally, the man who used the torch on the bank vault was accidentally killed the next day."[107]

Silvestre Terrazas's subsequent arrest in 1908 (a jefe político sued him for libel because *El Correo* had printed accusations against the jefe by a disgruntled citizen) fueled suspicions that the governor was trying to hide the truth by muzzling the opposition press. Two weeks later, Silvestre Terrazas was released and resumed his attacks on the Creel administration. The case has never been entirely cleared up, and in spite of the fact that for years after the revolution, the courts continued to deal with it, its most bizarre aspects still baffle researchers. Did Juan Creel in fact break into his own bank? Was there substance to the rumors that he stole the money to pay off gambling debts? Was it an insurance scam? Did he want to circumvent his own brother and the other owners of the bank? Was Enrique Creel involved in any way? Why did the robbers send 100,000 pesos to Silvestre Terrazas? While a final answer to these questions may never be found, there is little doubt that the case had a powerful impact on Chihuahua's public opinion in the years immediately preceding the revolution. It contributed to undercutting the legitimacy of Creel's and Terrazas's rule over Chihuahua and to uniting an extremely heterogeneous opposition against them.

What made this internal crisis in Chihuahua so dangerous for the administration of Porfirio Díaz was that it coincided with a national crisis that his government was facing. That national political crisis between 1908 and 1910 linked the Chihuahuan opposition to opposition movements in the rest of the country and gave it a very distinct direction.

The Emergence of Francisco Madero

The national crisis began, as prerevolutionary crises frequently do, with a conflict within the country's upper class. New presidential elections were due in 1910, and while most people expected Díaz to stand for reelection, there was a possibility that he might not survive his term in office because of his advanced age. Within Mexico's elite, two groups were vying to control the succession, each one hoping that Díaz would name their candidate vice president (who would succeed the dictator if he died). The first group, Mexico's financial elite, were called *científicos*, a designation based on their espousal of the "scientific" principles of positivism and social Darwinism. Their vice-presidential candidate was an unpopular politician from the northern state of Sonora, Ramón Corral. The second group included parts of northern Mexico's economic elite as well as important segments of the army. Its leader and vice-presidential candidate was one of Mexico's most powerful generals, Bernardo Reyes. For a brief period in 1908 and 1909, Reyes had become the focal point of middle-class opposition to Díaz.[108] Fearing that Reyes might overthrow him, Díaz had sent the general into exile. In order to weaken the opposition led by Reyes, Díaz was ready to tolerate the activities of other opposition groups whom he considered harmless. He even encouraged them by giving an interview to an American newspaperman named James Creelman in which he stated that he would not run for office in 1910, and that he would welcome any opposition groups that might form in Mexico.

One man who immediately availed himself of this opportunity was the scion of one of the wealthiest families in the northeastern state of Coahuila, Francisco I. Madero. Neither Díaz nor Madero's family took him seriously. He seemed at first glance the absolute antithesis of a revolutionary caudillo. He was a small man, a spiritist, a teetotaler with a squeaky voice, full of good-hearted intentions. In 1908, he published a book, *La sucesión presidencial en 1910* (The Presidential Succession in 1910), in which, while recognizing the merits of Díaz, he advocated a reform that would only allow a president to remain in office for one term. To the astonishment of Díaz and his científico advisors and of his own family, both disgruntled members of the middle class and members of Mexico's lower classes took Madero seriously, and soon thousands of people were coming to listen to his speeches and rallying to his campaign. His anti-reelectionist party grew dramatically once Reyes had gone into exile.

In January 1910, Madero made a brief campaign trip to the state of Chihuahua. Although thousands came to hear him in the state's main cities—Ciudad Juárez, Ciudad Chihuahua, and Hidalgo del Parral—his campaign there seemed at first glance less successful than in the neighboring states of Coahuila and Sonora. In those states, disgruntled members of the upper class who had supported Reyes, men such as Venustiano Carranza in Coahuila and José María Maytorena in Sonora, rallied to Madero's cause. Reyismo was never strong in Chihuahua, and no member of the upper class in that state joined the Madero movement. This may have been one of the reasons why Creel underestimated Madero's impact on his native state, writing Vice President Ramón Corral that Madero's rallies had only been attended by "the curious, who [queue up] for an exhibition of a rare animal or some company of clowns."[109]

Creel obviously shared Porfirio Díaz's conviction that no successful revolution could take place in his country without the support of dissident members of the upper class. He was mistaken. The middle-class leadership of the anti-reelectionist party, headed by the impoverished scion of a former wealthy family, Abraham González, would prove to be far more formidable opponents than most upper-class dissident leaders.

When elections were approaching and Díaz recognized that Madero was more dangerous than he had initially thought, he had him imprisoned and faked the elections, in which officially Madero received all of 183 votes. Nevertheless, Díaz continued to underestimate Madero, and, in response to pleas from his family, freed him from jail. Madero immediately fled into exile in the United States, where he issued a revolutionary plan, called the Plan of San Luis Potosí, the last city where he had stayed before crossing the border into the United States. In his plan Madero assumed the provisional presidency of Mexico and called for a general uprising against Porfirio Díaz to begin on November 20, 1910. It was a plan primarily aimed at securing the support of Díaz's middle- and upper-class opponents. It called for political reforms: non-reelection of either the president or other powerful officials, genuinely free elections, a free press, and an independent judiciary. The plan contained few clauses dealing with social reforms. Nothing was said about labor, and only one paragraph dealt with the peasantry. It stated that lands taken from peasants because they were considered to be vacant land should be returned to their former owners, or, if these lands had in the meantime been sold to a third party, the former owners should be compensated for them.

This paragraph was very limited in scope, since only a part of the peasantry had lost its holdings under the federal Law of Vacant Lands. The plan was also vague about the modalities for the return of expropriated holdings. Yet this vague promise was sufficient to provoke the largest rural uprising in Mexico's history since the rebellion of 1810. This was not what Madero had wanted or expected. He had hoped that very different forces would constitute the pillars of his movement: that in addition to his retainers, clients, and friends in his native state of Coahuila, the forces that supported Reyes—parts of the army, the middle classes, and dissident members of the upper classes—would transfer their support to him.

On November 20, 1910, none of the forces on whom Madero had pinned his hopes rebelled. With one significant exception, there were only a few sporadic uprisings, generally of small groups of men, in various parts of Mexico. The only serious revolt that took place in November and December of 1910, when most of the country was still quiet and peaceful, occurred in the state of Chihuahua. But what did occur in Chihuahua was more than a simple armed movement or an uprising. It was a genuine mass insurrection.

To Revolt or Not to Revolt: The Dilemma Facing Mexico's Revolutionaries

When Francisco Madero issued his call for revolution throughout Mexico in November 1910, he may have been mistaken in his assessment of the forces that would constitute the core of the revolution, but he was essentially correct in his judgment that Mexico had become ripe for a revolutionary upheaval. Every revolution in history is different from every other, and the results are even more diverse, yet on the eve of a revolutionary upheaval, certain common conditions tend to occur.

On the eve of revolution, there has to be a widespread dissatisfaction with political, economic, and social conditions affecting not just one segment or class of the population but a wide variety of social classes and social groups. This was the case in Mexico in 1910. While expropriation of peasant land may not have been as generalized and as widespread throughout Mexico as has been assumed, it was nonetheless extensive enough to produce resentment and dissatisfaction among peasants in a number of key areas of the country. Even where land tenure had not been affected, the end of the open range, as well as the loss of autonomy, with increasing centralization and interference by the central government, had affected large segments of the peasantry. These peasant grievances were not new, although they had greatly increased in the final years of the Porfirian dictatorship. In the 1890s, in many parts of Mexico, peasants had risen against the government, but their rebellions had been crushed when no other social groups except a few caudillos supported them. By 1910, dissatisfaction was rampant among Mexico's middle classes and industrial workers as well. Lack of democracy, which meant lack of access to political power and subordination to an all-powerful state bureaucracy, increasing taxation, and resentment at the privileges accorded to foreigners, in addition to a generational conflict, profoundly affected Mexico's middle classes. While in the 1890s, industrial workers, many of whom had been hacienda peons, favorably compared labor conditions in industry with the way they had lived in the countryside, a new generation of industrial workers had other points of comparison: living conditions of workers in the United States and the rights accorded to foreign workers in Mexico, who received higher wages for similar work. Dissatisfaction alone, however, was far from sufficient to produce a revolutionary climate.

Another precondition for revolution is a widespread politicization of the people. Politicization in this context means not only awareness that conditions as they exist must change, and that large numbers of people share that opinion, but also a widespread political mobilization in which people hitherto estranged from or uninterested in politics are suddenly willing to participate in the political process. Such a politicization can come about in very different ways. In some cases, it has been brought about by war—this was the case after Russia's defeat at the hands of Japan in 1905, and again in Russia in February 1917, when after three years of world war that had cost millions of lives, the problem of peace began to dominate people's thinking. In other cases, politicization resulted from a dictatorial government suddenly opening up political spaces. This was the case in France in 1789, when the government allowed elections to the States General and permitted people to voice their grievances openly. A similar process happened two centuries later when Gorbachev's *glasnost* policy suddenly opened up a new political space for the peoples of the Soviet Union. This also occurred in Porfirian Mexico. Díaz's interview with Creelman and his tolerance, although limited, of the Madero movement created such a political space. The Madero campaign in Mexico politicized hundreds of thousands of people.

A third precondition for revolution is a sense by increasing numbers of people of the illegitimacy of the existing government. That sense of illegitimacy receives a powerful impulse from the opening up of the political process. Grievances can now be voiced more openly, and the negative aspects of the existing regime can be exposed in a way that was not possible before. In unprecedented fashion, speakers at rallies of Madero's anti-reelectionist party, as well as opposition newspapers, laid bare many of the injustices of the Porfirian administration. Public perceptions of the illegitimacy of the existing political system tend to reach a high point when the government, sensing the negative consequences of the way it has opened up the political process, tries to close it down again. The people of Paris rose on July 14, 1789, when rumors began to spread that the king was bringing troops into Paris in order to dissolve the national assembly and put an end to the political opening that had emerged in France. The attempt by conservative military officers, led by General Kornilov, to take power in Russia in July 1917 radicalized large segments of the Russian population and helped the Bolsheviks to seize power in October that year. The attempted coup by conservatives within the Communist party in August 1991 put an end to any kind of legitimacy that the Communists had enjoyed in the eyes of the majority of Soviet people. Díaz's manipulation of the 1910 elections had been so blatant that a widely shared perception that the Díaz government lacked legitimacy emerged in Mexico.

A fourth and decisive precondition that can transform an uprising into a revolution is the appearance of a clear alternative to the existing regime. In 1910, Madero was seen as such an alternative by a majority of Mexico's population. Nevertheless, one often-cited precondition for revolution, the perception that the government is weak and irresolute, seemed to be absent in Mexico in 1910, although it had existed for a time. The divisions within Mexico's upper class between the supporters of Reyes and the científicos had, perhaps for the first time since Díaz assumed power, created the impression that the government was not monolithic. The Creelman interview and Díaz's toleration of Madero's opposition movement in 1909–10 may have strengthened the impression that the government was not strong enough to impose its rule upon the country. In the eyes of many people, however, Díaz seemed to have dispelled the notion that his government was weak and irresolute in the latter part of 1910. The banishment of Reyes, the arrest of Madero, and the manipulation of the elections without provoking active opposition convinced many supporters and opponents that Díaz had regained control of the country. The festivities that took place on September 15–16, 1910, on the occasion of the hundredth anniversary of the beginning of the country's independence movement, enhanced the image of a strong and stable government enjoying international recognition. Parades by elite troops through the streets of various cities reinforced the impression of government strength, while the arrival of delegations from all over the world seemed to give Díaz international legitimacy.

CHAPTER TWO

The Revolution That Neither Its Supreme Leader Nor Its Opponents Expected

The Chihuahuan Revolution, 1910–1911,
and the Role of Pancho Villa

Camino real de Durango	On the royal road of Durango
adornado con nopales;	Full of nopales
huye Doroteo Arango,	Doroteo Arango
lo persiguen los rurales.	is fleeing from the rurales.
Lo siguen por un delito	They are pursuing him for a crime
para llevarlo a prisión;	and want to imprison him;
en el rancho Gogojito	at the Gogojito ranch
herido dejó al patrón.	he wounded the owner.
El patrón quería mujer	The boss wanted a woman
con intenciones malsanas;	for his own vile purposes
entonces pensó escoger	and he thought he could pick one
entre una de sus hermanas.[1]	from among Arango's sisters.

With Porfirio Díaz seemingly in firm control of Mexico in November of 1910, many would-be rebels were loathe to rise against him. They waited either for a sign of weakness within the regime or for a successful challenge to its power by a revolutionary group. Thus a vicious circle developed, with nearly everyone waiting for everyone else to make the first move. The one revolutionary movement that broke this vicious circle, exposed the weakness of the government, and finally triggered revolts all over Mexico was centered in the state of Chihuahua. In this respect, Chihuahua would play a role similar to that of Boston in the American Revolution of 1776, Paris in the French Revolution of 1789, Petrograd in the Russian Revolution of February 1917, and Moscow and Leningrad in the defeat of the attempted conservative coup of 1991.

We should not, however, take these comparisons too far. Paris, Petrograd, and Moscow became the ideological centers of revolution in their countries, which was never the case with Chihuahua. What the Chihuahuan revolutionaries had in common with the men who stormed the Bastille in Paris on July 14, 1789, or the demonstrators against the coup in Moscow in August 1991 was that they managed to show that the government was weaker than anyone had dared believe. The relative ease with which the rebels in Paris captured the Bastille contributed to the outbreak of peasant revolts all over France. The incapacity of the coup plotters in Moscow to disperse the demonstrators in front of the Russian parliament was a decisive factor that led to their defeat. In the same way, the incapacity of the Díaz administration to put an end to the Chihuahuan rebellion provoked uprisings in many parts of Mexico.

It is not easy to explain the unique role Chihuahua played both in 1910–11 and again in 1913 as a catalyst of the Mexican Revolution. Certain factors that triggered revolutionary upheavals in other parts of the world were scarcely present. While the state of Chihuahua was one of the main recipients of foreign and, above all, U.S. investment in Mexico, there is little evidence that nationalism was of decisive importance in the outbreak of the 1910–11 revolution. Mormon colonists were the object not so much of attacks as of expropriation of goods by revolutionaries, and relatively little harm was done to American estates or American mines in the first phase of the revolution in Chihuahua. This is especially significant, since during the first few months of the revolution, no central authority exercised any clear control over the men who rebelled, and thus, had there been a strong, spontaneous xenophobia, no one could have kept these men from attacking foreign properties. While fear of U.S. reprisal certainly affected their conduct, they were also influenced by the fact that foreign investors, especially foreign hacendados, had been forced to attract their laborers with higher wages, better conditions, payment in cash and not in scrip, and full freedom of mobility. Most Mexican hacendados, and especially the Terrazas, refused to grant their peons such benefits.

It cannot be said either that the rulers of Chihuahua were outsiders with no roots in the state they ruled, as was the case in some other parts of Mexico. No one had deeper roots in Chihuahua than the Terrazas. Nor did any charismatic leader emerge to rally all dissatisfied elements around him. Pancho Villa would play such a role in a later phase of the revolution, but not in 1910–11. Pascual Orozco, the most important military leader of the initial stage of the revolution in Chihuahua, never had that kind of influence. There is no doubt that Madero was such a leader, but his influence was national, he did not come from Chihuahua, and his influence certainly does not explain the unusual role of Chihuahua in this first phase of the revolution. It cannot be said either that the state administration was in disarray or was showing signs of weakness on the eve of the revolution. Bolstered by their close connection with Díaz, Terrazas and Creel seemed more powerful than ever.

The factors that made for revolution were of a different kind. One element that helped to create unity among the state's heterogeneous social groups was the degree of economic, social, and political power—unusual even by Mexican standards—that Terrazas and Creel had gathered into their hands. As a result, the most diverse segments of society were united against them.

Chihuahua had also been more affected by the cyclical economic crisis of 1907–10 than most other states of Mexico. This was partly owing to the concentration in Chihuahua of foreign investment: foreign-owned businesses were more dependent on international economic fluctuations than other enterprises in Mexico. Above all, however, it was because that crisis coincided with three years of drought and bad harvests, which sent food prices skyrocketing and impoverished large segments of the peasantry, who then began to look in vain for work in industry or in mines that had closed. The return from the United States of thousands of migrants who had lost their employment north of the border deepened this crisis. One important characteristic of the Chihuahuan revolutionary movement was the fact that it was the only opposition movement in northern Mexico not led by dissident members of the upper classes. Terrazas and Creel had succeeded in either ruining or co-opting all the hacendados who in former times had opposed them. Dissident landowners in other states, such as Venustiano Carranza in Coahuila and José María Maytorena in Sonora, were hesitant about taking up arms against the Díaz administration and did so at a relatively late stage of the revolution. The middle-class leadership of the Chihuahuan revolution had no such compunction.

Of decisive importance for all revolutionary movements in the north was the proximity of the United States and the possibility of acquiring arms there, whether legally or illegally, and smuggling them across the largely unguarded border.

Yet the most important element that helps to explain the outbreak of the revolution in Chihuahua was the fighting capacity and the self-confidence of its inhabitants. They had vanquished the Apaches, and at Tomóchi they had repeatedly defeated government forces far superior in numbers and in equipment.

One advantage that these former military colonists enjoyed was that they were closer to the urban middle class than were villagers in many other parts of Mexico. They shared a similar ethnic background. Most of the former military colonists were mestizos or whites. Tarahumara Indians, the largest indigenous group in Chihuahua, participated only marginally in the revolution. The military colonists and the urban middle class in many respects shared a similar class background. Before losing their lands, these colonists had been middle-class rancheros, without the traditions of indigenous communal organization that predominated in central and southern Mexico. In addition, during the years of Apache warfare, they had been popular heroes, whose exploits were sung all over Chihuahua, and who were received in triumph in the capital city of the state after every successful Indian campaign. The sympathy that these militant villagers encountered all over Chihuahua greatly boosted their morale.

The Course of the Chihuahuan Revolution

The revolution that broke out in Chihuahua expressed the pent-up hatred of the state's free villagers for the Terrazas and the Creel clan, as well as for the local officials they had appointed. But, in spite of these profound hatreds, the uprising was in its earliest phases a gentle revolution. There was no resemblance between the Chihuahuan revolution and the classic French Jacqueries, in which French peasants of the Middle Ages expressed their pent-up hatred for their masters by staging a local revolt, killing their lord, his family, and retainers, and burning the manor house to the ground. With few exceptions, the Chihuahuan revolutionaries of 1910–11 carried out no executions, burnt no houses or haciendas, and engaged in no massive destruction of property. What occurred was a massive upheaval of civil society against a regime that had come to be considered intolerable by the majority of Chihuahua's inhabitants.

The first revolutionary uprising both in Mexico and in Chihuahua took place in the small village of Cuchillo Parado in northeastern Chihuahua. Toribio Ortega, who in 1903 had led the peasants of his native village in their attempt to recover their lands, had become the head of the anti-reelectionist party in Cuchillo Parado.[2] His former colleague, and later rival, Ezequiel Montes, who had joined him in 1903 but had then defected to the government side and been appointed by Creel as mayor of the village, attempted to intimidate Ortega by imprisoning his nephew. When this reprisal had no effect, Montes endeavored to confiscate the ballots the villagers had cast on the day of the presidential election and to replace them with ballots of his own. Ortega became convinced that there was no other way out for him or for his villagers than revolution, and he promised his full support to Abraham González when he called for a general uprising in support of Madero. Ortega and his supporters had made plans to revolt on November 20, but a week earlier, on the evening of November 13, word reached them that the authorities had learned of their plan. Orders had been given to have Ortega arrested. On November 14, he decided to take the initiative. As a village chronicler put it, "Toribio Ortega . . . at the head of 60 men, most of them without arms, decided to defy the dictator. . . . On this same morning, Ezequiel Montes, the evil and hypocritical cacique, seized by indescribable panic, fled from the village. Fully dressed, he crossed the river, which crested at this time of the year, and he was seen in a neighboring field trembling, covered with mud, without a hat. . . . Ortega could have taken him prisoner; because of his generosity and his magnanimous heart, Ortega let him go, forgetting the evil he had done."[3]

Toribio Ortega's men were soon joined by the inhabitants of the villages of San Antonio and San Carlos, who had so desperately attempted to use every means at their disposal to save their lands. In the mining town of Parral, Guillermo Baca, a wealthy merchant, led 40 men in an attack on the residence of the jefe político. Within a short time, he was joined spontaneously by over 300 men, many of them unarmed. While they could not prevail against the town's well-disciplined police force, they could not be defeated either. Over 100 men joined Baca when he took to the hills to wage a guerrilla struggle against the Porfirian authorities. The insurrection spread throughout the former military colonies and mining towns both of western and southern Chihuahua. In Namiquipa, on November 20, the local revolutionaries gathered early in the morning; "the moment has come to carry out the revolution," their leader told them. "Our situation is intolerable, our sacred rights have been infringed upon, we have a powerful enemy, but this does not matter. Righteous causes are never defeated." As a veteran of that uprising remembers it, there was an enthusiastic response to this speech: "Long live the revolution, long live Madero, death to Porfirio Díaz."[4]

The revolutionaries proceeded to attack a government garrison of 25 men sent to Namiquipa by the authorities, who had heard rumors of an impending uprising. Shooting went on all day, but the revolutionaries could make no headway against the well-entrenched garrison and ceased their attack by nightfall. The local police commander, Félix Merino, was so sure that he had put an end to the rebellion that he decided to go home for the night. Taking only one of his men with him, he proceeded to his house, located more than three miles away from his headquarters. The revolutionaries were waiting for him and killed him on his way home. At that point, the government defense disintegrated, Merino's soldiers threw down their arms, and the revolutionaries took control of Namiquipa.[5]

In adjoining Bachiniva, victory came with even greater ease. Hearing that a revolt had broken out in a neighboring town, the mayor had taken all his loyal men with him and left Bachiniva the night before. On November 20, under the leadership of Heliodoro Arias Olea, the revolutionaries occupied the municipal palace and set up new authorities. Arias Olea was elected both mayor and military commander, and the town proclaimed its loyalty to Francisco Madero and to the principle of no reelection.[6]

Neither in Namiquipa nor in Bachiniva were there any massive reprisals against the supporters of the Terrazas-Creel administration. Nor was there looting or any burning of houses.

Local rebellions similar to those of Namiquipa and Bachiniva now broke out all over the mountain ranges of western Chihuahua. As their predecessors had done in the 1890s, nearly twenty years before, the rebellious villagers attempted to occupy their communities and to replace unpopular local authorities. If resistance by these authorities proved too strong, or if government troops were in the area, the rebels would fade into the mountains and wage guerrilla warfare from there. Decisive differences nevertheless emerged between the tactics of the rebels of the 1890s and the 1910 revolutionaries. The wave of rural uprisings that had swept Chihuahua twenty years before had been uncoordinated. Each village had acted on its own and had tended to wage defensive rather than offensive warfare. They had retreated into the mountains waiting for government troops to attack them. This time it was different: the revolutionaries rallied to regional chieftains and waged relentless offensive warfare against government troops. The two men who emerged as the main military leaders of the revolution in western Chihuahua, Pascual Orozco and Francisco (Pancho) Villa, had both been recruited into the revolutionary ranks by the leader of the anti-reelectionist party in Chihuahua, Abraham González.

What González had originally had in mind for both of them were subordinate functions in the military hierarchy of the revolution. The two men who in González's opinion ought to head the revolutionary movement were two of the most prominent political leaders of the anti-reelectionist party: Albino Frías, a businessman and rancher from the town of San Isidro, and Castulo Herrera, the head of the boilermakers' union, who had been head of the anti-reelectionist party in the capital city of Chihuahua. Both men had been first-rate political organizers, but as the revolution progressed, they showed themselves to be inept in military terms. The military leadership soon passed to their subordinates, Pascual Orozco and Pancho Villa. Orozco, a tall, lanky 28-year-old scion of one of the region's oldest families, lived in the town of San Isidro. He was a member of Chihuahua's growing, enterprising, self-confident middle class. His father, Pascual Orozco Sr., was described by a Protestant missionary who visited him shortly before the outbreak of the revolution as "not strictly wealthy, though he does own cattle, lands and several houses."[7]

His son, Pascual Jr., after finishing the local primary school, began working in the family store. He soon decided to go into business for himself and chose a profession that was at once dangerous, lucrative, and prestigious: he organized and led convoys transporting precious metals through the mountain regions of western Chihuahua. The talents necessary to carry out this kind of work and the capacities it developed tended to convert him into a natural leader of a revolutionary movement: he knew all the nooks and crannies of the mountain ranges of Chihuahua. He had constantly to be attuned to danger. He had to be not only a good rider and a good shot but also a leader of extremely tough men. He had established contacts all over western Chihuahua. The money he had accumulated in this profession—in a report to Porfirio Díaz his worth was estimated at 100,000 pesos—gave him additional power and prestige.[8]

Orozco's home town, San Isidro, had a long history of conflict with neighboring hacendados and with the local cacique and military commander of the region, Captain Joaquín Chávez, who ruled with an iron fist.[9] (This was the man whose tyrannical rule had provoked the uprising of Tomóchi twenty years earlier.) There is no evidence that Orozco had participated in San Isidro's struggle against Chávez, but he obviously shared the villagers' hatred for their cacique. He must have resented Chávez's domination, for he showed a strong interest in the rebellious ideas of the Flores Magón brothers, and, in 1907, the local authorities reported that he was reading subversive literature. His resentment must have reached a high point shortly before the outbreak of the revolution: Chávez, who was also in the business of conveying precious metals, took a lucrative contract away from him.

Orozco may also have been influenced by the local Protestant minister in the regional capital of Ciudad Guerrero. Twenty-four years before the outbreak of the revolution, the Orozco family had converted to Protestantism. The U.S. missionary who had baptized them, James Eaton, was no revolutionary. In fact, he maintained very good relations with Enrique Creel, who even gave him money to proselytize in Chihuahua. The Mexican pastor who resided in Ciudad Guerrero, on the other hand, was a convinced revolutionary and joined the revolution as soon as it broke out. His ideology, which he propagated long before the revolution began, was clearly expressed in a letter he sent to Eaton: "Brother, I will say with certainty and with frankness that if God in His love should come down to the world to pacify this, he would not succeed. . . . You yourself know that we have labored by means of the law, justice, meekness, right, democracy, etc. and we have suffered vexations, insults, mockeries, prisons, death. . . . Nothing remains for us but war."[10]

Opposition to the existing power structure and resentment at the personal losses he had suffered were not the only motives that impelled Orozco to revolt. He soon developed political ambitions. His capacities both as an organizer and as a military chieftain transformed the heterogeneous rebel groups who joined him into a coherent and effective military force. In fact, only one day after he revolted, he laid siege to the district capital, Ciudad Guerrero.

When Orozco and his men began their movement in San Isidro, a second group of revolutionaries were meeting on a small ranch called La Cueva Pinta in the mountain ranges of the Sierra Azul, not far from the city of Chihuahua. As a witness recalled two years later, "At dawn on November 20, 1910, various groups of armed men sat around camp fires in the main square of the Cueva Pinta. As soon as the light shone through the darkness of the night, all the participants formed a large circle." The meeting had been organized by the anti-reelectionist party. Antonio Ruíz, a local official of that party and the author of these memoirs, began to read the Plan of San Luis Potosí to them.

As they heard the moving words of the plan, the faces of these simple peasants who were listening showed enormous satisfaction and unending enthusiasm. Some had suffered from the egotism of their masters their whole lives long, and the latter had taken their last cent from them; others, small landowners, had been eternal victims of the despotism of authorities who forced them to pay enormous taxes on their small holdings; others had seen their small properties confiscated by the powerful with the full sanction of the government; others had been persecuted their whole lives for having avenged the honor of their sisters or wives, violated by the rich and by corrupt authorities. . . . Once the reading of the plan was finished, we all brandished our arms and hands and cried out, "Down with the tyrants, long live freedom for all, long live Francisco Madero!" and full of enthusiasm we embraced each other, swearing to die rather than to give up our aims.

The participants then proceeded to elect their military chieftains.

Castulo Herrera, the head of the boilermakers' union in Chihuahua, and the man who had led the anti-reelectionist party in the state's capital, was elected to lead the group, since "he was the best-known of the participants." After two other party officials had been designated to share power with him, the group proceeded to elect the more subordinate leaders who were to head the four companies into which the men who had decided to revolt were now divided. The first company consisted of "First Commander, Francisco Villa; Lieutenant Eleuterio Armendariz and six corporals commanding four men each."[11]

Thus Pancho Villa entered the history of the Mexican Revolution as a minor leader of 28 men, but also as a man elected to this position by dedicated revolutionary activists. It is doubtful whether anyone in this revolutionary assemblage that met at the Cueva Pinta, including perhaps Villa himself, suspected the role he would soon be called upon to play.

This contemporary description (it was written in November 1912, only two years after the outbreak of the revolution) casts doubt on some of the main aspects of all three legends about Villa: the black legend, the epic legend, and the white legend.

Had Villa indeed been the common bandit and multiple murderer that the black legend has made him out to be, it is difficult to conceive of an assembly of responsible citizens electing him to a position of leadership in the revolutionary movement. The fact that this position was of a subordinate nature—he was placed under the command of Castulo Herrera and headed only 28 men, a quarter of the assembled revolutionaries—indicates that he was scarcely the idol and acknowledged leader of thousands of peasants, the scourge of the Terrazas empire. It also refutes Villa's own description of his activities, his insistence on his complete independence from anyone else except González and Madero, and his claim that he was one of the revolution's main leaders from the outset.

A closer look at Villa's life prior to 1910 also shows that it differed considerably from what all three legends have made it out to be.

There is no doubt that Villa was born Doroteo Arango on the Rancho de la Coyotada, belonging to the hacienda of the López Negrete family in Durango, on June 5, 1878. In his autobiography, he briefly describes himself as a sharecropper, but in another account, written by a supporter, he is portrayed even at an early age as a kind of young entrepreneur attempting to supplement his income as a sharecropper by buying and selling goods.[12]

The first reference by Porfirian authorities to Doroteo Arango occurred when he was 21, on November 1, 1899. On that day the jefe político of San Juan del Río, Manuel Díaz Couder, reported to the government that bandits had been sighted in his district, among them Estanislao Mendía and Doroteo Arango, "who were riding in the direction of Guagojito, where Arango and Mendía have family."[13]

Less than one and a half years later, in January 1901, Arango was arrested. The crimes he was accused of committing were of a relatively minor nature: he had stolen two burros and the merchandise they were carrying. Nevertheless, the state authorities ordered the official in Canatlán in charge of the prisoner to turn Arango over to Octaviano Meraz, the head of the mounted police in Durango, who had a reputation for effectiveness in combating banditry, as well as for executing outlaws and dissidents without benefit of a trial by applying the *ley fuga*—that is, shooting a prisoner and then stating that he had been killed while attempting to escape.[14]

At this point an event that in some respects was unusual in Porfirian times took place. A local judge placed a restraining order on Meraz and ordered the local official to return Arango to Canatlán. The official complained bitterly about the behavior of the judge: "When I put Arango at the disposal of Meraz, I was carrying out the orders of the government, and I never acted in an arbitrary way, but this *licenciado* has shown strong objections to the way I proceeded. The judge stated that he was going to try me should the prisoner not be returned."[15] The man who in all probability induced the judge to save Villa's life was a local cacique, Pablo Valenzuela, with whom Villa had had some business dealings, and to whom he may have sold stolen cattle.[16] Two months later, the judge freed Arango for lack of evidence.[17] "Arango is of very bad conduct and one of those who are part of the gang of the bandit Estanislao Mendía, a fact very well known to Don Octaviano Meraz; and since this individual is now being freed, there is little doubt that he will continue to conduct himself the same way, which he may correct if he enters the army," an indignant Porfirian official declared.[18]

Four days later, on March 8, Arango was arrested again, this time for having assaulted Ramón Reyes and robbed him of two guns that he was carrying. The authorities now inducted him into the army, in which he seems to have served for one year. Doroteo Arango was too independent a man to continue to serve indefinitely in Porfirio Díaz's army, however, and on March 22, 1902, the jefe político of San Juan del Río reported to the governor that he had "deserted from the 2d regiment and that I have given instructions to the authorities of this district to capture this man." He called Arango a "dangerous bandit."[19] The experience Villa acquired in the Porfirian army, even though it was only that of a lowly common soldier, would be of assistance to him in his revolutionary days. It was an experience he shared with other popular leaders of the revolution such as Emiliano Zapata and Calixto Contreras.

The contemporary account of Villa's life as an outlaw in Durango casts even more doubt on all three legends about his early life. Did he wound the hacendado López Negrete and kill several rurales, as he says in his memoirs? Did he commit all the murders that the black legend imputes to him? These facts would have emerged once a local judge had examined his case after his capture. Instead, the only crimes he was accused of were of a minor nature. There is no evidence either that he possessed any great backing among the lower classes in Durango, as the epic legend suggests. He seems to have been a minor outlaw, roaming the Durango countryside.

While this account contradicts Villa's story that he seriously wounded López Negrete, and that a warrant was out for his arrest, it does not necessarily invalidate his story that he was defending the honor of his sister. Rapes of peon women by hacendados were common on haciendas, and after an altercation with the hacendado, Villa might very well have felt that life on the hacienda was impossible for him. On the other hand, throughout history, outlaws have protested that they were obliged to break the law for the sake of honor. The story of Robin Hood is but the best known of many cases in which banditry was not only explained but justified in such terms. The stories were frequently true, but just as frequently were invented by the outlaws to justify their acts.

Doubts about Villa's story are deepened by discrepancies between the memoirs he dictated to Bauche Alcalde and the accounts given of the same episode by other people who knew Villa well. For some, the culprit was not the hacendado but his son; for others, it was the administrator of the hacienda, and according to still others, it was either a sheriff or another worker on the estate.[20]

There are many other reasons that might have impelled a highly intelligent, entrepreneurially minded, independent, and frequently violent young man such as Doroteo Arango to become an outlaw. In 1892, the jefe político of San Juan del Río spoke of the considerable increase in the number of prisoners "because of the general poverty that exists in this district."[21] Equally important was the *leva*, forced induction into the army for many years, which amounted to virtual slavery. In theory, a lottery was supposed to determine who would be drafted. In practice, things were very different. In 1907, Pedro Marín, a lawyer for men inducted into the army in Durango, wrote the governor that the lottery was in fact a joke. "In reality, the lottery is a mere pretext to allow men of influence to get rid of persons they do not like and against whom they are carrying out reprisals."[22] The same opinion was voiced by the jefe político of San Juan del Río, who stated that "the hacendados tend to attribute pernicious characteristics to individuals who do not possess such characteristics simply because they dislike them."[23] Many of these men preferred the life of a bandit to that of a soldier, either fleeing into the hills before they were inducted or deserting from the army.

In addition, the authorities of San Juan del Río and those of Durango in general had very little legitimacy in their people's eyes. In April 1911, the British vice-consul in Durango painted a devastating picture of conditions in that state:

The governor has been appointed from Mexico; he in turn has appointed as jefes políticos men who, to say the least, could never be elected. Such men, badly under-paid, and with absolute power, have established a traditional "caciquismo;" the administration of justice has been very unsatisfactory and dilatory and the incidence of state taxation most unequal, falling heavily on the miners and small merchants and lightly on the great estates and haciendas. The members of congress, both state and federal, are appointed, not elected, and I doubt if one per cent of the inhabitants could tell their names.[24]

Such conditions obtained throughout the Porfirian period. Pablo Soto, who had been mayor of Canatlán and then became the head of the *acordada* (police force) of that town, was a habitual drunkard who was repeatedly accused of murder. At one time the governor attempted to have him removed from his position, but the jefe político protested that Soto was his most efficient policeman, and the order was rescinded.[25]

Another factor that attracted men to banditry in Durango was the success that many of these bandits had attained. A notorious example was Heraclio Bernal, who spent ten successful years alternating between political rebellion and robbing stagecoaches and attacking mines, until he was finally killed by the state police headed by Octaviano Meraz.[26]

In 1883, Bernal was joined by five Parra brothers, one of whom, Ignacio Parra, became as famous in Durango as Bernal had been and managed to survive even longer, until he too was killed by Octaviano Meraz sometime in the 1890s.[27] What allowed these men to survive for a long time without being captured by the authorities was that they were able to establish good relations both with the lower classes of society and with important men in their region. On his home ground, Bernal made sure that he paid for everything that he took and never bothered the inhabitants of the region.[28]

Ignacio Parra maintained good relations with Guillermo Brinck, who represented the peasants of Yerba Buena,[29] and he also lived for several months in the house of Pablo Soto, the chief of police charged with catching bandits. He had entered into an agreement with a man close to the governor, a wealthy hacendado named Antonio Bracho, who granted him his protection for a time.[30] Such relations were widespread. In 1892, the secretary of the court in San Juan del Río was accused of favoring bandits and freeing them.[31] Porfirian officials repeatedly complained of the leniency of judges to bandits, which might be linked to the judges' fear of reprisals that the bandits might take against them.[32]

It thus is not surprising that after several months of leading a lonely, precarious life in the mountains of Durango, only occasionally helped by some family members, Villa decided to join Ignacio Parra. This led to a rapid reversal in his fortunes, and Villa had soon accumulated the huge sum of 50,000 pesos. Villa insists that he spent this money to support both his family and poor friends and acquaintances. The one such case he singles out was that of Antonio Retana, for whom he set up a small sewing shop. After eleven months, his money was spent, and Villa went back to life as an outlaw.

Villa's account is not improbable. In later years, those who knew him would stress his generosity, but in this case, it was not entirely disinterested. Villa had probably learned from Bernal and Parra how important it was to have a popular base. Subsequently, in fact, he was able to hide for some time in Retana's house.[33] Another lesson Villa had learned from the experience of Durango's most prominent outlaws was the need for powerful protectors, and to that end, he now established cordial relations with the merchant Pablo Valenzuela.

Relations with Parra, while profitable, were not very cordial, however, and Villa soon broke with him. Villa insists that the main motive for this break was the fact that Parra allowed one of his subordinates to kill a harmless old man who had refused to sell bread to the outlaws.[34] Whatever the motives for the break, it was a wise decision on Villa's part, since he was not there when Parra was finally tracked down and killed by Octaviano Meraz.

There is no information concerning Estanislao Mendía, whose gang, according to the authorities of San Juan del Río, Villa joined after breaking with Parra. The fact that he left so little trace seems to indicate that he was scarcely a prominent outlaw.

Pancho Villa in Chihuahua

It was probably after he deserted from the army in 1902 that Villa decided that life in Durango had become too dangerous for him and fled to Chihuahua. Nevertheless, he did not want to stray too far from his native state, and he settled in Parral, a town near the Durango border.

For Villa, the move to Chihuahua represented a new and difficult beginning. He did not know the state, had no family there, and lacked both the infrastructure of friends he had so carefully built up in Durango and the protection of powerful men that he had acquired in his native state. In addition, bandits seem to have been far more negatively regarded by the public in Chihuahua than in Durango. There is no record of popular outlaws comparable to Heraclio Bernal in the history of Chihuahua.

Villa's claim that he began life in Chihuahua in very modest circumstances as a mason working for a local entrepreneur, Santos Vega, is by no means improbable. He insists that he would have continued in this line of work had he not been forced to flee once again because the Durango police had found his trail in Parral. If this was indeed the case, it was the last time he was identified as Doroteo Arango, since he soon changed his name to Francisco Villa. His main reason was probably to escape both the federal army, which was searching for him as a deserter, and the Durango authorities. Why he chose the name "Francisco Villa" is still a hotly debated issue. According to one account, Arango adopted the name of a famous bandit, Francisco Villa, who operated mainly in the state of Coahuila. Such a man had in fact existed, and he had operated in Durango as well as in Coahuila. But Villa's own explanation in his memoirs—namely, that his father, Agustín Arango, was the illegitimate son of a wealthy man called Jesús Villa and that he simply took his grandfather's name—is the most plausible one. This would help explain why his brothers also adopted that name.[35]

It is at this point that a large discrepancy emerges between contemporary documents on the one hand and Villa's autobiography and the legends about him on the other. All of the latter describe Villa as leading the life of a persecuted outlaw and constantly having to flee from one region of Chihuahua to the other. Villa and his enemies concur in insisting that he was one of the state's most wanted men, with a huge reward on his head, although they obviously give very different reasons for this. The most revealing document that contradicts these legends is a short report in the archives of the district capital of Guerrero in Chihuahua, which were for many years practically unknown and inaccessible. On June 29, 1910, Eduardo Castillo, an obscure official of the small town of Madera, wrote to the jefe político at Ciudad Guerrero:

I have the honor to answer your letter of June 24, in which you asked me for a report about a complaint that Francisco Villa has sent you, and in accordance with your orders, I would like to report the following: On the night of the 23d, the guard at the train station, José María García, put said Villa in jail for an offense he committed. An hour later, more or less, he was freed and given back the money that was taken from him: 225 pesos in bills and 27 pesos in change, and the next day his handgun was returned to him. No sentence or fine was imposed upon him in view of existing circumstances, and so I do not understand on what Villa bases his complaint, since I have treated him with excessive respect.[36]

While this does not say why Villa was arrested, it could only have been for a minor offense. What the document does reveal is that in June 1910, Villa was not a wanted man in Chihuahua. Wanted men are not released and given back their guns. While it is conceivable that the minor official who arrested him did not know that Villa was on the wanted list, or that he was either bribed or intimidated by Villa, the last thing Villa would have done, had he known that the authorities were looking for him, was to complain to the jefe político, an important Porfirian official, who had access to all the relevant information. It is even less likely, had Villa been a wanted man, that the jefe político would have transmitted his complaint to a lower official and not had him arrested.

In any case, this report indicates that in June 1910, Villa enjoyed some kind of legal status in Chihuahua and was not being sought by the authorities for the multiple murders and other offenses that have been alleged against him.

It is also difficult to conceive that Abraham González, who by all accounts was not only an honest man but had a deep knowledge of western Chihuahua, would have recruited a man known to be a murderer into the ranks of the revolutionary army.

There are indications that apart from banditry, which he doubtless committed, Villa led a more prominent legal existence than any of the legends attribute to him. That legal existence, about which Villa says nothing in his memoirs, seems to have been largely based on employment by foreigners and foreign corporations in Mexico. This was no coincidence. Foreigners frequently tended to pay better wages than Mexican entrepreneurs, since they had to compete for scarce labor. In addition, Villa may also have wanted to replicate what he had successfully done in Durango—that is, to gain some protection from the law with the help of people with influence. The domestic power structure in Chihuahua, dominated by Creel and Terrazas, was closed to him, but even if that had not been the case, since his days on the López Negrete estate, Villa had conceived a profound hatred for hacendados. Thus it was no coincidence that he concentrated his efforts on finding employment with foreign companies, which soon recognized his multifarious talents as a leader of men, and that he was completely reliable when he gave his word. When Villa was imprisoned in 1912 and questioned by a judge, he said that "on more than one occasion, he had been responsible for carrying large sums of money, such as 700,000 pesos, for the paymasters of the mines on the Northwestern Railroad, and on another occasion was responsible for transporting thirty-six bars of silver and six bars of gold and he never took a cent from these large sums."[37]

These statements by Villa were borne out by the many foreigners who remembered hiring him and being satisfied with his work. A wealthy Englishman named Furber who hired Villa in the years before the revolution wrote: "I know Villa personally. He worked for me several years ago and was in charge of a mule train for about eighteen months. He is a Mexican peon with what that implies to anyone who knows the true character of a Mexican peon which is very bad. The work he had to do for me called for a rough man, as it was in a rough country, and even in President Díaz' time, known as one of the bad parts of the country. Consequently when I picked him out to be put in charge, I had to choose a man who was known for his roughness."[38]

Furber had acquired a large silver mine in Durango. "The wagons carrying the concentrates over the long rough road to Durango were drawn by mules," he recounts in his memoirs. "I needed a good man to take charge of the teams and drivers en route. By good I mean good in a fight in case the drivers quarreled or in case the wagons were held up. I chose a tough specimen who gave me his name as Pancho Villa."[39]

The American tycoon Arthur Stilwell, who built a railway line in Chihuahua, wrote: "Pancho Villa . . . had been one of my contractors. He had twelve teams. I used to let him a mile or two of work and when he had finished I would let him another mile or two."[40]

An American businessman named Burkhead, who headed a sales agency for Cadillac automobiles in El Paso and on the side raised fighting cocks, met Villa in 1909 in El Paso. He was so impressed by Villa's knowledge of cocks and cockfighting that he employed him in his pens. "Villa knew many promoters in Mexico and was soon getting me lists of prospective customers. We built up a big business in shipping fighting cocks south of the border."[41]

What all the statements by foreigners who hired Villa have in common (with the possible exception of Burkhead's) is that they recognized his qualities as a leader of men and hired him primarily for that purpose. And none of them accused Villa of breaking his word or of stealing from them while he was in their employ.

One of Villa's main ambitions in this period of his life seems to have been to set up a butcher shop and lead a legal life in the city of Chihuahua. He did in fact establish a small store, but he soon found that using the slaughterhouse owned and controlled by the Terrazas family was practically impossible. Villa insisted that he was "killing cattle in an honest way," although he does not say where the cattle came from.[42] He was deeply resentful of the fact that the two men in charge of the slaughterhouse always found fault with his cattle, asserting that the brands were not correct or that there were other defects, which he calls a pretext. After refusing to allow him to slaughter his animals, they then offered to sell him meat of their own to resell in his shop. Villa thus abandoned his plans for a butcher shop in Chihuahua, although not his interest in cattle.

The fact that in June 1910, Villa was not on the Chihuahuan authorities' list of wanted men does not mean that he had entirely given up life as an outlaw. Rather, he seems to have switched from robberies and holdups to a less unpopular activity in Chihuahua: cattle rustling. This was no coincidence. Banditry in Chihuahua, with the exception of cattle rustling, was less widespread and less romanticized than in neighboring Durango. While in Durango bandits such as Heraclio Bernal became popular and romantic figures, whose exploits were sung in ballads, no similar figure emerged in Chihuahuan history. In part, this may have been because Chihuahua is further north than Durango and was more exposed to raids by nomadic Indians, so that even bandits found it too dangerous to roam its countryside. Also, if Eric Hobsbawm is correct in seeing social banditry as a form of pre-political protest,[43] Chihuahua had a long history of genuinely popular lower-class uprisings—protests that were anything but pre-political. The negative attitude of many members of Chihuahua's lower classes toward bandits is perhaps best exemplified by the resentment that the inhabitants of Tomóchi felt when the mayor labeled them bandits and prevented a convoy of silver from passing through their village.

Cattle rustling, by contrast, was a very different affair and met with widespread social approval. For nearly two centuries, the public lands of the state had been an open range, where wild cattle could be hunted and killed or appropriated by anyone willing to make the effort. When the Terrazas and other hacendados appropriated both the open range and the wild cattle, large segments of Chihuahua's population saw it as a violation of age-old custom. Stealing cattle from these hacendados was thus viewed, not as a crime, but rather as the restoration of traditional rights. "Why should I respect as Terrazas's property what he did not know, did not raise, and was born outside of his domain?" Villa told Elías Torres, who came to interview him in the 1920s. "Every year, Terrazas sent many peons to collect the wild cattle that had been born there and to put his mark on them. . . . My brothers and I, as well as all of those who followed me and were as poor as we were, had the same right to collect whatever cattle we could and market them under our brand. Why should only rich old men have these rights?"[44]

Villa now entered into partnership with a somewhat shady rancher and business man from the city of Parral, Miguel Baca Valles. The latter had a ranch as well as a butcher shop, in which meat from Villa's stolen cattle was sold. This fact, as well as the proximity of Parral and its adjoining region to Villa's native Durango, may explain why he operated largely in southern Chihuahua. Nevertheless, Villa never remained in only one part of the state. Although based in the south, he seems to have roamed throughout Chihuahua and established a net of contacts all over the state, which would stand him in good stead once he joined the revolution. It is not surprising that many of the members of the lower classes with whom Villa came in contact did not consider him an outlaw, but rather a man who was reinstating a traditional right, and thus did not denounce him to the Porfirian authorities.

In mid 1910, Villa was neither the much-wanted murderer his enemies have made him out to be nor the legendary Robin Hood, the idol of the peasants who struck terror into the hearts of the hacendados, that some of his admirers have portrayed him as being. Unlike other major leaders of the Mexican Revolution, Villa had not prior to 1910 been involved in any of the revolts, rebellions, or protest movements in Chihuahua during the Porfirian era. Nor was he linked to communities fighting for their lands like Emiliano Zapata, Toribio Ortega, and Calixto Contreras.

One of the greatest mysteries about Villa's early life is the strange coexistence of legal and illegal existences. Why did the authorities not arrest Villa? How could he be so self-assured that he even complained about his mistreatment to higher officials, obviously sure they would not arrest him? Some of the explanations that spring to mind can immediately be discarded. Certainly, this does not indicate that Villa had always been a peaceful, law-abiding citizen who never committed any acts of banditry. He himself makes this clear, not only in his memoirs, but in the many interviews that he gave to journalists and friends. While Villa frequently operated under aliases, it cannot be assumed that the authorities knew nothing of his activities. Too many stories were circulating about him, many of them exaggerated. Nor can Chihuahua before 1910 be likened to Chicago in the 1920s, where Al Capone for many years operated with impunity, since the authorities could not gather sufficient proof against him to convince a jury to convict him. The Porfirian authorities observed no such legal niceties. If they wanted to arrest someone, especially for banditry, they did so. Creel's judges would have had no regard for the laws of evidence; and even if they had, the government had other means at its disposal. At the very least, it could have impressed Villa into the army, as had previously been done in Durango, or, if that was not felt to be final enough, could have resorted to the ley fuga; few would have doubted that he was genuinely trying to escape when shot. The fact that these things did not happen, and that Villa, in spite of his acts of outlawry, led a legal existence in Chihuahua, shows that he availed himself of the one means by which one could avoid arrest in Porfirian Mexico: links to powerful protectors.

The most powerful protectors one could have in Chihuahua were obviously the Terrazas and Creel families, but there is no evidence that Villa had any links to them, and the hatred that he felt for these families for many years indicates the contrary. Villa's protectors were probably the men for whom he worked for many years and who entrusted large sums of money to his care: the foreign companies in Chihuahua. They were influential enough to gain impunity for one of their employees as long as the crimes he committed were kept within limits. This might have been the case with Villa. His relations to foreign companies and the protection they gave him may also explain his positive attitude toward Americans until 1915, and also his negative attitude toward the Magonistas and the Industrial Workers of the World (IWW), who tried to organize the workers in foreign enterprises. In the long list of crimes committed prior to 1910 that Villa himself mentions in his autobiography, or that his enemies attributed to him, attacks on foreign companies or foreigners do not occur.

A second reason that may explain why Villa was not more actively persecuted by the Chihuahuan authorities was a tradition in Porfirian Mexico that continues to exist in much of present-day Mexico. Since people from the lower classes mistrusted both the police and the judiciary, they tended to settle conflicts among themselves. At times, they would let local leaders they trusted make decisions; at times, they would resort to violence. The upper classes and the authorities frequently showed little interest in clearing up conflicts and killings among the lower classes of society as long as these killings did not affect the elite. Thus the authorities may have shown little interest in some of the killings that Villa probably carried out.

On June 24, 1910, only one day after Villa was released in the Guerrero district, the attitude of Chihuahua's authorities toward him changed. In another part of the state, in the Hidalgo district, a warrant was issued for his arrest. Villa was accused of having stolen 28 head of cattle from the ranch of Santa Rita, which belonged to a Señora Guadalupe Prieto, and of having delivered them to the slaughterhouse in Santa Barbara with a bill of sale signed by Antonio Flores. The authorities found another receipt for cattle signed by Francisco Villa and, comparing the two documents, came to the conclusion that Flores was Villa's alias. On June 24, a warrant was issued for his arrest, in which he was described as "a white man of regular stature . . . clear gray eyes . . . with a blond mustache, married and approximately 28 years old."[45]

There is no evidence at first that Villa was pursued with great energy by the authorities, but their attitude soon changed. By the latter part of 1910, he was being relentlessly pursued by the Chihuahuan police and had emerged as both a prominent outlaw and a revolutionary. It is not entirely clear whether these two roles were related, at least in the beginning.

Two events seem to have put Villa on the Chihuahuan authorities' Most Wanted list. The first was his killing of Claro Reza, a man who according to the governor of the state had been a member of its secret police.[46]

Reza was a former companion of Villa's in bandit activities. After being captured by the Chihuahuan police, he not only became an informant for them, but went one step further and joined Creel's secret police. He informed the authorities of Villa's plans and whereabouts and led an unsuccessful expedition with the aim of capturing his former companion. The kind of information he gave the authorities, and thus the immediate reasons for his killing, are still a matter of dispute. Villa's opponents claim that Reza was revealing Villa's cattle-rustling plans, but in his memoirs, Villa gives an entirely different account of Reza's activities. The latter was spying on secret meetings between Villa and Abraham González and came to Villa's house at a time when González was scheduled to arrive there. Villa's killing of Reza thus had a political purpose. While the motives for Reza's killing are still subject to debate, the killing itself has been well documented and has become an integral part of the Villa legend. All accounts seem to agree on how Villa rode into Ciudad Chihuahua at a leisurely pace to find Reza. Some include the detail that he first bought a big ice-cream cone and was munching it when Reza stepped out of a bar he frequented, Las Quince Leguas. Villa shot him and then, at an equally leisurely pace, rode out of town, with no one daring to pursue him.[47]

The second event that greatly alarmed Chihuahua's authorities was an attack on the hacienda of Talamantes by 22 men looking for money, in which Villa had allegedly participated. The jefe político of the Jiménez district was convinced that Villa and a small rancher from Parral, Miguel Baca, were connected with the attack. The jefe político described Alfredo Villa, Francisco Villa, and Abelardo Prieto as "members of a gang of bandits roaming through the Benito Juárez district and the municipalities of Balleza, Olivos, and El Tule, and in the neighboring state of Durango, carrying out robberies and assaults."[48]

It is not clear whether these events were mere acts of banditry or were already part of Villa's revolutionary activity. It was either shortly after or shortly before this event that Villa was recruited into the ranks of the Madero revolutionists by Abraham González.[49] The circumstances of this meeting strongly impressed González, as he later told Silvestre Terrazas. González had contacted Villa, and they had agreed to meet at a specified date, after dark, at the headquarters of the Anti-Reelectionist Party in Ciudad Chihuahua. When González arrived at his office, he found two men, Villa and a companion, Feliciano Domínguez, their faces covered by *sarapes*, waiting in the dark for him.

"Good evening, gentlemen," he told them.
"Good evening and God be with you, Don Abraham."
"Come in."
Without shaking their hands, González put his hand into his back pocket in order to take out the key to the room and matches to light the oil lamp located in the middle of the room. This gesture, carried out in the dark, was noted by both Villa and Domínguez. When he struck a match and tried to light the lamp, Don Abraham found two pistols pointing at his head. Without showing the least sign of nervousness, his hand not trembling in the least, he quietly lit the lamp and smilingly and jokingly told them: "You're very smart. . . . You can put back your guns, since you have nothing to fear."
These words and his extreme calm, without fear and irresolution, so strongly impressed Villa that years later, he told me about it with great admiration, and said that this fearlessness of González had enormously impressed him and increased the confidence he had in that man so sincere and full of goodwill that he developed an affection for him that was to last throughout his life.[50]

At this meeting, González gave Villa a brief lesson in Mexican history, told him of the aims of the Anti-Reelectionist Party and of Madero, and asked him to join the planned revolution. Villa agreed, and from that moment on, he began recruiting men for the planned uprising. It is not at all clear what induced González to enlist Villa in his movement. It has been assumed that González saw Villa as one of the main leaders of Chihuahua's villagers and thus felt that he needed him to gain popular support. But if, as this book has tried to show, Villa was not a major peasant leader prior to the revolution, what could have induced González to recruit him? The question is all the more interesting in that Villa was the only outlaw whom the revolutionary leader asked to join his movement.

The most probable explanation is that the two men had known each other previously. González had once tried to export cattle from Mexico, and it is quite possible that one of the men with whom he had dealings was Villa. There is no evidence that González made any commitments to Villa, but it is quite possible that he promised him that if the revolution succeeded, no criminal proceedings of any kind would be instituted against him. Villa had at least two good reasons for wanting amnesty from a new revolutionary government. The first was the charge of desertion from the federal army hanging over him, and the second was the killing of Reza. If Villa had killed Reza for personal reasons and not because the latter was betraying his participation in the revolution, then he would have had a strong incentive for accepting a promise of amnesty by González. If this was not the case, Villa's motives are more difficult to explain.

Unlike Pascual Orozco, Villa at that time had no political ambitions. Unlike Toribio Ortega or Emiliano Zapata, he had never been a peasant or community leader, and the interests of such a constituency did not determine his actions, although his Robin Hood–like actions prior to 1910 and his massive distribution of goods to the poor after 1910 were to show that he was by no means indifferent to the fate of Mexico's have-nots. Outlaws at times join revolutionary movements in the hope of acquiring loot. While some looting may have gone on, most observers were impressed by the extraordinary discipline Villa kept among his men. The strongest motive for Villa's participation in the revolution was probably an element that was to play a key role throughout his whole life: hatred and desire for revenge. Although in mid 1910, Villa was not a hunted fugitive, he had had many conflicts with both hacendados and the Porfirian authorities.

The López Negrete family had a reputation for ruthlessness. The expropriation of the lands of the Ocuila Indians by a member of that family on the eve of the revolution, carried out with a brutality that stood out even in Porfirian Mexico, was to trigger a major social upheaval in the state of Durango.

Even if the owners of the estate were better disposed toward their laborers than the López Negretes, sharecroppers on large northern haciendas working marginal lands were the most rebellious element on these estates. No one has described this better than Patrick O'Hea, who was himself an administrator of a large hacienda in Durango, not far from the one where Villa had grown up:

On the upper lands where the irrigation water could not reach were straggling patches of maize and beans, precarious crops sown with the summer rains where the drift of rainfall over the land might to best advantage be deflected across the soil. . . . It was particularly in regard to the claim made by me, as representative of the owners of the hacienda, upon these outlying rainfall farmlands that I felt the resentment of the toiler at yielding any part of his produce to another merely because that other held some document of title. . . . I never invoked the civil power against them nor used high-handed methods; but on other haciendas men such as these, traditional squatters, were persecuted viciously to the slow and brooding growth of vindictive hate that at last bursts forth in revolution. Then they strove with reckless bloodshed, and striking blindly, to break the fetters and crush the power of the landlord and his law.[51]

The revolution offered Villa a chance for revenge. In addition, he was not indifferent to the plight of Chihuahua's villagers. Although he had never been a peasant leader, he seems to have maintained close contact with one of the oldest military colonies in the state, San Andrés, and, in the course of the revolution, he was to marry a girl from the town, Luz Corral. San Andrés had been the scene of Macario Nieto's peasant movement (see chapter 1) and of a large-scale tax revolt in 1909. While Villa did not participate in these movements, he probably not only knew of them but shared in the villagers' hatred for the Porfirian authorities. Villa recruited a sizable number of men for the revolution in San Andrés.

Villa may also have been influenced by a tradition of outlaws in Durango actively participating in politics. This was certainly the case with the most famous outlaw who had roamed the hills of Durango and Zacatecas, Heraclio Bernal. Parra had been a part of Bernal's band, and he in turn recruited Villa into his own band.

In 1910, when he joined the ranks of the Madero movement, Villa was 32, in the prime of life. "In personal appearance, he is about 5 feet 10 inches in height," an American doctor who knew him well reported to U.S. military intelligence,

weighs about 170 lbs., is well developed in a muscular way; has a very heavy protruding lower jaw and badly stained teeth; a rather dandified moderately heavy moustache of a heavy villain variety; crispy kinky black hair of the Negro type, which is generally tousled. He has the most remarkable pair of prominent brown eyes I have ever seen. They seem to look through you; he talks with them, and all of his expressions are heralded and dominated by them first; and when in anger or trying to impress a particular point, they seem to burn, and spit out sparks and flashes between the hard drawn, narrowed and nearly closed lids.

He is a remarkable horseman, sits on his horse with cowboy ease and grace, rides straight and stiff legged Mexican style, and would only use a Mexican saddle. He loves his horse, is very considerate of his comfort, probably due to the fact that they have aided him in escaping from tight places so many times. He has often ridden over a hundred miles within a twenty-four hours over the roughest mountain trails. He is untiring on horseback and boasts that he is generally further away in the morning than his pursuers expect him to be.

He dresses very commonly, has none of the Latin desire for pomp or show of any kind, and is never so happy as when he is performing some rough riding stunts or attending a cock fight, one of his pet diversions.[52]

Villa had the reputation of being one of Mexico's greatest gunfighters. "For Villa, the gun was more important than eating and sleeping," a subordinate wrote about him. "It was a part of his person indispensable to him wherever he was, even at social occasions, and one can say that it was only very rarely that he did not have the gun ready to be drawn or placed in his gun belt."[53]

Silvestre Terrazas, the author of this description, one day took a walk with Villa to the outskirts of the city of Chihuahua:

Far away, perhaps 100 to 200 meters away, a small lonely branch of wood was floating in the water. . . . And it seemed to have been placed there to test the marksmanship of General Villa, as I indicated to him.

"Well, General," I told him, "I have never seen you shoot your gun and your reputation states that no one can be compared with you. There you have a piece of wood," I showed it to him, "and if you hit it, you are a very good shot. . . . "

General Villa without saying a word, calmly took out his pistol and very quietly, with perfect aim, first raised the gun as high as he could, and then slowly lowered it, aiming at the very small target, he shot with such accuracy and with such a firm hand . . . that he divided the small branch into two exactly similar pieces.[54]

Villa neither smoked, drank, nor took drugs. He could be enormously generous and might weep publicly when emotion overtook him. When seized by a burst of fury, he was also capable of acts of great cruelty. He was loyal to the men he respected, but if he felt betrayed, he became relentless in his hatred, frequently extending it to the families of his victims. He was a passionate lover, fathering children with girlfriends and wives throughout Chihuahua. He had no compunction about being married to several women at the same time and some have speculated that he may have been influenced by Mormon colonists who had settled in Chihuahua to escape U.S. laws against polygamy. Even after leaving the women he lived with, he supported them and acknowledged and cared for his many children.

He had little education, and it is still a matter of dispute as to whether he could read and write when the revolution broke out. Perhaps for this reason, he had a deep respect for education and during the brief time that he exercised power in Chihuahua in later years, unprecedented amounts of money were spent on schools.

Friends and foes alike agreed that he had a sharp and penetrating intelligence, which became clouded only when he was seized by one of his bouts of fury.

In the eyes of González and the leadership of the Anti-Reelectionist Party, Villa was a valuable asset as a guerrilla fighter, but it is doubtful whether they believed he could be more than a subordinate leader of the revolution. His lack of education, his lowly social origin, his political inexperience, his lack of a large family network in Chihuahua, and his reputation as a bandit seemed formidable obstacles to achieving primary importance in the ranks of the revolutionary movement. Yet within a few months, Villa would emerge as one of the most important military leaders of the Mexican Revolution, second only to Pascual Orozco in Chihuahua in power and influence. He possessed qualities that more than made up for his weaknesses: he was a living dynamo imbued with a unrelenting energy. He constantly attempted and frequently succeeded in carrying out offensive actions and taking the initiative in military operations.

His prestige among Chihuahua's revolutionaries soared after the outbreak of the revolution, since he was the first of its leaders to be involved in an armed clash with government supporters and the first to defeat regular government troops. On November 17, three days before he joined the group of armed men commanded by Castulo Herrera, Villa and a group of fourteen men he had recruited, largely from among associates from his cattle-rustling days, attacked the hacienda of Chavarría in order to obtain money, horses, and supplies. They had to fight their way into the hacienda, killing its administrator, Pedro Domínguez, who had attempted to resist them.[55]

On November 21, Herrera, Villa, and their men occupied the old military colony of San Andrés without encountering any active resistance. On that same day, news reached Villa that a train carrying federal troops was on its way to San Andrés. With a small group of men, Villa went to the railway station, and when the soldiers began disembarking, the revolutionaries opened fire. The commander of the federal troops, Captain Yepez, was killed, along with several of his men, and the survivors retreated.

In military terms, this was a minor clash, but its psychological impact was enormous. For the first time, revolutionaries had fought federal troops and forced them to retreat. Hundreds of volunteers, primarily from San Andrés but also from surrounding villages, joined the revolutionary army, and the contingent of Herrera and Villa soon numbered 325 men. In theory, Herrera was their commander. In practice, Villa was assuming more and more leadership functions. Herrera had been a good politician, but he was not a military leader and proved incapable of controlling his men. When his contingent entered San Andrés, the men began to celebrate their victory by firing their guns into the air. Not only did this shooting spree frighten the civilian population, it was also a waste of ammunition. Villa tried to persuade Herrera to order a stop to it. Perhaps because he felt too insecure, Herrera refused to control his men. It was Villa who had to order an end to the shooting and to discipline the troops.[56] This was the beginning of the shift of authority from Herrera to Villa.

In the early days of every revolution, there is a surge of what could be called a wild exuberance, a boundless optimism, a feeling that with a minimum of sacrifice, everything is possible. The Chihuahuan revolutionaries were no exception. They had captured their first villages practically without fighting and had repelled the first attack of federal troops. Why not attack the state capital and thus obtain a decisive triumph once and for all? It was a wild scheme that nearly led to total disaster for Villa and his men. Their ranks swollen to 500 men, the revolutionaries advanced on Ciudad Chihuahua. They set up camp within a few miles of the state capital, and Herrera sent 40 men out on a reconnaissance mission. Villa, who commanded these men, divided them into two groups. The first, comprising 30 revolutionaries, reached the hilltop of El Tecolote, where they saw 700 federal soldiers advancing on them. Instead of returning to their main contingent, they decided to fight. It was an unequal struggle, and within half an hour, they were forced to retreat. By a clever trick, however, they succeeded in delaying pursuit by federal troops. On the mountain top, they had placed a large number of sombreros, and the federal soldiers were convinced that a revolutionary was lurking beneath every one of these hats, so that they advanced very cautiously, shooting off their ammunition at the fictitious soldiers.[57] While the 30 revolutionaries were thus retreating, without having suffered any casualties, Villa and his remaining 10 men arrived on the scene and immediately attacked the 700 federal soldiers. It was a brave, but as Villa later recounted it, absolutely foolhardy act, and he and his men were on the point of being killed when the 30 retreating members of his command returned and counterattacked.

After keeping the federal troops at bay for nearly an hour, they managed to escape and to elude federal pursuit, thanks to the sombreros, which the federal troops still took to be soldiers. The federal troops could not conceive that only 40 men had attacked them. Villa and his men had held out for so long against the far superior federal forces in the hope that Herrera and his men would join them, and that from the vantage point of the hilltop they might prevent the federal troops from moving into the mountain range of western Chihuahua, where the main forces of the revolutionaries were concentrated. Herrera had refused to move. As a result, increasing bitterness developed between him and Villa.[58]

The Díaz Administration
and the Chihuahuan Revolution

In the early days of the uprisings in Chihuahua, Díaz was optimistic that he could crush the Chihuahuan revolutionaries and decided to do so without any effort at compromise. Evidence of discouragement among Chihuahua's revolutionaries in the early phases of the revolution strengthened Díaz's optimism and his resolve to crush the uprising at any cost.

For many revolutionaries, these first days of December had proved a time not only of triumph but also of disappointment. They began to realize that they stood practically alone in Mexico, for only a few local skirmishes had taken place outside of Chihuahua. Madero was still in the United States, unable to enter Mexico. All the might of the federal government was now concentrated against the people of Chihuahua. At the same time, the success of the revolutionaries had brought home to parts of the Chihuahuan elite (though not to the Terrazas) the fact that they were dealing, not with a few isolated bandits, but with a genuine popular uprising. A group of prominent Chihuahuans (it is not clear whether they acted with the tacit support or tolerance of either the state or the federal government) began to negotiate with the revolutionaries. Villa and a number of other leaders were at least willing to consider the possibility of four weeks' armistice. The members of the elite who made the proposal hoped that negotiations might put an end to the revolution. After four weeks of seeing that the rest of the country was not revolting, the negotiators hoped that the revolutionaries would finally lay down their arms. For their part, the revolutionaries may have anticipated that within four weeks, other movements would develop elsewhere in the country, and that once they resumed operations, they would not have to bear the brunt of the fighting anymore.

The revolutionary leaders in Chihuahua were not ready to sign such an accord on their own. They decided to send Castulo Herrera to the United States to find out whether González and Madero agreed to such an armistice. Before the latter could make a decision, however, Porfirio Díaz rejected any kind of compromise with the revolutionaries.[59] News of the Chihuahuan revolution had made headlines all over the world and had undermined the confidence of financiers and banks in the stability of the Mexican government. The finance minister, José Yves Limantour, who had gone to Europe to negotiate for a reconversion of the Mexican debt, wrote that repayment terms offered by banks and other financial institutions had worsened as a result of news of upheavals and unrest in Mexico.[60] Díaz felt that a decisive victory was needed so that the financial markets would regain confidence in the ability of his government to control the country. In addition, since the main forces of the revolutionaries were concentrated in Chihuahua, he believed that it should not be too difficult to crush the uprising.

Díaz decided on a two-tiered strategy. He sent reinforcements consisting of more than 5,000 federal soldiers into Chihuahua. He placed these troops under the command of a longtime associate whom he greatly trusted, General Juan Hernández. Hernández had been stationed in Chihuahua for many years and knew the terrain and local conditions well.

At the same time, Díaz decided to utilize whatever resources the Terrazas could mobilize to fight the revolution. Rumors were reaching the Mexican president that the Terrazas were repeating their old game of duplicity that they had successfully played in 1879 and in 1892: officially supporting the government while surreptitiously helping revolutionaries in order to secure more concessions from the administration. There was, he felt, a way to force the Terrazas' hand, and that was to name a prominent member of the family as governor of Chihuahua. On December 6, Governor José María Sánchez, who had been appointed by Creel and was Terrazas's and Creel's creature, was replaced by Alberto Terrazas.

No one could have been closer to both Luis Terrazas and Enrique Creel than Alberto Terrazas. Not only was he Luis's son, but having married Enrique Creel's daughter, he was also the latter's son-in-law and the husband of Luis Terrazas's granddaughter, his own niece.[61]

This appointment was a grievous mistake, for which Díaz would pay a high price. Even without one of their own being appointed state governor, the Terrazas-Creel clan would have fought with all of their resources against the revolutionaries, since they had everything to lose and nothing to gain from a rebel victory. They realized that the revolution was directed primarily against them. By identifying himself completely with the Terrazas, Díaz put oil on the fire.

At first glance, the Mexican president's hopes and calculations seemed reasonable. The number of revolutionaries in Chihuahua by the beginning of December was estimated at about 1,500 men. Little revolutionary activity had taken place in the rest of the country. The combination of 5,000 federal soldiers and the huge resources of the Terrazas empire made it seem easy to crush the rebels. The better organization, better armament and training, and the superiority in numbers of the federal army could be expected to enable it to defeat the revolutionaries in regular battles. The Terrazas in turn, by mobilizing their retainers, clients, peons, and supporters both on haciendas and in small towns, would isolate the remaining revolutionaries, cut them off from any supplies, and prevent them from waging guerrilla warfare.

For several weeks, Díaz may have thought that his strategy was successful. Federal troops penetrated the mountains of western Chihuahua and occupied the larger towns that the revolutionaries had briefly held: Ciudad Guerrero and San Andrés. They defeated Orozco in December at the battle of Cerro Prieto and prevented the revolutionaries in eastern Chihuahua from occupying the town of Ojinaga. Díaz received a steady stream of reports exuding optimism from Governor Alberto Terrazas. On December 14, Terrazas wrote Díaz that he had succeeded "in changing the opinion of the people living in some of the regions that had been prey to seditious ideas." He further reported that his agents had gone into some of the districts where revolutionary activities had taken place and had "returned full of hope based on the expectation that their propaganda would prevent the cancer of revolution from progressing further."[62] On January 7, 1911, the governor's brother, Juan Terrazas, wrote Díaz that he had organized a meeting in Ciudad Camargo in which all participants had pledged allegiance to his regime. He told of setting up groups of volunteers to fight against the revolutionaries in a whole series of villages in that district.[63]

Only one day later, the governor wrote Díaz that one of the leaders of the revolutionary movement, Apolonio Rodríguez, wanted to surrender to the Terrazas' troops, and that he was sure that Rodríguez's example would be followed by other revolutionaries.[64] Within two days, the governor's optimism grew even more. He reported to Díaz that Pascual Orozco was on the verge of surrender.[65]

Even when, only a few days after Alberto Terrazas's optimistic report, it became abundantly clear that Orozco did not in the least contemplate surrender, the governor expressed the hope and the expectation that as soon as government troops occupied those parts of the western mountain region of Chihuahua still occupied by revolutionaries, they would be able to count on massive popular help. In late January, however, the governor's optimism became more muted; he was obliged to report an ever-increasing number of attacks by revolutionaries, while the "boundless enthusiasm" of his own supporters that he had described in such detail in earlier letters was suddenly absent from his reports.

The Collapse of the Terrazas Strategy

Not only Alberto Terrazas but his father Luis and Enrique Creel were soon forced to realize that their strategy for defending their power and interests was on the verge of collapse. That strategy rested on four pillars: the state and municipal officials whom Terrazas and Creel had appointed; the thousands of peons on their estates, whom they hoped to arm to defend their interests; men hired to fight for them, consisting primarily of members of those factions within villages and military colonies whom the Terrazas had favored and who had benefited from the land law of 1905; and, finally, the state's hacendados, who were all either intermarried with or economically linked to Terrazas and Creel.

The first of these pillars proved to be extremely weak; the three others collapsed.

While a few of the state and municipal officials, such as the mayor of Namiquipa, attempted to fight, most simply fled. Those who fought did not resist for long. They soon saw how isolated they were and how ineffective the other bases of Terrazas's power, on whose help they had counted, proved to be.

The peons on the Terrazas estates not only refused to fight for their masters; most of them sympathized with the revolution. "I have been trying to arm the people on my haciendas," Terrazas wrote sadly to Creel on January 20, 1911, only eight weeks after the outbreak of the revolution, "but frankly I have to tell you again that the peons themselves have been contaminated and I can only count on a very small number who are loyal. To arm those who are not loyal, as you can imagine, would be counterproductive since they would join the enemy with their arms and equipment."[66]

Terrazas's hope of recruiting mercenaries and volunteers above all from those factions within the villages and the former military colonies that Creel's policies had favored and who had benefited from the land law of 1905 proved equally elusive. "I have not been able to secure men," Terrazas complained, "although I offered to pay them two pesos a day and to provide them with horses and arms at my expense." Those men who did join the Terracista auxiliary forces—Alberto Terrazas optimistically reported in January 1911 that he had recruited 1,175 men—effectively refused to fight.[67] Terrazas complained to Díaz that when a rebel commander, Práxedis Guerrero, attacked the town of Janos with only 27 men, the mayor and several loyal retainers were forced to fight off the revolutionaries alone, since neither the townspeople nor the members of the local police force joined in the defense.[68] Not even the remaining members of the state's oligarchy, above all its hacendados, so closely linked to the Terrazas by both family and financial ties, came to their defense. Creel complained bitterly of the "incredible egotism of the hacendados." The state government had asked them to arm some retainers on their haciendas to protect their estates from the revolutionaries and had offered to defray the cost. The hacendados had refused, however, fearing that the revolutionaries would take reprisals against them, "killing their cattle and destroying their haciendas." With great indignation Creel wrote that "as a result of this fear, remote as it may seem, the feelings of patriotism and personal dignity have disappeared . . . and these poor people do not understand that with this indifferent attitude they are contributing to the destruction of what is their ideal, i.e., their fortune."[69] The passivity of the hacendados primarily reflected their hope that if they did not actively oppose them, the revolutionaries would concentrate their hatred on the Terrazas.

There is no single explanation for the sudden collapse of these pillars of Terracista resistance. The rebelliousness of the Terrazas peons was partly owing to the fact that Terrazas, in contrast to most foreign landowners, had maintained the system of debt peonage on his haciendas. The old caudillo's unwillingness to break with traditional forms of servitude was combined with his capacity to avoid doing so. Because of his enormous economic and political power, Terrazas had the means, which few other northern hacendados possessed, to enforce an increasingly unpopular system of debt peonage among his recalcitrant laborers. The Terrazas peons contrasted their situation not only with that of their counterparts on foreign-owned states but with ranches across the border as well. In addition, traditional patriarchal bonds that had existed on these estates for many years were beginning to break down. This was not because of any lack of effort to maintain them. Luis Terrazas made it a point to visit each of his haciendas at least once a year. On those occasions, a holiday was declared, and the peons lined up to receive him and the gifts he brought. He went to great pains to remember the name and history of each peon.

But the transformations that his empire had undergone tended to vitiate those efforts. First, a traditional patriarchal relationship was strained by the growth of the landholdings of Terrazas and other barons of the north, which made it more and more difficult for the landowners to establish personal relationships with their peons. Second, the patriarchal relationship had been drained of much of its meaning with the defeat of the Apaches in 1884. Until then, the hacendado, like the medieval lord in Europe, had been able to offer protection from attack by taking his peons into his fortified *casco* (the central residence of the hacienda, which in northern Mexico had been built as a refuge and a fortress) and by sending out retainers to fight the wandering Indian bands. With the end of the Apache wars, that protection was no longer needed, and the hacendados began losing much of the legitimacy they had hitherto possessed among their peons.

It is at first glance more difficult to explain why the free villagers, many of them from the old military colonies, whose support Creel had been courting either by granting them political power or by making them beneficiaries of his 1905 land law, preferred not to fight and to remain as passive as possible. Some, sensing the weakness of the Terrazas and the strength of the revolutionary movement, refused to be drawn into the conflict. Others were increasingly bitter toward Creel, feeling that he had taken back with one hand what he had given with the other. In the case of San Andrés, even those who had benefited from land seizures were victims of the huge tax increases the state administration had imposed in 1908 and 1909.

The failure of the Terrazas strategy was a disaster for the federal government's attempts to suppress the Chihuahuan revolution.

The Failure of the Military Option

Traditionally, when dealing with local uprisings, Díaz had relied on a combination of federal troops and local auxiliaries. The locals knew the terrain, had a good knowledge of their area's rebels and their hideouts, could count on at least some degree of local support, and made for an efficient counterguerrilla force. With the failure of the Terrazas' counterguerrilla strategy, Díaz would have to rely on federal troops alone. The few efforts at counterguerrilla strategy that Díaz initiated from U.S. territory had no great success.[70] The federal troops did not know the terrain and were generally unpopular in Chihuahua. Above all, there were too few of them.

One of Díaz's most important commanders in Chihuahua, García Cuellar, had come to the conclusion that "this revolution is identical to the Boer insurrection [in South Africa,] and England could only dominate it when it sent ten soldiers for every Boer. This fact, which may seem laughable to some, is the truth, and this is what we shall have to do."[71]

The number of federal soldiers in Chihuahua was only between 5,000 and 10,000 men. The total size of the federal army was about 30,000 men, but Díaz could not send the whole Mexican army to Chihuahua at a time when revolutionary upheavals threatened to erupt in other parts of the country.

The first solution to this problem that occurred to Díaz was to rapidly increase the size of the federal army. He soon realized that finding recruits was an impossible task. That was the gist of the reports that his governors sent him from all over Mexico. In Campeche, the governor, who expressed his full support for Díaz, did not see how he could comply with the president's instructions and recruit 100 men to form the garrison of his capital city, "in view of the general opposition of the people to military service, especially under present circumstances, since every call for the service is seen as a means of sending troops out of the state."[72] In a similar vein, the governor of the state of Zacatecas reported on the difficulties his officials had in finding volunteers to fight for the regime.[73] The governor of Durango was even more explicit. "For some days I have been attempting to set up guerrillas to actively pursue the revolutionaries who have invaded the state; this is creating difficulties for me, for there are not many people of sufficient goodwill to do this."[74]

Some of Díaz's governors were in a quandary when they attempted to explain the lack of popular enthusiasm for fighting for the regime. They did not want to admit that the inhabitants of their states might be dissatisfied with Díaz, or with their own administrations, and so they looked for other explanations for their inability to recruit volunteers. "The reason for this," the governor of the state of Tamaulipas wrote after describing his difficulties in finding men ready to volunteer for service in Díaz's auxiliary troops, "is the present situation of our people, who are only interested in working, caring for their families and enjoying the benefits of peace. When someone is drafted, he deserts; many find work in other villages or ranches that need men for agricultural work. . . . This is especially the case near the border, where these deserters pass onto the American side, which leads to a reduction of the number of inhabitants."[75] The governor of Queretaro found a particularly original excuse. The people of his state were too "timid" to fight.[76] The governor of Puebla attributed his difficulties in securing volunteers to their fear of being sent out of the state, especially to Chihuahua or to Yucatán.[77] Other governors were more honest and outspoken. "I would like to repeat to you what I have already said in my telegram," the governor of Sonora wrote to Díaz: "from day to day, the number of enemies is increasing, while the number of our troops is decreasing and sympathy for the revolutionaries grows in the whole state."[78]

The difficulties Díaz had in finding volunteers for his auxiliary troops were compounded by the even greater difficulties he encountered in replacing federal casualties. The traditional method of recruitment, the leva, which consisted of impressing either dissidents, personal enemies of local officials, or the poorest segments of society into the army, was so unpopular that the government, which realized that this was one of the major causes for the outbreak of the revolution, was reluctant to use it. Yet no other method was open to the Díaz regime. When it did apply the leva, the results were often catastrophic. In the city of Tula, in the state of Tampico, the rural police, whom Díaz's officials had hoped to mobilize to fight the rebels, preferred to shoot their way out of the city rather than to go into battle against the revolutionaries.[79] The governor of Campeche nearly caused a revolt in his state when he impressed 28 men for army service. "These measures caused great unrest and alarm among the population of this state. In many villages, men liable for military service went into hiding, while others emigrated to Yucatán, Quintana Roo, or Tabasco so as not to be subjected to conscription. In some villages, signs of rebellion were evident, and I became afraid that a grave conflict might erupt."[80] The governor, who feared that further conscription would provoke an uprising in Campeche, suspended the military draft.[81] In Yucatán, the governor reported that men sent to serve in the national guard were going into hiding. "The organization of such national guards has led those who were to form it to stage uprisings in some villages, while in others, they simply disobeyed without taking up arms."[82]

Some governors now envisaged desperate strategies to recruit soldiers. The governor of Yucatán considered recruiting Indians from the Huasteca, who had been drafted to work on the sisal fields, into the army. He was convinced that they would prefer six months' military service, with a guaranteed return home afterward, to continuing work as contract laborers on the henequen plantations of Yucatán.[83] General José María de la Vega in León, Guanajuato, suggested to Díaz that an advance payment should be offered to prospective soldiers, who would thus be lured into government recruiting offices. There, "they would not be allowed to leave and be sent to the army immediately."[84] On the whole, these strategies had little effect, and as the revolution proceeded, the number of troops at the disposal of the government could not be substantially increased.

In Chihuahua, the failure of the Terrazas strategy and Díaz's inability rapidly to increase the number of federal troops in the state induced Díaz's military commanders, particularly the man the Mexican president had designated to crush the uprising in Chihuahua, General Juan Hernández, to advocate a policy of compromise and conciliation.

At first, after his arrival in Chihuahua, Hernández had been optimistic. He spoke of sending troops to Ciudad Guerrero, which was the center of the uprising. He was convinced that "if we can exterminate the revolutionaries [in Ciudad Guerrero], the rest will certainly become demoralized" and the revolt would be finished.[85] A week later, he became even more optimistic after the revolutionaries had suffered a minor defeat. Hernández now believed that the end of the revolution was near: "from the reports I have obtained, it is clear that the revolutionaries have been profoundly impressed by their defeat and many have been convinced that they cannot fight against the government and thus decided to abandon their evil cause."[86] As the revolutionary movement, in spite of temporary defeats, gathered more and more momentum, Hernández began to revise his opinions. He was impressed when in the town of Carretas, "thirteen revolutionaries plundered the city, which has 2,000 inhabitants, and no one resisted them." He had become convinced "that the revolutionaries have many sympathizers among the people here, who speak with great fervor of the triumph of their cause."[87]

A few days later, Hernández was even more explicit. "I have to inform you with all due clarity that the problems that have come up here and that have caused so much bloodshed have one main origin: the general dissatisfaction among the inhabitants of the state with conditions since the government has been taken over by the Terrazas family, a family they hate. Since they believe that their rulers can only remain in power with your support, they make you responsible for this situation."[88]

An anonymous report that Hernández transmitted to Díaz amounted to a devastating indictment of the Terrazas and a somber preview of what the revolution could bring for the Díaz regime if changes were not rapidly instituted. The main causes of the revolution, in the opinion of the anonymous author, were "ancient conflicts over the distribution of communal lands, frequent disappearances of unmarked cattle, excessive pressure by prefects and mayors with a low degree of education, increasing taxes, which small businessmen have to pay above all, and increases in individual taxes." Madero only utilized for his own ends the dissatisfaction of Chihuahua's population, which was directed primarily against "General Don Luis Terrazas, the richest man in Chihuahua, who controls all large and small enterprises, including public urinals." There was a generalized feeling that the Terrazas "would absorb all capital and energy in Chihuahua."[89]

Attempts at a Political Solution

General Hernández was a notable exception among the Porfirian military in that he advocated a political and social solution to the Mexican Revolution rather than a purely military one. His ideas were also different from those of Porfirian politicians who in the later stage of the revolution came to advocate a compromise with the upper-class leadership of the Madero movement. Hernández was in favor of a compromise with the rebellious lower classes in Chihuahua so as to prevent them from joining Madero.

This does not mean that Hernández rejected repression. On January 19, 1911, he described the policies he was advocating in a letter to Porfirio Díaz. "I must tell you again," he wrote the Mexican president, "that the whole state sympathizes with the present revolution and that a great amount of work will be necessary to change the situation; work of a moral and material nature is necessary. On the one hand, some must be convinced, others must be treated with great energy, while the most rebellious of the state's inhabitants should be dealt with inflexibly. For many, being placed under arrest by district courts is not sufficient; it would be much more practical and much more positive results would be obtained if they were sent to Yucatán or perhaps even better, to the territory of Quintana Roo, in the same way that we dealt with the pernicious rebels in Oaxaca and Puebla. If you would authorize me to do so, we would remove many seditious elements from the state who by their presence are helping the revolutionaries."[90]

In an order sent to his subordinate, General Juan Navarro, who was advancing with federal troops into the Guerrero district, Hernández admonished him to fight "these rebels, these evil people who, as really ingrained scoundrels, have refused to recognize how much we owe our president. . . . I want you to activate your operations to give no more time to these murderous bandits to win converts and to organize . . . to bring about their complete destruction."[91] Navarro seems to have understood his chief's instructions correctly: he began to carry out massive executions of revolutionary prisoners, and Hernández never restrained him or admonished him to desist from such killings.[92]

Hernández's advocacy of repression was not substantially different from Alberto Terrazas's call to Díaz to carry out massive punishment of revolutionaries or from the suggestion made by Luis Medina Barrón, a federal commander sent to Chihuahua by the head of the federal forces in neighboring Sonora, who in December 1910 had called for the implementation of a state of siege in the rebellious Guerrero district and large-scale executions of revolutionaries.[93] What distinguished Hernández from these men was his advocacy of reform and limited compromise. In his eyes, two men were to be instrumental in implementing the new policy: the former governor Miguel Ahumada and the dissident newspaper editor Silvestre Terrazas.

It comes as no surprise that Hernández should have thought of Miguel Ahumada as the candidate best suited to replace Alberto Terrazas and to make some kind of deal with the revolutionaries. Ahumada, who was serving as governor of Jalisco at the time, was a loyal Porfirian politician. From 1892 to 1903, for eleven years before Luis Terrazas reassumed political power in Chihuahua, Ahumada had been governor of that northern state. At the time, his tenure had been controversial (it was he who had mercilessly crushed the uprising in Tomóchi). Nevertheless, in comparison to what came later, his image steadily improved, and in the minds of many Chihuahuans, he had become "the good governor." While land expropriations had taken place during his tenure, they had occurred on a much smaller scale than the large-scale destruction of peasant property during the Terrazas-Creel rule. While Ahumada had allowed the Terrazas more leeway than they had achieved before, he still permitted other groups within the state to maintain a degree of political and economic power. He had attempted to conciliate the state's middle classes, and in spite of his harshness toward the rebels of Tomóchi, he had preferred mediation to confrontation.

It is more surprising that Hernández should have shown an interest in Silvestre Terrazas, Chihuahua's maverick opposition editor and journalist. When revolution broke out in Chihuahua, Silvestre Terrazas's newspaper, *El Correo de Chihuahua,* had published long, detailed reports on the rebellion in the state, thus indirectly encouraging it. Governor Sánchez had admonished him to stop publishing this kind of information. When Terrazas refused, he had been arrested and sent to prison in Mexico City. The newspaperman blamed Creel for his arrest.[94] He was right.

It is possible to imagine what made Silvestre Terrazas such an important figure in Hernández's eyes. He enjoyed enormous prestige in Chihuahua because of his long-standing opposition to Creel and Terrazas, a prestige that was especially great among the regime's opponents. That prestige only increased once Silvestre Terrazas had been imprisoned and sent to Mexico City. At the same time, Hernández believed that Silvestre Terrazas was only intent on toppling the Terrazas-Creel dynasty and had little interest in national politics or the overthrow of Díaz. Silvestre Terrazas maintained very friendly relations with Ahumada, and the bishop of Chihuahua interceded on his behalf, which must have convinced Hernández that the editor might become an intermediary, trusted by both sides. Such a person could reestablish peace in Chihuahua.

Porfirio Díaz responded positively to Hernández's suggestions. At the end of January, Alberto Terrazas was removed from office and replaced by Miguel Ahumada. In a bitter letter to Luis Terrazas on January 24, Creel wrote to his father-in-law: "Porfirio Díaz is highly alarmed at the news that public opinion in nearly the whole of the state is in favor of the revolution. He has been told that a change of administration might remedy this situation."[95]

A few days later, at the request of Hernández, Silvestre Terrazas was not only released from prison but granted a lengthy interview with Porfirio Díaz, in which the Mexican president assured him that he wanted peace, although it is not clear whether Díaz suggested any kind of compromise to Silvestre Terrazas.[96]

In spite of the measures he took, it is doubtful whether Porfirio Díaz really understood the nature of the revolution that was directed against him. In a lengthy interview with a British representative in February 1911, Díaz stated, "the trouble in the north was very difficult indeed to suppress, on account of the nature of the country; the rebels were greatly aided by the good breed of the Chihuahua horses, of which they were always able to obtain a supply by theft or otherwise." The revolutionaries, in Díaz's opinion, "were merely armed men, who fought under no political banners; they were mere desperadoes who had every-thing to gain and nothing to lose by disorder, but the root of the whole matter was the encouragement they received from Madero."[97]

A few days after Ahumada had assumed office in Chihuahua, Hernández re-ported optimistically to Díaz that the state had finally turned the corner, and that an end to the revolution was in sight, writing, "Since Señor Ahumada has taken charge of the government of this state, the situation has changed totally, at least in the capital, and I believe that the same will happen in the outlying districts."[98]

Hernández was mistaken. By February 1911, whatever chances of a compro-mise might have existed before had disappeared. In the intervening months, the revolutionary army had doubled in size. The revolutionaries were no longer iso-lated; the revolution was spreading throughout the country. Above all, on Feb-ruary 14, Madero had entered Mexico from the United States to assume personal command of the revolution. It thus acquired a new dimension.

In military terms, the situation between the outbreak of the revolution and the arrival of Madero in Chihuahua in February 1911 can best be summarized by saying that the federal army was winning most of the battles, while the revolu-tionaries were winning the war. After suffering a series of initial defeats—including the battle of Pedernales, where a federal contingent was decimated by Orozco's troops, and the battle of Malpaso, where the head of the federal troops, Colonel Martín Luis Guzmán, was killed and his troops were forced to retreat—the federal army proved to be more effective in its encounters with large contin-gents of revolutionaries. It defeated them in the battle of Cerro Prieto, recap-tured the larger towns, such as Ciudad Guerrero, from the revolutionaries, and prevented them from carrying out plans to occupy cities such as Ojinaga, Ciu-dad Juárez, and Ciudad Chihuahua. These defeats, however, did not prevent the revolutionaries from steadily growing in numbers and importance. While the fed-eral troops occupied the towns, the revolutionaries roamed practically at will through the countryside, controlling much of it.

The almost universal hatred for Terrazas and Creel was not the only factor that explains the persistence and the growth of the revolutionary movement. The na-ture of the terrain of Chihuahua made it easy for the revolutionaries to retreat into the mountains, where their adversaries were not able to find or even pursue them. Thanks to the closeness of the U.S. border, arms were constantly being smuggled to them, largely owing of the efforts of Abraham González. Mexican volunteers from across the border swelled rebel ranks. Even more important was the enor-mous wealth of the great haciendas belonging to the oligarchy. The revolutionar-ies simply swooped down on the estates and confiscated horses, food, arms, and money from their owners. Since the federal army could not station troops on all estates, and since the peons were unwilling to fight for their masters, the hacen-dados gave the revolutionaries whatever they wanted without any resistance.

Guerrilla Strategy and Federal Incompetence

The federal forces were not well equipped to wage an effective counterguerrilla campaign. Many of the soldiers were recruits forcibly impressed into the army and unwilling to fight. Only a short time after assuming command of the military forces in Chihuahua, Hernández wrote Díaz, "Nearly all of the sixth battalion is composed of recruits who have only been in the service for two months and do not yet love the military career, so that they would desert at the first opportunity."[99] Many of Díaz's generals, such as one of the leading federal commanders in Chihuahua, Juan Navarro, were old and lacked initiative. "I have been urging Juan [Navarro]," Hernández reported to Díaz, "to become more active in the pursuit of the revolutionaries whose center of operation was in the Guerrero district. I have called on him to do so, as a friend, as a brother, as a commander, as you will have seen from the instructions that I have sent him in letters and telegrams of which I have sent you a copy. But since Juan has been indifferent to these instructions, I thought of proceeding in a different way. . . . My explanation for this indifference on Juan's part is the natural tiredness of old age, for very few men always keep their vigor and activity like you."[100]

In other cases, corrupt officials had padded the payroll and used money intended to equip soldiers for their own ends. Major Mauricio Cavazos, a personal confidant of Díaz's who had been sent to Ciudad Juárez to take command of the border guards, bitterly complained that "there are mounted guards who receive their salary without owning a horse, a saddle, or arms, and for these reasons, do not inspire great confidence in me."[101]

The federal troops had the greatest difficulties in coping with the kind of guerrilla warfare waged by the revolutionaries. Some of the strategies the revolutionaries employed are perhaps best described in a letter that the federal authorities intercepted, written from San Antonio, Texas, by a man named Andrés, and directed to a Mariano López Ortíz, a revolutionary from Coahuila, whom he addressed as "Papacito."

From the letter, it seems that "Papacito" was operating in the state of Tamaulipas and that Andrés was supplying him with ammunition. Andrés had contacts with leaders of the Madero movement: he mentions a meeting with Alfonso Madero and with Francisco Vázquez Gómez. In addition to writing to "Papacito" about the ammunitions and arms he is going to smuggle to him, he gives him detailed instructions on how to operate. He calls on him to blow up bridges, destroy railway tracks and telegraph and telephone lines, and interrupt rail communications between Torreón and Chihuahua. "Naturally all this should be done secretly without having to fight anyone; that means that it should be done during the night."

Andrés calls on "Papacito" to send officers to the haciendas to supply his forces with money, arms, and ammunitions. The officers should "arrest and capture the owner of a hacienda or the administrator and keep him as a prisoner until he gives as much as he can as a ransom; he should under no circumstances be killed, but he should rather be treated well. At the same time, you should respect foreigners and their families." The instructions that Andrés gives "Papacito" are very detailed. He is to remain in his camp and post guards between 700 and 1,000 meters from the camp, so that they can never be surprised by an enemy. "Your soldiers," he tells him, "should not be tired out, and they should be kept as satisfied as possible, for this purpose they should be given a certain degree of freedom when haciendas are captured, but abuses should not be tolerated. In all operations, as far as possible, armed confrontations should be prevented, except when there is no other way out; you should never attack people who are barricaded and ready to repel you or whose numbers are larger than yours; rather, you should retreat and force the enemy to follow you where you find it convenient." Finally, Andrés warns "Papacito" not to expose himself to enemy fire or to take risks, but rather to wait until he has sufficient men, arms, and ammunition.[102]

The effectiveness of this strategy is best described in a letter sent to Díaz's secretary by a federal commander in the field. "This revolution in Chihuahua," he wrote his friend,

is far more important than it is assumed in Mexico. . . . The present way of fighting this revolt is fundamentally wrong. Infantry columns cannot destroy this enemy, who is light on his feet, flees, and only fights when he finds himself in impregnable positions, from which he causes us many losses. The only benefit of the infantry columns who are operating at present is that they do not allow the revolutionaries to capture villages or cities and can expel them from the towns; but they can never destroy them or finish them off. The only way to destroy the enemy is to pursue him with cavalry, and certainly not with the army cavalry, which is inefficient. Because of the fear that its members have of their own department and its regulations, they take their tired and emaciated horses with them, since if they were to abandon them, they would have to pay for them. Our cavalrymen do not dare to take fresh horses from the haciendas, since they have no authorization to do so.

The officer called for more freedom for battalion commanders to provide their men with fresh horses and supplies. One telling example of bureaucratic inefficiency he gives is that only 30 cents a day was allotted to feed the mules of his battalion. The officer felt that 40 cents was the minimum needed to provide a decent meal for a mule. He sent a request for the 40 cents to the treasury and after a month received a questionnaire asking him why he wanted 40 cents per mule. Before obtaining anything, he had to fill out a long questionnaire. "Isn't this discouraging to military leaders who, like me, are fighting out of patriotism and out of the wish to serve the government?" he asked.[103]

The Problems of Control: Francisco Madero and the Chihuahuan Revolutionaries

On February 14, 1911, the Mexican Revolution took a new turn. Francisco Madero, who until then had remained in Texas, finally crossed the border into Chihuahua to assume command. For several months, he had hesitated to do so, and it was only after a warrant for his arrest was issued by the U.S. authorities, accusing him of violating U.S. neutrality laws, that he finally decided to proceed to Chihuahua. His earlier hesitation was by no means due to cowardice but rather to his hopes of entering Mexico on more familiar terrain and under conditions more congenial to him. On November 20, he had planned to cross into Mexico through his own native state of Coahuila, where he had innumerable relatives, friends, and clients. This was a state he knew very well and where everyone knew him. His uncle, Catarino Benavides, had promised him that several hundred men would be waiting for him when he arrived at the border between the United

States and Coahuila, but only seven turned up. After his expectations of assuming the leadership of a large revolutionary movement in his home state were dashed, he seems for a brief period of time to have entertained the hope of entering Mexico at the head of rebellious segments of the national army, to whom he had addressed a separate proclamation. Much of the army had been supporters of General Bernardo Reyes, and Madero hoped that the military Reyistas would rally to his cause in the same way that many of Reyes's civilian supporters had. He was mistaken: Reyes was one of their own; Madero was a civilian whom the army despised. Not even when he became president would the army remain loyal to him. On the contrary, in the end, it would destroy Madero.

Another plan of Madero's for entering Mexico, a project to travel by sea from New Orleans to the port city of Veracruz and to enter Mexico from there, proved equally unrealistic. There was no major revolutionary outbreak in Veracruz.

There is a puzzling contrast between these unrealistic plans of Madero's to enter Mexico and his reluctance to alight in that part of the country where a genuinely large revolutionary movement had broken out against the Díaz regime, the state of Chihuahua. The reasons for this are not entirely clear. In part, his hesitation to cross into Chihuahua was probably because it was not his native state, and because except for Abraham González, with whom he maintained close relations, he did not know most of the leaders of the revolution personally. In addition, the kind of social revolution that was taking place in Chihuahua was not entirely congenial to him, and he must have considered many of the aims of the rebels there as far too radical. The main reason, though, was probably that he wanted to resolve the main problem he faced in Chihuahua before entering that state: in fact he exercised only a very limited degree of control over the revolutionary forces that were sweeping over Mexico's northernmost and largest state.

Madero's lack of effective control over most of the revolutionaries in Chihuahua was linked to the fragmentary nature of the movement. It was split by deep ideological, regional, and personal divisions. A substantial minority of the revolutionaries were adherents of the Partido Liberal Mexicano, led by the Flores Magón brothers, who refused to recognize Madero's leadership. In the Galeana district of western Chihuahua, the PLM had succeeded in broadening its base beyond its traditional constituency of miners and industrial workers and began winning substantial support from the area's free villagers. The villagers in the Galeana district had become more radical than those in other parts of Chihuahua, including the center of the revolution in the Guerrero district. Unlike in the rest of Chihuahua and most of the rest of Mexico, American settlers had colonized the region. If there is one rule of thumb that can be applied to colonial and dependent countries, it is that settlers are always met by the local population with more hostility than are foreign capitalists or investors. This was true for Algeria, Rhodesia, and South Africa, and it was equally true for Chihuahua. Foreign capitalists are less visible than foreign settlers; they do not displace locals as much as settlers do, and even if this is the case, their links to this process are less visible than in the case of foreign settlers. Foreign capitalists do not introduce an alien culture in the same massive way that settlers do. The settlers who penetrated the Galeana district were mainly Mormon farmers who had left Utah after the U.S. authorities forced the Mormon church to ban polygamy.[104] Well organized, well endowed with capital, and highly industrious, the settlers began displacing both local rancheros and local merchants.[105]

In the Galeana district, unlike the rest of Chihuahua, Mormons rather than members of the oligarchy were the main beneficiaries of the expropriation of village lands resulting from Creel's land law of 1905. In Casas Grandes, the largest town of the district, the Mormons controlled most of the medium-sized and large enterprises. Five of seven lumber factories were in their hands, as were most food-processing enterprises. In 1900, five of seven flour mills in the district had belonged to Mexican owners. By 1905, five of these mills were in American hands, four of them belonging to Mormon entrepreneurs. Economic conflicts, as well as cultural, religious, and nationalist tensions, contributed to opposition to the Mormons. Paradoxically, many of Galeana's inhabitants had acquired their radical ideology across the border in the southwest of the United States, where they worked as temporary laborers and were strongly influenced by the radical Industrial Workers of the World (IWW), with which the PLM was closely linked. The PLM's leaders, the Flores Magón brothers, had called on their followers to revolt in 1910, at the same time as Madero, but they had denounced Madero as a rich capitalist who wanted to utilize the revolution for his own ends and called on their followers not to accept his leadership of the revolution.[106]

This ideological split was not the only cause of the fragmentation of the revolutionary movement. Regional and local divisions were equally important. While acknowledging Madero's supreme leadership, many villagers gave their loyalty first and foremost to the men they elected to lead them. Some of these men, such as Toribio Ortega, were their traditional spokesmen and political leaders. Others were men whose leadership qualities only manifested themselves in battle when they turned out to be the best military leaders. Most had close family ties to those who followed them. Some of these local leaders refused to subordinate their forces to regional chieftains; others did so but on their own terms. They would join a regional chieftain for a limited time but leave him if he was not successful enough, if he could not provide them with sufficient arms, if their own villages were threatened, or even if they were needed at home to bring in the harvest.

Only one man had emerged as a statewide leader with a relatively large following: Pascual Orozco. His traditional authority had been bolstered by the support of the numerous members of his extended family, which was spread throughout the Guerrero district, and of his many friends. In a worried letter to the president's secretary, one of Díaz's generals described him as "very popular and well known in these parts. He was a kind of commission agent who maintained relations with all the Americans involved in railways and mines. He is a great shot."[107] His popularity and power were enhanced by the fact that he turned out to be the most capable and successful military leader of the Madero revolution. It was his troops that had captured the first city in the state to fall into revolutionary hands, Ciudad Guerrero. While he had not been able to hold it indefinitely, he had again and again defeated government troops. In spite of these successes and his prestige, and in spite of the fact that he led the largest force of revolutionaries in Chihuahua, Orozco by no means controlled all of the state's revolutionaries. Other leaders, such as Pancho Villa, might temporarily cooperate with him in joint actions, but they did not bow to his authority. Orozco, in turn, had political ambitions of his own and was by no means ready to give unconditional obedience to Madero.

Madero's lack of effective control over the forces revolting in his name was owing not only to his absence from Mexico but also to his incapacity to put large economic resources at their disposal. While some arms were smuggled from the United States to the revolutionaries, the number was small—certainly not sufficient to equip the many men who had rallied to Madero's call for revolt.

In January and early February 1911, Madero believed that he had finally evolved a strategy that would allow him to assume effective leadership of the revolutionary forces and to make a triumphant return to Mexico. He ordered all the revolutionary forces in the state to northern Chihuahua to seize the border city of Ciudad Juárez. Its capture would have allowed Madero to set up his government on Mexican soil. The customs duties would have financed the revolution, and he hoped that he could then legally import arms for his forces from the United States. He would then be able to assume effective control over his supporters both economically and politically. Large numbers of revolutionaries led by Orozco heeded Madero's call and advanced on Ciudad Juárez. Nevertheless, the plan failed. The revolutionaries lacked sufficient arms to carry it out.

In addition, many of them became demoralized when they heard that federal reinforcements were pouring into Ciudad Juárez. There are also indications that Orozco lost enthusiasm for the plan when he learned that Madero wished to subordinate him and his forces to a commander-in-chief whom Madero had named, José de la Luz Soto. Madero sent a delegation to secure Orozco's agreement to relinquish control of his men; a witness to the meeting graphically describes Orozco's reaction:

Orozco awaited us, standing up, his lean tall figure outlined against the low fire. He received us courteously enough, offered coffee all around, but I felt the Latin hostility in his manner. We exchanged news back and forth. He told us of conditions in the interior of Chihuahua, while we gave him information about the plans of the Madero junta; while talking, he seemed to relent somewhat, but when Eduardo Hay acting as our spokesman, came to the point of asking him to act on our orders, he became immediately distrustful again. His officers had come up to listen to our talk, and I noticed that they too did not like the idea of relinquishing their freedom of action.

Perhaps, I thought, this attitude was merely an expression of the free spirit of revolt. Being mountaineers and plainsmen, they resent placing themselves under the control of city bred leaders. We are the type of men they had suffered under for so many years.

Orozco gave us his answer, "Yes, we go to fight for the common cause to the finish, the cause of the people. But we will fight it in our own way." And turning to his own men, he said, "I will have nothing to do with these men."

A murmur of approval greeted the sentiment and without another word, they mounted their horses and rode away into the darkness.[108]

Soon after this fruitless exchange, Orozco and his men withdrew from the border and returned to their mountain district of Guerrero. It is not clear whether this withdrawal was primarily owing to Orozco's resentment of Madero's efforts to supersede him in command or to the fact that his soldiers were becoming demoralized by lack of arms and food and the news that federal reinforcements were arriving at Ciudad Juárez.

It is thus not surprising that when Madero finally crossed the border into Chihuahua on February 14, 1911, he found only a small fraction of the revolutionary army waiting for him. Moreover, many of the assembled rebels represented some of that army's most unreliable elements from his point of view. A substantial number of the few hundred men who had come to meet him were commanded by Prisciliano Silva, a Liberal commander, who declared that his primary allegiance was to the Flores Magón brothers and not to Madero. Tensions between Madero and the revolutionaries he encountered at the border arose from the Magonista sympathies of some of the revolutionaries and to nationalist resentment of some of the volunteers that Madero had brought with him from the United States. Half of the hundred or so men who accompanied him were American, and the military man he trusted most was an Italian, Giuseppe Garibaldi, the grandson of Italy's most famous revolutionary. Yet Madero was undaunted by the relatively small number of men who met him and by the refusal of some of them to heed his authority. When Silva declared that he would not recognize Madero's leadership, Madero harangued the commander's soldiers, who proceeded to disarm Silva and a few of his loyal followers; they agreed to follow Madero, forcing Silva to flee to the United States.[109]

In spite of the few men he commanded and his complete lack of military experience, Madero decided to undertake a military campaign on his own rather than to await Orozco, Villa, or any other of the more experienced revolutionary leaders. In an effort to score a victory and to install his administration in an urban setting, he attacked the town of Casas Grandes. The attack was a dismal failure. Despite the fact that his largely inexperienced troops showed great courage in storming a heavily garrisoned town, Madero had failed to heed the arrival of federal reinforcements, who attacked him from the rear. His forces were routed, but Madero impressed his followers by his physical courage. He was in fact the last to leave. "I told myself that this man either does not know that bullets kill or he is extremely courageous," his bodyguard, Máximo Castillo, wrote.[110] Fortunately for Madero, the revolutionary dedication of his men was such that they did not desert as a result of their defeat and respected his orders to retreat to the hacienda of Bustillos, to which the federal army, for reasons that are not entirely clear, hesitated to pursue them.

Díaz and his supporters briefly expected that Madero's defeat would turn the tide in their favor. Madero's failure, they hoped, would discourage would-be revolutionaries in other parts of Mexico from rising and would prevent Chihuahua's revolutionaries from joining him. They hoped that Madero had been thoroughly discredited by his failure at Casas Grandes. Moreover, Díaz and his military commander, Hernández, instituted political changes in Chihuahua, which they felt might satisfy the demands of many of the state's inhabitants for the removal of the Terrazas clan from political power.

Within a few weeks, it was apparent how unfounded their hopes were. Madero's arrival in Mexico had in fact unleashed a revolutionary force that no one could now repress. Nationwide, government reports that Madero had been defeated were ignored, and in many cases not even believed, while the news that Madero was now in Mexico inspired new revolutionary outbreaks. By March 1911, events in Chihuahua had ceased to be an exception.

From Revolt to Revolution: The Maderista Upsurge

Revolts now occurred all over Mexico. They were diverse in size, in social composition, and in the degree of control that the Maderista leadership exercised over them. In some states, only small guerrilla groups emerged, but even these were dangerous for the government, since they tended to have large-scale popular support and managed to occupy much larger numbers of federal troops. In other states, such as Morelos, revolutionary armies of several thousand coalesced.

Their leadership and social basis differed. In Morelos, a genuine peasant leader had emerged in the person of Emiliano Zapata, whereas in the two northern states adjacent to Chihuahua, Sonora and Coahuila, the revolutionary movements were led largely by hacendados opposed to Porfirio Díaz. On the whole, Madero exercised more control over the revolutionaries in the north than over those in the south, who, while nominally Maderistas, to a great extent pursued their own strategies and their own policies. Díaz's attempts to contain these movements both by military means and by promising reform proved to be a dismal failure. In much of Mexico, his troops at best managed to hold on to large cities, while the revolutionaries controlled an ever-increasing part of the countryside.

Díaz's reform promises began on April 1, 1911. In his annual report to the nation, he announced that there would be no more reelections of either the president or other officials of his government. A land reform would ensure the division of large estates among the peasants. Local autonomy would be restored to towns and villages. Díaz accompanied these promises by a series of concrete measures: a number of unpopular governors and jefes políticos were removed. The cabinet was revamped. While Limantour remained as minister of finance, Díaz removed other unpopular figures closely linked to the científicos. On April 12, the unpopular vice president, Ramón Corral, was persuaded to leave the country. These promises and changes did not deter the revolutionaries. On the contrary, many Mexicans saw them as a sign of weakness—an expression of the fact that Díaz's regime was unraveling.

This was certainly the case in Chihuahua, where Díaz's commanders soon realized that their policy of "reform" had been a complete failure. Shortly after Madero crossed the border into Mexico, Díaz's commander in chief in Chihuahua wrote in a pessimistic vein to his president that

the news that we have in the capital is the following: that the people in general, and even part of the middle class, not only sympathize with the rebels, but are in constant touch with them when they enter this city or come close to it. They are obsessed by the idea of destroying the Terrazas and Creel families and their haciendas, holdings, and the Banco Minero.

In addition, the instigators of the rebellion have offered their supporters that once this city [Ciudad Chihuahua] is taken, they will allow them two or more days of general looting; for this reason, people anxiously await the day when they will able to rob.

Hernández went on to describe an episode that in his opinion expressed "the feeling of these inhabitants." An "uprising had broken out in the state penitentiary. The prisoners had gotten hold of arms and were trying to shoot their way out. Some of them had already taken to the streets when federal troops arrived to subdue them. A large crowd had gathered in front of the penitentiary, and when the soldiers arrived, the crowd chanted, 'Death to the federals! Viva Madero!'"

At the same time, a bullfight was taking place, and when the spectators heard of the shoot-out [between federal troops and the escaped convicts], they began to shout, "Long live Madero and death to Creel." From all this, it is clear that the people only await an opportune moment to rise in arms and join the ranks of the bandits headed by Madero.

Since I understand this situation, I am keeping a regular federal force in this city to counter such an eventuality, and it must be said that if these bandits try to attack the city, we shall have to kill many people. I must say, Mr. President, that I am happy to see the enthusiasm of our troops, who are always ready to fight against this rabble.[111]

For a brief period after Madero's defeat at Casas Grandes, both Hernández and Díaz had hoped that a reversal of the situation in Chihuahua might now occur: Madero's popularity might sag, and in view of his defeat, some of his military commanders might now refuse to submit to his authority. Within a very short time, however, it became clear to both Hernández and Governor Ahumada that these hopes were misplaced. Not only did Madero's popularity increase as a result of his having entered Mexico, but nearly all of the revolutionary commanders, including Orozco, joined him at the Hacienda de Bustillos, where he had set up his headquarters, and recognized him as commander in chief. By March 21, less than two weeks after Madero's defeat, Hernández wrote Díaz that the federal army was in full retreat. "The authority of the government," Hernández said, in what constituted an admission of defeat, "is limited to the radius occupied by federal forces; where there are no federal forces, there are no authorities. The districts of Guerrero and Benito Juárez are occupied by rebels. . . . They control the whole of the Galeana district with the exception of Casas Grandes."[112]

Not only had the federal troops withdrawn to a few large cities and left the countryside to the revolutionaries; their strategy, which had been offensive a few weeks before, now became purely defensive. This was partly because uprisings were breaking out all over Mexico, so that the federal government could not send any more reinforcements to Chihuahua, and the number of federal troops there had been depleted to 4,000.[113] A factor of even greater importance was the increasing popular opposition to the regime.

General Lauro Villar, who had been sent by Díaz to replace Hernández, reported to Díaz: "General Hernández says that he did not send troops to attack Madero in Bustillos since 85 percent of the population consists of supporters of Madero, a view shared by the governor, and he was afraid that if his forces left the city to attack Madero, the population of this capital would rise and attack the now weakened garrison of Chihuahua."[114] As a result of this federal retreat, Madero not only controlled most of the state of Chihuahua, he could now proceed to transform his motley array of guerrillas into a well-disciplined fighting force. But in doing so, he faced a formidable and problematic task. None of his men were professional soldiers. Their armament varied—some had rifles, others pistols, and some only machetes. They were not used to military discipline. Many felt they could go home at any time. While acknowledging Madero's leadership, many volunteers only obeyed their local and immediate superiors. Others were supporters of the Flores Magón brothers' PLM and refused to recognize Madero's authority. Even more worrisome to Madero than the attitude of the soldiers was the command structure of his army. Of the military commanders, the man Madero seems to have trusted most and at first invested with the greatest military authority was Giuseppe Garibaldi. But in a country as nationalistic as Mexico, a foreigner had little chance of gaining the kind of recognition that a military chieftain of revolutionary troops needed. Compounding the problem, Garibaldi simply did not have the technical skills or the kind of personality that the few foreign revolutionary leaders who did gain this kind of authority in Latin America, such as his grandfather or Che Guevara in Cuba, have possessed. Garibaldi had no outstanding military capacities and in addition was vain and conceited. As a result, more and more local chieftains refused to accept his authority. On the other hand, Pascual Orozco, the most capable and popular revolutionary leader, to whose authority most commanders were ready to submit, was not entirely trusted by Madero. He had political ambitions of his own, and only a few weeks earlier he had refused to subordinate his troops to a commander named by Madero.

Despite all these difficulties, Madero soon realized that the Chihuahuan guerrillas had one great advantage over many revolutionaries in the center and south of the country: a rich fighting tradition. Not only had their grandfathers fought against the French (in that respect, Chihuahua was no exception to the rest of Mexico) but they had a long tradition of fighting the Apaches.

Initially, Madero had hoped to mold these volunteers into something akin to Mexico's regular army. To this end, he had brought three former federal officers into his ranks, the most prominent of whom was Rafael Aguilar. Aguilar proposed that the army be divided into companies of 30 men each, which in turn would be divided into squads. Competent military men would be designated to lead them. Madero soon understood that his volunteers would never accept this structure. They wanted to remain in their original companies, frequently consisting of friends and relatives from one village, and they wanted to serve under the men they had chosen to lead them. After some initial hesitation, Madero showed flexibility in this respect. He dismissed Aguilar and recognized all existing officers. Their ranks depended on the number of men they had been able to enlist. The original companies were kept intact, and Madero even recognized the right of every soldier to leave the army, as long as no battle was in progress and he returned the horse and the arms that had been given him. Only if he left during a battle was it considered desertion. Madero set up additional incentives to keep the men under his command. Every soldier was paid one peso a day and assured that in the event of his death, his widow would receive a pension. Once the revolution ended, it was promised, all former soldiers would receive grants of public lands owned by the government. Disciplinary courts were set up to try men accused of indiscipline, pillage, or desertion. Only a few sentences were handed down, however, and most of these were quietly revoked, with the prisoners being allowed to rejoin the army when battles took place. There was only one clearcut case in which a deserter was shot: this was a bandit, Juan Carrasco, who had joined Toribio Ortega and José de la Luz Blanco and attempted to desert while the siege of Ojinaga was taking place. He was tried, sentenced to be shot, and executed by a firing squad.[115]

Madero's personal prestige, his ability to arm and pay his troops, and the stories of the courage he had shown at Casas Grandes enhanced his authority and made it difficult for subordinate leaders to challenge him. Men who recognized only the leadership of the Flores Magón brothers did not, however, accept his command and heed the call to join his army. It was when he attempted to deal with the Magonistas that Madero also felt the limits of his authority over his own subordinates. When he ordered Orozco to either force the dissidents to join his army or to disarm them, Orozco refused, and it seemed at first that there was no one else to whom Madero could turn to impose his authority.[116] Garibaldi, who was equal in rank to Orozco and had no political objections to proceeding against the Magonistas, lacked the prestige, the authority, and the power to do so. Once again, Madero's authority over his army seemed in doubt. A few days later, this situation was drastically reversed when Pancho Villa with 700 well-disciplined men joined Madero in his camp at Bustillos.

The Emergence of an Ambiguous Relationship: Madero and Villa

In the months between the outbreak of the revolution in November and the time he rejoined Madero in March 1911, Villa had emerged as commander of a guerrilla force second in numbers only to Orozco's. This is all the more remarkable, and in some ways puzzling, in that Villa's military record was inferior to Orozco's. He had achieved no brilliant victory comparable to those that would give him worldwide fame in later years. In fact, he had suffered more defeats than victories. After a quarrel with Orozco, Villa withdrew to the village of San Andrés, from which he hoped to ambush a federal convoy carrying ammunition that was supposed to pass nearby.[117] Since most of his men came from San Andrés, he allowed them a few hours' leave to rejoin their families. He disregarded a warning that federal troops were approaching, thinking that the person who warned him had the ammunitions convoy in mind. As a result, when a federal striking force carried out a surprise attack on the town, Villa's forces, scattered throughout San Andrés, were incapable of waging effective resistance. With a few followers, he barricaded himself in the railway station, holding out until the evening, when he managed to escape into the mountains with what remained of his troops. In the process, he had lost most of his horses and supplies.[118]

In spite of his defeat and the cold and freezing weather in the mountains, many of his scattered men rallied to him, and new recruits joined his forces. Villa now resupplied his troops with over 400 horses taken from a neighboring hacienda, belonging to one of the wealthiest members of the state's oligarchy. Before proceeding with his next military action, Villa occupied the hacienda of Santa Gertrudis, where he obtained large amounts of money, arms, and supplies, and then entered the mining town of Naica, where the company manager also put food and money at his disposal.

This "friendly" attitude of hacendados, administrators, and mine owners toward the revolutionaries was generally not owing to sympathy for Madero's supporters. According to a prominent hacienda administrator in Durango, Francisco Gómez Palacio, the hacendados simply had no choice. At first when the revolution began and seemed relatively weak, Gómez Palacio had called on the hacendados "to get together and with or without the sanction of the government to raise sufficient forces to face the revolutionaries." Such a policy, though, only made sense as long as the revolutionaries were weak, Gómez Palacio felt. "Such a defense of their properties by the hacendados," he wrote, "will only be possible as long as the revolution maintains its present proportions; if unfortunately its scope begins to broaden, it will not be possible to do this, and even if this were to be the case, it would not be prudent for private citizens to attempt to contain it."[119]

Villa now felt strong enough to attack Ciudad Camargo, one of the larger towns in Chihuahua. For hours, Villista troops stormed the city, which was fiercely defended by federal troops. When they were on the verge of occupying the last barracks in the town from which the defenders were still firing, federal reinforcements arrived, and Villa had to retreat once again. He was equally unsuccessful in his attempt to occupy the town of El Valle de Zaragoza. He hesitated in attacking it because of the fortifications its federal defenders had erected. After vainly calling on the federal troops to come out and fight him in the open, he withdrew again. His lack of success did not daunt Villa. On the contrary, he now set his sights higher. He decided to make an attempt to occupy Parral, one of the largest towns in Chihuahua, where he had lived for many years, and for which he had a special predilection. To prepare for the attack, Villa undertook an action that was rash in every possible sense. Together with an officer of his command, Albino Frías, he went to Parral himself to reconnoiter its defenses. This was a risky step, in view of the fact that Villa was known to dozens of people there. He was in fact recognized by an old enemy, who alerted the garrison. Instead of fleeing, he took refuge on a friend's ranch, where according to his memoirs, he was attacked by 150 soldiers.[120]

Villa's description of the way he and Frías shot their way out would delight any Hollywood producer. Perhaps the account is exaggerated, but Frías and Villa did manage to escape, each along a different road. When Villa finally reached the camp where he had asked his troops to wait for him, he found it deserted. In the next village, he located some of his soldiers and officers, who told him that Frías, who had also made his way out of Parral, had told them that Villa had been killed. At this point, they had decided to give up on the revolution and go home. When they heard that Villa was alive, they quickly rejoined him, and he was soon leading an even larger force than the one that he had initially commanded. By some accounts, his force at this time numbered 700 men. Villa now achieved his first victory since his retreat from San Andrés. At La Piedra, he defeated a force of 150 federal soldiers who were pursuing him and took much of their equipment and arms.[121] In March 1911, he went to Bustillos to put himself and his troops at Madero's disposal.

Villa's lack of military success is reflected in the little attention that the Mexican government, U.S. consuls reporting on the revolution, and the U.S. news media, which were avidly looking for news of the upheavals in Mexico, were paying to him. In the reports from civilian and military officials that reached Porfirio Díaz, Villa is only mentioned twice and briefly. Alberto Terrazas mentioned in one of his reports that the "bandit Villa" had now joined the revolution, and an unnamed official from the state of Zacatecas expressed fear that the "formidable bandit, Francisco Villa" might enter his state and raise havoc.[122] It was not Villa but Orozco who was constantly mentioned in all reports and newspaper articles as the heart and soul of the revolution and referred to as the most capable military leader it had produced.

It seems at first glance puzzling why Villa was able, in spite of his lack of military success, to raise a force of men second only to that of Orozco in strength and power. One of the reasons military leaders who lose battles nevertheless manage to retain their following is that they are ideologues or men with a religious appeal. This was true of Madero but certainly not of Villa. Another hypothesis might be that Villa remained a bandit and his men stuck with him because he allowed them to plunder at will. There is some evidence that at the very beginning of the revolution, when Villa's command was small and consisted of a disproportionate number of companions from his bandit days, some pillaging took place. One revolutionary leader who participated in the successful attack by Maderista troops on the town of Santa Isabel describes Villa's men plundering one store after the other in the town.[123] As Villa's strength increased, however, he seems to have made a dramatic reversal in this respect. Not only are there no further reports of plunder and pillage but, on the contrary, most contemporary observers described Villa's troops as the best-disciplined in Madero's army.

One of the first contemporary descriptions of Villa in this early period of his revolutionary career originated with Ignacio Herrerias, a correspondent for *El Tiempo*, a newspaper published in Mexico City, at a time when the Díaz regime was still firmly in control of the capital. "This Don Francisco Villa," Herrerias wrote,

is the man the revolutionaries respect most. While they love and obey Orozco blindly, they fear Villa more, since they know that he will have no inhibition if he wishes to impose his authority.

It is said that he committed many offenses before he took part in the revolution, but it is stated that since he joined, he has become one of the most honest and incorruptible leaders, who prevents his men from committing offenses.[124]

To say that Villa was a born leader, a charismatic personality who could inspire his men, is to say much and nothing at the same time. Such definitions do not show what it was that inspired his men to follow him and to accept his leadership with the kind of unquestioning loyalty that few other revolutionary leaders inspired. One important element of Villa's leadership was doubtless his audacity. With few exceptions, such as the time when he was surprised by enemy troops in San Andrés, it was always Villa who took the initiative. He did not shy away from tackling steep odds, as when he attacked a superior federal force with only a few men under his command at the battle of Tecolote.

While such actions were by no means always successful, especially not in this first phase of Villa's career, they were not very costly in terms of human life either. During the Madero revolution, in contrast to Villa's future campaigns, the loss of life among Villa's men was relatively small, thanks in part to the element of surprise that Villa brought to most of his actions, and to his leadership. His qualities as a gunfighter and personal courage also inspired his men.

His attack on a much larger federal force at Las Escobas (and the fact that most of his men got away unscathed) and the risky decision he took to go into Parral, where the danger of his being recognized was high, seemed to confirm the stories and legends that were beginning to circulate about him. In addition, Villa attempted to establish a personal relationship with his men. Desiderio Madrid Carrasco, a soldier who joined him in 1913, was impressed by the way Villa treated him as well as the other soldiers. Carrasco first joined a local leader, Porfirio Ornelas, who had few means at his disposal and could not supply his men with arms, clothes, or money. Ornelas finally decided to join Villa and to put his men under Villa's command. Carrasco's description of their meeting with the revolutionary leader characterizes the type of relationship that Villa attempted to establish with his soldiers. "Villa asked us to stand at attention. He greeted each one of us with a handshake and asked of each of us: 'How are you my boy, what is your name, from where are you, do you have a family?' Then he gave us arms, ammunition, clothing, and food." It was no coincidence that Villa carried out extensive raids on large estates before every battle. Paying his soldiers well and attending to their needs was a cornerstone of his policy. This was one of Villa's traits that most strongly impressed Carrasco: "I remember that every week Villa ordered us to be paid fifteen pesos in gold. I had never even seen gold before. . . . After every battle Villa organized meetings to see how many men were absent, who had been killed and who had been wounded. He personally attended all those who needed something and gave them more ammunition and paid them. He treated us very well."[125]

Impelled by the desire to establish closer links to his men, and perhaps also making it more difficult for him to be poisoned by a regular cook, Villa would frequently show up at a campfire where his men were eating and, after asking for permission, partake of their food with them. But prestige, friendliness, and care about his men were not the sole underpinnings of his authority. Villa was a strict disciplinarian and ruthlessly executed anyone who disobeyed his orders.

There is no doubt that the authority that Villa enjoyed over his men and the strict discipline he maintained impressed Madero. It strengthened Madero's conviction that he might be the one revolutionary chieftain who had both a large following among the Chihuahuan revolutionaries and could be relied upon to follow orders. Madero soon put this conviction to a test. Shortly after Villa's arrival in his camp, Madero's relations with the Magonistas had reached a breaking point. When he ordered the Magonista leaders to join him in an attack on Ciudad Juárez, the latter openly defied him, saying that they would only participate in the attack if Madero allowed their troops to loot the city for three days after it was taken.

Madero's authority over his troops was now decisively threatened. That threat increased when Orozco defied him by refusing to obey his instructions to disarm the Magonistas. Orozco's attitude was probably not only owing to his traditional sympathies for and links with the Magonistas but also to his wish to weaken Madero's authority. At this point, Madero saw only one way out of this dilemma. He called on Villa to disarm the Magonistas, but insisted that this should be done without any bloodshed. This was not only because of Madero's humanitarian feelings but also because he realized that a bloody confrontation among the revolutionaries would help to discredit him and greatly benefit Porfirian propaganda.

At this point, Villa proved his loyalty to Madero and demonstrated his ingenuity as well. He made a show of embarking his troops at a railway station, which drew the attention of curious Magonistas officers and soldiers, who were puzzled by Villa's behavior. At a given signal, Villa's soldiers jumped on the Magonistas, who had not brought along their arms, and disarmed them by physically overpowering them without killing a single man.[126]

Villa's readiness, in contrast to all the other revolutionary commanders, to proceed against the Magonistas had two different origins. One was the admiration for and fascination with Madero that took hold of Villa after the two men first met. Again and again, Villa would reiterate his first impression of Madero. "Here is one rich man who fights for the people. He is a little fellow, but he has a great soul. If all the rich and powerful in Mexico were like him, there would be no struggle and no suffering, for all of us would be doing our duty, and what else is there for the rich to do if not to relieve the poor of their misery?"[127]

Madero possessed four qualities that Villa admired: he was an educated man, and Villa always had a great respect for education and feelings of inferiority because he himself had had so little of it. This made him particularly sensitive to the arrogance of men who knew more than he. Madero's lack of arrogance—"he seemed to love everyone and returned the friendliest greetings to every man"— seems to have particularly struck him. In addition, he believed Madero to be scrupulously honest, and he admired the physical courage the little man had shown at the battle of Casas Grandes.

The other reason for Villa's readiness to obey Madero's orders to disarm the Magonistas was that, unlike Orozco and most other military leaders of the Maderista movement in Chihuahua, he had never been involved in radical politics before 1910. All those who had in one way or the other fought against Creel and Terrazas before 1910 had established some kind of cooperation with the Magonistas and were now reluctant to proceed against their erstwhile allies.

In the long run, Villa's attack on the Magonistas would initiate the opposition of many Mexican and later U.S. radicals to Villa. In the short run, it convinced Madero that Villa was not only a first-rate military commander but could serve as an effective counterweight to Orozco as well.

One of the first decrees Madero signed in Mexico as provisional president of the country was to name Villa a major in his army. Within a few weeks, he was promoted to colonel. In order not to alienate Orozco, Madero made sure that he was always one rank above Villa: when Villa was appointed a major, Orozco became a colonel, and when Villa became a colonel, Orozco was promoted to general. Madero knew that appointing Villa to such a high rank in his army might be costly. The government had been labeling the revolutionaries bandits, outlaws, and rebels. The emergence of Villa as a colonel in the Madero army added fuel to government propaganda against the revolution. To counteract this, Madero sent a letter to the *El Paso Morning Times* stating that Villa had never really been a bandit, but had been forced to become an outlaw because of the repressive policies of the Porfirian government.[128]

The letter was both a justification by Madero to Mexican and U.S. public opinion for having accepted Villa into his ranks and an implicit promise of amnesty for the revolutionary chieftain. It also marked the birth of the Villa legend beyond the narrow confines of certain regions of Chihuahua. By likening Villa to a Robin Hood, Madero's letter contributed to the process by which Villa became a focus of interest for both the U.S. and the Mexican press.

To a large degree, thanks to Villa's help, Madero had been successful in the few weeks he spent at Bustillos in imposing his authority and in creating a unified and disciplined army out of the heterogeneous guerrilla forces that had rallied to him. The reports of an American who visited Madero at this time provide a picture of the new revolutionary army. Charles C. Harris was an American photographer who spent some time with the revolutionary troops and then described his observations to the U.S. consul in Chihuahua. Harris was impressed by the armament of the revolutionaries, their discipline, and their ideology.

In the matter of arms and equipment, the rebels to all appearances were quite well off. . . . In regard to the matter of discipline and morale, Mr. Harris said that strict order prevails throughout the camp and that the men appear to be cheerful and in good condition generally. Madero maintained a provost guard, one of the principal duties of which was to see that all liquor was kept out of the camp. Mr. Madero told my informant that he had taken much pains to weed out undesirable men. In this connection he said that he had on occasion to have one man shot, and quite a number of others had been released. In cases of the latter kind, the men are beyond the danger of arrest.

It was the ideology of the revolutionaries that struck Harris above all. "Mr. Harris expressed himself as impressed with the orderliness of the camp and the general appearance of [orderliness] on the parts of individuals with whom he conversed from time to time. The leaders spoke very hopefully of the situation and of the final triumph of the ideas for which the revolutionaries were struggling which, as expressed by them, were the opportunity for land-ownership, the abolition of the jefe político system and the destruction of other related methods of government which are at variance with the guarantees of the Mexican Constitution, and changes in the operation of the election laws."[129]

One of the reasons Madero may have been successful in disciplining his men was that most of them, unlike the future revolutionary armies of Mexico, consisted of mature heads of families with a clear idea of what they were fighting for. This fact impressed Ignacio Herrerias, the first and only correspondent from

Mexico City who was allowed to visit Madero's army and to report on it while Porfirio Díaz was still president of Mexico.

"A curious detail that I observed," Herrerias wrote, "is that the majority of the revolutionaries are men of 35 or older. There are few young men among them, and the explanation that was given to me is that people in this part of Mexico have great respect for their fathers and that the latter leave their sons to take care of their lands and their family and they go out to fight. There are hundreds of men of 40 or older."[130] The impression that Herrerias wanted to convey, without saying so, was that this was not a revolt of desperadoes, of bandits, of marginals, but rather of respectable heads of families.

It is at first glance not easy to explain why these respectable heads of families would have held a man who prior to the revolution had "committed many offenses" in such awe. But four factors may help to explain Villa's standing in the revolutionary army. The first was doubtless the audacity and lack of fear that he had shown during the military campaign. This was something that many of his men, descendants of Apache fighters, who knew the value of unconventional fighting capacities, could appreciate. The second element that contributed to Villa's prestige was that, possibly in order to counteract his image as an outlaw, he maintained stricter discipline and more control over his men than any other revolutionary commander. Madero's confidence in him also bolstered his popularity, while his lower-class origins may have convinced many of the revolutionaries that after victory, he would not turn against them.

Pancho Villa had emerged as one of the four main military leaders of the revolutionary army, together with Orozco, Giuseppe Garibaldi, and José de la Luz Blanco. In practice, his prestige and power within the army was second only to that of Orozco. In the eyes of the Terrazas, Villa had become the most dangerous revolutionary leader in Chihuahua. "Even if Madero is ready to compromise," Luis Terrazas Jr. wrote to his father, "Villa will not submit to him."[131]

Decision at Ciudad Juárez

In April 1911, his confidence bolstered by news that more and more uprisings were occurring throughout Mexico, Madero decided to take Ciudad Juárez. The capture of this second largest city in the state of Chihuahua would not only give the revolutionaries a psychological boost but would also allow them to control traffic to and from the United States. As a result, they might hope to be recognized by the Americans as belligerents and thus have free access to American arms. Within a few days, the revolutionary army was laying siege to the city, isolating its 700-man garrison from the rest of Mexico, although not from El Paso on the other side of the Rio Grande.

In some respects, the strategy of the revolutionaries seemed to correspond to the wishes of the federal generals. The federal commanders had voiced their frustrations at the guerrilla tactics of the revolutionaries. Instead of facing them and fighting a regular battle, they would skirmish with the federals and then melt into the mountains or into the countryside. Now for the first time, the revolutionaries constituted a regular army ready to meet the federal forces in regular battle. Instead of meeting this challenge and advancing on Juárez to catch Madero in a pincer movement between the well-fortified garrison and the attacking federals, however, the government commanders sat tight in Ciudad Chihuahua. The fear of a popular uprising in Chihuahua entertained by the governor and the federal commanders was a powerful motive for not leaving the city. The gradual demoralization of the federal troops may have been another.

On April 7, 1911, Madero's army began its march northward. The army was headed by two columns of 500 riders each, one commanded by Pascual Orozco and the other by Pancho Villa. Behind the two columns came 1,500 riders led by Madero. The revolutionary army had ceased to be a guerrilla force. The tactics it now used were those of a regular army. Until it arrived at Ciudad Juárez, it met with little resistance from the federal army. Its advance seemed like a triumphant march.

The revolutionaries occupied Temosachic without firing a shot and were greeted by a jubilant population. Casas Grandes, the scene of their greatest defeat only a few weeks before, was occupied with little resistance. In Bauche, twenty kilometers from Ciudad Juárez, a federal garrison attempted to make a stand. After a bloody battle, it too was overrun. The next day, Madero's army began to lay siege to Ciudad Juárez, encircling it from three sides. The city was now cut off from communication with the rest of Mexico, and its only link to the outside world was through El Paso in the United States. Madero called on the federal commander of the garrison of Ciudad Juárez, General Navarro, to surrender. The latter refused, perhaps believing that the fortifications he had erected would allow his 700 men to resist a revolutionary onslaught. Above all, he hoped that Madero and his troops would hesitate before carrying out a full-scale attack, in view of the possibility that stray bullets might cross the border into El Paso, endangering the lives of Americans and thus provoking a U.S. intervention. This was one of two factors that transformed Madero's initial enthusiasm for the capture of Ciudad Juárez into hesitation and reluctance. The second factor was a skillful "peace offensive" by the Díaz government, with the support of prominent members of Madero's family.

This newfound desire on the part of the Díaz administration to negotiate with the revolutionaries was largely triggered by the fear, sometimes amounting to panic, that had taken hold of Mexico's hacendados and financial elite. No one has better expressed the attitude of Mexico's upper class than a member of its "reformist wing," Jorge Vera Estañol, who had been appointed by Díaz as secretary of education in a move to broaden his cabinet so as to make it more acceptable to the country's opposition. In a memorandum to the minister of foreign affairs, Vera Estañol wrote that in his opinion, two kinds of revolution were taking place in Mexico.

One was what he called a political revolution, which only existed in the northern states of Sonora, Chihuahua, Durango, Sinaloa, and Zacatecas. The main demand of these political revolutionaries, he stated, was the implementation of the principles of no reelection and genuinely free elections. The government should attempt to make peace with these revolutionaries by subscribing to the principle of no reelection, allowing genuinely free elections to take place, and paying them some monetary compensation. Such concessions, coupled with an amnesty, should be sufficient, he felt, to make peace with the political revolutionaries. He did not advocate giving them positions in the cabinet or turning governorships over to them, and Díaz's resignation was out of the question.

Vera Estañol felt that such an agreement was absolutely necessary in order to crush the revolution in the rest of the country, which he subsumed under the general name of anarchy, with the utmost energy. "Every day the newspapers carry news of new rebel bands being organized in different parts of the country. . . . They carry out pillage, they commit murders, they destroy the railroads and telegraph and telephone communications; they take money and food in the cities, and horses, arms, and other supplies in the countryside." These bands, he felt, were proliferating rapidly, and unless the army's strength was drastically increased, the revolutionaries would soon dominate the countryside, and the government would only control the large cities. In that case, he said, "anarchy would dominate the country; this would mean the destruction of the national wealth that has been obtained with such great efforts and with such sacrifices during the last quarter century; it would mean personal insecurity, and a period of real barbarism in the midst of civilization." Such a situation, in turn, would inevitably lead to the intervention of foreign powers, led by the United States.

"Anarchy," he wrote, "cannot be destroyed through proclamations, reforms, or government plans; anarchy can only be dealt with by force, using the most radical means of annihilation." This, he felt, "could only be obtained if the government could rapidly increase its military's strength. This, in turn, could only be achieved if the government was able to make peace with the political revolutionaries and concentrate all its efforts on destroying anarchy."[132]

What Vera Estañol was advocating and most of Mexico's upper classes wanted was reconciliation of the upper classes, the co-optation of at least part of the dissident middle class, and a joint effort to crush the largely peasant uprisings that were taking place all over the country. The basic aim of these conciliatory elements of Mexico's upper classes was the maintenance of the federal army and most of the structure of what can best be called the Porfirian state.

Within the Díaz administration, the main advocate in favor of striking a deal with the revolutionaries was José Yves Limantour, the minister of finance. The main opponents of such a policy were Díaz's military leaders, above all General Victoriano Huerta. From his exile in Paris, Bernardo Reyes expressed similar views, telling Limantour that he had "the secret hope of being called upon to destroy the revolutionary movement, something he felt could easily be accomplished. . . . In his opinion repression should be carried out with the greatest energy, punishing without any pity anyone participating in the armed struggle."[133]

These differences of opinion were no coincidence. Financiers whom Limantour represented feared that a continuation of Mexico's revolution and civil war would irreparably damage Mexico's international credit. The hacendados, who shared Limantour's conciliatory view, wanted an agreement at any cost, since the federal army was incapable of protecting them. The army leadership on the other hand was deeply worried by the possibility that in the event of some kind of conciliation with the revolutionaries, armed forces composed of former revolutionaries could emerge as a potent rival and undermine the army's power. In addition, any deal with the revolutionaries would be a blow to the army's pride, an acknowledgment that it had been defeated.

What is striking is the contrast between the optimism of the army leadership and the pessimism of the commanders in the field, such as Hernández and Lauro Villar. In the case of Reyes, who lived in exile in France and who had no access to reports from field commanders, excessive optimism is understandable. Not so in the case of Victoriano Huerta, one of the highest federal commanders, who did receive reports of how the fighting was really proceeding.

The attitude of Huerta and other members of the federal high command may in part have been due to arrogance. They had, after all, defeated all popular insurrections during more than 30 years of Porfirian dictatorship, and they felt they had reason to be confident that they could do the same with the present uprising. In addition, some of the commanders felt that they could make use of Mexican nationalism for their own purposes. A dramatic step taken by the United States seemed to offer them a chance to do so.

In March 1911, Porfirio Díaz's growing internal problems were compounded by new and dangerous pressure from the United States. On March 8, 1911, U.S. President William Howard Taft ordered 20,000 U.S. army troops to proceed to the Mexican border and ordered U.S. ships to patrol the Mexican coastline. Taft assured the Mexican ambassador, "with great energy and with an attempt to show the sincerity of his government," that the aim of this mobilization was "to show the effectiveness and good state of readiness of the American army . . . to help our government morally and to make vigilance along the border more effective, to prevent arms smuggling and . . . to intimidate badly intentioned adventurers." After a long talk with Taft, the Mexican ambassador, Francisco de León de la Barra, reported to Díaz that he tended to accept Taft's explanation. Nevertheless, he was worried about the U.S. mobilization. "In spite of my conviction [that the mobilization was not directed against Mexico]," de la Barra wrote his chief, "I believe that it is absolutely necessary to watch events in this country very closely, because it seems to me that the measures taken by President Taft can have very serious consequences, since they are encouraging the 'jingoes,' of whom there are so many in the United States."[134]

Díaz's civilian advisors, above all Limantour, were deeply troubled by these measures on the part of the Taft administration, which by giving the impression that Mexico was unable to put its house in order lowered the country's credit rating. In addition, they seem to have harbored genuine fears of U.S. intervention. Some of Díaz's military leaders, on the other hand, discounted that possibility and used the mobilization of U.S. troops to fan the flames of nationalism. "We should not fear a Yankee intervention," General Gerónimo Treviño wrote Porfirio Díaz on April 22, six weeks after Taft had mobilized his troops on the border and nothing had happened, "since I continue to believe that such an intervention will not occur unless something very unexpected takes place. It would nevertheless be very useful to propagate the idea that such an intervention is possible in order to awaken the patriotism of the Mexicans and to utilize this impression in defense of the government."[135]

Díaz rejected the policies advocated by his military leaders and heeded Limantour's advice instead. He sent emissaries to Ciudad Juárez to negotiate with the revolutionaries.

The same kind of division between civilians and military men that existed within the Díaz administration seems to have emerged among the revolutionaries. As a humanist who abhorred bloodshed, Madero was more amenable to a compromise with the Díaz forces than his military leaders. Moreover, he was under pressure from the conservative elements of his family to arrive at some kind of a compromise. At least in part, he shared the Mexican upper classes' fear of anarchy. As his future attitude toward Emiliano Zapata would show, he was worried that the peasant movements in central and southern Mexico, which officially spoke in his name but in fact were not controlled by him, might get out of hand. He also shared the fear of much of Mexico's political class of a possible U.S. intervention. His middle- and lower-class military leaders had no such fear of anarchy but did have a very real fear of the federal army, which, were it maintained intact, might very well turn against them and attempt to exterminate them, as in fact it did some time later.

Madero at first disregarded the opinion of his military leaders and after much prodding from his family agreed to a temporary cease-fire, which would prevent his troops from attacking Ciudad Juárez. At the same time, he seemed ready to accept a compromise that would have not only kept the federal army and large segments of the Porfirian state in power but allowed Díaz himself to remain in office. He agreed to peace in return for the government's acceptance of the principle of no reelection, concession of fourteen governorships and four cabinet posts to the revolutionaries, and evacuation by the federal forces of the states of Sonora, Chihuahua, and Coahuila. Díaz's resignation was not included in these conditions.[136]

Madero's delay in attacking Ciudad Juárez, the cease-fire he implemented, his negotiations with government representatives, and his willingness to accept conditions that would have left Díaz in power stirred unrest both among the military leaders of the revolution and among their followers. Madero did not make his agreement with Díaz's emissary public, but rumors that some kind of a deal was being struck emerged in the American press in El Paso, which was closely following events across the border. The cease-fire, for which Madero could give no convincing reason, added new fuel to these rumors and began to lead to demoralization in his army, the morale of which had undergone an unprecedented surge only few days before. As the revolutionary army had proceeded from Bustillos toward Ciudad Juárez, it had gained a new kind of legitimacy in the eyes of the great majority of Chihuahua's population. This was no longer a motley array of guerrilla bands but a well-organized, well-armed regular contingent, led by a man whose popular appeal was greater than that of any Mexican since Benito Juárez. It could now freely roam through the state of Chihuahua, and an irresistible momentum seemed to be carrying it to victory.

Their successful march towards Ciudad Juárez, the consciousness that they were now a regular fighting force, able to confront the federal forces head-on instead of utilizing the hit-and-run tactics to which they been limited until now, the retreat of the federal army from large parts of Chihuahua, and Madero's leadership had buoyed the spirits of the fighting men. There was a feeling that a major victory was in the offing and that the Díaz regime was doomed. All along the way to Juárez, new men joined the revolutionary army. This optimism and effervescence suffered a sharp decline once the cease-fire started and the troops were subjected to days of uncertainty and inactivity. Lack of sufficient food and supplies, as well as arrears in their promised pay, further dampened their spirits. Worried by the effects of Madero's policies on the army, Juan Sánchez Azcona, one of Madero's close collaborators, wired the vice-presidential nominee, Francisco Vázquez Gómez, who was at the time in Washington: "It is urgent that you come here, to counteract enemy influences. Promulgation of armistice constitutes great danger since soldiers who are impatient are beginning to desert."[137]

A further indication of the unrest that Madero's decision to postpone the attack on Ciudad Juárez produced in his army was a letter sent by the three main leaders of the revolutionary forces, Pascual Orozco, José de la Luz Blanco, and Francisco Villa, to the editor of *El Paso del Norte*, a newspaper published on the U.S. side of the border. It stated:

It has come to our attention that a certain newspaper printed in English in that city has printed the falsehood in its columns that there has been insubordination in the ranks of the forces under the command of the provisional president of the Mexican republic, Mr. Francisco Madero, on account of the delay of the attack on Juárez. . . . The undersigned who are the commanders of the various units which are operating under the command of Mr. Madero consider it necessary to make public that no insubordination in that sense has taken place, or will take place, as all the men under our command obey the instruction and orders of Mr. Madero, with all due subordination, and we are the first to do the same.[138]

The fact that the military leaders found it necessary to so vehemently deny the story, as well as the fact that only a few days later they would be insubordinate to Madero, indicates that there was a basis to the rumors of dissatisfaction with Madero's policies in the army.

The letter also indicates that by this time Pancho Villa had become one of the three main military commanders of the revolutionary army. Villa's increasing status within the revolutionary leadership was shown on April 30 and May 1, 1911, when, together with eleven other men, including two other military leaders, he was invited to participate in a meeting of "the most prominent members of the anti-reelectionists party" to decide on a dispute that had arisen between Francisco Madero and some members of his family, on the one hand, and the vice-presidential candidate, Francisco Vázquez Gómez, and prominent members of the anti-reelectionists' leadership, on the other.

At issue was whether the revolutionaries should accept peace along the terms agreed to by Madero and representatives of Limantour on April 22, which did not call for the immediate resignation of Porfirio Díaz. During the meeting, Madero stated that he had agreed not to insist on including a clause for Díaz's resignation because he had been confidentially told that Díaz would resign anyway. Vázquez Gómez, who represented the attitude of the majority of both the political and military leaders of the revolutionary movement, insisted that no agreement should be signed that did not call for the immediate resignation of

Díaz. "A part of the insurgent revolutionary forces would not abide by the treaties, which they might not find satisfactory," he stated. The meeting practically forced Madero to change his stand and to demand the resignation of Díaz as a condition for any peace settlement.[139]

Vázquez Gómez's position indicates a particularly strong military opposition to Madero's compromise proposal. It probably came less from Orozco than from Villa and Blanco. Only a day before, while engaged in a private discussion of other matters with his vice-presidential nominee, Madero had called in Orozco to ask whether in his opinion the resignation of Díaz should be a precondition for peace. "Don't ask me these things," Orozco replied, "since I understand nothing about them. Tell me that the enemy is coming from somewhere, and I shall see what I can do; but these things I know nothing about; you know what you should do."[140]

When Madero told Francisco Carvajal, the government representative who had come to meet him and to sign a peace agreement along the lines proposed by Limantour, that any agreement between the government and the revolutionaries would have to include Díaz's resignation, the peace negotiations broke down, and the armistice ended on May 7. Madero was now free to attack Ciudad Juárez, but he refused to do so, apparently convinced by the arguments of Díaz's two representatives that such an attack would bring about U.S. intervention. These representatives had good reason to do anything in their power to delay an attack on the border city. Its fortifications were inadequate, and its garrison was demoralized by the strength of the revolutionary army, the lack of ammunition and supplies, and the fact that the revolutionaries had cut off its water supply. The main military leaders of the revolution, Orozco and Villa, now decided that the time had come for insubordination. A retreat southward, they felt, would provide a morale boost to the government and demoralize their own forces. They decided to attack Juárez without informing Madero, making the attack seem to be a spontaneous, uncontrolled conflict between the federal troops and the revolutionary army. Once it had begun, they believed, Madero would have no choice but to throw all his forces into the attack on the border city. This was precisely what happened.[141]

On instructions from both Orozco and Villa, an officer of the revolutionary army, Reyes Robinson, ordered his men to fire at the federal troops. The federals responded, and fighting soon became general. Madero desperately attempted to stop it. He sent a message to the federal commander, General Navarro, asking him to order his men to hold their fire. Navarro, who was in a desperate position, agreed, and his men effectively stopped shooting. The revolutionaries did not. They continued advancing on the city and did not heed the order for a cease-fire from an emissary Madero sent with a white flag. The fighting again broke out, as more and more revolutionaries joined in and Navarro's men began shooting again. In the afternoon, Madero made a last attempt to stop the fighting and sent Castulo Herrera with a white flag to put an end to hostilities. Like Madero's previous emissaries, he was disregarded. According to some accounts, Villa and Orozco had crossed the border into El Paso so that Madero would not be able to reach them during the first hours of fighting to force them to stop the shooting, since they did not want an open break with Madero. When Orozco finally went to see the provisional president, he told him that the fighting had now reached such a stage that it could not be stopped, and that the best decision Madero could now make was to order a general attack on the city. He also assured Madero that Ciudad Juárez would be occupied by his troops within a few hours.

The conviction that victory was imminent, and the fact that he had done everything in his power to stop the fighting, and that despite the heavy combat no U.S. intervention had occurred, led Madero to agree to Orozco's suggestion. Madero ordered his troops to take the border city. Fearful of hitting the thousands of Americans lining the border to watch the attack on Juárez as if they were attending a football game, the revolutionaries attacked the town along the river parallel to El Paso and thus did not fire in the direction of the United States. While Orozco and his men moved into the city from the north, Villa's men attacked it from the south. Fighting was heavy, and casualties ran high on both sides, but it soon became clear that the revolutionaries were winning. Timothy Turner, an American correspondent who had crossed over into Juárez to watch the fighting, was greatly impressed by the revolutionaries' unconventional military tactics.

We sat up there on the hill and saw the river oaks swarming with insurrectos moving into Juárez. They moved in no formation whatsoever, just an irregular stream of them, silhouettes of men and rifles.

Thus they began to move in and to move out along that road throughout the battle. They would fight a while, and come back to rest, sleep and eat, returning refreshed to the front.

The European-trained soldiers raved at this, tried to turn them back, to make everybody fight at one time. But that was not the way of these chaps from Chihuahua. They knew their business and they knew it well.

That way of fighting, I think, more than any other thing, took Juárez. For by it, the insurrectos were always fresh with high spirits, while the little brown federals with no sleep and little food or water, with their officers behind them ready with their pistols to kill quitters, soon lost their morale.[142]

To counteract heavy machine-gun fire from the federal positions, the revolutionaries had developed a new and original tactic, which impressed Turner, who had now gone down from his hilltop to join the revolutionary troops in their assault.

I heard somebody calling me, and in the doorway was an insurrecto officer I knew, an erstwhile schoolteacher from the state capital, and I ran to where he was and then to the house. He was with some men who carried axes and crowbars in their hands, with their rifles swung onto their backs, and I saw what they were up to. They were cutting their way from one house to the other, chopping through the adobe walls dividing the structures. Thus one could walk a whole block without ever going outside a house.

This made a fairly safe way of moving through the center of the town, except, of course, when one had to run across three intersections to the next block of buildings. Nobody was in any hurry.[143]

The fighting continued until May 10. By mid-morning of that day, Navarro's position had become desperate. His remaining troops were concentrated in only a few buildings, their water supply cut off. As Madero put it a few months later when an inquest by the federal army into Navarro's conduct during the siege took place, "the forces of General Navarro had spent two days without drinking water, and it was impossible for them to resist anymore. The situation was desperate in yet another respect: my troops had come so close to them that hand grenades had become more effective than their cannon, their machine guns, and their Mausers."[144]

The Rebellion of the Military Leaders Against Madero

At 2:30 on May 10, 1911, Navarro surrendered, and the revolutionaries achieved their greatest and decisive victory. While this victory was the result of a conscious act of insubordination to Madero on the part of Orozco and Villa, they had endeavored to prevent this from leading to an open confrontation with the immensely popular revolutionary leader. Three days later, however, another act of insubordination occurred that did lead to such a confrontation.

It is still not entirely clear whether what happened was simply an attempt by the military leaders to exert pressure on Madero to obtain limited goals or a much more substantial move by the military to control, or at least to veto, the decisions of the civilian administration, or perhaps even a genuine attempt at a coup to eliminate Madero politically or physically. There are disagreements among contemporary observers and historians about what actually happened, although a much greater degree of consensus exists about Villa's motives.

The federal leader most hated by the revolutionaries was the commander of the garrison of Ciudad Juárez, General Juan Navarro, who had ordered the prisoners his army had taken after the battle of Cerro Prieto bayoneted to death. What had angered the revolutionaries was not just the execution of their comrades or the brutal manner in which it had been carried out, but that this manner of proceeding was in stark contrast to the way they dealt with federal prisoners, whose lives they almost invariably spared. One of the slogans observers heard revolutionary troops shouting again and again when they entered Juárez was "Death to Navarro!" They were all the more convinced of the legitimacy of their demand for Navarro's head in that Madero's Plan of San Luis Potosí stated that federal commanders who violated the laws of war and executed prisoners should themselves be prosecuted and executed. Instead of acceding to his soldiers' demands and calling for the court-martialing of the federal general, Madero unequivocally stated that he would protect Navarro's life and in fact later personally escorted him across the border to El Paso. Many soldiers of the revolutionary army became angry and dissatisfied with Madero's leadership because of his leniency to Navarro, as well as because they had not been paid for many weeks, and supplies were running low.

When Orozco went to see Villa and suggested that they should jointly force the president to hand over Navarro to them, he found Villa very responsive. The two agreed to confront Madero at 10 o'clock in the morning on May 11. "At the appointed hour, I presented myself with 50 men," Villa says in his memoirs. "Orozco was there with his troops. He called me aside and said, 'I am going to ask them to deliver Navarro to us. If the answer is no, disarm the president's guard.' I answered, 'Very well.'"[145]

Accounts of what then happened are highly contradictory. According to Villa's own account, he waited outside while Orozco went into the house to talk to Madero.

He entered the office and after a moment appeared at the door and shouted, "Disarm them." I consequently understood that Señor Madero was opposed to the execution, but had no recourse except to give my order. I gave the order to disarm the guard, and it was executed. Señor Madero rushed [out] and saw what I had done.

"So you are against me too, Pancho?"

I made no answer but waited for orders from Orozco. All he did, however, was to come out, behind Señor Madero and say, "No, Señor, let's understand each other."

They went on speaking. I could not hear what they were saying for the whispering of the troops. But I saw them embrace, and this naturally surprised me at first. One of two things must have happened. Either Orozco had lacked the courage to order the execution of Navarro in opposition to the president, or Señor Madero had persuaded him. In either case, Orozco owed me an explanation. I rearmed the guard and returned to my quarters.[146]

Most other accounts differ from Villa's. They describe Villa and Orozco jointly entering Madero's headquarters and Orozco demanding that Navarro be handed over to a court-martial (which would in fact have been the proper procedure under the Plan of San Luis Potosí) and that Madero pay his troops. In addition, Orozco expressed opposition to Madero's appointment of a civilian, Venustiano Carranza, a former prominent supporter of Reyes and a Díaz senator, who had joined the revolution at a relatively late date, as his secretary of war.

When Madero refused to accede to his requests, Orozco put a gun to his chest and told him he was under arrest. One of Madero's collaborators took out a gun and threatened Orozco with it. At this point, Villa rushed out to call in his 50 men. Madero ran outside, rushed past Orozco, who did not use his gun on him, and brushed off Villa, who, according to an account by a federal officer, threatened him in obscene terms. He jumped on top of a car and addressed both Villa's and Orozco's soldiers, who had been stationed outside his headquarters and had no clear idea of what going on. After listening to Madero for a few minutes, they began to cheer him. At this point, Orozco capitulated, the two men shook hands, and, by some accounts, Villa did the same.[147] Other accounts have Villa publicly crying and asking Madero for forgiveness. The mutiny had ended with Madero a clear victor. He personally escorted Navarro across the border to El Paso. Madero had emerged triumphant from this confrontation, rejecting Orozco's two main demands concerning Navarro and the appointment of Carranza. The only concession he was willing to make was to withdraw money from an El Paso bank to pay Orozco's soldiers.

There is little controversy among historians and eyewitnesses concerning Villa's motives. Punishing Navarro was his primary concern. He had always had a strong sense of revenge toward those he felt had betrayed him or had violated what he considered basic norms of behavior, as Navarro had done by executing his prisoners. Villa was probably also expressing his exasperation with what he perceived as Madero's readiness to make compromises with the Díaz forces. Political ambition was not, however, among Villa's motivations.

The same cannot be said of Orozco. He had pronounced political ambitions and may have hoped to be named secretary of war in the revolutionary government, since he was the revolution's highest and most successful military commander. The fact that Carranza, a relatively unknown civilian, whose revolutionary credentials were by no means impeccable, was now his nominal superior must have galled him. His confrontation with Madero may very well have been designed to force the Mexican president to give him a major post in the cabinet.

There is, however, another, much more Machiavellian interpretation of Orozco's conduct, which Villa came to believe. "I learnt the black story," he wrote in his memoirs:

Orozco, expecting a sum of money from Don Porfirio's agent, promised to assassinate Señor Madero and wished to involve me. Having disobeyed the president's order, I would have to go along with the rest, or at least I would have difficulty in proceeding in any other way, as I now understood.

At the last moment, Orozco lacked the courage to go through with it, or to go all the way, and knowing my violent character, he planned for me to disarm the guard, so that I would appear to be the principal instigator of the shooting and the president would challenge me face to face and I would draw my gun and kill him, and everything would be done with Pascual Orozco uninvolved, and me, Pancho Villa, apparently the true and only assassin.

It was a devious plot.[148]

These allegations cannot be proven, but they are not entirely without foundation. Orozco met at least four times, between the time Ciudad Juárez was captured and his confrontation with Madero, with Porfirio Díaz's representatives, Oscar Braniff and Toribio Esquivel Obregón. Madero himself in a letter spoke of outside influences on Orozco.[149] Villa's charge that Orozco was mainly motivated by financial considerations is improbable, however, notwithstanding that U.S. agents had heard that the Díaz regime had offered Orozco 50,000 pesos to kill Madero. If, indeed, he wanted to eliminate Madero, Orozco had higher aims than money. He was not only the most successful military leader the revolution had produced but its most popular figure after Madero. If Madero had disappeared, it was quite possible that his designated successor, Abraham González, who was unknown outside of Chihuahua, or his vice-presidential nominee, Francisco Vázquez Gómez, who had stayed outside of Mexico during most of the revolution, would easily have been replaced by Orozco in popular favor.

If this was Orozco's aim, imprisoning or killing Madero would have been counterproductive. Had he imprisoned him, the president's adherents would quickly have freed him. Had he killed him, it would have destroyed both Orozco's prestige and legitimacy. On the other hand, if Villa, a man with a reputation as a former bandit, had done the killing, things might have been different. Orozco's troops would not have hesitated to kill Villa. Villa would have emerged as a murderer and Orozco as the man who, in spite of personal disagreements with Madero, had avenged his leader's murder. Orozco must also have realized that the only issue that would sufficiently incense Villa to break the loyalty that he had shown Madero up to then was his outrage about the way Madero was attempting to spare Navarro's life. This may have been the main reason why either the execution or the court-martialing of Navarro was Orozco's main demand.

The motives for Madero's generosity toward the defeated federal commander are not entirely clear. Obviously, he could not simply have had him summarily shot. Even if he had wanted to, to have done so would have destroyed his credibility as the representative of a new, more humane and lawful order in Mexico. On the other hand, to have court-martialed Navarro would have been in accord with his own Plan of San Luis Potosí and with the Geneva Convention, which outlawed the execution of unarmed prisoners.

Once the military leaders presented him with this demand, Madero's wish to assert his authority may have prevented him from accepting it, even if he agreed with it. All indications, though, are that he simply did not want to subject Navarro to a court-martial. His personal sense of humanity—Madero always tended to respect the lives of those who fought against him—certainly is one explanation for his conduct. Another motive for Madero's clemency toward Navarro may have been that he felt and perhaps knew that a peace agreement would soon be reached, and that he then wanted to be able to rely on the federal army. By sparing Navarro's life, he probably hoped to ensure the federal army's loyalty to him. In fact, one of the main clauses of the peace agreement signed between Madero and the Díaz administration on May 9, 1911, was the maintenance of the federal army under the same leaders who had fought against Madero. The treaty of Ciudad Juárez, as it came to be known, stipulated that both Díaz and his vice president, Ramón Corral, would resign and be replaced by Díaz's foreign minister, Francisco de León de la Barra, who would assume the provisional presidency and preside over free elections within a few months. Madero and his people were allowed some influence in the formation of the government. They were to approve the cabinet, as well as name fourteen provisional governors, but the Porfirian state would remain practically intact. The revolutionary troops were to be demobilized as soon as possible, and the federal army was to constitute the main armed force of Mexico. Judges, mayors, and policemen, as well as "elected" bodies such as state legislatures, were to remain in office. The one concession to the revolutionary army contained in the agreement was that some of its members could apply for membership in the rurales. At the same time, provisions were made to provide pensions for widows and orphans of soldiers who had died in battle. There was no mention of immediate social reform.

It is remarkable how similar the clauses of the treaty of Ciudad Juárez are to the memorandum that Vera Estañol had formulated in 1911. The memorandum had stated that it should be the main aim of the government to make some kind of peace with the "political" revolutionaries in the north in order to concentrate on fighting "anarchy" in the rest of the country. Although this aim was never specifically stated in the peace treaty, this was in fact its objective result. In the north, the federal government made very clear-cut concessions to the revolutionaries. The federal army was withdrawn from some of the northern states, which implicitly meant that former revolutionaries would remain armed and would be entrusted with the task of keeping law and order in the north. On the other hand, nothing was said about withdrawing the federal army from the rest of the country or about maintaining the armed forces that the revolution had produced outside the north. The treaty of Ciudad Juárez implied that if the revolutionaries in southern and central Mexico did not lay down their arms, the federal army would force them to do so.

The similarities between the clauses of the peace treaty and the views of Vera Estañol do not mean that he had become influential in Mexico and that both the government and Madero had been converted to his views. Rather, Vera Estañol was reflecting a consensus among the federal authorities and Madero. The Porfirian elite and the revolutionary elite shared a fear of "anarchy," which to them meant something akin to the popular revolution a century before, when Father Miguel Hidalgo had been incapable of controlling his forces, who began massacring all Spaniards found on their triumphant path. This fear of an Indian revolt leading to anarchy had been fueled by the Caste war in Yucatán in 1847, when the Maya Indians had risen against all non-Indians and threatened either to massacre them or to expel them from the Yucatán peninsula. These fears were perhaps best reflected in the way Mexico's elite viewed the Zapata revolt in southern Mexico. In the government press, Zapata was called the Attila of the south, and his soldiers were depicted as Indian hordes who destroyed everything non-Indian they could find.

To a certain degree, Madero seems to have shared these views. It seems at first puzzling why he should have shown such confidence in the federal army, none of whose members had shown the least indication of wanting to join him in the revolution. The revolutionary chieftain may have been inspired by the example of Porfirio Díaz 35 years earlier, when he staged the coup that brought him to power in 1876. When Díaz rebelled against President Sebastián Lerdo de Tejada in 1876, most of the federal army remained loyal to the president. After achieving victory, Díaz did not dissolve that army but integrated it with his own forces, and the army remained loyal to him until his fall in 1911. Why should Madero not expect the same kind of loyalty? What Madero failed to realize was the fundamental difference between the armed movement that brought Díaz to power in 1876 and the one that allowed Madero to triumph in 1911. Although some peasants did follow Díaz, his basic support came from former soldiers who had fought with him during the war against the French and from caudillos closely allied to him. These men inspired no fear among Mexico's elite, whereas the peasant revolutionaries who brought Madero to power certainly did.

In addition, if Madero was really inspired by the example of Porfirio Díaz in 1876, he failed to learn a lesson from the caudillo's behavior. Díaz had made sure that his support was not limited to one kind of armed force. As a counterweight to the army, he set up the rurales, the rural police force, which depended upon the Ministry of the Interior and was independent of the Ministry of War. He also set up a multiplicity of local forces under jefes políticos and governors who to a large degree were appointed by him. Madero's aim by contrast, except in northern Mexico, was to disarm all the revolutionary forces, making him exclusively dependent upon the federal army. It was a fatal mistake. Not only would the federal army overthrow Madero and assassinate him two years later, in February 1913, but its leaders were opposed to the treaty of Ciudad Juárez.

Shortly after the fall of Ciudad Juárez, a dramatic confrontation had taken place in Díaz's residence between Finance Minister Limantour and two of Díaz's most important military commanders, General Victoriano Huerta and Minister of Defense González Cosío. Both sides were trying to influence Díaz, who was suffering severe pain from a toothache, and even when that pain eased had difficulty understanding what was being said because of a loss of hearing. When Huerta entered Díaz's residence, an agitated Limantour asked him what he thought of the "decisive event," meaning the fall of Ciudad Juárez. Huerta did not answer Limantour directly but proceeded to where Díaz was sitting and yelled into his ear that in his opinion, the capture of Ciudad Juárez was irrelevant; revolutionaries had captured another border town, Agua Prieta, before and had been expelled from it, and the same could easily happen with Ciudad Juárez. He told Díaz that a number of columns would have to be sent to Chihuahua in order to expel the revolutionaries from Ciudad Juárez, "to pursue them and to exterminate them." When Limantour stated that the government simply did not have the soldiers and the means to pursue such a large campaign, Huerta asked him what the financial reserves of the government were. When Limantour answered, "the treasury has a surplus of 72 million pesos," Huerta replied that this was "a lot of money for such a small thing." When an increasingly agitated Limantour expressed fears that if all the government's troops were sent to the north, the southern revolutionaries would overrun the capital, Huerta, supported by the minister of defense, treated them with contempt. He told Díaz that with 1,500 men, he could contain the southern revolutionaries and with 2,000 riders, he could exterminate the Chihuahuan rebels. Díaz was at first convinced by these arguments and gave instructions to Huerta to start a campaign of extermination against the southern revolutionaries. Before the campaign could begin, however, Díaz had changed his mind and agreed to resign and accede to the compromise that was reached at Ciudad Juárez.[150]

The opposition of Huerta and González Cosío was based on an unrealistic assessment of the respective strengths of the federal army and the revolutionaries. Huerta could never have exterminated the northern revolutionaries with 2,000 cavalrymen as he boasted to Porfirio Díaz. Both Limantour's attitude and Díaz's willingness to listen to the advice of his finance minister were because of an exaggerated fear of U.S. intervention and a realistic appraisal of the military situation in Chihuahua, with its social and political consequences.

The strong opposition of many revolutionary leaders to the treaty of Ciudad Juárez was based on a more realistic understanding of the military and political situation in Mexico. They felt that the military situation made such a compromise unnecessary. By mid-May 1911, the revolutionaries not only controlled most of the Mexican countryside but had occupied Cuernavaca, Chilpancingo, Durango, and other large cities as well. They felt that the federal army was on the verge of collapse, and that a few more weeks of fighting would give them complete control of the country. Leaving the Porfirian state practically intact and allowing a provisional president hostile to the revolution to control it would doom the revolution. Venustiano Carranza told Madero that he was "delivering to the reactionaries a dead revolution, which will have to be fought over again."[151]

Among the military leaders of the revolution, the one who most strongly expressed his opposition to the treaty of Ciudad Juárez was Pancho Villa. He did this in a way, though, with which even Madero's upper-class opponents within the revolutionary movement would scarcely have agreed. According to a story that Villa told many years later, he had prophesied to Madero, then preparing to sign the treaty of Ciudad Juárez, that such an agreement would lead to his death. This happened at a banquet in the customhouse of Ciudad Juárez in 1911. "I attended because he asked me to, but already I felt a deadly hatred for all those elegant dandies [*perfumados*]. They had started in with

espiches [Spanish in original] and that bunch of politicians talked endlessly. Then Madero said to me, "And you, Pancho, what do you think? The war is over. Aren't you happy? Give us a few words." I did not want to say anything, but Gustavo Madero who was sitting at my side, nudged me saying "Go ahead, Chief. Say something." So I stood up and said to Francisco Madero, "You, Sir, have destroyed the revolution." He demanded to know why, so I answered, "It's simple: this bunch of dandies have made a fool of you, and this will eventually cost us our necks, yours included." Madero kept on questioning me. "Fine, Pancho. But tell me, what do you think should be done?" I answered, "Allow me to hang this roomful of politicians and then let the revolution continue." Well, seeing the astonishment on the faces of those elegant followers, Madero replied, "You're a barbarian, Pancho. Sit down, sit down."[152]

Whether this episode occurred as Villa relates it or not (no other source confirms it), there can be little doubt that Villa strongly opposed the treaty of Ciudad Juárez. On May 18, three days before it was signed, when Madero's propositions became known to the public, the *New York Times* reported that Villa seemed to be the only military chieftain in Chihuahua opposed to these terms. The *Times* correspondent wrote that Orozco "himself says that he is satisfied with the terms on which peace is now being negotiated," and that as far as Blanco was concerned, "there seems to be no reason to doubt his loyalty to Madero." The *Times* wrote in entirely different terms about Villa: "As for Villa, the most hot-headed chieftain of them all . . . he appears to be completely out of sympathy with everything." On that same day, the *Times* reported that "Madero himself announced this afternoon that Villa had quit the insurrecto army."

Was Villa forced out of the army by Madero or did he resign voluntarily? In his memoirs, he describes himself as so ashamed over his attempt to imprison Madero on May 13 in Ciudad Juárez that he offered his resignation to the revolutionary leader. It was immediately accepted, which shows that at the very least Madero was not unhappy to see Villa leave the army. Madero now offered Villa 25,000 pesos as a bonus. "I answered that I had not fought for money," Villa writes in his memoirs, "but only for the victory of the people and would retire to work for my living if the guarantees he had made were honored now that the revolution had triumphed."

Madero said, "Pancho, you shall see them honored and so shall the people, I promise. But now if you are unwilling to take all I offer you, accept a small amount. I shall have 10,000 pesos turned over to you." Villa accepted this amount "in obedience to the president's wishes."[153]

The reasons for Villa's dissatisfaction with the treaty of Ciudad Juárez seem to have been twofold. The first reason was his lack of confidence in both the federal army and the federal bureaucracy, which he felt, rightly as it turned out, would turn against both the revolution and Madero.

The second reason he expressed some years later in an ironic letter to one of Chihuahua's richest hacendados, in which he stated that the most stupid thing Mexico's ruling class had done was to turn against Madero. "You wanted to overthrow the government of the people, which was that of Maderito, and when he was assassinated, all of you were very happy. . . . You did not understand that this government would not have disturbed you and you would have continued to be the masters, since Maderito's family and he himself had ties to all members of the high aristocracy, and these ties would have allowed you to remain where you were."[154]

Villa was probably also disturbed by the fact that in the treaty of Ciudad Juárez, nothing was said about any measures to be taken against Terrazas and Creel. He would express such feelings vehemently in the weeks to come. It is also probable that he resented the fact that nothing was said about land reform, especially for his soldiers. It was around this time that he went to see Abraham González, demanding that the expectations of the revolution's soldiers should be met and land should be granted to them.

Finally, in personal terms, he was frustrated that his own important contribution to the revolution had gained so little recognition. If the *New York Times* is to be believed, Villa's anger and frustration at this fact were expressed in a somewhat bizarre way.

Armed with two guns, Villa crossed over from Ciudad Juárez to El Paso looking for Giuseppe Garibaldi. The two men had clashed only three days before, when Villa, for reasons that are not entirely clear, disarmed Garibaldi's American volunteers. Madero forced him to return their arms and to apologize to Garibaldi. The *Times* reported that Villa was jealous of Garibaldi's reputation as the man who had in fact vanquished Navarro in Ciudad Juárez and received his sword as a token of surrender. Garibaldi had repeatedly said that both Orozco and Villa were cowards, who had not participated in the fighting at all. In his account of the battle, Garibaldi stated that he had single-handedly conquered Juárez with his men, in spite of the cowardice of Orozco and Villa.[155]

In the eyes of the American press, Garibaldi thus became the victor of Ciudad Juárez, a reputation deeply resented by Villa.

It was about 1:30 o'clock this afternoon, when Villa accompanied by two men appeared at the Hotel Sheldon in the city. He was dressed in plain clothes. An angry glitter in his eyes was noted by many. He strutted about looking for someone, and his manner attracted the attention of federal secret agents.

In a secluded corner was Major Roque González Garza, who had been designated as the historian of the Battle of Juárez and for reasons such as those furnished by Villa today is anxious to lose the job. Villa saw him and in the absence of larger game gave him attention. He wanted to know whether he was to get proper credit for his part in the capture of Juárez. He also made it plain that he would not enjoy an account of that struggle which gave too much credit to Garibaldi. Seated opposite Villa while he was telling Garza how to write a history of the battle was one of the secret service agents. He soon knew that Villa had two pistols and was looking for Garibaldi. . . . Garibaldi, who had been out taking pictures, strolled in the hotel in his jaunty way. His camera was strung across his shoulders. Although a secret service man had told him of the danger, he smiled and greeted his friends. As he reached the center of the lobby, Villa came up from the Grill Room with Gustavo Madero.

When Villa caught sight of Garibaldi's back, his face was a picture of rage. But at the same time, he met the cold gaze of the three secret service men and understood that it was not the time for any mischief he may have intended. Gustavo Madero took in the situation at a glance, and pushed Villa into the elevator and went up to his room.

When, a few minutes later, Villa reappeared with Gustavo Madero in the lobby of the hotel, the mayor of El Paso decided to expel him from his city. "Villa," said the Mayor, "I had made up my mind to lock you up, but for good and sufficient reasons, I have determined to send you back to Juárez. I have issued orders that you shall not be allowed to cross over the river again if you are armed. If you do, I will put you in jail and the American courts will do the rest. Now you are going back to Juárez. Come on."

Villa was put into a carriage, which left him in the middle of the international bridge. "The secret service men told Villa to get out, and he did so. He was furious but his face was pointed south, and that was the direction he went."[156]

In the opinion of the *New York Times,* the episode was so important that it wrote an editorial on Villa's behavior. Its author doubted whether Villa had really wanted to kill Garibaldi:

That Colonel Villa went over from Juárez to El Paso thirsting for the life of his adopted or adoptive brother-in-arms, Colonel Garibaldi, is rendered just a little doubtful by two facts; first that his nominal purpose was so well advertised that he could count rather confidently on effective interference, and second, that he killed nobody, though the interference he did encounter was not such as would have prevented a really determined man from at least trying to shoot.[157]

The reason for the *Times's* interest in Villa was distinctly expressed in the same editorial, in which the leaders of the revolution were warned to be careful about recruiting such men as Villa. "As for Colonel Villa himself, he is one of the dangerous weapons that the leaders of revolutions so often consider themselves forced to use, tolerating their faults in the day of need and doing what they can after that day has passed to minimize the consequences of having followers hard to control."

In spite of his opposition to Madero's policies and his personal frustration, Villa would never publicly or openly oppose the Mexican president. In fact, less than a year later, when most of the military leaders of Chihuahua's revolution turned against Madero and rose up in arms against him, Villa was the only major military leader of the Chihuahuan uprising who remained loyal to him and took up arms on his behalf. In the meantime, Villa withdrew from public life in order to utilize his newfound legal status, his freedom from military obligations, the money he had received from Madero, and the prestige and power he had acquired in the course of the revolution, to become a successful businessman.

On the whole, Villa's contribution to the victory of Madero's forces seems to have been more important from a political than from a military point of view. Militarily, the 700 men he commanded, about 12 percent of the Chihuahuan revolutionary forces, certainly played an important, but by no means a decisive, role during the revolution. Villa's military achievements were overshadowed by those of Orozco. In political terms, though, Villa played a decisive role in helping Madero to gain control of his army at a time when his authority was fading because of his inability to discipline the Magonistas. It also seems to have been Villa more than Orozco who objected to Madero's initial attempts to effect a reconciliation with the Díaz forces, and it probably was Villa who more than anyone else pushed for initiating the attack on Ciudad Juárez in spite of Madero's reluctance, and he thus played a decisive role in the achievement of the one great victory that turned the tide in Chihuahua.

Whatever Villa's activities and lifestyle might have been prior to the revolution, his behavior during the revolutionary upheaval showed no traces of a bandit past or a bandit consciousness. It was that of a radical revolutionary, demanding an end to the existing power structure but also maintaining strict discipline among his troops. Perhaps more than any other of the main military leaders of the revolution in the north, he had become the spokesman for the demands, fears, and expectations of his soldiers.

The Fruits of Revolution and the National Scene

Like many moderate reformers before and after him who had called on the people to revolt, Madero soon realized that he could not control all the forces he had set in motion. He achieved his greatest success among segments of the middle classes, many of whose members enthusiastically welcomed his political reforms, which gave them new access to power at the national, regional, and local levels. Industrial workers too either supported him or at least did not oppose him, since Madero, while not openly favorable to labor, had allowed them to form unions and tolerated strikes.

It was in the countryside that the old order was shaken in a way that Madero had neither wished for nor anticipated, and in large parts of Mexico a situation emerged that he could not control. The best-known expression of the demise of the old order was the uprising in Morelos of Emiliano Zapata, who became disillusioned with Madero when he refused to return lands confiscated from villages and to allow the Zapatistas to exercise political influence in their native state. In addition to the one in Morelos, smaller uprisings occurred, but even where no larger revolts took place, there was a kind of cultural and political transformation of the attitude of free peasants and also of hacienda peons, traditionally the most docile part of Mexico's rural class. Not only regions that had been at the center of the Maderista revolution were affected, but even those where only small armed upheavals had taken place. This was the case in the southeastern state of Oaxaca, where few peasants had joined the Maderistas. Their attitude changed once the revolutionaries secured their military triumphs. A case that proved to be typical of the situation in large parts of rural Mexico occurred on the Hacienda de Dos Bocas in Oaxaca. A few peons from that estate, which belonged to an Englishman, Woodhouse, had gone to see for themselves the triumphant entry of revolutionaries into a neighboring city and had expressed their sympathy with them. That prompted Woodhouse to shoot at one of them and to threaten them with expulsion from his estate. Before the revolution, his control of his peons had been absolute, but this time they rebelled against him and forced him from the hacienda. Woodhouse was unable to persuade the authorities to take radical action against his peons, since, as a government commissioner told the British minister in Mexico, who had intervened on Woodhouse's behalf, "the troubles complained of by Mr. Woodhouse are more or less chronic on all haciendas throughout the state."[158]

At the other end of the Mexico, at the Hacienda de Santa Catalina in the state of Durango, the peons of the estate, which had been ruled with an iron hand by its administrator, Gómez Palacio, began an unprecedented strike. They demanded an increase in wages from 37 centavos to one peso, the abolition of the company store, payment in money instead of in kind, and a shorter working day, from dawn until 2:00 P.M.[159]

Such movements occurred all over Mexico and created a feeling of panic among both Mexican and foreign landowners, which expressed itself in a virulent hatred of Madero. "We Catholics know that certain spiritist phenomena such as relations with spirits are only an expression of contacts with the devil," Antonio Castro Solorzano, the administrator of the haciendas of Mazaquiahuac, El Rosario, and El Moral, wrote to his cousin in Rome after hearing of Madero's death. "I believed since the beginning of the revolution that Madero and his supporters were agents of the devil, and the events that we have seen cannot be explained rationally, but have to be seen as the results of a superhuman influence of a higher intelligence, that of the devil. . . . The last conflict in which the ex-president and the ex-vice-president lost their lives, whether in a real or a simulated attempt to save them, though it may appear inhuman, was a wonderful event for the peace of the nation."[160]

A similar hatred of Madero, although with a different cultural bias, was expressed in a letter that more than twenty long-time American residents of Mexico sent to President Woodrow Wilson in early 1913, after Madero had been assassinated. After describing Mexico's peons as both inhuman and irrational, they wrote with regard to Madero that:

a man who should start a rebellion, among the peons, is a thousand times more of a knave or a fool than one who smokes cigarettes in a powder factory, or builds a bonfire in a drought scorched forest. This is exactly what Madero did, offering the peons a vote and a free distribution of land.

Suppose a wealthy white man in Alabama had started in arming the Negroes a few years after the War, offering each a pure democracy, 40 acres and a mule, if they would make him governor. How long would the intelligent whites hesitate in stringing him to the nearest telegraph pole, especially if the Negroes there outnumbered the whites three to one?

And if, suppose conditions were such that he succeeded, he sat supine in his gubernatorial chair, while his black cohorts kept on robbing farm houses, outraging women, wrecking trains and paralyzing businesses, and when people went to him with demands for some actions, he blithely chattered, "Well, if you have not yet got peace, you have liberty, haven't you?" How long would the vigilance committee of southern gentlemen postpone his lynching? This is an exact parallel to conditions here due to the Madero's misguided criminal performance.

And would the President of the United States decline to recognize the situation and help stop the rapine and robbery, because the succeeding Governor of Alabama was suspected of belonging to the lynching committee and in any event had obtained his office "by force"? Would he demand an armistice and a full and "free" election? Is there a white woman in the south who did not approve of the legal doings of the Ku Klux Klan? Similarly if there was a good woman, regardless of nationality in this part of Mexico, outside the Madero family who did not breathe a sigh of relief when Madero's death became known, she was either ignorant of the true conditions, or was politically blind.[161]

Mexico's upper classes attributed Madero's failure to put down Zapata's uprising and to quell rising peasant restiveness either to his incapacity to do so (the majority thought he was too weak; the minority considered him too humane) or to his unwillingness to put a stop to rural unrest (rumors were spread of a secret deal between Madero and Zapata).[162] Their suspicions were fueled by the fact that Madero had curbed Juvencio Robles, the general appointed by the provisional government to subdue Zapata. Robles had practiced a systematic policy of terror: he had burned rebellious villages, deported their inhabitants, and carried out mass shootings and executions. Madero had dismissed Robles and replaced him with the head of the military college, Felipe Angeles, an artillery officer, who was one of the very few federal officers who sympathized with the revolutionary president.

Angeles waged what might be called a "gentleman's war," ending most acts of reprisal against the civilian population and treating prisoners well. This kind of restraint, the majority of Mexico's upper classes felt, could not lead to victory. What they did not want to see was that Robles's strategy had not only not produced victory but had actually strengthened Zapata's movement. Resentment and fear of Robles had led thousands of peasants who would not otherwise have joined Zapata to do so. Angeles's restraint had in fact persuaded many Zapatistas to lay down their arms, since they now felt that they would not be subjected to reprisals.

More acute observers, even if they shared the hacendados' opposition to peasant revolts, felt that Madero had no choice in the matter, since the Mexican state was simply too weak to carry out the kind of harsh policy Madero's conservative opponents advocated. Thus, the British consul in Torreón, Cunard Cummins, defended the restraint practiced by Francisco Madero's brother, Emilio, who commanded the revolutionary troops in the Laguna area. Emilio Madero had warned that too harsh a policy by the government "could develop into violence by the armed 'poor' against the defenseless 'rich,' irrespective of nationalities." Cummins defended this view:

Mr. Madero's most severe critics voiced the opinion that a strong man will improve the situation; on the other hand, Mr. Madero's policy here has found many strong supporters, it being contended and rightly so, that without an inner knowledge of the full situation, it is eminently unfair to criticize with decisiveness the action of the authorities, that the present temper of the turbulently inclined does not dispose them to tolerate extreme harshness now, and that, it may well be argued, stern measures would aggravate a delicate situation, and more over, perhaps, assist to give revolutionary movement to the grindstone with which others may wish to share new seditious acts.

Treatment to be effective and not liable to produce worse conditions would have to be overwhelming in strength and applied with decision.

The steadiest men among the Maderists cannot with safety be put to the test against their present or late brothers in arms.[163]

Mexico's upper class did not realize, nor did they want to realize, that the powerful state that Porfirio Díaz had so laboriously built up was disintegrating, and that no one, neither Madero nor anyone else, had the power in the short run to restore its repressive capacity.

The Díaz regime had never developed the kind of all-powerful secret police that emerged in many countries later in the twentieth century. Its repressive organs constituted a kind of multilayered pyramid. Its basis was formed by the hacendados and local authorities: mayors, judges, and jefes políticos. It was these authorities who first dealt with dissent on a small scale. They could count on local policemen, the state rurales, private retainers of the hacendados, and the acordada, a semi-official militia largely financed by estate owners. Small-scale rebellions would be quelled at the local level either by impressing their participants into the army (the leva), by deporting them to Yucatán or to other tropical regions of the country, or, in more serious cases, by imprisoning them in the dungeons of San Juan de Ulúa or resorting to the ley fuga. Larger rebellions would be quelled at a higher level of the pyramid by both the army and the national rurales (perhaps the best-trained police force in Mexico, although it numbered only 3,000 men), but these rarely acted alone and generally mobilized local forces to assist them.

With the exception of the national army, in many though not all parts of Mexico, every layer of repression had been undermined by the Madero revolution. Many mayors and jefes políticos had been ousted and replaced by men sympathetic to the revolution. Even when this was not the case, officials who had formerly been able to exercise repression without any risk to themselves now felt intimidated and hesitated to resort to the harsh policies of the Díaz period. The same was true of the judiciary, although it contained far more holdovers from the Porfirian period than the administrative sectors of the government. In some parts of the country, the acordada had disappeared, and the effectiveness of both the state and national rurales as instruments of repression had been undermined by the thousands of former revolutionaries who had joined their ranks. Only the federal army had remained largely intact. Few of its officers sympathized with the revolution, and few revolutionaries, if any, had joined it. Its effectiveness had nevertheless also been curtailed. In much of Mexico, the leva had been abolished, and there were few volunteers willing to join. Some army units had been demoralized by their defeat during the revolution. When it did have to carry out repressive functions during the Madero period, the army found itself alone, bereft of the help of its traditional auxiliaries, whom the jefes políticos and mayors had always mobilized in the past.

The hacendados reacted in various ways to the surge in peasant rebelliousness and to the simultaneous weakening of the central, regional, and local state. In southern Mexico, especially in the states of Chiapas, Tabasco, and Yucatán, where the Madero revolution had been relatively weak, they were most successful in maintaining the status quo with the help of federal troops. They still controlled some state governments with retainers of their own. For years, they had used co-ercion against the hacienda peons, who lived in a state of debt peonage akin to semi-slavery.

In central Mexico, a very different situation had arisen. There the hacenda-dos' power rested on much shakier ground. The Zapata uprising had begun to spread from Morelos to the surrounding states, and many hacendados had fled from their estates. Even where this was not the case, as word of the growing Za-patista movement spread, a new spirit of assertiveness manifested itself not only among free village communities but also among hacienda peons in regions not directly affected by the Zapata movement. In many cases, the hacendados were forced to make concessions. As their situations worsened, their hopes focused more and more on the only force they felt could restore the old status quo, the federal army.

In the state of Tlaxcala, where a peasant uprising had also occurred, the situa-tion was somewhat different. There the peasant leaders had tried to work within the system and had in fact succeeded in having a man favorable to their interests elected as governor of the state. The hacendados set up a political organization of their own, however, and with federal help, they soon succeeded in toppling the governor and replacing him with their own man.[164]

Hacendados in central and southern Mexico could ultimately rely on the help of federal troops. In northern Mexico, however, the hacendados faced an entirely different situation. Following the Madero revolution, federal troops had either been withdrawn from the north or were at most weakly represented there. As a result, the hacendados found themselves forced to make deals with the revolu-tionaries. This proved to be easiest in those states, Sonora and Coahuila, where revolutionary hacendados had assumed state power. In spite of differences be-tween conservative and revolutionary landowners over the spoils of power and concessions to the middle classes and industrial workers, both sides agreed on the need to curb peasant rebelliousness. When the Yaqui Indians in Sonora who had joined the ranks of the Madero revolution in order to regain their land tried to force the revolutionary governor, José María Maytorena, to meet their expec-tations, he sent troops against them.[165]

It was in the states of Durango and Chihuahua, where strong revolutionary movements that were not controlled by hacendados had emerged in 1910–11, that the traditional landowning oligarchy encountered their greatest difficulties. In Durango, they attempted to bribe and subvert one of the main revolutionary leaders in the state, Calixto Contreras, but failed.[166] Even if they had succeeded, it is doubtful whether it would have meant very much, since no one leader in Du-rango had emerged as the supreme chieftain of the revolutionary forces.

However great the regional differences faced by most of Mexico's hacendados, they had one attitude, one strategy, in common: in the last instance, they believed that their salvation would come from the federal army, which, they were con-vinced, would sooner or later overthrow Madero and reestablish the old order. The last thing any of them considered was aligning themselves with former rev-olutionaries against the federal army.

One state was an exception to this rule, as it had been an exception during the

1910 revolution. There the hacendados made an alliance with former revolutionaries and attempted to fight both the federal government and the federal army.
This was Chihuahua. As in 1910, events there would affect all of Mexico. This
exceptionalism was the result of a long historical tradition; of what some would
call the arrogance and others, more favorably inclined, the daring of the Terrazas-
Creel clan; and of the policies of the revolutionary governor of the state, Abraham González.

CHAPTER THREE

Disillusion and Counterrevolution

Chihuahua, 1912–1913

> I believe in nothing but the partition of land among the people that was promised to us by Madero. . . . I waited two months, three months, six months. I saw the peonage binding the chains deeper and deeper upon my people. Sick at heart, I gathered my old band together, and on the 2nd of February, 1912, I was again in the field.
>
> —Máximo Castillo, a former Maderista, on his reasons for joining the Orozco revolt[1]

González and the Oligarchy

Among the many Maderista upheavals, which had engulfed much of Mexico, the Chihuahuan movement remained unique. It was the strongest and best-disciplined military force the revolution produced. It was also unique in its social composition. Unlike the other large popular movement to emerge in 1911, the Zapatista revolt in Morelos, its influence reached beyond the peasantry. Unlike its counterparts in the adjacent states of Coahuila and Sonora, no members of the upper class, except for Madero himself, played any significant role in its leadership. Very soon after the triumph of the revolution, however, the multiclass unity that had allowed it to achieve victory fell apart. Like Madero, Abraham González was subjected to increasing pressure from both sides of the social spectrum: the oligarchy on the one hand and the peasants on the other. Unlike Madero, his failure to maintain the alliance that had brought him to power was not the result of any illusions about Mexico's upper classes or family connections to them (he had none); rather, he was a victim of his loyalty to his chief, who at every step prevented him from implementing radical social policies that might have allowed him to maintain the support of the popular classes.

During his term in office, Madero pursued a policy of damage control. After his initial transformation of Mexico's political structure, which created more political democracy than Mexico had ever known before, Madero's main aim was to contain the social revolution he had initiated in 1910. In many respects, this aim was identical with that pursued by Mexico's upper classes. But, in contrast to them, Madero was not willing to institute a dictatorship in the pursuit of such a policy or to rely on repression alone. Rather, he tempered his policies with concessions, although these were mainly directed at the middle classes and the urban working class. In many respects, González seems like a local replica of Madero. This was no coincidence; the two men were close. Shortly before the battle of Casas Grandes, Madero had selected González as his successor were he killed. In late 1911, Madero named González to what was perhaps the most important post in the revolutionary cabinet, making him *secretario de gobernación* (i.e., minister of internal affairs).

The similarities between them were striking. Both came from the north, and they shared a conception of progress and modernization modeled on the United States and western Europe. Both had spent many years north of the border. Both believed that one of Díaz's main errors had been his failure to open up the political process to the rising middle class, and both were sincerely committed to altering this aspect of Díaz's policies. Both were willing to make concessions to the urban working class, and both were wary of the lower classes of rural society. Both were convinced that lower-class "anarchy" could seriously impede foreign investment, which they clearly thought important. Once the treaty of Ciudad Juárez was signed, both set about demobilizing and disarming the peasants who had played such a decisive role in the revolution. And, in the end, both would pay a high price for this decision.

While the two men were very different physically, they had one thing in common: they did not conform to the macho stereotype of the Mexican revolutionary or caudillo, which led their conservative opponents to hold them up to ridicule. Madero was a small man with a squeaky voice; González was large and portly in appearance, the embodiment of middle-class respectability. Yet appearances were deceptive. While neither was a military man, both possessed extraordinary physical courage. Both were deeply humane men whose trust in the humanity of their opponents would lead to their deaths. Both would fight a two-front war, against both radicals and conservatives, but it was at this point that differences that would become more and more pronounced over time manifested themselves. From the moment he signed the peace agreement with the federal government until the day he was overthrown by a military coup, Madero considered the radicals, and especially the peasant revolutionaries, as his main enemy. He felt that his conservative opponents, such as Bernardo Reyes and Félix Díaz, who unsuccessfully attempted to overthrow his regime, were less dangerous. They had, after all, no mass popular support. He was either unable or unwilling to see the genuine basis of conservative support: the upper classes of society and the army. To the end, he believed that these forces would remain loyal to his regime. This attitude was owing both to his naïveté and to his social origin as a hacendado. If he ever forgot his origins, the many conservative members of his family were there to remind him that they and he were related by marriage to some of the most important hacendado families in Mexico, including the Terrazas.

Partly because of his social origins, Abraham González did not share Madero's favorable view of Mexico's traditional upper classes and the federal army. Unlike Madero, González came from the middle classes and had no personal or family links to Mexico's oligarchy. Long before the revolution began, he had been a victim of the Terrazas clan. He had fought the Terrazas during the revolution and was to meet their undying opposition until he was killed. He knew no compromise with them was possible. They had never resigned themselves to the idea that anyone not under their control would govern Chihuahua. And they had forced such powerful men as Benito Juárez and Porfirio Díaz to accept their rule over their native state. In part, too, the differences between Madero's and González's attitudes arose from the different aims of the two men in making the revolution. Madero had considered Porfirio Díaz as his primary enemy, and once Díaz was gone, he felt he could now turn his energies toward combating the radical revolutionaries. For González, the main enemy had been the Terrazas-Creel group, and they were still very much a presence in Chihuahua. Although Luis Terrazas and Enrique Creel had left the state, their sons and many of their retainers were still there. The remnants of their political organization had by no means dissolved, and their huge economic empire had largely survived the revolution.

González's measures to demobilize the revolutionary army, which were in line with the interests of the Terrazas-Creel clan, earned him no thanks from the Chihuahuan oligarchy. They would fight him until he was assassinated. Their policies greatly contributed to gradually changing González's focus. While, like Madero, he continued to fight a two-front battle against both radicals and conservatives, González, unlike Madero, directed his main attacks not at the radicals but at the conservatives, and he finally faced a unique situation in Mexico in that some radicals and the conservatives united against him.

The differences in approach between Madero and González were sometimes subtle, sometimes sharply delineated.

Both men were firmly convinced that one of the revolution's most important tasks was to absorb the middle class into the political process. They regarded the fact that Díaz had not done so as one of the main causes of his defeat. Madero basically believed that political reform would give the middle class more voice in government affairs, and that more freedom would in itself ensure its support and make it an effective counterweight to both conservative and radical opponents to his regime. González felt that more active steps against the conservative opposition were needed.

Unlike his chief, who kept a large number of holdovers from the Díaz administration in his government, González removed as many officials as he could from the Terrazas-Creel period, replacing them with former revolutionaries. González also proposed abolishing one of the most hated types of official, the jefe político. While González's measures basically affected the internal oligarchy of the state, another measure he took dealt with foreign influences there. He abolished company towns—that is, towns where officials had not been elected but were appointed by the company (generally foreign) that had obtained a concession to exploit the lands where the town was situated. González now allowed these communities to elect their own officials.[2]

Further down on the social scale, the differences in approach between the two men increased. When a wave of strikes broke out after Madero became president, he was quite willing to legalize unions and allow strikes, but he did not show any favoritism to industrial workers. González, by contrast, gave overt support to strikers and forced companies to accept compulsory arbitration by a committee composed of one representative of the workers, one of the owners, and one of the state. Decisions were taken by majority vote, and González generally instructed his representatives to favor the workers.[3]

The greatest differences between Madero and González were either directly or indirectly linked to the land question and to González's attitude to the state's traditional landowning oligarchy. González informed the hacendados that he was opposed to any kind of debt peonage or forcible detention of peons on their estates. "Don Panfilo Rodríguez, who worked as a laborer on the hacienda 'El Sauz,' told me that after he left the hacienda, he attempted to take his family from there, but Don Guillermo Terrazas prevented him from doing so, telling him that he would not allow his family to leave the hacienda. For this reason I ask you," he wrote to a hacendado, "to use your influence with Don Guillermo to get him to allow Rodríguez's family to leave the hacienda."[4]

While González had issued no laws or decrees implementing the return of confiscated lands to their former owners, he had elaborated a plan linking tax and land reforms in a way that in other countries might have seemed mildly reformist, but that in the Mexican context could well be called revolutionary. It became one of the main causes of a counterrevolutionary uprising in Chihuahua.

In contrast to Madero, whose plans for agrarian change were limited and vague and would not have hurt the oligarchy (Madero contemplated buying some large estates and selling them off in monthly installments to poor peasants, as well as doing the same with most of the land the government still owned), González had a plan that the oligarchy considered more dangerous and harmful. "Very soon after taking office," the U.S. consul in Chihuahua, Marion Letcher, reported to the State Department, "he [González] announced that he was going to see that a law was passed taxing progressively the big land-holdings to such a degree that after some 20,000–30,000 acres, a man could not afford to own more." While such measures only had long-range effects and seemed inadequate to expropriated peasants who wanted the immediate return of their properties and to landless laborers who needed immediate access to lands, they were resented by the oligarchy. "It is easy to understand," Letcher continued, "that such a measure would not win the support of people owning a 1,000,000 or more acres, as several wealthy individuals in the state do."[5]

This measure would primarily have benefited the agrarian middle class, which had the financial means to buy these parcels. The measures González actually took against the oligarchy were less radical than his earlier pronouncements had indicated, yet they were sufficient to trigger a wave of hatred against him among the entire Chihuahuan oligarchy. Rather than increasing the tax rate, González simply carried out a somewhat more realistic assessment of the tax value of the oligarchy's property, assessments that nevertheless fell far short of the haciendas' real worth. "The just value of Luis Terrazas's properties," González wrote to Madero, "lies between 50 and 100 million pesos. . . . Before the victory of the revolution of 1910, his properties were merely estimated at 1,702,438 pesos. The state actually estimates them at 9,156,610 pesos and 80 centavos, which as you can see is less than a fifth of their value."[6]

González in fact felt that he had made a major concession to Terrazas by not immediately assessing his properties at their full value, and only increasing the taxes to a limited degree. Neither Terrazas nor the other members of the clan who were affected shared these views, and they felt that these tax changes were merely the beginning of a long-range campaign to destroy the supremacy they had achieved in their native state.

With relentless energy, the clan now proceeded to fight González. They first attempted to prevent him from assuming the governorship of Chihuahua; when this failed, they sought to bribe him. When these initiatives brought no results, they sought to overthrow him with the help of foreign and domestic forces. They became so desperate that they finally attempted to align themselves with lower-class revolutionaries, many of whom were profoundly committed to agrarian reforms that were anathema to them.

The means at their disposal for achieving these aims were considerable. Not only had all of the members Terrazas and Creel clan survived the Madero revolution, but they had held on to their economic empire. Large segments of Chihuahua's upper classes that had disassociated themselves from the Terrazas during the armed phase of the revolution now rejoined them in their fight against Madero. As González succinctly put it, "as far as the upper classes [of Chihuahua] are concerned, part of them support me, but if their most important members are against me, that is not owing to the fact that I am treating them badly, or that I did not listen to them, but because, unfortunately, when they have come to see me, they have come to ask me to do things that are contrary to the law and contrary to my conscience, and since I have naturally not agreed to them, they have turned against me and condemned me."[7]

The oligarchy's hope of mobilizing American support for their fight against González met with only limited success until the end of 1912. Only American entrepreneurs, businessmen, and landowners closely linked by personal and financial deals with the Terrazas-Creel group supported them. The most outstanding of these supporters was Albert Bacon Fall, senator from New Mexico, who had inherited large amounts of land in Chihuahua by marrying the daughter of the American investor William C. Greene. Fall, who was also the lawyer for Terrazas and Creel, became the most vociferous advocate of U.S. intervention in Mexican affairs.[8] Many other Americans who had invested money in Chihuahua, though, did not share the views of the domestic oligarchy at this time. When they had invested their money in Chihuahua, they had received generous tax exemptions, and González made no move to lift or abolish them.

With skill and insight, the oligarchy attempted to exploit the contradictions, rivalries, inadequacies, and insufficiencies of the revolutionaries for their own ends. Some of their most important support—sometimes indirect, sometimes direct—came from Madero himself, whose national policies and interference in Chihuahuan affairs created obstacles that González found more and more difficult to overcome. In his eagerness for a reconciliation with Mexico's traditional upper classes, Madero allowed the Díaz-appointed state legislatures to remain in office until new national elections could be held. In Chihuahua, the first result of this was that the state legislature refused to ask for the resignation of the Porfirian governor, Ahumada, and to appoint Abraham González as provisional governor. Only when revolutionary troops began marching on Chihuahua did Ahumada finally resign and the legislature name González governor; but the Porfirian forces were not resigned to their defeat. They had utilized Madero's concessions for their own ends, and they attempted to do so again, although in a different way. The basic principle of the revolution had been no reelection. For this very reason, Madero had resigned as provisional president and turned over the provisional presidency to León de la Barra, a Díaz holdover, until new elections could be held at the end of the year. On the basis of the no-reelection principle, which they themselves had never observed, and of Madero's example, the conservatives who dominated the legislature hoped to force González into an insoluble dilemma: either he would have to resign as provisional governor, in which case the legislature would appoint one of its own to fill his post, giving them at least a breathing space and further demoralizing the revolutionaries, or he would remain as provisional governor and so not be able to become a candidate. For a brief time, González hoped to abide by the rules the revolutionaries had established and to force the legislature to name a provisional governor from the ranks of the revolutionaries. The conservative legislators refused, and González decided that he would not submit, that he would remain provisional governor and still be a candidate for governor. He was finally elected to that post in August 1911.

The activities of the Chihuahuan conservatives in the state legislature were a kind of rearguard action. They probably did not believe that González would relinquish power, but they sought by these maneuvers to discredit him. González's loss of popularity, they hoped, would redound to the benefit of a man whose vanity and ambitions they had begun to court, and who had played a decisive role in the military victory of the revolution, Pascual Orozco. "He was cultivated assiduously from the time that he came to Chihuahua after the fall of Juárez," Letcher reported. "He was urged by his new friends to run for the governorship against Abraham González."[9]

These new friends were members of the Creel and Terrazas families, who now established ever-closer relations with Orozco. Although he briefly did contemplate declaring himself a candidate, however, Orozco staunched rumors of his candidacy before the election took place. This was partially because legally he could not be a candidate, since he was not yet 30, the minimum age for a governor. But Orozco also realized that he did not yet have the support needed to win the governorship and probably hoped that failure to fulfill his promises would in time discredit González, and that he would then be able to replace him.

When it became clear to the oligarchy that their efforts to prevent González from taking office were doomed to failure, they began to think more and more of a "national" solution.

Their hatred and resentment at the revolution were perhaps best expressed in a letter that Enrique Creel sent to Porfirio Díaz, then in exile in Paris, in September 1911:

I cannot yet resign myself to the great misfortune that our country has suffered, to the ingratitude of the Mexican people, to the enormous injustice, to the disloyalty of some men, and to so many things that have happened to this country, so unexplainable, so unexpected, so futile and so disruptive, like an earthquake which in one instant destroys the work of many years. . . . The general situation of the country is very bad, there is no respect for the constitution, for private property, for political rights and free suffrage, but rather we have the rule of the brutal force of the lower classes armed with rifles, full of passion, with communist ideas and full of hatred against the upper classes. Uprisings continue to take place in many states. . . . Many haciendas are occupied by revolutionaries.

Mexican society, Creel said, was divided into two classes:

The first, very numerous group consist of the lower classes; workers and employees who are in favor of Madero, who are fanatic and obstinate. This class is the active one, and they will make Madero president. . . . The other class is composed of capitalists, intellectuals, and the upper classes of society. All of them who should be very powerful will not do anything because they have no organization, no civil courage, and the instinct of self-preservation and egoism are the basis of all of their actions. This class sympathizes with General Reyes, whom they consider capable of giving them guarantees, but since this is a passive class, it will not actively intervene in the electoral process, and even if it wanted to do so, Madero's supporters would not allow it.

Creel was pessimistic about the likelihood of Reyes winning an election against Madero. He called Reyes's situation "desperate since he was publicly assaulted and stoned in the Avenida Juárez and the press has called him a coward and a murderer."[10]

Neither Creel nor Reyes believed in the possibility of a Reyes victory in a free election. Reyes, however, was convinced that he could successfully carry out a coup against Madero, and that the army and the upper classes would rally to his cause. Creel seems to have shared both of these hopes, for agents of the U.S. Bureau of Investigation (the predecessor of the FBI) reported Reyes telling an informant that Creel was giving financial support to his movement.[11]

If Creel had indeed pinned his hopes on Reyes, his capacities of analysis were as flawed as they had been on the eve of the 1910 revolution. The Reyes revolt literally fizzled out. Reyes crossed the border in late 1911, calling for the people to revolt in his favor. No one responded, and Reyes and the few men who were with him were captured by federal troops. Fortunately for him, Madero was no Porfirio Díaz,[12] and Reyes was imprisoned in comfortable quarters, where he was allowed to see friends, relatives, and supporters and to plot a new revolution with considerable freedom of action.

If the Mexican army could not restore law and order, why not have the Americans do so? By the end of 1911, segments of Mexico's upper classes and members of the Chihuahuan oligarchy began to pin their hopes more and more on U.S. intervention.

In September 1911, U.S. Secretary of War Henry Stimson sent two secret agents from the general staff of the War Department, captains Charles D. Rhodes and Paul B. Malone, disguised as correspondents for the *Washington Times*, to Mexico to find out whether U.S. intervention might be necessary. They carried letters of introduction from the War Office to U.S. diplomats, who talked candidly and openly to them. The U.S. consul in Chihuahua, Marion Letcher, told them that while both the majority of the Americans in Chihuahua and the majority of the people were against U.S. intervention, there were some exceptions. They were (1) a small group of científicos, adherents of Díaz who had enjoyed concessions and other privileges under the old regime, who would invite annexation to thwart the present government, and (2) possibly the Catholic hierarchy in Chihuahua because of the very subordinate position it occupied under Madero and the fact that Madero's platform pledged a still further separation of church and state. The bishop of Chihuahua had confidentially told a friend that he would welcome annexation to the United States as a step toward bettering the status of his church in Mexico.[13]

A few months later, in February 1912, agents of the U.S. Bureau of Investigation reported that Terrazas was doing everything in his power to bring about U.S. intervention.[14]

When their hopes of securing either a Reyes victory or U.S. intervention faded, the Terrazas-Creel clan did not give up. They had a long tradition of relying on their own forces and triumphing in the end. They were confident that even without Reyes or the Americans, they would be able to change the power structure in Chihuahua, and perhaps in all of Mexico as well.

Their first and simplest step was to use a means that had proven enormously effective so frequently in the past: buying and bribing their opponents, as well as leading officials. Why not do the same with Abraham González? Such an attempt was made shortly after the state government of Chihuahua decreed a tax increase for Terrazas. "General Terrazas tried to bribe me," González wrote Madero, "through a lawyer very close to him who at the time was also a friend of mine, who told me what would finally happen if I did not accede and offered me on a regular basis a sum of money as long as I reduced the taxes of Señor Terrazas."[15] González's refusal led them to put into practice a more ambitious plan: a revolt with the aim of toppling not only González but Madero as well.

One of the reasons Terrazas and Creel may have thought that they had a chance of bribing González was that they felt the governor was no longer as strong as he had been in the heyday of the Madero revolution. This was in fact the case. González's power to resist the increasing onslaughts on his administration had been undermined, partly as a result of Terrazas-Creel maneuvers and machinations, but above all, as a result of Madero's policies in general and in Chihuahua specifically. González had lost some lower-class sympathy as a result of Madero's policies of rapidly demobilizing the revolutionary army and at the same time stifling progress in satisfying the peasants' demands for land. Other results of Madero's policies had also been harmful to González. In the treaty of Ciudad Juárez, Madero had implicitly recognized the legality of the state legislature, which both Madero and the anti-reelectionist party had always declared lacked legitimacy, because its members had never been chosen in genuinely free elections. For all practical purposes, it had been appointed by the Creel administration. Nevertheless, this patently illegitimate, vanquished state assembly had retained the right to name the governor.

González did not feel daunted by these obstacles, since he felt he had a weapon at his disposal that he could use at any moment to strike a decisive blow at the recognized leader and most intelligent member of the Terrazas-Creel clan: Enrique Creel himself. This was the Banco Minero scandal that had rocked Chihuahua only a few years before, had become a cause célèbre, and had undermined the legitimacy of the Creel administration. The affair had been quashed during the Díaz dictatorship as a result of Creel's close connections to both the administration in Mexico City and the legal authorities in Chihuahua. Now if the matter were taken up again, it might not only undermine whatever prestige Creel had left, but also weaken the economic power of his clan, and perhaps even lead to Creel's imprisonment, or at least to a criminal sentence. This case was the strongest weapon González had, and he had hoped to utilize it to intimidate the Creel-controlled state legislature and perhaps finally get a genuine trial under way. To his dismay, the rug was pulled from under him when Madero sent him instructions to discontinue any kind of investigation of the matter.

Madero was motivated by personal, social, and political considerations. While they fought Madero at every step along the way, Terrazas and Creel had no compunction about utilizing family and business connections, as well as Madero's obvious wish to reconcile Mexico's upper classes to his regime, for their own ends. In this case, they were successful. After Creel came to see him to ask him to intervene in the Banco Minero affair, Madero sent a long letter to González in which he stated his conviction that Creel was innocent. "It is impossible to attribute to Señor Creel or to a member of the family responsibility for the robbery, since four-fifths of the capital of the bank belongs to them, and it is illogical that they would rob themselves by perpetrating such an open scandal."[16]

Although Madero did not give a direct order to González to drop the case, he wrote him that Creel had convinced him that the judge who was in charge of the case, one of the few judges who had not bowed to Creel during his administration and had for that reason been dismissed by him, was partial, and that he wanted to replace him with another federal judge.[17] For González, Madero's letter, which in fact was an order, came as a blow. It not only deprived him of the most effective weapon he had in fighting the Terrazas, it also undermined popular confidence in his regime. One of the main planks of the anti-reelectionist party had been honest judges who would judge cases irrespective of the power and wealth of those affected. The Banco Minero scandal, many Chihuahuans felt, was a test case for the possibility of having an honest judiciary in Chihuahua.

González acceded to Madero's request, since he wanted to avoid a break with his chief, for whom he had great respect, but to deflect responsibility from himself, he released Madero's letter to the press.

The blows Madero unwittingly directed at González continued. Around the same time that Madero's popularity in Chihuahua was plummeting as a result of his intervention in the Banco Minero investigation, Madero further antagonized many of his erstwhile supporters by changing his vice-presidential nominee for the coming elections in November 1911. During the campaign against Porfirio Díaz, the anti-reelectionist vice-presidential nominee had been a physician, Francisco Vázquez Gómez, a man with whom Madero had had increasing differences during the revolution, but who enjoyed a great deal of popularity in Chihuahua. When Madero dropped his candidacy in favor of a politician from Yucatán, Pino Suárez, indignation against him in Chihuahua mounted. González, who attempted to win Chihuahuan anti-reelectionists over to the new ticket that Madero proposed, felt its repercussions through both divisions in and a weakening of the political party that had brought him to power.

The Growing Disillusionment of Chihuahua's Lower Classes

González had not yet recovered from these blows when Madero's very confidence in him and friendship for him weakened his power in Chihuahua even more. In November 1911, Madero prevailed upon a reluctant González to join his cabinet as Secretario de Gobernación, one of the most important posts in the Mexican government. González finally accepted Madero's request, and since he did not want to give up the governorship of Chihuahua, he asked for and received a leave of absence from the state legislature. This was a serious mistake. Doing so was highly unpopular in Chihuahua because of precedents during the Creel and Terrazas administrations. Both men after having been elected governor had taken long leaves of absence and turned over the position to far less competent subordinates, who were incapable of making crucial decisions. More important, González's temporary replacement, Aureliano González (no kinsman), lacked his chief's initiative and popularity, as well as his personal contacts with popular leaders in the state. While the state government remained passive between November 1911 and February 1912, the Terrazas-Creel clan was able to recoup its losses and to win over the second most popular political figure in the state, Pascual Orozco, with whose help they hoped to stage a counterrevolution.

Orozco counted not only on his own popularity but on the disillusionment of many of Chihuahua's villagers with both Madero and González. The Chihuahuan governor found himself in a paradoxical situation. His long-range plans with regard to the land question had antagonized the state's upper classes. His refusal to implement any dramatic changes in the short run had antagonized significant numbers of the state's free villagers and hacienda peons.

The Chihuahuan revolutionaries had risen at a time when most of Mexico thought that their enterprise was utopian at best, mad at worst. For nearly two months, they had almost single-handedly faced what was generally considered to be one of the strongest states in Latin America. They had borne the brunt of the fighting in these first months, and exposed the weakness of the Porfirian regime to all of Mexico and the rest of the world. When the rest of Mexico began to follow suit, it was still they who achieved the decisive victory that forced the Mexican dictator to resign. It was consciousness of this achievement that led thousands of inhabitants of Ciudad Chihuahua to give the victorious revolutionary troops a triumphant welcome when they entered the city in June 1911. For most of the soldiers of the revolutionary army, it was the last triumph and the last measure of recognition that they would experience in a long time. Only a few days later, Madero and the newly appointed governor, González, began to carry out a massive program of demobilization and disarmament of the revolutionary troops. Although a few contingents were kept on as state rurales, the vast majority of revolutionary soldiers were sent home with a bonus of 50 pesos apiece (and 25 more if they turned in their rifles), train tickets to their villages or towns, and the right to keep their horses.[18] Few, if any, thanks were expressed to them by the authorities, and scant provision was made to care for the widows and orphans of men killed in battle or for wounded or disabled soldiers. The reality they found at home, while not identical with what they had left, was far from the expectations that had led them to join in the revolution in the first place. In most cases, the mayor, whose autocratic rule they had hated, was gone. In most cases, the same was true of the jefes políticos, or if not, their authority was far more limited than before. Many other state authorities, such as the judges, had, however, remained in office. Most distressing, the haciendas had remained largely intact, and their enormous wealth and power was still at the disposal of Chihuahua's oligarchy.

But the returning soldiers, who had fought and defeated the oligarchy at the national and state levels, were not ready to acquiesce to the old order at the local level. As in the rest of Mexico, large segments of those classes of society who had hitherto been excluded from political and economic power were becoming conscious of their power and were being gripped by a new rebelliousness. Strangely enough, in contrast to other regions of Mexico where major rural insurrections had taken place, in Chihuahua, in the first months after the signing of peace, it was the urban sectors of the population far more than the rural ones that defied the traditional authorities. Chihuahua's middle classes—teachers, doctors, lawyers, small businessmen—began to assert their power, taking more and more elective and appointed offices, at both the local and the regional level, from the members and supporters of the traditional oligarchy. At the same time, a tax reform was instituted that shifted some of the burden of taxation from small businessmen to large enterprises. And Chihuahua's middle class appreciated and exercised a greater degree of freedom of the press in the state than ever before in its history.

Industrial workers also defied the old order. A wave of strikes gripped the state. Streetcar workers, miners, railwaymen, and the employees of meat-packing factories struck and, for the first time in many years, secured significant victories, forcing the owners to grant them large wage increases.[19]

For a time, Chihuahua's country people seem to have been less rebellious than their counterparts in Morelos, or even in Durango. Although until August 1911, revolutionaries and former revolutionaries continued to confiscate and slaughter Terrazas cattle, there are few reports of land occupations or invasions similar to the ones that occurred in Morelos or on the estates administered by Gómez Palacio in Durango. In Namiquipa and Cuchillo Parado, and probably in a number of other towns, villagers did take back some of the lands they had lost as a result of Creel's 1905 land law.[20] But the lands they occupied were mainly those that other villagers who were protégés of the Creel administration or village caciques had taken from them, not the lands that hacendados had confiscated. This picture of rural passivity vis-à-vis the hacendados may be erroneous and owing to lack of trustworthy information like that which we now have for other states. Nevertheless, in a series of bitter letters to Madero, Terrazas complained only of cattle, money, and some objects being taken from his estates and never mentioned land occupations. Nor did Chihuahua's free press report anything of the kind. This seems to indicate that there was little, if any, seizure of land from estates at the time, which is difficult to explain. Why did the men who had so strongly complained of the loss of their lands to the large estates on the eve of the revolution, and who had, to a large degree, taken up arms to reverse their losses, not occupy the lands they claimed? This was what Zapata's peasants, as well as the peasants in the Cuencamé district in Durango, were doing. Was it the awe in which Chi-

huahua's country people still held the huge power of the oligarchy? This is unlikely, since they had defeated that oligarchy. What is far more probable is that
villagers trusted the men who had led them into the revolution, Abraham
González and Pascual Orozco, who had respectively assumed the political and
military leadership of the state, to carry out their promises and take the necessary measures to grant them redress. Divisions within the peasantry may also
have led to passivity. In addition, many countryfolk were willing to give the government time and continued to have confidence in it, since some of the benefits
that primarily affected the urban middle classes and the industrial workers had
trickled down to them, although to a very different degree.

All benefited from the fact that they could now elect their own municipal authorities. Only those who held property substantially benefited from the tax re-
ductions the government had decreed, however, and only those who worked part-
time in industry profited from the wage increases that newly founded unions
were securing. But the number of these beneficiaries was substantial, and many of
them continued to support the state government.

The main popular opposition to the González administration came from the
district that had been the traditional basis of support for the PLM: the Galeana
district, where the Mormons had settled. When calls to expel the foreign settlers
from Mexico found no echo within the state government, many of Galeana's peasants were ready to heed the Flores Magón call to resume revolutionary warfare.

Their dissatisfaction was soon echoed by members of the one social group that
had benefited least from the revolution: the peons on the state's large haciendas.
Time had stood still on the Terrazas estates. In October 1911, a newspaper reported that the hacienda peons were still only getting 50 centavos a day, which
was not even paid in cash, but in scrip redeemable only at the company store.[21]

Although a kind of stalemate between hacendados and peons was characteristic of the period from June to about October 1911, it no longer applied to the situation that had arisen by the end of 1911 and the beginning of 1912. Encouraged
by the increasing unpopularity of the state government, its loss of prestige, owing
not only to failure to keep its social promises but to Abraham González's absence
from the state, the hacendados felt that the time had come to carry out a counteroffensive against those peons on their estates who had been rebellious. On November 20, 1911, one year from the date when the revolution had broken out, the
inhabitants of the hacienda of Humboldt bitterly protested that "every day we
undergo attacks and discrimination by the German Pablo Hoffman, and since
no one has protected us from these reprisals, we again ask for justice, since we
believe that we do not live in the period of the past administration, which protected every kind of attack on Mexicans."[22]

The protests of the workers on six haciendas whose spokesman was Cástulo
Herrera, Villa's former chief and one of the first revolutionaries to take up arms in
Chihuahua, were even more bitter. "Because some of us went into the revolution
to fight tyranny, we are now the object of discrimination and bad treatment by
the owners of these haciendas," they declared. Moreover, the hacendados were
trying to force them to bear the burden of the destruction that the fighting had
brought about. Because of the revolution, only part of that year's crop had been
harvested, and the hacendados sought to force their peons to hand most of it over

to them, depriving the laborers of the minimum needed to survive. "Convinced that the government that resulted from the revolution would carry out the clause of the Plan of San Luis Potosí consisting of land division to small landowners, many of whom were robbed of their lands by the illegal government of Porfirio Díaz, and weary of the owners and hacendados profiting from our energy without even treating us well, we call on the government to take the necessary measures to help us in our difficult situation," Castulo Herrera and others petitioned.[23]

On the hacienda of San Felipe, an unprecedented strike of hacienda workers had lasted for two months, since the administrator of the estate was asking the sharecroppers to turn over to him a far larger part of their harvest than ever before.[24] The Terrazas, by no means intimidated by the success of the revolutionaries, sought to recoup the losses they had suffered during the revolution at the expense of peasants who rented pastureland from them. Prices for renting pastureland in the vicinity of Ciudad Chihuahua increased from one peso a year to six, eliciting bitter denunciation from the *Correo de Chihuahua*.[25]

Discontent even spread to some of the military colonies, which had been the backbone of the Madero revolution. "We are worse off now than before and . . . the caciques have only changed names," Porfirio Talamantes, the village leader who during the Díaz dictatorship had attempted with such determination—and lack of success—to fight for municipal autonomy and for the return of the lands lost by the village of Janos, now wrote to the *Correo de Chihuahua*. The man named mayor by the new jefe político, Pacheco, "was a revolutionary in the presence of revolutionaries, and a government supporter in the presence of federal troops." He accused Pacheco of stealing wheat that the state administration had sent to be divided among the inhabitants of Janos. "I and many others will lose our harvest because Pacheco is refusing to give us water to irrigate our fields," he said.[26] "I have a feeling of despair, since I have twice complained against the authorities of Janos, and although Governor Abraham González has told me that I might hope for a change, I do not see anything occurring. I ask myself, why is this happening? When I try to answer my question, I must stifle the melancholy of my heart, since I have not yet lost faith that sooner or later my words will be listened to."[27]

Talamantes was finally successful. A few weeks later, the governor ordered the jefe político of the Galeana district to remove the mayor about whom Talamantes had so bitterly complained.

While Abraham González was thus able to diffuse discontent at Janos, it continued to smolder in the military colony that had been one of the cradles of the 1910 revolution, the village where Pancho Villa had recruited most of his original adherents: San Andrés. In February 1912, the *Correo de Chihuahua* reported that since Madero had not carried out the promises he had made, discontent was such that many "would prefer the Porfirian dictatorship, which at least did not try to hide the facts. . . . privileges for a few favorites are again the order of the day."[28]

The mood of many of Chihuahua's villagers was perhaps best expressed by Máximo Castillo, a peasant leader who had led a detachment charged with ensuring Madero's personal security during the revolution. In 1914, he gave a revealing interview to the *El Paso Morning Times*. "Máximo Castillo," the reporter who interviewed him wrote, is a spare wrinkled, shrunk figure, the moustache and beard almost white. He is well educated, extraordinarily well read for a Mexican farmer, and has a gentle and cordial manner. Castillo says that he is over sixty years old. "I believe in nothing but the partition of land among the people that was promised to us by Madero," he told the *El Paso Morning Times*. "I am not a socialist. I know nothing about it. I am one of the few independent farmers left in the state of Chihuahua. I own a little rancho at San Nicolás de Carretas, which my father owned before me and his father before him. That happy life is all I want in this world. But I could not sit still and see my comrades robbed under Porfirio Díaz's criminal land law, their homes taken away, themselves turned naked into the streets by federal soldiers, that their miserable little holdings might go to swell the great estates of Don Luis Terrazas."

Castillo had been very enthusiastic when the Madero revolution, with its promise of land reform, broke out. He returned home after victory in the hope that Madero would finally do what he had so eloquently promised. "I waited two months, three months, six months. I saw the peonage binding the chains deeper and deeper upon my people. Sick at heart, I gathered my old band together, and on the 2nd of February, 1912, I was again in the field."[29]

The Orozco Revolt

As more and more news of unrest, revolts, and uprisings arrived from Chihuahua, Abraham González decided he could no longer remain in Mexico City. He resigned his position as secretario de gobernación and returned to Chihuahua in order to resume his duties as governor of the state and to do everything in his power to avert the new revolt that seemed to be in the offing. By now, González had understood the reason for the increasing dissatisfaction among his erstwhile supporters in the state. "I can assure you," he wrote in an open letter to the citizens of Chihuahua, "that the government will attempt as quickly as possible to solve the agrarian problem, which is the root of an eminently healthy discontent."[30]

At the instigation of González, the state legislature passed a law appropriating six million pesos for irrigation works and the purchase of haciendas in order to redistribute some lands.[31] González also asked the federal government for funds to survey public and village lands and establish their borders. Once again, the central government in Mexico City sabotaged his efforts, stating that there was no money available for this purpose.[32] In any event, these measures were long-range, and many peasants felt them to be too little, too late.

In February 1912, a series of riots and local peasant revolts broke out in Chihuahua. The movement achieved a new quality when on February 27, the garrison of former revolutionaries at Ciudad Juárez revolted and seized the town. Some of these men were members of the PLM, and a few called themselves Zapatistas, but most regarded Emilio Vázquez Gómez as their leader. A curious and in some respects contradictory personality in the history of the Mexican revolution, Emilio Vázquez Gómez was the brother of Madero's vice-presidential candidate during his first campaign against Díaz, Francisco Vázquez Gómez. Emilio, a high official in Madero's anti-reelectionist party, emerged into the limelight when

Madero forced the provisional president, León de la Barra, to take him into his cabinet as secretario de gobernación as a representative of the revolutionaries. He rapidly gained the sympathy of many of Madero's armed supporters by striving to prevent the provisional president from demobilizing them, and he finally resigned in protest after federal troops massacred former revolutionaries in Puebla in 1911 and thus gained even more popularity among former revolutionaries.[33]

Emilio Vázquez Gómez was nevertheless less popular among the newly emerging revolutionaries in Ciudad Juárez than Orozco, whom they considered one of their own, and the rebel garrison indicated to Orozco that they would follow him if he would join their revolution but would repudiate him if he did not. Orozco now faced a difficult choice. He had not initiated this revolt, and it was not clear that he was ready at this point to rise against the government. But if he did not join them, he would lose all influence over these men, and his chances of leading a successful revolution would be in jeopardy. Madero still hoped that Orozco would remain loyal to him, and there are indications that he was ready to offer him the governorship of Chihuahua. This might have given Orozco a unique opportunity to implement a radical land-reform program if it had been his wish.[34] But Orozco refused Madero's offer. There is still much debate concerning his motivations. Some historians believe that he did so because of his close links to the Chihuahuan oligarchy, which urged him to assume the leadership of the revolt. Others feel that he was responding to pressure from his men. A minority believe that he was genuinely interested in reform and was convinced that under the leadership of Madero, such reforms were not possible, but that he, Orozco, could make use of the oligarchy for his own ends. Whatever his motivations, when Madero ordered him to retake Ciudad Juárez and reestablish government authority in the state, Orozco resigned from his post as commander of the state's rurales, and on March 2, 1912, he declared for renewed revolution.[35]

Although Orozco initially sought some kind of accord with Emilio Vázquez Gómez, who was living in the United States, he soon broke with him and assumed the leadership of the movement himself. In the Plan de la Empacadora, issued a few days later, Orozco called on the people of Mexico to revolt once again. He accused Madero of having broken all the promises he had made in his original call for revolution and of having set up a corrupt dictatorship with no intention of carrying out any of the social reforms for which so many revolutionaries had fought in 1910 and 1911. Orozco called for far-reaching reforms for both industrial workers and peasants. His plan demanded higher wages, abolition of company stores, and recognition of unions, but above all he insisted on the need for agrarian reform. Land illegally taken from peasants would be returned to them, and the state would expropriate, although it would pay compensation for them, all the lands of large estates that were not being cultivated.[36]

This radical program gained Orozco the endorsement of Zapata in the south (who had already stated in November 1911 in his Plan of Ayala that Orozco was his choice to head a new revolution) and of the PLM in the north. On March 6, six days after Orozco had decided to revolt, Juan Sarabia, one of the leaders of the PLM, came to Ciudad Chihuahua on a fact-finding mission. He was effusively received by Orozco and other leaders of his movement, and Orozco issued a new proclamation stating "that we have no other ideals than those of the great and glorious PLM."[37] Sarabia was impressed and extended to the movement a kind of official party blessing by stating that "the present armed movement . . . is clearly liberal in nature."[38]

In his proclamation and plans, Orozco assumed the mantle of a radical revolutionary, a man in many respects akin to Zapata, a kind of Zapata of the north.

The reaction both of large segments of the lower classes and of the state's upper classes to Orozco, though, was far different from the reaction of the same social groups in southern Mexico to Zapata. In Morelos, the great majority of peasants, especially the former inhabitants of free villages, supported Zapata, while the oligarchy desperately sought federal help to contain the revolutionary tide.

Things were different in Chihuahua. While villagers affiliated with the PLM, whose main stronghold was the district of Galeana, rallied to Orozco in great numbers, the same was not true of Orozco's own people in the Guerrero district. This region in the western mountains of Chihuahua, which was Orozco's home turf and where he had recruited most of the revolutionaries who finally defeated Díaz, now remained largely quiescent. In February 1912, Abraham González wrote Madero that "the whole district of Guerrero remains loyal, this is very significant and I believe I can mobilize troops to support the government there."[39] Indeed, volunteers from Guerrero joined government ranks to fight against the very man who seemed to have been the incarnation of their revolt only a few months earlier.

The stance of the people of Guerrero was partly owing to the fact that they trusted González, who was one of their own, and that they had benefited from the limited reforms he had already carried out and were willing to believe his promises that he would finally solve the agrarian problem. Their support of the government was also owing to the attitude of the oligarchy to Orozco. Whereas in Morelos the hacendados were fleeing their properties and desperately calling on the Mexico City authorities to help them, Chihuahua's hacendados rallied to Orozco and threw their support to him. They set up a rump legislature composed of their supporters that gave unqualified support to Orozco. At the same time, 1,200,000 pesos were raised mainly from the oligarchy for Orozco's rebellion.[40]

Two problems puzzled contemporary observers and continue to puzzle scholars and historians. Why did Orozco align himself with the Chihuahuan oligarchy, and, conversely, why was the Chihuahuan oligarchy willing to risk an alliance with a movement in which revolutionary villagers played a prominent role?

There is widespread agreement among both contemporary observers in Chihuahua and historians that Orozco was linked to the Chihuahuan oligarchy. The evidence is clear on the financial, diplomatic, social, and political support that he received from both the Terrazas-Creel group and other members of the oligarchy. What is still controversial is the question of why Orozco went along with his erstwhile enemies. Was he a genuine social reformer who hoped to utilize the resources that the oligarchy was putting at his disposal for his own reformist purposes? Or did he, as his enemies accused him of doing, sell out to Chihuahua's ruling class?

There are a long history and many precedents in Chihuahua of villagers aligning themselves with members of the oligarchy, each side hoping to use the other for its own purposes. The last such instance had been the 1910–11 revolution itself, when peasants had rallied to a wealthy hacendado, Francisco Madero. Could not the Orozco alliance with the state's ruling class be considered in the same vein?

This was not the opinion of the U.S. consul in Chihuahua, Marion Letcher, or of the radical peasant revolutionary Máximo Castillo, initially an enthusiastic supporter of Orozco's. Describing the origin of Orozco's revolt, Letcher reported in April 1912 to the State Department:

The first steps taken to further loosen the hold of Madero upon the people were the circulation of reports about the corruption of the Madero brothers and the careful cultivation of non-fulfillment of promises sentiment. It may be noted that those in charge of this propaganda did not want to see any of the promises of Madero fulfilled, nor did they expect them to be fulfilled. The seed of discontent was sown with careful hand by master politicians, the husbandmen of the old days. . . . It seemed to me at one time that Orozco had been led to believe that he would be made president. I do not think so now. I believe he will be satisfied with the money consideration. . . .

To sum up the present situations: the revolution is the result of intrigue pure and simple, and takes advantage of the ignorance of the people. It is fostered and backed by the wealthiest men of the state. The fulfillment or the non-fulfillment of promises credited to Madero have nothing to do with it. These have been mere incidents availed of in a propaganda to discredit him with the masses.[41]

Máximo Castillo, one of the most radical agrarian revolutionaries in Chihuahua, was even more explicit with regard to Orozco. Because of his credentials as an agrarian revolutionary, Madero had sent Castillo, together with a number of other delegates, to Morelos to negotiate with Zapata. This visit influenced Castillo enormously. "There I saw my dreams accomplished," he said. "Two vast states, Morelos and Guerrero, after being in continuous revolution for more than three years, are building up at their centers an agricultural republic. I saw how Zapata divided the greatest estates into little farms and gave them to the people, who were at once farmers and warriors who have risen to protect their land."

This was the ideal Castillo sought for Chihuahua, and when Orozco proclaimed his revolution, Castillo felt that social change and land reform might finally come to Chihuahua. "I saw a copy of his [Orozco's] Plan of Tacubaya and it fired me with immense enthusiasm. It promised the division of the lands. . . . At Estación Gallego, I joined my forces with those of [José Inés] Salazar and we united with Pascual Orozco near Chihuahua. There we took a solemn oath to uphold the Plan of San Luis Potosí. By March we were marching south, a real peasant revolt. We took Chihuahua." But Orozco disillusioned Castillo as much as Madero had:

Then came the bitterest time of my life. I found out that Orozco was a traitor, a coward who had been bought by the rich. Everywhere the wealthy people gave them dances, banquets. He became a society hero. He accepted presents of money from the very robbers who had left the poor without a foot of ground they could call their own. One day he told me that he did not altogether believe in the division of the land. Salazar, Rojas, and I immediately left him after a public denunciation before the whole army.[42]

Castillo's assessment of Orozco was borne out when about two weeks after he joined the rebellion, Orozco issued orders, according to informants of the U.S. Bureau of Investigation, that the property of Luis Terrazas was not to be touched under any circumstances.[43] The administration that Orozco's party appointed to govern Chihuahua went a step further and reduced Terrazas's taxes to 50 percent of what he was paying under González. This, according to González, was the major reason why Terrazas supported the Orozco revolt.[44]

One of the most succinct characterizations of Orozco's revolt was given by an agent of the U.S. Bureau of Investigation in March 1912. "Every businessman in Chihuahua," he wrote, "supports Orozco's and the científicos' policy of disarming all of Mexico and using an iron hand like that of Díaz to hunt down rebels."[45]

Nevertheless, saying that Orozco "sold out" simplifies a much more complex situation. It implies that at some point Orozco had been a peasant leader, who then went over to the other side. This was never the case. Orozco came from a relatively well-to-do family, which owned land and a substantial transportation business. The family holdings have been estimated at anywhere between 50,000 and 100,000 pesos.[46] Before 1910, Orozco had never shown any interest in agrarian questions. He was not a peasant leader, although for a short time he declared that agrarian reform was one of his aims, but rather conformed to the general pattern of a local Mexican cacique, who when fighting rivals or the central government would alternately align himself either with the lower classes of society or with other caciques. This was precisely the policy he had pursued between 1910 and 1912. He had sided with the villagers in 1910 and with the oligarchy in 1912, with the consistent aim of increasing his own power.

One explanation of why Orozco's radical followers should have been willing to go along with Chihuahua's oligarchy is that in some cases they simply did not know about Orozco's relationship with Terrazas and Creel, and when they did find out, as was the case with Máximo Castillo, they broke off relations with him.

In other cases, some radical leaders may have felt that they were simply using Chihuahua's upper classes for their own ends. They had aligned themselves with Madero, a wealthy hacendado, in 1910–11, so why not do the same with Chihuahua's elite, utilizing the elite's resources but making no concessions to it? This might also have been the stance of another radical leader, José Inés Salazar, who had his troops put the branch office of Creel's Banco Minero in Parral to the torch when his troops occupied the town, making it very clear that whatever help he might have received from the oligarchy, he was not ready to make any concessions in return. Others may have been so personally involved with Orozco that they were ready to follow him whatever decision he took.

An even more intriguing problem is why the Chihuahuan oligarchy was willing to align itself with a movement in which their sworn enemies, revolutionary peasants, participated. Why was it practically the only important oligarchy in Mexico to do so?

The most obvious explanation is that the oligarchs had not initiated the revolt. In fact, it is doubtful whether by themselves they would have taken such an initiative. The men who first revolted—Antonio Rojas, Salazar, and Professor Braulio Hernández—seem to have been genuine radicals. There was a clear possibility that they would turn against the oligarchy. If Orozco, with whom the oligarchy had in fact a close relationship, assumed the leadership of the movement, the radicals might be brought under control. There were historical precedents that might justify such optimism on the part of the oligarchy. In 1879 and 1892–93, the Terrazas clan had successfully utilized village revolts for their own ends. In 1910–11, Madero had without too much difficulty brought the Magonistas under his control. Why should Orozco not be able to do the same?

While the oligarchy thus believed that by having Orozco take the leadership of the movement, it would diminish the potential risks that such an uprising represented for its interests, it was probably also convinced that the cost of surreptitiously supporting such a rebellion were minimal.

The revolt presented several possible scenarios, each of which, in one way or the other, could turn out to be favorable to the oligarchy's interests. The first, and most improbable, scenario was a straight victory by Orozco, who might defeat the federal army and take Mexico City. In that case, Orozco, a man the oligarchy now considered as favorable to their interests, would assume national power. In view of the regional nature of the revolt and the strength of the federal army, such a scenario seemed extremely unlikely. It was more likely that the federal army, which disliked Madero, would utilize the Orozco uprising to stage a revolt, take power, and then reach some sort of compromise with Orozco. This would allow the oligarchy to achieve its real aim, which, according to Consul Letcher, was to replace Madero, not with Orozco, but with Francisco León de la Barra, former minister of foreign affairs under Porfirio Díaz, who had been provisional president after Madero's victory and had shown his partiality for Mexico's upper classes.[47]

A third scenario was stalemate, with the Orozco movement controlling the north, or at least Chihuahua, while the federal government continued to control most of the rest of the country. In that case, a compromise, or better perhaps, a deal, similar to the one that was struck in 1891–92 between Díaz and the oligarchy after the Tomóchi uprising, could also be arrived at. The federal government would agree to remove González as governor and replace him with a man closer to the oligarchy who would have no objection to federal troops entering Chihuahua and, perhaps with the support of Terrazas and Creel, wiping out the rebellious peasants.

A fourth scenario, the defeat of the Orozco movement by federal troops, would have had no negative impact on the oligarchy either. It would have meant the return to Chihuahua of federal troops, who were far more conservative than the former revolutionaries who now garrisoned the state.

A fifth, more improbable but not impossible, scenario, U.S. intervention and the occupation of Chihuahua by U.S. troops in the event of depredations against American properties, would, according to U.S. Bureau of Investigation informants, have been welcomed by Luis Terrazas.[48] It is no coincidence that during the whole of the Orozco revolt, Senator Fall, with his close ties to Luis Terrazas, constantly urged the U.S. government both to support the Orozco uprising and to intervene in Mexico.

In the final analysis, whatever the end result of this revolt, there was one outcome that the oligarchy was sure to be happy about: revolutionaries would be killed. Nevertheless, the involvement of the oligarchy in an uprising that included radical peasants did entail a number of risks. The first, which the oligarchy did not consider very serious, was the possibility of reprisals against them or their properties by the Madero or González administrations. The Terrazas had had much successful experience in dealing with this kind of danger. When revolts in Luis Terrazas's favor, or revolts surreptitiously financed by him, had occurred in Chihuahua in 1879 and 1891, he had never become directly involved. Although Porfirio Díaz knew of his involvement, as long as Terrazas did not directly and openly side with the revolutionaries, Díaz had been loath to take direct action against one of the richest and most powerful men in Mexico. Madero, related as he was to the Terrazas family, could also be expected not to proceed against any of the clan's members.

It is not clear whether Luis Terrazas and Enrique Creel were directly involved in the revolt or whether the initiative came from younger members of the family.[49] As Abraham González saw it, there was little doubt about Terrazas's guilt. In a letter to Madero, he wrote that "Terrazas would have been happy if the Orozco rebellion had triumphed because he wanted a supporter to govern Chihuahua; not only to elude taxes as he had done in the past . . . but also to secure contracts and concessions et cetera, in other words, to govern the state through another person."

While González did not say that Terrazas had directly intervened in the rebellion, he did mention that a grandson was fighting in Orozco's forces, while a son, who at first volunteered to do so and at the last moment withdrew, had offered a large financial contribution instead. "Another son," González wrote, "helped [Orozco] repeatedly post bond for all those accused of violating the neutrality laws, and here in Chihuahua, all the representatives of General Terrazas who did not take an active part in the armed movement were untiring propagandists for the idea of revolt, and I am convinced that far from propagating socialist ideas, they openly worked for a Porfirian científico reaction, which would be favorable to their interests, with the aim of securing at least a change in local government in order to evade the tax rate on their agricultural and urban property."[50]

"In the period between 1910 and 1915, Luis Terrazas the elder essentially worked through his sons, thus succeeding in apparently keeping himself aloof from public affairs," reported Andrés Ortiz, governor of Chihuahua in 1918, who had been charged by the Mexican government with investigating Terrazas's activities during the revolution. After Orozco rebelled in 1912, according to Ortiz, his movement proceeded to levy a voluntary loan of 1,200,000 pesos. "A large number of the bonds were taken over by the Terrazas family, to the amount of 500,000 [pesos] (as well as by local banks, which the family controlled almost totally)."[51]

The oligarchy's confidence in Madero's goodwill was largely correct. Madero never took any reprisals against them, and in November 1912, he urged Abraham González to allow Luis Terrazas, who had been living in Los Angeles, to return to Chihuahua, where he would exercise full control over his vast economic empire.[52]

A second, more serious potential risk faced by the oligarchy was that the revolutionary movement, which it sought to control, might get out of hand and turn against their interests. To a certain extent this happened when Salazar either lost control of his men or directed them to burn the local offices of Creel's Banco

Minero after the capture of Parral. Far more dangerous for the oligarchy was Máximo Castillo's radical agrarian policy. In the first phase of the movement, though, Castillo's actions and Salazar's loss of control seem to have been exceptions rather than the rule. The oligarchy attempted to control the Orozco movement not only through its influence on Orozco but by increasing control of the movement's purse strings. The oligarchy designated one of its men, Gonzalo Enrile, as its representative within the leadership of the Orozco movement, and he seems to have played an ever-increasing role in dispensing money to Orozco and his men.[53]

Control of rebel finances helped the oligarchy in another way: it allowed them to recruit mercenaries, who were paid two pesos a day, considered a very high wage at the time. These men were not interested in agrarian reform; they gave their loyalty to those who paid them. As González put it, the Orozco revolutionaries "paralyzed the main industries of the state, and then offered to pay the enticing wage of two pesos a day to all of those who joined their ranks; many did so forced by needs, and others without understanding what they were doing."[54]

On the whole, the oligarchy's risk of losing control was limited in the first weeks and month of the uprising, when it seemed to be victorious. When in the summer of 1912, it was defeated, the remnants of the movement split. Some of them, under the leadership of Máximo Castillo, became radical land reformers, distributing the lands of six Terrazas haciendas among their laborers.[55] Other Orozquistas seem to have turned to banditry and began indiscriminate attacks upon Chihuahua's wealthiest men, including the oligarchy that had supported them in the beginning.

The greatest risk the oligarchy faced was that before the movement got off the ground, it might be defeated, not by the federal army, but by local forces loyal to González. These forces might conceivably, without asking Madero for permission, impose reprisals upon the state's upper classes. Only one former revolutionary in Chihuahua had the strength, prestige, and military capacity to challenge Orozco and possibly defeat him without federal assistance. That was Pancho Villa.

CHAPTER FOUR

An Unrequited Love

Villa and Madero, 1912-1913

En Santiago Tlatelolco	In Santiago Tlatelolco
lo metieron tras las rejas,	they put him behind bars,
como el tiempo no fue poco	and since he had much time
ahí conoció las letras . . .	he learned to read . . .
Francisco Villa "se pela"	Francisco Villa "escapes"
de la prisión militar,	from the military prison,
pasa frente al centinela	he passes in front of the guard
que ni lo llega a notar.	who does not recognize him.

Villa Enters Civilian Life

One of the main results of the Madero revolution was the entrance of men from the lower rungs of society into the ranks of Mexico's political class. Few made it into the higher echelons of political life, which still largely remained the domain of the upper class. The new men often became local leaders of those units of the revolutionary army that had not been demobilized and exercised some kind of local or regional power. This was the case of such men as Calixto Contreras in Durango. Others, such as Toribio Ortega, became mayors of their towns. Still others, such as Emiliano Zapata, continued to fight the government as leaders of revolutionary groups. Pancho Villa, by contrast, had no political or military power but entered the ranks of the middle class. According to Luz Corral, the most articulate of his many wives, Villa's career was a classic rags-to-riches story. The former outlaw had become a respectable middle-class pillar of society. He married the girl of his choice, set up a household in Ciudad Chihuahua, became a successful businessman, and enjoyed the respect and support of Governor González and President Madero.[1] His only political activities consisted of carrying out a number of missions for Madero. According to his enemies, all this was a front for continuing his bandit activities behind a legal cover. The small-time robber and murderer had now become a big city gangster.[2] Different and opposite as these two accounts are, they nevertheless have one thing in common: both of them assert that Villa's main preoccupation at the time was making money—in one case legally, in the other illegally. They project the image of a man who felt no identification with the frustrated hopes of the lower classes of society, and who did not object to Madero's conservative social policies.

The reality was in fact more complex than these two accounts would indicate.

There is little reason to doubt Luz Corral's story of Villa's brief courtship and elaborate wedding to her, although the validity of that marriage ceremony is still in doubt. They first met in the stormy days after the outbreak of the Madero revolution. Luz Corral lived with her widowed mother in the town of San Andrés, where Villa had made his headquarters for a time, and her family had great difficulty making ends meet. For this reason her mother was deeply shaken when the head of the anti-reelectionist party in San Andrés asked her for a "voluntary" contribution to the revolutionary cause. Afraid of being branded a counterrevolutionary, and unable to pay the sum allocated to her, Señora Corral went to see the revolutionary leader who exercised ultimate authority in San Andrés, Pancho Villa. Contrary to her fears (she had heard of the shooting of Claro Reza and had an image of Villa as a brutal man), he proved quite soft-hearted and accommodating. After going to her house and seeing for himself the poverty in which she lived, he agreed that all she had to do was to give some coffee, corn, and tobacco to his men. She directed her fearful, shy, and attractive daughter, Luz, to choose the items from the small store's shelves to be handed to the troops.

Villa, as Luz Corral recounted with pride, could not take his eyes off her. The next day, he came to see her, telling her that he had known her for a long time and had been captivated by her since he had seen a portrait of her that hung in the house of one of San Andrés's inhabitants. Villa went straight to the point— no long courtship, no guitars strumming in the street, no serenades. He asked Luz if upon the victory of the revolution, she would be willing to become his wife and establish a new home.

Luz agreed. Her mother, however, did not share her feelings, although she seems to have been afraid to express her opposition openly. She thought she had finally found a way to prevent the marriage, when Villa came back the next day and asked Luz Corral to make a shirt for him. The mother felt that her daughter was being put to a test. Villa obviously wanted not only an attractive wife but a good housewife and seamstress as well, and the shirt request was seen by both Luz and her mother as a kind of test. The mother now did everything to ensure that her daughter flunked this test. Luz knew nothing of sewing, and when she asked her mother for help, the latter refused, obviously hoping that the ill-fitting shirt might dissuade Villa from marrying her daughter. Villa's standards were not those of Parisian haute couture, however, and the shirt seems to have fitted. Villa's feelings for Luz Corral did not change.[3]

Her mother's hope that Villa might find another girl in another town was quite justified. In spite of the arduous nature of the revolutionary campaign, Villa had made scores of promises of marriage to girls all over Chihuahua. Nevertheless, he came back to Luz Corral, and an elaborate wedding ceremony took place in a Catholic church soon after the signing of the treaty of Ciudad Juárez. A minor hitch developed on the eve of the marriage when the priest who was to officiate the next morning asked Villa if he would not confess himself before the ceremony. "Look," Villa replied to the priest, "in order to hear my confessions, you would need no less than eight days, and as you see, everything has been arranged for the marriage to take place tomorrow."[4]

Villa had obviously convinced the priest that spending eight days or even eight minutes with him was not the most attractive of propositions, and he married Villa in a great ceremony, attended by his military chiefs and by a representative of the governor, the next day. Luz Corral soon found that Villa had a very big heart. When they settled down in Ciudad Chihuahua, scores of letters from girls to whom he had proposed marriage streamed into their home. In her memoirs, she relates these facts with considerable pride; after all, she had been the one he chose to marry. Her memoirs sound less happy in later years, when Villa married other women without having divorced her. She nevertheless felt herself to be his first, and thus only legally married, wife. She may have been mistaken, since there are indications that a few years earlier, in Parral, Villa had forcibly abducted and married another woman, Petra Espinoza.[5] Luz Corral was perhaps the only one of the many women in Villa's life who played a certain role in his political career.

The official church wedding was but one of the trappings of middle-class respectability that Villa now assumed. A smallish house that he had bought before the revolution was now rebuilt, refurbished, and enlarged. Together with his brothers, Antonio and Hipólito, whom he had brought to Ciudad Chihuahua, Villa set up a successful meat business. He bought modern refrigeration equipment in the United States and within a few weeks had set up four butcher shops in Chihuahua, which supplied large parts of the city with meat.[6] He was quite well off, as a complaint he wrote to Madero in 1912 indicates. He described to the Mexican president the properties that Orozco had confiscated from him in 1912. They included 200 horses, 200 cattle, and 115 mules, as well as 1,700 pesos and quantities of corn and beans.[7]

Was this image of a rising young successful businessman embracing middle-class values all there was to Villa at this time? Did he in fact leave politics to the governor and the president, concentrating exclusively on his own life and career? Did he identify in any way with those social groups in Chihuahua who felt that the revolution had not achieved the aims for which they had fought? Had he gone back to his old ways of cattle rustling? Was that the basis for the success of his business ventures?

The first of these questions is easiest to answer. To a large degree, Villa retained the attitudes he had held during the revolution. The same reasons that had driven him to oppose Madero at Ciudad Juárez in May 1911 now led him to criticize both Madero and González. He had nearly rebelled against Madero in May 1911 because of what he considered the latter's indulgence toward the leaders of the old regime—namely, Madero's refusal to have General Navarro court-martialed. Madero, Villa felt, was guilty of the same kind of behavior when he interceded with Abraham González to prevent Enrique Creel from being prosecuted for his part in the robbery of the Banco Minero. In a strongly worded letter to Madero, Villa wrote him to "remind him once more of the promises he made to all his supporters during the revolution." Villa insisted that

now that you have assumed supreme power in the republic, in view of the fact that one of the main causes for which we fought was the lack of guarantees and the op-

pression that the Chihuahuan people suffered because of the behavior and the brutality of the Creel dynasty, of which we were all victims, you will do everything you
can in accordance with your responsibilities to see that justice is carried out in the
scandal of the robbery of the Banco Minero.

While the three men who had been convicted of the robbery were still imprisoned, Villa said, those who were really responsible for it were still enjoying their
freedom. He requested that the three convicted men be freed and that "the
law . . . be applied in its full dimension to those who are really responsible for the
robbery, without any regard for individuals or their status."[8]

Apart from Madero's treatment of Navarro, another reason that had provoked
Villa in May 1911 was that his soldiers had not been paid. It was again payment of
his soldiers that led Villa to challenge, although in a very mild way, the man for
whom he felt the greatest respect and affection in the revolutionary leadership:
Abraham González. Shortly after the signing of the armistice in Ciudad Juárez,
some of Villa's men went to see González and asked him when they would get
the land they had expected to obtain after the victory of the revolution. González
told them that laws to this effect would have to be drafted, and that land distribution might take some time to be implemented. Dissatisfied with the governor's
answer, the soldiers went to see Villa. A new conference with González, in which
Villa participated, now took place. Villa asked him what would happen with the
land, and González again asked the soldiers to be patient. After reminding
González of the promises that had been made to the soldiers, Villa then endorsed
González's call for patience.[9]

Villa attempted to find other ways to pay his men. During the course of the
revolution, the revolutionaries had supplied their needs by confiscating products
from large estates, especially those of the Terrazas. In spite of the treaty of Ciudad Juárez, which clearly established that conditions should return to "normalcy"
and requisitions were to stop, the revolutionaries were reluctant to return to the
prerevolutionary status quo, and especially to respect the property of Luis Terrazas, who in their opinion was the prime cause of the revolution, and against
whom they had fought. In a bitter letter to the secretario de gobernación, Terrazas declared that he had hoped that once the revolution ended,

things would more or less return to their normal state, and that once the peace treaty
was signed, the ex-revolutionaries, in accordance with the principles they had advocated, would respect the right of private property. My hopes were partly frustrated.
While some of them have returned to normalcy, others have not respected these
treaties and like warlords dispose at their convenience of my property, disobey the
authorities, and, on some occasions, even refuse to recognize the latter's instructions.[10]

Terrazas singled out Villa as one of the main culprits and accused him of taking
60 mules from his hacienda of Torreón. Villa obviously felt that such exactions
were justified. In his memoirs he relates that after his return to San Andrés, "the
wives and widows of soldiers who had fallen in my campaign came to see me;
and as they had nothing to eat, being from a town that had given everything to
the revolution, I had 1,500 [hectoliters] of corn brought from the Hacienda de
Ojos Azules and distributed it."[11]

Madero and González both clamped down more and more on such exactions, and Villa was now forced to put pressure on the government to pay his men. In August 1911, he went to Mexico City to "present different demands in favor of his men. Some of them," the minister of finance wrote González, "could be paid, since their veracity could be duly proved." The minister sent other requests to González to be endorsed by the Chihuahuan government so that Villa's men could finally be paid.[12] Villa was only partly successful in his endeavors, for some time later, he reported to Madero that he himself was supporting three families of revolutionaries who had been killed in battle, since the government refused to do so.[13]

Loyalty to his men was to be typical of Villa throughout his life. A few weeks after the treaty of Ciudad Juárez was signed, Villa showed this loyalty in a less controversial way. He went to El Tecolote, the scene of one of his first battles, to retrieve the bodies of the men he had not been able to bury then. "Villa gave us the sad news," the *Correo de Chihuahua* reported, "that all the dead have disappeared."[14]

The most intense but also most ambiguous conflict that Villa had with Chihuahuan authorities, although it only marginally involved Abraham González and Madero, was again closely linked to both the fate and the activities of his men. After the treaty of Ciudad Juárez, many of them refused to accept the right of the hacendados to resume control of the huge wealth they had accumulated. Some of them were rustlers and simply went back to their old trade, while others had been convinced by the revolution of their right to dispossess Chihuahua's upper class. Complaints began to come in from different parts of Chihuahua that Villa's former soldiers were not respecting private property. In September 1911, an official from Satevo wrote González that there were:

scandalous amounts of acts of banditry and cattle rustling in the district I am responsible for, because of the support Villa gives to all kinds of men who do not submit to the authorities and who like to live off other men's properties. A completely unjustified reason they give for their acts is that they participated in the revolution and for that reason, can have their way with haciendas that do not belong to them. The majority of them do not accept and respect the authorities; they are not willing to go along with them, [and] they do not want to accept the law, but only do what they wish to do.[15]

The attitude of these men might have been different had Madero treated Villa in the same way that he had treated other local and regional revolutionary leaders. Most of them had been given some kind of local or regional power, of either a military or a political nature, and were thus able to take care of their men. Villa, who had commanded one of the largest revolutionary units, had no such power and thus had no legal possibility of helping or supporting them. It is not surprising that he clashed with local authorities when he attempted to do so. This was above all the case in Parral, a city very close to his heart, where he had lived for many years and had many friends and supporters. There Villa's attempt to protect his men led to an increasingly violent feud with the revolutionary chieftain who had become military commander of Parral and considered Villa a dangerous potential rival. This was José de Luz Soto, an older man, who had fought against the French in the 1860s, joined Porfirio Díaz during his uprising in 1876, and then turned against his erstwhile chief when he felt that the latter had become too much of a dictator. Like practically all of the senior military leaders of the Madero revolution in the north in 1910–11, he was made a commander of state troops. Soto was wary and fearful of Villa's popularity among many of Parral's inhabitants.

The conflict between Villa and Soto burst into the open when Soto accused several of Villa's men of having committed acts of banditry. Two died while resisting arrest by Soto's men, and another was killed while attempting to break out of prison in Parral.[16]

González was caught in the middle. Initially, he seems to have favored Villa, and as a result he received a violent letter, displaying an uncharacteristic lack of respect, from Soto, who wrote that he had received a letter from the governor's secretary "that young Pancho Villa" was coming to Parral on private business, and that the secretary asked Soto to help him. Soto had heard that Villa himself was boasting that he would come to Parral on orders of the governor to reestablish peace in the region. These rumors, Soto reported, had created indignation in Parral. He quoted people saying, "You have repeatedly told us that the governor is an immaculate, just, and clean person without reproach; it is impossible to believe that a person who has such qualities could lower himself to put the church in the hands of Luther; it is impossible to believe that he could put society under the rule of a man who only a year ago carried out barbaric acts in this region. What guarantees did the revolution bring us? Did it simply mean replacing white-collar thieves with bandit thieves?"

Soto accused the governor of showing Villa preferential treatment, and he reminded González that he, Soto, had "never robbed, never murdered. I have never established friendship with a bandit or had any other close relationship with one."[17] After accusing González of a "lack of reliability," he told him, "I did not, I had no intention of offending you, but if you think that I am offending you with this letter, I repeat, I am ready to take a stand in front of the supreme tribunal of public opinion." Perhaps because of Soto's letter, but more likely because Villa's men were infringing the status quo, González reversed his attitude. He now took Soto's side, writing Madero, "on the basis of the reports I have received from impartial observers and which I believe to be true, I have been assured that these killings were justified under the circumstances."[18]

For González, the Villa-Soto conflict was particularly onerous, since he needed the support of both men. There was no sign of conciliation, though. On the contrary, the conflict escalated when Soto attempted to imprison a protégé of Villa's, a "compadre," Major Agustín Moreno.[19] When he found that González was unwilling to take his side, Villa appealed directly to Madero. He asked him to intervene in his dispute with Soto. He likened Soto's behavior to "the arbitrary conduct of some caciques in the state of Chihuahua who still follow the discredited methods of the old regime."[20]

Villa's letter was written at a particularly bad time for the Madero and González administrations. The first uprising of former revolutionaries against González and Madero had taken place in Chihuahua, and the two men had strong reasons to doubt Orozco's loyalty, since he had just resigned from his position as head of the state rurales there. Under these circumstances, Villa's loyalty was of great importance to the Madero administration. On the other hand, they also wanted to maintain Soto's support.

Madero now attempted to mollify Villa by instructing his secretary, Juan Sánchez Azcona, to write a long, friendly but noncommittal answer to Villa's complaint. He wrote that the president had taken note "of the alleged arbitrariness" of some caciques in Chihuahua and had ordered an investigation. Coupled with assurances that Madero would do "everything in his power to apply the principles of the revolution" was an appeal addressed directly to Villa, telling him that the president hoped "to be able to count on the clear cooperation of all those who were his companions in the struggle for the ideals of the revolution, in which you played such a distinguished role."[21]

In another letter, written on the same day, to Abraham González, Sánchez Azcona expressed his concern about the meaning of Villa's letter. "I know Villa somewhat, and I believe that at present someone is whispering in his ear, and since this could have dangerous consequences in the long run, I felt it to be convenient that you should know of this letter, so that with your well-known prudence, you could do what you consider most convenient."[22]

Villa was not placated, and after writing Madero, he did something he had never done before. He resorted to the press and voiced his complaints in public, although in a veiled form, without mentioning any names. On February 15, 1912, the *Correo de Chihuahua* published an open letter that Villa had addressed to the people of Chihuahua on February 10. In it he said that "our dear country is suffering from a long and painful illness, and it is deplorable that it should suffer so much. What is its cause? Is it not perhaps a lack of guarantees caused by personal ambition and ignorance of the people? We believe it is necessary because it is in the public's interest to say that I have gathered our troops since our people does not have guarantees in this part of the Mexican republic."[23]

Villa noted that civil protections were lacking in the state of Chihuahua, and "that it was not just that because of a few ambitious men the people should suffer and lack those guarantees that it justly deserves. . . . If someone attempts to deceive the people and hypocritically put on a mask . . . he is a traitor to our homeland."[24]

For the average reader of the *Correo*, and for the average citizen of Chihuahua, this proclamation must have seemed vague and ambiguous. Villa did not spell out the kind of civil protections he meant, nor did he name the ambitious men he attacked. There is little doubt, though, that he was referring to Soto and perhaps also accusing González and the Madero administration of allowing such caciques as Soto a free hand in Chihuahua.

In view of Villa's complaints to Madero and his open letter to the people of Chihuahua, it is not surprising that both González and Madero should have harbored increasing doubts as to Villa's loyalty to their administration. Rumors circulating in Chihuahua that Villa might rise against the government had already reached agents of the U.S. Bureau of Investigation in the summer of 1911.[25] González had probably heard news of secret negotiations between Villa and Orozco (who had not yet rebelled against the government, but whose loyalty was more and more in doubt). Such negotiations had in fact taken place, although Villa and his enemies gave two completely different accounts of what had happened. "Do not forget," Villa wrote Madero in July 1912, "that I have not been seduced by the money that Orozco's father offered me in my own camp, and this is well known by many people."[26]

Both contemporary and later historians hostile to Villa tell a different story, of Villa attempting to join Orozco and the latter refusing his support because he considered Villa a bandit.[27] This version is rather improbable in view of Villa's hostility to Orozco, and since many months later, when Villa had more reason to rebel against Madero than he had in early 1912, he did not do so. In addition, Orozco never showed any sign of discriminating against any follower who had a reputation for banditry or lack of discipline.

It is thus not surprising that González felt he faced a dilemma when the Orozco rebellion broke out in early 1912. Should he entrust Villa with the command of the militias that he was raising to fight Orozco? On the one hand, the arms and money he would give Villa could be used against the government. On the other hand, by not supporting him he might drive Villa into the arms of the opposition and lose the support of one of the best and most influential military chiefs of the revolution in Chihuahua. González voiced his doubts when he wired the *subsecretario de gobernación*, Federico González Garza, "In answer to the wire you sent me yesterday in which you tell me that money has been assigned to me to recruit up to 900 men in accordance with the instructions of the president, I have named Colonel Francisco Villa as chief, who received 1,500 pesos; but there are rumors that although he has gone out with his men, he will not carry out the president's instructions but will join the revolutionaries." He finally decided to continue to support Villa but "for obvious reasons," as he wrote to Madero, ordered him to reduce his forces to 250 men.[28]

In the final analysis, González was convinced that Villa would remain loyal to the government. "He has reiterated his support to the government and to me personally," he wrote Madero on February 16.[29] He was right. Only a few days later, on February 29, Villa wrote another open letter, this time condemning the uprising in Chihuahua. It was addressed to Braulio Hernández, a high official in the González administration who had become one of the leaders of the Vázquez Gómez uprising.

"Do you think that there is no better means to carry out the promises of the Plan of San Luis than an armed uprising?" Villa asked Hernández. "Will it be a consolation to those who became widows and orphans during the last revolution to have their ranks swelled by new widows and orphans? Is it a sign of patriotism if we kill each other every time an ambitious man wants to take power?" He accused Hernández not only of fighting out of personal ambition, but of corruption as well, and finally of being in the pay of the Americans. "When the government sent you to . . . Madera to settle problems dealing with land, why instead of siding with the Mexicans did you side with the Americans? It was said at the time that you received a bribe of several thousand pesos that the Americans gave you so that the lands they then occupied and are still occupying would not be expropriated."[30]

Why did Villa, in spite of all the differences of opinion and even conflicts he had had with Madero and González, finally decide to take up arms on their behalf? On the one hand, there is little doubt that he continued to have feelings of admiration for and loyalty to both González and Madero, which he repeatedly expressed during the rest of his life, in spite of the many doubts that he harbored about their policies. In addition, it must have been clear to him that he could not remain neutral in the armed confrontation taking place in Chihuahua. As long as he did not join the rebels, they would remain suspicious of him, even if he did not support the government, and they might very well proceed against him. Moreover, he hated Terrazas and Creel, and his relations with Orozco had been tense ever since Villa became convinced that Orozco had duped him into rebelling against Madero at Ciudad Juárez. In addition, if the government was successful, Villa would emerge as its most important military leader in the state.

Conversely, if the government won, and he had not responded to its call, his standing in Chihuahua would suffer great harm. In addition, he was on bad terms with all the major forces that had revolted in Chihuahua. His relations with the radical Magonistas, who originally sparked the uprising against Madero, had been strained ever since he had proceeded against the Magonista forces at Madero's behest.

The two open letters reflected a new eloquence Villa had never manifested before. During the Madero revolution, he had never issued any letters or proclamations, and neither had he ever talked to reporters. When the Mexico City reporter Ignacio Herrerias arrived at Madero's camp in 1911, Villa was the only one of the major revolutionary leaders who refused to speak to him. Villa granted no interviews to the American reporters who flocked into the revolutionary camp during the siege of Ciudad Juárez.

Villa's newfound eloquence was a sign of increasing self-assertiveness and self-confidence, which reflected the fact that he had now become the government's prime military leader in northern Mexico. By mid-February 1912, even though Orozco had not yet joined the revolt, it was becoming increasingly clear that a kind of revolutionary momentum was building in Chihuahua. Even people who were not opposed to the government and might not revolt against it were becoming increasingly wary of supporting González or Madero, since they felt that everything was moving toward a new revolution, and that they might end up on the losing side if they expressed support for the government. Villa now felt that the time had come to break that momentum and to show that forces loyal to the government not only were present in Chihuahua but could be very effective. At the end of February, Villa and his men marched into the mountain region of western Chihuahua, whose inhabitants had formed the core of the revolutionary forces that overthrew the Díaz dictatorship.

The correspondent of the *Correo de Chihuahua* who followed Villa reported that while some doubts had initially been raised about his loyalty, they were soon dispelled. "Persons who knew him well stated that he would support the government, since, as they said, 'One can have all kinds of opinions about Villa, but he is a loyal man, he is true to his word of honor, he is not a traitor.'" The correspondent was impressed by the way Villa was received by the inhabitants of western Chihuahua and by the discipline of his troops:

The peaceful inhabitants of that region have placed their hopes on him, and believe that he is best able to master the situation and give guarantees to the people. The best evidence of this is the enthusiasm and goodwill that have been shown him in all the places where he has been. What has helped him most to gain sympathy and inspire confidence among the inhabitants of those villages and ranches is the order that he keeps among his men. They are very well organized.

Again and again the correspondent stressed the discipline maintained by Villa's men. They were divided into groups of 100, with officers and noncommissioned officers. Villa also had a paymaster, a quartermaster, secretaries, and so forth. "When they arrive in a town, all bars are closed, and the sale of liquor is strictly forbidden. Each major billets his men where the colonel tells him to. He receives supplies from the quartermaster, and their owners are immediately paid for the animals he kills." Villa also showed himself to be a good propagandist:

Last Sunday, Colonel Villa remained in San Andrés. In the afternoon, he gave orders for a band to be brought to the main square, where it played for the inhabitants. Since he had just received the last proclamation of Governor González, he ordered his men to proceed to the main square and to listen to the manifesto. It was listened to with great attention and very well received by the soldiers and inhabitants of the village, who shouted "Long live the governor, long live the legal government, long live Colonel Francisco Villa!"

This seems to be one of the first occasions on which a cry that was to mark the Mexican Revolution for many years to come was heard in a Mexican town. Villa was clearly beginning to develop military ambitions. "It must be noted," the correspondent wrote, that his men have unanimously agreed to call Señor Villa 'general' and demand from the government that he be given this title. . . . It is remarkable how much confidence and sympathy for Villa can be found among the inhabitants of this region, so that it was easy for him to find sufficient men to serve in his command."[31]

Only a few days after this report appeared in the *Correo de Chihuahua*, Villa's fortunes suffered a reversal. Orozco, whom the government had called upon to fight the Vázquez Gómez insurgents who had seized the border city of Ciudad Juárez, refused to comply with Madero's orders and instead resigned. It was becoming clear that he would soon join the revolt. Since there were no federal troops in Ciudad Chihuahua, and most of the former revolutionaries who were still under arms were men selected by and loyal to Orozco, González urgently called on Villa to enter Ciudad Chihuahua, so that he might have loyal troops at his disposal. Villa's imminent arrival provided Orozco with the pretext he needed to switch sides. He told the inhabitants of Chihuahua that he would mobilize them to prevent Villa from entering the city and plundering it. The black legend about Villa was revived, including both genuine details of his earlier life as a bandit and unproven rumors. Orozco's troops and volunteers who feared that Villa would plunder the capital forced Villa to retreat. He withdrew to the Valle de Zaragoza and remained on the sidelines until the end of March, except for a brief skirmish with Orozco's troops.

March was the high point of the Orozco uprising. The movement spread from Chihuahua to other parts of the north, especially to the Laguna area of Durango and Coahuila. Disillusioned revolutionaries led by such former Maderista leaders such as Emilio Campa and Benjamín Argumedo, a tailor, who had been one of the most successful military leaders of the Madero revolution, joined Orozco with thousands of men who had gained experience fighting the federal army in 1910–11. The Madero government attempted to suppress the uprising before it could gather momentum. The secretary of defense, José González Salas, a relative of Madero's, assumed personal command of whatever troops he could muster and set out to defeat Orozco. The two armies met in the small village of Rellano, in the state of Chihuahua. After hours of indecisive skirmishing and fighting, Emilio Campa had a brilliant idea. He loaded a locomotive with dynamite and let it roll against the federal troop train. The ensuing explosion not only killed hundreds of federal soldiers but created such a panic that the federal troops retreated in wild disorder. The impact of the defeat seemed even greater when it became known that González Salas, unable to face up to the consequences of his defeat, had taken his own life.

Orozco was now urged by his supporters to march on Mexico City. New volunteers swelled the ranks of his army from day to day. Some were disillusioned Maderistas who felt that the day of reckoning had come. Others jumped on what seemed to be a victorious bandwagon. For the unemployed, the lure of two pesos a day seemed irresistible. With the exception of a few scattered villages where leaders such as Pancho Villa or Toribio Ortega were still holding out, and the city of Parral, which was still loyal to Madero, Orozco controlled the whole of Chihuahua, and his bands were spreading all over the north. Orozco had now broken with Vázquez Gómez, whom he originally seems to have supported, but his unlikely coalition of radical revolutionaries and the Chihuahuan oligarchy, although increasingly fragile, was still held together by the lure of victory. Nevertheless, Orozco faced an obstacle that prevented him from exploiting his victory fully and marching south toward Mexico City: an embargo on the sale of ammunition and arms to the revolutionaries imposed by the Taft administration in Washington.[32]

There was a strong pro-Orozco lobby in the United States, composed primarily of men who held large properties in Chihuahua. Among them were the newspaper magnate William Randolph Hearst, who owned the huge hacienda of Babicora in Chihuahua, and Albert Bacon Fall, newly elected senator from New Mexico.[33] They were, however, unable to persuade the Taft administration that a new revolution would not disrupt Mexico's economy, harm American investors, and possibly make necessary military intervention by the United States, which Taft definitely did not want. Shortages of arms and ammunition owing to the U.S. embargo were only one factor that prevented Orozco from marching on to Mexico City, but in the long run the embargo would be of decisive importance in bringing about his defeat. Nevertheless, early in 1912, Orozco had a chance of partially circumventing the consequences of the U.S. arms embargo by making full use of his victory and the demoralization of the federal troops.

Orozco set his sights on an occupation of the rich and wealthy city of Torreón, Coahuila, which would have provided him with new sources of revenue, as well as some arms and ammunition that were stored there. In view of the support he enjoyed in the countryside around Torreón, the demoralization of the federal troops stationed there, and the fact that it would take several weeks for federal reinforcements to reach the northern city, Orozco had a good chance of taking this major industrial center. Its capture would have been a major victory in both financial and psychological terms. It might have persuaded the federal army, whose loyalty to Madero was superficial at best, to switch sides.

The unexpected obstacle that prevented Orozco from taking Torreón was Pancho Villa. Up to that point in time, Villa's activities during the Orozco campaign had been far more of a liability than an asset for the Madero administration. He had been defeated in his attempt to capture Ciudad Chihuahua, and the fear his name inspired had contributed to rallying large sectors of the middle class to Orozco. He had carried out no further military actions against the rebels, probably because his forces were plagued by desertions. By the end of March, only 60 men remained under his command.

At this point, neither Orozco, the federal government, nor any impartial observer could have believed that Villa was still a force to be reckoned with. Throughout his revolutionary career, however, Villa would show an uncanny ability to do the unexpected. With equal ease he plucked victory from the jaws of defeat and defeat from the jaws of victory. He was least dangerous for his opponent when he had achieved a major victory and most dangerous when he seemed on the verge of annihilation. He showed a far greater ability than any other leader in the Mexican Revolution to recover from defeat. In March 1912, when his force had been reduced to almost nothing, he achieved just such a dramatic recovery.

Pancho Villa's Lone Resistance

By the end of March 1912, Parral stood out as the only city in Chihuahua still loyal to Madero. The great majority of its population supported both Madero and González, and it was this that prevented the military commander of the city, Villa's archrival, José de la Luz Soto, from openly supporting Orozco. For several weeks he wavered, but when Orozco seemed to be winning and had assumed control of most of Chihuahua, Soto finally threw his support to the insurgent leader. Not all of the former revolutionary troops garrisoning Parral agreed with Soto. An important contingent, led by a young ranchero, Maclovio Herrera, remained loyal to Madero, and when he heard of the divisions in the ranks of the local garrison, Villa felt that he now had an opportunity to regain his strength and to strike a decisive blow against both Soto and Orozco. In military terms, he hoped the attack on Parral might hold off Orozco's capture of Torreón and give the government valuable breathing space. It would also allow Villa to replenish his ranks with volunteers, and, above all, obtain supplies and money to pay for them, in a city that up to then had remained unscathed in the turmoil of the Orozco revolution. When Villa and his 60 men slipped into Parral, he was soon joined by Maclovio Herrera and those of his men who were still loyal to Madero. With very little fighting, Soto's men were disarmed and Soto himself captured.

The Siege of Parral

In view of Soto's feud with Villa and disloyalty to Madero, everyone in Parral expected Villa to have him shot on the spot. Instead, he sent Soto under armed escort to Mexico City, where he was imprisoned by Madero. As a German representative who was present in Parral reported, people were pleasantly surprised by Villa's behavior:

When Villa entered Parral, everyone was trembling and believed his last hour had come, since the reports in the press about Villa and his men had given rise to great fears.

In truth I must say that Villa behaved with great decency toward foreigners. He forced Mexicans, not always in the friendliest of ways, to give him arms, horses, and money. But he did not molest them in any other way. Villa took nothing from foreigners, and if his men on their own confiscated any of their property, a short conversation with Villa was sufficient to obtain the return of stolen property. The troops maintained perfect order, and absolutely no looting took place.[34]

Villa confiscated whatever arms and ammunition he could find, and he forced the wealthiest men of the city to give him a total of 150,000 pesos. With one exception, he acted just as he and other leaders of the Madero movement had acted during the Madero revolution: he gave receipts for the money he took and assured the wealthy citizens of Parral that he had full authority from the governor to take these forced loans, and that as soon as the federal government won, it would repay the money. Villa, who knew Parral well, had drawn up a list of wealthy citizens and the sums each had to pay. Those who demurred were imprisoned in Villa's headquarters until they agreed to pay. All did. A few months later, when Villa was put on trial by the federal government, some of these men complained that Villa had kept them without food until they complied with his demands.

In the case of the Parral branch office of the Banco Minero, which belonged to Enrique Creel and his brother Juan, Villa departed from his usual norm of granting receipts, however, since he felt that the money should under no circumstances be repaid. He obviously felt that since Creel and Terrazas were behind the Orozco uprising, he had a legitimate right to take their property. In the receipts he gave the bank manager, Sánchez Domínguez, for 50,000 pesos that he took from the bank, he wrote that he considered this money "spoils of war." Villa had also proceeded with far greater harshness against the bank manager than against anyone else in Parral. "Villa came to our bank," Sánchez Domínguez wrote,

and, furious since he only found 3,500 pesos there, treated me and my son as if we were criminals and led us under military escort to the provisional prison he had prepared for us in his headquarters; there he told me that I would have to give him 50,000 pesos immediately, and if we did not do so, he would force us, the same night, to be at the very front of the military forces who were readying for the fight against the revolutionaries who attacked this town on March 2. When he saw that these threats did not intimidate us, he became even more furious and threatened us with things that were worse than death and seemed very intent on carrying out these threats.

Villa's intimidation was obviously successful, for Sánchez Domínguez finally agreed to pay the 50,000 pesos Villa asked for.[35]

Villa's forces had now been swelled, not only by the addition of several hundred men, but also by the arms, horses, equipment, and money that he had confiscated in Parral. But Maderista Parral was still an island in an Orozquista sea. A vastly superior force commanded by Orozco's General José Inés Salazar now set out to attack Parral, and Villa was faced with the choice of resisting overwhelming odds or retreating either to wage guerrilla war or to join government forces further to the south. Villa decided to stand and fight. For a time, his stand was surprisingly successful. He inflicted an unexpected defeat on Salazar's advancing troops. Like many of the town's inhabitants, Carlos Roth, the German representative in Parral, witnessed the battle which was being fought on the outskirts of the city.

We were awakened around 4 A.M. on April 2 by heavy cannon fire: Orozco had sent 1,000 men, two machine guns, and a cannon, expecting that it would be easy for him to take the city. The garrison of the city nevertheless offered a desperate resistance and attempted to keep the fighting on the outskirts of the city as far as possible, so that their families and uninvolved civilians would not suffer in the battle.

By 8 A.M., it seemed as if the Orozquistas were on the verge of winning. Six mules with their cannon were halfway up the mountain that dominates the city, and the intention probably was to bombard Parral, when a machine gun of the rurales manned by an American named Tom Fountain began to shoot with deadly results. Fountain concentrated all of his attention on the cannon, and he must have been a very good shot, for once the fighting had stopped, the six mules were found to be dead, and the artillery officer had been hit in the head and was lying beside the cannon, which his men had left behind.

The inhabitants of Parral, who were watching the fighting from the roofs of the their houses through field glasses, were relieved when the cannon suddenly came to a halt and could not be brought up to the mountaintop; it was clear to everyone that if the Orozquistas had bombarded the city from the top of the mountain [the Cerro de la Cruz], not much would have remained of Parral. . . . In the morning, the Orozquistas began to withdraw. Most of them did so in orderly fashion toward Jiménez, while some groups that were cut off from the main column had to fight their way out with every means at their disposal. Shots could still be heard by 6 P.M., although the fighting was further and further away from the city.

Parral had survived this battle, although everyone feared the consequences of that victory.

"The inhabitants of Parral knew," as Roth noted, that "Orozco absolutely had to take Parral before he could march further south. . . . The days following the battle of the 2d of April were the saddest that I have witnessed. Most stores were closed. No one dared to go into the streets. Everyone who had something to lose was full of fear for his property, even for his family's lives; the most terrible rumors circulated in the town concerning the way Orozco would take revenge on Parral."

By the afternoon of April 4, 2,500 Orozquistas were besieging the city, and Villa and his outnumbered men could no longer hold them off. When night fell, they withdrew, leaving Parral to its fate.

There was a striking contrast between Villa's orderly occupation, notwithstanding his impositions on its upper classes, and the aimless and generalized terrorism of the Orozquistas once they occupied Parral. Their arrival brought about the two most terrifying days in its history. "Like ants, the Orozquistas entered the city," Roth reported, "constantly firing their guns without seeing a single enemy."

Everyone who had been fighting against Orozco had fled, and only unarmed citizens and families had remained in town.

Once they had entered the city, the Orozquistas split up into small groups and ran yelling through the city, constantly firing their guns. Their first work of destruction was to break into every store in which they believed alcohol could be found, and after the troops were drunk, things really began to warm up.

It was around 10 P.M. We were in our apartment, which is somewhat distant from the downtown area, and where fortunately there are no stores. The bells of the church were tolling. We all became panicky, since rumors had been spread that Orozco, because of the defeat he had suffered before, would burn down Parral. . . .

The bells continued tolling eerily in the night. The streets were dark, since most electric wires had been cut in the fighting. All doors and windows were closed, [and] there were no lights in any house. Sometimes one could still hear cannon firing; the Orozquistas were shooting at the fleeing enemies from the mountains. And from the downtown part of the town, noises of shouting and revels could be heard as far as our house, as if hell had broken loose. Hundreds of shots were fired, and at the same time, one could hear the explosion of hand grenades and dynamite bombs.

The Orozquistas were busy in the center of the city. By 11 P.M, there was not a single Mexican store that had not been broken open. The branch office of the Banco Minero was burning, shots were fired at the church tower . . . since the soldiers believed that Villa's men were hidden there. They soon began to enter the houses asking for money, arms, jewelry, alcohol; they destroyed the furniture and caused panic among families. To underline their demands, these drunken men entered the living rooms with the safety catch pulled off their rifles. . . . Without hesitating much, the Orozquistas forced many rich Mexicans to kneel in their own houses in the presence of their families and told them that they would be shot, since they were friends of the government. Finally, they released them if they paid a certain sum of money. There were cases where money did not help. Two wealthy brothers called Martínez were dragged into the street by the Orozquistas and shot down like dogs.

By the next day, the city looked as though a hurricane had swept over it. On the Plaza Hidalgo, where the Palacio Municipal is located, things looked terrible. Nothing remained intact; all the stores located on the squares had been completely plundered, all doors and windows broken in, and pieces of the stores' furniture littered the streets. . . . The cement of the square had been sprayed with red wine, which looked like blood.[36]

When Roth went to see General Salazar, the commander of the Orozquistas in Parral, the latter intimated to him that he had in fact lost control of his troops. This loss of control was to boomerang against Orozco. As news of the sack of Parral spread throughout Chihuahua, Orozco's popularity began to ebb. Events in Parral hurt Orozco in another way as well. They strengthened the hostility of the U.S. government to him in spite of the efforts of his supporters in the United States, particularly Hearst and Fall, to muster support. This hostility was reinforced by the summary execution by Orozco's men of Thomas Fountain, the American soldier of fortune who had contributed to the Orozquistas' defeat a few days before. As Roth described it, Fountain had not had time to flee with Villa. When the Orozquistas entered Parral, he hid in a drugstore that had a door going out toward the mountain and hoped to find a moment when he could flee. When the owner of the drugstore came to his store [on] Sunday morning, he found Fountain hiding [there], half dead of hunger. The poor man had not been able to eat anything for three days. The drugstore owner immediately told Salazar of his discovery, and a group of Orozquistas was immediately sent to the drugstore to capture Fountain.

Fountain surrendered to the troops, who "without any hesitation shot him immediately."[37]

The fighting in Parral had proved so disastrous for its inhabitants that, according to Roth, a quarter of the population fled the city after the fighting. Events in Parral turned out to be a great boon to the government as well, since Villa had succeeded in detaining the Orozquistas at a crucial moment for the Madero administration.

"Villa's actions were of decisive importance," González wrote Madero. "I would like to remind you that if after the retreat of [federal] General Trucy Aubert, Villa had not called attention to himself in Parral by defeating Campa [who commanded the Orozquistas' first attack on Parral] and later distracting Salazar with more than 2,000 rebels, they would have utilized their initial success by marching immediately on Torreón when the government did not yet have time to concentrate enough troops there to stop them."[38]

From Glory to Prison

Madero was impressed both by Villa's loyalty and by his unexpected military success. His was the first victory, however temporary its character, that government forces had achieved against Orozco. Madero sent a letter of congratulations to Villa, praising his loyalty and saying: "I am really happy about your conduct, and I can assure you that apart from the legitimate satisfaction that you must feel in serving a just cause and being loyal to me, I shall see to it that you are rewarded for the services that you have rendered the republic."

Madero's letter to Villa shows that the Mexican president shared Abraham González's respect for Villa's military capacities. It also showed, though, that the two men differed with respect to the means of securing Villa's loyalty. When he dismissed Villa from the revolutionary army, Madero had offered him 10,000 pesos, hoping to thus keep him quiet and prevent him from rebelling against the government. This time, he again held out the promise of some kind of reward if Villa would only fight against the Orozco rebellion. In contrast, González, both in his letters to Villa and in his extensive correspondence with Madero concerning Villa, never mentioned monetary rewards. Villa's loyalty, he felt, was not motivated by money or an offer of reward but by a traditional frontier code of loyalty and reciprocity, to which, he felt, Villa absolutely adhered. Far better than Madero, González had understood Villa's motivations and psychology. As long as he felt that his attitude was reciprocated, Villa would remain loyal to both his superiors and his subordinates.

Madero's letter was not only a letter of thanks to Villa for supporting the government. It asked Villa to give up his extensive military independence—while nominally subordinate to Abraham González, Villa in fact was not under the orders of any military commander—and to join the federal army corps under the command of Victoriano Huerta that was preparing to go to Chihuahua to fight Orozco. Madero told Villa: "Your help will be very important and effective, not only because of your courage and that of your soldiers, but also because of your knowledge of the terrain."[39]

Madero's request to Villa to fight alongside the federal army was part of a comprehensive policy he had adopted. Madero realized that if he sent only the federal army out to fight against Orozco, he would face the same insurmountable obstacles that Porfirio Díaz had faced in 1910–11. Díaz had lost the north largely because he had had to rely on the federal army and had no local auxiliaries who could wage an effective counterguerrilla war against the revolutionaries. In order to have such a force, Madero decided to call on the former revolutionaries. This was risky. Many of Madero's former supporters were disillusioned by his moderate social policies and might take reprisals against Mexico's upper classes. Even more dangerous was the possibility that the federal army might turn against Madero if it felt that he was giving too much support to the former revolutionaries. In order to counteract both of these dangers, Madero resolved to place his former supporters under strict control by the federal army.

It was a decision that provoked great resentment among the former revolutionaries. They had defeated Porfirio Díaz's army and now they were to be placed under the orders of its commanders. They did not trust the federal generals and had no reason to do so. The federals seized every opportunity to turn against their former enemies. They had no compunction, after peace had been signed in Ciudad Juárez, in massacring Zapatistas, or, on a smaller scale, in killing former revolutionaries in a sports stadium in Puebla.[40] In the "joint campaign" they were waging against Orozco, the federal commanders would in fact do everything in their power to weaken the contingents of former revolutionaries. Sometimes they would attempt to dissolve revolutionary units, integrating their men individually into the federal army. In other cases, they would send them into the most dangerous battle zones in order to spare their own troops.

One of the federal generals who harbored the most virulent hatred for the former revolutionaries was Victoriano Huerta. He had been one of Díaz's most successful generals, having helped to crush rebellious Maya Indians on the Yucatán peninsula at the beginning of the twentieth century. During a conference with Díaz shortly before his resignation, Huerta had voiced his contempt for the Chihuahuan revolutionaries, saying that with 2,000 men he could defeat them. It was Huerta who, against Madero's wishes, had provoked an armed confrontation with the Zapatistas. In addition, Huerta had a political agenda of his own, one opposed to that of Madero. He wanted a reconciliation with the oligarchy, and he was in favor of removing González from office.[41] It is thus not surprising that a conflict soon developed between him and Villa. Nevertheless, when Villa joined Huerta with his men, he did not realize that he was walking into the lions' den.

Relations between Villa and Huerta were cordial at first. In Huerta's eyes, Villa was a bandit, and he had learned from Porfirio Díaz that bandits could be bought. Why not buy the loyalty of Villa? To do so, Huerta decided to flatter his ego. At his suggestion, Madero appointed Villa an honorary general. The mea-

sure proved counterproductive, however, for Huerta's commanders took every occasion to show their contempt for Villa and to poke fun at him.

Years later, Villa bitterly described to Felipe Angeles, one of his closest collaborators, how inhibited he had been, wearing the new general's uniform Huerta
had ordered for him, when confronted with the hostility of the officers of
Huerta's staff—men more fortunate than he, born under better circumstances,
who had studied at good schools—and of how they had laughed and exchanged
glances when Huerta formally introduced him as General Villa. "I would have
liked to be a friend of those boys, but they never allowed me to get near them,"
he told Angeles. "Only [General Antonio] Rábago had some liking for me. I understood that they were worthless, and that they had no real motive for treating
me so badly. It was clear to me that they were opposed to me without knowing
why, and that they would in the final account annihilate me, kill me, although I
did them no harm. But they would certainly do so."[42] Villa resented the attitude
of these federal officers all the more inasmuch as he was fascinated by military
technology and had hoped to learn from them.

The federal officers' contempt for Villa was but one manifestation of the hostility between the federal army and the revolutionaries, who had fought one another the year before and would do so with even greater ferocity the next year.
That hostility reached a climax early in May when Huerta ordered the arrest of
one of Villa's lieutenants, Tomás Urbina. The probable reason was that Urbina
had violated the norms of both the federal army and the revolutionary army by
occupying and plundering a large estate belonging to the Anglo-American
Tlahualilo Company. He had taken some horses, requisitioned some arms, and
threatened to shoot one of the company's employees if a ransom of 1,500 pesos
was not paid for him.[43]

Although the Tlahualilo Company was primarily a British concern, and the
British minister to Mexico had lodged no protest with the Mexican government,
U.S. Ambassador Henry Lane Wilson, who hated Madero and all former revo-
lutionaries, sent a strong protest to Huerta, who promised that he would have
Urbina executed immediately.[44]

Huerta had Urbina arrested but could not carry out the planned execution,
since Villa and all other leaders of volunteer units fighting in the ranks of
Huerta's División del Norte protested and threatened to pull out of the military
campaign if Urbina were shot.[45] Huerta capitulated and released Villa's lieutenant. It was an affront Huerta would not soon forget.

The clash between Villa and Huerta was more than a conflict of personalities.
It was a clash over jurisdiction and, above all, over the extent of the power and
authority of the federal army. The former revolutionaries saw themselves as temporary rather than permanent members of that institution. Huerta and the other
federal commanders did not accept this stance. This difference in attitude would
lead to conflicts not only in Chihuahua but throughout the entire north, where
former revolutionaries and federal officers were engaged in a fragile collaboration
against the Orozquistas. Huerta considered Villa's behavior an affront to his authority. But since he still needed the support of the former revolutionaries to vanquish Orozco, he capitulated. He was, however, firmly resolved to exact revenge.

Huerta now took every occasion to harass Villa. When a minor altercation over a horse that Villa had requisitioned and that a federal officer wanted for himself erupted, the conflict between the two men reached a climax. On June 3, Villa sent a telegram to Huerta stating that he and his men could no longer fight under his command and were therefore leaving Huerta's División del Norte.[46] According to the norms of the Maderista army of 1910–11, such conduct did not constitute an act of desertion, since the revolutionary contingents were only required to remain with the army when a battle was in progress. At any other time, they were free to withdraw from the army.[47] Villa probably also felt that he was no longer needed, since in May Orozco's troops had been defeated by Huerta's División del Norte, with the full participation of Villa and his men, in two decisive battles.

Villa's decision came as a godsend to Huerta, who had been searching for a pretext to eliminate Villa for some time and chose to construe his telegram as an act of rebellion. "I have been informed that Villa intends to start an uprising," he told one of his officers, Guillermo Rubio Navarrete; "take whatever forces you need and destroy the quarters of that man, leaving no one alive."[48]

Fortunately for Villa, Rubio Navarrete was neither a killer nor an enemy of his. As his troops were encircling Villa's headquarters, expecting to be met by resistance from heavily armed soldiers, he found both Villa and his men fast asleep and no sign of any impending insurrection. Rubio Navarrete did not feel that under these circumstances he was justified in attacking Villa and returned to his headquarters in order to ask for further instructions from Huerta. For Huerta, the execution of several hundred men was such a routine matter that he had gone to sleep, not even waiting to hear what the results of his orders had been.[49]

When Villa awoke the next day and saw that federal troops had encircled his compound, he made no effort to arm his men or to prepare for a fight. His reaction was to proceed to Huerta's headquarters, where the army's telegraph office was located, and to send a telegram to Madero telling him that he wished to resign from Huerta's command, stating that "he wanted to operate alone, surrender his arms, or do whatever the Mexican president asked him to do."[50] By proceeding alone and unprotected to federal headquarters, Villa had in fact placed himself in the lions' den, and Huerta had him arrested. Huerta made no effort to speak to Villa, or even to carry out a court-martial, but ordered his immediate execution.

Once more it was Rubio Navarrete who saved his life. As an execution squad was on the point of shooting Villa, Rubio Navarrete intervened:

I saw Villa kneeling and weeping, loudly begging not to be shot and to be allowed to see General Huerta. He was kneeling, holding one foot of Colonel O'Horan, and behind the group, consisting of him and Colonel Castro was the execution squad with their arms at rest. Without speaking to anyone, I rapidly went to headquarters in order to see General Huerta. But when I turned around before leaving, I saw that the situation had changed, since Villa was already standing with his back to the wall, and the execution squad was readying its arms . . . I returned immediately, gave orders to suspend the execution, and brought Villa to headquarters.[51]

Huerta first threatened Rubio Navarrete himself with immediate execution for having violated his orders. His attitude began to change when Rubio Navarrete explained that he had found no indication or sign that Villa was planning an uprising.[52] Huerta's decision to desist from executing Villa derived not so much from what Rubio Navarrete had to say, however, as from telegrams, probably including one from Madero, asking him to spare Villa's life.[53]

Huerta now decided to send Villa under a military escort to be imprisoned in Mexico City and at the same time dissolved Villa's unit and forcibly inducted its men into his army. In a lengthy telegram, he explained his conduct to Madero. He accused Villa of theft and rebellion. The theft consisted of stealing two horses from their owner; when Huerta asked him to return them, "he went to his barracks, which are located 200 meters from general headquarters, armed all the men under his command, and told his soldiers to be ready to disobey the orders of my command, which consisted in ordering all the troops to Santa Rosalia."[54] The statement that Villa had armed his men and was preparing to resist Huerta's orders is contradicted by the observation of Rubio Navarrete. But it was the only justification Huerta could muster for his decision to shoot Villa on the spot.

Huerta concluded his message to Madero by stating that he felt no hostility toward Villa. "I personally have a great regard for Villa, but as the commanding general of the division, I believe that he constitutes a danger to its discipline."[55] The letter to Madero, though, seems to have been merely a smoke screen for Huerta's real intentions. He knew that he had made a deadly enemy of Villa, and he was resolved not to allow him to reach Mexico City alive. He instructed his subordinates to apply the ley fuga to Villa. In the case of Villa, with his well-known violent temperament, such an accusation might even look believable. Unfortunately for Huerta, his plan miscarried. He had first ordered the head of the garrison in Torreón, Justiniano Gómez, to execute Villa, but when Gómez consulted his immediate superior, General Gerónimo Treviño, the latter countermanded Huerta's orders. Huerta did not give up. From Torreón the train carrying Villa proceeded to San Luis Potosí, and Huerta wired the head of the garrison there to carry out the execution. But this commander too consulted headquarters in Mexico City and was given orders to send Villa to the capital.

Villa never knew of this second failed attempt on his life, but he arrived in Mexico City a humiliated man. He had knelt in front of federal officers and begged for his life. In his memoirs, Villa tried to rationalize this, writing: "At the time, I hardly knew whether I was weeping from mortification or from fear, as my enemies said. I leave it to the world to assess whether my tears in these supreme moments were due to cowardice or to despair at seeing that I was to be killed without knowing why."[56]

Another humiliating fact in Villa's eyes was that he had been caught unawares. He had always prided himself on his ability to shoot his way out of danger even when he faced the greatest odds. In 1911, he and a companion had fought their way out of a house in Parral that was besieged by dozens of federal soldiers. This time though, in the midst of hundreds of his own armed men, he had let himself be captured without offering the least resistance.

As his train steamed into Mexico City, Villa was nevertheless optimistic. He had taken up arms for Madero, and he clearly expected, as his letters were to show, that the Mexican president would reciprocate his loyalty and soon free him from prison. His hopes were soon dashed. Madero would make no effort to free him.

Madero was under pressure from at least three sides to keep Villa in prison: from Huerta, from U.S. Ambassador Wilson, and from the Chihuahuan oligarchy. Huerta not only was conscious that he had made a deadly enemy of Villa, he also saw him as a potential obstacle in his efforts to make a deal with the Chihuahuan oligarchy and to remove Governor Abraham González from power. Wilson was equally adamant in his efforts to keep Villa in prison and, if possible, to have him executed. His hostility to Villa even earned him a rebuke from the State Department in Washington.

According to his (not always reliable) memoirs, Wilson went to see Madero after Urbina's attack on the Tlahualilo estate and demanded that Villa be arrested. "He [Madero] questioned the reliability of my information, saying that Villa 'was a patriot and an honorable gentleman.'"

Wilson then carried out another investigation and again went to see Madero. "To my astonishment, he again impugned the character of the testimony which had been given me and seemed inclined to maintain his position; I then quietly but formally requested him to again 'arrest Villa and have him tried by court-martial.'" At this point, Wilson decide to use the threat of military intervention against Madero.

When he demurred to my request, I said to him that he was forcing me to the unpleasant course of asking my own government to send troops to furnish protection to American citizens which he declined to give. The president then observed that this would mean war. I said to him that "When soldiers in the uniform of the government attacked the persons and property of a friendly government, and reparation was denied by the offending government an act of war had been committed." As I announced this dictum a perceptible change took place in his manner and he said, "Very well, Mr. Ambassador. I will have the man arrested and tried." This was promised and was carried out. Villa was arrested and tried by a court-martial over which General Huerta presided. He was found guilty of the crimes charged and sentenced to be shot at daybreak the following day. Madero however interfered and commuted his sentence to imprisonment in the military penitentiary in Mexico City.[57]

There is no evidence that Villa was arrested on Madero's orders or that a court-martial against him had taken place. But there is little doubt that Wilson did intervene with the Mexican authorities and that his intervention had some effect. On May 6, 1912, the U.S. ambassador had sent a letter to the Foreign Ministry in Mexico requesting the detention and trial of Villa. Only one day after this took place, on June 5, the minister of foreign affairs told Wilson "that he had some pleasant information to impart" and reported that Villa had been arrested. "It appears," a U.S. embassy official reported to the State Department,

that upon the receipt of the Ambassador's note to the Minister . . . an investigation was promptly begun on the conduct of Francisco Villa at the time of the attack upon the Tlahualilo hacienda.

This investigation soon established the fact that not only had Villa's acts in connection with the Tlahualilo matter been attested in the Ambassador's note but that Villa had been guilty of numerous acts of brigandage and savagery against foreign interests.[58]

In fact, these accusations were greatly exaggerated, for Villa had not even been present at Tlahualilo. This was probably the reason why the British minister to Mexico, whose citizens were primarily affected, since the Tlahualilo Company was predominantly controlled by British interests, refused to protest to the Mexican Foreign Ministry. When Wilson went ahead and did so on his own, his action was rebuked by the State Department, which considered it "hasty" since he had not gone along with the British minister. With characteristic arrogance, Wilson dismissed the State Department's reservations by stating that "the British Minister is a person of very leisurely habits and seems incapable of taking the initiative in situations requiring immediate and vigorous actions" and insisted that "the bandit Villa who is a federal soldier only in name" threatened American lives.[59]

It is remarkable how relentless Wilson was in his determination to have Villa arrested, going so far as to threaten military intervention, a threat that was clearly not supported at that moment by his superiors in the State Department. It was a manifestation of Wilson's implacable hostility to Madero. The imprisonment of Villa would weaken Madero's standing among the popular classes, while a trial of Villa would show the world that Madero's support was based on bandits and riffraff.

As a result of these pressures, and perhaps also because of his own reservations about Villa, Madero remained inflexible and refused to help Villa. Villa in turn became more and more disillusioned with the Mexican president, although he remained loyal to him until the end.

Villa never realized the extent of the pressures on Madero. While he suspected that both Huerta and the oligarchy were attempting to influence the president, he never seems to have been informed of the role of the U.S. embassy in the whole affair. In fact, in the first weeks after his arrest, Villa felt he had reason to be optimistic. His first defense lawyer, Adrián Aguirre Benavides, was a supporter of the revolution and a distant relative of the Maderos. Francisco Madero's brother Gustavo attempted to keep in touch with Villa and regularly sent his secretary, Luis Aguirre Benavides, to visit him in prison.[60] All this seemed to indicate a favorable disposition toward Villa on the part of the Madero family.

Above all, Abraham González had sent him a letter of support and voiced the expectation that Villa would soon get out of prison. In addition, Villa felt that the accusations leveled at him would be easy to disprove.

Villa soon found out that while the military prosecutors were unable to make a coherent case against him, the army was not about to let him go. The one person who could have intervened on his behalf, Francisco Madero, refused to do so. The Mexican president not only would keep him in prison, but, what was even more serious in Villa's eyes, he left him at the mercy of the federal army.

Villa would spend the next seven months in prison, with Madero refusing to intervene on his behalf and González, who did attempt to help him, unable to achieve any results. In the meantime, the military proceeded to prepare a case against him at a leisurely pace. In a series of hearings from June through September 1912, the military prosecutors of the Ministry of War attempted to establish a case against Villa based on Huerta's charges. They repeatedly confronted Villa with accusations and at the same time allowed him to respond to charges formulated against him by a series of hostile witnesses. This investigation, during which Villa remained imprisoned, dragged on at a slow pace because it was very difficult for the prosecutors to make a case against Villa, since Huerta did not respond to any of the questionnaires that they sent him.[61]

Huerta's attitude may have been deliberate. In part, he could not have had sufficient information to bolster the charges he had brought against Villa, and in part the status quo may have been convenient for him. A trial of Villa might have put his own credibility on the line; it might even have resulted in Villa being acquitted, and even if this had not been the case, Madero might have granted him amnesty. As long as the investigation dragged on, these dangers could be avoided. In addition, the Mexican general may have believed that sooner or later, Madero would fall, and that at that point he might be able to dispose of Villa at his leisure, without the risks that a trial might entail.

The most serious charge that Huerta had leveled against Villa was that of massive disobedience and rebellion. According to the later statements of Rubio Navarrete, the officer whom Huerta sent to attack Villa's headquarters, however, these charges were untrue.[62] It is thus not surprising that the military prosecutors had trouble making them stick. Villa denied that he had armed his men with the aim of resisting an order by Huerta to return a horse and other property. The matter of the horse, Villa stated, was a minor affair. One of his assistants had told him that it had been brought to his headquarters from Jiménez and that a federal officer had taken it. Since Villa felt that no one could take anything from his headquarters without his consent, he sent some men to take the horse back. He denied that he had mobilized his men to resist Huerta and that he had instructed them not to obey the federal general's command to proceed on the next day to Santa Rosalía.[63] The prosecution suffered a setback when two of their own witnesses, two former soldiers of Villa's who had been brought to Mexico City to testify against Villa on another aspect of the case, confirmed Villa's statement. Both Encarnación Márquez and Blas Flores, two former aides of Villa's, stated that Villa had in fact told them that the next day his units would march together with the whole División del Norte to Santa Rosalía, and that they had never heard Villa giving any orders to the contrary.[64]

The one basis for the accusation of insubordination the prosecutors felt that they could prove was Villa's own statement that on June 3, one day before he was arrested, he had wired Huerta that he would not continue to serve under him, and that one day later he had sent a telegram to Madero asking him to be relieved of his command. Villa's declaration transformed the case from that of a simple act of insubordination to a political problem. Before a coherent case could be established, the government would have to decide and specify to what degree and to what extent irregular troops were subordinated to the military command and to the laws of war.

As it became more and more difficult for the prosecution to establish proof of Villa's alleged insubordination, it concentrated on the one field where it felt it would be easiest to make a clear-cut case against Villa, the accusation of theft. Villa's reputation as a bandit and robber would constitute a good basis for this. The prosecution's case against Villa was based on three points: he had taken 150,000 pesos from wealthy men in Parral, he had done so by resorting to threats and violence, and he had used the money to enrich himself rather than in order to finance his military campaign.[65]

To prove the case, the prosecutors obtained statements from a number of the men in Parral whom Villa had forced to give money to his military unit. They accused Villa of threatening them with execution and of imprisoning them in his headquarters until they paid. The head of the Banco Minero, who had been forced to contribute the largest sum of money to Villa, and who had suffered most at Villa's hands, personally came to Mexico City to present his accusation against Villa.[66] He described how Villa had threatened to put him and his son in the first line of defense against the Orozco invaders unless he paid up immediately. The prosecution also confronted Villa with two of his former lieutenants, who stated that Villa did not pay his troops regularly but only when his soldiers asked for money, and thus implied that he was using the sums he had confiscated for personal ends.[67]

Villa denied all the charges leveled at him. He stated that it was with the knowledge and consent of the state authorities that he had carried out his confiscations of money and arms in Parral. He denied that he had used threats to obtain money and stated that he had paid his troops regularly, and that only officers and men close to him were paid at irregular intervals. He insisted he was not a thief. He said that he personally paid every soldier 1 peso a day and gave a list of the persons to whom he had paid the money that he had not used to supply or pay his troops. He nevertheless did provide an opening to the prosecution by stating, "since he did not want to appear to be a thief, he wants to declare that in the mountains of Santa Barbara, there is a place that he knows but cannot identify by description where he buried 5,000 silver pesos before the battle with Orozco in Parral."[68]

The prosecution attempted to bolster its case by locating and identifying whatever criminal charges existed against Villa in any part of Mexico. In these endeavors, the prosecutors enjoyed the full support of the conservative opposition press, which depicted Villa as a bandit and criminal who had been granted amnesty by Madero despite warrants for his arrest in several Mexican states. In a letter to Madero, Villa denied that he was a wanted man:

I shall now refer to what the newspapers state, that accusations are pending against me that are documented in the archives of Zacatecas. No legal proceedings have been undertaken against me in any part of the country and should this have been the case, they should be made public, since I do not want it to be said that either you or the judges are trying to wash their hands of the matter, in a sense. I have always acted legally, and no one can accuse me of appropriating capital that belongs to others. All of these journalists who make these accusations are just scum.[69]

Villa seems to have been correct in his assessment, for neither the court nor the newspapers were able to prove that criminal proceedings had been initiated against him in any state in Mexico.

The acts that the prosecution accused Villa of committing, and that in its eyes constituted criminal behavior, were in fact the norm among participants in the 1910–11 Madero revolution. Levying forced loans to finance the revolution had been standard practice during the 1910–11 uprising. In his letter to "Papacito," Andrés had called on revolutionaries to intimidate supporters of the old regime into paying the costs of the revolution directed against them.[70] Revolutionary leaders had to arm and feed their men, and they had never been asked for a detailed accounting of the sums that they had taken. It had been standard practice for the revolutionaries to give receipts for whatever they took. And Villa had acted no differently in Parral. In case of disagreement between soldiers and leaders, or between local and regional leaders, it had also been standard practice to allow both soldiers and local leaders to leave the revolutionary army, unless a battle was in progress or was imminent. This was the procedure that Villa had followed when he attempted to resign from Huerta's command.

The problem of Villa's guilt or innocence was a political rather than a judicial one. If Villa's actions were judged by the standards of the 1910–11 revolution, there was no basis for filing charges against him. If Villa was considered as belonging to the federal army and his actions were judged by its standards, it was a very different matter.

It was finally up to Madero to decide what judicial norms to apply. In Villa's eyes, putting his case under the jurisdiction of a federal military tribunal was unjustified, since most of the actions he was accused of had been committed while he was a member or a subordinate not of the federal army but rather of the state authority of Chihuahua. Most of the charges against Villa were related to his occupation of Parral at a time when he was directly subordinate to the governor of Chihuahua. In fact, the federal bureaucracy itself provided Villa with evidence that he was not part of the Mexican army and thus did not fall under its jurisdiction. Shortly after being arrested, Villa had asked that since he had been appointed an honorary general, he should receive a general's pay as long as he was officially in the army. The Ministry of War replied that it had no record either of Villa's being made an honorary general or of his having any kind of military appointment. In a sarcastic letter to Madero, Villa observed that he was then not subject to any kind of military discipline, and he implied that a military court had no authority to try him.[71]

Villa clearly realized that his problem was political, and he appealed to both González and Madero for help. It was, after all, in order to support them that he had taken up arms in 1912, and both of them, having led the 1910–11 revolution, knew very well what the norms had been at that time. Nevertheless, Villa did not disregard or boycott the judicial proceedings against him.

His main hope lay in persuading González and Madero to quash the accusations against him, or at least to grant him freedom on bail. The two men reacted very differently. While González attempted by every means at his disposal to help Villa, Madero showed an inflexibility toward Villa that he had never shown toward federal commanders such as Navarro, accused of far more serious crimes in 1911 than the ones Villa had committed.

"I would like to insist again about the matter of Villa," González wrote Madero, "and hope that the government will show indulgence toward him." González declared that Villa's campaign had achieved "transcendental results." Had Villa not defeated Campa's forces in Parral and distracted those of Salazar, the Orozquistas would have attacked and captured Torreón. González insisted that the confiscations Villa had carried out in Parral were justified, since the resources that Villa took "were not made available to the enemy." The Chihuahuan governor stressed that Villa had made great sacrifices in order to support the government. The four butcher shops he owned had suffered, and two of his brothers had been arrested by the Orozco forces. González argued that Villa's loyalty to both himself and Madero had been demonstrated in February 1912, when Orozco's father had visited Villa and suggested that he join the Orozco revolt, but he had remained loyal to the government. González did not ask that all proceedings against Villa be quashed, but asked Madero to show him leniency. "It would be a bad precedent not to ask Villa to account for the loans he demanded in Parral, and for that very reason, all I ask for, is that leniency be showed him compatible with the services he has rendered the government."[72]

This was the only reference critical of Villa's behavior that González ever made. As time went on, his support for Villa solidified more and more. In response to a call for help from Villa, González wrote him, in a letter that began with the words "My dear friend," that he had intervened several times on his behalf with Madero, and he confirmed Villa's statement that he had acted on behalf of the governor, and on orders of the governor, when he demanded forced loans in Parral. González specified that the one limitation he had imposed on Villa was not to require contributions from foreigners. He closed his letter by saying, "I am disposed to help you in every way I can. I hope that your difficulties will soon find an end."[73]

On the same day González's letter was written, Villa sent a second letter to the governor containing a desperate plea for help, saying:

I greet you with the affection I have always shown you, and that will last until I am laid down in my grave, and I hope that God finds you happy when you receive this letter. . . . I would be very grateful to you if you could help me to recover my freedom, since this war has left us in poverty. I have to work to be able to live. . . . Every sincere man should act as I did, and though I am not a man of culture, deep in my heart, I love my friends and my country and have only feelings of affection and gratitude for them. I am not saying any more, since I do not want to dwell on the injustices of life. I send you my deepest affection from the depth of my heart.[74]

González continued in his efforts to help Villa. When Villa's defense lawyer asked González to testify in Villa's behalf, the governor not only agreed but sent a letter in which he once again stated that Villa had acted on behalf of the government and on his orders, as well as those of his deputy, Aureliano González, when he carried out his confiscations in Parral. He closed his letter by saying that he would in his testimony "be more explicit about all these points and render justice to Villa, who in my opinion should come out very well from the trial which he will face."[75]

Unfortunately for Villa, the final decision as to his status did not rest with González but with Madero, who was less favorably disposed toward him than the governor of Chihuahua. Villa made three requests of Madero, all of which were refused. He first asked the Mexican president to free him either on bail or permanently, and volunteered to fight against any enemies the president wanted him to, including Emiliano Zapata in Morelos. When this offer was turned down, Villa asked the Mexican president to free him from the jurisdiction of the military court. When that request too received a negative response, Villa asked Madero that he be sent into exile to another country, preferably Spain. In this case, Madero hesitated, but he finally refused. His attitude toward Villa became somewhat more positive in the last weeks of Villa's imprisonment, however. Until November 1912, he refused to intervene in any way in Villa's case, did not grant his request for an audience, and did not answer most of his letters, and in the two cases where he did answer, the replies were cold and impersonal. In spite of Madero's behavior, Villa continued to send warm letters to the Mexican president, although at times tinged with despair and traces of resentment. As his behavior after his successful escape in January 1913 was to show, these feelings of loyalty were not contrived but real.

Villa's nearly one-sided correspondence with Madero began a few weeks after his imprisonment, in July 1912. In his first letter to Madero, on July 11, Villa insisted that he was no criminal and that newspaper reports that he was wanted by the authorities in Zacatecas were wrong. He stressed his loyalty to Madero. "I have been a loyal friend of the government," he concluded, "and I swear that I shall always tell you the truth and I am not a man with two faces such as our good friend, Orozco. Farewell."[76] A day later, he again wrote to Madero insisting on his loyalty:

I am one of your friends who wishes you happiness. Though I do not know how many bad things they have told you about me, I swear to you that I shall be loyal. . . . You will never hear signs of adulation from me, since I am a man of firm convictions who knows how to suffer. I suffer from the depth of my heart, but I am not complaining to you about my suffering, since man was created to suffer.[77]

The lack of any response from Madero may have moved Villa to offer more concrete proofs of his loyalty. "Do not forget," he wrote Madero a few days later, "that I have not been seduced by the money that Orozco's father came to my own camp to offer me. Many people know this. I have never been seduced by money. There are persons who speak about me, but who do not understand the feelings in my heart. I am a man of firm convictions and if they have not been understood, I must suffer."[78]

There was still no reply from Madero, and on July 30, Villa asked Madero to see him for a short time. The demand seemed warranted to Villa, since Huerta was on a visit to Mexico City, and Villa felt that the time had come to clear up the accusations against him. "In the name of justice, I would ask you to grant me an audience of three minutes now that my General Huerta is here. All I ask from you and from the general is justice, and I hope that you will solve my problems, since I am victim of ingratitude in this jail. Farewell, Sir."[79]

At the beginning of August, Villa received his first reply from Madero, a cold refusal to meet him, not even written by the Mexican president himself, but on his instructions by his secretary, Juan Sánchez Azcona, who wrote:

The president has charged me to tell you in response to your letter of July 30, that since General Huerta had to leave immediately, to take charge of the northern campaign, it was not possible for the president to accede to your request for a conference with the general and with the president; he did speak in detail about you with General Huerta, and you can be sure that full justice will be granted you since as you know, the president has a positive commitment that the law, and only the law, be applied in all cases submitted to the courts under the new regime.[80]

The reference to "the law, and only the law" being applied carried two meanings. On the one hand, Madero was telling Villa that he would not let himself be influenced by outside considerations. What was more important for Villa on the other hand was that Madero implied that he would not intervene, and that the courts, which in this case meant a military court, would make the final decision as to his fate. Villa's answer to Madero's refusal to see him was a new profession of loyalty that contained an attempt to defuse any negative comments Huerta might have made about him. "I do not know what my general will have told you about me, but if he is a person with a conscience, I am convinced that he will not have spoken badly about me. I would be happy if they let you read the telegram I sent you from Jiménez [alluding to the telegram of resignation he had sent to Madero, in which he offered to continue fighting for the Mexican president on his own], but I do not believe they will do so." Villa not only insisted on his loyalty to Madero but said that he did not want to criticize Huerta. "I will not speak badly about the general either in letters or in your presence, since God has not brought me into this world to do so."[81]

Villa's despair deepened a few days later when he received news that his brothers, who had first been detained by Orozco's troops and removed from Ciudad Chihuahua after their return to the state capital (it is not clear whether they had escaped from the Orozquistas or had been freed), had been arrested again by the state police. "I would like to ask you," Villa wrote Madero,

why we are victims of so much abuse, since the secret police has detained my brothers and accused them of being Orozquistas, after Orozco had imprisoned them for nearly five months. Now the employees of the government are arresting them. What will happen to us? I believe we shall all be martyrs. I believe that I have not dealt in such a way with the government to deserve such treatment, and I hope from you that you will help my brothers . . . that you will free them so that they can support both my family and the two families from the revolution that I am supporting, which consists of one family with three young girls and the mother, and the other of four children and the mother. I say farewell to you and offer my sincere respects.[82]

It is not clear why Villa's brothers had been arrested. On July 24, the *Correo de Chihuahua* had reported that both of Villa's brothers, who had been arrested by the Orozquistas, "who wanted revenge for the actions of Colonel Villa, who did not sympathize with Orozco and tried to mobilize people in favor of the legitimate government, had been able to flee from Casas Grandes, where they had been detained." It is not clear on whose orders, if at all, the Chihuahuan authorities arrested them, but at any rate, they must soon have been freed, for on September 18, the same newspaper reported that Hipólito Villa was traveling to Mexico City to visit his brother.

In spite of Madero's refusal to grant him an audience, Villa continued to hope that the Mexican president would intervene on his behalf and continued to write him letters professing his loyalty and stressing his services to the government. He insisted that if he had not fought Orozco, the latter would have taken Torreón, and "they would have obtained more than a million pesos and much more supplies and they would have become very powerful. . . . As a result of his efforts to take Parral, Orozco was left without ammunition, was not able to take Torreón, since in the two battles I waged against him, I gave the government time to organize its troops in Torreón."[83] In his eagerness to show his loyalty to Madero, Villa went one step beyond stressing his past merits. He told Madero that he was again ready to fight for him, not only in Chihuahua but against Emiliano Zapata as well.

Villa's readiness to fight Zapata, with whom he became so closely identified in later years, is not entirely surprising, for Zapata had recognized Villa's greatest enemy, Orozco, as the supreme leader of the revolution.

Madero finally replied to Villa's letters, but in the same cold and impersonal way as before, without making any promise to intervene on his behalf. "The president of the republic has read your letter of September 7, and with his agreement," Madero's secretary wrote Villa, "I am answering you to tell you that you should not be afraid, since in your case, as in all others, full and ample justice will prevail."[84]

Even though Madero's reply said nothing new and was cold and noncommittal, the simple fact that he had replied seems to have encouraged Villa to become more and more insistent. On September 6, for the first time, he explained his action in Parral to Madero, insisting that not only did he have instructions from the state government to impose forced loans to supply his troops, but the main victims of those forced loans had been enemies of the government, such as the Banco Minero belonging to Juan Creel and Castulo Baca. Villa stressed that he was not the only leader who carried out confiscation of property in the name of the government. He reported to Madero that on Huerta's orders, he had confiscated, for the benefit of the army, 600 head of cattle belonging to private owners.[85]

Villa's hopes that Madero would finally intervene on his behalf were dashed when on September 24 the military tribunal refused to grant his lawyer's request that the charges of robbery against him be dismissed, although González had confirmed that in imposing forced loans, Villa had acted on the orders of the government.[86]

It is easier to understand González's support for Villa than Madero's coldness and reluctance to do anything to help the revolutionary leader. González's interventions in favor of Villa were inspired, not only by his friendship with the latter and by his conviction that Villa was a man he could depend on, but also by his own increasingly precarious situation. At first glance, it would seem that González's position had been strengthened in the summer of 1912. In June of that year, Orozco's forces suffered a decisive defeat at the battle of Bachimba, and his army ceased to be able to act as a coherent, united military force. Agrarian revolutionaries such as Máximo Castillo left Orozco to fight on their own, while other members of his army fled to the United States and wrote bitter proclamations to the effect that Orozco had betrayed them, saying that they had been told that all of Mexico was rising against Madero, "that there would be no resistance when we march[ed] on the city of Mexico, which would fall into our hands on March 7." While thousands of soldiers died in battle against the federal army and their families were suffering from hunger, they wrote, Orozco "was participating in orgies and drunken sprees in his special train coach ten kilometers from the line of battle." They accused Orozco of having deposited 500,000 pesos in an El Paso bank and called on those still fighting to lay down their arms.[87] Other Orozquistas dispersed into smaller groups, waged guerrilla warfare, frequently turning against the civilian population, and began to lose more and more support in the state.[88]

In August 1912 the last important stronghold of the Orozquista faction, the border city of Ciudad Juárez, fell into government hands. Nominally, González was again in control of the state of Chihuahua.

In reality, however, it was only Orozco, not the oligarchy, that had been defeated. As they had always done in the past, the Terrazas again seemed on the verge of transforming defeat into victory. The oligarchy felt they now had a much more potent ally in the state than Orozco could ever have been: the federal army. They were not mistaken. Huerta set out to accomplish what Orozco had vainly sought to achieve: the removal of Abraham González as governor of Chihuahua. In this endeavor, he enlisted the help of Madero's conservative uncle, Rafael Hernández, who had become minister of finance in the federal government and who wrote his nephew that he and Huerta concurred in believing that peace in Chihuahua could only be reestablished if González were removed as governor.[89]

Although Madero refused to sacrifice his old friend and companion from revolutionary days, he went along with virtually every other demand of the oligarchy, thus undermining González's position more and more. He forced the governor to accede to Huerta's request to grant a broad-based amnesty to Orozquista rebels that was so generous that it signaled to them that they could resume their political activities in the state with impunity and victimize revolutionaries loyal to the governor. In the village of Santo Tomás, González reported to Madero, his own supporters were being persecuted by former Orozquistas who had accepted the government's amnesty. They had all returned to the village and outnumbered the men loyal to the governor, most of whom were still participating in the army's efforts to disperse the remaining bands loyal to Orozco. Newspapermen and editors who had joined Orozco in his rebellion, after accepting a government amnesty, had begun ferocious attacks on both González and Madero.[90]

The patriarch of the Terrazas clan, Luis Terrazas Sr., had left Chihuahua for the United States once the Orozco revolt broke out. Although González wrote Madero that Terrazas had sympathized with the Orozco revolt and that many members of his family had actively supported it, the Mexican president forced the governor to allow Chihuahua's most powerful hacendado to return to the state and resume control over his vast economic empire.[91]

The strongest attacks on González's power and authority came from the federal army. Its soldiers and officers openly declared that they were opposed to both Madero and González, thus encouraging potential opposition to the revolutionary government. According to the U.S. consul in Chihuahua, they refused to pursue the Orozquista bands and even undertook secret negotiations with them.[92]

All this undermined González's authority, both in military terms and because it prevented an economic recovery of Chihuahua. At the same time, it gave the federal troops an excuse to remain in the state. The state militias González had raised, which were loyal to the revolution and were willing to fight against the Orozquistas, suffered constant discrimination and at times persecution by the federal army. In addition, Madero refused to grant any federal funds to pay for these troops, thus drastically limiting their number.[93]

In social terms, the federal government also undermined González's efforts at reform. González became so frustrated by this policy of both the federal government and the Madero administration that he sent his highest official, Isidro Fabela, to Mexico City to persuade Madero to reverse his policies and to give more money to support state forces in Chihuahua.[94]

In this increasingly desperate situation for González, Villa would have been a considerable asset. None of the commanders of the state's militia loyal to Madero in Chihuahua enjoyed the kind of prestige and authority that Villa had, and neither did they possess his military capacities. The accusations formulated by conservative newspapers that González wished Villa to return to Chihuahua and lead the fight against the Orozquista rebels were probably correct. For this very reason, both the federal commander, Huerta, and the oligarchy exercised considerable pressure on Madero to prevent Villa's return to Chihuahua. They were successful. Madero refused to free Villa and never contemplated utilizing his services in Chihuahua.

The contrast between González's positive attitude and Madero's negative attitude to Villa is at first glance surprising. After all, Madero was aware of the role Villa had played in the campaign against Orozco and had in fact written him a warm letter of congratulation after the battle of Parral. Madero's man in Chihuahua, his closest collaborator, Abraham González, was asking for clemency for Villa. Yet Madero remained adamant in his refusal to do anything for him. It might be argued that Madero, as a genuine democrat, was, as he stated, unwilling to interfere in a pending judicial process. But in other cases involving enemies whose offenses were more serious than Villa's, Madero had had no compunction about influencing a judicial process. Although Navarro had violated the norms of civilized warfare and the Plan of San Luis Potosí by executing revolutionary prisoners in an especially gruesome way, Madero had refused to submit him to a court-martial or even to an investigation. He had intervened in another judicial process to quash accusations against Creel, his longtime enemy and a close collaborator of Porfirio Díaz's. In fact, he did contemplate intervening in the judicial process against Villa, but only in later months, when it seemed politically feasible and expedient to do so. Nor is there evidence that Madero's reluctance to help Villa was because he feared that he might join the insurgents. He seems to have shared González's conviction that this was something Villa would never do.

The differing attitudes of the president and his governor had more profound roots, of both a personal and a social nature. In personal terms, Madero does not seem to have shared González's liking for and confidence in Villa, perhaps because of the latter's insubordination after the attack on Ciudad Juárez. Madero tended to treat Villa like a mercenary. He had offered him money after his resignation from the army, and in his congratulatory letter after Villa's battle with the Orozquistas in Parral, Madero again spoke of granting him a financial reward. Nevertheless, Madero's personal attitude toward Villa was not the main reason for his conduct. It seems to have been linked above all to his relationship with Huerta, the federal army, and the Chihuahuan oligarchy.

While it is possible that Madero intervened to save Villa's life and prevented him from being shot on Huerta's orders, he seems thereafter to have subordinated his attitude toward Villa to his desire to conciliate Huerta. Immediately after Villa's imprisonment, Madero issued a press communiqué stating that there had been no disagreements between him and Huerta with respect to Villa's treatment.[95] In spite of Villa's entreaties for help, Madero refused to answer his pleas and letters before Huerta came to Mexico City in July 1912. Up to that time, Madero had harbored increasing doubts about Huerta because of his slow prosecution of the war, rumors that Huerta was seeking to remove González from power, and allegations that he was intriguing against the Mexican president.[96] After the two men conferred in July, either these doubts were dispelled or Madero felt that they were outweighed by Huerta's military capacities. After the visit, Huerta again returned to Chihuahua as military commander. Villa's continued imprisonment seems to have been a price Madero was willing to pay for conciliating Huerta. It was after Huerta's visit to Mexico City that Madero sent Villa his first cold letter refusing to give him an audience or to intervene in any way to end his imprisonment by the military. It was only after he changed his mind with respect to Huerta and finally dismissed him in October 1912, because of the general's continuing intrigues against his administration,[97] that Madero seriously considered intervening in the judicial process against Villa and substituting exile for his imprisonment.[98]

Unfortunately for Villa, Madero's attitude toward him was linked not only to his relations with Huerta but to a broader conflict pitting the northern revolutionary governors against the federal army. It was a conflict in which Madero was caught in the middle, but in which he tended to favor the army.

The Orozco uprising was at once an opportunity and a danger for the increasingly conservative federal military establishment. As a result of the 1910–11 revolution, most federal contingents had been withdrawn from the three northern states that had risen most dramatically against Díaz. Control of these states had been assumed by paramilitary forces composed of former revolutionary soldiers, who were now subordinated to the revolutionary governors. As a result, until the Orozco revolt, the federal army been unable to implement the same policies in the north that it had begun to apply successfully in southern and central Mexico. In those two regions, its main aim had been to disarm the revolutionary contingents, or at least to bring them under its control. It had provoked a conflict with Zapata, initially against the wishes of Madero; and in Puebla, federal troops had massacred a contingent of revolutionaries. In both cases, Madero, after some initial hesitation, had gone along with the army. The Orozco revolt gave the federal troops a unique opportunity to return to the north. It also created a danger for them, since the northern governors were recruiting militias of their own, subordinate only to them. The federal commanders were intent on either assuming control of or destroying these newly founded militias and establishing themselves firmly as the main military force in northern Mexico. In this respect, Huerta had been the most radical of the military chieftains, arresting Villa, forcing his volunteers to become draftees in federal contingents, and even intriguing to remove Governor González from his post.

Villa's Escape

Villa probably never realized all the political and social implications of his case, but after the military court refused to dismiss his case in September 1912, it had become clear to him that González could not and Madero would not release him.

The despair and resentment he felt at this point are evident in the letter he wrote to Madero after he learned of the court's decision. It is the only letter written during his imprisonment in which he attacked the Mexican president and even uttered threats against him. He emphasized his adherence to Madero ("I have been loyal to you and I shall remain so since I am not swayed by money") and reminded him of the importance of his services in the campaign against Orozco ("Without my campaign the government would have lost half a million pesos"). Then Villa stated that he was a victim of ingratitude and bluntly and angrily wrote the Mexican president,

I do not know why you allow all this [Villa's further imprisonment]. I ask you for justice; I am tired of doing so and if you cannot grant it to me, I ask you in the name of justice to have a meeting of ministers so that it can be established who was right. One of the reasons for my bad luck is that I am a man without culture and I do not know how to defend my right. I ask for justice and I say good-bye to you with love and respect as always. Farewell, Sir.

This last expression of affection was contradicted by a postscript containing a kind of veiled threat: "If you do not want me to speak out against you, give me an audience of five minutes by telephone from here."[99] Another expression of Villa's despair was a botched escape attempt that he undertook around the same time.

Even before the court rendered its negative verdict, Villa had been contemplating escaping. The most immediate problem he had to deal with was the isolation in which he had been kept for several months. As long as he believed that Madero would soon free him, he had behaved like a model prisoner. Now he felt the time had come to act. One day, when he was being returned to his cell after a hearing by the prosecuting judge, Villa undertook what was possibly the only act of passive resistance in his life. He refused to go. He explained this to his jailer by saying, "No law or ordinance authorizes jailers to hold a man incommunicado for more than three months when he is awaiting trial."[100]

He refused to give in when the jailer brought in reinforcements and the guards threatened him with force if he did not return to his cell. The authorities did not want to provoke an open conflict with Villa. They may have been worried that if they did, public pressure on the government to free Villa might mount, or that Madero himself might feel obliged to help him. They therefore acceded to his demands that he be allowed to circulate more freely and to establish links with other prisoners. Thanks to his charismatic personality, to the legends that surrounded him, and to his largesse with money, Villa soon became a popular figure both among the common criminals and among the jailers. But it was clear to him that if he wanted any help in escaping, the most reliable accomplices would be the political prisoners housed in the same tract as he was. He soon established friendly relations with two such prisoners, both Zapatistas. One was Gildardo Magaña, a young Mexico City intellectual who in later years was to become one of Zapata's most important intellectual advisers and a general in his army, and would succeed him in 1919 after Zapata was assassinated. The other was Abraham Martínez, a commander of revolutionary forces in Puebla who had clashed with federal forces when he believed they were planning to assassinate Madero in Puebla in 1911. Martínez had been imprisoned by Madero because his retreating men had killed three German employees of a textile factory, who were apparently firing on the revolutionaries.[101]

An expression of the despair Villa now felt is that in spite of all the plans they had made, the one attempt Villa and Magaña made to escape had all the earmarks of a desperate, unplanned venture, in which, according to Magaña, Villa misled his companions. Villa had acquired duplicate keys for some of the cells and told Magaña that he had purchased the goodwill of the jailers, who would look the other way if an escape attempt was made. The prisoners opened their cells with Villa's keys. They made their way to an adjacent guardroom, which was regularly visited by jailers, but which, according to Villa, should now have been empty, because he had bribed the guards. This was not the case. At the last moment, they were able to return to their cells without being noticed by the guards. "Only then did I realize the magnitude of the danger I had faced," Magaña wrote.[102]

Magaña now lost confidence in Villa's escape plans and did not join him in any further endeavors to escape from prison.

At this low point in his life, when Villa felt that his friends had abandoned him to the mercy of his enemies, help seemed to beckon from men he had considered his enemies and from whom he had least expected it: conservative forces attempting to overthrow Madero. The first sign of conservative interest in Villa manifested itself only a few weeks after his arrest. Villa's first defense lawyer had been a prominent attorney closely linked to the revolution and to the Madero family, Adrián Aguirre Benavides. Within only a few weeks, however, two other men began to play an ever-increasing role in Villa's defense, while that of Aguirre Benavides receded.

One of Villa's new defenders was a lawyer named Castillo, about whom little information exists, and the other was Antonio Castellanos, who came from Villa's home state of Durango and had been a member of Porfirio Díaz's secret police. He had supported Bernardo Reyes's unsuccessful coup in 1912 and had later established links to Félix Díaz. While he called himself a *licenciado*, he apparently never really earned this title.[103]

In September 1912, conservative interest in Villa sharply increased. Just when the military court was rejecting Villa's demand to be freed, José Bonales Sandoval, a lawyer closely linked to Porfirio Díaz's nephew Félix Díaz, who was on the verge of staging a coup against Madero, joined Villa's defense team.

There was no clear reason for Villa to take on a new lawyer, since he already had two defenders. Bonales Sandoval did not undertake Villa's defense for financial reasons either. In a letter to Madero's secretary, Villa praised Bonales Sandoval for having taken up his case for "philanthropic" reasons without gaining anything from it.[104]

However, Bonales Sandoval's interest was anything but philanthropic. It was probably linked to Félix Díaz's projected uprising against Madero. What makes Bonales Sandoval's activities especially suspicious is that he did not involve himself in Villa's court case. That was left entirely in the hands of Castillo.

Bonales Sandoval intervened on Villa's behalf on two occasions, in each case apparently in connection with Félix Díaz's bid for power. Thus, a few weeks before Félix Díaz occupied the city of Veracruz and called on the army and the people to rebel against Madero, Bonales Sandoval applied to have Villa freed on bail. With the coming trial hanging like a Damocles' sword over his head, Félix Díaz might have offered Villa amnesty in return for joining his insurrection if he had been free on bail. Bonales Sandoval may have hoped that in Chihuahua, Villa would be able to revive the quasi-moribund Orozco uprising and thus cause trouble for Madero.

In the eyes of the conservatives, Villa was nothing more than a bandit, and they saw no reason why financial inducements coupled with amnesty should not persuade him to change sides, all the more so since he had been so badly treated by Madero. There were many precedents for such turnabouts. Porfirio Díaz's famous rurales had largely been made up of former bandits who had been persuaded by the dictator to change sides. Orozco himself had done so. While there is no clear proof that this was Bonales Sandoval's aim in September, his later activities clearly suggest that this was indeed the case.

When Bonales Sandoval once again intervened in favor of Villa in November, Félix Díaz's situation had changed dramatically. His coup in Veracruz had fizzled out, and he had been captured by federal troops.

While many of his supporters urged Madero to execute Díaz, the Mexican president showed an unusual degree of generosity toward his enemy. Félix Díaz was sent to the military prison of Santiago Tlatelolco, where Reyes was also kept. When he arrived at prison, he quickly established contact with Reyes, and the two prepared a new plot to overthrow Madero. Unlike the Chihuahuan conservatives, who wanted Villa kept in prison at any price, Reyes and Díaz felt that Villa, if they helped him to escape, could cause enormous trouble for Madero in the north and thus make it easier for them to topple the Mexican president.

This seems to have been the background for Bonales Sandoval's second intervention on Villa's behalf. The lawyer, who had kept in the background during Félix Díaz's uprising in Veracruz, now petitioned Madero to have Villa transferred to the military prison of Santiago Tlatelolco.[105]

This petition was written with the full acquiescence of Villa, who a few weeks earlier had made a similar request to Madero. On October 7, he had written to the Mexican president asking to be transferred to the military prison from the penitentiary "for important reasons that I shall explain in time."[106]

In this petition, written only three days after Villa's angry, frustrated, and even threatening letter to Madero on October 4, there is no mention of the earlier threats and demands, and the anger is all but gone from it. Was the earlier letter written during one of the furious moods for which Villa later became famous? Did Villa understand that he was in no position to threaten Madero? Or did Bonales Sandoval convince Villa that the only way to gain conservative help was to be as friendly as possible to the president in order to persuade him to transfer Villa to Santiago Tlatelolco?

It is significant that between October 7, when Villa made his first request for a transfer to the military prison, and November of that same year, when Bonales Sandoval reiterated it, the matter was dropped for several weeks. This was probably no coincidence, for in October the possibility of Villa's release from prison with Madero's help suddenly emerged again. In October 1912, Madero removed Villa's greatest enemy in the federal army, Victoriano Huerta, from his position as commander of the federal forces in Chihuahua after hearing countless rumors about Huerta's disloyalty to him. As a result, Villa now felt that the Mexican president might change his attitude. On October 24, Villa wrote Madero in order to congratulate him on the defeat of Félix Díaz's attempted coup. The letter contained the same expressions of sympathy and affection that Villa had so strongly emphasized in all his communications to Madero before the court had given judgment against him. Again, Villa insisted on his profound loyalty to Madero, saying, "Even if I suffer from injustice, I have not stopped from having the highest regard for you even if you do not act loyally toward me."

He reiterated his affection for Madero and called on the president to ask "the directors of the prison about the way I express myself about you, and the way I am attacked by the enemies of the government. But if God put me into the world in order to suffer, I shall have to suffer. But I shall be consoled by the fact that I have not been loyal to one party yesterday and to another today. And even if you do not comply with your duty, I hope that God will help you. I say farewell to you with love and respect as always. Good-bye, Sir, your friend who appreciates you deeply, Francisco Villa.[107]

This letter was a kind of prelude to a new request that Villa now presented to Madero, stating that "in view of the sad situation in which I find myself because of the intrigues and *attacks* of which I have been the target on the part of people without feelings, I recur to you, Mr. President, to ask you to transfer me to Spain until the pacification of the country has taken place, since my humble services have brought about conflicts, and that to some people in high positions."[108]

In spite of the relatively bitter tone of Villa's letter, the Mexican president's response to this was much more favorable to Villa than hitherto. In his earlier letter, Madero had simply stated that justice would be done. This time, on his instructions, his secretary, Sánchez Azcona, wrote: "The president has charged me to tell you that he is grateful for your assurances of support and affection and you can be convinced that he has always known that you are a loyal friend of his." He told Villa that a trial would soon take place, and that in the meantime, Madero would accede to his desires that he be transferred to a military prison.[109]

Two days later, Madero went one step further, telling Villa, "We are studying the way in which, in accordance with existing legislation, you can be transferred to Spain as you wish."[110]

Madero never gave any explanation for his sudden change of heart, but it was certainly not unrelated to the fact that Villa's major enemy in the government, Huerta, had been dismissed from his position only a short time before. It is also probable that Madero's brother, Gustavo, who exercised a strong influence on the president, had intervened on Villa's behalf. Gustavo Madero was more of a realist than his brother and was also more distrustful of the federal army. Perhaps for this reason he had made it a point to visit Villa in prison and to send his secretary, Luis Aguirre Benavides, to visit Villa on those days when he could not do so himself.[111]

Perhaps Madero was also noticing the discrepancy between his treatment of Villa on the one hand and his handling of the rebellious Orozquistas and the Chihuahuan oligarchy on the other. He had granted a wide-ranging amnesty to most Orozquistas who had fought against him. He had been extremely lenient toward prominent members of the oligarchy, including Luis Terrazas, in spite of González's insistence that Terrazas had at least tacitly supported the Orozco revolt. The idea that he was rewarding his enemies and punishing his friends probably influenced Madero's action. Nevertheless, Madero was not consistent, and Villa's expressions of joy and gratitude proved premature. Without giving any explanation to Villa, Madero never again responded to his request to be sent to a foreign country.

The main reason for the reversal of Madero's attitude seems to have been his fear of antagonizing the Chihuahuan oligarchy. Only two days after Madero had written Villa that he was considering the possibility of sending him to a foreign country, the president's brother, Emilio Madero, who commanded a large contingent of revolutionary troops in the north, sent him a letter of warning: "People have written to me from Chihuahua, telling me about rumors that Francisco Villa will be freed, and that this will provoke a disastrous reaction in the whole state, and they assure me that there are persons who are resolved to rise in arms against the constituted government should this happen."[112]

While Emilio Madero never named the potential insurgents to whom he was referring, there is little doubt that they were primarily supporters of Orozco and clients, relatives, or supporters of Terrazas and Creel. Madero must have taken these warnings all the more seriously in that he was in the midst of trying to effect a reconciliation with Terrazas. Madero wrote Terrazas, who had fled from Mexico after the outbreak of the Orozco revolt, that he was willing to offer him every possible guarantee for both himself and his properties if he returned to Chihuahua.[113] Similar offers were made to Sánchez, who had been the Creel-appointed governor of the state when the revolution of 1910 broke out.[114] In both cases, Madero pressured González to allow Terrazas and Sánchez to return to Chihuahua and to take no reprisals against them. These measures were part of Madero's policy of conciliation toward the federal army and the Orozquistas, but they proved fruitless. Madero did not gain the loyalty of any of these men or their supporters, nor did he even manage to secure their neutrality. Only a few weeks later, the army would topple and kill him, and the Chihuahuan oligarchy and the Orozquistas would joyously join the new rulers of Mexico.

What Madero's policy did produce was an increasing alienation of his revolutionary supporters. These policies probably helped to convince Villa that he had little to expect from Madero, and that his only chance of ever leaving prison alive was to escape. Since all escape attempts from his penitentiary had failed, he must have hoped that another prison might provide better possibilities of escape. This was probably the reason why Villa instructed Bonales Sandoval to submit a second petition for his transfer to Santiago Tlatelolco.

Of the many requests made by Villa or on his behalf during his imprisonment, this was the only one to which the president acceded, and Villa arrived at the military prison in November. Shortly afterward, Villa began to organize his escape. He made friends with Carlos Jauregui, a young lower-level clerk in the prison administration who was attached to the military court. Villa showered him with both gifts and attentions and held out the promise of rich rewards if Jauregui would only help him escape. Jauregui proved a loyal and resourceful helper. In order to enable Villa to slip out of the courtroom, whose windows were secured by iron bars, Jauregui brought a saw to the prison; while a band in the neighborhood was playing folk songs, thus drowning out any noise, Villa sawed through the window bars.

Nevertheless, at the same time that he was preparing his escape, Villa still hoped to avoid such a risky undertaking by persuading Madero to restore his freedom. To this end, he first attempted to influence public opinion. On December 11, 1912, two weeks before his prison break, Villa gave an interview to a large Mexico City newspaper, *El Pais*. Villa's demeanor impressed the newspaperman who interviewed him: "Villa wears a black suit, is quiet in his behavior and in his speech and there is nothing in his demeanor to indicate the ferocious revolutionary that he was pictured as being in 1910." Villa insisted that he had no military ambitions, that the title of "General" had been conferred on him by Madero, but that he himself did not consider himself as such. He even deprecated his former rank of colonel: "'In 1910, I was named colonel by the men under my orders, but this rank was simply aimed at having someone lead the men, but during fighting all of us are equal; my men like me a lot.'"

Villa denied that he had ever committed an act of insubordination. "'Everything has been a black cloud that has descended upon me. I have always respected General Huerta, whom I admire because of his courage and his knowledge.'" Villa spoke of the ingratitude that had been shown him, "He remembered his last campaign and showing a book of notes exclaimed, 'Here are my campaigns, they were of no use to me. As you can see, I am imprisoned, far from my family and far from my boys, whom I like so much.'" Villa insisted that he had raised the 150,000 pesos he took in forced loans from wealthy Mexicans in Parral on instructions of the governor of Chihuahua and that he had used that money to supply his soldiers. He ended the interview by telling the reporter, "I am quiet, I hope that justice will be done in my case, I am not the Francisco Villa that many believe me to be, I am a human being and I am sorry that my words cannot help me."[115]

Two days before he escaped, Villa wrote a final letter to Madero. It can be seen as a desperate plea for help and an attempt at a reconciliation with Madero, a proof of loyalty in case he escaped, and a political testament in case he died during his flight.

Dear Mr. President, the man who writes you from the center of this prison has the same ideas and the same principles as always to defend your government.

I believe that my enemies want to influence you so that I can remain here to suffer the bitter blows of misfortune, but I do not believe that you will allow them to influence you; I have confidence in the greatness of your soul and in the goodness of your heart.

Mr. President, if you still want me to serve you in some way in Chihuahua, in order to contribute to the pacification of that state, I swear and I give you my word of honor to carry out such a campaign and, unless I die in battle, to capture in one way or another the traitor Orozco, whom I deeply condemn as a man who is disloyal.

If you want me to die at the hands of my enemies, and if God wills me to die, I shall resign myself to doing so, always shouting 'Long live the clear-sighted democrat who risked the vagaries of war in order to reestablish the rule of law and of justice.' 'Long live the apostle of democracy who broke the dictatorship of General Díaz.' These will be my last words if I fall into the hands of my enemies.

Mr. President, they accuse me of having stolen the money of Parral. I took it in order to sustain my troops. I took this money from my enemies and I did so with full authorization of the supreme government.

Villa told Madero that he was sending him all the relevant documents proving that he had in fact acted on orders of the Chihuahuan government. "You are my only hope. . . . I hope that you will find the generosity to order that I be freed so that I can go and fight for you, or I hope that you will send me to a foreign country. I am awaiting your answer to know how I stand. I remain your useless friend and loyal servant."[116]

The next day, Christmas Day, Villa finally escaped, having sawed through all the window bars of his cell and put on a suit such as most lawyers wore, which Carlos Jauregui had brought him. Both men slowly walked through the prison courtyard. Hiding his face behind a handkerchief and seemingly engrossed in a conversation with Jauregui about court cases, Villa slipped past the guards and entered a waiting automobile. Villa had wanted to escape in the same way he always had in his days as an outlaw—on horseback with mounted companions at his side. He had instructed his brother, Hipólito, to bring both the horses and armed men to Mexico City. But Jauregui had convinced him that such an undertaking in a region he did not know, located so far from his own northern home ground, would be risky and prolonged. The automobile took Villa and Jauregui to the city of Toluca in the neighboring state. Then they took a train to the Pacific port of Manzanillo and there boarded a ship bound for the port of Mazatlán, on Mexico's northern Pacific coast.[117]

It was an exciting trip. All over Mexico the police had been alerted and were looking for Villa. He was nearly discovered on the ship, on which a former paymaster of the northern division who knew him well was also traveling. It was only by secluding himself in his cabin, bribing a ship's official, and obtaining a boat to leave the ship before the health authorities of the port of Mazatlán boarded it for inspection that Villa was able to escape detection. From Mazatlán, Villa had no difficulty in making his way to El Paso, Texas, where he arrived at the beginning of 1913.

He immediately attracted the attention of the U.S. press. A correspondent of the *El Paso Herald* wrote that Villa was "in fine fettle with plenty of dinero. Dressed as a Spanish bullfighter or priest, Villa put in his appearance Saturday afternoon in El Paso. He wore a hard hat and a long black cape beneath which rumor has it is his cutlery and artillery both heavy and light. He had an enjoyable day Sunday. He rode around with his young wife who accompanied him."[118]

The "fine fettle" and good humor were at best a very short-term expression of relief at his successful escape. In the coming days, he would grow increasingly bitter, since in many respects his situation was worse than it had been on the eve of the revolution. Then at least he had been in his native country; now he was in exile. Then it had been his enemies who had imprisoned him; now it was Madero, a man whom he had revered and for whom he had fought. Although Madero had granted the Orozquistas, the very men who had risen in arms against him, a wide-ranging amnesty, he had kept Villa in prison at the mercy of a hostile federal army. That Villa had risked his life in two campaigns for the revolution had counted for nothing. Nor had Madero taken into account the personal sacrifices Villa had made, since his business in Chihuahua had been destroyed by the Orozquistas. The only people who had effectively helped him during his imprisonment were a faction of Mexico's conservatives. They had both provided him free legal assistance and helped him escape.

There is no evidence that Villa felt that he owed any debt of gratitude to these conservatives. From the moment he arrived in El Paso, Villa's primary aim was to persuade both González and Madero, at first by expressions of loyalty and finally by threats, to allow him to return to Chihuahua and to assume a military command in his adopted state. In order to convince the two men of his loyalty, he publicly and privately told them of the help he had received from the conservatives, but linked these revelations to profound expressions of loyalty. "We can say that the help granted the guerrilla leader in his flight was based on the understanding that he should come to Chihuahua in order to raise men and rebel against the present government," the *Correo de Chihuahua* reported on January 10 after interviewing him. "In return, he was offered a thousand things, which Villa with his natural cleverness and his natural good sense, which we know, accepted, [and] profited from the means of escape he was offered but did not assume any obligation to the enemies of our country. When the time came and he could flee, he used these means."[119]

Villa sought to prove his loyalty to González and Madero by disclosing to them the identity of the conservatives who had helped him. The name he revealed to González's emissary was "Escandón." When he received a letter from González with that name, Madero assumed Villa was referring to Guillermo de Landa y Escandón, a close confidant of Porfirio Díaz's who had been mayor of Mexico City. "I am very puzzled that Villa states that Guillermo de Landa y Escandón has helped him in his escape," Madero wrote González, "since this gentleman has been in Europe for some time. Perhaps Villa is referring to some brother of this man, and I have already ordered that a corresponding investigation be carried out."[120]

The matter so intrigued both González and Madero that they questioned Villa about it again. Villa responded that he had never seen or spoken to Escandón, but that two men, Rodolfo Valles and an engineer whose name he did not remember, told him that they had come on Escandón's behalf. This Escandón was the one who had been arrested in Morelos and accused of helping Zapata, and he had been imprisoned for a few days in October.[121]

The Escandón to whom Villa was referring was in all probability Pablo Escandón. It is an irony of history that the same man who had been arrested for helping Zapata should have been involved in helping Villa escape. Pablo Escandón had done more than anyone else in Mexico to provoke Zapata's revolt in Morelos in the first place. He had been the governor appointed by both the planters and Porfirio Díaz in 1908, whose support for land confiscations and repression of the peasantry had been the final spark that ignited Zapata's uprising. The aid he had given Zapata did not represent a sudden conversion to revolutionary ideals, but rather a desperate attempt to strike a deal with the Morelos revolutionaries that would allow him to keep his haciendas and continue working them.[122] He was not the only Morelos planter who had made such an attempt and provoked the enmity of Madero and parts of the federal army in the process. It is not entirely clear in what way the conservatives had helped Villa to escape. Had they only provided the money to bribe Jauregui and to pay for the rental of the car in which Villa escaped? Or was Jauregui himself a gift of the conservatives to Villa? There are some indications that Jauregui was a godson of Reyes.

The conservative faction that helped Villa had probably offered him financial help and arms if he would rise against Madero. Their hopes were not completely illusory. Villa did consider such a move against Madero if the Mexican president did not allow him to return under conditions of full amnesty to Chihuahua. On January 20, 1913, Villa sent a bitter letter to Madero that amounted to an ultimatum to the Mexican president. While Villa began his letter with a friendly greeting and hopes that Madero was enjoying "complete happiness," the tone of the letter soon changed. Bluntly, Villa wrote that

looking at the situation which the state of Chihuahua is undergoing and at my own situation, I believe that it is just that I should as soon as possible be given all necessary guarantees to cross the border into that state, and that these guarantees should be published in the "newspapers" of the capital, since I believe that my petition is just, and if this is not the case, the many enemies I have made through my defense of your government will force me to rise in arms to obtain the guarantees I need, and in that case no one should call me either a traitor or a bandit, since I shall have had no choice but to defend my rights. Do not forget, Mr. President, that I am one of the men who brought you to power and I am still loyal to you.

Villa then warned Madero "that this time you should make use of what elements I can dispose of, since although I am a man who makes little noise, I can assure you that I am the first who can help you. But if this does not take place within a month, you will have no right to count on me in any way." And he added a prophetic warning:

Remember that the persons in your cabinet who surround you will not defend you, and that men who will do so in critical times are not easy to find. Do not believe that the reason that I have not crossed the border into my country is that I cannot sustain myself and give myself guarantees. The reason is my care for your prestige. But I have come to a time when I am becoming a man. I am patient, but, as I told you before, that patience will only last for one month, and once that period has passed you cannot count on me for anything, and three months later you will see the results. Your government will be discredited. I, Mr. President, am telling you what I told you when I was a prisoner, I shall tell you again now that I am a free man: I do not need a favor either from you or from the disgraceful judge who questioned me nor from any authority of the republic. All I need is justice. . . . Although I understand that you find yourself between the devil and the deep blue sea, insofar as I am concerned all you have to do is put on your pants [i.e., bite the bullet], since all you should do with regard to me is to comply with justice and no civilized nation will be able to criticize you in any way. . . . What I ask for is justice.

I bid you farewell, sir, with the affection that I have always shown you, and you should consider the respect I have for you and I hope that you will not force me to lose that respect for lack of justice. Please accept, sir, a firm embrace, as sincere as the ones I sent you while I was a prisoner. Farewell, sir.

Villa added a postscript asking that the same civil protections that he requested be given to the man who had helped him to escape from prison, Carlos Jauregui, "since I will not allow this man to be victimized because of me."[123]

Villa never resorted to implementing his threats. In part, he continued to feel loyal to the Mexican president. But above all it was owing to the efforts of Villa's greatest friend within the Madero administration, the Chihuahuan governor, Abraham González.

Some weeks before, four days after crossing the border into the United States, Villa had written Governor Abraham González from El Paso. Referring to himself as a "friend who suffers and has suffered unjust persecution," he asked González to come and see him personally, "in view of the circumstances I find myself in, and the infamous calumnies of which I was a victim." He felt that such an interview would be "of interest to the government as well as to my dear homeland."

"Do not forget," he admonished the governor, "to be a friend of justice and do not forget the man who has suffered for it, and I want you to be assured of the sincere affection I have for you to the death, and I profess these feelings now that I am free in the same vein that I did when I was a captive."

He ended his letter with both an admonishment and a warning: "I would like to repeat to you that many important things will depend on our interview, since I shall never deceive you and will not allow myself to be seduced by powerful persons who are interested in worsening the situation of our country."[124]

González himself did not meet with Villa, perhaps because he feared the political fallout of such a meeting, but he sent one of the his closest confidants, Aureliano González, who had been his deputy as governor while he was minister of the interior, to see Villa in El Paso.

After extensive meetings with Villa, Aureliano González sent a report to the governor saying that Villa's attitude to him was extremely positive. "Villa has the greatest admiration for you, and from my talks with him, I have the feeling you can do with him whatever you want." Nevertheless, "Villa was very resentful of the federal government and might even rebel if nothing is done for him." Aureliano González's conclusion was ambiguous; he described Villa as "somewhat beaten down, but full of good wishes for the government in spite of the many sufferings that it has inflicted on him and for which he might very well seek to avenge himself, as he himself stated, but he declared that he did not want to darken his military record."

Aureliano González contrasted Villa's resentment toward the federal government with his feelings of affection and loyalty for Governor González. But, he warned, "Villa's intentions have been good up to now. In order to prevent him from revolting, everything should be done not to make him desperate." Aureliano González drafted a telegram to Madero co-signed by many residents of Ciudad Juárez and El Paso asking for an amnesty for Villa. He also intimated that in such a case, Villa might take command of the state militia in Chihuahua and eliminate the remnants of the Orozco rebellion.[125]

Governor González became increasingly worried about his protégé's behavior if Madero did not make some conciliatory gesture, all the more since the conservatives had by no means given up their efforts to induce Villa to revolt, and he wrote Madero:

The fears and vacillations of our friend [Villa] have been strongly influenced by the behavior of one of his defenders, Lic. José Bonales Sandoval, who in a letter that he wrote me on December 7 of last year told me that "if Villa did not obtain his freedom, it was due to the fact that some members of Señor Madero's family had suggested to you that it would be dangerous to free him."[126]

González observed that Bonales Sandoval had said the same things to Villa's brother in Mexico City, and he told Madero to ask Villa's other defender, Adrián Aguirre Benavides, to counter these intrigues by Bonales Sandoval. The greatest difficulty in responding to these accusations (González may not have known this) was that they were essentially true. It was after receiving a warning from his brother Emilio that the Mexican president went back on the implicit promise he had made earlier to Villa to let him go into exile in a foreign country. Bonales Sandoval was in fact playing a Machiavellian game. While attempting to stir up Villa against Madero, he was simultaneously trying to turn Madero against Villa by suggesting that now that he had escaped, Villa had in fact become his enemy.[127]

Through his emissary, the Chihuahuan governor granted Villa as much as it was in his power to grant. He offered to pay him his salary as an honorary general, allowed and perhaps instructed his emissary to sign the petition directed at Madero, and in all probability promised to intercede with Madero in Villa's behalf. He also went out of his way to visit Villa's family and assured them that no reprisals would be taken against them if they visited Villa in El Paso. But while he was basically loyal to both González and Madero, Villa had obviously had enough of promises and wanted more. On January 16, a worried Aureliano González wired the Chihuahuan governor that Villa was coming under increasing pressure to rebel.[128]

It was only after Villa's ultimatum of January 20 reached him that Madero finally relented. He now gave Abraham González full powers to deal with Villa and to promise him his freedom, for on February 6 he wired the Chihuahuan governor, "Fully agree with measures you have taken in respect to Villa."[129] At the same time, Tomás Urbina, Villa's old crony from bandit days, who had also been imprisoned by the federal government, was ordered freed.[130]

Before these things could be done, however, Madero was dead, toppled by a military coup led by Huerta, and in the wake of his murder, Abraham González was also killed by the federal military.

PART TWO

From Revolutionary to National Leader

CHAPTER FIVE

From Exile to Governor of Chihuahua

The Rise of Villa in 1913

Válgame Dios de los cielos,	God in heaven, help me,
válgame Dios, que haré yo,	God, what shall I do,
ahi viene Francisco Villa	Here comes Francisco Villa
que buen hueso me quitó . . .	Who kicked me off the gravy train . . . [1]

The Fall of Madero and the Rise of Huerta

As Villa sat in his dingy hotel room in El Paso impatiently waiting for Madero to grant him the clemency he had sought for so long, events took place in Mexico that would change the face of the country and allow Villa a comeback that neither he nor anyone else in Mexico had ever dreamed of. Between February 9 and 18 of 1913, a coup took place in Mexico City. Madero was taken prisoner by the federal army, forced to resign, and shot, together with his vice president, Pino Suárez, probably on orders from the leader of the coup, Victoriano Huerta.[2]

In many respects, the coup against Madero was the forerunner of the many similar twentieth-century coups in which reform-minded presidents, such as Romulo Gallegos in Venezuela, Jacobo Arbenz in Guatemala, and Salvador Allende in Chile, would be toppled by the military with varying degrees of covert or even overt support from foreign, mainly U.S., sources. Unlike his reformist successors in other Latin American countries who, from the first day they took office until their fall, faced armies that jealously guarded their monopoly of armed force, Madero had been in a far better objective situation. His revolutionary forces had defeated the federal army, and Madero could have converted them into a formidable alternative to the federal army had he wanted to. He did not do so. While keeping on some of the revolutionaries as state troops and utilizing them to fight the Orozco uprising, Madero had supported all efforts by the federal army to weaken its revolutionary rivals. After having demobilized most of the former revolutionary troops, and having done so in a way that created resentment of his perceived ingratitude, he went on to take a variety of actions that undermined the position of the minority of former revolutionaries he retained under arms. He reduced or eliminated their budgets; he acquiesced in the imprisonment of some of their leaders, such as Pancho Villa; and he supported attempts by the federal army to have them subordinated to federal commanders. Whenever armed clashes between the two occurred, he supported the federal army. The federal commanders did not reward this policy with support for Madero. They saw it as merely a sign of weakness, and it would in the end contribute decisively to the fall of Madero's government and cost him his life.

The coup, when it finally occurred on February 9, 1913, was by no means unexpected, although its denouement came as a surprise to most of Mexico and to much of the rest of the world.

On the morning of February 9, 1913, a group of military cadets and other supporters freed Bernardo Reyes and Félix Díaz from their military prison and marched on the national palace, whose garrison they expected would join them. They were mistaken. The commander of the garrison, General Lauro Villar, was loyal to the government and ordered his troops to fire on the conspirators. Reyes was killed, and the remnants of his supporters fled into an old fort located in the center of Mexico City, the Ciudadela.

The revolt seemed to have petered out. Its participants did not constitute a major military force, and they were now closed up in a fort, where they could be easily be starved out, blockaded, or reduced by concentrated artillery fire. No other army units had risen to second the uprising in Mexico City in the rest of the country.

When the revolt first broke out, however, fear seized many revolutionary chieftains, who now expected the federal army to strike out at them. In Chihuahua, Abraham González asked the U.S. consul in Ciudad Chihuahua, Marion Letcher, to take charge temporarily of 180,000 pesos that the state treasury still held, while he went into the hills to join former revolutionary troops.[3] Then, when it seemed clear that the revolt was confined to a few hundred men in Mexico City, González decided to remain in Ciudad Chihuahua and expressed his confidence that the coup had been crushed in a series of optimistic reports to state officials in different parts of Chihuahua.

"The government continues to be in firm control of the situation, as reports coming from the capital show, and they are very favorable," González informed the mayor of Ciudad Guerrero and other officials of his administration on February 11.[4] "Situation has improved," he wired the same officials on February 15. "General Huerta is every day more successful in besieging the Ciudadela, the rest of the city is quiet. Rumors about the resignation of the President are wrong. All fears of intervention have disappeared. The government has full confidence in the patriotism of the people."[5] And on the morning of February 18, only a few hours before Madero was arrested, he sent his most optimistic telegram: "The city is entirely quiet and the majority of its inhabitants are going about their daily occupations. An enormously strong reaction in favor of the government is taking place."[6]

González's attitude is not surprising, since Madero himself was blind to what was going on and remained optimistic until the last moment. Only a few hours before he was toppled, the president gave a highly optimistic appraisal of the situation in Mexico City to the German minister in Mexico, Paul von Hintze, who noted: "President says that west side of Citadel was intentionally given up to allow Díaz's numerous conspirators opportunities to escape. And while he did not wish to engage in prophecy, he feels the whole affair would be over in three to four days."[7]

What Madero had not anticipated, although he had been repeatedly warned of it, was that his commander-in-chief, Victoriano Huerta, would betray him. Throughout the fighting in Mexico City, known as the Decena trágica (the ten tragic days), Huerta had secret dealings with both Félix Díaz and the U.S. ambassador to Mexico, Henry Lane Wilson. The ambassador encouraged Huerta to overthrow Madero and told him that the United States would recognize a government arising out of such a coup. Huerta now came to a secret agreement with Díaz to end hostilities, and units of his army arrested Madero and his vice president, Pino Suárez. He promised to spare their lives if they resigned, but after they did so had them shot, stating that they had been killed while their supporters were attempting to rescue them.

The new military government of Mexico headed by Huerta seemed to be in a highly favorable position, and U.S. Ambassador Wilson's view that calm and order would soon be reestablished throughout Mexico probably reflected the opinion, not only of the diplomatic corps and the military government, but of most foreign and domestic observers of the Mexican scene as well.

The military government was able to cover itself with the trappings of legality. After he was promised that his life would be spared if he resigned, Madero tendered his resignation, and, in accordance with Mexico's constitution of 1857, Secretary of State Pedro Paredes Lascurain assumed the provisional presidency. He then immediately resigned in favor of Huerta, who became the legal head of the country. In the first days after Huerta took power, the divisions that had existed within Mexico's upper classes and among the business interests of the foreign powers in Mexico seemed to have disappeared. They all rallied to Huerta's support. The church hierarchy also expressed support for the new president, the church bells in Mexico City tolled on the day the fighting stopped, and the archbishop celebrated a solemn Te Deum in the presence of Huerta. Most state governors, bureaucrats, and deputies rallied to the military government. The federal army, which had scarcely suffered during the fighting in Mexico City, was unanimous in its support of the new military ruler.

The Constitutionalist Revolution

In contrast to the newly unified conservatives, the former revolutionaries seemed divided and demoralized. After the deaths of Madero and Pino Suárez, there was no revolutionary leader left with the kind of national recognition and national prestige that Madero had enjoyed. Of the military leaders the revolution had produced, only three had national reputations: Emiliano Zapata, Pascual Orozco, and Pancho Villa.

Zapata would have had great difficulty in rallying a national constituency. He had been fighting Madero for more than a year, and the latter's supporters were naturally wary of him. Moreover, since he had been depicted in the national press as the Attila of the South, intent like the Maya Indians of Yucatán in the nineteenth century on a kind of caste war in which all non-Indians would be killed, the middle class was afraid of him. Orozco had also been fighting Madero's government, but he soon made his peace with Huerta and mobilized troops to fight for the new military dictator. Pancho Villa was not only living in exile in El Paso but, the new regime hoped, had been discredited by his arrest by the Maderista administration and by the accusations of banditry leveled against him. In addition, the force he had commanded prior to his arrest had been dissolved, and its members had been drafted and dispersed among the federal army.

The one political Maderista leader who did enjoy a measure of national recognition, and whom many considered Madero's spiritual heir, was Abraham González. The fear that González would spark a new uprising against the federal government led Huerta to order his arrest. González, who had never shared Madero's naive belief in the loyalty of the federal army, had nevertheless been lulled into a false sense of security by his confidence in the integrity and decency of the federal commander, General Rábago, who had promised that he would not arrest the Chihuahuan governor. As a result, González refused to heed the warnings of friends that his detention was imminent and did not flee Ciudad Chihuahua. After his detention by federal troops, he was sent to prison in Mexico City. On the way, the officers escorting him stopped the train in which they were traveling, shot him, and then had his body run over by the same train. Officially, it was stated that he had been killed while supporters of his were trying to rescue him.

Madero left no viable political organization that could challenge the new government. The anti-reelectionist party, which prior to his assumption of power had been a genuine mass organization, had fallen apart long before Madero was deposed. Many of its supporters, especially in the countryside, abandoned it after Madero's conservative social policies began to be recognized. It was replaced by a more traditional type of client-oriented political organization based on patronage and directed by Madero's brother, Gustavo.

Parts of the former revolutionary army had survived the Madero years, especially in northern Mexico, but had been badly battered and demoralized by Madero's opposition and neglect. In addition, during the fighting in Mexico City, Huerta had done his best to further weaken them. He had sent many of these contingents on suicidal attacks against the Ciudadela, where, with his full connivance, they had been exposed to murderous machine-gun and artillery fire from the fort's defenders.[8]

Madero had not only alienated large segments of the peasantry that had originally supported him, but in his last month in office that alienation had extended to important middle- and upper-class supporters. Only a few weeks before he fell, Madero's most radical supporters in parliament, who called themselves the *renovadores*, the renewers, had written a bitter memorandum to the Mexican president, saying that "the revolution is heading toward collapse and is pulling down with it the government to which it gave rise, for the simple reason that it is not governing with revolutionaries. Compromises and concessions to the supporters of old regime are the main causes of the unsettling situation in which the government that emerged from the revolution finds itself. . . . The regime appears relentlessly bent on suicide."[9]

The hopes and expectations of the military rulers seemed at first to be justified. In Mexico's largest cities, there were no strikes, no demonstrations, no signs of any overt opposition to the coup. Within only a few weeks, however, it became clear to both Henry Lane Wilson and to the new military government in Mexico that whatever hopes they had had of stabilizing the situation in the country and preventing a new large-scale revolt from breaking out had been misplaced.

The new series of revolutions that now encompassed Mexico largely began in the same regions that had been the center of the Madero revolution of 1910–11. While many of its leaders and participants had been involved in the earlier Madero revolution, this second revolution was no mere replica of the first. It was more radical, bloodier, and more all-encompassing, but in many respects far less spontaneous.

Its radicalism was linked to the fact that both sides realized that the kind of compromise that had occurred in 1911 could not be duplicated. In return for the resignation of Díaz, the 1911 treaty of Ciudad Juárez not only had left the social structure of the country more or less intact, but had also preserved the federal army and dissolved revolutionary units. Because they envisaged such a compromise, Mexico's upper classes had provided little military support to the Díaz administration in 1910–11. After the rural unrest of the Madero period, however, the upper classes, especially the hacendados, were far more fearful of the possible results of the new revolution and became far more involved in directly helping the new government. And after deposing and killing Madero, the federal army feared that it would not survive a new revolution.

In some respects, the increasing radicalism of the second phase of the Mexican revolution conformed to patterns evident in other major social revolutions, especially those of France and Russia. As in those two cases, the radical phase of the revolution started with attempts by the army and the traditional upper class to topple the moderate revolutionary leadership. But in France (the attempted flight of Louis XVI from France) and in Russia (the Kornilov putsch), the military counterrevolution failed. In Mexico, Huerta's coup succeeded.

In all three cases, the radical revolutionaries would demand and finally carry out the destruction of what might be called the traditional state—that, is the old army, the old police force, the old judiciary, and, to a large extent, the traditional local administration. In all three cases, the radical revolutionaries would make use of the property of the old ruling class in order to finance the revolution. In all three cases, the radical phase of the revolution was bloodier and more violent than its moderate predecessor—as in France and Russia, the radical revolutionaries would wage battles among themselves that at times became more violent than their conflict with the old regime.

Nevertheless, there were differences as well, which make it difficult to compare the radical phase of the Mexican revolution to that of France or Russia. Unlike France and Russia, where foreign armies intervened on a large scale in order to destroy the revolutionary government, the role of foreign governments was far more ambivalent in Mexico. For a long time, the dominant foreign power, the United States, aligned itself with the revolutionaries. When it turned against them, it did so in a milder way than the foreign opponents of the French or Russian revolutionaries. U.S. military intervention in Mexico was on a more limited scale in both time and place than foreign intervention in France and Russia and would have fewer consequences. One of the most fundamental differences between the second phase of the Mexican revolution and those in France and Russia was the fate of the traditional ruling class. Not only were there no massive executions of its members, as was the case in the other two countries, but most of them regained their properties, although frequently only in the short run. Finally, it took longer for the Mexican revolutionaries to reconstruct a strong state than it did their counterparts in France and Russia.

The increasing radicalism of all factions in Mexico led to far bloodier reprisals by both sides against each other than during the first revolution. The small-scale guerrilla fighting that had predominated throughout most of the Madero revolution was replaced by large regular armies fighting each other in battles with large numbers of casualties. The cities, most of which had been spared revolutionary fighting in 1910–11, now became the scene of savage fighting that resulted in large numbers of civilian victims. In economic terms, the disruption caused by fighting would lead to widespread starvation and famine in many parts of the country.

In one respect, nevertheless, the 1913–14 revolution was similar to its 1910–11 predecessor: the same five states that had constituted the core of the Madero revolution now constituted the initial basis of the second Mexican revolution, generally designated the constitutionalist phase. They were the states of Morelos, Coahuila, Sonora, Chihuahua, and Durango.

In two of these states, Sonora and Coahuila, the revolution was not a popular insurrection as it had been in 1910–11 but a state-organized enterprise largely directed by state administrations led by a coalition of hacendados and middle-class revolutionaries. Military action was based on regular state contingents that had either survived the Madero revolution or been organized to fight the Orozco rebellion. In Morelos, no new social movement emerged, and the second revolution was simply a more radical continuation of the first Zapatista revolt. In Durango and Chihuahua, by contrast, new and extremely powerful popular insurrections took place without the initial support of any revolutionary state administration, incorporating the dispersed remnants of revolutionary state militias that had survived both the Madero revolution and Madero's and Huerta's attempts to dissolve or subjugate them.

It is not surprising that the first regions where the second revolution broke out were those where an existing state or an existing revolutionary army was ready to assume its leadership: Coahuila, Sonora, and Morelos.

The first, and for a time the only, high official of the Madero administration to refuse publicly to recognize Huerta and to call on the people of Mexico to take up arms against him was the governor of the northern state of Coahuila, Venustiano Carranza. He was in many respects an unlikely leader of a second, more radical Mexican revolution. Fifty-five years old, and with a long, flowing white beard, he was very different from practically all the other revolutionary leaders, who were in their twenties and thirties and led a mainly youthful revolutionary movement. Carranza also lacked the populist presence of men such as Madero and Villa. Those who met him for the first time were struck by his aloofness.

Isidro Fabela, who came to be his closest collaborator and greatest admirer and defender, felt devastated after his first meeting with Carranza. After escaping from Huerta's police and making his way with great difficulty to Sonora, Fabela was looking forward with great anticipation to joining Carranza, who by that time had arrived there. He asked for an audience with the "First Chief," as Carranza was now called. The meeting took place on a train en route to the state capital of Sonora, Hermosillo. Fabela was bubbling over with enthusiasm, telling Carranza what he had done for the revolution, expressing his wish to do whatever Carranza thought he could do.

> He allowed me to speak without even opening his lips and looked at me with clear attention. . . . After my brief words, the First Chief continued as mute as he had been before, so that a few minutes later, with his agreement, I left him.
>
> The reception Carranza gave me left me completely disconcerted. I, who admired him so much for his historical achievement, which would endure through posterity; I, who hoped that the illustrious patrician would pronounce a few words of approval for my conduct, or would at least make a well-meaning gesture and show some expression of political or human sympathy for my young and romantic love for freedom and the revolution, met with an icy silence that left me surprised and perplexed.[10]

Carranza's social origins and political history were different from those of most of the revolutionary leaders who took up arms in 1913. He was a hacendado (although some considered him merely a wealthy *ranchero*) and one of the few leaders of the Madero revolution who had held important political posts under Porfirio Díaz, if not the only one. He had been closely linked to two highly influential personalities of the Porfirian era: Bernardo Reyes, the longtime Porfirian military commander in northeastern Mexico and governor of Nuevo León, and Miguel Cárdenas, the Porfirian governor of Coahuila. With their help and support, Carranza had held different positions in Coahuila, and for a time, he had been a senator in the powerless Porfirian senate. Up to 1908, he had had no serious differences with the Díaz administration.[11]

Carranza's break with Porfirio Díaz came in 1908 when Díaz turned against Reyes and his supporters. Governor Cárdenas was forced to resign, and his supporters, who included a large part of the Coahuilan elite, named Carranza as their candidate to succeed him. Díaz prevented his victory, and Carranza became an embittered opponent of his. He was a fervent Reyista until Reyes was forced into exile; then he joined Madero. His participation in the Madero revolution had not been outstanding, but Madero nevertheless rewarded him by supporting his candidacy for the governorship of Coahuila.

In the approximately two years during which he was governor of his native state of Coahuila, Carranza generally followed Madero's policies. With regard to the land question, Carranza was at least as conservative as Madero. Like his president, he made no effort to change agrarian structures, to meet the demands of villagers who asked for the return of expropriated lands, or to address the problems of those landless peasants who hoped to acquire properties as a result of the revolution. His policies met with the overwhelming support of the state's elite and in fact, with one significant exception, corresponded to the policies advocated for many years by his former mentor and protector, Bernardo Reyes.

Like Reyes, and unlike Madero, Carranza did not have much respect for genuine elections and democratic niceties. Like Reyes, Carranza believed that modernization implied granting certain minimal rights to workers, and like Reyes
(probably to a greater degree than Madero), Carranza was a nationalist. These
attitudes were reflected in his social and fiscal policies. When workers struck
against a foreign company, they could generally count on Carranza's aid. He supported striking mine workers against the foreign-owned Sabinas Coal Company.
He was less supportive of workers who struck against Mexican businessmen. In
December 1911, he allowed Sierra Mojada merchants to form a volunteer corps
against striking workers.[12]

It is thus not surprising that Carranza's policies enjoyed the support of
Coahuila's elite. That support did not significantly waver when he shifted part of
the state's tax burden from the middle to the upper classes. The elite must have
felt that this was, after all, a relatively small price to pay for middle-class support
and for being able to weather the effects of a social revolution without any further
sacrifices.

Carranza's nationalism, because of its limited scope, also appealed to the native
elite. Carranza never advocated expropriation or nationalization of foreign property, and neither did he want to put barriers in the path of foreign investment
that would have cut the state's elite off from foreign financial support. His nationalism mainly manifested itself in attempting to extract more from foreigners
than either Porfirio Díaz had done or Madero was willing to do. He forced foreign companies to pay more taxes and higher wages, and he frequently got them
to make other concessions, such as building schools for their employees.

There was one significant way in which Carranza did differ from Madero. Unlike the latter, he understood the logic of revolution and realized that as long as a
mainly unchanged federal army was the most powerful armed force in the country, the revolution would be in deadly danger. He expressed these thoughts to
Madero in a letter he sent him after the treaty of Ciudad Juárez, and both in theory and practice, he continued to air these views until Madero's death. In 1912,
when the Orozquista uprising broke out, he organized a state militia from Coahuila to fight it. With great energy and obstinacy, he opposed efforts by Madero
to subordinate these militias to the federal high command.[13]

Increasingly worried about the possibility of a coup by the federal army, Carranza invited the governors of five states who were considered genuine revolutionaries to a hunting party in Coahuila. Governor Rafael Cepeda of San Luis
Potosí attended, and the governors of Sonora, Chihuahua, and Aguascalientes
sent representatives. While it is not entirely clear what was discussed, a common
policy in the event of a military coup was probably on the agenda.[14]

When Carranza received a message from Huerta on February 18 stating, "Authorized by the senate, I have assumed the executive power, the president and his
cabinet being prisoners,"[15] he immediately summoned an emergency meeting of
the Coahuilan state assembly, which refused to recognize Huerta's assumption of
power and called on all Mexico's other state governors to do the same.

Carranza very soon found out, however, that he stood alone. The governor of
Chihuahua, Abraham González, who would have been willing to fight Huerta,
had been murdered. The governor of San Luis Potosí, Cepeda, had been arrested,

and his counterpart in Aguascalientes, Alberto Fuentes, had been removed from his position. José María Maytorena, the governor of Sonora, was the one in the best position to fight Huerta, since very few federal troops were stationed in his state and he commanded the loyalty of many of the state's troops. Instead of leading the fight against Huerta, however, Maytorena, a hacendado who had played a prominent role in the Madero revolution of 1910–11, opted for a leave of absence, officially for reasons of health, and took up residence in Tucson, Arizona.

Maytorena doubted that a new revolution would be able to defeat Huerta. In addition, in his memoirs, he explains his decision to leave Sonora by saying that when on February 24, 1913, the civilian and military leaders of Sonora decided

to defy General Huerta . . . I could not countenance the methods that were advocated, nor the measures that I would be forced to take. . . . They included a general confiscation of property, which would include the properties of people who had no political interest and had not participated in the events in Mexico City . . . forced loans . . . detentions and executions of peaceful citizens whose only crime was their wealth and the fact that they did not adhere to our cause.[16]

His secretary, Francisco Serrano, put it more succinctly: "Don Pepe [as Maytorena was often called in Sonora] does not want to assume the responsibility of dragging the state into the revolution. The state has no money to finance a war. Don Pepe is related to all the wealthy men and thus feels that he cannot hurt their interests."[17] When a Sonoran official came to see him in Tucson, asking him to reconsider his decision, Maytorena refused to return to Sonora, saying, "In this fight I would have to pressure the rich to take money from them, since only with money can a revolution be carried out, and I have too many obligations to do so."[18]

Maytorena's departure from Sonora did not mean that the state now recognized Huerta. The legislature elected a provisional governor, who called on the people to fight against the military dictatorship. Nevertheless, the consequence of Maytorena's decision was that Carranza was now the only remaining constitutionally elected governor who was both willing and able to call for resistance to Huerta.

After finding that he stood alone, Carranza seems to have prevaricated, and he pursued an ambivalent policy in the two weeks following Huerta's coup. While continuing to make defiant speeches against the new military rulers of Mexico, he told U.S. Consul Philip Holland that he was willing to compromise with Huerta and sent two emissaries to negotiate with the new authorities in Mexico City. The emissaries asked Huerta to maintain Carranza as governor and not to send troops to the state capital of Saltillo.

Carranza's motives in negotiating with Huerta are still the subject of hot debate. While his opponents, and some historians, maintain that he was genuinely interested in reaching a compromise—he had never been an ardent supporter of Madero's or had a profound belief in democracy—his supporters maintain that was playing for time.[19] He had no money to start a revolution, and the few state militias at his disposal were scattered in other parts of Mexico. Carranza did in fact immediately recall the state militias under the command of Pablo González and those headed by his brother, Jesús Carranza, to Saltillo. At the same time, he imposed a forced loan of 75,000 pesos on the state's banks, and on March 3, he made it unmistakably clear that he would fight Huerta.

It required courage to be the only governor to openly defy the military regime. In part, Carranza was certainly impelled by ambition. History had suddenly thrust the chance of assuming the presidency into his lap. He probably also felt that he had no choice. The murders of Madero, Pino Suárez, and González could well be seen as foreshadowing his own fate.

Other reasons as well probably explain Carranza's behavior. The one ideology to which he remained committed throughout his life was nationalism. The large role that U.S. Ambassador Wilson had played in the overthrow of Madero helped convince Carranza that Mexico's independence and sovereignty were at stake. While he certainly did not know of the report that the German minister in Mexico, von Hintze, had sent to Berlin—"The American embassy, without much attempt to hide the fact, rules through the provisional government, whose principal figures, General Huerta and Minister de la Barra, are morally and financially dependent upon U.S. support"[20]—he probably shared this view.

Carranza was more realistic than Madero in his assessment of the federal army, but he was just as naive with respect to the role and attitude of Mexico's ruling classes. He felt he could win them over to his cause. The Plan of Guadalupe (named after the hacienda where he announced it to delegates from Coahuila and representatives of other states) under which Carranza assumed the provisional leadership of the country called on the people of Mexico to repudiate the dictatorship and rise against Huerta. It condemned Huerta's seizure of power as usurpation and demanded a return to constitutional rule, but went no further. In social terms, it was even more conservative than Madero's Plan of San Luis Potosí. Madero had mentioned the agrarian question, however briefly and vaguely, but Carranza made no social demands whatsoever. "Do you want the war to last for five years?" he asked his more radical supporters, who sought to include promises of land distribution, labor legislation, and the like. "The less resistance there is, the shorter the war will be. The large landowners, the clergy, and the industrialists are stronger than the federal government. We must first defeat the government before we can take on the questions you rightly wish to solve."[21]

Carranza obviously had the example of the Madero revolution in mind. With a single, generalized demand, Madero had succeeded in opening the ruling classes to compromise and in winning over the peasantry to his cause. But the two years of the Madero period had made a deep impression upon both the ruling classes and the peasants. The former were convinced that even the slightest concession to the revolutionaries might endanger their power; the peasants were no longer willing to go into battle for general demands that did not address their specific interests.

Carranza's refusal to engage in what might be called revolutionary warfare contributed to his defeat in his home state. He had limited himself to strengthening the state militia by levying new taxes and waging a conventional war against Huerta. He made no attempt to win a mass base for the revolutionary movement in Coahuila by means of reforms or even promises of reforms. Nor did he try to build a significant guerrilla force. The better-equipped and more numerous

Huerta troops could easily defeat the state militia in a conventional war, and that was precisely what happened. In 1913, Carranza's army was beaten three times in Coahuila—at Anhelo, Saltillo, and Monclova—and Carranza decided to leave the state, which was now largely controlled by Huerta's troops, and to seek refuge in Sonora, large sections of which were dominated by the revolutionaries.

The 1913 Revolution in Chihuahua and the Return of Pancho Villa

That armed resistance broke out in both Coahuila and Sonora did not much surprise the Huerta regime. After all, both states had played important roles in the Madero revolution, and both were dominated by revolutionary administrations with their own armed forces. What neither Huerta nor his domestic and foreign supporters expected was that Chihuahua would again become one of the main centers of revolution. Its revolutionary movement had been badly divided after the outbreak of the Orozco rebellion. Abraham González, its most important leader, had suffered a sharp loss of popularity and prestige as a result of his inability to restore peace and his unwillingness or incapacity to carry out the social reforms that many of his erstwhile supporters had expected of him. His death and Orozco's support for the new military administration of Mexico were considered by many in the government as the final blow to any revolutionary movement in Chihuahua. Indeed, Chihuahua was now viewed as a mainstay of federal strategy. Located as it was between Sonora and Coahuila, it would prevent the revolutionary movements of those states from uniting their forces. From Chihuahua, federal troops and their Orozquista allies could proceed to the two neighboring states and destroy their burgeoning revolutionary movements.

In the course of only a few weeks, these expectations would prove to be mistaken. Within a very short time, Chihuahua would again become one of the main centers of the new revolutionary wave sweeping Mexico. There is no single reason to account for this astonishing revival of revolutionary energies in Chihuahua. It was owing to a mixture of anger and resentment, fear, and hope. In a state whose inhabitants were especially proud of their long tradition of independence, autonomy, and self-reliance, the military regime's decision to appoint an outsider, Federal General Rábago, as governor of the state provoked intense resentment. It heightened their fears that one of the main gains they had achieved during the Madero administration—autonomy from federal control and genuine municipal autonomy—would again be taken from them.

Although Abraham González's popularity had declined during his last month in office, his murder made him into a martyr. It also persuaded many of his former supporters that the federal government and Orozco would exact revenge from them for having supported Madero. These fears were combined with the conviction of many Chihuahuans that their forces could defeat the federal army, as they had at Tomóchi and during the 1910–11 revolution. Many villagers felt that now that González's restraining hand was gone and a counterrevolutionary federal government was in power, the time was ripe to carry out some of the radical social transformations that had not been undertaken during the Madero years. In March 1913, the village council of Namiquipa decided that the time had finally come to divide up the lands among the traditional inhabitants of the village, which outside immigrants had taken from them under Creel's 1905 land law.[22]

Elsewhere in Chihuahua, as well as in parts of Durango, a similar wave of radical attacks on many elite social and economic structures that had survived the Madero revolution now took place. Such revolutionary movements, frequently led by men who had already participated in the 1910–11 revolution, and often based on the militias that had been raised in the state in 1912 to fight Orozco, emerged all over Chihuahua. It would require the charismatic presence of Pancho Villa to forge these local movements into a coherent whole and to recreate the unity of the Chihuahuan population that had temporarily emerged during the Madero revolution. It was under Villa that the loose array of guerrilla forces would be transformed into a regular army and guerrilla warfare would be replaced by regular warfare. To the surprise of both Chihuahuan and non-Chihuahuan observers, Villa emerged as a kind of consensus candidate to reestablish the coalition of lower- and middle-class forces that had brought Madero and Abraham González to power.

That surprise is understandable. Not only did Villa have a past as an outlaw, but he had made no ideological pronouncements during the Maderista uprising. His few statements to the press in 1912 indicated no ideological interest or capacity. What decisively contributed to changing Villa's outlook was his imprisonment, which strengthened his hatred of those he considered responsible for his plight—Huerta, Terrazas, and Creel—and the institutions they represented. "Persons who visit me have very clearly stated that Terrazas and Creel have said that as long as they are alive, I shall not leave prison, and they will do whatever they can to achieve this aim; as you know they are very powerful," Villa wrote in 1912.[23]

For most revolutionaries, imprisonment constitutes an experience that shapes their lives, their thinking, their ideology, and their behavior in decisive ways. In prison, they frequently meet other revolutionaries of different backgrounds and persuasions, whom they might never have met outside. Most revolutionaries tend to be men of action, for whom prison provides an enforced leisure time in which they can study, reflect, and deal with the problems of aims and ideology. In emotional terms, the special kind of confrontation with their enemies that prison brings about tends to have profound effects, at times transforming moderates into radical revolutionaries, and generally reinforcing already-strong emotions and hatreds.

It was in prison that Villa probably became convinced that the revolution could only triumph if both the federal army and the hacendado class in Chihuahua and Durango, and perhaps in most of the rest of Mexico, were eliminated. Prior to 1913, he had shown little awareness of the need for land reform, except as far as his soldiers were concerned. His contacts in prison with the Zapatista ideologue Gildardo Magaña and another Zapatista leader, Abraham Martínez, may have greatly enhanced his understanding of that problem, although in all probability they were less important for Villa's awareness of the agrarian problem than his later alliance with the northern revolutionaries Toribio Ortega and

Calixto Contreras, who were traditional peasant leaders and would strongly influence Villa's outlook (see below).

It is unlikely that Villa first learned to read and write in prison, as some of his biographers have asserted. His primitively spelled letters to Madero while he was still being held in isolation show that he knew the rudiments of reading and writing, and a presiding judge remembered lending him *The Three Musketeers* by Alexandre Dumas *père*. It is doubtful whether the exploits of D'Artagnan, Athos, Porthos, and Aramis sharpened Villa's revolutionary consciousness, but the manual of Mexican history that Magaña supplied him with probably did so. Perhaps his outlook on life was also transformed by reading Cervantes's *Don Quijote*. Magaña seems to have imbued him with a strong sense of Mexican history. Prior to 1913, Villa had shown no great resentment of Spaniards, something that would constitute a decisive element of his policies in later years. Conversely, Villa showed no anti-American tendencies until 1915, perhaps largely because of his positive experiences as an employee of American companies.

Prison strengthened the ambivalence Villa had always felt toward Madero. He had rebelled against his chief in Ciudad Juárez because he felt that Madero was letting the federal commander off too gently. In 1912, he believed that he himself was the victim of Madero's conciliatory policies, since the main reason for his imprisonment was to placate Huerta. Moreover, Villa felt that Madero was again attempting to conciliate Creel at his expense.

Finally, Villa was deeply hurt by what he regarded as Madero's lack of gratitude. He had, after all, taken up arms to save the president when things seemed hopeless for Madero in Chihuahua. Now Madero had amnestied his enemies, and Villa was still kept at the mercy of the federal army.

Madero's death fully rehabilitated the martyred president in Villa's eyes. (Until the end of his days, he would speak of "Maderito" with the greatest respect and affection.) Things were restored to the coloration Villa preferred: black and white. His enemies were now the antagonists whom he had always hated: Huerta and the federal army. The leader who had called on him to fight the new military rulers of Mexico was a man for whom he had the greatest respect and affection: Abraham González. The Chihuahuan governor not only asked Villa to join him but also offered him money and resources to mobilize troops.

Villa immediately began to revive his old contacts in Mexico. The wife of an El Paso hotel owner remembered Villa frequently coming down to a bar and club her husband owned, the Emporium. "The club was a meeting place for revolutionary leaders, reporters, spies and others looking for information for what was going on in Mexico."[24] She remembered Villa as a man

of unstable temper . . . who liked ice cream and got it almost every day at the elite confectionery. He was also very fond of peanut brittle and always carried a supply in his pocket. Though he was always eating candy, Pancho said he had a very delicate stomach and had to almost live on squab. He kept a box of live pigeons in his rooms at my father's hotel. That was accepted as one of his little personal oddities and no one thought much about it. As my husband used to say, in the state of nervousness that Pancho lived in at that time, it was no wonder he had a tender stomach. Later we found out the pigeons were really homing pigeons and that Villa was sending messages down to friends in the ranch country of Chihuahua.[25]

Villa's plans for a smooth return to Chihuahua were placed in jeopardy when the news of González's murder reached him. His hatred of Huerta increased, but he suddenly found himself alone, without any resources to undertake a campaign against both the powerful federal army and the Orozquistas in Chihuahua.

At the beginning of March 1913, when he heard that the governor of the state of Sonora, José María Maytorena, who had refused to recognize Huerta as president of Mexico, was in Tucson, Arizona, Villa decided to seek him out and to appeal to him for help. After his arrival in Tucson, before he had a chance to meet with Maytorena, Villa was visited by another of the revolutionary leaders from Sonora, Adolfo de la Huerta, who suggested that he join the revolutionary forces in Sonora. "Why don't you come with me to the state of Sonora?" he asked Villa.

"No, my boy, no, no. No way," Villa answered.

"In your state, I am worth nothing. I do not know the people there; I don't know the land; no. In my state, which is Chihuahua, although I was born in Durango but consider Chihuahua as my home, that is where I am worth ten times more than in Sonora. No, no, no. Get me some money from Maytorena and I will go to El Paso, Texas, and from there I will see how I will return to my own country."[26]

De la Huerta may have convinced Villa that the only way to get some support and financial help from the Sonoran revolutionaries was to go to Sonora. So when he finally interviewed Maytorena, whom he had met before in 1911 during the siege of Ciudad Juárez and with whom he had gotten along well, Villa suggested that he was willing to go and fight in Sonora. What he did not realize was that this was the last thing Maytorena wanted. It was clear to the governor that if Villa ever got to Sonora, he would have no compunction about carrying out the one measure that Maytorena opposed most: the expropriation of the wealth of the richest inhabitants of the state. He thus told Villa to do exactly the contrary of what de la Huerta had suggested and encouraged him to go and fight in Chihuahua, giving him $1,000 for that purpose.[27] From Maytorena's point of view, this was a stroke of genius. For the small sum of $1,000, he had kept Villa away from Sonora, given him the means of crossing into Chihuahua, and ensured his friendship and loyalty. Villa was a man who never forgot his debts or those others owed him. He would live to attempt to repay the debt he felt he owed both Maytorena and de la Huerta. The first repayment would decisively contribute to his defeat, the second to his death.

With the money he had obtained from Maytorena, Villa paid his hotel bills, bought nine rifles, rented nine horses, and on the night of March 6, with eight supporters, crossed the muddy and shallow waters of the Rio Grande into Mexico. Apart from the rifles and horses, the expedition had 500 cartridges per man, two pounds of coffee, two pounds of sugar, and one pound of salt.[28]

Eight months later, he would return to the border, this time at the head of several thousand men and in control of most of the state of Chihuahua.

In March 1913, though, Villa's later success was by no means a foregone conclusion. In some respects, the situation of all the revolutionaries in Chihuahua was more difficult in 1913 than it had been in 1910–11. In addition, Villa's authority was not recognized by all other revolutionary leaders in early 1913, and he had no means to enforce it. In 1910–11, the Chihuahuan oligarchy had been caught by surprise by the uprising, and many hacendados preferred to stay on the sidelines, hoping that they would be spared if they did so. Madero was, after all, one of the wealthiest hacendados in the north and not a fiery agrarian revolutionary. One of the consequences of the hacendados' reluctance to defend the Porfirian regime was that Alberto Terrazas managed to raise only a few hundred men to support the federal campaign against the revolution, allowing the revolutionaries to wage classic guerrilla warfare. They controlled the countryside, the initiative was in their hands, and when they felt strong enough, they proceeded to attack the large towns and cities.

In addition, financial help from Madero had enabled the revolutionaries to be well supplied with arms from across the border. In 1913, by contrast, the federal government had at its disposal thousands of armed local auxiliaries ready to fight for the new military regime. They consisted of the many battle-trained veterans of Orozco's army and of the armed retainers that many hacendados were now willing to mobilize. The hacendados now believed (and rightly so) that, unlike Madero, the lower-class revolutionaries who were taking up arms would spare neither their properties nor their lives.

This disadvantage of the 1913 revolution in Chihuahua vis-à-vis the 1910–11 movement was offset by an enormous advantage. In 1910–11, for several months, the Chihuahuan revolutionaries had stood practically alone. This time, revolutionary movements had broken out in Coahuila, Sonora, and Morelos too.

The multiplicity of regional rebellions and the overconfidence of the federal government and its military leadership led them to send Orozco's forces to crush revolutionary movements in other states instead of utilizing them against the revolutionary wave that began to sweep Chihuahua in early 1913. The Chihuahuan movement's leadership came mainly from among the commanders of the revolutionary forces in 1910–11. These men had either retained command of ex-revolutionary forces incorporated into the state militia as rurales after Madero's victory or had taken up arms for Madero with their own followers after the outbreak of the Orozco rebellion. Wherever these core groups went, they immediately found much popular support.

On February 24, Manuel Chao, a former schoolteacher who had taken up arms for Madero in 1910 and who commanded a battalion of volunteers against Orozco in 1912, attacked the town of Santa Barbara. Not only did his men outnumber the garrison but at the height of the battle the townspeople rose and began shooting from their houses at the federal troops. The federals lost all morale and surrendered or were captured by Chao's men. A similar popular uprising took place when Chao's troops laid siege to Parral. The federal commander bitterly complained of the "infamous help, so valuable to our enemies, of all of the lower classes of society, who from the time fighting erupted began to shoot at our troops from their houses in a perfidious way."[29]

In spite of the widespread support he enjoyed in the town, Chao had to retreat when federal reinforcements arrived on the scene. Retreat, however, did not mean defeat. Chao's troops melted into the countryside and availed themselves of the great wealth of the large estates, which the Madero revolution had not destroyed. In March and April, they waged what was essentially guerrilla warfare, briefly occupying towns, recruiting volunteers, and destroying railway tracks to impede the movements of government troops. When federal troops reoccupied a town, the revolutionaries destroyed the railway tracks all around it to prevent supplies from getting in. Meanwhile, other revolutionary contingents attacked towns where federal garrisons were either weak or nonexistent. Similar movements headed by former commanders of Maderista troops included that led by a rancher from Parral, Maclovio Herrera, who had also led troops against Orozco, and that led by Toribio Ortega, the peasant leader from Cuchillo Parado. Both constantly harassed federal troops. One of the most successful of these revolutionary leaders was Tomás Urbina, Villa's former crony and lieutenant, who had fought against the Orozco uprising. Urbina, whose bases were in the state of Durango, had revolted there in the town of Inde and then moved to southern Chihuahua, where he occupied the town of Jiménez.

It took less than two months for these guerrilla leaders to transform the nature of the fighting in Chihuahua. Increasingly harassed by revolutionary forces, short of money, arms, and ammunition from the government in Mexico City, and largely dependent on conscripts who were scarcely willing to fight, the federal army retreated into a few large cities. They left most of Chihuahua, including some of the larger towns, in the revolutionaries' control. Chao again temporarily occupied Parral, Urbina captured Jiménez, and Ortega for a time controlled the border town of Ojinaga, where he collected customs duties and smuggled arms into Mexico from the United States.[30]

In the neighboring state of Durango, a similar situation had arisen, and Calixto Contreras again dominated his native region.

In its first stages, this new radical revolution that was sweeping both Chihuahua and Durango lacked centralized control and centralized leadership. While most of the revolutionaries from these two states recognized Carranza as the supreme leader of the revolution, he had no means of exercising effective control over them. The same was true of Pancho Villa in the first month after his return to Chihuahua.

His return did not lead to his immediate preeminence in the state's revolutionary movement. Villa had hoped that both his popularity and his revolutionary credentials would persuade the other revolutionary leaders in the state to accept his authority. After the murder of González, the defection of Orozco, and the execution of José de la Luz Soto in a prison in Mexico City, Villa was the only senior military commander of the 1910–11 Madero revolution in Chihuahua who was still alive and still a revolutionary. Many of the local leaders who had taken up arms in Chihuahua after Madero's assassination had been his direct subordinates. Nevertheless, only a very small number of his former commanders, such as Fidel Avila, once a foreman on a hacienda and an officer in Villa's contingent during the Madero revolt, joined him. Most other insurgent leaders in Chihuahua not only did not do so but then refused to obey his command to stage a feint attack on Ciudad Chihuahua in order to allow him to capture the town of Casas Grandes.[31]

They had defeated the federal army on their own without Villa's help or advice, commanded more men than he did, and initially controlled more resources than he did. Until June 1913, they had scored far more important victories than Villa since his return to Mexico. While local revolutionary chieftains in Chihuahua had recognized Carranza's authority as First Chief of the revolution, Carranza was far away and exercised no direct control over them. Although the revolutionary chieftains would temporarily join forces to attain some military objectives, most of them refused to subordinate their authority to a higher leader on a permanent basis. They behaved at this time as caudillos or as peasant leaders had so frequently behaved in history, not only in Mexico but in other countries. They were interested above all in maintaining the control they exercised over their local district. For a time it even seemed that some local leaders such as Chao had begun to negotiate with the Huerta government for some kind of a deal whereby federal troops would leave them alone and they in turn would not attack the government units.[32] According to one historian, Chao even received some subsidies from the federal government.[33] Whether this indicated a real desire for negotiations or was just a clever deception is difficult to say.

In September 1913, only a few months after most local chieftains in Chihuahua had made a show of independence and refused to heed Villa's command and to subordinate their troops to any supreme leader, they elected Villa as commander of the Chihuahuan revolutionary army. It came to be known as the División del Norte and became subordinate to him in a way that for most of them would have been unthinkable only a few months earlier.

The primary cause for this dramatic change of attitude among the Chihuahuan revolutionaries was the irresistible rise in Villa's popularity and strength. There were several reasons for this. The first was that he chose to operate not in his traditional haunts in Durango and southern Chihuahua but mainly, although not exclusively, in the northwestern part of the state. This was no coincidence. In his former hunting grounds in Durango, his former partner and lieutenant Tomás Urbina held sway and showed no sign of being ready to subordinate his forces to Villa. The same held true for Manuel Chao in Parral. Northwestern Chihuahua held many advantages for Villa. It was the center of the military colonists who had constituted the backbone of the Maderista army in Chihuahua. In spite of the fact that Orozco came from the region, many of its inhabitants had remained loyal to Gonzáles and Madero during the Orozco rebellion, and many more had been disillusioned by Orozco's behavior. Villa had established many contacts with inhabitants of northwestern Chihuahua in the 1910–11 and 1912 campaigns. Northwestern Chihuahua was also close to the U.S. border, and American arms would thus readily be accessible to Villa. Another advantage that the region presented was that no other Maderista leader was currently operating there.

In order to gain support in a region where he both had only operated for a limited amount of time and had no strong family ties, as well as elsewhere in Chihuahua, Villa undertook an original political campaign. He did not issue the traditional manifesto that was the hallmark of rebellious Mexican politicians. It was not his style, and it is doubtful whether it would have had much impact on the Chihuahuan countryfolk. Nor could he do what the Maderista revolutionaries, including Villa himself, had done two years earlier: replace unpopular local mayors, judges and officials, and jefes políticos with popular local men. Most of this work had already been done during the Madero administration. Huerta had often not had time to replace them with his own men yet, and where he had done so, Villa restored the Maderista authorities. What Villa now carried out in many parts of Chihuahua were Robin Hood–type acts of social justice that strongly appealed to the sense of fairness and justice of Chihuahua's rural population. A few days after his arrival in Mexico, he occupied one of the largest Terrazas haciendas in Chihuahua, the estate of El Carmen. Its administrator was particularly unpopular among the estate's peons. Not only did he claim for himself the right to sleep with the peons' wives the first night after their marriage, but he was also notorious for having recalcitrant peons lashed to stakes outside the main building of the hacienda. Debt peonage, largely abolished in many parts of Chihuahua, still existed on this estate, and the debts of parents were transmitted to their children. Villa publicly executed both the administrator and an aide, opened up the granaries of the hacienda, and distributed large amounts of food to the peons. He made a speech to the assembled estate laborers, telling them not to tolerate similar treatment in the future and to elect a representative who would oversee the distribution of food from hacienda provisions. He carried out similar acts of retribution and redistribution on the estates of San Lorenzo and Las Animas at Saucito, where the increasingly familiar cry of "Viva Villa!" was accompanied by "May God shield and protect you!"[34]

In the town of Satevo, it was not an estate administrator but the local priest who became the object of Villa's wrath. A young girl came up to Villa after he had occupied the town and bitterly complained that the priest had locked her up in his church and raped her. Moreover, she said, he refused to recognize the child he had fathered, asserting that its real father was Pancho Villa. When Villa had the priest brought before him, the latter at first denied any responsibility, either for the child or for the allegation that Villa was its father. Villa felt he had irrefutable proof: the child had the priest's head and protruding ears. When the priest caved in and confessed, Villa ordered him shot. Unlike in the case of the administrator of El Carmen, however, whose execution had been greeted with joy by the estate's peons, the priest still enjoyed great popularity among the inhabitants, above all among the women. Hundreds came to Villa and begged for the priest's life. Villa agreed to spare him if he made a public confession in the town square. From the church pulpit, in the presence of a large number of Satevo's inhabitants, the humiliated priest accordingly repented his sins of the flesh.[35]

Acts of redistribution were at least as frequent as acts of retribution. In San Andrés, which had practically been Villa's home base during the Madero revolution, large amounts of food were distributed to the population after Villa captured the town.[36] And when he occupied Camargo, Villa confiscated all the goods in the large store of Sordo y Blanco, which belonged to Spanish merchants, distributed much of the food among the soldiers, and sold the rest at low prices to the townspeople.[37]

Another reason for Villa's popularity was his relentless pursuit of bandits. The constant fighting that had taken place in Chihuahua had caused a breakdown of both traditional and revolutionary authority, leading to the rise of what might best be described as pure banditry. Many of those involved were Orozquistas, who found crime far more attractive than fighting for a cause that offered fewer and fewer rewards. Alden Buell Case, an American Protestant missionary who spent most of the revolution at his mission in the Valle de Buenaventura in Chihuahua, described the whole region by the end of 1912 and the beginning of 1913 as

infested by bands of Colorados [red flaggers, or Orozquistas] who although often led by "generals," "colonels," and "captains," continually occupied themselves in works of destruction and robbery rather than in fighting which they avoided . . . Villa . . . was especially energetic and effective in his hostility to the bandit elements wherever en countered. The "Colorados" who refused to accept amnesty in laying down their arms or joining his own troops, were treated as outlaws and hunted down like beasts. Never had Porfirio Díaz in the days of his iron rule exhibited more relentless vigor or success in the suppression of brigandage than Francisco Villa in the brief era of his supremacy.[38]

Villa did not limit his protection from banditry to Mexicans. Even at this early stage of his career, when he had not yet established relations with the U.S. authorities, Villa was intent on protecting American properties. He wanted to prevent a possible U.S. intervention and to gain access to American arms. This attitude was clearly evident in his dealings with a bandit named Francisco Moreno, known as El Mocho. El Mocho had killed an American named Griffin, and Villa decided to have him shot. As he was being led to his execution in front of a firing squad in the town of La Ascensión, which Villa had captured, he was allowed one last favor: the right to address most of the people of La Ascensión and Villa's soldiers who were stationed in the town. It was a favor Villa came to regret. In an eloquent speech, El Mocho told the soldiers "that they and he were fighting for the same cause—their rights—that he was being executed for killing a foreigner who had no more rights in Mexico than any of the Mexicans." The speech "excited the soldiers to such an extent that Villa was afraid to order his execution by the usual firing squad and . . . the execution was actually performed by two captains and a lieutenant."[39]

Another man whom Villa treated like a bandit was nothing of the sort. This was Máximo Castillo, the one genuine Zapatista that Chihuahua produced. Although he himself does not seem to have had any serious grievances against the Creel administration—there is no evidence that the small ranch he owned in San Nicolás de Carretas had ever been confiscated—land reform was his main aim when he joined the revolution. After acting as Madero's bodyguard during the battle of Casas Grandes and practically saving his life, he became disillusioned when the Mexican president refused to carry out land reform. Castillo joined Orozco, became disillusioned with Orozco as well when no reforms were forthcoming, and began a campaign of large-scale redistribution, above all of Terrazas haciendas, on his own.

In the short term, Villa did not want these estates broken up, however, since he hoped to use them to finance his army. What bothered him even more was that Castillo refused to recognize the need to conciliate the United States, which Villa considered crucial to the success of the revolution. Instead, Castillo began demanding large sums of money for his army from American and other foreign-owned companies, singling out the Mormons.[40]

In view of Castillo's Orozquista past, Villa felt no loyalty to him and did not see fighting him as waging civil war against another bona fide revolutionary. He ruthlessly pursued Castillo, wiped out most of his supporters, and forced him to seek asylum in the United States.

Villa not only pursued men considered to be bandits but enforced the strictest discipline among his own troops. These actions created an impression of respectability that allowed him to shed his image as a bandit. Villa became so popular in Chihuahua that he had no trouble finding and recruiting volunteers for his army. His main problem was obtaining arms to equip his men and money to pay them. In this respect, Villa's capacity for organization was supplemented by luck. Only a few weeks after he reentered Mexico, he captured a train carrying a large amount of silver, with which he proceeded to buy arms and ammunition in the United States. This was no easy undertaking, since the U.S. government had banned arms sales to Mexico. In view of the length of the border and the limited number of U.S. officials guarding it, however, this embargo was practically unenforceable. In addition, many American arms dealers, eager to sell their products, sometimes helped in the smuggling. Local officials sympathetic to the revolution, or simply sympathetic to business, frequently closed their eyes to contraband arms. "Hundreds of Mexicans, among them women and children" smuggled munitions. "For this work," the El Paso Times reported, "they received $8.00 per 1,000 for cartridges and when only 50 or 100 were smuggled they received 2¢ and 3¢ a cartridge."[41]

At some point, the Woodrow Wilson administration, increasingly hostile to the Huerta regime, became more and more lax in its enforcement of the arms embargo against the Mexican revolutionaries. While smuggling in the first weeks of the revolution was a small-scale affair carried out by local volunteers, many of them women, its organization was soon taken over by a revolutionary junta in El Paso composed mainly of intellectual supporters of Madero's, such as the newspaperman Silvestre Terrazas and Aureliano González, Abraham González's deputy, who had fled from Chihuahua after Huerta's coup.

A piece of luck provided Villa with a man capable of training his troops. This was a former federal officer, Juan Medina, who had joined Villa and turned out to be an extremely effective instructor of both the men and the officers of Villa's army in the art of warfare. Only three months after his arrival in Mexico, Villa led what was considered a substantial force by Chihuahuan standards: 700 well-trained and well-equipped men. A few weeks later, when Toribio Ortega, who commanded 500 men, decided to place himself under Villa's direct orders, it became the largest revolutionary force in the state.[42]

It is not clear what prompted Ortega's decision. It may have been that unlike some of the other Chihuahuan leaders, such as Chao or Urbina, Ortega never aspired to lead the revolutionary movement in the whole state. He came closest to being what might be labeled the classic peasant leader produced by the Chihuahuan revolution, and Villa probably seemed to offer the best guarantee that the old order would not return to his native village of Cuchillo Parado and the other villages from which his force had been recruited. His men and his prestige proved a great boon to Villa.

Nevertheless, Ortega's support was at first insufficient to ensure Villa's preeminence in Chihuahua. In the first month after he returned to Chihuahua, his military successes by no means overshadowed those of other leaders in the state.

When Villa first captured an important town in Chihuahua, Nuevas Casas Grandes, in June 1913, Chao had already occupied the much larger city of Parral. In contrast to leaders who managed to maintain control over the towns they had occupied, Villa did not hold on to Nuevas Casas Grandes for long. The most significant victory he did score, the capture of San Andrés and the defeat of a government force of over 1,300 men led by General Félix Terrazas in August 1913, was dwarfed by a more important victory achieved several months earlier, in June 1913, by a coalition of revolutionary troops from Durango led by Urbina, who had stormed and sacked the capital city of Durango, held by large contingents of federal troops.

The relatively large number of men Villa controlled was perhaps a more impressive credential in the eyes of these leaders than his military operations. Nevertheless, all of this would not have convinced the semi-autonomous military chieftains of the north to place their men under someone else's control and to limit their newly acquired power. What influenced them most was a conviction best summed up by Benjamin Franklin when he said of the American revolutionaries of 1776: "We must all hang together, or assuredly we shall all hang separately."

In July 1913, the federal government had initiated a counteroffensive that shattered the self-confidence of many northern revolutionary leaders, especially those in the south of Chihuahua, who had been most obstinate in refusing to subordinate their troops to any higher command. At that time, Pascual Orozco, whose commitment to the Huerta regime never waned, was sent together with 1,000 men from the government-controlled city of Torreón to reinforce the federal garrison in Ciudad Chihuahua. In order to reach the state capital, he had to march through the southern part of Chihuahua held by the revolutionary contingents of Chao, Rosalio Hernández, and Trinidad Rodríguez. Although the revolutionaries outnumbered his men, Orozco showed that his military capacities were no less formidable than in 1911, when he inflicted defeat after defeat on the federal troops. This time he smashed through the revolutionary forces. He defeated Rosalio Hernández in Ciudad Camargo, killed 170 revolutionaries in Mapula, on July 11 captured a supply train from the constitutionalists, and finally obtained his greatest triumph when he defeated the troops of both Manuel Chao and Trinidad Rodríguez in Santa Rosalia.[43] A few days later, he entered Ciudad Chihuahua in triumph.

In August 1913, a new dimension was added to the federal counteroffensive. The Chihuahuan hacendados were directly mobilized as participants in the counterrevolution. Every hacendado was required to send a contingent of ten men to reinforce the federal troops.[44]

These measures finally convinced the revolutionary commanders in both Chihuahua and Durango that they had no choice but to unite under a common commander. The identity of that commander was not a foregone conclusion. Carranza's choice was Manuel Chao. While nominally recognizing Carranza's leadership, however, the revolutionary chieftains of Chihuahua and Durango were unwilling to allow him to make that kind of a decision. The majority supported Villa, who spared them the embarrassment of having to choose between him and Chao by personally "convincing" Chao to withdraw his candidacy. As described by a confidant of Villa's, the confrontation between the two men was the stuff of

Hollywood cowboy movies. They met at Jiménez, where Villa asked Chao to recognize him as supreme commander.

When he hears Villa, Chao becomes red in the face; he does not like Villa's proposal,
becomes less and less diplomatic and more and more irritable. He finally decides to
answer Villa by putting his hand on his pistol holster; he does not see that Villa's
movements are far more rapid than his, and suddenly Villa's gun is pointed at his
chest and two piercing eyes intimidate him. He now gently listens to Villa's arguments, and the latter suddenly becomes very friendly; he embraces him and calls him
by his first name and treats him like a boy who has been naughty and now regrets
what he has done.[45]

Chao's withdrawal was not only owing to Villa's powers of persuasion. A soft-
spoken schoolteacher of middle-class origin, he could not have competed with
Villa's immense popularity. Chao also lacked the traditional network of personal
and family ties that had, for example, helped Abraham González, who had also
been of middle-class origin. He did not even come from Chihuahua but had
been born on the Atlantic coast near Tampico.

Villa had another rival for the post of supreme commander who, like Villa,
came from the popular classes and whose military successes in the 1913 revolution had been greater than those of his erstwhile chief. This was Tomás Urbina.
Under his leadership, the revolutionaries from Durango had scored their greatest
success, the capture of the capital city of Durango. It was precisely this victory,
however, which bore all the hallmarks of Urbina's style, that led most revolutionary chieftains in the north to oppose him. The capture of Ciudad Durango had
been followed by an orgy of killing and plunder. "The victorious army, of about
8,000 men entered the city without order, without leaders," Pastor Rouaix, one of
the main revolutionary leaders in Durango sadly wrote,

and, like an avalanche that descends from the mountain, fused their forces with those
of the lower classes, full of desires for vengeance, destruction, and plunder, and began
to assault stores, carrying out shameful acts of plunder, while other groups, animated
by the natural lack of confidence of the peasants, were shooting at fictitious enemies,
and dynamite explosions and rifle fire could constantly be heard. The sack of the city
was followed by fire, and the night of June 19 was more horrendous than the day of
combat, since the city was lighted by the sinister glow of the flames that had engulfed
twelve of the main stores in the city.[46]

These reprisals had not been unprovoked. Durango was one of the few cities
where the upper classes had decided take up arms themselves and not leave all
the fighting to federal troops or mercenaries. They had constituted a military unit
called the Defensa Social, which had not only fought the besieging revolutionary
troops but had begun to execute revolutionary sympathizers inside the city. This
sparked ferocious reprisals by the revolutionaries.

It became increasingly clear to the revolutionary chieftains of the north that
they could not afford another victory like Durango. It would cost them whatever
middle-class support they had, and more to the point in Chihuahua, which was
so close to the U.S. border and contained such large American investments, such
an undisciplined orgy of looting might very well provoke U.S. intervention. If

there was one thing that Villa had always been noted for, in contrast to Urbina, it was the discipline he was able to instill into his troops.

The Formation of the División del Norte and Villa's First Capture of Torreón

On September 26, 1913, the main military commanders of Durango and Chihuahua met in the town of Jiménez and elected Villa to command them in an expedition whose aim was to capture Torreón, one of the most important and wealthiest cities in Mexico. Since Torreón was also the hub of railway communications in the north, taking it would provide the revolutionaries with supplies and money for their troops, while helping to cut off supplies to the federal forces in Chihuahua.

Apart from the growing belief that unity was their only means of survival, there was another factor that helped persuade the Chihuahuan revolutionaries to accept Villa's leadership. This was the possibility of joining forces with an even larger contingent of revolutionaries: the men from the Laguna area of Coahuila and Durango, as well as revolutionaries from other parts of Durango. For these men, Torreón was the key to the control of their region. Since July 1913, they had vainly attempted to capture this well-fortified city and had been repulsed with enormous losses. They now called on Villa to bring up reinforcements and offered him the leadership of the combined attack. Torreón was at least as important for the Chihuahuan revolutionaries as for the men from the Laguna and Durango, inasmuch as all the federal reinforcements from central Mexico to Chihuahua passed through Torreón.

Taking "the pearl of the Laguna," as Torreón was called, offered Villa substantial benefits. In addition to assuring him of control of Chihuahua, it would give an additional boost to his prestige, since Carranza had failed to capture Torreón when he assumed the leadership of the besieging army in July. Villa would have 6,000 to 8,000 men under his command, a force far larger than any he had ever commanded before, and one of the largest, if not the largest, of the revolutionary armies, and Torreón itself would put huge financial means at his disposal, allowing him to arm and equip his army.

The risks of this operation were also enormous. Villa had never led an army of that size. He had little experience in waging regular warfare; on the few occasions when he had done so, it had been under other commanders. He lacked one of the main prerequisites for an attack on a large city: a strong and well-organized artillery. He only had two cannon, which his troops had captured in San Andrés, and he had scarcely any well-trained artillerymen to service them. In addition, the revolutionary troops from the Laguna and Durango were notorious for their lack of discipline.

This lack of discipline was one of the main reasons why Carranza had been unable to capture Torreón and had given up hope of leading these men, proceeding to Sonora instead. When an officer of Carranza's staff had attempted to stem a rout of Calixto Contreras's troops by shooting two of their panic-stricken officers, who were leading the flight, the revolutionaries had threatened Carranza's life if he did not hand his officer over to them to be executed.[47]

A potentially even greater risk for Villa, although it is not clear to what degree he was conscious of it, was a plan by the federal army to take advantage of the siege of Torreón to destroy the core of Villa's División del Norte. The federal commander in Chihuahua, Salvador Mercado, had sent out a large contingent of troops under General Castro with a view to catching the revolutionaries in a kind of pincer movement. Mercado assumed that after having been as unsuccessful in capturing Torreón as they had been in July, the weakened and demoralized revolutionaries would retreat northward. There they would meet Castro's large contingent and be cut to pieces by his superior artillery and the superior discipline and organization of his troops.[48]

In less than a week, Villa was able to overcome every obstacle he faced, to capture Torreón, and to bring to naught the federal plan to destroy his forces. Within a few weeks, he would gain control of all of Chihuahua.

His success was owing to his strategy, to the control he was able to assume over his men, and to the ineptness and cowardice of the federal commanders. Further aiding him was the unwillingness of many of the federal troops, particularly the conscripts from southern Mexico, to fight.

The federal commander in Torreón, General Eutiquio Munguía, so overestimated his own strength and so underestimated the fighting capacity of the revolutionaries that he sent one of his generals, Felipe Alvírez, with 500 men to the town of Avíles on the outskirts of Torreón to attack a far larger contingent of revolutionaries. Alvírez's force was cut to pieces, and he died in the battle along with most of his command. Munguía desperately attempted to keep this news from his men, but it spread to Torreón, and the federal forces became demoralized.

Munguía had pinned his hopes for victory on the superiority of his artillery, which he had stationed on a series of hills surrounding the approaches to Torreón to pour fire on the advancing revolutionaries. Instead, in a series of night attacks, which were to be a hallmark of his strategy, Villa and his troops overran one hilltop after another, capturing the federal guns. Once the hilltops and the artillery stationed there were in Villa's hands, the situation of the defenders of Torreón had become critical. At this juncture, Munguía not only decided not to defend the city but did not even attempt an orderly retreat. His forces fled in panic. He did so at the same time that he ordered a subordinate general, Luis G. Anaya, to counterattack and recover the hills that the revolutionaries had occupied. Anaya in fact scored initial successes and attempted to persuade Munguía to send him further reinforcements. Anaya later reported to Huerta's Ministry of War:

When the fighting had subsided for a moment, I went to the San Carlos hotel to inform the commanding general of the situation, but I did not find him and was told by one of his subordinates that he had left by car at 5 P.M. and had not returned; I immediately went to the headquarters of the 5th regiment to see whether there was any information there about the whereabouts of General Munguía, but to my great surprise, I found the headquarters abandoned; I went [back] to the San Carlos hotel and found it empty too, and no one knew where the general was.[49]

A federal court-martial later convicted Munguía of cowardice.

Federal General Castro, who was advancing on Torreón from the north, proved to be at least as inept, although not as cowardly, as Munguía. He had placed his artillery in such a way that its first shells decimated his own infantry and nearly provoked a rebellion. He failed to capture the city of Camargo, garrisoned by a much smaller force of revolutionaries. Nothing is more revealing of the problems and the structure of Huerta's federal army than the report on Castro's activities by his superior in Chihuahua, General Mercado:

Unfortunately, the command of operation was in the hands of General Castro, a leader who lacks the most elementary military knowledge and the most rudimentary instruction. It may be asked why, knowing of Castro's ineptitude, I allowed him to assume command of the expeditionary force. I simply did so because military law demands it, since his rank was superior to that of all the other officers who led this force, and one has to respect the law in order to be able to judge the men by it.[50]

Yet federal ineptitude was not the only reason, perhaps not even the main reason, for Villa's success in Torreón. After all, only a few months earlier, the same officers had successfully repelled a revolutionary attack on the town. Villa succeeded because of the strategy he adopted and his ability to transform groups of men who had little military training, and even fewer traditions of discipline, into a well-organized, highly disciplined whole. His strategy of relentless attacks by day and by night overcame the federal fortifications and superiority in artillery and finally demoralized both the federal officers and their men. Villa could be far more drastic in imposing discipline than Carranza ever was. He had no compunction about shooting on sight men or officers he suspected of cowardice or of disobeying his orders. Nevertheless, the revolutionary peasants of Durango as well as his own contingents in Chihuahua accepted this without protest. He was one of their own, and they felt that he had a right to take such measures. The kind of discipline he was able to impose upon his troops came out most clearly when he occupied Torreón. Many of the men who now entered this richest city in northern Mexico thought they could repeat what they had done only a few months previously when they had sacked, looted, and pillaged the city of Durango.

When the first revolutionary troops entered Torreón on the night of October 1, the inhabitants' direst fears of robbery and pillage seemed about to be confirmed. "During the night, a number of stores on Calle Ramos Arizpe and Avenida Hidalgo were almost totally sacked and several others partially sacked," George Carothers, the U.S. consul in Torreón, reported. "I visited these places personally and traces of the rebels were everywhere—old hats, shoes and clothing left on the floor, showing the clothing had been substituted where they were sacking." Within only a few hours, according to Carothers, the situation had completely and dramatically changed:

At eleven o'clock, I went in a carriage through the city on a tour of inspection . . . splendid order prevailed in the city at that time. There were guards placed at all the stores that had been sacked or partially sacked, and the order was out to shoot anyone who attempted to steal anything. I consider that 500,000 pesos will cover the actual loss from sacking. This is less than five percent of what was expected by the people of Torreón in the event of the capture of the city, and everyone expressed great praise of General Villa as a leader in being able to maintain such order.[51]

These impressions were shared by U.S. Consul Walter C. Hamm from Durango, who had been in that city when the revolutionaries had stormed and sacked it, and who had now gone to Torreón to inspect the situation there:

Upon my arrival in Torreón on the 9th instant, I was no little surprised at the almost perfect order which prevailed, and by the fact that business was being transacted under conditions approaching the normal, and could not help to contrast the complete desolation of Durango with the few evidences of destruction and violence visible in Torreón. Several stores were more or less completely sacked during the first flush of victory, but this was quickly stopped by General Villa and the other leaders and very fair discipline established. Practically the only buildings burnt were those ordered set on fire by federal officers before abandoning the city for the purpose of destroying munitions of war.[52]

In some respects, Villa's occupation of Torreón was his calling card to the world. Much of that world, both Mexican and American, was pleasantly surprised. This was not the brutal, ignorant bandit indiscriminately looting and pillaging whom many had expected. The U.S. representatives praised not only the order he kept but even more the way he attempted to protect Americans. Consul Hamm lauded Villa for having "shown himself very well disposed towards Americans and their interests."[53]

Another of Villa's policies made a very different impression upon both domestic and foreign observers: that of executing all federal officers, and all Orozquistas, whom he took prisoner (federal enlisted men had the option of joining Villa's army, and sometimes he even freed them). The U.S. publication *Review of Reviews* reacted to these executions in a way that was characteristic of many foreigners, saying, "the Constitutionalists have disgraced their cause."[54] Many defenders of the revolution reacted by either denying that such executions were taking place or by stating that unfortunately they were commonplace and routine in Mexico.

Execution of prisoners was in fact the norm on both sides during this second Mexican revolution, but it had not been characteristic of the Madero revolution only a short time before. The great majority of prisoners taken by the Madero forces had not been executed, and even the federal army had only sporadically killed its prisoners. It will be recalled that one of the reasons that Villa and Orozco had rebelled against Madero in Ciudad Juárez in 1911 and had asked for the execution of the federal General Navarro was precisely that the latter had violated what they considered a unspoken norm of warfare by killing his prisoners.

One of the main reasons for the "gentleness" of the Madero revolution was the assumption on both sides that some kind of compromise would finally be found. After his victory, Madero continued to believe that all Mexico's problems could be settled by reasonable men in a reasonable way with a minimum of violence. This attitude, as well as his personal gentleness, led him to reprieve all upper-class and middle-class opponents of his regime who plotted against him or carried out uprisings. Instead of being shot, Félix Díaz and Bernardo Reyes were incarcerated in comfortable conditions in a military prison. Madero was less gentle toward his radical lower-class opponents, and for several months federal troops carried out search-and-destroy operations against Zapata's forces in Morelos. But Madero eventually changed his policies in Morelos too, sending General Felipe Angeles to replace Juvencio Robles, whose policy had involved wholesale deportations and executions. Angeles waged the war against Zapata in a much more humane way, largely sparing both the civilian population and the prisoners he took (see below).

The federal officers who took power in early 1913 felt that no compromise could or should be reached with the revolutionaries, and that in order to win, they had to wage a war of extermination. The brutal executions of Madero, Pino Suárez, and Abraham González, which contrasted so sharply with the way these men had treated their opponents, were only the tip of the iceberg.

This was characteristic of the way the Huerta regime treated both its civilian and military opponents. The German minister to Mexico, Paul von Hintze, who was quite favorably disposed toward Huerta, painted a gaudy picture of nightly executions of opponents of the regime:

The phantoms of those executed each night are stalking Huerta. After making some careless remarks, Huerta's collaborator the former governor of the Federal District, was taken in February 1913 from the president's chambers to the suburb of Tlalpam and was killed without ceremony. The leader of the Catholic party, Somellera, was first detained in San Juan de Ulúa, then freed, but was forced, under threat of death, to hand over a considerable sum of money and to leave immediately for Europe. The methods of the government correspond roughly to those employed in Venice in the early Middle Ages, and we could look upon them with equanimity were they not occasionally extended to foreigners.[55]

John Lind, Woodrow Wilson's special representative to Mexico, painted an equally grim picture of the way Huerta's army treated its prisoners. Since, unlike the German minister, he strongly opposed Huerta, the tone of his description is much more hostile, but the substance is very similar. "Reporting on Villa's executions of prisoners," he wrote Wilson,

his [Villa's] acts in this regard should be judged by Mexican standards. In so far as he allowed any captives to escape death, to that extent he is more humane than the commanders of the federal forces. They murder all captives. After six months of continuous warfare, there is not one constitutionalist commander in a federal prison. Explanation is those captured have been shot, every one. Likewise, the privates, except that in a few instances their lives have been spared on condition that they enter the federal service. The federals shot over thirty rebels in their cots in the hospital at Gómez Palacio in the presence of an American doctor. Blood covered the floor an inch deep. You wonder why these things had not been reported. I have not had time to report all. Isolated instances would only minimize the viciousness of the whole. The federals, where they have captured towns in which there were no *científicos* to be injured, have razed and destroyed every home and every structure. They have shot or hanged all the men and sent the women and children into captivity.[56]

The Orozquistas, who were fighting on Huerta's side, seem to have been particularly brutal in this respect. A detachment of Orozco's forces was sent to a plant of the American Smelting and Refinery Company, located in the Laguna region of Mexico, to protect it from revolutionary attacks.

The second in command of the irregulars one of the plant managers reported was hospitably entertained at ASARCO, then had a prisoner brought up to the Club of the Americans where he was drinking, and guilty or innocent, put him up against the wall amongst the houses, shot him badly with his own hand, then continued to pump bullets into the squirming body. . . . To give further proof of valor he returned drunk that evening and shot out the lights in the scale house inside the plant, went through the peons' houses like a scourge of God and ended with a naked dance in Pedriceña where all manner of obscenities were committed.[57]

The reaction of the revolutionaries was no less violent and bloody. Soon after assuming the leadership of the revolution, Carranza declared Benito Juárez's law of January 25, 1862, mandating the execution of anyone caught fighting against the Mexican republic was again to be applied. As a result, the execution of prisoners became the rule rather than the exception for most revolutionary commanders. Many of these commanders, while accepting the need to shoot prisoners, were shocked when they actually witnessed such executions. Describing the aftermath of the battle of San Andrés, where a federal column under General Félix Terrazas had been cut to pieces by Villa, a revolutionary officer reported on the scenes of horror that followed:

Terrazas's column was completely destroyed. Of the 900 men, only he and about 30 others were able to escape and make it back to Ciudad Chihuahua. Those who did not die in battle were either taken to the execution ground or departed, never to rejoin the traitors again. The next day witnessed a macabre, Dantesque spectacle. Enormous piles of human flesh were erected, covered with firewood, and set alight. Rigid hands, fists clenched, were raised to heaven, as though gesturing despairingly. There were craniums with eyes bulging out of their sockets, scorched hair, half-burnt intestines gaping out of bellies, and trunks separated from the rest of the body.[58]

Neither Carranza nor Villa seems to have shared the shock that this officer of the revolutionary army experienced when he heard and witnessed these executions. Villa regularly sent reports to Carranza such as the one he dispatched to the revolutionary chieftain after the capture of Torreón stating that "nineteen prisoners were taken, who were all executed in accordance with the law of January 25, 1862, which was declared to be valid by the supreme leader of the constitutionalist army."[59]

Carranza objected only once to such a report by Villa, when the latter wrote him that he had spared some prisoners who were artillerymen, whom he wanted to use in his own army. "I have seen the decree of amnesty that you issued," he wrote Villa, "and I am writing you to tell you that it is wrong to give any amnesty now to those affected by the law of January 25, 1862."[60]

Carranza made his position with respect to execution clear in responding to a protest by the governor of Arizona, W. B. Hunt, against Villa's shooting of federal officers whom he had captured in Ciudad Juárez only a few months after the capture of Torreón. Hunt's letter had protested the killing of unarmed prisoners and declared that "the continuation of summary executions by insurgent commanders would horrify the people of the United States and alienate their sympathies." In his reply, Carranza assumed full responsibility for the executions and declared that it was he who had revived Juárez's law of January 25, 1862, considering all those who were fighting against the legitimate Mexican government as subject to execution. He emphasized that the federal army not only had attempted to destroy all legitimate democratic institutions in Mexico but was also executing all prisoners it took. "It is true," he wrote,

that the established principles observed in international war grant to prisoners the privilege of pardon or immunity from bodily harm, but in civil struggles the most civilized nations at all ages have employed more rigorous and bloody means even than the ones we have been compelled to adopt. And with reference to the executions of the officers in the city of Juárez, these should be perceived not as any needless cruelty visited upon prisoners of war, but merely such punishment as was prescribed by the law applicable to offenders against the public peace and safety.

The Mexican people in the beginning of this civil struggle initiated by Francisco I. Madero exhausted all their powers of clemency and forgiveness but experienced as the only result of their magnanimity tyranny in their country's interior, the loss of prestige outside of its borders.[61]

While Villa's executions of prisoners were no exception, he tended to be more brutal and more open about them than other revolutionary leaders. In one of the most memorable and gruesome scenes in Mexican literature, Martín Luis Guzmán, one of Mexico's greatest writers, who fought alongside Pancho Villa, describes how one of Villa's henchmen, Rodolfo Fierro, personally executed hundreds of Orozquista prisoners.[62]

Villa did not kill all the prisoners. He concentrated his hatred on Orozquistas and federal officers and frequently spared enlisted soldiers who had been impressed into the federal army and were willing to join his own forces. He also spared men who had a particular knowledge he could utilize for his own army, such as artillerymen. When one of his most brutal commanders, Tomás Urbina, captured a federal military band and applied for authorization to execute all of its members, Villa refused, saying that they could be used to constitute a revolutionary band. Urbina insisted, stating that the revolutionary army already had many bands and did not need one more. Villa prevailed, however, and the musicians were set free and incorporated into the revolutionary army.[63]

What differentiated Villa from other revolutionary commanders is that whereas they tended to carry out executions in the dead of the night, he did so openly. One day, while Villa was having lunch with his secretary and with a high official of Carranza's government, Jesús Acuña, his men brought two captured Huerta officers into his presence, and Villa ordered them to be shot immediately. He not only refused to heed the pleas of one of the officers, who begged for his life, saying that he was ill and that it was in order to support his family that he had enlisted in the army, but also rejected a request by Acuña that if the executions were to be carried out, it should not be done in his presence. "Villa," his secretary remembered, "replied that he could not accede to his wishes, that this order had to be summarily carried out; that it was very hard to have to do this, but that our struggle was without quarter, and that if unfortunately we had fallen into the hands of the enemy, we would have undergone the same fate. The order was carried out in our presence, and we went on to eat as if nothing had happened."[64]

The Capture of Ciudad Juárez
and Villa's Occupation of Chihuahua

Villa's victory in Torreón provided him with larger amounts of arms and enabled him to add a potent artillery section to his army. His troops had only possessed two cannons when they attacked the town. He now captured eleven cannons, among them the largest piece of artillery used in the northern campaign, which was to become the centerpiece of Villa's artillery, a huge gun known as El Niño. In addition to the small arms and ammunition he captured, Villa imposed forced loans amounting to three million pesos upon the rich in Torreón, especially targeting the banks. The banks tried to elude this by giving him checks drawn on U.S. banks, which the latter refused to honor. Very clearly articulated threats by Villa finally persuaded the bankers to comply.

The capture of Torreón not only provided Villa with national and international prestige, it also marked a turning point in the history of his movement and of the revolution as a whole. In an important part of Mexico, guerrilla warfare would be replaced by regular warfare, guerrilla forces would be transformed into a regular army, and the revolutionaries would exercise real power over a vast and wealthy territory. It was a result neither the federal government nor most foreign and domestic observers in Mexico had anticipated, and even after Villa's occupation of Torreón, they continued to believe that nothing would really change and that his victory had in fact been a fluke. It was owing, they felt, to the cowardice and incapacity of a few elderly federal generals; fresh contingents of federal troops under more capable generals should easily be able to reverse the tide. After all, with one exception, the revolutionaries had never been able to hold onto large territories, especially to a big city. Carranza had lost control of most of his native state of Coahuila, and his general, Pablo González, who led the remnants of the state's troops, was making little headway. While Zapata controlled large parts of rural Morelos, he had not managed to control any major cities. The lone exception was Sonora, where Alvaro Obregón had been able to assume control of much of the state. But Sonora was sui generis. It was so isolated from the rest of Mexico that federal reinforcements could only be sent either by sea or through the United States.

The revolutionaries, the federal government as well as many foreign observers felt, would never be able to unite. Even in Sonora, dissension had broken out between various factions vying for power. In spite of his enormous popularity and personal appeal, Madero had never been able to control his adherents effectively in the 1910–11 revolution. Many of his nominal Chihuahuan supporters had refused to join him in the attack on Casas Grandes and had attacked Ciudad Juárez against his express orders; some of his contingents had even attempted to rebel against him after the capture of that border city. His whole administration had been plagued by unrest and dissension among his supporters. Why should things be different now? The heterogeneous array of revolutionaries that had captured Torreón, the government hoped, would soon fall apart. After all, many of these troops, especially the contingents from the Laguna, were notorious for their lack of discipline. Some of their commanders, such as Calixto Contreras, had great difficulty in enforcing their authority. But even in those cases where the troops did obey their commanders, most revolutionary officers were averse to submitting to command. They might do so temporarily for a particular military expedition, but they had never done so on a regular basis. Neither Francisco Madero nor his brother Emilio, who had been in nominal command of these troops during the Madero revolution, nor Venustiano Carranza, whom the revolutionaries recognized as the supreme commander in the summer of 1913, had been able to impose their authority on these recalcitrant soldiers and officers. Why should a semiliterate former peon and bandit like Villa, with no formal military training, with scarcely any education, without political experience and knowledge, be successful where all others had failed? As soon as Villa suffered his first defeat, which the federal government felt was inevitable, his army would fall apart and he would revert to leading the life of a bandit or a local guerrilla chief at best.

Villa's next military actions seemed to confirm the Huerta regime's optimism and many observers' skepticism about his military capacities. He was now set on capturing Ciudad Chihuahua in the same way that he had captured Torreón, by a series of frontal attacks. He proceeded to try to do so in spite of the warnings of a number of his military commanders that not only was Mercado, who commanded the federal troops in Chihuahua, a better and braver general than the hapless Munguía, who had fled in panic from Torreón, but the troops making up the garrison of Ciudad Chihuahua were different from those he had faced at the "pearl of the Laguna." Munguía's army had consisted largely of unwilling southern conscripts, whereas battle-hardened Orozquista veterans from the mountains of Chihuahua formed the bulk of Ciudad Chihuahua's garrison. In addition, the federal troops not only were well fortified but had a distinct superiority in artillery and far more ammunition at their disposal than Villa's troops.

Nevertheless, for three days, Villa attempted to storm Ciudad Chihuahua. Eventually, his attacks broke down in the face of withering fire from federal machine guns and artillery. When Villa finally decided to abandon the attack, the federal garrison in Chihuahua were triumphant, firmly convinced that they had broken the back of Villa's movement. Mercado reported to his superiors in Mexico City:

I have the honor to report to you that yesterday at 6 P.M., the enemy was expelled from his last positions and thrown back by our courageous troops to Mapula, where, under conditions of greatest confusion and disorder, they fled in trains, on foot, or on horses. . . . After our important triumph, bands of the heroic division of the north [the federal division of the north, which had the same name as Villa's División del Norte] marched through the streets of this city, hailed by the delirious enthusiasm of its inhabitants, since this music told them that they were free from murder, rape, and robbery, and they cheered the army, the minister of war, and the president of the republic.[65]

His defeat in Chihuahua was potentially a major blow both to Villa's leadership and to the revolutionary movement in Chihuahua and in the Laguna. It weakened Villa's authority and endangered the fragile unity he had created between the revolutionaries of Chihuahua and those of the Laguna and Durango. It now seemed to many federal commanders and to many observers that Villa had nowhere else to go. He could not proceed southward to attack the federal army in the center of the republic as long as he had to contend with the powerful federal garrison in Chihuahua. An attack northward by the revolutionaries against the border city of Ciudad Juárez, the largest urban agglomeration in Chihuahua, would be dangerous. Not only was the town well fortified, but it was located along the Rio Grande opposite El Paso. Shots fired during an attack on the city could easily cause casualties on the U.S. side of the border and lead to a U.S. intervention. Villa, who had been one of the Maderista commanders during the attack on Juárez in 1911, realized the difficulties he would face. He must also have realized that this time his situation might be more precarious than that of Madero two years earlier. When Madero had attacked and besieged the northern border city, he had no reason to fear an attack from federal troops coming from Ciudad Chihuahua. Its garrison was so weakened and demoralized that the federal commanders were not ready to leave the capital city. This time, Villa could be quite sure that federal troops from the south would march north toward Ciudad Juárez and attempt to envelop him in a pincer movement. After his devastating experience with federal artillery superiority in Ciudad Chihuahua, he must have been conscious of the great danger of being caught in a pincer movement between two contingents with far more firepower than he had. Nevertheless, he saw no other way to snatch victory from defeat than to attempt to attack the border city. At this point, luck and genius combined to allow Villa a victory that propelled him to world fame in a matter of days. He captured a train that ferried coal and other supplies between Ciudad Chihuahua and Ciudad Juárez and forced the conductor to wire his headquarters in Ciudad Juárez that Villa's troops were in the vicinity and ask for instructions on what he should do.

Predictably, headquarters told him to return immediately with his train, but to confirm his movements and the fact that he still controlled the train at every station along the way. Villa now loaded 2,000 of his men on the train and at every station, with Villista soldiers holding guns to their heads and a Villista telegrapher controlling the contents of the message, local telegraphers wired Ciudad Juárez that the train was on its way. The train, with its deadly load of 2,000 Villista soldiers, with Villa at their head, was thus allowed to proceed without hindrance into Ciudad Juárez itself. As a newspaper report from neighboring El Paso put it,

The attack upon and the capture of Juárez was a complete surprise. Pancho Villa and his command reported last night surrounding Chihuahua City, and the federal officers retired to their barracks believing themselves in absolute security. Shortly after two o'clock this morning, a freight train rolled into the Juárez yards over the Mexican Central, and from it poured hundreds of rebels. That the surprise was complete is proved by the fact that not a shot was fired until the rebels had penetrated into the very heart of the city. The train was allowed to proceed without interference. . . . Taken completely by surprise, the federal garrison made but little resistance. The cuartel fell by four o'-clock and the remainder of the city, with the exception of a group of volunteers in a house near the Juárez race tracks gave up their arms by five. This last group of defenders fought desperately and gave up only when their ammunition was exhausted.[66]

Not only were the defenders taken by surprise, but according to General Mercado, the supreme commander of all federal forces in Chihuahua, many officers and men of the garrison would have been incapable of resisting even if they had been warned in time. They were busily engaged in the many amenities Ciudad Juárez had to offer: its countless bars, brothels, and gambling joints.[67]

With the capture of Juárez, Villa's fame grew by leaps and bounds both in Mexico and north of the border. He was depicted by many newspapers in the United States as the greatest general and the greatest revolutionary in Mexico. They praised the discipline he kept in Ciudad Juárez but showed disgust and resentment at the executions of prisoners, which he made no effort to conceal. One of the few exceptions to his executions was the commander of the federal forces in Ciudad Juárez, General Francisco Castro, who had interceded with Huerta in order to save Villa's life in 1912.[68] Villa gave firm orders to his troops that he was not to be harmed and was to be allowed to cross unscathed into the United States.

While the capture of Ciudad Juárez increased both his fame and the morale of his troops and provided him with some additional funds and additional military matériel, it did not assure his final victory and domination over Chihuahua. In fact, in many respects his position seemed precarious.

In 1911, the capture of Ciudad Juárez by Madero had ended the armed phase of his revolution. By striking a deal with Madero, both the federal authorities and Mexico's upper classes had hoped to salvage by political means what they could no longer hold by military might. This time, neither Huerta nor the revolutionaries were ready for such a deal. The federal military authorities both in Mexico City and in Chihuahua were convinced that they could soon reverse the situation. A strong federal force under General Refugio Velasco was on the march toward Torreón, which they hoped to reconquer within a few weeks. The federal garrison of Ciudad Chihuahua, flushed by its recent triumph over Villa, felt that it could now take the offensive, and a large force set out to recapture Ciudad Juárez. Villa faced a difficult dilemma. Should he resist the federals in Juárez itself, or should he leave the city and fight elsewhere? The first alternative presented some advantages—Ciudad Juárez had been fortified by the federal army and these fortifications had fallen intact into Villa's hands; Villa's army would have all the advantages of a defensive position against an attacking outside force. But these potential advantages were outweighed by disadvantages. As always, a major battle along the U.S. border might cause casualties in neighboring El Paso and lead to U.S. military intervention. This might happen even if both sides did their best to avoid such casualties. It was all the more likely if the federals, as some observers suspected they would, purposely fired into El Paso to provoke an American attack on those troops closest to the U.S. border, namely, the Villistas in Ciudad Juárez. Another consideration that probably impelled Villa not to hold out in Ciudad Juárez was that his troops lacked both the ammunition and the provisions to withstand a long siege. What he needed was an immediate victory, and he decided the best way to achieve it and to minimize the risks of a U.S. intervention was to force the federals to fight thirty miles from Ciudad Juárez, near the small railway station of Tierra Blanca. "Long before dawn, on November 23rd," Ivar Thord-Gray, a Swedish mercenary who had joined Villa and would participate in the approaching battle, remembered,

all troops were aroused noiselessly in their billets, that is, in the open behind walls of houses, the church, the plaza pavilion or whatever shelter had been found in the bitterly cold wind. Except for a few senior officers, no one seemed to know what it was all about. The men were told to eat and be ready to march at dawn in full marching order and "without women." Rumors soon began to spread of a large enemy force marching against us and not far distant. The men accepted the news with calm and austere fortitude, but some did show elation in their stoic Indian nature.

Just before sunrise, this ill equipped little rebel force of about 5,500 men, with bandoleers three-quarters emptied, moved out of Juárez. The column was most unusual and colorful, but I was moved by a strange sympathetic sadness towards these brave little peons and Indians.[69] Their cause seemed so helpless against such great odds. Some of them didn't even have a gun, but proudly carried their machetes and vicious looking long knives, many of them bowie knives. . . .

The women camp followers had orders to remain behind, but hundreds of them hanging onto the stirrups followed their men on the road for a while. Some other women carrying carbines, bandoleers and who were mounted, managed to slip into the ranks and came with us. These took their places in the firing lines and withstood hardship and machine gun fire as well as the men. They were a brave worthy lot. It was a richly picturesque sight, but the complete silence, the stoic yet anxious faces of the women was depressing, as it gave the impression that all were going to a tremendous funeral, or their doom.[70]

Both Villa and his soldiers knew the odds were heavily stacked against them. From their defeat at Ciudad Chihuahua, they knew how great the federal superiority in artillery was and how devastating the impact of that artillery could be. In contrast to the federal troops, they were short of ammunition. In other battles, such disadvantages had been compensated for by superior numbers and by superior morale, in contrast to that of the generally unwilling and forcibly recruited federal conscripts, who had come from very different parts of the country. This time the numbers on the two sides were roughly equal, and the federal army consisted largely not of conscripts from the south but of Orozquistas, who, like the revolutionaries, came from the north, mainly from Chihuahua, Durango, and Coahuila. Whatever had driven them to join Huerta, and whatever they had hoped to gain by doing so, was outweighed by what they now stood to lose. They had reason to doubt that they would ever be able to return home if they were defeated, even if they were not shot by Villa. Their will to resist and to fight was thus almost as strong as that of the revolutionaries.

Another difficulty with which Villa had to contend was the lack of integration of his revolutionary army. Most of these men had belonged to a fighting unit for only a few weeks. This was reflected even in the way they marched. The troops moved not in units but "in a gypsy kind of formation," Gray noted. "Only one regiment, Villa's own, and perhaps one more, marched in anything resembling military order."[71]

In 1911, when the newspaperman Ignacio Herrerias had first visited a camp of revolutionaries in Chihuahua, he was greatly impressed by the maturity of the men, who were generally heads of families who had left their homes for the serious business of fighting. This time, observers noted the number of children, frequently boys of ten or eleven, who were part of the revolutionary army. As the army moved toward Tierra Blanca, Thord-Gray was moved by the sight of "young boys among the group" and especially by

one little fellow in particular, for he was not over ten years old. When he came walking by me, he looked hungry and tired, so I offered him a tortilla and some water which he gulped down. He told me he came from Lake Guzmán in northern Chihuahua and did not know whether his father or mother was alive, but thought his father had been shot by the federals because he refused to be drafted into the army.[72]

A few weeks earlier, an American reporter had been deeply impressed by the number of young boys he found among the revolutionary troops:

These boys are now fighting, they are now undergoing the lot of a soldier accepting his chances, reaping his glory, paying the only price in defeat. They are visible in every camp, in every town. . . .

Juan Dozal, late lieutenant or chief of staff of Pancho Villa, rebel commander, said the other day that but for one thing he would rather have a regiment of boys than old men. Dozal himself is a proved fighter and his word should carry weight.

"They do not know what danger is," he explained, "they will go forward against anything, machine guns and artillery, up the sides of mountains or down the bullet swept streets, just as cheerfully as they will return to camp. They only thing against them," and Dozal shook his head mournfully, "is they can't shoot. They won't aim and they waste an awful lot of ammunition."

Upon this all are agreed that a boy of fourteen, demoralized by a military life can be the most heartless, most cruel, most relentless human being on earth. Savagery and grief become his first nature.[73]

These boys could also be extremely courageous when facing death. After the battle, Thord-Gray found the ten-year-old boy to whom he had given his tortilla mortally wounded. He tried to save him by having his assistant amputate his arm, but to no avail.

When we were about to place him on the limber, he came to and his weak smile of recognition was a wonderful thing to see. His gun which had been placed by his side was there when he made an effort to find it and again this graceful smile, full of understanding. Then he took something out of his pocket, gave it to me and said, "I got this from my mother a long time ago, will you please keep it for me?" It was brightly polished American twenty-five piece.[74]

It was at Tierra Blanca that this army, whose soldiers and supreme commander were unused to regular battles, awaited the attack of the federal forces. Villa had chosen his position well. The revolutionary troops were stationed on low, rising hills overlooking sand dunes, through which the federal troops would have to pass in order to attack, and where their cannon might easily become stuck.

The fighting began on the night of November 23, when federal troops left their trains and attacked the revolutionary lines. For two days the battle continued, consisting of a series of charges and countercharges, with each side trying to outflank the other. The superior firepower of their cannon, their greater number of machine guns, and, above all, their larger supplies of ammunition allowed the federal troops to relentlessly pound the revolutionary lines and to inflict ever-greater casualties on them. Villa's troops nevertheless held their positions. By the third day of fighting, the Villistas' situation had grown desperate. Their ammunition was giving out, and the pounding by the federal artillery and machine guns continued ceaselessly. At this point, Villa made a bold and desperate move. He ordered his troops to charge into withering enemy fire and at a crucial moment of the fighting, his cavalry attacked the federal flanks, causing a panic among the federal troops. The panic was heightened when the Villistas sent a locomotive loaded with dynamite into a federal troop train, causing a tremendous explosion. A rout now occurred, and the government troops left most of their artillery in Villista hands when they fled toward Ciudad Chihuahua.

The battle of Tierra Blanca showed both the strengths and the weaknesses of Villa's strategic thinking. His choice of Tierra Blanca as a battleground and his occupation of the heights had been well thought out. He was able to maintain the morale of his troops in the face of intense enemy fire. His cavalry charges, carefully designed to surprise his enemy, demoralized and routed them. At the same time, however, according to a military expert who participated in the battle, Villa had no concept of reserves and threw practically all of his troops into battle. When he had to send reinforcements to any sector, instead of taking them from the reserves, he had to weaken one part of the front in order to strengthen the other. In addition, the same expert felt that Villa was not coordinating the battle enough and was giving too much leeway to individual commanders. This was in the tradition of guerrilla fighting but was contrary to what was expected of the commander of a large army on the battlefield. Finally, the expert felt Villa had no real concept of how to deal with enemy artillery or to how to place and maximize his own artillery forces.[75] In later battles, Villa was able to eliminate some of these mistakes and to obtain experts in such fields as artillery and to follow their advice. Some of these weaknesses, however, would persist and would contribute to Villa's final defeat in 1915.

The commander of the Ciudad Chihuahua garrison, Mercado, who had remained behind during the battle, now faced an extremely difficult dilemma. Should he stay and fight in Chihuahua after a defeat in which his troops had been demoralized and had lost much of their equipment to the revolutionaries, or should he evacuate the capital city of Chihuahua and retreat toward the U.S. border? The city's upper class, who had done everything in their power to support the federal army and were desperately afraid of what Villa might do if he entered Chihuahua, implored Mercado to stay. They offered him money to pay his troops, and Mercado could take encouragement from the fact that a strong federal relief column was advancing toward Torreón. Once Torreón was retaken (it was in fact reoccupied by federal troops at the beginning of December 1913), he could reasonably expect his communications with central Mexico to be reestablished in a short while. Mercado nevertheless decided to evacuate Chihuahua. The reason he gave was that he had begun to lose control of an essential part of his troops, the Orozquistas, who had become demoralized as a result of their defeat at Tierra Blanca and were beginning to resort to banditry and to turn against Chihuahua's oligarchy and upper classes.[76]

Leaving 200 men to keep order in the city until Villa's arrival, Mercado's troops thus abandoned Ciudad Chihuahua and, accompanied by a large part of the state's oligarchy, including Luis Terrazas and Enrique Creel, set out for the border city of Ojinaga, the only part of Chihuahua that would still be under the control of federal troops at the end of 1913.

CHAPTER SIX

Four Weeks
That Shook Chihuahua

Villa's Brief but Far-Reaching Governorship

> The rich with all their money
> Have already got their lashing,
> As the soldiers of Urbina
> Can tell, and those of Maclovio Herrera.
> Fly, fly away, little dove,
> Fly over all the prairies,
> And say that Villa has come
> To drive them out forever.
> Ambition will ruin itself
> And justice will be the winner,
> For Villa has reached Torreón
> To punish the avaricious.[1]

On December 1, the first of Villa's troops, orderly and well-disciplined as they had been in Torreón, entered Ciudad Chihuahua. A few hours later, Villa followed them. Masses of people lined the streets to greet him, shouting, "Viva Villa! Viva Carranza! Viva la revolución!" In the Red Room of the state palace, the Chihuahuan merchant Federico Moye, who had assumed provisional power for the transitional period from federal to revolutionary control, officially handed the city over to Villa. He stated that he had no ambition to exercise any kind of political office and was now retiring to private life. The ceremony was interrupted by the cheers of the thousands who lined the streets facing the palace. Villa went onto the balcony and extended his greetings to his "brothers" (*hermanos de raza*), who responded with renewed tumultuous cheers. When he returned to the ceremony, Villa thanked Moye, assuring him that the 200 soldiers of the federal army who had remained in the city to keep order would be well treated and allowed to go anywhere they wished. He told Moye that he himself had no political ambitions either and would retire to private life as soon as the fighting was over.

For many of Villa's soldiers, this was the second time they had entered the state capital in triumph. They had done so two years before, after the victory of the Madero revolution. Then as now thousands of people had come out to greet and cheer them. In 1911, many of these soldiers had not had more than these cheers, 50 pesos, and a horse to show for the risks they had taken. This time they expected more. Meeting such expectations was but one of the many problems that Villa now faced. This former peon and outlaw, who only a few months earlier had commanded nothing more than a few guerrillas, now confronted daunting tasks. He had to integrate his heterogeneous force of former guerrillas into a coherent, well-disciplined whole, capable of meeting a renewed federal threat. South of Chihuahua, the federal general José Refugio Velasco had recaptured Torreón, while in the northeast of Chihuahua, in the border city of Ojinaga, the former commander of the garrison in the state capital, Mercado, had gathered the remnants of his troops, more than 3,500 men, with whom he hoped to support an expected offensive by Velasco from the south.

To a large extent, Villa's ability to deal with the military situation would depend on the way he dealt with the political and economic problems that confronted him: how to administer the state of Chihuahua, one of the largest and wealthiest entities in Mexico, and in so doing how to be successful where Abraham González had failed in maintaining the unity of the very heterogeneous forces that had brought him to power.

The problems that the administration of such a complex state as Chihuahua presented to this semiliterate revolutionary were enormous. Neither he nor his commanders had any administrative experience. Most of them were uneducated men. Their knowledge of economics was nil.

Chihuahua was in a very difficult situation. Except for a few months in the latter part of 1911 and the early days of 1912, the state had endured nearly three years of continuous fighting. Much of the railway system on which it so heavily depended had been destroyed. Many American companies had ceased operations and laid off their workers. In many parts of the state, food was scarce and people were on the edge of starvation.

There also was a shortage of money. People were hoarding silver, as people always do in times of crisis. Much of the paper money had been taken away by the retreating members of the oligarchy, and many of the notes that had been accepted until then as legal tender, such as those issued by Creel's Banco Minero, were now being rejected by many merchants and businessmen because it was not clear whether the new government would honor the old notes.

In addition, the state's population was more divided politically than it had been in 1910–11, when all of civil society had rebelled against Terrazas and Creel and Porfirio Díaz. Many members of the state's lower classes had sided with Orozco, and a large segment of the middle class was wary and fearful of what Villa would bring. It was a volatile situation and might easily lead to riots and uprisings, with attendant plunder and pillage such as had taken place in Durango. Riots would not only tarnish the image of the revolution but squander resources. In Durango, much of the wealth of the city, instead of being utilized to finance the revolution, had been plundered by soldiers and the city's poor, as well as by greedy generals such as Tomás Urbina. Much of it had simply gone up in smoke. More important still, in the eyes of Villa and Silvestre Terrazas, was that in Chihuahua, where so much American money was invested, with such a large number of American residents, and with such a long border with the United States, indiscriminate rioting and pillaging might easily trigger what every revolutionary in Mexico feared most, U.S. intervention.

If Villa wanted to maintain order in Chihuahua, he had to meet the hopes and expectations of his soldiers and of the lower classes of society in general, many of whom had been disillusioned by how little they had gained during González's governorship. Many of them supported Villa, expecting great things from him, but some still sympathized with Orozco. If Villa wanted to maintain and broaden his popular support, he would have to give both his soldiers and Chihuahua's lower classes far more than the promises and policies they had received under González and Madero.

In addition, if Villa wanted to rule and control the northern region his troops now occupied effectively, lower-class support was not enough. He also needed to attract the middle classes to his cause, and this was a far more difficult undertaking. In the eyes of many of Chihuahua's merchants, artisans, bureaucrats, doctors, and teachers, Villa was the embodiment of the fearsome traditions of Mexican history. They feared a violent uprising of the lower classes, leading to a mindless and general massacre. The slaughter of city inhabitants by Hidalgo's supporters during the Independence War of 1810–11 and by the Maya Indians of Yucatán during the Caste War of 1847–48 were very much present in the minds of Mexico's middle classes. While Indian rebels scarcely existed in Chihuahua, general fears of lower-class excesses had been fueled by the Orozquista sack of Parral in 1912 and by the even more gruesome scenes of pillage and looting carried out by Urbina's men and the city's lower classes in Ciudad Durango in 1913. Exacerbating such fears were Urbina's close ties with Villa and Villa's own bandit image, now greatly embroidered by the conservative press in Ciudad Chihuahua.

Yet their initial fear of Villa was not strong enough to drive Chihuahua's middle classes into the arms of Huerta, for a genuine revolutionary potential still existed among them. Many of their members had joined the Madero revolution; many more had sympathized with it. They had hated the monopoly of political and economic power exercised by the Terrazas-Creel clan. They wanted more democracy, a desire closely linked to their wishes for upward mobility. Some members of the middle classes, especially in the Galeana district, where the Mormons resided, had developed strong nationalistic feelings and resented the rights and privileges of both American settlers and American enterprises in Mexico.

González had in fact satisfied many of the demands of this middle class. He had created the most democratic government Chihuahua had known since independence. He had reestablished much of the municipal autonomy that Terrazas and Creel had practically abolished and thus returned to many teachers, merchants, lawyers, well-to-do rancheros, and local officials the kind of power they had lost when the state government had begun to assume control of local administrations. He had decreased the tax burden imposed on the middle classes and attempted to make the judiciary as well as the police more autonomous vis-à-vis the state's oligarchy. While definitely not anti-American, González had dented some of the privileges that Americans had enjoyed in Chihuahua by restoring municipal autonomy to company towns, and Madero's decision to replace American railroad employees in Mexico, who frequently did not know Spanish, with Mexican railwaymen was a very popular measure in Chihuahua.[2]

But, while supporting González, some members of the middle classes had also expressed dissatisfaction. They resented Creel's effective immunity from prosecution in the Banco Minero affair. They resented even more the fact that the oligarchy's huge economic empire had scarcely been touched by the González administration. In addition, they were increasingly worried by the inability of Madero and González to reestablish peace in Chihuahua. But despite having made peace with Orozco, Huerta could not capitalize on this middle-class dissatisfaction. The imposition of an outside military governor on a people as proud and jealous of their independence as the Chihuahuans; the murder of González, which meant that anyone who had sympathized with Madero might meet the same fate; and Huerta's inability to restore peace and close links to Terrazas and Creel all contributed to an increasing sympathy for the constitutionalists in Chihuahua.

In addition to reorganizing his army and gaining the sympathy of the Chihuahuan people, Villa was faced with another problem of equal importance: how to obtain the support or at least the neutrality of the United States. Chihuahua had one of the longest borders with the United States, and thousands of Americans had settled there, some of whom owned vast properties. Villa not only feared U.S. intervention; he had become more and more dependent on American arms. By the end of 1913, the U.S. government had become more favorably disposed toward him, and it seemed to be doing less and less to inhibit the smuggling of arms to his troops. In fact, there was talk that the U.S. arms embargo, which was still officially enforced with respect to all factions in Mexico, would soon be lifted, thus increasing Villa's dependence on U.S. supplies.

Finally, the administration of Chihuahua would have to take place in such a way that it would not lead to a break with Carranza, whom Villa had nominally recognized as the supreme chief of the revolution. Since Huerta was far from being defeated, such a break could have had disastrous consequences.

It is not surprising that in view of the problems confronting him, Villa was at first reluctant to assume the governorship after the Chihuahuan leaders of his army named him military governor of Chihuahua. After all, leading and reorganizing his División del Norte was a gigantic task in itself. One option that Villa had in theory, but that he was not willing to implement, was to withdraw completely from the political field and to put the administration of Chihuahua into the hands of Carranza's nominee, Manuel Chao.

Carranza, while leaving much of the military leadership to his commanders, was attempting to take political power wherever the revolutionaries held sway. Villa not only mistrusted Carranza, he was also conscious of the fact that in the eyes of Chihuahua's inhabitants, he would ultimately be held accountable for the administration of the state. Chao, perhaps because of his previous confrontation with Villa, perhaps because he felt that Villa could not in the long run simultaneously be governor of Chihuahua and commander-in-chief of the División del Norte, was one of the generals who elected him to that position.

One alternative Villa envisaged was to name someone who was well educated and experienced, whom he trusted, but whom he could also control, to play a decisive role in the administration of Chihuahua. The reservoir of such people was limited. It consisted of those officials of Abraham González's administration who had fled to El Paso after his assassination, who had set up a constitutionalist junta there that supported Villa both by making propaganda for him and by smuggling arms to his army. The junta's most prominent members were Aureliano González, Abraham González's former deputy; Sebastian Vargas, a former high official of the treasury department in Chihuahua, and the newspaperman Silvestre Terrazas.

Of these men, Silvestre Terrazas was the one Villa trusted most. The reasons for this are not entirely clear. Silvestre Terrazas had the least administrative experience of anyone in the junta, and he had never occupied any government position in Chihuahua. That may, in fact, have been one of the main reasons why Villa chose him. Moreover, Silvestre Terrazas's newspaper, *El Correo de Chihuahua*, had always reported positively about Villa, and Villa had entrusted large sums of money to him to buy arms. When the two men met after Villa's capture of Ciudad Juárez, the revolutionary leader was impressed by the newspaperman. Silvestre Terrazas also offered Villa important political advantages. For a decade his newspaper had been something like the conscience of Chihuahua. He enjoyed great respect among the state's middle classes, and Villa realized that having the cooperation of Silvestre Terrazas was a first step toward gaining middle-class support. In addition, Silvestre Terrazas was not a military man; he had no troops and no military constituency of his own. Thus dependent on Villa, he could be counted on not to rebel against him.

Villa's confidence in the newspaperman was so great that he was willing to relinquish the office to which he had just been elected by his commanders in favor of Silvestre Terrazas. Only a few hours after his army had occupied Chihuahua, Villa called the newspaperman into the executive room of the palace and told him, "I now want you to become governor of the state." In his memoir *El verdadero Pancho Villa*, Silvestre Terrazas recalled:

My surprise was such that it took me a few seconds to respond, and then I told him:
   "No, General, I cannot and should not accept."
   "Why?" he asked me.
   "Because among the people who follow you, there are many who would not show any respect to a civilian authority such as I would be, and this should be prevented. They now obey only you, and for that reason you, or someone close to you, should be military governor of Chihuahua. I have always been a civilian."
   "But I shall grant you a high military office."
   "And what use will this be to me, since I do not deserve it and I have not even been a plain soldier?"
   "Fine. At any rate, I want you to help me in the government. Are you ready to become general secretary of the government?"
   "I accept," I told him. "But under the condition that I shall only be dealing with the civilian branch, for which I agree to assume responsibility, without having to do anything with the military branch."[3]

In accepting such a high position in Villa's administration, the newspaperman had come a long way. He had always fought for the removal of the Terrazas-Creel clan from power, but he had never advocated the kind of social transformations that he and Villa would now embark on. In fact, while he had been sympathetic to the anti-reelectionist party, he had never joined the Madero revolution. Even in early 1911, he had still been convinced, as he wrote Porfirio Díaz, that if only Terrazas and Creel were removed from power and a number of other changes instituted in Chihuahua, a solution might be found whereby Díaz could be allowed to retain national power.[4]

It is not clear from his memoir what moved the newspaperman to alter his attitude. Certainly the closing of his newspaper by the Huerta administration and his outrage at the assassinations of Madero and González must have played a role in his decision to participate in the government of Chihuahua. Also, it was clear to him that as long as Huerta remained in power, he would not be able to resume publication of his newspaper, and his own life would be in jeopardy if he remained in Chihuahua. His support for a revolution in which Villa and the more moderate Carranza were still cooperating was quite understandable. It is less understandable why he was willing to become such a high official in Villa's administration, something that could turn out to be quite a risky affair. Villa had a bloody reputation. In addition, Silvestre Terrazas's assumption of an office meant that he had to abandon, at least for a time, his life's work as a newspaper publisher. Was it the lure of power? Or was it the conviction that by assuming the position of general secretary of the government, he would be able to restrain Villa and in fact become a kind of tribune of the middle classes? Without ever spelling it out in detail, this was how he portrays himself in his book—as a man attempting to restrain Villa and to lead him along the path of moderation.

Was Villa serious when he hesitated about accepting the governorship of Chihuahua or was he simply displaying the self-deprecating attitude he often assumed when speaking with educated outsiders? Whenever he was interviewed, either by politicians or by reporters, Villa would emphasize that he was but a poor, ignorant man of the people who was incapable of really assuming responsibility and preferred to leave high office to more sophisticated men.

There is no reason to assume that Villa's initial refusal to accept the governorship of Chihuahua was only a theatrical gesture. While it is true that Villa was frequently given to such gestures, these occurred in a public context where he was attempting to impress either important outsiders or the general population. He had no reason to resort to such theatrics to impress a subordinate. It may have been the same lack of confidence in his abilities to administer a complex economy or his contempt for civilian politicians that prevented him from attempting to assume the presidency of Mexico over the following two years. It was an attitude that was not confined to Villa. None of the lower-class military leaders of the revolution had ever exercised any real administrative power over large parts of Mexico, and there is no evidence that any of them in this early period of the revolution, except Zapata and Orozco (who cannot be termed a "lower-class leader"), had even aspired to it. Even in 1911, all the "revolutionary" governors of the northern states, where the revolution had triumphed, had either been hacendados like Carranza and Maytorena or members of the middle class such as Abraham González.

Why would Villa have assumed civilian responsibility when the military problems he faced were enormous and may at times have seemed insurmountable? Villa now led a regular army of nearly 10,000 soldiers, many of them poorly armed, many poorly disciplined, and their loyalties not clearly defined between their immediate chiefs and the central army command headed by Villa. These masses of men had to be integrated, trained, fed, clothed, and armed. All this had to be done in a military situation that was growing more and more precarious. The only way Villa could ensure his control of Chihuahua and the other regions of the north he controlled was by recapturing Torreón. This time the federal troops were commanded by one of Huerta's best generals, José Refugio Velasco, who was building an impressive ring of fortifications around and within the city and concentrating some of his best soldiers there. Villa would not be able to count on the element of surprise that had played such an important role in the first capture of Torreón and his victory in Ciudad Juárez.

The Chihuahuan revolutionaries in some respects confronted a situation similar to the one they had faced in November and December of 1910, when they had been the only major revolutionary force in Mexico to challenge Porfirio Díaz. This time there were other forces in the field: Zapata was fighting in the south; Pablo González was skirmishing in the northeast; and one of the most brilliant generals the revolution produced, Alvaro Obregón, was slowly advancing southward in Sonora. But it was still against the Chihuahuan revolutionaries that the federal government sent the best-trained, best-equipped troops it could muster. Why would Villa, given the difficulties the military situation presented, have taken upon himself the additional burden of governing Chihuahua? He could scarcely read and write, had never held any public office, and had never had any administrative responsibility.

He had only limited means to respond to the challenges that governing Chihuahua presented. Unlike Madero in 1910–11, he had no political organization on which he could depend. Unlike the situation in Sonora, where the revolutionaries could count on an intact state administration, in Chihuahua, after the murder of Abraham González, the bureaucracy had been disorganized, partly decimated, and partly co-opted by the Huerta administration. There were few intellectuals or men with administrative experience in Villa's movement who could compensate for its leader's lack of education and administrative experience. But Villa nevertheless decided to take on the challenge that the governorship of Chihuahua presented.

There are a number of reasons that might help to explain why Villa so rapidly changed his mind and accepted the governorship of Chihuahua. In psychological terms, it must have given him a particular satisfaction to become the supreme arbiter of the law in a state where he had been an outlaw. There were practical advantages as well. As governor, Villa constituted a direct challenge to the power of Carranza, whose authority he had ostensibly accepted. Although Carranza was nominally the First Chief of the revolution, he had in fact been forced to concede practical control of their armies to his military chieftains. What he tried to retain was control of the civilian administrations of the territories ruled by the revolutionaries. By giving his army chiefs the final say in who was to be governor instead of letting Carranza make the decision, Villa clearly indicated to the First Chief where the limits of his power lay. Consciousness of the probable brevity of his tenure may have been one of the factors that led Villa to accept the governor's position even though he knew that in the final analysis, it would be difficult for him to exercise civilian power and simultaneously dedicate his energies to organizing and commanding the División del Norte. By appointing men loyal to him during the first few weeks of revolutionary power in the state, he might be able to shape its nature and limit the eventual power of his successor. Above all, it was the realization that the administration of Chihuahua and the military problems he faced were inextricably linked that led Villa, if only for a brief period, to assume the political leadership of the state and to attempt to solve all the state's problems.

In these endeavors, Villa could count on some real assets. His popularity among Chihuahua's lower classes was enormous. For many of them, his rise to power had made him into a living legend. In addition, much of the wealth the oligarchy had accumulated in Chihuahua was still there for the taking. Most of Luis Terrazas's cattle still roamed his vast estates, and while the members of the oligarchy had taken large amounts of paper money with them in their precipitous flight, they had been unable or unwilling to remove the substantial amounts of precious metal that their banks had stored. Rumors reached Villa that much of it had been hidden somewhere in the Banco Minero.

There was no one in Chihuahua who could challenge Villa's power and authority. Most members of the oligarchy that had so effectively prevented González from carrying out his reform program had fled the state, and Carranza did not have the power to intervene in internal Chihuahuan politics in the way Madero had done.

In addition, the Wilson administration in the United States was far more favorably disposed toward the Mexican revolutionaries than the Taft administration had been, and as long as Villa could control the situation in Chihuahua, the likelihood of U.S. intervention seemed limited.

Villa's Reformist Strategy

Within three weeks after Villa became governor, he and Silvestre Terrazas elaborated and implemented a policy that transformed Chihuahua and allowed Villa, in the short run at least, to resolve some of the most immediate dilemmas he faced. Villa and Terrazas's measures would allow the new government to gain the support of both the lower and middle classes and, at the same time, to obtain the necessary means to transform his army into the best-disciplined and best-equipped force among the revolutionaries. In terms of the United States, it would put Villa in the unique position of gaining the simultaneous sympathies of American radicals, American capitalists doing business in Mexico, and the Wilson administration. It would, in addition, allow Villa, for a brief time at least, to shed the bandit image that had followed him for so long.

The cornerstone of the strategy Villa now implemented was a decree issued in December 1913 that represented a radical departure from the policies that both Madero and Abraham González had pursued in Chihuahua. They had sought to eliminate the political power of Terrazas and Creel, while only nibbling at their economic power by taking away some of their prerogatives and increasing their taxes. It was a strategy that had failed on two counts. It alienated both the lower classes, who felt that Madero and González had not gone far enough, and the oligarchy, which resented the limited losses it had to suffer. Villa's decree, by contrast, was an act of radical surgery. It ordered the confiscation of the lands and other properties of the wealthiest and most powerful Mexican landowners in Chihuahua, the most prominent of whom were the Terrazas, Creel, Cuilty, and Falomir families.[5]

The decree made no mention of foreign-owned properties. Villa not only refused to confiscate them or to increase their taxes but protected them (with the significant exceptions of the holdings of Spaniards and Chinese) in every possible way.

In the short run, the profits from operating these haciendas were destined for the public treasury, which really meant the army, and to pay pensions to the widows and orphans of those soldiers who had died during the revolution. In the long run, the decree stated that after the victory of the revolution, laws were to be passed that would fundamentally change the ownership of the lands of the oligarchy. A part were to be divided among the revolutionary veterans, another part were to be returned to former owners from whom the hacendados had taken them, while a third part were to remain at the disposal of the state, with the primary aim of paying the pensions of the widows and orphans. Until the final victory of the revolution, these lands were to be administered by the State Bank of Chihuahua.[6]

In some respects these measures were not very different from those taken by revolutionary leaders in other parts of Mexico. In spite of initial opposition by both Carranza and the Sonoran governor, Maytorena, revolutionary leaders in Sonora and in northeastern Mexico were occupying estates and properties belonging to real or perceived enemies of the revolution and utilizing the proceeds to finance their armies and the costs of revolution. What differentiated Villa's decree from the measures taken by generals close to Carranza, both in Sonora and in Coahuila and Tamaulipas, was that in those states, the occupation of large estates (with one conspicuous exception in Tamaulipas) was never linked to land division and expropriation. The occupation of estates was called "intervention," a term that implies a temporary state of affairs. Villa, by contrast, clearly stated that the expropriation he had carried out would be final, and that others would become beneficiaries of these lands. What made this promise so dangerous in the eyes of the more conservative revolutionaries was, not only that Villa was setting a precedent, but that a promise made to soldiers in the field was not something that could easily be broken without risking unrest.

While these decrees were drafted by Silvestre Terrazas, they bore the stamp of Villa's hatred for the state's oligarchy and the care he had always shown for his soldiers. His troops and their families would be the first beneficiaries of his decree. The second group of beneficiaries would be the inhabitants of the former military colonies, such as San Andrés, who had strongly supported Villa throughout his campaigns. It is significant that neither landless laborers nor hacienda peons were even considered in these decrees. Nevertheless, Villa did give them the possibility of becoming beneficiaries. All they had to do was to join his army; then they would automatically become eligible for grants from his government.

Although Villa only promised, and did not actually distribute, land to the peasantry, he did succeed in gaining large-scale support within this class of society. This support might seem surprising, since Chihuahua's peasants were wary of promises. Madero had promised land; but after assuming power, he did nothing for them. Villa's promises, however, were more convincing. His social origins may have impressed the peasants; but, mainly, his credibility was enhanced by the fact that he had confiscated the largest haciendas in the state and had expelled their owners from Chihuahua. An additional factor was the establishment of a state agricultural bank to provide the peasants with credit.

There was an element of tradition that made the Chihuahuan villagers ready to accept some postponements of land distribution. The ownership of land by military colonists had always been linked to the obligation to "earn" it by fighting. In their eyes it was thus quite appropriate that land division should be linked to service in the revolutionary army. Villa's promise to give land to revolutionary veterans reinforced this attitude. Soldiers in the field would object strongly to agrarian reforms being carried out before they returned from the war. In addition, Villa's decree also gained him the support of the urban poor, since much of the revenue from confiscated estates was redistributed to them, either in the shape of subsidized low-cost food or through outright gifts.

A decree issued by Villa as governor drastically reduced the price of meat. "The price of meat in Chihuahua is fixed at 15 cents, Mexican money, a kilogram instead of one peso formerly charged in federal reign," according to the *El Paso Times*. "The Government is operating the meat market and each day a detachment of soldiers is sent out to one of the Terrazas ranches and a herd of cattle is rounded up and brought into the city and slaughtered. The meat is then distributed to the various markets in the city."[7] A few weeks later the same newspaper reported: "Unemployed Mexicans of the devastated lumber camps and mines are being given daily rations . . . Madera, Pearson, and Casas Grandes are daily provided with rations by the Constitutionalist Army. Townspeople are unable to secure employment because of the closing down of industries caused by the Revolution. . . . They call at the Constitutionalist Army Commissary and are provisioned under arrangements made by Villa, and the Constitutionalist Army bears the whole expense of providing for these people."[8]

Villa's measures benefited the poor and unemployed in yet another way. Thanks to the resources he now had for paying and equipping his troops, thousands of Chihuahuans joined the army. As a result, despite the fact that many enterprises had closed down because of revolutionary turmoil, unemployment was drastically reduced in his state.

Villa's redistributions had a tremendous psychological impact on Chihuahua's poor. It was the first time ever as far as they could remember that a government had given them anything.

During the few weeks that he was governor of Chihuahua, Villa's popularity soared to new heights. In fact, no other leader of the revolution, with the possible exception of Madero in the days following his victory, would ever achieve the kind of prestige and mass appeal that Villa attained at this time. More than any other leader, he had become a legend in his lifetime. This was by no means only a rational response to the measures he was taking. In popular thinking, Villa conformed to a series of deeply ingrained popular traditions and images, some of them characteristic of all of Mexico, some of them peculiar to its lower classes.

Villa epitomized the traditional Mexican macho image: he possessed all the fighting qualities that machismo demanded, he was courageous, he was a first-rate fighter, his ability with the gun was proverbial, and his capacities as a rider were so great that bards wrote ballads about his horses. His interest in cockfighting and his reputation as a womanizer were essential parts of that image. So was his cruelty, which also fitted the macho pattern.

He also fitted another image, that of the avenger of the poor, the man from the lower classes who had made it big but never forgot his origins and punished those who had made him suffer. This tradition was closely intertwined with the Robin Hood social bandit image that Villa presented—above all, as a result of his activities in early 1913—of a man who took from the rich and gave to the poor. These two traditions were not always identical, since some social bandits came from the upper classes. In Villa's case, however, they were. Villa also conformed to traditions and images specific to the northern frontier. In Chihuahua, with its two-century-old tradition of savage combat against nomadic Indians, fighters enjoyed a special prestige. Joaquín Terrazas is still remembered today as the man who defeated Victorio's Apaches at the battle of Tres Castillos. And even while they were fighting the rule of Luis Terrazas in Chihuahua, the opinions of many of its inhabitants about him were still ambivalent. Although many saw him as a tyrant in 1910, they also remembered that it had been under his governorship that the Apaches suffered their greatest defeat.

Another tradition of the northern frontier was that of the good caudillo. As the central government of Mexico proved incapable of protecting the frontier from marauders, or even of ruling, it was to regional leaders, caudillos such as Santiago Vidaurri in the northeast and Luis Terrazas in Chihuahua, that people looked for protection. Traditional links of mutual obligation, underlined at times by marriage ties and much more frequently by ties of *compadrazco*, created bonds that were broken only around the end of the nineteenth century when the caudillos became capitalists and "forgot" their traditional obligations.

Not only did Villa's persona naturally fit these patterns, he also made a conscious effort to enhance his image. While his government distributed food to the poor, Villa made it a point to give money and gifts to the needy personally. Many families whom Villa did not even know called on him to be godfather of their children, and he frequently accepted, showering them with gifts. He had an uncanny memory for people and names, remembering not only all those who had ever done him a favor, but even chance acquaintances. He would frequently bypass existing judicial structures, personally meting out rough justice to those accused of wrongdoing to people he considered poor or oppressed. Even those who frowned upon his womanizing were impressed by the way he cared for all his wives and children. In all the interviews he gave, Villa would repeatedly emphasize his humble origins and, as he did in his memoirs, even exaggerate the degree of persecution he had suffered in order to emphasize that his career as an outlaw had been forced on him.

Villa's activities as governor, the image he presented, and the amnesty he offered allowed him to rally the lower classes of society to his cause not only in Chihuahua but in Durango and Coahuila as well. Many of those who had supported Orozco and his generals now joined Villa, both because he was the victor and because he seemed able to implement the promises Orozco and his men had made but never carried out.

Villa and Chihuahua's Middle Class

Many of the elements of the Villa image that endeared him to the poor had a very different effect on Chihuahua's middle class, to whom these elements confirmed their idea of Villa as a ruthless and bloodthirsty bandit. Their fear of Villa was so great that many had rallied to Pascual Orozco in 1912, when the latter began his revolt against the Madero administration under the pretext of defending Ciudad Chihuahua against the hordes of Pancho Villa, whom Governor González had called to his aid. Only a few weeks after becoming governor, Villa was able to defuse his negative image. Not only would large segments of Chihuahua's middle classes view him in a better light; many would embrace his cause. Villa had made sure, at least in the early stages of his rule in Chihuahua, that his confiscations and expropriations affected only the oligarchy and not the middle class. In fact, the latter would profit from the large-scale redistribution of wealth that took place in Chihuahua. Even more important was the contrast that the orderly Villa administration presented to the arbitrary, undisciplined, and violent image of the Huerta regime in Chihuahua. Villa's well-disciplined troops stood in stark contrast to the increasingly undisciplined Orozquistas, many of whom had resorted to banditry after Orozco's defeat in 1913. Above all, Villa immediately took actions that served to defuse the bloodthirsty image broadcast both by his wholesale executions of Orozquista prisoners and by the propaganda of his enemies.

One of his first official decisions as governor of Chihuahua was to offer an amnesty to all those who were fighting him if they laid down their arms. The amnesty was directed at both the lower and middle classes. It aimed at undercutting support for Orozco by allowing those of his supporters who were ready to lay their arms to do so, instead of forcing them to fight on to avoid execution by Villa. It also assured both bureaucrats and lawyers and teachers who had continued in their jobs during the periods of Orozco's rule and the Huertista military administration of the state that no reprisals would be taken against them.

For a short while after Villa's occupation of Ciudad Chihuahua, it nevertheless seemed to Silvestre Terrazas that his efforts to win the middle class over to the new regime might end in failure, and that a wave of terror might sweep Chihuahua. Attempts by individuals to use the cover of revolutionary turmoil to settle personal accounts are characteristic of all revolutionary upheavals, and in view of Villa's bloody reputation, a number of people in Chihuahua thought that the time had come to settle old scores and kill off personal enemies or competitors. In the days following Villa's capture of Ciudad Chihuahua, letters denouncing real or purported enemies of the revolution poured into his headquarters. Fortunately for the intended victims, the man who first examined these letters was the general secretary of the state government, Silvestre Terrazas. Terrazas was not a bloodthirsty man and had personal relations with many of those denounced; indeed, he also would have had very much to lose if mass executions had taken place in

Chihuahua. It was clear to him that if his name were ever associated with a massacre, he would never be able to resume a normal life in his native state after Villa was gone. He would become the object, not only of hatred on the part of the victims' families, and public opinion in general, but probably of personal revenge. Thus Silvestre Terrazas tried to ignore most of these denunciations and above all refrained from telling Villa about them.

There was, nevertheless, one denunciation that Silvestre Terrazas soon discovered he could not ignore: an anonymous letter listing "many of the best-known businessmen and employees of the most important local institutions. . . . Their hiding places where they had taken refuge from possible violence were described . . . and the accusations against them were detailed with such assurance that if they had been followed up, a real massacre would have taken place, and its victims would have been some of the best-known merchants and industrialists in Chihuahua." The anonymous writer denounced these men for supporting the military, opposing González, saying derogatory things about Villa, and so on.[9] What made these accusations particularly dangerous for the accused is that some of them were probably true.

Fearing a wholesale massacre of much of Chihuahua's upper and middle classes, Silvestre Terrazas tried to ignore the letter and to keep it from Villa. As day after day passed and nothing happened, the letter's author, in a way that Silvestre Terrazas could not exactly determine, alerted Villa to its existence. At a meeting with his secretary general, Villa asked him to produce the letter. Silvestre Terrazas told him that he did not think it very important, but would bring it to him the next day. That same night, Silvestre Terrazas dictated a "sanitized" version of the letter to his secretary. It contained only the most harmless accusations and referred only to people Silvestre Terrazas made sure did not have the standing or the antecedents to incur Villa's wrath.

The next morning, much to his relief, Silvestre Terrazas found Villa to be in good humor. This meant that he was amenable to suggestions and arguments. "Read it to me." Villa ordered his general secretary. After Silvestre Terrazas had read ten or twelve names of the "sanitized" version of the letter, Villa began to lose interest. "This is nothing but gossip and it is really unimportant," Villa told Silvestre Terrazas. He instructed him to have Manuel Chao, who was to succeed him, take care of this by at most imposing forced loans on some of the men mentioned in the letter.[10]

Terrazas believed he had prevented a "wholesale" massacre of Chihuahua's educated elite. Had he? Or would Villa have refrained from such executions even if he had read the unadulterated denunciation? Villa had no compunction about killing his enemies, but he was intelligent enough to realize that such executions might cost him the support of the state's middle class and the goodwill of the United States, and he needed both. In addition, while Villa hated the Chihuahuan oligarchy, he never shared the aversion to the educated classes that characterized many peasant revolutionaries, including some of his followers. Silvestre Terrazas nevertheless obviously feared that Villa in a fit of fury might ignore all such rational considerations. His fears were exaggerated or, rather, premature. During Villa's rule of Chihuahua, there were no massacres of civilians as long as his star was on the rise. Only during the last months of his rule, when his fortunes were in decline, and he felt that those he had trusted were betraying him and that he had nothing to lose, did Villa allow the killing of civilians in addition to prisoners and military opponents, whom he had always executed. These killings would increase in number during the bloodiest period of Chihuahua's history, the guerrilla warfare that took hold of the state between 1915 and 1920.

The fact that Villa did not carry out wholesale massacres of his purported enemies did not mean that no civilians were being killed at all. Although their number was limited, Villa secretly had civilians whom he disliked executed. According to Silvestre Terrazas, during a dinner at Del Monico's Restaurant in Ciudad Chihuahua, soon after Villa's occupation of the town, one of the rare official dinners that Villa ever attended (he was so afraid of being poisoned that during the meal he regularly exchanged plates with one of his neighbors), close associates of Villa's came up to him and indicated by sign language—by raising a half-closed hand to the brow and turning it around—that his orders for an execution had been carried out.[11]

Deciding whether to execute someone was not a problem over which Villa agonized for long or about which he carried out extensive investigations before coming to a decision. Guadalupe Galván had been mayor of the town of Valle de Allende during the Porfirian era. According to Silvestre Terrazas, who called him "educated and correct in his actions,"[12] Galván had been one of the better Porfirian mayors. Nevertheless, he had arrested and imposed fines on men who now fought in Villa's ranks. They ordered his arrest soon after the occupation of Chihuahua and attempted to have him shot. His desperate family called on Villa, asking him to stay the execution until Galván could defend himself. In this respect, their interests and those of Villa coincided, for he had given strict orders that no executions were to be carried out without his approval. Once Galván had been brought into his presence, he called in Silvestre Terrazas. "Do you know this man?" he asked him.

> "Yes, General. It is Señor Galván."
> "Is he a good or bad person?"
> "He is a good person."
> "Does he deserve to be punished or badly treated?"
> "No, Sir."
> "Does he deserve his freedom then?"
> "Yes, Sir."
> "Good," Villa said. "Let him go."[13]

His decision to execute someone could be equally summary.

The limited number of reprisals that Villa undertook against the civilian population of Chihuahua assuaged the middle class's fears and served to improve his image in the United States, although that image suffered from other reprisals short of executions that Villa took after he occupied Ciudad Chihuahua. They were directed against the city's Spanish residents and against the lone male member of the Terrazas family who had remained in the state capital, Luis Terrazas Jr. Both cases provoked diplomatic intervention by U.S. representatives.

One of Villa's first actions on assuming power in Chihuahua was to call together all the Spaniards he could find in the city to tell them that in view of the support they had given Félix Díaz and Huerta in the overthrow of Madero, they were all being expelled from Mexico. An edict issued by Villa and signed by Silvestre Terrazas on December 9, the day Villa assumed power in the state, decreed not only the expulsion of the Spaniards but the confiscation of all their property in retaliation for their political activities. The confiscated property would be used to support the widows and orphans of soldiers and to finance the revolution.[14]

This decree brought forth a storm of protests by foreign representatives in Chihuahua. The first to voice such objections was the British consul, a man named Scobell, who represented Spanish interests in Chihuahua in the absence of the Spanish consul. In view of Britain's overt support of Huerta, Villa dismissed Scobell's objection out of hand. He was friendlier but in the final account equally uncompromising when American representatives, first the U.S. consul in Chihuahua, Marion Letcher, and later the U.S. consul in Torreón, George Carothers (soon to be U.S. special representative to Villa), attempted to convince him to cancel these measures.[15] Officially, the American intervention came in response to a request for help by the Spanish ambassador in Washington, but the U.S. position was based on more than the simple wish to comply with diplomatic niceties. If Villa was allowed by one stroke of the pen to expel a whole community of foreigners, it could set a precedent for other nationalities as well. In addition, these measures created such a bad image for Villa abroad that they made it more difficult for the United States to undertake a policy more favorable to the revolutionaries. Woodrow Wilson seemed intent on supporting the revolutionaries after Huerta had defied him by dissolving the national assembly and having himself reelected president in the fall of 1913.[16]

Silvestre Terrazas too, he tells us, protested against Villa's measures against the Spaniards, and against the decree he himself had signed, telling Villa that the Spaniards had been completely integrated into Mexican life and were working for the progress of Mexico, and that besides not all Spaniards had supported Félix Díaz and Huerta.[17]

Villa remained adamant. The only concession he was willing to make to Terrazas was to allow a few Spaniards and, above all, a few Spanish nuns who were working as nurses in a hospital, to remain in Ciudad Chihuahua. He was a little more conciliatory in his talks with American representatives, promising them that after their expulsion, those Spaniards who could prove that they had not intervened in Mexican politics or supported the Huerta dictatorship might be allowed to return.

Villa defended his measures against the Spaniards by stating that they had played a large role in the overthrow of Madero. He told Silvestre Terrazas that while he had been in prison in Mexico City together with Reyes, he had heard of many Spaniards offering to help Reyes in his plots against Madero. According to John Reed, Villa also gave historical reasons for his measures against the Spaniards.

They have not changed in character since the Conquistadores. They disrupted the Indian empire and enslaved the people. We did not ask them to mingle their blood with ours. Twice we drove them out of Mexico and allowed them to return with the rights of Mexicans and they used these rights to steal away our land to make our people slaves and to take up arms against the cause of liberty. . . . It was the Spaniards who framed the plot to put Huerta into power. When Madero was murdered, the Spaniards in every state of the Republic held banquets of rejoicing.[18]

There is little doubt that many Spaniards had in fact supported the coup against Madero. The Spanish minister had asked for the president's resignation, and there were fourteen Spaniards among Félix Díaz's troops when he attempted to overthrow Madero. There is no doubt either that the great majority of Spaniards in Mexico were opposed to Madero and welcomed Huerta's rise to power. As the Spanish minister to Mexico put it in diplomatic language in a confidential report to his government,

The merchants, industrialists, agriculturalists, and property owners in general had lost all faith in the government of Señor Madero, and this attitude was shared by all the foreign residents of Mexico. It is not surprising thus that all or nearly all the members of the Spanish associations had the same attitude, with the added fact though that we like to express our opinions, we speak the same language as the Mexicans, we easily identify with their problems, and, as a result, we become very passionate. As everyone knew, the associations came to be centers of anti-Maderismo.[19]

Most Spaniards in Torreón and Chihuahua had supported Huerta's military government, and there are some indications that a number of Spaniards had joined the Defensa Social, the armed volunteers mobilized in Durango by the city's upper classes to fight the revolutionaries.

Other foreign residents of Mexico had also been enthusiastic in their support of Huerta and had hated Madero. Yet Villa made it a point to touch neither them nor their properties. The fact that he singled out the Spaniards was certainly also linked to the circumstance that Spain was a far weaker country than France, Great Britain, or the United States. It would scarcely be able to intervene in Mexico to protect the properties of its citizens. More important, perhaps, was the fact that Villa's actions and opinions concerning the Spaniards reflected the attitudes of large parts of the lower and the middle classes of northern Mexico. A disproportionate number of Spaniards tended to be hacienda administrators or small merchants, who had frequent conflicts with the lowest classes of Mexican society, and many of them were unpopular. Villa felt, and he was probably right, that this measure would increase rather than decrease his popularity in Chihuahua. The same can be said of another repressive measure Villa took that attracted a considerable amount of attention both domestically and internationally: the arrest of the son of Mexico's wealthiest hacendado, Luis Terrazas.

Villa and Terrazas

Unlike the rest of his family, Luis Terrazas Jr. had remained in Ciudad Chihuahua. He had fled to what he considered would be the safety of the British consulate, which enjoyed diplomatic immunity, and from where he could operate at his leisure.

According to an anonymous report sent to Silvestre Terrazas, the reason that Luis Jr. had not joined the rest of his family on their long and arduous trek with the federal troops retreating to Ojinaga, which would finally allow them to find freedom and asylum in the United States, was that he "wanted to have the pleasure of buying off the state government and General Villa himself."[20]

This is quite plausible. In the eyes of the Terrazas, all revolutionaries were bandits. The Terrazas had attempted to buy off all the revolutionary leaders. While their efforts in regard to Abraham González had been unsuccessful, they had managed to buy Orozco's support. Why should it be more difficult to woo Villa, who after all had been a real outlaw for so many years?

At first glance, if they did intend to leave one of their clan in Chihuahua, Luis Terrazas Jr. was probably the best candidate. Unlike most other family members, he had not been involved in the political administration of the state. According to Silvestre Terrazas, who had no reason to like the family of his distant relative, Luis Terrazas Jr. was "a good man, who, in contrast to the other members of his family, enjoyed a certain degree of popularity in Chihuahua City."[21] In addition, since he seems to have overseen the administration of all Terrazas haciendas, he may have been considered by his family to be the man best qualified to continue to keep an eye on their properties. Nevertheless, whether he was induced by the family to remain behind to supervise their holdings or whether he did so on his own, it proved to be a miscalculation that would cause him much suffering and entail enormous costs to his family. Villa showed no respect for the diplomatic immunity of the British consulate. His men invaded it and arrested the younger Terrazas.

Villa's victories in Ciudad Juárez and Tierra Blanca and the decision of the federal commander, Mercado, to evacuate Ciudad Chihuahua came as such a surprise to the Creel brothers and their associates that they did not have time to evacuate the gold holdings of their Banco Minero from Chihuahua. They were obviously convinced that to transport such a huge fortune under the dubious protection of Mercado's demoralized soldiers was to run an unacceptable risk. Accordingly, as a report by the board of directors of the bank stated, "We hid $590,000 in gold in a column in our office building."[22]

As one of the directors of the bank, Luis Terrazas Jr. knew of this hiding place. Unfortunately for him, Villa suspected that the bank could not have sent all of its money out of the state and also knew that if the bank had any secrets, Luis Jr. would certainly be apprised of them.

Villa resolved to extract this secret from him. He first tried gentle persuasion. He sent two of his trusted upper-class followers to find common ground with him to try to persuade him to reveal his secret. They were an engineer, Andres Farías, and Francisco Madero's brother Raúl, who had just joined Villa. Then Villa himself confronted Terrazas. "They all exercised great pressure on me to give them the amount of $500,000 they wanted for my freedom," Terrazas later reported to his associates. "I told them that I had no money at my disposal, and that for that reason I could not give them anything, and they could do with me whatever they wanted, since I could not respond to their demands."

Villa now decided to use other means of persuasion. As Terrazas recalled:

On the night of the same day on which this conference took place, around 11, Madinaveitia [an officer of Villa's], Manuel Baca, and Pascual Tostado came to my prison and ordered me to go with them in a car. I assumed that they would shoot me, and I had resigned myself to die. . . . Near a tree, they made me get out of a car. There they asked me again for money, and again I refused to give it to them since I had none. After I had left my car, Pascual Tostado began to whip me and continued to hit me in the same way. Manuel Baca put a rope around my neck and I understood they wanted to strangle me. Madinaveitia said, "What are you waiting for, Don Pascual? Let's go to work." Madinaveitia and Tostado pulled the rope, and I became unconscious and have no recollection what happened then. After three hours, I was conscious again and found myself in my prison and saw that my throat had become inflamed and I had the greatest difficulties in speaking and drinking water. The next day, Raúl Madero and Andres Farías came to my prison and made new accusations against me, not only as far as I personally was concerned, but with respect also to my family, since my mother, my wife, my daughters, and nearly all my sisters were still in Chihuahua. . . . At this point, I understood that the only way to save my mother, the other members of my family, and myself would be to hand over the gold that belonged to the Banco Minero.[23]

In his statement, Terrazas insisted that both Villa and Raúl Madero promised him that in return for revealing his secret, both his family and he himself would be freed. Bitterly, he added that this promise was never kept.

After several hours searching the bank—Terrazas did not exactly know in which column the gold had been buried—a team headed by Raúl Madero and Villa's secretary, Luis Aguirre Benavides, finally found the gold the Creels had hidden.

They delivered the gold to Villa, who put most of it away in a safe. Some of it, though, Villa personally distributed to his generals. Villa told Aguirre Benavides to take 10,000 pesos for himself. "If we have to go to hell in this enterprise, in which you too are taking risks," he told his secretary, "it would not be right that you should leave your family without anything."[24]

From a practical point of view, it was by no means surprising that Villa, if he indeed promised Luis Terrazas Jr. that he would free him, refused to keep his promise. The old hacendado's son was still of great value to him. While Villa had confiscated the huge Terrazas holdings and could now dispose of the old caudillo's vast cattle herds, their value to him would be limited if he could not sell them on the open market in the United States. If Luis Terrazas Sr. had really wanted to, he had effective means at his disposal for preventing such sales from occurring, or at least for creating enormous obstacles to them. He could sell his properties to Americans and thus cause tremendous problems for Villa. If Villa refused to surrender the properties to the new owners, they could attempt to embargo the cattle when they reached the American border and could provoke conflicts between him and the U.S. authorities, which, in view of his reliance on American arms, he wanted to avoid at all costs. Even if Terrazas were unwilling to sell his properties, he might still recur to U.S. courts and declare that the cattle that Villa's men were bringing over the border were stolen property. Such recourse might not prevent but could delay the sale of Mexican cattle, the proceeds of which Villa desperately needed.

It was in order to prevent such reprisals from taking place that Villa decided to keep Luis Terrazas Jr. as a hostage. He did so in spite of a torrent of protests, entreaties, and demands for Terrazas's release by U.S. officials, politicians, and diplomats whom the Terrazas clan had been able to mobilize, although the Americans had no official reason to protest, since Terrazas was a citizen of Mexico. When George Carothers, the U.S. special representative, went to see Villa and among other things interceded on Luis Terrazas Jr.'s behalf, Villa solemnly promised not to shoot his prisoner.[25] Since he had no intention of doing so anyway—Terrazas was far too valuable as a hostage—he was giving nothing away while seeming to make a great concession to the Americans.

What Villa really wanted comes out in an unsigned letter, dated December 1913, in the archives of Villa's secretary of state, Silvestre Terrazas, which reads in part:

in view of our blood ties, we are asking you respectfully to spare the life of our Luis Terrazas Jr.

If you accede to grant us such an important favor, we the undersigned solemnly pledge to separate ourselves absolutely from the revolution carried out by General Victoriano Huerta, in which, blinded by political passions we have participated.

The letter says that Villa "is expressly authorized by us to dispose of whatever he needs of our property to sustain his army during the struggle that you are carrying out to maintain the constitution. . . . In addition, we shall send you 300,000 pesos, Mexican money, every month." It concludes by stating that this agreement "is subject to approval by the first chief of the constitutionalist army, Venustiano Carranza."[26]

The letter, which the Terrazas were meant to sign, is obviously only a draft, but it indicates the kind of ransom that Villa demanded of them in order to spare their son's life.

While the Terrazas may have been naive in assuming that Villa would not violate the diplomatic immunity of the British consulate in order to capture their son, Villa was equally naive in assuming that the Terrazas would simply accede to his demands. They were far too tough for that. A deal was finally struck in which Villa ended by paying money to Luis Terrazas Sr. instead of the latter paying Villa. It was a complex and secret deal managed on Villa's side by one of his representatives in the United States, a shady businessman from Torreón, Lázaro de la Garza, with several American buyers, which established that Luis Terrazas would receive part of the proceeds from the sale of his cattle.[27] These agreements, as well as concern for the safety of his son, may explain why Terrazas, despite the confiscation of his properties, refused an offer by an American company to buy his more than 6,000,000 acres of land at one dollar an acre.[28]

In spite of continued American pressure to free Luis Terrazas Jr., Villa continued to hold the son as hostage. Nearly a year after Luis Terrazas Jr.'s arrest, in November 1914, Fidel Avila, the military governor of Chihuahua, who had been appointed by Villa, seems to have suggested some alleviation of his conditions of imprisonment. Villa acceded but cautioned Avila. "You may do as you wish in the matter of Luis Terrazas Jr., but I want to clearly tell you it is absolutely necessary to keep him in complete security and prevent his escape, since his imprisonment prevents his family from acting against our cause."[29] In late 1915, Luis Terrazas Jr. finally succeeded in escaping from Villa's control and in rejoining his family in the United States.[30] He died a short time after. According to his father, his death was due to the stress he had suffered while Villa's captive.[31]

While Villa's expulsion of the Spaniards from Chihuahua and his imprisonment of Luis Terrazas Jr. provoked some strains with the U.S. government and led to a number of negative articles in the American press, it had little adverse effect on his standing and popularity in Chihuahua itself. The Spaniards had never been popular among either Chihuahua's poor or its middle class, and popular hatred for the Terrazas continued to be very strong.

What harmed Villa far more than these steps was the conduct of many of his military officers, who proceeded to occupy the elegant houses and villas that the oligarchy had either abandoned or from which their remaining members had been expelled on Villa's orders. Instead of turning over the property of the oligarchy to the state treasury, some of Villa's officers appropriated it for themselves. Villa issued repeated decrees that any confiscations of properties of people considered enemies of the revolution could only be carried out by his order and with his consent. The very frequency of these decrees—the fact that they were issued again and again—indicates that they were not always observed.

Since civilian authorities of the state had no power over them, these military men had little difficulty in carrying out such expropriations. The military governor, who did have such power, frequently hesitated in disciplining his commanders and preferred to leave the matter in Villa's hands. Even when Villa wanted to restrain his commanders, his decisions frequently took time in arriving, since he was more and more often away on military campaigns and occupied with military affairs. At times, his loyalty to his subordinates overrode whatever objections he may have had to their behavior and he sanctioned what they had done.

What frequently disturbed Chihuahua's middle classes was the way these nouveaux riches dealt with the unfamiliar properties they had acquired. Many revolutionary officers found large libraries, including extremely valuable books and incunabula, which the former owners had not been able to take with them when they precipitously fled their homes. Many of these books were now used as toys by the children of the new occupants. Others were used to light and fuel kitchen fires. More entrepreneurially oriented owners sold them as scrap paper to butchers, merchants, and other businessmen in Chihuahua. The gradual disappearance of some of Chihuahua's finest libraries deeply offended both Silvestre Terrazas and the middle class's cultural sensibilities, and their eardrums were frequently assailed by a wild cacophony of sounds coming out of many of these newly occupied houses. Silvestre Terrazas wrote:

I heard of the sad way in which children and even men with beards handled the pianos, jumping on them with their feet so that they could play more loudly with the speed of several kilometers per hour, and they created a pandemonium for those who did not belong to the "new rich" and whose nerves were in a state of constant crisis because of these very strange "musical notes." . . . In addition some women used wood from the pianos as fuel for their ovens.[32]

Silvestre Terrazas was so incensed at what he considered a waste of cultural resources that he went to see Villa and asked for his help. Villa immediately acceded, and squads of Silvestre Terrazas's men, frequently forced to brave the guns of the recalcitrant occupants of the houses, proceeded to take all books to the state archives and deposited the pianos in the state conservatory in Ciudad Chihuahua.[33] These measures helped to dispel some of the fears that Chihuahua's middle classes harbored toward Villa.

Villa's Resignation as Governor and the Balance of His Brief Administration

On January 7, 1914, only a little more than four weeks after he had become governor of Chihuahua, Villa resigned from that position. Officially, he did so in response to a suggestion from Carranza that Manuel Chao become governor. "As you know," he wrote Carranza,

I am a man who obeys your orders in accordance with my duties. I understood that your letter saying that General Chao should become governor, although couched in form of a suggestion, was in fact an order of yours. I am putting General Chao at the head of the government so that you will find things easier when you come here and also so that I can resume my march southward.[34]

Even if Carranza had not ordered him resign, Villa would probably have done so anyway. It was very difficult, if not impossible, for him to assume administrative responsibilities at the same time that he was preparing his army for the attack on Torreón.

Villa's resignation as governor of Chihuahua did not mean that he was giving up real power in the state. In the few weeks that he had controlled Chihuahua, he had implemented basic social and economic measures that were to affect the state not only during the two years his faction continued to control it but for many years afterward. In addition, Villa had made sure that he would still control Chihuahua both de facto and de jure. De facto control was assured by having his own man, Silvestre Terrazas, play a decisive role in ruling the state. De jure, Villa had issued a decree to the effect that ultimate power in Chihuahua rested not with the civilian but with the military administration. This was not only the case at the governor's level but also at the local level, at which mayors and civilian administrators were subordinated to the *jefe de armas*. Moreover, Villa's successor, Manuel Chao, had been appointed military governor of the state and was thus under the direct orders of Villa.

When Villa left the governorship, most foreign and even domestic observers agreed that the impact of his policies had been enormous: he had extracted more from the rich in Chihuahua than any comparable revolutionary leader, with the possible exception of Zapata. And he had done so with a minimum of waste and a maximum of effectiveness by limiting pillage and looting both by his own men and by the poorest segments of society.

He had effectively succeeded in making these measures into a great ideological asset by redistributing part of the proceeds from his confiscations to the poor and to the population in general and by promising to redistribute much of the land he had taken from the hacendados after the victory of the revolution.

He had succeeded in recreating the social consensus—the unity of the lower and middle classes—that had been the hallmark of the Madero revolution in Chihuahua. He had also managed not to alienate the Americans but, on the contrary, to gain the goodwill of American residents in Chihuahua, and of the U.S. authorities, by respecting American property and by the discipline he kept. His popularity with the Americans increased both his power and the resources at his disposal. Many U.S. officials passively tolerated arms being smuggled to Villa in the early weeks of 1914. In March of that same year, Woodrow Wilson revoked the arms embargo against Mexico, and Villa could legally buy as much as he could pay for in the United States.

The increasing confidence of Americans in Villa's capacities was also reflected in another way. The paper currency that he now began to print at a furious pace was accepted, if not at par, at a very high value north of the border, so that many Mexicans could make up for the destruction of much of the local economy by buying supplies and other goods in the United States. Villa's newfound power allowed him to establish such firm control over Chihuahua that the year and a half in which he effectively controlled the state would constitute practically the only period of peace that this much-battered region of Mexico would know between 1910 and 1920.

It has at times been argued that Villa had never really been in charge of the administration of Chihuahua. He was, it was assumed, far too inexperienced in administrative affairs, far too ignorant to have ruled such a highly developed state. According to this version, Silvestre Terrazas and a few other bureaucrats ruled the state and drafted the laws and decrees, and Villa did nothing but acquiesce to their decisions. Contemporary observers paint a very different picture of Villa's administration. In his memoirs, Silvestre Terrazas shows a man very much in charge. This is also the picture that John Reed draws of Villa:

It has often been said that Villa succeeded because he had educated advisors. As a matter of fact, he was almost alone. What advisors he had spent most of their time answering his eager questions and doing what he told them.

I sometimes used to go to the governor's palace early in the morning and wait for him in the governor's chamber. About eight o'clock Silvestre Terrazas, the Secretary of State, Sebastian Vargas, the State Treasurer, and Manuel Chao, the interventor, would arrive, very bustling and busy, with huge piles of reports, suggestions, and decrees which they had drawn up. Villa himself came in about eight-thirty, threw himself into a chair, and made them read out loud to him. Every minute he would interject a remark, correction, or suggestion. Occasionally he waved his finger back and forward and said, "No sirve." When they were all through he began rapidly and without a halt to outline the policy of the State of Chihuahua, legislative, financial, judicial, and even educational.[35]

While there is little doubt that Silvestre Terrazas drafted most of the laws, they were not complicated legal documents that only lawyers could understand. The most important decrees issued in this time, such as the confiscation of the properties of the oligarchy, were very much in line with Villa's policies and were not difficult for anyone to understand.

Villa's greatest personal achievement in these first weeks was not so much these decrees as the creation of conditions that made it possible to implement such decrees. Villa was the first and perhaps only leader of the northern revolution who managed to control and to direct the popular forces that the revolution had aroused. In spite of his enormous popularity, Madero had failed to control the popular forces he had called to arms in the north. Most Chihuahuan revolutionaries did not follow him when he first attacked Casas Grandes, and the leaders of the revolutionaries had attempted to rebel against him after the capture of Ciudad Juárez. The first step that both Madero and González took after achieving a nominal victory over Porfirio Díaz was to send most of their erstwhile allies home and to do so with haste.

The Chihuahuan oligarchy in early 1912 had believed that it could control many of these popular forces. After all, it had done so in the past, and the most popular leader, Orozco, was on their side. They too failed. The sack of Parral by the Orozquistas was but the first proof of the oligarchy's lack of control over its nominal allies. As their revolt progressed, many Orozquistas would set out to plunder and pillage the property of some of the most prominent members of the oligarchy, including the Terrazas.

The military leaders of the revolution in Durango proved either unwilling to discipline their forces, as in the case of Urbina, or incapable of doing so, as in the case of Contreras. Sacking Ciudad Durango not only harmed them domestically and internationally but prevented them from using the city's wealth to consolidate their army and systematically win popular support. Carranza, too, had failed to control these popular revolutionaries when he tried to command them in the siege of Torreón and had given up in disgust, proceeding to Sonora, where a well-structured state was waging a far more conventional war against Huerta's troops.

Villa, by contrast, was the only leader who had managed successfully to control the popular forces of both Chihuahua and the Laguna. Not only had he prevented pillage, but he managed to mold his heterogeneous forces into what was probably the best-organized and most effective fighting machine of its time in Mexico. This was owing to his charismatic personality and the appeal he exercised over the lower classes of society, and also to a clever mix of immediate rewards and long-term promises that he implemented. Were these measures only pragmatic responses to immediate needs or were they the result of a more profound ideology? There is no doubt that pragmatic factors, the need to gain popular support, secure enough resources to arm and equip his army, and maintain the goodwill of the Americans played a decisive role in the decrees Villa issued. Nevertheless, they were also in accordance with his deeper convictions. He had always hated the oligarchy and advocated proceeding against them. His hatred had increased immeasurably during his imprisonment, for which he largely blamed Terrazas and Creel. He had always sought to reward his soldiers with pensions, goods, and land, and this was precisely what his decree proclaimed.

The one element that was new in his plan was the promise to return lands to villages that had been deprived of them. These villages were above all the former military colonies. This is no surprise. From the first, Villa maintained close contact with the men from these colonies, such as his earliest supporters in San Andrés. In fact, the old northern tradition of military colonies came to constitute his ideal of how an agrarian society should be structured. In a conversation with John Reed, Villa told him:

When the new Republic is established there will never be any more army in Mexico. Armies are the greatest support of tyranny. There can be no dictator without an army.

We will put the army to work. In all parts of the Republic we will establish military colonies composed of the veterans of the Revolution. The State will give them grants of agricultural lands and establish big industrial enterprises to give them work. Three days a week they will work and work hard, because honest work is more important than fighting, and only honest work makes good citizens. And the other three days they will receive military instruction and go out and teach all the people how to fight. Then, when the *patria* is invaded, we will just have to telephone from the palace at Mexico City, and in half a day all the Mexican people will rise from their fields and factories, fully armed, equipped and organized to defend their children and their homes.

My ambition is to live my life in one of those military colonies among my *compañeros* whom I love, who have suffered so long and so deeply with me.[36]

In the four weeks during which he ruled Chihuahua directly, Villa achieved tremendous short-term successes: he assumed control of vast resources and by imposing strict discipline on his army prevented the destruction of most of this wealth by looting. He gained much popular sympathy by both expropriating the property of the oligarchy and redistributing part of it to the lower classes of society. He successfully earned, if not the support, at least the respect of large segments of the middle class, whose sensibilities he had respected and whom he had granted an amnesty.

Transformation of these short-term successes into long-range ones was a much more complex affair. To a large degree, it would depend upon factors over which Villa had only limited control: the quality of the men with whom he worked; how successful he was in transforming his guerrilla army into a regular fighting force, and the ensuing results in the field; his relations with the United States and with other revolutionary factions (above all, with the revolution's First Chief, Venustiano Carranza); and, finally, on the changes in the evolution of his own personality and the way it was affected by the increasing power that Villa gathered into his hands.

CHAPTER SEVEN

The Villista Leaders

"Drink, but never get drunk; love without passion;
steal, but only from the rich."
—Villa to Agent Grey.[1]

Villa the Administrator

In the years between 1910 and 1913, Pancho Villa probably acquired more varied and broader military experience than any of the senior commanders of the revolutionary armies that swept through Mexico from 1913 onward. Like most other revolutionary military commanders, he had had extensive experience in guerrilla warfare, both in 1910–11 and in 1913. Unlike most of them, he also had experience in regular warfare. His forced impressment into the federal army in 1901–2 must have given him some insights, albeit at the lowest level of military organization. He had participated as a leader in the siege of Ciudad Juárez in 1911, and during the time he spent as a subordinate of Victoriano Huerta's in the campaign against Orozco, he had had the opportunity to study the organization and tactics of the federal army at a higher level than in 1901–2. When the military commanders of the División del Norte elected him as their leader, they thus not only selected the man with the greatest prestige and the best Maderista credentials among them but also the commander with the greatest experience in regular warfare, a quality they desperately needed in order to capture the well-garrisoned fortified city of Torreón.

When his Chihuahuan commanders elected him governor of Chihuahua, Villa could look back upon no similar experience in civilian administration. In this respect, he had far less experience than many of his subordinate officers. Many of them, such as Toribio Ortega, Porfirio Talamantes, and Calixto Contreras, had long experience in a political struggle to protect the lands of their communities. In the process, they had dealt with state authorities, federal authorities, and the courts. During the Maderista period, they had been military commanders of state rurales in their respective regions and had de facto exercised a large measure of civilian control. Villa had none of this experience. He had not participated in politics before 1910, and he had spent the Maderista years as a businessman, as a military leader in the fight against Orozco, and as an inmate of a federal jail.

During his first few weeks as governor of Chihuahua, Villa was quite conscious of his limitations. While his repeated statements to journalists that he was but a humble, ignorant man, willing to learn from anybody, should be taken with a grain of salt, there is no reason to doubt Villa's very real insecurity when he offered the position of governor of Chihuahua to Silvestre Terrazas. In the first months of his administration, he was willing to listen not only to Silvestre Terrazas or to Chao, with whom he discussed most cases, but to other former members of Abraham González's administration who had fled to El Paso after González's murder.

Villa discovered when he assumed the governorship of Chihuahua that the limits placed on his authority were smaller and less visible than those he had to face as commander in chief of the División del Norte. His army was composed of volunteers, whose loyalty he had to retain if they were not to abandon his cause. Many of his senior officers were semi-autonomous caudillos, whose men were primarily loyal to them, and whom Villa had to consult and conciliate. Thus in his career as commander of the División del Norte, Villa constantly had to consider the limits placed on his power by his subordinates, and to a more limited degree by Carranza, his commander in chief.

There were some clear political boundaries that Villa never considered transgressing as governor. He knew that he could not touch American property without antagonizing the United States and thus endangering supplies for his army. He respected the local power of those military leaders, such as Ortega, the Herreras, and Talamantes, who were at the same time local political figures in their native regions. Apart from these military leaders, however, there were no powerful civilian leaders whose opinions he had to respect. The one civilian leader who had enjoyed real power and popularity in Chihuahua, Abraham González, was dead. Others, such as Braulio Hernández, a prominent former Maderista, had joined Orozco and thus had become unacceptable for any political office in Villa's eyes. There was no state legislature to challenge him or to discuss his ideas. The bureaucrats on whom he depended, former members of the González administration and Silvestre Terrazas, who had fled to El Paso and formed a revolutionary junta there, now became some of the most important members of his administration, but they had no political constituency of their own. Carranza did try to limit Villa's civilian authority, but except for the brief appointment of Chao, Villa scarcely heeded him, and in this respect he could count on the support of the vast majority of Chihuahua's inhabitants, who rejected any kind of outside influence on the administration of their state.

As his power grew, his willingness to listen diminished and he brooked less and less contradiction.[2] This increasing power led to Villa's almost single-handed control of Chihuahua's substantial economic resources. It did not, however, lead him to focus primarily on acquiring personal wealth.

Some contemporary observers speculated that allowing Villa to control Chihuahua was like putting the fox in charge of the henhouse. They were mistaken. Villa never set out to build an economic empire or to deposit large sums of money in foreign banks, the way traditional Latin American caudillos such as Batista in Cuba, Trujillo in the Dominican Republic, and Somoza in Nicaragua subsequently did. His main interest was to strengthen his División del Norte and to win the war. In addition, he used much of the money he controlled to make gifts to his friends, to his soldiers, and to the poor in general. This does not mean that he disdained money or the good life. Once he settled down in Chihuahua, he gratefully accepted a Packard automobile as a "gift" from his representative in the United States, Lázaro de la Garza, in which he proudly rode through the streets of Chihuahua.[3]

"General Villa, this afternoon, gave as a present to Mrs. Juanita Torres de Villa, his wife, the packing house of Juárez formerly the property of Roy S. Sherman and John S. Weaver," the *El Paso Morning Times* reported on March 13, 1914. "Villa reportedly paid 20,000 in gold for this property and Mrs. Villa said today that the profits will go to the Constitutionalist cause." In 1916, the U.S. authorities found Villa's brother Hipólito, who had fled to Texas after his brother's defeat, in possession of several hundred thousand dollars.[4] While this money may have been Hipólito's alone—he was notoriously corrupt—relations between the two brothers were such that part of it at least must have belonged to Pancho Villa. It is nevertheless not clear whether this money was to be used for personal purposes or whether Villa intended it as a reserve to buy arms and ammunition in the United States.

Once he returned to Chihuahua, Villa had a mausoleum erected for himself in the city's largest cemetery, but most of the money he took in was probably destined for his increasingly numerous and complex family. He built or expropriated houses for some of his wives,[5] gave money to his mistresses, recognized all of his children, and did his best to support all of them.

The Intimate Life of Pancho Villa

When Luz Corral decided to marry Pancho Villa, it is doubtful, in view of Villa's reputation and the tradition of machismo in Mexico, that she expected her marriage to be a simple, conventional, monogamous affair. It is unlikely, however, that she was quite prepared for the stream of mistresses, girlfriends, and "legal" wives and children that she was to encounter in the years that she spent as Villa's wife. According to her memoirs, written many years later, she regarded Villa's love affairs with great equanimity. "My love for him never diminished. I want to firmly state my belief, and this is also my profound conviction, that for a housewife, the love affairs of her husband should be of no importance as long as the wife is loved and respected in her home, which is her sanctuary."[6]

When she returned to Chihuahua in early 1913 from El Paso, Luz Corral found that Villa had fathered at least three children by three different women. Perhaps because after the death of her daughter she could not have any more children, or perhaps because she wanted to show Villa how broad-minded and good-hearted she was, she succeeded in establishing very close links with these children. The oldest one was Agustín. Very little is known about his mother, Asunción Villaescusa. Agustín spent many hours every day in Villa's home, mainly at the side of Luz Corral, who became, as she described it, a kind of second mother to him.

Luz Corral soon discovered the existence of another of Villa's daughters, Reynalda, who was living with Villa's sister, Martina. For several days, Luz Corral had noted that Villa was making unexplained visits to the home of his sister, although the sister was visiting Luz Corral at the time. Martina finally revealed to her that he was visiting a daughter of his who was staying with them. Luz Corral never mentions the identity of the latter's mother, nor the reasons why Reynalda was staying with her aunt. When she discovered these facts, Luz Corral decided while Villa was away directing a military campaign to take Reynalda into her own home. She made this decision without saying anything to Villa and surprised him with the news when he returned from battle.

I waited for him at the door of my house with Reynalda at my side; he entered, greeted me as he usually did and then looked at me; he then looked at Reynalda as if he wanted to ask her something. He did not do so and suddenly turned around and tells me,

"What have you done, Guera?" [the name by which he addressed his wife] I assumed he was referring to Reynalda and I answered:

"I have just taken your daughter to live with us, which is where she should be; I hope that you will not object to this," and he answered, "If this is what you want, it is fine with me."[7]

Now that he realized that his wife would not only tolerate his escapades but accept his children as well, Villa showed much less reticence about revealing their existence. "One day he arrived home holding his daughter Micaela by the hand, and he told me that from now on she was going to live with us."[8] He had made this decision after discovering that Micaela's mother, Petra Espinosa, had had a secret affair with one of his officers.

Luz Corral maintained her equanimity in the face of Villa's increasingly numerous love affairs as long as she was convinced that she would be his only official wife, and that all the other relationships were subordinate and temporary. Her attitude changed when she discovered that Villa had a much deeper, more permanent, and even more official relationship with another woman, Juana Torres, who also called herself Señora Villa, and whom he had in fact also married.

For several weeks after capturing Chihuahua, Villa kept Luz Corral in El Paso, telling her that he did not want her to return before he was able to build a beautiful new house for her, which was to be called the Quinta Luz. Finally, tired of waiting, she decided she would come anyway. "Upon my arrival in the capital, I understood that the reason my husband did not want me to come to Chihuahua was not so much because my house was not finished, but for a very different reason," she later wrote. "Señora Juana Torres who called herself Señora Villa was living with him and had succeeded in gaining part of his affection."[9]

For several months the two women competed fiercely for Villa's attentions. Villa himself had no compunction about living with both and maintaining separate houses. While there is no reason to doubt Luz Corral's statement that she loved Villa's children by other women, her attitude toward these children was probably also inspired by her desire to impress her husband with her loyalty and affection for him in the ongoing battle with Juana Torres.

Fortunately for Luz Corral, an unexpected controversy seems to have put an end to the relationship between Villa and Juana Torres. Villa had deposited a large sum of money in her house, and when he came to pick it up, he found that 40,000 pesos were missing. Although he could find no definite evidence of it, he believed that Juana Torres's mother and sister had stolen the money, and he ordered them to be put in prison. Juana Torres was so incensed at this treatment of her family that together with a parcel of food that she sent them to prison, she included a letter in which she called Villa a bandit and deplored the fact that he had forced her to live with him. The prison authorities found the letter and sent it to Villa, who became enraged when he saw it.

Villa, who frequently gave vent to his rages, showed a surprising amount of restraint in this case. Before confronting Juana Torres, he asked his secretary, Luis Aguirre Benavides, for advice. The secretary told him to show some understanding for Juana Torres's attitude. After all, he had imprisoned her mother and sister, whom she considered to be innocent. "I advised him to pardon all of them," Aguirre Benavides recalled. "He partly followed my advice. As he later told me, he went to see Juana and showed her the letter. She became extremely pale when she saw it; he forced her to read it out loud several times, which she did weeping and full of terror, and after this moving scene, he was noble enough to free the prisoners and to give them money to go to Chihuahua."[10] After this episode, relations between Villa and Juana Torres cooled off considerably, and they seem to have ended soon thereafter.

Nevertheless, any hopes that Luz Corral may have entertained that Villa would limit his extramarital activities to short-term affairs and not enter into any long-term official relationships would soon be dashed. She seems to have remained his only official wife until his defeat in late 1915, when he resumed guerrilla warfare and sent his family abroad. She spent the five years during which Villa fought his desperate guerrilla war in the hills of Chihuahua first in Havana and later in El Paso. In the meantime, Villa married and established some kind of more permanent relationship first with Soledad Seáñez, a young girl, in 1917, and then with Austreberta Rentería at a later date. When he finally made his peace with the government in 1920, both of these women came to live with him. Luz Corral also briefly joined him in 1920, but he broke with her definitely in 1921.

Villa was a good father. He loved children and was tender and generous toward his own. He could be a tender lover but he could also be harsh, insincere, demanding, and jealous of the women with whom he had affairs. Although Villa lived with several other women and had in fact never married Micaela's mother, he became so furious when he discovered that she had had an affair with another man that he punished her by taking away her daughter.[11] His imprisonment of Juana Torres's mother and sister based merely on suspicion is further evidence of this harshness.

Villa could be extremely jealous. His secretary tells the story of how he picked up a young woman whom his secretary considered to be a kind of prostitute during his stay in Torreón. Before she met Villa, she had been the mistress of Dario Silva, one of Villa's most loyal officers, one of the eight men who had crossed the Rio Grande with him in March 1913. Villa was so jealous of this affair, which had taken place before Villa even knew the girl, that he humiliated Dario Silva in front of both his girlfriend and his officers, forcing him to act as a waiter and to serve food to all of them.[12]

If Villa wanted a woman, he did not rely on his charm or his prestige alone. One expedient he used to win her favor was to fake a marriage. As he traveled from Ciudad Juárez to Chihuahua, after his troops had occupied the capital city of that state, Villa asked Silvestre Terrazas for advice and how to proceed in a delicate affair.

Don Silvestre, I would ask you to give me the advice of a friend. When I was in Torreón, I had an affair with a secretary and in order to accede to her wishes, I simulated a marriage with her. This marriage was a fake since I persuaded a judge to carry out the marriage ceremony and to write up an official certificate, but then I ordered him to destroy it immediately, and I believe that was done. But I regret what I have done. What do you advise me to do now?

Silvestre Terrazas suggested that Villa should tell the girl the truth, that he was already married, and to console her by giving her a large sum of money. Villa never told him how he finally handled the matter.[13]

This was by no means the last simulated marriage that Villa entered into. In a bitter letter to President Abelardo Rodríguez of Mexico asking for help in educating her children, Villa's wife of later years, Soledad Seañez, wrote ten years after her husband's death:

I have grown up in an atmosphere of honesty and work, which I can prove to anyone; during this period of our history, Francisco Villa exercised a reign of terror among the inhabitants of this part of the republic, which he dominated, and all of us, as is well known, depended on his will and whims. In this situation, destiny put me within reach of the claws of Villa, who utilized his control of civilian authorities to simulate a marriage with him in the presence of witnesses and the judge of the civilian registry of Valle de Allende. There are still witnesses alive who were present when the marriage document was signed, but this document can nowhere be found now that I have tried to obtain a copy, and I understand now that all this was just a simulated legal marriage in order to persuade me to live with him.[14]

And yet, in spite of what they had endured at his hands, both Luz Corral and Soledad Seañez continued to have fond memories of and feelings of great warmth for Villa. Luz Corral spent practically her whole life attempting to defend the memory of her husband and in so doing earned the respect and admiration of one of Mexico's great intellectuals, José Vasconcelos, who for a time had become one of Villa's bitterest enemies.[15]

In Soledad Seañez's later years, she remembered Villa far more fondly than in the letter she wrote President Rodríguez in 1933. Describing her first meeting with Villa 30 years after the event, she makes no mention of his having forced his attentions upon her or of any kind of violence:

Pancho told me he first saw me in 1917 in Villa Matamoros, Chihuahua. He was wounded in the leg at the time and was passing through town in a carriage. I was sitting on a porch, where I had taken some sewing to do in the good light. After seeing me on the porch, Villa asked around town till he found a cousin of mine and became acquainted with him. I only knew Villa by name at that time. My cousin had a small picture of me, which Villa asked for. It was very romantic. Villa carried my picture next to his heart until it was almost worn to pieces. He showed it to me when we finally met, two years later. He was still carrying my picture when he was assassinated.[16]

She describes Villa as an ardent lover who sang romantic songs to her and called her by her pet name, "Chole," and as an affectionate, caring husband, who spent hours with her telling her the tragic story of his life and, when she became pregnant, sent her across the border to El Paso so that she could get the best medical attention.

With one exception, none of his wives seem to have participated in political deliberations or to have had any kind of influence upon the decisions Villa took. The one exception was Luz Corral, whom he sometimes consulted and who exercised a moderating influence on Villa, above all with regard to executions.

The Villista Leadership

When Fidel Castro triumphantly entered Havana on New Year's Eve of 1959 and began to take control of Cuba, he headed a team of men he had led for nearly two years, who knew each other well and had a history of close cooperation. The same was true of most revolutionary movements of the twentieth century. When Lenin's Bolshevik Central Committee assumed power in Russia in October 1917, its members had also known one another for many years.

The same cannot be said of the leaders of Villa's movement who took control of Chihuahua in December 1913. They did have certain things in common: most of them had participated in the Madero revolution, many had exercised some kind of civilian or military power at the local level during part of Madero's rule, and most of them had fought Orozco in 1912. Nevertheless, many of them did not know one another, their cooperation had been only sporadic, and Villa had been their leader for only a few weeks. Integrating these men and their followers and molding them into a coherent political and military organization would prove a difficult task, which Villa nevertheless managed to accomplish, at least temporarily.

In contrast to what might be called the core of the leadership of Carranza's administration or of the Zapata revolution in the south, in which intellectuals played a prominent and ever-increasing role, the Villista leadership initially consisted of military men. The one prominent exception was Silvestre Terrazas, who, however, concentrated his efforts more and more on administration and abdicated more and more of his intellectual functions, especially those of an ideologue. The two years in which he was a high official in the Villista administration constituted practically the only period in his active life when Silvestre Terrazas stopped writing for newspapers.

The military leaders of the Villa movement can be divided into two broad categories: those who had an independent power base and those who derived their power entirely from Villa.

This first category was by no means homogeneous. They came from all walks of life: members of former military colonies, independent rancheros, teachers, merchants, and even a member of the hacendado class. Some had been popular leaders before the revolution broke out, others assumed those functions only during the Madero upheaval.

The three men within this group who could most clearly be labeled popular leaders were Toribio Ortega, Calixto Contreras, and Orestes Pereyra.

The prestige of Ortega, who for many years had led the inhabitants of his native village of Cuchillo Parado, and who had been the first to rise in the state of Chihuahua during the Madero revolution, was such that within a few weeks of his taking up arms against the Díaz administration, hundreds of men from neighboring communities had rejoined him, and he had become a prominent regional leader. After Madero's assassination, he was one of the first revolutionaries in Chihuahua to take up arms against the Huerta administration. John Reed provides a vivid portrait of Ortega, "a lean dark Mexican who is called 'the honorable' and 'the most brave' by his soldiers. He is by far the most simple hearted and disinterested soldier in Mexico. He never kills his prisoners. He has refused to take a cent from the Revolution beyond his meager salary. Villa respects and trusts him perhaps beyond all his generals."[17]

Ortega's men largely consisted of dispossessed former military colonists from the northeast region of Chihuahua. By contrast, Calixto Contreras, the other major peasant leader of the Villa movement, led troops from the Laguna area, and their composition was far more heterogeneous. They comprised dispossessed peasants from villages such as San Pedro Ocuila and Peñon Blanco, as well as peons from estates such as Santa Catalina, which belonged to the wealthy Martínez del Río family.

Like Ortega, Contreras had a long history of resistance to the Porfirian authorities. For many years, he had been the spokesman of the inhabitants of his village, San Pedro Ocuila, in their fight to retain their lands against the encroachment of the Hacienda de Sombreretillo, belonging to the López Negrete family. He had paid a higher price than Ortega for his resistance to the Porfirian authorities, having been forcibly impressed into the federal army for several years. Later, during the Madero era, he was the military commander of a region including both his native village and one of the largest haciendas in Durango, the Hacienda de Santa Catalina. During that time he earned both the hatred of the hacendados and much sympathy, not only from the villagers of his own community but from the laborers of the Santa Catalina hacienda. The administrator of that estate complained "that the tenants have been loudly stating that they will not surrender to the hacienda that part of the corn and bean harvest they owed since Contreras told them that everything belongs to them."[18]

The inhabitants of Peñon Blanco, a community that for many years had a land dispute with that same hacienda, regarded Contreras as "a simple man of good faith."[19] Having been impressed into the Porfirian army, he was one of the very few leaders of the Madero revolution who had had some previous military experience. Nevertheless, his qualities as a military commander seemed to have been inferior to his capacities as a political leader. He was one of the few generals of the División del Norte who had serious problems in controlling his men.

"General" Calixto Contreras never was able to maintain any but a poor discipline; horses, saddles, bridles, and accouterments had to be guarded against communal theft. To do them justice, the troopers despoiled one another as indiscriminately as they would me and to my protests, Don Calixto would reply with a sly wry smile: "But Don Patricio, the boys are playful like that. You know them as well as I do. Would you have me order them shot?"[20]

This description by Patrick O'Hea, hacienda administrator, British vice-consul in Torreón, and longtime opponent of Contreras (although he had a grudging respect for him), may have somewhat exaggerated the anarchy among Contreras's troops. It was nevertheless a serious problem, and Contreras did not view it with the equanimity that he displayed when talking to O'Hea. It was not easy for Contreras to endure the contempt that many of Villa's officers felt for his troops and that was perhaps most clearly expressed by one of Villa's henchmen, Rodolfo Fierro, when he called them "useless, those simple fools of Contreras."[21] Contreras became so desperate that he finally sent a delegation to Carranza asking him to name a chief of staff who enjoyed his confidence and who would be capable of organizing his forces.[22]

Shortly after Villa suffered his greatest defeats in 1915 and had gone back to being a guerrilla leader in the mountains of Chihuahua, his former secretary, Enrique Pérez Rul, writing under the pseudonym Juvenal, attempted to give an assessment of Villa and his movement based on his own observations. Pérez Rul divided Villa's generals into two groups, those he called honorable and those he labeled dishonorable.[23] Among the first he named Ortega, Contreras, and the third popular leader of the Villa movement, of whom far less is known, Orestes Pereyra. Pereyra, a tinsmith from the Laguna area, was one of the few revolutionary leaders outside of Chihuahua who had already taken up arms against the Díaz regime in November 1910. He participated in one of the most audacious military operations in this early phase of the revolution. Together with another young revolutionary, a former streetcar operator, Jesús Agustín Castro, he managed, with a few dozen men, to occupy the second-largest city in the Laguna area, Gómez Palacio. This victory was short-lived—federal troops soon forced him to leave the city—but it sent a powerful signal, and Pereyra soon led large numbers of peons who lived and worked in the vicinity of the great Anglo-American estate of Tlahualilo.[24]

In the words of a military commander who fought against him during the civil war of 1914–15, Pereyra was "a man who looked like the heroes of the war against the United States, with his long hair falling to one side over his mutilated ear in order to hide this physical defect; he was a man always correctly dressed and equally correct in his actions; always fair in his appreciations, humble and conscious; a pure revolutionary without any defect; his hands were never stained by murder or theft nor was his conscience stained by any crime."[25] Pereyra had commanded a detachment of rurales during the Madero period, had fought against Orozco, and had taken up arms against Huerta when the latter seized power in Mexico.

While all three of these men were popular leaders with constituencies of their own and a long history of opposition to the Díaz regime, the social bases of their forces were by no means identical. Ortega's men showed the greatest homogeneity. Most of them were members of the free village communities of northeastern Chihuahua. Contreras's forces were far more heterogeneous in nature, comprising both inhabitants of his own community of San Pedro Ocuila and a large number of laborers from the Santa Catalina hacienda. The most heterogeneous of these forces, in which independent peasants played the smallest role, were those of Orestes Pereyra, comprising both miners and temporary workers on Laguna estates.[26]

Other popular leaders representing their communities, with similar histories of long-standing opposition to Porfirio Díaz, also fought in the División del Norte, although they held lower rank. They included such men as Porfirio Talamantes, who had led the villagers of Janos in their long struggle to keep their lands, and Contreras's deputy, Severiano Ceniceros, who for many years had been his assistant in his struggle on behalf of San Pedro Ocuila.

In later years, none of these men, with the exception of Ceniceros, would ever turn against Villa. Talamantes died in battle, and Ortega of a fever. Contreras and Pereyra and his son were all shot by Carranza's troops because they remained loyal to Villa even after the latter had suffered his most devastating defeats.

In contrast to these three men of humble origins, Manuel Chao and Maclovio Herrera, whom Pérez Rul also includes among his list of honorable men, could clearly be labeled middle-class revolutionaries.

In view of his social origins and his activities on the eve of the revolution, it is not surprising that Manuel Chao was Carranza's favorite military commander in Chihuahua, the one with whom he felt he could identify most closely. Chao's parents belonged to the elite of the port city of Tuxpan in the state of Veracruz. When he was 17, in 1900, his father took him along on a trip to the northern state of Durango. Manuel decided that he would stay in the north and not return with his father to the Atlantic coast. He accepted a teaching post in Durango, and in later years he taught in several towns in Chihuahua. Like many other underpaid government employees in Mexico, Chao supplemented his salary by going into private business. He set up a shop along the railway yard near the town of Baqueteros in Chihuahua, where he taught school. This "friendly, middle-sized man, whose traits were anything but warlike . . . was well read and of outstanding goodness."[27]

Chao was one of the first in Chihuahua to respond to Madero's call to arms. He revolted on November 20, 1910, leading a group of men from Baqueteros and its surroundings into the revolution. His "lack of a warlike physiognomy" did not prevent him from becoming a highly successful and recognized military leader of the Madero revolution in Chihuahua. After the end of the Madero revolution, Chao decided to become a full-time military leader rather than to go back to teaching. He became a lieutenant colonel of the state rurales, the traditional police force of the Porfirian regime, which had been transformed by the Madero administration into a corps consisting mainly of former revolutionary soldiers.

Chao was very good at his new profession. When Orozco revolted in 1912, he was one of the few local commanders who not only remained loyal to the government but succeeded in achieving a victory. He defeated the Orozquista commander Blas Orpinel at the battle of Balleza and was promoted to colonel of the state militias.[28] He was equally successful when he revolted against Huerta in early 1913 and became the first revolutionary leader in Chihuahua to capture a major city in the state, occupying Hidalgo del Parral.

Having attempted to set up his own "División del Norte,"[29] Chao was resentful of Villa, who forced him to recognize his supreme leadership of the revolutionary forces in Chihuahua. When Chao escorted Carranza through southern Chihuahua on his way from Coahuila to Sonora in August 1913, he complained about Villa's behavior. According to one witness, he even asked Carranza to remove Villa from power, which Carranza obviously could not do.[30]

Chao's attitude impressed Carranza, who saw in him the best Chihuahuan antidote and counterweight to Villa and did everything in his power to strengthen his position. He pressured Villa to name Chao governor of Chihuahua, and in January 1914, Villa acceded to this request.

Maclovio Herrera, another officer of the División del Norte, also accompanied Carranza through Chihuahua in August 1913. Carranza showed more interest in Chao, who was older, better educated, and came from a higher social class than Herrera, and thus seemed to correspond more to the type of man that Carranza thought should administer Chihuahua, and for that matter, the type of man who should emerge triumphant from the revolution. Yet it was Maclovio Herrera who would become Carranza's man in Chihuahua. Although he had joined the anti-reelectionist party in Parral in 1909, there is no evidence that Herrera had been a popular leader of comparable stature to Ortega or Contreras prior to the 1910 revolution.

A ranchero of relatively modest means, Maclovio Herrera owed the great prestige and popularity he enjoyed in Parral to his increasingly legendary courage, audacity, and military capacities. He was 31 when the Madero revolution broke out. In November 1910, he took up arms under Guillermo Baca, one of Parral's most respected personalities, who was the leader of the revolution there. When Baca was killed in February 1911, Herrera assumed command of his troops. It was during the Orozquistas' siege in early 1912, when together with Villa he defended Parral against far superior forces, that Herrera earned Villa's respect and a large degree of popularity there.

Like most of the other main revolutionary leaders under Villa, Maclovio Herrera had been a commander of rurales throughout the Madero period. When Huerta carried out his coup, he too disavowed the new regime. At the battle of Tierra Blanca, he headed the desperate cavalry charge that broke the back of the federal army and helped to decide the battle. His military prowess and blood ties with an old, well-established family in Parral gave him a solid basis of support in and around his native city.[31]

The commander of Villa's Zaragoza Brigade, Eugenio Aguirre Benavides, should have been closest to the kind of revolutionary Carranza hoped for, in terms of his social origin and liberal education. He came from the First Chief's native state of Coahuila, of a well-known, prosperous family of businessmen. Aguirre Benavides's social advantages were erased in Carranza's mind, however, by his close connections to the Madero family. He was related to them, had business links with Francisco Madero's father, and his deputy as commander of the Zaragoza Brigade was Francisco Madero's younger brother, Raúl.

In view of their close links to the Maderos, it is not surprising that both Eugenio and his brother Luis joined the anti-reelectionist party and the small group of men in the Laguna area who decided to take up arms in response to Madero's call for revolution on November 20, 1910. When news reached them that another planned uprising on that day by Maderistas in Puebla, led by Aquiles Serdán, had been crushed by Díaz's forces, "We were gripped by real panic," as Luis later recalled it, "and fearing the worst, my brother Eugenio and I decided to flee to Eagle Pass, Texas. The other participants in the conspiracy, more courageous and more resolute than we were, fulfilled the obligation they had imposed upon themselves and rose up in arms on November 20, 1910."[32]

Their momentary panic and flight harmed neither of the Aguirre Benavides brothers. Once they arrived in the United States, they immediately contacted the leaders of the Madero movement and became part of an activist group. They first worked in the publicity department of the movement, and when Madero later entered Mexico, they accompanied him and fought at his side in the Chihuahua campaign. Luis soon became secretary to one of the most influential members of the Madero family, the president's brother Gustavo. One of the tasks Gustavo entrusted him with in 1912 was to pay regular visits to Villa while the latter was imprisoned in Mexico City's penitentiary. When Madero was overthrown and Carranza issued his call to arms, the two brothers immediately reported to Carranza, who kept Luis on as a member of his staff but sent Eugenio to his home region in the Laguna, where Carranza hoped he would be able to recruit a significant number of men to fight Huerta. Like all other revolutionaries in the Laguna area, Eugenio Aguirre Benavides accepted Villa's leadership when the latter came to attack Torreón. In spite of his upper-class origins, it was probably easier for Eugenio to subordinate himself to Villa than for many other Laguna leaders to do so. Villa greatly liked Luis because the latter had visited him in prison in Mexico City during the period that Villa considered his darkest hour. He would soon make Luis his private secretary. Eugenio not only benefited from Villa's regard for Luis but also from the fact that another relative, Adrián Aguirre Benavides, had been one of Villa's defense lawyers in 1912.

Above all, what attracted Villa to the commanders of the Zaragoza Brigade was its deputy commander, Raúl Madero, the younger brother of President Francisco Madero. Raúl's relationship with the murdered president would in itself have been sufficient to inspire affection and respect in Villa. In addition, Raúl was free of the arrogance that characterized much of Mexico's upper class and was, according to a witness, "enormously loved and popular among the troops, since he fraternized with everyone including the most obscure revolutionaries, without manifesting any kind of presumption, vanity or pride."[33] Raúl Madero and Villa had become friends during the Madero revolution. It was Raúl who had served as intermediary in the reconciliation between Francisco Madero and Villa after Villa's attempt to depose the president in the aftermath of the capture of Ciudad Juárez.

Another Villista general who had established close links to Eugenio Aguirre

Benavides and basically shared his views was José Isabel Robles. He had been a primary schoolteacher on one of Madero's haciendas when the revolution broke out, and at 20, he mobilized a small group of men and took the field against Porfirio Díaz. What distinguished him from all the other generals of the División del Norte was that he had not remained loyal to Madero, but participated in the Orozco uprising. When Orozco joined forces with Huerta, however, Robles refused to follow him and persuaded his 300 followers to switch sides and to join the forces of a relatively obscure revolutionary, Gregorio García. García was more than happy to have the reinforcements that Robles offered and enthusiastically welcomed him into his army. When García fell in battle, Robles succeeded him. At 23, Robles was one of the youngest of Villa's generals and also one of the most intellectually engaged. His favorite reading on his campaigns was *Plutarch's Lives*. His charms, and perhaps his military capacities, were so great that Villa, who was usually extremely wary of anyone who had fought alongside Orozco, showed no compunction about accepting Robles into his army.[34]

There was one general among Villa's commanders whom no one, no historian, no journalist, no observer, ever called "honorable." This was Tomás Urbina, Villa's crony from his bandit days. Urbina's aim in joining the revolution was perhaps most aptly described by one of his adjutants, who explained to American correspondent John Reed why he had taken up arms. "This *revolución*. Do not mistake. It is the fight of the poor against the rich. I was very poor before the revolución and now I am very rich."[35]

Urbina, a "broad medium size man of dark mahogany complexion, with a sparse black beard up to his cheekbone that didn't hide the wide, thin, expressionless mouth, the gaping nostril, the tiny small humorous animal eyes," seems to have had one ambition in life—namely, to become a wealthy hacendado and to set up an economic empire similar to that of the Terrazas. The hacienda of Las Nieves, which he had occupied, was the cornerstone of this proposed empire. "The town belongs to General Urbina, people, houses, animals and immortal souls. At Las Nieves, he and he alone wields the high justice and the low. The town's only store is in his house."[36]

Pérez Rul describes Urbina as a dissipated, arrogant drunkard with an extremely bad character. "At the high point of Villa's career, Urbina controls an important part of the country, which is subject to no other law than Urbina's whims or those of his numerous corrupt favorites, and no one can escape his disastrous immorality because Villa believes that everything that is being said about his 'compadrito' are simple calumnies and hearsay."[37]

And yet while Urbina came closest among Villa's generals to being a pure bandit, he nevertheless must have had other talents. He was one of the few among Villa's former cronies who had made it on his own. He had headed an important fighting force composed of miners, peons, and peasants during the Madero revolution. During the Orozco rebellion, he had been one of Villa's lieutenants, but he had gone off on his own when the new revolution against Huerta broke out. He had been so successful in recruiting men and in waging guerrilla warfare against the federal forces that the commanders of the revolutionary forces in the state of Durango had elected him their chief when they decided to attack the state's capital. They won, and that victory marked the end of any respect he enjoyed among the majority of his fellow generals. His inability and unwillingness to control his troops when they entered the city, the looting and pillage that ensued, and his own participation in it when he held many of the town's citizens for ransom and pocketed the money for himself created fears among most revolutionary leaders that he would so discredit the revolution that it would be unable to make any genuine advances. Fortunately for him, Villa trusted him blindly and refused to hear anything against him. It was a loyalty that was not reciprocated. A year and a half later, when Villa's fortunes were at their lowest ebb, Urbina tried to abandon him. He would pay for this disloyalty with his life.

The relationship between these hitherto independent military chieftains and Villa was in many respects ambivalent. On the one hand, they accepted Villa's authority in military matters, especially on the battlefield. They were well advised to do so. When one of the lesser-known commanders, Domingo R. Yuriar, in a drunken stupor, refused to heed one of his commands, Villa had him executed. None of the other commanders objected to this execution, since Yuriar had clearly violated military discipline.

Nevertheless, off the battlefield, these chieftains attempted to retain as much autonomy as possible from both Villa and Carranza. While recognizing Carranza's authority as leader of the revolution, they clearly showed their independence by electing Villa both commander of the División del Norte and governor of Chihuahua without consulting the First Chief. Their assertions of autonomy with respect to Villa were more subtle. They attempted to inculcate into their soldiers the idea that while Villa was commander in chief, their primary loyalty should be to them. It was quite characteristic of this attitude that when John Reed came to visit one of Contreras's units and identified himself with a pass signed by Villa, the soldier to whom he showed his credentials told him, "Francisco Villa is nothing to us. . . . we are of the Brigada Juárez, Calixto Contreras' gente."[38] At times they subtly attempted to balance one leader against the other. This explains why Contreras, who until the end of his life remained one of Villa's most loyal generals, nevertheless asked Carranza rather than Villa to send an officer to train and discipline his troops.[39]

While it was Villa who largely supplied his generals and their soldiers with arms and ammunition, they attempted to preserve a certain degree of economic independence from their commander. For example, they staked their claims to certain haciendas, which were administered in their names and were not subject to the Office of Confiscated Property, which was headed by Silvestre Terrazas and was directly under Villa. Their independence was further enhanced by Villa's policy of allowing many of his generals to retain political control over their regions of origin.

In contrast to these generals, who since the days of the Madero revolution had carved out independent power bases of their own, there was a second group of men around Villa whose power derived mainly from him, and with whom he maintained very different relations. They might broadly be labeled technicians, executioners, and military men, although the three categories at times overlapped.

It is not surprising that once Villa became governor of Chihuahua and attempted to transform his forces from a band of guerrillas into a regular army, he needed technicians to help him in this complex administrative and organizational task. Four men formed the core of what one might call the Villista cabinet, although at this early stage of Villista rule, this term was never used by Villa or his subordinates.

Of all the civilians who joined Villa, Silvestre Terrazas was the one who stayed with him and served him longest, from December 1913, when he assumed power in Chihuahua, until he lost control of the state in December 1915. Although he served only as secretary-general of the government (he was interim governor for a very brief span of time), Terrazas's civil power grew steadily. In the first months of Villista rule, during the governorships of Villa himself and of Chao, the power he exercised was limited. Villa took a keen interest in Chihuahuan affairs, and Chao was a cultured and highly educated man, with a keen understanding of the problems he faced, and was not dependent on Terrazas's advice. When, a few months later, Chao was replaced by Fidel Avila, a former hacienda foreman with a low level of education, Terrazas assumed a more central role. He was better educated than his new chief and had a better knowledge of Chihuahua.

Villa remained interested in Chihuahuan affairs, but he was so frequently away on military campaigns that Silvestre Terrazas's freedom of action increased. It was also enhanced when a few months after he became secretary-general of the government, Villa named him chief administrator of confiscated properties. Terrazas, the only high official of the Villista administration other than Villa himself who left memoirs, describes his role in very limited terms. He insists that he was only an administrator, that he knew nothing of the repression that was going on during Villista supremacy, and that in fact one of his main objectives was to limit Villa's repressive tendencies. There is no reason to doubt that time after time, as he describes it in his memoirs, he attempted to restrain Villa; nevertheless, he knew far more about Villista repression, and may have been more involved in it, than he cared to admit:

He was one of Villa's chief advisers during the two years of Villista rule. It was Terrazas who drafted the main laws promulgated by Villa during his brief period as governor that aimed at reorganizing public administration and protecting the poor, especially as far as food was concerned; Silvestre Terrazas was the regulator of this incipient revolutionary government. It was also through him that all orders that Villa or his military governors dictated, both of a violent and a peaceful nature, were transmitted. He could at the same time sign an order to have an execution carried out and another to help the poor.[40]

It seems that it was not Villa's attempts at social reform that attracted Silvestre Terrazas. In fact, in his memoirs, Terrazas never mentions the issue of land reform. Like many members of Chihuahua's middle class, he was most impressed by the fact that Villa had put Chihuahua on the map. It was the men from Chihuahua who had scored the decisive victory that had brought Madero to power. Yet Chihuahua was soon forgotten once Madero became president. With Villa at the helm, Chihuahua would become the center of the new Mexican revolution.

Another "technician" who also ranked among the "cabinet officers" was Juan Medina, a former federal officer who had participated in Porfirio Díaz's campaign against the Yaqui Indians in Sonora in 1903. He had become so disgusted at the treatment meted out to the Indians that he resigned from the federal army and became a small businessman in Chihuahua. He joined the Madero uprising in 1911, and Abraham González appointed him to one of the most important offices in the state, that of jefe político of the Bravos district. He fled from the state once Huerta assumed power but returned to join Villa in 1913. Villa, who urgently needed a man with experience in dealing with a professional army, appointed Medina as his chief of staff, and Medina became centrally involved in the complex task of transforming Villa's motley array of guerrillas into a regular army.[41]

While both Silvestre Terrazas and Juan Medina were judicious and intelligent choices, the same cannot be said of the other two persons Villa appointed in early 1913 to equally responsible "technical" positions in his unofficial cabinet.

When Villa had occupied Torreón in November 1913, he had appointed a rather shady businessman, Lázaro de la Garza, to collect the forced contributions he had imposed on Torreón's wealthy Mexican businessmen. It is not clear why de la Garza was chosen. But since he assiduously collected the contributions that Villa had imposed, he gained the general's confidence, and Villa sent him to the United States as one of his most important emissaries. Villa entrusted de la Garza with large sums of money to buy arms north of the border and to have Villa's new currency printed on American printing presses. Villa also frequently charged him with diplomatic missions. It would prove to be a disastrous choice. A year later, Lázaro de la Garza would betray his chief at one of the most critical moments in Villa's revolutionary career.

Another "technician" whom Villa soon put in charge of purchasing arms and supplies in the United States, and who also administered the gambling concessions in Ciudad Juárez, was his own brother Hipólito. Pérez Rul called Hipólito Villa the Rockefeller of the revolution and said that his life deserved a biography by a historian of Plutarch's stature.[42] Since Hipólito could read and write, and Villa implicitly trusted his younger brother, he appointed him to head an agency in the border city of Ciudad Juárez charged with buying military supplies in the United States, which disposed of large sums of money. Hipólito also administered the large revenues from gambling and horse racing in the border city. "Hipólito was a very different kind of person than his brother," his former wife describes him. "Hipólito liked to have a good time. He loved to spend money and always seemed to have plenty. He was very handsome. He would always drive up to the picture house in a beautiful Cadillac."[43]

Albeit less bloodthirsty, Hipólito also lacked his brother's virtues and ability. He had none of Villa's social commitments and did not share his gift for leadership. Hipólito's organizational capacities were minimal. He was a playboy, and his love of spending money was matched only by the intensity of his desire to acquire it. For Pancho Villa, money was always a means to acquire more power and influence; for Hipólito, it was an end in itself and the means of maintaining his lifestyle. Through incapacity, lack of interest, or outright corruption, Hipólito repeatedly botched assignments to buy urgently needed supplies. Pancho Villa had a soft spot for his brother. He kept him on in his position and as far as possible kept him of out danger. In spite of his ineptness and corruption, Hipólito in his own way remained loyal to his brother to the end. But unlike Pancho, Hipólito lived out his life and died a natural death in Chihuahua.

The other prominent "technician" whom Villa chose for the most important position of railway supervisor was even more of a disaster. Although he never turned against his chief, Rodolfo Fierro, a former railwayman, would do more to harm his reputation than probably any other of his associates, including Tomás Urbina.

In history, legend and reality rarely concur. In the case of Villa and his movement, the disparity seems especially wide. But there is one exception to this tendency, one case where the two not only overlap but coincide, and it relates to Rodolfo Fierro. Fierro's "technical" capacities were limited. He had been a low-level railway employee and had never had to deal with the complex managerial problems that troop transports entailed. In fact, in some respects, Fierro was an unlikely member of the group assisting Villa, most of whom had been close to Madero, were related to Villa, or had either known Villa or worked with him in the days preceding the revolution. The two men only met in 1913, after the end of the Madero revolution.

Unlike most of Villa's close associates, Fierro was neither born nor raised in Chihuahua or Durango. He came from Sinaloa and had lived for many years in the western state of Sonora, where he had first served as a federal soldier, taking part in the campaign against the Yaqui Indians, and later as a railwayman. What primarily attracted Villa to him was not his dubious "expertise" about railroads but other qualities: his reckless courage, his ruthlessness, and his loyalty. It is not known by what act Fierro first drew Villa's attention, but it was probably similar to a brief one-man attack during the battle of Tierra Blanca that spread his fame throughout the División del Norte. As a train full of federal soldiers was gathering steam and began to pull out of Tierra Blanca, Fierro, in a ride that would have delighted any film producer, caught up with the train on his horse, rode alongside the locomotive, jumped on it, shot the engineers and stopped the train, which was then attacked by Villa's soldiers.

Besides this act of courage, Fierro showed other "qualities" that attracted Villa. His executions of prisoners became even better known in the División del Norte than his military actions. One of Mexico's greatest writers, Martín Luis Guzmán, has described how he single-handedly shot several hundred Orozquista prisoners taken in battle. Telling the prisoners that he was going to give them a "chance," he ordered them released into a yard in groups of ten, where he stood facing them with his pistols. If they made it across the yard and over the wall they would be free. They ran, they jumped, and they died. Only one of the more than 200 men finally reached the wall and jumped to freedom. Fierro became Villa's primary executioner, and he soon extended his activities from the "public" to the "private sphere." It was said that he once shot a stranger in Ciudad Chihuahua "to settle a bet on whether a dying man falls forward or backward. Fierro won the bet and the man fell forward."[44]

Any doubts that Patrick O'Hea, British businessman and consul in Torreón, might have entertained about the veracity of these stories were dispelled when he met Fierro for the first time. O'Hea was stopped by Fierro, "tall and swarthy but with a Mongolian cast of features," and a group of men on a street in Torreón. Fierro appropriated O'Hea's automatic pistol and began playing with it:

he pointed the weapon down at me. The blood-shot eyes were those of a man well-gone in liquor and fatigue, fixing my gaze with his, he slowly brought the barrel upward until I found myself looking fairly into its blue-black aperture and noticing as one will notice trifles at such instants, the grooves of the rifling around the weakened edges of the death-hole.

Very drunk must Rodolfo Fierro have been at that moment, for the barrel perceptibly jerked downward as he squeezed the trigger, using increasing force as the weapon failed to explode and to fulfill its intended purpose of sending me into eternity. With a baffled look he steadied the little weapon again, small in his vast palm, but again the hidden hammer failed to fall upon the cartridge again, and still I lived. . . .

By now I was smiling what manner of ghastly and fear-frozen grimace I cannot know but there was something in that wretched grin that made its appeal.

"Let me show you how it works," I said, grinning still.

Without relaxing his hold upon the weapon he allowed me to demonstrate the safety catch, almost invisible, that unlocked the hammer. He fired a sudden shot into the ground at our feet then looked into my smiling eyes and pocketed the automatic, his face relieved. His killing instinct abated when his companions explained to him that oh, he was a foreigner, and his execution might lead to complications. He gripped my arm, alcohol heavy on his breath, grinning now with his face close to mine said, "When it happens again, smile and it may again save your life."[45]

These methods of Fierro's were quite effective when it came to dealing with Villa's real or potential enemies. They were far less effective when it came to dealing with railroads. During the battle of Torreón, Villa apparently vented his rage on Fierro when a train carrying water and provisions was 35 minutes late. As an American newspaper correspondent reported it, Villa's "screams of wild rage could be heard across the camp, terrifying, maniacal, as he shook both fists at his subordinate's face. Fierro, a murderer by profession, green with passion remained silent, without lifting a hand against his chief. But half an hour later, when the delayed train pulled into its siding, Fierro cut short the conductor's explanation by shooting him dead."[46]

Fierro's "administrative style" led to increasing restlessness among the railway workers, who were staunch supporters of Villa's, and on whom the whole transportation system of the army depended. When Fierro, in a drunken stupor, killed a railwayman who had accidentally brushed against him on the street, resentment against him among railway workers reached such a pitch that Villa was finally forced to act. Until that point Villa had steadfastly refused to proceed against Fierro in any way, even when he killed members of his own party and tensions arose in the ranks, saying that if he were ever defeated and had to return to the hills, Fierro would be among the few who would follow him.

This time Villa felt that Fierro had gone too far. In view of the División del Norte's increasing dependence on railway transportation, loss of support among railroad workers would be a devastating blow. Villa dismissed Fierro as railway superintendent and had him replaced. He also agreed with Silvestre Terrazas's suggestion that a prosecuting judge should begin collecting evidence against Fierro so that he might be put on trial. Fierro's name inspired such terror that the chosen judge begged Silvestre Terrazas to remove him from the case. "You know," he told Terrazas, "how General Fierro, Villa's deputy, is. I fear him."[47]

He need not have been afraid, for unlike Fierro's dismissal as railway superintendent, which was very real, the investigation was a charade, destined above all to pacify the angry railwaymen. Villa had no intention of proceeding against his most trusted lieutenant, who was soon to become one of his most important generals.

In contrast to Fierro, most other members of Villa's inner circle have faded into oblivion. There was another executioner among them, probably as bloodthirsty but far less capable than Fierro. This was Manuel Baca Valles, a crony from Villa's bandit days, whose criminal record dots the pages of Chihuahuan archives. Although he had become a business associate of Villa's in 1912, Luz Corral was extremely wary of him and considered him a murderer.[48] Like Fierro, he killed personal enemies and random acquaintances, and Villa refused to punish him, although at times he did restrain him.

The other men around Villa were of a different caliber. While they could be brutal, they were neither executioners nor murderers like Fierro and Baca Valles. They were military men who formed the core of the personal strike force that Villa was setting up—an elite fighting unit whose primary loyalty would be to Villa himself and not to any of his generals. Unlike Fierro, most of them had joined Villa in the early days of the Madero revolution, had fought with him against Orozco, and had joined him when he called on them to revolt after he returned from the United States.

There is no common denominator to their social origins. Nicolás Fernández, who was 35 when the revolution broke out in 1910, could be considered a member of the state's upper middle class both because of his social origin and the kind of work he did. His grandfather was the brother of Lauro Carrillo, who had been governor of Chihuahua in the 1880s, and Fernández was administrator of several haciendas belonging to Luis Terrazas. It is not easy to understand why he took part in the revolution, and even less easy to explain why he joined Villa's forces. All he said in an interview he gave years later was that he was on good terms with Abraham González, and that Villa one day rode into the hacienda and asked him to join his forces. Was he so deeply shocked by conditions on the Terrazas haciendas that he was willing to sacrifice his own position in order to fight his former boss? Did he hold a personal grudge against Terrazas? Was he motivated by friendship for Abraham González? Or had he been a surreptitious associate of Villa's in his cattle-rustling activities?[49]

The same type of question arises with regard to Fidel Avila, a foreman on a hacienda before the revolution, who also joined Villa in the early days of the Madero uprising. Both men were very close to their leader. Nicolás Fernández remained with him until his death, while Fidel Avila was designated by Villa to succeed Chao as governor of Chihuahua.[50]

There are fewer question marks concerning the career of Martín López, a former baker who was 18 when he entered the ranks of the Madero revolutionaries. He first joined a minor chieftain, Guadalupe Gardea, whose forces were soon incorporated into Villa's detachment. Unlike Fernández and Avila, who were officers from the moment they joined the revolutionary army, López, like many others of his age group, rose through the ranks. He started as a private, and his audacity, courage, and loyalty so impressed Villa that within a few years he would become a general and one of Villa's most trusted aides.[51]

The Coming of Angeles

There was another man, who joined Villa later than Urbina or Fierro, who came to be as closely associated in the public mind with Villa as they, and who in many respects was their complete antithesis. He was not a peasant leader. He did not belong to any of the traditional intellectual professions—lawyer, teacher, newspaperman—whose members tended to join the revolution, nor did he have a long history of opposition to the Díaz regime. He was Felipe Angeles, a federal general who was an exception to every rule of both Porfirian and revolutionary Mexico.

Angeles was the only high federal officer who joined the revolutionary forces, and he was also one of the very few Mexican generals, either federal or revolutionary, who was also an intellectual in the broadest sense of the term. He taught mathematics and artillery science and wrote widely noted papers in both fields. He also showed a profound interest in literature and culture and was a well-read man. In addition, he was one of the very few military men who enjoyed both national prestige and national popularity in much of Mexico. Above all, he was one of the few ideologues the Mexican revolution produced. He would greatly influence both Villa and his army in several different ways: as an artillery specialist, as a strategist, as an organizer, as an ideological leader, and as an intermediary with the Americans.

At first glance, Angeles seems an unlikely revolutionary. He had never expressed any sympathy for the opposition to Díaz prior to 1910, and in fact after the triumph of the revolution, he continued to express his admiration for Díaz himself.

He came from a Porfirian middle-class family. His father, who had distinguished himself in the war against the French and Maximilian, was a Porfirian jefe político who enjoyed the full confidence of the authorities. He took care to give young Felipe, who was born in Zacualtipán in the state of Hidalgo in 1868, the best education then available in Mexico.[52] After completing primary school, Felipe Angeles attended the Instituto Científico y Literario of Pachuca, and at 14, he became a student at the Colegio Militar, one of the most prestigious institutions of higher learning in Mexico. Unlike the many young men during the Porfiriato who owed their careers to wealth, patronage, or nepotism, Angeles's rise was due to his intellectual talents. He was so good in mathematics that while still a student at the military academy, he was called on to replace those of his professors who were on leave. He specialized in ballistics, and his technical articles on that subject seem to have won acclaim far beyond the borders of Mexico. After graduating from the military academy, he soon received an appointment as professor at the prestigious institution. As an artillery specialist, he was sent to France in 1902 as a technical expert in a purchasing commission that was buying artillery pieces for the Mexican army. There he clashed with the Porfirian power structure. Angeles's personnel file states that "some disagreement emerged in France among the members of the commission, one of whom was Felipe Angeles . . . [and] the latter was ordered to return to Mexico."[53]

The man with whom Angeles seems to have clashed was his godfather, one of the most powerful and corrupt generals in the Mexican army, Manuel Mondragón. He was in charge of artillery procurement for the Mexican army and became extremely wealthy in the process. Germany's leading industrial company and producer of cannon, Krupp, reported to the German Foreign Office that in the course of negotiations, Mondragón had asked that the price of any cannon that Krupp sold to the Mexican government should be increased by 25 percent to cover the commission that Mondragón personally charged.[54]

Obviously, Angeles had refused to go along with Mondragón's schemes. Two years later, in 1904, he again seems to have clashed with procurement officials in Mexico. The undersecretary of war wanted to acquire a new type of gunpowder developed in the United States by an inventor, Hudson Maxim. A prominent científico, Rosendo Pineda, was involved in the deal and recommended purchasing the gunpowder. Angeles opposed it on technical grounds, and the deal fell through.[55] This was the last time that Angeles seems to have been involved in any kind of procurement deal. It may have been the long memory of the bureaucracy that four years later led to his being confined to quarters for eight days for having written an article critical of the low quality of education given to noncommissioned officers in a new school established to train them.[56]

One year later the government sent him to France to study artillery techniques at two artillery schools in Fontainebleau and Mailly.[57] Was this a promotion to groom Angeles for a high position in the Mexican military, or was it intended to prevent him from interfering once again with lucrative arms deals? The latter hypothesis is more probable, since study missions seem to have been one means by which the Díaz administration sent recalcitrant military men into a kind of golden exile under the best possible conditions in Europe but as far away as possible from Mexico. Bernardo Reyes (with whom Angeles had no relations) was likewise sent on a study mission to France when Díaz wanted to eliminate him from public life.

When the Madero revolution broke out, Angeles was still in France, and in November 1910, he offered his services to the Mexican government to fight against the revolutionaries.[58] The government refused to recall him to Mexico—partly because it was still overconfident, partly because his recall would have given the impression in France that the government took the Madero revolution seriously, which in 1910 was still not the case.

Angeles's rise to prominence occurred during the Madero administration. Perhaps because he was less controversial than other officers of the Díaz army, since he had not fought against Madero, he was named chief of the Colegio Militar. Madero frequently asked him to escort him on rides outside of the capital, and the two men became friends. Angeles became a committed Maderista, and Madero trusted him more than any other military leader. It is thus not surprising that the Mexican president charged Angeles with two important tasks. He largely succeeded in the first and failed in the second.

His first task was to fight the Zapata revolt in Morelos in a manner commensurate with Madero's ideology. Angeles's predecessors in the campaign against Zapata had applied bloody counterinsurgency tactics. Generals Huerta and Juvencio Robles had burned villages suspected of Zapatista sympathies to the ground and massacred their inhabitants. Zapatista prisoners were routinely executed, frequently after being forced to dig their own graves. The result of this campaign of terror was that many peasants hitherto unwilling to join Zapata now joined his cause both out of a desire for revenge and because they felt that it was the only way to survive. After expressing his disgust at the methods his predecessors had utilized, Angeles applied a completely new tactic. To a large degree, he gave up burning villages, reprisals against civilians, and executions of prisoners. The results were gratifying to both Madero and Angeles. Not only did the bloodthirstiness of the campaign that had disgusted both men end, but in military terms, its results were also impressive. Many peasants, realizing that they had no reprisals to fear, returned home and, although not defeated, Zapatismo was greatly weakened.[59]

In the process of fighting Zapata, Angeles became sympathetic to the aims of his opponents. He continued fighting the Zapatistas, however, because he believed that only Madero could resolve their problem. "I am a general, but I am only an Indian," he told an acquaintance. "I would give anything . . . to show these people the mistake they are making. President Madero is doing his best for them but he needs cooperation. The Conservatives, using all the tricks of politics, fight him at every step, and how can he force through his reforms if the people he wants to help will not back him?"[60]

If Angeles chalked up something of a success in Morelos, he failed in the other even more important task with which Madero charged him, that of making sure that the federal army would not turn against him during the revolt of February 1913. During the uprising, Angeles was faced with a Machiavellian situation with which he could not cope.

After the initially unsuccessful revolt by Félix Díaz and a few hundred supporters against Madero in Mexico City, the Mexican president had named Huerta supreme commander of the federal forces in charge of fighting the rebels. Madero's trust in Huerta was limited, however, and he took the risk of traveling with only a few aides through Zapata-held territory to Cuernavaca to persuade Angeles to come to Mexico City with his troops and to become a kind of army chief of staff overseeing the operations against the Ciudadela rebels. Angeles complied and came to Mexico City with a large part of his command, but he soon found that his services were not welcomed by the leaders of the federal army. In spite of Madero's endeavors, Minister of War Angel García Peña, a friend of Huerta's, refused to accede to Madero's wishes to nominate Angeles as chief of staff on the grounds that his rank in the military hierarchy was too low.[61]

Madero caved in to the wishes of his minister of war, perhaps fearing that otherwise the army might turn against him. Angeles was relegated to a secondary role, commanding an artillery unit in one section of Mexico City. The situation the general faced was strange and difficult. While Angeles had no knowledge of Huerta's real aims, during the Decena trágica, he soon realized that something was deeply wrong with the way the campaign against the rebels was being waged. "Poor Castillo and his men," Angeles told a friend a few weeks later, "ordered by Huerta to the corner of Balderas and Morelos, where he knew they would be blown to pieces. . . . Imagine if you can, Señora," he told the same friend, "the moment when I opened fire on the Ciudadela and discovered that the focus of my cannon had been secretly destroyed."[62]

While Angeles may have briefly mentioned some of his doubts to Madero, there is no evidence he made any serious attempt to warn Madero of the dangerous situation in which he found himself. A few weeks after Madero's fall, he told his lawyer, Manuel Calero, that "because of military discipline and because [he] did not want to appear as an intriguer, [he] had not insisted enough with the members of the government about the fact that Huerta was carrying out the operations against the Ciudadela in such an incompetent way that his conduct seemed more than suspicious." That fact is one of the reasons for the continuing, heated historical controversy over Angeles.[63]

Angeles's arguments to Calero, that he did not want to be considered by the president and the cabinet as an intriguer, and that in addition, as a military man, he was so strongly convinced of the need for discipline that he did not want to override the chain of command, are not sufficient to explain his conduct: in both later and earlier periods, he had been willing to challenge his superiors when he felt that it was necessary. Probably he entertained serious doubts whether Madero would support him if he challenged Huerta. After all, Madero had undertaken the perilous journey to Cuernavaca to suggest to Angeles that he become chief of staff, yet when the military objected, Madero had caved in. In addition, Angeles was plagued by another problem that he never mentioned either to his friends or to other officers: it was not at all clear whether the troops he had brought from Morelos would effectively support him in a conflict with other sectors of the military.

Time and time again, Angeles had been faced with rebellion among his own troops. "Part of the 11th regiment, which garrisoned Yautepec, rebelled," Angeles reported to Madero on October 31, 1912, "and another part was close to rebellion so that I was forced to disarm it." He also reported that he had been forced to instruct another battalion, the 32d, to leave the city of Jojutla, which it was garrisoning, and to send it to Mexico State, because it was threatening to destroy an important aqueduct.[64]

An even more serious mutiny against Angeles occurred during the Decena trágica itself. A Mexican deputy, García de la Cadena, who was visiting Angeles's headquarters, later testified at Angeles's trial in 1913 that "the latter's troops were deeply resentful because of the death of their colonel which they attributed to the imprudence of General Angeles. For that reason his soldiers were waiting for him to come down from the roof of the building where he had been staying and wanted to kill him." With the greatest difficulty, the deputy and a captain of Angeles's troops succeeded in convincing the soldiers that Angeles was not responsible for the death of the colonel, but that he had just been following orders when he set up his command post at the place where the colonel had been killed.[65]

The reasons for Angeles's unpopularity among many of his soldiers are not difficult to comprehend. Under his predecessors, Huerta and Robles, they had been allowed to plunder at will and kill civilians who opposed them. Angeles had sharply restricted such behavior, a fact that the underpaid and forcibly inducted soldiers, whose main compensation had been whatever they could loot, deeply resented.[66]

The soldiers' perception that they had been placed in a particularly exposed position was in fact correct. Huerta, the commander of the federal troops, did everything in his power to decimate those troops whose commanders he felt would not join him in a coup, while sparing those whose leaders were ready to conspire with him. Thus the troops of Aureliano Blanquet, a commander closely allied to Huerta, and who later arrested Madero, were kept out of Mexico City and remained in the suburbs as long as the fighting lasted. By contrast, Angeles's troops were sent to particularly exposed parts of the city. Angeles continued to obey orders, however, and did not alert Madero to these facts.

It is dubious that if he had done so, he would have persuaded Madero to depose Huerta as federal commander. One day before President Madero was toppled, his brother Gustavo, who had heard rumors of secret meetings between Huerta and Félix Díaz, arrested Huerta and told the president of the disloyalty of the federal commander. It was the last chance Madero had of saving his government and his life. Not even his brother could shake Francisco Madero's deep-seated confidence in the federal army and its commanders, and after Huerta promised to order a final offensive the next day, Madero released and reinstated him. Would a warning by Angeles have made a difference? Perhaps, although it is not very probable.

While Angeles was not ready to proceed against his superiors on his own initiative, the situation would have been drastically different if he had received news of the arrest of Madero and Pino Suárez while still in command of his men. He could easily have become the center of resistance against the coup and rallied the many soldiers still loyal to Madero. This was obviously the conclusion reached by Huerta, who, on the same morning that he had Madero and his vice president arrested, summoned Angeles to his headquarters to receive orders and there arrested him. Angeles had obviously not anticipated such a possibility, and he had left no instructions to his subordinates to come after him should he not return on time.

Angeles was detained in the same room as Madero and Pino Suárez. Márquez Sterling, the Cuban representative in Mexico, and the only diplomat allowed to visit the prisoners, was struck by Angeles's deep pessimism:

Sitting on a sofa General Angeles had a sad smile on his lips. He is a distinguished looking man; tall, slender, serene; large expressive eyes; intelligent face and very good manners. When he was ordered to turn against Madero he refused to obey. He just had changed his uniform for civilian dress. He was the only one of all those who were present at our meeting who had no confidence in the illusion of a trip to Cuba [Madero had been promised by Huerta's representatives that if he resigned he would be allowed to go to Cuba together with his vice president and his family]. One hour later he told me in his military language of his suspicion of a horrible end: "they will murder Don Pancho."[67]

Vice president Pino Suárez was more optimistic. "The only danger we face is for our freedom, not our lives. . . . killing us would lead to anarchy."

He was especially optimistic as far as Angeles was concerned. "They will not dare to touch him. The army likes him because he is such a valuable man and because he was a teacher of many of its officers. Huerta is an astute man and he will not antagonize the army, his only support, by shooting Angeles."[68]

Pino Suárez was mistaken as far as his own fate and that of Madero were concerned, but he was right about that of Angeles. Huerta did not dare to have him executed. The military dictator's uncertainty was reflected by his inconsistent attitude toward Angeles. At first he was ready to send him into golden exile. Angeles was appointed Mexican military attaché in Brussels, a city close to France, which Angeles loved.[69] Only a few days later, however, Huerta reversed his stand. He felt that he had found a good motive for imprisoning Angeles and thus decisively neutralizing him, as well as discrediting him in the eyes of Mexico's public opinion.

A few weeks after he was freed from prison, in early April, the government accused Angeles of ordering the killing of an innocent child during the fighting that took place during the Decena trágica. It is not clear whether Angeles was captured by the police or by Huerta's troops, or whether he turned himself in to respond to these charges, but he was present during the trial.

The child turned out to be the son of a prominent Mexico City official, an 18-year-old boy, who at the height of the fighting against Félix Díaz had harangued Angeles's troops and called upon them to join the rebels. Angeles had thereupon ordered his arrest, and one of Angeles's subordinates had had him executed. The defense argued that Angeles had not given the order for the boy's execution, and that even if he had, he would have been justified, since calling for troops to rebel in the midst of a battle was an act of treason.[70]

The fact that Angeles was proved innocent did not greatly help him. Huerta planned to apply the same tactic to him that he had used on Villa—drag the trial on so that he would be able to keep him in prison indefinitely.

Fortunately for Angeles, he had influential backers. The most powerful of them was U.S. Ambassador Henry Lane Wilson, who had voiced no objection when Huerta executed Madero but strongly objected to possible reprisals against Angeles.[71] Another powerful protector of Angeles's life was Manuel Calero, an equally influential conservative politician, who took on Angeles's defense. Calero not only exercised a great influence on Mexico's conservatives but also maintained close links to one of the most powerful American oil companies doing business in Mexico, Doheny's Mexican Petroleum Company. Both Wilson and Calero had supported Huerta's coup, but both believed that he should turn the presidency over to someone else. Wilson hoped that this would be Félix Díaz; Calero was thinking of himself. In both cases, gaining the sympathy and support of an influential military man such as Angeles would have given a great boost to their political projects. The pressure of these men persuaded Huerta to suspend the trial and send Angeles out of the country, ostensibly on military research mission.[72]

Soon after arriving in Paris, Angeles established contact with a representative of the constitutionalists in that city, Miguel Díaz Lombardo, and offered his services to the constitutionalist cause. All he asked for was that he be paid $2,000 to support his family.[73] Because of his scrupulous honesty, Angeles had not made any money from the deals that were so common during the Porfirian period.

When Angeles arrived in Sonora, Carranza welcomed him with open arms and named him secretary of defense in his cabinet. Soon, however, relations between the two men deteriorated. Revolutionary officers such as Alvaro Obregón objected to a former federal officer being named to such a high position in the revolutionary cabinet, and their pressure led Carranza to demote him to undersecretary, which in practice meant that he had no effective power. In addition, ideological conflicts with Carranza soon developed. Unlike the First Chief, Angeles firmly believed that part of the federal army could be induced to change sides.[74]

Carranza had no confidence in that army and did not want to have it join his forces. In addition, Angeles was repelled by Carranza's overt anti-Maderismo. He was thus ready to accede to a request by Villa to join his army as chief of artillery. Carranza, who was still allied with Villa at this time, seems to have been happy to get rid of Angeles.

Once he joined the División del Norte, Angeles acquired an ascendancy over Villa and his generals that went far beyond his technical expertise. This was partly owing to the deep respect for highly trained military men that Villa had already manifested when he met Reyes in prison. Probably more important, however, was Angeles's closeness to Madero, which in Villa's eyes and those of his associates, in contrast to those of Carranza and the Sonorans, counted for a great deal.

In addition, Angeles was unlike the federal officers Villa and his associates had known in the brief period that they fought together against the Orozco rebellion. He lacked their arrogance and their contempt for the officers of the revolutionary forces. In addition, he was a mestizo, and unlike most of them, he constantly emphasized his Indian heritage.

Villa and some of his officers also seem to have believed that Angeles could confer the kind of legitimacy that Carranza had initially provided for them. Like Carranza, he had been a high official in the Madero administration. The fact that, unlike Carranza, he never had been elected to public office had no impact on Villa's opinion. In fact, Villa seems to have for a time envisioned having Angeles and not Carranza become president of Mexico.

Angeles was not only a military man but an ideologue, in the sense that he had developed what he felt was a national agenda for Mexico. That agenda was largely Maderista in nature, since Angeles was in many respects Madero's spiritual heir. Like Madero, he had a profound belief in democracy. He was more committed to social reforms than Madero had been—in later life he considered himself a socialist—but like Madero he believed that whatever reforms were instituted should be gradual in nature, and that the sanctity of private property should be respected. He strongly opposed confiscations of private property.

The obvious question that emerges is how Angeles hoped to implement this agenda, knowing that many of its points were not shared by Villa. As he had shown in Chihuahua and in the territories occupied by the División del Norte, Villa was not opposed to confiscations. And as Angeles himself noted, Villa was no democrat. Finally, Angeles had behind him neither an organized political party nor a constituency aside from the men of the División del Norte, the vast majority of whom shared Villa's ideas and ideals.

There are three possible ways in which Angeles might have hoped to achieve his aims. The first was what might be called the Machiavellian road. This was the course Obregón was convinced Angeles envisaged. It involved having as many former federal soldiers and officers as possible rally to the División del Norte, who would subordinate themselves to Angeles and overthrow Villa if he did not accede to Angeles's plans. There is no evidence that Angeles made any efforts or preparations for such an eventuality. While he did favor the inclusion of federal soldiers and officers in the División del Norte, he never made efforts to set up separate units composed of former members of the federal army, which would have been the best way of establishing a separate striking force. The one time such a possibility emerged, when the leadership of the federal army proposed to Villa that its remnants join his División del Norte, Angeles dissuaded Villa from taking such a course (see below).

The second possibility that Angeles may have envisaged was that with Villa's help he would become either president or a high officer in a Villista-sponsored national government. In that case, while he might not persuade Villa to apply democratic procedures in Chihuahua and the northern regions he controlled, he might very well get Villa's agreement to do what he thought best in the rest of Mexico.

Independent of such considerations, the most important way in which Angeles hoped to influence Villa was by forging and strengthening an alliance between Villa and the United States. In Angeles's eyes, Woodrow Wilson was the ultimate apostle of democracy and social reform and, by becoming increasingly dependent on the United States, Villa might be persuaded to carry out the kind of democratic reform that Woodrow Wilson advocated and that Angeles thought Mexico needed.

Angeles's increasing importance in the councils of the División del Norte was reflected in at least four ways. In military terms, he did not limit himself to organizing the army's artillery but played an important and perhaps, according to some Villista veterans, decisive role in transforming Villa's guerrilla force into a regular army. In addition, he drafted the tactics and strategy for one of the most important battles that Villa's troops would wage, the attack on Zacatecas. He would be the architect of Villa's alliances both with the conservative Sonoran governor José María Maytorena and with Emiliano Zapata. At the same time, he drafted some of the most important ideological pronouncements of the Villista faction.

Angeles and Silvestre Terrazas were doubtless the two intellectuals who had the greatest influence on Villa, but they were not the only intellectuals to join his ranks.

Villa and the Intellectuals

Intellectuals, Villa once said, were "disloyal cowards and potbellied profiteers."[75] When he spoke of intellectuals, however, Villa by no means meant all educated persons. In fact, he had respect for teachers, whom he constantly lauded, and whom his regime attempted to help as much as it could. The men Villa called intellectuals seem to have been, above all, lawyers, journalists, and bureaucrats. Villa's attitude doubtless reflected the fact that in the Mexican revolution, unlike other twentieth-century revolutions, intellectuals, according to Daniel Cosío Villegas, played a very minor role.[76] Only a small minority of the country's professors, lawyers, and artists participated in it. One of the social groups most prominently involved in twentieth-century revolutions, students, were noticeably absent from the Mexican revolution. Their participation was minimal, and the vast majority of professors and students at Mexico's largest institution of higher learning, the National University in Mexico City, had opposed Madero and at least for a time supported Huerta.[77] Yet, as Alan Knight notes, looking only at prominent intellectuals and men so designated because of their position in the social hierarchy would mean leaving out one group that has played a major role in every social movement: the group Antonio Gramsci called "organic intellectuals"—that is, men who often held no "intellectual position" yet were thinkers who tended to strongly mold the ideology of the factions which they supported.[78]

The majority of intellectuals who participated in the revolution were in one way or another linked to the Carranza faction. Indeed, Carranza's most prominent intellectual supporter, Luis Cabrera, played a decisive role in fashioning and putting together the Carrancista national coalition. The intellectuals' affinity for Carranza's movement was no coincidence. The Carrancistas were, after all, the most middle-class and urban faction, with the highest number of literate supporters, and they thus attributed great importance to newspapers. Two of Mexico's most prominent journalists, Heriberto Barrón and Félix Palavicini, were in fact among Carranza's closest advisors. The Carrancistas turned to newspapers and newspapermen both because the print media were far more important to the middle classes than to the largely illiterate peasantry and because Carranza had none of Villa's or Zapata's charisma and therefore lacked the "traditional" means of communication that these leaders had established with their followers.

The fact that neither Zapata nor Villa turned to intellectuals to mobilize support among their most important constituency, the inhabitants of Mexico's countryside, does not mean that they rejected intellectuals or had no use for them. The relatively small number of radical intellectuals Zapata had gathered around him were used to write proclamations destined for the rest of Mexico, as intermediaries with other factions and at times with the United States, and as administrators during the brief period when the Zapatistas participated in a national government.[79]

Villa had a somewhat broader use for intellectuals than Zapata. Since his urban constituency was larger than that of Zapata in Morelos, and since the degree of literacy in Chihuahua was among the highest in Mexico, the Villistas published a newspaper, *Vida Nueva*. At first, Villa had little interest in or respect for newspapers, so when young, enthusiastic journalists, first from Chihuahua and later from Guadalajara, asked for his support in order to set up a regional newspaper to propagate the ideas of the Villista faction, he rebuffed them.[80]

Apart from newspapermen, who never achieved any prominence in the ranks of Villismo (the lone exception was Silvestre Terrazas, who significantly relinquished his position as a journalist during the Villista period), Villa used his intellectual supporters mainly for four purposes: to give respectability to his movement; to draft laws and proclamations; as intermediaries with other factions and with the United States; and as administrators.

The intellectuals who contributed most to giving Villa and his movement both internal and external respectability were prominent former high officials of the Madero government who had been close to the murdered president and who had assumed key ideological functions in his administration. For that reason, either

Carranza had refused their services, or, if they had joined him, they were soon re-pelled by the anti-Maderismo that both Carranza and his most prominent sup-porters displayed. They had no other choice but to join Villa, if they had not done so in the first place. Apart from Angeles, the most prominent of these intellectu-als were Manuel Bonilla, Miguel Díaz Lombardo, and Federico González Garza.

Bonilla had been an engineer and administrator during the rule of Porfirio Díaz. For many years, he did not oppose Díaz. In fact, he was named a judge on the supreme court of Sinaloa. In 1909, he backed a candidate for governor whom Díaz did not like, and as a result he was stripped of all his offices by the dictator. Bonilla then became head of the anti-reelectionist party in Sinaloa and editor of an opposition newspaper. His open opposition both to the state government and to the Díaz dictatorship led to his imprisonment. Madero had such confidence in Bonilla that he named him his representative in the provisional government headed by de la Barra, in which Bonilla became minister of communications. Once Madero had become president, Bonilla occupied an even more prominent post, that of minister of development.[81]

Like Manuel Bonilla, Miguel Díaz Lombardo, a lawyer, was also profession-ally successful during the Díaz period yet nevertheless opposed the dictator. In contrast to Bonilla's middle-class origins, Díaz Lombardo had an aristocratic background. His maternal aunt had been the wife of one of the emperor Maxi-milian's most prominent generals, Miguel Miramón, who was executed together with Maximilian after Juárez's victory in the war against the French and the Mexican Conservatives. Thanks to his background and intelligence, Díaz Lom-bardo had a successful professional career during the Díaz dictatorship. He be-came professor of law at the School of Jurisprudence in Mexico City, the coun-try's most distinguished law faculty. It may have been his family ties or simply the fact that Díaz did not consider universities to be dangerous that allowed him to retain his post as professor in spite of his mounting criticism of the dictator-ship in his lectures. After Madero became president, Díaz Lombardo was named minister of public education. Shortly before Madero was toppled, he sent Díaz Lombardo to France as his ambassador. Madero needed a prominent intellectual as his representative in France to counteract the influence of Porfirio Díaz and high officials of his administration who had taken refuge there. Once Madero was murdered, Díaz Lombardo immediately expressed his opposition to the Huerta dictatorship and became the representative of the constitutionalists in France. His greatest success was in preventing French financiers from granting a loan to Huerta. Subsequently, he gave up his comfortable life in Paris in order to rejoin the revolutionary administration in Mexico. He too became disillusioned with Carranza and joined Villa.[82]

In comparison to Bonilla and Díaz Lombardo, Federico González Garza had been far less successful professionally during the dictatorship. Although he stud-ied law and finally received his degree, his career was marred by constant financial worries after the death of his father. To support himself and his family, he worked for many years as a telegraphist at the post office. González Garza was older than Bonilla and Díaz Lombardo, and he also had a far longer history of resistance to the Díaz dictatorship. He was first arrested for opposition to the regime in 1893, when he opposed Governor Garza Galán, who ruled his native Coahuila with an iron fist. González Garza was one of the earliest supporters of Madero and played a prominent role in formulating and disseminating the ideology of the anti-reelectionist party in newspapers and in manifestos. Once Madero became president, González Garza became a member of his cabinet. He was first secretary of justice and then governor of the federal district.[83]

After the coup that toppled Madero, González Garza became convinced that the only way the revolutionaries could regain power was by gaining the support of Mexico's peasantry. This could only be done by radical agrarian reform. He wrote a letter to Carranza, whom he naïvely assumed shared his ideas, and offered his services to the First Chief. He attempted to convince Carranza that he had given up his moderate political opinions and was now in favor of agrarian reform. So successful was he in persuading Carranza of his radical opinions that the latter refused to give him any post in his administration. But González Garza established links with one of Villa's prominent officers, Fidel Avila, who first administered the frontier city of Ciudad Juárez for Villa and later was named by his chief to be governor of Chihuahua. González Garza followed Avila into Ciudad Chihuahua as his main political advisor.[84]

All three of these men became centrally involved in the formulation of Villista ideology. González Garza helped to write proclamations, Bonilla was charged with elaborating a land law for Chihuahua and later a national land-reform project, and Díaz Lombardo in 1915 became one of the nominal heads of Villa's northern administration and drafted many of its decrees.

Two men who in later years were numbered among Mexico's greatest writers, Mariano Azuela and Martín Luis Guzmán, also joined the Villista faction. Neither seems to have played a very important role in the Villa movement, however, and neither did they have any significant personal influence on Villa. Azuela at best only met Villa once or twice. He was a doctor who had joined the leader of the Villista faction in Jalisco, Julián Medina, and for a time became head of public education for that state. After the defeat of the Villistas in Jalisco, Azuela fled north to Chihuahua, where he seems to have lived in the last months of Villista rule without exercising any official function, and in December 1915, he accepted an amnesty granted to all Villistas, with the exception of the top leaders, and returned to his native Jalisco.

Martín Luis Guzmán knew Villa better than Azuela. In March 1914, he went to Ciudad Juarez. During the rule of the conventionist administration of Mexico, he became adviser to Minister of War Robles, secretary of the National University, and director of the National Library. After Eulalio Gutiérrez broke with Villa, Guzmán too abandoned Villismo, going into exile in Spain. While the role of these men in the Villista movement was limited, the books that they subsequently wrote would play a decisive role in the way millions of people viewed both Villa and Villismo.[85]

Only three Villista intellectuals—Felipe Angeles, Silvestre Terrazas, and Díaz Lombardo—had a closer personal relationship with Villa and were able to exercise some kind of influence on him. This was no easy task, for in spite of Villa's repeated public statements that he was an ignorant man just waiting for educated men to tell him what to do, in reality he brooked no overt opposition. According to his former secretary Pérez Rul, great talent was required to influence Villa. An able and discreet advisor does not openly oppose Villa's decisions. . . . This would be the worst of all ways to influence the revolutionary chieftain. He needs to seem completely submissive; he has to study his passions, his hidden aims, and his different reactions. Once he knows him, and this is somewhat difficult, he has to be "opportune." Not one inadequate gesture, not one extra word, not one inopportune gesture. No attitude of arrogance, no presumptions, no attitude of violent opposition or of rigid censorship. The able advisor needs not to speak when he should not, not give any opinions when he is not asked to, and especially not to get "involved" in what does not concern him.[86]

There was no consistency to Villa's relations with these intellectuals. While he might listen to them one day, he might rely on the advice of men such as Fierro or Urbina the next. Moreover, Villa was extremely susceptible to flattery. Two intellectual adventurers, Manuel Bauche Alcalde and the Peruvian poet José Santos Chocano, gained Villa's attention by the kind of sycophantic behavior that Villa's chief intellectual followers would not have considered.

Manuel Bauche Alcalde was a teacher and school principal. After the outbreak of the Mexican revolution, he became a fervent supporter of Madero. He was one of the first intellectuals to join Villa. He soon managed to gain both the chieftain's sympathy and confidence. He achieved this aim largely by fostering for Villa what in modern parlance might be called a personality cult. Pérez Rul recalled a meeting in Chihuahua's Theater of Heroes at which, as soon as Villa entered, Bauche Alcalde got up and shouted to the large audience: "Everyone get up. In the presence of the leader of the people, of the immortal Francisco Villa, all women should stand up; the men should take off their hats and stand in an attitude of reverence."[87]

Villa appointed Bauche Alcalde, who had no experience in this field, as editor in chief of the official newspaper of the División del Norte, *Vida Nueva.* Villa had such confidence in Bauche Alcalde that it was to him that he dictated his memoirs. These measures by no means ensured Bauche's loyalty. In early 1915, when Villa's fortunes seemed to be ebbing, Bauche switched sides and rejoined Carranza, who sent him on missions to several states in Mexico. Bauche's unique talents for flattery evidently worked again on another revolutionary general, since the commander of the division of the northeast, Pablo González, appointed him as his private secretary.[88]

Bauche Alcalde obviously felt that revolutionary Mexico was not a restful and convenient place to stay, however, and sought a more comfortable post, where he would not be troubled by the consequences of revolution and war. This was not easy to find, for most of Europe was then convulsed by World War I, which the United States was soon to enter. Bauche used his talents to secure a position in one European country not involved in the war, where life was still agreeable. This was Switzerland, to which Bauche was appointed consul, probably thanks to the influence of Pablo González. The salary of a Mexican consul was apparently not sufficient to enjoy the bounties of Switzerland's neutrality, however, and Bauche decided to make some money on the side. According to an indignant official of the Swiss Foreign Ministry, he began writing pornography. Feeling that this did not accord with the duties and rights of a diplomat, the Swiss government asked the Mexican ambassador to have him recalled to Mexico. Bauche's influence in

Mexico continued to be so strong, however, that instead of being recalled, he was sent to the Mexican embassy in Germany.[89]

José Santos Chocano was another intellectual who managed to gain Villa's confidence for a time. Santos Chocano was considered a great poet not only in his native Peru but throughout much of Latin America. But being a poet was not enough for Santos Chocano. He dreamed of becoming the Bolivar of the twentieth century. The Peruvian poet had come to Mexico during Madero's presidency and soon became a fervent admirer and close friend of the president's. Shortly after he assumed control of the Mexican government, Huerta had Santos Chocano deported from the country. He was forcibly placed on a Spanish ship, whose captain was instructed to take Santos Chocano all the way to Europe and only there to give him back his freedom. The Peruvian poet had many friends and sympathizers in the Caribbean, however, and their influence enabled him to secure his release once the ship docked at Havana. From there the poet first corresponded with Carranza and then decided to join him in Hermosillo, the capital of the state of Sonora. He was firmly convinced that under his guidance, revolutionary Mexico would free all of Latin America from foreign domination and create an entirely new order. To a friend, he wrote that he intended to give a series of lectures on "the two Americas in ten years." "You will see," he wrote. "Behind every word that I say, there will be a bayonet to sustain it. . . . I will be the verb, Carranza will be the action. Finally! . . . I have found our man." Carranza was to organize 500,000 soldiers, whom Santos Chocano was convinced would realize his dream, "the union of Central America and Antillian confederation, the federal Bolivarian confederation."[90] In a letter to his mother, he wrote, "you cannot imagine the gigantic role that I am playing by corresponding with Carranza and with President Wilson, who is my personal friend, and with the governments of Cuba, Santo Domingo, and Central America. Soon the state of Veracruz will be under the control of the revolution, and that will be the end of things; all of this will have been achieved by me."[91]

After he arrived in Sonora, it soon became clear to Santos Chocano that Carranza had no intention of recognizing him as the Bolivar of the twentieth century and handing power over to him. At this point, the Peruvian poet decided to join Villa. When a friend later asked him why he had preferred Villa to Carranza, Santos Chocano said: "Villa was a superior man of action; I would take care of the thinking. . . . I understood that Villa was the man for me, for my aims about the organization not only of Mexico but of this whole sick America. The shadow of Bolivar inspired me."[92]

After arriving in Chihuahua, Santos Chocano published a long article in the official newspaper of the state in which he expressed what he considered to be the aims of the revolution. It was neither a very new nor a very radical program, but the Peruvian poet made sure that it included a number of demands that Villa had previously articulated. He called for the establishment of military colonies and a state bank to finance agrarian reform, and he advocated the primacy of the revolutionary army, calling it "the suffrage of the revolution." Modestly, he stated that he wanted to become "the verb of the revolution." This article made a very favorable impression on Villa, all the more so since at its beginning Santos Chocano had called Villa "an impressive soul, full of mystery, miracles and glory who has roots in the most profound layers of collective grief and raises its flow-cry roots to the clouds of the great human dream." He also called him "the guardian angel of principles against the attacks and intrigues of the enemies of his people."[93]

Santos Chocano continued to see Villa as a guardian angel as long as he expressed his generosity by making large sums of money available to the Peruvian poet. But when Villa refused to give him 200,000 pesos "to work on some mines" and $300 to help him pay medical costs and to confront "the great demands of life," Santos Chocano turned against Villa.[94] Soon afterward, Santos Chocano wrote a long letter to Carranza asking the latter for financial help.[95] When he was unsuccessful in getting it, the Peruvian poet accepted the hospitality of another influential friend, the president of Guatemala, Estrada Cabrera, whose endeavors to recover some of the territories that Guatemala had lost to Mexico in the nineteenth century he actively supported.[96] In fact, Santos Chocano's first trip to Mexico and his first contacts with Madero arose from a confidential mission that the Guatemalan president had given him to sound out Madero about the possibility of negotiations with Guatemala to get back the territories. Madero refused to consider these suggestions, but this did not prevent him from becoming friends with Santos Chocano.

Among the highly influential but frequently shadowy figures that the revolution produced were the private secretaries of the revolutionary leaders. They were especially influential when the leaders were illiterate or semiliterate and left it to their private secretaries to draft letters, messages, and proclamations. To a certain degree, they controlled access to the leader. Some of them were opportunistic and corrupt in the extreme. This does not seem to have been the case with the two private secretaries that Villa had, although both of them would leave Villa, one of them at a high point of Villa's career, the other after Villa's defeat in Sonora in 1915. Both were men who had a history of opposition to the Díaz regime prior to 1910 and had joined the Madero revolution at an early date.

They were Luis Aguirre Benavides and Enrique Pérez Rul. The fact that Villa chose Luis Aguirre Benavides as his secretary was no coincidence. Since his earliest childhood, the latter had had close relations with the Madero family. After attending a commercial academy, he had worked for different members of the Madero family, joined the Madero revolution in 1910, and soon became secretary to the member of that family who was closest to Villa, Francisco's brother Gustavo. Gustavo had always been more favorably disposed toward Villa than his brother Francisco, and during Villa's imprisonment in Mexico City, Gustavo repeatedly sent Luis to visit Villa in prison. When the constitutionalist revolution broke out, Luis joined Carranza, who sent him to Chihuahua as secretary to his minister of foreign affairs, Francisco Escudero. After Escudero lost his position because of a drunken conflict with Villa, the latter asked Luis Aguirre Benavides to become his private secretary.[97] The choice may also have been influenced by the fact that his brother Eugenio was one of Villa's generals. In January 1915, when part of the conventionist faction, which included Eugenio Aguirre Benavides, broke with Villa, Luis abandoned his chieftain, hid in Mexico City, and made his peace with Obregón when he occupied Mexico's capital. At Obregón's suggestion, he wrote articles sharply critical of Villa in the constitutionalist press and U.S. newspapers. In his later memoirs, he admitted that "this was a mistake that I shall regret all my life of which I openly state that I am deeply ashamed."[98]

Villa then named Martín Luis Guzmán, who was to become one of Mexico's most famous intellectuals and Villa's most talented biographer, as Luis's successor. He did not know that Guzmán was a supporter of Gutiérrez's. Guzmán accepted the position but told Villa that he wished to visit his ill mother in Chihuahua before he started, to which Villa agreed. Guzmán did not return, however, and instead left Mexico for Spain.

Villa's last secretary was Enrique Pérez Rul, who may have gained Villa's sympathy because he was both an officer in the constitutionalist army and professionally belonged to the one category of intellectuals that Villa deeply respected: he had been a teacher prior to the Madero revolution. He stayed with Villa until his last great defeat in Sonora and then fled to the United States.[99]

It is difficult to determine the exact extent of the influence of these private secretaries on Villa, but it probably was substantial. They drafted Villa's letters and controlled access to their leader, and at times Villa would ask them for advice. In his memoirs, Luis Aguirre Benavides says that time and time again he was able to moderate Villa's more violent impulses. Enrique Pérez Rul claims that it was he who suggested to Villa the composition of the northern revolutionary government that Villa established in 1915. Both Luis Aguirre Benavides and Enrique Pérez Rul published books about Villa that depict him as a revolutionary, and not the common bandit his enemies made him out to be, but at the same time show his brutality and question whether he was fit to be the leader of Mexico. Aside from Martín Luis Guzmán and Mariano Azuela, none of the Villista intellectuals were to play a major role in Mexico's political or intellectual life after Villa's defeat.

Villa's relationship with the intellectuals drawn to his banner was different from that which both Carranza and Zapata maintained with their most influential intellectual advisors. For the most part, Carranza's and Zapata's most important intellectuals shared their leaders' views. By contrast, the most prominent intellectuals who supported Villa were far more committed to democracy, a strong central government, and the sanctity of private property than he was. And with the significant exception of Federico González Garza, they were far less committed to radical expropriation of haciendas and agrarian reform. Of the three major leaders of the Mexican revolution after 1913, Villa had the least interest in ideology, and he was thus ready to allow intellectuals with opinions far different from his own to draft intellectual pronouncements in his name, which very frequently contradicted his views. In some cases, this may have been a conscious strategy in order to gain support for his movement in the United States. In other cases, as in the discussions at the convention meetings in Toluca and Cuernavaca in 1915, where Villista delegates espoused such conservative views that they contributed to a break with the Zapatistas, this may have been because of benign neglect or contempt for political debate.

CHAPTER EIGHT

The División del Norte

Yo soy soldado de Pancho Villa,	I am a soldier of Pancho Villa;
de sus dorados soy el más fiel,	of his Dorados, I am the most loyal.
nada me importa perder la vida,	Losing my life means nothing to me,
si es cosa de hombres morir por él.	since it is a manly thing to die for him.[1]

The División del Norte is the institution most closely identified with Villa in people's minds and the aspect of Villismo that has sparked the least controversy.

The problems that Villa faced in transforming the motley array of revolutionaries from Durango and Chihuahua into an effective fighting force are clearly revealed by the state of the División del Norte shortly after its establishment, when it captured the city of Torreón. The British consul in that city, Cunard Cummins, who observed the army at close range and came to know most of its leaders, very much doubted whether it could have any military significance in Mexico, notwithstanding its triumph at Torreón. In December 1913, he painted a devastating picture of disunity and reluctance to fight, writing: "There is no general loyalty and obedience to one head; nor is there cohesion and unity among themselves; they cannot 'pull together.'" Only a small number of the men directly under Villa were primarily loyal to him. At most, they numbered 3,000. The rest gave their primary allegiance to other regional and local leaders, who constantly quarreled among themselves:

Pereyra declares that Urbina is a barbarous bandit and Yuriar a born traitor and that he will place trust in neither of them. Ex-deputy García de la Cadena rated all but himself as ignorant robbers, as black souls incapable of harboring a noble sentiment yet he himself was little better than the worst and was recently executed by the other leaders in Torreón. Notwithstanding the previous arrangement, the Arrieta brothers quarreled with Natera whilst they were attacking Zacatecas, the former retired with their men leaving Natera to continue the fight; in consequence, Zacatecas was saved [from the Villistas].

Probably with reference to the sack of Durango, Cummins described the revolutionary soldiers as a hoard of locusts, looting and stealing from rich and poor alike. "The continuance of the revolution is marked by more frequent and more cruel assaults against the defenseless, more sweeping destruction and clearer signs of degenerating ultimately into anarchy of the worst form," Cummins wrote. Furthermore, many soldiers refused to leave the confines of their native region. "Contreras in reply to commands asserts that his men do not fight outside their own territory." Many others were reluctant to fight. "The men do not distinguish themselves by natural braveries," Cummins observed.

In order to go into battle, they usually find it necessary to indulge in much shouting, as it were to encourage each other. It does not seem to be customary to assist courage by alcohol, though resort to stimulants is not unknown. During a battle, skulking is very noticeable, many men carefully avoiding the danger zone; nevertheless, in certain instances when the men have become worked up to a high pitch of excitement, a somewhat general bravery has become evident. During some of the attacks delivered against Torreón, fierce rushes were made almost to the mouth of the cannon. As a rule, however, an encounter at close quarters is the result of accident, the rebels and the government irregular forces preferring to exchange rifle fire at a very great distance from each other.

Cummins was convinced that the revolutionaries were not up to facing regular troops:

When the regular infantry of the government are engaged, matters are different, because under the immediate lead of their officers, they continue to advance, sometimes employing volley firing with the almost invariable result that the rebels are put to flight. . . . Only in the most exceptional cases do the revolutionaries show themselves able to stand against the disciplined advance of the federal infantry, even if their numbers are many times those of the government force; and in this connection we are not taking into account the demoralization that may have been caused by a previous federal artillery.[2]

Cummins, whose hatred of the revolutionaries was almost obsessive, is perhaps not the most reliable of witnesses, but his observations coincide closely with those made by Carranza and his chief of staff, Juan Barragán, when they for a short time in July 1913 attempted to take command of these same troops (minus the Chihuahuan contingent) and organized a failed attack on Torreón (see above).

Only seven months later, Edwin Emerson, a newspaperman who in fact was a secret agent for the U.S. chief of staff, Leonard Wood, drew a completely different picture of the División del Norte, with whom he spent several months, witnessing its greatest battles. Instead of the hodgepodge of badly equipped, ill-clad revolutionaries that Cummins had described half a year before, Emerson called the men of the División del Norte "the best set-up, best armed, best mounted, best equipped, best clothed, best fed, best paid, and generally best cared for troops I have yet seen in Mexico." In contrast to October 1913, when it was not clear whether any leader would be able to control the newly formed División del Norte, there was not the least doubt about who was in charge. The authority Villa exercised over his men deeply impressed Emerson:

Villa's greatest asset is his personality. As a former outlaw and bandit, who successfully stood his ground against Porfirio Díaz' soldiers and *rurales* for over ten years, Villa is idolized by all the lower classes of Mexico. His reported exploits, true or false, such as shooting a judge on the bench, shooting a federal colonel in the midst of his staff, shaking his fist in Huerta's face, shooting an Englishman out of hand almost in plain sight of the impotent gringos, and finally his enormous exploits of stealing pretty women, have brought him a renown among Mexicans like the old legends of Robin Hood or Dick Turpin. Anyone who has ever seen him on horseback knows that he is a splendid rider, a thing that all Mexicans set great store by, and he is also taking pains to spread and emphasize a universal belief that he is "a dead shot." He has further endeared himself to the lower classes and to his followers by his manifest lack of fear (never bothers about having guards around him or escorts), by his frank manners and speech, by his simple dress, simple habits, and rough unadorned speech set off by very forceful profanity and quaint obscenities. In all press interviews or public gatherings, he always makes it a point to lay stress on the fact that he is a simple, uneducated, unlettered man who never has had any advantages of culture. If he had a Machiavelli for an advisor he could not have found a surer way to the hearts of his followers, nine-tenths of whom are absolutely ignorant pelados.

Emerson painted a picture completely opposite to Cummins's dire predictions. "During all the time that I was with them [Villa's soldiers] in the field, I never saw an act of violence committed against natives, only against Spaniards, foreigners, or out and out federal sympathizers, who invariably belonged to the upper classes." Emerson felt that

Next to Villa's personality which completely overshadows that of Venustiano Carranza or any other rebel leader, his second greatest asset is the temper of the common people of northern Mexico, who in their sentiments are thoroughly against the federal government and against the people of the center and south. This feeling extends as far down as Zacatecas, and is an inestimable advantage to Villa's army since it brings them a constant flow of recruits, supplies and valuable information, and makes it unnecessary for them to resort to the forceful measures which make soldiers hate it [the Central Government].

There was another factor, according to Emerson, that was at least as important as his personality: "Villa's strongest card with his followers is his known irreconcilable hatred for Huerta, and Huerta's known irreconcilable hatred for Villa, on most intimate personal grounds, which preclude the possibility of Villa ever selling out his men to the gobierno, a species of treachery otherwise common among other Mexican rebel leaders of the past and present. Therefore Villa's followers know they can trust him to stick."[3]

What further attracted many of Villa's soldiers to him was that he was not aloof but attempted to establish as many personal links with them as he could and to show how much he cared for them. Not only were they paid regularly, but he also made it a point to give them relatively large sums of money after every victory. When a soldier was in urgent need of money for family purposes, he would go and see Villa, who would personally hand it to him.

Frequently, Villa would suddenly turn up at one of the campfires where his soldiers were preparing their food. He would ask if he could join them and then sit down and partake of whatever they had prepared. This was not just a populist gesture to endear him to his troops but also a way of avoiding being poisoned, since no one knew where he was going to eat.

But the tremendous authority that Villa exercised within the army and the hold that he had on his soldiers did not derive only from his charismatic personality or from the prestige that his victories had given him. Villa also took concrete measures to overcome the natural reluctance of peasants to fight outside their native region and to force his commanders to cooperate with one another and to respect his authority.

Persuading reluctant peasants to fight far from home was all the more difficult because Villa had to rely on volunteers and instituted no compulsory military service, which had been one of the most hated features of the Porfirian regime. One means he used to get them to do so was to recruit as many individuals as possible who had few kin and whose roots in their home communities were not yet very firm—primarily boys of 14, 15, and 16, who did not yet have families of their own. In July 1914, Villa made every effort to recruit miners for his army. "Every mining camp in the district has been visited by recruiting officers and hundreds of hardy mountaineers of the remote districts who have hitherto manifested little interest in the revolution have been induced to take up arms," the *El Paso Morning Times* reported.[4]

Villa gave his men economic incentives to join his army. He had promised them land; since many of his soldiers identified with him, and since he had confiscated the properties of the oligarchy, many believed that he would in fact comply with his promise. His soldiers were regularly paid. In addition, to prevent them from looting, he carried out large redistributions of money and goods from properties confiscated from "enemies of the revolution" after each victory.

Another measure that both Villa and other commanders of the revolutionary forces in the north took in order to persuade recalcitrant peasants to fight far from their native regions was to allow them to take their wives, girlfriends, and mistresses along. These women were known as *soldaderas*, and sometimes as *adelitas*, a name derived from one of the most popular songs of the Mexican revolution.

In many respects the Mexican revolution was not only a men's but a women's revolution. Like the men, the women came from highly various walks of life. On the whole, historians have paid far less attention to them than to the men. With a few exceptions, the only women to emerge from obscurity belonged to the middle class and played a prominent role in the political movement that led to the revolution; some of them also participated in the armed movement, at times even as leaders of men. The great mass of poor peasant women who joined the revolutionary armies in the most different capacities—some as camp followers, some as sweethearts, many as fighters—have remained far more anonymous than their male counterparts.

The tradition of women following the army went back a long way before the outbreak of the revolution, and a large number of women and children followed the federal army as well. When the federal troops from Chihuahua, commanded by General Salvador Mercado, crossed the border and sought asylum in the United States, the army included 3,357 officers and men, 1,256 women, and 554 children.

The federal high command allowed so many women to accompany the army for several reasons. In part, it was because these women constituted army support units by performing essential functions such as cooking, foraging for food, and tending the wounded. Above all, though, the participation of women was also a consequence of the type of recruitment that the federal army traditionally carried out in Mexico. The soldiers were neither volunteers nor short-term conscripts, but men forced into the army through an unjust recruitment system that forced the poorest and most unpopular men (from the point of view of the authorities) into a kind of semi-slavery, in which they remained for many years. The rate of desertion was, not surprisingly, enormous. One of the ways of attempting to keep the men in the army was to allow their women to accompany them.

There is little evidence of a similar massive participation of women in the Maderista armies. While some women, above all those of middle-class origin, played a prominent role in its leadership and at times even directed some of the troops, the descriptions of Maderista armies do not mention large contingents of soldaderas. Indeed, most Maderista forces operated near their native regions, and the women stayed at home, frequently providing the men with food and other help when they came to their native villages. Women's participation was also limited in Chihuahua and elsewhere in the Madero revolution because of the manner in which the rebels prosecuted the war: most Maderista forces consisted of cavalry, and since food and horses were in short supply, the Maderista horsemen tended to leave women behind when they went on campaign.

The situation completely changed in 1913–14 with the appearance of the large armies of the constitutionalist revolution. Unlike the Maderista soldiers, the constitutionalists would fight further and further away from their native homes. It is thus not surprising that many soldiers wanted to take their wives, sweethearts, and at times even their children with them. What allowed the constitutionalist leaders to acquiesce to this demand is that unlike the Maderistas, who relied primarily on horses for transportation, the constitutionalist armies were based on railroads. Thus the price the army had to pay for transporting women and even children was far smaller than it would have been had each of these camp followers had to be supplied with a horse. In addition to cooking and foraging, women frequently acted as nurses, and as along as the embargo on arms from the United States lasted, many of them smuggled ammunition and arms across the border. Others, frequently in opposition to the wishes of the army leadership, fought alongside the men.

Since trains played a greater role in the transportation of the División del Norte than in that of most other armies—there were no railroads linking Sonora to central Mexico, which forced Obregón's army to rely on horses for a large part of its southward march—women seem to have been particularly numerous in the ranks of the División del Norte. Perhaps for this reason, Villa, of all the major military leaders of the revolution, seems to have shown the greatest reluctance to allow soldaderas into his army. He could not prevent them from joining and riding along on the military trains, but he did try to limit their number. His elite Dorados were not allowed to bring women along, and by setting up a regular quartermaster corps and a hospital train, Villa sought to supply some of the functions that women were playing in the army. Based on descriptions of the División del Norte in its heyday, it is doubtful whether Villa was very successful in this respect. "Of glamour, Mexico today has its full share," Gregory Mason, a correspondent for the journal *The Outlook*, wrote.

Nowhere has warfare ever been so picturesque: the excitement of the start for the front, when as the long trains gather momentum, the men stand up on the swaying cars, shooting as wildly as they yell, but with more danger to bystanders while their sweethearts, yelling also, wave sarapes or the men's sombreros, or wrest a rifle from a lover's hands and join the fusillading; the happy hours of the dusty journey when booming guitars soothe compañeros with heads pillowed on the laps of their ladies; long drowsy waits in the heat of noon with the engines drinking at the water tanks, all talk stopped for the siesta hour and the only sound the hum of the cicada undaunted by the rocking heat of the desert that rises in billows above the grave outline of the mountains; evenings around boisterous fires after a meal of tortillas and jerke, the shrill chatter of the children, the subdued conversation of wives and the loud laughter of the other women who follow camps, the boastful bickerings of the men and deep sleep for everyone and the quiet over the silver desert broken only by the occasional quavering bark of a coyote and far off the faint bell-like notes of the mockingbird.[5]

As long as the haciendas that the revolutionary troops occupied on their way south remained stocked with large amounts of food, there was no problem in feeding both the soldiers and the soldaderas, and the latter in fact were excellent foragers, who managed again and again to find hidden supplies of food. Villa's soldiers were greatly impressed by the way he cared about them. "General Villa did everything he could to help the widows and the families of those who had fallen in battle," one of his soldiers stressed, adding that he also sent hundreds of poor children to get an education either in Ciudad Chihuahua or in the United States.[6]

Villa's care for his wounded soldiers is one part of his legend that is fully justified. For this purpose, he organized one of the most modern hospital trains in Mexico. "And surely it was a magnificent thing to see," John Reed wrote. "The hospital train lay right behind the work train now. Forty box cars enameled inside, stenciled on the side with a big blue cross and the legends 'Servicio Sanitario' handled the wounded as they came from the front. They were fitted inside with the latest surgical appliances and manned by sixty competent American and Mexican doctors. Every night shuttle trains carried the seriously hurt back to the base hospitals at Chihuahua and Parral."[7]

One right that his men forced Villa to grant them was the right to remain in units derived from their home communities. There was one instance when Villa attempted to abolish this right and failed completely. He had decided he needed an effective infantry. While his whole army stood at attention he picked out every man who did not have a horse and assigned him to an infantry unit, which would be commanded by one of Angeles's closest collaborators, Gonzalitos. When Gonzalitos one day later came to review his unit, he found no one to review. All the men had simply rejoined their old unit, and Villa was wise enough not to try to enforce his previous decision.[8]

Villa's popularity and the incentives he offered men to join his División del Norte attracted an increasingly heterogeneous group of volunteers whose motives for joining the army were various. When John Reed spoke with soldiers of Villa's army in 1914, he was struck by the diverse motives that people gave for joining the revolution. A Captain Fernando told him: "When we win the *revolución* it will be government by the men, not by the rich. We are riding over the lands of the men. They used to belong to the rich but now they belong to me and the *compañeros*."[9]

When Reed asked him, "What are you fighting for?" Juan Sánchez, a plain soldier in the army, answered: "Why, it is good fighting. You don't have to work in the mines." Another soldier, Manuel Paredes, said, "We are fighting to restore Francisco I. Madero to the presidency." He had obviously not heard that Madero had been killed in the meantime. Another, Isidro Amayo, stated, "We are fighting for *libertad*." When Reed asked him, "What do you mean by *libertad*?" Amayo responded, "*Libertad* is when I can do what I want." At this point, Juan Sánchez asked Reed, "Is there war in the United States now?" "'No,' I said untruthfully. 'No war at all.' He meditated for a moment. 'How do you pass the time then . . . ?'"[10]

In interviews carried out by a number of scholars many years later when the participants of the revolution were already very old, a similar variety of views emerged.

Two brothers who soon became two of Villa's most famous commanders, Martín and Pablo López, joined his army, according to a surviving brother, "because of the bad treatment they suffered at the hands of Catholic hacendados." They felt exploited by the hacendado Jesús Acosta at the ranch of El Pajarito, where they worked. Acosta not only paid them very small wages but repeatedly hit Martín López with a stick and at other times tried to do the same to Pablo.[11]

The motives that impelled Desiderio Madrid Carrasco to join the revolution were quite different. "I was very young," he told an interviewer, "and I was a tramp, very lazy; I didn't like to work. I loved dances, girls and drink. My father had repeatedly warned me but I never listened to him. One day when I was very drunk, my brothers expelled me from my house. At this point, I participated in the war, and I said, 'Let them kill me now so that the coyotes will devour me.'"[12]

Pedro Romero was a peon on the hacienda of Bustillos when the revolution broke out. When he was asked by the interviewer when he was born, he did not remember the exact date but he said, "I was born in the period of slavery." While it is not clear what he meant by slavery, the term probably referred to his status as a debt peon. He was working the land and was about 15 at the time, when four men, one of whom was Villa, rode over to him and asked him to tell another peon, Pablo Martínez, that "Pancho Villa tells him that the time has come, and that I am waiting for him here." When Romero transmitted this message to Martínez, "it seemed as if I had told him that God had spoken; he threw everything away, ran to his house, saddled his horse, and we galloped back. When he arrived, he embraced Villa and told him, 'Here I am, my general, at your disposal.'" As they were leaving, Villa turned around and asked Romero, "'How old are you, boy?'"

"Fifteen."
"Don't you want to come with us?"
"Where?"
"To war."

"Why?"

"To put an end to injustice."

"Will we also end slavery?"

"Slavery too, but for this we have to fight. Come with me boy, and I'll give you arms."

I turned around to see my mother's reaction to all this, but she understood that I would leave with Villa, and she blessed me. This is how I met Villa, how I went to war with him. Later we recruited and armed the men of the neighboring ranches.[13]

Rogelio Rodríguez Saenz was a son of the owner of the hacienda of El Pichague and the nephew of Trinidad Rodríguez, an old crony of Villa's from his bandit days who had become a general of the División del Norte. While his father, for obvious reasons, wanted nothing to do with the revolution, the influence of his uncle seems to have been one of the main factors that led him at 14 to become a soldier in one of Villa's brigades.

Lauro Trevizo Delgado was a member of the old military colony of Namiquipa. The reasons he gave for going to war were "land, freedom, and justice."[14]

For obvious reasons, very few hacendados joined Villa. The four Murga brothers were a conspicuous exception. Not only did this family own the large hacienda of San Juan El Duro, located in the vicinity of San Andrés, but members of the family had been highly unpopular caciques in the village whose inhabitants formed the core of Villa's first revolutionary guerrilla band. It is thus not surprising that the participation of the Murgas in the División del Norte was not a wholly voluntary affair. An uncle of theirs who lived in San Andrés had a longstanding conflict with Villa over debts that the revolutionary general had not yet repaid. When Villa sent two emissaries to the uncle to ask for help in providing for the revolutionary troops, Sabas Murga shot them as they were on the way to his ranch. When Villa heard of this, he ordered his troops to wipe out the whole of the Murga family. Villa's troops surprised the four Murga brothers, Juan, Ramón, Aurelio, and Encarnación, who had not at all been involved in the conflict between their uncle and Villa, as they were tending their fields. As Villa's men prepared to execute them, Juan Murga asked that he be allowed to talk to Villa. He told Villa that if he spared his life, he, Juan, would immediately enlist in the División del Norte, and his three brothers would follow as soon as the current crop was harvested. Villa agreed, and the Murgas kept their word. While they had originally joined Villa, as the lone surviving brother told an interviewer in 1976, "to protect our families and property,"[15] they became so deeply attached to Villa that they remained loyal to the revolutionary chief even after his great defeats in 1915 and the dissolution of the División del Norte.

Villa did not only attract recruits from Chihuahua. As his fame spread through Mexico, men from distant states made the long journey north to join his army. Federico González Jiménez, a landless peasant from the Altos de Jalisco, came from a poor family. From the age of 10 on, he had worked the fields of a hacendado for five centavos a day. He joined the revolution "because of the terrible conditions in the countryside."[16]

Pablo Baray, who joined the División del Norte from the old military colony of Bachiniva, which had a long history of conflict with the Porfirian authorities, may have had additional reasons. In his eyes, fighting for the revolution was the good life, and he proudly stated that during his army service his weight had increased from 64 to 75 kilos.[17]

While most of the fighters in the División del Norte were volunteers, there was one conspicuous exception to this rule: captured members of the federal army were frequently given a choice between joining Villa's forces or being shot. Most of them had been impressed into the federal army against their will, and the relative freedom, better pay, and better living conditions of the División del Norte formed a stark contrast to their treatment in the federal army.

While the social origins of Villa's men varied tremendously, their perceptions of Villa showed great similarity. Jesús Pérez, the well-educated son of a mining administrator, who had been secretary to Emilio Madero and had joined Villa, described him as a man "endowed with the gift of leadership who was given absolute obedience by his men. He was a great organizer, so that his soldiers had great respect for him rather than simply fearing him."[18] Pérez had joined the División del Norte because, had he not done so, "federal troops would have shot him. All of those who joined at that time had done so for similar reasons."[19]

José Dolores Figueroa, from the former military colony of Bachiniva, was impressed by "the electricity" in Villa's eyes and by the fact that the people loved him.[20]

Another volunteer from Bachiniva considered Villa "a good man who never changed sides."[21]

Porfirio Adrian Díaz, a carpenter whose parents were relatively well-to-do peasants, came all the way from the southern state of Oaxaca to join Villa, whom he considered "very brave. He was very good to the common people."[22]

Lieutenant Colonel Victorio de Anda, the son of relatively well-to-do peasants in Jalisco, had joined Villa against the wishes of his father. He felt that Villa's authority derived from his courage and the fact that he could always be seen in the first line of combat.[23]

There was a consensus among those of his former soldiers who were interviewed about Villa's characteristics as a social revolutionary. A few described him as an agrarian revolutionary who would redistribute the land. Most of them used a more general designation and called him "a friend of the poor." Pedro Romero, the former peon, saw Villa as "a general who fought for the poor."[24] Lucio Alvarado Portillo, who worked in a munitions factory in Chihuahua that made ammunition for the División del Norte, considered Villa "the benefactor of the poor."[25]

The former Villista colonel Federico González Jiménez was impressed by the fact that after taking a town, Villa "gave corn and other help to the poor."[26] Francisco Muro Ledesma, who joined Villa at 13 because he sought revenge for the murder of his father by federal troops, felt that "the common people loved Villa. Wherever he went he distributed corn, beans, etc."[27]

Most of Villa's former soldiers insisted that the ex-bandit kept better discipline and better order among his troops than any other general in Mexico. They all stated that looting was absolutely forbidden and that anyone caught plundering or robbing would immediately be shot. Secundino Vaca insisted that bandits who robbed the poor frequently declared that they were Villistas in an attempt to discredit the revolutionary leader. "Villa," Secundino Vaca declared, "never took from the poor but only from the rich."[28]

The one exception to this consensus was Francisco Muro Ledesma, who had joined Villa at 13, and said that Villa sometimes allowed his soldiers to loot for three minutes. Anyone caught robbing after that would immediately be shot. He also insisted that when looting did occur, it was mainly done by the troops of Tomás Urbina and Maclovio Herrera, which were not under Villa's direct command. His men also expressed the conviction that Villa took nothing for himself.[29]

In order to maintain the discipline of his army, Villa relied not only on his popularity and the incentives that he gave his soldiers but on harsh measures of control as well. The man in charge of these policies, Manuel Banda, was a former employee of a collection agency in Torreón, who had joined Villa after he captured the city. Unlike Villa's other killers, he had given no indication in his pre-revolutionary life of the violence he would practice as an officer of the División del Norte. He was, as a former school friend remembered, "one of those quiet, relaxed, good pupils who never picked a quarrel and was on good terms with everybody." When his friend met Banda again during the revolution, he could not believe the change that had come over him. "What is your role?" he asked him.

"To force people into battle at the point of a gun."
"Did you have to hurt some of them?"
"Hurt? No, kill. I do not wound, I kill. . . . A wounded man is cured someday and can kill me anytime. . . . I shoot to kill and if I do not do so immediately, I continue to shoot until the man is dead."
"Have you killed many?"
"Many. I have killed many; in some battles I may have killed as many of our men as the federal troops have done. That's the system of General Villa, and I tell you that it's the only system that has had success, above all with these people from Durango."[30]

Banda had concentrated his efforts on Contreras's men, insisting that before Villa assumed command, they had run from firefights like "sheep" in every battle. They had sparked such contempt among their enemies that instead of calling them the Brigada Contreras, the federal soldiers had named them Brigada Carreras (the Running Brigade). According to Banda:

They now know me, and they are gripped by panic when they see me on my motorcycle with a pistol in my hand. They immediately go on the attack. In this way we took Torreón. Now Contreras's men are completely transformed; they fight at least as well as the other brigades, perhaps even better; they know that if someone is not killed by the federals in front, he will be killed by us in the back.[31]

Banda and his men were but one of the units that Villa created to enforce his will upon recalcitrant soldiers and officers. The Dorados (men of gold) were the most important of these. At first they served only as Villa's bodyguard. But soon they became an elite unit utilized for various purposes, ranging from serving as adjutants to Villa to executing his enemies, or, like Napoleon's Old Guard, to intervening in a battle when the odds had become desperate. When the Dorados were created after the battle of Torreón, they consisted of three units of 32 men each. Their number soon rose to 400. Villa chose all of them personally, on the basis of their loyalty to him and their prowess in battle. The Dorados included many of his relatives, since he felt that he could count on their unconditional loyalty (which was not always the case). Whenever Villa heard of a soldier or an officer who had distinguished himself by a particular act of bravery or of resourcefulness, he would recruit him into the Dorados. For example, Candelario Cervantes attracted Villa's attention when during an attack on the hacienda of Santa Clara, in which the Villistas had no artillery to support them, Cervantes loaded a few pieces of wood on a mule train, approached the enemy lines, and loudly gave orders for his soldiers to prepare an artillery attack on the hacienda. The federal soldiers panicked and surrendered.

Carlos Gutiérrez Galindo's experiences also captured Villa's imagination and led to his incorporation into the Dorados. Gutiérrez Galindo had been wounded and his horse killed during an unsuccessful Villista attack. After his unit retreated, federal soldiers swarmed over the battlefield, killing all the wounded and prisoners. Gutiérrez Galindo gutted his dead horse and hid for hours under its skin until Villista troops advanced once again, when he was able to emerge from his hiding place.[32]

Why these men were called Dorados is still a matter of controversy. Some believe that it was because they wore a golden insignia on their hats, others that it arose from the gold coins in which they paid for many of the goods they acquired, while others see an analogy to a famous nineteenth-century group of bandits called *los plateados*, the silver ones.[33]

In some respects, it was more difficult for Villa to maintain and secure the loyalty of the different generals of his army than that of their soldiers. Many of these generals had become regional warlords and were reluctant to give up their autonomy. They had done so only when it became clear that only by uniting under a strong chieftain could they repel federal attacks. Later, Villa's victories had greatly enhanced his standing and his influence among them. Nevertheless, many still smarted from their loss of autonomy. Others, such as Urbina, resented the discipline Villa imposed, which meant that they could not return to their traditional ways of enriching themselves and securing the loyalty of their troops by allowing them to plunder whatever city they conquered. These tendencies to autonomy were all the more dangerous for Villa, since Carranza attempted to foster them. At the same time, Carranza was wooing two of Villa's generals, Maclovio Herrera and Manuel Chao.

Villa showed great shrewdness in counteracting his subordinates' plays for greater autonomy. The first and simplest step he took was to increase the number of men under his direct command and to transform at least some of them into an elite fighting unit. In June 1914, when Villa's División del Norte had reached the high point of its development, Carrancista officials estimated that of its approximately 12,000 soldiers, 3,000 were directly under Villa and unconditionally loyal to him.[34]

In order to maintain the loyalty of his generals and their troops, Villa made substantial concessions to them. Part of the estates confiscated from the oligarchy was placed under the control of Villa's generals. They did not have to account directly for the revenues from these estates, but they were obliged to use the income to feed, clothe, and supply a certain number of their men. Some of the generals, such as Urbina, received these lands as compensation for income that they and their men lost when Villa ordered them to stop pillaging conquered cities.

In other respects as well, the different units of the División del Norte maintained a large degree of independence. When General Juan García, the commander of the Madero brigade, fell in battle, it was not Villa but the officers of the brigade who designated his successor.[35] Moreover, regional chieftains could maintain control over their home regions. Villa had decreed that in Chihuahua and Durango, the orders of local military commanders—who were largely beholden to the regional chieftains—would supersede those of civilian officials appointed by the governor.

Villa never attempted to appeal to the soldiers of the División del Norte over the heads of their generals. Nevertheless, he did try to establish some kind of personal rapport with the soldiers, and his personal charisma and legend strengthened his popularity among his soldiers. They would go in to battle shouting "Viva Villa!" instead of the name of the local or regional general who commanded them.

Villa secured even greater loyalty from the troops of the División del Norte in the spring of 1914. Many of the men who joined at this time were far more influenced by his personal prestige and success on the battlefield than by personal links to local leaders.

Until late 1914 and early 1915, when a new civil war broke out among the revolutionaries, Villa with two exceptions never attempted to execute any of his highest officers or to take violent reprisals against them. General Domingo Yuriar's drunken refusal to join a battle was one exception. Villa's subsequent execution of Yuriar met with no opposition within his army. The situation was very different when Villa attempted to execute Governor Manuel Chao for disloyalty. In that case, Villa was forced to relent.

While Villa had made substantial concessions to some of his generals and to their subordinates by providing them with haciendas and by allowing them to maintain a large degree of control over their native regions, he tried in other ways to make them dependent upon him. He attempted to maintain complete control over the acquisition of arms, ammunition, and uniforms. He was also very careful in restricting his subordinates' access to the American market. Thus while the generals could dispose of the goods of their haciendas without asking Villa's permission, they were required to obtain a special license from him if they sought to export cattle or other goods across the border to the United States. He also maintained some control over the purse strings of his army by controlling the production and the supply of the paper money he printed.

When Villa began issuing such money, American merchants across the border accepted it at a relatively high value, since they were confident that sooner or later Villa would win, and that his currency would then increase in value and be redeemable at par.

Perhaps the easiest of the many complex tasks that Villa faced in attempting to streamline and reorganize his army was the procurement of arms and ammunitions once the U.S. embargo had been lifted by Woodrow Wilson in February 1914. Although Carranza already had representatives in place in the United States who were charged with buying arms, Villa did not want to be dependent on the first chief and sent agents of his own to the border and to the United States to procure arms and ammunition. His main agents were the Torreón businessman Lázaro de la Garza, Felíx Sommerfeld, a German adventurer and former head of Madero's secret service in the United States, and his own brother, Hipólito. The first two of these men were knowledgeable and capable businessmen, who would work for Villa efficiently as long as it suited their interests, but would otherwise betray him. Hipólito Villa was loyal to his brother, but this loyalty was frequently overshadowed by his greed and incapacity.

Until August 1914, when World War I broke out, the arms and ammunition market in the United States was a buyer's market, and Villa had no difficulty in securing whatever supplies he needed. Nor in this early period did he have any problems paying for the goods he acquired. Largely through Lázaro de la Garza, he sold the cattle from estates confiscated from the Mexican oligarchy across the border in the United States. In addition, Villa received tax revenue from American companies whose businesses were located in the zone he controlled.

Villa's monopoly over the acquisition of arms and ammunition was not the only way he was able to control his potentially rebellious generals. Another was through direct control of the technical branches of his army, such as artillery, in which most of his commanders and soldiers lacked expertise. Villa made sure that these technical units were commanded by men who were not dependent upon his subordinates, who had no constituency of their own, and whose primary link was to him. But finding trained soldiers to fill these units was no easy task. There were only two sources from which Villa could acquire such experts: the federal army or foreign countries. Both presented risks.

With the exception of Juan N. Medina, who became Villa's chief of staff, few federal officers voluntarily enlisted in the División del Norte before Felipe Angeles joined Villa's ranks in March 1914. The great majority of former federal officers or soldiers who served in his ranks in the first months after the formation of the División del Norte were prisoners captured from the federal army and offered the choice of serving in the revolutionary forces or being shot. While most of them, for obvious reasons, elected to serve, their loyalty was by no means guaranteed.

Foreign soldiers of fortune and volunteers presented a different problem for Villa. He had no ideological opposition to using foreigners in his service. After all, Madero had done the same. Although Villa had criticized Madero's use of foreigners in 1911, he had not done so as a matter of principle but rather because Madero seemed to trust Garibaldi more than he trusted most of his Mexican officers and had given him a position of decisive responsibility. This was something Villa never did. He used foreigners as experts but never gave them a place in his war councils or among his generals.

Foreigners presented two problems for Villa. First, if he disciplined them, or even if they were killed in battle, complications with foreign governments might ensue. Second, he had no way of checking the credentials of the foreigners who came to him. They would cross the border from the United States, come to his headquarters, and claim to have great experience in military affairs and to have fought in many battles. Villa had no way of knowing whether they told the truth.

There were no agencies that hired these men, no letters of reference on which he could depend. If he found they had lied, he could dismiss them, but punishing them in any other way, especially shooting them, might again entail diplomatic problems. As a result, Villa's experiences with foreign mercenaries were of a very mixed nature. John Reed describes meeting five American mercenaries who had fought with Villa for a time, and whom the revolutionary leader had practically forced to leave his army. Of these, only one had real military experience; all the others had falsified their records when they enlisted.[36]

The one way Villa tested his recruits was to put them in charge of technical branches of his army and judge them on the basis of their performance. Thus, Villa named an American soldier of fortune who had fought in the U.S. Army, but had no artillery experience, as head of his artillery prior to the battle of Tierra Blanca.[37] At the time, the artillery consisted of only two guns, which Villa had captured in Torreón. Fortunately, another officer who had more experience in battle than the American, Ivar Thord-Gray, arrived in Mexico hoping to offer his services to its revolutionaries. He had fought in the Boer War in South Africa, as well as with the British Army in India, and had gone to China to try his fortune with warlords there before alighting in Mexico. He was a cavalry expert, but Villa felt that while he needed no one to tell him how to run his cavalry, he was in urgent need of artillery officers. Thord-Gray was no artillery expert, but he did know something about guns. When the two guns that Villa had captured in Torreón did not fire and seemed to be completely out of service, Thord-Gray, unlike the American soldier of fortune who was in charge of artillery, had no difficulty in diagnosing the problem. The federal gunners had taken away the firing pins and the range sights before abandoning the guns, thus disabling them. Thord-Gray slipped across the border and had some firing pins made, so that the guns could at least fire, although without sighting ranges, their aim was erratic. Nevertheless, when, in Villa's presence, Thord-Gray showed that he could fire these guns, Villa walked up to him

and to my amazement gave me a Mexican embrace (abrazo), words shot from his lips like bullets from a gattling gun; I had suddenly become his friend (amigo) and companion (compañero).

A few minutes later he proclaimed me as his chief of artillery with the rank of first captain (capitan primero). My command consisted of two seventy-five millimeter field guns, no officers, no non-coms. There were a few half-wild Apache gunners who knew nothing about guns and some could only speak their own language except for a little pidgin-Spanish.[38]

In this case, Villa's improvised hiring of Thord-Gray turned out to be positive, as did his enlistment of another adventurer, Captain Horst von der Goltz, a German.

Horst von der Goltz, who according to his memoirs had worked as an agent of the German secret service in different parts of the world, wandered into Mexico looking for adventure. He arrived in Ciudad Chihuahua when it was still occupied by federal troops and was immediately imprisoned by federal commander, Mercado, as a possible revolutionary spy. He was only freed when Villa's army occupied the city. Von der Goltz immediately volunteered his services to one of

Villa's generals, Trinidad Rodríguez, some of whose officers he had befriended in jail. He told the revolutionaries that he had long military experience. This was a lie; he had never been in battle. The only military training he had was the obligatory service that any German of military age had to render. The little training he had and the reputation of Germans as great fighters, as well as a series of bluffs and coincidences, soon enabled von der Goltz to rise rapidly in the ranks of Villa's army and to assume a leading technical position, for which in reality he had neither the training nor the expertise. His reputation as *el diablo alemán* (the German devil) was made when during an infantry attack, he got lost and, not knowing where he was, and trying to get away from the battle, he inadvertently fled toward the front. As he was advancing, his detachment had received orders to retreat, and when, after long wanderings, von der Goltz, coming from the front, met the rearguard detachment, its commander was impressed. "'But,' cried the colonel suddenly warming into emotion, 'you—where have you been? You brave German refused to come back with the others. All by yourself you have been fighting single-handed. Let me embrace you.'"[39]

Rodríguez was now convinced that von der Goltz was a battle-tried war veteran and decided to utilize his services in a technical capacity.

Chief Trinidad Rodríguez got twenty machine guns down from the United States and turned them over to me. "Train your gun crews and get the platoons ready for field service," he ordered. "You can have three weeks. Then I shall need them."

Without a word I saluted and turned on my heel. I could not very well tell my general that I had never in my life applied even the tip of one finger to a machine gun.[40]

While von der Goltz may have had no inkling of machine guns, his basic training and resourcefulness led him to a success he himself had not expected. He hired a former American bank robber named Jefferson, who had escaped from jail in El Paso, recruited a few Mexican gunners, and finally set up an efficient machine-gun company.

Von der Goltz must have possessed unusual learning skills, for only a few months later, an agent of the U.S. war college, posing as a war correspondent, carefully examined Villa's army and lavished praise on the organization of his artillery, for which he credited the German soldier of fortune.[41]

Some of the mercenaries whom Villa hired were real experts and had no need to bluff their way into his army.[42] One such, with much fighting experience in his chosen field, machine guns, was Sam Drebben, "internationally known as the 'fighting Jew.'" According to Patrick O'Hea who knew him,

he had fought in the U.S.A. war against Spain, in the Marines in Nicaragua at least, and on a condottieri basis in the other republics of Latin America. Of medium height but rather heavy build, in age on the happy side of the half-century, there was nothing of the expected bluster and blasphemy to his mouthed speech as he asked for any unwanted newspapers that I could lend him, no matter how old, the better to pass the lonely hours.

The antithesis of a swashbuckler, he was silent and diffident concerning his feats of arms but took a sort of modest pride in his profession as might any other artificer or master craftsman.[43]

One of the strangest of the men said to have served with Villa was the American short-story writer and satirist Ambrose Bierce, who was 71 when he entered Mexico. It is not clear why he went there, and it is still less clear in what capacity he rode with Villa's army, if indeed he did. One purpose of his trip may have been to put an end to his life. Shortly before he left the United States, he wrote his niece that "if you hear of my being stood up against the Mexican stonewall and shot to rags please note I think that I think that a pretty good way to depart this life. It beats old age, disease or falling down the cellar stairs. To be a Gringo in Mexico—Ah!, that is euthanasia."[44]

By Bierce's own account, he crossed the border from El Paso to Ciudad Juárez sometime in November 1913, shortly after Villa had captured the city, and rode south with Villa. He probably participated in the battle of Tierra Blanca, where Villa defeated federal troops sent to retake Ciudad Juárez. During that battle, at least temporarily, Bierce's status changed from mere observer to combatant. He took a rifle and shot at the federal troops, killing one federal soldier. The Villistas were so delighted that they gave him a large sombrero. On December 16, he sent his last letter from Ciudad Chihuahua, which Villa had captured not long before, stating that he expected to go to Ojinaga, where the last federal troops in the state of Chihuahua had holed up and were resisting attacks by Villa's troops. This was the last communication he ever wrote. What later happened to him, when and where he died, remains one of the great mysteries of American literary history. One theory, accepted by many of his biographers, is that he died during the battle of Ojinaga. Other authors believe that he stayed for some time with Villa and then angered him either by criticizing him or by saying that he intended to join Carranza, and that Villa then either shot Bierce or abandoned him in the desert.[45]

Villa's way of dealing with the specialized and technical branches of his army and the quality of those services dramatically improved when Felipe Angeles joined the División del Norte.

As Villa achieved one victory after another, his strategic abilities and the fighting qualities of his army became the subjects of intense debate in the press in the United States. On a very different level, they also became a preoccupation of the U.S. military, which was contemplating the possibility of an American military intervention and trying to gauge the kind of resistance U.S. troops would encounter.

In the press, the discussion largely focused on Villa's personality, with John Reed clearly expressing the opinion of large segments of U.S. public opinion. "On the field too Villa had to invent an entirely original method of warfare," Reed wrote, "because he never had a chance to learn anything of accepted military strategy."

In that he is without the possibility of any doubt the greatest leader that Mexico has ever had. His method of fighting is astonishingly like Napoleon's. Secrecy, quickness of movement, the adaptation of his plan to the character of the country and of his soldiers, the value of intimate relations with the rank and file and of building up a tradition among the enemy that his army is invincible and that he himself bears a charmed life. These are his characteristics.[46]

The U.S. secret agent Edwin Emerson was also impressed by Villa's ability to generate loyalty among his soldiers and to mold them into a fighting whole, but he did not believe that this warranted the American press calling Villa "a consummate Napoleonic strategist." Branding such descriptions "moonshine," he wrote:

as for strategy he has merely the inborn cunning of any Indian on the warpath, with an almost inexhaustible fund of intimate personal knowledge of the north country, gained during the strenuous years when he was chased all over the lands as an outlaw, besides which he has the invaluable quality of energy, dash and initiative which as you know is exceedingly rare among the Mexicans. Maps are quite lost on him, for he can no more read a map than an owl. This last also applies to most of his officers except for a few of his highest staff officers. . . . What glimmers of apparent strategy Villa has shown in this campaign were either simple Indian cunning or were the result of the advice of some of the educated soldiers around him, to whom he is always willing to listen—another great military virtue. These professional soldiers include General Felipe Angeles, Marshall P. Martil Poole, an American civil engineer, and young von der Goltz.[47]

Emerson was only willing to concede "three innovations in Villa's military organization which excited most comment among Mexicans and foreigners resident in that region . . . his supply service, his commissary and quartermaster department, and his medical department, all of which depended wholly on the railway service and never made any effectual attempt of getting away from the railway. Whenever they did so they invariably broke down but while with the railway they did good work, in fact surprisingly good work judging by Mexican standards."[48]

A committee of U.S. military men of which Emerson was part, many of whom had also spent time with the División del Norte, came up with a much more favorable view of Villa's strategic innovations. His strategy, they felt, was based on the dependence of the federal garrisons in large cities on supplies brought in by railroad, as well as on the federal army's incapacity to take offensive action: the federals had no mobile units for this purpose, and the soldiers impressed into that army largely lacked the will to fight.

The enemy's bread line is cut where it is impossible for him to repair it in time; the hungry insurgents watch on the hills for a sign of weakness and as soon as one appears an attack is made; if successful the federals evacuate with practically their whole force. No pursuit is made by the Constitutionalists, because, in the first place the towns taken contain too much loot to be abandoned to anyone else, and in the next place, the federals' line of retreat is stripped bare of food, animals and often of water. If the attack is unsuccessful the federals make no vigorous prolonged counterattack, and the Constitutionalists retire unmolested to the hills, resume the policy of watchful waiting and prepare for the next attack. Each time a town is taken the insurgents, unmolested by the enemy, become stronger, better equipped and their next operation takes place against a stronger force of federals. . . . there is nothing complicated about the strategy; but it is hard to beat in northern Mexico.[49]

The commission was also greatly impressed by Villa's strategy of night attacks on large cities, which had paid off at Torreón.

Emerson tried to analyze the effectiveness of the División del Norte. He was not much impressed by the infantry, which he designated as "Villa's weakest arm." He felt that "in a horse country like northern Mexico people who have to go afoot are generally scorned, therefore nobody serves in the infantry by choice but only those poor devils who could not get themselves mounted. During the latter part of the Torreón campaign all the federal deserters and prisoners who were incorporated in Villa's army were stuck into the infantry." Nor, in spite of Angeles's leadership, was Emerson impressed by the quality of Villa's artillery.

These negative ratings were overshadowed by the praise that Emerson heaped on the División del Norte. Its three greatest assets were its cavalry, its mobility, and the fighting spirit and resilience of the Mexican soldiers. The strength of Villa's cavalry was attributable in part to the quality of the horses bred in Chihuahua and Coahuila. "The best horses come from the ranch of the Zuloagas, a Spanish family near Chihuahua who had for many years been importing Arab stallions and mares, barbs and some English and Kentucky and California thoroughbreds." With the help of these horses, Villa's cavalry achieved "a remarkable mobility . . . in moments of stress. This mobility was enhanced by the fact that Villa's cavalry when engaged in hostile operations, moves unhampered by any impediment such as wagons or pack trains, the men carrying nothing but their arms, ammunition, canteen and one blanket, their invaluable practice being to make the country supply them and their horses with subsistence."[50]

The same mobility applied to Villa's military train. Emerson compared Villa's march south from Chihuahua to Torreón with a similar northward movement by Huerta's troops two years earlier, when Huerta was in charge of the campaign against Orozco. "It took Huerta's army, 7,500 fighting men (15,000 people) two months. Huerta as you may recall had twenty railroad trains. Villa this time had nineteen trains and two additional short trains which he used for communication purposes and Villa carried practically the same number of people but it took Villa only ten days." What impressed Emerson most and boded ill for a possible U.S. invasion of Mexico was the fighting spirit of the División del Norte:

You know from your own observations in Mexico that the average Mexican pelado is a pretty sturdy creature, who can stand more privation and hardship, such as cold, heat, wetting, hunger, thirst, vermin, than any white people could put up with. I was agreeably impressed while serving with Villa's men by the generally cheerful and contented demeanor, without any of the grumbling so usual among our own troops. During the battle days and at other times when I came in contact with the wounded men, I was filled with admiration at the stoical way in which they bore their hurts. Men who were not seriously wounded, almost invariably continued their service in the field, and I saw many instances of men who were really quite seriously hurt—shot through the shoulders or elbows or hands or wounded in the head—who held their places in the firing line and stayed with their commands, refusing to go to the rear. The conduct of the women who came along on the railway trains and many of whom accompanied their men into the firing line around Torreón was also notably heroic.[51]

Can the División del Norte be called a revolutionary army in the fullest sense of the term? Revolutionary armies in history have tended to have certain common characteristics. They have tended to be composed largely or entirely of volunteers, with most soldiers conscious of the aims they were fighting for, and civilian society has closely identified with the army and exercised either control or at least a profound influence over that army.

There was one army during the Mexican revolution whose revolutionary credentials according to these criteria no one has ever doubted. This was the Liberating Army of the South, headed by Emiliano Zapata. Such a "perfect" revolutionary army was only possible in a guerrilla setting where the men fought near their communities, remained peasants to a large degree, and did not become professional soldiers.

The northern revolutionary armies were of a very different nature. While they too were composed of volunteers, their social composition was more heterogeneous, and the links to their communities were different, since, unlike the Zapatistas, they fought further and further away from their homes and native communities.

It is difficult to determine either the revolutionary consciousness or the civilian link of the northern revolutionary soldiers and officers. There was no system of political commissars or political parties to indoctrinate them, as was the case with communist revolutionary peasant armies. Nor were there religious leaders to carry out similar labor, as in the Iranian army. Unfortunately, very few surveys of the mentality of these revolutionary soldiers and officers were ever carried out, and the few that were took place when most of them were in their late seventies or early eighties. Nevertheless, one can speculate on the character of the armies' revolutionary consciousness and links to civil society on the basis of the way these armies were formed and the social characteristics of the regions from whence they came.

In both Coahuila and Nuevo León, where the most important contingents of Carrancista troops originated, the core of the revolutionary armies came from professionalized state militias, which absorbed those former Maderista revolutionaries who wanted to become professional soldiers and were greatly strengthened during the Orozco rebellion.

In this respect, the composition of the División del Norte was very different. In contrast to what happened in Sonora and Coahuila, the professional state militias that had been set up in Chihuahua after the victory of Madero largely disappeared in the Madero years as a result of the Orozco rebellion. The bulk of these state militias had joined Orozco, and the majority of the units that had remained loyal to the government and had been headed by Pancho Villa were dissolved after Villa's arrest. Thus, once the constitutionalist revolution broke out, a new popular army had to be raised. Its core was not composed of professional militias but of men recruited from their communities, with which they still had links. These links were so strong that attempts by the leadership to disrupt them were doomed to failure in spite of Villa's prestige.[52]

In addition, Chihuahua and Durango were the core areas of agrarian discontent in the north, rather than Sonora, Coahuila, and Nuevo León, and men either from expropriated communities or from communities that had seized hacienda lands constituted an important part of the División del Norte. Since military units frequently came from one community, as did their leaders, their links to civil society, at least as far as their home regions were concerned, were still strong.

The División del Norte was by no means exclusively a peasant army, however.

Cowboys, miners, and drifters also joined. In addition, many of the peasants who came from other regions of Mexico joined as individuals and not as communities, sometimes out of revolutionary consciousness, sometimes just to survive by becoming soldiers. They received regular pay, with bonuses after each victory, and for some of them at least, the army had become a way of life in itself. Since many of them were boys aged between 12 and 16, the extent of their revolutionary consciousness is debatable.

What is not clear is how the revolutionary armies were perceived in regions where they did not originate. To a large degree, this depended on the amount of discipline they were able to keep and to what degree the leadership could prevent the soldiers from looting. By all accounts, at least until the end of 1914, it was the División del Norte that kept the strongest discipline among its men and thus probably gained the greatest degree of popularity even in parts of Mexico far removed from its native region.

The Battle for Torreón

In February 1913 Woodrow Wilson lifted the arms embargo that had prevented the revolutionaries from legally acquiring arms in the United States. As a result, a few weeks later, the well-armed northern revolutionaries began their offensive southward. In the east, Pablo González's army set out toward Monterrey and Tampico, and in the west Obregón advanced south from Sonora. Neither of these armies was considered an immediate or serious danger by the federal army. Pablo González's military record had not hitherto been very impressive, and the southern progress of Obregón's army would be hampered by Sonora's lack of railway links with the south.

It was Villa, the federal command believed, who presented the greatest and most immediate danger. If he could be held back or even defeated at Torreón, then the tide of war could be reversed. The federal command and the government expressed optimism that the "bandit" armies of Villa would finally meet their match in Torreón.

That optimism reflected the views of Huerta's general staff, as well as his commanders in the field. They knew that Villa had never faced the kind of situation that would now confront him in Torreón. His first capture of that city was frequently considered a fluke, due to the ineptness and cowardice of the federal commander, Munguiá. At Ciudad Juárez, Villa had surprised the garrison, and at Tierra Blanca he had fought only against irregular troops and had been able to choose the site of battle. The one time Villa had attacked a well-fortified city commanded by a competent general, his attempt to take Ciudad Chihuahua by storm at the end of 1913, he had failed.

This time the situation would be different. One of the federal army's best commanders, Refugio Velasco, commanded the nearly 10,000 federal troops in and around Torreón. They had fortified not only the city itself but a host of smaller towns around it. In Gómez Palacio, fortifications nearly as strong those in Torreón had been erected. Well-placed federal cannon, frequently located on hills, and machine-gun nests were formidable obstacles, designed to obstruct

Villa's famous cavalry charges. The federal high command hoped and expected that these strategic measures would offset Villa's superiority in numbers—Villa had sent 16,000 men. They were not unduly worried by the fact that Villa now disposed of an artillery contingent, which he had lacked when he had attacked Ciudad Chihuahua. They were convinced that Villa was incapable of organizing well-trained artillery in the few months that had elapsed since the battle of Chihuahua. According to Emerson:

This artillery . . . was not too well handled in the field, but at least it was promptly brought into action, largely through the efficiency of the railroad and the noise it made as well as the artillery prestige of General Felipe Angeles, who was generally believed to have personal command of it (not always the case), had much to do with breaking down the morale of the federals at Gómez Palacio, Torreón, and San Pedro. . . . [Nevertheless the] positions of the guns were generally ill-chosen, single pieces often getting separated from their batteries and even from their own caissons. This was because no competent artillery officer went ahead to choose the ground. When the artillery first went into action north of Gómez Palacio, they did so after nightfall, each gun by itself, floundering about in the uneven ground, trying to find a suitable firing position. When daylight came they were found strewn all over the landscape, some in the most impossible positions, in canals and exposed slopes or out in the open spots directly under the guns of the enemy.[53]

What more than made up for the federal superiority in artillery was a new strategy that Villa now developed, consisting of night attacks, which was much admired by U.S. military observers.

"Although [the revolutionaries'] fire was poor in the daytime, it was much worse at night," William Mitchell noted. It "was not effective over five hundred yards and it was very difficult to make them cross the fire-swept zone in the daytime and engage the enemy at a range of two hundred yards or closer." At night the situation would be much better for the revolutionaries. "The insurgents crawled up to close range with few casualties, delivered their fire with almost as much effect as in the daytime, and the federals expended even more ammunition than in the daytime. The insurgents had more or less regular lines of federals to fire at while the federals had to fire at the flashes of the insurgents' firearms scattered all over the sides of the hills and in no particular formation." In addition, federal commanders feared that their units might become scattered and even fire upon each other, so no counterattacks at night were carried out by the federal army.[54]

The night attacks also had disastrous effects on the morale of the federal army. Unlike the revolutionaries, who could temporarily withdraw from the battlefield, and thus find some rest, the federal troops could never do so. By day, they were pounded by the artillery; by night, the Villista infantry attacked. The siege was extremely bloody, since the night attacks, which brought the revolutionaries into such close proximity to the federal lines, led to savage hand-to-hand fighting. The terror of that fighting was enhanced by the darkness.

Federal ammunition and federal morale seem to have given way simultaneously. The army first evacuated Gómez Palacio, and then its battered remnants, consisting of about 4,000 men, withdrew from Torreón.

The federal high command did not give up. It sent about 6,000 fresh federal troops to the city of San Pedro de las Colonias, not far from Torreón, hoping that these troops, combined with the remnants of Velasco's army, would finally be able to crush the revolutionary troops, wearied by more than ten days of incessant fighting. They were mistaken. Velasco's demoralized men from Torreón infected the fresh troops with their fears and pessimism, while the euphoria of victory more than made up for the weariness of Villa's men. San Pedro de las Colonias too was stormed, and the remnants of the federal army withdrew to the south.

CHAPTER NINE

Villa's Emergence
as a National Leader

*His Relations with the United States
and His Conflict with Carranza*

His victory at Torreón made Villa a national leader. He now controlled more resources and more territory than any other revolutionary commander, his army was the strongest among the revolutionary forces, and his prestige was unequaled by that of any other military chieftain the revolution had produced. In the United States, public opinion, and perhaps even the Wilson administration, considered him a national leader whose decisions might decide the fate of the Mexican Revolution. Carranza's enemies in the revolutionary movement hoped, and Carranza feared, that Villa was out to replace him as leader of the revolution. Villa himself was long uncertain about what role he should play. Whatever his hesitations, however, his newfound status transformed his relations with the United States, with Carranza, and with non-Carrancista factions in the Mexican revolutionary movement.

Villa and the United States

One of the greatest successes that Villa initially achieved was the relationship he was able to establish with different forces in the United States. For a time, he was able to gain the support of institutions and individuals whose views on most issues were divergent and who frequently clashed with one another. The Wilson administration, important segments of big business, leaders of the military, and liberal and radical intellectuals, as well as some radical organizations, all sympathized with Villa, and many of them considered him the potential savior of Mexico.

In the eyes of Woodrow Wilson and his secretary of state, William Jennings Bryan, who were looking for alternatives to both Huerta and Carranza, Villa emerged into prominence at just the right time. Wilson had been inaugurated as president only a short time after Huerta's coup, and he was appalled at the killing of Madero. He closely identified with the murdered president, whose commitment both to democracy and capitalism he shared. "I will not recognize a government of butchers," he said. He firmly rejected calls for Huerta's recognition by the U.S. ambassador to Mexico, Henry Lane Wilson, who had done so much to overthrow Madero, and by important U.S. business interests.[1] His opposition to Huerta was further fueled by indications that both the British government and British oil interests strongly supported the new military dictator of Mexico.[2]

Nevertheless, when in August and September 1913, leading members of Mexico's upper classes offered Wilson the same kind of compromise they had offered Francisco Madero two years before, he was quite ready to accept it. The compromise took the form of the holding of new presidential elections in Mexico in which Huerta would pledge not to become a candidate. The preferred candidate of Mexico's elite was Federico Gamboa, a conservative politician who had been Huerta's secretary of foreign affairs and was supported by the Catholic party. What made the compromise so attractive to Mexico's upper classes was that it would have preserved the federal army and the federal bureaucracy. In fact, nothing in their offer precluded Huerta from remaining commander in chief of the army.

Both Wilson and Bryan were enthusiastic when they were told that Huerta had accepted the compromise. "I think our troubles in Mexico are over," Bryan wrote Wilson. The Wilson administration called on the revolutionaries to participate in the elections and rejected the argument that honest elections were impossible as long as the federal army controlled most of the country. They warned the revolutionaries that if Gamboa were elected, the United States would support him even against the constitutionalists. Unfortunately for Mexico's upper classes, neither Huerta nor the Mexican military were willing to serve the elite as they had during the rule of Porfirio Díaz. For the first time in many years, the military had taken control of the country, and it was by no means ready to relinquish it. The military was further encouraged in its attitude by the British minister to Mexico, Sir Lionel Carden, who gave Huerta and his generals to understand that Britain would support Mexico even against the United States. In open defiance of Woodrow Wilson, Huerta dissolved the one legacy of the Madero period that he had hitherto respected, the Cámara de diputados, the Mexican legislature, when it decided to investigate the assassination of a politician who had been sharply critical of Huerta. Opposition deputies were rounded up and imprisoned. At the same time, new presidential elections took place, in which Huerta had himself reelected with the help of massive electoral fraud.

Wilson now resolved to do everything in his power to topple Huerta. He decided to throw his support to the revolutionaries, but he was worried that allowing them to win on their own would entail great loss of life and property and the possibility that the United States would lose control of the movement it was sponsoring. The "short-cut" that Wilson had in mind was for U.S. troops to occupy the largest cities in northern Mexico, as well as some port cities, while Carranza's troops marched southward to conquer Mexico City.[3] It was the kind of compromise that no Mexican politician, even if he had wanted to, could have acceded to without being considered a traitor by most Mexicans. Carranza's abrupt rejection of this plan when it was presented in November 1913 was not only a matter of expediency but an expression of his profound nationalism.

At precisely this moment, when the Wilson administration was unalterably opposed to Huerta and beginning to have doubts about Carranza, Villa emerged into the limelight. Did he represent a genuine alternative to both Huerta and Carranza? It was a question Woodrow Wilson and top officials of his administration would examine and ponder with increasing interest. On the one hand, there were the reports of Villa's bandit past, stressed by U.S. representatives in Mexico City, who embellished them with information provided by the Huerta administration, to the effect that Villa had been convicted of over 100 murders.[4] Villa's wholesale execution of prisoners, his expulsion of the Spaniards from Torreón and Chihuahua, and the way his troops had violated the diplomatic immunity of the British consulate in Ciudad Chihuahua when they arrested Luis Terrazas Jr. seemed to confirm this bandit image. On the other hand, there was the evidence of his great military capacities and of the popularity he enjoyed both among his troops and among the lower classes of society in northern Mexico. There was also the evidence of the discipline he was able to keep among his troops when they occupied Torreón and Chihuahua and of the protection he had granted Americans.

There were two main criteria that Americans and Europeans applied to politicians from Mexico and other countries they called backward: could they keep order, and could they protect foreign interests? Villa seemed to meet these criteria. Wilson had added three additional criteria by which he assessed Mexican politicians. First, would they carry out land reform? Wilson had become convinced that some kind of agrarian reform was necessary to stabilize Mexico, although he would always balk whenever American property was affected by such reforms. Villa's lower-class origins, his confiscations of the properties of Terrazas and Creel, and his pledge that he would divide up those properties once the revolution was triumphant seemed to make him a credible agrarian reformer. The legal justification that Villa gave for his confiscations of hacendado estates, that he was not carrying out expropriations but simply collecting overdue taxes, may have further endeared him to Wilson, in whose eyes respect for private property was a cornerstone of civilization. Wilson's second criterion was that Mexican leaders should be democrats, willing to implement the same kind of democratic system in Mexico as existed in the United States. The credibility of Villa's pledges that he was in favor of civilian administration and genuinely free elections was bolstered by his insistence that he could never be president of Mexico because of his lack of education and ignorance.

When it became more and more apparent that Angeles was one of Villa's preferred candidates for the presidency of Mexico, Wilson's belief in Villa's commitment to democracy was further strengthened. Wilson's representatives in Mexico had repeatedly stressed Angeles's pro-American attitude; his commitment to democracy, as well as to the sanctity of private property; and his restraining influence on Villa.[5]

Wilson may also have been influenced by statements by Villa expressing admiration for the United States. "What I want," Villa told an American newspaperman, "is peace in Mexico. Not the kind of peace we had under Díaz, when a few had all and the many were slaves, but such a peace as you have in the United States where all men are equal before the law and where any man who is willing to work can make such a living for himself and his family as only the very wealthy in Mexico can enjoy."[6]

Wilson's final criterion for judging Mexican politicians was the way in which they responded to his paternalism. Were they willing to listen to his suggestions and to his advice? Carranza had rejected Wilson's suggestion for a joint military campaign in Mexico, but Villa seemed more responsive and friendly whenever U.S. representatives approached him (although it must be said that this was relatively easy for Villa, since Wilson never asked him to accede to the same proposals for joint military operations against Huerta that he had made to Carranza).

In December 1913, when Villa had just begun to administer Chihuahua, Woodrow Wilson was already expressing his high regard for the Mexican revolutionary. "Speaking of Villa," the French military attaché reported, after a conversation with Wilson in December 1913, the U.S. president "expressed his admiration that this highwayman has gradually succeeded in instilling sufficient discipline into his troops to convert them into an army. Perhaps, he added, this man today represents the only instrument of civilization in Mexico. His firm authority allows him to create order and to educate the turbulent mass of peons so prone to pillage."[7]

The image that Wilson and some officials of his administration had of Villa was strongly inspired by traditions of the American frontier. In January 1914 the French ambassador in Washington reported on conversations with a "leading official" (in all probability, Wilson himself or Secretary of State Bryan):

In contrast to what is generally said, my interlocutor told me, Villa is hardly a man of no property. His parents had a ranch and enjoyed a certain affluence. His education was limited to grammar school, but he at least got that far; he is not the illiterate the newspapers describe; his letters are even well formulated.

He is, like Huerta, of Indian origins, an excellent horseman, and a crack shot. Without fear of physical danger or the law, he already led the life of a "rancher" at a very early age. It is the same life many of us led until recently in the distant areas of the west, in areas that lie outside of the power of the authorities, where every man was his own master and sometimes controlled others, sometimes had followers and created his own law. . . .

Villa wins popularity easily and makes sure his popularity lasts. He takes care of his soldiers, he helps them, he sees to their needs and is quite popular among them. The romantic story of the marriage that he supposedly had with a young girl from Chihuahua during the occupation of that city is not true. He is married and is not separated from his wife.

He would be unable to rule but could create order quite nicely if he wanted to. If I were president of Mexico, I would entrust him with this task; I am completely convinced that he would do it masterfully; he would also compel all the rebels to remain peaceful. In Mexico's current situation, I see no one besides him who could successfully manage this task.[8]

Not only Woodrow Wilson but American businessmen as well were impressed by Villa's personality, although their reasons for supporting him were in some respects at odds with those of the U.S. president.

The vast majority of American businessmen neither wanted nor believed in the possibility of a democratic regime in Mexico. Only a dictator in the mold of Porfirio Díaz, they felt, would be able to rule Mexico effectively. When some American companies, particularly oil interests, turned against Porfirio Díaz, it was not because they resented his dictatorial ways but because they felt his policies were too pro-European. But they resented Madero's democratic reforms, which for the first time allowed workers to organize and to strike, and they initially expressed their strong support for Huerta. In a petition sent to Woodrow Wilson shortly after Huerta had assumed power in Mexico, all large American companies doing business in Mexico advocated recognition of the Mexican dictator by the United States.[9]

When it became apparent Wilson would not comply with their request, and when Huerta began flirting with European interests, including British oil companies, many U.S. business interests reversed their position and looked for another strongman capable of ruling Mexico with whom they and Wilson could live. More and more, Villa seemed to fit this mold. He imposed such severe discipline upon his troops and was so relentless in his pursuit of bandits that he provided foreign business with a greater degree of protection than any other leader of the revolutionary forces was able to give them. Until the end of 1914, he imposed no forced loans on Americans, and the taxes he demanded of them were far lower than those Carranza requested in the territories he controlled.[10]

The two revolutionary leaders' policies reflected their social views as well as those of their respective movements. Both men needed large amounts of money to finance the revolution. In the absence of loans, which at this stage no one was willing to grant them, the revenues of the revolutionaries could only come either from wealthy Mexicans or from foreigners. Since Carranza sought to gain the support or at least secure the neutrality of Mexico's upper classes, he tried to shift much of the burden of paying for the revolution onto foreigners. This policy was also in line with his nationalism. By contrast, Villa, who had confiscated all the properties of the Mexican oligarchy, felt he had sufficient means at his disposal, at least until late in 1914, to finance his revolutionary warfare and his domestic projects in Chihuahua without increasing the taxes paid by foreign companies. This policy, he hoped, would gain him sympathy and support in the United States. Since Villa had always been hostile to the Partido Liberal Mexicano (PLM), which had close links to the Industrial Workers of the World (IWW), American businessmen hoped he would not tolerate strikes, or at the very least would not encourage them. It is thus not surprising that representatives of the largest American company doing business in Villista territory, the American Smelting and Refining Company (ASARCO), expressed their enthusiastic support for Villa.[11]

In the eyes of many of the U.S. business interests, Villa's reputation as a bandit was an asset rather than a liability, for they harbored plans that no reputable Mexican politician could acquiesce to. Representatives of U.S. oil and banking interests, including ASARCO's most important director interested in Mexico, John Hays Hammond, openly stated that their aim was to annex the northern part of Mexico to the United States.[12] The financier Otto Kahn was somewhat more modest. All he wanted was for northern Mexico to become an independent nation, as Texas had done less than a century before, and as Panama had separated from Colombia only a few years earlier.[13] Others demanded veto power by the U.S. administration over the appointment of key officials of the Mexican government and the right to station U.S. troops in Mexico. Regardless of their long-range aims, all of these large corporations were snatching the properties of medium-sized American companies and of Mexican land, mine, and oil-field owners up at bargain prices. Many Mexican owners, fearing that the revolutionaries would confiscate their holdings, were willing to sell at any price. For their part, the foreign companies knew that the Mexican revolutionaries, as long as they needed U.S. support, would not touch American-owned properties.

In time they would find out that Villa would acquiesce to none of their long-term plans for dividing Mexico, and his large-scale confiscation of the properties of Mexico's oligarchy would prove a major obstacle to their acquisition by U.S. companies. In the short term, however, Villa's banditlike image and the more than dubious character of some of the intermediaries he used in his dealings with the United States encouraged them in their belief that he was the best choice they had in Mexico.

For a long time, Villa had no trusted advisor or intellectual he could send to the United States and so relied on paid intermediaries who were not part of the revolutionary elite, owed no loyalty to him, and thus tended to be highly corruptible. The only exception to this pattern was his brother Hipólito, who, although inept and corrupt, was genuinely loyal to Villa. Most of his other representatives to the United States would at some point rob him, betray him, and turn against him. This was certainly the case with Lázaro de la Garza, and it was also true of the man many contemporary observers considered Villa's most important intermediary, the U.S. consul in Torreón, George Carothers. Villa trusted him not because he was honest but precisely because he was corrupt.

Relations between Villa and the portly 38-year-old grocer, real estate agent, and part-time U.S. consul became close after Villa occupied Torreón. Carothers, who in 1912 had described Villa as a common bandit, was now full of praise for the order that Villa was keeping in Torreón and for the protection he was giving U.S. citizens. The relationship became so close that Carothers had access to Villa any time he wanted, and Villa assigned him a special carriage in the military trains in which he traveled when on campaign. In view of his close relationship to Villa, Carothers was promoted by the State Department to the post of Wilson's special agent with Villa.[14]

The basis for the close relationship between Carothers and Villa is perhaps best described by a French representative in Mexico who understood both the dynamic between them and the relationship that other special representatives of Wilson had developed with the Mexican leaders to whom they had been assigned:

all of them have only one aim—the victory of the chief to whom they are accredited. They are similar to election managers going from door to door and from location to location to canvas in favor of their candidates.

They have all signed secret pacts with the chieftains to whom they are accredited, which in case of his victory would provide them with substantial profits.

They did not even belong to the second set of the United States political world. . . . Mr. Carothers was an agent for an express company. . . .

Their intellectual capacities did not prepare them for these tasks. They have all the faults of Americans of their class: lack of culture, lack of delicacy, narrowness of views, excessive pretentiousness, and, above all, lack of tact, comprehension for finer feelings, and subtleness, which might be explained by some Germanic origin.

Thus Mr. Wilson's confidential agents might perhaps have been good salesmen for a Chicago canning factory, but they are out of place as diplomats in the great drama taking place in Mexico.[15]

Accusations of corruption followed Carothers throughout his career. In 1913, the State Department was on the verge of dismissing him from his post because of the large gambling debts he had incurred. His effective measures in protecting American properties from depredations during the successive occupations of Torreón and later his close relations with Villa persuaded the State Department to reconsider its earlier decision. Still, charges of corruption, lewd morals, and of being in the pay of Villa continued to dog him. "Since I have been in Mexico," another U.S. diplomat reported to Secretary of State Bryan, "I have heard Carothers described as a crook, blackmailer, gambler and woman-chaser." Americans in Mexico accused him of receiving lucrative business concessions from Villa, and a few months later Carranza's representatives accused him of serving "as a political attaché and advisor of Villa in international matters."[16]

The relationship between Carothers and Villa was by no means unilateral. While Carothers depended on lucrative concessions that the revolutionary leader awarded him, Villa in turn counted on positive reports that Carothers sent to Washington, which he hoped would exercise a favorable influence on Woodrow Wilson.

American business interests were only too happy to use Carothers's leverage with Villa in their favor. A consortium organized by the newspaper owner William Randolph Hearst, who also possessed large haciendas in the state of Chihuahua, was established to acquire Mexican properties in Chihuahua at cut-rate prices, with Carothers serving as intermediary.[17] J. Brittingham, owner of a large soap factory and of several haciendas in the Laguna area, was able not only to protect his properties but to secure very advantageous conditions from Villa by naming Carothers as his manager.[18]

Carothers was not the only channel through which U.S. interests hoped to influence Villa. Some large U.S. interests resorted to what might perhaps most aptly be called the "Hopkins connection." Few better fit the shady and shadowy portrait of the behind-the-scenes operator and manipulator of revolutions than Sherbourne G. Hopkins, although he is all but forgotten in the literature on the Mexican revolution. In December 1910, the leaders of the Madero revolution were looking for lobbyists to represent them in Washington. One of the names that was suggested to them was that of Hopkins, who was a lobbyist for several South and Central American governments. Hopkins's involvement in Latin America had begun in 1891, when he smuggled arms to "Chilean revolutionaries" seeking to overthrow their government on a schooner. In 1898, he had commanded a U.S. warship during the Spanish-American War.[19]

Hopkins's reputation as an effective lobbyist was probably one of the determining factors that led the Maderista revolutionaries and Francisco Madero's brother Gustavo to employ him as representative and lobbyist. It was by no means the only reason they paid him the fabulous sum of $50,000—8 percent of the $700,000 that was the estimated cost of the Madero revolution.[20] Hopkins was also in the employ of one of the major business leaders interested in Mexico, Henry Clay Pierce, the head of the Pierce Oil Corporation. Pierce was strongly interested in Mexican railroads, was affiliated with the Standard Oil Company, and was the greatest rival and competitor of Lord Cowdray's Mexican Eagle Oil Company, which enjoyed the favor and support of the Díaz administration.[21]

It is by no means clear what services Hopkins really performed for the revolutionaries—rumor has it that he persuaded U.S. oil interests to contribute $300,000 to the Madero revolution,[22] although no proof of this has ever been found—but he must have been extremely effective. After the outbreak of Carranza's revolution, Carranza also hired Hopkins, who once more was in the employ of Henry Clay Pierce.

In the first month of the Carranza revolution, Hopkins was the main representative of the Mexican revolutionaries in the U.S., although his shady reputation soon began to alienate more and more revolutionaries. They discovered what was also noted in a confidential memo of the State Department on Hopkins: "There seems to be no doubt that Hopkins has been the advisor and confidential agent of practically any Mexican or Central American revolutionist plotter who had sufficient money to pay for his services. . . . It apparently makes no difference to him for which side he is working and he is believed to be not above selling the secrets of one party to another."[23]

When tensions developed between Villa and Carranza, Hopkins followed Pierce's lead and sided with Carranza. This came out clearly after a mini-Watergate occurred in Washington in 1914. Anonymous burglars broke into Hopkins's office, stole his documents, and revealed them to Washington newspapers. It came out that Hopkins had promised Henry Clay Pierce that he would again become the dominant figure in Mexico's northern railways and that one of the means by which he hoped to achieve this end was to name Alberto Pani, a close confidant of Carranza's, as railway chief for northern Mexico. This measure was strongly opposed by Villa, who wanted to keep his own man, Eusebio Calzado, as superintendent of the northern Mexican railways.[24]

In order to maintain his influence with Villa, Hopkins sent a shadowy character to spy on him. Born in Germany, Felíx Sommerfeld was, as a Justice Department official who interviewed him in 1918 put it, "a soldier of fortune." A dropout from his mining and engineering studies at the University of Berlin, Sommerfeld came to the United States at the end of the nineteenth century, joined the U.S. Army to fight in the Spanish-American War, deserted to return to Germany, after having stolen $250 from a roommate to pay for his passage, and later joined the German expeditionary corps sent to China to fight the Boxer Rebellion. He returned to the United States at the beginning of the twentieth century and soon wandered off to northern Mexico, hoping to make a fortune in mining. (He was unsuccessful.) Among many other occupations, Sommerfeld was a stringer for the Associated Press. From this relatively lowly position, he rose within a few months to become one of Madero's most influential advisors and representatives. This was due in part to an astute knowledge of which direction the political wind was blowing from. At a very early stage during the Maderista revolution, when few intellectuals had joined Madero's forces, Sommerfeld convinced the revolutionary leaders of his profound sympathies for their cause. As the U.S. consul in Chihuahua, Marion Letcher, who knew Sommerfeld well, reported, the sympathy was faked, but Sommerfeld's demagogic capacity for expressing it was very real. He could talk "with eloquence and earnestness about democracy in Mexico. Deep in his heart, however, as confidential discussions with him indicate, he is a convinced monarchist and absolutist, who firmly believes that monarchs and absolutist governments are the only ones which make any sense." Sommerfeld's eloquence served him well. "He relied on Madero's gullibility, inexperience and pliability and quickly exercised a decisive influence on Madero which continued until the latter's murder."[25] Sommerfeld soon became head of Madero's secret service along the borders of the United States and, unknown to Madero, was also a confidential advisor to the German minister to Mexico, Paul von Hintze, who arranged for his departure from the country after Huerta's coup.[26]

The high office Sommerfeld had held under Madero and his connection with Hopkins soon paid dividends. On Hopkins's instructions, he rejoined Carranza and soon arranged negotiations between Carranza and Wilson's special representative William Bayard Hale. Carranza had so much confidence in Sommerfeld that he sent him to Chihuahua to work with Villa and spy on his activities. Sommerfeld's eloquence and position in the Madero administration served him equally well with Villa, and he soon became one of Villa's main representatives, as well as buyer of arms and ammunitions in the United States. The connection to the Mexican revolutionaries proved lucrative for Sommerfeld. He had an exclusive concession for importing dynamite into the country, which brought him a profit of $5,000 a month.[27] This did not prevent him from spying on Villa, but rather than passing information to Carranza, he provided it to the German secret service, with which he soon established contacts through the German naval attaché, Karl Boy-Edd.[28]

Carothers, Sommerfeld, and, through the latter, Hopkins (although Villa does not seem to have known this) became Villa's main intermediaries for dealing with both the U.S. government and U.S. businessmen. In the long run, these men would prove harmful to Villa. Their loyalty was to their pocketbooks rather than to Villa, to the revolution, or to Mexico. Unlike Carranza, who sent prominent intellectuals to represent him in the United States and thus could counterbalance whatever information his U.S. intermediaries provided him with or gave Americans about him, Villa sent no reliable representatives of the same caliber north of the border in 1913 and 1914. Villa's two main Mexican representatives to the United States, the corrupt businessman Lázaro de la Garza and Consul Enrique Llorente never proved a counterweight to Sommerfeld, Hopkins, and Carothers. In their reports to U.S. politicians and businessmen, they undoubtedly attempted to portray Villa in a favorable light up to the end of 1914, but their reports to Villa on U.S. policy have unfortunately not been preserved. In view of their conservative ideology and their continuing links with parts of the oligarchy, it is likely that they attempted to convince Villa that the only way to win U.S. support was to adopt a policy more conservative than that of Wilson and Bryan. The conservatism of these men was reinforced by the conservatism of the one U.S. politician with whom Villa maintained close relations, who had sincere admiration for the Mexican revolutionary, and for whom Villa in turn professed feelings of sympathy and respect. This was the commander of the U.S. forces along the southern border with Mexico, who was later to become chief of staff of the U.S. Army, General Hugh C. Scott.

The first meeting of the two men took place on the international bridge between Ciudad Juárez and El Paso. Scott told Villa in no uncertain terms that his shooting of prisoners would alienate public sympathy for his cause in the United States and the world. On that occasion, Scott gave him a pamphlet detailing the rules of war and the agreements of the Geneva convention on treatment of prisoners.[29] After this meeting, Scott developed strong feelings of sympathy and admiration for Villa, which never wavered, even after Villa attacked Columbus, New Mexico. Scott described Villa in glowing terms. His admiration for the Mexican revolutionary chieftain is perhaps best expressed in a private letter he wrote his wife:

I have been struggling for fame ever since coming into the service nearly forty years ago and have at last arrived at the result that my title to consideration in Washington is that I am seen as a friend of Villa's—that is my distinction—they all thought me crazy when I came up from the border a Villista last April but the Spanish and English ambassadors have both told me that they have come around to my view and have so informed their governments. Villa himself seems to have taken a romantic regard for me and I have sent him word once in a while to keep him staunchly on his course. The last time I sent word that if he continues on his course in insisting on constitutional government and putting his personal ambitions aside he will be considered as the "Washington" of Mexico and so he will without any doubt.[30]

Scott's regard for Villa seems surprising at first, since the general was anything but a radical. On the contrary, he was a staunch conservative and had greatly admired Porfirio Díaz. He shared the idea of many American politicians that only a strongman could put Mexico in order, however, and the only real strongman in sight was Pancho Villa.

Scott's regard for Villa was also based on his own personal and military experiences. Few U.S. officers had as much experience in dealing with the groups commonly referred to as "natives" by contemporary Americans. For many years, Scott had fought on the Indian frontier of the United States, and he had subsequently participated in the Spanish-American War and been an administrator of the U.S. military government in Cuba for a time. He had then gone on to the Philippines, where he had fought against the Moro insurgents, who refused to accept American domination. These 40 years of fighting Indians, Cubans, and Filipinos, and at the same time aligning himself with some of them and making deals with others, had influenced his attitude toward what might be called third-world countries. On one hand, he firmly believed in the current ideology of "the white man's burden." Only enlightened Westerners could guide these people toward modernization and civilization, and he had little respect for intellectuals from these subject peoples. On the other hand, he never became converted to the kind of racism that was so prevalent along the American frontier and that so strongly influenced American attitudes toward nonwhite peoples. He never believed the maxim that "the only good Indian is a dead Indian"; on the contrary, he repeatedly protected Indian tribes from pillage and depredations by corrupt Indian agents. In line with this contradictory ideology, Scott had little respect for Cuban intellectuals and sharply censored Cuban editors who attempted to print articles critical of the U.S. military government, but evinced profound respect for the Moro Sultan Hassan, with whom he had made an alliance.[31]

Pancho Villa fitted the profile of the nonintellectual kind of native chief Scott respected. In addition, as a cavalryman, Scott admired Villa's military tactics and his use of cavalry charges as the backbone of his strategy. His support of Villa was not completely disinterested. Unlike Carothers, Scott did not seek financial reward (although his influence with Villa helped to protect an American mining company in which his son was employed as a mining engineer), but, as his letter to his wife indicates, he did hope to gain political leverage from his influence on Villa.

It is by no means clear how great Scott's influence on Villa really was and to what degree the Mexican revolutionary reciprocated the American general's feelings. There is no reason to doubt that Villa felt some sympathy with and admiration for Scott. Villa always respected professional military men, especially when they did not look down on him, as most of Huerta's officers had done during the 1912 Chihuahuan campaign. Because of Scott's long experience on the American frontier, the two men may have shared a similar code of honor, regard for mutual obligations, and deep respect for promises once given.

Nevertheless, there is no evidence that in the frequent negotiations that Scott had with Villa, the American general secured any concessions from the Mexican revolutionary beyond those that Villa would have been forced to grant him anyway by virtue of his dependence on American arms and because of the strength of the United States.

Like many other Mexican and American political figures who came into contact with Villa, Scott may have been led to overestimate his influence on the Mexican revolutionary chieftain by Villa's outward humility, his constant assertion that he was only an ignorant farmer who needed the guidance of men with more education than he. While Villa did allow himself to be influenced at times, these statements were more of a theatrical performance than a real sign of humility.

These intermediaries between Villa and the U.S. administration played a major role in determining how Villa reacted to U.S. policy. They played a smaller role in the way the United States viewed Villa. It was not so much these intermediaries but the American media that determined how American public opinion and even the U.S. administration viewed Pancho Villa.

Villa and the American Left

One of Villa's most remarkable achievements was that he won not only the support of conservative businessmen, generals, and the Wilson administration but also the admiration, for a time, of substantial segments of the American left, which opposed the businessmen who regarded Villa so highly. It was an admiration based on Villa's popular origins, the popular character of his army, his confiscations of the properties of the oligarchy, and his redistribution of goods, as well as the erroneous notion that he had already redistributed land from the state's haciendas to the peasantry of Chihuahua.

The man who most decisively contributed to Villa's standing among substantial parts of the American left was one of the country's most influential, most talented radical journalists and intellectuals, John Reed.[32] Although he was only 26 in 1913, many considered Reed already part of America's intellectual elite. At Harvard, where he had studied, he had become editor in chief of the *Lampoon*, and after graduating, he wrote a series of short stories that had widespread appeal. He was perhaps best known for his reports on a strike that thousands of textile workers had staged in Patterson, New Jersey. His descriptions of police brutality against the strikers and against himself—he was beaten up and imprisoned for four days—aroused nationwide attention.

Reed's intellectual capacities and political opinions strongly differentiated him from practically all other correspondents in Mexico. He was a socialist, originally strongly influenced by the radical milieu of Greenwich Village and later by his personal experiences and the many people he met in Patterson. Moreover, he combined these intellectual and political traits with physical courage.

These characteristics led Reed to do things in Mexico that no other correspondent did. Like his colleagues, he was interested in Villa as a leader and as a man, but in contrast to most of them, he was also interested in his followers. He refused to see the revolutionaries the way most correspondents did, as a gray, undifferentiated mass of ignorant peons to be manipulated by their leaders. He was not the only American correspondent who ventured deep into Mexico, although those who did were a minority in comparison to those who preferred the safety of the hotels of El Paso to the dangers of Mexico. Unlike his colleagues who did cross the border and join Villa's campaign, however, Reed mostly traveled alone, outside the protection that Villa's staff and Villa personally afforded.

No one has better described Reed's approach than a contemporary observer whose ideas generally tended to be diametrically opposed to Reed's, Patrick O'Hea. A former Cambridge student who had migrated to Mexico and become a hacienda administrator, O'Hea had a profound contempt for most foreign correspondents in Mexico. "However," he wrote, "I have to recall, with grudging admiration, at least one exception in the person of John Reed, a special correspondent, I think, of the *New York American* who personally achieved a position of mutual respect with Villa such as I found remarkable, as also the manner in which he lived the hard life of the fighting men, yet always within a frame of sobriety and restraint."[33]

Reed felt that in Chihuahua the foundations of a socialist society as he envisioned it were being laid. The oligarchy had been expelled from the state, every inhabitant who wanted it had the right to a piece of land, and the state assumed responsibility for the welfare of the poor and the unemployed. Reed saw Villa as a man with a vision who wanted to transform and reform Mexico through division of the lands of the rich and through education. He downplayed the ferocious side of Villa's personality, although he did show that Fierro was a killer and that Villa let him do whatever he wanted.

Reed's reports found an overwhelming response in the United States, ranging all the way from literary critics to President Woodrow Wilson. The *Metropolitan* newspaper, in which Reed's articles appeared, heralded them with large advertisements in other newspapers, which were suggestively headed: "John Reed in Mexico. Word pictures of war by an American Kipling."[34] Walter Lippmann wrote him:

Your . . . articles are undoubtedly the finest reporting that's ever been done. It's kind of embarrassing to tell a fellow you know that he's a genius. . . . you have perfect eyes and your power of telling leaves nothing to be desired. I want to hug you, Jack. If all history had been reported as you are doing this, Lord—I'd say that with Jack Reed reporting begins. Incidentally . . . the stories are literature.[35]

Woodrow Wilson seems to have read Reed's articles with great interest and as a result invited him to the White House for a long conversation, in which he gave Reed to understand that he would in fact have no objection if Villa were elected president of Mexico and tried to implement a major agrarian reform.[36] Reed's reports not only endeared Villa to Wilson and to American liberals but also gave the revolutionary a legitimacy he had not possessed before, and would soon lose, in the eyes of the American left.

John Reed's favorable view of Villa was not shared by all the leading figures of the American left. Lincoln Steffens had reservations about Villa, which would later turn into outright hostility. The basis for Steffens's contempt was precisely the admiration for Villa that some American businessmen were expressing. Steffens came to see Villa as an instrument of Wall Street; to him Carranza was the real nationalist and revolutionary.[37]

The hostility to Villa of another prominent figure of the American left, John Kenneth Turner, whose book *Barbarous Mexico*, written and published during the Díaz period, had for the first time revealed to a large public the terrible conditions under which many hacienda workers lived, was based on different considerations.[38] Turner had always maintained close relations with the PLM, whose leaders, especially Ricardo Flores Magón, were strongly opposed to Villa. Their opposition was based on Villa's hostility to the members of the PLM in Chihuahua. When Madero had called on Villa to disarm the rebellious members of the armed contingent of the PLM in 1911, he had immediately responded. In 1912, Villa had again fought against members of the PLM who had joined forces with Orozco. Turner's hostility to Villa was for similar reasons shared by many leaders and members of the IWW.

John Reed was nevertheless not entirely alone among American radicals in his favorable assessment of Villa. Mary (Mother) Jones, a prominent and legendary figure of the American left, was also a fervent admirer. Jones had worked for many years as an organizer for the United Mine Workers of America. She had first been active in the Appalachian coalfields and later went west and helped to organize the Western Federation of Miners. She was more than an organizer. She was a first-rate speaker, and during strikes and periods of conflict, her fiery oratory helped to rally the miners. Although she was repeatedly jailed, she continued her militancy into her eighties and even nineties. While working with miners in the southwestern United States, she became strongly interested in Mexico and in the fate of Mexican miners. She protested the poverty and the atrocious conditions under which Mexican miners lived in the Díaz era, in part because these conditions made it possible for American mine owners to recruit strikebreakers from Mexico. Mother Jones collected large sums of money to help the leaders of the PLM after their arrest in 1909, and in 1911 she went to Mexico and obtained Francisco Madero's approval of her endeavors to speak to Mexican miners and prevent them from acting as strikebreakers in the United States. In 1913–14, she crossed the border once again and went to see Pancho Villa, who gave her an interpreter and allowed her to address Mexican miners in Chihuahua with the same message.[39]

In 1914, Mother Jones was imprisoned once again in the United States. The socialist newspaper *Appeal to Reason* published a letter from Villa to Woodrow Wilson proposing to exchange Mother Jones for one of his own prisoners, Luis Terrazas Jr. When Wilson had asked for the latter's release, according to the *Appeal to Reason*, Villa wrote Wilson that he would free Terrazas if Wilson

would show the same regard for humanity toward one of your own citizens, a woman past eighty years who is being illegally deprived of her liberty by General Chase, Commander-in-Chief of the Colorado division of the Rockefeller forces. I refer to Mother Jones. . . . I may take the liberty to remind you that about two years ago Mother Jones made an organizing trip for the Western Federation of Miners through Mexico under the full protection of President Madero. . . . Will you do as much for Mother Jones?[40]

Villa's offer may have come as a response to an appeal that Mother Jones had addressed to him from jail:

Let the nations know, and especially let my friend General Francisco Villa know, that the great United States of America, which is demanding of him that he release the traitors that he has placed in custody, is now holding Mother Jones incommunicado in an underground cell surrounded with sewer rats, tin soldiers and other vermin.[41]

For a time both John Reed's views and those of Mother Jones reflected and influenced the opinions of some sectors of the American left about Villa. But this positive attitude would not last very long, and by 1915 and 1916, U.S. leftists had turned to Carranza and became more and more opposed to Villa.

Villa and the American Media

It is remarkable how profoundly a semiliterate man like Villa understood the importance of public relations and of influencing the media on behalf of his movement. Not only did he frequently grant interviews to Reed and other newspaper correspondents, he also had a special car full of newspaper correspondents attached to his military train. Villista agents seem to have surreptitiously paid a border newspaper, the *El Paso Herald*, to give favorable coverage to Villa's movement.[42] In addition, Villa signed a film contract with a leading Hollywood producer.

On the whole, Villa's public relations efforts paid off. John Reed's articles had a tremendous impact on U.S. public opinion. Reed's opinions were reflected in a number of American newspapers. The *Charleston News and Courier* saw Villa as a necessary instrument of reform. "The Mexican people need a leader," the paper remarked, "and what is required of that leader is not so much that he shall have clean hands as [that] he shall sympathize with necessary reforms calculated to secure the emancipation of the common people and that he shall have the brains and the strength to carry out these reforms. . . . Who can say that Villa is not such a man? There have been cut-throat emancipators in history; there have been ruffian liberators; there have been ruthlessly cruel benefactors of the downtrodden serfs."[43]

By no means all of the American press was favorable to Villa or the Mexican revolutionaries. The Hearst papers, which advocated U.S. intervention in Mexico, tended to describe all Mexican revolutionaries as bandits (although for a brief period of time they expressed support for Villa). A number of American newspapers adhered to traditional preconceptions and clichés about Mexico. In their eyes, Mexican revolutionaries were comic-opera bandits, ruthless, uncouth, and uncivilized. For *Sunset*, a magazine then published by the Southern Pacific Company, for example, the Mexican revolution was nothing but a comic-opera revolution and Villa a comic-opera general:

The war in Mexico has lasted more than three years; "battles" innumerable have been fought, scores of "armies" have been annihilated, wiped out, blown up, massacred and wholly destroyed according to the glowing reports of the commanders on either side, but the supply of cannon fodder does not appear to have diminished appreciably. Its quantity seems to depend largely upon the regularity of the ghosts' monthly promenade. . . . Never was there war of equal duration in which more gunpowder went off with less harm to the opposing forces.

This from a purely humanitarian standpoint very happy result is due to the Mexican private's sensitive shoulder. He hates to have his anatomy hurt by the recoil of the rifle. Therefore when he goes into action, he rests the butt of the gun on the ground, inclines the muzzle at an angle of forty-five degrees, firmly seizes the barrel with the left hand and with the right works trigger and ejector until the magazine is exhausted. This method of firing saves both his eyesight, his shoulder and the enemy's skin. Sometimes he varies the proceedings by lying flat on his back behind the earthworks, firing over them in the general direction of the adversary without exposing an inch of his precious cranium. . . . After Villa's great victory below Juárez more graves were found on the city's execution ground than on the twenty-mile battlefield.[44]

Other newspapers saw Villa as a bloodthirsty bandit: "Everything that has been told of Villa," the *World Herald* wrote, "shows him as a monster of brutality and cruelty. His entire history is that of a robber and assassin, lifted now, by the fortunes of war, into a conspicuous position which he has filled with such signal military ability as to give him a coating of semi-respectability."[45] Such attacks on Villa were frequently part of attacks by Republican-oriented newspapers on Woodrow Wilson's policy of opposition to the Huerta regime.

Others felt that Mexico was not civilized enough to be ruled by anyone but a dictator, and that Villa was in fact a second Porfirio Díaz. In the *Pittsburgh Dispatch*, Alexander Powell wrote:

Whether this former outlaw who, less than a year ago slipped out of El Paso with a revolver in his belt and seven dollars in his pocket and who is now at the head of twenty thousand victory-elated men, will ever sit in the presidential chair, only time can tell. Far stranger things have happened below the Rio Grande as those who are familiar with the history of Porfirio Díaz know. And Villa is but following the path that Díaz trod.[46]

Whether American journalists admired or opposed Villa, one tendency common to most of them was a patronizing note when they dealt with the revolutionary chieftain. When an American newspaper published a report that Villa had ordered a bathtub costing $1,000, the press pounced on this news to make fun of Villa. "No more convincing proof of the Americanization of Mexico could be given," the *Birmingham Herald* jeered,

> than this act by the rebel leader who aspires to take his morning "bawth" in a receptacle that is rivaled by the tubs of a few millionaires. It is reported that when Villa reaches Mexico City he will cast General Huerta's bathtub on the junk pile and install his new tub in the Mexican palace.
> Time was and not long since when the redoubtable Villa reeked not of such luxuries as ornate porcelain bathtubs. There are very good reasons to believe that he did not indulge in the matutinal dip any more than he did in the evening shower. A wild, rough life was led by Pancho. He had little time to take a bath, even had he been so disposed, and practically no facilities.[47]

This patronizing attitude was also reflected in the way many American newspapermen gathered information for their reports. Some who were stationed in El Paso did not even bother to cross the border into Mexico but wrote their reports based on fantasy and rumors that were crossing the borders.

Villa and Hollywood

Villa understood not only the importance of favorable coverage by newspapers for his movement but also the impact that an entirely new medium, the movies, was beginning to have on U.S. public opinion. Not only did he allow film correspondents to accompany him on his campaigns but he also signed a unique kind of contract with a Hollywood producer.

Villa's deals with Hollywood proved to be highly profitable enterprises in every sense of the word. They burnished his image and increased his popularity in the United States. They also produced urgently needed dollars, which Villa used to arm and supply his troops. On January 5, 1914, only a few days after his troops had occupied Ciudad Chihuahua, and even before they were in full control of the state, Villa signed a contract with Harry E. Aitken of the Mutual Film Company. On January 7, the *New York Times* reported:

> The business of General Villa will be to provide moving picture thrillers in any way that is consistent with his plans to depose and drive Huerta out of Mexico and the business of Mr. Aitken, the other partner, will be to distribute the resulting films throughout the peaceable sections of Mexico and the United States and Canada.
> To make sure that the business venture will be a success, Mr. Aitken dispatched to General Villa's camp last Saturday a squad of four moving picture men with apparatus designed especially to take pictures on battlefields.

For the film industry, this contract was very important. Newsreels were a relatively new genre, and the film industry was greatly interested in their development. For the first time, people who had never been involved in a war could actually see what war was like. Coverage of the Balkan War in 1912 and 1913 had enormously increased the popularity and appeal of newsreels. Now a war was taking place much closer to home, in a region adjoining the United States south of the border, and films on the war in Mexico promised to attract a great deal of attention.[48]

Like everything else related to Villa, the story of his relations with the film industry became an inextricable mix of myth and reality. Stories soon began to circulate in the press that the contract contained some very peculiar clauses: "If the camera man did not film good battle scenes, then Villa would reenact them. . . . [Villa] agreed to carry out his attacks during the daylight hours."[49]

Such tales, which attracted worldwide attention, reinforced the negative image that many in the United States had of both Villa and Mexico. It was the image of a barbarian leader unscrupulously ready to sacrifice the lives of his men in order to gain publicity. The actual contract in fact contained no such clauses. There was absolutely no mention of reenactment of battle scenes or of Villa providing good lighting. What the contract did specify was that the Mutual Film Company was granted exclusive rights to film Villa's troops in battle, and that Villa would receive 20 percent of all revenues that the films produced.[50]

The directors of Mutual felt that Villa offered such good copy that they decided to combine their newsreels with a fictional film, *The Life of General Villa*. The plot was a typical Hollywood concoction. Reality was sacrificed to what the producer assumed were the tastes of American film viewers. The scriptwriters obviously felt that poor people do not make good heroes. So instead of being sharecroppers working on a hacienda, Villa's family are transformed into relatively well-to-do independent ranchers with land of their own. Two federal officers are the villains rather than a hacendado. They pursue two of Villa's sisters while he is away, and one of them kidnaps the younger, rapes her, and leaves her to die. When Villa returns and learns what has happened, he seeks revenge. After fierce pursuit, he kills the culprit, but is unable to do the same to his companion, who escapes. Pursued by federal troops, Villa flees into the mountains swearing to kill the second officer involved in the rape of his sister. It is in the battle of Torreón that he finally encounters and shoots him—the climax of the film. Raoul Walsh, a well-known actor, who later became one of Hollywood's most famous producers, was brought to Mexico to play the young Villa in the first part of the film. In its later parts, Villa played himself, and actual newsreels of the battles of his army were included in the fictional film.[51]

Villa had no objection to this embellishment and "gentrification" of his early career. He was willing to accommodate Mutual Films in other ways as well. When the producers felt that his regular dress, a slouch hat and a sweater, detracted from his prestige as a military man, he was ready to wear a uniform provided by Mutual Film Company, which continued to be the property of the film makers.[52]

The film was shown in several U.S. cities and seems to have been a great success, partly because it was shown at a time when Villa had reached the apex of his popularity in the United States. It came out after U.S. troops had occupied Veracruz and a war between the United States and Mexico appeared a very real possibility. Villa was the only major Mexican leader who declared that he did not resent this occupation and would not fight the Americans.

Villa broke with the United States only a short time after this film was produced, and Hollywood would drastically alter its image of the Mexican revolutionary. In April 1916, after Villa had attacked the town of Columbus, New Mexico, a film titled *Villa Dead or Alive* was released by the Eagle Films Manufacturing and Producing Company, which proclaimed in its advertising:

> That's what President Wilson said, and that's what we are going to do.
> Is the United States prepared?
> Go and see Uncle Sam's troops in action.
> See your flag cross the border to punish those who have insulted it.

Advertising for another film, *Following the Flag in Mexico*, produced by the Feinberg Amusement Corporation, announced: "Villa at any cost. $20,000 reward, dead or alive. Mexican bandit bands in action."[53]

The favorable treatment that Villa received in films and other media in 1914 was of great importance to his standing both in Mexico and in the United States. By treating him as a national leader long before there was a basis for this, the media facilitated his rise to national and international prominence. The widespread approval of his movement that Villa had achieved by early 1914 in the United States was threatened, however, by what has come to be known as the Benton affair.

The Benton Affair

On February 17th, 1914, William S. Benton, a British citizen and the owner of the Los Remedios hacienda in Chihuahua, entered Villa's house in Ciudad Juárez. A British soldier of fortune, Frances Michael Tone, who had lent his services to the División del Norte and was taking an inventory of arms in a room in Villa's house adjoining the one where Villa and Benton were talking, overheard them shouting at each other:

> Mr. Benton: Give me money for my cattle, sir.
> Villa: Mañana, hombre.
> Benton (in English): I am a damned sight better man than you, any way you'd like to take it.
> Villa: No, muchacho.
> A second or two later a shot was fired and . . . Mr. McDonald and I rushed through the folding doors which were ajar, into Villa's office with our revolvers drawn. Villa was standing behind his roll-top desk which was placed at an angle in the corner of the room formed by the partition and the outer wall of the house. Mr. Benton was lying in front of the desk with his feet toward it and his head towards a bench in the corner opposite the desk. Blood was coming from a wound in his right breast, he appeared to be dead and his eyes were glazed. There was blood on the carpet and a hole in the back of the desk through which the bullet had evidently passed,

showing that Villa must have been sitting at his desk when he fired. Mr. Benton's handkerchief was partly out of his right hip pocket.[54]

The controversy between Villa and Benton that led to this bloody denouement was the result of a conflict between Benton and the inhabitants of the village of Santa María de Cuevas, which adjoined his hacienda, as well as of a preceding altercation with Villa in 1912.

In June 1910, some months before the Mexican revolution broke out, Chihuahua's opposition newspaper, *El Correo de Chihuahua*, published a report in which the inhabitants of Santa María de Cuevas bitterly complained that Benton had appropriated for himself, with the help of the authorities, a piece of land that the inhabitants claimed had always belonged to them. Benton had fenced off this pastureland, on which the villagers had formerly grazed their cattle, and if any animals belonging to the inhabitants of Santa María de Cuevas strayed in any way onto this land, Benton, together with the mayor of the village appointed by the government, charged them exorbitant fees. When a village spokesman protested, Benton attempted to slap him in the face. He then somehow got the state government to send 65 armed men to protect his property.[55]

The ease with which Benton obtained help from the state government reflected his close links to Terrazas and Creel. Perhaps the best reflection of this relationship was the experience of a geologist and mining engineer, Luis Hernández, who had been commissioned by a mining company to investigate a site in the Sierra Madre. When Hernández reached the village of San Rojas, where he planned to begin, he was met by Benton, who told him that Creel and Terrazas had instructed him to allow no one to do any research or prospecting. When Hernández showed Benton that he had an official permit to do the kind of work he wanted to carry out, Benton told him that he would have to desist, because "God ruled in heaven and Terrazas and Creel ruled Chihuahua."[56]

Benton's close connection to Terrazas and Creel, as well as the hatred he had aroused among the peasants of Santa María de Cuevas, may have convinced Villa in 1912 to except Benton from a rule he otherwise scrupulously observed: not to impose any forced loans on foreigners. Seeking money and resources to fight the Orozquistas,

Villa came to Benton's ranch near Santa Isabel on the twentieth and demanded money. Benton said he had no money for him. Villa insisted, and Benton said he would not give him a cent. They took him a short distance from his house, and again demanded money, to which Benton replied that they could kill him if they pleased but that he would not give them a cent. Villa said he wanted the money for the government and Benton told him the government did not get money that way. They then searched his house and took all his arms and ammunition, eight horses and saddles, and left. . . . Benton says he is going to place the matter before the governor tomorrow and demand a guard, as he was always given protection by the government. He says that if he is refused protection, he is going to tell the governor that he is going to get it from another government.[57]

After Huerta's coup, Benton repeatedly and publicly voiced his support for the military dictator, his contempt for the revolutionaries, and his admiration for Porfirio Díaz.

When Villa finally assumed control of Chihuahua, he told Benton that he could not assure his safety if he remained in Mexico and requested that he go to the United States. Villa promised that he would not expropriate Benton's land and would safeguard his property. Villa had been very careful not to confiscate properties belonging to foreigners other than Spaniards and Chinese. He refused, however, to prevent the inhabitants of Santa María de Cuevas from reassuming control of the pastureland they considered their own and from grazing their cattle there. In the process, some of Benton's cattle seem to have strayed from his property or to have been appropriated by the villagers, and perhaps even by Villa's men.[58] Arrogant and stubborn, but also courageous, Benton decided to confront Villa, to demand payment for his lost cattle, and to request the expulsion of the villagers' cattle from the land he claimed as his own. In deciding to confront Villa in his own home, Benton may have been encouraged by the fact that he had done so in 1912 and Villa had backed down. This time the confrontation with Villa cost him his life, although the manner in which Benton died is still a matter of controversy.

Adrián Aguirre Benavides, who had been Villa's defense lawyer in 1912 and was close to him, told Carranza that in the heated discussion with Benton, Villa had offered to buy Benton's ranch on condition that he stayed in the United States. Benton had refused, raised his voice, called Villa a bandit, and attempted to draw his gun, at which point Villa hit him on the head. When Fierro came in a few moments later, Villa told him to execute Benton. Fierro took him to the railway station of Salamayuca, where he shot and buried him.[59]

Many months later, in a conversation with the British vice-consul in Torreón, Cunard Cummins, Villa gave a different version of what had happened. "He was, with difficulty," he told Cummins,

dominating a large force of armed men, composed of criminals and desperadoes, men from whom he could not permit a disrespectful word and hold his position as commander. A foreigner entered his headquarters and in loud, unmeasured terms upbraided and defied him. Suddenly the foreigner, on whose head the perspiration was visible, passed rapidly his hand to his hip pocket, and Fierro, the man who acted as Villa's bodyguard, believing Benton was about to draw a pistol, immediately shot him. It then appeared that the victim had reached for his handkerchief. Villa admits anger had arisen and high words were being exchanged.[60]

Cummins later told the Foreign Office that he was convinced that this explanation was true. It does conform to Tone's account, with the significant exception that Tone had it that Fierro was not even present in the room, and that it was Villa who had shot Benton.[61] Tone was probably correct, and for obvious reasons Villa was not ready to confess to the British that it was he himself who had done the killing.

Villa probably never anticipated the storm of controversy that Benton's killing would arouse. Only a few months before, the Wilson administration had forced the British, against their will, to withdraw their support for Huerta. On February 1, Wilson had taken a major step in favor of the revolutionaries by lifting the arms embargo against Mexico. One of the justifications he gave for his actions was that the constitutionalists had agreed to guarantee the rights and properties of all foreigners there. Both British and American opponents of Wilson's policies saw the Benton killing as a welcome opportunity to show that the constitutionalists were nothing but bandits and could not be relied upon to respect the lives and properties of foreigners. The British press and members of the British Parliament vehemently protested against Wilson's policy. So did a number of newspapers and politicians in the United States. While the British hoped that Benton's killing might force Wilson to reimpose an arms embargo on Mexico, some American opponents of his policies went a step further and argued that the only way to guarantee the safety of foreigners in Mexico was an armed intervention by the United States. Villa was disconcerted by the storm he had aroused, and his reaction was clumsy at first. Talking to George Carothers, the U.S. special representative, he first denied any knowledge of Benton's whereabouts, but two days later, he reversed himself, saying that Benton had pulled a gun on him, that a court-martial had taken place, and that Benton had been sentenced to death and executed. The brief proceedings of this court-martial were also made public. They were, in fact, faked, although Villa's detractors had no way of proving this.[62]

Taking this tack was an intelligent move on Villa's part, since courts-martial are generally not public affairs. In order to convince the enemies of Wilson's policies toward Mexico that Villa was telling the truth, however, Wilson's representative asked him to ship Benton's body to the United States, where an autopsy could be done to determine whether he really had been executed by a firing squad. It seems that Villa seriously contemplated doing so for a time and ordered Fierro and his henchmen to pump the body full of holes to simulate an execution. Being ignorant of forensic science, he could not know that this was useless.

Villa was so disconcerted by the repercussions of the Benton affair and the constant interventions by U.S. diplomats that resulted from it that he was more than happy when Carranza told him that he was assuming full responsibility in this matter and instructed him not to speak to foreign representatives about the Benton affair anymore, but to refer them to the First Chief.

For Carranza, the Benton killing represented both a boon and a risk. It was a boon because for the first time he was able to demonstrate both to Mexico and to the world at large that it was not Villa but he who was the supreme commander of the revolution, and that Villa had clearly recognized him as such. He also realized, though, that the risks he was incurring by placing himself at the center of the affair were very great. Part of the international resentment that hitherto had been directed at Villa would now be deflected to him. In addition, he knew that the proceedings of the court-martial on which Villa's justification rested were a fake, and that if this came out, he had no means and no power to discipline Villa, which would expose the weakness of his position. In addition, he had no wish at this point to break with Villa, whose forces he desperately needed in order to defeat Huerta.

On the whole, Carranza handled this complex affair adroitly. For weeks, he refrained from taking any action, claiming bureaucratic delay, in the hope that public interest in the matter would abate. When he was finally forced to do something, he appointed a Mexican commission of inquiry to examine the whole affair but refused to heed the advice of his representative in the United States to name an international commission of inquiry. He also rejected the advice of some of the members of his commission to hire an American forensic specialist to examine Benton's body.

The commission Carranza had appointed soon found out that the purported trial of Benton had been a fake, but it did not publicly announce this. Instead, it sought unsuccessfully to prove that Benton, who had lived in Mexico for 30 years, had in fact become a naturalized Mexican, and thus did not rate foreign diplomatic protection. This could never be established. The commission succeeded better in uncovering Benton's record as an extremely brutal hacendado: it revealed such facts as the whipping by Benton's men of two Tarahumara Indians who had strayed onto his land, his closing of a public road, and his threat to shoot muleteers who attempted to use it.[63] It is not clear, though, to what degree these facts were ever made public.

The most important thing Carranza did was to challenge the U.S. interpretation of the Monroe Doctrine, which was risky but proved rewarding. In all their complaints about the Benton affair, the British had refused to deal directly with the revolutionaries and had addressed their demands to the U.S. State Department, which in turn referred them to Villa or Carranza. This conformed with what has generally been called the Roosevelt Corollary to the Monroe Doctrine. In 1905, President Theodore Roosevelt had announced that in all conflicts between European powers and Latin American countries, it was not up to the Europeans but to the United States to enforce the Latin Americans' compliance with international law. This doctrine was naturally opposed by most Latin American countries, and when U.S. officials complained to Carranza about the Benton affair, he finally told them that he would not deal with them, but only with the British.

On the one hand, by doing so, Carranza risked alienating the Wilson administration, which could have reestablished the arms embargo against his forces. On the other hand, he created a situation in which the British would either be forced to extend de facto recognition to him or to bear the onus for not clearing up the Benton killing. His gamble paid off. The Benton affair did not lead the Americans to reimpose the arms embargo on Mexico. The investigation into the background of the killing was never pursued, since the British refused to negotiate with the revolutionaries. Carranza's supremacy within the revolutionary movement was clearly established, and he had demonstrated independence from the United States. Conversely, Villa, who would become his main competitor, emerged from the Benton affair with damaged prestige. That damage, however, was far from permanent. Only two months later, when U.S. forces occupied Veracruz, and Villa, unlike Carranza, refused to condemn the attack, his prestige with the Wilson administration rose once more.[64]

Villa and Carranza: From "Honeymoon" to Conflict

"I am organizing my army for the march southward, but in order for this march to take place, your presence in this state is indispensable, so that I can leave without any worries," Villa wired Carranza.

"And now all I want to do is ask you . . . that you tell us something about your health so that we can be reassured, since I do not know what we would do without you." Carranza replied, "I hope that the roar of your cannon will be heard in the capital of the republic so that the great work that we have undertaken can be completed, a work of which you are one of the main architects."[65]

This cordial exchange of telegrams gives the impression that the relationship between Villa and Carranza was a replica of the relationship between Villa and Madero: Villa loyal and full of affection; Carranza friendly, while making it clear that he was in charge. The reality was more complex. Long before the two men met, conflict had already simmered between them, and the cordiality of their initial exchanges of telegrams did not reflect the true state of their relations. Legend has it that the relationship only soured when they finally met, and Villa found that unlike Madero, who had been friendly, hearty, and open-minded, Carranza was cold, aloof, and duplicitous.

There is little doubt that Carranza was a colder personality than Madero. There was also a generational gap between Villa and Carranza. The Mexican revolution was a young man's war, with many generals only in their twenties. A man in his thirties, like Villa, was considered already to be middle-aged. When Villa first met Carranza, who was in his fifties, had a long flowing beard, and seemed to be slow and ponderous in his movements, his initial impression of the First Chief was, "This man cannot lead us to victory; he has already given in life everything he could give."[66]

In the first weeks of the revolution that he initiated, Carranza already felt that Villa might constitute a deadly danger to his movement. "Villa is a great warrior, a great organizer and a great general, and I am in fact convinced that we shall soon see him at the head of a large group of men," he told Adolfo de la Huerta, a revolutionary leader from Sonora who had come to Coahuila in April 1913 to express the support of the Sonoran revolutionaries for Carranza. "Villa also has a very strong personality, he is a terrible man, and a man without any visions, someone who is not conscious of what he is doing; he is enormously dangerous and we must be prepared." Carranza was remembering that one of the reasons that Villa and Orozco had rebelled against Madero in Ciudad Juárez in May 1911 was because the revolutionary president had appointed a civilian, Carranza, as secretary of war. "I cannot forget the look in Villa's eyes at the time, which showed me that he wanted to go even further than Orozco."[67]

From the very beginning of the revolution, Carranza attempted to subordinate Villa to leaders whom he considered far more reliable and to limit his authority in Chihuahua and other territories he controlled. Apart from Villa's immense popularity, however, Carranza faced another difficulty in his effort to limit Villa's power: he himself had no political or social network of support in Chihuahua. He was practically unknown in the state, and since he had not been a national politician before the outbreak of the second phase of the Mexican revolution, he had never spoken at or participated in political rallies or activities in Chihuahua.

Carranza tried to remedy this situation in mid 1913 when he crossed Chihuahua on the way to Sonora by establishing cordial relations with two of the state's military leaders—Maclovio Herrera and Manual Chao. It was Chao, the former schoolteacher and the best-educated of the popular leaders in Chihuahua, who became Carranza's favorite candidate for leader of the Chihuahuan revolution. Carranza first attempted to designate Chao as the supreme military leader of the Chihuahua revolutionaries. This attempt failed when Villa not only refused to accept him but intimidated Chao into recognizing his own leadership, and when the majority of Chihuahua's revolutionary leaders clearly showed that it was Villa whom they wanted to command the revolution.

Carranza's next attempt to limit Villa's power was a rather clumsy effort to subordinate him to the commander of the revolutionary forces in the neighboring state of Sonora, Alvaro Obregón. When he sent a delegation to Villa in August 1913 to that end, however, Villa absolutely refused, using an argument that clearly reflected his ideology. "Don't send me foreign generals. I have been told that they want to send a General Obregón and who knows who else to Chihuahua . . . but here all of us are from Chihuahua."[68] Not only in Villa's eyes but in those of his soldiers as well, anyone from outside Chihuahua, and possibly Durango, was a foreigner.

For Carranza, the need to control Villa took on a new urgency once the División del Norte had become master of Chihuahua. In Carranza's eyes, it was a matter of principle that while the military leaders of the revolution were given a wide leeway as far as organization and control of their armies was concerned, the civilian administration of liberated territories should be under the supreme authority of the First Chief. If that principle were violated in Chihuahua, it might set a precedent for the rest of Mexico. If Carranza could not impose his authority on Chihuahua, his government might remain a purely nominal, shadowy administration without any real authority. In addition, Carranza wanted to have at least partial control of the large revenues that rich states such as Chihuahua generated. Above all, he feared that radical social measures that Villa might take might jeopardize his own program, which was designed not to antagonize Mexico's ruling classes.

With this in mind, Carranza named Chao as governor of Chihuahua and warned Villa not to carry out any radical social changes. Carranza called on Villa to refrain from carrying out any land distribution and even demanded that the Villistas return to their former owners the few lands that Abraham González had divided among peasants. Villa was incensed at Carranza's request, stating that this would mean that he would have to take from the widows of men who had fallen in the Madero revolution the one means they had of surviving.[69]

Carranza's attempts to limit Villa's social policies elicited a strong and in some respects prophetic warning from one of his main intellectual supporters in the United States, Manuel Urquidi. In a letter to one of Carranza's other representatives in the United States, Roberto Pesqueira, Urquidi wrote: "The First Chief is in a difficult situation right now, and since the smallest hesitation could be disastrous, men like you who are morally closer to the chief should convince him to fully sanction and accept the actions of his subordinate chieftains. Any attempt to limit Villa's measures . . . would be an error that would divide the constitutionalist movement into two camps, and Villa and Zapata would have a much more popular platform than that of [the Plan of] Guadalupe, and they would be victorious."[70]

In a sense, this was a prophetic announcement. Urquidi was anticipating an alliance that was not even in the offing when he wrote this letter. He was right in the kind of split that would develop among the revolutionaries; he was wrong only as far as the results were concerned.

Carranza's instructions probably backfired and may have been one of the reasons, though certainly not the only one, why Villa decided that he personally would assume the governorship of the state. In addition, by having himself elected governor by the Chihuahuan generals (even including Carranza's nominee, Chao), Villa openly questioned Carranza's right to appoint the governors of newly liberated states.

While continuing to pressure Villa to relinquish the governorship of Chihuahua in favor of Chao, Carranza sent some of his highest officials to Chihuahua to attempt to keep Villa in line. Luis Cabrera, one of Carranza's most intelligent and influential advisors, went to Chihuahua and attempted to persuade Villa not to issue his own currency but to let the First Chief make the final decisions in all economic matters. Carranza also sent his secretary of foreign relations, Francisco Escudero, to Chihuahua. While it is not entirely clear what instructions Carranza gave him, Escudero's mission was probably to attempt to reverse Villa's expulsion of the Spaniards from Chihuahua and to emphasize to Villa that Carranza was ultimately in charge of all foreign relations of the revolutionary movement. Another high Carrancista official, Meza Gutiérrez, was named by the First Chief to assume control of all federal dependencies in Chihuahua, with authority to appoint some of the most important federal officials in the state.

Carranza also attempted to gain the support and loyalty of Villa's most important civilian official, Silvestre Terrazas. He warmly congratulated the newspaperman on his appointment as secretary of the government of Chihuahua and thus gave him to understand that although Villa had appointed him, Carranza was ready to support him in that position.[71]

Carranza's attempts to impose his agenda and his officials on Villa had very little success during the crucial period of Villa's governorship of Chihuahua. Villa received Cabrera and another high Carrancista official, Eliseo Arredondo, with the greatest courtesy and friendliness, but he continued to print his own currency in Chihuahua.[72] Escudero's mission to Villa was even less of a success. At a banquet given in his honor, the high Carrancista official became so drunk that he insulted Villa by telling him that he would soon betray the revolution and become another Pascual Orozco. "Listen, General. I have been told that you are a great killer. Well, let's see whether you have the guts to kill me," he told Villa at the same banquet. Villa finally lost patience, got up from the table, and before leaving told Escudero, "You are not a man, you are not courageous, you are nothing more than a disgraceful drunk who is annoying me, and the only reason that I am not having you shot on the spot is out of respect for my chief, Don Venustiano Carranza."[73]

Meza Gutiérrez, who had been appointed by Carranza as *jefe de hacienda* (i.e., the man in charge of economic affairs in the state), had been received by Villa with the greatest friendliness and cordiality and completely caved in to the revolutionary chieftain. Instead of naming his own people, he confirmed all of Villa's appointees and even hesitated to displace the man Villa had appointed to his own job of chief of economic affairs. "I have not dared to impose my presence in an energetic way since I feared not to be successful in my intention to gain the sympathy and respect both of Villa and his supporters," he wrote Carranza.[74]

On January 9, 1914, Carranza finally seemed to have secured a decisive victory. After having vainly asked Carranza to appoint anyone but Chao to the governorship of Chihuahua, Villa finally acceded to Carranza's wishes, resigned from the governorship, and allowed Chao to become his successor.[75] Chao's appointment was not, however, the victory for which Carranza had so hoped it would be. With Chao in command, the first chief hoped to reassert his authority in Chihuahua and if possible to reverse some of the changes that Villa had instituted. Even if Chao had wanted to accede to Carranza's wishes, he would have had great difficulty in doing so. He was surrounded by men appointed by and loyal to Villa. This included his highest civilian official, Silvestre Terrazas, who, although he for a time tried to conciliate both revolutionary leaders, finally sided with Villa. At the local level, Villa had given supreme power to the military commanders, who superseded all local civilian middle-class officials who might have supported Chao. Officially, Chao's position was ambiguous. As governor of Chihuahua, he was in some respects Villa's superior, but as an officer of the División del Norte, he was Villa's subordinate. A far more important obstacle to Carranza's imposition of a conservative regime in Chihuahua was Chao himself. He was neither a conservative nor a blind adherent of the First Chief.

One of Chao's first acts as governor was to write a long letter to Carranza justifying all of the social and economic measures that Villa had taken as governor of the state. His next step, probably with Villa's assent, was to promulgate a municipal land law that, while it did not affect the great estates, constituted one of Chihuahua's most important agrarian laws. Chao's report was probably an enormous disappointment for Carranza, since the latter's aim was to force Villa to return much of the property he had confiscated, including that of the Terrazas, to its former owners.[76]

Carranza finally became convinced that there was only one effective way of imposing his agenda on both Villa and Chihuahua, and that was to transfer his government and his seat of power from Sonora to Chihuahua. By the end of March 1914, with Villa's official assent, Carranza and his federal government accordingly moved to Ciudad Juárez. Soon afterward, open conflict broke out between the two men.

On the whole, it can be said that until April 1914, Carranza had taken the offensive and Villa had been on the defensive in their mutual relations. Although Villa had resisted Carranza's attempts to subordinate him to another military leader and to prevent him from carrying out his social agenda, he had done so with moderation. This is all the more surprising in view of Villa's innately suspicious nature and his volatile and sometimes ferocious temperament. In his reports to Carranza and in personal conversations with Carranza's representatives, he had always stressed his loyalty to the First Chief and had even offered to help fight Carranza's rivals in Sonora. "Tell my general," Villa told an emissary from Carranza in November 1913, "that he should not fight with any one of these people; he should send anyone who disturbs him to me and I'll take care of him." In this conversation, Villa was harshly critical of the Sonoran governor, José María Maytorena, whose relations with Carranza had become increasingly tense, and expressed his admiration for the Carrancista generals Pablo González and Obregón.[77] Villa's letters to Carranza were warm and effusive, and in all his interviews and conversations with journalists, Villa again and again reiterated his loyalty to Carranza.

While not all of Villa's declarations were necessarily sincere, there is no evidence that he was in any way plotting to depose Carranza. He himself was not ready to assume the leadership of the revolution or the presidency of Mexico, and until April 1914, he had no alternative candidate for those positions. When tensions did arise with Carranza in those months, Villa tended to comply with the First Chief's wishes. In spite of his reservations, he named Chao governor of Chihuahua and complied with Carranza's instructions in the Benton case.

Villa's relationship to Carranza would change after Carranza's arrival in Chihuahua, when he felt that the First Chief threatened what he considered his most vital and essential interests: his control of his core areas of support, his control of his army, and his access to supplies from the United States.

The first direct conflict between Villa and Carranza broke out soon after the latter's arrival in Ciudad Juárez as the result of another conflict that pitted Villa against Carranza's protégé, Chao. In Sonora, Carranza had enhanced his power by successfully playing off the governor of the state, Maytorena, against the military leaders of the revolution. Villa was afraid that Carranza would do the same in Chihuahua and soon became suspicious that Chao was willing to become Carranza's instrument in such a maneuver. The fact that Chao had appointed some of his own men to high positions in the Chihuahuan state government, and that Carranza was showing him special signs of respect and affection, fueled Villa's suspicions. They were reinforced by members of Villa's entourage, who intimated to him that Chao was aiming to have him assassinated and to assume the leadership of the División del Norte.[78]

In an attempt to weaken Chao, to better control him, and perhaps even to kill him, Villa ordered him and his troops to come to the Laguna and to participate in the campaign in and around Torreón. Villa felt that as head of the División del Norte, he had the authority to issue such a command. Chao, on the other hand, believed that as governor of Chihuahua, he had a right to make his own decision. He consulted with Carranza, who was only too glad to support Chao in his rebellious attitude. Villa now became so incensed that he went to Ciudad Juárez, arrested Chao, and ordered him to be shot.

Chao's life was finally spared, but accounts greatly vary as to how this was achieved. Silvestre Terrazas, who was present at this meeting, tells of a confrontation between the two men, in which Villa exploded into one of his famous and dangerous rages. "With indescribable fury, Villa hurled terrible charges against Chao and his subordinates, and we believed that the order would come for the execution of the military governor of Chihuahua at any moment," Terrazas later wrote.[79] Villa accused Chao of wanting to kill him in order to replace him at the head of his army and intimated that he was doing this in agreement with Carranza.

According to Silvestre Terrazas, Chao remained quiet, convinced of his innocence, and "his impassive face, the fact that his expression did not even change, led Villa to become calmer and calmer. Once Villa's rage had faded, Chao managed to convince him that he had never plotted against his commander and had remained loyal to him all the time." Carrancista sources give a very different view of these events. They describe a dramatic confrontation between Villa and Carranza after the First Chief heard that Villa wanted to execute Chao. Carranza was prepared for an armed confrontation; two aides with drawn pistols were hidden in his room, while he himself had a gun hidden under his seat.[80]

Carranza abruptly ordered Villa to give immediate orders to suspend the execution and refused to listen to Villa's justification that Chao deserved to die because he had violated military discipline by refusing to heed Villa's orders to proceed to Torreón. Villa complied with Carranza's orders, not only because he did not want a break with the First Chief but also because only a small number of men directly loyal to him were in Ciudad Juárez. The great majority of the troops there were either Carranza's or Chao's men. Officially, a hearty reconciliation took place between the three men. Silvestre Terrazas gave a banquet that same night in which the three leaders made a great show of mutual cordiality. As far as Chao and Villa were concerned, the cordiality was real. When the break between Villa and Carranza came, Chao, in spite of all their earlier conflicts, went with Villa.

The conviction that Villa was an unpredictable loose cannon, whom no one could control, which Carranza had expressed in the first days of the revolution, was now confirmed in his eyes, first by the Benton affair and then by Villa's refusal to heed his authority in Chihuahua and the violence that he had shown toward Chao. Carranza's aim now was to prevent Villa from being the first of the revolutionary leaders to reach Mexico City. He knew that whatever revolutionary army first reached the capital would have enormous advantages. It could at the very least dispose of the large arsenal held by the federal army. Because of the influence of Angeles in the Villa camp, Carranza believed that there was a genuine danger of an alliance between Villa and the remnants of the federal army. In addition, the first army to reach Mexico City could move further south and profit from the rich, hitherto scarcely tapped resources of Mexico's southeastern provinces. The occupation of Mexico City would also confer enormous prestige and legitimacy upon the leader who first entered it.

The hostility that Carranza felt toward Villa was deepened only a few weeks after the events of Ciudad Juárez when the first open and public difference of opinion between him and Villa emerged after the U.S. occupation of Veracruz.

Villa and the U.S. Occupation of Veracruz

On April 21, 1914, U.S. troops landed in Veracruz and occupied the city after breaking the spontaneous resistance of civilians and naval cadets, who had taken up arms against the foreign invaders without the help of the Mexican federal army, which had withdrawn from the city rather than fight the Americans. The occupation was the result of a small local conflict, which President Woodrow Wilson had purposely escalated in order to find a pretext to strike at Huerta.[81]

When a German ship bringing arms and ammunition to Huerta was on the verge of arriving in the port and unloading its cargo, Wilson decided to move. His aim was to hasten the end of the Huerta regime and at the same time to gain more leverage on Mexico's political evolution. Although Wilson's action was at least in part destined to help the constitutionalists, Carranza strongly protested against the occupation in a sharply worded note to Woodrow Wilson that held out the threat of war between the two countries. "Your invasion of our territory and the permanency of your forces in the port of Veracruz and the violation of the rights that constitute our existence as a free and independent sovereign entity will drag us into an unequal war, which we desire to avoid." Carranza called "the acts committed at Veracruz . . . highly offensive to the dignity and independence of Mexico and contrary to your reiterated declarations of not desiring to sever the state of peace and friendship with the Mexican nation."[82]

Carranza's reaction to the invasion was both the result of his ideology—nationalism was his most deeply held conviction—and the political situation in which his movement found itself. In view of Wilson's support for the revolutionaries, the Huerta regime had called Carranza an agent of the United States, and he feared that the label would stick unless he protested against the invasion. Such fears were all the more justified inasmuch as his natural constituency, the Mexican middle class, was highly nationalistic. For similar reasons, most of his generals and officers shared his attitude and clearly indicated their support for his uncompromising stand. Some even started negotiations with federal officers to coordinate joint action in the event of war with the United States. Pancho Villa was the one significant exception to this consensus of revolutionary leaders (even Zapata had said that he was ready to fight the Americans).

Only one day after Carranza had issued his sharply worded note of protest to the U.S. government, Villa proceeded to the border, met with the U.S. representative George Carothers, and told him "that as far as he was concerned we could keep Veracruz and hold it so tight that not even water would get in to Huerta and that he could not feel any resentment. He said that no drunkard, meaning Huerta, was going to draw him into a war with his friend; that he had come to Juárez to restore confidence between us." Villa did imply, however, that if the United States extended its occupation to other parts of Mexico, there would be fighting. The Mexicans might succumb to superior force "but that they would do much damage and fight as long as they could continue to exist on herbs and live in the hills.[83]

Two days later Villa sent a personal note to President Wilson, distancing himself in even clearer terms from Carranza's protest. "It is true," he wrote Wilson, "that the situation has been aggravated by the form of the note of the Constitutional governor of Coahuila and first chief of the revolution, but this note was entirely personal and the attitude of one person measuring what his momentary authority may be cannot carry such weight as to bring on a war between the two countries who have premeditated continuing peace, thereby promoting the machinations of Huerta, whom we both consider a common enemy."[84]

Villa's attitude was partly due to practical considerations. His army depended on arms and ammunition from the United States. In addition, in contrast to Carranza, Villa saw the world more in terms of personalities than of ideas. He believed Wilson's idealistic declarations far more than Carranza did. His attitude was also influenced by his largely rural constituency, which, unlike Mexico's middle class, saw Veracruz as a remote region that held little of interest.

Villa's attitude may also have reflected his lack of political experience. In contrast to Carranza, who had had a long political career, Villa was not used to distinguishing between rhetoric and reality. It was far easier for Carranza than for Villa to understand the tremendous distance that separated threats against the Americans from war with the United States.

Perhaps even more important than all of these explanations was the fear, which Villa shared with large segments of Mexico's lower classes, that in a conflict with the United States, they would simply be used by the upper classes for their own ends. This was the gist of a letter that Villa wrote to Marcelo Caraveo, a former Maderista who had joined first Orozco and then Huerta, and who had written Villa, offering to fight the Americans under his command:

Today the cursed reactionaries and científicos, who are descendants of the Conservatives of the period of Benito Juárez, have provoked an intervention, not European but American, in the belief that all Mexicans will be deceived, just as you have been, and will unite to fight against aggression. If we constitutionalists were dumb enough to unite with the científicos and reactionaries, we would only succeed in being sacrificed, so that later these forces would make an agreement with the Americans, and we would finally be vanquished by Huerta's men.[85]

There is little doubt that Villa was also influenced by Angeles, who had in fact drafted the personal letter from Villa to Wilson in which for the first time he voiced open criticism of Carranza.[86] Angeles's attitude was not only due to his favorable attitude to the United States but also to his wish to bring about a break between Carranza and Villa.

As a result of Villa's refusal to condemn the U.S. invasion of Veracruz, he was regarded more favorably by the Wilson administration than ever before, and the Benton case was practically forgotten. Carranza now considered Villa a threat not only to his social aims but to Mexico's independence as well. From this moment on, his aim seems to have been to eliminate Villa from Mexican political life altogether.

In contrast to Carranza's implacable hostility to him, Villa's attitude to the First Chief was more contradictory and at times still showed strong tendencies to conciliation. Between the Chao episode in March 1914 and Villa's open and public break with Carranza in June of that same year, Villa manifested very contradictory tendencies. On one hand, he felt that he had won in the conflict that erupted when Carranza set up his headquarters in Ciudad Juárez. He had firmly retained his control of Chihuahua, and in fact Carranza made no further efforts to influence events there. Since Villa himself had no ambitions to become president of Mexico, he was quite ready to allow Carranza to rule over the rest of the country as long as Villa was assured control over his bailiwick of Chihuahua, Durango, and the Laguna area. On the other hand, powerful anti-Carrancista forces among the revolutionaries, as well as within his own División del Norte, sought to persuade him that no coexistence with the First Chief was in fact possible. These forces included Zapata, Maytorena, and Angeles.

Villa and the Zapatistas

The first group of anti-Carrancista revolutionaries who established links with Villa were the Zapatistas. Zapata, the head of the Liberating Army of the South, was haunted by the fear that after all the fighting and bloodshed, the constitutionalist revolution would bring forth another Francisco Madero, who, like his predecessor, would attempt to repress the southern revolutionaries. In Zapata's eyes, Carranza seemed more and more like Madero. The First Chief's social origins, his reluctance to implement any agrarian reform while governor of Coahuila, and his refusal to include any plank on agrarian reform in his Plan of Guadalupe had all fueled these fears. They were decisively increased when Carranza forced one of his generals, Lucio Blanco, to give up his command in northeastern Mexico because he had begun the implementation of a program of land division. One of Zapata's closest collaborators, Gildardo Magaña, had gone to Matamoros, Lucio Blanco's headquarters, and reported firsthand to Zapata that Blanco had been prevented from carrying out agrarian reform by the First Chief.

Zapata thus proved to be extremely receptive when, sometime in the fall of 1913, he received a letter from Villa in which the latter told him that he planned to carry out a massive land reform once he became master of Chihuahua. It is not clear what had impelled Villa to write this letter.[87] Was he already looking for support in case of a future conflict with Carranza? Or did he hope to gain the support of scattered groups of northern revolutionaries who called themselves Zapatistas and proclaimed their support for the southern revolutionary chieftain?

Zapata's response to Villa contained a veiled warning about Carranza, an admonition to follow the principles of Zapata's Plan of Ayala, an expression of confidence in Villa, and a muted offer of alliance. Without mentioning Carranza by name, but obviously referring to him, Zapata wrote, "We should not let ourselves be deceived by our enemies. We should be careful of those false idealists who finally turn into furious, self-seeking individuals. We should be careful about these self-seeking individuals who under the guise of idealism ruin our country." In case his meaning had not been grasped, Zapata made it clear that it was inside the revolutionary movement that Villa should look for these self-seeking individuals. Zapata called on Villa to scrutinize with the greatest attention "our companions and false supporters so that we should not be surprised, so that our cause will not be betrayed and the people's hopes will not be foiled."

The part of Villa's letter that had most impressed Zapata was a statement that it would be necessary to destroy all "corrupt elements who are enemies of the people, who can be designated as cientificism, militarism, and clericalism." Zapata enthusiastically welcomed that idea and called for massive reprisals once the revolutionaries occupied Mexico City, saying:

We must carry out these executions to put an end to the enemies of our country, for only in this way will there be peace. . . . Remember that the revolution that began on November 20, 1910, failed for one and only one reason. When it entered Mexico City, it did not decapitate its enemies, and it was they who in the final account triumphed. After having been vanquished, they became victors. The same would happen now if some kind of '93 [Zapata is obviously referring to the terror practiced by the French revolutionaries in 1793] did not take place in order to purify this corrupt society, which is the real cause of the sufferings of our country.

Zapata called on Villa to carry out agrarian reform in accordance with his Plan of Ayala and expressed his confidence in the northern revolutionary, saying: "I am confident that you perhaps will be the only one in the north whose interest is progress for the people and who will carry out in those regions the division of the lands and the division of the great monopolies as it is indicated in the Plan of Ayala."

Zapata's letter effectively offered Villa the kind of alliance against Carranza that the two men would conclude in the fall of 1914. He expressed the hope that Villa's troops would reach the capital, so that the two of them would be able to march triumphantly into Mexico City, "and then the revolution will hoist on the National Palace the flag of reform, freedom, justice, and law."[88]

While Zapata's warnings to Villa about Carranza were veiled and never spelled out, his emissary, Villa's old cellmate Gildardo Magaña, seems to have been far more direct. Before visiting Villa, Magaña had been in Matamoros in northeastern Mexico, where he had spoken to Lucio Blanco, and he gave a detailed report to Villa on how Carranza had prevented the agrarian reform that Blanco had attempted to implement. Magaña was obviously interested in undermining Villa's links to the First Chief.[89]

Zapata would continue these efforts throughout the spring of 1914. When two emissaries of his arrived in El Paso in April 1914, they made it clear to newspaper reporters: "With Villa, yes; with Carranza, no. Our General Zapata does not recognize Señor Carranza, whom he considers a usurper, as the leader of the revolution. . . . Our general recognizes General Villa as the chief of the Army of the North and we have no objection to telling you that General Zapata, chief of the Army of the South, wishes through us to come to an agreement with General Villa to march on the capital of Mexico."[90]

While there is no evidence that the Zapatistas played a decisive role in the events leading up to the first split between Villa and Carranza in June 1914, the possibility of an alliance with Zapata was a factor that neither Villa nor Angeles ignored when they decided to oppose Carranza.

Villa and Sonora

In the end, the faction that most influenced Villa's break with Carranza was not part of the División del Norte but a geographically, politically, and militarily separate entity. This was a political and military faction led by Maytorena in Sonora. The strategic location of Sonora, Maytorena's own personality, and the influence of his most active proponent within the División del Norte, Felipe Angeles, all contributed to the split.

Six months after he had decided to take a leave of absence from his functions as governor of Sonora and to remain in the United States, Maytorena returned to his native state in the fall of 1913 to resume his functions as constitutional governor. His return was viewed with hostility by the younger military leaders of the revolution who had assumed control of the movement during his absence. They were a group of highly intelligent, highly talented men of middle-class background. The most important of these leaders was Alvaro Obregón, the young owner of a middle-sized ranch, who had worked as a mechanic, a schoolteacher, and a tenant farmer. Obregón was not a veteran of the Madero revolution. His only military experience prior to the constitutionalist revolution had been in setting up a corps of volunteers from the city and region of Huatabampo to fight invading Orozquista troops from neighboring Chihuahua. In spite of his lack of military experience, he had successfully defeated the Orozquistas at the battle of La Dura. Once the constitutionalist revolution broke out, he managed to expel all federal troops from his native state, with the exception of a federal garrison in the port city of Guaymas. He would turn out to be one of the best generals the Mexican Revolution produced, perhaps even the greatest of them.

Other military men who had emerged as leaders of the revolutionary movement in Sonora included Plutarco Elías Calles, who at various times had been a schoolteacher, a municipal employee (he was dismissed for alleged fraud), a hotel supervisor, and administrator of a small hacienda and a flour mill. Salvador Alvarado had pursued many occupations, among them those of pharmacist, shopkeeper, tenant farmer on a ranch in the Yaqui Valley, and innkeeper.[91]

These men resented Maytorena's return. They felt that the governor had abandoned them in their most difficult hour and believed that he had no right to claim the spoils of a victory for which he had done so little. Carranza at first strongly supported Maytorena's right to return. After all, Maytorena was the constitutionally elected governor of the state, and it was by virtue of the same status that Carranza had claimed leadership of the revolution. The First Chief soon began to support Maytorena's rivals, however, above all, Obregón. In part, this may have been a manifestation of the policy of divide and rule that he was to exercise throughout his presidency. Moreover, Obregón had become the strongest military chieftain outside of Chihuahua, and Carranza realized that Obregón was the only genuine obstacle to the supremacy of Villa and the División del Norte. Maytorena did not, however, allow himself to be simply shunted aside. Part of his political organization still existed, he still enjoyed popularity among part of Sonora's middle class, and many Yaquis still considered him their protector and were willing to fight on his side. In spite of his support by the Yaquis, the conflict between Maytorena and his rivals cannot be called a social struggle. None of them was a radical revolutionary, their social ideas were quite similar, and Obregón and Calles had strong family ties to hacendado families, while Maytorena was himself a hacendado.[92]

Their conflict was a power struggle, perhaps with regional overtones. As Carranza began more and more overtly to support his enemies, Maytorena realized that the only possible source of help from outside of Sonora was Villa. This was his only interest in Villa, for in social terms the two men could not have been more different. Villa had confiscated all the estates of the oligarchy and had clearly said that he was going to break up the large haciendas after the victory of the revolution, whereas one of the main reasons that Maytorena had left Sonora was precisely because he did not want to confiscate the lands of the hacendados. In fact, one of his first acts after he resumed the governorship of Sonora was to return the properties that the interim rulers of the state had taken away from some estate owners. Maytorena probably hoped that the help and support he had given Villa shortly before his return to Mexico in March 1913 would in some way be reciprocated. It was the kind of obligation that Villa valued highly. Nevertheless, in the fall of 1913, Maytorena had not been able to count on such reciprocity from Villa. On the contrary, Villa expressed himself in very harsh terms about Maytorena and offered Carranza his help in subduing any enemies he might have.[93]

In early 1914, however, Villa's attitude toward Maytorena began to change, not only because of increasing tensions with Carranza and a series of measures that Maytorena had taken in order to influence Villa on his behalf, but primarily owing to the intervention of the newly arrived general of the División del Norte, Felipe Angeles.

Only a few weeks after his arrival in Chihuahua, Angeles engaged in secret negotiations with two representatives of Maytorena's who were stationed in El Paso, Texas: Alberto Piña, a deputy in the Sonoran legislature and one of Maytorena's closest confidants; and a Licenciado Rosado, the editor of a small Spanish-language newspaper in El Paso, the *Correo del Bravo*, which was financed by Maytorena. The aim of these talks was to organize an alliance between Villa and Maytorena. Angeles promised to lobby Villa in favor of this project.[94]

The campaign was in fact waged by the *Correo del Bravo*.[95] Headed by Rosado, the paper constantly teetered on the edge of financial collapse until the next subvention arrived from the Sonoran governor. It is indicative of the importance that Maytorena had attached to gaining Villa's support that he should have founded a newspaper not in a border city of the United States facing his own state of Sonora, which might have influenced members of his own constituency, but in El Paso, far away from Sonora, where its only target could have been Villa and his faction in Chihuahua. It is difficult to understand how Angeles pinned such hopes on this obscure newspaper, which was not even allowed to circulate in Chihuahua, and whose potential readership, even if it had been allowed to circulate, was limited by the fact that the majority of Villa's supporters and many of his commanders were illiterate. Nevertheless, Angeles was optimistic in this respect, stating that the "campaign undertaken in this respect by the *Correo del Bravo* has been very well received by the Maderista elements which constitute an immensely popular and powerful party."[96]

The reason for Angeles's optimism was that the newspaper concentrated its anti-Carranza campaign on an issue that he and Maytorena felt was of such concern to the Chihuahuan revolutionaries that smuggled copies of the paper and word-of-mouth reports on its contents would be sufficient to influence Villa and his supporters. That issue was land reform.

On April 15, 1914, the *Correo del Bravo* launched a series of articles intended to show that Carranza was an enemy of agrarian reform, and that if he became president the people would have fought in vain:

The people does not believe in promises from magnates anymore. . . . The Plan of Guadalupe promises nothing and will grant nothing. . . . The Plan of Guadalupe is a bastion behind which the First Chief is hiding, who has named himself without understanding the enormous responsibility that rests on his shoulders. . . . It seems that we are fighting only to make one or the other magnate president of the republic.

But one thing should be well understood: the people is not fighting to secure a new master. It has not shed its blood on the battlefield so that a tyrant can take power; it has not gone to war in order to create a dictatorship. . . . It fights in order to remove a criminal from power and it fights to receive the lands that the rich have taken from them.[97]

The editorial's most important message was that Villa and Zapata, rather than Carranza, were the saviors of Mexico, and that they would carry out a broad program of land reform. In the following weeks and months, the paper continued in the same vein. On April 21, an article demanded, "Why Does Señor Carranza Prevent the Division of Lands?" On April 22, "The Mexican Agrarian Question" was raised. On May 1 and 2, the paper published anti-Carranza articles along the same lines signed "Danton and Robespierre." It continued to carry such articles throughout 1914.

From Secret Rivalry to Open Break

In spite of Maytorena's and Angeles's constant warnings that Carranza could not be trusted, Villa still hoped for a reconciliation with the First Chief. He had achieved his aim of consolidating his hold on Chihuahua and Durango and on his own División del Norte, and he hoped by making substantial concessions to Carranza to persuade the First Chief to accept a modus vivendi with him.

In return for recognition of Carranza's supreme leadership of the revolution, Villa expected the First Chief not only to accept his control of his region and his army but also to refrain from placing any obstacles in the way of his march on Mexico City. What he failed to realize was that Carranza would not, and probably could not, accept such a compromise. If the División del Norte were the first to reach Mexico City, Villa would become the national leader of Mexico in the eyes of both domestic and international public opinion. Carranza was willing to use any means at his disposal to prevent this. First, to slow down Villa's advance on Mexico City, he asked him for substantial concessions. Hoping to conciliate Carranza, Villa was willing to go a long way toward meeting the First Chief's demands. After Villa's troops captured the major railway center of Torreón and occupied the surrounding Laguna area, Carranza named his own man as superintendent of the highly developed northern railway system, replacing Eusebio Calzado, Villa's extremely capable chief. Villa's acceptance of this decision was a major compromise on his part. The railways were of decisive importance for his military strategy, since troop trains constituted the basic means of transportation for his army, including his cavalry. Villa also allowed Carranza to interfere in the administration of the Torreón slaughterhouse, at the cost, according to one Villista official, of "famine among the poor."[98] And to allay the First Chief's fears that he had national ambitions, Villa dismissed Manuel Bauche Alcalde as editor in chief of his newspaper, *Vida Nueva*, because he had praised Villa far more than the First Chief in its columns.[99]

Moreover, Villa was ready to go even further in order to conciliate Carranza. The remnants of the federal army that had opposed Villa in Torreón had fled to Saltillo, the capital of Carranza's native state of Coahuila, and to Paredón, a fortified town nearby. Carranza now asked Villa to proceed with his army to free Saltillo instead of marching south and attacking Zacatecas, where the strongest federal garrison was located, which constituted the gateway to Mexico City. Villa objected that an attack on Saltillo would delay his march to Mexico City, and that in addition Carranza's general, Pablo González, the commander of the Army of the Northeast, was in fact much closer to Saltillo and should be the man to capture the capital city of Coahuila. Carranza was adamant, and Villa complied with his wishes. Forcing Villa to march to Saltillo not only delayed his advance on Mexico City, but it would be Villa's troops, rather than González's men, who were loyal to Carranza, who would suffer the high casualties resulting from an attack on 15,000 federal troops.[100]

The commanders of the 6,000-man federal army stationed in Paredón had hoped that by destroying about 20 kilometers of railway tracks leading to the town, they would prevent or at least greatly delay Villa's troop trains from bringing his army to Paredón and Saltillo. They were mistaken. Villa disembarked his cavalry from the train, and 8,000 riders stormed Paredón, creating a panic among the federal troops, already demoralized by their defeat at Torreón. It was another triumph for the División del Norte. Of the 6,000-man garrison of Paredón, 500 died, among them two generals, and 2,500 were either taken prisoner or wounded. Villa captured more than 3,000 rifles and ten cannon. The remaining federal troops in Saltillo preferred to retreat rather than to fight Villa, and the División del Norte made its triumphant entry into the Coahuilan capital. Villa made no effort to retain control of the newly occupied territories himself, but handed both Saltillo and the surrounding countryside over to Carranza, who now set up his headquarters in the capital city of his native state.[101]

Villa had hoped that these considerable concessions on his part would conciliate Carranza and make the First Chief amenable to a compromise. With this in mind, he sent Silvestre Terrazas to Saltillo to negotiate on June 8. What Villa wanted above all was to regain control of the northern railway system in order to make an unimpeded advance southward to Zacatecas, the largest and most important remaining federal bastion in the north, where Huerta had concentrated the elite of the federal army. In addition, Terrazas was to negotiate on several other points, such as the disposal of "intervened" haciendas and other confiscated properties, as well as the issuance of paper money by Villa. Carranza refused to accede to any compromise on even the most minimal point.[102]

One of the main reasons for Carranza's obduracy was that the last thing he wanted was for Villa and his División del Norte to occupy Zacatecas. Such an occupation would have constituted a decisive blow to a strategy that Carranza had devised in order to prevent Villa from winning the race to Mexico City. Carranza had encouraged all northern revolutionaries who were opposed to Villa to join another army corps that he had established, the Army of the Center. He named Panfilo Natera, a former subordinate of Villa's, as the commander of that army and gave him the same rank as his former commander, which was an obvious slap in the face to Villa.

Carranza then instructed Natera to attack Zacatecas, opening the way to Mexico City. Together with the troops of Alvaro Obregón, who was advancing from the west, he would then occupy the capital, and Villa would be restricted to his bailiwick in the north. Carranza's plan failed, for Natera failed. Although his troops again and again attempted to storm Zacatecas, they were no match for the federal artillery and machine guns. Carranza now faced a dilemma. The only army that was strong enough to take Zacatecas was the División del Norte, but Carranza did not want Villa to achieve that victory and to be able to proceed to Mexico City. He now decided on a stratagem that would allow Natera to take Zacatecas and weaken Villa at the same time. He ordered the head of the División del Norte to detach 5,000 of his troops and to place them under Natera's command in order to attack Zacatecas.

Fearing the disintegration of his División del Norte, Villa hoped to persuade Carranza to rescind the order. This was part of the mission that he had entrusted to Silvestre Terrazas. When Terrazas returned to Chihuahua and reported to Villa that Carranza had not given in on a single point, Villa flew into one of his rages. "No, no. There's nothing else we can do," Villa yelled. "We will march on Saltillo and hang the old man and his accomplices. I can't stand him anymore. With 7,000 men I can encircle them and hang them all." Villa's rage was such that for a moment Silvestre Terrazas feared for his own life. "It would be impossible to describe the tremendous impression this explosion of rage of General Villa made on me; for a moment I believed that I too would be his victim. His fury was such that I thought of a savage animal being threatened and chained."[103]

When Villa raised the question of whether he should march on Saltillo with some of his closest advisors, most of them, especially Angeles and Roque González Garza, strongly objected and managed to persuade him to give up any such project.

Villa's explosion of rage was not only because of Carranza's intransigence and his own volatile temperament, but also because he realized that he had been tricked. He had made genuine and substantial concessions to the First Chief: he had given him control of the northern railroads and, more important, control of his own native state by handing Saltillo over to Carranza's nominees. He had thus delayed his own march south to Mexico City and had received nothing in return.

After the failure of Terrazas's mission, Villa became convinced that an agreement with the First Chief was impossible, that their differences were irreconcilable. At this point, his main actions were designed to convince his generals that Carranza was perfidious, and to get them to go along with a break. He knew that some of them were supporters of the First Chief, and that others, who were not, did not want a break in the ranks of the revolutionaries. He also knew, however, that most of them were opposed to the dismemberment of the División del Norte that Carranza had ordered. Above all, he knew that neither his generals nor his soldiers had great confidence in Natera, who had just been defeated in his efforts to take Zacatecas; if, indeed, they were to make the sacrifices necessary to take the strongest bastion the federal army had erected in Mexico, they would do so under a general they trusted to lead them to victory—that is, under Villa. He believed that the best way to gain the support of his generals was to involve them directly in the negotiations with the First Chief. On June 11, he designated a commission consisting of Angeles, Contreras, and Ortega to negotiate with Carranza.[104] Their mission, however, never got off the ground. On June 12, one day after the commission was named, and before it could go to Saltillo, the

First Chief managed to alienate all the generals of the División del Norte. Even those most hostile to Villa and most closely linked to the First Chief dissociated themselves from Carranza.

The confrontation began when Villa initiated a telegraphic conference with the First Chief by asking the latter once more, as he had done through his intermediary Silvestre Terrazas, to reconsider his order to send reinforcements from the División del Norte to Natera at Zacatecas. Villa obliquely criticized Carranza by suggesting that Natera's attack on Zacatecas (which Carranza had ordered) had been an error, which necessarily resulted in the latter's defeat. He suggested that sending reinforcements from his own division to Natera, as Carranza wished, would be disastrous. His men would be uselessly slaughtered, and the attackers would still be defeated. There was only one way, in Villa's opinion, that Zacatecas could be taken and the greatest and largest federal army still in the field could be defeated. That was by Villa himself taking the lead in the attack on Zacatecas at the head of his whole División del Norte. In his reply, Carranza refused to heed Villa's arguments and once again ordered him to send 5,000 men to reinforce Natera.

At this point, Villa offered his resignation to Carranza. "Señor," he wired the First Chief, "I resign command of this division. Tell me to whom to deliver it."[105]

It will never be clarified whether this resignation was the result of a momentary rage or pique or of a premeditated plan. Whatever its motive, it was a stroke of genius from a tactical point of view. It forced all of Villa's generals, even the most recalcitrant ones, to rally behind their leader. The man who organized this rally, and who extracted every ounce of political capital that could be extracted from it, was Felipe Angeles. According to his recollections, Angeles knew nothing of what had transpired between Villa and Carranza until Villa had him called into the telegraph office. There he found many of Villa's generals profoundly worried and preoccupied. Villa himself

told me to sit down in a empty chair facing him. "See what you can do with these troops, General," he told me. "I am leaving."

Since I did not understand I did not know what to answer; but the attention of the general was distracted and he did not seem to expect any answer.[106]

Once he was apprised of what had happened, Angeles took control of events. He was convinced that if Villa really gave up command of the División del Norte, the results would be disastrous. His army would either dissolve or rebel. The already-demoralized federal troops would be encouraged to resist, and the war might drag on for a long time to come. These considerations were shared by Villa's generals. Some had hoped until the last moment that Carranza would reject Villa's resignation and had not believed Angeles when he told them that he was convinced that Carranza would accept it. Once Carranza's reply came in, in which he accepted Villa's resignation, appointed him governor of Chihuahua, and asked his generals to appoint an interim commander in chief, many were gripped by anger and despair. "I will go into the mountains and live off roots," Angeles heard one of Villa's generals, Trinidad Rodríguez, exclaim.[107]

Angeles now drafted a short but courteous telegram to Carranza, asking him to reconsider his decision, since "it would lead to a serious loss of morale and great trouble for our cause, not only inside our republic but on the outside."[108] Carranza now made a fateful decision, refusing to heed the general's wishes, and insisting again that Villa had to resign. At this point, the generals were forced to choose sides, and they did so unanimously. They went to see Villa and asked him to reconsider his resignation. Villa agreed and once more became head of the División del Norte.

When the generals apprised Carranza of their decision, he was incensed. He sent them a telegram in which he refused to accept Villa's renewed command of the División del Norte. He threatened Villa's generals with the imposition of a commander without consulting them, and finally asked for five generals to come to Saltillo to confer with him on the situation. He did not ask the generals to designate that commission but named it himself. It would have consisted of Angeles, Tomás Urbina, Maclovio Herrera, Toribio Ortega, Eugenio Aguirre Benavides, and Rosalio Hernández.

Carranza's choice of names was carefully planned. While some of the generals were loyal to Villa, the list of six included two men, Maclovio Herrera and Rosalio Hernández, who were sworn enemies of Villa's and had secretly suggested to Carranza in March 1914, after Villa had threatened to execute Chao, that Carranza should order Villa to be shot.[109] Another of the generals, Eugenio Aguirre Benavides, had had disagreements with Villa. Carranza obviously hoped that at the conference he would be able to create divisions among Villa's generals. His maneuver failed, however, and the conference never took place. Instead, all the generals signed a telegram directed to Carranza, drafted by Angeles and much more harshly worded than any they had sent before. In all their previous communications, the generals had been highly respectful of the First Chief, and while they had questioned Carranza's decision to remove Villa, they had never questioned his leadership. This time they were openly and harshly critical. "We consider your measure a violation of the laws of politics and war and the duties of patriotism," they told him.

We say further that among all those who defend our cause, General Villa is the chief with the greatest prestige, and if he should obey your order and retire, the people of Mexico would be right in blaming you and realizing your very great weakness, and they would accuse you of being the cause of a great loss. We say this and much more, Señor: We know very well that you are looking for the opportunity to stop General Villa in his action because of your purpose to remove from the revolutionary scene the men who can think without your orders, who do not flatter and praise you or struggle for your aggrandizement but only for the rights of the people.[110]

The generals concluded their telegram by stating that they would all march south—to Zacatecas.

This was the first personal attack on Carranza by Villa's generals, but, harsh as their words were, they did not yet repudiate Carranza's leadership. They only said that they refused to accede to his orders to remove Villa and implied that whatever his decision, they would march on Zacatecas.

The harsh tone of the letter may very well have been inspired by Villa himself. He had not intervened (at least not directly) in the generals' deliberations before they asked him to resume command of the División del Norte. Once he had done so, he revealed to his generals the whole history and antecedents of his differences with Carranza, which doubtless contributed to their acceding to the harsh tone of the letter that Angeles had drafted. The generals' decision officially at least to maintain the unity of the revolutionary movement meant that their conflict with Carranza was never publicized.

From Villa's point of view, the results of his clash with Carranza could not have been more gratifying. All his generals, including his enemies Maclovio Herrera and Rosalio Hernández, had signed the letter to Carranza and reiterated their loyalty to Villa. Two generals, Robles and Ceniceros, whose troops were not officially part of the División del Norte, now asked for their incorporation into Villa's army, and Chao, who was on his way to rejoin Carranza with 300 men who were to constitute the First Chief's personal escort, expressed his solidarity with Villa and decided to remain within the División del Norte.[111]

The break between Villa and Carranza was now irreconcilable, although it was not made public. The División del Norte now set its sights on Zacatecas, hoping not only that it would defeat Huerta's army but also to win the race to Mexico City.

The Battle of Zacatecas

The battle of Zacatecas was the largest and bloodiest battle that took place during the revolution against Huerta. Zacatecas was an old mining town of 30,000 inhabitants that impressed both its attackers and its defenders by its natural beauty and picturesque qualities. When he first looked down at the city from the top of a hill, Angeles was struck by "a beautiful panorama. Down at the right the very large valley of Calera y Fresnillo with many small villages shining in the radiant light of morning. Facing it, part of the city of Zacatecas, between the hills of El Grillo and La Bufa, two formidable fortified positions."[112] The beauty of Zacatecas also impressed Ignacio Muñoz, a federal officer who entered the city with the last train of reinforcements to arrive before it was encircled by the revolutionaries.

This was the first time I visited Zacatecas. The city, far from presenting the aspect that one would assume in a city on the eve of one of the most furious battles of our history, seemed like a town that had not undergone any changes. . . . like an enchanting miniature we were discovering the city lost in the middle of deep ravines. . . . Streetcars hauled by mules were waiting at the station. Numerous persons mainly dressed in black could be seen on the street and gave the city a visibly religious character.[113]

Unfortunately for the city's inhabitants, Zacatecas was of great strategic importance to both sides. It was a railway junction that any attacker from the north had to capture before being able to advance on Mexico City. According to James Caldwell, the British consul in Zacatecas, the federal commander of the city, General Medina Barrón, "was very confident that he would be able to defend the town successfully."[114] His optimism was based on the great natural obstacles that Zacatecas presented to any attacking force. It was surrounded by high hills, which any attacker would have to storm before he could successfully take the city. This meant that Villa would not be able to use his "classic" tactic of massive cavalry attacks to overrun Zacatecas. Medina Barrón had placed his artillery on top of two of the highest hills surrounding the city, El Grillo and La Bufa. He was confident that attacking infantry, which would slowly have to climb up these hills, could easily be decimated by concentrated fire from his artillery and by his massed infantry. This tactic had proved successful in repelling all the attacks by the troops of Natera, and Medina Barrón was confident that he could do the same with Villa's attacking forces. His confidence was bolstered by the several thousand fresh troops that had arrived to reinforce his garrison, now numbering about 12,000.[115]

Another reason for Medina Barrón's confidence in the fighting capacity of his army was the morale of his troops. While some of his soldiers were unwilling conscripts, others were volunteers, who had joined Huerta's troops in the mistaken belief that they would be sent to fight U.S. invaders. Many did not know that it was Villa's troops and not the Americans they were fighting. Others still were battle-scarred Orozquista veterans, commanded by experienced generals such as Benjamín Argumedo, who knew that Villa would execute them if they were ever captured.

It is nevertheless doubtful whether Medina Barrón still believed that the original plan of the federal army, the aim of which had been nothing less than the total destruction of the División del Norte, could still be implemented. According to one of its drafters, General Rubio Navarrete, that plan involved exhausting Villa's troops for several days in a fruitless attempt to take Zacatecas. Once his troops had been sufficiently weakened and demoralized, a federal counteroffensive would set in. The federal División del Bravo, stationed in Mexico's northeast, would cut off the División del Norte from its rear base in Torreón, while 15,000 fresh federal reinforcements would then go on the attack, catching the División del Norte in a pincer movement between the two federal divisions. That strategy was scotched by the U.S. invasion of Veracruz, according to Rubio Navarrete. There were no arms to supply the federal reinforcements at Aguascalientes, and the División del Bravo was kept in reserve along the border with the United States for use in the event of a Mexican-American war.[116]

Villa realized that the capture of Zacatecas would require different tactics than those he had used in taking Torreón. He commissioned Angeles to draft a plan of attack.[117] After having carefully reconnoitered the surroundings of Zacatecas, Angeles proposed a strategy the essence of which was that the División del Norte should make full use of its superiority in both artillery and numbers so as not to be forced into a lengthy siege. The attacking troops should surround the city and storm it simultaneously from all sides. The División del Norte's artillery should be concentrated near the federal artillery emplacements of La Bufa and El Grillo either to destroy the federal artillery or to draw its fire onto itself while the infantry stormed the two hills.

Since Pascual Orozco was expected to lead a strong detachment of reinforcements for the garrison of Zacatecas from the city of Aguascalientes, where many federal troops were stationed, revolutionary troops were to be concentrated along all exits from the city, especially near the town of Guadalupe, which was located on a road linking Zacatecas to Aguascalientes. These troops should prevent reinforcements from getting in, and above all prevent the federal garrison from evacuating the town, as the federals had been at least partially successful in doing at Torreón.

Villa approved Angeles's plan and it proved brilliantly successful. The first contingents of the División del Norte arrived near Zacatecas on June 19, and some scattered fighting took place in the following days. The revolutionaries were under strict instructions from Villa not to attack the town, and the fighting consisted mainly in the attackers attempting to repel federal skirmishers sent out to harass them. Villa arrived on June 22 to take command of the siege. "We saw him as always affectionate and enthusiastic, mounted on a spirited horse belonging to General Urbina," Angeles recalled.[118] Villa decided not to remain behind the lines to coordinate operations but rather to head one of the attacking columns himself.

On June 23, at 10:00 A.M., the revolutionary attack on Zacatecas began simultaneously all around the city. The most important objective of the revolutionaries was the capture of El Grillo and La Bufa, where the federal artillery was concentrated. Once they had captured these heights, the revolutionaries not only would have eliminated the federal artillery but would be able to dominate the city. It was on these two hills that the bloodiest fighting took place. Medina Barrón had personally gone to La Bufa to take charge of its defense. His presence may have impelled its defenders to present a stronger resistance to Villa's troops than the men holding the adjacent hill of El Grillo, who proved incapable of resisting the constant attacks by Villa's infantry, supported by withering fire from 29 of Angeles's cannon placed around the two hills. By 1:00, El Grillo had fallen. Panic now gripped the federal troops. "About 1:00 P.M. we began to see federal soldiers running in the streets in great disorder," Caldwell reported,

without rifles of any kind and very soon the news spread that El Grillo had been taken by Villa's men. From the time of that first defeat, panic seemed to go through the federal army, and soldiers and officers who up to that time had fought bravely, lost their heads completely and thought of nothing else but of saving their own lives. The men got into any hole or corner they could find, while hundreds of them undressed in the streets, throwing away uniforms, rifles, cartridge belts, etc., etc. The officers rode about collecting their belongings, making ready for the retreat, and it is hard to imagine such a scene of wild disorder as took place in the streets of Zacatecas at that time.

While all this was going on, the fighting on La Bufa was terrible, but finally all the federals were driven from that position too, arriving in wild confusion in the Plaza de Armas.[119]

As panic swept through the federal army, a very different atmosphere reigned in Villa's headquarters. Villa and Angeles were having lunch in a hut overlooking the city of Zacatecas. As Angeles described it,

My assistant Baca brought us the food that we shared with General Villa and with other officers who were present.

We ate happily in a house whose roof had been torn apart by our grenades. I have never seen such destruction with more pleasure.

In order to have a good digestion, Cervantes and I went to take a walk.[120]

Convinced that Zacatecas was lost, Medina Barrón now ordered all remaining troops to evacuate the city. Their plan was to take the road leading from Zacatecas to Aguascalientes, where they would join the other federals. The main obstacle they faced on their way were 7,000 troops of the División del Norte that Villa had stationed in the town of Guadalupe. The retreating federal column which passed here must have been composed of about 1,500 men, four cannon, and a number of machine guns. "It was a sorry sight," the British consul wrote,

to see these people who only a few hours before were respected and looked up to by everyone, leave Zacatecas riding away in such confusion, men women and children—the poor soldaderas—running along, carrying all their worldly possessions on their backs. Many of the horses carried two officers, everyone taking the last chance to save his life. When they left the town they went out under a regular shower of bullets but as their only chance of escape was through Guadalupe, and as 7,000 rebels were there to attack them, the poor federal garrison which defended the town so gallantly up to a certain point was simply slaughtered. They say that between here and Guadalupe the road and hills are simply covered with dead bodies.[121]

In their desperate attempt to flee through Guadalupe, the retreating federal troops were decimated but not yet annihilated. The survivors attempted to leave the city by two other routes, were repelled both times, and finally returned, as Angeles described it, "in one last desperate attempt to be able to leave where they first attempted to do so, through Guadalupe. We now witnessed the most complete disorganization. We did not see them fall but we knew that they did. I must confess without embarrassment that I witnessed their annihilation with the greatest joy."[122] For the inhabitants of the city and for the remaining federal soldiers, Zacatecas now became an inferno. "Anyone capable of descriptive writing," of which the British consul was obviously capable, "would have found material for several books in what took place between 1:00 and 4:00 P.M. that afternoon and I must confess I was completely scared and as nervous as a cat. We all sat upstairs in the doctor's house, of which as you know the walls are practically all windows, until it became so hot for us with bullets coming in that we decided to seek cover downstairs in one of the little back rooms."[123]

This was just the beginning of the wave of destruction and carnage that overtook the town. "We had not been there for more than five minutes when the most terrific explosion took place, shaking the house to its foundations; the little window in the room where we were was blown completely in and we were smothered in dirt and debris." This explosion was a federal commander's destruction of the federal headquarters, the *jefatura de armas*, where large amounts of ammunition had been concentrated. According to Muñoz, the lieutenant colonel of cavalry who was the commander of the ammunition dump had committed an act of supreme heroism by preferring to blow himself up together with revolutionary troops who were entering the building rather than to surrender. He called this commander "an example of honor and sacrifice similar to the artillerymen of ancient times who after rendering their cannon useless took their own lives."[124]

Both Caldwell and the inhabitants of Zacatecas saw things in a very different way. "This will go down in history as one of the most cowardly, dastardly acts ever committed by the federals, and it is hard to believe that they could have found a man so base and so utterly devoid of feeling as to explode this mine right in the heart of town," Caldwell observed. "We saw Colonel Bernal (late *jefe político*) ride up in the direction of the Jefatura after the federal column had evacuated the city and later on it was proved that he was the brute who was responsible for this great calamity."

The whole block of buildings beginning with half of the Bank of Zacatecas right up to the "La Palma" (which is also badly wrecked) is one heap of ruins. The Hotel de la Plaza, Nacho Flores' house, and as far down as the Correo de Mexico on the opposite side of the street is also so badly damaged that the buildings will probably have to be taken down. There are hundreds of bodies buried in the debris as at the time of the explosion a great number of federal soldiers were still in the Jefatura and the rebels were also entering in great numbers. Above the Botica de Guadalupe the whole family of Lic. Magallanes (twelve or thirteen in number) were blown to pieces. When I passed there next morning on my way to the Hotel Francis where I had been urgently called, I had to simply jump over dead bodies and dead horses. The streets were full of them everywhere; it was dreadful. On the Plaza the dead were lying everywhere, in many places one on top of the other.[125]

Anyone who after the explosion panicked and attempted to flee his house soon returned, prey to even more fear. "About 5:00 a hail of bullets fell in the town, something impossible to describe except by comparing it to a very severe hailstorm. I was told next day by General Almanza that at that time 20,000 rifles were being fired into the town from the heights surrounding Zacatecas."

In his description of the battle of Zacatecas, Angeles shows himself to have been strangely callous, rejoicing in the slaughter "from an artistic point of view." But that callousness stopped when specific lives were at issue. Soon after the capture of Zacatecas, some revolutionaries began to carry out a massive execution of prisoners.

Ignacio Muñoz was one of the federal officers who arrived in Zacatecas on the eve of the battle with the last federal reinforcements to be sent to the embattled city. Once federal resistance had disintegrated, Muñoz shed his uniform and put on civilian dress, hoping thus to elude capture by the revolutionaries. This hope proved to be vain; Muñoz was identified by a Villista officer and placed in a convoy of prisoners. The prisoner platoon, consisting of about 500 men, was taken to a nearby cemetery. There plain soldiers were separated from those from the rank of corporal upward who had exercised any kind of command in the federal army. The commanders stood in line waiting to be executed. "Some men, in all probability Villista chieftains, seized the prisoners by the arm, by their jacket, put a pistol to their head, and shot them. If the wounded man gave a sign of life he was shot again while he was lying on the ground and then he was dragged and thrown on a mountain of bodies."[126]

Like an Aztec victim waiting at the foot of the pyramid to be sacrificed, Muñoz waited his turn to be shot.

For a few minutes I must have lost the notion of time. I advanced automatically. . . . I thought of my mother. . . . I thought of my girlfriend in San Luis Potosí. . . . I even thought of fleeing, but there was no possibility of doing so. . . .

The sun was going down in the west. It sent its last rays on the hilltops on this spring afternoon. And the groups were still advancing.

Suddenly, when only a few men had to be shot before it was my turn and that of Zarate [a friend and companion of Muñoz's], I heard the sound of galloping horses.

A group of men arrived at the door of the cemetery. It was headed by General Felipe Angeles wearing a Texas hat . . . followed by a group of officers of his staff. . . .

He harshly upbraided the murderers; with the greatest energy he condemned these vile killers and ordered that those of us who were still alive should be brought to the station facing the Pullman in which he had installed his headquarters.[127]

Humanitarian concerns and adherence to what he considered to be the rules of war doubtless played an important role in Angeles's decision to curb the execution of prisoners. There were other factors motivating him too, however. It was rumored that his nephew was one of the prisoners who had been taken by the revolutionaries, and that Angeles hoped to save his life.[128] In addition, Angeles felt that he could use the retrieved prisoners to strengthen the División del Norte and perhaps even his own influence in it. Muñoz, his colleague Zarate, and all other retrieved prisoners were inducted into the Villista forces. At first they were reduced in rank to plain soldiers, but soon, because of their technical knowledge, many of them became officers again.[129]

The battle of Zacatecas proved to be the bloodiest in the history of the revolution against Huerta: 6,000 federals and 1,000 constitutionalists had died, 3,000 federals and 2,000 constitutionalists had been wounded, and a large number of civilians had been injured or killed.[130]

"In the streets of the town alone 850 bodies have been collected; I don't know the number of horses but there must have been several hundred," Caldwell noted. "Between Zacatecas and Guadalupe they are burning the dead, and I am told that an estimate of 3,000 had been handed in to the Governor as the number killed in that section."[131]

CHAPTER TEN

The Elusive Search for Peace

The Aftermath of the Battle of Zacatecas

The battle for Zacatecas was the greatest victory that any revolutionary army achieved in the campaign against Huerta. The way now seemed clear for Villa to march on Mexico City. The demoralized remnants of the federal army were no match for Villa's triumphant División del Norte, whose morale had been enormously bolstered by their victory. Huerta now realized that he was defeated, and only a few weeks later, he would resign and flee from Mexico. Nevertheless, Villa would not be able to achieve his aim of being the first of the revolutionary leaders to reach Mexico City.

It was not the federal army but the policy of the United States and his former ally Carranza that were the main impediments to Villa's continuing his triumphant march on the capital.

In a desperate move to stop Villa, Carranza embargoed all shipments of coal to the División del Norte. Since Mexico's main coal mines were located in Carranza-controlled territory in Coahuila, Villa found himself in a very difficult position, since he did not have the fuel for his troop trains. Nevertheless, this was not the main obstacle that he faced. He could have bought coal in the United States. His real problem was that the Wilson administration had embargoed all shipments of arms to Mexico in the days following the invasion of Veracruz.

Wilson's arms embargo was part of a strategy all U.S. administrations had followed and would continue to follow from the moment the Mexican revolution broke out. That strategy consisted in using the right to buy arms in the United States to influence events in Mexico on behalf of factions that the United States favored. In 1910–11, the Taft administration had refused demands by the Díaz government that it prohibit the sale of arms to Madero's revolutionaries. In 1912, in the hope of preventing Orozco from toppling Madero, President Taft had decreed an arms embargo against all revolutionary factions in Mexico. That embargo was maintained by President Wilson in the first few months after Huerta's coup, when the U.S. president still hoped that Huerta would resign in favor of a conservative candidate, such as the foreign secretary, Federico Gamboa, whom Wilson could support. It was only after the break between Huerta and the Wilson administration that the U.S. president shifted his sympathies to the constitutionalists and first made it easy for them to smuggle arms across the border and then, in February 1914, revoked the arms embargo, thus allowing the constitutionalists to buy unlimited amounts of arms and ammunition in the United States. This decision by the U.S. president was enthusiastically greeted by Villa, who called Wilson "the most just man in the world. All Mexicans will love him. . . . We [the Villistas] will look upon the United States as our friend."[1]

It is doubtful whether Villa's enthusiasm for Wilson remained as strong after the reasons for the renewed U.S. embargo were explained to him by the U.S. special envoy, George Carothers. He was told that it was owing to Carranza's aggressive anti-American declarations, and that if the constitutionalists modified their behavior, the United States would change its policy.[2] Why, he must have asked himself, was the embargo being extended to him, who after all had been the one revolutionary leader who had refused to go along with Carranza's anti-American pronouncements?

Villa must have been even more puzzled and indignant when he learned that only a short time after having decreed a general embargo on arms to Mexico, the Wilson administration had partially lifted it, but only in favor of Carranza, not of Villa. Limited shipments of U.S. arms were now allowed to proceed to the Mexican port of Tampico, which was controlled by Carranza's faction, but no arms were allowed to cross the border by land into Villa-held territory. Villa now attempted to both pressure and persuade Wilson to change his policies. The pressure consisted in telling Wilson that Villa's División del Norte would withdraw to Chihuahua and would only be able to resume operations against Huerta once "the American government allows the importation of all material to the custom houses, which are under the control of our forces in the state of Chihuahua."[3]

Villa obviously believed that Wilson wanted Huerta defeated as rapidly as possible, and that he might be persuaded to change his policy to enable Villa to proceed with his campaign against the Mexican dictator. At the same time, Villa tried to reassure Wilson and quiet his fears that such a measure might lead to a new civil war between his forces and those of Carranza. "For my part I protest in the most solemn manner that no personal ambition influences me in this fight. . . . I protest likewise that we have no intention to fight with the forces addicted [sic] to Mr. Carranza which are fighting for the same ideals and aspirations. We shall only defend ourselves in case we are attacked," Villa wrote Wilson.[4] The U.S. administration refused to alter its policy, however, and Villa halted his advance on Mexico City.

The Wilson administration's motives are still hotly debated. Why would the U.S. government embargo all arms to the one faction that had supported its attack on Veracruz while it lifted the embargo against Carranza, who had so vociferously condemned U.S. intervention? One interpretation is that the U.S. government, worried by the popular nature of Villismo, had swung its support to Carranza. This is doubtful, since only a few months later, the arms embargo against Villa was lifted, and it would not be reimposed during the civil war between him and Carranza. What is more likely is that after Carranza's vehement protest against the U.S. invasion of Veracruz, the Wilson administration had become convinced that it had no way to really control any faction in Mexico, and that the only way it could exercise influence was to prevent one faction from becoming dominant by playing off the factions against each other. This was probably also the primary reason why the Wilson administration tried for a time to salvage the remains of the federal establishment and to bring together the remnants of Huertismo, Carranza, and Villa in a coalition government, which would not have been possible had Huerta been decisively defeated by Villa, and had Carranza been shunted aside.[5] In addition, a move southward by Villa might have led to a civil war among the revolutionaries before Huerta was decisively defeated, which would also have been undesirable in Wilson's view.

Villa now had several options. The first was to withdraw from the revolution, to consolidate his hold over Chihuahua and Durango, and to resist any attempt by either Carranza or any other faction in Mexico to drive him out of his bailiwick. Such an option was fraught with risks. If Carranza dominated the rest of Mexico, and if his government were recognized by the United States, which would give him the exclusive right to buy arms, Villa's control of Chihuahua and Durango might prove impossible to maintain. Villa therefore never opted to do this.

The second option was very different. Villa could attempt to make a deal with the federal army for its arms, and possibly to recruit a large number of its men into his own forces. For a brief period of time, he seriously considered such a deal.

With its army reeling from successive defeats, and after the U.S. occupation of Veracruz, it was clear to the conservative establishment in Mexico City that it would never win in the field. It nevertheless still had hopes of repeating its successful strategy of 1911, when, in spite of military defeats, it had by negotiation salvaged both the federal army and much of the federal bureaucracy. Such hopes at first glance seemed illusory. Not only had the federal forces suffered far greater defeats than in 1911, but in 1914 the U.S. government, in contrast to its stance in 1911, seemed absolutely opposed to the Huerta regime. The conservatives nevertheless pinned their hopes on the divisions among the revolutionaries and the cooling of relations between the Wilson administration and the revolutionaries after the U.S. invasion of Veracruz.

The first focus of their efforts was the United States. After the U.S. occupation of Veracruz, Wilson had proposed a conference to mediate the dispute between Mexico and the United States. It was to include representatives of the United States, and of the three largest and most important South American countries—Argentina, Brazil, and Chile—acting as mediators, as well as representatives of both the Huerta administration and the constitutionalists. The conference, which the constitutionalists refused to attend, took place at Niagara Falls. Huerta's delegates suggested that the United States should approve a plan whereby a neutral government would be established in Mexico. Wilson was absolutely opposed to such a plan. He knew that the revolutionaries would never accept it, and that the only way the United States could impose it would be by force. Nevertheless, he did consider a different scheme that would still have allowed the conservatives to retain a measure of influence in the country. Wilson's plan was for an armistice between the federal government and the revolutionaries. At least in the short run, that would have meant the preservation of the federal army. A provisional president, who would be a constitutionalist, but who would not be either Villa or Carranza, would be named and would conduct elections for the presidency of Mexico. His authority would be shared with "a board of three persons, acceptable to the revolutionaries, but one of whom should be a conservative, not actively identified with the revolution."[6]

The revolutionaries absolutely refused to accept any plans for an armistice with the federal government, however, and Carranza insisted on unconditional and absolute surrender of the federal forces.

As the revolutionaries continued their advance on Mexico City, Huerta, fearing that his life was in imminent danger, resigned on July 15 and fled Mexico, naming Francisco Carbajal, chief justice of the supreme court, as provisional president to succeed him. Carbajal had been one of the negotiators who had arranged for the compromise between Madero and the Porfirian authorities in Ciudad Juárez in 1911. This time, Carbajal hoped to exploit the increasing conflicts between the revolutionaries. He first attempted to make a deal with Carranza. His emissaries suggested to the First Chief that an armistice be signed between the two sides and the old Maderista legislature that Huerta had dissolved be recalled into session to elect a provisional president and declare a general amnesty. Carranza flatly rejected this proposal and demanded unconditional surrender.[7]

The failure of Carbajal's plan by no means ended the attempt by the leadership of the federal army to ensure its institutional survival. A few days after Carranza had refused to accept Carbajal's terms, General Refugio Velasco, the commander of the federal forces, offered the services of his army to Carranza. He implied that unless Carranza accepted these services, the federal troops would allow Zapata's army, which was closest to Mexico City, to occupy the capital. Rumors also began to circulate in Mexico City that the federal commanders were contemplating a deal whereby they would join Villa's División del Norte.[8]

These rumors were not unfounded. Acting as Carbajal's emissary, Juan Hernández, an engineer whose father had for a time commanded the federal forces in Chihuahua during the Madero revolution in 1911, had in fact offered José María Maytorena, the governor of Sonora, the surrender of the federal army. Maytorena refused to accept the surrender and instead sent Hernández to Chihuahua, escorted by his confidant Alberto Piña, to talk with Villa. Villa received Hernández, and, according to Piña, who was present, Villa was at first very receptive to his suggestions. Hernández told Villa that the federal army was ready to surrender to him. There are differing accounts as to what the army wanted in return. According to Piña's account, Hernández asked only that the lives of the federal officers and soldiers be spared.[9] According to other accounts, they wanted much more, hoping to be integrated into the División del Norte under the command of Felipe Ángeles.[10]

According to these accounts, Villa seems to have reached some kind of an accommodation with the federal representative and ordered a telegram be sent to Carbajal asking him to remain in office and to refuse to make any deal with Carranza.

Villa evidently soon had second thoughts about the agreement. The acceptance of the surrender of the federal forces posed major logistical, strategic, military, and political problems. Villa's army was concentrated in the north, separated by hundreds of miles from Mexico City, where the bulk of the federal forces were stationed. The troops of the Army of the Northeast, loyal to Carranza, stood between Villa and the federal capital. The only way Villa could have accepted the surrender of the federal forces was through an armed conflict with his fellow revolutionaries. The federal troops could have fought their way north, Villa could have fought his way south, or both could have attacked Pablo González's army simultaneously. Villa now consulted Angeles, who strongly objected to the pact, saying, "Our enemies, the Carrancistas, and the revolutionaries in general might regard our reaching an agreement with the Huertistas as suggested as a betrayal of our cause." Villa was hesitant, saying that if he did not sign such a pact, Carranza would do so and use the federal troops against him. Angeles finally persuaded him, however, and the telegram, which had already been sent, was canceled. Hernández returned empty-handed to Mexico City.[11]

There was, interestingly, one possibility of a peaceful agreement with the federal army that Villa never considered. That was for the federal forces to surrender to Zapata, whose army was after all closest to Mexico City, and who in theory could have accepted that surrender. Villa seems never to have considered this. Perhaps, since he had not yet made any agreement with Zapata, he saw no reason to allow the latter to occupy Mexico City; perhaps he believed that the federal army, which had been fighting a bloody war against the peasantry of Morelos, considered the Zapatistas to be their most deadly enemies and would never have surrendered to them.

Villa's fear that the surrender of the federal army would greatly strengthen Carranza and that he would make some kind of a deal with the federal army was not unjustified. Only a few days after Villa rejected Carbajal's offer, Obregón signed the treaties of Teoloyucan with the federal commanders. The federal army was to surrender all its arms and equipment to the Carrancistas, and although in the end they were all to be demobilized, federal troops were to man the defenses of Mexico City against the Zapatistas until they could be replaced by Carrancista troops. On August 15, 1914, Obregón's troops triumphantly entered Mexico City.

Villa's Political and Military Counteroffensive

With Carranza strengthened by Obregón's occupation of Mexico City, Villa now had only two options left if he did not want to remain isolated and marginalized in his northern stronghold. The first was to resort to politics and the second to wage a kind of proxy war in Sonora.

Villa's political aim was to elaborate a national program that would convince the Americans that Villa did not want national power for himself, that he was in favor of peace, and that he both ardently supported land reform and respected the principle of private property. This program was also addressed to all of Carranza's enemies within the revolutionary movement, to all the revolutionary caudillos who were not affiliated with any faction, and to Carranza's generals: it was aimed at creating a national anti-Carrancista coalition.

In a long conversation with one of Woodrow Wilson's special representatives to Mexico, Paul Fuller, Villa described his national plan for Mexico. In his report to Wilson, Fuller, who was greatly impressed by the northern revolutionary, wrote: "Villa is an unusually quiet man, gentle in manner, low-voiced, slow of speech, earnest, and occasionally emotional in expression, but always subdued, with an undercurrent of sadness with . . . no outward manifestation of vanity or self-sufficiency." Fuller felt that Villa stood in great fear of what Carranza would do to Mexico. "He then expressed his dread that the struggle for constitutional regeneration would end in disorder and in the substitution of one master for those of the old regime who had been displaced at the cost of four years of conflict and bloodshed."[12]

In this conversation with Fuller, Villa outlined a social and political program that he felt could transform Mexico and guarantee peace among the revolutionary factions. The cornerstone of Villa's social program was agrarian reform. "The oppression of the worker by these wealthy landowners is inhuman," he insisted in his talk with Fuller. He attempted to reassure the U.S. envoy that he had no intention of simply taking away the properties of the rich. "We will not confiscate; the government will take the lands for the public good and make just compensation; they will pay the owners their valuation, attested by them for the purposes of taxation; if they insist that the newer valuation they insist upon today is a true value, they may have the alternative of paying the arrears of taxes on the real value which they have hitherto concealed."

In Villa's agrarian plans, his soldiers played a special role. He told Fuller that he had 27,000 men under his command. "To disband these men and set them adrift would be a cruelty to them and a disadvantage to the community. Most of them would find it difficult to get remunerative labor; in the best of times their wages were not sufficient even for the most frugal maintenance; unemployment would create distress, breed habits of indolence, and fritter away the high spirit of service and self-reliance which patriotic opportunity and strict military discipline have bred in them." Villa repeated his aim of creating military colonies, "giving each an allotment of land on some homestead principle which would require them to utilize it in order to acquire title, or putting a price upon it, payable by small yearly installments upon an amortization plan. For a time they would remain subject to military discipline, with a few hours of military drill and instruction each day, keeping up the spirit of obedience and of public service."

The political solution that Villa envisaged both to resolve the short-term conflicts among the revolutionary factions and to create a new political structure was to recreate the Mexican state from below. "All that he and the majority of the Constitutionalist party were insistent upon was that an election of municipal, state, and federal officials, including the president, be proceeded with at once."[13] In later statements Villa would make it clear that municipal and state elections should precede that of the federal authorities. This would make it very difficult for the central government to impose its candidates as it had done in the past.

The program that Villa offered to Fuller was addressed both to Woodrow Wilson and to other factions within the revolutionary movement, including factions loyal to Carranza, as well as to the popular forces of the revolution. It offered each audience much of what it wanted to hear and what it hoped to derive from the revolution.

Woodrow Wilson had stated that he wanted a combination of democratic elections and land reform, but also respect for the principle of private property. Villa's program offered all that. There would be elections at every level, the large estates would be divided but there would not be expropriations, since the landowners would have the option of paying the huge back taxes they owed the state on the basis of the real valuation of their property. For example the assessed value of the Terrazas' property for tax purposes was 1,700,000 pesos, while the real value was 50,000,000. Since it is likely that other landowners' tax assessments were calculated in the same way, the government would have few problems in confiscating large estates and maintaining the fiction of absolute respect for private property. And by constantly insisting that he respected the principle of private property, Villa quieted Wilson's fears that he might apply the same principles to American landowners in Mexico.

To the other factions within the revolutionary movement, Villa offered de facto control of their respective regions. Since local and regional elections would precede national elections, there would be no national authority to supervise the quality and honesty of these local elections. In regions where popular forces were in control, as in Morelos, genuine popular elections could be expected. In other regions, where caudillos had assumed power, they would have control of local authorities. This plan was in fact a recognition of the military status quo, with each faction exercising control over its own region. It also implied that the central government that would emerge from all of these elections would have to have the approval of all factions and would de facto be an extremely weak government.

Apart from decentralization, the strongest incentive for the popular forces to join or remain in his camp was Villa's insistence on land reform. In later formulations of his program, he would nevertheless largely leave the type, amount, and structure of land reform up to the different regions—that is, up to each revolutionary faction.

This program, whose main tenets were regional autonomy, a weak central government, and land reform, would constitute the basis for all of Villa's future negotiations with other factions. Again and again, he insisted that he himself did not want to be president of Mexico, and that he was genuinely in agreement with initiatives that would bring a neutral and perhaps even a Carrancista (although not Carranza himself) to the presidency of a weak government of Mexico.

While this program constituted Villa's third option and was in effect the carrot offered to all other factions, Villa's fourth option was of a very different nature. It consisted in waging a proxy war in Sonora, one of the main bastions of the Carranza movement, and thus aimed at forcing Carranza or his lieutenants to compromise with Villa on a national scale. After the break with Carranza, Villa not only openly encouraged Maytorena to take control of the state of Sonora but went one step further. When Carranza decided to send his troops to subdue Maytorena, whose forces numbered under 2,000 men, Villa stated unequivocally that if that happened, his own forces would enter Sonora. Carranza desisted, and a regional conflict in which fewer than 2,000 men were engaged on each side suddenly became central to the Mexican Revolution. With the help of the Yaqui Indians, Maytorena soon gained the upper hand and assumed control of most of the state. The forces loyal to Carranza, headed by Plutarco Elías Calles and Benjamin Hill, were forced to retreat into a narrow corridor along the border with the United States.

For the Carrancistas, Sonora was of enormous importance. It was the home state of some of their most important leaders, above all of Obregón. It was from there that they drew their strength, and it was from there that a disproportionate number of their soldiers and officers originated.

The situation in Sonora was one of the chief factors that brought Carranza's generals to the negotiating table with Villa, but it was not the only one. Carranza and Villa considered their break to be irreconcilable, but the vast majority of the Mexican people and of the revolutionary armies were not ready for renewed war. The conflict between Villa and Carranza had only emerged into the open in June 1914, and apart from squabbles over the structure of the army, there seemed to be no real ideological differences between the two leaders. In addition, both sides needed to impress upon the Americans that they were the ones who wanted peace.

In the latter part of June 1914, the generals of the Division of the Northeast, in spite of the fact that they were closest to Carranza, suggested to Villa and his generals that they arrange a conference in which some kind of agreement between their respective forces could be reached. They warned Villa that "at a moment when the whole world looks upon us it would be a crime to fight among ourselves." Only the federal army, which they had vanquished in the field, would profit from such a division.[14]

Villa accepted, and eight emissaries, four from each division, met in the city of Torreón on July 5–6. They signed an agreement, ratified by both armies, that dealt with the immediate causes of discord between Villa and Carranza, with the nature of the postrevolutionary regime, and with the long-term solution of Mexico's problems. For the short term, it was agreed that Villa would recognize Carranza as the First Chief of the revolution and that Carranza would in turn recognize Villa's leadership of the División del Norte and give all the military commanders substantial freedom of action in waging their campaigns. The delegates also called on Carranza to resume deliveries of coal and ammunition to the División del Norte.

This agreement amounted to a kind of armistice between the two factions. The delegates decided to go further, however. As soon as the federal army was defeated, the First Chief was to convoke a convention of revolutionary leaders to determine the future of the revolution. Only the revolutionary forces would be represented at it, with one delegate for each 1,000 soldiers. It was not the soldiers, however, but the military leaders who would determine who the delegates would be. This was clearly a measure that would subordinate Carranza to the authority of the revolutionary armies. As a counterweight to this supremacy of the military, the agreement stipulated that no military man could be elected to the presidency of Mexico. In addition, it stated that one of the first tasks of the interim president would be to organize national elections for president of the republic and to conduct local elections in every part of Mexico.

The agreement also contained a somewhat ambiguous statement about conditions in the state of Sonora. On one hand, it emphasized that Maytorena's authority as governor should be respected. On the other, it suggested that he should resign if that was in the interests of peace. The resolution of the conference ended with a clear call for social and economic reform that had been lacking in Carranza's Plan of Guadalupe. "Since the Divisions of the North and the Northeast understand that the present struggle pits the powerless against the powerful," the Declaration of Torreón concluded, "both commit themselves to fight for the complete disappearance of the ex-federal army, which will be replaced by the constitutionalist army; they commit themselves to set up a democratic regime in our country, to punish the Roman Catholic clergy, which has openly aligned itself with Huerta, and to carry out the economic emancipation of the proletariat through an equitable distribution of land, and by securing the welfare of industrial workers."[15]

Although this plan provided a genuine blueprint for a temporary truce, as well as an accord for the future of Mexico, neither Carranza nor Villa was ready to abide by it. Through a clever political maneuver, Carranza had made sure that he would be able to circumvent any clause of the agreement with which he did not agree. The delegates of the Division of the Northeast had come to the conference with his agreement but not as his official emissaries. Thus the First Chief did not feel bound by their agreement and soon said so openly. While he agreed with the idea of a convention, he clearly stated that to a large degree he would determine its composition and thus prevent any majority of hostile military chiefs from dominating it. He did not feel bound by the social and economic agenda the conference had proposed, since he felt that it did not have the right to determine the program of the revolution. While he agreed in theory to the practical compromises the delegates had suggested, he never sent the promised ammunition, arms, and coal to Villa.[16]

Perhaps because he anticipated Carranza's reaction, perhaps because he felt that he had a better plan for Mexico, Villa did not feel bound by the decisions of the conference either. None of the three full delegates he sent to the conference was a member of his inner circle. Two, Manuel Bonilla and Miguel Silva, were prominent Maderista intellectuals, and the third, General José Isabel Robles, was a man not really close to him. The only member of the delegation who was in any way close to Villa was its nonvoting member, Roque González Garza, a colonel who had little influence in the División del Norte, although he did have good relations with Villa.

In a letter written only a few days later to Maytorena, Villa tried to convince the governor that in spite of what had been agreed on at the conference, he was by no means ready to sacrifice him. An emissary from Villa and Angeles assured Maytorena that "as far as the conferences that have recently taken place in Torreón in relation to the Villa-Carranza conflict as well as concerning its results, they [Angeles and Villa] are telling you through me that their only aim was to simulate for foreign consumption that there are no divisions between Villa and

Carranza; their real aim is to prepare the radical elimination of Carranza through a well-studied and articulated plan."[17]

The plan represented a shift by Villa from a southern strategy to what could be called a western, or a Sonoran, strategy. What is remarkable about this plan is that in many respects Villa and Angeles wanted to take measures in Sonora that only a few weeks later Carranza would carry out in Mexico City.

The first part of the plan consisted of accepting an offer made to Maytorena by the head of the only remaining federal garrison in the state of Sonora, in Guaymas, to surrender to the Sonoran governor. In secret negotiations with the federal commanders, Maytorena's confidant Piña would establish the terms of surrender. Officially, such negotiations would never have taken place. Maytorena himself was to go to Guaymas, assume the leadership of the besieging troops, personally call on them to attack the federal garrison in Guaymas, and ready them for the attack. Then he would accept the surrender of the federal troops. Obviously, the impression would emerge that the federal army had capitulated to his superior forces, and his prestige would thus be greatly enhanced. With his troops now relieved of the task of besieging Guaymas, he would then proceed northward, attack the remaining units loyal to Carranza, and imprison their leaders.

Once he was in complete control of Sonora, Maytorena was to sponsor a conference "of several of the governors who had been deposed by Huerta and eliminated by Carranza in order to sign, together with you, a manifesto to the whole nation, which should also be circulated outside the country, in which the participants would disown Carranza as First Chief of the revolution. The participants would then convene a convention of genuine revolutionaries . . . whose primary objective will be to designate someone to replace Carranza." The División del Norte would give its full military support to the decisions of the conference, and Villa and Angeles proposed sending 5,000 to 10,000 men to reinforce Maytorena in Sonora, insisting that "it would be more convenient if the civilians initiated the process of nonrecognition of Carranza, so that any suspicion of a military coup could be dismissed."[18]

Although the first part of the plan, the surrender of the federal garrison to Maytorena, was in fact carried out, its second and third parts, the convocation of an anti-Carrancista convention in Sonora and the arrival of Villista troops in the state, were never implemented.

While there is no evidence to indicate the reasons for the plan's failure, it is likely that Maytorena was not enthusiastic about it. The last thing he wanted was for outside troops to occupy his state. This would have meant a significant curtailment of his power and authority. In addition, he did not need them. After the surrender of Guaymas, he had in fact assumed control of most of Sonora, and troops loyal to Carranza were confined to a few northern towns along the border with the United States. In addition, he was never interested in securing national power.

When this plan failed, Villa began to realize that Maytorena was not a pawn in his hands, and that the Sonoran governor was in fact using him as much as he was using Maytorena. This realization may have led to a brief but dramatic shift in attitude by Villa toward his Sonoran ally. What brought it about was a second meeting with the Carrancistas, which seemed of greater significance than the first. This time it involved Villa personally, as well as the most important general in Carranza's forces, Alvaro Obregón. Of all of Carranza's generals, Obregón had the most to lose if Maytorena assumed control of Sonora. The bulk of the forces that were loyal to him came from Sonora, and if he were deprived of his hinterland, he would be tremendously weakened and in fact completely dependent on Carranza's goodwill.

A Dramatic Confrontation: Villa and Obregón

Obregón now resorted to a desperate expedient that many of his supporters considered an act of lunacy, since it put him completely at Villa's mercy. He decided to proceed to the lion's den, and with a small escort of no more than 20 men he traveled to Ciudad Chihuahua to meet with Villa. Villa at first did not take the meeting very seriously and considered it a charade, destined mainly for foreign and domestic public consumption, as he had the conference at Torreón.

Villa warmly welcomed Obregón with a huge guard of honor upon his arrival in Chihuahua, invited him to stay at his home, and sent a telegram to Maytorena asking him to suspend hostilities with Carranza's troops, but his real intentions were quite different. Only five days after having called on Maytorena to end the fighting in Sonora, he sent him a private wire telling him the exact contrary. "Do not heed my telegrams concerning the suspension of hostilities," he wired him, "since they have been sent under special circumstances." He assured Maytorena of his "unconditional support," offered him arms, and told him to "recover from the usurpers all the cities they are still holding . . . proceed with all energy against our common enemy." Villa ended his telegram by reassuring the Sonoran governor that Obregón's mission would have no effect on his attitude to the conflict in Sonora. "General Obregón is coming here today asking me to accompany him to Sonora to put an end to the conflict that they have provoked; you can be sure that I shall not come with him, and should I go to Sonora, I shall do so alone, since I want things to be arranged in a just manner, and that can only be achieved by completely eliminating those elements who with such injustice have attacked and continue to attack your government."[19]

Thus reassured by Villa, Maytorena refused to cease hostilities and was laying siege to the frontier town of Nogales, where the bulk of Obregón's supporters, led by Calles, were concentrated.

Only one day after Villa had encouraged Maytorena to fight on, promised him unconditional support, and declared that he would never support Obregón's efforts to find a compromise, Villa's attitude to the Sonoran problem underwent a dramatic shift. He decided to join Obregón in a mission to Sonora in order to reach a compromise that would both prevent Maytorena's complete control of the state and avoid the complete elimination of Obregón's forces in Sonora. The reason for Villa's change of heart was less Obregón's proverbial charm than the fact that Obregón had now outlined the kind of deal he was willing to make and told Villa that he would support him in his endeavors to prevent Carranza from becoming president of Mexico.

At Obregón's suggestion, Villa arranged a meeting with Maytorena and the latter's two main military commanders, the Yaqui leaders Urbalejo and Acosta. At that meeting, Obregón unleashed all his rhetorical skills against Maytorena. "I ask you, here in the presence of General Villa and of these other gentlemen," he relates in his memoirs, "to state all the charges that you as governor of the state can make against me."

Obregón then asked Maytorena to produce any telegrams or any proof that would show that Obregón had urged his supporters not to recognize Maytorena as governor. Since Maytorena could produce no proof of Obregón's disloyalty, the latter now asked the governor "why he called me a traitor, if he had no concrete accusations he could level at me."

Maytorena remained silent; then Villa, taking part in the conversation, addressed Maytorena, telling him, "Answer, Mr. Governor."

Maytorena answered, "I have a custom of not immediately answering questions that are asked of me."[20]

Maytorena's silence was certainly not because he had no charges he could level against Obregón. After all, Obregón had supported Calles in his efforts to topple Maytorena. Maytorena's silence was probably because he was puzzled, confused, and did not know what to make of this conference. Only five days earlier, Villa had told him that he would never join Obregón in his peace mission and that he should disregard every message in favor of compromise that he sent him. As the conference proceeded, the Sonoran governor became more and more uncertain as Villa failed to provide him with the "unconditional support" that he had promised. Whatever hope he may have had that all this was only a charade disappeared when Obregón suggested a compromise and Villa pointedly said: "If no agreement is signed, it will be because you do not want one. . . . look at the generous proposal that Obregón is making."[21]

Under pressure from Villa, Maytorena signed an agreement suggested by Obregón that at first glance had all the characteristics of a genuine compromise. It stipulated that the Sonoran governor would recognize Obregón as his commander in chief, and Obregón would appoint him commander of all military forces in the state of Sonora, including those he had been fighting.

It was a compromise that satisfied Villa and Obregón but that none of the parties who were doing the fighting really wanted. For Maytorena, it meant that he had lost his independence. Since he was now subordinate to Obregón, what was there to prevent his commander in chief from deposing him? That was in fact Obregón's intention. "I did not for a moment assume," he wrote in his memoirs, "that the difficulties had been solved by naming Maytorena military commander of the state of Sonora; but I was convinced . . . if I gave orders which he would not obey I could remove him from his command."[22] Maytorena had hoped with Villa's support to completely defeat his opponents in the state, and now he was forced to cease all operations against them. The fact that they had been nominally placed under his command meant very little as long as Obregón could countermand any order he gave to disarm them.

Conversely, the leaders of Obregón's forces in Sonora, Calles and Hill, were worried that even their nominal subordination to Maytorena might allow the governor decisively to weaken them. Perhaps they were also afraid that Obregón might sacrifice them in order to come to a full agreement with Villa.

It is thus not surprising that the agreement did not last even 24 hours. Only a few hours after it had been signed, supporters of Maytorena published a pamphlet containing a violent denunciation of Obregón:

> The people of Sonora have been insulted, and the person most responsible is General Obregón, who exiled many constitutionalists from Mexico. . . . Alvaro Obregón and his followers are the bastards of Sonora, they are parasites and like a new Nero want to slash the belly of their mother country, destroying its breast, and they are not worthy to live among us.
>
> Sonorans, shall we allow those who have fought against the sovereignty of the state to continue to insult us and to live among us?

It was signed by "various citizens of Sonora."[23]

While Maytorena disclaimed all responsibility for the pamphlet, Obregón was convinced that he had in fact engineered its publication. That gave him a pretext to reject an agreement that his own supporters were extremely unhappy with.

Villa at this point became convinced that Maytorena was an obstacle to the kind of agreement he wished to reach with Obregón, and he was willing to sacrifice his erstwhile ally. On September 3, without consulting Maytorena, Villa and Obregón agreed that one of the few Sonoran revolutionaries who had remained neutral in the conflict between Maytorena and Obregón should become governor of Sonora. This was Juan Cabral, the only Sonoran revolutionary leader who had called for the implementation of major agrarian reform throughout the state,[24] which may have been one of the main reasons why Villa was ready to accept his candidacy.

In return for Villa's sacrifice of Maytorena, Obregón was ready to sacrifice Carranza. The two men reached an agreement, largely along the lines of the program of compromise and unity that Villa had suggested to Woodrow Wilson's representative, Paul Fuller, only a week before. Carranza would become provisional president but would not be allowed to be a candidate for the presidential elections, which were to be held within a few weeks of the signing of the agreement. The same applied to all the military leaders of the revolution. National elections would be preceded by local and regional elections, which meant that the national government would have difficulties in imposing its own candidates. The agreement was not only political in nature. It called for the interim governors to set up commissions in every state composed of representatives from local districts to study the agrarian problem and elaborate reform projects that would be submitted to the state legislatures.

In return, Obregón agreed to a corresponding "sacrifice" of his own troops. As soon as Cabral took command of the military forces in Sonora, the troops led by Calles and Hill would be withdrawn to the town of Casas Grandes in Chihuahua, where they would be located in the midst of Villa's territory. The sacrifice of his own men was only a small part of what Obregón was willing to concede to Villa in order to sack Maytorena. Far more important for Villa was the fact that Obregón was willing to sacrifice Carranza.

When Villa and Obregón bade farewell to each other, they did so in an optimistic spirit. They were convinced they had found a way to solve Mexico's problems and to maintain peace. Obregón probably shared the sentiments Villa had expressed to him on the first day the two men met: "The fate of our country in is your hands and in mine; if we unite, it won't take a minute for us to dominate the country."[25]

What both men had underestimated was the unwillingness of the sacrificial lambs to be sacrificed. The first negative reaction came from Carranza. In a letter to both Obregón and Villa, Carranza bluntly told both military chieftains that he did not accept their proposals. He did agree to the first clause of their agreement, which was a major concession to him, that he should assume executive power for the present. He also voiced some vague agreement with the decision to carry out local elections. All the other provisions, including the restrictions imposed on his electability as president of Mexico and the commitment to agrarian reform, were, he stated, too important to be decided by a few men alone.[26] Only a much broader forum with a far greater degree of representativity, could make decisions on such important issues. That forum he decided to convoke on October 1, 1914. Its composition was not based on the agreement of Torreón whereby only military leaders selected to represent every 1,000 members of the revolutionary army would participate. Instead, it was a forum constituted by Carranza. It would include the governors he had appointed as well as all the military chieftains of the revolution, again to a large degree chosen by Carranza.

In Sonora, too, both parties to the conflict vehemently rejected the Villa-Obregón accord. Maytorena, who had fought for years to be governor of the state, was not about to relinquish his power to any compromise candidate. He told Angeles that he was opposed to Cabral's taking over the state and asked Angeles to make this fact known to Villa.[27] Calles and Hill not only feared that their planned withdrawal from Sonora would jeopardize their political ambitions but were even more worried at the idea of being evacuated to Chihuahua and placed at Villa's mercy. In the event, both sides did their best to sabotage the Villa-Obregón agreement by breaking the cease-fire and resuming fighting.

Although he had not been able to deliver on Villa's most important demand, that Carranza should not be a candidate for president, Obregón returned to Chihuahua in the hope of persuading Villa to make a unilateral concession—namely, to replace his ally Maytorena with the neutral Cabral. Villa would get practically nothing in return except for the withdrawal of the forces directly subordinate to Obregón and commanded by General Hill from Sonora. Villa probably felt duped and must have suspected Obregón of coming to Chihuahua with very different aims than the ones he proclaimed. This was in fact the case. One of the main aims of Obregón's journey was to undermine Villa's authority among some of his generals and troops. As he later wrote in his memoirs, Obregón had gone to Chihuahua "to remove from Villa some of the good elements who had joined him in the fight against the usurpation but who repudiated many of the actions of their leader."[28] This was a dangerous undertaking with any leader under any circumstances, but doubly dangerous with a man as deeply suspicious of treachery as Villa. Villa's suspicions increased when he received news that hostilities had broken out between Maytorena's forces and those of Obregón's General Benjamin Hill.

Villa's suspicions produced one of the best known and most dramatic confrontations in the history of the Mexican revolution. As he was having a friendly dinner with Raúl Madero, Obregón was suddenly summoned to Villa's presence.

Villa broke out in one of his ferocious rages. He demanded that Obregón immediately order Hill to evacuate Sonora, accused him of betraying him, and ordered a firing squad to stand by so that Obregón could be executed as soon as Villa gave the order to do so.[29]

Soledad Armendariz de Orduño, a young girl who had been hired as Villa's secretary a few months before, who was present in an adjoining room, and who had generally known Villa as a quiet man who rarely used profanity, was profoundly shaken when she saw him with "his eyes blazing in fury and using very harsh words." According to her, both men used equally harsh language and both were on the point of drawing their guns.[30]

As Villa was telling him, "I will have you shot in a moment," Obregón, according to his memoirs, kept calm. "As far as I personally am concerned, you will do me a lot of good, since through such a death you will give me a personality I do not have, and the only one to suffer from this will be you."[31] Hearing of the planned execution, Raúl Madero and Angeles attempted to dissuade Villa. Angeles went to see Luz Corral, who with great difficulty persuaded Villa that executing Obregón in his own home would brand him in the eyes of future generations as a man incapable of respecting the rules of hospitality.

She told him that if he executed Obregón, the foreign press would write the next day: "'Francisco Villa has ordered the assassination of his colleague and friend, and above all of his guest,' and you know that hospitality is sacred in all parts of the world, and [if] in 100 years they will say, 'Francisco Villa was right in shooting Obregón,' for many years more, though, Francisco Villa will be the murderer of his companion, the friend and the guest."

"I thought," Luz Corral wrote, "that he would tell me that what he did was no concern of mine."[32]

To her surprise, Villa said nothing. After resting for a moment, he got up, canceled the planned execution, and called for a train to take Obregón back to Mexico City. Obregón describes him as tearfully telling him: "Francisco Villa is not a traitor; Francisco Villa does not kill men who cannot defend themselves, and even less will kill you, *compañerito*, who are my guest. I shall prove to you that Pancho Villa is a man, and that [even] if Carranza does not respect him, he will fulfill his duty to his country."[33]

Villa then left the room. On his way out, he saw his trembling secretary. He looked at her and said, "The only thing I regret is that this young girl should have heard me saying everything I said. I am very sorry that she became so fearful." He then ordered two glasses of orange juice, offered her one to calm her nerves, and asked her, "Can you excuse me, my girl?"[34]

Obregón continued to retain his calm. The two men had sat down at dinner, and Obregón joked as if nothing had happened. That same evening a previously planned dance for the generals of the División del Norte took place, and Obregón danced until four in the morning. When asked by one of his subordinates, Carlos Robinson, what had happened, Obregón told him, "I really don't know. I was thinking how to obtain a safe conduct from the Don Venustiano in heaven."[35] He was obviously referring to St. Peter, whose beard was reputed to be as long as that of Carranza.

Although Villa loved to dance, he did not attend the celebration. This was a sign to Obregón that things were not yet over. Villa's generals were profoundly divided on the advisability of executing Obregón, and both groups attempted to influence Villa. The group seeking to spare Obregón's life was mainly made up of Villa's civilian and military middle-class backers: Robles, Angeles, Aguirre Benavides, Raúl Madero, Roque González Garza, Miguel Silva, Angel del Caso, Díaz Lombardo, and, surprisingly, Manuel Madinaveitia, who generally had the reputation of being one of Villa's more ruthless generals. Those advocating Obregón's execution were Urbina, Manuel Banda, and Fierro, all of whom belonged to what might be called the murderous element in the Villa movement.

Villa threw his support to the middle-class faction. He realized that the hardliners who advocated Obregón's execution would remain with him even if he spared Obregón's life, while his middle-class supporters might decide to abandon him if he committed an act that they felt would dishonor their cause. Once he had decided to spare Obregón's life, Villa proved surprisingly conciliatory. Although Carranza's planned conference in Mexico City was contrary to all the agreements that the latter's generals had signed with Villa, the Chihuahuan chieftain agreed to send his representative to it. This agreement, though, was not unconditional. In a joint letter to Carranza, Villa and Obregón established several preconditions for the participation of the División del Norte in the Mexico City conference: Carranza would have to assume the title of provisional president, which meant that he could not be a candidate for the presidency of the country; elections would have to be carried out as soon as possible; and an agrarian reform would have to be approved. Villa and Obregón were in fact reiterating the same basic proposals that they had made, and Carranza had rejected, only a few weeks earlier. Apart from limiting Carranza's term in office to the few weeks of his provisional presidency, the two basic principles that the letter propounded were decentralization and agrarian reform.

Whatever fears of Villa Obregón may have entertained seem to have been unfounded. Obregón was allowed to board a train for Mexico City and once again seemed to bring a message of peace to his battered and devastated country. Obregón had reason to be satisfied with this trip. Not only had he furthered the cause of peace, he had also come closer to fulfilling two other aims for which he would fight in the weeks to come: the simultaneous removal from power of both Carranza and Villa. Villa's participation at the forthcoming Mexico City conference, and thus peace in Mexico, was now dependent upon Carranza's agreement not to be a candidate for president. This might finally induce the First Chief to give up his presidential ambitions. In addition, Obregón had undermined Villa's leadership of the División del Norte by intrigues and secret agreements with some of his generals.

It is quite possible that Carranza realized what Obregón's real aims were, and it is even more probable that Villa did. This explains both leaders' subsequent attempts on Obregón's life. Without waiting for Obregón's return, and without attempting first to secure exact information on what had occurred in Chihuahua, Carranza ordered all communications interrupted between Zacatecas, which was occupied by Villa's troops, and Aguascalientes, where his own troops were stationed. He instructed General Natera to tear up the railway tracks between those cities. Carranza said he was doing this because of the way Villa had treated Obregón and the way he had threatened his life.

This was the most overt act of hostility that Carranza had yet taken against the División del Norte. It was an expression of Carranza's fear that Villa would advance southward and threaten the control that his troops exercised over much of southern and central Mexico. It was also a means by which Carranza, thinking that Obregón was still in danger, sought to put pressure on Villa to spare his life. On the other hand, it might also be seen as a Machiavellian measure designed to provoke reprisals by Villa against Obregón, in whom Carranza was slowly losing confidence, and thus to discredit Villa in the eyes both of most Carrancista generals and of the United States. Villa's reaction to the measures taken by Carranza were swift and predictable. Deciding that any compromise with the First Chief was now impossible, he drafted a manifesto in the name of the División del Norte withdrawing recognition from Carranza as First Chief of the revolution. This signified a complete break between the two men and their respective forces, but it was not yet an act of war.

Villa's manifesto accused Carranza of wanting to implement a new dictatorship in Mexico. After reviewing in detail the agreements that Villa had signed with Obregón and Carranza's Division of the Northeast in Torreón, it described Carranza's opposition to all of these accords. It accused the First Chief of wanting to perpetuate his role by packing the convention in Mexico City with his supporters. It called on the Mexican people to oust Carranza and replace him with a provisional president who would immediately conduct elections and "adopt sufficiently effective measures to guarantee the solution of the agrarian problem in a sense favorable to the popular classes."[36]

Villa's manifesto does not seem to have been primarily addressed to the mass of the Mexican people. It lacked the clarity and simplicity of Madero's Plan of San Luis Potosí or Zapata's Plan de Ayala. The great majority of Mexicans, who were not familiar with the detailed history of the negotiations among the revolutionary chieftains, would scarcely have been able to follow the intricacies of the Torreón agreements or of the accord between Obregón and Villa. The main addressees of this manifesto seem to have been Zapata and the other independent revolutionary leaders who had emerged in many parts of Mexico, and whose allegiance to one or the other side was not yet clear. It also played to the United States.

Villa must have known that, on September 3, attempts by Carranza to reach an understanding with Zapata had failed and a Carrancista delegation sent to Morelos had returned empty-handed from Zapata's headquarters. What Villa was offering both Zapata and the local revolutionary leaders was a far weaker president than Carranza and a strong commitment to local and regional rule (which meant that they would be able to remain in power), as well as a commitment to agrarian reform.

Another implicit aim of the manifesto was to convince the Wilson administration in Washington that Villa had done everything in his power to reach a peaceful agreement with Carranza, and that it was the First Chief who had rejected every accord that Villa had signed with Carrancista generals. It may have also been with the U.S. government in mind that Villa included in his manifesto a reference to a subject that he had never touched on before: religious freedom.

He accused the Carrancistas of exaggerating "the just resentment of the constitutionalist party against the members of the Catholic clergy who played an important part in the coup and in the support of the dictatorship." This "exaggeration" consisted in "profoundly hurting the religious feelings of the people through acts that are contrary to civilization and law."[37]

This paragraph might have been addressed both to Wilson, who was under strong pressure from the U.S. clergy to protect the Mexican church, and to the Zapatistas, many of whom carried the picture of the Virgin of Guadalupe on their hats.

The break between Villa and Carranza once more put Obregón's life in jeopardy. The train on which he was traveling to Mexico City was recalled to Chihuahua by order of Villa. Obregón was again brought to Villa's house and according to his memoirs, Villa again threatened to execute him. Once again the problem of what to do with Obregón created profound divisions among Villa's generals. While Urbina and Fierro called for his execution, Villa's middle-class supporters, above all Raúl Madero, Eugenio Aguirre Benavides, and José Isabel Robles, opposed Obregón's execution and seem to have threatened to withdraw their support from Villa should Obregón be shot. Villa was thus caught in a dilemma. On one hand, he did not want to lose the support of his middle-class generals. On the other, he was convinced that in the event of a civil war (which seemed imminent), Obregón would be his most formidable opponent. "Obregón," he told one of his secretaries, "will cause far more bloodshed to our republic than Pascual Orozco; in fact, he will cause more harm than Victoriano Huerta."[38] After some hesitation, Villa seems to have rejected the moderates' position and decided to execute Obregón.

So as not to be accused of breaking his hospitality, and perhaps in the hope of hiding his responsibility, Villa ordered that the execution was not to be carried out in Chihuahua. Obregón was put on a special train returning to the capital of Mexico, and Villa instructed one of his generals, Mateo Almanza, to stop the train on the way and shoot Obregón. This decision probably explains why Villa refused to heed Raúl Madero's call for a group of generals of the División del Norte to accompany Obregón to make sure that nothing happened to him. He nevertheless agreed to have one of his commanders, Roque González Garza, join Obregón on his trip back to the capital.

It was Villa's commanders, according to Obregón, who saved his life.[39] Almanza, the general ordered by Villa to execute Obregón, had stopped his train, waiting for Obregón's train to pass. He obviously did not notice when the train went by, and when Villa learned of this, he telegraphed an order for Obregón's train to stop, to wait for the execution squad under Almanza, which was approaching. Roque González Garza ordered the train to proceed, however. But Obregón was still not safe. Villa had ordered that an execution squad should wait for him on the train station at Gómez Palacio. Before Obregón's train reached that station, another train carrying high officers of two of the generals who most opposed Obregón's execution, and were in fact conspiring with him against Villa, Eugenio Aguirre Benavides and José Isabel Robles, reached Obregón's train, and thanks to their help the Sonoran general finally arrived in the city of Aguascalientes, which was garrisoned by troops loyal to Carranza.

While Obregón had failed in his endeavors to regain control of his native state of Sonora, he had succeeded in one of the main purposes of his trip: creating divisions among Villa's generals. The enormous risk Obregón had faced when he went to seek out Villa had not been entirely in vain. In fact, Villa's secretary, Luis Aguirre Benavides, had openly told Obregón that he would leave Villa at the first possible opportunity and implied that his brother, the general, might do likewise.[40]

This success encouraged Obregón to hope that he would be able to find a solution that would simultaneously eliminate Villa and Carranza from power. Such a solution, he hoped, would bring peace to Mexico and perhaps also supreme power in the country to himself.

The clear and open repudiation of Carranza by Villa did not lead to an immediate outbreak of fighting between the two factions. Hostile acts were still very limited in nature. Each side arrested a few prominent supporters of the other whom it had captured, and Villa ordered Calixto Contreras to occupy the capital city of Durango after the Arrieta brothers, who occupied most of the state of Durango, had refused to express their wholehearted support for the chieftain of the División del Norte in his struggle with Carranza. It was a peaceful changing of the guard: the Arrietas simply withdrew from the capital, and Contreras made no move to follow them.

Partly owing to the opposition of the vast majority of the Mexican people to a new civil war, neither side could yet afford to attack the other. This opposition was not only linked to the wish of the people for a peaceful new beginning after the long-drawn-out war against Huerta, but also because there had been no ideological or psychological preparation for the split that had now occurred. Until Villa officially repudiated Carranza, both factions had constantly insisted on the unity of their movement. Before waging war, both sides needed to gain some new legitimacy and to persuade public opinion of the evil nature of their rivals. In addition, both sides worried about American reaction to an outbreak of hostilities. As tension mounted in Europe and the Far East and World War I broke out in August 1914, keeping Mexico quiet became an increasingly important priority of the Wilson administration. In addition, Wilson had staked much of his political prestige on a Mexican policy that promised to restore peace to the country once the revolutionaries had triumphed. A renewed civil war in Mexico would deal a great blow to Wilson's prestige, both inside and outside the United States, and he might easily turn against the Mexican faction he judged responsible for it.

The opposition of a significant number of the military leaders of the revolution was, however, what chiefly blocked the outbreak of hostilities. This opposition could be found within both factions. A number of the Villista generals of predominantly middle-class origin, such as José Isabel Robles and Eugenio Aguirre Benavides, had indicated to Obregón that they would not support Villa in a civil war with Carranza. It is not clear whether Villa knew of this opposition—these generals signed Villa's proclamation against Carranza—but in view of their opposition to Obregón's execution, he must have suspected that they would not blindly obey his orders. The brothers Maclovio and Luis Herrera had been even more vehement in their opposition to Villa and had clearly shown their sympathy for Carranza.

Opposition to a renewed civil war was even stronger in the ranks of Carranza's army, especially among Obregón's Division of the Northwest. Obregón's commanders had accepted Carranza's authority because, as the highest official of the Madero administration who had revolted against Huerta, he conferred legitimacy on them. They also found Carranza a convenient arbitrator of the differences among them. He was not, however, one of their own. Many of them, such as Lucio Blanco, who had carried out the first measure of agrarian reform during the constitutionalist revolution, were far more radical in their social policies than Carranza and thus had no compunctions about sacrificing him if that were the price of peace and reconciliation.

The Initiative of the Generals:
Renewed Attempts at Reconciliation

With a view to reconciliation, Lucio Blanco and 49 other Carrancista generals founded a *junta de pacificación* (pacification committee), which took the initiative of contacting the generals of the División del Norte in order to find a way of peacefully resolving their mutual differences. Carranza had reluctantly given his approval to their initiative to negotiate with the División del Norte. He could not afford to antagonize these men, and even less so when his most capable and powerful general, Alvaro Obregón, joined the junta.

The junta's first act was to write Villa and his generals telling them that "a break between the members of the revolutionary army in the present circumstances would lead to the collapse of the revolution, which is not yet victorious, and to the victory of our enemies, who have not yet been defeated."[41] They called upon the Villista generals to resolve the conflict between their factions by peaceful means and to cooperate in the pacification of Mexico. Only a few days later, in a letter to both Carranza and to the members of the junta, Villa and his generals offered their suggestion for the reestablishment of peace between the revolutionary factions. They suggested that the conflict that divided the revolutionaries would quickly disappear if Carranza were to resign and be replaced by a liberal Mexican politician, Fernando Iglesias Calderón, whom they called an "incorruptible liberal."[42]

Iglesias Calderón was the son of a former supreme court justice of Mexico who had contested Porfirio Díaz and Sebastián Lerdo de Tejada for the presidency of Mexico in 1876. The younger Iglesias Calderón had been an opponent of Díaz and had refused to recognize Huerta. He had not joined the revolution and was thus not identified with any of its factions. In his message, Villa indicated that neither he nor his generals aspired to the presidency or vice presidency of Mexico.

Carranza rejected the message out of hand, stating that a group of generals had no authority to force him to resign. Only the representative convention that he had called upon to meet in Mexico City had that authority. For Carranza's dissident generals, however, Villa's message struck an encouraging note. He would not force his own candidate upon them—Iglesias Calderón was a genuine neutral—and he had made it clear that he favored a weak central government. Iglesias Calderón had no social, political, or military constituency of his own.

The junta sent a number of its members, including Obregón, to Zacatecas to negotiate with Villa's generals, and an agreement was reached to convene a convention of revolutionary chieftains in Aguascalientes, which was considered neutral with regard to the two revolutionary factions, to find a solution to the problems of Mexico. Only military leaders, and no civilians, unless they represented a military leader, were to be admitted to the meeting, and it was the number of troops of each side that was to determine the number of delegates it could send to the convention.

This was a slap in the face to Carranza, since it restated to a large degree the agreements of Torreón between Villa's División del Norte and the generals of the Division of the Northeast, agreements Carranza had repudiated. The First Chief did not accept these proposals, but neither did he openly reject them. Instead, he wanted and needed his dissident generals to participate in the convention of civilian administrators and revolutionary leaders that he had called for October 1 in Mexico City. The members of the junta agreed to attend Carranza's meeting, but they also declared that whatever decisions that meeting took would in their view be subordinated to the decisions of the convention at Aguascalientes. The stage was now set for two meetings that would decisively influence the fate of Mexico.

The Carrancista Convention

Carranza's convention met on October 1, 1914, and it was heavily stacked in favor of the First Chief. In addition to the military commanders of the Division of the Northwest and the Division of the Northeast and some independents, all of the governors whom Carranza had personally appointed were either present or represented. So were a number of civilian advisors to the First Chief, among them Luis Cabrera, his most important political advisor and ideologue.

The deep rifts between the members of the junta de pacificación and Carranza's military and civilian backers became more and more apparent as the convention progressed. On October 3, in a clever political gesture, Carranza submitted his resignation to the members of the convention and put his fate in their hands. It is doubtful whether he really had expected the convention to accept it. Not only did his close supporters constitute a majority of the participants, but the members of the junta did not want his immediate resignation either. For them he was a bargaining chip to be used at the convention at Aguascalientes. Carranza's resignation was thus rejected by all participants, although they did so in very different ways. While his supporters rejected it unconditionally, the members of the junta attempted to do so on a provisional basis, leaving it up to the Aguascalientes convention to make a definitive decision. Through a series of parliamentary procedures, Carranza's supporters thwarted this tactic, however, and the First Chief's resignation was unconditionally rejected. Nevertheless, in the eyes of many contemporary observers, this seemed a Pyrrhic victory. The pressure for peace in Mexico was so strong that a resolution calling for all the military participants at the convention to go to Aguascalientes was accepted by an overwhelming majority of the delegates.

On October 5, the meeting ended, and the vast majority of the military delegates set out for Aguascalientes. Some of the civilian participants, such as Luis Cabrera, who had originally expressed the wish to go to the convention, were barred from doing so by the military. "In the north we signed a pact of honor with Villa and his generals, and as a result of this pact, the civilians will not go to Aguascalientes," Obregón explained.[43]

The Revolutionary Convention of Aguascalientes

On October 10, 1914, the first preliminary meeting of what came to be known as the Convention of Aguascalientes took place in the Morelos theater, the largest public gathering place in that city.[44] The term *convención* that was used to designate the meeting of revolutionary chieftains was no coincidence. Those participants and organizers who knew their history sought a conscious identification with the National Convention in Paris that had drafted some of the main reforms and social changes implemented by the French revolution and successfully organized the defense of revolutionary France against the united kings of Europe. But the organizers of the Convention of Aguascalientes chose to ignore the fact that the French revolutionary Convention had also been the scene of profound factional conflicts that led to savage massacres of revolutionaries by other revolutionaries. Ironically, this was perhaps the greatest similarity between the two conventions, since the bloodiest fighting of the Mexican Revolution broke out in the aftermath of the Aguascalientes meeting.

Unlike its French predecessor, the Aguascalientes gathering was not a meeting of intellectuals and representatives of political parties but of military men. The military leaders of the revolution were either present themselves or had designated a representative, who also had to be a member of the revolutionary army; in all 57 generals and governors and 95 representatives of revolutionary leaders, all of them either colonels, lieutenant colonels, majors, captains, or lieutenants, participated. At first glance, it could be called an unrepresentative military gathering. No common soldier participated and no election of delegates took place. On the other hand, a large number, although by no means all, of the military leaders owed their power and their authority to their soldiers, who had elected them as leaders precisely because of their revolutionary credentials. Unlike their French predecessors, their deliberations would not be influenced by the population of the city where they met. Even if they had wanted to, the people of the small provincial town of Aguascalientes, known above all for its mineral waters and textile industry, could never have played a role similar to that of the sansculottes of Paris who so frequently imposed their will on the French National Convention of the 1790s. It was soldiers and not civilians who filled the streets of Aguascalientes. Every general brought along members of his staff and a greater or smaller number of soldiers as bodyguards and escorts. Some stayed in the few overcrowded hotels in Aguascalientes; others found lodgings with wealthy families in the city, who felt that this was the best protection they could secure from roving bands of soldiers, while many others brought their special trains, complete with lace curtains, beds, kitchens, and accommodations for girlfriends, spouses, and escorts. What differentiated this convention most from its French predecessor is that its debates did not augur the bloody conflict that would soon ensue. There was widespread agreement both on ideological and, to a lesser degree, personal issues. It is the apparent contradiction between this degree of agreement and the ensuing bloodbath that puzzled not only contemporary observers but historians as well.

At its outset, the Convention of Aguascalientes can be said to have broadly comprised three factions, whose degree of cohesiveness was not identical.

The most cohesive group were the Villistas. They made up a minority of only 39 delegates among the nearly 150 who initially attended. Their moderation impressed most contemporary observers. In the agreements of Torreón, the representatives of the División del Norte had asked that one delegate be named for each 1,000 soldiers. This would have given them a relatively large number of delegates, although probably not a majority. Woodrow Wilson's special agent with Villa, George Carothers, had reported that Villa told him that he wanted to expand his army so that the División del Norte would dominate the Convention by the number of delegates.[45] This was not the case. In fact, the División del Norte proved extremely conciliatory when it came to accepting the credentials of delegates representing the other revolutionary factions. They did not ask for any proof that the Carrancista generals represented or led 1,000 men, and they accepted the credentials of any general or governor whom the Carrancistas proposed as a delegate to the Convention.

The conciliatory attitude of the Villistas went much further. On the second day of the meeting, at the initiative of Alvaro Obregón, all the delegates swore by signing the Mexican flag to uphold the decisions of the Convention at whatever cost to themselves. Although they were a minority in a convention dominated by Carrancista delegates, all the Villista representatives solemnly took the oath and signed their names on the Mexican flag. Two days later, Villa himself, who was not a participant at the Convention, but who had sent a personal representative, also came to sign. During a surprise appearance at a very emotional ceremony, Villa personally affixed his signature to the Mexican flag and stated that he too would respect whatever the Convention agreed to. "You will hear from a completely uneducated man the sincere words that his heart dictates. . . . I must tell you that Francisco Villa will not be a disgrace for conscientious men because he will be the first not to ask for anything for himself."[46]

Why did the Villistas go to such extraordinary lengths to swear to adhere to the decisions of an assembly that they not only did not control but whose members were made up mostly of potential enemies? Did they do so, as some have assumed, because they hoped that once Zapata's delegates joined the Convention, they would be in a majority? That was very unlikely, since no one knew how many representatives the Zapatistas would have. Was their oath merely a Machiavellian gesture, which they were quite willing to disregard if the Convention did not meet their demands? This is possible but unlikely, since breaking their oath would have discredited them both inside and outside of Mexico.

It is far more probable that their conciliatory attitude was above all because of the nature of their demands and of their strategy. When Villa insisted that he did not want national power for himself, he was absolutely sincere. Only a few weeks later, when he could have become president of Mexico, he made no move to do so. Neither Villa nor the Villistas attempted to impose their candidate on the Convention. In Aguascalientes, Villa's strategy remained what it had been all along: a basically defensive one. He wanted to maintain the military and political status quo and to retain military control of the División del Norte and political control of Chihuahua and the adjacent regions. The key to achieving these aims, the Villistas felt, was the removal of Carranza from power. Both Villa and the Villista delegates at the Convention made it abundantly clear that they were willing to accept a candidate who was a member of either the Division of the Northeast or the Division of the Northwest. The Villistas were convinced that the vast majority of representatives from the other revolutionary armies would not attempt to imperil peace in Mexico by keeping Carranza in power as long as they knew that Villa would not seek to impose either his person or a candidate of his choice as president of the country. The conviction of the Villistas that the majority of Carranza's supporters were willing to sacrifice the First Chief on the altar of peace was strengthened by obvious signs of disunity among the Carrancista delegates and by the fact that several of those delegates were clearly lobbying to secure the presidency for themselves.

The two other demands that the Villistas would make in the course of the Convention and that most of the remaining delegates had no problem in accepting were that delegates from Emiliano Zapata's Liberating Army of the South should be admitted to the Convention and that some kind of commitment to agrarian reform should be proclaimed.

The two leaders of the Villista faction at the Convention were Villa's personal representative, Roque González Garza, and Felipe Angeles. In Villa's eyes, González Garza had impeccable political and military credentials. Although only 29 at the time, he could nevertheless look back at a long career of opposition to the Díaz regime, of early and close cooperation with Madero both before and after his revolution's triumph, and of very early opposition to Carranza. He had also cooperated with Villa during the Madero revolution and was one of the few civilian politicians who was also a military man.[47] González Garza was Villa's chief spokesman at Aguascalientes, but he always deferred to Angeles, who was in fact the leader of the whole Villista delegation.

One of the most interesting and revealing characteristics of the Villista delegation at Aguascalientes is the paucity of its ideological pronouncements. Unlike a number of Carrancista delegates, and unlike the Zapatista delegation, which joined the Convention at a later date, the Villistas scarcely participated in ideological debates. This was owing in part to the agreements of Torreón, which excluded civilians from the Convention. Villa's main ideologues, Federico González Garza and Silvestre Terrazas, were civilians and therefore did not attend the meetings. Roque González Garza, who shared the liberal outlook of his older brother, Federico, was nevertheless no ideologue, and his numerous interventions at Aguascalientes were practically all dedicated to procedural matters. A more profound cause for this lack of ideological discussion was that the Villista faction, except for a general but vague commitment to agrarian reform, had developed no national agenda. One of the main points Villa had insisted on in his discussions both with Paul Fuller, Wilson's representative, and with Obregón was that each revolutionary faction should have the right and freedom to develop its own policies.

There was nevertheless one Villista ideologue at Aguascalientes who did have a national agenda of his own. This was Felipe Angeles. Angeles's aim at the Convention, though, was not to impose his ideology—his representatives would attempt do so at later meetings—but rather to forge an alliance between the Villistas and the Zapatistas. And so Angeles's ideological pronouncements were limited to complete identification with the views of the Zapatistas (which in many respects he really did not share).[48]

The other end of the political spectrum of the Convention was constituted by a faction that might best be described as the die-hard Carrancistas. They had not collaborated in the work of the junta de pacificación, and their main aim was to keep Carranza in power. They had only reluctantly participated in the work of the Convention of Aguascalientes and their reluctance was clearly expressed, insofar as very few of them attended in person; most only sent representatives.

The most important members of this group were Pablo González, Francisco Coss, Ramón Iturbe, Jesús Agustín Castro, Cesareo Castro, Ignacio Pesqueira, Fortunato Maycotte, Jacinto Treviño, Francisco Murguía, and Manuel Diéguez. Both the social origins and the political antecedents of these men were extremely diverse. Only a minority came from the upper classes, such as Carranza himself and his brother Jesús; Manuel Barragán, scion of a wealthy landed family in San Luis Potosí; Ignacio Pesqueira, who belonged to a family of hacendados in Sonora; and Jacinto Treviño, a professional military man with a wealthy background. In contrast to these men, Pablo González had been an industrial worker, Francisco Coss a miner, Jesús Agustín Castro a streetcar employee, Manuel Diéguez an employee of a mining company, and Francisco Murguía an itinerant photographer. The one thing that most of them had in common in social terms (with the exception of the hacendados) was an urban background; not one of them had been a peasant or a peasant leader. Their political backgrounds also varied greatly. While Carranza himself had been a Reyista, many of these men had been radicals active in the PLM. This was the case with Francisco Coss, Pablo González, and above all with Manuel Diéguez, who had been one of the organizers of the great mining strike of Cananea in 1906, which had led to his imprisonment by the Porfirian authorities in the dark cells of the fortress of San Juan de Ulua.

What these men had in common were their links to Carranza. At a very early date they had established strong personal ties to the First Chief, and most of them belonged to Pablo González's Division of the Northeast. That division had scored the fewest military successes and yet had secured the greatest amount of political plums in the shape of Carranza-appointed governorships in central and southern Mexico. By no stretch of the imagination could most of them be called of bourgeois origin, but by the end of Carranza's term in office, many of them had accumulated enough wealth to be considered part and parcel of a new bourgeoisie.

There was a very important difference between this new Carranza bourgeoisie and what could also be called the new Villista bourgeoisie. The Villistas' main source of wealth was the confiscated estates, which either they administered or were administered for them. The most conspicuous such case was obviously Villa's companion from bandit days, Tomás Urbina. These estates were generally located in the regions from which both the Villista leaders themselves and most of their followers originated. As a result, the Villista bourgeoisie was subjected both to traditional, local restraints and to the need to share the proceeds, and at a later date probably the land, with their followers, whose loyalty they would otherwise lose. Thus their rule was subject to strong limits; even Urbina could not afford to be only a tyrant in his home region.

The Carrancista bourgeoisie was far less subject to such restrictions. Carranza had appointed them as governors and military leaders in states frequently far removed from their native regions. They were in many respects conquistadores in foreign lands rather than leaders in the regions where their followers originated. They could thus afford to be far more ruthless and far more tyrannical in accumulating wealth than their Villista counterparts.

By no means all of the Carrancista leaders supported the First Chief because of the opportunity for enrichment that he offered. Some of them firmly believed that only a strong central government such as Carranza advocated could force the most backward regions of Mexico to carry out reforms. During their tenure as governors, men such as Heriberto Jara carried out far-reaching social reforms. Others were convinced that only a strong central government led by a nationalist such as Carranza could maintain the integrity of Mexico in the face of U.S. pressure. Others feared Villa and considered him a dangerous, uncontrollable bandit.

What these die-hard Carrancistas had in common with the Villistas was that they too did not offer a coherent ideological program to the Convention. The reasons were partly similar. Their main ideologues too had been excluded from the Convention because they were civilians. In addition, most die-hard Carrancista generals were not present at the Convention and were represented only by stand-ins. Their ideological reticence, though, unlike that of the Villistas, did not mean that they had no national agenda; rather, it reflected the nature of that agenda. The Villistas had offered a genuine compromise to the Convention. In return for the resignation of Carranza, they were willing to allow another Carrancista to assume the post of provisional president, and above all they were ready to recognize the political and military status quo in Mexico. They were willing to allow every revolutionary faction to exercise control in the regions it dominated and did not seek to extend their own power to those regions. Carranza, on the other hand, laid claim to national supremacy and demanded that both the Villistas and the Zapatistas submit to his authority. The Villista proposals held out the possibility of compromise; the Carrancista agenda inevitably led to war.

It was difficult to formulate such an agenda at a conference that had met to find a compromise between the different revolutionary factions. That the die-hard Carrancistas attended the Convention of Aguascalientes at all was owing in part to the pressure of Mexican public opinion and to the fear of seeming uncompromising in the eyes of the Wilson administration. The main reason for their attendance, however, was the realization that they could only triumph if they won over the majority of the third and largest group at the Convention, the members of the junta de pacificación. It was the wish to regain the support of this group, which seemed to be defecting from Carrancismo, that led both Carranza and his die-hard supporters, in spite of their opposition to the Convention of Aguascalientes, not to repudiate it at the outset of its deliberations.

The third force at the convention did not consist entirely of members of the junta de pacificación. It was far more heterogeneous in nature and in the aspirations of its members than either the Villistas or the Carrancistas. Its motley array of members included representatives of the Division of the Northwest, mainly from Sonora; radical, reform-minded intellectuals; and genuine independents whose revolutionary movement had developed outside and independently of the main revolutionary factions. The one common aim of these delegates was the elimination from the national scene of both Carranza and Villa, but their motives in this were by no means identical. Some leaders of the group, such as Antonio Villareal and Eduardo Hay, who openly propounded their candidacy for the post of provisional president, as well as Obregón, who did not, probably hoped to assume the leadership of the revolution themselves. Others feared that Carranza would impose a conservative regime on Mexico, whereas Villa would become a tyrant. Others only wanted a weak central government that would leave them alone in their home regions.

It was the third faction that dominated the deliberations of the Convention until the arrival of the Zapatistas. In general, the delegates they proposed and the procedures they suggested were accepted by both the Villistas and the die-hard Carrancistas during the initial phase of the Convention. It was a member of this group, Antonio Villareal, a former radical and member of the PLM, who made a keynote ideological address that met with near-unanimous approval from the great majority of the delegates at the Convention.

Villareal's speech constituted a kind of ideological manifesto of the third force. It called for peace, not only because Villareal considered fratricidal struggle, leading inevitably to an enormous number of victims, as senseless, but also because in his opinion the unity of the revolutionaries was the only means by which the Americans could be persuaded to leave Veracruz. "We must confess that we bear a great share of responsibility for the fact that the flag of the Stars and Stripes is still waving over Veracruz," he said.[49] Furthermore, his call for a radical expropriation of the rich was a clear slap in the face to Carranza, who had firmly opposed such radical confiscations.

These words of Villareal's reflected the opinions of all factions at the Convention. Most of them, including some of Carranza's most loyal followers, had engaged in massive confiscations. Many of these confiscated properties had not, however, been used, or had only partially been used, to finance the revolution. Many if not most went mainly to enrich their administrators. Here Villareal was somewhat more reticent. "We have attempted to take from the rich what the rich had taken from the hungry; but this has not been done in an orderly way, and what has been taken has not greatly increased the wealth of the republic. We must do this in an orderly way, we must do it wisely, so that with these riches we can pay all the war debts . . . and ensure the economic future of our country." The statement was so vague that no general stood accused of robbery or corruption.

In yet another way, Villareal's speech reflected the views of the third force. He was very concrete and clear with respect to the abolition of peonage and wage increases for industrial workers. "This revolution," Villareal stated, "will not have achieved its aims until the slaves that we had in Yucatán and in the south until a short time ago have disappeared and until starvation wages have been eliminated from our factories."[50]

Villareal was far more vague with respect to agrarian reform, simply calling on Zapata to join the other revolutionary groups so that "the land division can be carried out that will make a free man and a happy citizen of every peasant."[51] Villareal said nothing more concrete about the kind of agrarian reform he envisaged. By contrast, he was extremely concrete when it came to attacking both Villa and Carranza:

We will tell Carranza and Villa: the revolution has not been carried out so that one man should occupy the presidency of the republic; the revolution has been carried out to put an end to hunger in the Mexican Republic. . . . We must have the courage to say that principles are more important than leaders; we must have the courage to state that it is better that all the caudillos die if we can save the welfare and the freedom of our country.

Instead of shouting vivas to the caudillos who are still alive and who have not yet been judged by history, we should shout, "Gentlemen, long live the revolution!"[52]

The general acceptance of Villareal's speech was but one more confirmation that the third force had to a large degree gained control of the Convention. They had forced the reluctant die-hard Carrancistas to attend the deliberations, and they had persuaded the Villistas to give in on two crucial points: the acceptance of all the delegates the third force proposed, irrespective of whether they did or did not represent 1,000 men as agreed on in Torreón, and the agreement of the Villistas to accept the sovereignty of the Convention, which meant accepting the decisions of the third-force majority. There was one potential threat to this third-force majority: it was the participation of Zapatista delegates at the Convention. Since the Convention had come together to make peace, it could not ignore one of the most important revolutionary factions in Mexico, and all participants thus agreed with Angeles's demand that the Zapatistas be invited to participate in the deliberations in Aguascalientes.

None of the three factions initially represented at the Convention can be considered a homogeneous bloc. Some of the Villista generals had clearly communicated to Obregón their opposition to Villa and their readiness to defect from his army. At the Convention, however, they continued officially to act in unison with the Villista delegation as a whole. Even among the die-hard Carrancistas, there was some wavering. At one point, Pablo González, considered the general most loyal to Carranza, contemplated turning against the First Chief if Villa resigned his command.[53] The third group was even more divided. While all of its members wanted the removal of both Villa and Carranza, once a split between the two of them occurred, the third group itself split, and the two halves ended up on opposing sides of the civil war. For some generals, the most decisive criterion on whom to join was not so much ideology or even personal loyalty as their perception of which side was stronger and which would turn out to be the winner. The hope of swaying these waverers by creating a seemingly irresistible Villa-Zapata alliance was certainly one factor, although by no means the only one, that led Angeles to consider the participation of the Zapatistas at the Convention one of his main priorities. He succeeded in having the Convention appoint him as the head of an official delegation sent to Morelos in order to persuade the Zapatistas to attend the Convention.

It was ironic that Angeles, the general who for more than a year had fought the Zapatistas in Morelos, and had been most successful at it, would be the architect of the Villa-Zapata alliance and would persuade the Zapatistas to send representatives to the Convention. Angeles believed that in Morelos he had earned, if not the sympathy, at least the respect of Zapata and his revolutionaries:

I am profoundly convinced that I am an Indian from the lowest classes of society and that because of my character and my independence those who deal with me like me, although those who are far from me may hate me. . . . I know that I may be the worst choice to go there, since I have been the leader of the forces that have operated in that region, but I shall undertake that effort with pleasure, and if I should be sacrificed there, I would be happy to die, because I strove to do something for my country. Nevertheless, I do not believe there is a great probability that I shall be sacrificed; I know very well that when I was there carrying out my campaign in Morelos, I frequently walked along with my aides, and the Zapatistas perhaps saw me pass and said, "Let him pass. This man will not harm us."[54]

Angeles's optimism was more than justified by the reception Zapata granted him. When Angeles and the delegation from the Convention arrived in Cuernavaca, Zapata told him: "General, you do not know how glad I am to see you. You were the only one who fought honestly against me, and by your acts of justice you succeeded in gaining the goodwill of the people of Morelos and even the sympathy of my men."[55]

Zapata's sympathy for the delegation that accompanied Angeles was reinforced by its composition. Whereas the delegation that Carranza had sent some weeks before to negotiate with Zapata, which had completely failed in its attempts to come to an agreement with the southern chieftain, had not included a single peasant leader, the delegation of the Convention of Aguascalientes did.

Among the representatives that the Convention had selected to meet Zapata together with Angeles was Calixto Contreras, the man who more than anyone else in the north could be called a peasant leader, and with whom Zapata identified immediately. "I am also happy to see you in Morelos, General," Zapata told Contreras, "since being a son of the poor and a fighter for land, you are the revolutionary in the north who inspires the greatest confidence in me." The other two delegates of the Convention had also been carefully chosen to gain Zapata's confidence. Castillo Tapia was an engineer who had participated in the first land division that Lucio Blanco had carried out in early 1913, which had been strongly opposed by Carranza. In addition, he had constantly emphasized his sympathy and understanding for the southern revolution. Rafael Buelna, the youngest member of the delegation, could be called the representative on the delegation of the third force at the Convention. Although originally a student, with no history as an agrarian reformer or agrarian revolutionary, he was the leader of the third force who had made the greatest show of independence from its leadership. He had gone so far as to arrest Obregón for a short period of time.[56]

Zapata was in a quandary. He did not want to submit his movement to any outside authority. He had done so twice, recognizing the leadership first of Madero and then of Orozco, and the results had been disastrous. Madero had turned against him, and Orozco had turned to Huerta. Submitting to the authority of a convention in which the Carrancistas held a majority was anathema to him. He was deeply worried that a victorious Carranza would pursue the same policy toward him, perhaps with even more brutality, as Madero had done. The only man capable of defeating Carranza was Villa, and from November 1913 on, Zapata had systematically sought a rapprochement with Villa and had with equal energy attempted to separate the latter from Carranza. If he now refused to attend the Convention, to which Villa through Angeles was inviting him, that alliance was placed in jeopardy. After consulting with his military chieftains, Zapata elaborated a compromise. He decided to send 26 representatives to the Convention, but they would not be official delegates, in the sense that they would not recognize the sovereignty of the Convention until that body had officially adopted the Plan of Ayala and Zapata and his chieftains were convinced that the Convention really meant to implement a far-reaching program of reforms.

None of the main Zapatista military leaders went to the Convention. Instead, Zapata sent intellectuals upon whom he had conferred military rank to Aguascalientes. He made it abundantly clear that his delegation's interest was primarily in Villa and far less in the Convention itself. The Zapatista delegation first went to Villa's headquarters before attending the meetings at Aguascalientes. Villa promised the Zapatistas his support, and some kind of an agreement with Zapata's main representative, Paulino Martínez, was reached. Only then did the Zapatistas attend the Convention, to which they introduced a new ideological dimension. Their main aim at the Convention was to strengthen their links to Villa, to persuade the Convention to adopt the Plan of Ayala, and to secure the removal of Carranza as leader of the revolution and his replacement by someone whom they did not consider an enemy.

In his inaugural speech at the Convention, Martínez made it abundantly clear that the only northerners he considered to be genuine revolutionaries were Villa and his followers:

The genuine representatives [of the revolution] were General Emiliano Zapata with his forces in the south and General Francisco Villa with his men in the north.

Both of them are Indians, and in their faces can be seen the traits of this noble race to which they belong, and they both feel in their hearts the pain and suffering of this humiliated race.[57]

With the help of Angeles and the Villista delegates, the Zapatistas persuaded the Convention to adopt as its own the Plan of Ayala. The Convention now went on record as favoring the most radical plan for the redistribution of the land that Mexico had ever known. That moment could in some respects be called Angeles's finest hour. He had taken the initiative in persuading the Convention to invite the Zapatistas, he had gone to Morelos and persuaded Zapata to send a delegation, and it was at his initiative that the Plan of Ayala was adopted at Aguascalientes. The relationship of forces in the Convention had thus fundamentally changed. Obregón and his supporters, and even the die-hard Carrancistas, had gone along with these measures. This was after all a meeting to reestablish peace, and they simply could not exclude from it one of the most important revolutionary factions. Opposing the Plan of Ayala would have been very difficult, and everyone now wanted *agrarista* credentials. In addition, adopting a plan in Mexico did not mean very much. Throughout Mexican history, innumerable plans and constitutions had been proclaimed, and only very few had been implemented.

What really interested Obregón was the question of power, and on October 31, his great hour seemed to have come. On that day the majority of the Convention, largely at his initiative, adopted a resolution calling on both Carranza and Villa to resign. To a large degree, this resolution came as a response to a letter that Carranza had sent to the Convention in which he stated that he would contemplate resigning if Villa and Zapata did the same, although he never said he actually would resign. This letter had shattered the illusion that some delegates had still retained that Carranza would simply bow to the wishes of the Convention. It gave Obregón the necessary argument to state that only the simultaneous resignations of Carranza and Villa (Obregón did not insist on Zapata's resignation) could bring peace and harmony to Mexico. It would also in all probability have brought Obregón to power. He was, after Villa, the most successful military leader the revolution had produced, and many of Villa's generals had clearly indicated to him during his journey to Chihuahua that they were ready to rally to his cause. The resolution was adopted with the vote of both the third force and the Villistas, with the exception of Villa's personal delegate, Roque González Garza. Only the die-hard Carrancistas voted against it.

Two days later, Obregón seemed to have scored an even greater triumph. The Convention voted to replace Carranza with the candidate that Obregón had selected as provisional president of Mexico. The representatives of the División del Norte had favored the candidacy of Juan Cabral. Cabral was a Sonoran, but he was neither a Villista nor a supporter of Villa's protégé, Maytorena. He was a genuine independent. This may be the reason why Obregón rejected him, although during his visit to Villa in Chihuahua, Obregón had proposed Cabral as governor of Sonora to replace Maytorena. In Sonora, Obregón may have felt that he had little reason to fear Cabral's agrarian radicalism. While the latter had been the only Sonoran revolutionary leader who proposed sweeping agrarian reform in the state, the Sonoran legislature, doubtless influenced by Obregón, as well as Maytorena, had rejected these proposals.[58]

Obregón may well have feared that once he had become president of Mexico, Cabral's agrarian radicalism would be far more difficult to control. Obregón's candidate, Eulalio Gutiérrez, was a minor regional leader with close links to the Carrancistas. Until Obregón suggested his name, no one had thought of Gutiérrez as a presidential candidate. He was little known and commanded few men, a very small force of guerrillas, operating mainly in San Luis Potosí. This may have been precisely the reason why Obregón nominated him. He was weak enough to be manipulated. Obregón also had reason to be satisfied with one of Gutiérrez's first choices as defense minister. This was José Isabel Robles, a Villista general, who had nevertheless indicated to Obregón during the latter's stay in Chihuahua that his loyalty to Villa was by no means unconditional. The success of Obregón and the Convention would nevertheless prove to be short-lived if Carranza and Villa could not be persuaded to accept the decision of the Aguascalientes assembly.

Officially, Villa acquiesced. To thunderous cheers from the Convention, Angeles read a communication from Villa not only saying that was he willing to resign but suggesting a rather "unconventional" way of being removed from office: the Convention should have both him and Carranza shot.

By contrast, Carranza hedged on his reply. As long as he was in Mexico City, which was occupied by troops nominally under his command, but in reality headed by Lucio Blanco, one of the leaders of the third force, who it was assumed was loyal to the Convention, Carranza was equivocal. On November 1, with the ostensible pretext of going on an excursion to the pyramids of Teotihuacán, he fled to Puebla, which was controlled by one of his most loyal generals, Francisco Coss. Carranza then became more adamant and more outspoken in his opposition to the resolution of the Convention. He expressed strong doubts (which in many respects were quite justified) as to whether Villa had really resigned. He offered to resign and leave Mexico for ten days and surrender his authority to Pablo González if Villa would do the same with the command of the División del Norte, which would be taken over by Gutiérrez. Since Gutiérrez was a man close to the Carrancistas, who had been elected with the votes of Obregón's faction, while Pablo González was a close supporter of Carranza's, this was obviously a suggestion biased in favor of the Carrancistas, which Carranza probably assumed Villa would not agree to. Then for many days Carranza refused to receive a delegation headed by Obregón that came to apprise him of the decisions of the Convention, and he finally stated that he did not recognize the authority of that body to remove him from office. At the same time, his most loyal generals withdrew their representatives from the Convention and announced that they only recognized Carranza as the First Chief of the revolution. After giving Carranza until November 10 to make up his mind whether to respect the decisions of the Convention, Gutiérrez finally declared him in rebellion against the legitimate revolutionary government of Mexico and appointed Villa as commander in chief of the forces of the Revolutionary Convention. The latest and bloodiest part of the Mexican revolution now began.

The personal responsibilities of the two main leaders of the revolution and the underlying causes of the bloody conflict that now developed constitute one of the most enduring and controversial subjects of Mexican historical debate.

While at first glance it would seem that Carranza was clinging to power and Villa was ready to resign, strong doubts have been expressed in this respect. Unfortunately, few of the men who were close to Villa and were later to write memoirs about their experiences with the northern revolutionary were with him during the crucial days of the Aguascalientes Convention. They were either at Aguascalientes or in Chihuahua, while Villa was at the head of his troops in the town of Guadalupe in the state of Zacatecas, 100 miles from Aguascalientes.

José Vasconcelos, one of Mexico's leading intellectuals, who in 1914 joined the Conventionist faction, only to recoil a few months later from Villa, whom he considered a homicidal barbarian, has given an account showing Villa flying into a murderous rage once he heard of the decision of the Convention to depose him. Vasconcelos describes himself as a member of the delegation sent by the Convention to advise Villa that his resignation had been accepted. Villa received the delegates in the railway car where he had established his headquarters. After Vasconcelos, the spokesman for the delegation, had told him that the Convention had decided to remove him and Carranza from office, the eyes of the general became red and bloody as they did, I have been told, when a homicidal fury took hold of him. But he managed to control himself.

"Good," he said after a long pause. "Good. Tell them," he said without looking at his generals, "tell them that Pancho Villa is leaving. . . . I leave everything . . . this division that I have formed. . . . I shall only take 20 men. . . . Organize your government, but let me tell you one thing. . . . I want to warn you about that. If I capture one of your mayors, I shall hang him. . . . " I was irritated by the abrupt and savage threat. . . . The three of us left convinced that the promises of obedience to the convention would only be a farce.[59]

This account by Vasconcelos is improbable. Vito Alessio Robles, one of the secretaries of the Convention, says that Vasconcelos was not even a member of the delegation that came to see Villa.[60] What makes Vasconcelos's account even more improbable is that if Villa had really so strongly objected to the vote of the Convention, he would not have allowed his generals to vote for his resignation. While some of them, such as Eugenio Aguirre Benavides, may genuinely have wanted him to resign, many of his commanders were fanatically loyal to him and would certainly not have voted the way they did if they had even remotely suspected that they were acting against the wishes of their chief. In all probability, Villa was taking a gamble, convinced that under no circumstances would Carranza resign. Villa wanted to show public opinion in Mexico, the undecided revolutionary generals, and the Washington administration that it was he who was ready for a compromise, and that if war broke out again in Mexico, Carranza would bear the main responsibility.

Would Villa have given up command of his troops if Carranza had resigned? No clear answer can be given to that question. What in the final account makes it improbable that Villa would have resigned is that such a resignation would have amounted to a capitulation, although Villa had not been defeated in battle and in fact seemed to many observers to head the best army in Mexico. It was Villa's charismatic personality, his tremendous popularity, and his reputation for invincibility that held the División del Norte together. Had he resigned, that division would have fallen apart. Carranza's main commanders, Pablo González and Alvaro Obregón, would not have resigned and would have remained in command of their troops. Obregón would have become the most powerful man in Mexico. Villa had reason to assume that some of his generals, who had unabashedly shown their sympathy for Obregón, would have rallied to him had Villa left. The result in Villa's eyes would have been that practically without firing a shot, the Carrancistas, this time led not by Carranza but by Obregón, would have taken power in Mexico, and that Villa would have abandoned his armies and his supporters. In addition, there is also strong evidence that Villa was recruiting men, importing weapons, and preparing for battle. This was not the conduct of a man contemplating his resignation. Depending on which leader they trust most, historians have believed that either Carranza or Villa was more ready to resign, and have thus attributed the responsibility for the ensuing civil war to either one or the other. In all probability, neither of the two men was really ready to resign, not only because they wanted power but because both were convinced that once they left, the Mexican Revolution would go down in defeat. Carranza considered himself the one bulwark of civilian rule against military predominance. In addition, he was convinced that if the Villistas and Zapatistas triumphed, Mexico would fall back into anarchy, the central state would fade away, and the country would be at the mercy of the United States. In Villa's eyes, Carranza was a dictator who would reverse all the changes that he had implemented in Chihuahua and Durango, and who would vent his ire on the men to whom Villa felt he owed the greatest loyalty: the soldiers, officers, and generals of the División del Norte. Yet when assessing responsibility for the final break, one fact should not be ignored. Carranza's demands all along had been for national power for himself and the absolute subordination of both the Villista and Zapatista factions to his rule. Villa by contrast did not want national power and had advocated a compromise solution under which each faction would retain control of the territories it dominated, thus ensuring a military status quo.

The final break between Villa and Carranza put a temporary end to Alvaro Obregón's hopes of assuming the inheritance of both leaders. The setback was only temporary. Within a year, Obregón would defeat Villa, and within five years, he would remove Carranza from power and become president and supreme arbiter of Mexico's destiny. In November 1914, however, Obregón's star seemed to be on the decline. He had risked his life by going to Chihuahua and had engaged the whole force of his personality at the Convention, thus clearly alienating Carranza by promoting a solution that would remove both main leaders of the revolution from power.

Obregón had even been willing to back that demand with military force. In a secret conference with Manuel Diéguez, who was nominally under Obregón's command and who commanded the strongest contingent of troops of the Division of the Northwest, concentrated in Jalisco, Obregón had proposed a radical course of action.[61] All troops loyal to Obregón should be concentrated in Jalisco and should indicate to both Villa and Carranza that they would proceed by force of arms against whichever of the two refused to resign. Obregón obviously hoped that he would be joined in this endeavor by dissidents from the División del Norte who had secretly promised him their support, and that Pablo González and his relatively weak Division of the Northeast would be unwilling to risk an armed confrontation with Obregón for the sake of Carranza. But Obregón had overestimated his control of his division and the loyalty of his commanders. Carranza, fearing such a reaction by Obregón, had in fact split up the Division of the Northwest into a series of contingents spread out over hundreds of miles, from Sonora to Mexico City. Above all, Obregón's commanders were not willing to go along. Calles and Hill in Sonora and Diéguez in Jalisco had indicated their loyalty to Carranza.

In spite of Diéguez's refusal to go along and his increasing weakness, Obregón still harbored hopes that he might succeed in his bid for control of Mexico. He agreed to participate in a delegation sent by the Convention to officially notify Carranza that his "resignation" had been accepted. That Obregón accepted such a commission indicates that he did take Villa's resignation seriously and now hoped to induce Carranza to do the same. Carranza had a more realistic appraisal of the correlation of forces than Obregón. It is doubtful whether Carranza really believed that Villa had resigned, but even if he had, Carranza knew that if he hedged on his own resignation, Villa would certainly not show the other cheek.

He knew that once the issue was between joining Villa and remaining loyal to the First Chief, Obregón would scarcely hesitate. Once Obregón arrived at Querétaro, which was in Carranza-held territory, the First Chief kept him practically in detention for two days and refused to see him until Obregón had made clear that he recognized the supreme authority of Carranza.

Three reasons have generally been given to explain Obregón's decision to join the First Chief. First, his closer ideological and social affinity to Carranza and his "petty bourgeois" origins made him ideologically and socially closer to the bourgeoisie, as represented by Carranza, than to the peasants, whose spokesmen were Villa and Zapata. Second, he hated Villa because of the treatment he had received in Chihuahua. Finally, most of his commanders would not have gone along had he joined Villa. These reasons were certainly of great importance in shaping Obregón's decision. Nevertheless, even if these factors had not been present, Obregón would have had no choice but to join the First Chief. Every revolutionary leader in Mexico derived his primary strength from control of his own region. Without it, he was left dangling in the air. Obregón could not play the role he did without control of his native state of Sonora, where his power base lay. This was the one thing that Villa was unwilling to give him. By backing Maytorena to the hilt and thus depriving Obregón of the control of his native state and the source of his strength, Villa left him no choice but to join Carranza. Carranza understood the dilemma and the situation in which Obregón found himself very well, and despite Obregón's apparent readiness to depose him, he was thus ready to entrust the most talented military man the revolution produced with the supreme command of his troops. It was a decision that played a decisive role in the Carrancista victory in the bloody civil war that would once more engulf Mexico.

What It Was All About:
The Villa-Carranza Controversy in Perspective

The conflict that now pitted the forces of the revolutionary convention, led by Villa and Zapata, against the armies of the constitutionalist faction, whose main leaders were Carranza and Obregón, is perhaps the most debated and controversial issue in both the history and the historiography of the Mexican Revolution. In the eyes of many contemporary observers, this conflict, which led to the greatest bloodshed in the history of the Mexican Revolution, was also its most senseless episode. Two revolutionary factions proclaiming similar aims were fighting each other. Both had opposed the dictatorship of Huerta and both were advocating democracy for Mexico, the nonreelectability of the president, a larger degree of national sovereignty over the country's natural resources, and some kind of land reform. Other issues connected with the Mexican Revolution have gradually faded away; the Villa-Carranza controversy constitutes one of the main points of debate among historians and others interested in its history. This is no coincidence. Debates about conflicts between revolutionary factions are by no means limited to Mexico. In the history of most revolutions, it is precisely the conflicts among revolutionaries that have generated the longest, most heated, and most acerbic controversies. For a long time, one of the most controversial, perhaps the single most conflictive, issues dividing historians of the French revolution was the debate between supporters of Danton and of Robespierre. The same holds true for the Stalin-Trotsky debate in the case of the Russian Revolution. Distortions of facts are more frequent from both sides in those debates than in those between supporters of the old regime and those of the revolution. Both revolutionary factions in conflict have great difficulties in explaining how their respected comrade, companion, and fellow revolutionary of only a short time before has suddenly been transformed into a traitor and counterrevolutionary.

In both the Soviet and the Mexican cases (although not in the French), one revolutionary faction was victorious, and for a long time the victors wrote the official history of their conflict. In addition, the extraordinarily thick web of legend that always surrounded Villa, to which he himself actively contributed, rendered a serious and objective assessment of his controversies with Carranza and with other factions in the Mexican Revolution extraordinarily difficult.

The many explanations of the new civil war that engulfed Mexico once again can be divided into several broad categories. Quasi-official Mexican ideology long held that Villa was a rebel against the legitimate authority of Carranza and bore full responsibility for the civil war. Jesús Silva Herzog asserts that "some educated men who lived under his shadow had awakened his ambition. . . . Villa dreamed of becoming president of the republic."[62] Charles Cumberland, however, sees Villa's resentment at "the insults and slight" inflicted on the División del Norte by Carranza as "the key to the Villa attitude."[63] These authors do not see Villa as an agrarian leader or a man dedicated to land reform, since in Chihuahua he in fact distributed no land. Some authors have felt that Villa's attitude reflected the social composition of his movement, which did not essentially consist of peasants, but rather of drifters, muleteers, and cowboys.

Other historians present a completely different point of view. In their eyes, Villa's movement was essentially a peasant movement, in many respects similar to that of Emiliano Zapata in the south, and the conflict between Villa and Carranza was basically a conflict between peasants on the one hand and the middle class and a new bourgeoisie, which Carranza represented, on the other. This perception is based on Villa's social origins as a hacienda peon, his proclamations in favor of land reform, and his alliance with Zapata, as well as on John Reed's—erroneous, as it turned out—reports of large-scale division of hacienda lands in Chihuahua.[64]

Alan Knight offers a new and highly ingenious theory. He rejects both the notion that the Villa-Carranza conflict was one of personality and the perception of it as a class struggle. In his eyes, there was no real difference between the social bases of the two movements. Northern peasants, whom Knight calls *serranos* (mountaineers), in contrast to their southern counterparts in Morelos and its adjacent regions, constituted the core of both the Villista and Carrancista parties. Basically, serranos were peasants from remote regions whose main conflict with the state was not over land but over the state's attempt to absorb and control them. What they wanted was to maintain their autonomy. In a few cases, they were involved in land problems, but these tended to be with local caciques, rather than with landowners. With the outbreak of the revolution, these problems had been solved. The caciques had fled, the state had been destroyed, and as a result these peasants had no clear ideological affinity with one or the other side. Their revolutionary affiliation depended on other factors, such as patron-client relations and personal loyalties. The real difference between the Villa and Carranza movements lay in the characters of their local and regional leaders. Knight does not see any social reason for this difference of attitude. It seems rather that like attracted like: parochialists joined Villa, while leaders with a more national orientation fought for Carranza. As a result, the Carrancistas wanted a strong national government, while Villa and his supporters wanted a weak federal administration and a large degree of regional autonomy.[65]

What makes a final determination of the validity of these theories so difficult is that each one identifies an element that contributed to the conflict between Villa and Carranza. No simple one-dimensional explanation is adequate.

Independent of the motives that impelled the different groups and factions to fight one another, it should be stressed that in the history of most revolutions, bloody fighting among revolutionary factions after the demise of the old regime is not the exception but the rule. The outbreak of revolutionary violence is but a symptom of the failure of traditional mechanisms of consensus and peaceful solution of conflicts. Once these mechanisms have disappeared, a power vacuum seems to have emerged, and large segments of the people have come to see violence as the only means of resolving their differences, it follows that very heterogeneous factions who have united to topple the old regime resort to force to impose their solution to the country's problems.

What greatly contributed to the outbreak of such violent confrontations in the Mexican case was that each of the main revolutionary movements had to a very large degree arisen independently of the others. "Because the big revolutionary armies had developed in materially and socially different regions, northeast, northwest, north and south, each represented a particular array of social forces," John Womack observes.[66] Unlike the Maderista revolution of 1910–11, there was no common political organization and no recognized charismatic leader whose authority had been established by a long political campaign before the outbreak of the revolution.

Personal rivalries and profound cultural differences between Carranza and Villa were certainly important factors that precipitated the outbreak of the new civil war. Limiting the motives for the conflict to personal rivalries, though, would liken them to the kind of traditional caudillo rivalry that had existed in many parts of Latin America throughout the nineteenth and twentieth centuries.

The problem with this interpretation is that the traditional caudillo armies, while they called themselves revolutionary, had never been the product of a social revolution. They were relatively small armies composed of professional soldiers or men closely linked to their respective caudillos by traditional ties—they were either their retainers or their clients—or temporary allies that caudillos had made. How could a movement that had begun as a social revolution so rapidly degenerate into traditional caudillo politics? Why would hundreds of thousands of Mexicans let themselves be manipulated by the ambitions of Villa or Carranza? The clearest proof that the new civil war was by no means exclusively the product of personal rivalries between Villa and Carranza is that long after Villa ceased to be a national leader, anti-Carrancista movements continued to persist throughout Mexico.

There is little doubt that in many respects the controversy between the supporters of the Convention and those of Carranza was a conflict that went back to the nineteenth century: a conflict between centralism and federalism, between a strong national state and regional aspirations for autonomy.

It is significant that Villa never attempted to impose on the rest of Mexico the kind of regime that he had set up in Chihuahua. Nor did his administration attempt to assume direct economic and political control of regions outside the Chihuahua-Durango-Laguna axis. When he withdrew from the state of Zacatecas after achieving one of his greatest victories, Villa left control of the state to a local leader, Panfilo Natera. Even in Durango, so close to Villa's heart, it was local leaders and not Villa himself who exercised control. Villa never wanted national power. When it was thrust on him, he declined it. What he wanted was control of his bailiwick of Chihuahua, the Laguna region, and perhaps of Durango. It was when Carranza interfered with that control that conflicts between the two men began to emerge.

Carranza's aim on the other hand was to reestablish a strong, centralized, powerful Mexican state. He was convinced that only the existence of such a state could guarantee Mexico's independence and its development into a modern capitalist nation. In 1913–14, such an aim seemed extraordinarily difficult to achieve. The Mexican state, which Porfirio Díaz had to a large degree created, had survived the Madero period and been broadly co-opted by Huerta. Most of it had been destroyed by the constitutionalist revolution: the federal army, the police, the judiciary, and most of the bureaucracy had been eliminated. As a result, Carranza's second aim, the creation of a supreme civilian authority (although not necessarily a democratic one), seemed even more difficult to achieve, and Villa in his eyes epitomized military control over civilian society.

Carranza had no national political organization on which he could rely, and at least in the first months of his revolution, he disposed of no army of his own after his fighting forces in Coahuila had been largely defeated by the federal army. He neither would nor could embrace the federal army and rely on it for support, as Madero had done. In this complex situation, Carranza relied on three means to restore the power of the central state: he played off his generals against each other so that he could act as arbiter; he attempted to assume at least partial control of the civilian administration of the territories liberated from federal rule; and he attempted to obtain as many resources as he could for his government in order to control the purse strings of his movement. All three of these policies necessarily brought him into conflict with Villa. He played off Villa against both Chao and Obregón; he attempted to impose a man of his choice as governor of Chihuahua; and finally he attempted to take control of the expropriated haciendas, on which Villa relied both to supply his military needs and for his social policies, away from the northern revolutionary leader.

Of all the explanations put forward to explain the conflict between Villa and Carranza, this issue, centralization versus regionalism, is probably the least controversial. The problem that has sparked the greatest amount of controversy concerns the issue of class. The class issue to which most authors refer concerns the question of land reform. Was this the main issue that differentiated the Conventionist movement from its constitutionalist rivals? Few historians and observers have doubted that this was one of the main issues separating the Zapatistas from Carranza and his followers. For Zapata, the Mexican Revolution was eminently a class struggle. The land issue had always been central to the revolution in Morelos. Zapata's army was composed of peasants demanding the return of their expropriated lands; he himself had been a peasant leader before the revolution; and his program, the Plan of Ayala, was the most explicit agrarian document that the Mexican Revolution produced. Above all, Zapata had both returned their expropriated lands to peasant villages and divided the remaining hacienda lands among landless peasants.

Was Villismo in the last instance also an agrarian movement, with land reform constituting one of its main demands, and can Villa be called an agrarian reformer?

What for many years made this problem so difficult to answer was the lack of basic information. Little was known about what actually happened in Chihuahua under Villista rule. Chihuahuan census data were so bad and misleading that for many years reputable historians assumed that few small landowners existed in the state, or that there were no agrarian issues of any importance. Since no statistical data exist on the socioeconomic makeup of the División del Norte, François-Xavier Guerra assumed that it was not peasants but miners who constituted its core.[67] For a time I myself believed that the Villista movement could be called a "cowboy revolution."

Nothing better illustrates this confusion than the fact that two well-known American radicals of the day, both sympathetic to the Mexican revolution, voiced diametrically opposed opinions with regard to Villa and the agrarian issue in Chihuahua. John Reed reported that Villa had divided Chihuahua's haciendas among the state's peasants, whereas John Kenneth Turner, who had written a highly influential book exposing the Díaz regime's oppression of Mexico's rural population, but who had never set foot in Villista Chihuahua, said that Villa had turned the Chihuahuan haciendas over to his generals, who now made up a new landowning class.[68] In fact, as the next chapter will show, Reed and Turner were both wrong.

What also complicates the class explanation of Villismo is that many of the arguments that are frequently used to prove that Villa was a bona fide agrarian reformer, such as his birth as a peon on a hacienda, are not very convincing. The personal origins of a leader are not necessarily reflected in his social and economic views. Villa, it is true, had been a peon, but he had also been an outlaw, a mule driver, a butcher, and a successful businessman, and if one were to attribute his social attitudes to his social origins, the question of which of these activities finally influenced his political consciousness arises. While Villa's alliance with Zapata constituted an important indication of the way the two men and the two movements viewed each other, it is not a definite proof of Villa's agrarianism either. Alliances during the Mexican Revolution frequently had very little ideological content. Villa had allied himself with Maytorena, and Zapata for a time contemplated an alliance with Félix Díaz.

Neither do Villa's repeated declarations in favor of land reform constitute proof of his final intentions. For that matter, Carranza, who was profoundly opposed to land reform and never allowed any significant land redistribution to take place during his presidency, had made similarly radical statements and promises.

What can clearly be stated is that in its social composition and in the personality of its leaders, Villismo was far more of an agrarian movement than its northern counterpart led by Carranza, whose supporters came mainly from the northeastern and northwestern frontier states of Mexico. In Chihuahua the number of villagers owning land and farming it on a full- or part-time basis was far greater than long assumed. These villagers had an extraordinary impact on the public consciousness of Chihuahua because of their traditional reputation of defenders of civilization against Apache incursions and their long military experience.

It was only in the homeland of Villismo that massive land expropriations, both by caciques and by hacendados, occurred. In the case of Sonora, Héctor Aguilar Camín found that with the significant exception of the Yaqui Indians, land expropriations were at best of a minor nature.[69] A recent study concerning the state of Nuevo León, from which Pablo González's Division of the Northeast drew many of its soldiers, suggests similar conclusions.[70] This study found that military colonies had been established there, as they had been in Chihuahua, at the end of the eighteenth century, but that these colonies had never lost their lands. The same seems to have been the case in Coahuila, where outside of the Laguna area, a bastion of Villismo, relatively few complaints of land expropriation could be found.[71]

The second argument that tends to support this view is that with very few exceptions those northern chiefs who can be identified as peasant leaders in the traditional sense (i.e., men who had led their supporters in conflicts with hacendados long before the revolution began) all rallied to Villa's side. Such leaders included Calixto Contreras and Toribio Ortega.

The third argument has to do with the confiscation of the haciendas. While in practice the differences in attitude between Villa and Carranza were not reflected in massive differences in land distribution, the one practical difference concerned the confiscated estates. Carranza had objected to their confiscation in the first place. When he could not prevent his generals from occupying haciendas, he was successful in preventing any kind of link between the confiscation of these estates and promises of later land division. Finally, he would return most of the confiscated haciendas to their former owners. Villa by contrast had made it clear that the hacendados would never get back their haciendas and had linked their fate to land reform.

The importance of this issue in the Villa-Carranza conflict was best expressed in a letter that Silvestre Terrazas sent to a number of revolutionary leaders to define one basis of the conflict between Villa and Carranza. "One of the leaders wants to act very radically, confiscating the properties of the enemy and expelling the corrupt element; the other disapproves of his conduct, proposes the return of some of the confiscated properties and allows himself to be influenced by an infinite number of enemies, who day after day estrange him from the aims, principles, and goals of the revolution."[72]

While it can be unequivocally stated that Villa's core constituency was far more agrarian in character than that of the Carrancistas, Villa's attitude to land reform is still subject to much controversy. His agrarian aims were more limited than those of Zapata, who saw his Ayala Plan as applicable to most of the peasantry, not just in Morelos, but throughout Mexico. Zapata insisted again and again that every leader with whom he dealt should apply the clauses of that plan to his region and to his district. Villa never showed any such commitment to agrarianism other than on behalf of his soldiers and the military colonists or outside of Chihuahua, the Laguna, and Durango.

There is no evidence, except in one case in Sonora,[73] that Villa ever pressured his allies to carry out significant land reform. While he held power in Chihuahua and the Laguna, he made no significant distribution of land (but as the next chapter will attempt to show, he had little choice in the matter). Had he won, it is extremely doubtful whether he could have resisted, even if he had wanted to, the enormous pressure from his constituency for the division of the large estates. Both Villa and his generals had undergone the traumatic experience of the Orozco revolt. They had seen how many of the men they had led into the revolution rose against Abraham González and Madero when those men had been unwilling to keep the promise the peasants had felt they had made of dividing up the large estates. This promise would have been all the easier to carry out inasmuch as the old hacendados had left and only a minority of generals, seven in all, had been able to get their hands on confiscated estates: a powerful Villista bourgeoisie with de facto control of the large estates in Chihuahua did not exist.

The means by which Villa would have been able to carry out his promise of land reform was his control of the confiscated estates. The division of these estates among his soldiers was an aim that Villa consistently advocated from the moment he assumed the governorship of Chihuahua when still an obscure provincial chieftain to the days when he was at the height of his power.

Beyond his commitment to grant land from the confiscated estates to his soldiers, Villa had emphasized another agrarian aim: the return of expropriated lands to villagers who had been deprived of them by hacendados. The main victims of such expropriations had been the former military colonists, who were one of the main bases of Villista support. For this reason, Villa's commitment to these villagers is very believable.

Carranza's attempt to force Villa to give up control of the confiscated estates had multiple motives. In part, he hoped that by successfully doing so, he would allay the fears of the hacendados, who feared that notwithstanding Carranza's protestations, he would be unable to stop Villa from confiscating all the estates that his armies occupied. In part, Carranza hoped that these estates would provide sufficient resources for him to set up an effective central administration and to strengthen the Mexican state, which he was attempting to reestablish. If land was to be divided, Carranza firmly believed, the central government should do so, not the local chieftains. Above all, though, as he was to show very soon, Carranza was intent on returning the estates to their former owners, which he felt was the only way in which Mexico's modern economy could be preserved from the backwardness of peasant proprietors.

Apart from the issues of centralization and agrarian reform, there was a third issue that divided Villa and Carranza and played a major role in their split: their respective attitudes to the United States. Carranza was a genuine nationalist, deeply worried by the increasing U.S. economic and political influence in Mexico.

These fears were compounded by the fact that the European states' close links to Huerta had discredited them in Mexico, weakened their economic and political positions, and thus prevented them from becoming a counterweight to the United States. Carranza feared that his own revolution was bringing about an unprecedented degree of U.S. influence in Mexico. This doubtless constitutes one explanation for his violent denunciation of the U.S. occupation of Veracruz, although this to some extent also reflected the attitude of Carranza's constituency, which was composed of the most nationalistic sector of the Mexican people— the nation's urban population. Villa saw the Americans in a far more favorable light, doubtless reflecting the fact that anti-Americanism was far less widespread in the countryside than in the cities.

These differing attitudes also reflected economic realities in the territories controlled by Carranza and Villa respectively. In Chihuahua, American mine owners had stopped work on many of their properties because of the fighting there, which had destroyed some property but above all had made railway communications with the United States much more difficult. As a result, the mines produced no income, and Villa's main interest was in persuading the Americans to resume work. He was thus quite willing to make substantial concessions to the mine owners. In Sonora, the situation was very different. Some of the richest mines were located close to the U.S. border, and work thus suffered far fewer interruptions than in Chihuahua. Carranza thus felt that he had no economic reason to favor the Americans, and that he could safely impose higher taxes on them. That attitude became even more pronounced when Carranza's troops occupied the city of Tampico, which controlled access to the oil fields. Throughout the revolution, oil production had been increasing, and Carranza saw no reason not to attempt to get more revenue for the Mexican state from these foreign properties. Paradoxically, Villa's more favorable attitude to the Americans was linked to his social radicalism. After confiscating the properties of the local Mexican oligarchy, he felt for a time at least that he had sufficient money to finance his revolution and so did not need to pressure the Americans, which might have limited his access to U.S. arms and supplies.

Villa's view of Woodrow Wilson and his administration was not that of a diplomat or a politician. He judged Wilson and his representatives in relation to his personal code of honor. For a time, Villa considered Wilson a kind of American Madero and took his moralistic declarations as seriously as he had taken Madero's idealistic statements. The personification of the Wilson administration in Villa's mind was General Hugh Scott. Perhaps because of his long experience in dealing with American Indian leaders and Filipino rebels, Scott spoke a language that Villa understood. What Wilson had implied in writing and Hugh Scott seemed to confirm orally was that a kind of tacit mutual agreement to which both sides were honor-bound existed between Villa and the Americans. Villa felt that if he respected American property, listened to Wilson's advice, observed the rules of war, and carried out some political and social reforms, the United States would support him, although no such reciprocal agreement was ever expressed in writing.

Any doubts Villa may have had on this subject were rapidly quelled by the four men who advised him on U.S. policy. Three of these—Wilson's special representative George Carothers and two of Villa's representatives in the United States, Lázaro de la Garza and Felíx Sommerfeld (at least until the latter became a German agent)—had strong personal stakes in maintaining good relations between Villa and the United States. All three were involved in business deals between the two sides that netted them large profits. Villa's fourth, and perhaps most important, advisor in this respect was not a businessman and was not interested in money, but he had a very strong ideological commitment to an alliance between Villa and the United States. This was Felipe Angeles, who was one of the architects of Villa's informal alliance with the Americans.

Carranza and many of his nationalistic supporters viewed Villa's increasingly close cooperation with the Americans with the deepest suspicion. Many of them saw Carothers as an agent of U.S. expansionism, manipulating Villa like a puppet.

CHAPTER ELEVEN

Villismo in Practice

Chihuahua Under Villa, 1913–1915

Villa's greatest initial achievement after taking power in Chihuahua was to recreate the unprecedented unity of the great majority of Chihuahuans that had existed in the five months of the Madero revolution, from November 1910 to April 1911. That unity broke apart soon after Madero's victory, when the demands of the lower classes of rural society were not met. The most tangible expression of this breakdown was the Orozco rebellion. That disunity was still apparent throughout the state when Villa crossed the border from the United States in March 1913 but had largely disappeared by March 1914.

Villa's success was achieved even though he neither ever fully reestablished the democracy that Madero and González had instituted nor implemented the agrarian reforms for which so many in Chihuahua's countryside had fought. Three elements held together the extremely heterogeneous coalition of Chihuahuan forces that had united against Díaz, Terrazas, and Creel in 1910–11 and were now again largely united under Villa's leadership. The tremendous victories of the División del Norte, in which thousands of Chihuahuans voluntarily fought, were the first of these elements. The second was the fact that every social group that had remained in Chihuahua benefited in one way or other from the expropriation of the huge Terrazas-Creel fortune, and to many in Chihuahua this expropriation meant that Villa would in the final account carry out the changes he had promised, and that both Madero and González had failed to implement. Finally, the support that the Americans were giving Villa increased the Chihuahuans' perception of his power and at the same time increased the economic means at his disposal to conciliate most social strata in Chihuahua.

When the victorious Maderista revolutionaries in Chihuahua had returned home in the spring of 1911 after having been demobilized, they found that most of the hated caciques who had been imposed upon them by Terrazas and Creel were gone, but that economic reality, if they lived in the countryside, had scarcely changed. The hacendados and their haciendas still existed, and although not as powerful as before, still dominated the Mexican countryside. Neither wounded or disabled veterans nor the widows of fallen soldiers received much compensation from the state.

In the spring of 1914, after Villa gained control of Chihuahua, the situation of the revolutionaries was quite different. Most of them had not been demobilized. On the contrary, they had been persuaded to remain in the División del Norte and were convinced that their invincible leader was taking them on a triumphant journey throughout Mexico. Wounded veterans who returned to Chihuahua were cared for by the state in a very different way than under González and Madero. They received pensions and frequently free deliveries of food, and they could buy cheap meat from the haciendas, which the Villistas were selling at extremely low prices throughout Chihuahua. The soldiers in the field appreciated the fact that the Villa administration, unlike those of his predecessors, was giving financial help to their families.

In the few weeks during which Villa held actual power as governor in Chihuahua, a feeling of euphoria emerged among large segments of the state's population. In a region that had been torn by civil war and ravaged by banditry for nearly three years after November 1910 (except for a few months in the latter part of 1911), Villa seemed to inaugurate the first real period of peace. He had expelled the federal troops from the state and practically eliminated the Orozquistas as a political force in Chihuahua. To those who were ready to surrender, he offered a general amnesty. Those who refused to accept this amnesty were either exterminated or forced into exile. Villa dealt in the same way with the bandits that had emerged in Chihuahua in the period of civil war.

There is no evidence that in his first weeks as governor, Manuel Chao attempted in any way to challenge Villa's power or to reverse his measures. Quite the contrary. Although Chao had been Carranza's candidate for the governorship of Chihuahua, and although within a few months he would be forced to leave office as a result of increasing conflicts with Villa, he never attempted to reverse Villa's radical measures. In a long memorandum to Carranza, which Chao and Silvestre Terrazas drafted together, he attempted to justify the measures that Villa had taken in the weeks he had ruled Chihuahua. Chihuahua, in the last few years, Chao wrote Carranza, had been "a foul and stinking mess comparable only to the capital of the republic." Chao told his chief that this state of affairs was mainly due to "científico money," which had exercised a profoundly corrupting influence. For this reason, "it had to be purified for our national good, and we had to punish those responsible for this state of affairs." Both the interests and the lives of the guilty were liable to be forfeited. "In accordance with the Plan of Guadalupe," Chao insisted, Villa, "by near unanimity," had been designated military governor of Chihuahua. Chao said that he himself, together with Villa and the other generals commanding the División del Norte, felt that two basic measures had to be taken in order to pacify Chihuahua. The first was to grant a broad amnesty to all those willing to lay down their arms and resume peaceful lives.

The second was to confiscate the property of the "enemy." If such confiscations did not take place, Chao wrote to Carranza, the enemy, in spite of the military victory by the revolutionaries, would be able to return, "well rested after fleeing the country [and] would find us weakened and enfeebled by the consequences of a long struggle . . . and would again begin with his intrigues, hiring murderers and paying in gold for treason in order to gain supremacy over the poor and help-less social classes with the aim of eternally solidifying the reign of injustice, ex-tortion, and crime."[1]

Throughout the two years during which it dominated Chihuahua, the Villista administration of the state was torn between the demands of the many thousands of people who had participated in the revolution on the one hand and the im-peratives of war on the other. When they heeded Madero's call to arms in No-vember 1910, Chihuahuans had had very clear demands in mind: the overthrow of the Terrazas and Creel; a return to the municipal autonomy that both cities and villages had enjoyed for most of the nineteenth century; and a drastic reduction in taxes. In addition, the inhabitants of the former military colonies wanted their expropriated land back; landless peasants wanted access to public land still held by the government; and urban workers wanted the right to form unions, the right to strike, and an end to government support for employers.

Abraham González had sympathized with most of these demands and had done whatever he could to meet them, but the means at his disposal were ex-tremely limited. González was able to do most for the urban workers. Not only did he legalize unions and allow strikes, he also made it clear to the contending parties that his administration would not favor the employers as his predecessors had done.[2] González had also responded to middle-class demands by changing the tax structure of Chihuahua and lowering the taxes paid by the lower and mid-dle classes. Furthermore, he had sought to end government control of municipal offices and had reestablished local control of villages through free elections.

As long as the oligarchy held on to its properties, and thus essentially contin-ued to control the economic life of Chihuahua, the extent of González's reforms was, however, limited. The Achilles' heel of the González administration had been its absolute inability to carry out any kind of social transformation in the countryside. The many thousands of hastily demobilized revolutionary veterans returned home to find that despite the many dangers they had endured, the prospect of having their lands returned to them was still extremely distant. More-over, they found that some of the hacendados they had fought were back in con-trol of their estates. González's inability even to begin to solve the land issue was owing less to ideological reservations than to the limits imposed on him by the national leadership of the revolution, and above all by Francisco Madero himself.

The Villista administration of Chihuahua faced similar demands and, for very different reasons, was also unable firmly to implement the reforms that so many of its supporters demanded. Its order of priorities, though, would be very differ-ent from that of the González administration, and it would go much further than its predecessor in destroying the state's existing political, social, and economic structure.

Like González, Villa was faced with a national leader profoundly opposed to agrarian reform. Like Madero, who had opposed any radical redistribution of hacienda lands, Carranza had both refused to include agrarian demands in his Plan of Guadalupe and attempted to pressure Villa into returning confiscated estates to their former owners. But this attitude of the national leadership was a far smaller obstacle for Villa than it had presented for González. Carranza did not have the authority and power that Madero had had in late 1911, and, above all, Villa never took the same subordinate stance with Carranza that González had with Madero.

But, unlike Villa, González had assumed the governorship of Chihuahua when it was at peace and the armed phase of the revolution had ended. Under Villa, the revolution was just beginning to assume larger proportions. The imperatives of war and revolution, far more than the opposition of the national leadership of the revolution, determined the way Villa applied or did not apply reforms and changes in Chihuahua. González had had no hesitations or compunction about tolerating strikes. They were after all directed against industries mainly controlled either by the oligarchy or by foreign entrepreneurs. Under Villa, the state assumed control of most of the industries formerly controlled by the oligarchy, and any strike would not only have diminished the revenues the state needed to conduct the war but might have weakened the war effort itself in those cases where peacetime industries had been converted to war production.

González had had no difficulty in reducing the taxes paid by the poor and the middle classes, but had faced enormous problems when he attempted to increase the taxes to be paid by the wealthy to compensate for this loss in revenue. Villa at first faced no such difficulty; he simply confiscated the properties of the domestic oligarchy. He thus disposed of resources of which González could not have even dreamed. However, he also faced expenses that had never confronted González. He had to finance not just a local revolution but the national revolution against Huerta. For a time, Villa managed to pay for both guns and butter—that is, both carry out large-scale redistribution of goods and finance the war effort—but he could not do so indefinitely, for the resources at his disposal were finite. They consisted of the cattle on the large estates in Chihuahua and Durango and of the cotton harvested on Laguna haciendas belonging either to Mexican landowners who were hostile to the revolution or to Spanish capitalists.

One of the most profound changes that Villa carried out in contrast to González was the way he dealt with one of the most vocal and profound demands of the Chihuahuan revolutionaries: municipal autonomy. Villa reestablished the municipal councils elected or appointed under Madero, which the Huerta administration had unseated, but he subordinated all civilian authorities to military commanders, the *jefes de armas*. This was in part because he hoped to retain control of Chihuahua even after leaving the governorship, but also because of differences between his movement and those of Carranza and Zapata, who both not only also led military forces but controlled important civilian infrastructures.

In Morelos, where Zapata was waging guerrilla warfare, local civilian authorities and guerrilla units were so closely enmeshed that neither was able to control the other, and Zapata was able to establish an equilibrium. In the Carranza-controlled states of Coahuila and Sonora, the erstwhile Carrancista authorities had been able to inherit an intact civilian infrastructure that to a degree at least counterbalanced the power of the military. In Chihuahua, first the Orozco uprising and later the military administration of the state had largely destroyed the revolutionary civilian infrastructure, so that the only "revolutionary organization" at Villa's disposal was his army. It is thus not surprising that this was the only organization he trusted and the only one he felt could guarantee a revolutionary administration in Chihuahua. In some respects, this meant that the Villa government was perhaps the most militaristic of all revolutionary administrations. In another respect, though, it also meant that the municipal councils, which had hitherto largely been controlled by the upper and upper-middle classes, had now come under the supervision of army men, who generally came from the lower or the lower-middle classes of society and had frequently been elected by their soldiers. Thus military control of the administration could also mean stronger popular control. Which of these two tendencies predominated—militarism or popular control—differed from region to region. In those cases where local revolutionary leaders had assumed control of their home regions, one might probably speak of a predominance of popular control. In those cases where Villa named an outsider as military commander, a new kind of militarism began to emerge. On the whole, as the army became more and more professionalized, the drift of Villismo seems to have been away from popular control and toward militarism and military control. It was an issue that had the potential for increasing tensions between large segments of the civilian population and the Villista authorities, since one of its consequences was the postponement of municipal elections in the whole state.

The contradictory types of military rule that emerged in Chihuahua and the very different types of military commanders in the state are perhaps best expressed in the divergent attitudes of the local population toward a highly popular military commander in Ciudad Guerrero on the one hand and a local tyrant in the mining town of Cusihuiráchic on the other.

Julio Acosta, the military commander in the old revolutionary and agrarian town of Ciudad Guerrero, was so popular that people even came to him with family problems. For example, Piedad Pérez de Olveda, whose husband had abandoned her, wrote to Acosta asking that "my husband, Trinidad Olveda, who is living in adultery in this town with Señora Dolores Córdoba, be obliged to fulfill his obligations to his family," and that the "scandalous prostitute" should be banished to a remote part of the state.[3]

It is doubtful whether the inhabitants of Cusihuiráchic felt the same kind of confidence in either their mayor, Lt. Col. Alberto Chacón, or his son, the military commander of the town, Pedro Chacón. Both men were hated by a large part of the population for having established, as a secret agent of Silvestre Terrazas's noted, a monopoly over the right to slaughter animals. "No one, absolutely no one, is allowed to kill even one animal. If someone, in order to help the poor, kills a cow or a bull, he must as a punishment give the hide to the mayor."[4]

Increased popular resentment of military rule led to repeated demands for both local and even statewide elections. In February 1914, the *El Paso Morning Times* reported on the formation of political parties in Chihuahua for an upcoming gubernatorial election: "Two parties have already been organized, one being known as the Liberal party, supporting attorney Aureliano González as a candidate for governor of the state and the other is called the Liberal Radical Party and will support Juan Bautista Baca Sr., a prominent Parral man[,] for the governorship." One of the candidates was Abraham González's former deputy and temporary governor of the state in 1912, while the other, Juan Baca, was the constitutionalist manager of a department store that had been confiscated from its Spanish owners and was now being managed for the benefit of the army. The newspaper doubted whether this campaign would be allowed to continue: "It is feared that Villa will put a stop to this political activity because of the necessity of first winning the country from the federal controls before the opening of political campaigns."[5]

The *El Paso Morning Times* was right. Villa soon quashed this political campaign. Yet the demand for at least local elections came up again and again. Obviously in answer to such pressure, Silvestre Terrazas drafted a municipal election law in October 1914. This date was carefully chosen. Huerta had been defeated, and the Convention Aguascalientes was in session. Terrazas's draft law called for elections in Chihuahua on the last Sunday of November, and its stated aim "was to put into practice the promises of the constitutionalist revolution." Nonetheless, the law seems to have done away with the secret ballot. Voters were required to sign the ballots on which they wrote their choice of municipal officials.[6]

One such municipal election was held without being authorized by the Villista authorities. The town council sent documents to the regional authorities that listed the name of every voter as well as the candidate for whom he had voted.[7] The election was invalidated not because of its open character but because Governor Fidel Avila, and obviously Villa, refused to hold municipal elections as long as the civil war lasted.

In April 1915, after promising that municipal elections would soon be carried out, Fidel Avila explained this policy by noting that "a large segment of Chihuahua's citizens who are fighting in the glorious División del Norte have not yet returned home and we have waited for their return to carry out these elections, so that they will not be determined by the present inhabitants alone." Avila added that some towns and villages "were so anxious to carry out elections that they did not wait for the state government to allow them but had done so without official permit. These elections were annulled."[8]

The main reason for Villa's refusal to allow elections was his wish to maintain complete control of the state as long as the war continued. But the argument given by Avila in his report, that many soldiers had not yet returned, was doubtless an important factor and constituted more than just a pretext for postponing the elections. Villa's most ardent supporters were in the army, and the results of the elections would obviously be affected by their absence. Moreover, Villa did not want to demoralize those of his soldiers who were fighting far from their communities, and even from their native state, by making them feel that they were being penalized for having joined the army. Some might want to be candidates for municipal office, and others would want to participate in important decisions. If elections took place in their absence, it was precisely those who had not volunteered to fight or who could not fight because of their age who would determine the shape of things to come.

The same contradiction between the demands of the population of Chihuahua and the imperatives of war affected the way in which the Villa administration dealt with an issue that was even more important to large segments of the population than the question of municipal autonomy: land reform.

Villa and Land Reform

From the moment he assumed control of the state of Chihuahua, Villa had indelibly associated himself with the land issue by promising that land that had been taken from village communities and individual villagers would be returned to them immediately after the victory of the revolution. In addition, large parts of the confiscated estates would be divided among his soldiers. In theory, once he controlled Chihuahua, Villa could immediately have returned expropriated lands to their former owners and divided the large estates among the peasantry of the state, as Zapata was doing in Morelos. This would have strengthened Villa's enormous popularity among rural Chihuahuans even more, and would have given him irreproachable revolutionary credentials both within Mexico and outside of the country.

Such a policy would have undermined Villa's war effort, however, and would have entailed unacceptable political costs. The same argument that the Villistas had given for postponing municipal elections in Chihuahua was even more valid with respect to land division. Thousands of the main potential beneficiaries of such a reform were far away from their native state, fighting the armies of Victoriano Huerta. As one Villista official put it:

Let us suppose that we can divide the land. Well; but these peasants who should obtain it at this moment are fighting, and they would face the alternative of either abandoning the fight or, if they do not do this, not receiving land, and this would be completely unjust and inequitable. If those who are risking their lives on the battlefield for the reforms and principles about which we are talking here do not deserve a piece of land, who does? Are those who have remained at home either as a matter of convenience or through cowardice to be the only ones to get land?[9]

He added that the only way to carry out a just division of land would be to call back all soldiers so that they could participate, which was obviously a military impossibility as long as the fighting went on.

In this respect, Villa's situation was profoundly different from that of Zapata. Zapata was essentially waging a defensive guerrilla war. His peasant soldiers continued to live in or near their villages and could thus easily participate in land division. Indeed, receiving land enhanced their determination to fight, since they now had much more to fight for. In contrast, Villa's troops were fighting an offensive war far from their villages.

These considerations were by no means the only obstacle that Villa would have faced had he immediately carried out radical land reform. In Morelos, the peasants who had received land from the large estates substituted subsistence farming, mostly of corn and beans, for cash crops, especially, sugar. This had a limited effect on Zapata's fighting capacities. Had the large estates in Morelos continued to produce sugar, Zapata could have done little with it. He could have sold some of it in Mexico City, but he had no border with the United States, with its huge market for Mexican goods and its enormous supply of arms. In addition, by reverting to subsistence agriculture, the peasants could now feed themselves, and Zapata's troops thus became more and more independent of outside suppliers.

A very different situation existed in the north. Every hacienda that Villa confiscated was a potential source of arms, since Villa could sell both their cattle and their cash crops across the border. In fact, these sales constituted the basis for supplying his soldiers with arms and with ammunition. In addition, the revenues from these estates made it possible for Villa to redistribute part of them to the large nonpeasant population of Chihuahua. He gave food to unemployed miners and industrial workers, granted regular pensions to the widows and orphans of soldiers, and sold cheap meat in the markets of Chihuahua's towns. In Morelos, where peasants constituted the overwhelming majority of the state's population, Zapata faced no such dilemmas.

An immediate division of the large estates might also have entailed unacceptable political costs for Villa. It could easily have led to a confrontation with Carranza, who opposed any such land reform. An important consideration, too, was certainly the fact that Villa did not have to pay any high political price for delaying agrarian reform in Chihuahua. It was part of the historical consciousness of the inhabitants of the former military colonies that land was earned by fighting. Their ancestors had received land in return for fighting the Apaches, and they would now receive and deserve it by fighting the counterrevolution.

The main problem that Villa faced with regard to the expropriated estates in the first few months of his rule in Chihuahua was not whether to divide them immediately but rather how to administer them. In contrast to other twentieth-century revolutionary leaders, Villa had no political organization when he assumed state power, and neither did his movement in its first stages include a large number of qualified intellectuals and technicians. The only way to administer the large estates was thus to maintain the status quo. As one high Villista official put it:

In Chihuahua . . . once a town is taken or a region has been conquered, all the haciendas, all properties of our enemies are intervened, and the first thing that has been done in the state of Chihuahua, and that I consider highly intelligent, was to continue the cultivation of these lands, which in most cases were left in charge of or administered by the same administrators who had taken care of them for our enemies, and the aim of this policy was that work on the estates should not cease for even one day.[10]

When Villa decreed the expropriation of the large estates in Chihuahua, he stated that it would be up to the Bank of Chihuahua to oversee all the confiscated properties, both urban and rural. But the bank was absolutely unprepared for this task. It had neither the personnel nor the experience to carry it out. As a result, Villa shifted control of the confiscated properties from the bank to a newly formed Administración de Bienes Intervenidos del Estado de Chihuahua, headed by Silvestre Terrazas. The administration of the confiscated properties turned out to be a much more complex affair than Villa and his generals had foreseen.

The only survey in existence regarding the confiscated haciendas reveals a complex pattern of control and administration.[11] Seven were administered by the

Administración General de Confiscaciones del Estado de Chihuahua, headed by Silvestre Terrazas. Eleven properties were directly subject to the authority of the state government, while thirteen others were controlled by local and regional boards. The military commander in Ojinaga controlled five estates, an exceptional situation with respect to other military commanders, perhaps because Ojinaga lies at the extreme eastern end of Chihuahua, far from the state capital.

Seven haciendas were directly controlled by generals of the División del Norte. Two of them were administered for Villa. The hacienda of San Miguel de Babícora, consisting of 200 *sitios de ganado mayor*, was "managed by Lieutenant Colonel Maximo Márquez, with special orders from General Francisco Villa to take care of his interests, authorizing him to sell the cattle he believes necessary to cover the costs of the people working there." Villa directly controlled another of Terrazas's largest properties, the Hacienda del Torreron, "whose livestock and agricultural business is under the direct charge of Señor Francisco Villa, his manager being Señor Refugio Domínguez, who as far as we know receives his costs from the general treasury."[12]

Other generals for whom haciendas were administered were Manuel Chao and Tomás Urbina. The destination of the proceeds of the haciendas administered directly for the generals are not entirely clear. In the case of Urbina, which may have been characteristic of all of the others, 50 percent of the profits were to be turned over to the state.[13] It is not clear whether Urbina was obliged to feed and equip his troops from the remainder.

These seven cases were exceptions, however, and the vast majority of confiscated estates seem to have remained under the control of diverse state agencies.[14] Obviously, such an administration provided manifold possibilities for corruption, and Silvestre Terrazas was repeatedly accused of having appropriated large amounts of money for himself.[15] On the whole, the most valid appraisal of what happened to the proceeds was given by Dean David Barrows of the University of California at Berkeley, who traveled to Chihuahua in the final days of the Villa regime in July 1915. "Opinion differs as to the effectiveness and honesty of this administration," he wrote, "but the government has derived its main support in food for its armies from cattle, *de facto* the revolution has been fought largely on beef."[16]

The properties under state control were administered in various and different ways. The large Hacienda de San Isidro was supervised by a government official, Salomé Espinoza; its 2,000 head of cattle and 1,000 horses were under direct government control. The irrigated lands, as well as those on a rancho belonging to it, were rented out to two tenants, Pedro Dávila and Lucio Meléndez, who paid 25 percent of their respective crops of 5,000 hectoliters of wheat and 3,000 hectoliters of maize and 1,000 hectoliters of wheat and 1,500 hectoliters of maize to the administrator.[17]

While the cattle on government-controlled properties were taken over by the administration, the lands themselves were nearly always rented out. The renters were both wealthy tenants and poor sharecroppers. On the one hand, there were such tenants as Manuel Fernández, who had rented the large Rancho de San Vicente y la Palma from the government for an indefinite period of time in return for 33 percent of its proceeds.[18] On the other hand, there were sharecroppers, as on the Rancho de San José in Chihuahua, who paid one-third of their crops for the lands they worked, or the 134 partners of the Hacienda de San Carmen, who paid half of their crops to the administration.[19]

What evidence is there of revolutionary changes on the haciendas, apart from the fact of their confiscation from the original owners? Is there any evidence of jacqueries, of large-scale occupations of lands by peasants? Was there any great change in the internal organization of the hacienda? Were the peasants represented in any way in the new administration? Did labor conditions, the terms of tenantry or of sharecropping, change substantially? The records indicate that very few, if any, changes in this direction took place until mid 1914 in Chihuahua and until the end of Villista rule in the Laguna.

Only one instance of hacienda land occupation by dispossessed peasants is recorded. The Rancho de Matachines was part of the Hacienda de Orientales, which had formerly belonged to Enrique Creel and was now being administered by a Captain Benigno Quintela on the instructions of the "*jefe de armas* in Ojinaga, Colonel Porfirio Ornelas. It was occupied by Roque Aranda, Albino Aranda, Lucás Aranda, and Manuel Aranda, who declared that they are the owners and that they were dispossessed of the property by the former proprietor of the hacienda, Señor Creel. They are now ready, so they say, to present their title deeds to the estate to the government of the state, for which reason they do not give the hacienda any part of their harvests."[20]

The report from the expropriated Mancomunidad de Ciénaga de Mata in Chihuahua, which had formerly belonged to Miguel Soto Villegas, stated: "It is common knowledge that most of these properties, which used to belong to poor folk, were taken from them during the Porfirian period to give possession to Señor Soto Villegas. It is these people who at present are negotiating for the return of the properties and who simply await the complete stability of the legal government to obtain justice, since once the case is resolved, they are ready to regain possession of what belongs to them and from which they were so villainously expelled by the government of the dictator." Unlike the Aranda family in Matachines, the peons of this hacienda had not occupied their former lands, and the hacienda "was being administered by a Sr. Ignacio Montoya, who had been left there by Señor Ernesto García, the person to whom General Francisco Villa had entrusted the administration of his properties."[21]

The same kind of reluctance to act was shown by the peons of the expropriated Rancho de San Vicente y la Palma. They bitterly complained about the tenant, Manuel Fernández, who had rented the rancho from the state for an indefinite period of time and was exacting very harsh terms from them.[22] There is no evidence that anything was done about this, either by the state administration or by the peons.

Except for the fact that many hacienda administrators had worked as such in prerevolutionary times, very little is known about them. There are no indications that the laborers on the haciendas had anything to do with the designation of the administrators or that they participated in any way in the administration of the confiscated estates.

There is no evidence in these reports prior to mid 1914 of any marked improvement, in comparison with the prerevolutionary period, in labor conditions and terms of tenantry or sharecropping to benefit the poorest groups on the haciendas. Many estates were rented out to wealthy tenants, such as a Sr. Márquez, who administered the Hacienda de Sombreretillo. He kept 40 percent of the harvest for himself and gave 60 percent to the government.[23] Much of the property confiscated from Miguel Guerra in the district of Camargo was rented to a Sr. Sacarías for 1,600 pesos a year.[24] Some of these wealthy tenants, such as Carlos Flores, who had rented a large part of the Hacienda de Hormigas, sublet their lands to small tenants.

There is some evidence that in Chihuahua in mid 1914, after Silvestre Terrazas had taken control of a large part of the expropriated estates, some changes in favor of poor tenants were implemented. In an undated memorandum written sometime in 1914 and entitled "Matters to be dealt with by General Villa," the first point on the agenda was "Measures to cultivate confiscated lands, either by renting or by leasing without rent during the first year."[25]

Terrazas's proposed reforms probably reflected economic as well as social motives. The reports from the haciendas in Chihuahua (in contrast to the Laguna region) continually speak of an acute labor shortage. Even well-irrigated lands were not worked owing to lack of laborers. Terrazas's proposals seem to have been implemented, and in his memoirs he later wrote:

In order to find work for the Tarahumaras, log-felling was organized to cut railway cross-ties, with which entire sections of the old Central North-east, Santa Eulalia, and Kansas City lines were repaired, under the direction of D. Rafael Calderón Jr. To find work for the peasants of the Sierra, they were supplied with arable lands on confiscated haciendas for sharecropping, on very generous terms and at times without any payment. The one condition was that they must actually produce, so as to avoid any shortage of crops of prime necessity, it being this rule that ensured that during the Villista regime that there was no shortage of wheat or maize or beans or any other indispensable produce.[26]

Silvestre Terrazas's memoirs may not be entirely objective, but foreign observers were also impressed by the way the Villista regime, in spite of all difficulties caused by the war, managed to avoid famine. In February 1915, the U.S. collector of customs at El Paso, Zach Lamar Cobb, noted the "startling fact" that "various parties who have come in here from all portions of the Villa territory, state that there is a large supply of these foodstuffs in the country and that the prices of the same are reasonable." Cobb concluded that "it appears that the bulk of the Mexican people in these particular sections have been at work, planting and harvesting their crops in spite of the state of war that has existed."[27]

It would be a great mistake to conclude from these reports that all of the peasantry of Chihuahua and Durango, as well as the Villa administration of those states, remained mired in passivity with respect to land reform for the whole of the period in which Villa ruled there. In contrast to the peons on the haciendas, the inhabitants of the free villages were much less passive in enforcing their demands for land, although these were not primarily directed at the hacendados. The latter had not been the only ones who had seized lands from villagers during the long rule of Porfirio Díaz. In many communities, wealthy inhabitants had made use of Creel's land law of 1905 to appropriate large amounts of village land for their own use. The social characteristics of the victims and of *los ricos*, as the more affluent were generally called, varied from village to village. In San Andrés, the victims of expropriation tended to be Indians, while those who took their lands were wealthy white and mestizo inhabitants of the community (see chapter 1). In Cuchillo Parado and Namiquipa, the village aristocracy that appropriated the lands of its former military colonists consisted above all of immigrants from outside, who were encouraged in this course by the state authorities.[28] In the Galeana district in northwest Chihuahua, there was a different kind of village aristocracy, consisting of wealthy merchants who had taken advantage of Creel's land law and the debts that many peasants owed them to seize much peasant-owned land.[29] Both in Cuchillo Parado and in Namiquipa, the traditional villagers, organized into a *sociedad agrícola* and a *sociedad de agricultura* respectively, had already begun to reverse the effects of Creel's 1905 land law under the González administration. After Villa assumed control of Chihuahua, they carried out a wholesale attack on the beneficiaries of Creel's law, mostly returning lands to their former owners.

The Villista administration had no intention of protecting Creel's erstwhile supporters, and neither was it ready to "intervene" these lands in the same way that it had "intervened" the haciendas of Chihuahua's oligarchy. Such a move by the state into village communities would have been ineffective and highly unpopular. On the other hand, the Villistas were not ready either simply to allow the villagers to take the initiative and decide who should get the repossessed properties. It wanted to impose its own priorities on this division and at the same time gain popularity among the mass of Chihuahua's villagers by finally abrogating the highly unpopular law that Creel had imposed on the state in 1905. The new government decree, signed into law on March 5, 1914, by Chao as military governor (only a few weeks after he had assumed the governorship) and Secretary of State Silvestre Terrazas, stated that the prime beneficiaries of municipal lands should be soldiers whose families laid claim to lands for them, widows and orphans of soldiers who had died in battle, and poor, landless laborers. They would receive the land free of charge. The maximum that any individual could receive was 25 hectares, which could not be sold to outsiders, or sold at all for at least ten years. To make sure that these provisions were observed, the decree stated that all land titles would have to be ratified by the Villista authorities. Since many communities had lost all of their land, the decree stated that once the fighting ended and a constitutionalist victory was assured, every community would have a right to municipal lands, which the state would give to them.[30]

This was a law that respected the imperatives of war, insofar as its prime beneficiaries were the soldiers fighting in the field, who would be represented by their families and their widows and orphans. But it was in some respects also more radical even than Villa's proclamation of December 1913, when he had declared that all large estates would be expropriated and the lands taken from the peasants returned to them after final victory was won. In Villa's decree, poor peasants had not been singled out as beneficiaries. In this decree, the poor were specifically mentioned and given priority in the acquisition of land. There is unfortunately no detailed information regarding to what degree this law was really implemented and what effects it had on land tenure in the Villista countryside. In all probability, it legalized the reversal of Creel's land law that some villages were already carrying out, and it may have been the basis for some division of either public or commonly held municipal lands.

Villa seems to have actively participated in implementing some of these reforms. On November 12, 1914, he sent one of his officers, Colonel Gabino Duran, to the districts of Rayon Arteaga and Andres del Rio to "immediately divide lands . . . putting them in the hands of poor people so that they can cultivate them and subsist on their proceeds."[31] While hacienda lands do not seem to have been divided, at least not on a massive scale, the Villista administration does seem to have reestablished the traditional unwritten law that permitted villagers to graze their cattle on hacienda lands. In fact, it was a decision of that nature that precipitated a conflict between Villa and the British hacendado William S. Benton (see chapter 9 above).

Villismo and *Agrarismo*: Plans and Decrees

Land reform was a major issue that constantly recurred both in Villa's pronouncements and in the two newspapers that his administration published, *Vida Nueva* and the *Periódico Oficial*. The Villista newspapers again and again reported on measures dealing with the agrarian situation taken by revolutionary authorities in other parts of Mexico. Without any comment, the newspaper published decrees of revolutionary authorities from southern states such as Tabasco abolishing debt peonage, establishing a minimum wage, and putting an end to company stores.[32] Without saying so, the editors of the newspapers obviously meant to suggest that similar measures should be taken in Chihuahua and Durango. What is significant is the absence from the columns of these newspapers of the opinions of those most closely and clearly affected by the agrarian issues: the villagers themselves. No reporters seem to have gone into the villages to ask how their inhabitants viewed the solution of the agrarian problem. The newspapers limited themselves to publishing essays, by authors both from Chihuahua and from other parts of Mexico, insisting on the need for agrarian reform.

Unlike Zapata, and in this sense much more like Carranza, Villa obviously felt that decisions affecting the lower classes of society should above all be taken from above and not from below. Nevertheless, both he and his administrators were serious about the need for agrarian reform. Every time it seemed that the fighting might soon end, plans and laws were discussed in Chihuahua for profoundly transforming the patterns of land tenure.

The man mainly responsible for the project of an agrarian law for the state of Chihuahua was neither a traditional peasant leader who fought on Villa's side nor his most radical intellectual advocate of agrarian reform, Federico González Garza. Rather, he was a far more conservative former high official in Madero's government, Manuel Bonilla. Bonilla, who had been first minister of communications and later of economy in Madero's administration, had, unlike a large part of Madero's cabinet, been an active participant in the 1910 revolution. He had remained loyal to Madero throughout the coup that toppled him in February of 1913, and although he was present when Madero was arrested by Huerta's soldiers, he had managed to get away from the National Palace. On his way north, he had been captured by Huerta's troops and brought back to Mexico City. Huerta did not consider him very dangerous, however, and in view of the outcry that the murders of Madero and Vice President Pino Suárez had produced, Huerta hesitated to have him either imprisoned or killed. Instead, he consigned Bonilla to Mexico City and allowed him to resume his seat in congress. When Huerta dissolved the congress in October 1913, Bonilla fled north and joined Venustiano Carranza. He did not stay very long with the First Chief. While the concrete reasons that made him leave are not known, he was probably a victim of Carranza's dislike and disregard for those who had been close to Madero. Bonilla went into exile in Los Angeles, but he had no intention of remaining in the United States.[33]

His friend and former colleague Federico González Garza, who had in the meantime rejoined Villa and become advisor to Fidel Avila, wrote Bonilla suggesting that he too join the Villa faction.[34] Bonilla agreed, came to Chihuahua in May of 1914, and soon afterward became head of the Chihuahuan agrarian commission, which was charged with drafting an agrarian reform law. By September 1914, the commission had completed the draft of such a law, and it was published in November and December 1914 in the official newspaper of the state, not yet as a final law but rather as a draft bill.[35] On the whole, it was more conservative than Villa's decree of December 1913, Chao's municipal lands law, and Zapata's Plan of Ayala were, and than Carranza's decree of January 1915 and the agrarian paragraphs of the Mexican constitution of 1917 would be.

Bonilla's draft seems to have been largely inspired by Madero's conservative ideas. While the draft law did state that the revolution had to a large degree been fought to change the land-tenure system of Mexico, and while it did recognize that lands taken from communities should be returned to them, it also provided that this should be done through the judiciary. This could easily mean long delays, since the judicial system in Mexico had traditionally been hostile to peasants, as well as corrupt and inefficient. While the draft stated that every family head in Chihuahua should have the right to a piece of land, it also declared that only uncultivated lands from large haciendas should be expropriated. The main aim of this law, Bonilla said, was to have all cultivable lands worked in Chihuahua. If the hacendados did so, there was no reason to expropriate them. One of the reasons why members of the commission believed that cultivated lands should not be expropriated was that after a preliminary survey, they had concluded that there was sufficient uncultivated land for all of Chihuahua's landless peasants. Bonilla and the co-authors of the draft wrote that there had been a long discussion in the agrarian commission as to whether the lands should be given or sold to the beneficiaries of agrarian reform. The majority of the commission decided that the lands should be sold, and that the former owners would have to be compensated for the expropriated property. Peasants would be allowed to pay for the land in installments. The draft law also asserted that giving land to peasants was not sufficient. To be able to work it, they would also have to be provided with credit, agricultural implements, and water. In fact, Bonilla and his associates proposed that the state build a series of dams and other means of irrigation to this end.

The draft law largely reflected the attachment of both Madero and traditional nineteenth-century Mexican liberals to the sacredness of private property. No property should be confiscated without compensation. All claims by communities for the return of expropriated lands should be carefully weighed by the judiciary so that the property rights of landowners should not be infringed on without cause. The draft also reflected the ideas of nineteenth-century liberals in another way. It prohibited communal ownership of land, the basic form of land tenure of Indian communities in Mexico.

In central Mexico, such a law would have evoked a storm of protest from village communities that had held lands in common for centuries. In Chihuahua, however, communal ownership of land was confined to a few Indian communities. The majority of those peasants who had land of their own had either been individual owners or members of agricultural colonies in which each member had a parcel of land that clearly belonged to him. Such colonies, according to the law, were to be allowed and even encouraged.

In many ways, the law basically articulated the traditional fears and even contempt of Mexico's upper and middle classes for the country's peasants. If control of the land were turned over to these primitive groups, all they would do would be to work as much as they needed for their own subsistence, ignoring the needs of towns and cities, and Mexico would thus revert to backwardness. To avoid this taking place, productive land should not be expropriated, and those who got land would have to pay for it. This meant that they would have to produce more than their subsistence needs in order to meet their installment payments.

Bonilla's ideas were probably shared by Chihuahua's urban middle classes and by parts of the agrarian middle class as well, but they ran counter to the wishes of expropriated communities for the rapid return of their lands and to the demands of landless peasants and revolutionary veterans, who felt that they had a right to free distribution of land. After all, when the Spanish colonial administration had first granted lands to the military colonists who were to fight the Apaches in the eighteenth century, it had not only not asked for payment but, on the contrary, exempted the new colonists from taxes for many years. Villa's soldiers felt that like their ancestors who had fought the Apaches, they had earned the right to land by their sacrifices in battle.

In his proclamation of December 1913, Villa had intimated that he shared these ideas, and he had also made it very clear that he would never compensate the Chihuahuan oligarchy for the lands he had taken from them. The main reason he gave was that in consequence of understating the value of their holdings, and thus underpaying their taxes, Chihuahua's oligarchy owed the state so much money that they had in fact forfeited the right to their estates.

The contradiction between Bonilla's and Villa's ideas may explain why Bonilla's draft remained a draft and was never accepted into law. Nevertheless, the Chihuahuan state authorities did adopt preparatory measures that would be necessary either for the implementation of Bonilla's law or for the implementation of much more radical agrarian reform. In December 1914, agrarian surveyors were recruited from the agricultural school of Chapingo in the vicinity of Mexico City and sent to Chihuahua, where they were met at the railway station by the governor of the state. They then undertook the large project of surveying all arable lands in Chihuahua.[36]

The differing debate among the agrarian commissioners as to whether land should be sold or distributed free of charge to peasants, and the differences between Bonilla's projected land law and the earlier decrees of Villa and Chao, indicate that there were greatly varying opinions among the Villistas as to the kind of agrarian reform that should be carried out in Chihuahua.

Not only did Bonilla's project run counter to many of Villa's ideas, but a few weeks later, Villa's newspaper published a critique of another of his pet projects: the creation of military colonies. The author of the article wrote that military colonies in which the peasants tilled the land three days of the week and underwent military training for the other three days was quite unfeasible. If the colonists were primarily soldiers and tilled the land on the side, agriculture in these colonies would be extremely inefficient, not only because of the inefficiency of the military per se, but because the soldiers would have no incentive to work the land intensively. If the colonies consisted primarily of peasants doing military training on the side, three days a week would still be far too little for efficient farming. In fact, any kind of intensive military training would detract from the efficiency of agricultural production.[37]

It is an open question why Villa's official newspaper was able to publish articles expressing views in many way diametrically opposed to Villa's. It was certainly not the case that as Villa became more powerful, he became more tolerant of opinions that contradicted his own. There is no evidence of such a change in his character. He might not have wanted to wound the pride of the author of Chihuahua's agrarian law, Bonilla. But such reticence on Villa's part is highly improbable. What is even more unlikely is that he had become a convert to Bonilla's ideas. It is inconceivable that he should suddenly have decided to compensate Terrazas or Creel for any of the lands that he had taken from them, or that he would have refused to expropriate any of the lands they had cultivated. Nor is it likely that Villa had decided to violate the implicit promise to his soldiers that after the victory of the revolution, they would receive land free of charge.

One explanation for Villa's tolerance is that he simply did not read *Vida Nueva*. In addition, he might have considered these decrees part of the "imperatives of war." In November and December 1914, when these laws were being published, Mexico was in the full throes of a civil war. Villa was desperately seeking to gain support in the United States. This law was one way of assuring both American landowners and Woodrow Wilson that no expropriation would take place without compensation. It may also have been directed at landowners in southern and southeastern Mexico, many of whom had refused to accept the authority of the troops Carranza sent to subdue them. Villa may have been telling them that in the southern areas, he would not confiscate their estates without compensation, in contrast to what he had done in northern Mexico.

Another reason certainly was that even if he had read the decrees, he did not much care what the *licenciados* were saying. He would apply his own law. This is in fact what happened. In mid 1915, he ordered Governor Avila to go ahead with land reform, but to exclude from it all the Terrazas haciendas, which were destined for his soldiers. There was no mention here of only distributing unproductive land on these haciendas, the richest in Chihuahua.[38]

In May 1915, Villa issued a comprehensive national land-reform law. All estates above a certain size were to be divided among the peasants. The owners would receive some form of indemnity, and the peasants would have to pay in small installments.[39] Bonilla's idea that only unproductive land should be confiscated was again completely disregarded. As far as Chihuahua was concerned, Villa had clearly stated that since the state's oligarchy owed huge tax debts to the government, they would receive no compensation for their expropriated properties.

Foreign-owned properties (with the significant exception of those belonging to Spaniards) were not affected by Villa's decrees. Villa neither interfered in the administration of these estates nor imposed high taxes on them. The only significant tax was an export payment due on all cattle exported to the United States. As cattle, and to a lesser degree agricultural products, from state-controlled haciendas were being rapidly depleted by the needs of Villa's war machine, the foreign properties emerged as islands of prosperity in an increasingly impoverished environment. As a result, in a period of increasing scarcity, foreign-owned haciendas could put goods at the disposal of their employees and workers that frequently could not be found elsewhere.

It is difficult to assess how Chihuahua's villagers perceived Bonilla's draft law. On the one hand, the idea that decisions about return of confiscated lands would be made by the judiciary, rather than by the Villa administration, and the possibility they would have to pay for the land they received may have alienated many peasants; this in turn may explain why the law was never ratified. On the other hand, the fact that Bonilla sent out questionnaires to many villages in which the villagers were asked to spell out their claims to land, and in which nothing was said about the peasants having to pay for it, may have given them the feeling that the Villista administration was sincere in its desire to carry out an agrarian reform once the revolution was over.[40] In addition, some of the clauses of the proposed land reform, above all the idea that there would be no communal property, and that everyone would personally own the land he obtained, was highly popular in Chihuahua. The great majority of Chihuahua's peasants had always rejected the *ejido* concept of communal property, which had originated in central Mexico.[41]

It is not clear how Chihuahua's villagers reacted either to the postponement of land reform or to Villa's refusal to touch foreign-owned properties. By the way they acted and fought, most of the Villa's peasant soldiers clearly showed that they did not object to his policies. Not only did they trust their leader; they also knew that they had been singled out as the prime recipients of land once the revolution was won.

For very different reasons, many workers on foreign-owned estates were also willing to accept the status quo. The wealthy foreign owners of Mexican haciendas made it a point to pay their employees wages that were frequently higher than those paid on estates owned by Mexican nationals.

There was an additional factor that persuaded many villagers to accept the delay in land reform and still remain loyal to Villa. This was the fact that at least temporarily, the revolutionary leader had another way of gaining the support of a large part of Chihuahua's inhabitants, and especially of his soldiers, as well as of many peasants, without giving them land.

This was the money that he printed at an ever-increasing rate. As long as it was accepted both in the territories he controlled and across the border, what easier way to gain support, without all the problems of rivalries that land divisions might create, than simply to give away bills of ever-higher denominations, which the printing presses were churning out at the rate of 3,000,000 a day? Whenever Villa occupied a new town, he handed out his bills. More profound reforms were postponed until the victory of the revolution.

Nevertheless, popular support for Villa's measures was by no means unanimous. Frequent references in Villista newspapers and foreign consular reports to "bandits" who raided estates and attacked trains is a clear manifestation that there was some dissatisfaction with Villa's measures in the Mexican countryside. The term *bandidos* was employed in an extremely broad sense. It referred both to genuine outlaws, interested only in robbing and killing, as well as to agrarian revolutionaries who rejected Villa's "moderate" policies.[42]

Villa and the Radicals in Chihuahua

Villa faced a similar problem to that of radical revolutionaries in other countries who had to deal with factions in some respects more radical than they were. These factions demanded immediate large-scale reforms and rejected reasons of state given by the revolutionary authorities for postponing them since they did not accept the legitimacy of the revolutionary state, and in many cases of the state at all. Revolutionary leaders tend to be particularly harsh when dealing with such rebels on their left. During the French Revolution, Robespierre proceeded against Jacques Roux and his supporters when they demanded far harsher measures against the wealthy than the Jacobins were willing to grant. The Bolsheviks reacted with similar hostility to Machno's anarchists and the sailors of the military fortress at Kronstadt who rejected the dictatorship of the Bolshevik party.

In the case of Villa, the best-known radical leader to his left was Máximo Castillo. Castillo, a ranchero before the revolution (see chapter 3), had joined first Madero, then Orozco, because he hoped they would return the peasantry's stolen lands. He left each of them when they did not keep their agrarian promises. During the last month of Abraham González's administration in Chihuahua, and in the first years of Huertista rule in the state, Castillo continued the revolutionary fight on his own.[43]

Villa and Castillo pursued similar aims in some ways, but the two never joined forces. In many respects, Castillo was an anarchist, unwilling to subordinate himself to anyone else. Above all, though, Castillo seems to have been unwilling to accept one of the basic tenets of Villa's strategy in 1913–14: respect for foreign property. Castillo demanded tribute from American estate owners, and if they refused to pay, he would attack their haciendas and seize their cattle.[44] He was especially hard on the Mormons, whose properties he constantly raided. Villa could not tolerate this, which would have cost him the goodwill both of the U.S. administration and of American businessmen, and would have prevented his acquiring arms in the United States. After he assumed control of Chihuahua, he was still less able to tolerate this kind of behavior on Castillo's part, since much of his popularity abroad was predicated upon his ability to put an end to "banditry" and to exercise complete control over Chihuahua. He repeatedly sent out troops to hunt down Castillo and at one point succeeded in capturing half of his force. They were immediately shot.

Nevertheless, Castillo was popular in Chihuahua's countryside. He enjoyed the same kind of Robin Hood reputation that Villa had enjoyed. For many peasants who were not interested in considerations of higher policy, Castillo's looting of American estates was quite popular. So was his commitment to agrarian reform. In addition, in spite of a contrary reputation, Castillo in many respects seems to have been a gentle man. Reporting on a train holdup by Castillo, American authorities stated: "When the train was stopped it was run in on a siding and the express mail baggage cars were looted, everything of value being taken. The passengers, who included between twenty-five and thirty Americans, many of them Mormons returning to their abandoned colonies, were not deprived of their possessions or harmed in any way."[45]

Castillo even earned Villa's reluctant gratitude when shortly after Villa's men had massacred half of his force, he allowed Villa's wife, Luz Corral, to pass unmolested through the territory he controlled. Once Castillo had heard that she was in the vicinity of his camp, he had her brought to him. At first she was worried, for she was forced to spend the night in the camp surrounded by Castillo's soldiers, who were shouting "Death to Villa!" Castillo, though, was very courteous to her. After greeting her, he told her about the recent fight that he had had with Villa, saying, "He nearly exterminated my people, but where families are concerned, things are very different." Castillo not only treated her well but escorted her to the U.S. border so that she would not be mistreated by anyone else. Villa was so grateful that, according to his wife, he decided to suspend any attack on Castillo, at least for a time.[46]

What finally caused Castillo's downfall was not Villa but the most bloody attack on a train in the history of Chihuahua, which, according to most accounts, was wrongly attributed to him. Bandits set fire to a railway tunnel called La Cumbre shortly before a passenger train entered it and blew up both exits of the tunnel, so that the passengers were either burned to death or suffocated. The attack occurred in a region where Castillo operated, and it was attributed to him, although he always denied having had anything to do with it. Mexican scholars have since identified the perpetrator of the attack as a local bandit named Gutiérrez.[47] As a result of these accusations, Castillo lost whatever popular support he had, many of his men deserted him, and he was forced to flee across the border to the United States, denying any responsibility for the La Cumbre massacre until the end.[48]

Villa and the Foreign Mine Owners

As they had in the case of the large estates, the imperatives of war also led the Villista administration to very contradictory policies with respect to the second-most-important sector of Chihuahua's economy, mining.

In contrast to the agricultural sector, the vast majority of mines and smelters in Chihuahua were foreign-owned, but the fighting in Chihuahua, as well as reduced demand for ore on international markets, had led most mining companies to curtail or abandon mining altogether in Chihuahua. Villa's main interest was to have the large foreign companies, above all the American Smelting and Refining Company (ASARCO), resume work in Chihuahua. Villa had two options for achieving this. The first was to grant the mine owners every possible condition they could wish for to resume operation. The second was to threaten them with the occupation of their holdings and state operation of the mines if they did not.

During most of the time that he controlled Chihuahua, Villa for the most part chose the first road. He obviously felt that the most important way in which he could simultaneously improve the living standard of the people and raise money was by persuading many of the American mining companies who had suspended operations in Chihuahua to return and begin work once again. He accordingly offered them wide-ranging guarantees. There would be no confiscation of their ores. Although trains were urgently needed for the military operations of the División del Norte, Villa guaranteed the companies that they would have sufficient facilities to transport the ores they had mined to the United States. He was willing to go one step further and to prevent union agitators from the United States, above all members of the IWW, from organizing their workers and carrying out strikes.[49] Villa managed to gain a large amount of sympathy among mining operators, and in February and March 1914, many of them had begun to resume operations. Only a few weeks after Villa had gained control of Chihuahua, a representative of ASARCO arrived in Chihuahua to confer with him. "It is said," the *El Paso Times* reported, "that Villa had promised the smelter official every protection if they will resume work and has given his promise that the railroad line between Juárez and Chihuahua will be kept open so that coal and coke can be transported from the border to Chihuahua for the fuel of the smelter."[50]

It is not clear how ASARCO responded, but in April and May 1914, it suspended operations, together with most other American mining operators in Mexico, after U.S. troops had occupied Veracruz and the possibility of a Mexican-American war loomed. Villa made every possible effort to persuade American companies to again return to Chihuahua. He publicly stated that he would never participate in a war against the United States and on June 23, he publicly declared, "I wish again to state that the persons and properties of foreigners in the territory controlled by the troops of my command will have every guarantee of protection."[51] The largest mining companies doing business in Chihuahua seem to have responded positively to Villa's offers. ASARCO soon resumed production and operated most of its mining properties until September 1915. The same was true of another large company, the Batopilas Mining Company.[52]

For those mining companies whose response was sluggish, the Villa administration for the first time did not limit itself to offering enticements but added a stick to the carrot, threatening companies that did not resume work with higher taxes.[53] It was still a very light threat in view of other measures to which Villa could have resorted. In theory at least, he could have declared (and later would) that if the mining companies did not resume operations, he would do so himself and have the state operate American-owned mines, as it did Mexican-owned mines. Such a measure would, however, have entailed very high costs, which Villa, at least at that time, was unwilling to accept. It would have brought about a rapid deterioration of his relations both with American business interests and with the Wilson administration, and would thus have posed a serious threat to his supplies of arms and ammunition. In addition, the months of July and August 1914 were a time when relations with Carranza became more and more strained and civil war loomed as a serious possibility. The support, or at least neutrality, of the United States was crucial to Villa at this time.

The fact that many American mining companies did not resume operation certainly limited the revenues of both a large number of affected Chihuahuans and of the revolutionary state. But it did not cause mass unemployment. That problem had been taken care of by the army, which more and more able-bodied men from Chihuahua joined. In fact, the labor shortage became such a problem that many mining companies gave this as their primary reason for not resuming operations.[54]

Villa's Panacea for Mexico: Education

There was one type of reform, though, that was far less controversial than agrarian reform, and that in some respects may have been even closer to Villa's heart: education. This was, in fact, the field in which Villista reforms manifested themselves most concretely. While many of the self-deprecatory statements that Villa frequently made constituted more of a posture than reality, there is no reason to doubt him when he expressed his profound regret at never having had an education. As his power increased, he must have been more and more conscious of the discrepancy between his ambitions on the one hand and his lack of education on the other. Villa's dedication to and belief in education was expressed both by spontaneous acts of his own and by the policies of his Chihuahuan administration.

It has often been said that Villa and the peasant leaders of the Mexican Revolution wanted to recreate the past—that is, to establish a society based on free peasants—while Carranza and the men who followed him wished to modernize the country, largely patterned on the United States and the industrial countries of western Europe. This disregards Villa's ability to gain the trust and support not just of peasants and the poor of the north in general but of large segments of the northern middle class as well. Above all, Villa was as much and probably more of a modernizer than any other northern revolutionary leader with respect to education. In his interviews and speeches, Villa again and again insisted on the importance of education and on his tremendous admiration for teachers. Doctor Francisco Uranga Vallarta, who witnessed the revolution in Chihuahua as a child, has vivid memories of going with his adoptive mother, a teacher, and two of her colleagues to Villa's headquarters in a railway car where they had been summoned by the revolutionary leader. "What I admire most in life," he told them, "is the capacity to express oneself. I lacked instruction and I only learned to read and write when I was already an adult. The profession I admire most is yours." This speech was followed by gifts of food, above all, corn, coffee, sugar, and flour, from the supplies of his troop trains. "The only thing I can offer you is the food I have on my trains," Villa said.[55]

Villa repeatedly showed his interest in and dedication to education both in speeches and in acts of generosity to both teachers and children. Francisco Gil

Piñon was a fatherless child in 1913 when Villa and his men occupied his native town of San Buenaventura. The town's leading citizens had panicked when news that Villa was on the way reached them. They were afraid of being caught in an insoluble dilemma. Villa came to San Buenaventura shortly after crossing the border into Chihuahua in 1913, when he did not yet dominate any large part of the state. The town's leading citizens were afraid that if they welcomed Villa, the federal authorities might take reprisals against them. On the other hand, if they simply ignored the revolutionary chieftain, the latter might very well consider them enemies of the revolution and act accordingly. The best way they felt they could solve the dilemma was by having a small child who had no father who might later become the victim of reprisals make a speech welcoming Villa. When Villa had entered the town, Francisco Gil Piñon addressed him in the name of its citizens, not with the words of a child but rather in bombastic terms that one of the town's revolutionary leaders had made him learn by heart:

General—my childish heart is deeply moved by your great personality and in the name of this village that admires you I offer you our most cordial hospitality. This town today is proud to receive a distinguished citizen who without fear and hesitation held high the flag of democracy to redeem our country, who will live forever in the annals of our town's history. Sir, welcome and I hope that your stay among us will be agreeable and happy.

Villa was deeply moved by the speech, got off his horse, embraced Francisco Gil Piñon, and promised him that once he had the power to do so, he would take care of his education. He kept his word. Once he was in control of the whole of the state of Chihuahua, he sent Gil Piñon, together with another boy, Eustaquio Rivera, to be educated in a military school in the United States.[56] It might be argued that this was more a case of personal sympathy—Gil Piñon became Villa's adopted son—than of policy. But Villa behaved similarly to children he did not even know. When he went to the Mexico City and saw children sleeping on the street, he was so moved that he had hundreds of them brought to Ciudad Chihuahua to be educated at the state's School of Arts and Crafts.[57]

Silvestre Terrazas once invited Villa to witness an artistic performance by children from a nursery school administered for the poor by Catholic nuns. Villa at first refused to attend the performance when he heard that the school, a charitable foundation called the "Friend of the Working Women," was run by nuns. With great difficulty, Silvestre Terrazas persuaded him to attend the event. When he finally did, Villa was so enraptured by the performance of the children that he jumped on the stage, embraced all of them, and then gave orders to Silvestre Terrazas to regularly supply the nuns with food, who had been completely dependent upon individual charities.[58]

Villa's commitment to education was expressed not only in personal and spontaneous acts of generosity but also in a systematic policy by his administration to aid and further education. In their report to the people of the state on the first year of Villista rule in Chihuahua, Governor Fidel Avila and Silvestre Terrazas proudly stated that more than 100 new schools had been built during this time, that the education budget had been enormously increased, teachers' salaries raised, and new teachers recruited from other parts of Mexico. "After land division," they wrote, "public education constitutes one of the most important promises of the revolution."[59] Apart from primary education, the Villista administration had begun to develop professional education and to make plans for institutions of higher learning. The School of Arts and Crafts profited from the confiscation of the oligarchy's property. Many of the printing presses taken from men considered "enemies of the revolution" were brought to that school to serve as learning instruments for its pupils. Plans were made to set up an industrial boarding school for the children of soldiers killed while fighting in the revolutionary armies.

The Villista administration had begun work on an even more grandiose project: the transformation of Terrazas's richest hacienda, the Quinta Carolina, where he and his wife had lived, into a university called the Universidad Fronteriza. Construction for the university had already begun when the Villistas were defeated in Chihuahua.[60] Plans for transforming Terrazas's sumptuous residence into a center of education were then abandoned once and for all.

Daily Life in Villista Chihuahua

With the exception of a few months after González initially assumed the governorship, Chihuahua was at war for ten years, between November 1910 and May 1920. For eight of these years, the war was fought inside Chihuahua; for two years, it took place outside of the state's borders, providing a period of respite and rest for its inhabitants. These were the two years during which Villa controlled the state. In comparison to what had come before and to what would come afterward, it was in many respects a period of peace and tranquillity for the state's civilian inhabitants, although the traces of war could be found everywhere. The destruction that the fighting had brought to Chihuahua was massive. "The wreckage of three revolutions lines the track," noted Herman Whitaker, an American reporter traveling in Villista Chihuahua, who described his impressions in 1914:

A black spot ahead develops into the wheels and the scorched ironwork of a burned passenger train. Again our train plunges down into a "shoo-fly," a piece of track built around a burned bridge. Miles of bent and twisted rails tell the tale of track destroyed and rebuilt, sometimes two or three times. Between and around them are strewn more grisly mementos—carcasses of dead horses, desiccated by desert heat, and here and there a small cross made of two twigs that marks the resting place of the riders.

They are really pathetic, these nameless graves. The car rolls on over the hot face of the desert with its blue hedge of distant mountains and endless procession of crosses, burned bridges, wrecks; a vivid impression of the cyclonic passion which has devastated this unhappy land is forced in upon one. The destruction is enormous.

The correspondent, though, was impressed by the speed and efficiency with which the Villa administration had restored the net of railway communications that spanned northern Mexico:

Meanwhile—and this is one of the remarkable features of the situation—the Mexican Central has been rebuilt and is in operation with trains running on a fairly fast schedule, from Juárez to Torreón, a distance of 570 miles. Between Torreón and Durango, the line has also been rebuilt for the third time, and at the time of writing the road has just been reopened to Monterrey. All this has been accomplished by Mexicans without any American help.[61]

Villa's assumption of control in Chihuahua meant that the civilian population would be far less affected by the consequences of war than before, but it did not mean that the human cost of the revolution would drastically diminish. On the contrary, as the revolution extended into other parts of Mexico, the casualties suffered by the División del Norte increased as the battles became larger and bloodier. The number of wounded being cared for in the hospitals in Ciudad Chihuahua and the number of cripples roaming the streets of the state capital were but one manifestation of the increasingly bloody cost of the revolution. The state's administration did its best to care for these men and their families: it provided hospital care for the wounded, pensions for those completely disabled, railway tickets for families wishing to visit their wounded relatives, and the promise of land grants once the revolution was victorious.

Apart from redistribution of goods, there were other ways in which the Villista administration tried to help Chihuahua's poor. Every month the state-supported Miguel Salas hospital proudly sent the Chihuahuan municipality a report on all the nonmilitary indigent patients that it had treated that month, noting, for example, that "M. H., an indigent woman, was admitted to the hospital on January 2, occupying bed no. 8. She suffered from hemorrhagic endometritis. She was operated on on January 3, and after having been cured, she left the hospital on January 12." There was a similar detailed public report on every patient admitted to the hospital, whether poor or not. The anonymity of patients was secured by only giving their initials. Even the slightest cases were reported to the authorities, such as that of E. M. a poor patient admitted on January 3: "Occupied bed no. 18. Hypochondriac. Left hospital January 4." While a few "distinguished first-class patients," who paid 6 pesos a day for their stay in the hospital, contributed some of the operating costs of 1,312 pesos and 82 cents for the month of January, the brunt of the expenses, 1,200 pesos, was borne by the state government.[62]

The Miguel Salas sanitorium was an entirely civilian institution. Soldiers and those wounded in battle were treated in different hospitals. It is not clear whether Miguel Salas was the only hospital of its kind in Chihuahua, or whether other similar hospitals taking in poor patients existed both in the capital city and in the rest of the state. Raising money for hospitals was a very popular affair in Villista Chihuahua, and special fund-raisers frequently took place. On one such occasion, a horse race was organized in order to raise money for the constitutionalist hospitals. Villa and his staff attended in gala uniforms, officers of his army were the racing jockeys, and a military band played popular melodies.[63]

The greatest, and in the final account most intractable, problem Villa had to deal with in Chihuahua was of an economic nature. Chihuahua had paid a high price for the three years of civil war it had undergone. "In Chihuahua, where the car stopped for a day," Whitaker reported,

more signs of economic disintegration are to be seen. Since the revolution began the foreign population has dwindled from about 800 in the city and 4,000 in the surrounding districts to some eighty souls. This means far more than the figures indicate. The majority of those who left the country were employers of labor, some on a large scale. Undoubtedly the number of Mexicans directly or indirectly dependent upon them would total 30,000 and it requires no large efforts of the imagination to picture the result attendant on the cutting off of such a large payroll.[64]

During the first few months of Villista rule in Chihuahua, Villa's policies of redistribution more than made up for these economic problems, at least as far as the poor were concerned. As Alden Buell Case, an American Protestant whose mission was located in a rural area of Chihuahua called El Valle, put it,

The revolution came to El Valle as a great leveler. The rich were relieved of their superfluous wealth, and the poor, for the time being at least[,] lived in plenty. Men well-to-do financially and not known to be in sympathy with the revolution were called upon to contribute heavily to the cause they detested. Sums of 3,000, 5,000 or 10,000 pesos were "squeezed" from certain individuals and in a few cases contributions of large size were repeatedly demanded of the same person. . . . On the taking of El Valle, the matter of meat supply, not only for the soldiers but for the entire population as well, was taken in charge by the military. A drove of fat beeves from these large herds was brought in daily, slaughtered whenever convenient—at first on the main streets—and sold to the townspeople at a very low price. This helped to fill the treasury of the revolutionists and at the same time tended to make them popular with the common people.

Many of the soldiers, although not all, soon found quarters with private families all through the city. No money was tendered for board, but fresh beef was supplied to these houses in prodigious abundance. In the sacking of the stores quantities of groceries were secured by the men, and those families who were so fortunate as to have revolutionary boarders, were under no necessity of buying sugar, coffee, lard and the like for some time to come.[65]

The main problems that Chihuahuans faced in the later months of Villista rule in 1914 were shortages and inflation. The reasons are not difficult to explain. Not only were revenues from mining shrinking, but the state's main source of wealth, its best-known and most important resource, its cattle herds, were slowly being depleted. Cattle paid for imports from the United States, and cattle were being used to feed the increasing number of troops that made up the División del Norte. In addition, much of Chihuahua's not very great agricultural production was being exported from the state to feed the troops.

The more immediate reason for the shortages and inflation that afflicted Chihuahua, however, was to be found in the huge amounts of paper money that Villa's printing presses were churning out. While the Villista peso had been worth about U.S. 50¢ in early 1914, it had rapidly fallen to 20¢ by midyear.[66] Inflation naturally went hand in hand with the drop in value. The Villista authorities did not know how to react to this alarming situation. The tendency was to blame it exclusively on rapacious merchants who were hoarding goods or selling them at outrageous prices.

The enormous economic problems that Chihuahua faced were perhaps best expressed in a dramatic confrontation that took place on September 15, 1914, between some of the wealthiest merchants of Ciudad Chihuahua on the one hand

and the mayor and members of the city council on the other. The meeting came on the heels of a sharp rise in the prices of some of the most essential products that the people of Chihuahua needed in order to survive. This led to an increasing number of complaints, especially from the poorest sectors of the population, which in turn began to concern the Villista administration. The mayor declared that one of the main aims he had in mind when he called the meeting with the city's most important merchants was to stabilize the prices of basic goods such as coffee, sugar, butter, flour, rice, salt, soap, oil, candles, and matches. He stated that the military government was deeply worried at "the difficult living conditions of the proletarian class." He appealed to the patriotism of the merchants and stated that their 20 percent profit margin on basic goods was far too high. Other members of the city administration evoked the authority of Villa, "who wished to improve the lot of the poor and prevent their exploitation by merchants."[67]

The two representatives of Chihuahua's merchant class, Juan Manuel Gurrola and Pablo Martínez, insisted that it was not greed but the fall in the value of Villista currency that was the basic cause of price increases. They brushed aside suggestions by a city councilman that they should buy more Mexican goods and thus become independent of the price fluctuations of American products, which were the result of the fall in value of the Villista currency. Mexican goods, they said, were difficult to obtain because of the enormous problems that internal transportation presented, and in fact Mexican products were generally more expensive than American ones and frequently sold only by American companies. They insisted that a profit margin of 15 to 20 percent was not too high considering the risks to which they were subjected as a result of the constant change in value of the Villista currency.

In the end, the two sides agreed on a 30-day price freeze.[68] Both sides also agreed that there was very little in reality that they could do about the increasing price rises and shortages in Chihuahua. All the government could promise was that at some point in the not-too-distant future, a new bank would be created in Chihuahua and a new paper currency based on gold would be instituted. In the meantime, the living standard of the population continued to decline, and dissatisfaction continued to increase.

In war-torn Europe, governments faced with increasing shortages of food and other prime necessities had instituted rationing to provide at least a basic subsistence minimum for their populations. The Villista administration never attempted to resort to rationing in Chihuahua. Had it done so, it would probably have very rapidly reached the conclusion that it lacked the European countries' well-organized bureaucracy, capable of taking charge of rationing. In addition, throughout much of 1914, large segments of Chihuahua's population were by no means as drastically affected by the deteriorating economic situation as the urban proletariat. The countryside, in which the majority of Chihuahua's inhabitants lived, still managed to feed itself. Banditry had been largely eliminated, and throughout 1914, the government did not impose levies on the agrarian population that might have caused starvation. Those foreign mining companies that operated in Chihuahua imported their own food—they had no dollar shortage and were not affected by the fluctuations of the Mexican peso—and sold it to their workers at company stores.[69] The many Chihuahuans who had joined the army were well supplied with basic necessities, both by living off the land and from large amounts of food and other supplies bought in the United States. It was basically the urban population of Chihuahua, which was not employed by foreign companies, that suffered most from increasing prices and shortages.

From the eighteenth century to the twentieth, aside from rationing, redistribution, and confiscation, revolutionary governments facing problems like that confronting the Villista administration—a deteriorating economic situation that it could not solve, at least not in the immediate future, combined with the need to wage continuing warfare—have resorted to two kinds of measures to stay in power notwithstanding increasing popular dissatisfaction and possible disillusionment. On the one hand, they have greatly increased what their supporters have called political education and their enemies political propaganda; on the other, they have resorted to control and repression. Chihuahua was no exception to this rule. But the amount of both political education and propaganda and of repression was less than under other revolutionary regimes.

Villista Propaganda

The main instruments of revolutionary propaganda were two newspapers published by the state government, the official organ of the División del Norte, *Vida Nueva*, and the *Periódico Oficial del Gobierno Constitucionalista del Estado de Chihuahua*.

Vida Nueva primarily contained news of the war. It published detailed descriptions of battles, interviews with generals, biographies of revolutionary leaders, constant praise of Villa as one of the greatest generals in history, attacks on Huerta, news of American support of the revolution, and, very rarely, ideological assessments of the aims of the revolution. *Vida Nueva* carried little local news, and, unlike earlier Chihuahuan newspapers, relatively few letters to the editor. It did not very much deal with ideology, and when it did, it propounded radical programs. Apart from discussions of land reform, the newspaper's main ideological content was a kind of personality cult: "Viva Villa! Torreón Is Ours" was the headline in *Vida Nueva* on the day that Torreón fell to the División del Norte. It was followed by an article entitled "Citizen Francisco Villa":

Multitudes can acclaim the hero whose courage, whose tenacity, whose talent, whose faith, whose energy has led his legions to the summit where the brilliant sun of victory shows the gigantic figures of our soldiers of the people.

The multitudes will come to put flowers at the feet of the victorious champion and thus show him their profound affection.

The great general, the invincible general, the all-powerful warrior who began to fight with nine men, with nine candidates for suicide, now heads the greatest army that this republic has ever seen in its history, which never believed that one man would be able to lead 25,000 soldiers. . . . Citizen Francisco Villa deserves to be studied by history, by the brain of a scholar and the soul of a moral philosopher.[70]

The *Periódico Oficial* was a much more sober publication, which basically contained the decrees and laws published by the government, as well as a series of ideological articles. For a time, one of its main ideologues was the Peruvian poet José Santos Chocano, who thus hoped to become "the brains of the revolution."

The Villista administration did not rely on newspapers alone to carry out its information policy, however. Several times a week, telegrams containing news, excerpts from U.S. newspapers, and comments were sent to regional and local officials throughout Chihuahua.

Villa's news media were never able to achieve a monopoly of information. Many literate Chihuahuans also had access to American publications from across the border, chiefly from El Paso, which were published in English but also contained Spanish-language sections. Frequently, *Vida Nueva* published articles in response to editorials or news stories published by the *El Paso Morning Times*. It is not clear to what degree, in a state where most people, and hence the great majority of Villa's constituents, were illiterate, a newspaper could actively have influenced their ideology.

Not surprisingly, therefore, the Villista administration also resorted to other forms of political propaganda, which it hoped would more effectively influence the illiterate lower classes of society. On festive occasions, both on traditional patriotic holidays and on days when the División del Norte had achieved major victories, the government organized patriotic ceremonies. The most visible such political manifestations were mass meetings organized by the Villista administration to honor both Villa and his army, which combined traditional middle-class political ritual, popular music, and above all popular enthusiasm.

Intellectuals and politicians sent out invitations to large segments of the population to attend a "literary musical ceremony" in the Teatro de los Héroes, one of Ciudad Chihuahua's largest auditoriums, on January 15, 1914, for example, "to express public homage, admiration, gratitude and sympathy to the great general Francisco Villa and to the generals, leaders, officers, and constitutionalist soldiers who have gained a great glorious triumph in the Ojinaga campaign by annihilating the hosts of despotism and tyranny and by freeing the heroic state of Chihuahua from traitors." In addition to speeches by notables such as Professor Matías García, the ceremony would include poems such as "Viva Madero," recited by Señorita Emma Nogueira, and "Verb of Apotheosis," read by the poet himself, Villa's secretary, Professor Enrique Pérez Rul. Señoritas Margarita Romero and Carmen Corral would give a piano recital from Verdi's *Il Trovatore*, and the Sala Wagner quintet would play the waltzes "Sound from the Valley" and "Rose Mousse." Finally, there would be some new music composed in honor of Villa and his soldiers: a march called "Villa," performed by the constitutionalist band, and a polka, "El Dorado," played by Professor Pablo Gama.[71]

While the Teatro de los Héroes event suggests some conventional form of political ceremony, this was not the case. John Reed, who attended one such meeting, has given a convincing glimpse of the enthusiasm these programs invoked, especially during the first month of Villista rule in Chihuahua. Reed describes a ceremony organized by the artillery corps of Villa's army, two weeks before he set out for Torreón, to present him with a gold medal for personal heroism on the field. It took place in the audience hall of the governor's palace in Chihuahua. Inside the palace, it was a military affair:

The officers of artillery in smart blue uniforms faced with black velvet and gold, were solidly banked across one end of the audience hall with flashing new swords and their gilt-braided hats stiffly held under their arms. There was a double line of soldiers presenting arms along the staircase leading to the palace. On the streets the people of the capital were massed in solid thousands on the Plaza de Armas before the palace.

"Ya viene," here he comes, viva Villa, viva Madero, Villa the friend of the poor.

The roar began at the back of the crowd and swept like fire in heavy growing crescendo until it seemed to toss thousands of hats above their heads. The band in the courtyard struck up the Mexican national air, and Villa came walking down the street.

Villa obviously felt no need to adapt too much to these rituals. "He was dressed in an old plain khaki uniform, with several buttons lacking. He hadn't recently shaved, wore no hat and his hair had not been brushed. He walked a little pigeon-toed, humped over with his hands in his trouser pockets. As he entered the aisle between the rigid lines of soldiers he seemed slightly embarrassed, and grinned and nodded to a compadre here and there in the ranks. At the foot of the grand staircase, Governor Chao and Secretary of State Terrazas joined him in full dress uniform."

Civilians and military men competed as to who could lavish greater praise on Villa. "Señor Bauche Alcalde stepped forward, raised his right hand to the exact position which Cicero took when denouncing Catiline, and pronounced a short discourse indicting Villa for personal bravery on the field on six counts, which he mentioned in florid detail. He was followed by the chief of artillery who said: 'The army adores you. We will follow you wherever you lead. You can be what you desire in Mexico.'"

An experienced politician counseled by a dozen media consultants could not have been more effective than Villa when he got up to answer all the praise lavished on him:

He looked at the medal, scratching his head and in reverent silence said clearly: "This is a hell of a little thing to give a man for all the heroism you are talking about." And the bubble of empire was pricked then and there was a great shout of laughter.

His speech of acceptance of the medal was then couched in two sentences. "There is no word to speak. All I can say is my heart is all to you."[72]

Was Villa reluctant to speak owing to shyness, to lack of experience, or, on the contrary, which seems far more probable, because he realized that two such sentences would strike a deeper chord among his listeners than any long and florid speech that he might make?

Unlike other revolutionary societies, Villista Chihuahua did not create any new political organizations to mobilize the population in its favor. There was no Jacobin Club as in revolutionary Paris, no Communist Party as in revolutionary Russia, and no committees for the defense of the revolution as in Cuba. This does not mean, though, that the army was the sole revolutionary organization in revolutionary Chihuahua. A host of civilian organizations, some of which had already emerged during the Porfirian period and others that had been created during the governorship of Abraham González, continued to exist and strongly supported the Villista administration.

In April 1914, when Carranza first visited Chihuahua (relations between him and Villa were, at least officially, still very good), a great meeting was held to greet the nominal chieftain of the constitutionalist revolution. Apart from a host of high military and civilian officials of the Villista administration, the meeting was also attended by a large number of representatives of workers' organizations, including, according to *Vida Nueva*, the Great League of Mexican Carpenters, the Union of Mexican Mechanics, the Union of Construction Workers, the Union of Typographers Gutenberg, the Cuauhtemoc of Workers, the Zaragoza of Tailors, the Morelos Society of Shoemakers, the Mutual Self-Help Organization of Coach Drivers, and the Miguel Hidalgo Society of Painters.[73]

While these organizations supported the government, it is not clear what role they played in the political activities of the Villista administration. The government had clearly set limits on their activities: strikes were practically forbidden, and none took place during the first year of Villista rule in Chihuahua. There is no evidence, though, that the Villista administration attempted to control or to manipulate these organizations.

Villa's Secret Police

While political and/or military mobilization of large segments of the population constitutes one essential characteristic of revolutionary societies, vigilance and repression are other equally inevitable characteristics of such societies. The type of vigilance and the type and extent of repression, though, can vary enormously from one revolutionary society to another. Vigilance can be broad and very encompassing or extremely limited in its scope. In some societies very large segments of civil society are called upon to participate in this vigilance, which at times has the aim of embracing the whole of the population. In other revolutionary societies, surveillance may extend only to groups perceived as real or potential enemies of the revolution and is practiced only by bureaucrats and by the secret police. This seems to have been the case in Villista Chihuahua.

The first call to vigilance and surveillance was contained in a memorandum sent to all heads of office (*jefes de oficina*) by Silvestre Terrazas on March 13, 1914, only a few months after the revolutionaries had assumed control of Chihuahua. It called for all higher Villista officials (all those who headed a department, an office, or an institution) to attempt to find out what their subordinates thought of the constitutionalist cause and how committed they were to it, but also how good they were at their work. This admonition by Silvestre Terrazas to the "office heads" was coupled with a clear warning. The head of any government office that employed enemies of the revolution would immediately be removed from office and "punished in a more serious way if his responsibility were found to be great by the war council of the state."[74]

Such decrees and warnings to the bureaucracy would have had very little effect unless the state government had ways to control the bureaucrats aside from simply relying on either their goodwill or their fears. This was one of the main aims of a newly constituted secret police unit, the Policia Reservada of Chihuahua, which reported directly to Silvestre Terrazas. One of its main tasks was to weed out enemies of the revolution and to prevent corruption in the bureaucracy, which tends to arise very easily in times of civil conflict and scarcity of goods.

The secret police were very active. For example, Silvestre Terrazas's agents denounced Enrique Villalpando, who was an assistant to Terrazas's driver, as a member of the Red Cross of the Orozco army who was in charge of cleaning the hospital. The report on him stated that after the Orozquistas had left Ciudad Juárez, he had crossed the border into El Paso, where he was sharply critical of the constitutionalists.

Another police report stated that Albino Velázquez, who rented a house that had originally belonged to Creel and was now administered by the revolutionary state, refused to pay any rent unless he had written instructions by Enrique Creel to do so.

The agents also closely watched a Captain Antonio Aldonna, who was officially in charge of one local office of confiscated properties. They described him as making large gifts of furniture and other merchandise that officially belonged to the state to his friends and of carting off the finest pieces of the confiscated furniture to his house in Parral. The secret police reported, too, on officials drastically cutting the pensions of widows and, when the latter complained, telling them that this was done on the orders of Pancho Villa.

Police agents regularly traveled on the train between Chihuahua and Ciudad Juárez monitoring the passengers and attempting to eavesdrop on their conversations. Correspondence was regularly checked and opened, and the agents sent Silvestre Terrazas reports on every suspicious letter.

"Suspicious letters" ranged from simple criticism of the constitutionalist authorities to expressions of sympathy for Huerta to more concrete attempts to circumvent constitutionalist laws. One and the same police report might list a letter from Patricia Avila, "who expressed critical thoughts about constitutionalism and our money", the fact that Lázaro Leyva had been sent clippings of the pro-Huerta newspapers by his sister; and a letter received by a widow Chávez from her compadre, Fernando Chávez, a member of the federal army who was interned in Fort Bliss near El Paso (Chávez wrote that he hoped to leave Fort Bliss as quickly as possible in order to join Orozco and put an end to the activities of the bandit Villa).

Except for one case—Velázquez, the tenant who refused to pay rent to the revolutionary government and was arrested—it is not clear what consequences these reports had either for the corrupt bureaucrats or for the writers of intercepted letters considered suspicious.[75]

Villa did have corrupt officials shot on occasion, but there is no evidence of this in the cases that the secret police reported to Silvestre Terrazas. As for the letter writers and letter recipients (the secret police provided a long list of names), there is no evidence of large-scale arrests of civilians during the Villista administration. In April 1915, in his report on the first year of revolutionary rule in Chihuahua, the Villista governor, Fidel Avila, proudly noted that the number of prisoners in the state penitentiary had not exceeded 100, and that most prisoners from local jails had been brought to the capital.[76]

Avila contrasted this number with the more than 600 prisoners that had been the norm in the prerevolutionary period. Obviously, this report cannot be taken at face value. The Villista authorities could conceivably have applied the *ley fuga*, so popular in Porfirian times, of shooting prisoners before they were brought to prison and then stating that they had been shot while trying to escape. If this had been the case, though, the El Paso newspapers, which carefully monitored events in Chihuahua and were in touch with inhabitants of many of its towns and villages, would have reported on such killings. They would also have been mentioned in the confidential reports drafted every week by American observers and officials along the Mexican border.

This does not mean that Villa or his lieutenants did not execute civilians whom they considered their enemies. Such executions did take place, above all in the first weeks of the regime. Nevertheless, the number of these executions seems to have declined thereafter, although they never ended and they increased again during the final months of the Villista administration. On the whole, violence of all kinds in Chihuahua seems to have reached its lowest ebb during the two years of Villista rule in the state.

The lower number of prisoners in the penitentiary may indicate a predictable reduction in crime levels. Many potential criminals and violent men had joined the army voluntarily. Criminals who had already been caught may never have entered the penitentiary because they had been given to understand that they had a choice that to some of them at least was more attractive: they could join the División del Norte. Others were summarily executed.

Villista Chihuahua: An Overview

It is extremely difficult to give any general coherent social, political, and economic characterization of Villista Chihuahua in its heyday. In many respects, it is easier to say what it was not than what it was. It was not a society of bandits and gangsters, where law and order had broken down and looting, robbery, and murder were the order of the day. Even in July 1915, when Villa had already suffered his greatest defeats and Villismo was on the decline, Berkeley's Dean Barrows was pleasantly surprised when he crossed the border into Villista-held territory. "I found the state of Chihuahua well governed by the military forces of Villa. I had anticipated anarchic conditions in places, but found the contrary."[77] Neither is it appropriate to define Villista rule as "institutionalized social banditry," as Alan Knight does,[78] since an effective state administration existed in Chihuahua.

It was not a state where Villista generals had taken over the holdings of the old oligarchy and become a new breed of hacendados. While some such cases existed, they were not common. Only seven of the large number of confiscated haciendas in Chihuahua or Durango were under the direct control of Villista generals. Among them, some generals, like Tomás Urbina, had in fact assumed the trappings of traditional hacendados. Urbina controlled the hacienda of San Ignacio, appropriated cattle from adjoining state-administered haciendas,[79] and had the ambition of becoming a new Terrazas.

In Chihuahua, Urbina was the exception rather than the rule. There were other corrupt Villista officials who appropriated goods for themselves and even became wealthy, such as Villa's brother, Hipólito, and Villa's representative in the United States, Lázaro de la Garza. Yet these men never managed to own a substantial part of Chihuahua's economy as their counterparts in Carranza-controlled states did.

With the exception of Urbina, and perhaps Villa himself (if one assumes the revenues from the two haciendas directly administered for Villa's benefit were destined for his personal use and not for his army, which is doubtful), no Villista general ever accumulated the type of wealth that Obregón did in his native Sonora.[80]

An even more significant difference between what could be called the embryonic Villista bourgeoisie and the far more developed new Carrancista bourgeoisie was that the Villistas exercised power in their own regions. Urbina's "empire" was located in part in Chihuahua but above all in his native Durango. Many Carrancista generals, such as Francisco Murguía and Jacinto Treviño, who for a time occupied Chihuahua, or Jesús Agustín Castro, who was military governor of Chiapas, enriched themselves in states in which they had absolutely no roots. This contrast was significant. The Villista generals ruled in a region from which their constituency and most of their troops originated, and thus however tyrannical they were, they had to conciliate the interests of that constituency. Carrancista generals operating far from their native states were not subject to such imperatives.

Nationalism, especially anti-American nationalism, was far weaker among the Villistas than among the Carrancistas. This was reflected in both the tone and the content of the Villista newspapers. Taxes on foreign-held companies were far lower in Villista-held regions than in Carrancista territory. In practical terms, on the other hand, the Villistas' far greater readiness to confiscate the property of the wealthy meant that hacendados in Villista-held territories would have far greater difficulty selling their holdings to Americans than did hacendados in Carrancista-held regions. As a result, Villista policy may have been a greater hindrance to expansion by American companies than Carrancista policies, despite the First Chief's genuine nationalism.

Villista society was not democratic. There were no elections, the press did not criticize the government, and criticism of Villa was unheard of. Military leaders, the *jefes de armas*, constituted the highest authority in Chihuahua. Yet Villista society cannot be characterized as a military dictatorship. While the army was the supreme arbiter of power, it was still far from being a professional military force, tightly controlled from the top. In Chihuahua, it remained to a very large degree a coalition of local revolutionary bands, many of them led by village leaders, whose loyalty to Villa was generally no greater than their loyalty to local and regional leaders. They were largely dependent on popular support. It was some of these local leaders, closely linked to their agrarian constituency, who provided the checks and balances that neither political democracy nor the judicial system was able to provide.

One of the most profound differences between Villista-held territories and those under Carrancista sway was that under Villismo, there had been a final and irreconcilable break with the traditional oligarchy. No steps were ever taken, or even remotely contemplated, by the Villistas to return the confiscated properties to their owners, as Carranza would do. Moreover, there were strong elements of socialism in its social democratic sense in Villista Chihuahua—that is, of state ownership and state influence on the economy, as well as a commitment to the welfare state. When Duval West, Woodrow Wilson's special envoy to Mexico, had a long discussion with Villa and his officials in 1915, he came away with the impression that the basis of Villa's ideology was "that the property of the rich ought to be administered by the government for the benefit of the masses, and even if not clearly articulated, the socialist ideal appeared to dominate the movement."[81]

These opinions were articulated very directly in Villista newspapers.

On April 11, 1914, long before any official break between Villa and Carranza, *Vida Nueva* attacked one of Carranza's highest officials, Isidro Fabela, who had said that private property was inviolable. The editors of *Vida Nueva* did not agree. They felt that capitalist property could not be inviolable.

Capitalism must doubtless be fought through the social revolution, which is affecting all of us, if we want this revolution to respond to national needs and not to limit itself to being a masquerade, which according to General Villa would only benefit cabinets.

Two types of transformation and reformation will affect Mexican capitalists: the expropriation of the properties of the capitalist enemy while the properties of friendly capitalists will be bought and subdivided. The first process has already been applied and constitutes the financial basis of the triumphant revolution.

Foreign capitalism, which has been neutral, will only and exclusively be transformed through buying and selling and subdivision.

The one foreign group that *Vida Nueva* excepted from this rule was Spanish "capitalism," which had not been neutral.

"One of the great enemies that we are fighting," *Vida Nueva* reiterated, "that directly affects the emancipation of the people is capitalism, this capitalism that in our country can be designated as cientificismo and that includes all forms of cacique rule, feudalism and slavery."[82]

In many respects, practice conformed to theory. In Chihuahua, the Villistas erected the most comprehensive and generous welfare state to be found anywhere in revolutionary Mexico. The extremely low subsidized prices of foodstuffs destined for the masses that marked the beginning of Villista rule in Chihuahua seem to have continued throughout the Villista administration. In July 1915, shortly before the Villista regime collapsed, Berkeley's Dean Barrows reported that "the government . . . controls the prices and sale of the 'prime necessities of life' . . . all meat is slaughtered by the authorities and sold for very low prices. . . . at Chihuahua City every third day a long 'breadline' purchases corn at police headquarters at 25 cents paper for 5 kilos."[83]

This system of food subsidies was complemented by food for the unemployed (at least in the initial stages of Villista rule), free medical care, development of education, boarding schools for homeless children, and a wide range of benefits for wounded soldiers and for widows and orphans of those who had fallen in battle.

Villa's policies achieved his aim of securing large-scale popular support. One of his fiercest enemies, Patrick O'Hea, the British vice-consul in Torreón, reported to the Foreign Office in London that "this section of the Republic is so solidly in favor of General Villa, that, for the present, at least, no other faction would stand a chance in the popular favor and without popular favor it would not attain any successes."[84]

Villista society was also very different from that of the one other state where radical transformations had taken place in the structure of society and that constituted one of the cradles of the popular revolution in Mexico: Morelos under Zapata. There, not only the land but political authority had been returned to the villages, and the state, except in its military shape, had been greatly weakened. In Chihuahua, the state had not only not begun to wither away—it had probably become stronger than ever before, since it had never before exercised the kind of economic control that it now practiced under Villa.

Chihuahua under Villa in 1914 was a revolutionary society from which the revolutionaries had temporarily taken leave of absence while fighting far from Chihuahua for the victory of the revolution. As a result, after the first great transformation—the expropriation of the oligarchy's land and redistribution of food and other goods (but not land) to the lower classes of society—further social, economic, and political changes were put on the back burner until victory could be achieved. These delays were accepted by the majority of Chihuahuan society, which in many respects had assumed the characteristics of a society engaged, not in a civil war, but in a war with an outside force, a war the great majority of the population approved of. This popular consensus existed during the war against Huerta and probably in the first few months after Villa's break with Carranza. It explains both the limited opposition that Villa encountered to his rule and to his policies, the readiness of much of society to wait for social transformations until the achievement of victory, and Villa's resulting ability to exercise power in Chihuahua with a minimum of violence. All this would change within a year when genuine civil war broke out in Chihuahua, with all its attendant savagery and bloodshed.

Chihuahua was the only state on whose internal evolution and policies Villa attempted to exercise systematic influence. In the other states that he controlled, mostly only for a short time, he left the administration as well as the decisions on what policies to implement to local leaders. This was even the case for the state with which Villa maintained the closest connections apart from Chihuahua, his own native state of Durango. The history of the revolution in Durango goes beyond the scope of this book. The villagers of Durango, like those of Chihuahua, had suffered from massive expropriations of land in the Porfirian period, and rural uprisings were as characteristic of the 1910 and 1913–14 revolutions in Durango as they were in Chihuahua. The greatest difference between the revolutionary movements in both states was that no centralized authority emerged either during the Maderista revolution or during the constitutional revolution in Durango, as it had in Chihuahua. In part, this may have been a matter of personalities. A centralized revolutionary authority developed in Chihuahua during the Maderista revolution only when Madero himself took command of the armed forces of the state in 1913. It was the emergence of Villa that led to a central command both in civil and military terms. No such personality emerged in Durango, and Villa made no effort to control affairs in that state with the same intensity as in Chihuahua.

It may also be that revolutionary leaders in Chihuahua were better able to control their forces because of the closeness of the American border, which allowed them to exercise substantial control over the supply of arms and ammunition to their troops. In the Villista period, Durango was ruled by caudillos, each of whom had his own areas of support, and each of whom instituted very different measures. In the Laguna area of both Durango and Coahuila, conditions in the countryside were similar to those in Chihuahua. A commission headed by one of Villa's upper-class supporters, Eugenio Aguirre Benavides, administered confiscated estates in the same way that Silvestre Terrazas did in Chihuahua. The Cuencame area was firmly controlled by Calixto Contreras, and there extensive expropriation of hacienda lands and their occupation by both rebellious villagers and peons took place. These movements had the approval of the Villista governors of the state. Other parts of Durango were controlled by Tomas Urbina, who hoped to establish a hacienda empire similar to that of the Terrazas in Chihuahua, while in yet another part of the state, the Arrieta brothers, who were loyal to Carranza, held sway. On the whole, the very weakness of the central government in Durango favored peasant seizures of hacienda lands in a way that did not occur in Chihuahua. Villa was not directly involved in these land seizures, but he did not prevent them, and this may in fact be one of the reasons, although it was by no means the only one, why in the years after the conclusion of the armed phase of the revolution, he was more popular in Durango than in Chihuahua.

CHAPTER TWELVE

The New Civil War in Mexico

Villismo on the Offensive

The Meeting of Villa and Zapata

As in the history of most revolutions, the bloodiest phase of the Mexican Revolution occurred not when revolutionaries were fighting the old regime but when they began to fight one other. That was no coincidence. In most revolutions the adherents of the old regime tend to be a minority supported by some segments of the old upper classes and foreign allies. The rival factions within the revolutionary movement, by contrast, have a mass following, and their leaders tend to be highly capable, since what they have achieved has generally been through their own talents, be they military or political, and through charismatic appeal rather than through family connections or birth. In the eyes of Robespierre, Danton was infinitely more dangerous than Louis XVI had ever been. In Stalin's Russia, Trotskyists frequently suffered a worse fate than those who had fought in the White armies against the Bolsheviks during the civil war. In the new civil war that now engulfed Mexico, revolutionaries would at times deal far more harshly and brutally with their former allies than they did with the federal commanders who had supported Huerta, many of whom were amnestied after their final defeat.

There were other differences between this new interrevolutionary conflict and the former struggle of all the revolutionary factions against Huerta. In 1913–14, when they fought against the federal army, revolutionary volunteers confronted mostly unwilling, forcibly impressed conscripts. This time volunteer would fight mostly against volunteer. In the long-drawn-out struggle against Huerta, very few leaders or units switched sides, although individual soldiers from the federal army sometimes deserted to the revolutionaries, and few captured officers, when faced with the alternatives of joining the revolutionaries or facing a firing squad, would have chosen to be executed in order to prove their loyalty to Huerta. In the interrevolutionary wars, switching of allegiances was a frequent occurrence, which often depended on personal decisions by leaders or on the perception of who would finally win.

In the war against Huerta, the revolutionaries to a very large degree could take popular support for granted. Their main propaganda efforts in fact were directed less at Mexico than at the United States, from which they hoped to obtain arms, ammunition, and diplomatic support. This time the revolutionaries, and particularly the weaker Carranza faction, were forced to carry out a much larger propaganda and political mobilization in order to gain popular support.

When hostilities between the revolutionary factions broke out in late 1914, most observers were convinced that Villa would soon and easily triumph. This expectation was more than confirmed by his seemingly irresistible offensive in the first weeks after the outbreak of the civil war. His first important decision was to order his troops to march upon Mexico City, so that the Convention could assume control of the country in both real and symbolic terms. The advance proceeded without difficulty. The Carrancista garrisons along the way, belonging mainly to Pablo González's Army of the Northeast, were swept aside. Their demoralized remnants fled either to Veracruz, which the Americans had evacuated and turned over to Carranza, who had concentrated the bulk of his troops there, or to the northern regions still controlled by the Carrancistas.

On the way to the capital, Villa was received with jubilation in the villages and towns he occupied. "The populace without exception was delighted at Villa's arrival," Wilson's representative George Carothers reported, "and the complaints against the treatment they had received at the hands of the Carrancistas were most frequent. The storekeepers accused the Carrancistas of never paying for anything that they took and [said] that during their short regime there was nothing but disorder. Upon the arrival of Villa's troops the shops were opened and business resumed immediately. Villa's orders were most strict against looting and the sequestering of any private property, and his solders were compelled to pay for everything that they purchased."[1]

On November 28, 1914, the advance units of the División del Norte arrived at Tacuba, a suburb of Mexico City. They did not proceed any further, for in the meantime the troops of the Liberating Army of the South under Emiliano Zapata had occupied the city, and Villa did not want to do anything without first securing Zapata's consent.

The first Conventionist leader to enter Mexico City after Zapata was President Eulalio Gutiérrez, who unobtrusively occupied the National Palace, where Zapata's brother Eufemio showed him around. There was no parade, no jubilant crowd, no great reception to welcome the new president to Mexico City. This obviously reflected both the fact that he was practically unknown in the country and the relatively low esteem in which the Zapatistas who occupied the capital held the new president. Villa's reception was very different. His first, historic meeting with Zapata occurred in the village of Xochimilco on the outskirts of Mexico City, where the southern leader awaited him. Schoolchildren with flowers in their hands greeted the two leaders, who then proceeded to a Xochimilco public school, where they held their first conference. Fortunately, a record of the meeting was preserved for posterity both by a stenographer who was present and by León Canova, an American representative whom Villa had invited to witness it. Reporting back to the U.S. secretary of state, Canova noted:

After the exchange of a few greetings these men who had never seen each other before but who had been working in accord for some months locked arms and went to the municipal school building where they were to hold a conference. They were ushered into a large upstairs room which was immediately crowded with about threescore persons intimate with the leaders. There were only a few chairs in the room, Generals Villa and Zapata sat at a large oval table, the two men making a decided contrast. To my left sat Paulino Martínez, one of General Zapata's confidential men and a delegate to the convention. Next to him was General Villa, tall, robust, weighing about 180 pounds, with a complexion almost as florid as a German, wearing an English helmet [i.e., a topee], a heavy brown sweater, khaki trousers, leggings, and heavy riding shoes. Zapata, to his left, with his immense sombrero, sometimes shading his eyes so that they could not be seen, dark complexion, thin face, a man very much shorter in stature than Villa and weighing probably about 130 pounds. He wore a short black coat, a large light blue silk neckerchief, pronounced lavender shirt, and used alternatively a white handkerchief with a green border and another with all the colors of the flowers. He had on a pair of black tight-fitting Mexican trousers with silver buttons down the outside seam of each leg. Villa did not have a sign of jewelry on, nor any color in any of his personal adornment.[2]

The contrast between the appearance of the two men, Zapata's elegance and Villa's informal dress, was not reflected by their respective armies. In fact, the opposite was the case.

The appearance of Zapata's men reflected their status. They were primarily peasants and only secondarily soldiers. They mainly wore the white cotton shirts of the southern Mexican peasants, as well as their characteristic sandals, known as *huaraches*. Villa's men, by contrast, reflected their greater degree of military professionalization. They wore khaki uniforms newly supplied from the United States and their arms were much more standardized than the motley assortment of rifles and guns carried by the Zapatistas.

Fortunately for history, León Canova had been a newspaperman and was a competent writer. (This may have been the reason why William Jennings Bryan appointed this man, who turned out to be one of the most corrupt officials in Wilson's State Department, to a high post in his administration.) Canova has given us an unforgettable portrait of that first meeting. "It was interesting and amusing to watch Villa and Zapata trying to get acquainted with one another. For a half-hour they sat in an embarrassed silence, occasionally broken by some insignificant remark, like two country sweethearts."

Zapata attempted to loosen the atmosphere by having a bottle of cognac brought in and proposing a common toast. Villa, a teetotaler, at first refused, but finally, under pressure from Zapata, acceded. "Villa reached hesitatingly for his glass, then apparently decided. He clutched it and drank with Zapata. He nearly strangled. His face contorted and tears sprang to his eyes while he huskily called for water." What broke the ice was not the cognac but a reference to "a character neither liked—Carranza."[3] In the ensuing conversation, both men showed the ideas and the limitations they shared, and they hinted, although in a very veiled fashion, at what divided them. Each made it clear that he had no ambition to become president or to assume national power. "I don't want public posts because I don't know how to deal with them," Villa said. "I very well understand that we the ignorant people are the ones who do the fighting while the cabinets are the ones who have to make use of it."

Both men insisted that the "cabinets" who would exercise power should be carefully controlled by Villa, Zapata, and their respective forces. "We'll just appoint the ones who aren't going to make trouble," Villa said. And Zapata insisted, "I'll advise all our friends to be very careful—if not, they will feel the blows of the machete. . . . I am convinced that we shall not be fooled. We have limited ourselves to reining them in, to keeping a careful watch on them, and to continuing to reorient them."[4] What the two men meant when they said the national government was "not going to make any trouble" (Villa) and spoke of "keeping a very close watch on them" (Zapata) was that they would severely curtail national leaders' ability to take any decisions concerning the revolutionaries' own regions. Apart from duties of diplomacy and representation, the national cabinet's authority would be limited to foreign affairs and to control of those regions in which Villa and Zapata were not interested and whose regional leaders would agree to give control to the Conventionist administration.

What is also revealing and significant about both men is the limitations they shared. Outside of land reform, no major issue affecting Mexico was touched upon. They did not, for example, consider the problems of foreign policy, of relations with the United States, or of labor.

The conversation also vaguely identified a major difference between the two men that would soon contribute to weakening their alliance. In military terms, Zapata was a regional leader with military capacities at best limited to the control of his own region. His army was incapable of waging war outside of Morelos and of having a decisive military impact on Mexico's destinies. In political and social terms, however, Zapata was far more than a regional leader. He had a national agenda, reflected in the Plan of Ayala, that set concrete terms for land reform all over Mexico. From the moment he proclaimed the Plan of Ayala in 1911 until he met with Villa in 1914, Zapata had made it abundantly clear that he considered his plan a national agenda. With this in mind, he had first made an alliance with Orozco in 1911 and then systematically sought to make alliances not only with Villa but with other revolutionary leaders, both in the north (Contreras was but one example) and among the Tlaxcalan revolutionaries closer to home.

Villa, conversely, had an army that was capable of waging war on a national scale, as the División del Norte had shown. But Villa's social agenda was of a regional and not a national nature. In the program that he had developed in his conversation with Woodrow Wilson's emissary Paul Fuller and in the agreement he had reached with Obregón, he had insisted on the need for land reform. He had also stressed that this land reform should be determined by local councils and regional assemblies and not by a central administration.

These differences between Villa and Zapata were implied, although never stated, both in their conversations on land reform and in what they said or did not say about military matters. Villa made a general commitment to land reform—"all large estates are in the hands of the rich, and the poor have to work from morn till night. I am convinced that in the future life will be different, and if things do not change, we shall not give up the Mausers that we hold in our hands"[5]—and he accepted the Plan of Ayala in principle, but he said nothing concrete about when, how, and by whom land distribution would be carried out. For a long time, Villa would retain his commitment to allow each region to decide what agrarian reform to carry out or not to carry out. Only at a relatively late date would he issue a national plan for land reform, and it would be substantially different from the Plan of Ayala.

While Villa had a regional perspective with respect to land reform, in contrast to Zapata's national agenda, the opposite was the case when it came to military matters. Villa insisted on the victories of his armies and on its national capacities, while Zapata said very little about the military structure and possibilities of the Liberating Army of the South.

There is no evidence that at the more private meeting of the two men that followed the larger get-together, a broader national agenda was discussed. The private meeting boiled down to a decision to divide military responsibilities. Villa would be in charge of the north and Zapata of the south, and they would cooperate in a joint campaign against Carranza in Veracruz. A more controversial subject that they discussed in their private meeting was how to deal with enemies of each leader who had sought refuge in the armies of the other.[6]

Once their deliberations had ended, the two men led a parade of tens of thousands of their soldiers through the main streets of Mexico City, past huge cheering crowds of the capital's inhabitants. They paid a courtesy visit to President Gutiérrez in the National Palace, during which Villa jokingly sat down in the presidential chair for a moment, with Zapata sitting at his side. A photographer recorded the scene, and the picture was soon disseminated worldwide, giving additional proof in the eyes of many observers that Villa had become the real strongman and ruler of Mexico.

That day, November 28, 1914, was perhaps the apex of Villa's career. No one at the time expected that in little more than a year, the enormous armies of the Convention that had marched through Mexico City with a reputation of near-invincibility would be defeated, and that Villa and Zapata would become fugitives in their own states, forced to resort again to guerrilla warfare of a sort that both probably thought, on the day they occupied the capital, they had given up forever.

The Conventionist Alliance: Doomed from Its Beginnings?

The reasons for the unexpected and dramatic defeat of the forces led by Pancho Villa continues to be one of the most controversial aspects of the history of the Mexican Revolution. Was Villa's defeat due to subjective or objective factors? Was it inevitable? Objectively, it is not possible to exclude the possibility that Villa might have triumphed had he applied a different strategy and different tactics. Nevertheless, the odds were stacked against him.

Objective factors tended to favor Villa in the short run but the Carrancistas in the long run. As the new civil war broke out, observers were impressed by the very visible (although in reality short-term) advantages of the Conventionist coalition. Not only did the Conventionist forces control most of Mexico, their lines of communication were unbroken. From the U.S. border down to Morelos, the entire country was under Conventionist rule. The Carrancistas, on the other hand, controlled no such unified land mass but were divided into several enclaves, which at times could only communicate with each other by sea. The main contingent of Carranza's forces, as well as the Carranza administration, was concentrated in Veracruz and adjacent regions. They communicated with the Carrancista forces operating in northeastern Mexico mainly by sea. Contacts with the large Carrancista forces operating in western Mexico and centered in the state of Jalisco were equally precarious.

Carranza's forces only ruled over a small part of the two states from which they drew most of their men and most of their support, Sonora and Coahuila. In Sonora, the Carrancistas occupied a small area bordering on the United States, and most of Coahuila was held by Villa's adherents. While the Carrancistas controlled the state of Nuevo León, their support there was lukewarm. In many of the south-central and southern states that the Carrancistas had occupied, particularly in Oaxaca, Chiapas, Yucatán (until mid 1915), and to a lesser degree Veracruz, the Carrancistas were seen as outsiders, occupation forces from the north, and there were local uprisings against their rule.

Carranza lacked the popular appeal and the charismatic personality of either Villa or Zapata. He lacked their popularity among the Mexican people, and his personal authority within his movement's military forces was far weaker than that of Villa or Zapata with respect to their own forces. His alliance with Obregón seemed precarious. Shortly before joining him, Obregón had called for his resignation. His generals had never won any victories comparable to Villa's successes at Torreón and Zacatecas.

Another advantage of Villa's was momentum. He was perceived as a victor; his armies seemed irresistible. This resulted in deepening demoralization among Carranza's supporters. The most palpable expression of that demoralization was the withering away rather than the defeat of some of Pablo González's forces as Villa overran the garrisons that the Carrancista commander had set up to block his access to Mexico City.

Villa also benefited from the widely held perception, both in Mexico and in the United States, that the Wilson administration favored him. While this perception was harmful to Villa among a number of nationalistically minded Mexicans, many others perceived this as one more proof that Villa would emerge as the victor, and that it was time to rally to his cause.

These advantages, however, were of a short-range character. In the long run (calculated in months, perhaps even in weeks, rather than in years), the Carrancistas could count on increasingly important assets. Their coalition was more coherent, less heterogeneous and divisible than the Conventionist alliance.

As a result, the Carrancista coalition would manifest a far greater degree of military unity than its Conventionist counterpart. In addition, the economic resources at the Carrancistas' disposal were greater than those of their rivals. Furthermore, in objective terms, the policy of the United States would prove to be more favorable to them than to the Conventionists.

The objective advantages that the Carrancista coalition enjoyed were supplemented by a subjective one: the personality of Pancho Villa. He was far more regionally oriented than Carranza or the Carrancista leadership and never developed a national military or political strategy. Unlike the man who was to become his main adversary, Alvaro Obregón, he never learned the lessons that World War I taught military strategists. Above all, as his power increased, he became more and more arrogant and unwilling to accept criticism and advice.

A Brittle and Heterogeneous Alliance

The core areas of the Villa-Zapata alliance were their respective home regions, which they largely, although not completely, dominated. Zapata's territory embraced the state of Morelos and surrounding areas of adjacent states, particularly Guerrero and the state of Mexico. By late 1914, the Zapatistas had extended their control to parts of the state of Puebla, including its capital. Zapatismo was essentially a movement of the village communities that made up the majority of the population of Morelos. It enjoyed limited support among resident workers on haciendas and even more limited support among the state's middle classes. Although some of its intellectual backers were members of the Casa del Obrero Mundial, the Zapatistas did not evoke much urban working-class support and had made few efforts to win converts among industrial workers.

Villa's home region of Chihuahua, Durango, and the Laguna area, which included parts of Durango and Coahuila, was wealthier and larger than Zapata's home base. While Villa, like Zapata, controlled most of his home region, he faced a more active opposition than Zapata did. In Chihuahua, two former leaders of the División del Norte, the brothers Maclovio and Luis Herrera from the city of Parral, had declared for Carranza and, although reduced to a few hundred men, continued to oppose Villa. The same was true of the revolutionary faction in neighboring Durango led by the Arrieta brothers, who had also declared for Carranza. Although they had been forced to retreat to a small mountain region in Durango, Villa never managed to crush them.

Unlike the Zapatista movement in Morelos, Villismo in its core regions was a multiclass coalition. It included former military colonists, agricultural workers, miners, railwaymen, and other industrial workers, large segments of the middle classes, and even some revolutionary hacendados, mainly from states other than Chihuahua. The main Villista peasant leaders had been Toribio Ortega and Porfirio Talamantes from Chihuahua and Calixto Contreras from Durango. The peasant contingent in the movement was weakened by the deaths of Talamantes, who was killed at the battle of Tierra Blanca, and Ortega, who died of typhus. The main spokesman for peasant interests in Chihuahua, apart from Villa himself, was now an intellectual, Federico González Garza. The peasant leaders from Durango had all survived and still played a decisive role in the División del Norte.

The Villa-Zapata alliance exercised a powerful attraction on peasant movements that had developed outside of their core areas. Most such movements rallied to the Convention and not to Carranza. Such was the case with a major peasant movement that developed in the state of San Luis Potosí, which had experienced a classic conflict between hacendados and peasants. The encroachment of large estates on traditional village holdings had provoked ever-increasing resistance and converted San Luis Potosí into a base of support for the Madero revolution.

Wilfred Bonney, one of the few U.S. consuls in Mexico who felt that the revolution did not consist merely of rural bandits, gave a succinct analysis of the revolution that embraced San Luis Potosí once Huerta had taken power in Mexico:

The revolution in this district is aimed instinctively at the caste system of society and the feudal system of production rather than at purely political ends. While the agrarian question is often referred to as behind the revolution, it is believed rather a revolt against the feudal system of production, which system includes land tenure and which determines the markets, wages, and transportation and pervades the whole commercial and social stratification.[7]

Militarily and to a certain degree ideologically, the constitutionalist revolution in San Luis Potosí developed independently of its northern and southern counterparts. In March 1913, at a time when the movement in the north was scarcely beginning, Alberto Carrera Torres, a primary-school teacher from Tula, organized a guerrilla force on the border between the states of San Luis Potosí and Tamaulipas and proclaimed an agrarian plan that called for an end to debt peonage, confiscation of the large estates of the oligarchy, and ten hectares for each landless peasant. Carrera Torres added a surprising clause that no other revolutionary movement would ever consider: land should be given to each federal soldier who refused to fight for Huerta. Carrera Torres succeeded in attracting the support of a relatively wealthy family of rancheros who had been competing for laborers with a neighboring hacienda: the Cedillo brothers, Cleofas, Magdaleno, and Saturnino. The most influential and best-educated of the brothers, Saturnino Cedillo, attended the Convention of Aguascalientes, and upon his recommendation, Carrera Torres decided to throw his full military support to the Conventionist movement along with the Cedillos.[8]

A similar decision was made several hundred miles to the south of San Luis Potosí by another group of brothers directing a major agrarian uprising, the Arenas brothers in the state of Tlaxcala. In Tlaxcala, as in San Luis Potosí, peasant resentment had been fueled by the encroachment of haciendas upon their lands. In Tlaxcala, peasant dissatisfaction had expressed itself as it did in San Luis Potosí by massive participation of the rural population in the Madero revolution. In both cases, the Maderista administration had done very little to satisfy the demands of its peasant supporters. In San Luis Potosí, the Maderista governor, Rafael Cepeda, who had been elected with the votes of many of the peasant revolutionaries, gave government help to the state's hacendados to suppress peasant insurgents. In Tlaxcala, the situation had been somewhat different. The peasants had succeeded in having a man favorable to their demands, Antonio Hidalgo, elected as governor. When Hidalgo refused to turn against his erstwhile supporters and in fact advocated a program of radical agrarian change, the state's hacendados in conjunction with the Madero administration in Mexico City carried out a coup and had him deposed.

Like the Cedillos and Carrera Torres in San Luis Potosí, the Arenas brothers in Tlaxcala had become disillusioned at the attitude of the Madero government to their agrarian demands, but they soon realized that Huerta was more hostile to their interests and far more ruthless than Madero had ever been. Once Huerta assumed power in Mexico City, they rose in revolt. The experiences of the revolutionaries in San Luis Potosí and Tlaxcala during the Madero administration had strongly influenced them. In 1911, the revolutionaries in both states had gone home and laid down their arms, clearly hoping that the new revolutionary administration in Mexico would heed their demands and carry out large-scale land reform. After Huerta's coup, they waited for no one. In San Luis Potosí, Carrera Torres issued a radical agrarian plan in March 1913, at a time when the northern revolution had scarcely begun, and in Tlaxcala, the Arenas brothers began extensive redistribution of hacienda lands. They were wary of Carranza, whom many considered another Madero. Nevertheless, the Arenas brothers, together with another Tlaxcalan revolutionary leader, Máximo Rojas, joined Pablo González's Army of the Northeast when it became the first northern army to enter their state. Once the civil war between Carranza and the Convention broke out, the Arenas brothers left González's division, proclaimed their allegiance to the Convention, and established close links to Emiliano Zapata. Their attitude was influenced by the strong agrarian commitment of the Convention, as well as by Pablo González's decision to appoint Rojas, whom they considered a rival, to take command of the Tlaxcalan revolutionaries. Their personal popularity and the attraction of the Villa and Zapata movements were such that most of the revolutionaries joined them, and Rojas was left with only a few hundred men from his own native region.[9]

In the western state of Jalisco, where the agrarian problem was less acute than in Tlaxcala, Morelos, or San Luis Potosí, the largest popular movement was headed by a miner, Julián Medina, who had a strong commitment to land reform, having attempted in 1912 to divide hacienda lands.[10] It included a far larger percentage of industrial and agricultural workers than in Tlaxcala or San Luis Potosí. It, too, clearly sided with the Convention.

Within the Conventionist coalition, the counterweight to the agrarian revolutionaries was a strong conservative faction. Its main proponents were concentrated along the west coast of Mexico, in a region not directly controlled by Villa's forces. Their most powerful spokesman was the governor of Sonora, José María Maytorena. After the split between Villa and Carranza, Maytorena made a few radical pronouncements and even briefly attempted to depict himself as a populist by making promises of concessions to industrial workers and of land reform to the Yaqui Indians, but his basically conservative policies did not change.[11] The confiscated estates he had returned to their former owners remained in their hands. Although he had established strong links to the Yaqui Indians—he had protected them from government deportation prior to the revolution and as a result they were among his strongest supporters—he did nothing to return their expropriated lands to them.

Maytorena's closest ally and protégé was the governor of the neighboring state of Sinaloa, Felipe Riveros. Like Maytorena, Riveros was a relatively conservative

Maderista who had been elected to his post after the victory of the Madero revolution. Unlike Maytorena, who had left the country rather than accept the military coup, Riveros had recognized Huerta, but this capitulation had not saved him from imprisonment.[12] However, it had saved his life, since Huerta, who obviously considered him harmless, released him. Riveros soon joined the revolutionaries in his native state, many of whom refused to recognize his leadership because of his earlier endorsement of Huerta. It was largely thanks to Maytorena's help that he was able to regain his governorship. He remained identified with and committed to the Sonoran governor. Like his counterpart in Sonora, he faced strong opposition from local revolutionaries who had aligned themselves with Carranza, and it was this rivalry rather than any kind of social commitment that had driven him, like Maytorena, to make an alliance with Villa.

A third and more surprising member of this conservative bloc was Rafael Buelna, the young revolutionary leader who had assumed control of the territory of Tepic on Mexico's Pacific coast. Buelna represented a type of revolutionary common in twentieth-century revolutions but rare during the Mexican Revolution: the student revolutionary. A brilliant and audacious commander, he mobilized a large group of men. Most of these fighters hailed from his native region of Tepic, which had been the cradle of one of the greatest Indian uprisings in the nineteenth century. He triumphed against all odds and gained control of his native region. Once he had won, he deeply disappointed his lower-class supporters. They had hoped that he would become a protector of and spokesman for the Indian villagers. Instead, he made his peace with the strongest ruling family in the territory, the Casa Aguirre clan. As José Valadés, a biographer generally sympathetic to Buelna, puts it, the revolutionaries who had taken up arms in southern Sinaloa and in Tepic "had not done so because of military ambition. There were social and economic woes that led people to take up arms. They did not want a simple change of men. Buelna knew this very well. Nevertheless, corrupted by power, he forgot the hopes that many had placed in him. . . . He stopped being a promise for those who, although not expressing it systematically, believed in a transformation that would benefit the great masses of the population." On the other hand, he ingratiated himself with the local aristocracy in Tepic, who called him "Granito de Oro" (Little Grain of Gold).[13] In early 1915, instead of dividing the large estates that had been confiscated by revolutionaries in 1913 among the peasants, he proposed to the Convention that these lands be returned to their former owners.[14]

The Madero family also belonged to the more conservative wing of Villa's movement. Many members of the family were involved with Villa. Francisco's brothers Raúl and Emilio were generals in the División del Norte. Eugenio Aguirre Benavides, also a general of Villa's, was related to the Maderos, and his brother, Luis Aguirre Benavides, became Villa's secretary. In the United States, Salvador Madero and a company belonging to the Madero brothers were active in supplying Villa with arms.[15] Nevertheless, there was no unanimity within the Madero family as to what side they should join. Another brother, Julio Madero, fought in Obregón's army, and the Aguirre Benavides brothers had made it clear to Obregón during his visit to Chihuahua that they strongly opposed Villa; in fact, they would soon turn against him. The most significant influence that the Maderos exercised on Villa's policies concerned their own properties and the large estates in the rich Laguna district. Villa had exempted the Maderos' properties, and even those of related families, such as the wealthy Zuloagas in Chihuahua, who had intermarried with the Maderos, from confiscation. He had also entrusted Eugenio Aguirre Benavides with the administration of the confiscated estates in the Laguna, thus giving him a great influence on the economy of the region.[16] Raúl Madero became governor of Nuevo León. There is no evidence, however, that the Maderos exercised any significant influence on Villa's overall economic or social policies.

It has frequently been stated that the high Madero officials who joined Villa were also part of the conservative faction within the Conventionist alliance.[17] This was not true of all of them, and the profound differences between them were clearly expressed in a controversy that Federico González Garza had with Angeles and Miguel Díaz Lombardo. "When General Angeles and Licenciado Díaz Lombardo were here," Federico González Garza wrote his brother Roque, "they stated that in their opinion the main difference between us and the Carrancistas was that the latter wished to or promised to implement the revolutionary reform in the so-called pre-constitutional period while we desired to primarily reestablish the constitutional order before carrying out the reforms. In reality this was not the original motive for our break with Carranza, and when I left Chihuahua no one even mentioned this difference."[18]

To the already heterogeneous Villa-Zapata-Maytorena-Angeles alliance was added an element of even greater heterogencity—the remnants of the third force at the Convention of Aguascalientes, who now constituted the core of the government of the Conventionist faction. In political terms, their origins were very different. Some had been Carrancistas, others had been part of the División del Norte, while still others were genuine independents. In social terms, none of them had been peasants or had led peasant movements prior to 1910. President Eulalio Gutiérrez had been a miner with a long history of revolutionary activism. Born on a hacienda in Coahuila, he moved at an early age to the mining town of Concepción del Oro in the state of Zacatecas, where he found employment in a mine. At 19 he had his first brush with the Porfirian system when he supported an opposition candidate for local office. This experience may have impelled him to join the PLM, and he became so committed to it that six years later, at 25, he headed an uprising. His small force was soon defeated, and he had to flee to the United States, but he returned in 1911, participated in the Madero revolution, and rose in arms again after Huerta's coup. He never managed to become an important military leader, commanding at the most about 200 men.[19] Nevertheless, in a certain sense, the quality of his forces compensated for their lack of quantity. Many of his soldiers were miners with special expertise in explosives. As a result, one of their main activities consisted in blowing up trains, for which Gutiérrez became famous throughout the region of Coahuila, San Luis Potosí, and Zacatecas, where his forces operated. Though for a time he fought under the orders of Carranza's brother Jesús, he enjoyed a greater degree of autonomy than most other revolutionary leaders.

In military terms, the most important member of the third force was Lucio Blanco, a former general of Obregón and Carranza's northwestern army, who remained loyal to the Revolutionary Convention. Blanco harbored a deep resentment of Carranza. In the first weeks of the constitutionalist revolution, Blanco had been one of the most successful military leaders in northeastern Mexico and had succeeded in capturing the important town of Matamoros. Carranza had removed him from his command because he resented the land division that Blanco had carried out at the hacienda of Los Borregos, belonging to Félix Díaz, and because Blanco did not get along with Carranza's favorite general, Pablo González. Blanco thereupon went to Sonora, joined Obregón's Army of the Northwest, and became one of its most successful generals. His cavalry charges had become legendary.[20]

At the time of the break between Villa and Carranza, Blanco commanded the army of 10,000 that garrisoned Mexico City, all of whom joined the Conventionist forces. His counterparts within the División del Norte were two of Villa's generals, José Isabel Robles and Eugenio Aguirre Benavides. Both were educated men of middle-class origins; Robles was reputed to be able to quote Plutarch, while Aguirre Benavides was related to the Madero family and had in fact been employed by them prior to the revolution. Although officially belonging to the División del Norte, they had indicated to Obregón during his visit to Chihuahua that they were opposed to Villa, and they enthusiastically joined the Carrancista members of the third force at the Convention in Aguascalientes in demanding the resignation of both Villa and Carranza. These men formed the core of the new Conventionist government, officially recognized by both Villa and Zapata. They had recruited one of Mexico's most brilliant intellectuals, José Vasconcelos, who became minister of education in the new government.

Men such as Robles, Blanco, Aguirre Benavides, and Vasconcelos hoped that Carranza would soon be defeated by Villa and that they then could take over the effective governance of the country. It is not clear how they hoped to impose their will. Did they believe that Villa and Zapata would retire to their own regions and leave the Conventionist government in control of the rest of Mexico? Did they believe that once Carranza was defeated those elements of the third force that had supported him would now rejoin them and strengthen them against Villa and Zapata? Whatever their strategic concepts were, they soon would find out that none of them were achievable.

To this heterogeneous coalition of peasant revolutionaries, western conservatives, and middle-class military men must be added a diverse array of regional and local leaders who joined the Conventionist alliance either because it seemed to be the victorious faction or because it promised more autonomy from the central government than Carranza's administration. What rendered this Conventionist coalition even more heterogeneous and brittle were the attempts of segments of Mexico's traditional conservative forces to seek to come to terms with or even to join the Conventionist alliance.

Villa and the Forces of the Old Regime

The defeat of the federal army and Huerta's resignation created a new and precarious situation for Mexico's traditional establishment. The federal army, the hacendados, and the church now faced a difficult choice.

Should they join either of the revolutionary factions? Should they attempt to stay neutral? Or should they again support counterrevolution? In the first weeks after Huerta's resignation, most of the old regime establishment was still working to find a solution acceptable to all of its components. A few weeks later, this effort collapsed, and the country's economic and political elite fragmented.

Villa and the Federal Army

The sector of the traditional establishment most immediately threatened by the success of the revolutionaries was the federal army. In spite of the hatred it had incurred among the revolutionaries, its leaders still hoped that the army might survive the constitutionalist revolution, as it had survived the Maderista upheaval. They pinned their hopes on the divisions among the revolutionaries. Their hopes went unfulfilled. Villa refused to absorb the federal army into his forces. Obregón, who had briefly utilized the Mexico City garrison to prevent the Zapatistas from entering the capital, subsequently dissolved the federal army, granting amnesty to its officers and men. Nevertheless, a large segment of the federal officer corps had not resigned themselves to entering civilian life. Attracted by the presence of Angeles in the ranks of the División del Norte, many of them sought to join Villa's forces.

Villa's attitude toward these officers was contradictory. "Villa held a meeting with a large number of former members of the federal army and succeeded in attracting them into his army by offering to restore their former ranks," a Chilean diplomat reported from Mexico City in January 1915. "They enthusiastically accepted his offer in view of the precarious situation in which they found themselves."[21] One month later, on February 16, however, Villa's newspaper *Vida Nueva*, reporting that more than 100 federal officers had offered their services to Angeles, wrote, "We are sure that they will not be accepted into the ranks of the revolutionary army since they are remnants of the forces that supported the infamous coup [against Madero]."[22]

According to most observers, the Carrancistas were far more reluctant to welcome former federal officers and soldiers into their ranks than Villa was, although he later accused Carranza of having done exactly the same thing. This difference in attitude toward the federal army in part reflected the greater heterogeneity of the Conventionist faction. In view of the greater breadth of his coalition, Villa had less difficulty in accommodating federal troops than Carranza had. This difference in attitude also reflected strong personal differences and different military needs. Although Huerta had imprisoned him, Villa had a more positive attitude toward the federal army than Carranza had, which to a large degree was probably due to Angeles. While it is not clear to what extent Angeles attempted to influence Villa in recruiting federal officers, his own example as a former federal commander who was absolutely loyal to Villa was certainly not unimportant in shaping Villa's attitude toward his former enemies.

There was also another important difference between the División del Norte and the Carrancista armies that made federal officers more attractive to the Villista military. A far larger percentage of officers of the Carrancista armies came from the cities and were literate, in contrast to the many former peasants, a large number of whom were illiterate, who commanded Villa's troops. As a result, Villa had greater need of the technical expertise that the former federal officers could provide.

Villa was already used to dealing with federal soldiers and officers, since at least some of them had joined the División del Norte after being captured in battle. Although they had done so under duress (they would have been shot if they had not joined), most of them seem to have remained loyal to Villa. There is no evidence that the former federal officers who joined Villa ever exercised any great degree of influence in the División del Norte. Obregón's prediction that these federal officers and soldiers would be incorporated into a separate force by Angeles in an attempt to build up an independent power base within the División del Norte never came true.[23] It is thus not surprising that in a proclamation to the Mexican people in late 1915, Villa, on the brink of defeat, still justified his use of federal troops.

Those who erroneously call themselves constitutionalists have called us reactionaries. This accusation is wrong and despicable. We really did accept the services of some former generals, leaders, and officers of the former federal army when we became convinced of the purity of their intentions, the righteousness of their principles, and the fact that they had been slaves of their duty and had condemned treason in their hearts and had never taken reprisals against our brothers. It is true that among the honest former federal officers there were unfortunately some men who were unworthy; we have been eliminating these men, and now only a small group of former federal officers are still in our ranks, who are all men of high esteem. In contrast, within the ranks of the constitutionalist army can be found the most unworthy members of the former federal army; it contains a large number of officers and leaders who were bloodthirsty, cruel, and cowardly murderers.[24]

On the whole, it seems that only a minority of former federal officers and soldiers joined the ranks of any revolutionary faction. Many of the soldiers who had been forcibly impressed into the army simply went home. A rather large number of officers, on the other hand, joined the ranks of counterrevolutionary forces operating in the states of Veracruz, Oaxaca, and Chiapas.[25]

By 1915, in spite of temporary alliances by individual members or even units of the old federal army and deals that these individuals and groups made with different revolutionary factions, the federal army had ceased to exist as a coherent force. It would never reemerge, and its place would be taken by the new army that had come out of the revolution.

Villa and the Catholic Church

A second bastion of conservatives in Mexico, the Catholic church, seems to have maintained better relations with Villa than with Carranza. The Carrancistas considered themselves the heirs of the anticlerical liberals of the nineteenth century and reflected the anticlerical views of many of their largely middle-class and working-class supporters. Those views had been strengthened by the systematic opposition to Madero of a newly formed Catholic party in the years 1911–12 and

by the favorable attitude, at least for a time, of the Catholic party and some high
church officials toward the Huerta dictatorship. Villa's attitude toward the church
was ambivalent. While he was not against religion, and probably believed in
Catholicism, he had contempt for priests. "Is a priest God?" he rhetorically asked
in an interview with an American reporter.

They are not. They may be the teachers of the doctrines of Christ, but that does not
mean that because they are teachers of what is good they should themselves be permitted to break nearly all of the commandments as my experience teaches me they always do. The priests, such as I have found in the small villages and even in the cities
in the mountains of Chihuahua, are paupers in mind and body. They are too weak
mentally and physically to make a living for themselves.

They live like lice—on others. From what I am told they are elsewhere in Mexico
as they are in my state of Chihuahua. In the first place, there are too many of them.
Take for instance the city of Parral. There are fourteen churches, and God knows
how many priests. And all are supported by the poor people who have barely enough
to keep body and soul together, clothed in a few pitiful rags.

Don't I know them? Have I not seen that a priest makes no move unless it means
money to him? Bah—don't argue with me. If you are a Catholic I don't want to hurt
your feelings, *mi amigo*, but let me tell you if you are not as disgusted with them as I
am it is because the priests differ from the priests in Mexico.

In Villa's eyes most priests were exploiters and thieves:

You go into any one of our churches in Mexico and you will find collection boxes at
every door and on every wall—sometimes as many as twenty of them in one church.
They are labeled, "for charity," "for St. Peter," "for the suffering souls in purgatory,"
"for prayers for the dead," and so on.

The poor never get a *centavo* from the charity box. St. Peter doesn't need the poor
copper coins dropped by a starving people into the box that bears his name. You can't
buy a soul out of purgatory, and I doubt if you can buy prayers for the dead that will
do the dead any good.

Ah, priests! Your day of reckoning is fast approaching. Religion is a good thing,
possibly for those who have the education which enables them to understand it. But
a multitude of priests being supported by the poor does not make Mexico religious.[26]

Villa had one of his stormiest domestic quarrels with his wife Luz Corral
when he discovered, as he was showing his house to Obregón, that she had secretly built an altar in their home. "There is a bad smell to this, General," he told
Obregón. "I fear that the priests have taken hold of my wife's *rebozo* [shawl] and
are going to spoil her."

Villa immediately ordered the altar to be dismantled. He relented when Luz
Corral, doubtless the most intelligent and diplomatic of his wives, did not object
to his decision but on the contrary told him: "In order to pray to God for you, I
have never needed an altar, since every time all of you have gone to sleep, when
there is silence in the house, I get on my knees and with all my heart I implore
God to help you, and he has listened to me up to now, since nothing has happened to you."[27]

This mixture of tolerance for religion and conviction that the priests were exploiting the people influenced Villa's practical policies toward the church. After

capturing the city of Saltillo, for example, he staged a mock execution of a number of captured Jesuits in order to force them to pay a huge ransom.[28] However, when he occupied Guadalajara, he ordered a number of churches that the Carrancistas had closed to be reopened.[29] Moreover, his newspaper *Vida Nueva* attacked the Carrancistas for closing churches and preventing the free exercise of the Catholic religion. "It is justifiable to expel or persecute bad priests. It is clumsy and useless to shoot at religious representations, to burn altars, and to destroy crucifixes. . . . religion is not equivalent to the clergy, in the same way that Citizen Carranza does not represent the revolution."[30]

On the whole, his more positive inclination toward religion than that of his Carrancista counterparts to a certain point reflected the fact that Mexico's peasants were more religious than the country's middle and working classes.

Villa's attitude toward the church may have gained him some additional support among the country's peasants, but it did not gain him the support of the church. Some of the most important members of Mexico's clergy, including the archbishop of Mexico City, José Mora y del Río, had fled to the United States, and some of them seem to have become involved in a wide-ranging plot to carry out a counterrevolution in Mexico with U.S. support.[31]

Villa and the Hacendados

While Villa's attitude toward the federal military and the church tended to be somewhat more favorable than that of Carranza, such was not the case with regard to a third conservative element, the hacendados, who continued to exercise considerable influence in important parts of the country. To a large extent, they would manage to survive the revolution as a class, unlike the federal army as an institution. But they came out of it so weakened that when in 1934, 24 years after the outbreak of the Mexican Revolution, the administration of President Lázaro Cárdenas decided to expropriate most of Mexico's large landholdings, the hacendados would be unable to put up any decisive resistance.

The weakened position of the hacendados was primarily due to loss of economic and political power, not to physical annihilation. In this respect the Mexican Revolution differed from its French or Russian counterparts.

In the vast library of literary works that the Mexican Revolution has inspired, both in and outside of Mexico, there is no Mexican equivalent to Charles Dickens's *A Tale of Two Cities*, in which French aristocrats tragically and heroically ascend the steps to the guillotine. The Mexican equivalent of the guillotine was the firing squad, and the image of a man standing in front of a firing squad, sometimes blindfolded, sometimes directing his own execution, has become part of the literature and legend of the Mexican Revolution. Nevertheless, those men were very rarely hacendados. With very few exceptions, if a hacendado ever landed in front of a firing squad, it was most likely as the victim not of a real but of a simulated execution, a very effective means of forcing him to pay a high ransom for his release. In most cases, it worked, and the hacendado was able to go north of the border and find asylum in the United States. On the whole, with relatively few exceptions, Mexico's wealthy hacendado families managed to escape the revolution physically unscathed.

It is characteristic of the Mexican Revolution, and not without symbolic value, that whereas Francisco Madero, Emiliano Zapata, Francisco Villa, Venustiano Carranza, and Alvaro Obregón all met violent deaths, José Yves Limantour Jr., Luis Terrazas, Enrique Creel, and Pablo Escandón died of natural causes.

One would have looked in vain in the streets of El Paso or Los Angeles, where most exiled Mexican hacendados settled, for the Mexican equivalent of the down-and-out Russian aristocrats who worked as waiters, nightclub bouncers, or taxi drivers in Paris after having escaped from the Bolsheviks. Unlike their Russian counterparts, most Mexican hacendados had been able to bring large parts of their fortunes with them into exile. This does not mean that they had been unaffected by the revolution. Many had fled from their estates as the armies of Villa, Carranza, and Zapata closed in, and a large number of haciendas had been "intervened." However, such "interventions," as the confiscations by the revolutionaries were called, had rarely meant total ruin for them. In general, the advance of the revolutionaries had not been unexpected and many hacendados had been able to convert part of their properties into cash. Some had precipitously sold their crops and cattle. Many others had gone further and sold their estates, often at cut-rate prices, to foreigners, whose properties, especially if they were American, the revolutionaries were forced to respect.

By no means all and perhaps not even a majority of Mexico's haciendas had been confiscated at the time of Huerta's resignation. In the regions controlled by the revolutionaries, practically all foreign-owned properties, with the exception of those belonging to Spaniards, had been spared. Obviously, too, those hacendados who had joined the revolution had not been affected. When civil war broke out among the revolutionaries, however, those hacendados who sided with the Convention suffered greater reprisals from the Carrancistas than had their Porfirian or Huertista counterparts.

In two states central to the Mexican Revolution, Coahuila and Sonora, both Carranza and Maytorena had done their best to spare the hacendados. Carranza had prevented many confiscations in his own state, while Maytorena, after reassuming the governorship of Sonora, returned many confiscated estates to their former owners.[32]

Even Villa, who had decreed the confiscation of all estates belonging to the oligarchy, was willing to spare some hacendados who had not joined his movement. He never touched properties belonging to the wealthy Zuloaga family in Chihuahua, probably because they were intermarried with the Maderos. There are also stories that the Zuloagas had once granted hospitality to Villa, who had a long memory.[33] Other hacendados in the regions controlled by Villa had been able to strike some kind of a deal either with him or with one or other of his commanders. One of the most effective intermediaries in such deals was George Carothers, Woodrow Wilson's special representative to Villa, who seems to have made a fortune by brokering such deals, and whom Villa tried by every means to conciliate.

In Morelos and the adjacent regions controlled by Zapata, practically all of the haciendas had been taken from their owners. By contrast, in southeastern Mexico, where no revolution had taken place, the haciendas were still intact. The hacendados still controlled their estates, and in many cases their peons, when Huerta resigned.

Because the situations the hacendados faced in different parts of Mexico were so divergent, their tactics and their reactions also varied enormously. Obviously, those hacendados who had lost their properties behaved in a very different way from those who still controlled them. Some of Mexico's hacendados and members of the country's traditional oligarchy hoped briefly that Villa might become their man. He was in their eyes a bandit, so why should it not be possible to buy and co-opt him, in the same way that Porfirio Díaz had co-opted men whom they had also considered bandits? They knew that Villa's ally Maytorena had returned the confiscated estates in Sonora to their former owners. Some of them hoped that, in view of Villa's close links to the Americans, he might be persuaded to do the same in the regions he controlled.

The hopes, expectations, and disappointments with Villa on the part of segments of Mexico's oligarchy are reflected in the reports of the French chargé in Mexico, Victor Ayguesparse. He was a brother-in-law of one of Mexico's wealthiest men, who for a time had been a minister in Huerta's cabinet. His colleagues in the French diplomatic service believed that his interpretations of Mexican reality were influenced by this fact.[34] At first he had hoped that Carranza would "form a government of conciliation . . . to gain the support for the revolution of parts of the former federal army, capital, the land-owning aristocracy, and the clergy."[35] A few weeks later, after the Carrancistas had occupied Mexico City, Ayguesparse became deeply disillusioned with Carranza's movement. He characterized the first chief as

a sincere, moderate man who is nevertheless weak and not very intelligent and who cannot control his young generals, the leaders of bands who have fought during one year and who now as victors attempt to destroy everything that ever resisted them.

These generals are practically all Indians, but Indians from the northern states adjacent to the United States and thus more intelligent, more advanced than the other Indians within the republic. They have heard of abstract ideas of liberty and equality and they are applying them more or less in the same way as Robespierre did.

Ayguesparse was convinced that the Mexican Revolution, which in his opinion sought to imitate the French Revolution, was "certainly a social revolution, an uprising of the lower classes against all conservative elements—against capitalists, landowners, and the clergy, etc." He resented the fact that the revolutionaries had "imprisoned the majority of the large landowners, confiscated their properties, occupied their private residences, and confiscated their horses and their cars." Disenchanted with Carranza, Ayguesparse now pinned his hopes on Villa:

For some time now, Villa and his friend General Angeles (a former officer of the federal army) seem to have wanted to separate themselves from Carranza in order to seek a rapprochement with the best elements of the former Madero government, i.e., the moderates, the intellectuals, the "científicos," as they are called here, who constituted Madero's advisors.

For that reason, at the present time, Villa constitutes Mexico's hope.

All those who are dissatisfied, and there are many of them, all those who have been dispossessed and ruined, all the former members of the federal army who were dismissed by M. Carranza and are now dying of hunger, [and] all the former federal officials who have lost their jobs and are also dying of hunger, are rallying around Villa.[36]

The hopes that Ayguesparse had placed in Villa were soon dispelled. It did not take him long to realize that the northern revolutionary leader would never return their properties to Mexico's oligarchy. Only a few weeks after he had sent this optimistic report to Paris, Ayguesparse wrote in a very different vein about Villa and Zapata:

These two movements, Villismo, which comes from the north, and Zapatismo, which comes from the south, have similarities: they are too intransigent, too dogmatic, not sincere enough; they include too many personal hatreds, too many desires for vengeance, too many ambitions and personal deals, and both of them have a clearly anarchic and destructive tendency, which attacks capital wherever they find it and in whatever shape it presents itself. Under these circumstances, these movements present little hope.[37]

Many of the hacendados from northern and central Mexico whose properties had been confiscated by revolutionaries soon realized that Carranza represented the only hope they had of regaining their expropriated holdings.

In January 1915, Carranza issued a radical agrarian law, which in practice, however, would scarcely be applied during his administration. At the same time, he began a massive policy of returning expropriated haciendas to their former owners. It is thus not surprising that a number of hacendados in central and northern Mexico aligned themselves with his faction and in some cases were even willing to support him with armed force. This was the case in Jalisco, where Carranza's commander, General Manuel Diéguez, was able to mobilize hacendado-led contingents on his behalf.[38]

A different situation emerged in Mexico's southeastern states, Oaxaca, Tabasco, Chiapas, and Yucatán, where there had been no large-scale social revolution up to 1914. The Maderista uprisings that had taken place in some of these states, above all in Chiapas, were basically elite-led movements in which one group of hacendados hoped to utilize the Madero revolution to displace another group that had held power until then. Unlike their counterparts in northern and parts of central Mexico, the southern hacendados had not lost their land, since so few uprisings had taken place in their region. Only in a few very limited, generally isolated instances did more radical peasant revolts occur. None of them was successful.

When Carranza sent troops to control Mexico's southeast, many of these hacendados, particularly in Yucatán, Chiapas, and Veracruz, revolted. Even more than the taxes that Carranza might impose upon them, they feared his honest desire to abolish debt peonage, which was still prevalent throughout Mexico's south. To fight these hacendado revolts, Carranza sent some of his most radical supporters, such as Salvador Alvarado and Francisco Múgica, to the south, where they proceeded to liberate the peons from their debts.[39]

Some of these rebelling hacendados felt that the only successful way to fight Carranza was to make a deal with Villa. They would call themselves Villistas, and thus gain some legitimacy, and perhaps some armed support, but in fact never accept any instructions from Villa or the Conventionist administration.

In Chiapas, Tiburcio Fernández Ruiz, who had fought for a time in the ranks of the División del Norte, called himself a Villista while leading a conservative revolt in which hacendados had united with some peasants in order to ward off the "foreign Carrancistas" who were occupying the state.[40] Ruiz's links to Villa remained nominal, and there is no evidence that he ever accepted orders from the northern revolutionary leader after returning to Chiapas.

There was one other nucleus of conservative landowners in Mexico that briefly aligned itself with Villa. Like its counterparts in Chiapas, its links to the Convention were nominal, and its Villista affiliation was destined to hide its much closer links to other outside forces. This was a group of landowners headed by Manuel Peláez in the oil-producing region of Mexico's gulf coast. Peláez was a prosperous landowner (it is not clear whether his properties were large enough for him to be called a hacendado) who had sold some of his land to foreign oil companies, and who for a time was an employee of Lord Cowdray's Mexican Eagle Oil Company. Apart from the oil companies, he had maintained close links with Mexico's conservatives. He had supported Félix Díaz's uprising in 1912, gone into exile in the United States once it was defeated, and only returned when Huerta assumed power. He supported Huerta until it was clear that the military strongman was headed for defeat, and then set up an armed movement of his own. Once the split among the revolutionaries occurred, he called himself a supporter of the Revolutionary Convention. He obtained large sums of money from the oil companies, enabling him to equip and maintain a well-trained military force, which exercised a large degree of control over Mexico's oil fields, although not over the oil-exporting port of Tampico.

The Carranza government accused Peláez of being a tool of the oil companies, armed by them in order to keep the revolutionary forces out of the oil fields. While the oil companies never denied their payments to Peláez, they insisted that this was done under coercion, since Peláez threatened to set fire to their fields unless they acceded to his financial demands. The truth seems to lie somewhere in between. At first, Peláez forced the oil companies to pay him and to support his forces, but they soon came to realize that he was an effective bulwark against any revolutionary advance into their region and supplied him with whatever he needed. They were subsequently supported in this first by the British government and later by members of the Wilson administration.[41]

Peláez was more than just a tool of the oil companies. He seems to have enjoyed a large measure of genuine local popular support, since as the civil war raged on in Mexico, bringing destruction, poverty, and hunger to large parts of the country, the oil-producing region remained an enclave of prosperity. Operations were constantly expanding, and the oil companies provided their workers with regular supplies of food and other goods, which were easily imported, since the oil region bordered the Gulf of Mexico. Oil workers were a privileged elite, and many of them felt that Peláez was defending their privileges. His links to the Convention, like those of the Chiapas landowners, were purely nominal. No Conventionist administration was ever set up in his territory, and he never applied any of the reforms for which the Convention called.

The "Villista" hacendados of Chiapas and the oil region were thus an anomaly in revolutionary Mexico. The vast majority of Mexico's hacendados either supported counterrevolutionary forces or were ready to make a deal with Carranza. This was even true for some members of the old científico elite. Although much of their property had been confiscated by revolutionaries, the old financial elite retained a much larger percentage of their wealth than most hacendados, both because they had been wealthier at the outset and because of their international connections. Terrazas had made large investments in the United States, and Creel was a partner in a series of foreign enterprises, including a number of banks and the British-owned Mexican Eagle Oil Company. José Yves Limantour Jr. went into exile during the Madero period, and at a time when no confiscations were taking place, he probably transferred whatever liquid or movable assets he had to France, where he had set up his residence. In view of Carranza's policy of returning confiscated estates to their former owners, these men had reason to believe that Carranza would respect their claims. This was indeed the case. Carranza returned properties to Limantour and was inclined to do the same for both Creel and Terrazas, although he never succeeded in fully implementing this aim.[42] It is thus no surprise that Mexico's hacendados preferred Carranza to the Revolutionary Convention.

An Alliance Torn by Increasing Divisions

There is no clearer expression of both the heterogeneity and the contradictions within the Conventionist movement than the lack of a unified command. Officially, all supporters of the Convention recognized Eulalio Gutiérrez as president of Mexico and accepted his authority. In practice, Gutiérrez exercised no real authority, not even in Mexico City, where he occupied the National Palace.

Villa was the nominal leader of the armed forces of the Convention and without any doubt its most popular personality. Nevertheless, he only controlled his own División del Norte. Zapata did not consider himself a subordinate of Villa's and carried out only such military campaigns as he thought were necessary. While Villa had greater influence on Maytorena and the Cedillo brothers, they too tended to go their own ways. Not only was there no unified political or military command in the territories dominated by the Convention, there was no real economic unity between these regions either.

What may have undermined the unity of the Conventionist factions even more was Villa's inability (and perhaps unwillingness) to supply his allies with arms and ammunition. This problem was all the more serious in that except for Maytorena, whose state bordered on the United States, no other faction linked to Villa had direct access to the U.S. border.

The Conventionist coalition represented such a heterogeneous mix of social, ideological, and economic forces that a lasting alliance between them seemed inconceivable, and in fact, it would soon disintegrate. While Zapata's peasant supporters demanded an immediate division of hacienda lands, as did many of Villa's soldiers (although they were willing to wait until the triumph of the revolution for this to occur), Maytorena had just returned many of the confiscated estates to their former owners. There was an equally wide gap between Eulalio Gutiérrez's demand to exercise genuine national power in all territories recognizing his authority and the unwillingness of the main leaders of the Conventionist faction to give him more than nominal allegiance, since large segments of the Conventionist movement, especially its peasant components, were opposed in principle to attempts by any central government to control them, as well as to the nature of the Gutiérrez administration. Gutiérrez had never been a major revolutionary figure and never commanded a substantial number of troops. He had been elected as a compromise candidate between the third force at the Convention, whose main leader had been Obregón, and the Villistas and Zapatistas. But Obregón and some of the other leaders of the third force had rejoined Carranza, thus undercutting Gutiérrez's authority even more.

Unlike the agrarian issue and the question of the power of the central government, one other issue that was to play a major role in the Mexican Revolution as a whole created no significant divisions among the Conventionist coalition. No faction within the coalition espoused a radical program of anti-American revolutionary nationalism. In part, this was owing to Woodrow Wilson's strong opposition to Huerta and to his favorable attitude toward the revolutionaries. Peasant localism also influenced Conventionist ideology. Many peasants had had no dealings with foreigners or foreign companies and were to a large degree only interested in their own village and the adjacent regions. Some of the most important Conventionist leaders, like Felipe Angeles, were firmly convinced that Mexico would never be able to prosper without U.S. help. In addition to these obvious factors, two somewhat less evident motives had a strong bearing on the pro-American foreign policy of the Conventionist leadership. One was that the economic dependence of the Conventionist factions on the United States was increasing rather than decreasing. With the outbreak of the European war, the United States had become the only major source of arms for any faction in Mexico. Those arms had drastically increased in price, however, since Mexican revolutionaries now had to compete with Great Britain, France, Russia, and other participants in World War I for American supplies. The resources with which the Conventionist faction could pay for American imports were decreasing, although the Convention now controlled a larger part of Mexican territory than its factions had ever ruled before. The huge cattle herds that Villa had used to finance the revolution in early 1914 had been depleted by large sales to the United States. Cotton crops in the Laguna, which had served the same purpose, had fallen off sharply, and American mining companies, whose taxes had also greatly helped the División del Norte, had largely suspended operations in Mexico. The Conventionist factions, but above all Villa, now depended more and more on American goodwill. He had to conciliate foreign mining companies if he wanted them to resume production. He also had to find some way for American merchants across the border to continue to accept his currency, even though it was depreciating rapidly as his printing presses poured forth millions of new pesos. Such acceptance was closely linked to the perception of merchants that Villa would win because the U.S. government supported him. Any tensions between him and the United States might easily cause his currency to plummet, limiting his ability to buy supplies in the United States.

In the eyes of Villa's conservative supporters, links to the United States had another advantage. Such links might serve as a means of controlling Villa and of preventing him from carrying out policies that they considered too radical. They seem to have warned Villa that any radical social reform might antagonize the United States and thus endanger his military effectiveness.

The Carrancista Coalition

Like its Conventionist counterpart, the Carrancista coalition was an alliance of very diverse forces, but it was far more homogeneous. The main reason for this discrepancy between the two major contenders for power in Mexico was that the Carrancista coalition encompassed few entities that could be considered peasant movements. Individual peasants fought in the ranks of Carranza's army, but it included very few fighting peasant communities such as those that made up the bulk of Zapata's army and Contreras's forces, and that played such an important part in the División del Norte. It is significant that the most important advocates of peasant demands within the Carrancista coalition were intellectuals who, while disagreeing with Carranza on agrarian issues, had many other points in common with the Carrancista leadership, above all its nationalism, which allowed them to bridge the gap on agrarian issues. To a far greater degree than either the Zapatistas or the División del Norte, Carranza's forces constituted a genuine professional army, willing to fight anywhere in Mexico. This was not true of large segments of the Conventionist army, with the significant exception of the División del Norte. Many of the Conventionist commanders and soldiers operated in their native regions, which they were reluctant to leave.

Such an attitude would have been impossible among most Carrancista commanders, since the states they controlled were not their own and the forces that they led were stationed far outside their home territories. They could never have maintained control of the regions they occupied by relying on local support. They were dependent on the national success of the Carrancista armies. This dependency on national support also explains the far greater degree of centralization of the Carrancista movement during the civil war with the Convention in 1914–15. This centralization was compounded by the fact that Carranza's power over his supporters steadily increased as the civil war progressed, largely because of his control of Veracruz, the largest port city in Mexico, which gave him ever-increasing command of the purse strings of his movement. The Carrancistas ruled the most important export-producing regions of Mexico: the port of Tampico, from which oil was exported; the henequen fields of Yucatán; and the coffee areas of Chiapas. Unlike the export-producing regions of the north, the south and the oil region had not been affected by war and revolution; in fact, production there, above all of oil and henequen, had continued to increase at a time when the prices for raw materials were on the rise as a result of scarcities produced by World War I. Overall, the revenues the Carranza-held territories generated were twice as great as those that the Conventionists could secure from the parts of Mexico they dominated.[43]

In spite of the fact that the Wilson administration was perceived as favoring Villa, objectively, it would be far more helpful to the Carrancistas. In the early phases of the civil war, this help consisted in the evacuation of Veracruz by U.S. troops, who handed over to the Carrancistas both the city and the huge supplies of arms that were stored there. (Why this was done is dealt with elsewhere in this book.) These assets were an enormous boon to the Carrancista faction and strengthened Carranza's control over his army by helping him to control its supply of arms and ammunition.

In the course of the civil war, the Carrancista coalition proved more solid and coherent than its Conventionist counterpart. It too would finally fall apart, but only in 1920, five years after securing victory.

The Decline and Fall of the Conventionist Movement

As a result of the heterogeneous composition of the Conventionist movement, it is not surprising that even before Villa's armies were overwhelmed in a series of battles that began in the spring of 1915, the deep contradictions within the Conventionist alliance led to dissension and to a kind of ideological and political paralysis.

The process of decline began with a break between the Gutiérrez faction and the rest of the Conventionist movement, followed by increasing tensions between Villistas and Zapatistas. The Convention showed itself less and less capable of reaching out to the urban sectors of Mexico's population, above all its working class. While local reform programs were proclaimed and implemented in certain regions, the Conventionist movement showed itself incapable of applying any reform on a national scale or of proclaiming a national ideology. Both domestically and abroad, the Convention was unable to counter increasingly effective Carrancista propaganda. Finally, for reasons that to a large degree were not of its own making, relations between the Conventionists and the United States rapidly deteriorated.

The contradictions within the Conventionist movement were scarcely apparent to the many observers who witnessed the triumphant parade of Villa's and Zapata's forces through Mexico City. They soon emerged into the open as relations between Villa and Zapata on the one hand and Gutiérrez on the other reached a breaking point.

The break between Villa and Gutiérrez was probably inevitable. The Convention government, the result of a compromise between Villa, Zapata, and the third force, was condemned to an illusory existence. After Obregón's supporters had left the Convention, Gutiérrez no longer represented a real force. He had rallied to Villa and Zapata in the hope of controlling their movement, but they, in turn, wanted to use him only as a spokesman for the Convention and thereby to increase their influence. Neither Villa nor Zapata considered subordinating themselves to his leadership. In fact, they distrusted him. Nevertheless, the break would probably not have occurred as rapidly as it did had it not been for the blatant disregard by both Villa and Zapata of the authority of the Gutiérrez administration in the one place where it attempted to exercise effective power: Mexico City. This attitude was most clearly expressed by what might best be called the Mexico City Terror, which resembled the Terror in Paris in 1793 and 1794 in that both members of the old ruling class and dissident revolutionaries were executed. It was, however, much smaller in scope than its French predecessor.

Whereas from 10,000 to 15,000 people are said to have been executed in Paris, the U.S. representative León Canova estimated that the Villista Terror put about 150 people to death in Mexico City. To a larger degree than its French predecessor, the Villista Terror was geared toward members of the upper class and supporters of the Huerta regime. Some of the most prominent men who were executed were former commanders of the federal army, among them General Eutiquio Munguía, General Herrera y Caro, and General Canseco, or civilians closely associated with Huerta.[44]

There were nevertheless a number of conspicuous exceptions, revolutionaries who had rallied to the Convention and who by all the standards of the Conventionist movement should have enjoyed immunity, but who were nevertheless executed by the members of the Zapata or Villista factions.

One such was Guillermo García Aragón, who had originally fought alongside Zapata during the Madero revolution. He had refused to go along when Zapata revolted against Madero and had gone his own way during the Constitutionalist revolution. Zapata considered him a traitor and bore a deep grudge against him. That García Aragón was a member of the permanent commission of the Revolutionary Convention and had been appointed by President Gutiérrez as governor of the National Palace did not protect him from arbitrary execution.[45]

A similar fate befell two other very prominent members of the Revolutionary Convention, David Berlanga and Paulino Martínez. Berlanga, a prominent representative of the third force at the Convention, had clearly and openly criticized both Villa and Zapata, but he had refused to go along when the Carrancistas left the Convention. The immediate cause for his arrest and execution is not entirely clear. One story has it that while sitting in one of Mexico City's best restaurants, Sylvain's, he saw a group of drunken Villista officers refuse to pay their bill. Incensed at their conduct, which he felt violated the ethics of the revolution, he upbraided them and paid for them. One of these officers was Fierro, Villa's executioner, and it was he who killed Berlanga. Berlanga is said to have showed such calm and courage in the face of death that even the murderous Fierro was impressed.[46]

The most prominent of the revolutionaries executed during the Villista Terror was Paulino Martínez. His death is still shrouded in mystery. One story has it that Martínez was the victim of an agreement that Villa and Zapata had reached during their closed-door meeting at Xochimilco. Villa is said to have agreed to hand over García Aragón to Zapata, and Zapata in turn voiced no objection to Villa executing Paulino Martínez. The reason for Villa's enmity to Martínez was that the latter had been a prominent member of the Orozco movement, had fought against Madero, and had continued to attack Madero in the press. According to another account, the Villistas arbitrarily arrested and killed Martínez, thus incurring the wrath of the Zapatistas. In contrast to the public executions during the Terror in France, the arrests in Mexico City were mostly carried out at night, and the prisoners were executed in secret. Zapatista demands for public trials and public executions were never implemented.

It is not clear who gave the orders for all of these executions. In some cases, it was Villa or Zapata; in many others, they were the work of subordinates. Many observers feel that Urbina carried out most of the executions.[47] Even if this was the case, their subordinates were never repudiated by either of the revolutionary leaders, and Villa and Zapata explicitly protected the executioners when President Gutiérrez sharply protested against the killings. There was a chilling arbitrariness about the way these executions were carried out. Martín Luis Guzmán describes how a subordinate told Villa that five men charged with counterfeiting had been arrested. The news was communicated to Villa in the evening. Without listening to the accused or examining the evidence, he immediately gave orders that the five counterfeiters were to be executed next morning. When the families of the five men came to ask for clemency or at least for a hearing, it was to no avail. When Martín Luis Guzmán tried to intervene with Villa, he was told by the latter's guards that the general could not be awakened before nine o'clock in the morning—the time set for the executions. President Gutiérrez and the minister of war, José Isabel Robles, who both opposed arbitrary executions, did not even try to wake Villa up, since they knew that they would not be listened to.[48] In this case, Villa's harshness can in part be attributed to the fact that counterfeiting of his money had become a major headache for him. The steady deterioration of the value of his currency, a natural result of the fact that he was printing so much of it, was exacerbated by the huge amount of counterfeit money that was circulating. Drastic punishments were thus meted out to counterfeiters.

In another case involving the life of a prominent member of the Gutiérrez administration, Villa refused to uphold the authority of the provisional president. José Vasconcelos, already at that time one of Mexico's most prominent intellectuals, had been designated minister of education in the Gutiérrez administration. A revolutionary general, Juan Banderas, popularly known as "El Agachado," threatened to kill Vasconcelos. He accused the minister, who had been a lawyer in the Porfirian era, of having taken money from him to settle a law case and having done nothing in return. When Gutiérrez demanded of Villa, the nominal head of the Conventionist army, that he discipline Banderas and protect Vasconcelos, Villa refused and advised the hapless education minister to go north and flee Mexico. For Villa the life of an intellectual and minister was not worth the problems a break with Banderas, who commanded a large number of troops, might cause.[49]

Executions were just part of the reign of terror in Mexico City. Equally prevalent were kidnappings of rich men, who were threatened with execution unless they paid large ransoms. These incidents were to a large degree also attributed to Urbina, although Villa certainly participated. Urbina's methods were vividly described by Frederick Adams, Lord Cowdray's representative in Mexico City:

In Mexico Urbina established his headquarters on a train in the central railway station and among other crimes has committed the following:

Juan Carbo, a wealthy man of Puebla, was sequestrated in his house on the Reforma driveway, taken to said train, ransom demanded, and he was tortured until he consented to give up some 2,000 pesos which was all the money he had in his house. He was placed in front of a firing squad, hung by the neck until he lost consciousness, etc., finally being released.

Melchor Ayala, a farmer from Irapuato, his majordomo was killed, and his secretary made prisoner, 500 pesos ransom being paid in Irapuato for his release. The secretary was again imprisoned, it being thought that if 500 pesos had been paid for the secretary a greater sum might be obtained for the ransom of the principal. Guided by the secretary Ayala was captured in his residence on Londres street. They also took away Mrs. Ayala and in spite of the fact that she became very ill, she and her husband were kept under guard the entire day. The brother of Mrs. Ayala, Luis Covarrubias, who had been looking for them, was also captured and finally he was compelled to go under force of arms to the bank and withdraw and deliver to his captors 17,000 pesos which he had there on deposit.

Ayala as well as Carbo had not been mixed at all in politics.[50]

Villa too utilized such methods, although in the one case that Adams reported, no torture was used. According to Adams, Villa "consigned Jesús and Antonio García of Zacatecas, in the basement of his house in Liverpool Street (the same in which Huerta lived) and has demanded a ransom of 500,000 pesos which they have been unable to raise. Finally he took them with him to Chihuahua. He will not receive any sort of paper money in payment of ransoms, only silver or gold."[51]

Forcibly extracting money from Mexico's wealthy classes was a procedure that all revolutionaries had followed and without which the revolution could not have been financed. Villa had done this in all the cities he captured, and Obregón, too, had attempted to obtain as much as he could from Mexico's upper classes after first occupying the capital. In previous cases, however, such measures had been taken openly. Villa would decree the confiscation of the property of the rich or impose forced loans upon them, as he had done the first time he took Torreón. Probably he now resorted to kidnappings and ransom in order to replenish the treasury of the División del Norte because he could not publicly impose contributions on the wealthy without openly infringing on the authority of the Conventionist government.

It is interesting to note that Villa took no reprisals at the prisons in which he had been incarcerated. It must have given him particular satisfaction to visit the penitentiary, "looking into the cell where he was confined when brought a prisoner from Chihuahua, after being arrested under orders of General Victoriano Huerta. While in the penitentiary General Villa chatted with Major D. Marines Valero, recalling the hardships he endured during his incarceration."[52] He neither executed nor imprisoned the wardens of the penitentiary. Had those who had held him prisoner fled, or had his treatment been so good that he did not want to take revenge on anyone?

Villa's contempt for Mexico City manifested itself in another, less destructive way. Villa forced the capital, which in his opinion was responsible for Madero's death, to rename one of its main streets Avenida Francisco Madero. On this occasion, an impressive ceremony was carried out, in which Madero's body was disinterred and buried once again. All stores and business houses were closed.

and the troops of the División del Norte paraded through the streets to the Spanish cemetery.

The troops formed a guard of honor around the tomb of Madero and the body of the slain president was disinterred and placed in a costly silver casket.

General Villa himself acted as master of ceremonies, while the band played the national anthem, and the crepe-draped flags of the army were lowered in salute to the dead.

Before the body was again consigned to the grave, General Villa addressed the multitude. He said in part: "The blackest mark that has ever stained the honor of Mexico was the assassination of the father of the new republic. Madero was the one man who at some day in the history of all nations rises up and saves his country from ruin and dishonor. He loved his people and fought for the honor and welfare of the Mexican race; he struck the chains from the ankles of his people and hurled the científicos from their places and power. But for Madero the científicos would still be kings and the plain people of Mexico abject slaves.

"Time will make Madero the greatest figure in the history of Mexico. I wish more could be done for him, but by this simple demonstration we prove that we still love and appreciate him. May his glorious example be ever before us in our work for the regeneration of our beloved country."

As General Villa closed, his eyes were filled with tears and his voice so choked with emotion that he was unable to give further utterance to his thoughts. The assembly was profoundly moved by the sight of the stern northern leader in tears, and the multitude remained standing in solemn silence for several minutes. . . . Later General Villa returned to town and personally mounted a ladder at each street corner of the Avenue San Francisco and replaced the old street signs with new ones bearing the name Avenida Francisco Madero, which had been removed during the days of the Huerta dictatorship.[53]

The reign of terror in Mexico City had two immediate consequences. It severely damaged Villa's image among both Mexico's upper classes and foreign diplomats and observers, and it led to a final break between Villa and Zapata, on the one hand, and with Gutiérrez and his government and supporters on the other.

The foreign observers' disillusion with Villa was perhaps best expressed by Lord Cowdray's representative, Adams, when he wrote his chief,

when he [Villa] entered Mexico everyone entertained the hope that he would be their salvation; although well known that he possessed arbitrary tendencies, it was thought that he would be sufficiently well advised, and was sufficiently capable, to understand that after the disorder and immorality which caused Carranza to lose the place that he had conquered, an aspect of order and morality would be required by whosoever desired to consolidate the government.

The release of houses that had been occupied, and discontinuance of confiscations of motor cars and horses, were things that confirmed this hope, but later we have been undeceived in an unmistakable manner. . . .

Generals Urbina, Fierro, and Medinaveytia, Villa's favorites, have been and are the dominating influence over him, assiduous companions in the cockpit established in San Cosme, where every day considerable sums are wagered, and in other diversions even more scandalous by means of which the marked weaknesses of the General are flattered thus dominating his actions.[54]

Adams had not entirely given up on Villa, since he felt that it was the bad advisors who were primarily responsible for the reign of terror. The same opinions were voiced by the U.S. representative León Canova, who also felt that the absence from Mexico of such leaders as Angeles and Raúl Madero contributed to Villa's arbitrariness.[55]

Foreign resentment of Villa was exacerbated by another episode of a very different kind. While shopping in a store owned by a Frenchwoman, a cashier caught Villa's eye. He made amorous advances to her and intimated that he would return the next day and hoped that she would be receptive to his wishes. The cashier was seized by panic and the owner of the store told her to stay at home and took her place the next day. When Villa arrived in the store as he had promised, not only did he not find the girl but he was met by the snickers and laughter of the employees and felt that his machismo was threatened. He seized the French owner of the store, and it took long expostulations to free her.[56] The event escalated into an international scandal.

It is not clear how much these events influenced or affected Mexico's lower classes. They were more impressed that Villa had taken up more than 60 homeless orphans who roamed the streets of Mexico City and sent them to Chihuahua to go to school. That episode greatly enhanced Villa's Robin Hood reputation.

For Gutiérrez and his government, Villa's reign of terror in Mexico City was only the tip of an iceberg. It had become clear to them that neither Villa nor Zapata would ever really respect their authority either in their home territories or even in the capital city where the Conventionist government was located. The result was a final break between Villa and the remnants of what had been the third force at the Aguascalientes Convention.

Gutiérrez's aim was to recreate the unity of the third force that had secured his election to the presidency. The majority of its members, headed by Obregón, had rejoined Carranza, although a minority, including some former Carrancistas, such as Lucio Blanco, and some of the generals of the División del Norte, such as Robles and Eugenio Aguirre Benavides, had remained loyal to the Convention. Gutiérrez began sending messages to different Carrancista commanders intimating that he would be ready to fight against both Villa and Carranza if they would join him. None of them was ready to break with Carranza, but they did encourage Gutiérrez in his course. When rumors of Gutiérrez's possible resignation or defection reached Villa in late December while he was at Guadalajara, he ordered all train service cut between Mexico City and the rest of the country. At the head of several thousand men, he made a "surprise visit" to Gutiérrez and a dramatic confrontation between the two men took place. Villa threatened to shoot Gutiérrez if the president resigned, but he remained unbowed. He told Villa that he could not effectively govern the country as long as assassinations and extortions were being committed in Mexico City. He also stated that Villa and Zapata were preventing him from exercising any real authority over the country. They continued to control the railroads, telegraph communications, and the printing of paper money. He was especially incensed at the murder of David Berlanga, who as a member of the Convention should have enjoyed complete immunity. Villa reportedly showed no remorse and said: "I ordered Berlanga killed because he was a lap dog who was always yapping at me. I got tired of so much noise and finally took care of him."[57]

Villa had the power to execute the president, but he hesitated to do so. He still had no definite proof of Gutiérrez's treachery. Moreover, the execution of the president would have undercut his legitimacy and threatened his relations with the United States. A strange kind of compromise between the two men was reached. On the one hand, Villa told Gutiérrez that he had ordered his troops to resort to all means to prevent the president from leaving Mexico City. On the other, he placed his troops under Gutiérrez's nominal control.

This confrontation only strengthened Gutiérrez's resolve to break with Villa. In a series of letters to Obregón and other Carrancista generals, he made it clear that he was ready to fight Villa and Carranza, if only the generals would join him. One of the Carrancista generals with whom Gutiérrez had been corresponding was Antonio Villareal. When Villareal's troops were routed by Angeles, some of the correspondence fell into Villa's hands. He wired José Isabel Robles, who was minister of war in Gutiérrez's cabinet but also a general of the División del Norte, to execute Gutiérrez immediately. Robles refused and showed the telegram to Gutiérrez, who decided to leave Mexico City with all troops who were still loyal to him.[58]

Gutiérrez had made some preparations for the crisis that he now faced. He had brought a number of troops loyal to him to Mexico City in order to protect him from the units that Villa had left in the capital. He had also sent Eugenio Aguirre Benavides, like Robles a general of the División del Norte who had strong sympathies for the third force, to San Luis Potosí as governor and military chieftain. It was in San Luis Potosí that Gutiérrez planned to establish his government. He still naïvely hoped to become the leader of a potent reconstituted third force that would eliminate Villa, Zapata, and Carranza and give him the presidency of Mexico. On the night of December 14, he collected all the troops loyal to him, as well as whatever money was left in the national treasury, and surreptitiously left Mexico City. Troops loyal to Villa and Zapata were taken by surprise, and they were too few in number to oppose him. On the next day, Gutiérrez published a scathing manifesto written by his most brilliant intellectual supporter, Vasconcelos, denouncing Villa and Zapata and officially deposing both from their commands. The reasons he gave for his defection were the same that he had orally given Villa at their meeting only three weeks earlier. He attacked Villa and Zapata for the reign of terror they had imposed on Mexico City and for the fact that they had not allowed the Conventionist government to exercise any kind of control over their regions, their economy, and the railroads and communications they controlled. He accused them of printing endless amounts of paper money without consulting the central government and of carrying out their own foreign policy with respect to the United States.[59]

Gutiérrez's hopes of reconstituting the third force proved an illusion. The Carrancistas gleefully published Gutiérrez's manifesto, hoping thus to demonstrate both to Mexico and to the world the weaknesses and rifts in the Conventionist faction. None of Carranza's generals was willing to break with the First Chief. Gutiérrez proved too weak a force to attract them. On the contrary, his defection renewed their hope that it would be possible to defeat Villa and Zapata.

Gutiérrez's hope of rallying Villa's middle- and upper-class supporters to his cause also failed. A few days after he left Mexico City, Eugenio Aguirre Benavides had a conference with the two Madero brothers, Raúl and Emilio, both generals in the División del Norte, as well as with Orestes Pereyra, hoping to persuade them to join his cause and take up arms against Villa.

Aguirre Benavides felt that he had some reason for optimism, since he was related to the Maderos, and Raúl had been his deputy as commander of the Zaragoza Brigade. He was not entirely mistaken. Both Raúl Madero and Orestes Pereyra showed some sympathy for his views but finally decided to remain loyal to Villa, on the advice of Raúl's elder brother, Emilio. According to Aguirre Benavides, Emilio's reasons were his personal obligations to Villa, as well as "his belief that our country must be ruled by a tyrant." Aguirre Benavides nonetheless still hoped to reverse his fortunes dramatically by gaining Angeles's support, and he called on Angeles to support him in his fight against the "unconscious tyranny of Villa, which because of its unconscious nature will be worse than every preceding tyranny."[60]

Angeles was more adamant in his opposition to Aguirre Benavides's proposals than the Maderos had been, however, saying: "I do not fight for a dictatorship but for democracy, and I am deeply sorry that you are hurting the revolution and its sacred ideals, which will be damaged through your personal ambitions and your folly. . . . As long as you were with us, you went from victory to victory, even against your wishes; from now on everything will go downhill with you."[61]

Angeles's words were prophetic as far as Gutiérrez and his supporters were concerned. Eugenio Aguirre Benavides had ensconced himself in San Luis Potosí in the hope that this state, which had been Gutiérrez's power base, would become a stronghold from which he and his associates would be able to defeat both Villa and Carranza. He soon realized that he had completely misjudged the general situation of Mexico, the relationship of forces in the country, and the loyalty of his own troops. When Villista contingents headed by Urbina approached San Luis Potosí, most of his troops refused to fight, and Aguirre Benavides retreated from the state's capital. Urbina's forces caught up with him at San Felipe Torres Mochas, most of his demoralized troops refused to fight, and Aguirre Benavides was decisively defeated. He attempted to flee to the United States but was intercepted by Carrancista forces and summarily executed by the Carrancista General Emiliano Nafarrete, although he carried a safe conduct from another Carrancista general. Lucio Blanco, also abandoned by most of his troops, did manage to make his way to the United States, where he was for a time interned by the U.S. government. He was killed in 1922 in an attempted revolt against Obregón.

Harassed by Villista forces and plagued by constant desertions, Eulalio Gutiérrez finally reached the obscure little town of Doctor Arroyo in Nuevo León, where he attempted to set up his capital. Abandoned by all but a few of his supporters, he soon realized the impossible situation he was in, resigned his presidency, and made his peace with the Carrancistas.

José Isabel Robles, who for a long time had been one of Villa's favorite generals, was the only Conventionist leader who for a short time continued to exercise some influence in Mexico. He made his peace with Villa, who pardoned him on the basis of his old sympathies. Until Villa was defeated in 1915, Robles fought on his side. Afterward, he rejoined Carranza, who accepted his services and sent him to Oaxaca to fight southern conservatives who had revolted against the Carrancista government. A man as charming, cultured, and civilized as he was inconsistent, Robles in 1917 again changed sides, suddenly throwing his support to the Oaxacan revolutionaries. Captured by the Carrancistas, he was summarily executed. Appeals by friends of his to Obregón for clemency, reminding the latter that Robles had saved his life when Villa threatened to execute him, were of no avail.[62]

The defection of Gutiérrez and his supporters had profound political and military consequences for the Conventionist faction. In political terms, Gutiérrez's accusations had a negative impact both on foreign governments, especially that of the United States, and on segments of Mexico's middle classes. More important than Gutiérrez's accusations, his defection put an end to even the appearance of a centralized Conventionist administration capable of ruling the whole country. This does not mean that a Conventionist central government ceased to exist. On the same night that Gutiérrez left Mexico City, Roque González Garza, Villa's highly respected delegate to the Revolutionary Convention, of which he was president, assumed the reins of government, and the remaining Conventionist delegates of both the Villista and the Zapatista factions confirmed him in his office.

González Garza's power was extremely limited, and only two weeks after Gutiérrez had left Mexico City, Villa established his own administration for northern Mexico, claiming that communications with the center were interrupted or at best very difficult to maintain. While he clearly stated that this was provisional, and that his administration was ultimately responsible to the Convention, in practice he had established a second government. For the first time since he had been governor of Chihuahua, Villa assumed a political post. He became the head of the northern administration, and three prominent intellectuals, all of them former Maderistas, Juan Escudero, Miguel Díaz Lombardo, and Luis de la Garza Cárdenas, became ministers of foreign affairs, economics, and communications respectively.

These men enjoyed some prestige inside and outside of Mexico because of their links to Madero, but on the whole they constituted a weak government. With the possible exception of Díaz Lombardo, they were not close to Villa, and it is doubtful whether they had any chance of really influencing him. None of them had a real power base of his own, and their authority derived completely from that of Villa. They lacked the intellectual potential of their counterparts both among the Zapatistas and the Carrancistas. None of them had the intellectual potential of either Antonio Díaz Soto y Gama or Luis Cabrera and Isidro Fabela nor were they radical social reformers. Villa's northern government never showed itself capable of elaborating a national agenda or a national policy. The end of any effective central Conventionist administration came at precisely the moment when the Carranza government in Veracruz took steps to show that it was a real national government with a national policy. It issued broad plans for agrarian reform as well as for a series of other social reforms in Mexico.

In some ways, Gutiérrez's defection also exacerbated the fragile and precarious relationship between the Villistas and the Zapatistas. González Garza soon faced problems similar to the ones Gutiérrez had had to deal with. The Zapatistas, jealous of their autonomy, and with vivid memories of what had happened to them when they had trusted Madero, refused to permit any central government to exercise authority in Morelos. At the same time, they demanded more and more resources and help from the central government. The result was a series of conflicts between Roque González Garza's Villista-dominated administration and the Zapatistas. This conflict aggravated tensions between the two factions but did not reflect the root causes of the differences between them. Those deeper causes were linked to ideological differences, which within a few weeks burst into the open in the deliberations of the Convention (see below).

Even more important were military considerations. During their meeting in Xochimilco, Zapata and Villa had decided to carry out a set of mutual obligations. The Zapatistas would wage offensive warfare against the Carrancistas in the south, while Villa would provide them with large amounts of arms and ammunition. Both sides proved to a large degree incapable and to a smaller degree unwilling to carry out these obligations. Zapata's peasant soldiers were unwilling to fight outside of their native region, and Zapata himself made little effort to persuade them to do so. Villa on the other hand was perennially short of ammunition, and in view of the limited fighting capacities of the Liberating Army of the South, supplying it with arms and ammunitions was not one of his main priorities.

The Mexico City Terror, Villa's attitude toward Gutiérrez, and his reluctance to supply Zapata with arms were more than just expressions of his hatred for Mexico City, contempt for central government, and lack of respect for Zapata's military capacities. They also reflected a newly found arrogance of power. Until he became supreme chief of the Conventionist forces and took Mexico City, Villa had been extremely careful about his image. He had maintained an iron discipline when his troops occupied Chihuahua and Torreón. He had always insisted on his respect for legal institutions and on his willingness to subordinate himself to civilian authorities. Prior to making any important decisions in the field of military, civilian, economic, or foreign affairs, he had always consulted with his intellectual advisors: Silvestre Terrazas, Angeles, and at times Carothers. In Mexico City, he had made decisions unilaterally, seemed to care little about the effects of those decisions, and did not seem concerned about the relationship between the costs and benefits of the steps that he decided on. In part, this was probably because much of the original Villista leadership that had been with him until his arrival in Mexico City was now dispersed throughout the country. Angeles was in the north; Silvestre Terrazas was in Chihuahua; and many of his generals were campaigning in other parts of the country. In a sense, this reflected the overconfidence that Villa always felt after a victory, but in another sense, it reflected the corruption of power. Inordinately popular charismatic leaders constantly surrounded by admirers, and increasingly by sycophants, have an especially strong tendency toward such arrogance, finally resulting in the belief that they and they alone incarnate the will of the people.

The Mexico City Terror and the break with Gutiérrez tarnished Villa's image both at home and abroad. Ever since the capture of Ciudad Juárez, he had tried his best to banish the image of Villa the bandit and outlaw. The events in Mexico City revived it, and an extremely able Carrancista propaganda machine magnified this image with unremitting intensity and energy.

The Propaganda War

In the shadow of the armed conflict that soon engulfed Mexico, a quieter kind of warfare was also raging: a propaganda war that pitted the twentieth century against the eighteenth, modern methods of propaganda and public relations against traditional forms of mass mobilization, methods used in the largely literate urban world against those that appealed to the rural, largely illiterate part of Mexico.

The Carrancistas turned out to be the greatest masters in the art of modern propaganda during the Mexican Revolution. Their propaganda concentrated on the image of Villa as a common bandit who was the tool of the reactionaries.

In their propaganda war against the Convention, Obregón and Carranza faced a problem that revolutionary leaders in practically all revolutions have faced: in the rapidly shifting patterns of alliances and conflicts that are characteristic of every revolution, revolutionary leaders have to convince not only their own followers but the population of the country as a whole that the ally and revolutionary hero of yesterday has become the counterrevolutionary traitor of today. This was the dilemma that Robespierre faced during the French Revolution when he labeled Danton a counterrevolutionary in the service of the forces of reaction, and that Stalin faced when he called Trotsky an agent of counterrevolution. The technique that both Robespierre and Stalin used was to describe genuine weaknesses and negative traits of their enemies, combine them with other more imaginary failings, and assert that whatever positive things their enemies had ever done had in reality been merely a smokescreen. Danton enjoyed the good life. He ate well, loved to live well, and was, according to many accounts, tainted by corruption. He had demanded that the terrorist system that was spreading all over France be limited. The technique that Robespierre used was to charge that Danton's convictions did not reflect genuine differences of opinion and interpretation but rather demonstrated that he had been bought by the forces of reaction. Over a century later, Trotsky cooperated with the Mensheviks, a faction in the Russian Social Democratic Party opposed to Lenin's Bolsheviks, before the 1917 revolution. He later joined Lenin and become one of the main leaders of the 1917 Bolshevik revolution. Once differences with Stalin emerged, the latter began to allege that all these differences showed that Trotsky had been a Menshevik agent within the Bolshevik party all along.

The same tactic was used by Obregón and Carranza against Villa. Once a bandit, they argued, always a bandit. One element of the Carrancista propaganda was to point out constantly that Villa's real name was Doroteo Arango. This was designed to be a reminder that beneath the glorious Francisco Villa lurked the bandit and murderer Doroteo Arango, and that Villa had changed his name precisely to escape from his horrendous past. This bandit, the propaganda said, was controlled by two evil men who personified the forces of reaction: Felipe Angeles and José María Maytorena.

The Carrancistas used a similar tactic against Angeles: once a federal officer, always a federal officer; since he had been a high official of the federal army before the revolution, he continued to act as such during the whole course of the revolution. Obregón went even further with his accusations. He implied that Angeles had joined the revolutionary army with the full consent of Huerta in order to undermine it from within and to serve as an agent of reaction within the revolution.[63] Obregón initially offered no proof to substantiate his accusations.

Soon afterward, the Carrancistas did offer "proof" of their accusations, which seems to have been the result of an extremely clever campaign of disinformation. In the spring of 1915, the propaganda office of the Carranza government in the United States, the Mexican Information Bureau, released copies of two letters that it claimed Angeles had left lying around while on a visit to Baja California.

The first was a purported letter by Porfirio Díaz to Angeles written in June 1913, calling on Angeles to save the federal army from annihilation. It was, Díaz declared, "an institution which to me is sacred, having devoted to it my greatest efforts. You are a member of that institution and know what it is worth."

The February happenings placed the army in this terrible dilemma. Either the army overcomes the fury of the people which is already roaring in a threatening manner and establishes peace and perhaps the only stable government in Mexico, or else the people will annihilate the army. The salvation of the army is a simple matter and you are most well-suited for carrying out this work, which maybe signifies the salvation of the country.[64]

The second letter that Carranza's agents "found" in Baja California purported to have been written nearly one year later by José Limantour, Díaz's finance minister, to Francisco Léon de la Barra, the former provisional president, addressed to him in Havana, Cuba. According to the Carranza information bureau, Limantour had written de la Barra that Angeles represented the only hope the conservatives still had of saving the federal army. "You know that the northern division [División del Norte]," Limantour wrote,

has no political or social aim in view, since it is commanded by an ambitious man, eager for money and power; on the other hand, one of our men is serving in his ranks with a highly significant military grade. It is impossible for Felipe Angeles ever to forget the great services which he owes to General Porfirio Díaz. We can satisfy the ambition of the former with our gold and use to advantage the gratitude of Angeles with our ability. Once this has been done we will advise Villa how to draw Zapata to him and thus give our new order of things a revolutionary and re-vindicating aspect which for the time being is what we need. We will faithfully carry out the Plan of Ayala, distributing lands only in the state of Morelos and compensate ourselves for this munificence with concessions and lands in other less tumultuous states. We will then organize a powerful army, selecting the most conspicuous members of the federal army and placing the Villa-Zapatista army under its command and in this manner we will again rule in Mexico.[65]

The editors of the *New York Times* were so impressed by these letters that they printed both of them, thus making them widely known both in the United States and in Mexico. At the same time, though, the *Times*'s editors published an editorial saying that the correspondence certainly did not prove that Angeles was a tool of the conservatives:

Its receipt by Felipe Angeles certainly does not prove that Angeles is working to restore *científico* rule. Nor does the expression of Mr. Limantour's belief in the undying gratitude of Angeles in his letter to Mr. de la Barra published at the same time prove anything. . . . it is only fair to say that there is not a particle of proof as yet that General Angeles is in sympathy with its projectors. Suspicions of his lack of sympathy with the revolutionaries he associates with are based solely on a superior education and social standing. He is the Philippe Egalité of the Mexican Revolution.[66]

Philippe Egalité was the nickname of Louis-Philippe, duke of Orléans, who became a revolutionary and renounced his title, calling himself Citizen Egalité; despite voting in the Convention for the execution of his cousin Louis XVI, he was arrested and later guillotined himself after the desertion of his son, the future King Louis-Philippe, to the counterrevolution. The comparison of the two men may not have been entirely unwarranted but the letters were in all probability forgeries. In a letter written to the *New York Times* only a few days later, Limantour stated that he had never written such a letter. While the denial by itself is not necessarily convincing, another part of the letter certainly is. "Mr. de la Barra was not in Havana in May 1915 nor did he spend a single day there during the whole of that year," Limantour wrote to the *Times*. "He was in Paris and I had occasion to see him there at the time I was supposed to have written from that city to Havana. Second, the letter attributed to General Porfirio Díaz in which references are made to mine is of the 18th of June 1913, one year before the date of that which bears my name."

Villa's representative in the United States also denied the authenticity of the letter, stating that Angeles had never been to Baja California. Also, it is improbable that in June 1913 Díaz would have written such a letter. This was a time when the revolution seemed to be petering out. Carranza had been defeated in Coahuila and had been forced to leave his native state, Villa was the leader of what was still a relatively small band in Chihuahua, and the Sonoran revolution was torn by disarray, Maytorena having left only a few weeks before for the United States. All the European powers had recognized Huerta, and it was not at all clear yet what course President Wilson would pursue with respect to the revolutionaries and the federal army. No copy of such a letter is to be found in either the Díaz archives or the Limantour archives.[67]

One manifestation of the sophisticated character of Carrancista propaganda was that the former Magonista Antonio Villareal hired John Kenneth Turner, author of *Barbarous Mexico* and an ideological enemy of Villa's since 1911, to write a scathing exposé of Villa. Turner and Villareal had probably known each other before the revolution, since both were closely linked to the Partido Liberal Mexicano, headed by the Flores Magón brothers. Villareal paid Turner $1,000 and offered him $1,000 more upon the completion of his manuscript. He also invited Turner to Veracruz, where he would be provided with all necessary information about Villa.[68]

There is no reason to assume that financial consideration played a primary role in Turner's decision to attack Villa. But in light of Turner's links with Magonismo and the Industrial Workers of the World, both of which Villa had undermined during the Orozco rebellion, many American radicals close to the IWW who were intimately linked to the PLM were extremely distrustful of Villa. They remembered that he disarmed the Magonistas at Madero's behest in 1911, opposed Orozco, whom the liberals had supported, and expelled IWW organizers from Chihuahua. Turner never attempted to enter any area under Villista control.

Turner's exposé included every accusation of banditry and murder that had ever been leveled against Villa. Turner denied that Villa had become a bandit because his sister had been raped by a hacendado, saying that he had no sisters. He condemned Villa's executions of prisoners taken from the federal army without mentioning that this had been done at the express orders of Carranza. Turner also denied that Villa had any reformist tendencies, asserting that all Villa had done was to transfer ownership of the haciendas of the oligarchy to his own generals.[69]

Turner's articles were published in both English and Spanish and aimed at both an American and a Mexican readership. In addition, the Carrancistas carried on a successful press campaign, sending articles free of charge to large numbers of American newspapers.

The Carrancista propaganda offensive was complemented by an equally effective ideological offensive. Urged on by intellectuals in his faction, Carranza began to make radical pronouncements and to issue radical decrees. At the end of 1914, in a series of additions to the Plan of Guadalupe, he declared that profound social changes would take place in Mexico. More concretely, on January 6, 1915, he decreed that lands expropriated from villages would be returned to them, and that large estates could be expropriated in order to give land to the landless. Local, regional, and national agrarian commissions would be set up to oversee these measures. In all regions controlled by the Carrancistas, and especially in Mexico's southeast region, debt peonage was declared illegal and the former peons emancipated.

The Carrancistas also wooed Mexico's working class. Carranza's governors and commanders frequently supported strikes by industrial workers, especially if they were directed against foreign enterprises. The largest Mexican union federation, the Casa del Obrero Mundial, was given semi-official status, allowed to organize freely in areas under Carrancista control, supported in conflicts with employers, and subsidized, occasionally with cash, but more often with confiscated houses for their offices.

It is not easy to assess the effect these measures had. It has frequently been stated that Carranza's agrarian law of January 6, 1915, resulted in the majority of Mexico's peasants rallying to the Carrancista faction. There is little evidence that this was the case. The majority of Mexico's peasants, insofar as they were affected by the revolution, identified with Villa and Zapata and traditionally distrusted the country's politicians. It is doubtful whether Carranza's agrarian decree swayed the peasantry, because it was not applied on a wide scale. It did encourage some peasants to take preliminary steps to set up agrarian commissions and to make demands upon the Carrancista leadership, but there were few cases of organized peasants rallying to Carranza.

Carranza's reform decrees had more concrete consequences in those cases where they were followed by practical steps. In the states of southeastern Mexico, where debt peonage was prevalent, the Carrancista military commanders effectively freed the peons from bondage, and in those regions, especially in the states of Yucatán and Tabasco, they gained widespread support. Moreover, the Carrancistas scored their greatest success with Mexico's working class. Carranza and Obregón signed a pact with the Casa del Obrero Mundial, which, in return for concessions, set up so-called Red Battalions, consisting of more than 6,000 unionized workers, which joined the Carrancista army in fighting both the Zapatistas and the Villistas, participating in the battles of Celaya.[70] In parts of Mexico controlled by the Carrancistas, political organizations and parties were established.

Coherence and unity were the hallmarks of the Carrancista propaganda effort to explain the outbreak of a renewed civil war to Mexico's people. While profound divergences did exist within the Carranza faction, they never manifested themselves in Carrancista propaganda or ideology during the civil war. The same cannot be said of the Conventionist faction. Its far greater heterogeneity was reflected in a lack of unity and even contradictions in its propaganda efforts.

The first great difficulty that the propaganda of the Conventionist faction encountered was that it had not one but at least three centers of power: the Conventionist government in Mexico City headed by González Garza, the headquarters of Zapata's movement in Morelos, and the Villista administration in the north.

The Zapatistas were the one faction in the Conventionist movement that maintained the same coherence that it had had from the first day that it emerged and needed to perform no ideological somersaults. The Zapatistas had never trusted Carranza or declared their support for him; in fact, they had always warned their people that he might very well turn out to be another Madero. Thus they had no great hurdles to overcome. Their propaganda was more limited in scope than that of the Carrancistas or the Villistas and basically addressed one issue: the agrarian problem. The gist of their propaganda campaign was best expressed by a proclamation written by Zapata's intellectual adviser, Antonio Díaz Soto y Gama, after the failure of Carranza's effort at reaching an understanding with Zapata, before the start of the Revolutionary Convention. "The country wants something more," Soto y Gama declared, "than the vague utterances of Señor Fabela supported by the silence of Señor Carranza. It wishes to crush feudalism once and for all." The constitutionalists had little to offer the poorest segments of the Mexican people. "Reforms in administration . . . complete integrity in the handling of public funds, a scrupulous insistence on official responsibility, freedom of the press for those who cannot read, freedom to vote for those who do not know the candidates, an equitable administration of justice for those who have never had any business with a lawyer. All these beautiful democratic principles, all these grand words, with which our fathers and grandfathers delighted themselves, have today lost their magical allure and meaning for the people." The Zapatistas made it clear that they closely identified Carranza with Madero: "With elections and without elections, with effective suffrage or without it, with Porfirian dictatorship or with the democracy of Madero, with a muzzled or a libertine press, the poor's portion is bitterness. They continue to suffer poverty and humiliations without end."[71]

Villista propaganda lacked the coherence of that of its Carrancista opponents and its Zapatista allies. It reflected the contradictions among the heterogeneous elements that made up the Villista coalition. In the proclamation that he issued in September 1914, before the meeting of the Convention of Aguascalientes, Villa cited Carranza's opposition to land reform as one of the primary motives for repudiating the leadership of the First Chief. The Convention itself went on record as supporting Zapata's Plan of Ayala. Yet in the explanations that the most important Villista newspaper, *Vida Nueva*, gave for the new civil war that had broken out in Mexico, the land issue was not even mentioned.

Vida Nueva attributed the new civil war above all to Carranza's illegitimate presidential ambitions, his unwillingness to bow to the will of the great majority of the revolutionaries as expressed in the Convention of Aguascalientes. It was Carranza's personal ambitions, according to *Vida Nueva*, that threatened to plunge Mexico into another bloody civil war. Carranza had disregarded the message that the Convention as a whole and then Gutiérrez in its name had conveyed to him:

You came to power on the basis of your tacit designation by a minority of revolutionary chieftains; today, after a huge majority of revolutionary leaders has repudiated you, you should step down from power. We bring this resolution to your notice so that you may submit to it. But since ambition has made you deaf to the voice of reason and of affection, we unite our voices with the solemn mandate of our brothers who died on the battlefield and in their last moments . . . cursed those who would violate the ideals of the revolution.[72]

Perhaps an even more important facet of the Villista explanation for the break with Carranza was the accusation that the First Chief was attempting to steal the fruits of victory from those who had in fact achieved it. That idea, that the División del Norte had been the main force to defeat Huerta, and that Carranza was attempting to be the beneficiary of a victory he himself had not achieved, had already been a major tenet of Villa's manifesto of September 1914. *Vida Nueva* now again took up this theme, and it would constantly recur in Villista propaganda. This idea was clearly reflected in the contempt that *Vida Nueva* showed both for the civilian leadership of the Carranza movement and for many of its military figures. "They have never seen the face of victory . . . and they will be incapable of obeying a Fabela or a Palaviccini who have never fought, nor know how to fight, nor have ever triumphed, nor know how to triumph."[73]

The subject of stability and order, completely absent in Zapatista propaganda, but extremely important in all Carrancista manifestos, played an equally important role in Villista propaganda. Not Villa but the Carrancistas constituted the real bandit element of the Mexican Revolution, according to *Vida Nueva*. "If General Villa does not come with his invincible division to destroy Carrancismo, the most terrible anarchy will take place and everyone will curse the revolution." The only salvation for Mexico, the only hope of reestablishing a decent, civilized order were "the courageous men who have known how to fight and have known how to triumph . . . who will bring back order to the country, allow people to work in a climate of freedom that has been so brilliantly secured. They will free the people from the sad condition it finds itself in and they will allow Mexico to develop as it deserves to do."[74]

The most remarkable aspect of Villista propaganda in the first few weeks after the break with Carranza was the absence of any reference to the land issue or even any mention of the far-reaching reforms that Villa had in fact carried out in Chihuahua: the expropriation of the lands of the oligarchy, the redistribution of some lands and many goods to the poor, the development of education, and the like. This was no coincidence. It reflected the profound divisions among Villista intellectuals between radical reformers such as Federico González Garza and more conservative men, including Angeles and the head of the Villista administration in the north, Miguel Díaz Lombardo.

More and more, *Vida Nueva*'s editorialists concentrated their propaganda on a kind of Villa personality cult:

Villa certainly had a divine revelation, he was anointed by our Good Lord for the salvation of his people, and with his head held high and his eyes on another world, he never vacillated, he never hesitated because of any obstacles he had to face, but marched toward the high mountains, where the ideals of the people were to be found. And Villa will arrive and will give his people the treasure that had been taken from them.

In his eyes, there is but one clear road: the law; and one conquest: freedom; destiny has given him one duty: justice. For this reason, having been chosen and predestined, whatever he does will always be invariably profound and fructiferous.

After having proven and constantly proving that he is a leader of his people in war, he has proven and is proving and will prove that he will be a leader in peace. There on the battlefields, he is destroying armies. Here in the vast region where there is no disorder anymore, he is organizing governments and building administrations.[75]

The editorialist of *Vida Nueva* was in fact stating that Villa would make the best president of the country. Such an implication was in stark contrast to an interview given by Miguel Díaz Lombardo, Villa's highest civilian official, to an American newspaper and republished in *Vida Nueva*.[76] Díaz Lombardo stated that he believed that the Convention would soon move to Chihuahua, that the appointment of González Garza as its president was provisional, and that the feeling among most military leaders of the Villista movement and of Villa himself was that Angeles should become provisional president. This was a slap in the face to González Garza, to Zapata, who had not been consulted, and to the possible presidential aspirations of Villa himself. One day later, Díaz Lombardo was forced to retract, saying that the American correspondent had misunderstood him. Díaz Lombardo now stated that he had not spoken as an official of the Villista administration but only given a personal opinion. That personal opinion was that since González Garza was the president of the Convention but not the interim president of Mexico, Felipe Angeles would be one of the best candidates for that post. Díaz Lombardo did not rule out the possibility that Villa might one day become president: "As far as General Francisco Villa is concerned, on various occasions he has stated that for now he is not thinking of accepting a political post since he wants to dedicate all his energies to the pacification of the country by personally directing all military operations."[77]

By promoting this kind of personality cult and even implying that some day Villa might become president of the country, the editorialists of *Vida Nueva* were building on strength. Villa's immense popularity in Mexico was still the strongest asset of the Conventionist movement.

For Zapata, as long as he operated in the countryside, his lack of modern propaganda techniques presented no problems. By giving municipal authority back to elected village representatives and by returning land to the villages, he had done more to win their allegiance than any modern propaganda could have done. When his troops occupied Mexico City, however, they were incapable of finding a common language with the city's large and important labor movement, although some of the Zapatista leaders were in fact members of the Casa del Obrero Mundial and knew something about the workers' grievances.

Villa had more experience in occupying cities and dealing with their lower-class populations than Zapata had. He did so in terms of nineteenth-century caudillo traditions rather than with the message of modern propaganda. While military bands played in the main squares of the newly occupied city, Villa would distribute food, clothing, and other goods taken from Mexican and Spanish-owned stores to the city's poor. That gave him a great deal of popularity. But it was frequently a one-time affair, and he was incapable of forging the kind of political links with organized lower-class urban groups that Obregón was establishing. Yet in spite of Carrancista propaganda, Villa by all accounts continued to enjoy the greatest popularity among Mexico's lower classes, above all in the countryside.

If one compares the explanations furnished by the Carrancistas and the Villistas for the renewed outbreak of a civil war, a series of remarkable similarities emerge. Both sides addressed themselves in those early weeks to a limited audience: their immediate civilian and military constituency, the undecided local revolutionary factions, and the Wilson administration and American businessmen. The main issues they stressed were legitimacy and stability. References to social reform were conspicuously absent from their propaganda. The gist of Carrancista propaganda was that the Conventionist faction had nothing to offer but anarchy, reaction, or a combination of the two. Inspiring fear rather than hope seems to have been the main tenor of Carrancista propaganda until mid-January 1915, when the First Chief finally came out with a positive program of reforms that promised to transform Mexico. Obregón and Carranza's radical supporters, who had insisted on the proclamation of such reforms, seem to have encountered a large amount of resistance before they were able to persuade the First Chief to accede to their demands. Carranza came to realize that his support among the mass of the Mexican people was weak and that the lower classes of society by no means shared his fear of Villa. Hence he would have to make concrete promises in order to gain their support.

The themes of legitimacy and stability were also cornerstones of early Villista propaganda. Whereas the Carrancistas attempted to legitimize their movement by stating that their opponents were bandits and reactionaries, the Villistas did so by insisting that they represented the vast majority of revolutionaries as embodied in the Convention of Aguascalientes, and hence that they were the only genuine democrats in Mexico. They also emphasized that only Villa, thanks to his great prestige and authority, could bring order out of chaos.

To a far greater degree than the Carrancista leadership, Villa appealed to the pride of his soldiers. This was reasonable. They had won the major battles of the revolution, they had suffered most, they had made the greatest sacrifices, and now, having won, it might all have been in vain. This appeal to the pride of his soldiers was linked to another characteristic theme of Villista propaganda, its appeal to regional pride. The core of the División del Norte was composed of men and women from Chihuahua and Durango, and even opponents of Villa's in these states felt that "foreigners" from other states were attempting to steal the fruits of victory from them.

One of the most striking deficiencies of Villista propaganda was that for a long time it did not react to the ideological and legislative offensive of the Carrancista faction. In part, this resulted from Villa's general lack of interest in ideological problems. There was relatively little reason for him to show any. He realized that, although unlike other revolutionary leaders, he had issued no plan and no substantive legislation, he was by far the most popular leader that the revolution had produced. In addition, he had always been a proponent of decentralization. Each state was to issue its own social laws. He may also have feared that in view of the heterogeneity of his movement, any law he might issue would immediately lead to disagreement. In addition, by allowing the Convention to continue to legislate in ideological matters, which he considered unimportant, Villa may have hoped to prove both to his allies in the south and to domestic and foreign public opinion that he still respected the sovereignty of the Revolutionary Convention.

Unlike Villa, the delegates at the Convention were worried about Carranza's ideological offensives. "Here you have Venustiano Carranza issuing agrarian decrees, while we are losing our time," a delegate to the Convention noted.[78]

The majority of the Convention, composed mainly of Zapata's delegates, reacted very rapidly. On February 8, they proposed that all estates that had been confiscated and were being administered by the state should immediately be divided among the peasants living on the haciendas and in the adjacent villages. Every village was to set up an agrarian commission elected by all the villagers, which would then supervise the distribution of the lands. On February 18, the Convention majority submitted a broad program of political and social reforms, proclaiming universal suffrage and wide-ranging rights for labor, including the right to establish unions, the right to strike, and the right to carry out boycotts against employers. It also gave rights to women and refused to recognize any difference between legitimate and illegitimate children.

These decrees were an effective response to Carranza's proclamations, but their adoption was delayed for many months because of the strong opposition of northern delegates, especially those representing Angeles and Maytorena, to the most radical provisions of this plan. They objected to any immediate land redistribution. Their main arguments probably reflected Villa's own views. An immediate land reform would discriminate against those who most deserved to obtain lands, the soldiers of the revolutionary army. As one delegate put it, "The soldiers who are now fighting in our ranks will strongly object that the land should be given to those who are not fighting and who would doubtless get the best lands, since they felt that it was they who should be the main beneficiaries since they had risked their lives in this struggle that has caused so much suffering in our country."[79]

This argument reflected the differences between the northern and southern armies. Zapata's guerrillas, who were fighting near their native villages, had no trouble in being present when land was being distributed. Villa's soldiers, frequently fighting hundreds of miles away, had no possibility of returning home to claim land. If land were to be distributed, there was a danger that many soldiers would desert and return home in order to participate. A second argument important only for the north was the fear that once land distribution began on a large scale, foreign property would be affected, and that this might arouse hostility, above all in the United States, to the revolutionaries.[80] This argument was irrelevant for the Zapatistas, since there were few foreign-owned properties in Morelos.

A third argument advanced by the northerners was that immediate land distribution would cause economic hardship, because production would fall drastically. Once the lands were turned over to the peasants, they would revert to subsistence agriculture instead of planting cash crops. This had in fact happened in Morelos, where sugar, the traditional staple of that region, had been replaced by corn and beans. Such a development entailed less hardship for the Zapatistas than for the northerners. They had limited means of disposing of sugar, since they had no common borders with a foreign country. In the north, by contrast, cotton and a number of other cash crops could be sold across the border in the United States and were used to buy arms, ammunition, and other supplies. Without such arms and supplies, the División del Norte could not continue to be a viable military force. While such practical considerations reflected the situation in northern Mexico and Villa's own views, some northern delegates went further and objected in principle to dividing up the large estates. Maytorena's representative Castellanos stated that "honestly acquired" latifundia (i.e., large haciendas) should not be divided among peasants. There was, he insisted, sufficient vacant land belonging to the state that could be a basis for agrarian reform.[81]

A series of northern delegates, including Maytorena's representative and Angeles's delegate Federico Cervantes, spoke out against another part of the reform project: universal direct suffrage. Treviño, a northern delegate, pointed out that 90 percent of Mexico's population were illiterate, that many Indians did not even speak Spanish, and that these people should not be allowed to participate in direct elections of deputies. Only those who could read and write should be able to do so. These objections were rejected by the majority of the Convention.

Northern delegates objected to another paragraph of the planned political and social reforms guaranteeing workers' right to strike and their right to carry out boycotts against employers. One of the northern delegates, Velázquez, stated that the right to strike would be misused by agitators, who would constantly provoke unjustified strikes. Another northerner declared that if the workers' right to boycott was accepted, Mexico would practically be destroyed.[82] Cervantes objected to the Mexican state officially recognizing the legitimacy of trade unions.[83] In this connection, the delegates dealt for the first time with the issue of socialism. In order to counter Zapata's most important delegate, Soto y Gama, Angeles's representative Cervantes stated that socialism was an extremely dangerous doctrine, since it declared that capitalists were exploiters and advocated the theory that under capitalism "man is exploited by man."[84] No decision was made on this issue.

There was no unanimity among the northern delegates when problems of family law were discussed. In the plan for social and economic reforms that a commission had proposed to the Convention, equal rights were to be granted to illegitimate children. While Cervantes strongly supported this project, another northerner, Marines Valero, thought it would result in polygamy. José Casta, also a northern delegate, went even further, saying that granting equal rights to illegitimate children meant that free love would now be officially sanctioned.[85]

Far greater differences of opinion emerged when a paragraph of the new political, economic, and social program legalizing divorce was examined. It stated that the right to divorce was essential to the emancipation of women. While the delegates from the south as well as Cervantes were in favor of this paragraph, Enrique Cepeda from the north objected. "What do we achieve with divorce? We open the door to those who break a solemn obligation, to those who commit perjury by breaking their oath. Divorce will destroy our bonds rather than unite them, will bring social ruins and depravity."[86]

In all cases, the objections of the more conservative delegates from the north were rejected by the majority of the Convention and the original proposals won majority approval, with some small modifications.

Did the conservative opinions of the northerners reflect Villa's own position? This is not easy to determine, since Villa showed little interest in ideological matters and his representative at the Convention, Roque González Garza, did not participate in the ideological discussions. This may have been because González Garza was the president of the Convention and thus officially had to assume a neutral position.

There is little doubt that the northerners who opposed agrarian reform were not speaking for Villa. He had made it clear that he was committed to massive land distribution at the expense of Mexico's large landowners. It is not clear what Villa's attitude toward labor was. He had recognized the unions that existed in Chihuahua but outlawed strikes. When unions and workers demanded higher wages in late 1915 and threatened to strike, Villa never repressed them but tried to be conciliatory.[87] It is doubtful that Villa was a great supporter of the emancipation of women. Yet he did give his name to all of his illegitimate children.

Carrancista and Villista Agrarian Policies

Villa's abstention from matters of ideology and social legislation on a national scale ended in May 1915, when he decreed an agrarian law. It is certainly no coincidence that this law was proclaimed after Villa had suffered his two great defeats at Celaya. He and his advisors probably felt that such a law was a way of restoring his waning internal and external support. All estates beyond a certain size were to be divided among the peasants, and the owners would receive some form of indemnity from the peasants, who would have to pay in small installments. And although this was a national law, it still reflected Villa's commitment to decentralization, since the state governments, rather than the federal government, were to implement the law. The communal property of the villages was not mentioned. Finally, the law reflected the heterogeneous and divergent character of the Conventionist movement: in order to maintain the unity of the factions that supported him, Villa allowed the states wide leeway in the application of agrarian reform.

The law also reflected the wishes and desires of the northern peasants, the majority of whom had never been organized in communal villages, in contrast to those of southern and central Mexico. One of the main provisions of the law was best defined by Zapata's adviser Soto y Gama. "When one compares the northerners' and southerners' opinion regarding agrarian problems, one sees that they were and are very different."

The restitution and settlement of communal lands to the people was the main preoccupation for the south. The Plan of Ayala, a true reflection of southern thought, confirms this.

For the northerners, from San Luis Potosí, Jalisco, and Zacatecas northward, the solution lay in the division of the enormous latifundia and in the creation of a great many small properties, large enough to support the cost of good agricultural development, achieved with enough resources to guarantee abundant production and future prosperity.[88]

In theoretical terms, Villa's law was in some ways more conservative than Carranza's agrarian decree. Carranza's law provided that the peasants would receive their lands free of charge, while Villa's law specified that they would pay small installments. By giving the states more leeway in determining agrarian policies, Villa's law made it easier for recalcitrant state governments to impede land distribution. In practical terms, however, there was an sharp contrast between Carranza's and Villa's attitude toward land reform. At the same time that he was issuing a radical agrarian decree, Carranza was quietly returning most of the confiscated estates to their former owners. Little land distribution actually took place. Among a number of radical supporters of Carranza, such as Francisco Múgica, these measures led to an increasing feeling of despair and hopelessness. In a letter to another Carranza supporter who was also his superior, General Salvador Alvarado, Múgica wrote in August 1916:

I do not agree with the general policy that is being carried out. . . . A great agrarian commission has been created to watch over the functioning of this law. It has ended in a complete fiasco; in spite of the fact that the first steps are only being taken to solve the agrarian problem, measures are already being taken to put an end to these first steps before they have been undertaken. When I was in the capital of Mexico in February and March of this year I saw that the Villistas, Zapatistas, and members of the Convention were persecuted far more than the supporters of Huerta. . . . Where does all this lead us to, my dear General?[89]

Unlike Carranza, Villa was fundamentally opposed to returning any confiscated estates to Mexico's hacendados, except in a few cases where he could not control conservative supporters such as Maytorena. Again and again, *Vida Nueva* reported on preparations for land reform carried out in many parts of the country under Villista rule. Within the short span of about two weeks, from March 10 to March 26, 1915, *Vida Nueva* wrote that in the Laguna area the military commander had decreed the closing of all factories producing alcoholic beverages, and in order to allow the workers at these factories to make a living, they would all be given land from the large estates. One day later, on March 11, the newspaper stated that the Villista administration had sent surveyors to the haciendas of Santa Ana del Conde, La Sandia, Jalpa, Atotonliquillo, Maravillas, Coecillo, Otates, and San Pedro del Monte in order to prepare a land reform. Six days later the same newspaper reported that in the state of Durango, preparations for a massive land reform were being carried out, and on March 26 *Vida Nueva* went into more detail, stating that surveyors had been sent to the hacienda of Aviles in order to prepare the division of its lands among peasants.

Villa went one step further in the summer of 1915 by sending an emissary to Sonora and attempting to influence Maytorena to begin carrying out land distribution.[90] But the region in which Villa showed the greatest interest was Chihuahua. In the fall of 1914 and the beginning of 1915, *Vida Nueva* carried advertisements every day asking for agricultural engineers who could survey lands prior to their distribution. In early 1915, questionnaires were distributed to peasants asking them to state what land they wanted to obtain. In August 1915, Villa asked that the Chihuahuan agrarian reform commence,[91] and Governor Fidel Avila signed a law ordering its implementation. Villa instructed Avila to not to partition the Terrazas's haciendas yet, though, because they were to be given to Villa's soldiers: "Regarding requests for land distribution, I wish to tell you that because soldiers and members of the army cannot go to Chihuahua to make their requests, please reserve all the Terrazas haciendas for them and distribute the rest."[92] But Villa's move came too late. By then his forces had been routed, and it is doubtful whether the peasants were willing to accept land from his defeated administration. It would brand them as Villistas and discredit them in the eyes of the victors.

The most striking difference between Carrancista and Villista propaganda, apart from the degrees of coherence, was that Carrancista propaganda was more radical than Carrancista practice, whereas Villista propaganda was more conservative than Villista practice. The Carrancistas never mentioned that at the same time they were promising land for the peasants, they were returning most of the confiscated estates to their former owners. Conversely, the Villistas never mentioned that they had expelled the traditional oligarchy from large parts of Mexico, and that they had redistributed large amounts of goods to the poor throughout Villista territory.

The War of the Revolutionaries

In military terms, in waging regular warfare (as opposed to his guerrilla period), Villa had reacted rather than acted. It had been the federal army that had determined the sites of the División del Norte's greatest battles. When the war between the revolutionary factions broke out, Villa found, however, that he could decide where to fight battles. In making his choices, Villa now for the first time disregarded Angeles's advice, with disastrous consequences.

Angeles was the one leader of the Conventionist faction with a clear perception of the military situation—of the Conventionists' initial advantages but long-term disadvantages. Since it was he who had largely forged the Conventionist alliance, he understood its fragility. Having dealt with many of the Carrancista leaders at Aguascalientes, he also knew their strengths and weaknesses. He probably understood better than Villa what the limitations of the economic resources at the disposal of the Convention were. He may also have feared that in a long-drawn-out war, the only resource left to the Convention would be to turn to the properties owned by foreigners, which up to then had scarcely been taxed. Such a move against foreign-owned properties would probably alienate the United States and thus destroy a cornerstone of Angeles's political vision of Mexico's future.

By all means at his disposal, Angeles tried to persuade Villa not to tarry in Mexico City but to continue his advance upon Carranza's headquarters in Veracruz. Villa's momentum was such that he would have been able to persuade Gutiérrez and his supporters, and even the Zapatistas, so reluctant to fight outside of their home grounds, to join him in an attack on Veracruz. Pablo González's army was demoralized by desertions and defeat, and Obregón had not yet been able to reorganize the Carrancista forces. Initially, Villa seems to have agreed with Angeles, but his attitude changed when he received a wire from his commander in the northern city of Torreón, Emilio Madero, that Carranza's forces were approaching and were threatening the city. As soon as he received Madero's message, Villa called Angeles and ordered him to march north to relieve Torreón and to capture the northern cities of Saltillo and Monterrey. Angeles strenuously objected (few other generals of the División del Norte would have dared to do so). "General," he told Villa, "our base of operations is the capital and not Torreón. With the forces he disposes of, Emilio Madero has sufficient men to defend that city. For us, the most important thing is to attack Carranza, who is the head of everything. One always has to attack the head." Villa refused to listen. He again ordered Angeles to proceed north, telling him that Zapata would certainly be able to crush Obregón.

Angeles made one last attempt to dissuade Villa from giving up on the idea of attacking Veracruz. "Once you destroy the head, you destroy everything," Angeles told Villa. "If you see a hanger on which several hats are suspended and you want to throw all of them down, you do not take off each hat individually; it is far easier to tear off the hanger so that all the hats fall. Carranza, you should not forget, is the hanger. The armed forces of the south have neither the organization nor the necessary arms to overcome the resistance of Carranza, whose forces would not be able to resist a common advance of the División del Norte together with the Liberating Army of the South."[93] Villa refused to listen, however, and again ordered him to advance to the north, whereupon Angeles had no choice but to comply.

Angeles was right. An immediate attack on Veracruz was the one chance Villa had of overcoming his long-term strategic disadvantages and perhaps of achieving victory. When he decided to forgo that option, he gave the Carrancistas a new lease on life.

Several reasons prompted Villa to make this fateful decision. His regional outlook, inability to visualize Mexico as a whole, and conviction that only the north counted have frequently been invoked to explain his behavior. This was indeed the case. There is little doubt that Villa was far more concerned about being cut off from his home base than Obregón, who, although largely isolated from his home state of Sonora, was quite capable of operating successfully in other parts of Mexico.

Regionalism, however, was not the only factor that moved Villa to act as he did and to send his best generals to relieve a city that was not yet seriously threatened. He had a vivid recollection of how his advance south had been paralyzed when Carranza cut off supplies of coal for his trains from Mexico's sole coal-producing region, located in the state of Coahuila. By dominating this region, Villa would have the natural resource to continue his military operations. He may also have entertained doubts concerning the viability of a campaign in Veracruz. In all the other cities and states that he had captured, he had always been able to rely on the help of local allies. When he first ventured outside of Chihuahua and attacked Torreón, he had been supported by several thousand local men, commanded by Contreras, Pereyra, and Urbina. At Zacatecas, he had been able to rely on the help of local forces headed by Natera, and in Mexico City he had been joined by Zapata. There seem to have been no significant forces aligned with the Convention in Veracruz, and that may have been an additional factor deflecting Villa from marching into that state.

One of Angeles's closest advisers attributed Villa's decision to very different motives. At their secret conference, Villa and Zapata had agreed that Villa would restrict his military activities to the north, while Zapata would operate in the south. Zapata, according to this version, felt that by occupying Veracruz, and by marching through Puebla, which was held by troops loyal to Zapata, Villa would be infringing on his turf. Zapata may have had another reason for fearing a Villista march through Puebla. The Zapatista troops that occupied that city were not men from Morelos but former Orozquistas, whom Villa hated and who had rallied to Zapata. The southern leader may well have believed that once the División del Norte had marched into Puebla, Villa would simply slaughter his erstwhile enemies. Villa, according to Angeles's aide, did not really believe, as he told Angeles, that Zapata would be able to defeat Obregón and Carranza singlehanded. He rather felt that Zapata would suffer a defeat and would then have no choice but to call on Villa to succor him. In that case, Villa's supremacy within the coalition would be established once and for all.[94]

Villa's decision to send Angeles north was not a short-term interruption of his plan to attack Veracruz but rather a complete change of strategy. Villa left Mexico City, taking most of his troops with him, and decided to concentrate all his efforts on destroying the Carrancista forces in the north and in the west. It was a strategy that fatally underestimated Obregón, to whom Villa contemptuously referred as "El Perfumado" (the Perfumed One). While Villa and Angeles would achieve some significant victories in this campaign, they did not succeed in destroying and eliminating any of the Carrancista armies, while giving time to Obregón to organize his army and to choose his preferred theater of operations.

Few contemporary observers, with the exception of Angeles, anticipated this turn of events. Obregón, who firmly expected Villa to march on Veracruz, was pessimistic about holding on to this important port. He had made plans for withdrawing his army even further south, to the isthmus of Tehuantepec.[95] He was surprised and relieved when Villa failed to attack.

In the early phase of the new civil war, Villa's northern and western strategies seemed to be paying off. Within a few weeks, he scored two major victories, occupied the two largest cities of Mexico outside of the capital, Guadalajara and Monterrey, and his popularity soared to new heights, not only among the lower classes of society but among some segments of the middle and upper classes as well. This was clearly the case in the western city of Guadalajara.

The first revolutionary troops to occupy the city were Carrancistas headed by Manuel Diéguez, an old supporter of the PLM and one of the organizers of the great miners' strike in Cananea in 1906, which had been put down with great violence and bloodshed by the Díaz regime. After his troops occupied Guadalajara, Diéguez persecuted the clergy, encouraged workers to strike, shot or imprisoned a number of Huerta supporters, and confiscated many holdings of the oligarchy. Neither Diéguez nor his officers made any effort to allow the lower classes of Guadalajara to benefit from these confiscations. The contrary seems to have been the case. A not untypical occurrence, according to a French merchant and consular officer in Guadalajara, M. Cuzin, was the confiscation of 1,300 bags of wheat by Carranza's troops from a wealthy hacendado. The pretext for the confiscation was that they needed the wheat to feed their horses. In reality, the wheat was sold to a French entrepreneur in the city, Eduardo Colignon, for 8 pesos a bag. He resold them on the market for 43 pesos, double the price paid for wheat only a few weeks before. As a result of such measures, the Carrancistas suffered a drastic loss of support among both the upper and lower classes of society, which was only partially offset by Diéguez's genuine efforts to support industrial workers and employees when they presented demands against their employers, especially if the latter were foreigners. Cuzin was disturbed when his workers demanded a substantial wage increase and were intransigent when he offered them a compromise. "They feel they are unconditionally supported by the government," he noted.[96] He soon altered his opinion. The Carranza authorities were willing to compromise, but the workers were not. "The authorities believe that it is the Villistas and the clergy who have persuaded them [the workers] to be so intransigent."[97]

Diéguez's massive confiscations of the property of the rich, which did not benefit the poor in any way, his persecution of the clergy, and the arbitrariness of his soldiers—"wherever the soldiers are located they take whatever they want without paying"[98]—created a rare unity between the upper and lower classes of society. "It seems," Cuzin remarked, "that the Villistas are supported by the Americans, and that a large part of the Porfirista, Huertista, and Catholic element are joining them and support them."[99]

Many of the revolutionaries from the state of Jalisco, headed by one of the most important and influential local revolutionaries, Julián Medina, joined Villa. Their numbers were constantly increased by massive desertions from Diéguez's army, and when they were joined by Villa and a large part of the División del Norte, Diéguez was forced to evacuate Guadalajara, where Villa made a triumphant entry.

"Everyone was shouting 'Viva Villa!'" As Villa rode in a car from the railway station to the palace, "an immense, very enthusiastic crowd" greeted him. "When he passed through San Francisco Street confetti, flowers, and paper pieces were thrown at him. I have never seen such a crowd. The streets, the balconies were full as was the main square. One can say that he had been received by popular acclamation. What a contrast with the other who left two days ago."[100]

Although the conservatives appreciated the fact that Villa's troops were better disciplined than those of Carranza, and that anticlerical persecution had ceased, their enthusiasm for Villa rapidly waned. Soon after occupying Guadalajara, Villa called a meeting of the richest men of both the city and the state. After notifying them that he would impose a forced loan of one million pesos upon them, he declared:

Some of you believe that reaction has come here together with the División del Norte. You are wrong. We support the people, and woe to the rich who would give money to support a "revolutionary" movement [by "revolutionary" Villa in this case obviously meant a counterrevolutionary movement directed against him]. They would pay a high price for such behavior. As for the hacendados, let me warn you. You will suffer most. The time is gone when one could say that God was ruling the heavens and the rich ruled on this earth. Those of you who have such beliefs are mistaken. Such ideas would bring anarchy and we would be forced to set up a guillotine worse than that of the French Revolution.[101]

Jalisco's conservatives were not greatly disturbed when Villa and his wife went about Guadalajara distributing money to the poor. They were even impressed by Villa giving ten or fifteen pesos to unemployed former federal officers. What disturbed them were other measures that Villa was preparing. Guadalajara's newspapers were suddenly full of news about preparations for land reform. "The government has begun to study the division of the haciendas and land distribution, as it had promised, to soldiers, officers, etc. The haciendas of persons who were hostile to the revolution will simply be confiscated. As far as those who have remained neutral are concerned, the government will deal with them in order to buy their haciendas and pay them with bonds redeemable within a certain span of time."[102]

The hacendados were even more concerned because the Villa administration had closed one of the loopholes that had allowed many Mexican landowners to escape confiscation by nominally selling their properties to foreigners. A decree by the Villa administration made clear that those responsible for such measures would be punished and their properties confiscated. French merchants now became so fearful of Villa that they refused to participate in the kind of lucrative maneuvers in which men such as Carothers had engaged by putting Mexican properties under their own names.[103]

Not only hacendados were concerned by the Villista administration's measures. The administration wanted to force property owners who generally had understated the value of their properties for tax purposes to now declare their full value. In pursuit of this end, it employed its traditional expedient: should any property be confiscated in the public interest, the state would only pay the value that the owner had declared. "We now have a knife placed on our throats. If we make a complete declaration we will probably have to pay very high taxes, and if we give a far lower value than the real one we risk losing our properties."[104] Sadly, Cuzin remarked that Villa "was no Porfirio Díaz." He foresaw a bleak future for Mexico. "Imagine all those Indians who will have lands and will not have the funds to work them. We shall have no harvest for next year and life will become very difficult."[105]

Cuzin's colleague, the U.S. consul, Will Davis, was even more outspoken in his hatred for Villa and his contempt for Villa's governor, Julián Medina.

Heavens—the change from the old Díaz regime to the Carranza hoodlums was bad enough, but to have to treat with this thing—this ignoramus, this untutored Indian—how can it be done?

General Medina has formerly been a mechanic. But when speaking of tradesmen in Mexican parlance one must not think to compare them with the intelligent American craftsmen—oh no, that would never do.

General Medina looks the Indian—General Medina acts Indian—General Medina is an Indian—and worst of all, an untutored Indian.[106]

The sympathy of Jalisco's upper class for Villa was further reduced by a series of executions he ordered. They were fewer in number, however, than those carried out by Diéguez. In all nine persons, mainly high officials of the former Huerta administration, were executed. One was a former Huerta governor of Colima who had attempted to no avail to save his life by rallying at the last moment to Villa. Another was a high official of the Huerta administration who had ordered the execution of the brother of Medina, the Villista governor.[107] Among the lower classes of Guadalajara, enthusiasm for Villa remained enormous. He was greeted by cheers and applause wherever he showed himself.

Angeles's Northern Campaign and the Capture of Monterrey

The other great initial military triumph of the Conventionist armies was mainly the work of Felipe Angeles. It was the first military campaign he had undertaken on his own, and in both military and political terms it bore his stamp. It was carefully prepared and strategically conceived. In terms of the treatment of prisoners, it was the most humane campaign in the history of the Mexican Revolution. And Angeles attempted to follow up his military victory with a clear-cut political strategy.

In terms of armaments and men, neither of the two sides had a clear superiority. Together with the Villista troops in northeastern Mexico and commanded by Emilio Madero, Angeles had brought about 11,000 men from Mexico City. The Carrancistas, headed by Antonio Villareal and Villa's old companion, now a ferocious enemy, Maclovio Herrera, had roughly the same number.

Angeles decided to execute a feint. Ordering Emilio Madero to march toward the city of Saltillo, the capital of Carranza's native state of Coahuila, he put his own men on nineteen troop trains headed for a location far removed from Saltillo, Estación Marte. Angeles's feint succeeded. The bulk of the Carrancista army marched on Estación Marte to meet him. But Angeles did not await them there. Leaving 800 men to fight a rearguard action, most of his troops detrained and marched to reinforce Madero's troops near Saltillo. Together they attacked the town of General Cepeda, an advance position designed to protect the state capital. Its garrison of 600 men fled, and Angeles marched on Saltillo. Too weak to resist, the Carrancista garrison thereupon abandoned the state capital, and Angeles was able to occupy Saltillo without firing a shot.

Having captured the city, Angeles now posed a direct threat to Carrancista control of Monterrey, Mexico's third-largest city and one of its most important industrial centers. In order to stem Angeles's advance, the Carrancistas concentrated all their forces in the town of Ramos Arizpe, located about ten miles from Saltillo. The battle that took place there on January 8, 1915, was one of the strangest in the military history of the Mexican Revolution. The town was covered by such thick fog that friend and foe could frequently not distinguish one another, their uniforms being quite similar. The fog also made it difficult for the artillery officers to determine where enemy positions were located.

The results were sometimes grotesque. Raúl Madero was twice captured by the Carrancistas, who freed him, not recognizing that he was a commander on the opposite side. Villista officers, believing that they were dealing with their own men, were supplying Carrancistas with ammunition. While the Carrancista gunners were mistakenly firing on their own headquarters, Villistas gunners were decimating their own troops. When the fog lifted for a brief moment, Maclovio Herrera encountered his former comrade-in-arms Martiniano Servin, now a Villista general, and the two men shot it out with pistols. Servin was killed, but this personal triumph of Herrera's could not stem the demoralization of his troops, who fled, leaving huge amounts of ammunition, supplies, and prisoners in Angeles's hands. The Villistas captured more than 200,000 cartridges, fourteen locomotives, nineteen wagons, 11,000 artillery shells, and more than 3,000 prisoners out of an enemy army of 11,000 or 12,000 men.[108]

As a result of their defeat, the Carrancistas were forced to abandon Monterrey, which fell into Angeles's hands. In this one brief period when he had an independent command of his own, Angeles not only imposed his military strategy but his political and ideological concepts as well. After the battle, he lined up the huge number of prisoners he had taken, 25 percent of the Carrancista army, and told them that he considered them misguided brothers. He ordered all of them freed in return for one concession: they all had to give their words on honor that they would never take up arms again in order to fight the Conventionist armies. The first to give his solemn word of honor was General Ignacio Ramos, one of the highest Carrancista officers to have been captured. Two days later he had rejoined Pablo González's army and was fighting the Villistas once more.[109]

When Angeles entered Monterrey, he was received with jubilation by the population. There was resentment against the Carrancistas, who had burned the railway station before evacuating the city. The upper and middle classes of society were especially gratified by Angeles's announcement that full religious freedom would be reestablished, that there would be no large-scale confiscation of property, and that individual political and property rights would be respected. It is probable that these moderate policies of Angeles's did not sit well with the majority of Villa's officers. This might explain why in an election carried out by the highest officers of Angeles's army as to who should become military governor of Nuevo León, Angeles obtained only one vote to Raúl Madero's ten.[110]

A few weeks after Monterrey had been taken, Villa arrived in the city to impose his own style of politics there. At a meeting of the city's wealthiest inhabitants—its merchants and industrialists—Villa upbraided them, accusing them of raising prices to the point where many of the city's poor were on the verge of starvation. In punishment, he threatened to deport them to Chihuahua. After much supplication and negotiation, he finally relented on condition that they paid a million pesos to the state administration. That money would not be used for military expenses, as had been the case in Guadalajara, but rather to buy food for the poor. Such measures could not, however, prevent increasing food shortages, which resulted in the starvation of some of the poorest inhabitants of the city. The city was cut off from a large part of its hinterland, which was still occupied by Carrancista troops. Its usual source of food, the haciendas in the state of Durango, had been devastated by the civil war, and agricultural production there had fallen to an all-time low. In addition, according to the Spanish vice-consul in Monterrey, the administration of Raúl Madero did little to alleviate conditions in the city.[111]

Angeles's great victory had two immediate consequences for the Convention-ist movement. First, it revealed to Villa the full extent of Gutiérrez's duplicity. The Carrancistas had retreated with such speed that they left behind the incrim-inating correspondence between Obregón and Gutiérrez. Villa ordered Gutiér-rez's execution, but the embattled president managed to flee from Mexico City. Second, in economic terms, Villista troops were now able to occupy the coalfields of Coahuila and thus to assure the uninterrupted movement of their military trains.

These two great victories by Villa's troops, leading to the occupation of two major Mexican cities, as well as another victory by the Zapatistas, who managed to capture the city of Puebla, had no decisive consequences for the course of the war. The defeated Carrancista armies of Diéguez in the west and Villareal and Herrera in the east were shaken but not destroyed or demoralized. A large influx of new arms and money helped them to replenish their losses and reestablish their morale, which was further strengthened by the knowledge that their main force in Veracruz, commanded by Obregón, had not at all been affected by the Conventionist offensive, but on the contrary was preparing for an offensive cam-paign that would certainly relieve them.

The turn of the tide was brought about by Gutiérrez's defection. In the only analysis that he ever gave for the causes of his defeat, in a speech he made in No-vember 1915, Villa said that "the treason of Gutiérrez was the beginning of Car-ranza's rise to power, since it weakened the troops defending legality."[112] Villa was obviously not an objective observer, and blaming Gutiérrez for his defeat was a convenient way of ignoring his own failings. Nevertheless, Gutiérrez's defection was not only of decisive political importance but militarily significant as well, al-though that significance did not lie in the strength of Gutiérrez's forces. Villa had no difficulty in defeating them. Gutiérrez's supporters were demoralized and had no clear idea what they were fighting for. As a result, they posed little if any re-sistance to Villa. The refusal of Aguirre Benavides's troops to fight the Villistas at San Luis Potosí was only the start of a wave of surrenders of Gutiérrez's sup-porters. With only 18 men, Villa was able to disarm the Elizondo Brigade, con-sisting of more than 2,000 men, which was occupying the city of Querétaro and was on the point of joining Gutiérrez's forces, and 4,000 Villistas under Agustín Estrada were able to defeat more than 10,000 of Blanco's troops at San Felipe Torres Mochas.

Gutiérrez's defection robbed Villa of more than 10,000 men, however, and prompted him to evacuate all his troops from Mexico City in order to face what-ever danger Gutiérrez might present in the north. At the same time, while leav-ing a substantial number of troops in Guadalajara, he had taken some of the troops that occupied the capital of Jalisco north with him. The result was that Obregón easily dislodged the Zapatistas from Puebla and then entered Mexico City when Zapata's troops were unwilling to fight to defend the Mexican capital.

Obregón's conquest of the capital gave a tremendous psychological boost to the Carrancistas and weakened the momentum of the Conventionist faction. Nevertheless, it still did not destroy Villa's reputation for invincibility. It had been Zapata's, not Villa's, troops that Obregón had defeated. Villa's reputation was, however, affected when Diéguez succeeded in defeating the contingents of the

División del Norte that Villa had left behind in Guadalajara under the command of Calixto Contreras and Rodolfo Fierro. Both men had great difficulties with their troops, although of different kinds. Contreras had problems in disciplining his men, Fierro in gaining and maintaining their loyalty. Contreras's difficulties were linked to his reluctance to punish any of his men for infractions of discipline, whereas Fierro's own troops regarded him as a ruthless killer who had no regard for his own men. An episode related by one of Fierro's men best epitomizes the general's attitude. As he was passing a wounded soldier, Fierro stopped when he heard the man groan. "What is the matter?" he asked him. "It is the pain, General," the man replied. "I'll relieve you of that," Fierro said, and he pulled out his pistol and shot him.[113]

Diéguez's defeat of the Villista troops, according to one of Villa's most intelligent former secretaries, Enrique Pérez Rul, "although of little importance from a material point of view, greatly stimulated the Carrancistas, since they began to see that the soldiers of the División del Norte were not invincible as had been assumed; they began to lose their 'fear' of them."[114]

If there was one thing that Villa understood well, it was the importance of this reputation for invincibility. He therefore mobilized the bulk of his army and marched toward Guadalajara. Diéguez had set up fortified positions in the town of Sayula, hoping to counter Villa's expected cavalry charges. He did not succeed. For the last time in a major battle, Villa's desperate cavalry attacks succeeded in overrunning fortified positions. The Villistas' morale was strengthened both by their victory at Sayula and by their triumphant reception in Guadalajara, which the Conventionist troops occupied once again. Diéguez had instituted such a reign of terror in the city that the Villistas were perceived as liberators.

This was the last important victory that Villa would achieve in the war against the Carrancistas, however, and it was not decisive. Diéguez was able to retreat with most of his forces to the coast, and Villa did not follow him, since Angeles had summoned him to the northeast to destroy the remnants of Carranza's forces there.

This photograph of Villa was probably taken in 1915 when he was at the height of his power. (All the photographs are courtesy of the Southwest Collection, El Paso Public Library)

Villa and his first wife, Luz Corral. Photograph probably taken in Chihuahua in 1914.

Villa (center) seated in the presidential chair and (right) Zapata. Presidential palace, Mexico City, Nov. 28, 1914.

Villa (right) and
Rodolfo Fierro

Villa (right) with
Hugh Scott (center)
and another Ameri-
can officer during his
honeymoon with the
Americans

Venustiano Carranza (fifth from left) and some civililian and military officials

Francisco Madero

Francisco Madero (left) and Abraham González during the campaign in Chihuahua in 1911.

Villista cavalry just after leaving a troop train. While the horses rode on the train, the men rode on the roof.

Infantrymen such as those shown here frequently captured federal prisoners who preferred to fight for Villa rather than be executed.

The Rurales were crack units, frequently consisting of former bandits, that had been organized by Porfirio Díaz to fight against bandits, recalcitrant peasants, and revolutionaries. Just discernible at the feet of these Rurales are the bodies of executed prisoners.

Captured Villista soldiers hanged by Carrancista General Francisco Murguia sometime in 1918

Revolutionary troops execute a federal prisoner. Whereas the Huerta government executed all its prisoners, the Villistas only shot officers and Orozquistas and generally allowed ordinary soldiers to join their ranks.

Federal officers on the way to fight Villa.

Soldadera on the way to battle. Many women had joined Villa's Division del Norte. Most were nurses, cooks, or camp followers. Some, such as the woman in this photograph, actually participated in the fighting.

Frequently whole families joined the revolution to fight in the same unit. In this case father and son had joined the revolutionary contingent.

Villa was a superb rider, and ballads have been written about one
of his famous horses, Siete Leguas. It is not clear whether this
horse is Siete Leguas.

This photograph of Villa may be
from his days in Canutillo.

CHAPTER THIRTEEN

Snatching Defeat
from the Jaws of Victory

De aquella gran División del Norte,	Of the great División del Norte,
sólo unos cuantos quedamos ya;	Only a few of us are left;
subiendo cerros, cruzando montes,	climbing hills, crossing mountains,
buscando siempre con quien pelear.[1]	looking for someone with whom to fight.

Villa's Disastrous Decline in 1915

Villa's strategy of concentrating all of his offensive efforts against the Carrancistas in northern, northeastern, and western Mexico brought him only temporary success. In the northeast, he achieved no major victory, but he was able to extend his control over large territories in the states of Nuevo León, Coahuila, and Tamaulipas. Parts of Pablo González's Army of the Northeast had become demoralized and preferred to retreat rather than to fight the Villistas. There was only one region in the northeast where the Carrancistas were making a stand. This was at El Ebano, which controlled access to Mexico's rich oil-producing region. The Villista attacks there were clumsily led by Urbina, and the Carrancista commander, Jacinto Treviño, succeeded in repelling them all and finally inflicted a decisive defeat on Urbina's troops. It was clear to Carranza and Obregón that if Villa succeeded in taking control of that region, the balance of forces in Mexico would be decisively affected. The Carrancistas would lose the huge revenue that their control of the oil-exporting port of Tampico gave them, and Villa would be able to use it to buy new arms and ammunition, taking from the Carrancistas the one substantial advantage they had over the Conventionist alliance: their far greater access to financial resources.

Carranza and Obregón reacted in different ways to the difficult situation in which their supporters found themselves. Carranza suggested to Obregón that he should withdraw from Mexico City, destroy all communications with the north, and retreat to a more southern point to await Villa's attack. Obregón did not agree.[2] He felt that his best strategy was to take the offensive. This was the only way, he believed, that Villa's plan to attack the oil port of Tampico could be thwarted. At the same time, Obregón had carefully studied Villa's tactics. He had no difficulty in pinpointing the major weaknesses of Villa's military strategy. Villa relied primarily on massive cavalry attacks, and these were frequently not even coordinated with each other. Moreover, Villa had little understanding of the need to maintain reserves. Obregón had studied the strategy and tactics being applied by the contending armies in the great war raging in Europe. At the outset of World War I, all sides had still relied on cavalry, but it had soon become clear to the European general staffs that cavalry attacks were obsolete. Infantry, massed in trenches, behind barbed wire and supported by machine guns, simply mowed down attacking cavalry.

Obregón decided to apply these European tactics against Villa. To that end, he moved his army north as close as he could to Irapuato, where Villa's army was concentrated. The battle site Obregón chose, the town of Celaya and its surroundings, located in the Bajío, Mexico's breadbasket, was ideally suited to the tactics he planned to use. It was crisscrossed by irrigation ditches, which would impede concerted cavalry attacks, and Obregón's troops to a large extent did not even have to dig their own trenches, since many of the ditches were ideal for that purpose.

Obregón hoped to provoke Villa into massive cavalry attacks with disastrous results for the Villista forces. The plan carried great risks. The arms and ammunition that Obregón required to resupply his troops had to be transported by rail through territory in which hostile troops were operating. If the Zapatistas decided to carry out a concentrated offensive against Obregón's communications, he might soon find himself isolated from Veracruz and without sufficient ammunition to resist Villa. In addition, Angeles might persuade Villa to change his strategy and, instead of taking the offensive, to wait for Obregón to attack on his lines. Obregón was nevertheless optimistic. His agents were reporting to him from Mexico City that there were increasing disagreements between the Villistas and Zapatistas. They doubted whether Zapata would be willing to undertake a large-scale offensive against Obregón's communications and thought that he might not even be capable of doing so. Furthermore, Obregón had studied Villa's character and hoped that his stubborn pride would prevent him from retreating or from going on the defensive.

Villa's plans and strategy were spelled out in a letter he sent to Zapata a few weeks before the first of his major confrontations with Obregón. In his letter, Villa described the victories he had achieved in both the northeast and northwest and expressed confidence that the troops he had sent to Jalisco to pursue Diéguez, who was retreating from that state, would soon control all of northwestern Mexico. He expressed confidence too that Urbina, whom he had sent to El Ebano to attack the oil region, would soon gain control of Tampico. Villa himself had decided to take on Obregón. The main reason he gave for this decision was, paradoxically, lack of ammunition, and he noted: "A contract for 40 million cartridges has not come through while deliveries of another for 70 million cartridges have not yet begun." As a result, Villa "had resolved to take ammunition from the enemy, who was well provided with cartridges."[3] He apologized to Zapata, saying that because of this shortage of ammunition, he had not been able to send Zapata the supplies he had promised, but that he would soon be able to do so; in the meantime, he asked Zapata to do whatever he could to disrupt Obregón's lines of communication.

This letter is extremely revealing, for it shows how overconfident Villa was. He seriously thought that he could take the offensive on all fronts at once despite being short of arms and ammunition. He did not realize that the morale of the Carrancistas was very different from that of the federal troops against whom he had won his major victories. Moreover, Villa underestimated Obregón; calling him "El Perfumado" implied that he considered him a kind of dandified sissy. His contempt for Obregón was such that he decided to attack him with an insufficient amount of ammunition and only part of his army. Angeles, who had far more respect for Obregón's tactical capacities, tried to dissuade Villa from going on the offensive. Angeles understood how vulnerable Obregón was to any interruption of his lines of communication with Veracruz and hoped to force Obregón to advance further and further to the north, which would greatly increase his vulnerability. Villa refused, however, to heed Angeles's advice.[4]

Overconfidence, triggered by the successes he had scored, as well as by the flattery of those who surrounded him, was only one of the factors that led Villa to take the offensive. Another factor was his fear that if he gave even the appearance of retreating, his reputation for invulnerability would be threatened and many revolutionary chieftains who had joined him out of opportunism would change sides.

In addition, he was experiencing a very real crisis in securing arms and ammunition. As already noted, World War I had transformed what had been a buyer's market in arms and ammunition into a seller's market; the Allies in Europe were buying munitions in the United States on a huge scale. Many arms merchants refused to sell to Mexican customers. When Villa did manage to secure ammunition, he had to pay $67 per 1,000 rounds, in contrast to the $40–50 that the same ammunition had cost him before the outbreak of World War I.[5]

Both the Villistas and the Carrancistas faced these new supply problems, but the latter were better equipped to deal with them. The Carrancistas were able to meet a large part of their needs by setting up munitions factories in the territories they controlled. The arms industry that Villa attempted to set up in Chihuahua was never able to compete with that of his Carrancista enemies. In addition, the price of the main exports from the Carrancista territories—oil and sisal—had also greatly increased as a result of new demands created by World War I, and their revenues had thus kept pace with the increasing price of arms and ammunition.

The same was not true of the Villistas, whose revenues were to a large degree based on the sale and export of cattle, cotton, and mining products to the United States. The value of these exports was less in 1915 than it had been in 1914. The huge cattle herds that had roamed on the northern grazing lands prior to the revolution had been substantially depleted in 1914 to pay for the arms and ammunition Villa needed to defeat the federal army. The cotton harvest was far smaller in 1915 than in previous years because of the fighting in the north and the flight of many hacendados from the cotton region of the Laguna. Many mines had either drastically reduced their production or shut down altogether, because railway transportation of their products to the United States had become irregular, since trains were used to transport the troops of the different revolutionary factions. These objective economic problems were compounded by "personnel" difficulties. Villa's most important arms and ammunitions buyers in the United States were either incompetent or corrupt or both. During 1914, both Villa and some of his lieutenants complained about the poor quality of the arms that their most important representative in the United States, Félix Sommerfeld, was acquiring.[6]

Villa nonetheless kept Sommerfeld on his payroll, probably because of his close association with Madero (he had been the head of Madero's secret service in the United States). After the outbreak of World War I, Sommerfeld's usefulness to Villa was further reduced, however, because he was a German citizen. Many American producers feared that if they sold arms and ammunitions to Sommerfeld, their British, French, and Russian clients might boycott them. It is thus not surprising that Villa dismissed Sommerfeld in early 1915.[7]

Villa now put two men in charge of buying arms and ammunitions for his armies: his brother Hipólito, who was in charge of an agency in the border town of Ciudad Juárez that managed Villa's foreign currency assets, and a businessman from Torreón, Lázaro de la Garza, who dealt with American companies. De la Garza was probably the most corrupt official Villa ever employed. He had first gained Villa's confidence in October 1913 after Villa occupied Torreón. In April 1915, Villa wired de la Garza, who was in the United States: "You are the only man I trust. Buy as many arms and munitions as you can for me."[8]

Villa's trust in de la Garza was so great that he ordered Sommerfeld to turn over to the Torreón businessman a contract for 15 million cartridges that he had signed with the Western Cartridge Company. Only 700,000 cartridges ever reached the División del Norte, and a puzzled and desperate Villa wired de la Garza, "Why don't you answer my telegrams?"[9] After delivering the 700,000 cartridges to Villa, de la Garza had, in fact, offered the shipment to the Carrancistas, who were willing to pay a higher price, and had finally sold it at an even higher price to the Morgan Bank, representing the French government.[10]

Angeles's advice to Villa not to attack Obregón was based on more than strategic considerations. Angeles had just hurt himself by falling from a horse and was unable to accompany Villa on his march southward to meet Obregón. He was worried that, lacking his advice, Villa's rashness, his lack of a military education, and his increasing arrogance would drive him to defeat.

He was right. Within a few days of his conversation with Angeles, Villa suffered his Waterloo at the two battles of Celaya. To a much larger degree than Napoleon, Villa himself was responsible for his defeat. He made no effort to choose a battle site that would give him a strategic advantage. In fact, he did not even reconnoiter the region of Celaya where the decisive battle with Obregón was to take place. Moreover, as he had written Zapata, he went into battle knowing that he did not have sufficient ammunition. Finally, he made no effort to exploit the one strategic advantage he had: Obregón's extremely vulnerable lines of communication with Veracruz, from which he derived his supplies, his ammunition, and his reinforcements. Villa's contempt for Obregón, as profound as it was unfounded, contributed to his rashness. On the eve of the battle, Villa told a reporter for his newspaper *Vida Nueva* that Obregón was finished, saying, "This time Obregón will not escape me. I know that he will attempt to withdraw as he always does, but I shall force him to fight in order to destroy the forces that constitute an obstacle to military operations without being of any great use to the enemy."[11] This interview not only reflected Villa's overconfidence but his erroneous view that Obregón constituted a lesser danger than Diéguez, who commanded the Carrancista forces in Jalisco and continued to fight Villa's forces in that state.

At the outset of the first battle of Celaya, which began on April 6, 1915, Obregón committed one of his few tactical errors, which only strengthened Villa's overconfidence and rashness. Obregón had not reconnoitered well enough before he sent 1,500 men of his advance guard to occupy the hacienda of El Guage, located between Irapuato and Celaya, in order to cut the railway lines leading to Celaya and thus reduce the mobility of Villa's troops. He had thought that the bulk of Villa's troops were concentrated in Irapuato and had not realized that they were located near El Guage. Obregón's advancing troops were met by murderous attacks from an overwhelming Villista force and were threatened with complete extermination. Obregón had never lacked for bravery, and he personally took command of a troop train that steamed toward El Guage with the aim of deflecting the Villista attacks on his advance guard. While Obregón was a careful tactician, he was also a master at improvisation. He realized that his initial setback might be transformed into victory if he could lead Villa to attack the positions he had carefully prepared at Celaya.

Obregón hoped that Villa, whose obstinacy he well knew, would disregard the natural obstacles he faced and recur to his traditional mode of attack: massive charges by mounted or dismounted cavalry. Obregón's expectations soon proved correct. As Obregón's advance guard and his troop train retreated, Villa and his troops became convinced that victory lay in their hands. They now charged headlong into Obregón's fortified positions and were met by withering fire from the entrenched soldiers and from Obregón's machine guns. Their losses were enormous. Yet Villa's obstinacy did not allow him to give up. He was still flushed with victory, and his battle-hardened veterans were ready to follow him wherever he ordered. In all previous battles, after initial setbacks, Villa's charging troops had always proved invincible. According to Obregón (whose account might exaggerate his own success), Villa's troops charged Obregón's lines 40 times and with one exception were always repelled.[12] According to General Luis Gárfias, a keen military analyst of the battle of Celaya, one of Villa's greatest strategic errors lay in not attempting to overwhelm Obregón's defenses by concentrating a superior force in a single sector.[13] At one time, the Villistas did manage to penetrate the Carrancista lines, and Obregón's front was in danger of disintegrating. Obregón again showed his capacity for improvisation, however. He ordered his bugler, an 11-year-old boy, to sound retreat, and the Villistas, believing that the order came from their own headquarters, abandoned the position they had won at such a high price. They were now bloodied, exhausted, and finally demoralized.

This was the moment Obregón chose to launch a decisive counterattack. It was also the moment when Villa's ammunition began to give out. Villa's troops had been using two kinds of rifles: .30-30 rifles and Mausers. While they had sufficient ammunition for the .30-30 rifles, they were suddenly out of ammunition for their Mausers.[14] Obregón now ordered his reserves to attack the exhausted Villistas. Unlike Obregón, Villa had set up no reserves, and his tired troops had to retreat when Obregón's reserves were joined by soldiers who rose from the trenches to join the attack. Unlike his opponent, Obregón counted on a constant supply of new ammunition from Carranza. Instead of attempting to cut Obregón's lines of communication and thus preventing him from obtaining supplies, Villa had relied on Zapata to do so. But the southern leader, who had received no ammunition from Villa, did not want to commit the bulk of his troops to an attack on railway lines located far from Morelos and instead limited himself to carrying out a few small-scale sporadic operations.

The first battle of Celaya was Villa's first major defeat. It was attributed by him and by many of his leaders solely to his lack of ammunition. An observer sent by the head of the Revolutionary Convention, Roque González Garza, assessed the reasons for Villa's setback more realistically. In addition to the lack of ammunition, González Garza attributed it to Villa's refusal to maintain any reserves and to the defection during the battle of one of Villa's leaders, a man named Colin, who at the height of the fighting turned around and had his troops suddenly shoot at their erstwhile allies.[15]

Villa's reputation for invincibility was not yet broken. The Villista press strongly denied Carranza and Obregón's claim to victory. On April 10, after the battle, Villa's newspaper *Vida Nueva* asserted: "Obregón has failed in his attempt to break the Villista line of fire. Messages received in Washington indicate that the battle of Celaya was favorable to the División del Norte." Two days later, *Vida Nueva* was even more explicit: "Outside of Mexico as well as in Veracruz celebrations are being held for the triumph (?) of Obregón. This is being done by those who believe the lies of Carranza's lieutenant, who cynically transforms the defeats he suffered into victories. His forces refused to fight and had begun to evacuate Celaya."[16] Since the propaganda of both sides constantly emphasized that they were the victors, whatever the outcome of a battle had been, Carranza and Obregón's claims to victory in Celaya were met with great skepticism both inside and outside of Mexico.

Villa had suffered a defeat, but he had by no means been routed. Not only had he managed to retain most of his army and his arms but the morale of his troops was still high, and Obregón's overall situation was precarious. The Carrancista supply of arms and ammunition was running low, and Obregón was completely dependent on the ammunition that Carranza was regularly sending him by train from Veracruz. If Villa had recalled most of his troops fighting on the east and west coasts of Mexico, leaving only a rearguard to hold off the Carrancistas in those regions, if he had waited to fight until he got ammunition, and, above all, if he had been able to cut Obregón's line of communications, he would have had a chance of winning and destroying Obregón's army. Except for having his brother Hipólito ship some more ammunition to him, Villa did not pursue such a course. He left most of his troops fighting on the two Mexican coasts and made no serious effort to interrupt Obregón's communications with Veracruz.

But Villa did hope to lure Obregón out of his fortified positions in Celaya. To this end, he sent a letter to the Carrancista leader, stating that in order to spare the city and the people of Celaya from the bloodshed that his artillery might cause, he suggested that Obregón should leave Celaya and that the two armies should fight a battle outside the city. Villa's proposal was supported by the foreign consuls in Celaya, who sent a letter to Obregón asking him to spare the city from damage by fighting in another place.

Obregón had not the least intention of giving up his strategic superiority, however, and his army remained in Celaya. It is not clear whether Villa really believed he could lure out Obregón to fight in the open or if he simply hoped to impress foreign diplomats, especially the Americans, with his concern both for the civilian population and for foreign property. On April 13, Villa reverted to the same tactics he had used previously, and this time the consequences were even more disastrous. Obregón had prepared well for a Villista attack. He set up barbed-wire emplacements in front of the trenches that his soldiers occupied and increased the number of his machine guns. He also set up a reserve of 6,000 cavalry, who remained hidden in an adjoining forest. Once the battle began, Villa's cavalry charged again and again against the highly fortified trenches manned by Obregón's soldiers. The one advantage that the Villistas had enjoyed in the first battle of Celaya, their history of invincibility, was gone. Villa's soldiers were slowed down by the numerous irrigation ditches on their way and by the barbed wire that they had to cut. As they advanced, they were mowed down by Obregón's machine-gun fire. By ordering such frontal charges, Villa repeated the major error he had committed in the first battle of Celaya. He repeated his other errors as well. He made no serious attempt to interrupt Obregón's communications, although the Carrancistas' situation had become extremely precarious. "I have the honor to tell you that the fighting has become desperate," Obregón wired Carranza on April 14. "We have no reserves of ammunition and we only have sufficient bullets to fight a few hours more. We will undertake every effort to save the situation."[17] Neither did Villa make any effort to reconnoiter the terrain of the battlefield carefully, and he thus did not know about the cavalry force of the 6,000 men, under General Cesareo Castro, hidden in an adjoining forest. Once again, he left no reserve to which he could turn in the hour of need. As a result, Villa's troops suffered an even greater defeat. After his men had become exhausted from continuous charges over two days, Obregón's hidden cavalry forces counterattacked, and Villa had no fresh reserve that he could throw into battle in order to contain Obregón's troops.

This time, defeat turned into a rout. "I escaped and managed to climb to the top of a hill," one Villista officer sadly reported. "I shall never forget what I saw from there: I saw whole battalions who seemed poised to attack Celaya again, but in reality they were prisoners. On top of the hill, artillery pieces had been abandoned, and in front of them a torrent of people passed without stopping, without thinking of anything. What they wanted was to flee, to flee as far as possible."[18]

After the battle of Celaya, Obregón asked all captured Villista officers, many of whom had dressed as plain soldiers, to identify themselves, promising that no harm would come to them. One hundred and twenty Villista officers did so and they were all immediately shot.[19] Obregón's triumph was overwhelming. According to the account Obregón sent Carranza, Villa had lost 32 cannon, 3,000 of his men were dead, 6,000 had been taken prisoner, and Obregón's troops had secured 5,000 rifles and about 1,000 horses.[20]

It is not clear why Villa repeated the errors of his first battle at Celaya in the second one. Angeles's absence certainly contributed to the disaster. So did Villa's machismo. He felt not only that retreating was dishonorable but that if he did not confront Obregón again, his reputation for invincibility would disappear. In addition, he seems to have been a captive of his own propaganda, which attributed the loss of the first battle to the lack of ammunition. This time Villa's defeat was so unmistakable that his own press could not ignore it. Yet since Villa had never openly acknowledged his defeat *Vida Nueva* had great difficulty in dealing with the results of the battle. On one hand, it likened the rumors of Villa's defeat at Celaya to the many erroneous rumors spread by the Carrancista press. In an editorial titled "Let Us Have Faith," the editorialist reminded his readers of "the dozens of times that they have taken Chihuahua, Torreón, and even Ciudad Juárez and Ojinaga; it would be worthwhile to remind everyone how many times they have killed General Villa, shot General Chao, and annihilated the División del Norte."[21] On the other hand, *Vida Nueva* tried to address those who did believe that Villa had been defeated.

Let us examine the worst scenario. Let us suppose that the Conventionist army has not been able to take Celaya: should we forget that General Villa's retreat from Chihuahua was followed by the brilliant capture of Ciudad Juárez?

And who was Villa then? The leader of less than 5,000 men who had just captured Torreón. What was his army? It was composed of thousands of badly armed men who had never been in battle, and he won and they won against thousands of soldiers who were veterans and who had been very well equipped and armed by Huerta's dictatorship.[22]

It is doubtful whether many military leaders would have continued to fight had they suffered defeats of such magnitude as the ones that Villa suffered at Celaya. Villa, however, seems to have had unlimited amounts of self-confidence, courage, and endurance. Above all, he had such charismatic appeal that his soldiers were willing to continue the fight and that he was even able to win new recruits for his army. Villa now recalled most of his troops fighting in other parts of Mexico and was soon joined by Angeles, who had completely recovered from his injury. He told Villa that a victory over Obregón was still possible, but that in order to secure it, Villa would have to carry out a complete change of strategy. The División del Norte should withdraw further north to Torreón or perhaps even to Chihuahua. Such a maneuver would give Villa's troops sufficient time to recover from their defeat at Celaya and at the same time would stretch Obregón's lines of communication further. In addition, Villa should refrain from carrying out offensive warfare, but should go onto the defensive and force Obregón into a lengthy battle in which his troops would be tired and his ammunition exhausted. Villa rejected this advice.[23] Instead of retreating northward into his own country, he decided to make a stand in central Mexico near the city of León in the state of Guanajuato. He refused to listen when Angeles told him that the site he had chosen for the coming battle was problematic, since his troops could easily be outflanked by the enemy. Villa did, however, at least temporarily, heed Angeles's advice to go on the defensive, and he had his troops entrench themselves along a line roughly 20 kilometers long between León and Trinidad. The Villista press was again exuding confidence that victory was at hand:

The greatest troop concentration of the Carranza faction on the one hand and an important part of the Conventionist forces on the other are facing each other.

General Villa will defeat General Obregón; but that is not the most important fact; what is above all significant is that his triumph will mean the destruction of Obregón, the destruction of the only army that dares to fight the people's army.[24]

As a result of Villa's new defensive tactic, the battle of León, as it came to be known, lasted for nearly 40 days and began to resemble the long and indecisive battles that European armies were fighting in World War I. Both sides attacked each other with limited forces, attempting to gain strategic advantage but not carrying out a full-scale attack. Obregón was waiting for Villa to carry out the kind of general attack that had led to his defeat at Celaya, so that he could mow down Villa's cavalry with the help of his machine guns. Villa refused to oblige, however, and Obregón's generals began to worry more and more that Villa might exhaust their ammunition and finally cut off their communications from Veracruz and thus their access to new arms and ammunition.

Adding to the Carrancistas' fear of being cut off, Zapata now for the first time sent large contingents of troops to attack Obregón's lines of communication. After Villa's defeat at Celaya, Zapata became worried that a decisive defeat of Villa would allow Carranza's troops to concentrate all their efforts on "pacifying" Morelos. Zapata's troops lacked the arms, the organization, and perhaps even the will to wage offensive warfare on a large scale outside of Morelos, however, and for inexplicable reasons, Villa made only half-hearted efforts to interrupt Obregón's communications with Veracruz.

Nevertheless, a number of Obregón's generals, above all Francisco Murguía, were worried about the course the battle was taking. A kind of standstill had developed in which neither side seemed strong enough to defeat the other. Murguía was concerned that if the situation continued, it would redound to the benefit of the Villistas. "The enemy had made the decision to remain in the defensive, attempted to cut off our communications with the south, and since he has sufficient ammunition, if he forced us to remain longer without advancing on León, the result would be that our ammunition would give out and if the enemy succeeded in completely isolating us from Veracruz, we would be defeated."[25]

Murguía urgently called on Obregón to go on the offensive. He was supported in this by Diéguez and a number of other generals, but Obregón was reluctant to take such a step. He still hoped that Villa would attack and thus allow him to repeat the successful strategy that had brought him victory twice at Celaya. Obregón, who had closely studied Villa's impetuous character, was convinced that if he only held out long enough, Villa would become impatient and finally carry out an all-out attack. As the pressure from his generals mounted, Obregón finally made the decision to attack on June 5. Three days before that date, Villa complied with Obregón's fondest hopes and decided to go on the attack. Not only was Villa himself impatient and unaccustomed to the long delays brought about by trench warfare, his soldiers were slowly becoming demoralized by the difficult conditions in which they found themselves.

There are a great number of unburied bodies, and their smell has become intolerable. After our "mistaken brothers," the Carrancistas, our worst enemies are flies, lice, and rats. The flies are a beautiful green color, and there are thousands of them, who after eating from the eyes and mouths of the dead attempt to devour our food. The rats are so voracious that in spite of the fact that they have enough to eat with the bodies of the dead, they come and eat our few provisions. . . . [and] even if we bathe, after two or three days, we are full of lice.[26]

Against the advice of Angeles, Villa took all of his reserves and attacked the Carrancistas from the rear. He was at first successful and captured the city of Silao. Other Villista contingents, though, failed to take a Carrancista position that was of decisive importance for Obregón's planned counterattack against the Villista positions: the hacienda of Santa Ana. The Villista attacks on it caused huge casualties and contributed to the demoralization of the División del Norte. Villa's attack did score one significant success: on April 3, as Obregón stood on the hacienda's tower reconnoitering the battlefield, a Villista shell exploded, shattering his right arm. Convinced that he was bleeding to death, Obregón tried to commit suicide by shooting himself in the temple. Fortunately for him, his adjutant had cleaned the pistol the night before and removed the cartridges. Obregón's men took the gun and brought him to the hospital.

Obregon's temporary incapacity did not paralyze his army. Villa's withdrawal of reserves from the front lines made his men extremely vulnerable to an attack by Obregón's troops. This was the moment the Carrancistas had been waiting for. Led by Obregón's deputy Benjamin Hill, his troops went on the offensive, and the weakened Villista lines could not hold them back. On June 5, the Villistas suffered more than 3,000 casualties and retreated in disorder from León.

The defeat of León destroyed Villismo as a national force. Villa nevertheless refused to give up. He still believed that Obregón could be defeated and decided to make his last stand in central Mexico, in the city of Aguascalientes. He concentrated all his remaining troops there and made his main priority the interruption of Obregón's communications with Veracruz. Despite his increasing weakness, he was able to do so. He sent two large cavalry units, one led by Rodolfo Fierro and the other by Canuto Reyes, behind Obregón's lines to disrupt railway traffic and force Obregón to withdraw part of his army from the attack on Aguascalientes to pursue the Villista raiders.

The maneuver was successful. Fierro proved that he was not only a butcher and murderer but also a first-rate guerrilla fighter. He captured León from the Carrancistas by sending a forged telegram to the commander of the garrison instructing him to abandon the city and also succeeded in temporarily occupying the city of Pachuca, where he was joined by some Zapatista troops. This occupation so greatly worried Pablo González that he evacuated his troops from Mexico City.

Fierro's success was nevertheless ephemeral. A few weeks later, he was defeated by a much larger contingent of troops that Obregón had sent to pursue him. Before his defeat, however, he had succeeded in his main purpose, which was to interrupt railway communications between Obregón and Veracruz and to prevent new supplies from reaching the main Carrancista force. Had this happened during the battle of Celaya a few weeks earlier, it might have been the margin of victory. Now it came too late. Once he realized that his ammunition would only last for a few days, Obregón ordered a general attack on Villa's lines at Aguascalientes. The remnants of the División del Norte, weakened and demoralized by three large defeats, scarcely resisted and fled northward toward Torreón and Chihuahua. The División del Norte had ceased to be a major military force.

Villa's Defeats: An Analysis

Ever since Villa's catastrophic defeats in central Mexico, debates have raged, first among contemporary observers and then among historians, as to whether these defeats were primarily the result of objective or subjective factors. Could Villa have triumphed, or were his military defeats inevitable? Was his inferiority in terms of ammunition and supplies, as well as in number of troops, so great that he could never have won?

There is no evidence that this was the case. While lack of Mauser ammunition certainly played an important role in Villa's defeat in the first battle of Celaya, this shortage was not an immutable fact. Villa chose to go into battle even though he lacked sufficient ammunition, because he underestimated Obregón. Had he waited, he could have acquired sufficient supplies—he did not lack ammunition in the later battles he waged against Carranza's forces. There is no evidence either that Villa's armies numbered fewer soldiers than Obregón's.

Villa's military defeats were primarily owing to gross strategic errors. Villa's greatest strategic error consisted in not heeding Angeles's advice and attacking Veracruz at a time when the Carrancistas had not yet been able to reorganize their forces, and when Villa was at the height of his power. His second great strategic error consisted in attempting to wage war on all fronts at the same time, instead of concentrating his forces against each of Carranza's armies in turn. His third great strategic error was not to heed Angeles's advice to draw Obregón further and further north and thus make his lines of communication more vulnerable.

These errors of strategy were compounded by equally serious tactical errors. At Celaya, Villa chose to attack Obregón at a site that was extremely favorable to his enemy. He did not reconnoiter the terrain in advance; he did not concentrate his forces on one front but attacked everywhere simultaneously, thus limiting the pressure on any one point of the Carrancista line. Despite having seen how devastated his cavalry was when it tried to attack Obregón's well-entrenched infantry, protected by barbed wire and machine-gun nests, at the first battle of Celaya, he repeated this error in all subsequent battles. It may be understandable that during the first battle of Celaya, Villa relied on Zapata to interrupt Obregón's communications. What is not understandable is that once Zapata failed to deliver, Villa did not attempt to sever Obregón's communications with Veracruz with his own troops, as he would finally do during the battle of Aguascalientes, when it was too late. Finally, Villa again and again repeated his error of not setting up a reserve capable of meeting Obregón's fresh troops once his own men were exhausted by hours of battle.

Villa's errors in part resulted from his limited northern perspective, which deterred him from attacking Veracruz. In part, too, they were the result of his lack of education. Unlike the far better educated Obregón, he did not read newspapers and knew nothing of the new strategies and tactics that were being developed in Europe during World War I. Hitherto he had compensated for this lack of education by his willingness to heed advice, above all from Angeles. Once he became head of the armies of the Convention, and in fact the undisputed leader of the Conventionist faction, however, he became so arrogant that he refused to do so. He was far less willing than Carranza or Obregón to discuss his options with his subordinates.

Villa was not a man given to self-criticism, and there is no evidence that he ever understood the profound strategic and tactical mistakes he had made. In the only account he ever gave of his defeat in the first battle of Celaya, he put the blame squarely on Angeles's shoulders. His main accusation against his hitherto favorite subordinate was that the latter, who had a short time before occupied Mexico's most important northeastern city, Monterrey, had given in to panic when he felt that a superior Carrancista force was threatening him. He had called on Villa to come to his rescue immediately, and Villa had interrupted his victorious campaign against Diéguez in Jalisco to come to Angeles's aid. Villa felt that Angeles had not, in fact, needed help—that he had by far overestimated the strength of the force under Pablo González that was threatening him, putting its number at 20,000 men, whereas in fact it amounted to no more than 6,000. Villa felt that if Angeles had not diverted him, "Diéguez would have been exterminated, and Obregón would not have had time to organize the army with which he fought in the Bajío, since I would have thrown all my forces against him. For this reason General Angeles is, in fact, responsible for the disaster in Celaya."

Villa was probably right in his assumption that Angeles could have held out without his help, and that had Villa destroyed Diéguez's forces, he would have had far more ammunition than he had in the first battle of Celaya, as well as more troops, since he would not have had to leave so many men behind to continue the Jalisco campaign. His men would also have been fresher and more relaxed, since they would not have had to crisscross Mexico first from the West to the East to rescue Angeles and then to march once again to the Bajío. On the other hand, it is doubtful whether Villa would have resorted to any other kind of tactic than the disastrous calvary attacks that contributed so decisively to his defeat.

Villa's second accusation against Angeles was far less justified. At the battle of León, Angeles had commanded the infantry when Villa, against his advice, after 40 days of stalemate, took his whole cavalry to attack Obregón from the rear, while ordering Angeles to hold the line and resist any Carrancista attack. "And what did General Angeles do?" Villa is said to have asked his subordinate Alfonso Gómez Morentin. "He could not resist the pressure from the Carrancistas, they destroyed his lines, and my charge, with which I decisively weakened them, bore no fruit."[27] What Villa failed to see was that his troops had become demoralized after his two major defeats at Celaya, and that he himself had kept no reserves that could be thrown into battle to reinforce the infantry.

After his disastrous defeats in central Mexico, Villa retreated to his northern bailiwick, where he still hoped to maintain himself. As his later actions indicated, he realized that whatever chances of survival he had depended more than ever on his relations with the United States.

From Sir Galahad to Bandit: The Stormy Relationship Between Villa and the United States

A central and puzzling characteristic of the policy of the U.S. administration toward Villa is the contrast between pro-Villa statements and actions that seemed to favor Carranza. This discrepancy would not be as puzzling if it only reflected the usual contradiction between public statements and realpolitik. In this case, however, the statements were not destined for public consumption but seem to have reflected the real opinions of members of the administration, as well as of influential businessmen. Yet U.S. policy, at least at first glance, does not seem to have been commensurate with these statements.

Shortly after U.S. troops occupied Veracruz and Villa expressed his opposition to Carranza's protest against this occupation, Secretary of State William Jennings Bryan wrote to George Carothers, the U.S. special representative with Villa, "we are earnestly desirous that the most friendly relationships should exist and are greatly pleased and reassured by what you report General Villa as having said. It shows a largeness of view on his part and a comprehension of this whole situation which is greatly to his credit."[28] Around the same time, Bryan referred to Villa for the same reason as "Sir Galahad."[29]

On August 30, 1914, after the split between Villa and Carranza had come out into the open, Woodrow Wilson's confidant Colonel Edward House wrote in his diary: "We went into the Mexican situation carefully and agreed that Villa is the only man of force now in sight in Mexico. We are afraid Carranza is not equal to the situation."[30] A few weeks later, on October 8, 1914, General John J. Pershing wrote to Chief of Staff Hugh Scott: "Villa seems to be a strongman and maybe the man of the hour."[31] And in December 1914, in a letter to Wilson, Bryan expressed optimistic views with regard to Villa, saying: "The situation seems to be clearing up in Mexico. Villa and Zapata are working in harmony and Gutiérrez seems to be about to assume control over most of the country. The occupation of Carranza is not likely to last long."[32]

On May 4, 1914, an editorial in William Randolph Hearst's *New York American* sharply criticized the Wilson administration for seeming to support Villa against Huerta. It stated, "You do your neighbor a service if you call a policeman to drive a sneak thief from his house, but you serve him ill if you send in a red-handed burglar and murderer to drive the lesser criminal away." Less than three months later, Hearst completely reversed his stand. In an editorial in the same newspaper, signed by Hearst himself, he wrote:

The one man in this Mexican conflict and crisis who has appeared to tower above all others in personal power and capacity, in the magnetism to lead, the mastery to command, and the ability to execute, is Francisco Villa. . . .

If Villa is made president he will remain as president and establish a stable and reliable government.

If another man is made president by foreign interference he will have to reckon with Villa and with the masses who believe in Villa.[33]

A representative of Villa's in the United States informed him that John Hays Hammond, who headed ASARCO's operations in Mexico, had "defended you very strongly, praising you in every way, stating that whatever you promised you carried out and that he was profoundly impressed by what different Americans who had spoken to you had told him. He stated that in his opinion the interests of Americans in Mexico enjoyed better guarantees than anywhere else and that he would have no compunction about carrying out any kind of business in the state of Chihuahua, where that business would enjoy absolute security."[34]

Despite these favorable statements by government officials and businessmen, and despite Villa's refusal to join Carranza in condemning the U.S. invasion of Veracruz, American arms shipments to Villa, but not to Carranza, were embargoed by the Wilson administration in the weeks following the occupation of Veracruz.[35]

The discrepancy between the administration's pro-Villa statements and its anti-Villa actions has no clear and easy explanation. There is no reason to doubt the sincerity of the pro-Villa statements made by members of the Wilson administration. They were made in internal memoranda, not destined for public consumption. Could the discrepancies between word and action have been due to differing opinions within the bureaucracy and to different policies being applied by different men or departments? There are some indications that this may have been the case with respect to the arms embargo imposed upon Villa, but not Carranza, in May and June 1914. When Carranza threatened the United States with war after U.S. troops had occupied Veracruz, Wilson imposed a general arms embargo upon Mexico. That embargo was relaxed when huge shipments of European arms were delivered to Huerta in May 1914. The relaxation of the arms embargo, however, was selective. The U.S. authorities wanted to prevent the balance of power from shifting too much in favor of Huerta, but they did not want to give the Mexican revolutionaries an unlimited supply of arms. The implementation of this policy seems to a large degree to have been left to Woodrow Wilson's special representative in Mexico, John Lind, a man very favorable to Carranza. He explained to representatives of the Mexican revolutionaries that the decision to allow some arms to be sent to the port of Tampico but not to other parts of Mexico was primarily a public relations ploy. The Wilson administration did not want to advertise its resumption of shipments to the revolutionaries, officially claiming that the arms that reached the Mexican port were destined for Cuba.[36] But since Carranza controlled Tampico, all of these arms fell into the hands of his forces. No similar techniques were elaborated for sending arms to Villa, which may very well have been owing to Lind's sympathies for Carranza and to the hostility of many U.S. customs officials along the Mexican border to Villa.

Even if lower-level officials made the decision to embargo arms to the División del Norte, the problem must have reached Woodrow Wilson's desk by June 1914, when Villa in a personal letter had asked him to lift the embargo against his forces so that he could march on to Mexico City.[37] Wilson did not respond to Villa's request, and no reason was ever given for this. In all probability, Wilson feared that a new civil war would result if Villa advanced on Mexico City at a time when the Carrancistas were on the verge of occupying it, and the U.S. administration wanted to avoid this.

The decision by the Wilson administration to hand over Veracruz and its huge resources in arms and finances to Carranza is more complex in nature. That de-

cision was made, not by middle- or lower-level bureaucrats, but at the highest
level of the administration. In September 1914, Wilson had indicated that he
wished to withdraw U.S. forces from Veracruz and return the city to Mexican
sovereignty. That decision was enthusiastically greeted by all revolutionary factions. Wilson's decision was partly based on the assumption, held by many observers in September 1914, that an agreement would be reached at the Convention of Aguascalientes, and that a united Mexican government would emerge.
The United States would then not need the port of Veracruz to influence events
in Mexico but would have other means at its disposal. Equally and perhaps more
important, World War I had begun only a month before, in August 1914. U.S.
officials feared that German submarines might endanger U.S. trade with Europe,
while Japan might become more aggressive in China.

Keeping a large part of the relatively small U.S. army in Mexico thus strongly
weakened the bargaining position of the United States with respect to the rest
of the world. Its evacuation was delayed, however, because the Americans had
set certain conditions for leaving Veracruz, which Carranza refused to accede to.
They demanded that no reprisals be taken against any Mexicans who had worked
for the occupation authorities, that inhabitants of Veracruz who had paid taxes
to the U.S. occupation authorities should not be forced to pay the same taxes
once again to a Mexican administration, and that Carranza give guarantees that
the more than 15,000 refugees who had poured into Veracruz would not suffer
reprisals. Carranza considered these conditions to be an infringement upon Mexican sovereignty and refused to agree to them. However, he consulted the Revolutionary Convention of Aguascalientes, which recommended that he accept the
American conditions so that U.S. troops could be withdrawn as rapidly as possible from Veracruz.

In November 1914, after the civil war between his forces and those of the Convention had broken out, Carranza finally acceded to the American demands.
Once it was clear that this obstacle to U.S. evacuation had been removed, the
Wilson administration became more and more convinced that it was time to
leave. Nevertheless, before making a final decision, it consulted Villa as to who
should take control of Veracruz. Not unexpectedly, Villa wrote back asking that
the city be handed over to a representative of the Conventionist faction. The
problem was that there were no Conventionist troops anywhere near Veracruz.
The adjacent region was entirely controlled by troops loyal to Carranza. Wilson
was now faced with the dilemma of either holding Veracruz until the Villistas
had defeated Carranza and could take it over, or transporting Villista troops on
U.S. ships to Veracruz, or handing the city over to Carranza. To Wilson and his
administration, the third option seemed the least likely to provoke an armed confrontation with Mexican forces. Had Wilson recognized the government of the
Convention and allowed Villista troops to enter Veracruz on U.S. ships, he might
very well have triggered strong anti-American actions by the Carrancistas and
then been provoked into intervening even more profoundly in Mexico. In addition, neither U.S. public opinion nor Americans interested in Mexico were entirely favorable toward Villa.[38] The second option, that of staying for a longer period of time in Veracruz, seemed equally risky. U.S. Secretary of War Lindley
Garrison wrote Wilson in November that if U.S. forces stayed in Veracruz, there

was a real possibility of their being embroiled in war with the Carranza forces.[39] As World War I increased in pace and intensity, Woodrow Wilson became even more wary of becoming tied down in Mexico.

It is not at all clear whether this widely accepted interpretation of Wilson's actions is a sufficient explanation for his withdrawal from Veracruz and his handing over of the city to the Carranza faction. Above all, it does not explain why Wilson refused to consider either destroying all the military matériel in Veracruz or removing it from the city, so as not to give an unfair advantage to any faction. If fear of being embroiled in a war in Mexico was the guiding principle behind Wilson's actions, it is not clear why he violated that principle only eleven months later in October 1915, when he recognized Carranza and allowed Carrancista troops to cross U.S. soil to attack Villa. At a time when World War I presented far greater risks to the United States than it did in 1914, he was ready to face the possibility—and ultimately the reality—of Villista reprisals against the United States.

Was Wilson's primary motive fear of Villista and Zapatista radicalism and hope that the more moderate Carranza would prevail in the civil war? That seems improbable. Wilson may have been wary of Villa and Zapata's radicalism, but he certainly cared just as little for Carranza's nationalism. It is also doubtful whether Wilson or any other high U.S. official at the time believed that even with the help of the arms stored at Veracruz, Carranza might be able to prevail in the coming civil war in Mexico. The general assumption of practically all foreign observers at the time was that the Convention was far superior in military and political terms, as well as in popularity, to the Carrancistas. What is more likely is that the Wilson administration simply did not want any one faction to become dominant in Mexico.

What Wilson had wanted all along in Mexico was a stable government, committed to the free-enterprise system and to U.S.-style democracy, that was responsive, if not completely subservient, to his suggestions. The best way of securing such a government was not to have one faction triumph in Mexico but rather to have a coalition of factions. This was in fact one of the main characteristics of Wilson's Mexican policies from the moment he assumed office until he recognized Carranza in October 1915. He had first attempted to effect a compromise between the more moderate wing of the Huerta regime, headed by Federico Gamboa, and Carranza. After Huerta resigned, he still hoped for a coalition regime that would include the revolutionaries as well as representatives of the conservative forces in Mexico that had supported Huerta.

It was with the same purpose in mind that in June 1915, when Villa was reeling from defeat to defeat, Wilson threw him a kind of life preserver. "We do not wish the Carranza faction to be the only one to deal with in Mexico," Secretary of State Robert Lansing wrote Wilson. "Carranza seems so impossible that an appearance at least of opposition to him will give us the opportunity to invite a compromise of factions. I think therefore it is politic for the time to allow Villa to obtain sufficient financial resources to allow his faction to remain in arms until a compromise can be effected."[40] Moreover, a series of other important factors persuaded Wilson to give up his hands-off policy as far as Mexico's civil war was concerned.

Doubtless the most important of these factors was World War I. Although officially neutral, the United States leaned more and more toward the Allies, and relations with Germany had become increasingly tense. The likelihood that the United States would be drawn into the Great War loomed on the horizon. The last thing Wilson wanted was for his attention to be diverted from Europe and the Far East toward Mexico. For economic reasons as well, Wilson needed peace south of the border. The Allies depended more and more on oil from Mexico, while the United States was becoming increasingly dependent on sisal from Yucatán, since its other sources of that raw material, such as German East Africa, were closed as the result of the hostilities.[41]

The risks that Mexico could present to the United States were starkly brought to the attention of the U.S. president when German plots to provoke a war between Mexico and the United States, precisely to prevent U.S. arms from being shipped to the Allies and to make sure that no U.S. intervention would occur, were uncovered. A German secret agent, Franz von Rintelen, was arrested by British authorities as he was returning from the United States to Germany. He was accused of having given $12 million to Huerta, who in return was said to have promised to undertake a coup in Mexico and, if he were successful, to attack the United States.[42]

Wilson was also influenced by a report from his special emissary Duval West. In April 1915, West had arrived at the erroneous conclusion that no party or faction could win in Mexico "without the aid or assistance of the United States."[43] West sharply opposed any U.S. military intervention and stated that the United States had other, more peaceful options for reestablishing "a condition of permanent peace and order and the establishment of a stable government."[44] He believed that the United States had three options: it could recognize and support one of the factions in the Mexican civil war; it could set up a candidate of its own, to whom the United States would throw its full support; or it could recognize a member of Madero's government who would constitutionally have succeeded Madero after his death. It was the latter solution that West advocated and that, at least for a time, Wilson looked into. His sense that something had to be done in Mexico as quickly as possible also stemmed from reports reaching him that the French government was contemplating a joint European intervention in Mexico, "regardless of American wishes in the matter," after the end of World War I.[45]

Thus motivated, Wilson dispatched a sharply worded note to the belligerent parties in Mexico, calling on them to come to terms as soon as possible, or the U.S. government would be "constrained to decide what means should be employed to help Mexico save herself."[46] Wilson did not state what this new policy might be, but most Mexican revolutionaries saw his note as a clear threat of intervention.

Carranza sharply rejected Wilson's note, but Villa must have considered it a godsend. If Wilson were energetic and threatening enough, Carranza might stop his advance and thus would not be able defeat him. Villa probably also hoped that the U.S. call on all factions for an immediate agreement would restore the morale of many of his troops, since it made Carranza's triumph by no means inevitable. While welcoming Wilson's initiative, Villa did not, however, want to support it publicly, which would have implied that he was recognizing the right of the United States to intervene in Mexican affairs. In a note to Wilson, he was cautious, stating only that Carranza was responsible for the outbreak of the new civil war in Mexico. In other ways, however, without saying so, he tacitly adhered to Wilson's point of view. He said publicly that if Carranza were willing to leave the country, he would immediately relinquish his leadership of the División del Norte and leave Mexico as well. In a note to Carranza, he argued that it was imperative for all Mexican factions to find a compromise to prevent armed U.S. intervention.[47] Carranza did not respond.

When it became apparent that Wilson's note had not had the desired effect, Secretary of State Lansing envisioned a conference of representatives of the United States, Argentina, Brazil, and Chile, the stated aim of which would be to bring about a meeting of lesser chiefs in Mexico, who would in turn create a new government. This new government would then be recognized by the United States and the three South American countries and provided with arms; simultaneously, arms shipments to the other parties would be cut off. The lesser chiefs alone, however, were not to choose the new president and his cabinet: in its proposals for the conference, the United States claimed for itself extensive co-determination rights. In fact, it appears that the Wilson administration had no intention of leaving such a momentous choice to the Mexican revolutionaries. It began to consider one candidate after another for the Mexican presidency, who could then be proposed to, and perhaps imposed on, the planned conference.[48] While Carranza refused to participate in the conference, Villa sent one of his most important officials, the former president of the Revolutionary Convention, Roque González Garza, as his delegate to Washington.

The life preserver that Wilson had thrown Villa came at a time when relations between the northern revolutionary and the United States had reached an unprecedented low. The days were gone when Villa considered Wilson as a kind of American Madero, an idealist and a friend of the poor. In January 1915, when Villa had a meeting with former officers of the federal army and invited them to join his División del Norte, he told them "that they should all prepare to fight for the integrity of Mexico; the United States was maintaining different confidential agents in Mexico who had only one purpose, which was to provoke dissension between him, Gutiérrez, Carranza, and Zapata; that it was indispensable to be ready to fight against the common enemy."[49] This statement was never published. Villa did not want to attack the United States publicly, but in private talks with U.S. representatives, he did not disguise the fact that his attitude toward Mexico's northern neighbor had undergone a profound change. When Wilson's special representative Duval West came to interview him in March 1915, Villa was blunt with respect to his aims and his attitude toward the United States:

Upon being questioned as to what extent foreigners would be encouraged to develop the country, [Villa] stated that there would be no disposition to prohibit such developments, except that in the case of lands foreigners should not, or would not, be permitted to own lands. That it was his idea that the country should be developed by Mexican capital, and that this capital should be compelled or required—did not say what or how or when—to employ itself in the establishment of the usual industrial enterprises.

I get the idea from the foregoing statement, and from the failure of General Villa to take the opportunity afforded by the question to make clear the wish of his followers to encourage foreign capital, that he is standing upon the popular demand that "Mexico should be for the Mexicans" and that an open door to foreign investors means ultimate danger to the nation.[50]

Relations between Villa and the United States deteriorated largely because it was clear to Villa that U.S. policy in practice contradicted Woodrow Wilson's idealistic pronouncements. What must have enormously heightened Villa's suspicion of U.S. intentions was "a long confidential note sent to General Villa through Consul [John R.] Silliman [in fact, vice-consul in Veracruz, and one of Woodrow Wilson's special agents] actually promising Villa recognition within a very few weeks (December 1914) providing that General Villa made several concessions imposed by the State Department: the use of lower California, Magdalena Bay, and the Tampico oil fields were subtly mentioned." According to the same informant, who reported this to U.S. Senator Albert Bacon Fall, Villa sent a letter to Zapata "mentioning this note and asking Zapata if he were willing to grant these concessions to the American government." Zapata told Villa "to go ahead and make any arrangements that he deemed best with the American government,"[51] but there is no evidence that Villa ever agreed to such concessions.

There is no evidence either to show that Silliman was acting on instructions of either Woodrow Wilson or Secretary of State William Jennings Bryan. Their papers do not indicate that Silliman in any way represented their intentions. Yet it is improbable that Silliman was only speaking in his own name. Other State Department representatives would make similar demands on Villa later. In all probability, Silliman represented a faction within the U.S. administration headed by Secretary of the Interior Franklin K. Lane, who maintained close contact with U.S. oil companies.

Villa's anger at and suspicion of the United States was doubtless heightened by the Iturbide conspiracy. Eduardo Iturbide was a wealthy landowner from the state of Michoacán, a descendant of Mexico's first emperor, Agustín de Iturbide, who was also close to Mexico's Catholic party. In an effort to improve relations both with the Catholic church and with Mexico's oligarchy, Huerta had named Iturbide governor of the Federal District and thus head of Mexico City's police. Unlike his chief, Iturbide had gone out of the way to be friendly to foreigners and especially Americans, and had his police extend them whatever protection he could. This had earned him much sympathy among Mexico City's influential foreign colonies, which was not shared by Mexico's peasants. According to the Zapatistas, Iturbide had either killed or sent to the army 80 peons from haciendas in Michoacán.[52] Moreover, he had sent his police to fight against the Zapatistas on the outskirts of Mexico City. It is thus not surprising that both Villa and Zapata hated him, and that he feared for his life once the Conventionist troops occupied Mexico City. Thanks to his good relations with the foreign establishment in Mexico City—and to a bribe of $5,000—he succeeded in persuading Woodrow Wilson's special representative León Canova to smuggle him out of Mexico.[53]

Learning that Canova had hidden Iturbide in his railway compartment, for which he claimed diplomatic immunity, Villa sent soldiers to arrest Iturbide, but they hesitated to enter Canova's compartment. When Canova lost his nerve and refused to protect Iturbide any further, the conservative politician jumped out of the train window and made his way to the U.S. side of the border.[54] There he was warmly received by influential American politicians and businessmen, who sought to stage a counterrevolutionary coup and put Iturbide at the helm of Mexico. The spokesman of the group was León Canova, who had become head of the Mexican Desk at the State Department.

Canova might best be described as the Colonel Oliver North of the Mexican Revolution. Like North, Canova attempted by covert means to carry out a counterrevolution. Like North, he was willing to bypass official channels and to violate the law of the land. Like North, he cooperated with business interests and shady adventurers in this process, Like North, too, he was willing to utilize his political activities for personal gain. And, like North's, his activities led to his dismissal from government service.

Canova was a journalist who spoke Spanish and had written some articles on Latin America, which had so impressed Secretary of State Bryan that he named him as one of Wilson's special agents in Mexico. Canova lacked the poise and charisma of Oliver North, however, and was held in contempt by many Mexicans and colleagues in the diplomatic corps, as well as by other foreign observers. "Canova is a cad of the first order, full of his own importance," a colleague said. "Dashing around there in delegation automobiles and always scheming to get himself in a prominent place. He has the ambassador bee in his bonnet, I think, for he was continually talking to me about how well he knew all these men and actually asking me if I did not think he got along with them so well."[55] An American journalist was no less critical of him, saying:

León J. Canova, another of Mr. Wilson's personal representatives, is of Portuguese descent. For no other reason than that he spoke Spanish, this man frittered around Carranza's cuartel as a representative of the great American people. . . . The day before Canova left with Señor Iturbide for the border, the Zapatistas in ransacking the former's house discovered a receipt for $5,000 made out to Edward H. Iturbide and signed by León J. Canova.[56]

A French banker disparagingly wrote that Canova "was probably a station master at some railway station."[57]

Canova's plan not only consisted of furnishing arms to the Iturbide group but suggested a form of support the United States used successfully in later years. It would supply the Iturbide group with stocks of food, which it could then distribute among the population. These gestures, it was hoped, would secure for Iturbide the popularity he lacked. In return for such help and in exchange for a large loan—$500 million was mentioned—from U.S. banks, the conservatives were to grant wide-ranging rights to the U.S. government and to U.S. bankers, including "American supervision of customs collection." The conservatives were also to accept the appointment by the United States of an "unofficial administrative advisor" with unspecified powers to "oversee the necessary reforms." In his memorandum to Secretary of State Bryan, Canova did not explain what he meant by "necessary reforms."[58] He did, however, stipulate in another memorandum, sent to Chandler Anderson, who frequently served as intermediary between the administration and business interests, that "all Church and other real property confiscated by revolutionary bands or others without proper or due process of law since February 13, 1913 shall be reoccupied by their legal owners."[59]

Canova's plot was more than an attempt by a high State Department official and a few Mexican and American associates to secure advantages in Mexico. The plan was backed by important segments of Mexico's prerevolutionary oligarchy, of whom Manuel Calero was a representative, and by U.S. business interests, for whom Chandler Anderson was spokesman.[60] Its purpose was to exploit disunity within the revolutionary camp in order to reestablish a Díaz-style regime that, unlike its predecessor, would be dominated by the United States.

In all probability, this plan was complemented by a secret agreement between the Mexican conservatives and the relevant American business interests (among which the oil companies played a dominant role), an agreement Canova did not reveal to the administration officials to whom he submitted his project. According to this secret pact, U.S. interests were to have decisive influence in selecting Mexico's secretary of foreign relations and secretary of finance. The United States was in turn to grant a large loan to Mexico and to supervise its finances. The United States was to be given naval bases in the Pacific, mainly in Magdalena Bay. And U.S. business interests were to share control of the Tehuantepec railroad, which hitherto had been under British control.[61]

The plan Canova submitted gained important support within the Wilson administration; most outspoken was Secretary of the Interior Lane, who in later years became closely identified with oil interests.[62] On his initiative, the plan was discussed at a cabinet meeting, but Bryan dismissed it, declaring that the United States "should not take up a man who would probably play in with the reactionaries."[63] Although Wilson did not voice any opinion at these meetings, he later expressed agreement with Bryan's position, and Canova's plan was discarded.[64]

Canova seems to have contacted some of Villa's generals to enlist their support. "I am assured that 20,000 men, mostly trained soldiers of the old federal army, coming largely from Villa's ranks, would adhere to it; but in all probability Villa's entire army will join the movement," he wrote Secretary of State Bryan.[65] He also approached Angeles, trying to enlist his support for the plan, which Angeles rejected with great indignation.[66] There is little doubt that Villa was informed of the Iturbide conspiracy either by some of his generals whom Canova had contacted or by Angeles. This could only have increased his suspicions of U.S. policy, since he was never told that Wilson had rejected Canova's scheme.

Villa's suspicions must have been further heightened when Canova (after his plan had been rejected by Wilson) once more attempted to persuade him to acquiesce to conditions along the lines of those Iturbide had accepted, which would have transformed Mexico into a de facto protectorate of the United States. The emissary Canova sent to Villa was a man very much like himself, a shady businessman named J. M. Keedy. In the words of a U.S. official stationed at the Mexican border, Keedy, a former U.S. attorney in Puerto Rico and in the Panama Canal Zone, was part of an "infernal stream of impostors and grafters who do no good for the government and who at best confuse the Mexican mind."[67]

Keedy had done some business with Villa and had thus gained his confidence. According to testimony he gave to a BI agent in September 1915, Keedy, in representation of both Mr. Paul Fuller and Mr. Canova of the State Department [was to use] his good offices and influence with Villa to have him name his cabinet as they wished in the event of [Villa's] recognition. Keedy arrived in Chihuahua during September and through Colonel Dario Silva, staff officer of General Villa, obtained a quick audience with the latter on these matters. After talking with Villa and making it plain to him how the (as he believed) best interests of the Mexican Republic could be served in naming his cabinet as per the outlines furnished him by Mr. Fuller and Mr. Canova, Villa told him, Keedy, after the conference that he would send for Díaz Lombardo and advise with him before he made up his mind on such important matters. . . . Keedy said he was put off several times in this way until he saw that Lombardo had turned Villa against his plans and it would be impossible for him to accomplish his mission with Villa so Keedy states that he returned from Chihuahua to Washington after the failure of his mission, traveling via El Paso.[68]

It is at first difficult to understand why Fuller and Canova, who were well informed about the situation in Mexico and knew that Villa was on the verge of defeat, were offering him recognition and showed so strong an interest in Villa's cabinet nominations. Did Canova and Fuller act on their own, or did they represent some larger group in the United States? It is likely that Fuller and Canova represented the same coalition of forces that was backing Iturbide: important members of the Catholic church, oil companies, and a conservative member of Wilson's cabinet, Secretary of the Interior Lane. This group was opposed to the recognition of Carranza. The members of the clergy were worried by his anticlerical attitude, while the oil companies had made a comfortable arrangement with Manuel Peláez, a "revolutionary" general who for a time had called himself a Villista, although he never had any close links to Villa, and claimed to be "protecting" the oil fields from the Carrancistas. The aim of these men was to have the United States impose a candidate for president of Mexico who would have the full backing of both the Wilson administration and American business interests. Their preferred candidate was Iturbide, but they were willing to support other candidates, such as Vázquez Tagle, a former minister in Madero's cabinet. Canova's great hope was to enlist both Villa and his army in support of whatever candidate the Americans named. Probably in order to show the administration that they could count on Villa and his army, they wanted him to name some officials belonging to this "new" conservative faction, so that they could prove to Wilson that their candidate enjoyed broad support in Mexico.[69] It may also have been a means to put pressure on Carranza.

Several months earlier, when Silliman had made such a proposal, Villa had at least considered it. This time, in spite of his desperate situation, he rejected Keedy's proposals out of hand. He had become more and more convinced that the real aim of the United States was to transform Mexico into a U.S. colony, and he was unwilling to acquiesce to such a project, even if it cost him U.S. support.

Economic factors also contributed to the deterioration of relations between Villa and the United States. As the war between the revolutionary factions progressed, as his resources such as the cattle from Chihuahua and the cotton of the Laguna were exhausted, and as his currency dramatically depreciated, Villa was less and less able to maintain his earlier policy of protecting the Americans from higher taxes. He now began to demand new taxes from American-owned and

American-controlled haciendas and to put pressure on U.S. mine owners who had stopped production because of the uncertainty the revolution had caused. He had already threatened these mine owners with expropriation unless they resumed work, provoking tensions with the United States.

Every time Villa issued such threats, U.S. officials protested vehemently, implying that he might lose the right to buy arms in the United States if he carried them out. Again and again Villa caved in, while the mining companies on the whole continued their policy of not working their properties, thus limiting Villa's tax revenues.[70] The only positive response the U.S. government was willing to make to Villa's conciliatory policy was to relax sanitary standards, allowing Villa to export more cattle and meat to the United States.

As a result of constant affirmation by U.S. representatives, Villa remained convinced that Carranza would not be recognized. He was reassured both by what Carothers and other representatives were telling him and by news he received from two lobbyists he had hired in the United States in order to promote his cause and to prevent the recognition of Carranza. These lobbyists were James Rudolph Garfield, a basically conservative man, the son of the former U.S. president James A. Garfield, who had good connections with the State Department, and a businessman, Nelson Rhoades.[71] In later years, Garfield would represent U.S. oil companies with interests in Mexico. He did not advocate recognition of Villa, and after his defeat at Celaya, Villa understood that such recognition was unlikely. Garfield advocated the "establishment of a new provisional Mexican government representative of all factions, Carranza's elimination, and U.S. political and financial support for the new Mexican government.[72]

Although the Garfield plan made no mention of Villa's elimination, Villa had publicly stated that if Carranza were to leave Mexico, he would do the same. When, in August 1915, the U.S. secretary of state and representatives of the largest Latin American nations called on all Mexican factions to send representatives to a conference to be held in the United States to decide on a provisional president, Villa was probably convinced that his lobbyists had played an important part in achieving this result. He now sent his most prominent intellectual representatives, Díaz Lombardo and above all Angeles, to the United States in order to persuade the Wilson administration to withhold recognition from Carranza.

Villa was rightly convinced that Angeles enjoyed a wide measure of support and even admiration within the Wilson administration. Wilson's emissaries to the different Mexican factions, first Paul Fuller and then Duval West, had described Angeles in glowing terms. In June 1915, Secretary of State Bryan wrote Wilson, "It is possible that it might be wise to encourage Angeles if he could show sufficient support."[73] That enthusiasm doubtless increased when Angeles wrote a letter to the U.S. president in June 1915 responding to Wilson's note to all Mexican factions. Angeles expressed his respect and admiration for Wilson, and added: "Now that you have in the name of humanity and through sympathy for the Mexican people proposed to effect within a short time the pacification of my beloved country, I feel certain that your acts will be inspired by the strict justice towards the contending factions, the members of each one of which are so numerous, and with a desire to secure for my country the greatest possible good."[74]

In July 1915, Wilson contemplated the possibility that "some man (perhaps Angeles) could be commended by our confidence to the trust of the rest."[75] Angeles hoped to meet Wilson and convey his wishes directly to the U.S. president. Wilson refused such a meeting, not because he was opposed to Angeles but because it would have been a clear signal to all Mexican factions that he favored the Villistas, or at least Angeles. Nevertheless, Angeles was able to meet with U.S. Chief of Staff Scott and with Secretary of the Interior Lane. While Scott remained noncommittal, he did express his admiration for Angeles in a letter he sent to Villa a few days later, saying, "I have forwarded his business as much as I was able."[76]

The highest official of the Wilson administration with whom Angeles was able to meet was Lane. During this meeting, Angeles told Lane that the United States should support a government headed by a former member of Madero's cabinet. He suggested Vázquez Tagle, "who had taken no part in political affairs since the Madero cabinet went out." When Lane expressed his skepticism as to whether Carranza would agree to such a proposal, Angeles suggested that the United States put pressure on Carranza. "I asked him," Lane reported, "in what shape this pressure should be applied, and he said by letting him know quietly that if he did not agree to the compromise for a provisional president, the United States would put an embargo upon munitions against him and regard his ships as pirates. I asked him if this would not antagonize the Mexican people, and he said that if it was known that an effort had been made by the United States to adjust the differences between the factions and that Carranza had stood out against the success of such effort, that the Mexican people would be glad that the president brought pressure to bear that would secure this result." Lane felt that this conversation was so important that he sent a memorandum about it to Woodrow Wilson.[77]

Angeles won the esteem of these officials of the Wilson administration not only by opposing Carranza's accession to any political office but by intimating that the same should be the case with Villa. He suggested that the Carranza faction name those who should be eliminated on the Convention side and the Convention name those of the Carranza faction. Such elimination was "to consist of renunciation of candidacy for any political post during the next constitutional term."[78] This aim was in accord with repeated statements by Villa that he did not want any political position. What is not clear is whether Angeles's aim was only to eliminate Villa from holding political office or whether he was ready to go further and demand that Villa give up the command of the División del Norte and leave Mexico.

Whatever hopes Angeles had that a final triumph by Carranza might be averted were soon dashed by the increasing military, economic, and political collapse of Villismo.

The Collapse

After winning his decisive victories against Villa in central Mexico, Obregón set out to drive Villa from his last bastions in the north. In spite of the defeats he had inflicted on Villa, Obregón was cautious and slow in his advance into the heartland of Villismo. This was partly because as he advanced northward his lines of communication became dangerously overextended. The raids by Fierro and Canuto Reyes had shown him how vulnerable he was in this respect. An even more important factor that restrained Obregón was the hope that Villismo would collapse and disintegrate of its own accord. His expectations were well founded.

The popularity of Villismo had rested on four foundations: Villa's reputation for invincibility; his extensive redistribution of goods and money to the lower classes of society; the promise he held out for land distribution after the victory of his armies; and, finally, the perception that he could not lose because the Americans were backing him.

After his decisive defeat, these foundations of Villa's power and popularity were shaken. For a brief time, Villa was able to conceal the extent of his defeat. His repeated denials that he had been defeated and the lack of belief in Carrancista propaganda worked for a time. In addition, the raids carried out by both Rodolfo Fierro and Canuto Reyes in central and southern Mexico, which briefly forced Pablo González to evacuate Mexico City, created the illusion that Villismo was on the rebound, that Villa again was inexorably advancing southward and stood a chance of becoming the victor in Mexico's civil war. By the end of June and the beginning of July, after both Fierro and Reyes had been routed by Carranza's troops and forced to flee northward, the full extent of Villa's defeat could be concealed no more. The result was a fall in the morale of his troops and, more important, the collapse of his currency, leading to a paralysis of economic life in the territories he controlled.

With the printing presses of all the revolutionary factions (with the exception of the Zapatistas) rapidly churning out more and more paper money, its value decreased day by day. Nevertheless, the decline of Villa's currency was limited as long as there was an expectation that he would finally triumph and in some way or other redeem the huge amounts of paper money he had issued. For a long time, people still accepted it in the territories Villa controlled firmly. Many foreign companies had bought huge amounts of Villista currency at discount prices in order to pay their taxes with it once his faction emerged triumphant. Once Villa was defeated, people lost confidence in his currency. Large foreign companies that had bought Villista pesos at a discount now confronted the possibility that it was Carranza to whom they would have to pay taxes and threw their large holdings of Villista money on the market. The result was that the Villista peso, which only a few months before had been worth 30 U.S. cents, dropped to 1 1/2 cents.[79] This led to rapid increases in the prices of all goods, both Mexican and imported. The buying power of Villa's currency reached an all-time low, and many merchants refused to accept it, while workers and soldiers clamored to be paid either in gold or in dollars. Villa at first gave in to the mine-workers' demands and forced foreign companies to pay them in hard currency. This created dissatisfaction among railwaymen, who threatened to strike, as well as among Villa's soldiers, who could buy less and less with their pay. Desertions from Villa's army sharply increased.

Villa, who had no inkling of economics, could not understand why his currency had fallen so drastically and attributed it to the greed of financiers who were speculating with his money and to the rapacity of merchants who increased prices to make larger profits. "The merchants of Chihuahua," Villa stated,

have exploited the people in a scandalous manner during the space of long months and the situation presents itself as really desperate and we were in serious danger of the people rioting on account of lack of food or rather because the merchants, having found an inexhaustible gold mine, exploited it at the expense of the needy on the pretext that the rate of exchange of our money had declined, day by day, which decline is due principally to shady manipulations of certain knaves; the merchants scandalously increased the prices of merchandise resulting that many articles cost twenty-five to thirty times more than the ordinary price and this too on merchandise produced inside the national territory. Many others hid their merchandise in order to produce an enormous increase in price or else exacted payment in silver, in Mexican gold and American gold, thereby contributing criminally to the depreciation of the paper money of the state. Notwithstanding all my efforts to suppress this ignoble attitude of the merchants they were sterile. The greatest abuses were committed by the foreign merchants who are the owners of the largest stores and of course the retail merchants necessarily had to sell at higher prices than the wholesalers.[80]

Villa was convinced that he could solve his economic problems by treating the merchants in the same way that he had treated Chihuahua's oligarchy—by intimidation and confiscation. In Ciudad Chihuahua, Villa put most merchants in prison and refused to give them food for 48 hours, so that they "should know what it means to be hungry."[81] He signed an order for the expulsion of all foreign merchants, saying they should "cross the border in order to seek gold there."[82] That order was rescinded, since Villa did not want to lose U.S. support, but he did confiscate the inventories of all Mexican merchants and of some foreign merchants as well. These products were then sold at very low prices to the people of Chihuahua and of the Laguna area around Torreón. The result was predictable. As Emilio Zapico, a Spanish observer, put it, Villa's measures "naturally, instead of solving the conflict, contributed to aggravating it, since all the merchants were afraid of arousing General Villa's ire, and since they could not sell at the prices he wanted, they did not sell anything, and for several days it was difficult to find any food, and at the same time an impossible situation was created for the future, since once the stocks that exist today are exhausted, no merchant will take the risk of bringing in new stocks of merchandise."[83]

The situation caused by the fall of Villa's currency was further aggravated by a drastic fall in agricultural production, owing partly to the demands of the huge armies of both factions. "A Mexican army of the irregular type of that led by General Villa," Patrick O'Hea, the British vice-consul in Torreón, wrote,

consisting almost entirely of mounted troops requires an enormous amount of food for horses and men which is increased by the graft and extravagance in the distribution of such food and by the fact that no commissary service exists but that wives and families accompany the men, even at the front, constituting so many additional mouths to feed. . . . to this must be added the very considerable tracts of land that lie at different points between the opposing factions and exposed to the requisitions of the opposing forces as also the very considerable amount of territory actually occupied by opposing armies where supplies have been seized and crops have necessarily been neglected or trampled out of sight.

O'Hea also noted that on many estates, after the landowning elite had fled, "the organization necessary in many cases in this republic for successful agriculture, particularly in regard to irrigation, has been destroyed and production under the changed conditions has been very much reduced."

An ever-increasing part of that diminished production was used to buy arms in the United States. The effect of these measures was particularly noticeable with regard to meat, which for centuries had been a staple food in central Mexico:

Cattle have been slaughtered in thousands and the carcasses left to rot, for the sake of the exportable value of the hides. Cattle have been sold across the border in tens of thousands or slaughtered in the packing houses in Juárez to realize the hides and the meat canned or on the hoof into gold currency. There is almost a famine of meat in this locality, yet but a few days ago I saw two trainloads of fat sheep pass through these towns on their way north, to the border undoubtedly, to be sold for U.S. currency.[84]

The result of these measures was increasing loss of popular support for Villa, as well as demoralization of his troops.

Demoralization was deepened by the changing character of Villa's army. Both its soldiers and its officers were very different in mid 1915 from the División del Norte that had stormed Torreón at the beginning of 1914. In early 1914, many of its units were composed of countrymen from the same region, frequently from the same village, many of them related. The officers to a large degree were leaders their men themselves had chosen, and who thus had profound ties to them. A significant number of Villa's higher officers were in fact peasant leaders, such as Toribio Ortega, Calixto Contreras, Severiano Ceniceros, and Porfirio Talamantes. By mid 1915, the División del Norte was far more heterogeneous in its composition. Many of the soldiers were prisoners of war, taken in battles against both the federal army and the Carrancistas. Others were recruits from central Mexico who had joined Villa's army as it advanced southward. A large number of people who had become unemployed as a result of the revolution—miners from closed-up mines, cowboys from cattle ranches most of whose stock had been sold across the border to the United States, men who simply wanted to escape the dreary life of provincial cities or their native villages—had all joined the División del Norte. Many of the officers now were not the elected leaders of 1914 but rather men who had risen in the ranks and whom Villa had promoted. Some of the most prominent peasant leaders, such as Toribio Ortega or Porfirio Talamantes, had died and been replaced by Villa appointees, some of them bearing more the traits of professional soldiers than those of popular leaders.

As the prospect of victory grew dimmer, and with Villa less and less able to pay in hard currency, the once-disciplined División del Norte, with its unique fighting spirit, began to disintegrate. Many soldiers simply deserted and went home. Whole units, such as the troops under the command of Pánfilo Natera, who had sided with Villa at the Convention, now joined the Carrancistas. Many of those who remained were less willing to fight and risk their lives than before and became more and more interested in pillage and killing. "It became impossible to speak with military officers," O'Hea reported from Torreón,

without the consciousness of perpetual menace and insomuch as the military dominated everything, including civil authorities, this state of affairs and this condition of life became well nigh intolerable. . . . There was a group of men, several hundred in number, who formed Villa's bodyguard, commonly known as the "Dorados." . . . It seemed to be the rule that they could kill with impunity and without subsequent questions of any sort and in fact at the last the unwritten law seemed to be that any official from colonel upwards might kill peaceful citizens in particular, without any fear of the consequences. . . .

Not a night would pass in Torreón without shooting affrays in the streets that sometimes seemed to the listener to assume the proportions of a small battle and one of the principal centers of discord was a gambling house run by a protégé of the northern chief. . . .

Joy-firing was the order of the day or rather of the night, and if you can picture to yourself dances going on, punctuated with pistol shots because the officer giving the affair preferred to order the musicians to stop or proceed by firing shots above their heads, if you can conceive a condition of firearms being discharged in this and other ways at every hour of the night and every man abroad carrying small arms upon his person, you may be able to understand the deadly readiness with which serious affrays arose, leaving scarcely a night without its quota of death and most nights marred by several murders in the town of Torreón."[85]

As his situation worsened day by day, Villa became desperate for money to pay his troops and purchase new supplies in the United States. There were only limited "reserves" on which he had not yet drawn. There were wealthy Mexicans whose property he had heretofore not touched, because they had not been involved in politics. There were hacendados, hacienda administrators, and peasants who had stockpiled the food they produced rather than sell it for the increasingly worthless Villista currency. There were a number of Mexican-owned properties that had avoided confiscations because their owners had nominally transferred ownership to foreigners, and, above all, there were the huge properties of foreigners, primarily Americans, whom Villa had protected during the first years of revolution.

Villa used the methods he had applied during his bandit days to intimidate wealthy Mexicans. In August 1915, he confiscated one of the largest factories in the Laguna area, the Compania Jabonera de la Laguna, which belonged to a partnership headed by an American entrepreneur, Juan F. Brittingham, who was associated with Luis Terrazas's son Juan and with Enrique Creel.[86] Finally, as the situation became more and more desperate, Villa levied additional taxes on American mine and landowners. He attempted to force American mine owners to give him a loan of $300,000 and at the same time threatened to have their properties worked by his government if they did not resume operation.[87] These tactics were a sign of how desperate Villa had become. It was a risky venture for him to alienate powerful American interests precisely at the time when he hoped the Wilson administration would bail him out and enforce a solution in Mexico that would impose the military status quo. The American mine owners were very conscious of the dilemma in which Villa found himself. They persuaded the Wilson administration to send the one man who generally supported Villa and for whom Villa had great respect, General Hugh Scott, to persuade him to cancel the forced loan and the decree affecting U.S.-owned mines that were not being worked, as well as the confiscation of the Compania Jabonera. Scott was successful in his endeavors: the forced loan was rescinded, and a few weeks after its confiscation, the Compania Jabonera was returned to the control of a representative appointed by Brittingham.[88]

The reaction of the U.S. government to the increasing pressure Villa was bringing to bear on American business interests was closely linked to discussions taking place in Washington on how to "solve" the Mexican problem after the Iturbide plan had been discarded. Two different options were being considered by the State Department, U.S. business interests, and the White House.

The first option, advocated above all by Secretary of State Lansing, was for the U.S. government to recognize one of Madero's ministers as the legal successor to the murdered president and to attempt to rally all revolutionary factions to his side. Both Villa and Angeles had stated that they would support such a plan, and while Lansing doubted that Carranza would support it, he felt that he could obtain the help of many of Carranza's generals and eliminate Carranza by withholding arms from him. "I think I can say," Lansing wrote,

that Carranza probably has ammunition . . . to last him two months and no more. If there should be an embargo placed on arms and ammunition, he could not continue [for long]. Furthermore, I believe that as soon as a government is recognized in Mexico, you will find that there are men in this country, not only Americans, but Mexicans, who will furnish the finances to carry on that government and will pay the soldiers in gold instead of paper money, you will see immediately desertions from all factions . . . so that the act of recognition will have a tremendous strengthening of those whom we decide to recognize.[89]

Lansing's plan was based on the assumptions that a military stalemate had been reached in Mexico and that no faction was strong enough to dominate the country. Carranza's nationalism and stubbornness had also provoked Lansing's opposition. By mid-August, however, Wilson had changed his opinion and no longer favored Lansing's plan. He had come more and more to the conclusion that the United States would have no choice but to recognize Carranza, whose military position was continually improving. In addition, Carranza's lobbyists in the United States made it clear that Carranza would protect foreign properties with all the means at his disposal. At the same time, American radicals and labor leaders were expressing full support for Carranza. The American Federation of Labor advocated the recognition of Carranza by the Wilson administration, as did one of America's most influential and radical muck-raking journalists, Lincoln Steffens.

In August 1915, Villa had no idea that such a change of policy was being contemplated by Wilson, although he did fear that if his military power shrank even more, the United States would recognize Carranza. He now decided on a desperate expedient. His plan was to concentrate the vast majority of his troops in the state of Chihuahua and to destroy all railway communications between Chihuahua and the rest of Mexico, which would greatly slow Obregón's advance.

In the meantime, Villa planned to move from Chihuahua to the neighboring state of Sonora, the greater part of which was occupied by the predominantly Yaqui troops of his ally Maytorena, who were renowned for their fighting capacities. No railway line linked Sonora to the rest of Mexico, so Carranza's troops would have great difficulty getting there. Moreover, unlike the states of Chihuahua and Durango, which had been ravaged by savage fighting, and whose re-sources had been largely exhausted, Sonora had come practically unscathed through the revolution. There had been little fighting there, since Huerta's army had only occupied the port city of Guaymas. As a result, Villa would have no dif-ficulty in feeding his army in Sonora and would also find resources he could sell to the United States in return for arms. Above all, the largest U.S. investments were in the two frontier states of Sonora and Chihuahua, and Villa hoped that even if he wanted to recognize Carranza, Wilson would hesitate to proceed against forces that controlled the greater part of the border region.

Villa's plan was to stay only briefly in Sonora and then head south from there. He wrote Zapata that he hoped to assume control of the states of Sinaloa and Tepic, as well as Michoacán and Jalisco. Finally, he would rendezvous with Zapa-ta, and both would then proceed to attack Mexico City.[90] This plan, Villa hoped, would revive his movement and put an end to the demoralization that was sweeping it. As his soldiers left one area after the other, however, many plundered the civilian population, in whose eyes Villa became more and more the man re-sponsible for their distress.

Not only was Villa's army disintegrating; what was even more disheartening for him was that many of his closest collaborators had begun to turn against him. The defection that probably mattered least to Villa was that of Peruvian poet and would-be ideologue José Santos Chocano, who in doing so simply lived up to Villa's stereotypical idea of intellectuals. After making one demand for money too many[91]—Villa had constantly been supplying Santos Chocano with funds and had gotten nothing in return—the Peruvian poet fled across the border to the United States. From there he began writing "private" letters to Villa's officials and finally printed a letter in the *El Paso Herald* that constituted a devastating critique of Villa and of all the efforts of the United States to set up a provisional government in Mexico with the help of Villa and his forces. "The president ad interim who might be named and recognized," Santos Chocano wrote to Manuel Bonilla, one of the candidates being contemplated by the Americans, since he had been a member of Madero's cabinet,

and if it were you, be supported by the Washington government, nevertheless still would be nothing but a figurehead. . . . The most formidable enemy to this artificial government would not be Carranza but Villa. Villa never obeys; he commands. Cir-cumstances have shown me this man clearly as he is, his primitive nature. With cul-ture he would seem to be a genius. Without it he seems merely a lunatic. His faculties are exuberant, but unbalanced. Psychologists studying the marvelous intelligence of this man would say "He may be a great man" but going deeper and seeing his will, which is quite unsteady and also ever first with him, proceeding always, always, al-ways with violence that is by "impressions" and not "reflections" would definitely con-clude "no, he is a simple eclectic."

A government built upon this man would be an innocent victim sleeping upon a grave peril. He listens to no one; he pays heed to no one; and what is more serious, he believes no one.

Santos Chocano went on to portray the man he had a few months before called a "divine guerrillero" as a beast of prey. "A wild madness of executions, a drunk debauch of assaults and kindred crimes, the desperation of a wild beast in the midst of a forest fire. At this moment he does not need ministers but simply executioners, and he certainly has them too! in his famous thugs (*puntales*, fighting bulls) as he calls them. Between what Díaz Lombardo suggests and what Fierro wants, Villa does not hesitate but does what Fierro wants. I may say to you that I now understand the defection of Eulalio Gutiérrez, Lucio Blanco, José Isabel Robles, and Aguirre Benavides."

Santos Chocano was intent on showing both Bonilla and public opinion in the United States that Villa was worse than Carranza. "Very well, the political campaign against Carranza has been simply 'Down with the dictator!' Very well, it is all farce. Effort is being made merely to change the dictatorship of Carranza for that of Villa. What a horror! I suspect that we who have been the sincere friends of Villa have, at any given moment, more protection and guarantees from Carranza than from Villa as he is now. To confess this is painful but just." All this was leading to a statement, largely destined for public opinion in the United States, that any effort to create a Mexican government with the support of Villa was doomed to failure:

Is it possible to eliminate Villa to set up a government which will be honorable, respected and solid? No. For then who would carry on the armed struggle against Obregón? Villa is the only one who wants to fight. His forces have not been defeated by Obregón but by "weariness," not to say that once it was by panic "for panic." Perhaps Angeles, our friend Angeles, cultured, fine, gentlemanly, able, is a long way from making himself into a military chieftain—and to continue the struggle there must be a chieftain who can inspire them, arouse their enthusiasm, carry them into the fight, for nobody wants to fight. At the moment Villa disappears, if we leave out his thugs, who are worse than he is, the rifles will have to shoot by themselves. Everyone—soldiers and civilians alike—feels the need of peace; the only one who wants to keep on fighting is Villa.

This means that for the government which results from the convention to succeed, it would be necessary—and here is the paradox—for Villa to be eliminated and yet for Villa also to remain, since he is a peril to the civil government but a necessity to the military arm. It has no solution as you can easily see.[92]

While the criticism of Villa that Santos Chocano voiced would probably have been shared by many of Villa's upper- and middle-class supporters, the poet was hardly a disinterested observer. Only a few weeks after publishing this letter, Santos Chocano offered his services to Carranza and immediately asked for money.[93] What Santos Chocano's letter suggested was that after his defeats, Villa had become more savage, violent, and unwilling to listen to advice than ever before.

This impression was confirmed by one of the men closest to him, and one of the few for whom he had genuine respect: Raúl Madero, the brother of the late president, who was a general in Villa's army. In September, he warned the Sonoran governor, Maytorena, that after his defeat at Celaya, Villa had become extremely neurotic and violent, that he was constantly fighting with his generals and officers, and that if Maytorena met Villa in Sonora, a conflict between the two men was likely.[94]

At the beginning of September 1915, Madero wrote a letter to Villa asking him to resign so as to "save our party which is collapsing more from day to day." He drew Villa's attention to the demoralization of his men. "They have no fighting spirit left, they do not want to fight anymore. They believe that it is time that this struggle should end, and the wish of the great majority of these soldiers is to return home." He linked the demoralization of Villa's troops to the fact that "the people as a whole is tired of this struggle since it cannot live anymore." "There is only one thing I can advise you to do," he wrote Villa: "make a public declaration that in view of the sufferings of the people and the interminable struggle that is going on . . . you are disposed to eliminate yourself, and that your subordinates are also disposed to sacrifice themselves for the good of the great majority."[95]

After writing this letter from his native state of Coahuila, Raúl Madero crossed the border into the United States, and three weeks later, he again wrote Villa urgently asking him to resign. He told him that this was in fact the only way to save the Conventionist party. If Villa resigned, Madero wrote, "our faction could make a public declaration in the following sense. 'The war has not brought any benefit to the country; although it is true that Señor Carranza's army has dominated in the republic, we are no closer to a well-founded organization that guarantees peace. As a result, since Señor Carranza only represents one faction without any legal support to be recognized, we cannot surrender to this faction so that he could rule the republic at his whim.'" Finally, Madero appealed to Villa's concern for his own soldiers:

One last consideration to take into account is in what situation you would place our soldiers and leaders, who have put their trust in you and have been so willing to sacrifice themselves, and who have faced and still are facing the greatest dangers. You know very well that the majority of the members of the División del Norte come from the state of Chihuahua. Can you imagine what would happen if the Carrancistas were to take over the state, and in what situation the soldiers would find themselves? The Colorados [this was the name by which the Orozquistas were known], who have been so strongly persecuted by us, will greet the triumphant enemy as a savior and will ally themselves with them in order to wreak vengeance upon our men; our soldiers will be calumniated and persecuted and their families will live in poverty.[96]

Madero did not say why he believed that Villa's army, which was already demoralized, would be able, once Villa was gone, to prevent the Carrancistas from controlling Chihuahua and the other northern regions dominated by Villa. What Madero was implying but not stating was that in such a case, the United States would force an agreement upon Carranza under threat of withholding recognition unless Carranza accepted the military status quo. In his letter, Madero told Villa that he was leaving his army for good. His brother, Emilio Madero, who was also a general in Villa's army, did the same.[97]

By September 1915, most of Villa's intellectuals and upper-class supporters had crossed the border into the United States. Most of them had done so with Villa's approval. He and they hoped that they would be able to influence the Wilson administration not to recognize Carranza but to throw its support to a government headed by a former member of Madero's cabinet. When they failed to do so, they decided to remain in the United States. None of them joined Carranza or issued declarations against Villa. A few remained loyal to Villa and attempted to support his cause in the United States. Manuel Bonilla, who had drafted Villa's agrarian law, said in September 1915 that he intended to withdraw from politics.[98] The brothers Federico and Roque González Garza continued to support Villa until his troops killed eleven American mining engineers in January 1916 (see chapter 14). Miguel Díaz Lombardo, the civilian leader of Villa's government, also stayed in the United States, but he remained loyal to Villa until his death and attempted to do everything in his power to further Villa's cause in the United States.

Angeles too left Villa in September 1915. With Villa's full accord he had gone to the United States in June and July in order to persuade the Americans to exercise all possible pressure on Carranza to accept a compromise candidate for president and to stop all hostilities. After speaking with Secretary of Interior Lane, and with Canova, it soon became clear to him that he was not going to be successful. In his talk with Canova, Angeles "stated that if the departure of Villa from Mexico until normal conditions were restored was necessary, he would endeavor to bring this about, and spoke as if he could do so."[99] After his unsuccessful mission to the United States, Angeles returned to the Villa-controlled part of Mexico, and by the beginning of September, news began reaching both Sommerfeld and U.S. agents in Mexico that Angeles had fallen out of favor with Villa and that his life was threatened. "I have well founded fear for his safety," George Carothers notified the State Department, and Villa's representative in the United States, Felíx Sommerfeld, wrote General Scott: "It is absolutely necessary that General Angeles leave Villa territory in order to save his life. . . . Most of Villa's generals are exceedingly hostile toward Angeles and one of these days he is going to be killed. Villa himself, although treating Angeles with respect, does not like him any longer due to intrigue and gossip."[100]

None of these reports give any reason for Villa's change of heart but it is quite possible that Angeles may have intimated to Villa what he had told Canova: that for the good of Mexico, Villa should, at least temporarily, leave the country. In addition, Angeles was probably opposed to Villa's planned campaign in Sonora, since he felt that Villa had lost the war and that the march to Sonora could only harm Maytorena, his close ally. At the beginning of September, Angeles told Carothers that he was very despondent over the outlook for the Villa faction and saw little hope. "Villa realizes that he has lost and must subordinate himself to someone," Carothers reported. "Angeles was deeply worried about the possibility of an American intervention and expressed to me his preference of recognition of Carranza as last resort if it would prevent intervention although firm in his belief that Carranza could never pacify nor govern the country."[101]

On September 13, Angeles received an urgent summons from Villa, who was in Torreón, to report to him immediately. The U.S. customs official Zach Lamar Cobb, fearing for Angeles's life, wrote the secretary of state, "If you consider it wise to suggest him not to go a telegram to Carothers would be in time."[102] It is not clear whether Angeles attended the conference or not, but only four days later one of his representatives made it clear that Angeles was on the verge of leaving Villa and had not yet done so and remained in Villa-controlled Ciudad Juárez only "because of anxiety for two dozen associate officers for whom he feels responsible and who would be thrown out destitute upon withdrawal of Angeles."

Moreover, "he has not received what is due to him in salary as promised by Hipólito Villa."[103]

A week later, on September 24, Angeles told an American newspaper correspondent that he had decided to make his home in the United States.[104] Angeles never made any public statement against his erstwhile chief, and until the end of his days, he continued to insist that he was proud to have served under Villa. It is significant that Villa never felt that Angeles had deserted him but, on the contrary, three years later quasi-apologized to Angeles for having driven him away.[105]

Once he settled in the United States, Angeles's main preoccupation was how to make a living. Unlike other supporters of Villa's who crossed the Rio Grande with large sums of money that they had managed to secure in the course of the revolution, Angeles had been scrupulously honest and left Mexico as he had entered it, a poor man. The few funds that he had, part of which Maytorena had loaned him, he used to buy a small ranch in Texas on the Mexican border, where he struggled to make a living farming and raising horses. He was the only prominent intellectual supporter of Villa's who returned to his chief's side in 1918—a decision he paid for with his life.

Villa's relationship with Maytorena was of a much more stormy nature. The Sonoran governor had expressed no enthusiasm about Villa's planned march into his native state. Maytorena was worried that Villa would destroy the kind of society that he sought to preserve in Sonora. One of his key aims had been to protect the property of the state's large landowners. Maytorena was afraid that Villa might confiscate the large estates, shoot their owners, and carry out an agrarian reform. Villa had in fact, some months earlier sent an emissary to Sonora asking Maytorena to carry out land reform, and Maytorena had refused.[106] Villa's planned march into Sonora threatened not only the property but even the lives of the state's upper class, including, perhaps, Maytorena's. His fears were increased by a letter Roque González Garza wrote him. While González Garza supported Villa's planned invasion of Sonora, he warned Maytorena that the troops of the División del Norte were completely demoralized and might constitute a public threat. He wrote that one of his "nightmares was the way our troops might behave in the state of Sonora."[107] In all probability, Maytorena indicated his fears and even his disapproval to Villa, and relations between the two men rapidly soured.

They became so tense that in September 1915, when Villa's troops were approaching Sonora, Maytorena fled rather than confront Villa. While Maytorena gave no public explanation for his departure, he later explained that one of the main reasons for his decision was Villa's desire to impose forced loans on wealthy merchants in Sonora and his own refusal to accede to such demands. According to Maytorena, Villa was becoming more and more convinced that the Sonoran leader's links to the upper class were discrediting the revolution.[108]

The depth of Maytorena's fear and resentment of Villa was expressed in secret instructions he gave his two most loyal subordinates in Sonora, the Yaqui generals Francisco Urbalejo and José María Acosta, to limit their support of Villa to their native state. If Villa should ask them to push southward, they were to tell him that their troops did not want to be too far removed from their families. Should Villa insist, Maytorena wrote, "you should tell him that you will do everything in your power to convince your troops. Instead of doing this, you should disperse them, telling them to keep their arms and ammunitions and await my instructions." Urbalejo and Acosta were then to go to the United States, where they would receive financial assistance from Maytorena.[109] While Villa did not know of these secret instructions, he had become so suspicious of the Sonoran governor that he executed the former deputy governor of Chihuahua under Abraham González, Aureliano González, whom he suspected of being an agent of Maytorena's.[110]

Rafael Buelna, the student revolutionary who governed the territory of Tepic on Mexico's west coast, also decided to flee to the United States rather than continue to support Villa. Buelna was one of the most capable and talented generals of the Mexican Revolution. In the summer of 1915, when Villa was reeling from defeat to defeat, Buelna still achieved victories in spite of the Carrancistas' superiority in numbers and Villa's refusal to send him the ammunition he had promised. In order to persuade Villa to resupply his troops, Buelna first sent his brother and then went himself to Villa's headquarters. He got the ammunition he wanted, but he was deeply disillusioned by what he saw there. "We are lost, both from a moral and material point of view," Buelna told his brother after returning to Tepic. "We are lost morally because Villismo has become no more than a group of ambitious men headed by Villa himself who has only one desire, that of becoming president of the republic; in material terms we are lost since it will be extremely difficult for the División del Norte to recover from the defeats of Celaya and León. Nevertheless, we have to fight. . . . It is a commitment we have taken, Brother, and I will try to fulfill it as best I can."[111]

By late summer 1915, however, Buelna decided that he had more than fulfilled his commitment. It had become clear to him that the Carrancistas were winning the war and that he was waging an isolated campaign in Tepic, unable to get reinforcements and unable to secure more arms and ammunition from a defeated Villa. Fleeing to the United States was a risky undertaking. Unlike Maytorena, Buelna controlled no territory along the border. Since he refused to switch sides and pledge loyalty to the Carrancistas, as many others did, his only way north was through Villa-held territory, and there was considerable risk that Villa might shoot him if he learned of Buelna's intention to defect. Buelna undertook a long and complex journey in which he first swore loyalty to Villa personally and then fled to the United States with a Villista firing squad on his heels.[112]

Buelna was an honest man and had very little money when he arrived in the United States. He at first wanted to buy a ranch, but having insufficient funds for this purpose, he acquired a small restaurant in El Paso. He did not do well. The burly former revolutionaries whom Buelna employed in order to help them, who had had no compunction about storming positions held by the federal army or by Carranza's troops, did not make for deferential waiters.[113] Nor did Buelna have it in his heart to refuse meals when exiled revolutionaries with no money asked him for food. Buelna managed with great difficulty to keep afloat until he returned to Mexico in 1923 to participate in a revolt against Obregón. The conflict between the two men finally ended in 1923 when Buelna was killed in a battle with government troops.[114]

The defections of Buelna and Maytorena were a great blow to Villa, but since these men had never been close to him or fought as his subordinates in the División del Norte, it was less painful to him to lose them than those members of his own immediate entourage who had fought on his side since the early days of the revolution. When Rosalio Hernández, who had participated in the battles of Paredón, Torreón, and Zacatecas, defected to the Carrancistas, Villa ordered his troops to execute Hernández and all of his soldiers if captured. "Chalio," Villa told Buelna, "was one of my best boys, but he has betrayed me and I will now show him what betrayal means."[115]

The defection that most deeply rankled with Villa was that of his compadre from bandit days, Tomás Urbina. They had ridden together long before the revolution, and when Urbina was wounded, Villa had nursed him until he recovered. Unlike Villa's other cronies from past forays, Urbina was a military leader in his own right. He had raised a force of his own, and as a result most of his men were primarily loyal to him. Throughout the revolution, he remained what he had always been—a bandit whose main aim in life was to accumulate as much wealth as he could. Urbina's hacienda of Las Nieves came to resemble a feudal fiefdom. At his estate, thanks to robbery, confiscation, extortion, and holding wealthy people for ransom, Urbina had accumulated huge amounts of wealth: large numbers of horses, mules, and 300,000 head of sheep. In addition, he had hoarded a large amount of jewelry and 54 gold bars in wells close to his hacienda.[116]

In every region that Urbina's troops occupied, he organized plundering expeditions and executed all real and potential enemies. For a long time, complaints about Urbina addressed to Villa both by civilians and by officers of the División del Norte fell on deaf ears. Villa continued to have unlimited faith in his former associate. His confidence began to waver, however, when the number of accusations mounted, and when it seemed that Urbina was less and less enthusiastic about fighting the Carrancistas. The final break between the two men came after Villa, advised that Urbina's chief of staff, Borboa, was implicated in several murders, decided to execute him.[117]

Urbina not only refused to hand Borboa over to Villa but withdrew with all his troops to Las Nieves and replied in "insolent terms," as one of Villa's former officers put it, to Villa's demands that he should return to the battlefield and hand over Borboa for punishment. At this point, Villa decided to make an example of Urbina and replenish his coffers as well. With the greatest secrecy, Villa assembled a squad of men to do so, who made their way by night to Urbina's hacienda. When they were woken by Villa's concentrated attack on the hacienda, Urbina's troops fought back, and when Villa finally managed to storm the hacienda, he found a wounded Urbina pointing a gun at him. Urbina was disarmed, and the two men repaired to a room for a long private talk. It seemed for a moment that Urbina had managed to persuade his leader and former comrade in arms to grant him his life, and Villa ordered him brought to his headquarters by Fierro. According to one account, Villa had promised Fierro that he could have the "privilege" of executing Urbina and decided to have Urbina killed when Fierro reminded him of his promise. Somewhere on the way between Las Nieves and Villa's headquarters, Urbina was shot by Fierro.

In a brief communiqué published in *Vida Nueva* on September 14, 1915, Villa said that he had been obliged to execute Urbina, who "ordered anyone shot whom he disliked." The gravest crime of which he accused Urbina was that he had killed several foreign nationals. Urbina had refused to give any account of his actions to the supreme military leadership of the División del Norte and had indicated "that he wanted to free himself from my leadership," Villa said. He had again and again attempted to persuade Urbina to change his attitude, but finally saw no other remedy than to attack him on his own estate, where Urbina and his men had shot it out bloodily with him. "I found that I had to recur to harsh and imperious measures and have Urbina shot," Villa said.[118] The execution met with almost universal approval.

Of the treasure that Urbina had hidden, Villa only managed to find three gold bars. He did not have time for a thorough search, so he left one of his officers, Ramírez, at Las Nieves with instructions to pay part of the treasure to one of Urbina's commanders, whose troops were stationed near Las Nieves, and whose loyalty Villa thus hoped to ensure. Villa also told Ramírez that if he found it, he could keep part of the gold as a reward. Ramírez did locate 50 gold bars that Urbina had hidden in wells near his estate, but fearing that once he handed over the gold, Villa would have him killed in order to keep his share, he deserted and gave his information to the Carrancistas. They managed to secure Urbina's treasure, and Ramírez waited in vain for a reward.[119]

As his troops became more and more demoralized and the number of defections increased, Villa pinned all his hopes on the planned Sonoran campaign. It would allow him to take the offensive again—Villa hated to be on the defensive—and the largely intact countryside of Sonora would allow him to feed his troops and to finance his new offensive. It would also give him more leverage than he now had with the United States. Not only would it convince the Americans that Carranza could never pacify Mexico; it would also mean that in addition to Chihuahua, where so much American investment was concentrated, Villa would control another state where substantial American interests were at stake.

Villa's state of mind on the eve of setting out for Sonora was expressed in an interview with a reporter for the *El Paso Morning Times*, which would prove to be the last he ever granted an American newspaper. "I am completely exhausted. My physical forces have reached the limit. The past month has been the most exhausting of my life," Villa said. He remained convinced that he had fought the good fight:

Never had I doubted the justice of our cause. Through twenty-two years of fighting for what I believe to be the cause of liberty, of human liberty and justice. When I was young I took cognizance of the great injustices being done to the great mass of my compatriots. I too was a victim of that oppression. In my roughness I saw fifteen million people who were being oppressed under the cruel talons, and that millions had to suffer for the few who became rich and lived luxuriously. I saw and felt that very deeply, even when I was in prison. I solemnly swore that I would escape, attack that system, and punish it severely, as severely as I could.

For the first time, Villa said he did not think he could win. "It can be seen that I am not the one to bring the fight to a successful conclusion." He was willing to shoulder some of the blame for his defeat. "It could be that my lack of education and experience has caused it. It could be that I have made mistakes in my affairs.

Undoubtedly, I have committed errors. It could happen that my perceptions respecting the more delicate questions in life are not what they should be. I don't make excuses."

A shift had occurred in his perception as to who was to blame for the outbreak of the civil war. Although Villa had nothing good to say about the First Chief, Carranza and his supporters were not primarily to blame. Indeed, Villa said,

I do not condemn the honored soldiers who were induced and supported Carranza . . . but I have no words to express my disgust for the men (and we know who they are) who without risking their lives on the line of fire, remaining at a good distance from danger, have attacked us in a more deadly way than all the armed, with wicked money. These men, refugees outside our country, sustained by economic interests allied to foreign lands, have given not their blood, but their gold to the end of weakening our forces and blinding our cause.

These words may have been inspired by the fact that the interview was given one day before the United States officially decided to recognize Carranza, and that rumors of the impending recognition had reached Villa. He warned the Americans that recognition of Carranza would "not bring order to Mexico. It will bring revolution after revolution, and revolution in its worst form. Compared to such revolution, the war of the last four years will be like child's play." Carranza's triumph "would signify the triumph of the reactionary movement and the complete failure of progressive movement in Mexico." Villa expressed his surprise that Carranza might be recognized, since "he has not taken into consideration the American interests and has been insolent with American authorities." Villa made one thing absolutely clear: he would never stop fighting and he would never leave Mexico. "Mexico is my country. I am in Juárez, but this is the most northern place to which I will come. I will not run from here. I will live and I will fight."[120]

Villa's decision to fight on regardless of what the United States did was shown in the days that followed, as he set out on his Sonoran campaign.

The Last Hurrah of the División del Norte

The Villista army that set out toward Sonora was a pale reflection of the División del Norte that had overrun Torreón and stormed Zacatecas. In its heyday, the División del Norte had numbered more than 50,000 men. Now it had shrunk to about 12,000, many of them demoralized by constant defeats and by increasing shortages of food, supplies, and ammunition. Some were still galvanized by Villa's will to fight on; others stayed because they feared reprisals by Villa against them or their families if they deserted.

Not only was the División del Norte greatly diminished, but few of the generals who had fought alongside Villa were still at his side. Angeles had decided to stay in the United States; Urbina had been shot; Rosalio Hernández had gone over to the Carrancistas; Toribio Ortega had succumbed to typhus. Yet this demoralized army had to face natural obstacles greater than ever before in its history. Villa's main means of transportation had always been troop trains, with their soldiers and soldaderas, their special cars for officers and reporters, and their hospital car. They had become a hallmark of the División del Norte. This time, how-ever, Villa's soldiers would have to ride or to walk to battle, since there was no railway line between Chihuahua and Sonora. The road to Sonora through the Sierra Madre was long and arduous. There was little water along the way, and there were no large estates where the army could replenish its supplies of food and clothing. Hauling artillery pieces through this barren terrain, and especially through the windswept and ice-covered Cañón del Púlpito, was a back-breaking undertaking. The morale of many of Villa's troops had been low from the start. They were no longer the invincible División del Norte but rather had gone from defeat to defeat. Desertions of officers as well as soldiers had become a common-place occurrence. The troops were further demoralized because for the first time, they were not accompanied by soldaderas. In view of the tremendous difficulties of the terrain, Villa had forced all the women to stay behind in Casas Grandes in Chihuahua.[121] It was a tribute both to Villa's capacities as an organizer and to the loyalty he could still inspire in some of his soldiers that the expedition ar-rived relatively unscathed in Sonora.

Along the way, Villa lost one of his most loyal lieutenants, a loss that gravely afflicted him, but that caused rejoicing among many in the División del Norte. Rodolfo Fierro, known to many as "the butcher," perished when his horse rode into a swamp and dragged Fierro into the quagmire.

Villa had assumed that once his men reached Sonora, his greatest difficulties would be overcome. When he left Chihuahua, most of Sonora had been in the hands of a friendly army, Maytorena's men, with only 3,000 Carrancista troops bottled up in the border city of Agua Prieta. Villa's plan was to have his army sub-due the garrison of Agua Prieta and then march south, living off the fat of the land, to be joined first by Maytorena's soldiers and later by scattered groups of Vil-listas in the neighboring state of Sinaloa and later in Michoacán and Jalisco. Since Sonora had a long border with the United States, it would be easy to resupply his troops from the other side, paying for American products with cattle from confis-cated estates, as well as forced contributions from American mining companies.

When Villa and his troops finally ended their hazardous journey and arrived in Sonora, they found that the situation had changed and was worse than Villa or any of his generals had assumed. Shortly before Villa arrived, two Carrancista armies had penetrated Sonora, one from the south through Sinaloa and one by sea, landing in the state's largest port, Guaymas. Demoralized by Maytorena's flight to the United States, his men had not put up any effective resistance, and Carranza's troops had had no difficulty occupying the state capital, Hermosillo.

Villa thus faced obstacles he had not anticipated when he decided to march into Sonora, but he had no choice but to go on. He could not retreat to Chi-huahua without risking the complete demoralization of his army. In addition, re-treat was anathema to him. He decided to proceed with his original plan of first overrunning the 3,000-man Carrancista garrison at Agua Prieta. Then, reinforced with arms taken from the Carrancistas, he would proceed south against Manuel Diéguez, who headed one of the Carrancista armies, and whom he had already defeated once before.

What Villa had not counted on was the recognition of Carranza by the Wilson administration and its implications. Not only did the Americans decree an arms embargo against Villa, they went much further in the help they granted to Carranza. In an unprecedented move, Wilson granted Carranza's request to let Carrancista troops pass through the United States on their way from Coahuila in order to reinforce the garrison at Agua Prieta. The troops that now entered Agua Prieta through Arizona were experienced veterans from the battle of Celaya, who had defeated Villa once and were convinced that they could do so again. They were soon followed by Obregón, who assumed command of the Sonoran theater of operations. According to an American correspondent, John W. Roberts, who maintained good relations with Villa, the latter knew nothing of the Carrancista reinforcements that had come into Agua Prieta. "Poor unsuspecting Pancho, believing that a garrison of but 1,200 defended the town ordered an immediate charge, first cautioning his soldiers not to shoot toward the American side. Three hours later his was a bleeding army, crushed, tired, helpless." The Carrancistas had set up deep entrenchments, protected by barbed wire and machine-gun nests every few feet. Villa thought that one of his famous nighttime attacks would blunt the accuracy of the defenders' fire, and that his troops would thus be able to break into Agua Prieta. What he did not anticipate was that as his troops advanced toward Agua Prieta in the dark of the night on November 1, 1915, searchlights would illuminate the battlefield, and his troops would face a withering fire from Carrancista machine guns, artillery, and rifles. It is still a matter of contention whether these searchlights were stationed on the Mexican or on the U.S. side of the border. Villa was convinced that the searchlights were on the U.S. side and saw in this another proof of Woodrow Wilson's perfidy. Roberts describes Villa's soldiers lying in the field begging for water:

Women camp followers flocked to the international fence with pails. Villa went with them. It was there that I met him. A startled, haunted look was in his eyes. I stood on the American side of the fence. He saw me and walked up quickly.

"My God, Roberts, what happened?" he asked, "I had positive information that there were but 1,200 Carrancistas here, but they have 6,000. Why? How? Tell me!"

I told him in as few words possible [and] I explained the situation.

Villa said nothing. His jaw dropped weakly and he hung his head in utter despair. I had expected a volcanic outburst. Just then, General [Frederick] Funston who had been sent to Douglas, rode up with a number of officers. I told Villa who he was. Villa merely stared. Funston dismounted and came forward.

"Is this General Villa?" he asked me, I nodded and introduced the two chiefs. Each stood in their own country and they shook hands over the barbed-wire fence.

Roberts did not witness their interchange but reported that Villa said afterward:

"I told General Funston to warn his chief that I would not tolerate the passage of more Carrancista troops through the United States. I want you to publish this. Tell the world that I have warned Señor Wilson that if such a thing occurs again I, Francisco Villa, will not feel responsible for the lives of Americans in my territory."

"What!" I exclaimed. "Will you kill them?"

"Worse than that," he replied, and walked away. I never saw Villa again.[122]

The defeated Villa now retreated from Agua Prieta toward the border town of Naco, which was still held by troops loyal to Maytorena. His attitude toward the United States had now undergone a complete change. He had always been intent on protecting American property and on preventing the plunder of American enterprises. He now radically reversed his stand. Dispatching troops to the large mining center of Cananea, whose mines were the property of the Cananea Mining Company, he threatened to destroy the mining installations unless the American company gave him $25,000 and a large amount of supplies.[123]

Villa's despair, bitterness, and rage were clearly expressed when he confronted two American doctors, Dr. R. H. Thigpen and a Dr. Miller, who had crossed the border from Arizona in order to treat the Villista wounded. "I have always extended guarantees to the persons and property of you Americans," he told them. "With my own eyes, I have safeguarded fortunes of precious metals for Americans; with my own hands I buried your treasures safely out of the reach of enemies. Your families have enjoyed my protection." And then he described to them what, in his opinion, Wilson's treachery at Agua Prieta had brought him. "For four days not a single bite of food has passed the lips of me and my men. We are starving; we are here, sacrificing our lives. For water we are drinking the discharge from your Douglas smelters. This, while you, whose families and treasure I have protected, lull [*sic*] in the lap of luxury. . . . your government is playing a high hand in its attempt at scuttling the peace, prosperity and freedom of Mexico."

Villa then revealed to the doctors that he planned an attack on Douglas, Arizona. Calling to one of his officers, he said: "My general, bring back the artillery, take it down there and turn it loose on these ———— in Douglas. . . . The Negroes are all ready to side with us. I did not want history to record our side as the offender, but the cowardly ———— has left us no other alternative." (The dashes probably stand for expletives that the doctors did not want to record.) "From this moment on," he told the doctors, "I will devote my life to the killing of every Gringo I can get my hands on and the destruction of all Gringo property."

Villa then ordered the doctors to be shot.

At the last moment, Villa relented. He did not attack Douglas, Arizona, and the two doctors, who were kneeling and praying and preparing for death as they watched an execution squad loading its rifles, were told that their lives would be spared.[124]

The role of the United States in the battle of Agua Prieta led Villa to formulate a new strategy and a new ideology, which were expressed in a manifesto that he issued in Naco on November 9, 1915. Published in *Vida Nueva*, it was the longest, most detailed, most bitter proclamation that Villa ever issued. It sought to refute the Carrancista charge that his faction was composed of reactionaries, it leveled new charges against Carranza, and it heralded a change of Villa's policy toward the United States. Villa dismissed the charge that his faction was "reactionary." That charge was based on the accusation that Villa had incorporated many federal officers into the División del Norte. He did not deny that some members of the federal army had joined his division but declared that their number was limited and that most of them were genuine patriots. It was Carranza, he stated, who was utilizing the services of deputies, senators, high officials, and journalists who had supported Porfirio Díaz. Not only did Carranza associate with reactionaries, he carried out reactionary policies. "He has begun to return the properties of the slave owners and slave merchants and he has returned their power to the overseers and to the caciques." Carranza, Villa said, "is protected by the gold of Creel and Terrazas and he has begun to associate with the most corrupt members of the científico clique." He had betrayed every person and every cause with which he had been involved. Carranza had planned to rise against Madero, Villa charged, because Madero had found out that he had stolen 50,000 pesos. Villa also accused Carranza of having betrayed Bernardo Reyes (he gave no explanation for this charge) and the constitutionalist revolution, by attempting to become dictator of Mexico, and added that Carranza had now committed the greatest betrayal of all by "selling our country" to the United States.

The manifesto raised the question why Carranza—who "had never given guarantees to Americans, who had plundered them, who had deprived foreigners as often as he could of the lands they owned in the eastern and southern parts of the republic, and who had always aroused the repugnance of the United States"—had suddenly obtained not only the recognition but also the active support of the United States. According to Villa, U.S. support to Carranza took the form of a $500 million loan and permission for Carranza's troops to cross into U.S. territory. The manifesto bluntly answered its own question: "The price for these favors was simply the sale of our country by the traitor Carranza."

The manifesto further charged that Carranza had agreed to eight conditions imposed by the United States: (1) amnesty for all political prisoners; (2) a concession granting the United States rights over Magdalena Bay, Tehuantepec, and an unnamed region in the oil zone for 99 years; (3) an agreement that Mexico's Interior, Foreign Affairs, and Finance ministries would be filled by candidates enjoying the support of Washington; (4) all paper money issued by the revolution would be consolidated after consultation with a representative named by the White House; (5) all just claims by foreigners for damage caused by the revolution would be paid and all confiscated property returned; (6) the Mexican National Railways would be controlled by the governing board in New York until the debts to this board were repaid; (7) the United States, through Wall Street bankers, would grant a $500 million loan to the Mexican government, to be guaranteed by a lien on the entire income of the Mexican treasury, with a representative of the U.S. government to have supervision over Mexico's compliance with this provision; and (8) General Pablo González would be named provisional president and would call for elections within six months.

Villa's policies in the next months were clearly presaged by passages in this manifesto. "Can foreigners, especially the Yanquis," Villa asked, "harbor the illusion that they can exploit 'peacefully while thanking God' the riches of Mexican soil?" He continued:

Can they be naive enough to assume that Carranza's government can give them effective guarantees?. . . . As far as I am concerned, I sincerely and emphatically declare that I have much to thank Mr. Wilson for, since he has freed me of the obligation to give guarantees to foreigners and, above all, to those who were once free citizens and are now vassals of an evangelizing professor of philosophy who is destroying the independence of a friendly people and who violates the sovereignty of the states of Arizona and Texas, allowing their soil to be crossed by the "constitutionalist" troops. This does not imply a feeling of enmity or hatred against the real people of the United States of North America, whom I respect and admire for their glorious traditions, for their example of order and economy, and for their love of progress.

Villa raised the possibility of an armed conflict with the United States, while he denied that that was his intent:

After such a clear-cut declaration, I wish to state that I have no motive for wishing a conflict between my country and the United States. For this reason, after all I have said, I decline any responsibility for future events, since the American people know perfectly well that I have always made superhuman efforts to give guarantees to each of their nationals who is living in our country. Let history assign responsibilities.[125]

What real substance was there to Villa's belief in the existence of a pact between Carranza and the United States? Had such a pact in fact ever been proposed by Wilson? Had it been hatched by members of his administration? Was it pure invention by Villa or his collaborators? Was it a scheme devised by U.S. business interests hoping to provoke U.S. intervention in Mexico? Was it a concoction of the German secret service, which hoped to distract U.S. attention from the European theater of war by forcing the United States to intervene in Mexico?

There is no evidence that Carranza ever signed such a pact. Of all the accusations Villa leveled against Carranza, only point 5 of the eight-point manifesto contained a grain of truth. Carranza had indeed agreed to examine U.S. claims for damages suffered during the revolution and was returning confiscated properties to their former owners. This, no doubt, was a major victory for the conservative forces. It was not, however, the result of U.S. pressure but of Carranza's own conservative convictions, to which he had held fast from the day he joined the revolution. His readiness to negotiate U.S. claims could scarcely justify the accusation that he had converted Mexico into a U.S. protectorate. Such a pact would have been entirely incompatible with his staunch nationalistic posture. Nor is there any proof that Woodrow Wilson proposed or contemplated such an agreement with any Mexican faction at any time during the revolution.

While Wilson never explained why he had recognized Carranza, three factors seem to have played a major role in his decision. The first was that it had become clear to him that Carranza had gained the upper hand and now dominated most of Mexico. The second factor was Wilson's desire to have peace and stability in his "backyard," so that the United States would be free to intervene in Europe if it decided to participate in World War I. Wilson's desire to "pacify" Mexico was intensified by the discovery of German plots to provoke war between Mexico and the United States. This idea was succinctly expressed by Secretary of State Lansing in his diary: "Looking at the general situation I have come to the following conclusion: Germany desires to keep up the turmoil in Mexico until the United States is forced to intervene; therefore we must not intervene.

Germany does not wish to have any one faction dominant in Mexico; therefore we must recognize one faction as dominant in Mexico.

When we recognize a faction as the government, Germany will undoubtedly seek to cause a quarrel between that government and ours; therefore we must avoid a quarrel, regardless of criticism and complaint in Congress and the press.

It comes down to this: our possible relations with Germany must be our first consideration; and all our intercourse with Mexico must be regulated accordingly.[126]

Finally, Carranza had given U.S. officials to understand that he was ready to carry out some reforms and at the same time would protect American property in Mexico. By contrast, Villa's increasing radicalism with respect to American properties made him less and less acceptable to Wilson and his administration.

While there is no evidence of a secret pact between Wilson and Carranza, Villa had some concrete reasons to assume such a pact had been signed. Most of the clauses contained in the secret pact that Villa had described, especially those most restrictive of Mexican sovereignty, had in fact been twice suggested to him, first by Silliman and then by Canova through Keedy.[127] Villa thus had reason to assume that if the United States had recognized Carranza, in spite of his frequent anti-American pronouncements and acts, this could only mean that he had accepted the kind of provisions that Villa had refused. Villa was strengthened in this conviction by a letter from Roque González Garza, his emissary to the international conference that Wilson was sponsoring to decide whom the United States and the Latin American states should grant recognition. "It was a great blow to me," Roque González Garza wrote Villa on October 29,

to see that you have always been miserably deceived; possibly this took place in good faith but you were always deceived. I was also deceived. . . . After arriving in Torreón . . . I was clearly told that, from the point of view of international political relations, our situation was very good; we were one step from recognition by the United States. . . . A few days went by and you received the clearest assurances that, from the point of view of international politics, everything was proceeding in your favor; that only a small effort on our part was required for the U.S. government to take us into consideration and that the original plan of the participants at the conference would be implemented with satisfactory results for us.

González Garza did not mention the name of the person who had given these assurances to Villa. That he left open the possibility of the intermediary's good faith indicates that he was probably referring to George Carothers, the U.S. special agent in the Villa camp, with whom Villa had had good relations.

Bitterly, González Garza then went on to describe how Villa's delegates at the Washington peace conference were treated by their American hosts:

Our situation was depressing. Everything turned out to have been a lie; we were very badly off; we were not even listened to. . . . October 9 arrived, and the participants at the conference decided to recognize Carranza. . . . This decision, communicated *ex abrupto* to the four winds, was an enormous humiliation for us, since we were delegates to the peace conference. We were not told anything and the solemn declarations made by Wilson at an earlier date were simply discarded. All historical precedents were ignored. Even common sense was not respected, since we had come to the conference ready to make peace but in an honorable way. This resolution was approved, and we suffered a great blow. . . . I have seen many injustices, but I have never thought that Carranza would triumph in the international political field after he played the comedy of being the most nationalistic of all Mexicans and after he provoked the United States two or three times. I do not entirely know what has been decided concretely, but I am convinced that something very dark has been agreed on; for I have no other explanation for the sudden change in U.S. policy against our group and in favor of Carranza.

"God knows how many secret pacts" Carranza had signed with the United States, González Garza exclaimed elsewhere in the letter.[128]

In his long proclamation, Villa said that Wilson had betrayed a de facto pact of honor between them. He listed what he had done for the Americans. He had protected both U.S. citizens and American property in Mexico. He stated that he had not wanted U.S. recognition of his forces, but that he at least expected U.S. neutrality. Wilson had betrayed Villa's trust, and betrayal was the offense he resented most.

Villa's proclamation marked a new turn in his policy. From now on, he would consider the United States as his main enemy.

In spite of the defeat that he had suffered in Agua Prieta, Villa was not yet ready to give up on his Sonoran campaign. When he heard that 2,000 men of Maytorena's army, mostly Yaqui Indians, would join him, he decided to attack the state capital, Hermosillo, which was defended by Diéguez's troops. Leaving 6,000 men under General José Rodriguez to contain Obregón's army and protect his rear from a surprise attack by the Carrancista garrison of Agua Prieta, he accordingly set out for Hermosillo. Again he used the strategy that had been so disastrous for him at Celaya, León, and Agua Prieta: frontal attacks by his cavalry against an enemy fortified in trenches and machine-gun nests behind barbed wire, and again he suffered a defeat. His troops began to give up hope, all the more so when a large part of Maytorena's troops defected to the Carrancistas soon after the Hermosillo debacle. The Carrancistas had succeeded in capturing a troop train carrying most of the wives and children of the Yaqui Indians, who now resolved to make a deal with them. Unlike Maytorena, Villa had no real claim on their loyalties.

At this point, Villa switched to a political strategy, banking on the patriotism and nationalism of Carranza's generals.

On November 22, 1915, after his defeat at Hermosillo, Villa sent a letter to the two commanders of Carranza's troops in that city, Manuel Diéguez and Angel Flores. In it he mentioned the eight provisions of the secret pact that he believed Carranza had signed with the United States, saying, "we are now in the hands of the North Americans; we have accepted a Yanqui protectorate." He added that Carranza had now converted the Conventionist movement (Villa and his allies) into the only group that defended the integrity and independence of Mexico, and, for this reason and in spite of all defeats, a Conventionist triumph was now inevitable. That the United States had allowed Carranza's troops to cross its territory meant that "when the United States wants or needs to, it can enter Mexican territory. Will you allow this?" Villa made no specific overtures to Diéguez and Flores; he only asked them to give their opinions on the charges. Probably, he hoped to enter into some kind of negotiations with Carranza's commanders. Although Flores did send a reply to Villa (the contents of which are not known), Diéguez declined to do even that, however.[129]

Villa's hopes that Carranza's generals and his soldiers would react to his charges of a secret Carranza–U.S. pact in the same way that many Mexicans, even those who were hostile to Huerta, reacted after the U.S. occupation of Veracruz, by offering to fight for Mexico, proved unfounded. He had given no proof of his accusations, and neither Carranza's generals nor his soldiers believed that the First Chief was capable of signing such a pact.

Thus, at the head of a defeated and demoralized army, Villa set out on the road back to Chihuahua. The changes that Raúl Madero had noted in Villa's character now took extreme form. The emotion that always triggered the strongest, most violent, and most brutal reaction in Villa was the sense of having been betrayed. He rarely, if at all, acknowledged that he bore any responsibility for his reverses. It was always someone who had betrayed him who bore the real guilt for his defeat. When some of the men who had been with him practically from the beginning began to turn against him, he pursued them with bloody single-mindedness. When he captured Mateo Almanza, who had fought at his side in the División del Norte and later defected to Gutiérrez, Villa ordered him hanged. A firing squad was too good for him, in Villa's opinion.

Villa's sense of betrayal reached a high point in Sonora. He vowed to execute Maytorena if he caught him. His sense of betrayal for the first time also encompassed the lower classes of society. As war-weariness took hold of an ever-increasing part of the civilian population, and as many of his common soldiers deserted, Villa began to feel that the common people too were repaying his generosity by betraying him. He had always been violent and vindictive, but his violence had spared the poor and the Americans. Now both became the targets of brutal reprisals.

Villa's anger vented itself on the men of a remote mountain village in Sonora, San Pedro de las Cuevas. As the civil war in Mexico progressed, government broke down, and many Mexican villages were ravaged both by advancing or retreating revolutionary armies and by gunslingers, deserters, and bandits. Frequently unable to rely on army or police for support, many villages organized militias of their own to repel marauders. When the inhabitants of San Pedro saw armed men riding toward their village, they thought they faced a renewed invasion by bandits, who had repeatedly plundered the town. The villagers hid in the surrounding hills, and when the armed men approached the village, they were met by a barrage of rifle fire. Several men died and, to their horror, the villagers discovered that their victims were not bandits but soldiers of the División del Norte. They tried to make amends and expressed their great regret to the commander of the Villista troops, Macario Bracamontes, himself a Sonoran. Bracamontes was sympathetic, and he had no intention of taking any reprisals, but the situation changed dramatically when Villa heard of the attack. Finally, he had found some of the traitors who had turned against him. When Bracamontes heard that Villa was approaching, he advised the villagers to flee into the hills.[130]

They did not heed his warning, and as soon as Villa entered the town, he ordered all its adult male inhabitants to be herded together. After keeping them in prison for one night, he ordered all of them to be shot. He made a few exceptions when a village priest kneeled before him and asked him to show pity for the villagers. At this point, Villa spared a few lives but told the priest never to show his face again. When the priest refused to heed this warning and came once again to ask Villa to show mercy to his parishioners, Villa pulled out his pistol and shot the priest himself. Sixty-nine villagers were shot by Villa, seven of whom managed to feign death and escape the massacre. This was the first time

Villa had ever vented his anger on the poor. The day after the massacre, he showed a profound sense of remorse and began to weep. Nevertheless, the massacre at San Pedro de las Cuevas would not be the last time that Villa struck viciously at the civilian population.

In many respects, Villa's return to Chihuahua from Sonora can be compared to Napoleon's return to Paris from his disastrous Russian campaign in 1812. Like Napoleon's failure in Russia, Villa's failure to conquer Sonora was followed by a disastrous retreat, although proportionately Villa lost fewer men than Napoleon had. Like Napoleon, Villa returned to a deeply divided, war-weary country, on which his enemies, stronger than ever, were advancing.

After crossing the inhospitable Sierra Madre mountains, where they were buffeted by icy winds and fed only by a few ears of corn gathered by the wayside, Villa and his men finally arrived in the Chihuahuan town of Madera. There, Villa learned that Carranza's troops had crossed the state's border and were advancing on its capital. Upon returning to Ciudad Chihuahua in the early morning hours of December 17, Villa soon realized how profoundly his situation had changed. Whenever he returned to that city on previous occasions, hundreds if not thousands of people had given him a delirious welcome at the railway station to express their support. This time not more than ten persons were present when his train arrived, all of them high officials of his administration and officers of his army. This tepid welcome and the fact that only 2,000 of the more than 10,000 men who had gone with him into Sonora were still with him left him undaunted, however. He had made plans for a new campaign, and the hope that buoyed him was that sooner or later the Mexican people would realize that Carranza had betrayed them to the Americans and part of Carranza's own army would rally to him. A few hours after arriving in Ciudad Chihuahua, he summoned all of his generals and leading officials to his home. There he expounded in great detail his plan for continuing the armed struggle against Carranza.[131]

Villa was convinced that he could still count on 15,000 men, whom he planned to deploy to defend the state of Chihuahua from the advancing Carrancistas. Like Napoleon after Waterloo, Villa failed to grasp the magnitude of his defeat after the disastrous end of his Sonoran campaign. He only did so when his generals, who in previous times would never have dared to contradict him, and would indeed have followed him to the end of the earth, began to speak up against him, one after another. Some said that their soldiers were simply not ready to fight, and that the idea that 15,000 men were still at Villa's disposal was an illusion. Others were even more open, saying that they saw no reason to continue fighting and to expose their men to death and mutilation any further. When he heard his officers turning against him, Villa grew more and more furious. Full of bitterness, he told them:

I have made this fight for my people. I thought you, my subordinate officers, were true to me, true to the cause, true to the people. I thought you were brave men and would die for your country. I think so no longer. I know I have been surrounded by traitors and thieves. Men who once supported me have deserted me. They clung to me only to rob me, and now they think I have nothing they can steal, and so they have left me. You yourselves are planning to leave me, to betray me and to go over to the enemy. I have called you here to tell you that I know your plans. I know what you intend to do. I am through with you. I will not lead a band of traitors. Now go when you will and do what you please, but remember that although everyone else may betray me, I will not betray myself. The time will come when you will need me as a leader again. When that hour strikes, I will not desert you. I will come to you and to others when you are fit to be led. I now release you from all loyalty to me and wash my hands of you, and whatever you do hereafter you will do on your own responsibility. I shall take my place in the ranks. I am no longer a general; I am simply a private.[132]

Villa may have hoped that his generals would react to this speech as they had only a year before when he had threatened to resign before the battle of Zacatecas and all of them had pleaded with him to resume his command. This time no such reaction ensued. Having realized that his situation was far more serious than he had initially thought, Villa interrupted the meeting to talk in private with his closest confidant, his long-time subordinate and military governor of Chihuahua, Fidel Avila. In private, Avila repeated to Villa what the generals had told him publicly: the army was demoralized, and the majority of the generals were unwilling to fight. He himself wanted to leave Mexico and go into exile in the United States, Avila said. At this point, Villa felt that he had no choice but to go along with the wishes of his generals. He allowed everyone who wanted to go home to do so and declared that he would make arrangements for the peaceful surrender of the two large cities his forces still held, the capital of Chihuahua and the border city of Ciudad Juárez.

Villa's will to continue fighting was nevertheless unbroken. Although he had officially dissolved the División del Norte, he persuaded 27 of his generals to meet with him a few days hence at the Hacienda de Bustillos.

A few minutes after the meeting ended, Villa went out on the balcony of the municipal palace of Chihuahua to address the people of that city one last time. A few minutes earlier, proclamations had been affixed to the walls of the city calling on the people to come to the main square to listen to Villa. Hundreds, if not thousands, came. Rumors were sweeping through the city. Some believed that Villa would now allow his soldiers to pillage and take whatever they wanted from the city's stores. Others believed that Villa had a hidden treasure that he would now divide among the population of the city.[133] Others simply hoped that the carnage would end and that Villa would tell them that he was going to surrender the city peacefully. This was in fact what he said, but he did so in a way that made it clear that the armed conflict in Chihuahua was by no means at an end. Villa did not acknowledge his defeat, although he did concede that he had made some unspecified mistakes. The gist of his speech, though, was that Carranza had betrayed Mexico to the Americans, and that his troops were simply the vanguard of a U.S. invasion. For that reason, Villa said, he was not willing to spend even one cartridge to fight against Mexicans but would reserve all of his forces to combat the Americans once they attempted to take over the country. He would go into the mountains, but when the people needed him he would return.

Villa's old companion and compadre Fidel Avila did not take Villa's promise to continue to fight very seriously. He thought that Villa had finally seen the light, and that after surrendering his army, he would be willing to into exile to the United States. Avila therefore sent a telegram to Woodrow Wilson stating: "Having done all that lay in our power and in a becoming form bent our efforts towards having Don Francisco Villa relinquish the supreme command of the Conventionist Army, we have at last prevailed on the said General Villa to agree to leave the country on the understanding that Your Excellency will extend full guarantees to him."[134] One day later the Wilson administration rejoined that it would "grant refuge to him [Villa] and will extend to him the full guarantees and immunity of a political refugee, provided he will in turn in his own behalf and that of such leaders as may remain on the other side of the border, extend full guarantees to all Americans in territory controlled by him and provided Americans reported detained at Chihuahua be immediately released."[135]

Rumors that Villa would cross the border seeped through to the United States, and some American entrepreneurs saw this as a golden opportunity to make money. Their proposals reflected the deep contempt in which they held the Mexican revolutionaries. Shortly after Wilson had recognized the Carranza administration, the *El Paso Herald* reported that "Cortney Riley Cooper, representative for Buffalo Bill's Wild West Show, was in El Paso today attempting to talk with General Villa. Mr. Cooper brings an offer for a job in the show for the general."[136]

It is not clear whether Villa commissioned Avila to make a request for asylum on his behalf or whether Avila did so on his own, presuming to speak for Villa. What is clear is that Villa had no intention of leaving Mexico. One day before Avila sent his message to Wilson, Villa sent a very different kind of message to the commanders of the Carrancista forces that were advancing on the state capital. To them, he proposed an alliance of all Mexicans against the United States. After reiterating his accusations against Carranza, he stated that because of this new development, his troops had stopped fighting the Carrancistas "so as not to shed Mexican blood." He proposed an alliance "that would unite all of us against the Yanqui, who because of racial antagonisms and commercial and economic ambitions is a natural enemy of our race and of all Latin countries." If such an alliance were concluded, he wrote, he would give up command of his troops.[137]

The letter never reached Carranza's commanders, since Silvestre Terrazas, whom Villa had commissioned to deliver it, was dissuaded by Villa's officers holding the front line against the Carrancistas from crossing into enemy territory. They told him that the Carrancistas were shooting anyone who attempted to enter the territory they controlled.

It is doubtful whether Villa's message, had it been delivered, would have made any difference to Carranza's commanders. In any case, the possible reply of these generals could not have dissuaded Villa from his firm determination not to leave Mexico, not to surrender to the Carrancistas, and to fight to the last. He did realize that he had no hope of keeping control of the state's largest cities, Chihuahua and Ciudad Juárez, and that a last-ditch resistance there would only alienate their inhabitants. He understood that he could not force the majority of his soldiers and officers to continue fighting against their will, and he agreed that those who wanted to lay down their arms could do so. But he refused to allow the men closest to him to surrender to the Carrancistas.

The last days of Villista control of Ciudad Chihuahua were by no means calm and quiet. Villa's increasing sense of betrayal manifested itself in killings. He personally executed one of his generals, Delgado, when he intercepted him in flight to the United States with a bag of money in his car. Fearing for his life, Villa's secretary Enrique Pérez Rul went into hiding, and squads of Villista soldiers scoured the city for him.[138]

Silvestre Terrazas himself escaped execution by a hair's breadth. As noted, Villa had sent him with a letter to the Carrancista commanders marching on Ciudad Chihuahua. Before Terrazas reached the last Villista outpost, however, Villa decided that he, too, was a traitor and a thief and ordered the commander of this last outpost, Cruz Domínguez, to shoot Terrazas as soon as he got there. Domínguez did not do so, however, and instead sent Silvestre Terrazas back to Ciudad Chihuahua. It is not clear whether this was his own decision or whether friends of the secretary's, above all Governor Fidel Avila, had intervened to save his life.

Villa subsequently sent Silvestre Terrazas on another mission to the Carrancistas, this time to El Paso, where he was to arrange for the surrender of Ciudad Juárez and Ciudad Chihuahua with the Carrancista consul. Having so narrowly escaped execution, Terrazas feared that Villa might once again decide to have him killed, and when Villa came to the station to bid him farewell, Terrazas assured him that he was his one civilian supporter who had always been loyal: "I say farewell to you and I can wholeheartedly say that I have been loyal to you until the end, something that many others who swore to be loyal to you until death had promised and then turned against you. You must know that I have been and am your friend."

"So am I," Villa replied. "We embraced each other and we said farewell for this life, each one taking a different road," Terrazas later wrote.[139] Terrazas would never turn against Villa. Some time after he left Mexico he published a Spanish language journal, *La Patria*. While the paper cannot be called Villista, it was clearly anti-Carrancista and on the whole tended to portray Villa in a more favorable light than most U.S. publications.

In his conversation with Silvestre Terrazas, Villa gave vague hints as to his future plans. When Terrazas suggested to Villa that he leave Mexico, perhaps in order to go to Europe to study new military techniques being utilized in World War I, Villa answered that he would instead retreat with a number of loyal men into the mountains, where he could easily elude hostile troops. "I shall never leave my country," he announced. "Here I shall stay and fight." He also intimated that he anticipated a possible revival of support and predicted that a conflict between Carranza and some of his generals, above all Obregón, would soon emerge and would create a new situation in Mexico. And he hinted at an even more important development that he expected. "Before six months have passed," he told Terrazas, "it will become clear that U.S. recognition of the Carranza faction was not disinterested but in fact depended on the same proposals that Washington had made as the price of granting me recognition, proposals that I rejected."[140] Villa did not reveal to Terrazas the meaning of his six-month timetable. That would only become clear three months later, when Villa attacked Columbus, New Mexico.

Villa was more forthright about his plans when he spoke to his 27 generals at the Hacienda de Bustillos, who had told him that they wanted to discuss the future of Villismo with him. He may have been impressed by the symbolic value of the setting. It was to the Hacienda de Bustillos that Madero had retreated in 1911 after his crushing defeat at Casas Grandes. Instead of demoralizing his troops, that defeat had led all the revolutionaries in the state of Chihuahua, including its main leaders Pascual Orozco and Pancho Villa, to rally to Madero. From that same hacienda, Madero had finally gone on to attain his great victory at Ciudad Juárez and to become president of Mexico. Villa may have asked himself whether this meeting with his generals would lead to a similar turnaround in his fortunes.

At the meeting, he told them that he was not ready to give up the fight and spoke of a coming conflict with the United States. One participant (whose statement was confirmed by no other) later told U.S. agents that Villa had suggested an immediate attack on El Paso by his troops.[141] But whatever hopes Villa may have had of the Bustillos conference quickly disappeared when 23 of the 27 generals made it clear that they had no wish to continue the civil war, and that they would either accept Carranza's offer of amnesty or seek refuge north of the border.

What must have discouraged Villa even more were negotiations going on at the same time in the border city of Ciudad Juárez between a number of his generals who had not come to Bustillos and Carrancista officials. An agreement was signed between these generals and representatives of Obregón and Carranza for the surrender of the bulk of the División del Norte.

Obregón agreed to grant amnesty to all of Villa's soldiers and officers and supporters, with the exception of five men: Villa himself, his brother Hipólito, and his three highest civilian officials, Miguel Díaz Lombardo, Luis de la Garza Cárdenas, and Francisco Escudero. All Villista soldiers would receive mustering-out pay, to which Obregón added ten dollars in gold, and they would have the choice of either joining Carranza's army or going home. Forty generals, 5,046 officers, and 11,128 soldiers thus laid down their arms.[142]

In the meantime, Villa, with a few hundred men, most of whom were part of his personal escort, the Dorados, faded away into the mountains. Neither the Carrancistas nor the U.S. government expected him ever to play any significant role in Mexico again.

Villa's decision to stay in Mexico and to fight on clearly differentiates him from most of the traditional caudillos in Latin American history. Men like Batista and Somoza, once their troops had been defeated, took millions from the state treasury and fled the country in order to lead the good life in exile. Villa could have done the same. In fact, he and his brothers seem to have brought $500,000 to the United States. "Villa and his brother Hipólito have $500,000 laid away for a rainy day, U.S. customs officials declare," the *El Paso Herald* reported in November 1915. "The money was stacked in piles of bills, with a small drawer filled with gold coins. None of the money was taken, as it was personal property."[143]

This was just a fraction of the money that Villa could have accumulated if money had been his main aim in life. He had controlled the finances of the División del Norte, and millions of dollars had passed through his hands. Even with the money that he had, he could have easily led a prosperous life as an exile. The United States and Cuba were both ready to grant him asylum, and other countries probably were too. This was the way traditional Latin American caudillos reacted once they were defeated. Instead, Villa chose to stay and wage five long and extremely harsh years of guerrilla warfare in Mexico, profoundly convinced that he was the only man who could prevent Mexico from becoming a protectorate of the United States. Instead of leading the good life, he seems to have used most of the money he had to pay his troops and to buy arms, either in the United States or on the black market in Mexico.

The Eclipse of Villismo: An Analysis

When the year 1914 ended, the vast majority of domestic and foreign observers of the Mexican situation were convinced that Villa's final victory was but a matter of time. Only a year later, however, Villa was a hunted fugitive, hiding out somewhere in the mountains of Chihuahua with a few hundred men. The reasons for this reversal of fortune generated much controversy during the Mexican Revolution and continue to do so today.

For the victorious Carrancistas, the answer was clear and simple: in military terms, Villa lacked the strategic acumen of Obregón, and in political terms, he represented a coalition basically made up of reactionaries, personified by Angeles, and bandits, personified by Villa himself, both secretly supported by Wall Street. In addition, the Carrancistas asserted that the Conventionist faction had lost support because it could offer nothing similar to the radical laws that Carranza had begun enacting at the beginning of 1915.

The explanations by Villistas and ex-Villistas for their defeat are less uniform. Villa himself was not given to offering lengthy analyses. In fact, he despised intellectuals who did so. Only three times did he refer to the causes of his defeat. After the first battle of Celaya, he said that his retreat had been basically owing to lack of ammunition. He never explained why, in view of this problem, he had nonetheless engaged Obregón in battle. In an interview he gave to the *El Paso Times*, he referred to errors he had committed, but he never specified what they were.[144] In his manifesto at Naco in November 1915, he dealt for the first and only time, although in a summary manner, with the reasons that led to all the reverses his forces had suffered, claiming that the turning point had come when Eulalio Gutiérrez and his supporters had rebelled against him. He never explained how and why Gutiérrez, whose support was limited, and who at most controlled about 10,000 men, exercised such influence on the destinies of the Mexican Revolution. In addition, he blamed the Americans and those of his generals who had deserted him for his defeat. With regard to the role of the United States, he referred only to the support it had given Carranza in his Sonoran campaign and made no mention of the fact that the Wilson administration had turned Veracruz over to Carranza. There was no self-criticism in Villa's assessment, and he made no mention of the strategic and tactical blunders he had committed in his battles with Obregón.

Enrique Pérez Rul, who was Villa's secretary until the end of the Sonoran campaign, and who then defected from Villismo, published a book under the pseudonym of Juvenal entitled *¿Quién es Francisco Villa?* In it the author is sharply critical of both Carranza and Villa. Pérez Rul, too, believed that Gutiérrez's defection had been the turning point in Villa's fortunes, and he is far more explicit about how Gutiérrez had harmed the División del Norte. He felt that dealing with Gutiérrez had distracted Villa from immediately taking on Obregón, thus giving the Sonoran general a breathing spell in which to organize and mobilize his army.

Angeles, who wrote many articles while in exile in the United States, never publicly assessed the causes for the defeat of the Convention. The likely reason for this attitude is that Angeles did not want to break completely with Villa, whom he would rejoin in 1918. In later years, Angeles's closest collaborator, and representative at the Revolutionary Convention, Federico Cervantes, gave a detailed assessment that in all probability reflected Angeles's views.[145] Cervantes felt that Villa's greatest mistake had been not heeding the advice of his brilliant subordinate. Villa did not listen when Angeles advised him to march on Veracruz immediately after capturing Mexico City, and he thus failed to defeat the Carrancistas while they were still weak and demoralized after the majority of the Convention had turned against them. In the same vein, Cervantes blames Villa for failing to listen to Angeles's advice not to engage Obregón at Celaya but to force him to march further north until his lines of communication had become so extended that Villa could easily cut him off from his supplies of ammunition and arms from Veracruz. According to Cervantes, Villa did not listen to Angeles's strong objection to confronting the Carrancistas at León either, when Angeles had again urged Villa to retreat northward until he could reorganize his forces.

The few times that Angeles himself dealt with the problem of the Conventionist defeat, he did so in political rather than in military terms. In an article he published in the United States, Angeles tried to assess the reason for "the errors of the 1913 revolution." Above all, Angeles blamed the "enemies" of the revolution, who had prevented its peaceful development by toppling and then assassinating the one man who could have led Mexico along the path of democratic reform, Francisco Madero. Another reason was the tragedy that the leader of the revolution (i.e., Carranza) was "a legitimate son of the Porfirian dictatorship who wanted above all to establish a despotic rule."[146] The third reason that Angeles cited was "the lack of culture of the lower classes of society," resulting in "the confiscation of property," which destroyed much of the wealth of Mexico and harmed the prestige and legitimacy of the revolutionary cause.[147] Without naming him, Angeles was certainly referring here to Villa. In private talks, he criticized Villa's "monomania of killing."[148]

Federico González Garza too saw Villa's attitude to expropriation as one of the keys to explaining his defeat, but he explained this in a different way from Angeles. Whereas Angeles felt that expropriation was per se harmful to the revolutionary cause, Federico González Garza believed that it was perfectly justified and had not gone far enough. "Since Huerta was ousted," he wrote his brother Roque in September 1915,

we have to agree, that from a practical point of view, if we had known how to conduct an orderly confiscation subject to strict rules, and if we had had a distribution of land guided by an intelligent plan and without violence, we would by now have created new interests that would have helped to sustain the new regime.

This is how the Constitutional Assembly proceeded during the first period of the French Revolution, seizing the land of the nobles and immediately redistributing it, and this constituted the basis for the resistance of the republican regime. Despite all the horrors that accompanied the Convention, neither the Directory nor the suc-ceeding Consulate dared to undo the work of the First Assembly; they did not dare to decree the restitution of the confiscated estates. Napoleon, himself converted a while later into a monarch, understood that in order to secure his power he could not meddle with the republicans' work, but on the contrary he had to ratify, confirm, and incorporate into laws the institutions that had been created and implemented dur-ing the violent period of the revolution. If we want to create a solid structure we must not forget the lessons of history.[149]

There is little disagreement among historians today that one of the main causes of Villa's military defeat was his lack of strategic and tactical ability on a par with Obregón's. The explanations given for this, however, are very different. Some view it in purely personal terms: Villa's conceit and lack of education are advanced as the main reasons why he was unable to understand, despite repeated fiascoes, that his strategy of frontal cavalry attacks against an enemy fortified in trenches had no chance of success. Others attribute the defeat of both Villa and Zapata basically to peasant localism: it was his limited regional view that pre-vented Villa from attacking Carranza in Veracruz and led him instead to fortify Torreón, which was one of the keys to control of the north.[150] For the same rea-son, Zapata was hesitant about taking large-scale military action outside of his native Morelos.

What is far more controversial today is whether Villa's defeat can be attrib-uted purely to military factors or should be ascribed to political factors as well. The effects of a military defeat to a large degree depend on other factors, above all of a political and social nature. In the nineteenth century, during the civil wars in Mexico between Liberals and Conservatives from 1857 to 1861, the Con-servatives had the better generals, won most battles, and yet lost in the end. The Liberals had a far greater degree of popular support and more resources at their disposal.

Similarly, in 1911, Madero suffered a crushing defeat at Casas Grandes, yet it had no effect on the revolution, which a few weeks later toppled Porfirio Díaz. Except in Chihuahua and adjacent areas, however, Villa's movement never re-covered from its military defeats.

Some have attributed Villa's defeats to loss of popular support because of the atrocities and killings he and his army committed. There is no evidence to indi-cate that Villa's troops were any more violent toward the civilian population than Carranza's. In fact, until the Sonoran campaign, Villista violence seems never to have been directed against the lower classes of society. By all accounts, even after his defeats at Celaya and León, Villa was still far more popular among Mexico's lower classes than Carranza or any of his generals. That popularity did not, how-ever, translate into the kind of massive guerrilla uprisings that Madero's popu-larity had generated all over Mexico in 1911. There is no single explanation for this phenomenon.

One important factor that made it difficult for Villa to translate his popularity into active support was that, unlike both the Zapatistas and the Carrancistas, he had not set up any political organizations. In Zapata's territory, power rested to a large degree with village councils, while the Carrancistas worked with trade unions and, in some parts of Mexico, such as Yucatán, sent political agitators to the large haciendas. Nothing similar took place in the regions controlled by the División del Norte, where absolute power rested with the military.

Villa's greatest weakness was doubtless the one that Federico González Garza identified: his failure to carry out far-reaching agrarian reform. This failure was partly linked to Villa's alliance with and later increasing dependence on the United States.

The effects of that alliance were paradoxical. On the one hand, his ability to buy arms in the United States allowed him in the course of a few months to do what other guerrilla movements in the world could only do after years of fighting: transform his guerrilla forces into a regular army. On the other hand, that very alliance with the United States made it more and more difficult for Villa to carry out any massive agrarian reform. This was both because Villa needed the revenue from the confiscated estates to finance his arms purchases in the United States and because Americans backed his paper money. The U.S. administration and American companies did not complacently opt to accept Villista currency. Rather, since the Wilson administration seemed to be backing Villa, American companies became convinced that he would be the victor in Mexico's civil war and thus began to buy up large amounts of his currency in order to pay eventual taxes with it and to redeem it later at a higher value when Villa had triumphed. Suddenly, Villa had come into possession of Aladdin's lamp—all he had to do was print money, and the Americans and, as a result, Mexicans too would accept it. Why divide up land and cause dissension within his movement and weaken his army if he could attain an even greater degree of popularity by simply distributing the paper money he printed? As long as this expedient worked, it was a highly effective way of gaining support and popularity. When, after his defeat, his paper money depreciated to nothing, his support dwindled and disillusion set in. Had he paid both his soldiers and his civilian supporters with land instead of with paper money, the quality of his support might have been very different, and the country people in the former Villista territories might have fought to keep their lands with the same energy as Zapata's supporters did in Morelos.

The transformation of his army from a motley array of guerrillas into a regular fighting force was the key to both Villa's success and his failure. Without a professional army, which the División del Norte was slowly becoming, he could not have defeated Huerta's regular forces. But a professional army had to be paid, and when Villa did not have the money to do so, many of his soldiers either deserted or switched sides. Once the United States swung against him, his ability to maintain a regular army disappeared.

PART THREE

From National Leader to Guerrilla Leader

CHAPTER FOURTEEN

Villa's Two-Front War with Carranza and the United States

Carranza in Power

With the surrender of most of what had once been the powerful División del Norte, Carranza had every reason to feel optimistic. He had defeated the only army that had for a time seemed powerful enough to challenge his grasp on national power. A reluctant U.S. president had been forced to grant him recognition. This meant that his faction would now be the only one that could secure arms and supplies in the United States. American banks and the U.S. government were contemplating the possibility of granting a large loan to his faction. American mining companies were planning to resume work in Mexico. As a result of the wartime boom in the United States, Mexico's raw materials, particularly oil and henequen, had sharply risen in price, and Carranza hoped that this would increase the revenues of his government. He now had reason to feel that he could implement the main points of his agenda. The first had been to secure the independence of Mexico. In that respect the country seemed to be better off than at any time since the outbreak of the revolution. There had been no foreign troops in the country since the U.S. evacuation of Veracruz. The European powers were embroiled in World War I and incapable, even if they had wanted to, of intervening militarily in Mexico. The United States too was getting more and more involved in events in Europe and thus less likely to exercise any military pressure on Mexico. In addition, in view of Carranza's victory, the strategy that Woodrow Wilson's administration had used before—attempting to play off one faction against the other—had ceased to be viable.

Restoring peace to Mexico also seemed a distinct possibility even though the country was still far from pacified. Zapata still controlled Morelos, and local Conventionist leaders such as the Cedillo brothers in San Luis Potosí and Calixto Contreras in Durango continued to fight in their native regions. Some conservatives, such as Peláez in the oil region and a former federal officer, Esteban Cantú, still refused to recognize the First Chief's authority. In Mexico's southeast, hacendado-led or localist factions attempted to maintain their military independence. Nevertheless, Carranza probably assumed that with the support of the United States, his victorious army could soon crush these forces.

Carranza's third priority was economic recovery, which he hoped to achieve with the help of substantial loans from American banks. Carranza's hopes of successfully implementing his strategy were dealt a decisive if not entirely fatal blow when on March 8, 1916, Pancho Villa, with 500 men, attacked the town of Columbus, New Mexico. That attack would stretch Carranza's relations with the United States to the breaking point, prevent him from gaining access to either U.S. money or U.S. arms, and shatter his hopes for a quick economic recovery, for pacifying the country, and for reducing the power and size of his own military. It would give a new lease on life to the popular forces fighting Carranza, above all Emiliano Zapata's Liberating Army of the South, and lead to an astonishing revival of Villa, which no one had expected once his mighty División del Norte surrendered. Villa's at least partial recovery from what had seemed a total defeat was to a large degree owing to the policies that the Carrancistas implemented in Chihuahua.

Carrancista Chihuahua

As Carranza's troops surged into Chihuahua and thousands of former Villistas laid down their arms and surrendered, Carranza was faced with the problem of how to administer and pacify the state that had been the hotbed of the Mexican Revolution. Its revolutionary forces had brought down Díaz, had played a decisive role in the defeat of Huerta, and had nearly toppled Carranza himself. There were two options for pacification that Carranza had rejected. One was to carry out the kind of land reform for which so many Chihuahuans had fought from 1910 onward, and that Villa had promised them. The other was to implement the kind of free elections in the state that Madero had allowed in 1911, which would have given the Chihuahuans the possibility of choosing their own leader. There would be no land reform, years would pass before elections were held in Chihuahua, and when they finally took place, they were followed by accusations of fraud and corruption. The two options that Carranza considered were either to treat Chihuahua as an occupied territory and rule it through outside politicians, supported by an army equally composed of outsiders, or to allow his Chihuahuan supporters to administer the state.

Carrancista policies in Chihuahua between 1915 and 1920 vacillated constantly between these two options, and the further fate of Villismo and of revolutionary movements in the state largely hinged on the policy the Carrancistas finally adopted.

A problem with the second option, that of turning power over to local supporters, was that until the collapse of Villismo, there had been very few Carrancistas in Chihuahua. The vast majority of the population had supported Villa. While many former Villistas were now quite willing to cooperate with Carranza, he did not trust them and was unwilling to appoint them to important political or military positions, although he did accept former Villista soldiers and officers into his army. Carranza was equally distrustful of the old oligarchy—the main social and political groups in the state that opposed Villa—above all, the Terrazas clan and its supporters. He distrusted them, both because they had supported Huerta and because rumors were reaching him that Creel hoped to provoke a U.S. intervention in Mexico.[1]

Nevertheless, after some time, Carranza attempted to make his peace with the oligarchy by restoring their properties, although not allowing them to regain political control of the state. Carranza was equally distrustful of the Orozquistas, who constituted the bulk of Villa's local opponents. Most of them had supported Huerta, and some had rallied to Zapata. Others had gone into exile to the United States. Eventually, Carranza would also make his peace with many of them, but he hesitated about turning over important political offices to former Orozquistas. At the time Villa and Carranza split, only a small number of Chihuahuan revolutionaries rallied to the cause of the First Chief. For example, Manuel Chao, the former schoolteacher on whom Carranza had pinned his hopes, whom he imposed on Villa as governor of Chihuahua in 1914, and whom he had saved from being executed by Villa, proved unexpectedly loyal to Villa and had repudiated the First Chief.

The only significant Chihuahuan revolutionaries who sided with Carranza at the time of the split with Villa in 1914 were the Herreras and their supporters in the Parral region of southern Chihuahua. Their number was relatively small, their support was only local in nature, and their most prestigious leader, Maclovio Herrera, who had participated in the Madero revolution and had the reputation of being one of Villa's bravest commanders, had been killed and replaced by a less well known brother, Luis Herrera. Perhaps because of the latter's limited local support, or perhaps because he was, as U.S. generals who came into contact with him noted, an illiterate,[2] Carranza was never willing to entrust the state to him. The man whom Carranza finally chose to administer Chihuahua, Ignacio Enríquez Jr., was, because of his social origins, his antecedents, and his ideology, close to the First Chief's heart. Enríquez belonged to a species that, unlike the rest of northern Mexico, was extremely rare in Chihuahua: he was a revolutionary of upper-class origins.

During the governorship of Miguel Ahumada from 1892 to 1903, Enríquez's father had occupied one of the most important political offices in Chihuahua. He had been jefe político of the Iturbide district, which included the state's largest city, Ciudad Juárez. His term ended when Terrazas once more became governor of the state in 1903. It is not clear whether this indicated any strong antagonism between the two men, but that might well have been the case, since Ignacio Enríquez Sr. became mayor of Ciudad Juárez in 1912 under the revolutionary administration of Abraham González and resigned from office as soon as Huerta carried out his coup.

Ignacio Enríquez Jr. did not participate in the Madero revolution. A few months before it began, he had returned to Chihuahua after completing a degree in agronomy at the University of Illinois. In spite of his youth, he had become administrator of the Hacienda del Rubio, which belonged to the Zuloagas, one of the wealthiest families in the state. The young Enríquez's involvement in politics began in 1912, when he joined the state militia fighting Orozco.

Soon after Huerta's coup, Ignacio Enríquez Jr. decided to take up arms against the Mexican dictator. Unlike all the other Chihuahuan revolutionaries, he and a number of men who joined him did not choose to fight in their native state, but instead went to Sonora, where on March 28, 1913, Enríquez became an officer in Obregón's Army of the Northwest. It is not clear what prompted his decision to go to Sonora. Did he find the Chihuahuan revolutionaries too radical? Or was he attracted to Sonora because a regular army already existed there, while only isolated guerrilla groups were fighting in Chihuahua? In any case, he soon established close links to Carranza and to Obregón, who rapidly promoted him, and to whom Enríquez would remain loyal until Obregón's death. Enríquez served on Carranza's bodyguard when he established his headquarters in Chihuahua, and the First Chief was obviously much taken with the young revolutionary, for he entrusted him with a series of important missions. For a time, he was Mexican consul in New York, and his responsibilities went far beyond the usual tasks of a consul; he was one of Carranza's arms buyers in the United States.[3]

One of the most important functions to which Carranza appointed Enríquez was that of head of one of the Red Battalions of workers that the Carrancistas had succeeded in mobilizing in order to fight the Revolutionary Convention. This command certainly played a great role in teaching him how to deal with the lower classes of society, but it did not turn him into a radical. His agenda—he became the first Carrancista governor of Chihuahua in January 1916—was a very conservative one. His first and most significant action as governor was to return a large number of urban properties and haciendas confiscated by Villa to their former owners. What probably deterred him from returning all of the oligarchy's property was Carranza's decision to take personal charge of this process and not to allow any governors to proceed on their own.[4]

Enríquez's conservative agenda was reflected in another way. While other Carrancista governors set up agrarian commissions to accept petitions for land from peasants, although very little land was in fact distributed, Enríquez did not even make a gesture in that direction. No agrarian commission was established in Chihuahua. He thus made it clear in 1916 that he had no intention of implementing the promises that Carranza had made in his agrarian decree of January 1915. He was equally conservative in his dealings with industrial workers and showed no sympathy at all for the union men he had only a short time before led into battle. He attempted to limit the activities of labor organizers of the same Casa del Obrero Mundial whose members had joined the Red Battalions. He proudly wrote Carranza that as commander of that battalion, he had learned how to control the workers, and he would do so either by reasoning with them or by force.[5]

It was nevertheless clear to Enríquez that such conservative measures alone could not win him the adherents he needed in order to govern the state. He complained to Carranza that he could not find sufficient people willing to assume political office in the state or to become administrators of the confiscated properties.[6] He attributed this less to lack of popular support than to fear of Villista reprisals. This situation may have induced Enríquez to take the one measure that, in spite of his social conservatism and lack of willingness to carry out any reform, would ensure him a large measure of popular support in the state and make him into a formidable opponent of Villa's. This was the decision to give arms to many of Chihuahua's villagers. Enríquez was one of the founders of an institution that was to play an important role in many parts of Mexico and a decisive one in Chihuahua: the *defensas sociales* (local militias).[7]

Like Carranza, Enríquez pinned his hopes on economic recovery as the primary means of pacification. By returning lands to hacendados, and by not threatening their status with the establishment of an agrarian commission, Enríquez hoped to persuade them to resume production. By preventing radical labor organizers from influencing labor, he hoped to induce American mine owners to resume operation of the mines. Both Carranza and Enríquez obviously based their hopes on the pacification of Chihuahua, on the expectation that if the new administration could bring about economic recovery and peace, the Chihuahuans, weary of five years of fighting, would give up the fight even though none of the reforms and social changes for which they had fought would be implemented. Whatever the validity of these assumptions, they could never be tested, for the Carrancistas failed to restore the economy and to reestablish peace. Economic recovery proved a more complex and long-range affair than they had assumed. And they fatally underestimated the potential that Pancho Villa still represented.

The thousands of Villista veterans who laid down their arms and returned home found that, except for an amnesty, the new Carrancista administration had very little to give them. They would not receive the land that many had expected to secure as a reward for their services in the División del Norte. Finding work on the large estates was more difficult than ever before, because many of the cattle herds that had been the backbone of ranching in Chihuahua had been depleted by years of revolution. Most mines were still closed, as were many industrial plants. In the public sector—that is, the state bureaucracy and the railroads—erstwhile Villistas were dismissed and replaced by Carrancistas, frequently from other parts of the country.

The one form of "employment" that the new Carranza administration held out for the veterans of the División del Norte was to enroll in the Carrancista army. On the whole, they soon discovered that this was an extremely unattractive option. The pay was low and irregular, and when Villa took to the field again, the risks associated with service in the Carrancista army were enormous. Not only would they have to fight their former leader, whose military capacities they still respected, but they knew that if they were captured, they would immediately be shot as deserters, and reprisals might be taken against their families.

For some former Villistas, as well as for the Carrancista administration, the United States provided a safety valve. The U.S. economy was booming as a result of World War I, and thousands of Mexicans found employment north of the border. That option became more problematic after the United States entered the war in April 1917, when many immigrant Mexican workers suddenly found themselves subject to the draft. At that point, many preferred to return to Mexico in spite of the economic distress south of the border.

Unemployment, which had been absent during Villista rule, was but one of the economic problems Chihuahuans now had to face. Even for those who were employed or who owned businesses or land of their own, Carrancismo brought great economic difficulties. They had hoped that the new administration would replace Villa's now worthless paper money with a stable currency. This did not occur. Carranza too had printed millions in paper money, and his currency was constantly losing value and was rejected by the mass of the population.

Carrancista policies in Chihuahua were one basis for an astounding resurgence of Villismo. The second basis was Villa's attack on Columbus, New Mexico, and the U.S. intervention in Chihuahua that it provoked.

A New Direction for Villismo

Pancho Villa was the main reason Carrancista pacification failed in Chihuahua. At the end of 1915, after Villa's disastrous Sonoran campaign, there seems to have been a widespread consensus among American observers, the Carrancista leadership, and most of Villa's generals that the former head of the División del Norte was finished in military terms.[8] Some U.S. officials believed that Villa would seek asylum in the United States. Governor Enríquez, who expressed no such view, felt that the forces under Villa's command who were roaming through Chihuahua were so insignificant that he asked Carranza for only 2,000 men for the task of containing the Villistas.[9] This was a vast underestimation of the potential for destruction that Villa represented. Within only a few months, more than 10,000 Americans and several thousand Carrancista soldiers would roam through Chihuahua, unable to capture Villa or to prevent his dramatic resurgence; by the end of 1916, Villa would again control a substantial portion of the state.

Villa's dissolution of the División del Norte by no means signified that he was now ready to give up fighting and to accept defeat. What he realized was that maintaining a regular army and waging regular warfare had by now become impossible for him. His men were demoralized, and he had neither the money nor the means to acquire arms and ammunition from across the border to sustain such an army. As he had implied in his last conversation with Silvestre Terrazas, he would now switch to guerrilla warfare. For this purpose, he initially only needed a small number of men. He was confident, as his actions in the future were to show, that if he should ever need his former soldiers again, he would be able to enlist them, either voluntarily or involuntarily, even though they had accepted an amnesty from Carranza. What he did hope was that the majority of his generals would now join him in the guerrilla war he was planning against both the Carrancistas and the Americans. When those hopes were frustrated at the Bustillos conference, Villa retreated into the mountains of western Chihuahua.

His arrival there must have been one of the saddest days of his life. Only a few hundred followers, mainly consisting of his elite guard of Dorados, were left of an army that had once encompassed between 30,000 and 50,000 men. All the trappings of regular warfare that had so strongly fascinated Villa—the troop trains, the sanitary trains, the artillery—were gone. Practically all of his generals had left him. After years of warfare that had ended in defeat, his popularity among the civilian population of Chihuahua had reached an all-time low. The possibility of securing arms in the United States was smaller than ever before, not only because of the U.S. arms embargo but even more because the resources he had used in earlier years to pay for those arms—the cattle from expropriated haciendas and the cotton of the Laguna area—had been depleted. In spite of this situation, Villa never even considered the possibility of giving up and going to the United States to accept the asylum that Woodrow Wilson had promised him. One important reason for Villa's decision was that he was not entirely without resources. He had hidden large caches of arms and ammunition in different remote parts of Chihuahua.

Although Villa had only a few hundred men, he knew that these men, mainly Dorados, were fanatically loyal to him. The same was true of the officers who now replaced the former generals of the División del Norte who had left him. These new officers tended to be young men, mainly Dorados who had risen from the ranks. With perhaps one exception, none of them had been a popular leader when the revolution broke out. The brothers Martín and Pablo López had joined Villa as plain soldiers but rapidly rose to be officers, thanks to their loyalty and their courage. The same seems to have been the case with Baudelio Uribe, while Nicolás Fernández, a former hacienda administrator, seems to have been a crony of Villa's from prerevolutionary days. One of the few exceptions to this rule was Candelario Cervantes. Cervantes had led over 100 men from his native village, Namiquipa, in February 1913 in their revolt against the dictatorship of Huerta. The loyalty to Villa that these men manifested and their legendary audacity (this was especially the case with Martín López) were matched by the ruthlessness and brutality they manifested toward their opponents and at times toward the civilian population. In 1916, one of Villa's own commanders protested against the depredations that Martín López was committing against the civilian population.[10] Baudelio Uribe was known for cutting off the ears of Carrancista prisoners, while Cervantes would force inhabitants of his own village, impressed into Villa's army against their will, to participate in Villa's attack on Columbus, New Mexico.

Questions about the aims that Villa pursued at this point in his life and the motivations that drove him constitute one of the most controversial issues in Mexican historiography, in part because Villa, although he lived for seven more years, would never acknowledge his actions at the time nor give any explanation for them. In the eyes of many Mexican historians, as well as contemporary Mexican and American observers, he had become completely irrational, driven only by his blind hatred for the Americans, who he felt had betrayed him and caused his defeat.

In the eyes of others, he had merely reverted to what he had always been: a bandit. He was driven by his desire for loot and gold and would do whatever he was paid to do. If someone paid him to cross the border and to attack Americans, he would do so, without the least regard for what this might entail for Mexico. In the eyes of a number of historians, the "someone" in question was the German secret service. For some contemporary observers, it was American business interests seeking to provoke U.S. intervention in Mexico.[11]

A third hypothesis, put forward by the Chihuahuan historian Francisco Almada, paints a picture of Villa as a kind of cornered beast. According to Almada, Villa had intended to seek political asylum in the United States, but was deterred from doing so when he learned that he would be prosecuted for the murder of William Benton (the British hacendado Villa or one of his men had killed in 1914).[12] At this point he had no choice but to remain in Mexico and to fight, and he would now take his revenge on the United States.

A fourth hypothesis, proposed by the historian Alberto Calzadíaz Barrera, is that Villa's main purpose in attacking Columbus was to punish an American merchant named Sam Ravel, to whom Villa had given a large amount of money to purchase arms, and who had refused to deliver these arms to Villa.[13]

In fact, the reasons for the actions Villa took in 1916 seem to have been far more complex than these theories suggest. There are two contemporary documents that, taken together, give an idea of what Villa's aims and motivations were.

The first of these documents is a letter that Villa wrote to Zapata on January 8, only a few days after leaving the hacienda of Bustillos. After describing his plans for the Sonoran campaign, he essentially blamed the Wilson administration for its failure. By allowing several thousand Carranza soldiers to cross U.S. territory to reinforce the Carrancistas at Agua Prieta, Wilson had been directly responsible for the defeat Villa incurred there. He wrote Zapata that his retreat from Sonora was provoked when the most important city he controlled in Chihuahua, Ciudad Juárez, was threatened by Carrancista troops whom the Americans had allowed to march into that city from the U.S. side of the border. The explanation that he gave for this was the secret pact that the U.S. government had allegedly signed with Carranza (see chapter 13). He had no choice but to remain in Mexico and to fight, and he would now take his revenge on the United States.

Villa concluded the letter by revealing his plans for the future and by asking Zapata to support them:

From the foregoing you will see that the sale of this country is complete, and under these circumstances, for reasons stated previously, we have decided not to fire a bullet more against Mexicans, our brothers, and to prepare and organize ourselves to attack the Americans in their own dens and make them know that Mexico is a land for the free and a tomb for thrones, crowns, and traitors.

With the aim of informing the people of the situation and in order to organize and recruit the greatest possible number of men with the aforementioned aim, I have divided my army into guerrilla bands, and each chief will go to that part of the country he considers appropriate for a period of six months. That is the time period we have set to meet in the state of Chihuahua with all the forces we shall have recruited in the country to carry out the movement that will unite all Mexicans.

The move we have to make to the United States can only be accomplished through the north, as we do not have any ships. I beg you to tell me if you agree to come here with all your troops, and on what date, so that I may have the pleasure of going personally to meet you and together start the work of reconstruction and improvement of Mexico, punishing our eternal enemy, the one that has always been encouraging hatred and provoking difficulties and quarrels among our race.[14]

In several ways, this letter is puzzling. Taken by itself, it would tend to confirm the hypothesis that Villa had become irrational, driven mainly by blind hatred for the Americans, and had resolved to take his revenge upon them whatever the costs to Mexico. Nowhere in his letter does Villa explain to Zapata what he expected to gain from an attack on the United States, a country vastly superior in resources and military strength to Mexico. Did he seriously expect Zapata, who had always been reluctant to send his troops out of Morelos and had not even done so when he could have interrupted Obregón's communications before the battle of Celaya, to suddenly lead his army hundreds or thousands of miles out of his native state through Carranza-controlled territory to attack the United States?

What is equally puzzling is Villa's time frame. Within a few weeks of writing the letter, he would lead a raid into Columbus, New Mexico, yet in his letter to Zapata he speaks of a delay of at least six months until sufficient men could be mobilized and rallied to attack the United States. Villa's real aims and purposes at this time become clearer in an interview given a few months later by one of his most important lieutenants, Pablo López, to an Irish correspondent after having been captured by the Carrancistas and shortly before he was executed:

My master, Don Pancho Villa, was continually telling us that since the gringos had given him the double-cross he meant not only to get back at them, but to try and waken our country to the danger that was very close to it.

Don Pancho was convinced that the gringos were too cowardly to fight us, or to try and win our country by force of arms. He said they would keep pitting one faction against another until we were all killed off, and our exhausted country would fall like a ripe pear into their eager hands. Don Pancho also told us that Carranza was selling our northern states to the gringos to get money to keep himself in power. He said he wanted to make some attempt to get intervention from the gringos before they were ready and while we still had time to become a united nation.[15]

The key words here are, "He [Villa] said he wanted to make some attempt to get intervention from the gringos before they were ready and while we still had time to become a united nation." What Villa wanted and finally got was a limited U.S. intervention similar to the one at Veracruz. There is little doubt that when Villa formulated his project, the experience of the U.S. landing in Veracruz was very much on his mind. After the Americans had landed in Mexico's eastern port city, thousands of Mexicans had volunteered to fight against the foreign invaders in the ranks of Huerta's army, even though Huerta was unpopular and had suffered one defeat after another. At that time, Carranza had been forced to issue a strongly worded anti-American declaration, which had led to the U.S. arms embargo against him by the Americans. The one obvious danger that an attack on the United States by Villa entailed was that the Americans might decide to occupy all of Mexico. Villa expressed the conviction to López that they would not do so. He had good reasons for his optimism. The Americans had not followed their attack on Veracruz by attempting to occupy all of Mexico. Wilson had not possessed the means to do so, and Villa was convinced, as his words to López implied, that this situation had not changed. He probably knew that the regular U.S. Army had no more than 50,000 men, and that in view of World War I, the United States was extremely reticent to commit a major portion its forces to Mexico. Both of these facts were public knowledge at a time when Villa still had many agents and representatives in the United States. Knowing Chihuahua as he did, he was probably convinced that he could easily elude any American pursuit.

One of the most hotly debated issues concerning Villa's attack on the United States is what role, if any, outside forces played in provoking it. In this respect, there are two main hypotheses, both falling into the category of conspiracy theories.

The first of these theories, widely accepted at the time of Villa's Columbus attack, was that American businessmen interested in provoking U.S. intervention in Mexico had paid Villa to attack Columbus. Even John Reed seems to have accepted it.[16] There is little doubt that a number of Americans with interests in Mexico were delighted when Villa attacked Columbus and hoped that Wilson would now be forced to intervene in Mexico and occupy large parts of the country. There is, however, no evidence for such a conspiracy, and only one author has attempted to reconstruct it. Bill McGaw believes that the Associated Press correspondent George Seese, who came to Columbus a few days before Villa, was in fact the bagman for the American interests that had organized Villa's attack.[17] McGaw has produced no tangible evidence to support this claim, however, and U.S. authorities have never expressed the least suspicion about Seese's motives.

The second set of conspiracy theories centers around Germany. Here the situation is more complex, for a German conspiracy to provoke Villa into an attack on the United States did in fact exist. In May 1915, Felíx Sommerfeld, long a munitions buyer for Villa and representative in the United States for Villa, decided to offer his services to the German Secret Service soon after Villa obliged him to give up his lucrative arms-buying activities in the United States.

As World War I progressed, Germany's leaders became increasingly worried about the impact on the war's outcome of the United States, which was neutral until 1917. From 1914 onward, American arms factories were selling arms, ammunition, and other supplies to the French, British, and Russians at an ever-increasing pace, but the Royal Navy denied Germany and its allies access to U.S. matériel. In addition, the Germans had become increasingly worried that the Wilson administration might finally enter the war on the side of the Allies.

To stop American arms sales to its enemies and keep the United States out of World War I, one of the measures that the leaders of Germany contemplated was provoking a large-scale U.S. intervention in Mexico. Such an intervention, the German leaders hoped, would prevent sales of matériel to Europe, since America's armed forces would require more and more arms, and it would have a good chance of preventing U.S. entry into World War I. To this end, German agents offered the exiled Victoriano Huerta $10,000,000 early in 1915 in order to carry out a coup in Mexico and then attack the United States.[18]

It soon turned out, however, that Huerta had too little support in Mexico to carry out such a scheme; moreover, he had been under surveillance from the moment he set foot on U.S. soil, and he was arrested before he was able to cross into Mexico again.

Just when the Huerta conspiracy seemed to have less and less chance of success, Felíx Sommerfeld suggested to Germany's representative in the United States, Bernhard Dernburg, that he would be able to manipulate Villa into attacking the United States. Sommerfeld believed, Dernburg reported, that although the administration wanted to avoid such intervention at any price, since it would prevent the United States from making its power felt in Europe and the Far East,

the military authorities of the United States . . . are for an intervention, and so are the governments of Texas and Arizona, which lie directly on the Mexican border. Roughly two months ago, there was an incident on the Arizona border that almost provoked an intervention. At that time, the chief of the American general staff was sent to the border by President Wilson, on the advice of Secretary of War Garrison, to negotiate with Villa. These negotiations took place with the mediation of Felíx Sommerfeld and at that moment, as he has repeatedly told me [Dernburg], it would have been easy for him to provoke an intervention. . . . This opportunity appears to be presenting itself again in the immediate future and Felíx Sommerfeld has discussed it with me.

Moreover, Sommerfeld pointed out, U.S. arms producers' contracts all contained a clause that rendered them null and void should the United States be drawn into a conflict.

Dernburg thought this a matter of such importance that he did not even report it to the German ambassador in the United States, but instead approached the German chief of naval staff, Admiral Hennig von Holtzendorff. The latter felt that he alone could not make such an important decision and consulted the German foreign secretary, Gottlieb von Jagow, who enthusiastically approved Sommerfeld's proposal, saying:

In my opinion the answer is absolutely yes. Even if the shipments of munitions cannot be stopped, and I am not sure they can, it would be highly desirable for America to become involved in a war and be diverted from Europe, where it is clearly more sympathetic to England. The Americans are not intervening in the Chinese situation, however, and hence an intervention made necessary by the events in Mexico would be the only possible diversion for the American government. Moreover, since we can at this time do nothing in the Mexican situation, an American intervention would also be the best thing possible for our interests there.[19]

After Villa's attack, the Germans enthusiastically endorsed it, and German agents seem to have supplied him with arms.[20] It is quite possible that either Sommerfeld or two Americans, J. F. Keedy and Edward Linss, who both seem to have had links to Germany, and who went to see Villa sometime in 1915, may have promised him German help should he attack the United States.[21] There is no proof, however, that the Germans played any role in Villa's assault. The German documents contain no such indication, and in early 1917, after the fiasco of the Zimmermann telegram and in the internal debates then raging in Germany, the Foreign Office and the German Navy would certainly have been interested in showing that they had persuaded Villa to attack the United States, but they never did so.[22] This does not mean that possible promises of aid by Germany played no role in Villa's determination, but it is extremely doubtful that they were a primary consideration for him.

Purely domestic considerations probably played a more prominent role in Villa's decision. At the very least, a limited U.S. intervention would provoke the same kind of reactions that the invasion of Veracruz had done: many Mexicans would rally to Villa as the champion of anti-Americanism, and Carranza would again be forced to issue a strong proclamation against the Americans, which would lead to a renewed arms embargo against him. If he did not do so, he would be exposed as a U.S. agent. As a result, in Villa's eyes, the secret pact between Carranza and Wilson, of whose existence he was absolutely convinced, would either cease to exist or be exposed to Mexican public opinion. Either way, it would be invalidated, and Mexico's independence would be safeguarded. Villa probably also assumed that if the danger of a Mexican-American war increased, Carranza's nationalistic generals might force him to come to terms with his domestic opponents in order to create a united Mexican front against the foreign invaders.

Thus Villa's real message to Zapata was that in the event of a national union with the Carrancistas against the United States, Zapata should stop fighting his domestic enemies and join in some way in an anti-American campaign. Whether Villa seriously expected Zapata to come north is doubtful. Villa may have judged it possible that in such a case Zapata would end hostilities against the Carrancistas and send a symbolic contingent to fight with the northerners against the Americans. It is also doubtful that Villa really wanted to wait for six months until attacking the Americans. The plan he submitted to Zapata was probably a long-range project, but Villa was doing everything in his power to bring about a conflict with the United States at a much earlier date.[23]

While Villa's main hope for the salvation of his movement lay in provoking U.S. intervention in Mexico, he did not entirely give up other strategies. He did not want to be merely a local leader fighting in Chihuahua; he wanted to remain a regional leader whose influence extended over large parts of northern Mexico. With this purpose in mind, he sent one of his generals, José Rodríguez, to Sinaloa to wage a guerrilla fight there, while Severiano Ceniceros, Contreras's former lieutenant, who had fought alongside his chief for many years during the Porfirian era to protect the land of the Ocuila Indians, was dispatched to Durango to prevent the Carrancistas from consolidating their hold on that state. Rodríguez never reached Sinaloa. He was first received and then betrayed by Maximiano Márquez, a former associate of Villa's who worked as an administrator on William Randolph Hearst's huge Babicora estate. Rodríguez was executed, and his body was shown throughout Chihuahua to remind former Villistas of the price they would pay if they continued to fight the Carranza administration.[24] Ceniceros did reach Durango, but instead of fighting the Carrancistas, he joined them and became one of the leaders of the state's counterguerrilla movement. Nevertheless, Durango remained a hotbed of Villismo. In contrast, Ceniceros's old chieftain, Calixto Contreras, continued to fight against Carranza in his native state.

A second major element of Villa's strategy was to repeat what the Maderistas had done in 1910–11 and what he himself had achieved in 1913. That was to make the state ungovernable by his opponents. Both in 1910–11 and 1913, this had been fairly easy. The revolutionaries had enjoyed a huge measure of sympathy in the Chihuahuan countryside. There had been genuine hope among the people that the revolutionaries would score a national victory, and that peace would then return to the country. In addition, the revolutionaries had increased their support by redistributing some of the huge wealth that had accumulated on the large estates belonging to Chihuahua's oligarchy. Sympathies shown the revolutionaries both by individual Americans and by some U.S. officials had increased popular feeling that they had been on the winning side. This time things were different. Villa was a defeated man; he had lost his reputation for invincibility and seemed to have no prospect of final victory. Not only had the Carrancistas won the war, they enjoyed the support of the great power north of the border.

There was very little left in the countryside to redistribute, since Chihuahua's cattle herds had already been depleted by the Villistas to obtain arms and ammunition from the United States. The lands on the estates that were still being worked were cultivated mainly by poor tenants and sharecroppers, whom Villa did not wish to antagonize.

The few remaining rich estates belonged to Americans, whom Villa had hitherto spared in the hope of preventing U.S. recognition of Carranza. Villa now sought to tap these to supply his army, and also to redistribute part of their property and thus gain popular support. When his troops occupied Hearst's Babicora ranch, he ordered a number of cattle slaughtered and the meat distributed to the peons on the hacienda.[25] The properties of foreign hacendados, however, were on the whole far too small to make up for the disappearance of the great wealth of the oligarchy's estates. In many cases, in order to survive, the Villistas had to take food from the peasants. At times it may have been given voluntarily, as Villa frequently paid for it in gold or silver, but at times his soldiers simply took it and thus created new enemies.

As his popular support dwindled, Villa resorted more and more to terror. In January 1916, when his troops defeated a large force of Carrancistas, he took more than 100 prisoners. These were carefully screened and divided into two groups. Those who had always been Carrancistas were allowed to join Villa's ranks, but more than 70 who had formerly been Villistas and had since joined the enemy were summarily executed.[26] This was a clear warning to any former Villista willing to join the armed forces of Carranza or the Carrancista civilian administration.

Another strategy of Villa's that was highly unpopular among large segments of the population was his attempt to prevent American entrepreneurs from returning to Mexico to reopen their mines and restart their businesses. By preventing economic recovery, Villa hoped further to weaken the Carrancista administration. Nevertheless, economic motives did not primarily determine the way he now dealt with Americans. Apart from revenge, Villa clearly wanted to demonstrate to the Americans that they would never be able to resume work in northern Mexico as long as they opposed him. This was an idea he had clearly intimated in his Naco manifesto. He may also have hoped that attacks on American businessmen in Mexico would help to provoke the U.S. intervention he was seeking.

The Massacre at Santa Isabel

Such considerations formed the background for the tragic events that took place on January 10, 1916, in the town of Santa Isabel in Chihuahua. On that day, a passenger train traveling from Ciudad Chihuahua to the mining town of Cusihuiráchic was stopped by a detachment of Villa's troops commanded by one of his most loyal lieutenants, General Pablo López. On board, together with many Mexican passengers, were eighteen American mining engineers and the American manager of the Cusihuiráchic Mining Company, who were returning to the town of the same name in order to resume work at the mines. They had been evacuated from the town at the height of the civil war in Chihuahua but were returning since the Carrancista authorities had persuaded them that they were in full control of the situation and that it was safe for them to resume work. The company's manager, C. R. Watson, had been dubious about the assurances of the Carranza officials and had asked for troops to accompany the train, but the newly installed Carrancista rulers of Chihuahua were so sure that they controlled the state, and that Villa had been reduced to impotence, that they refused to send any soldiers to guard the train.

This decision was fatal for the Americans. When the train suddenly stopped, they were puzzled but not greatly alarmed. Three of them, including Watson, got out to see what was happening. The rest remained in the compartment playing cards. Thomas B. Holmes, one of those who left the train, subsequently recalled:

We walked forward to see what the trouble was but saw nobody working around the derailed car, or attempting to get it on the track. We had reached a point about ten feet ahead of the rear end of the coach when the shooting began. Looking around the rear end of the coach I saw a line of Mexicans to the number of twelve or fifteen, standing in a solid line on the edge of the bank on the other side and above our train. How many others there were I could not say as my view was obstructed by the train. At this time I saw Mr. Watson just leaping off of the rear steps of the train. He landed right at the entrance of this cut on the riverside and ran directly away from the train, at right angles from the train toward the river. McHatton and myself were directly behind Mr. Watson when he started running. McHatton fell but I do not know whether he was killed then or afterwards. I ran diagonally away from the train towards the river and to the rear of the train. I tripped and fell at a distance of about 100 feet from the rear of the train and lay perfectly quiet in some small bushes so that I could look around and saw the Mexicans shooting in the direction in which Mr. Watson was running when I last saw him. Seeing that they were not shooting at me, I crawled into some thicker bushes nearby, ten or twelve feet. I made my way through the bushes to the river bank and along the bank to a point about one hundred yards' distance from the train. There I remained for about half an hour.

By staying hidden in the bushes, Holmes managed to survive. He was the only one of the Americans to do so.[27] After shooting the Americans who had left the train, López entered the compartment where the remaining Americans were sitting. "A tall man armed with a pistol and a rifle opened the door and directed a blow to my face," Cesar Sala, an Italian who was traveling with the Americans, and who was spared by the attackers because of his nationality, recounted.

I was the first one that had been assaulted. I afterwards learned that this man was Pablo López who struck me. I put up my arm to protect myself at the time and he said, "Get down, you gringo," and used another name. I told him I was not an American and said, "I am not a gringo." He then told me to sit down and cursed the president of the United States and Mr. Carranza and said they were after the Americans and commenced to take all the clothing off the Americans.[28]

The attackers then taunted the unresisting Americans. "I heard them cursing Mr. Wilson," Manuel Silveyra, a Mexican witness to the massacre recounted,[29] "and they were telling the Americans to call Mr. Wilson to protect them and Mr. Carranza to guarantee them safety, saying that the Americans were the originators of the trouble in Mexico. I saw Mr. Pierce, Mr. Robinson, Mr. Wallace, Mr. Anderson, Mr. Romero, and Mr. Newman stepping down, leaving the car with their clothes off except their underwear. I was sitting on the right-hand side and saw the killing of the Americans. They were executed just as they got down."

Some of the attackers then started robbing the Mexican passengers. "At the same moment Colonel Pablo López came into the coach and told these soldiers that they must stop that and told them that the harm was only intended to the Americans and no others, in accordance with the previous understanding and that other passengers would not be harmed," another of the Mexican witnesses recalled.[30]

López then made a speech to the Mexican passengers telling them that they should have no fear of him since his actions were only directed against Americans.[31] It is ironic that some of the Americans who had returned before undertaking their journey had been afraid of Carranza and convinced that Villa would not harm them. One day before leaving, W. D. Pierce, one of the mining engineers, wrote his brother: "Yet Carranza is more to be feared than was Villa. Villa at least had courage and enforced orders, which is more than I can say of Carranza. Carranza fears Villa more than anything else and if he can make any trouble for us Americans and at the same time make it appear that it was Villa who made the trouble, you may be sure that he will do it."[32]

Had Villa ordered the massacre, or was it an indirect result of his orders? After Woodrow Wilson allowed Mexican troops to cross U.S. territory, Villa had begun confiscating whatever American property he could, with the conspicuous exception of the Alvarado Mining Company in Chihuahua, one of whose employees was the son of General Hugh Scott. He had nevertheless hitherto spared the lives of most Americans he encountered, with the exception of a bookkeeper, P. Keane, on the Hearst ranch of Babicora.[33] A commission of the U.S. Army sent out to investigate Villa's actions concluded

that Villa's location at the time of the massacre was far from the scene where the act was enacted, that he was so situated and the circumstances attending the accidental arrival of the train bearing the ill-fated seventeen Americans were such that Villa could not have had first-hand advance information to have been able to issue direct orders to López to kill them. . . . There is reason to believe however that orders to rid Mexico [of Americans] were given López by Villa. . . . Orders from Villa to kill Americans could have reached López at any time of course, but it can be stated quite positively that Villa was not in the vicinity of Santa Ysabel at the time of the massacre, and further that when reports of the incident reached him by couriers he was inclined to deny its authenticity.[34]

The man who ordered the massacre, Pablo López, in the only interview he gave to a correspondent after being captured by Carranza troops, was ambiguous about the instructions he had received from his chief. López had at first refused to speak to the correspondent of the *El Paso Herald* since he refused to talk to Americans. After the correspondent explained that he was of Irish birth, López changed his opinion.

"Ah," said López, "you are not then a gringo. Well, that makes a little difference; you have revolutions in your own land. Is it not so? Yes, my friends keep me posted on outside news. If it was not for them I would starve. . . . Yes, since it is you, I might talk a little. . . . I do not care to say much about Santa Ysabel. You know that was different from fighting armed men in Columbus but you can imagine perhaps that when you are the devoted slave of a great leader you obey orders.

"Even so, things might not have gone as they did if it had not been that there were other jefes there among whom there was a spirit of deviltry. Perhaps we would have been content with only the Americans' clothes and money.

"But Señor, they started to run and then our soldiers began to shoot. The smell makes our blood hotter. The excitement and—ah well, Señor, it was all over before I realized it. Yes, I was sorry when I had time to cool down and reflect."[35]

As a result of this massacre, clamor for intervention in Mexico mounted in the United States, but the Wilson administration refused to budge, stating that it was an internal matter for Mexico to deal with. That attitude would undergo a dramatic change only a few weeks later.

Villa's Attack on Columbus, New Mexico

On January 18, 1916, Villa assembled 200 men, most of them members of his Dorado elite guard, at Los Tanques and told them that the time had come to strike at the Americans. "We will leave tomorrow to attack the border towns of the United States in the vicinity of Ojinaga. Large detachments of our troops will join us en route. I shall hold none of you after that venture, and I assure you that you will not regret participating in this last expedition with me."[36]

It is not clear why Villa chose the small American towns across the Rio Grande from Ojinaga as the targets of his first raid. The Texas border towns there, especially Presidio, were among the poorest in the whole of the United States, and little in the way of loot or supplies could be expected from them. Perhaps he reasoned that this part of the border was lightly garrisoned by U.S. troops, and so he could expect to score some success, all the more so since some of his most fervent supporters came from the Ojinaga region, especially from Cuchillo Parado, where Toribio Ortega's death had made no dent in the great support Villa enjoyed.

The projected march toward Ojinaga proved to be a disaster, as the small force of Villistas was plagued by recurrent desertions. As one Villista officer recorded:

January 25th. During the night of January 24th and 25th our forces are considerably depleted through desertions. Colonel Julián Pérez deserted us with a portion of his detachment. Colonel Cárdenas, a personal friend of Pérez, is sent after him with five men. Our march temporarily suspended in hopes of recovering some of the deserters.

January 26th, 27th, 28th: Our troops still waiting for the apprehension of the deserters.

Several more men deserted during the night on January 27 and 28, and desertions continued even during daylight. Colonel Cárdenas had not returned. The deserters from this camp numbered about 30.[37]

On January 30, Villa concluded that if he continued his plan to attack the Americans, even more desertions might ensue, and his army might disintegrate. He decided to return to San Gerónimo, from whence his expedition had started. In order to halt mounting demoralization, he decided to reward his soldiers. One day later, the Villistas stopped a passenger train from Ciudad Juárez. The passengers were forced to get out of the train, though none of them were harmed, and Villa's soldiers were allowed to plunder anything they found in the train. This "success" seems to have stopped the rash of desertions.[38]

The failure of Villa's initial expedition against the United States did not convince him that such an attack would be futile. He did, however, realize that openly proclaiming his aim of attacking the United States would not secure volunteers but on the contrary would lead some of his most devoted followers to desert. For his second planned attack on the United States, he used a very different tactic. For the first time, at least on a large scale, he decided to break with a tradition that had been essential to the strategy of the División del Norte: that of only accepting volunteers into his army. He now adopted the mode of forced recruitment. On February 20, he sent one of the most important of the leaders who had remained loyal to him, Colonel Candelario Cervantes, to the latter's hometown, Namiquipa, to draft a large force of men into his army. This was not yet the *leva*, forced recruitment as it had been practiced during the period of Porfirio Díaz. It did not affect all able-bodied males but only former soldiers of the División del Norte. In the orders given to Cervantes, Villa decreed "the immediate mobilization of all soldiers residing in the districts of Namiquipa and Cruces who have had previous service in the Conventionist army and their assignment to the detachment in command of Colonel Candelario Cervantes. Those who fail to join said detachment shall be shot. Those who conceal themselves and are not found, the families of these shall pay the penalty."[39]

Villa probably hoped that coercion would play only a minor role in mobilizing the men of Namiquipa for his cause. Namiquipa had been one of the centers of the Villista movement, and Cervantes was a local man who had handed out many favors, for which he now expected to be repaid. Villa had no compunction about brutally punishing former soldiers of his who hesitated to rejoin his forces. Lauro Trevizo Delgado was a former Villista soldier who had suffered a leg wound and returned to Namiquipa. He was drafted together with 30 other men and sent to Villa's camp, where he was told that he was to take part in a military operation. After arriving, Trevizo Delgado pleaded with his former chief to allow him to return home because of his wound, which made it difficult for him to ride, Villa did not believe him: "Look, Trevizo," he said. "When your people needed me, I helped you as much as I could, and now that I need you, you do not want to help me." Villa then ordered him shot. Trevizo Delgado was lucky. As he was being led by a firing squad toward a place of execution, he met one of Villa's most devoted lieutenants, Nicolás Fernández, whom he had known from previous campaigns, and who agreed to intercede for him. Villa retracted his order, and Trevizo Delgado joined the expedition.[40]

Fearing the reaction of his men if they heard that an attack on the United States was planned, Villa had told them nothing of the real target of the attack.

He thus hoped to prevent the kind of desertions that had frustrated his first anti-American foray. In order to make sure that the men from Namiquipa who had been forcibly impressed would not desert, he told them that if they left him "he would hang their families from the trees along the river."[41] When they were captured by the Americans a few weeks later, most of the men from Namiquipa who participated in Villa's attack on Columbus insisted that they had been forcibly impressed into his army and that he had left them no choice but to join him if they did not want to risk their own execution as well as that of their families.

The expedition under Villa's command that set forth on February 24 to attack Columbus, New Mexico, was a far cry from what the División del Norte had been in its heyday, with its thousands of men and volunteers flocking to every railway station to join Villa. It was also a far cry from the enthusiastic guerrilla contingents that Villa had led in the early days of the revolution. For the first time, he was leading a force partly composed of unwilling recruits, who, he feared, might desert him at any time. None of the generals who had sided with Villa when he broke with Carranza in mid 1914 were still with him. None of his commanders were regional leaders, as Contreras, Ortega, and Buelna had been. The López brothers, Martín and Pablo, and Candelario Cervantes from Namiquipa were men who had risen through the ranks; they felt they owed everything they were to Villa and trusted him absolutely, but they at best had only local followings.

There was, however, one way in which Villa's attacking force was a reflection, albeit a pale one, of the old División del Norte. This was in its geographical heterogeneity. Of the six contingents into which the strike force was divided, three came from Chihuahua; one was from Durango; one was from Sonora, including a number of Yaqui Indians; and the sixth, headed by Nicolás Fernández, Villa's old crony from his outlaw days, was composed of men from all over Mexico. They had fought under leaders who had deserted Villa, but instead of staying with their erstwhile chiefs, they had preferred to rejoin Villa, to whom they were fiercely loyal.[42]

For nearly two weeks, the expedition marched toward the U.S. border through remote parts of Mexico, frequently at night, in order to avoid detection by Carrancista troops and to prevent any warning of their arrival from reaching the Americans. The few people, all civilians, whom the expedition encountered along the way were taken prisoner. If they were Mexicans, they were released after a few days, and their property, including their horses, was returned to them. The few Americans whom Villa encountered before he reached the U.S. border were treated with uncommon brutality. Although Villa had plundered American properties and expelled Americans from Mexico, he had never wantonly killed them. This time it was to be different. Three American cowboys whom he captured on the way north, one of whom knew Villa from former times, and who had approached the Villista contingent confident that Villa would not harm him, since they had once been friends, were summarily executed.[43] Villa spared only an American woman, Maude Wright, whom he captured, forced to stay with his troops until the attack on Columbus, and freed after his troops retreated back into Mexico.

On March 8, 1916, Villa's expedition arrived at a point four miles from Columbus, New Mexico. It is not clear why this small town, consisting mainly of wooden shacks with a few hundred inhabitants and a U.S. garrison of nearly 600 men, had been chosen as the target of Villa's raid. In spite of lavish praise from the town's promoters—on September 1, 1911, a headline in the local newspaper read: "No boom wanted in this valley: just the steady, solid growth that we are having suits us: everything looks fine; irrigation farming is attracting the best people in our country"—the town did not have the kind of glitter to attract a raiding party. In fact, a member of its garrison, Lieutenant Ralph Lucas, characterized it as "mud, shacks, and rattlesnakes."[44]

It has frequently been said that one of Villa's main reasons for choosing Columbus was because it was the home of Sam Ravel, to whom Villa had given money to buy arms, and who had refused either to return it or to deliver the weapons.[45] This may have been one reason why Villa chose Columbus, but taking revenge on Ravel does not seem to have been his main preoccupation. His first choice of a target had been Presidio, Texas, across the Rio Grande from Ojinaga. U.S. intelligence officers who attempted to reconstruct both Villa's motives and the itinerary of the Villa expedition make no mention of Sam Ravel.[46]

In the eyes of the Villista leadership, Columbus and its garrison seemed small enough to be overrun without too many sacrifices by Villa's troops. If the raid was successful, it could prove quite profitable both in military and economic terms. The garrison's horses, machine guns, and Springfield rifles would certainly do much to replenish Villa's supplies. The town's stores had stocked large amounts of goods, and the banks held relatively large amounts of money, since ranchers and cattlemen both from the United States and from across the nearby Mexican border came to Columbus to buy supplies.

Villa had sent spies into town to reconnoiter the terrain, but his agents do not seem to have been very effective, for Candelario Cervantes told him that the garrison consisted of only 50 men, rather than 600, and could easily be overrun in two hours.[47] Before making a final decision on whether to attack the town, Villa himself went on a reconnaissance mission to a hill overlooking Columbus. He came back full of doubt. "He said in effect," as one of the expedition's members later reported, "that there was no need of sacrificing the lives necessary to take an unimportant town like Columbus. That the garrison there was very large and that better chances of success were to be had in fighting the Carrancistas."[48]

This time his commanders, generally blindly obedient to his orders, resisted. Cervantes insisted that the expedition could not fail, since the U.S. garrison was very small.[49] Cervantes and his supporters probably also told Villa that, since he had already withdrawn once from an attack on the United States, doing so again might very well demoralize those men who were still loyal to him. Villa finally acceded, and orders were given to attack Columbus during the night on March 8–9.

Before sending his men across the border, Villa felt that he had to give them some explanation for his decision to attack the United States. In his Naco manifesto, in letters to Carrancista generals, and in his farewell speech to the people of Chihuahua in December 1915, he had again and again accused Carranza of selling the country to the Americans, and had mentioned in detail all the provisions of the alleged secret agreement that both sides had entered into. They had evoked little response and little interest. Villa must have realized that telling his 400 mainly illiterate soldiers that he was attacking the Americans because Carranza had given the U.S. government the right to approve the naming of three cabinet officers and was turning the Tehuantepec railway over to U.S. control would scarcely move them. Chihuahua's peasants had never much cared who cabinet officials were, and most of them did not even know of the existence of the Tehuantepec railway. Villa understood the mentality of his soldiers very well. Even when he talked with the officer closest to him, Pablo López, he had "simplified" the terms of the alleged secret treaty by stating that Carranza had in fact sold the northern Mexican states to the United States. To López he had expressed the hope that the conflict with the United States would unite all Mexicans and might force Carranza to end the civil war.

He expressed no such thoughts when he made a rousing speech to his soldiers, calling them to attack the Americans. The only motive he mentioned was revenge. The United States, he said, had been responsible for their defeat at Agua Prieta in Sonora by allowing the Carrancistas to travel across its territory and reinforce the garrison. This accusation elicited a strong reaction from his men, many of whom had participated in the battle of Agua Prieta. Villa also accused the United States of sending defective arms and ammunitions to him and thus contributing to his defeat. He finally mentioned a horrendous incident that had taken place only two days before in El Paso. In what seems to have been standard practice, 20 Mexicans, who had been arrested by the local authorities for different reasons, had been soaked with kerosene in order to delouse them.[50] Someone, however, had set fire to the kerosene. It has never been proven whether this was by accident or by intention, but the 20 Mexicans were burned alive. Villa and his men had much reason to suspect that this was a deliberate act, for large numbers of Mexicans had been lynched in the lower Rio Grande valley in the preceding weeks.[51] Not everyone interested in the Columbus Raid confirms that Villa made such a speech. In fact, there are some indications that point to a very different situation: that Villa never told his soldiers that they were crossing the border, and that many continued to believe until the end that they were attacking a Mexican town garrisoned by Carrancista troops.

The raiding force was divided into two detachments. One was to proceed to the southern part of town and attack Camp Furlong, where the garrison was stationed. The other was to proceed to the center of Columbus, storm the bank, and, according to Mexican participants in the raid, shoot Ravel and burn down his properties. While Villa remained with a small reserve on the Mexican side of the border,[52] his main forces, after crossing into the United States three miles from the town, began storming Columbus at 4:45 A.M. on March 9.

The raiders managed to surprise the garrison, whose commanders had disregarded repeated warnings that Villa was approaching the border and might attack Columbus. Only two days before, the commanding general along the border, John J. Pershing, had been warned of this by General Gabriel Gavira, one of the Carrancista commanders in Chihuahua. Neither Pershing nor the commander of the Columbus garrison, Colonel Herbert J. Slocum, to whom Pershing relayed Gavira's message, took the warning seriously. There had been previous rumors about an impending attack by Villa on the United States, and it had never materialized. Slocum disregarded a similar warning from a U.S. commander along the New Mexico–Mexican border and was only a little more alarmed when a Mexican cowboy named Antonio, who was employed on an American ranch, told him that he had seen a large body of armed Mexicans near the border, who had captured one of his four men, an American cowboy named Corbett.

Slocum now found himself in a difficult situation. Strict instructions from Washington prevented him from sending his own men as scouts across the border. He decided to pay Antonio $20 to cross into Mexico again and try to discover the identity, or at least the location, of the armed Mexicans. Antonio never found them, or perhaps never attempted to, but he did report that he had found the trails of two columns of men moving away from the direction of Columbus. Antonio's report largely, although not entirely, reassured Slocum. He sent two detachments to keep watch at frequent crossing points along the border, but he did not put the rest of the garrison on alert. Most officers were thus allowed, as was the case when the garrison was not put on alert, to spend the night with their families in their homes, located in the northern part of town.[53]

Slocum's passivity was also in part owing to the contradictory nature of the reports that reached him from Mexico. There was a rumor that Villa did intend to come to Columbus, not to attack but rather to go to Washington and explain to President Wilson that he had had nothing to do with the attack on Santa Isabel, and that he might even seek asylum in the United States. These reports may have been given some credence by the presence of the Associated Press correspondent George Seese in Columbus. A Mexican connected to Villa had told Seese some weeks earlier that Villa intended to go to the United States to prove his innocence of any participation in the massacre of the American mining engineers to Wilson. Villa's alleged emissary had asked Seese to act as an intermediary in negotiations with the U.S. government. Before Seese could proceed with any such negotiations, he was prevented from doing so by the head of the Associated Press.[54] Seese had come to Columbus in part to see whether Villa might not turn up en route to see Wilson and partly because he had also heard rumors of an impending Villista attack.

Seese's story further contributed to Slocum's doubt that Villa seriously intended to attack the United States. Thus, when the Villistas struck at 4:45 A.M., firing indiscriminately into the army barracks, the soldiers, most of whom had been asleep, were caught completely by surprise. Only two officers were in the camp, contributing to the chaos. However, the officers soon managed to rally the soldiers to take the offensive, since the Villistas had committed a series of blunders. Underestimating the size of the garrison, only half of Villa's attacking force had struck at Camp Furlong. In addition, they mistook the stables for the sleeping quarters of the garrison and directed most of their fire there, thus killing horses instead of soldiers. While Villa's raiders were concentrating their attack on the stables, the commander of the garrison's machine-gun company, Lieutenant Ralph Lucas, marshaled his men and his machine guns to rake the ranks of the Villistas. In the face of superior American firepower, they began to retreat toward the central part of Columbus. There panic had broken out among the residents when the second column of Villistas rode into the town shouting "Viva Villa! Viva Mexico!" and wildly shooting into houses and at any civilian who emerged from them. They stormed into Sam Ravel's Commercial Hotel and killed four of its guests, some of whom had shot back at the Villista riders.

Villa's men vainly sought to find Sam Ravel, who was absent from Columbus, having gone to see his dentist in El Paso. The Villistas captured Sam's younger brother Arthur and two of the raiders forced him to take them to the family store. Fortunately for Arthur, both men were shot as they emerged from the hotel, and the younger Ravel was thus saved.

When Lucas's detachment reached the central part of Columbus, they found that another detachment of U.S. troops, commanded by the second officer who had remained in the barracks, Lieutenant James P. Castleman, had already begun a counterattack. It was hampered by the predawn darkness, in which both the raiders and civilians trying to escape ran through the streets. At this point, the raiders committed a grievous mistake. They set fire to the Commercial Hotel, thus lighting up the streets and enabling the American troops to distinguish the civilians from the Villistas. The U.S. troops opened withering fire, and at 7:30 in the morning, three hours after the raid had begun, a Villista bugler signaled retreat. The Villistas did not panic; taking most of their wounded with them, they began an orderly withdrawal into Mexico.

The Villistas were pursued by U.S. troops, who had no hesitation about crossing the border and followed them five miles into Mexico, but after fierce resistance by Villa's rearguard, they returned to Columbus. In military and economic terms Villa's raid had been anything but a success. While 17 Americans, most of them civilians, had been killed, more than 100 Villistas had died. Villa had not managed to get any supplies from the stores, money from the bank, or arms from the U.S. garrison. In strategic terms, however, Villa's raid would largely meet his expectations and give him and his movement a new lease on life.

The Renewed U.S. Invasion of Mexico: The Punitive Expedition

Villa's hopes that his raid on Columbus would provoke a U.S. intervention strong enough to cause a nationalist backlash in Mexico that would decisively weaken Carranza's popularity and his links to the United States, one that would allow a resurgence of Villa but at the same time not prompt a complete occupation of Mexico, proved to be more than justified. Villa's Columbus raid was and remains to this day the only case of a foreign military force attacking the metropolitan territory of the United States since the British-American war of 1812. After the Santa Isabel massacre, there had already been a strong clamor for intervention by both the Hearst press and interventionist senators such as Albert B. Fall of New Mexico. Hearst's *Los Angeles Examiner* had written: "We are too proud to fight. . . . Why, even a little, despicable, contemptible bandit nation like Mexico murders our citizens, drags our flag in the dirt and spits and defies this nation of ours with truculent insolence."[55] The Wilson administration had resisted these calls, stressing that the State Department had warned the mining engineers not to return to Chihuahua because of the insecurity there, and that they had deliberately ignored this warning. The State Department had expressed confidence that Carranza would destroy Villa and his men. This time, however, the clamor for intervention was irresistible. Wilson was up for reelection in only a few months. In addition, he was afraid that if he did not take any initiative, Congress might force him into a full-scale intervention that would lead to war with Mexico. This was the last thing he wanted. The likelihood that the United States would enter the war against Germany loomed ever larger, and Wilson did not want to have his forces diverted to Mexico. As he told his secretary Joseph Tumulty:

Someday the people of America will know why I hesitated to intervene in Mexico. I cannot tell them now for we are at peace with a great power whose poisonous propaganda is responsible for the present terrible conditions in Mexico. . . . It begins to look as if war with Germany is inevitable. If it should come, I pray to God it may not, I do not wish America's energies and forces divided for we will need every ounce of reserve we have to lick Germany.[56]

Having a free hand to deal with Germany was not the only reason that Wilson was opposed to full-scale intervention in Mexico. He continued to feel sympathetic toward the Mexican Revolution:

It is not a difficult thing for a president to declare war, especially against a weak and defenseless nation like Mexico. . . . Men forget what is back of the struggle in Mexico. It is the age-long struggle of the people to come into their own, and while we look upon the incidents in the foreground, let us not forget the tragic reality in the background which towers above this whole sad picture. The gentlemen who criticize me speak as if America were afraid to fight Mexico. Poor Mexico with its pitiful men, women and children fighting to gain a foothold in their own land.[57]

This does not mean that Wilson did not want to shape the course of the Mexican Revolution. He had attempted to do so from the moment he took office, and, as the invasion of Veracruz showed, he had no compunction about resorting to armed force when it seemed likely to be efficacious. He would do so now, but the kind of intervention he envisaged was of a limited nature, would require only a modest commitment of troops, and would not lead to U.S. occupation of all of Mexico.

On March 10, one day after Villa's raid, Wilson announced: "An adequate force will be sent at once in pursuit of Villa with the single object of capturing him and putting a stop to his forays. This can and will be done in entirely friendly aid to the constituted authorities in Mexico and with scrupulous respect for the sovereignty of that republic."[58] Wilson gave orders for an expeditionary force of about 5,000 men to enter Mexico in pursuit of Villa under the command of John J. Pershing.[59]

Pershing's immediate superior in the United States, to whom he would report, was Frederick J. Funston, who had commanded the U.S. occupation force in Veracruz. Both Pershing and Funston shared a common characteristic: they had many years' experience in what would today be called counterinsurgency. They had participated in the U.S. Army's successful campaign against Filipino guerrillas. Funston had captured the head of the Filipino resistance, Aguinaldo, while

Pershing had been so successful at fighting the Moros (Filipino Moslem guerrillas) that Theodore Roosevelt had promoted him to general over the heads of 862 officers who had more seniority.

Most U.S. military leaders placed high hopes on the U.S. intervention for reasons that had little to do with the fate of Villa or of Mexico. In the United States, a traditionally antimilitaristic country, the armed forces had long been the stepchild of the nation. Unlike all of the European countries, the United States imposed no obligatory military service. The U.S. Congress was reluctant to appropriate large funds for the military, and a program to train volunteers for deployment if the United States became embroiled in a war had not gotten off to a very good start. U.S. military leaders hoped that a popular campaign such as the Mexican one would lead to more funds for the army, more volunteers, and more popular sympathy, and at the same time allow them to test both their tactics and their weapons.

They nonetheless felt uncomfortable with the limited aim that Wilson assigned them in his first public pronouncement: to capture Villa. U.S. Chief of Staff Hugh Scott later recalled in his memoirs that Newton Baker, Wilson's newly appointed secretary of war, had told him: "I want you to start an expedition into Mexico to catch Villa." "This seemed strange to me," Scott wrote, "and I asked,"

"Mr. Secretary, do you want the United States to make war on one man? Suppose he should get into a train and go to Guatemala, Yucatán, or South America; are you going to go after him?"

He said, "Well, no, I am not."

"That is not what you want then. You want his band captured or destroyed," I suggested.

"Yes," he said, "that is what I really want."[60]

In the instructions finally given to the Punitive Expedition, as it came to be called, the main aim was not the capture of Villa; rather, it was stated, "the work of these troops will be regarded as finished as soon as Villa's band or bands are known to be broken up."[61] The instructions also emphasized that the expedition was to respect the sovereignty of the Carranza government, and that unless it were attacked by Mexican troops, it was never to proceed against them.

This created a problem for the military that they never discussed either with Wilson or with members of his cabinet. The military knew that unless they had unusual luck and stumbled upon Villa's contingents, to break up his bands, which they knew enjoyed strong support in the Chihuahuan countryside, they would have to wage a counterinsurgency war. This meant, as it had in the Philippines, burning villages, taking reprisals against civilians, and shooting prisoners.[62]

There were only two ways in which such tactics could be applied: either by cooperating with the Carrancista authorities, should they be ready to do "the dirty work," or by assuming sole responsibility for the war and ignoring the authority of the existing Carranza administration. It soon became clear to the U.S. military that the Carranza government would never acquiesce in the first option. The Americans therefore began to prepare for the second one, which they felt would become necessary because it was the only way to destroy Villa's bands, and also because they were convinced that sooner or later Carranza would resist American penetration into Mexico. On March 23, 1916, the War College drafted a plan "for the occupation and pacification of northern Mexico." The plan called for 250,000 U.S. soldiers to occupy the northern states of Tamaulipas, Nuevo León, Coahuila, Chihuahua, and Sonora. In addition, the U.S. Navy would blockade all the ports in southern and central Mexico. The planners did not spell out how they would deal with Mexican guerrillas who resisted occupation, but in all probability they considered applying a tactic recommended three years later in another plan:

The period of active operations will be short, as compared to the period of guerrilla operations. The early disbandment of temporary troops is highly desirable. It is the testimony of all well acquainted with Mexican character that any number of Mexicans can be hired to fight against anyone and for anyone who will regularly pay and feed them. The Mexican soldier will be cheaper and more efficient against banditry than the American and the cost can be more easily charged against the Mexican government.
In addition an army can be established that will not be anti-American and which may, for many years in the future, exercise on the Mexican government an influence favorable to the United States.[63]

These plans were never implemented, since they were based on the assumption that a war would break out between the United States and the Carranza government. In the months to come, the two countries would several times be on the brink of war, but it was averted because neither Wilson nor Carranza wanted it. While both were rigid in their public pronouncements, they showed a surprising degree of flexibility in practice.

Upon hearing of Villa's raid, Carranza hoped to deflect a possible U.S. intervention by ordering a strong contingent of troops under Luis Gutiérrez to pursue him, while at the same time proposing an agreement to the Americans for the reciprocal pursuit of bandits across the border in case of future raids. One day later when the news of the planned U.S. intervention reached him, he sent a stern warning to Wilson that a U.S. military expedition into Mexico without the consent of the Mexican government might lead to war. This note worried Wilson, and there are indications that he might have refrained from sending Pershing into Mexico had Mexican troops at the border offered armed resistance.[64]

They did not, and on March 16, the first of two columns of Pershing's Punitive Expedition entered Mexico. It consisted of about 5,000 officers and soldiers, comprising cavalry, infantry, and artillery, as well as an air squadron of eight planes. By the end of March, it had marched deep into Chihuahua, reaching a point approximately 350 miles from the U.S. border. In spite of his sharp pronouncements against the entry of U.S. troops into Mexico, Carranza offered no resistance in March and secretly cooperated with the Americans. Officially, Pershing's troops were not allowed by Mexican authorities to be supplied by railroad, so the farther they were from the U.S. border, the more they would be hampered in their operations. In fact, through a subterfuge, Carranza did allow the U.S. troops to resupply themselves by rail. The supplies were officially not addressed to the expedition but to private individuals within it.[65]

In a proclamation to the people of Chihuahua, the Carrancista governor, Ignacio Enríquez Jr., essentially defended Wilson's actions and indirectly called on the people of the state to cooperate with the Americans. He stated that Wilson, far from wanting intervention, had always resisted it. Pershing's Punitive Expedition had penetrated into Mexico as a result of a reciprocal agreement between the Carranza administration and the U.S. government for the pursuit of bandits (a statement completely at variance with Carranza's attitude):

Under the provisions of this agreement, which grants equal rights to our forces, and owing to the presence of bands on the frontier of the state, the American troops have passed the line in pursuit of them, having due respect for our own forces, their movements being even controlled in accordance with the wishes of our chiefs. The attitude of this American force is considered opportune and behavior so far without reproach, no towns now garrisoned by our troops having been occupied by it. . . . What is the solution of this state of affairs? If Doroteo Arango, alias Francisco Villa, infernal monster, and worthy pupil of Victoriano Huerta, the instrument of the enemies of our people is to provoke such a situation, we must seek to employ all our forces to exterminate this bandit, and then there will be time enough to inform the Americans that the motive of their presence on our soil no longer exists and to demand their withdrawal from our country.[66]

Carranza and Enríquez not only wanted to prevent a U.S.–Mexican war, which would have been suicidal for Mexico, but also hoped that Pershing's well-equipped column might achieve its aim of capturing Villa, or at least destroy his forces.

By the end of March 1916, Carranza's hopes seemed to have become a reality. The Villistas had suffered a great setback, and most of them had dispersed. Villa himself was reported to be dead or gravely wounded, and there was talk that the Americans would now withdraw across the border. In fact, unbeknownst to Carranza, this was what Chief of Staff Hugh Scott was suggesting to Wilson. Nevertheless, by the beginning of April, it was becoming apparent to Carranza that the situation was developing in a far different way from what he had hoped.

Perhaps the main reason that Pershing was unsuccessful in his initial endeavors was the reaction of the people of Chihuahua to his expedition. In a bitter telegram sent to his superiors, Pershing largely attributed his lack of success to the

attitude Mexican people. Little doubt people assisted Villa evade American troops vicinity Namiquipa. Our best guides and interpreters familiar with Mexican people during long residence here completely misled and columns delayed through falsehood told by Mexicans. When Seventh Cavalry left Bachiniva on March 29 for Guerrero Mexican peons started by night from neighboring ranches to notify Villa. After Guerrero fight inhabitants without exception aided Villa escape openly giving apparently authentic information based entirely on falsehood.[67]

Only a few months later, in the fall of 1916, Villa would enjoy a dramatic resurgence that no one had remotely foreseen in March 1916. It was all the more unanticipated, since Villa and his forces suffered great reverses in the early months of that year.

Villa's Retreat

As Villa and the fewer than 400 men of his raiding force who had survived the attack on Columbus retreated into the mountains of Chihuahua, he was confronted with the most negative odds he had ever faced since embarking on the life of a revolutionary. More than 7,000 Americans had crossed the border into Mexico with the aim of capturing him and destroying his forces. They were equipped with a modern technology that neither he nor his Mexican enemies had access to. A squadron of U.S. airplanes flew over the mountain ranges and deserts of Chihuahua searching for him. In addition to the Americans, thousands of Carrancista troops were pouring into Chihuahua, attempting to eliminate him as rapidly as possible, while also preparing for a possible U.S.–Mexican war.

Morale was low among the Columbus raiders as they retreated into the mountains of western Chihuahua, slowed down by the many wounded they had to carry with them. They had suffered huge losses and gotten nothing in return. Villa himself was deeply disappointed by the results of the raid. At the first stop that the troop made after retreating from Columbus, Villa, Cervantes, and Nicolás Fernández gathered at the side of Cruz Chávez, one of Villa's officers who had been wounded at Columbus, and who would soon die. "Villa first turned to Cervantes and pointing to Chávez in an abject manner said, 'It has come to this, Cervantes; I gave way to please all of you.' Cervantes turned to Fernández and blamed him for insisting that the attack on Columbus would succeed. Colonel Martín López was heard to express the view that the attack had been a futile effort for a few dollars."[68]

Nevertheless, in spite of the disappointment and demoralization of many of his men, Villa kept them together and prevented any large-scale desertions, thanks to his charisma and the loyalty and terror he inspired. Villa did not give way to despair but, on the contrary, did everything in his power to capitalize on the wave of nationalism that he hoped the U.S. invasion of Mexico would inspire. He proposed a cease-fire to Carranza's generals as long as U.S. troops were on Mexican soil,[69] and when he passed through a village, he would harangue the inhabitants and call on them to fight the U.S. invaders and support his forces. At Galeana, several thousand people assembled on March 14 to hear Villa, who addressed them from a window facing the main square. He gave no explanation of why he had attacked Columbus. Saying that war had broken out between the United States and Mexico, and that the people should be ready to defend their country, he explained:

Brethren, I have called you together to inform you that in an endeavor to enter the United States I was stopped by the "gringos" on the line and was compelled to fight large numbers of them. I repeat to you, I shall not waste one more cartridge on our Mexican brothers but will save all my ammunition for the "*güeros*" [i.e., blonds]; prepare yourselves for the fight that is to come. I want to ask you to assist me in caring for the wounded I have with me, suffering for the good of our beloved country.

The reaction to Villa's call for humanitarian aid was overwhelming. "The people of Galeana responded to the words of Villa in rendering all assistance in their power to the wounded and when our column left Galeana," a Villista reported, "at 9:00 A.M. that day one express wagon load of clothing and food and even money had been collected and donated to us."[70] The response was less overwhelming when Villa asked for volunteers to join his army in order to fight the Americans. Only five men from Galeana joined his forces, and they seem to have been impressed by force.[71]

In the town of El Valle, Villa was much more forthright about what he really wanted from the townspeople:

I have wanted you all present here to inform you that the Americans are about to come to Mexico to fight us. War has already been declared and I desire to see how many of you will join me; how many of you are ready to take up arms. I have soldiers with me from all the pueblos except from your own and it is essential that your pueblo be held above criticism. Fear nothing, I promise you not to fire a single cartridge against Mexicans and if one day I do so you may say I am a barbarian.[72]

The men of El Valle showed little enthusiasm for joining Villa's army, and 40 of them had to be recruited by force.[73]

Villa's appeals seem to have evoked a greater response among Carranza's soldiers. On March 16, his men suddenly encountered a large Carrancista force only two miles away. The Carranza troops simply rode on and did not fire a single shot at the Villistas.[74] In the village of Matachic, there was a brief rising by the Carrancista garrison, which demanded to be sent to fight the Americans and not the Villistas.[75] At times Carrancista troops even helped Villistas who were fleeing the expeditionary force. In one case, a Villista hotly pursued by U.S. troops fell into the hands of a Carranza detachment. "Are you a Villista?" the Carranza commander asked him. "Today every Mexican should be a Villista," the fleeing soldier answered. The Carrancista commander did not reply but gave him a horse and allowed him to go on his way.[76]

A truce with Villa was the last thing either Carranza or his top generals wanted. Killing or capturing him and destroying his army had now become their main priority. It was, they hoped, the quickest way to get rid of the Americans. On March 17, a Carrancista force attacked Villa. He now felt there was no reason to keep his pledge not to shed Mexican blood. Attacking the Carrancistas was at that point his only chance of securing arms and ammunition and, as he soon found out, the best way to secure recruits. On March 27, his troops fell upon the town of Ciudad Guerrero and the villages of Miñaca and San Ysidro, Orozco's old home base. The Villistas easily surprised and overran the garrisons of Ciudad Guerrero and Miñaca but were repelled at San Ysidro, where the Carrancista general José Cavazos had his headquarters. When Cavazos attempted to retake Ciudad Guerrero, he was easily repulsed, and the Villistas secured a significant victory, capturing large numbers of weapons and persuading 80 Carrancista prisoners to join their ranks.

This success turned out to be a Pyrrhic victory, however, for in the fighting Villa was wounded in the knee. He suffered great pain, could not ride, and could only be carried slowly and with great difficulty. He decided that he had no choice but to go into hiding. The one way he had always escaped his pursuers was through constant mobility and through his knowledge of every nook and cranny in Chihuahua. He was not mobile anymore, and if he remained in one place with his troops, his location would soon be found out either by the Americans or by the Carrancistas, and his numerically inferior troops would soon be overrun. Villa now divided his forces into several detachments, which were to disperse to different parts of Chihuahua and Durango.

Villa himself, with an escort commanded by Nicolás Fernández, set off for a destination that he was careful to reveal to no one. It was a slow ride. Villa was alternatively carried in a carriage or on a litter and suffered excruciating pain in the process. There was no doctor in the detachment, and there were no medicines to relieve his suffering. At times he wept, at times he became delirious. The expedition proceeded until it arrived at the ranch belonging to the father of one of Villa's generals, José Rodríguez, who offered to help them in any way he could. To make sure of his continued loyalty, they did not tell him that his son had been killed three months before but rather described him as doing very well on a confidential mission for Villa.[77]

Villa recuperated for a short time at the ranch, but he had no intention of staying there: sooner or later the Carrancistas were bound to look for him at locations where either his sympathizers or their families had some property. He also felt that such a large escort would inevitably draw attention to itself. He therefore told Fernández to proceed to Durango, far south of the U.S. border, and to lie low there until he heard from him.

Only two men stayed with Villa, both of them first cousins of his. With great difficulty, they mounted him on a burro and proceeded to a cave known as the Cueva de Cozcomate, where he holed up for two months. The entrance to the cave was concealed by branches and leaves, and his relatives regularly provided him with food and water. From there he was able to watch Pershing's columns riding by one day. No doctor treated his wounds, but Villa slowly recovered, even though according to most reports the only treatment he received was when Francisco Beltrán, the only one of his commanders who had some knowledge of medicine, dressed his wound with a rudimentary bandage.

During the approximately two months that he hid out in the cave, Villa was completely out of touch with his men, which was probably good for his morale. It would certainly not have speeded his recovery had he learned that a significant part of the small group that had remained loyal to him had been wiped out. Only two detachments that had retreated to Durango, those led by the Sonoran General Beltrán and by Nicolás Fernández, had remained relatively intact. Those detachments that decided to remain in Chihuahua—it is not clear whether they were obeying Villa's orders or disregarding them by staying there—were soon decimated by internal conflicts, desertions, and attacks by both Carrancistas and U.S. troops. This was especially true of Villista units that ventured near or into regions where the Americans has established strong occupation forces.

Candelario Cervantes's detachment, which at the outset had consisted of more than 200 men, was hardest hit. Cervantes had quarreled with some of his commanders, who then left his detachment with their men. He refused to pay his men, and many of the Carrancista deserters who had joined him after the battle of Ciudad Guerrero now abandoned him as well. He was soon left with no more than 30 men, nearly all of them from his own village of Namiquipa or from neighboring Cruces. Many of them also left Cervantes after he had returned to his hometown only to find that a large part of its population had turned against him. Few of the village inhabitants were willing to listen to his impassioned calls for a rising against the Americans.[78]

As his force had practically disintegrated, Cervantes resorted to a desperate expedient. He decided to go into the lions' den. Although the Americans had established one of their strongest bases in Namiquipa, Cervantes decided to concentrate his operations there. It was after all his own hometown, and the men who still followed him came from the area. They had risen together with most of the villagers in 1911 against Porfirio Díaz, and he had led them in 1913 against Huerta and mobilized them in 1916 to march on Columbus. He now wanted to arouse the men of Namiquipa once more to fight against the U.S. invaders. At the same time, he harbored the expectation that the Carrancistas would not impede him in these efforts. In a proclamation addressed to "The Civil Chiefs of the Carranza Army," Cervantes declared: "We hope that if you do not unite with us like one great family, since by force we can succeed, at least you will leave us free to fight the miserable North American invaders; the only cause for our disagreement and national disgrace."[79]

The Carrancistas did in fact leave Cervantes alone, but his own people refused to follow him. In economic terms, the U.S. occupation had proved to be a bonanza for the people of Namiquipa. The Americans paid for what they bought in the village in hard currency and not in the worthless paper money that both the Villistas and Carrancistas, if they paid at all, had tendered. The Americans also armed part of the population and organized them in a local defense force capable of defending the town against any outsider. Indeed, Pershing was anticipating the recommendation to organize a Mexican force loyal to the United States that was made three years later in the U.S. plan for war in Mexico. The Namiquipa force proved so loyal that they turned over a large cache of arms that Villa had hidden near the village and informed the Americans of the identity of every villager who had participated in the attack on Columbus.

Not all of the villagers shared the pro-American enthusiasm of José María Espinosa,[80] son of a former leader of the uprising against Madero, and one of the main supporters of the Americans in the town, but very few of the villagers were willing to fight the foreign occupiers. Many of the local men who had followed Cervantes home now deserted, and as one of them, whom Cervantes called to rejoin his ranks, wrote him:

If it's a matter of combating the gringos, I'm ready when you call on me and when you need me. But only if I see that we can strike a massive blow. Otherwise, it's not in our interest, because as you know, first and foremost, the pueblos won't help us and there's no one who will say I have the will to offer my services as a Mexican, no one. On the contrary, they are always trying to help the damned gringos and because of this one sees that it's not worth trying to do the people this good because one sees they will not even cover for us let alone help us.[81]

Another Villista detachment, which like Cervantes's troops sought to put up a fight against the Americans, was decimated by a direct American attack rather than by internal conflict. The detachment was commanded by Julio Acosta, who in the years of Villista administration in Chihuahua had been in charge of the

Guerrero district. Acosta had accepted an amnesty from the Carrancistas in January 1916 and had not participated in the Columbus attack. He had nothing to fear from either the Carrancistas or the Americans, who told him that if he did not proceed against them, they would leave him alone. He decided nonetheless to rejoin his old leader. In the battle of Guerrero, he united with Villa's other forces in fighting the Americans. Like Cervantes, he called on the people to fight the foreign invaders. In a proclamation addressed "To the Sovereign Mexican Republic," signed by Acosta, another Villista general, Cruz Domínguez, and a Colonel Antonio Angel, they declared:

We have the honor to inform you that fatal circumstances befall our dear and beloved country due to the intervention and entry of Americans in our country. The Carranza government has proven itself a traitor by agreeing to permit this nation in arms to set foot on our beloved soil. . . . Let us recall, dear sons of Mexico, our ancestors and the venerable patriots of Dolores, Don Miguel Hidalgo y Costillos [*sic*], Allcade [*sic*], and Aldama, who, among other heroes perished solely to give us country and liberty and today we must follow their examples so as not to live under the tyranny of another nation.[82]

Acosta and his men also hoped that the Carrancistas would not interfere in their efforts to fight the Americans, and their expectations were met when the Carrancista garrison at the town of Ojos Azules surrendered to them without firing a shot.

Before the detachment could proceed to attack the Americans, the U.S. troops surprised them in Ojos Azules and inflicted a crippling defeat on them. Forty-one members of the detachment died, and a large number were wounded. It was the greatest victory that the Punitive Expedition would achieve during its stay in Mexico. Acosta nevertheless managed to escape. Defeated by the Americans, he concentrated his subsequent activities on fighting the Carrancistas.

Even more painful for Villa than the decimation and dispersal of his soldiers was the killing of a large number of his officers. They were far more difficult to replace than their men. Cruz Chávez, one of the leaders of the Columbus raid, had been so seriously wounded by U.S. soldiers that he died of his wounds on the way back from Columbus. Ramón Tarango, another participant in the attack, was killed during the battle of Ciudad Guerrero. Cruz Domínguez and Julián Granados were captured and executed by the Carrancistas.[83]

The three men whose loss was most painful to Villa were Manuel Baca, Candelario Cervantes, and Pablo López.

It is doubtful whether many people besides Villa mourned the death of Manuel Baca, a comrade from his bandit days, who had become one of Villa's most dreaded executioners. When Villa was wounded, Baca attempted to operate near his native village of Santo Tomás. Hatred against him ran so high there that the villagers themselves killed him.[84]

Candelario Cervantes, too, died a lonely death. After being abandoned by most of his men, he attempted to attack a U.S. cavalry troop. The Americans shot him; a trooper attached his body to his horse (one Mexican observer believes that Cervantes was still alive at the time)[85] and dragged him to U.S. headquarters to be identified. His face had become so mangled that he was unrecognizable, and a relative managed to identify him only by a small wound on his finger.[86] Only a dozen people attended the funeral.[87]

Pablo López died in a very different way, feeling until the end that the people were behind him. Wounded at Columbus, he had sought refuge in a lonely ranch in the Chihuahuan hills. His location was revealed to the Carrancistas, and when López saw them approaching, he fled into the hills. The Carrancistas could not find him but roamed through the region shouting: "López, you are surrounded. There is no sense in resisting. Give yourself up." After three days without food and water, completely emaciated, López responded, "If you are Americans, I refuse to surrender. If you are Mexicans, I shall give myself up."[88]

The Carrancistas took López to Ciudad Chihuahua, where they decided to stage a public execution. Such an execution was in line with the public showing of Rodríguez's body only a few months before. The Carrancistas wanted to intimidate Villa's remaining supporters and show the people of Chihuahua that they were really winning the war against Villa. They were also intent on proving to the Americans that they were serious about combating Villa, and that they had scored a major victory by capturing the man whom apart from Villa the Americans hated most. López had not only participated in the Columbus raid but was responsible for the massacre of the seventeen American mining engineers at Santa Isabel. López was determined to die in dignity, remaining convinced to the end that what he and Villa had done was for the good of Mexico. A few days before he was executed he told an Irish correspondent:

"I am only a poor ignorant peon, Señor. My only education was gained in leading the oxen and following the plow. However, when the good Francisco Madero rose in arms against our despotic masters, I gladly answered his call.

"We all knew Pancho Villa—and who did not? His exploits are recounted nightly at every fireside. He was the object of worship of all who were ground under the heel of the oppressor.

"When the call came, I was one of the first to join him and have been his faithful follower and adoring slave ever since. . . . I am bound for Santa Rosa [Chihuahuan execution place] when I am able to walk there. I would much prefer to die for my country in battle, but if it is decided to kill me, I will die as Pancho Villa would wish me to—with my head erect and my eyes unbandaged and history will not be able to record that Pablo López flinched on the brink of eternity."[89]

López maintained this conviction until the end. On the night before his execution, he wrote a letter of farewell to his parents. "I write this letter to bid farewell to my brothers and sisters and to you. You can be proud of me for your son does not die a traitor but dies because my Mexican brothers have sentenced him to obliteration as a concession to the enemies of my country. Please take care of my unforgettable wife, my son, and my brothers. I await you in my eternal resting place. Farewell, my parents."[90]

A day later, López died as he had promised. He smiled on the way to his execution, he smoked a cigar, he chatted with his guards, and when asked for his last wish, he requested that any American present to witness his death should be removed from the scene. He refused to have his eyes bandaged, and he himself gave the execution squad the order to fire.[91] He was buoyed in his last moments by the fact that many of Chihuahua's inhabitants who were watching the execution were openly expressing their admiration and sympathy for him and insulting the Carrancistas by calling them dogs.[92] This manifestation of sympathy for Pablo López was an expression of an increasing nationalist backlash in Chihuahua, which worried U.S. military and political leaders more and more.

Decision in Washington to Stay or Not to Stay

By the beginning of April 1916, several members of Wilson's cabinet were urging the withdrawal of the Punitive Expedition. Secretary of War Newton Baker told Woodrow Wilson's confidant Colonel Edward House that he was in favor of "giving up the Villa chase and bringing the troops back from Mexico. He thought the purpose had been accomplished, that is the Villistas had already been dispersed and it was foolish to chase a single bandit all over Mexico."[93] Chief of Staff Hugh Scott was even more explicit in this respect. "I do not know," he wrote two days later to a friend, "how long this thing is going to continue. It seems to me that Pershing has accomplished about all that he was sent for. . . . It does not seem dignified for all the United States to be hunting for one man in a foreign country. . . . If the thing were reversed, we would not allow any foreign army to be sloshing around in our country, 300 miles from the border, no matter who they were."[94]

The reasons for this attitude are clear. A major crisis had just erupted between Germany and the United States over the sinking of neutral ships by German U-boats. There was a distinct possibility that the United States would enter World War I on the side of the Entente, and neither Baker nor Scott wanted U.S. troops to be tied down in Mexico at such a juncture. Now that Villa had gone into hiding and his men had been dispersed throughout Chihuahua and Durango, Baker and Scott realized that if U.S. troops stayed in Mexico, they would have to do so for a long time and greatly expand the scope of their operations. In a memorandum he sent to his commanding officer, Pershing made this clear:

It is very probable that the real object of our mission to Mexico can only be attained after an arduous campaign of considerable length. . . . Villa is entirely familiar with every foot of Chihuahua, and the Mexican people through friendship or fear have always kept him advised about every movement. He carries little food, lives off the country, rides his mounts hard and replaces them with fresh stock taken wherever found. Thus he has had the advantage since the end of the first twenty-four hours after the Columbus raid occurred. . . .

Success then will depend upon a) our continuing occupation of as many distinct localities as possible in the territory to be covered, b) the establishment of intimate relations with a sufficient number of reliable inhabitants in each locality to assure their assistance in obtaining trustworthy information . . . d) the maintenance of ample and regular lines of supply, especially to the large extent of unproductive or mountainous territory; and a sufficient number of men and animals to occupy localities and keep fresh columns constantly at work. . . . The execution of the general plan has already been begun and will be pushed to completion as fast as possible.[95]

Such a policy was bound to provoke conflicts with Carranza and provoke a full-scale U.S.–Mexican war at a time when the United States could least afford it. Baker and Scott also felt that the political price Wilson might pay for withdrawal would be a very small one. After the defeat the Villistas had suffered at Guerrero, Washington could say that it had succeeded in its primary purpose of destroying Villa's bands. Even if the expedition stayed in Mexico, capturing Villa was extremely unlikely. Also, Carranza had agreed to sign an accord with the United States whereby, in the event of a future raid, U.S. troops would have the right to cross the border into Mexico.

If Baker's and Scott's proposals had been accepted by Wilson and if the Punitive Expedition had been withdrawn from Mexico, it is doubtful whether Villa could have recovered from the losses he had suffered. Carranza could have claimed that his steadfast attitude had prevented both a U.S.–Mexican war and forced the Americans to withdraw. At the same time, he would still have enjoyed all the benefits of having gained recognition by the United States as the legal ruler of Mexico. The Wilson administration chose instead to remain in Mexico and thus set off a train of events that within only a few weeks would lead to a dramatic and completely unexpected resurgence of Villa.

The motives that led those members of the Wilson administration whose opinion finally predominated to reject withdrawal from Mexico were varied. Secretary of Agriculture David Houston was concerned primarily with the political repercussions such a decision might have; "his argument was that if the troops were withdrawn from Mexico, Villa would come back and make further raids and we would have to go in again and thus indicate a weak and vacillating policy."[96] Secretary of the Interior Lane, who in an initial conversation with Colonel House had favored the withdrawal of the expedition, reversed his stand within a few hours, and House himself, who on April 6 had still been indecisive, one day later came out firmly against ending the military involvement in Mexico. House came to this conclusion after having "asked a good many of our friends with whom I could talk with some degree of freedom, concerning Mexico and the consensus of opinion is almost entirely against withdrawing the troops."[97] Since House and Lane were the two men within the administration most closely connected to U.S. business interests in Mexico, it is likely that the "friends" to whom House referred were precisely those interests and that these men had also influenced Lane.

Wilson's motivations for deciding to keep U.S. troops in Mexico were more complex. He repeatedly emphasized his contempt for interventionist American businessmen in Mexico and his opposition to their demands that the United States annex part of Mexico or attempt to rule the country by force. Yet the proposals that his administration finally submitted to the Carranza government in late 1916 as a precondition for withdrawing from Mexico would in effect have "Cubanized" Mexico by imposing something very close to a Platt Amendment, the proviso that allowed U.S. troops to enter Cuba unilaterally when the U.S. government considered such intervention justified. Mexico would in many respects have become a protectorate of the United States. In late 1916, the U.S. commissioners negotiating with the Carranza government for the withdrawal of the Punitive Expedition wanted Mexico to accept a clause that stated:

The Government of Mexico solemnly agrees to afford full and adequate protection to the lives and property of citizens of the United States, or other foreigners, and this protection shall be adequate to enable such citizens of the United States . . . (to operate) industries in which they might be interested. *The United States reserves the right to re-enter Mexico and to afford such protection by its military forces, in the event of the Mexican Government failing to do so* [emphasis added].[98]

Such a clause would have abrogated Mexican sovereignty. Although some of his delegates to a U.S.–Mexican conference had accepted these terms, Carranza unequivocally rejected them. Even before the Wilson administration made such demands, his attitude toward the United States became more and more hostile when he realized that the presence of U.S. troops in Mexico was not a short-term affair. The first practical step he took was to cease his unofficial cooperation with the Americans and to rescind the permission he had given them to use the Mexican Northwestern Railroad to supply their troops.[99] His second step was to replace Obregón, whom he considered too willing to give in to the Americans, as his representative in the U.S.–Mexican negotiating team with Luis Cabrera, the political figure closest to him and more of a hard-liner than Obregón.

Carranza was soon driven to even more radical steps by a surge of Mexican nationalism, primarily in Chihuahua but also in the rest of the country. On April 12, an American patrol entered the city of Parral, located in southern Chihuahua, far from the U.S. border. Some local people led by a woman named Elisa Griensen threw stones and began shooting at the Americans as well. What worried Carranza was that the people of Parral had not only shouted "Viva Mexico!" as they attacked the Americans, but "Viva Villa!" as well. It was time for more energetic measures. Hostility to the Americans, Pershing reported to his superiors, was growing by leaps and bounds.[100]

Finance Minister Luis Cabrera informed the U.S. representative in Mexico that "every high official of the de facto government insisted upon immediate withdrawal of American troops. . . . Generals Carranza and Obregón are determined to secure withdrawal at once."[101] In the face of an imminent threat of war with Mexico, the Wilson administration decided on a partial retreat. The U.S. troops would be withdrawn from most of Chihuahua and concentrated in the north of the state, near the Mormon colonies of Colonia Dublán. The main aim of these troops would not be to capture Villa but to be "maintained here indefinitely as an incentive to Carranza forces to kill or capture Villa."[102] From that point on, the Punitive Expedition ceased to be a serious danger to Villa, although it could still inflict casualties on Villista units that ventured near its zone of occupation.

The continued presence in Mexico of U.S. troops continued to generate tensions with the Carranza administration and to entail the danger of a U.S.–Mexican war, which was in fact nearly precipitated by a clash between U.S. and Mexican troops in the Chihuahuan town of Carrizal in June 1916. A major battle was averted only at the last moment, when both the United States and the Carranza administration showed extreme caution and flexibility.

The situation that now emerged was extremely favorable for Villa. The Americans could not proceed against him as long as he did not approach their occupation zone, but their continued presence in Mexico generated increasing anti-American hostility, of which he was the main beneficiary. Carranza was increasingly discredited in the eyes of both Chihuahuan and Mexican public opinion because of his inability to expel the foreign troops, and at the same time he lost the main advantage that U.S. recognition had conferred upon him: the possibility of acquiring money, arms, and other supplies in the United States. As relations with Carranza grew more and more hostile, the United States first imposed a ban on arms shipments to Mexico and later extended it to gold, credit, and even food.[103] With some interruption, these restrictions were maintained until Carranza's fall in 1920. They constituted a major obstacle to carrying out a successful military campaign against either Villa or the other forces, both radical and conservative, still fighting Carranza in many parts of Mexico.

The Carrancista "Invasion" of Chihuahua

Pershing's invasion of Chihuahua led to another "invasion" of the state that would exacerbate Chihuahuan resentment at least as strongly and greatly redound to Villa's benefit. This second invading force consisted of Carrancista troops from outside Chihuahua whom the First Chief concentrated in that state to fight Villa and to resist the Americans in case a U.S.–Mexican war broke out. In the eyes of many Chihuahuans, who had always been extremely proud and jealous of their autonomy, these troops constituted no less an occupation force than the Americans. Their commander, one of Carranza's most influential generals, Jacinto D. Treviño, was an outsider who had never had any links to the state but soon assumed complete control of Chihuahua. On May 12, Carranza, probably at the instigation of Treviño, recalled Governor Enríquez, who became a high official in Carranza's war office, and replaced him as governor with Treviño's brother, Francisco.[104]

Only a few weeks later, Treviño attempted to secure the arrest of Luis Herrera, who commanded the only significant Chihuahuan force to support Carranza in the state. Alleging that Herrera's forces were disorganized, that he ruled arbitrarily over his native district of Parral, and that he sent no funds to the Chihuahuan state government, Treviño suggested to Secretary of War Obregón that Herrera be recalled to Mexico City and there placed in indefinite detention. In the meantime, Treviño would assume complete control of his troops.[105]

Both Obregón and Carranza refused. They were not willing to sacrifice one of their few influential Chihuahuan supporters, but they tacitly gave a free hand to Treviño to treat Chihuahua like an occupied territory. Treviño lost no time in making himself felt, and in so doing, he alienated much of the state's population. Treviño's successor, Francisco Murguía, who behaved no better, described the rule of his predecessor as follows:

Instead of exterminating banditry, a legacy of reaction [these were the terms used by the Carrancistas to designate Villa and his forces], General Treviño and his forces encouraged banditry because of their attacks on the property of peaceful men intent only on making a living who now became armed enemies of his forces for the simple reason that their interests and their lives were better protected by the bandits than by those who because of their military occupation should have been obliged to maintain peace and order. . . . The bad government that exists in this state since General

Treviño's brother Francisco has become governor is notorious. Francisco Treviño, his brother Federico, the general treasurer of the state named Doria, and other speculators have assumed control of all commercial transactions in the state.[106]

Murguía's harsh judgment of Treviño's rule was more than confirmed by U.S. intelligence reports. "These new troops in Juárez are doing what they please," one observer reported. "They go into restaurants and after eating all they can, walk out and refuse to pay. The poor on the streets are furious at their conduct, saying the soldiers can fill themselves without paying but they themselves die of hunger. These troops are nothing but a plague."[107]

"Conditions in Juárez are dreadful," another report concluded. "The troops instead of preserving order keep the people terrified. Every morning bodies of people killed the night before are found, the murderers are not brought to light and no protection is given the citizens. Houses are robbed every night and people are assaulted on the streets."[108]

Colonel Díaz González, a Carrancista military commander of El Valle, was probably one of the men to whom Murguía was referring. In a brief but highly explicit report, James Ord, an American observer, described Díaz's rule of his district, listing 21 cases of extortion and murder carried out by Díaz:

Cesario Valverde. Captured at Galeana by Major Elisondo about November 5 and accused of having attacked a traveler on El Valle–Galeana road and robbed said traveler, this in December 1915.

In reality, he is the uncle of a girl Elisondo wished to marry and objected to the marriage.

Colonel Díaz threatened to execute Valverde and mistreated him viciously, hanging him by the thumbs and beating him. On intervention of father Muñóz Valverde sentence of death was changed to a fine of 1000 pesos.

Ramón Rodríguez, November 15, 1916. Uncle of Lupe Muñóz, a young girl of El Valle. This girl was wanted by Colonel Díaz; Ramón Rodríguez objected and was imprisoned by Díaz, fined and mistreated physically; then sent to American border under charges of being a Villista and a Columbus raider.

Margarita Acosta. Public prostitute, an employee of Carranza government. She was sent for by Colonel Díaz and expressed unwillingness to go. Díaz imprisoned her and ordered execution without trial for being a Villista spy. She was known to have money to the amount of $500 in her possession at the time of her apprehension. Executed 4:00 A.M., November 22, 1916 without trial.

Both the sister and the maid of Margarita Acosta were seized by Díaz and executed without trial on the same charges. Díaz forced all men passing through El Valle to have a pass issued by him. "Those leaving town without a pass and apprehended, to be fined heavily and imprisoned. . . . All persons taking cattle through El Valle paid $5 per head duty to Colonel Díaz or were imprisoned and all cattle confiscated by Díaz."

Even those who paid Díaz were not assured of immunity. The report cites the case of Loren Taylor, "wanted by Colonel Díaz on the charge of killing cattle belonging to Carranza government. This cattle having been sold to Taylor by Colonel Díaz himself."[109]

American reports confirmed Murguía's accusation that Treviño not only allowed his commanders to steal but did so himself, in a way that was particularly resented by the people of Chihuahua. At a time of increasing hunger, which threatened to escalate into a full-scale famine, Treviño was exporting food from the state's capital. "Day before yesterday," American observers reported, "Treviño began to rob the stores in Chihuahua and is sending his loot to Juárez. Yesterday thirty-two cars of merchandise, among them five cars of flour, arrived in Juárez and instead of being stored at the custom house warehouse were stored at the warehouse of Cuellar brothers. Treviño is a big thief and they say he is simply looting Chihuahua. He and Cuellar have an arrangement of some sort."[110] In comparison, the years of Villista rule seemed like a golden era to many Chihuahuans, for whom Villa thus became the defender, not only of national sovereignty against the Americans, but of state sovereignty against outside Carrancista forces.

CHAPTER FIFTEEN

The Resurgence of Villa
in 1916-1917

In April and May 1916, with Villa in hiding recovering from his wound, the Carrancistas and the Americans were convinced that he was finished—both in political and military terms. Some believed that he was dead, others that he was so seriously wounded that, without access to a hospital, to which he could not be brought, since he would then easily be captured by the Carrancistas, he could never recover. But even if he did, there was a consensus among American and Carrancista observers that his army had been crippled beyond repair. Three of his most important lieutenants were dead, and more than half of the men who had accompanied him to Columbus were either dead or had dispersed. A huge array of outside troops, nearly 10,000 Americans and an equal number of Carrancistas, occupied Chihuahua. It seemed inconceivable that in the face of such odds, Villa could again become a force to be reckoned with in Chihuahua. Even after Villa resumed operations, the Carrancista military commanders were convinced that, as the commander of Carranza's forces in Chihuahua, Jacinto Treviño, stated, "So far as Villa was concerned he was no longer a factor to be considered a Mexican problem."[1] The Carrancista commander in Durango, Francisco Murguía, expressed a similar opinion.[2]

The small number of troops who initially rejoined Villa when he again resumed command of his forces at the beginning of June 1916, as well as his physical appearance, might very well have confirmed their expectations. "I saw Villa seated on an armchair, a totally changed man since I last saw him at my own home at San Gerónimo," a U.S. intelligence agent whom Pershing's men had managed to sneak into Villa's headquarters reported. "His long untrimmed jet-black beard first attracted my attention and beside him were two crutches; he wore only one shoe, the right, the swollen left foot was covered with a light woolen sock. . . . The leg is considerably swollen from the knee to the toes so that Villa is unable to wear a shoe. For very short distances about the house he moves with the aid of crutches. The wound pains him considerably when he rides a horse and [he] does so only when necessary."[3]

In spite of his wound and the reverses he had suffered, Villa was not discouraged. Like all successful revolutionaries, he had boundless energy and an equally boundless belief in himself. There was probably no other revolutionary leader in Mexico who had suffered as many reverses and managed in one way or the other to recover from them. He was convinced he could do so once again by utilizing the tactics first applied by the Maderistas in 1910–11 and then by himself in 1913 in Chihuahua. Many years later Mao Tse-tung would characterize such tactics with the maxim that a revolutionary guerrilla army should first assume control of the countryside and then encircle the cities.

By the end of 1916, Villa had managed to occupy and control a substantial part of the Chihuahuan countryside and headed an army of between 6,000 and 10,000 men. He even briefly occupied the state's capital. But many of the tactics by which he achieved these successes, although rewarding in the short run, were detrimental to his cause in the long run and would, in the end, turn large segments of the Chihuahuan population against him.

Paradoxically, the greatest advantage Villa enjoyed when he resumed his campaign in 1916 was far better access to ammunition than the Carrancistas had. Carranza's administration was deeply affected by the arms embargo the Americans had decreed against him and could not make up for it by buying arms in Europe, which was in the throes of World War I. The munitions factories that Carranza was rapidly establishing in Mexico could not yet make up for the losses. Villa, by contrast, had hidden large caches of arms before the defeat of the División del Norte. The one in Namiquipa had been betrayed to the Americans, but others were still at his disposal. Also, as a result of his victories over the Carrancistas in late 1916, he secured large amounts of arms and ammunition at the expense of his enemies. Among the tactics he employed to achieve victory, the least controversial was certainly his unprecedented attempt to act as a political agitator. In every village through which his troops marched, Villa asked the mayor to assemble the population on the main square, where he addressed them, denouncing the Americans and warning that they threatened to annex Chihuahua to the United States. A tactic that proved more controversial in the minds of many Mexicans was that although he constantly called for the union of all Mexicans against the American invaders, Villa always attacked the Carrancistas, and never the Americans.

His Robin Hood tactic of redistribution of goods proved far more controversial in 1916 than it had in 1913. Then he had redistributed the goods of Terrazas and other members of the oligarchy. Since little of their wealth was left, he now turned to the properties of Americans and of the Chihuahuan middle class. Cowboys on American-owned estates might have no objection if Villa slaughtered beef and distributed it to their families, but they were less happy when he took away cattle to feed his army. The miners in American-owned mines were even more resentful when Villa forced the American owners to leave and to close the mines down. What created the deepest resentment among part of the population was when Villa, after occupying a town, allowed large-scale looting of stores, in contrast to what had happened in 1913 and 1914, when he had maintained the strictest discipline. This substantially affected Chihuahua's middle class.

What many Chihuahuans most resented was that Villista terror now not only affected the oligarchy, foreigners, and enemies of Villa but was also directed against large parts of the peaceful civilian population. In many cases, Villa forced unwilling men to join his army, threatening not only them but their families with execution if they refused. Some of these men would desert at the first opportunity. Others would remain with Villa as long as he achieved victories but leave him after his first defeat. Many of them were then so fearful of being branded deserters and punished as such that they took up arms against Villa. As more and more people turned against him, Villa took increasingly savage reprisals, not only against the men who had deserted but a few times against women as well. That in turn antagonized ever larger sectors of the population.

As the resources of Chihuahua's large haciendas were depleted, Villa to a large degree supplied his troops with food produced by the free peasants and the tenants on Chihuahua's haciendas. As long as the harvest was good and the peasants had a surplus they could sell beyond their immediate needs—as was the case in 1916—and as long as he was able to pay in gold and silver, Villa could supply his men without antagonizing the peasantry. If the harvest was bad or if he was unable to pay in gold or silver for what he took, resentment against him grew in the Chihuahuan countryside.

Only in mid 1917 did Villa feel a strong negative impact as a result of his tactics. As of late 1916, both General John J. Pershing and the Carrancista leaders noted that the majority of Chihuahua's population still supported Villa.

The military and political successes that Villa enjoyed by late 1916 took everyone by surprise. It was the most successful campaign he waged between the time of his defeat in December 1915 and his surrender in 1920. It would once again put him in control of large parts of the state of Chihuahua, and once more, for a brief time, he would establish the rudiments of a regular army. In no other campaign he ever undertook, with the possible exception of the early months of 1913, after he crossed into Chihuahua with eight men, did he make such a personal effort to win "the hearts and minds" of the people, to use a modern phrase of American psychological warfare. In his speeches to townsfolk, his explanation of why he was fighting both the Americans and the Carrancistas was based on purely nationalistic motives. No social issues were even touched upon. The most important part of his speech was always a reference to the secret pact that he had accused the United States and Carranza of entering into in his Naco manifesto of November 1915. In the speeches he made to Chihuahua's villagers, he added a new twist, which he had first mentioned to Pablo López: Carranza, he said, had agreed to sell both Sonora and Chihuahua to the United States.

During a meeting in the village of Río Florido, Villa attempted to justify attacking the Carrancistas and not the Americans by stating that as long as Carranza was in power, no effective resistance could be waged against the Americans. "Carranza must fall as a traitor to our country and I am here to urge you all to join me in overthrowing this usurper of Mexican rights and liberty; we shall then be free to challenge the United States of North America and demonstrate to them that the Mexican people will not allow themselves to be bought and sold in bondage."[4] The results of this political campaign are perhaps best described by a secret agent of U.S. intelligence who was present at his camp during the initial phase of his 1916 summer and fall campaign. "Although the speech lasted for about ten minutes, Villa repeated the above statement several times in different words. He is not gifted in elocution and frequently words fail him. In this effort, such as it was, between fifty and one hundred more recruits of Río Florido flocked to his standard."[5]

Villa made up for his speeches' failure to touch upon social issues by redistributing goods and land. When he occupied the hacienda of San Ysidro, which had formerly belonged to Terrazas, he "ordered it confiscated for the use of his forces and then proceeded to partition it among the peon tenants with the only reservation that they should furnish food to the detachments of his forces that happened to halt there on the march."[6] After he had occupied the town of Jiménez, he "decided that all of the stores should be looted and that all of the spoils should be distributed to the peons and dependent families. The families of the men who joined him were to receive double the allowance." On the way from Jiménez to the next town he occupied, El Valle, "the wagons containing loot followed the center column with Villa. The articles contained on these wagons are distributed gratuitously to the peons en route."[7] After occupying El Valle, "the stores of the rich were sacked here as in the other places and distribution of the loot made to the peons. The wagons laden with loot brought from Jiménez were all unloaded and the articles likewise distributed."[8]

In other ways as well Villa tried to win the adherence of Chihuahua's population. After occupying an American-owned hacienda, "he announced that as the ranch belonged to the 'gringos' all of the buildings there would be set on fire. In this however he was dissuaded by Gorgorio Beltrán [one of his officers] on the ground that the tenants there were Mexicans and that burning the houses would be doing harm to his own people. The produce, such as wheat, corn, etc., was all confiscated and the portion not used by his troops was divided among the tenants."[9]

Villa at this time was more "humane" toward his prisoners than the Carrancistas, although it is doubtful whether the recipients of this "humanity" or the civilian witnesses to it were fully able to appreciate it. Whereas the Carrancistas either shot or hanged all the Villista prisoners they took, Villa in one of his first engagements decided to allow some of the prisoners he had taken to go free. After killing all the officers and wounded, and before setting the rest of the prisoners free, one of Villa's generals, Baudelio Uribe, cut off part of the men's ears, telling them that if they ever took up arms against Villa again and fell into his hands, they would easily be recognized as erstwhile prisoners and immediately shot.[10] Uribe became known throughout Chihuahua as the "ear-cutter."

In spite of the increasing popular sympathies for Villa, Carranza's military commanders in northern Mexico refused to take him seriously until the dramatic events of September 15, 1916 (see below). Francisco Murguía, the commander of the Carrancista forces in the states of Coahuila and Durango, told American observers that "the Villa faction, as a political or military factor, is a thing of the past," saying, "politically Villa himself is at the end of his career. As a military factor he has no organization and no following from which to create one."[11] Jacinto Treviño, commander of Carrancista forces in Chihuahua, had a similar opinion.

This opinion was not shared by some of the more perspicacious foreign observers in Mexico. Patrick O'Hea, the British vice-consul in the Laguna area, a strong opponent of Villa, reported:

If, for instance, we compare the relations between the better classes and the authorities today with those that existed in Villa times, and if we take into account the absolute insecurity not only for property but for life as well that existed then, we can appreciate the change for the better than has been affected. But on the other hand, the Villa regime, cruel and intolerable as it was, at least possessed an element of strength, which to these people is lacking. That party [the Villistas] could count upon the support and allegiance of the masses, but this [the Carrancistas] cannot do so for whatever may be the indifference of the indigenous inhabitants of other parts of the republic to this regime, here in the north the people are one and all hostile to it, and it is a question whether it is not only hunger and want and the absolute lack of supplies in the rural districts that keeps revolutionary bands from getting together, and possibly overthrowing the authority of the present administration.[12]

O'Hea considered the activities of the Carrancista military one of the prime causes for popular resentment:

The soldiers of these forces have been permitted almost unlimited license in disposing at will of the poor man's possessions, in the matter of animals and grain, and the abuses committed in this regard have caused feelings of bitterness and hatred which cannot be appeased. Of course there are some who are not ill-pleased that the poor should, at last, learn something also of the significance of the depredations of revolution and if these acts had for their objects the complete disillusionment of the lower classes and their becoming disgusted with all forms of revolution, something would have been attained. Such however is not the case.[13]

O'Hea was deeply worried about the nationalistic message that Villa was conveying. "The army that now follows him, Villa has called to his standard like a mad *mullah*, preaching a holy war, a crusade against the foreigner, and particularly against the 'gringo.' Every speech of his that has reached our ears is a raving mainly upon the same topic upon the lips of this man with an American bullet in his knee, a fanatical declamation against the invaders."[14]

In spite of Villa's growing popularity in both Durango and Chihuahua, Murguía and Treviño's skepticism about his military capacities in the summer and early fall of 1916 is understandable. Villa had not yet scored a significant victory. He had been defeated once by the Carrancistas at Villa Hidalgo in Durango, losing a large part of his equipment,[15] and had secured two victories that had no major relevance. The first, at the hacienda of Salaices, was due to an act of treachery. Ignacio Ramos, a Carrancista officer who headed a detachment of 600 men, had written a letter to Villa's lieutenant Nicolás Fernández calling on him to stop fighting the Carrancistas and unite forces against the Americans. On instructions from Villa, Fernández replied that he was ready to enter into negotiations with Ramos, who awaited him at the Hacienda de Corrales. Villa had no intention of keeping his word and of negotiating. Instead, his forces surreptitiously approached the hacienda and then attempted to storm it. The Carrancistas were prepared for treachery, however, and a bloody fight ensued in which Ramos was defeated, although he managed to flee with about 300 men.[16]

It is not clear why Villa committed this act of treachery. His attitude may have been provoked by events a short time before, when a Villista officer, Hilario Ramírez, had accepted such an offer and rejoined the Carrancistas with the aim of fighting the Americans. Instead, Ramírez had been imprisoned and was subsequently shot. Villa may have been afraid that such a fate awaited him. Villa may also have believed that Ramos had not written to him directly but rather to Fernández simply as a device to persuade one of his most important leaders to defect to Carranza. Or he may simply have felt that there were no rules at all in dealing with the Carrancistas.

The turning point that for a brief span of time seemed to augur a revival of Villismo on a national scale came on the night of September 15, 1916, when Villa's forces attacked and partly occupied the capital city of Chihuahua.[17]

Villa's Major Offensive

In early September 1916, accompanied by only five men, Villa reconnoitered the approaches to Ciudad Chihuahua. For an hour he looked nostalgically at the bustling traffic in the state's capital, telling his secretary José Jaurrieta: "Isn't this a beautiful ranch? But we have to enjoy it in full security. Now it is full of monkeys [this was the term he used for the Carrancistas]. . . . I love Chihuahua; I was born in Durango; but my love for Chihuahua is so great that when people ask me from where I come, I proudly tell them from Chihuahua." After a moment of silence, Jaurrieta recounted: "Villa said, full of fury, 'If I feel like it I will pronounce the *grito* [cry] there on the 15th."[18] Clearly, Villa was considering an attack on the city, since Mexican state governors and municipal mayors have the honor of giving the *grito* of independence on September 15.

But Villa's decision to attack Chihuahua was not just a momentary whim. It was based on rational calculation. Villa had no intention of permanently occupying the capital; he knew he did not yet have sufficient forces to do so. The primary purpose of his attack was to free a number of political prisoners held by the Carrancistas in the state's penitentiary. Some were supporters of his, but the bulk were Orozquistas, whom he had pursued with relentless energy and cruelty in 1913 and 1914. The most famous of these prisoners was José Inés Salazar, who had commanded the forces against whom Villa had fought in 1912 in Parral during the Orozco uprising and in 1913 at one of Villa's most famous battles, Tierra Blanca, when Salazar had been allied with Huerta.

With the help of these men, whom he intended to rescue from the death sentences that the Carrancistas had imposed upon them, Villa hoped to gain the support of his erstwhile Orozquista enemies and their followers. A few days before the planned attack on Ciudad Chihuahua, Villa had a meeting with all of his commanders and told them that the main aim of the attack was to seize the penitentiary in order "to save his enemies [Marcelo] Caraveo[19] and Salazar from death, since now that Orozquismo was dead, they were Chihuahuan brothers."[20]

Villa realized that an attack on the state's capital, especially on Mexico's greatest national holiday, could enormously enhance his prestige and his reputation.

Surprise attacks had always been his hallmark. Yet it was also an enormously dangerous undertaking, since he commanded at most 2,000 men, while more than 9,000 Carrancistas were concentrated in the capital. It was the size of his garrison, the obvious discrepancy in numbers between Villa's forces and his own, as well as his contempt for Villa, that led Treviño not to take the most elementary precautions. He was twice warned that Villa was approaching Ciudad Chihuahua and was planning to attack but refused to put the garrison on alert.[21] He did concentrate a few pieces of artillery on a hill overlooking the city, but allowed most of his troops to revel and celebrate Mexico's Independence Day along with thousands of civilians. Villa's attacking columns had no difficulty in surreptitiously entering the city. Treviño's troops were celebrating, and those of them who were not took the Villistas for outside visitors coming to join in the capital's celebration.

Villa had planned the attack carefully. While his main detachment stormed the penitentiary, other Villista columns were to attack Carrancista military barracks and occupy the government palace. At midnight they went into action, shouting their traditional war cry, "Viva Villa!" Treviño was taken by surprise and fled to the hill of Santa Rosa, where his artillery was concentrated. Villa freed the political prisoners from the penitentiary. His men surprised the guards, killed all of them without themselves suffering any losses, and after a few minutes brought Salazar to Villa, who embraced him, saying, "I have come here for only one reason, to prevent you from being shot."[22] Caraveo, whom Villa had also hoped to free and to recruit, was not in the prison.

Villa now retreated with the freed prisoners, most of his troops, and some booty, consisting mainly of uniforms, without having sustained any significant losses. Two columns of Villistas were, however, unable to join in the retreat. They were the men who had occupied the governor's palace and surrounding buildings. Since these buildings were far from Villa's headquarters, he could send no messenger to advise them that he had sounded the retreat. It had been agreed that as soon as the firing subsided in the district where the penitentiary was located, these men would retire. But the firing did not subside, because the Carrancistas continued wildly shooting in all directions even after the Villistas had departed. It was only in the morning, when Treviño ordered his artillery to fire on the governor's palace, that the occupiers realized that they had to leave. They managed to fight their way through the Carrancista lines, but lost nearly three-quarters of their men on the way. In a report to Secretary of War Obregón, Treviño tried to depict the battle as a "brilliant" defense against Villa.[23]

Among the Chihuahuan population, the battle was seen in a very different light. With 10,000 American troops occupying parts of Chihuahua and 9,000 Carrancistas in the capital, Villa had managed to storm into Ciudad Chihuahua, free all prisoners, temporarily occupy the governor's palace, and then make his way out of the city with the bulk of his forces. His prestige now soared; the defeats of 1915 were forgotten, and he was again Villa the Invincible. "Villa is accredited with having over 1500 men," American observers reported, "and men from the whole mountain country are flocking to him and he is getting stronger every day while the majority of the people in Chihuahua are pro-Villista."[24]

From September 15, 1916, the day of the surprise attack on Ciudad Chihuahua, until December of that same year, Villa seemed to replicate some of the great successes he had achieved in 1913–14, and for a time his army once again became an irresistible juggernaut, sweeping from victory to victory. In the process, he would again manage to rally massive popular support, establish firm control not only over rural areas but over several cities in Chihuahua, and transform his army, although for only a brief span of time, from a guerrilla force into a regular army, which in November 1916 would once again capture Ciudad Chihuahua, this time through a regular siege, lasting several days.

Villa's withdrawal from Ciudad Chihuahua was thus not a retreat but rather the beginning of a major offensive. His first target was San Andrés, a town with which he had always had a special relationship, and from which many of his Dorados came. A relatively large detachment of Carrancista troops, mainly from Carranza's home state of Coahuila and commanded by Colonel Carlos Zuazua, had prepared a trap for Villa. While Zuazua, with about 60 men, was occupying the railroad station at San Andrés, "a detachment of about 300 Carrancistas under Colonel Maultos [part of Zuazua's regiment] had been purposely sent out by Zuazua with orders to remain in concealment in the immediate vicinity of the pueblo; Zuazua's plan being to inveigle Villa to attack the station and Maultos was to attack the Villistas from the rear during the engagement." At the last moment, however, Maultos lost his nerve or, as one observer more delicately put it, "overestimating the Villista strength [he] failed to deliver the expected attack." Left to fight on alone with 60 men against more than 400 Villistas, Zuazua continued to resist for six more hours, until 31 men had been killed. At that point he decided to surrender. Villa showed no mercy, and Zuazua and all his men were executed.[25]

Villa managed to lure another detachment of Zuazua's troops, consisting of 25 men, to San Andrés. Having obtained Zuazua's code, he wired the lieutenant in charge of the detachment to come immediately to his rescue. The lieutenant replied that he had just heard from a soldier who had managed to escape that Zuazua had in fact been defeated. Villa, posing as Zuazua, replied that the man was a deserter and that he should be executed immediately. The lieutenant, blindly obeying orders, executed the soldier who had warned him, marched to San Andrés, was promptly captured without firing a shot, and executed together with his whole detachment.

The remnants of Zuazua's detachment, the men under Colonel Maultos who had refused to attack Villa, now fled all the way to Coahuila. It was a terrible journey:

They marched across the desert Bolsón de Mapimi, losing 300 horses and forty men, women and children dead from starvation . . . and upon arrival in Cuatro Cienégas vicinity they killed cattle and raided fields to the extent that people were afraid they would die from eating so ravenously after being without food for so long. This band have disbanded and scattered from Cuatro Cienégas to Allende. Their colonel is at Múzquiz and says he will never go back to Chihuahua again; that he has had enough of fighting with reloaded ammunition and nothing to eat or wear.[26]

The battle of San Andrés marked the beginning of more savage treatment of prisoners by Villa than at the beginning of his campaign. Before his attack on Ciudad Chihuahua, he had frequently spared prisoners. Now executions were the rule. This new attitude was doubtless linked to Carranza's declaration of martial law and to the treatment of Villista prisoners taken in Ciudad Chihuahua. "They just marched by the office with seventeen [Villista] prisoners being taken to Santa Rosa hill," an American observer reported to the U.S. official Zach Lamar Cobb from Chihuahua, "each of whom had a pick and shovel to dig his own grave. . . . Wounded Villistas were executed. The boy Villista they had in hospital and another they captured were both put out of the way yesterday and that in the hospital."[27] "Not only captured Villista soldiers but sympathizers were also executed and 'milk peddlers' coming in from nearby ranches have been imprisoned because of their failure to inform the authorities of Villista activities," Cobb informed the U.S. State Department.[28]

The battle of San Andrés also marked the beginning of a string of Villista victories that gave Villa control of more and more of the Chihuahuan countryside. His next objective was the mining town of Cusihuiráchic. Villa warned Colonel José V. Elizondo, the commander of the Carrancista garrison in the town, that he was coming, and Elizondo decided to retreat. As his troops were leaving Cusihuiráchic, they saw armed men approaching and immediately opened fire upon them. After a bloody battle they found out that these men were Carrancistas under General Ramos, sent to reinforce them. When the two detachments finally discovered their mistake and united to face the approaching Villa, they were soundly defeated. Ramos and Elizondo managed to escape to Ciudad Chihuahua (Elizondo was so panic-stricken that he threw away his pistol, which came into the possession of the Villistas),[29] but most of their men were either killed or captured by Villa and then executed. Villa spared only a Carrancista military band, which thereafter played for his army and for the civilian population in each of the towns he captured.

Villa then proceeded to the town of San Isidro, where he celebrated his saint's day lavishly with horse races and cockfights while the captured band played in the streets. A few days later, near the town of Santa Isabel, he defeated a strong column of troops under General Marcial Cavazos that Treviño had sent out against him.

As Villa won one victory after another, a new legend of his invincibility began to emerge in Chihuahua. Villa himself would be its first victim. After defeating Cavazos, he became so overconfident that he allowed his troops to rest in Santa Isabel without posting the usual guards and taking the precautions that he usually took when he occupied a town. The result was that the Villistas scattered throughout Santa Isabel were surprised the next morning by a large column of Carrancista troops under General Andrés Osuna. Routed from their beds, most Villistas fled the town, but, fortunately for Villa, Osuna failed to follow up on his initial advantage, which was great indeed. Not only had he surprised the Villistas, but he had captured most of the horses they had brought with them to Santa Isabel, and the Villistas were forced to flee the town on foot. "For a brief time Osuna was in full control of the situation," according to Villa's secretary Jaurrieta, but he let the advantage slip through his fingers. Jaurrieta surmises that Osuna and his men were demoralized when they found hundreds of bodies of Cavazos's men strewn along the way to Santa Isabel.[30] When a small group of Villistas opened fire, they feared an ambush, and precisely when they could have caused havoc among Villa's men, they retreated and abandoned Santa Isabel. The

Villistas then recovered most of their horses, and the next day they charged into Osuna's troops, who had fortified themselves on hills surrounding Santa Isabel. The resistance of the Carrancista troops was brief. Soon their commander crowned his decision of the day before by fleeing back to Ciudad Chihuahua. Mounted on a good horse, he managed to escape. But his soldiers, riding undernourished and second-rate horses, were slaughtered by the Villistas.

Villa's military capacities and his relentless pursuit of offensive warfare were doubtless essential factors in the victories he secured. They were nevertheless due as much to the fear he inspired as to the lack of ammunition and to the incompetence and at times cowardice of Carranza's generals. At San Andrés, Maultos had failed to attack Villa from the rear, thus sacrificing Zuazua and his detachment. At Cusihuiráchic, Ramos and Elizondo had fought with each other instead of fighting Villa. At Santa Isabel, not only had Osuna failed to exploit the initial success of his surprise attack, but, more important, as Obregón pointed out, instead of taking advantage of their great numerical superiority, Cavazos and Osuna had attacked Villa separately, with the result that both were defeated.

After winning this string of victories, Villa took to the written word. He sent an ironical letter to Treviño and issued a manifesto to the people of Mexico. In the letter, he told Treviño, "As your subordinate you know that I always have to make a report to you," and told him to strike 300 men from the lists of troops he commanded. "Send us more," he told him,

since you have a factory for doing so. Traitor[,] . . . with the gringos on Mexican soil, why are you not fighting them? Isn't it because your constitutionalist government authorizes you as constitutionalist to allow the invader to remain in Mexico? You cannot constitute a government, because the people are not behind you, traitors, and the curse of history be upon you. I shall not tell you any more, since I know what a despot you are, and talking to you is like talking to a donkey who has never studied.[31]

His manifesto to the Mexican people, his first public written pronouncement since the attack on Columbus, was written in a very different language, with a very different content. It constituted both a kind of declaration of war on the United States and a nationalistic program for the future of Mexico. It contained no reference to the Columbus raid. Until the day he died, Villa would never publicly acknowledge his participation in that attack. His manifesto attacked both the Americans for occupying Mexico and the Carrancistas for not resisting them. It called for all Mexicans to make common cause against the foreign invader:

Our beloved country has reached also one of those solemn moments in which, in order to cooperate against the unjust invasion of our eternal enemies, the barbarians of the north, we should be united, imitating that group of heroes who, immovable and smiling, offered their lives in the holocaust to the sacred country in which they were born. . . . It is disgraceful that there cannot be unity, although our beloved country has patriotic and self-sacrificing men; however, it also has Carrancistas, who, unfortunately, today govern the destinies of Mexico, which impoverished, defenseless, and unable to guard its frontiers, delivers them to the invaders.

The manifesto contained a radical nativist program. All foreign property was to be confiscated immediately. In future, only foreigners who had been naturalized citizens for 25 years would be able to acquire real estate in Mexico. In addition, they would only be allowed to buy properties in the interior of the republic and not close to its borders. Americans and Chinese were to be excluded from that arrangement too and were not to be allowed to hold any property at all in Mexico. "In order to stimulate the development of home industry, all mercantile operations with the United States will be suspended, expecting with this measure to awaken the energy of the Mexican laborer and help in the perfection of the national products. Therefore the railroads and telegraph lines will be cut eighteen leagues from the border of the United States."

The plan that most strongly affected Mexicans was the implementation of universal military service and a declaration "that all Mexicans refusing to take arms in this special occasion, during which the national integrity is in danger, will be declared traitors and their property confiscated without chance of recovering it." The plan called for the election of a president, who could not be a military leader, and a congress composed of "persons of outstanding character and culture and of humble birth, those who are apt to know more about the wants of the people, the wants of that large, poor, suffering, much-enduring family."[32]

The plan is significant not only for what it contains but for what it does not. Unlike all of Villa's previous public pronouncements, there is no mention either of land reform or of any other social reforms, except for the vague reference to persons of humble origin constituting the majority of the Mexican Congress, so that they might understand the needs of the poor.

This omission was linked both to the timing of the manifesto and to the main audience to which it was addressed. The manifesto was issued at a time when Villa, having achieved significant victories in the mountain region of Chihuahua, was seriously preparing an offensive, first against Ciudad Chihuahua and then against Torreón, that might give him control of large parts of Mexico's north and would once again make him a national leader. The potentially most receptive audience for his nationalistic message was the most nationalistic segment of the Carranza movement: the army. His call in the manifesto for the confiscation of "the property of foreigners . . . in favor of the nation" to finance the war was a clear appeal to the Carrancista army leaders to seize the one source of wealth that had been least affected by revolutionary turmoil. At the same time, by excluding any military man from the presidency of Mexico, Villa was excluding himself and telling Carranza's military chieftains that he might agree to the choice of a neutral civilian as president.

Villa's hopes were not entirely unfounded. Not only was he winning in military terms, but scores of Carranza deserters were joining his ranks, and the Carranza regime in Chihuahua seemed to be disintegrating. As George Carothers wrote to the State Department:

Situation in Chihuahua is really desperate for Carrancistas. The city is isolated, the railroad having been cut and bridges burned south of line, to the north constantly menaced, and telegraph lines cut almost daily. Treviño has sufficient men to control situation if they would fight, but they are demoralized, poorly equipped, paid practically nothing and desert at the first opportunity. It is for this reason that Treviño does not send them any distance from Chihuahua City.[33]

In a desperate move to stave off a Villista attack on Chihuahua and a Villista breakthrough to central and southern Mexico, the Carrancista high command mobilized whatever troops it could muster in neighboring Durango and sent them to attack Villa in the mountain regions of western Chihuahua. These troops were headed by Fortunato Maycotte, who had played an important role in defeating Villa at Celaya, and by the Arrieta brothers, who had fought for years against pro-Villista guerrillas in Durango. Obregón hoped that having fought Villa before, these leaders would not be intimidated by him and would know how to deal with him.

The most important instruction that Obregón gave Maycotte was to attack Villa and not allow him to go on the offensive, since the federal troops would not have sufficient ammunition to resist a Villista attack.[34] "You know," Obregón wrote Maycotte one day later, "that Arango [Obregón always referred to Villa when they were fighting by his original name, so as to draw attention to his bandit past] must be dealt with the utmost energy, then he will turn tail as we have often seen him do."[35] Maycotte and the Arrietas took Obregón's instructions so literally that at La Enramada they suffered a devastating defeat.

As Maycotte's and Arrietas' troops slowly advanced on the Villista troops, who had set up positions at La Enramada, they were suddenly attacked by a small contingent of Villista troops led by "the ear-cutter," Baudelio Uribe. After only a few minutes of fighting, Uribe's greatly outnumbered contingent fled toward the Villista lines and the Carrancistas, believing that the Villistas were now in retreat, followed them in a wild pursuit without any discipline or organization. They were met by withering fire from the Villista lines, were decimated, and fled from the battlefield.

No one has described Villa's tactics better than his archrival, Obregón, who warned Treviño's successor, Murguía:

The tactic that Villa employed during this last campaign, and that has produced magnificent results for him, is the following: he positions his people for battle on a terrain that he has chosen beforehand and sends some of his men to challenge ours, who then feign a disorderly retreat to the place where Villa has established himself with the rest of his troops. This leads to the disorganization of our forces pursuing Villa's first column; they carry out an attack on Villa's disorganized forces, believing him to be fully defeated, [and] pursue his forces without any order. This tactic has given him magnificent results against the forces of General Treviño and a short time ago against those of Arrieta and Maycotte.[36]

Ever the diplomat, Obregón was careful not to be too harsh in his criticism of Maycotte and the Arrietas. Murguía had no such compunction and, in a blunt letter to Carranza, laid full responsibility for the defeat on the shoulders of Maycotte and the Arrietas, saying:

I have come to the sole conclusion that the disaster or complete failure of Arrieta and Maycotte was due to the absolute lack of both military tact and organization for combat and the complete absence of any disposition to counteract the defeat of his forces; it must be emphasized that they fought no more than ten minutes then turned around and without stopping fled from Santa Rosalia to Bermejillo, leaving more than 400 weapons with ammunition and prisoners in the hands of the enemy. From Bermejillo they withdrew without order.

Murguía accused the Arrietas of allowing a train full of horses and ammunition to fall into enemy hands in Santa Rosalia. In Murguía's opinion, the responsibility for that disaster was shared by the commander of the Carrancista garrison at Santa Rosalia, Mariano López Ortiz, whom Murguía called "a chocolate general."[37]

Villa's Ambivalent Situation: Victory on the Battlefield and Gradual Loss of Popular Support

After Maycotte's defeat, Treviño sent his wife and $47,000 to El Paso. He himself holed up in Ciudad Chihuahua and refused to go on the attack against Villa again. For him, Villa's summer and fall campaign had been an unmitigated disaster. According to one Mexican observer, who kept a record of the battles that had taken place between Carrancistas and Villistas in September 1916, "The record shows that the Villistas were successful in twenty-two different encounters in all of which they captured arms and ammunitions from the Carrancistas."[38]

Villa's situation was in many ways reminiscent of the one he faced three years before in the fall of 1913, on the eve of his successful attacks on Torreón, Ciudad Chihuahua, and Ciudad Juárez. As in 1913, he now controlled Chihuahua's countryside, while the federal troops were confined to the large cities. As in 1913, outside military governors and their troops had incurred the hatred of the people of Chihuahua. As in 1913, the U.S. government was hostile to Mexico's federal government and had embargoed all arms sales to it. This embargo was more effective than in 1913, since the European powers were involved in World War I and so were unable to provide an alternative source of arms to the Mexican government. As in 1913, revolts against the federal government were flaring up all over Mexico, so that it could not concentrate all of its forces on the revolution in Chihuahua. As in 1913, the federal army was plagued by corruption, demoralization, and desertions. According to his successor, Murguía, Treviño had padded the payroll in the same way that his Porfirian predecessors had done: the actual number of his soldiers was far smaller than the number he declared, and Treviño himself pocketed the pay for his phantom troops. While the Carrancistas never resorted to the leva, and their army, unlike its federal predecessors, consisted mainly of volunteers, those volunteers were different from the revolutionaries who had taken up arms in 1913–14. Then ideology had played a major role; now many Carrancista recruits were men who had been forced into the ranks by fear of starvation. They were largely underfed, underpaid, and unwilling to fight, and their commanders were afraid that at the first opportunity they might desert.

In spite of these similarities, there were significant differences that made Villa's situation in 1916 more precarious than it had been in 1913. Then he had been able to count on the benevolent neutrality of the United States—at times the U.S. authorities had tolerated shipments of arms to him, and by early 1914, they had lifted the arms embargo, so that he could buy whatever he wanted across the border. This time, as a result of his attack on Columbus, he had incurred the hostility of both the federal and local American authorities, and smuggling arms to him was an extremely difficult and risky affair. Vigilance on the U.S. border was greater than it had been in 1913, and Pershing's expedition, although immobilized, loomed like a kind of sword of Damocles; it might strike at him at any time.

In 1913, the Chihuahuan countryside had been immensely wealthy. Its riches afforded the basis both for redistributing wealth, and thus gaining popular support, and for equipping Villa's army. Now most of the wealth was gone, and Villa had far fewer resources at his disposal.

Above all, the attitude of significant parts of the population of Chihuahua toward him was changing. In many parts of the state, he was still immensely popular. When he came into a village or town, people flocked to greet him and to listen to the speeches in which he denounced the American invasion and the Carrancista government for tolerating it. Many doubtless accepted what he said again and again: that he could easily have become a millionaire, had he wanted to, instead of fighting a bloody guerrilla war in Mexico. Many looked back at 1914, the first year of Villista rule in Chihuahua, as a kind of golden age. There had been no fighting in the state then, they were governed by their own people, Villa was constantly redistributing goods, and his currency was accepted north of the border. In 1916, many hoped that Villa would consolidate his hold on the state of Chihuahua and offer them protection from the graft, corruption, and pillage of the Carrancista military.

They soon discovered, to their dismay, that Villa in the fall of 1916 was a very different man from Villa in the fall of 1913. The first to discover how changed he was were Chihuahua's middle classes. In 1913–14, he had directed his hatred at the oligarchy and wooed the middle classes. He had spared their properties and not required forced loans or other involuntary contributions of them. The same had been true of foreigners, with the conspicuous exceptions of the Chinese and the Spaniards. This time, with no domestic oligarchy left whose wealth he could expropriate, Villa demanded huge contributions both from foreigners and from Chihuahua's middle classes. After he took Parral, "fifty-two of the most prominent merchants were lined up before Villa himself. . . . Villa made them a stirring address, in which he abused the better classes in general, foreigners in particular, and 'los consules' (the consuls) most of all, making one exception in his speech in favor of the Germans only whom he stated to quote his own words, 'Tienen los huevos bien colgados' (i.e., had real balls). He demanded a large financial contribution from the merchants. In one respect they were lucky, for unlike the situation in other cities, no looting occurred in Parral. "There was no drunkenness nor disorder in the streets of Parral during the presence of Villa there as he continues to have the greatest aversion to alcoholic drink and keeps it from his soldiers as much as possible."[39]

Some of the merchants and other well-to-do citizens of Parral might have preferred looting to the measures that Villa now took against their sons. He forced all of them into a stockade, telling them that they would now have to live as the poor were living. The only food they were allowed was dried meat and corn, and their families were not allowed to have any contact with them. What worried the prisoners and their families most was not the food they were forced to take but the uncertainty they faced. Their fears were finally allayed when, before leaving Parral, Villa freed all of the stockade prisoners.

These measures were not just designed to intimidate the well-to-do and force them to pay the contributions Villa demanded. They were probably also a sign of his wrath against large segments of the middle class (especially merchants), which had clearly turned against him. Villa may also have hoped by these measures to increase his popularity among the poor, many of whom held the merchants responsible for the increasing inflation sweeping Chihuahua. He may also have hoped that the killings of Chinese that he perpetrated might appeal to the xenophobia of some of Chihuahuans.

Although the number of volunteers willing to fight in his army had greatly increased, Villa felt that he needed still more, and he now changed his policies toward the lower classes and instituted forced recruitment. This sparked a tremendous wave of resentment against him among the lower classes. After he entered the town of San Isidro, an eyewitness reported:

Villa went at once to the main plaza, bringing with him a music band from Cusi. The band played and many shouted, "Villa, viva Villa! Viva Villa!" etc. Then Villa made a speech, stating that the Americans were coming in from every direction into Mexico and that Carranza had sold most of the republic to the Americans, and urged all his beloved paisanos to assist him to run the gringos out of the country, etc. Some three hundred signed at once. The number was so small that he became vexed. He took dinner and left at 3:30 P.M. for the station at San Isidro. . . .

During the days that Villa was in San Isidro, Julio Acosta [one of Villa's lieutenants] gave orders that every man that could walk must present himself to him and leave with him and Villa to fight against the Americans, that everybody must come to help and those that did not come were sent for and brought in by force. Three men were shot because they refused to go and many were badly treated and tortured and beaten and hung up, etc. One of the Rico boys was badly beaten and others burned with hot irons.

All this was a great surprise to the peons, as they were certain they would have a free hand again.[40]

Popular resentment of forced impressment was greatly increased by the threats Villa issued that the families of men who deserted would suffer. There is no evidence that Villa ever carried out such reprisals at this time, but the threat was sufficient to generate a large amount of hostility to him.

The resentment of many of these forcibly impressed men grew when Villa informed them that he was not sending them against the Americans but first against the Carrancistas. This led to "great uproar and dissatisfaction among the men. Eight were shot at the station and the others departed."[41] Some deserted, although most remained to fight. Among many of his soldiers, Villa still evoked sympathy and admiration. His string of victories increased that admiration, and many thought that he might once again control Chihuahua and perhaps all of Mexico. Some, above all deserters from Carranza's army, were lured by the wage of one silver peso a day that Villa was paying his men, far more than the Carrancistas were paying.[42] Above all, Villa's march on Ciudad Chihuahua offered Chihuahua's villagers a chance to take revenge on Treviño and his soldiers for the abuse and extortion they had suffered. As an observer, W. M. Stell, put it in a report to Cobb:

discontent exists through western Chihuahua, with soldiers because of worthless Carranza money and among populace because soldiers confiscated their means of livelihood, for instance butchering milk cows, upon which families are dependent, to furnish beef for soldiers. I saw a petition which had been presented, prepared by 175 ranchers in vicinity Cusi appealing to governor to stop military depredations and carrying implied threat unless protection were afforded. Carrancistas through their abuses have lost friendship of populace.[43]

In some cases, resentment increased when Treviño failed to provide protection against Villa even when the local citizenry offered to fight for the government themselves:

It is known that he [Villa] is coercing natives to follow him, but men so impressed would probably not remain with him if there were any other alternative. When Villa recently resumed activities, the people in the towns along the northwestern railroad, including Madera, Guerrero, and other towns in that section, sent word through their leaders to the *de facto* government that they would gladly take up arms and help the government against him if supported, but no notice was taken of their offer.[44]

Villa's hold on his soldiers and their perception that he was winning increased when he took steps to transform his ragged guerrilla force into a regular army. History seemed to be repeating itself. After occupying Parral, he had uniforms made for all of his men,[45] and they now looked far more like a regular army than their ragged Carrancista enemies. Now that he controlled the whole region, Villa could once again pack his men into troop trains as in the heyday of the División del Norte.

Villa had become once again the Carrancista high command's main problem. The threat he represented was heightened by the presence of Pershing's expedition in northern Chihuahua. Carranza had been successful in obliging Pershing to retreat to his bases and not to venture outside of them. Negotiations between Mexican and American commissioners were under way in Atlantic City for the complete withdrawal of the Punitive Expedition from Mexico. If Villa succeeded in controlling all of northern Mexico, it was possible that Wilson would send Pershing against him. In that case, Pershing would have to push far further into Mexico's interior than he had ever done before, and Carranza would face an impossible dilemma. Carranza had clearly told the Americans that he would not allow them to march south into Mexico again. If Carranza did not keep his word, if he allowed Pershing to proceed south, not only would Villa be able to assume the mantle of the defender of Mexico's national sovereignty, but Carranza's own nationalistically minded generals might topple him. If he resisted, there was every chance that a full-scale U.S.–Mexican war would break out, which Carranza wanted to avoid at all costs.

The Disarray of the Carrancista High Command

The Carrancista high command sought frantically to assess the reasons for Villa's continual successes. Treviño was of no help in this. Not only did he underplay his defeats or fail to report them, he had only one constantly repeated explanation: lack of ammunition. This was indeed a very real problem. But neither Treviño's subordinates nor the Carrancista high command nor Treviño's colleague Francisco Murguía, the commander of the Carrancista forces in Durango, were ready to see lack of ammunition as the main reason for the catastrophic reverses that Carranza's troops were incurring.

Luis Herrera, the only important Chihuahuan general allied with Carranza, placed the blame for the Carrancistas' repeated military disasters squarely on Treviño's shoulders. Treviño, he felt, had no understanding of the nature of guerrilla warfare. "I am suffering the consequences of the fact that the great generals who have had successes in regular battles believe that the same tactics should be used against guerrilla attacks, as is the case with the hero of El Ebano [Treviño], who allowed the bandit to get where he is." He openly accused Treviño of not being interested "in the welfare of the republic but only in his own enhancement."[46]

Obregón shared Herrera's view of Treviño. What finally moved him to remove Treviño from his command and to admonish him in unusually blunt terms was a suggestion by Treviño that reeked of panic. Fearing an imminent attack by Villa on the state's capital, Treviño wired Obregón asking that troops to relieve the city be sent from Sonora across U.S. territory.[47] This was the last thing the Carrancista high command wanted. It would have meant asking for help from the United States, at a time when relations were at a breaking point, and amounted to confessing that without U.S. help, they could not vanquish Villa. If the Americans granted such permission, it would be grist for Villa's propaganda charge that there was a secret collusion between Carranza and the United States.

Treviño's proposal was the last straw for Obregón. With the support of Carranza, he now decided to wrest the command of operations in Chihuahua from Treviño and proceeded to do so in a particularly humiliating way. Murguía was instructed to head a relief column of more than 6,000 men and march immediately to Chihuahua. Treviño was to place himself under the command of Murguía, who was nominally of a lower rank. Obregón also wrote an unusually blunt letter to Treviño, saying:

The First Chief has shown me the message that you sent him, where you attribute the disasters you have suffered to the lack of ammunition. Allow me to make some clarification in this respect so that you do not attempt to escape from the responsibilities incumbent upon a man of your military stature by putting the blame on the lack of ammunition. The fact that I have never been informed of the defeats that you suffered and that you have always attempted to hide them has been one of the reasons why you were not able to take the necessary measures in time. The successes of Villa in this state have consisted in the way in which he has been able to surprise our leaders, the last of which was his sudden entry into the capital, occupying both the jail and the palace. The lack of ammunition was not a factor in allowing the enemy to surprise our forces. The contrary is the case. When one has little ammunition, vigilance should be all the greater.

Obregón stated that the defeats suffered by both Ramos and Osuna had not been because of lack of ammunition. It was the division of their forces into two columns that gave Villa the chance to vanquish them.

Obregón called on Treviño to take the offensive against Villa. "If the ammunition that you have to defend this city [Chihuahua] with is so limited, then you should concentrate all your troops and take the offensive when Villa attempts to attack the city, and you should secure victory before lack of ammunition gives it to the enemy. It is not my aim to judge the military operations that you have carried out," Obregón wrote Treviño, after having done just that. "Perhaps I would have made the same errors had I been in command, but I do want to put an end to the idea that you have that the lack of ammunition is responsible for the present situation."[48]

In his reply, Treviño tried to shift the blame as much as he could to his subordinates, to Obregón himself, and to the Americans. He had not informed the Carrancista high command of the defeats of his troops, he said, because his subordinates had hidden that information from him. A few days earlier he had called many of his subordinate commanders cowards, since they were afraid to engage Villa. Treviño wrote Obregón that Obregón himself was at least as much to blame as he was for the defeat of Maycotte and the Arrietas. Finally, the most important factor in Villa's successes was the presence of the Americans in Mexico:

I believe that the Secretariat of War has not understood that the bandit in order to recruit men has exploited with great success the fact that American troops are stationed on our territory, which has led to a great deal of confusion that can be seen above all in the mountain region where the bandit has still a certain measure of support; this constitutes the explanation why the bandit, who was defeated completely on September 16 in this capital, should suddenly a few days later dispose of more men and of new men in the northwestern part of the state.

Treviño now asked to be relieved of his command and to be granted a furlough in order to take care of private affairs.

Obregón refused to allow Treviño to escape from what could very well be a major disaster in Chihuahua. "You will remain at the head of your forces under the orders of General Murguía until the main forces of the Villistas are destroyed in the state. When this had been accomplished, you will receive the furlough you have asked for."[49]

Murguía was even harsher in his judgment of his predecessor than Obregón had been. He saw Treviño's corruption and vanity as the main causes for his defeats. By their exactions and corruption, Treviño and his brother had not only alienated the population of the state, they had also padded the payroll and neglected to take the most elementary precautions. "In a more general way," Murguía stated, "while the commercial spirit awakens in our generals and leads them to deal with personal affairs, others develop a passion to write about their wartime glories, publishing thousands of pamphlets to describe their personality, but at the same time they neglect their military activities."[50]

In October 1916, Hunter McKay, an American newspaperman, wired from Chihuahua "that Treviño is weakening and has been for weeks, that his regiments are short numbered, only carried on payroll, that his men are deserting to Villa, that his forces cannot be trusted beyond protected points, that he is short ammunition, that his forces have been whipped by Villa at San Andrés, Santa Isabel, and Cusi, that population is Villista, that he expects Carranza collapse in Chihuahua."[51]

Obregón's sharp rebuke and his dismissal from command of Chihuahuan troops did not yet constitute the low point of Treviño's military career. That occurred on November 27, when Treviño fled with the remnants of his command from Ciudad Chihuahua, allowing Pancho Villa once more to enter it in triumph.

Villa's Occupation of Chihuahua

As soon as he heard that a strong Carrancista relief column headed by Murguía was marching on Chihuahua, Villa decided to occupy the city before its arrival. It was a risky decision, for in the past, unless he could count on absolute surprise, as had been the case in Ciudad Juárez and during the first capture of Torreón in October 1913, Villa had only been able to lay siege to large cities and capture them with the help of sufficient artillery. This time he could not count on the element of surprise; Treviño was expecting him. He had no artillery, whereas Treviño was placing cannon on the hill of Santa Rosa, overlooking the city. In addition, if the siege dragged on too long, Murguía's relief column might arrive, and he could be caught between Treviño on the one side and Murguía on the other.

Villa had never been averse to taking risks, however, and had frequently paid dearly for his daring. This time he would be successful. After sending out troops to tear up the railroad tracks between Jiménez and Ciudad Chihuahua to slow down the advance of Murguía's troops, Villa, as in the heyday of the División del Norte, loaded his men aboard troop trains and steamed toward the city. On November 23, the siege began.

For four days, the fighting was bloody but indecisive. Villa's charging cavalrymen were mowed down by artillery and machine-gun fire from the hill of Santa Rosa. On the second day, Treviño personally led a counteroffensive, which produced an initial rout among the attacking Villista infantry. In a desperate charge, headed by Villa himself, his Dorados managed to repel Treviño's counterattack. Nevertheless, Treviño was convinced that Villa had been decisively defeated, and he began making preparations for a victory celebration. On the evening of November 26, four days after the siege had begun, "Treviño asked the usual crowd to his table and we were a merry company," an eyewitness reported. "During the meal we were all invited to a festive dinner to be given on next Tuesday, that is on the 28th, in celebration of the victory." When shooting occurred for a few minutes, Treviño was unperturbed and "explained to us that probably the Villistas who were corralled at the Avenida Zarco had tried to make a break and that no reason for excitement existed." Not all of Treviño's commanders shared his optimism. General González Cuéllar told an unnamed U.S. intelligence agent "that he personally did not think that the danger was over, on the contrary, he was expecting the final and most desperate attack on the same night. He felt very uneasy on account of shortness of ammunition and lack of close organization and he finished the talk saying: This night will bring the decision one way or the other."[52]

González Cuéllar was right. The Villistas launched a decisive attack on Santa Rosa hill, where Treviño's artillery was located. Around 1:00 A.M.,

a boy of 23 years, of a rachitic constitution, scarcely weighing 50 kilos, came to see General Villa. . . . He came with his arm in a sling and half his body, the thorax, draped in bandages. . . . This was Martín López. He got down from his horse without being able to hide the pain that his wounds were inflicting upon him and that were reflected in contractions in his face, and he presented the general with this disconcerting petition. "I want to ask you, General, for 300 men to storm the hill of Santa Rosa tonight."

When they heard this, "all those present were silent. Something like that was impossible: they had never seen a case where a wounded man would leave his hospital bed with three wounds in his body in order to risk his life in the same battle, as Martín López was doing when he asked for the command of the troop that was to storm Santa Rosa hill." Villa at first refused. López was his most valuable commander. When López insisted, Villa finally gave in. Within a few hours, López reported to Villa that Santa Rosa hill had been taken.[53] "We have now taken Chihuahua," Villa told his staff.[54]

An observer close to Treviño had come to the same conclusion.

Sharp at 3:00 as it is always Villa's custom to begin a morning fight, a most violent shooting started on the line spreading up to the hill of Santa Rosa. Shortly afterward the Santa Rosa guns began to boom and then it was clear to me that the dreaded general attack was taking place on the whole line. At 5:00 A.M. the firing stopped suddenly and the silence was not disturbed any more until the daylight, that is about 7:00, when the wild yells "Viva Villa!" plainly indicated that the town fell into Villa's hands. This supposition was soon confirmed: government soldiers began to run in a wild panic towards the central railroad station, Villa's riders following them closely. Between 6:00 and 7:00 A.M. four trains have left the central railroad station carrying infantry towards the north. It was known later on that most heroic fighting took place on the hill of Santa Rosa defended by the artillery colonel Silva Sánchez. Lieutenant Colonel Padilla, Captain Cuauhtémoc Aguilar and others were shot mercilessly and finally when everything was lost, Silva Sánchez blew his brains out, preferring death to falling into the hands of the cruel enemy.

A few hours later, Treviño gave up the fight for Chihuahua, "having gathered around him his staff and some of the cavalry he took on horseback the road toward the little town of Aldama and arrived at night-break to the hacienda of Dolores where the night was spent."[55] In his haste to flee, he had neglected to advise all of his troops that he was abandoning Chihuahua, and some of his men, including those guarding the penitentiary, were left to fight the Villistas alone. They held out for several hours, until Villa sent them an ultimatum offering them their lives if they surrendered and threatening to kill every one of them if they did not.

The commander of the Carrancista garrison accepted Villa's ultimatum, and shortly after the surrender, Villa himself came to address the prisoners; "with tears in his eyes he addressed them and invited them to go and fight against the gringos." Both the Carrancista commander and his men were incorporated into Villa's army; his officers were reduced to simple soldiers, but their lives were spared.[56] Within a few days, however, 48 of these men and their commander had rejoined the Carrancistas.

Treviño's sudden evacuation of Ciudad Chihuahua generated intense controversy, part of which would be made public in the summer of 1917. He justified himself by stating that he had run out of ammunition and that, had he continued to fight, his troops would have been sacrificed uselessly. His aim, he declared, had been to evacuate as many of his soldiers as possible in order to unite with Murguía and retake the city. He also blamed Murguía, whose column was advancing so slowly that it did not arrive in time to relieve Treviño's troops. There was no excuse, in his opinion, for Murguía's delay. Only a year earlier, in December 1915, Treviño at the head of 7,000 men, fighting all the way, had needed only 11 days to reach Chihuahua City, whereas Murguía took 25 days to march the same distance.[57]

Obregón was as critical of Treviño this time as he had been several weeks earlier when Treviño had presented a similar explanation for his earlier defeats. Obregón felt that Treviño's defeat derived primarily from his failure to take offensive against Villa.[58] He expressed his astonishment that "while a city was being attacked infantry . . . trains can leave it without the enemy preventing it."[59] In other words, he implied that Treviño's troops were leaving the city of their own free will rather than being forced to do so by Villa. Obregón's criticism of Treviño not only reflected his disappointment with Treviño's military errors and defeat but also revealed a factional struggle among Carranza's military men. Two factions, respectively led by Obregón and Pablo González, were competing for power in Mexico, and Treviño was one of González's most loyal adherents.

As sharp as Obregón's criticisms (which were never published) were, they were as nothing compared to the harsh accusations that Murguía voiced against his predecessor. Murguía accused Treviño of corruption—since he had padded the payroll, he had had far fewer soldiers than he should have had; of incompetence—Murguía further charged that Treviño had not put sufficient infantry on Santa Rosa hill to protect the artillery stationed there, thus making it possible for Villa to capture the hill; of having showed lack of care for his men—he had not warned many of his commanders that he was evacuating the city; of having lied, since it was not true that he had been short of ammunition; and, finally, of being a coward, because he had been the first to leave the city.[60]

Pershing and Villa

With the capture of Chihuahua City, Villa had scored his greatest triumph since the defeat of the División del Norte a year earlier. It was the apex of his post-1915 career. Nevertheless, in spite of this enormous success, he was in a precarious position. Murguía's powerful relief column was advancing from the south, while Pershing's forces might strike at any time from the north.

Villa intended to keep Pershing where he was. For that reason, although he constantly emphasized the need to drive the Americans from Mexico in his speeches, Villa did not attack Pershing's expedition. Between June 9, 1916, and Pershing's departure from Mexico in February 1917, very few clashes took place between Villistas and the Americans. In late 1916, Villa may have gone further in his attempts to neutralize the Americans. Two Americans who had had extensive business dealings with Villa reported that they were given the opportunity to have an exclusive interview with him. The two Americans, Frank Thayer and Brennan, one of whom had been a munitions agent for Villa in 1914–15, were brought to his presence by his brother-in-law, Regino Corral. Villa gave them a statement

to the effect that he was not responsible for the Santa Isabel massacre, that he did not know about it until four days later. That with the exception of several of his former generals who had been killed, there was nothing that happened during the revolution that had caused him deeper regret. That regarding the Columbus incident, he would neither affirm nor deny his having been there, but that he said that when the proper time came, he would prove where he was on that day by three American citizens.

Regarding his feelings towards Americans, he said that he would welcome them back in the country, as soon as he could keep communications open, that he had no hard feelings towards them, and that he realizes that Americans must be protected in Mexico, and permitted to work their properties for the benefit of the poor. That he has been credited with all kinds of barbarities but that they are circulated by the Carrancistas, and that when the truth is known, these charges will be disproved. That he had given orders to all of his men not to molest Americans, or any other foreigners except Chinamen, whom he claimed were a pest in the country, and would be run out of Mexico; that they came to Mexico with nothing and sent all their earnings out of it; and that they did not make good citizens.[61]

Villa also made other overtures to the Americans. In an interview with a U.S. agent, a Villista colonel and another "of Villa's prominent officers" said that Villa

would be glad to meet and confer with some U.S. government official and that he was anxious to know what the policy of the future was going to be in regard to himself and his people; he said that Carranza and his followers in their policy towards the masses had been more disastrous than that of either Díaz or Huerta and that his only ambition was to see his people liberated from the slavery and the evil condition that had been brought upon them by the tyrants of his country and that he expected to fight on regardless of consequences until this had been accomplished and that he hoped that he might be able to again gain the good will of his neighbors of the north as he realized that without their aid in opening up the industries that his people would have to suffer for a long time; that in reality he did not have the feeling of malice against the people of the north but against the policy and against those who inaugurated the policy of the recognition of Carranza.

Villa condemned Wilson but said that he believed that General Scott was "a great and good man and had this question been left to him and the military leaders of the U.S., it would have been settled long ago." The Villista officers told the U.S. agent "that they would be very glad of the privilege of taking to General Villa any information that the American government or officials of the government, either military or civil, might desire to have sent to him."[62] Carrancista agents who monitored these conversations were convinced that Villa had offered every possible guarantee to American citizens if the United States would refrain from proceeding against him and allow him to continue his fight against Carranza.[63] Indeed, Treviño was so convinced that a secret understanding between the Americans and Villa existed that he believed American munitions had allowed Villa to score his victory in Chihuahua.[64]

Villa's decision to attack neither the United States nor Pershing's troops was certainly one important factor that kept the American commander from undertaking any hostilities against him, but the restrictions imposed by Wilson, who was resolved to prevent a U.S.–Mexican war, were the main reason. These restrictions were deeply resented by Pershing and his subordinates, who repeatedly called on the U.S. president to give them a freer hand in Mexico. In April, Pershing had called for "our continuing occupation of as many distinct localities as possible in the territory to be covered."[65] In June, after U.S. and Mexican troops clashed at the Chihuahuan town of Carrizal, Pershing recommended to the administration that he be allowed to occupy all of Chihuahua.[66] In October, after Villa's first successes, General Frederick Funston, Pershing's immediate superior, probably upon his recommendation, "strongly urged" that U.S. forces should occupy the two largest cities in Chihuahua, the capital and Ciudad Juárez.[67] After Villa took Ciudad Chihuahua, Pershing was even more explicit. "In view of Villa's daring," he wrote his commanding officer, "and the comparatively inefficient Carrancista forces, Villa's power is almost certain to increase. . . . A swift blow delivered by this command should [therefore] be made at once."[68]

Pershing's increasing frustration was owing both to Villa's constantly increasing strength and to considerations of prestige, both that of the United States, as he perceived it, and his own. He expressed this openly in a letter to his superior. "I do not believe that the general public understands why this expedition has not caught Villa and his band. They do not appreciate the fact that we are now occupying a tactical position and that further movement would involve us in a war with a *de facto* government. I think in justice to yourself and this entire command, that the War Department should clear this up."[69]

Although Pershing himself was cautious about criticizing Wilson—this was one of the reasons why Wilson named him supreme commander of the American forces in Europe only a few months later—one of his officers who was relatively close to him, the young Lieutenant George S. Patton, had no such compunction. "I think that war is now the best for two reasons," he wrote to a friend:

First, it is inevitable, hence the sooner the better. Second, it will surely give us a better army for I doubt that over half of the militia muster in and even they will be too few. . . . It will not take many of us to beat the Mexicans in battle but it will take a lot to cover the lines of communication so that those who fight may also eat.

You have no idea of the utter degradation of the inhabitants. . . . One must be a fool indeed to think that people half savage and wholly ignorant will ever form a republic. It is a joke. A despot is all they know or want. So when they lost Díaz they set up bandit kings who were worse tyrants than he [Porfirio Díaz] ever dreamed of being.[70]

With respect to Wilson, he wrote, "He has not the soul of a louse nor the mind of a worm or the backbone of a jellyfish."[71]

In spite of the restraints that were imposed upon him, Pershing by no means remained inactive during his stay in Mexico. He regarded the region of northern Chihuahua where his troops had been concentrated as a kind of laboratory where he could try out the policies he would implement if his advocated occupation of all of Chihuahua or of all of northern Mexico by U.S. troops came to pass. To this end, he set up in embryonic form the kind of Mexican constabulary that the U.S. war plans envisaged and that U.S. occupation forces would soon establish in Nicaragua and the Dominican Republic. "Neutral natives Namiquipa at my suggestion organized a few days ago small detachment for protection peaceful inhabitants," Pershing reported to the adjutant general in Washington.

This detachment working in conjunction with our troops, furnishing guides and information. Location cache Villista arms pointed out by Columbus, New Mexico prisoner, arms found by local guard brought in yesterday. Cache consisted 400 small arms, various makes, and ten Colt machine guns. Organization local guards and their reliance on us illustrates attitude peaceably inclined people would assume in case of occupation. With protection assured until suppression banditry peaceable inclined citizens would assist us materially. Payment for supplies would distribute much-needed money to pauperized natives. Little doubt majority realize impossibility of stable government under present *de facto* personnel or any other of the contending factions. Many very solicitous that we remain here indefinitely and fearful of consequences at the hands of both bandits and Carranza forces after our departure.[72]

The people of Namiquipa were to pay a high price for accepting Pershing's "suggestion." They would suffer bloody reprisals at Villa's hands, and the feuds that their cooperation with Pershing engendered would last for many years. Seventeen years after these events, in 1933, when José María Espinosa, one of the leaders of the Home Guard who had played a prominent role in cooperating with Pershing, returned to Namiquipa, he was ambushed and killed by men who had neither forgotten nor forgiven his role in 1916.[73]

To a certain degree, Pershing succeeded in winning what later U.S. strategists would call "hearts and minds" of the people in the regions he occupied. He did so by paying for supplies in hard currency, which neither the Villistas nor the Carrancistas had done, by enforcing strict discipline among his troops, and by frequently protecting the inhabitants of the region where his troops were stationed from the depredations of Carrancista troops. His assumption that he could have replicated such a situation had the Americans occupied the rest of Chihuahua or for that matter all of Mexico is more than problematic. One of the main reasons that the situation remained quiet in the region Pershing occupied was that neither the Carrancistas nor the Villistas from June 1916 onward (in spite of Villa's anti-American rhetoric) made any serious effort to conduct guerrilla warfare against the Americans. Had the opposite been the case, the inevitable escalation of guerrilla activity, counterinsurgency, and reprisals would have created the same kind of popular resentment that the Americans had encountered in the Philippines and would later encounter in Nicaragua and in Vietnam. In addition, the fact that the expedition occupied only a small parcel of Mexican territory did not create the resentment and nationalistic reaction that a real occupation of a larger territory would doubtless have provoked.

The Fate of the Captured Columbus Raiders

During this period of enforced inactivity, Pershing scored two successes against the Villistas. The first, the discovery of the cache of arms, was a serious blow to Villa. The second "success" was more problematic and would lead to serious conflict among judicial authorities in the United States: with the help of local informants, U.S. troops managed to capture the men from Namiquipa who had participated in the Columbus Raid. It was ironic that the Americans should have captured precisely those members of Villa's expeditionary force who had been forced against their will to participate in it. These men were first imprisoned in the military stockade at Columbus, then transferred to Grant County Jail in Silver City and arraigned on February 21, 1917, in Deming, Luna County, New Mexico. They were the second group of Columbus raiders to be tried in the

United States. As they awaited their trial, they had time to ponder the fate of their six companions who had been tried a few months earlier, sentenced to death, and, with one exception, hanged.

The first trial had been anything but impartial and in many respects had the appearance of a legal lynching. Feelings in Luna County, of which Columbus was a part, were so aroused against Villa and his men that the U.S. Justice Department was convinced that the raiders could not get a fair trial there. On the eve of the trial, E. B. Stone, the head of the Bureau of Investigation's office in El Paso, went to see the presiding judge, Edward L. Medler, and told him that "he was directed by the Department of Justice to protest to the judge of the court against the trial of the seven Villistas the following morning." Stone received the support of the U.S. Attorney in Albuquerque, Burkhart, who called the judge and told him "that he had been instructed by the Attorney General to go to Deming and protest against the trial of these Villistas upon the ground that they would not receive a fair trial." When the judge protested and told him that such a statement was in contempt of court, the U.S. Attorney became more explicit, stating "that he meant that the state of public sentiment was such in Luna County that those seven men couldn't get a fair trial." The War Department protested against the trial too, stating "that it would involve the United States in international complications with Mexico." Telling a BI agent "that there would be no watchful waiting in that court," however, the judge, a friend and admirer of the interventionist New Mexico Republican Senator Albert B. Fall, went forward with the trial.[74]

The Villistas were accused of murdering Charles Miller, one of the civilians killed in the raid. The jurors took no notice of the raiders' statement they had been forcibly impressed into Villa's army, that they were soldiers obeying orders and did not even know that they had entered the United States, and that there was no proof that it was these particular men who had killed Miller. The jury concluded that the accused had "with force and arms, in and upon one Charles D. Miller, then and there being, unlawfully, willfully, feloniously, deliberately, premeditatedly, of their malice aforethought, and from a deliberate and premeditated design, then and there unlawfully and maliciously to effect the death of the said Charles D. Miller, did make an assault."[75] The outcome of the trial may very likely have been influenced by the attitude of their court-appointed defender, who, in a letter to a Deming newspaper, called critics of the trial "chicken-hearted" and said that he believed that the accused deserved hanging.[76]

At the request of President Wilson, State Governor MacDonald held up execution of these men for three weeks and, in order to gather supplementary information, sent a detective employed by the Ben Williams Detective Agency into the prison. The detective was put into a cell with the Columbus raiders and told them that he had been a spy for Villa and thus tried to gain their confidence. Talks with some of the raiders confirmed what they had told the court, that they had been forcibly impressed into Villa's army, had not known that they were in the United States, and had not wanted to fight the Americans.[77] The report had little effect on Governor MacDonald. He commuted the death sentence of one man, José Rodríguez, to life imprisonment. Rodríguez was a former Carrancista soldier who had been taken prisoner by Villa and forced to enlist in his army. The other five men were hanged.[78]

The chilling fate of their companions, as well as the terrible conditions under which they lived in the Silver City jail—sadistic guards gave them so little food that two of their number died of malnutrition[79]—probably persuaded the men Pershing had captured in Namiquipa to plead guilty to second-degree murder. It is not clear whether they received any legal advice before they did so. The men were sentenced to eighty years imprisonment and spent five years at hard labor in the New Mexico penitentiary. They were finally pardoned in 1921 by New Mexico's Governor Octaviano Ambrosio Larrazolo, who stated that they should have been considered as soldiers and not as murderers. Larrazolo explained his decision by saying that Villa

kept an army regularly officered as all armies are officered, maintaining and enforcing therein a degree of military discipline that requires and compels the rank and file thereof to obey the orders of superior officers; the above-named defendants belonged to that army and in obedience to the orders given to them by their superior officers they marched to a point of destination unknown to them and for a purpose of which they were equally ignorant, except that, in a general way because they understood it they were "going to fight the enemy." These men say that although they did not know where they were going, that the impression generally prevailed among their number that they were going to attack Carranza's garrison in the border town of Palomas in the state of Chihuahua, Mexico. It is a fact that when they in pursuance of superior orders attacked the town of Columbus not one of them knew that he was standing on American soil and attacking an American settlement; this plea adds further merit to their defense, and I use the words "further merit" advisedly because even although they had known that they were attacking an American settlement, still they would not be guilty of murder, because as above stated they were not responsible agents; they were acting under superior orders which they must obey under penalty of death.[80]

Feelings in New Mexico still ran so high against the Columbus raiders that this was not the end of their sufferings. While Larrazolo was briefly absent from the state, his deputy, Lieutenant Governor Pankey, revoked the pardon.[81] Larrazolo had no difficulty in reinstating his pardon but a new accusation of murder of other victims who died at Columbus was made against the remaining Columbus raiders, and they were once again arrested. The Supreme Court agreed with the arrest, and they were tried once again. This time, however, a reversal of public opinion had taken place and after only fifteen minutes of deliberation, the jury found them innocent. After five years of incarceration, they could finally return to Mexico, where they were welcomed both by representatives of the federal government and by Villa himself. Villa had in the meantime made his peace with the Mexican government, and all the soldiers who had been with him when he surrendered were treated as members of the regular Mexican army and paid accordingly. Villa made sure the returning prisoners were included in that agreement and given sufficient pay to begin with their lives once again.[82]

Poisoning Villa?

The arrest and trial of the Columbus raiders could scarcely make up for the frustration that Pershing, his subordinates, and other U.S. authorities felt at their incapacity to capture Villa. It is thus not surprising that two high officials of the U.S. government—Bureau of Investigation agent Stone and one of the heads of Pershing's intelligence department, a Captain Reed—decided to take an "unconventional" road to getting rid of Villa—namely, to poison him.[83] This plot involved Stone, Reed, and several Japanese living in Mexico. All of the Japanese had had good relations with Villa. Gemichi Tatematsu had been a personal servant to both Pancho Villa and his brother Hipólito and seems to have been in continuous contact with Hipólito's family. Others were known to Villa's wife, Luz Corral. Villa seems to have admired the Japanese, in contrast to the Chinese, whom he hated.[84] Posing either as men carrying messages from Villa's brother Hipólito or from Luz Corral or simply as former friends wanting to join his forces, they managed to gain Villa's confidence. They proved to be excellent scouts but bad poisoners. Their reports on Villa's operations and the composition of his army were excellent, but the effort they made to put poison into Villa's coffee failed. That project was first broached in a conversation they had with Stone. "Agent took up with informant Jah [Hawakawa] the matter of capturing Villa alive and delivering him to the border to agents; the matter was also taken up whether or not Villa could be delivered dead, on the border, if same was requested. Agent gave him no instructions whatever in this matter but merely put this proposition up to him with a view to seeing what could be done by them towards capturing Villa if the department would authorize such action through this office."[85] The Japanese were referred by Stone to the Intelligence Department of the Pershing Expedition. On September 23, two of these Japanese agents, Dyo and Sato, reported that they had placed poison in Villa's coffee. They stated that

they had been sent by Captain Reed of our American expedition in Mexico to General Villa's camp with the poison prescription, with instructions to administer it to General Villa and kill him. Dyo and Fusita state the prescription was given to Captain Reed by an American army surgeon with the Pershing Expedition for this purpose and that the medicine was known as a three-day poison—that his death should be effective three days after taking same. Further Dyo and Fusita state that in pursuance with instructions from Captain Reed they went into the camp of General Villa taking with them this poison, and that Dyo did put this dose of poison in a cup of coffee set in front of General Villa; but that Villa, having been suspicious that he might be poisoned through his food for a long time, poured half of this cup of coffee which contained the poison into another cup and handed it to a Mexican who sat on his right, and waited until this Mexican drank his portion of the coffee before he drank his own. Dyo and Fusita after noting the way in which this poison was taken, got away from Villa and his forces immediately and reported back to the American expedition not having learned at the time of their departure just how serious an effect the poison had on him.[86]

It is not clear why the attempt failed. Was the poison not good enough? The poisoner, Dyo, had in fact tried it out before setting out on his expedition. He "used two tablets (20 in a tube) on a dog with apparent good results. Circumstances did not permit more thorough test."[87] Was the poison so weak that Villa, by giving half of the cup of his poisoned coffee to one of his aides, prevented it from working, or did the Japanese report on an attempt they never really carried out? These questions cannot as yet be answered.

While the Japanese poisoners had little effect on Villa, they did incidentally succeed in poisoning the atmosphere in Washington and among U.S. officials linked to the Punitive Expedition. When a report by Stone on the poisoning mission reached Attorney General Thomas Watt Gregory, he sent a message to the secretary of war:

Herewith I enclose copy of a very startling report made by one of our secret service men and sent from El Paso.

The story seems to [sic] wild for anything but as it mentions Captain Reed of the expeditionary force in Mexico I thought you might care to run it down somewhat.[88]

Had the plot become public knowledge, there might have been serious moral and political consequences for President Wilson, who was up for reelection a few months later. Neither Wilson himself nor his cabinet nor significant segments of U.S. public opinion would have accepted assassination as a legitimate instrument of policy. For Pershing, this revelation entailed a grave risk. On September 22, he had applied for promotion to major general, which had been granted three days later. If the plot became common knowledge, he might easily become discredited. The assertion by the historians Charles Harris and Louis Sadler that all parties concerned now attempted to carry out a cover-up is quite convincing. The secretary of war instructed the Southern Command, of which Pershing's forces were a part, to carry out an investigation "with as little publicity as possible." Pershing himself seems to have been involved when he sharply upbraided subordinate intelligence officers for writing too many reports on the Japanese agents. The whole matter was quashed.[89] Two of the agencies charged with investigating these accusations cooperated in quashing them. Stone suddenly reversed the report in which he had originally implicated the Punitive Expedition in a plot.

Major Ralph H. Van Deman, who headed the Military Intelligence section of the Army War College, showed so little impartiality that even before seeing the evidence he wrote, "I am very sure that somebody is lying. . . . the story about the poison is simply absurd."[90] As a result, the story never reached the public, and Secretary of War Newton D. Baker in February 1917 cleared the U.S. Army and Pershing of any wrongdoing. "I have had the matter very fully investigated and am of the opinion that no officer of the expedition in Mexico had any knowledge or any connection with any such plan as was reported by the Japanese. It is entirely possible that these Japanese had some such plan of their own, but I do not believe that any of our officers knew of it."[91]

The Japanese plotters had offered their services not only to the Americans but to the Carrancistas as well. In March 1916, they contacted the Mexican consul in El Paso, Andrés García, one of the heads of the Mexican secret service in the United States, offering to poison Villa. García transmitted the offer to Carranza, who refused to have any part of it.[92] It is not clear why Carranza refused the Japanese agent's offer. Did he not take him seriously or did he have moral scruples? Such an attitude on the part of Carranza would raise a number of questions, since a few years later, in an operation that presented far greater moral problems to the Carrancistas—in the process they had to execute a number of their own men—they assassinated Zapata.

This bizarre conspiracy was the last active measure the Punitive Expedition took against Pancho Villa. From now on, Carranza, not Villa, became the main reason for its presence in Mexico. Woodrow Wilson hoped to use it as a bargaining chip to secure concessions from the Carranza administration. At no time perhaps were the contradictions of Woodrow Wilson's Mexican policy more apparent than in the fall of 1916, when his commissioners met those of Carranza in Atlantic City to negotiate for the withdrawal of the Punitive Expedition from Mexico. On one hand, Wilson repeatedly emphasized his contempt for interventionist American businessmen in Mexico and his opposition to their demands that the United States annex part of Mexico or rule the whole country by force. On the other, the proposals his commissioners offered Mexico as a condition for the evacuation of the American troops would have converted Mexico into a U.S. protectorate. While some of the Mexican commissioners at Atlantic City were so intimidated by the American demands that they were ready to bow to them, Carranza rejected them. He had, in effect, called the Americans' bluff, and the Wilson administration decided to withdraw from Mexico anyway.[93] War with Germany was becoming an increasingly distinct possibility, and Wilson did not want to have his troops bogged down south of the border.

The Consequences of the Punitive Expedition

Villa's attack on Columbus and the resulting Punitive Expedition have aroused much interest and some controversy among historians. The interest has centered on the fact that no one except Villa has ever attacked the metropolitan territory of the United States since the British did so in the War of 1812. The identity of the American participants also aroused great interest. Pershing would later head the American expeditionary force in Europe in World War I, while Patton was to play a very important role in World War II. The controversies have above all focused on the motives for Villa's attack, with some authors citing revenge as the primary factor that guided Villa, while others have thought of him having been paid and instigated either by the Germans or by large American corporations. While practically all contemporary observers and historians have condemned Villa for an attack that could have brought about a U.S.–Mexican war, or at least the long-term occupation of parts of Mexico by the United States, there is some controversy, above all among American historians, as to the consequences of the Punitive Expedition. Some American historians have felt that the expedition was a failure, since it did not succeed in capturing Villa. Others believe that its main aim, preventing Villa from ever attacking the United States again, was achieved. In addition, these historians stress the fact that the Punitive Expedition had given the U.S. Army an opportunity to exercise its weapons and tactics, thus providing a useful preparation for World War I. In addition, they feel that it helped to strengthen the preparedness campaign in the United States, whose aim was to alert the population to the need for a stronger army and a larger military budget. The prevailing view among American historians is that Villa's attack on Columbus and the resulting Punitive Expedition had the potential for bringing about a U.S.–Mexican war, thus significantly shaping the history of the two countries, but that since such a war did not occur, neither

Villa's attack nor the Punitive Expedition had any major impact on the history of either country.

This is a view with which I strongly disagree. The Punitive Expedition had a profound effect both on world history and on the internal development of the Mexican Revolution. The failure of the expedition to achieve its aims strongly contributed to two decisions by the German government that would decisively affect the outcome of World War I. Since 1915, once the United States began supplying Britain, France, and Russia with arms, ammunition, and other goods, a debate had been taking place within the German government as to whether Germany should unleash its submarines on American ships, a measure called unlimited U-boat warfare. While a significant element within the German military felt that to do so would destroy Britain's capacity to fight and force it to its knees, civilian forces within the German government were worried that it would bring the United States into the war and thus completely change the military balance. The failure of the Punitive Expedition in Mexico greatly helped the German military to persuade the adversaries of unlimited U-boat warfare, including the Kaiser, that a declaration of war by the United States would have no significant military impact, since the U.S. Army was not a force to be seriously reckoned with.

In March 1916, the press office of the German armed forces wrote that "the military incompetence of the United States has been clearly revealed by the campaign against Villa. . . . the United States not only has no army, it has no artillery, no means of transportation, no airplanes, and lacks all other instruments of modern warfare."[94] The Germans also tended as a result of the U.S.–Mexican crisis to overestimate Carranza's willingness to go to war with the United States and Wilson's willingness to respond to any attack on the United States from Mexico with renewed military intervention. The result was that the party in the German cabinet that favored unlimited U-boat warfare, which was sure to bring the United States into the conflict, gained more and more ascendancy.

The Punitive Expedition had an even more direct impact on a second German decision that also contributed to bringing the United States into World War I. This was the well-known Zimmermann Telegram, in which the German foreign secretary, Arthur Zimmermann, proposed an alliance with Carranza in January 1917, promising the return of Texas, Arizona, and New Mexico if Mexico attacked the United States following the latter power's entry into the Great War on the side of Germany's enemies. After being intercepted by British intelligence, Zimmermann's telegram was published in the United States and played a major role in turning isolationist U.S. opinion against Germany. Zimmermann's offer came as a direct result of a plea for help that Carranza had sent to the Germans after the Americans refused to leave Mexico. The very real possibility of a U.S.–Mexican war inspired Zimmermann to draft his fateful proposal.

The conflict generated by the presence of the Pershing expedition in Mexico also had profound consequences for the internal development of the Mexican Revolution. Carranza had hoped that U.S. recognition of his administration would give him two advantages that would enable him to destroy the popular forces still resisting him in large parts of Mexico and permit him to implement his program of returning the haciendas to their former owners. These potential advantages of American recognition were sole Mexican access (1) to U.S. war matéricl and (2) to loans and credits from American banks. The tensions between Mexico and the United States brought about by the Punitive Expedition led Wilson to embargo the export of arms and ammunition to Mexico, and his administration discouraged American banks from giving credit or loans to the Carranza administration. As a result the Mexican government was so weakened that its main enemies, Zapata in Morelos and Villa in Chihuahua, as well as smaller foes such as the Cedillo brothers in San Luis Potosí, were able to survive until Carranza was overthrown by Obregón in the 1920s and the latter reached a genuine compromise with all rebel forces that secured many of their social and political demands.

For Villa, his attack on Columbus entailed both great advantages and disadvantages. On the one hand, Villa's revitalization in 1916 doubtless arose from his ability to assume the mantle of a national leader resisting a U.S. invasion. When the expedition entered Mexico, Villa was at the head of a largely demoralized force of about 400 men. When it left, he controlled large parts of northern Mexico and had several thousand men under his command. In addition, for a short time, thanks to the arms embargo that Wilson had imposed on Carranza, Villa was better supplied with arms and ammunition than his rival, since many of these came from supplies that he had hidden before the final defeat of the División del Norte.

On the other hand, Villa's attack on Columbus led to an irrevocable break with the Wilson administration, which would never again, even when it became dissatisfied with Carranza, consider Villa a viable alternative. Even some U.S. officials who had been close to Villa reversed their attitude. "This is a different man than we knew," George Carothers wrote to U.S. Chief of Staff Hugh Scott. "All the brutality of his nature has come to the front, and he should be killed like a dog."[95]

Villa's attack also led to a complete break with the American left, which had never been uniformly enthusiastic for Villa in the first place. The National Executive Committee of the Socialist Party of America described Villa as an agent of Wall Street and his men as "Mexican mercenaries." The real responsibility for the attack on Columbus lay with "the same capitalist interests who have so freely hired gunmen to kill, to break strikes in the past."[96] The secretary of the Socialist Party, Walter Lanfersiek, stated that he had "reliable information that Mexican raids upon American territory are inspired by and paid for by American interests."[97] Louis Fraina, a leader of the Socialist Labor Party, demanded in his *New Review*, "The least that should be done is an investigation of the raid, and the punishment of the forces on the American side of the border that evidence seems to indicate were implicated in the raid."[98] Even Villa's long-time admirer John Reed expressed the view that someone had persuaded or hired Villa to carry out his raid.[99]

The conservative American business establishment in Mexico, after briefly flirting with Villa, had abandoned its support of the Mexican revolutionary once it realized he was unwilling to become another Porfirio Díaz. Now it saw Villa's attack on Columbus as a godsend, and it would continue to attempt to use him to force American intervention in Mexico. The manager of the Mexican Northwestern Railroad in Chihuahua wrote to his chief in Toronto:

Such men as C. M. Newman, who is interested in mines and ranches in northern Mexico, Donald B. Gillies, president of the San Toy and Cusi Mexicana Mining Companies, J. R. Enlow, manager of the American Smelting and Refining Company, H. F. Stevenson, vice-president and general manager of the Palomas Land and Cattle Company, E. C. Houghton, vice-president and general manager of the Corralitos Land and Cattle Company and a great many others with all of whom I have talked since the Columbus affair, and since the announcement that this government would send troops after Villa, are of the firm belief that for the interests in northern Mexico, and the clarification of the situation, the Columbus affair is the one thing that could have happened to bring about a stable condition.[100]

This conservative enthusiasm for Villa's raid does not, however, mean that these business interests had ever directly supported him. Nor is there the least indication that they would ever voluntarily send him arms, money, or supplies in the future, although they would try in one way or another to use him.[101]

CHAPTER SIXTEEN

Villa's Darkest Years

The Savage and Bloody Guerrilla Struggle in Chihuahua, 1917-1920

Nuestro México, febrero veintitrés,
dejó Carranza pasar americanos,
diez mil solados, seiscientos aeroplanos,
buscando a Villa, queriéndolo matar.

Pobrecitos de los americanos,
pues a sollozos comienzan a llorar,
con dos horas que tenían de combate
a su país se querían regresar.

Los de a caballo ya no se podían sentar
y los de a pie ya no podían caminar,
y Pancho Villa les pasa en su aeroplano
y desde arriba les dice:—Goodbye!—

Pues que creían estos rinches tan cobardes,
¿que combatir era un baile de carquís?
Con la cara toda llena de vergüenza
se regressaron otra vez a su país.[1]

Our Mexico, on February 23d,
Carranza let Americans cross the border,
10,000 soldiers, 600 airplanes,
looking for Villa, wanting to kill him.

Oh, those poor Americans,
they burst out sobbing and crying;
they had only been in battle for two hours,
and they were ready to go back to their country.

Those on horseback no longer could sit down,
and those on foot could no longer walk,
while Pancho Villa flew over them in his airplane
and from up there told them, "Good-bye!"

What did these cowardly *rinches* think,
that making war was like a fancy ball?
With their faces all full of shame
they returned once more to their country.

Mexico, 1917–1920

The unconditional departure of the Punitive Expedition from Mexico was one of Carranza's greatest triumphs. He had twice refused to sign agreements with the United States that his own representatives were advocating. The first of these, the Scott-Obregón Protocol, would at least temporarily have legitimated the presence of Pershing's expedition in Mexico. The second, in return for American withdrawal, would have allowed the United States to return to Mexico whenever it saw fit to do so. Carranza had thus twice safeguarded Mexico's sovereignty, yet the departure of the American forces did not strengthen his regime. Angered by Carranza's nationalism, the Wilson administration imposed an arms embargo on Mexico and set up strict limitations on trade between the two countries. These measures weakened Carranza both militarily and economically. In addition, now that the U.S. government had stopped supporting Carranza, American business interests began supporting and financing his conservative opponents. More overtly than ever, U.S. oil companies expressed their support for Manuel Peláez. Conservatives in other parts of Mexico were encouraged to revolt by the U.S. opposition to the Carranza regime.

Carranza could hope to counteract the mounting hostility of the United States in two ways. The first was to seek a reconciliation with the popular factions in Mexico. The second was to resort to the traditional expedient frequently used by Mexican governments, to play Europe off against the United States. He chose the second path by playing the German card and refused to reach out to his enemies and to forge some kind of consensus to defend Mexico's sovereignty.

While it is not clear how his enemies would have responded, Carranza never made any effort to conciliate them. About two weeks before Villa attacked Columbus, on the third anniversary of Madero's overthrow on February 22, 1916, two of his former supporters, Roque González Garza, the Convention's former head, and his brother Federico, one of Villismo's outstanding intellectuals, wrote an open letter to Carranza advocating reconciliation and a return to the democracy of Madero. Warning of the domestic and international consequences for Mexico if Carranza refused to heed this advice, they noted: "We have been vanquished on the battlefield, but unfortunately as far as the interests of the revolution are concerned there is no evidence yet that we have also been vanquished in the field of ideas."[2]

Although Villa's attack on Columbus and the Punitive Expedition had yet to occur, Federico and Roque González Garza feared that U.S. intervention might soon occur unless stability were reestablished. Stability was impossible, they argued, as long as the military dominated Mexico and created a general climate of insecurity. Only a genuine compromise based on the reestablishment of the kind of freedom that had existed during Madero's presidency and the implementation of the reforms that Carranza had promised would allow Mexico to put an end to the internal conflicts that were sweeping the country and thus avert foreign intervention. Carranza never replied to this memorandum, and he refused to accept the services of the numerous exiles who were willing to fight alongside his army for the independence of Mexico. He did tell them that in case of war, he might accept them into his ranks, but in the meantime he would not allow them to return and refused to grant them amnesty.

Reconciliation with his enemies would have entailed far more than an amnesty. He would have had to accept their control of their own regions and the reforms they had carried out, as Alvaro Obregón was to do five years later.

Nothing of the kind happened. Carranza waged unrelenting war on the Zapatistas and against other popular factions who were advocating a radical redistribution of land. His own promises of land reform were scarcely implemented. In August 1916, in a bitter letter to his superior, General Salvador Alvarado, Francisco Múgica, one of Carranza's most radical generals, expressed his profound disappointment at Carranza's lack of commitment to land reform:

I do not agree with the general policy that is being carried out. . . . a great agrarian commission has been created to watch over the functioning of this law [of January 1915]. It has ended in a complete fiasco; in spite of the fact that the first steps are only [now] being taken to solve the agrarian problem, measures are already being taken to put an end to these first steps before they have been undertaken. . . . When I was in the capital of Mexico in February and March of this year, I saw that the Villistas, Zapatistas, and members of the Convention were persecuted far more than the supporters of Huerta. . . . Where does all this lead us to, my dear General?[3]

Múgica's evaluation of Carranza was echoed at the other end of the political spectrum. Two years later, one of Lord Cowdray's representatives, A. E. Worswick, wrote:

A tendency to conservatism is observable now that the government is well established and is not so dependent on the radical military element. Undoubtedly Carranza is doing his utmost to free himself from the extremists, and the most hopeful sign is, that he is commencing to take into the government offices, some of the old regime. [Ignacio] Pesqueira told me that this is their defined policy, and when the hatreds engendered by the revolution die out, they propose to utilize the services of as many of the best of the old government as possible, thus consolidating their position and placating, what they call, the "Reaccionarios." . . .

You probably know that they have returned Don José Limantour's properties, also Ignacio de la Torres', and an amnesty law is promised in July which will bring back hundreds of the "émigrés," and we hope will make the City take on more of its old time appearance."[4]

Carranza showed himself to be equally conservative as far as the rights of labor were concerned. Although he had made extensive promises to labor unions when he called on workers to join the Red Battalions and to fight on his side in the civil war against Villa and Zapata, he attempted in 1916 with the utmost severity to break a general strike by workers who were demanding higher wages to compensate for rapid price increases. Not only did he declare the strike illegal, he arrested strike leaders and threatened them with execution.

Elections were held during Carranza's tenure in office, but most observers considered them a farce. Members of opposing factions were not allowed to be candidates, participation was extremely limited, and accusations of fraud were widespread.

Carranza relied on repression to maintain his power. Captured prisoners of anti-Carrancista groups were routinely shot. He had no compunction about having Zapata assassinated and Angeles shot after a mock trial. Rebellious villagers were frequently deported. Yet, on the whole, Carrancista repression was milder than that exercised by military juntas in Latin America or revolutionaries in other parts of the world. Carranza was no Pinochet, no Stalin, no Pol Pot. He did not institute death squads or establish gulags, and there were no wholesale massacres of the civilian population. Those who accepted amnesty did not have to recant their former opinions in public (unless they wanted a government position); nor were they forced to express "their joyous enthusiasm" for the new regime at meetings.

But on the whole, far from pacifying the country, Carrancista repression fanned the fires of discontent. Instead of becoming the main instrument of the pacification of Mexico and consolidation of the regime as the Carrancista leadership hoped, his army became the main obstacle to these aims. This situation was linked both to the policies of the Carrancista leadership and to the nature of its regime.

Since the Carrancistas were willing neither to share power with the myriad revolutionary movements that had supported rival factions in the Mexican civil war nor to implement the reforms for which many of these movements had fought, and that they themselves had officially proclaimed, resistance continued to smolder in many parts of Mexico. As a result, the size of the army constantly increased, as did the budget necessary to maintain it. Fewer and fewer resources were dedicated to economic recovery.

Another consequence of the Carrancistas' unwillingness to share power with local leaders who had not rallied to them in 1914–15 was that in many parts of the country, outsiders assumed control, and the forces they led came from another part of Mexico. For the locals, this smacked of foreign occupation.

This fact was one reason for the Zapatista peasants' ferocious resistance to Carrancista occupation of Morelos. It also explains why in parts of southeastern Mexico, especially the states of Chiapas and Oaxaca, peasants and landlords would at times forget their differences and unite against the common enemy from outside.[5]

In Chihuahua, too, outside occupation of the state would be one of the factors that contributed to a spectacular resurgence of Villismo. In certain regions of Mexico during the Maderista period, and in others during the heyday of the revolution, there had been a degree of autonomy from both the central government and any outside power that these regions had never experienced before. Now outsiders were attempting to assume control again. This was bound to provoke conflicts and resentment. When such occupations were linked with graft and corruption, the mixture proved explosive. Reports by foreign diplomats and by Carrancista military and civilian officials writing to their superiors provide a picture of multiple exactions that provoked deep popular resentment against the Carrancistas and frequently led to the outbreak of revolutionary movements against them where none had existed before. The simplest and most brutal form of exaction was to seize crops that peasants had harvested and their domestic animals on the pretext that the peasants were rebel supporters. As a result, many of these country people were converted into genuine rebels. Hacendados, too, were forced to contribute part of their crops to the army. While some of these seized goods were used to feed the military, others were sold for hard currency to the United States, at a time when hunger was stalking Mexico.

There were other ways in which the Carrancista military increased the misery of the civilian population. The generals exercised a virtual monopoly on the control of railway communications in their respective areas. Landowners wishing to send food to areas where the harvest had been bad were charged monopolistic prices by the commanding general to use the railroads, and this expense was passed on to the consumers. The military often made enormous profits from food imports. In 1918, butter sold at $8.50 in El Paso was sold at $17.50 across the border in Ciudad Juárez. Flour that could be bought at $13 in San Antonio was sold at $27 in Mexico.[6]

The activities of these military leaders were particularly onerous because their control over their regions was quasi-absolute. In most cases, appeals to the federal government brought no result. Carranza simply did not have the power to control his generals. While he himself was not corrupt, tolerating the graft and corruption of others was the price he had to pay to ensure their loyalty.

This graft and corruption was only partly due to cupidity and desire for self-enrichment by Carranza's generals. They needed these funds to ensure the loyalty of their troops, as well as of the civilian supporters and clients they recruited in the regions they controlled.

The regional military commanders, who had to a large degree become regional warlords, increased the size of their forces not only to maintain their power in relation to rival warlords but also because their enemies after the defeat of Villa's División del Norte had turned to guerrilla warfare as their main means of resistance. Antiguerrilla warfare, requiring an ever-increasing number of soldiers, led to an ever-increasing cycle of repression and counterrepression, and it also exacerbated opposition to the Carrancista government. All of these factors would play a decisive role in fueling five years of bloody civil war in large parts of Mexico.

These policies of Carranza's alienated not only his former enemies and neutral victims of his generals but even men who had staunchly supported him. His agrarian decree of 1915 had sparked hopes among the country people that the promises of the revolution would finally be kept. These decrees mobilized large segments of the peasantry, since the law required meetings of village communities, and often the election of representatives where they had not previously existed, in order to formulate demands for lands. Hundreds of such demands were sent to the government. Only a few were granted by Carranza. Many peasants who had begun to trust Carranza were disillusioned when their claims were disregarded. In order to prevent a further erosion of his bases of support, Carranza was willing to make some concessions to the radicals, although most were more nominal than real. As far as labor was concerned, after a military tribunal twice rejected the sentence of death that he had imposed on recalcitrant labor leaders, he finally freed them.[7]

Carranza was willing to grant in theory what he was not willing to grant in practice. This was reflected in a new constitution promulgated at Querétaro in 1917. Its radical provisions had been adopted to a large degree against Carranza's will. He had first submitted a draft that embodied few of the radical demands of the Mexican revolutionaries, even those he himself had proclaimed at the beginning of 1915, in his agrarian law of January 15, and his pronouncements on labor, to a constitutional convention. The radicals at the convention were dissatisfied with Carranza's draft and persuaded the majority to adopt a constitution that was at the time thought to be one of the most radical adopted anywhere. It advocated extensive land reform at the expense of the large estates, gave far-reaching rights to labor—the eight-hour day, the right to strike, protection from strike-breakers—and sharply limited the rights and prerogatives of foreign business interests in Mexico. The riches of the subsoil were to be considered as essentially the property of Mexico, and foreign-owned properties could be expropriated for the common good. Foreigners were not allowed to hold property along a wide strip of land fringing Mexico's borders and coasts. Carranza would apply the constitution in a highly selective manner, conservative with respect to land reform, far more radical with respect to foreign-owned property.

The Return of the Confiscated Haciendas

Carranza shared the conviction of the Porfirian elite that land reform would be a disaster for the Mexican economy and would sharply reduce both production and productivity. His conservatism was expressed in the way he dealt with the hundreds of estates and urban properties that both his own generals and the Villista administration had confiscated from their former owners. Some had been taken over by Villista or Carrancista generals, others were administered by state agencies. Carranza felt that the best way of rapidly resuming production in the countryside was to return the estates to their former owners. This process had political risks but could also bring great political benefits to the First Chief.

The risks were obvious. How could Carranza force his generals to return to their former owners the estates they had seized, which they felt belonged to them as a result of the revolution? Would the peasants allow the estate owners to reassume control of their estates, or would such a measure lead to a huge new insurrection in Mexico's countryside? Despite these risks, such a move might finally earn Carranza the support of Mexico's hacendados, for which he had long striven in vain. He hoped that the hacendados would revitalize food production, and that the taxes they paid would fuel his deficit-ridden budget. With this in mind, he prevented his governors and his generals from making unilateral deals with the hacendados and specified that all returns of confiscated property had to go through his central administration. To make sure that this was done, he decreed that all confiscated properties had to be turned over to a national Administración de Bienes Confiscados (Administration of Confiscated Property), which he controlled. This meant that he would make the final decisions about the return of these properties and that their revenues would flow to his administration and not to governors and regional military chieftains.[8]

If a hacendado wished to recover his confiscated property, he had to make an application to the federal government in Mexico City. Carranza would then consult with local authorities as to why the property had been confiscated, what role the hacendado had played in politics, and whether the local authorities were in favor of returning the estate. He would then make the final decision about the hacendado's request. If the hacienda was returned to the estate owner, he would have to sign a paper stating that he did not hold the Mexican government liable for any damages that the property had suffered while in government hands. Carranza carefully screened all applications. He was intransigent when it came to properties owned by hacendados who had supported other revolutionary factions. He decreed the confiscation of all properties of Maytorena and of the Maderos. He was equally adamant about returning estates that he found, in contravention to Mexico's liberal laws, to be the property of the Catholic church. Carranza was careful not to antagonize those of his generals who wanted to keep some of the estates they had occupied, and he was hesitant about returning properties when such a move could spark popular unrest, as in the case of the Terrazas family in Chihuahua.

The large-scale return of confiscated estates to their former owners took place with a minimum of resistance or violence, except in those regions where peasants were resisting the Carrancistas, as in Morelos. The reaction of hacienda peons and peasants to the return of the hacendados varied from place to place. Many preferred the traditional paternalistic relationship they had maintained with the estate owners to the unpredictability and voracity of Carranza's generals, who unlike the hacendados did not think in the long term, were not interested in preserving the integrity of the properties, and were quite willing to plunder everything. Others resisted, either by remaining on the lands of returning hacendados or, if they were sharecroppers or tenants, simply by refusing to hand over part of their harvest to the newly returned estate owner. Strikes, unknown in the Porfirian era, now proliferated on many haciendas.

In most cases, Carranza's generals were quite happy to return the expropriated properties to their former owners. Many had plundered and taken whatever they could and had no intention of investing any efforts or capital in these properties. Once the hacendados returned and got the properties going again, the generals would frequently force them to share their harvests with them. They did so at times through direct pressure but more frequently through economic means. The generals controlled the railroads, and whenever a hacendado wanted to ship his produce by rail, he was forced to pay high freight rates, in addition to the money the generals charged for "protection."

On the whole, the economic recovery of the haciendas was a slow process, and the hacendados never regained the power and the authority they had had in Porfirian times. Many haciendas had been ruined or at least seriously weakened in economic terms after having been occupied by the state and the military. Many hacendados did not have capital to invest in their estates. If they did, they were reluctant to do so in view of the general insecurity in the countryside. The reluctance of many hacendados to invest capital in their estates was strengthened by the high taxes that Carranza forced them to pay. As a result, a large number of haciendas were offered for sale to foreigners, and in some cases the hacendados tried to make arrangements with their tenants and peons to buy the land from them at favorable prices.

The infrastructure that had sustained the political power of the hacendados was either gone or weakened, while peasants' consciousness of their own power had increased. This does not mean that the hacendados lost all their influence. In some parts of the country, especially in western Mexico, the hacendados made alliances with the Carrancista military and managed to subjugate recalcitrant peasants once again.[9] In the central part of the country, where some Carrancista leaders had greater links to segments of the peasantry, such alliances were more difficult to forge, and the Carrancista military at times supported the peasants against the estate owners.[10] In general, Carranza's policies antagonized the lower classes without earning him the loyalty of the hacendados.

The only provisions of the constitution that Carranza vigorously implemented were those relating to foreign property. He attempted to apply those laws that gave Mexico sovereignty over its raw materials. He did not go so far as to confiscate foreign holdings, but he demanded that they submit to Mexican legislation and attempted to increase their taxes. The Wilson administration protested both the constitution and the taxes Carranza imposed on American property. As a result of the increasing tensions between the two countries, Washington continued the arms embargo it had imposed in 1916 on Carranza, discouraged banks from granting him loans, and set obstacles in the way of trade between the two countries.

The result of the cold war between Carranza and the Americans and the hot war between Carranza and the radical factions was that for three years there was a military stalemate in Mexico, in which Carranza was not strong enough to vanquish his enemies and the latter were too weak and disunited to overthrow his regime. Extensive fighting, coupled with drought, disrupted Mexico's agriculture to such a degree that a large-scale famine ensued in 1917 and in 1918. In many parts of Mexico, Patrick O'Hea wrote to the British Foreign Office in November 1917,

in regard to the conditions prevalent among the poorer classes, there is no doubt but what in the coming winter they will face worse conditions than have existed in the memory of the present generation.

Wages are still based more or less on the scale of pre-revolutionary 1913 while the cost of necessities of life has increased to three times as much on the average, as the value of the same indispensable articles four years ago.[11]

Weakened by malnutrition, hundreds of thousands of Mexicans became victims of epidemics of Spanish influenza and of typhus. Thousands died.

The Darkest Phase: Civil War in Chihuahua, 1917–1920

The years 1917 to 1920 were the most savage period that Chihuahua experienced during the revolution and one of the darkest episodes of Chihuahuan history of any time. Both soldiers and civilians were caught up in increasing violence. Many fell victim to federal soldiers from outside the state, who frequently considered civilians legitimate prey to be plundered, raped, or killed at will. Many others were victims of increasingly brutal reprisals on Villa's part. The increasing savagery was by no means limited to Chihuahua. It could be found in other parts of Mexico, as well as on a much greater scale in Europe, where World War I dragged on. In many respects this increasing violence was a "natural" outgrowth of years of war, with its attendant callousness, brutalization of all participants, and growing disregard for human life. In Chihuahua, the brutality of the civil war was heightened by the personal characteristics of the two leaders who largely shaped its course: Francisco Murguía, who led the federal army in the state for nearly two years, and Pancho Villa.

Francisco Murguía was a former photographer from Zacatecas who had been one of the first Maderista leaders in Coahuila to rise against Porfirio Díaz. He was without any doubt the most talented military leader that the Carrancistas sent to Chihuahua to fight against Villa. Unlike Treviño, who had rarely ventured out of the capital of the state, Murguía repeatedly took the offensive against Villa. He was the only federal commander fighting against Villa in the years 1916 to 1920 whom Villa respected and at times feared. He was also cruel, corrupt, and bore a particular hatred toward the people of Chihuahua. "Chihuahua has always been a nest of rebels and traitors," he wrote Carranza.[12] Treviño had shot all Villista prisoners he took, mostly surreptitiously, but Murguía hanged them publicly and left their bodies dangling in the wind. This earned him the nickname of Pancho "Mecates" (the equivalent of Pancho the Hangman: *mecates* are ropes made of maguey, which Murguía used to hang Villista prisoners).

Murguía was callous when Chihuahuan rancheros came to see him to protest against exactions and atrocities committed by his troops. A U.S. intelligence report noted:

A short time ago a reputable man among the small ranchers of the Guerrero Valley named Gutiérrez, went into Chihuahua, as a delegate for the small ranchers, for the purpose of seeing General Murguía to ask him for some relief in that section; he had an interview with the general and explained the situation to him and the fact that the crops were short and people were facing actual privation; and that they would suffer unless the troops were compelled to stop their confiscations, etc. This Gutiérrez told our informant that the general struck the table with his fist, cursed him for everything that he could think of; and told him that he could and would do nothing for the country people of Chihuahua—they were all rascals, bandits, and Villistas.[13]

Murguía had no compunction about speculating in foodstuffs in times of famine and hunger and thus increasing the suffering of Chihuahua's civilian population.

Unfortunately for the people of Chihuahua, too, Murguía's brutality was matched by an increasing brutality on Villa's part. It would not be an exaggeration to speak of a moral decline of Villa in these years. He had never been what one might call a gentle man. In the heyday of the División del Norte, however, his reprisals fitted the pattern typical of all factions during the revolution. In many respects, Villa had shown himself to be more humane and respectful of life than either the federal army or other revolutionary factions. It was Carranza who had issued the decree that all prisoners were to be shot, and when Villa reported to the First Chief, he always stated that he had executed his prisoners in accordance with Carranza's decree. While he took reprisals against members of the oligarchy, he had kept a greater discipline among his troops than practically any other revolutionary leader and had thus prevented pillage and looting in the cities he occupied. In spite of Carranza's orders, he frequently respected the lives of captured plain federal soldiers, and he himself never forced anyone (except federal prisoners) to join the División del Norte against his will. The U.S. secret agent Edwin Emerson, who carefully observed Villa's policies, stated that he would never harm the poor (see chapter 8, p. 289).

Villa's attitude began to change in 1915. The first dramatic manifestation of this change was his massacre of the male inhabitants of San Pedro de las Cuevas in Sonora (see chapter 13 above). In 1916, he forced unwilling recruits to join his army and allowed looting and plunder by his troops. In 1917, his violence extended to family members of his enemies, including women. While these policies were partly an outgrowth of savage traits in Villa's own personality, to a large degree they are observable in revolutionary leaders in many other parts of the world, who underwent a similar process of moral decline. This decline was in some cases linked to material corruption. Men who in bad times were willing to risk their lives for a revolutionary cause frequently discovered the lures of wealth and the good life. After being named head of the federal forces fighting Zapata's troops in Morelos, for example, Pablo González, who prior to the revolution had been a member of the Partido Liberal Mexicano and had been willing to confront the Porfirian police on behalf of industrial workers, had begun an unprecedented policy of looting the riches of the state and increasing his own personal wealth. González also pillaged in Mexico City.[14]

A more frequent element of moral decline, outside of Mexico, resulted from the absolute power acquired by such leaders as Stalin or Mao. Surrounded by sycophants, these men soon identified their own personal fate with that of the revolution and had no moral compunction about taking reprisals on a gigantic scale against their opponents, as well as against individuals and the families of people they considered *potential* opponents. But independently of whether they exercised absolute power or not, the moral decline of many revolutionaries often set in at a time when substantial segments of the population became disillusioned with the revolution and either withdrew from it or turned against it. At that point, in the eyes of the leaders, the former members of the "revolutionary masses," "toiling workers and peasants," turned into "counterrevolutionaries," "lackeys of capitalism," "running dogs of imperialism," or simply into "traitors" to the revolution. In 1921, when the sailors at the naval base of Kronstadt near Petrograd, who in 1917 had helped to bring about the Russian Revolution, protested against the Bolshevik monopoly on power and demanded a return of power to the elected councils (i.e., the soviets), they were mowed down by the fire of Red Guard troops sent there with the approval of the Bolshevik Central Committee. The sailors of Kronstadt were seen as pawns of reaction. It was no different in China when, during the period of the Hundred Flowers and during the Cultural Revolution, Mao turned against the intellectuals who had supported the Communist revolution in the darkest days of the Japanese occupation and the fight against Chiang Kai-shek.

Money, wealth, and the lure of the good life were not the reasons for Villa's moral decline. He had for many years had scope to accumulate enough money to become a millionaire and lead a comfortable life in exile wherever he chose. It was an opportunity he did not take. On the other hand, while he never held absolute power, he liked to be surrounded by sycophants; this frequently clouded his judgment and diminished his moral restraints. Like the Bolshevik Central Committee in 1921, Stalin, Mao, or the East German leader Erich Honecker in 1989, he felt he personified the revolution: when people turned against him, they had simply become traitors to the cause. But his mentality was not the same as that of the Communist revolutionary leaders. He did not feel that the people who turned against him had betrayed great abstract principles such as "the dictatorship of the proletariat" or "the cause of socialism"; rather, he felt in a more traditional way that they had broken a kind of covenant that both sides were obliged to honor. When one of the veterans of the División del Norte, Lauro Trevizo Delgado, refused to rejoin his army at Namiquipa, Villa had told him, "Look, Trevizo. When your people needed me I helped you as much as I could, and now that I need you, you do not want to help me," and ordered him shot.[15] Trevizo was nevertheless spared after Nicolás Fernández intervened on his behalf. Villa's reprisals could be extremely savage when he was in the grip of his uncontrollable furies, but he was incapable of the cold-blooded callousness or inhumanity of many other revolutionary leaders.

On the whole, during the bloody years of civil war in Chihuahua from 1915 to 1920, the atrocities committed by Villa were on a smaller scale than those of his Carrancista rivals. Whereas the Carrancistas executed all Villistas who fell into their hands, Villa at times released Carrancista prisoners. Villa sometimes committed bloody acts of reprisal against civilians, but these were the exception rather than the rule. It was the Carrancistas who systematically pillaged villages in Chihuahua, in the process frequently alienating their own allies in the state.

Villa's Last Victorious Campaign

From the moment he recovered from his wounds in June 1916 and discovered that Pershing was immobilized in northern Chihuahua and would not actively pursue him, Villa's main aim had been to secure control of large parts of Chihuahua's territory and to reconstitute a regular fighting force. He had achieved that aim by the end of 1916, when Treviño and his men were cooped up in a few cities, while most of the Chihuahuan countryside was firmly in Villa's hands, as it had been in 1913 on the eve of the capture of Ciudad Chihuahua. His renewed occupation of the state capital in November 1916 was the culmination of that strategy. Nevertheless, he knew that, unlike in 1913, he was not strong enough to hold on to the city. His main aim in capturing it was to secure supplies, both to equip his army and to maintain the loyalty of the people in the countryside, to whom he distributed some of the goods that he extracted from the capital. At the same time, it was a propaganda coup of the first magnitude, designed to show the people, not only of Chihuahua and the north but of all of Mexico, that Villa was still a force to be reckoned with.

It may have been his desire to impress public opinion or the fact that he was more magnanimous in victory than in defeat that led Villa to be less repressive and show more restraint in Chihuahua than he had in many of the small towns and villages he had earlier occupied. There seems to have been no forced recruitment of soldiers, and at least some of the prisoners he took were spared. Although the prisoners he took on Santa Rosa hill "were shot mercilessly" and "the wounded who were found in the field hospital at the Avenida Zarco" were executed, those "from the large military hospital were all pardoned and even visited and cheered up later on by Villa himself." Villa told representatives of Chihuahua's merchants that he would grant all foreigners his fullest protection, "excepting from the same the Chinamen and the white Chinamen, that is the Americans, as these ones are the only ones responsible for all the misfortunes of this country." While the few Americans in Ciudad Chihuahua managed to hide, the Chinese the Villistas found were mercilessly massacred.

Villa was heartened when the lower class of the population received his troops "with shouts of joy and cheers, which circumstance together with the later rapacious behavior of the civilian population has plainly demonstrated the sympathy of the majority of the inhabitants for Villa." In order to strengthen the popular sympathy he enjoyed among the city's lower classes, Villa initially allowed pillage on a large scale:

One of the first stores that was looted was the government shoe factory and saddlery situated in the next vicinity of the Chihuahua Foreign Club which was spared this time. After the doors were broken in the waiting mob rushed wildly in. The soldiers were taking mostly cartridge belts and rifle scabbards and the mob, composed mostly of women, went after everything that was in sight. Nothing was left, and the last woman leaving the place was carrying the empty box and the cobbler's stool. The mob spread quickly over the other parts of the town. Next to the Chinamen the mob directed its savage instincts to the business places of the Syrians, or the Arabs, as they are called in this country and who are particularly hated by the natives.

Although he allowed it at the outset, Villa was resolved to keep looting by the populace under control. By nightfall, troops were occupying most strategic points in the city, and it was Villa's forces who now systematically emptied the stores and put the loot on railway cars, which were sent to the countryside. Villa also imposed a tax on all merchants in the city. When the German consul, who was hoping for Villa's sympathy, protested, Villa told him that he was not going "to respect the wishes of the local consuls as they ought to be rather at the European warfront but that he would be very pleased to consider direct orders from the Kaiser himself." Villa also kept his troops under strict control:

drunkenness was prevented as far as possible, all saloons being closed. . . . Several circulars with guarantees for the town and inhabitants were posted and distributed and Villa's proceedings are somehow different from his previous ones. A certain tendency for capturing the confidence and the good will of the population is visible, and not one of his terrible outbreaks occurred this time. Has the tiger softened or is he gathering for an unexpected leap?[16]

As his troops were loading all they could on trains headed for the countryside, Villa was faced with the immediate problem of how to deal with Murguía's relief column, which outnumbered his forces by two to one and was rapidly approaching Ciudad Chihuahua. Should he withdraw from the city in the face of overwhelming odds without giving battle? Or should he lead all his troops in a desperate charge against Murguía's forces? This is probably what Villa would have done in 1913 or in 1915. His defeats had made him more cautious, but he did not want simply to retreat, not only because of his pride and his image but also because he needed time to take all the supplies he wanted out of Ciudad Chihuahua. He decided on a compromise. He sent 3,000 men on a delaying action against Murguía, but knowing how slim the chances of victory were, he charged Salazar with the task.

A strange relationship had developed between Villa and Salazar. They had twice faced each other in battle. It was Salazar who had commanded the Oroz-quista army that expelled Villa from Parral in 1912, and a year later the two men had again led opposing armies at the battle of Tierra Blanca, one of Villa's most notable victories. Salazar was something of a chameleon—his allegiances had frequently changed. Prior to the revolution, he had been a Magonista and had joined with one of the most famous Magonista leaders, Práxedis Guerrero, in an unsuccessful attack on Palomas in Chihuahua. When the attack was repelled, one of the Magonista leaders wrote, "José Inés Salazar became afraid and abandoned us in the middle of the desert, unknown to us."[17]

Salazar joined the Madero revolution in 1910, but he turned against Madero two years later during the Orozco rebellion of 1912. His allegiances continued to zigzag. In 1913, he first joined Vázquez Gómez in calling for a rebellion against Huerta, then joined Huerta against the revolutionaries, and then fled to the United States. There he offered his services to Carranza, and when they were rebuffed, he crossed into Chihuahua to attempt an anti-Carrancista rebellion together with other former Orozquista leaders. He was defeated by the Carrancistas, sentenced to death, and imprisoned in Chihuahua's penitentiary. Villa's hope that Salazar would rally the former Orozquistas to his cause was not so much because he believed in Salazar's innate loyalty but rather because he knew that Salazar had nowhere else to go. By entrusting him with the command of the army that was to fight Murguía, he was, on the one hand, showing his confidence in the former Orozquista leader but, on the other, was forcing him to bear the onus of an almost certain defeat. Salazar's 3,000 men were no match for the 8,000 or 10,000 soldiers commanded by Murguía, who had been reinforced by the troops that Treviño had evacuated from Ciudad Chihuahua.

The two armies met at Horcasitas, located close to Ciudad Chihuahua. When Salazar saw the enormous force that Murguía had arrayed against him, he knew that he could not win. Nevertheless, he had strict instructions from Villa to fight at any cost, and so he ordered his men to charge into the Carrancista ranks and the only instruction he gave to his officers was to set out to drink coffee in Bachimba. The canyon of Bachimba was located behind Horcasitas and in order to get there the Villista troops would have to smash Murguía's columns. The Villistas were repulsed again and again, yet nevertheless they managed to withdraw in good order with moderate losses. In fact, Treviño would later accuse Murguía of having botched a possible victory. "I must frankly tell you," Treviño wrote Murguía, "that I was surprised by your report of the battle of Horcasitas . . . since you say that the enemy had hundreds of dead, wounded, and prisoners, which is by far exaggerated since you should remember that nothing of the sort occurred. On the contrary, our victory was insignificant, with very few practical results, if we consider the arms at our disposal and our superiority in numbers."[18]

After the defeat of his troops at Horcasitas, Villa was forced to evacuate Ciudad Chihuahua. As he watched Murguía's troops entering the city from afar, his secretary observed that his face was full of rage and heard him muttering that he would trade Chihuahua for Torreón.

The "rage" that Villa now felt against the Carrancistas would express itself both in one of the greatest victories he was still to achieve, the capture of Torreón, and in one of the darkest episodes of his life.

As Villa's troops retreated in good order from the battlefield of Horcasitas, they had no difficulty in taking the city of Camargo and overwhelming its Carrancista garrison. As Villa was entering the town, which had been taken by his general Baudelio Uribe, a woman, her face full of tears, knelt in front of him. She implored Villa in the name of God not to kill her husband, who was only a paymaster in the federal army and had been captured by Uribe's troops.

When Villa asked Uribe what had happened, the latter told him that the paymaster was already dead.

When the woman heard this news, she flew into a rage and began hurling imprecations at Villa, calling him a murderer and asking why he would not kill her as well. Flying into one of his uncontrollable rages, Villa thereupon pulled a gun and shot her. But this was not enough to assuage his fury. Encouraged by some of his local supporters, who feared that the remaining Carrancista soldaderas might denounce them once the Carrancistas returned to Camargo, they called on Villa to kill all of the women who had accompanied the Carrancista garrison. Villa now ordered the execution of the 90 women they had taken prisoner. Even his loyal secretary was deeply shocked at the grisly scene that now ensued. It was with a sense of deep moral revulsion that he contemplated the bodies of the 90 women, their bodies lying one on top of the other, all of them killed by Villista bullets. The incongruity that stuck most was the picture of a two-year-old baby laughing and happily playing, his hands full of the blood of his dead mother, on whose body he was sitting.[19]

In moral terms, this execution marked a decisive decline of Villismo and contributed to eroding its popular support in Chihuahua, although it did not destroy it entirely. In military terms, the capture of Camargo furnished Villa with sufficient supplies, together with the ammunition and arms he had hidden before his defeat in 1915 and the booty he had taken from Chihuahua, to achieve his greatest victory since the end of the División del Norte in 1915: the capture of Torreón. In 1914, Villa's occupation of that city had been the turning point in the war against Huerta and had given the División del Norte access to central Mexico. The Carrancista leadership was deeply worried and fearful that Villa's capture of Torreón might enable him either to join forces with the rebels swarming all over central Mexico or to overrun the weak garrisons in other parts of the north and allow him to once again become the master of that vast region of Mexico.

Torreón was garrisoned by only about 2,000 men, headed by General Severiano Talamantes, and Secretary of War Obregón urgently called on Murguía to send cavalry units of 3,000 men to reinforce Torreón. Murguía refused. His primary aim, he declared, was to destroy Villa's base in the mountains of western Chihuahua. "Nearly all of the Guerrero district has taken up arms in favor of the bandit Villa," Murguía wrote Obregón, and he added that he was sending 3,000 men there "to put an end to banditry."[20] He explained that the reason for sending such a large force to Guerrero was "to be able to organize men willing to cooperate with us and to take this base away from Villa, to which he will doubtless return after having been defeated at Torreón."[21]

Murguía's only move to support the defenders of Torreón was to send a cavalry force, not to reinforce them, but rather to intercept Villa once he had failed to take Torreón and attempted to return to Chihuahua. All Murguía was willing to give Talamantes was advice. He reassured him that Villa had been so weakened in the battles with Murguía that he did not have sufficient ammunition to take Torreón, and that Talamantes should concentrate on repelling Villa's "famous charges . . . carried out in the early morning hours."[22]

Obregón was not persuaded by Murguía's argument and again ordered him to reinforce Torreón as quickly as possible. Again Murguía refused. It is not clear what induced Murguía to do so. Did he hope to single-handedly defeat Villa upon his return from Torreón and thus earn the glory, prestige, and power that such a victory would entail? Did he genuinely want Talamantes to be defeated? Murguía is known to have quarreled with some of Carranza's other generals and to have hated them at least as much as he did Villa, so that such an attitude on his part would not be surprising. Since he belonged to a Carrancista faction opposed to Obregón, he may even have wanted to discredit him and force him to resign as secretary of war.

Obregón now desperately tried to get troops from other parts of Mexico to reinforce the Torreón garrison. His inability to do so reflected the critical situation of the Carranza government in late 1916 and early 1917. The army was fighting rebels practically everywhere in Mexico, he told Carranza, and troops could not be spared to go north. The Carrancista commander in Tamaulipas had just told Carranza that rebels had taken an important railway junction, and he wanted to concentrate all his troops in Veracruz, San Luis Potosí, and Nuevo León to fight the rebels in the Tamaulipas mountains. In Guadalajara, Diéguez was worried that Villa's former supporter Buelna would land in Tepic and attack his forces. The Carrancista garrison of Campeche had just revolted, and General Salvador Alvarado wanted Obregón's authorization to send troops to there to put an end to the rebellion. General Gavira from Durango "urgently asks me to send him cavalry forces to fight against the rebels. . . . General Estrada of Zacatecas is asking me to send the first regiment of his division, which is now located in Jalisco, to help him, since he does not have sufficient forces to carry out an active campaign in the state." Bitterly, Obregón told Carranza that "if General Murguía had pursued Villa with all of his cavalry, without waiting for the repair of the railroad, leaving his infantry to protect Chihuahua . . . Villa would not be able to attack Torreón."[23]

Obregón's fears proved more than justified. On December 22, 1916, Villa's troops stormed and occupied Torreón, which was evacuated by Talamantes, with the trains and artillery in the city falling into Villa's hands.[24] Talamantes was so shaken by his defeat that he committed suicide. There was no pity in Murguía for his defeated colleague. In a letter to Carranza, his epitaph for Talamantes consisted in calling him a man "without spirit and energy, full of weakness and ineptitude."[25]

With his violent criticism of the dead Talamantes, Murguía was attempting to evade responsibility for one of the greatest successes that Villa scored in the post-1915 period. The capture of Torreón not only increased Villa's prestige, it demonstrated that he was the only one of the numerous rebel leaders still fighting the Carrancistas who was capable of achieving a major military victory. In Torreón, he captured large amounts of supplies and succeeded in extracting substantial amounts of money from domestic merchants and foreign companies in the city. The size of his army also increased significantly. Some of the new recruits were members of revolutionary groups that had continued to fight the Carrancistas in the Laguna area and now rejoined Villa. Some were volunteers from Torreón, impressed by Villa's rising star. But others were men forcibly inducted into his army. "The other day," an unidentified observer from Torreón reported, "when a big crowd of pelados were standing outside the Hotel Francia waiting to see and admire Villa, he came out with a pistol in hand and ordered everybody arrested and from the crowd he picked the ablest men, forcing them to be enlisted in his army."[26]

"Happily, apart from acts of vengeance, not many murders of natives were committed," Patrick O'Hea, the British vice-consul, reported from Torreón. "The abandonment of the defense by the government commanders in utterly cowardly fashion, deserting their soldiers fighting in the trenches without advice or other impulse than panic, at least had for its effect that the taking of Torreón was a relatively bloodless matter, and the invaders entered in less sanguinary spirit than might otherwise have been the case."[27]

Villa showed a certain "restraint," when he entered the French consulate at the head of 300 men and confronted the French consul, Bernadini. The consul, a wealthy hacendado, had an almost pathological hatred of Villa. In his report to the French Foreign Ministry, he called Villa a "hyena," and when he described Villa's arrival at the consulate, he spoke of the "jackal, together with 300 of his executioners." Villa accused the consul of holding 350,000 pesos in silver for a federal general, Fortunato Maycotte; of having stored Carranza's car in the consulate; and of having given refuge there to a number of Villa's enemies.

It was the consul's son who responded, by calling on Villa "to prove his accusations, and if they are indeed true, shoot me at once; if that is not the case, I want to change from an honest man into a bandit and I want to ask you to put some men under my orders to avenge my father and to kill the criminals who have so unjustly accused him."

Villa was so impressed by the young man that he told him, "You are a man of courage. Do you have a gun?" "Yes." "Throw it away, and I will give orders that you be respected."[28]

Villa's restraint did not include the Chinese, however, who were hunted down and killed. Villa never explained his hatred for the Chinese, which contrasted so strongly with his admiration of the Japanese. In all probability, he shared the xenophobic attitude that many northern Mexicans evinced toward Chinese immigrants. That attitude was owing partly to racism and resentment of an alien culture and partly to the fact that many Chinese were merchants who came into the most direct contact with Mexicans, who blamed the Chinese for the high prices of the merchandise they were selling.

Villa's restraint did not include the Americans either, but they had been evacuated from the city in a special train organized by Patrick O'Hea prior to Villa's entry into the city. The fear and hatred Villa engendered among the British and Americans, as well as the upper classes of Torreón, is reflected in the way O'Hea characterized him in his report to the Foreign Office in London. "His [Villa's] career is that of a dog in rabies, a mad mullah, a Malay running amok."[29] It is interesting that in his own report to the Foreign Office, O'Hea's immediate superior, E. W. P. Thurstan, did not agree with his vice-consul's description of Villa. "With respect to Mr. O'Hea's comments on the conduct of the Villistas, he is perhaps displaying an unnatural excess of acerbity. I am not aware that the Villistas are 'per se' any worse than any other parties in the field and it remains to be proved whether their rivals, if actuated by similar feelings of rage and disappointment, would display any nicer compunctions."[30]

One of the federal commanders who was killed in the battle of Torreón was Luis Herrera, who, together with his brother, Maclovio, had been the only important Chihuahuan revolutionary to take Carranza's side when the split between Villa and Carranza occurred in the fall of 1914. This had earned the whole Herrera family Villa's undying hatred, which was displayed even after Herrera's death. "The body of General Herrera," an observer reported from Torreón, "was hanged at the station for two days with a peso paper in one of his hands and a Whiskers picture in the other" ("Whiskers" was the nickname many Americans used for Carranza). Many observers felt that Villa had now become an irresistible force, and that he would soon dominate all of northern Mexico, and perhaps all of Mexico. "From what I saw and my military experience allows me to judge, I can say that there is not any Carranza army which will be able to stop the victorious march of Napoleon," this same observer observed.[31]

Unfortunately for Villa, he himself shared that opinion. He had ample reason to have confidence in himself. After all, only a year before, he had been a defeated and discredited leader whom only a few hundred men still followed. The bulk of his army had surrendered, and the majority of his generals and intellectual supporters had abandoned him. His access to American arms and ammunition had been abruptly cut off, and after his attack on Columbus, 10,000 new enemies had crossed the border to pursue him. Yet he had now again organized an army, had almost miraculously equipped it with arms and ammunition, partly from caches that he had hidden but mainly from supplies he captured from his enemies, and had taken the two largest cities in the north.

Villa was convinced that this time he would be able to defeat Murguía, whose troops were slowly advancing from the north on Torreón. Unlike the situation at the battle of Horcasitas, when Villa had known that he had no chance of winning because of the disparity of forces, there was now a real equivalency in troops and armaments between the two sides. The size of Villa's army had substantially increased in Torreón, while Murguía, himself overconfident after defeating the Villistas at Horcasitas, had divided his forces and sent 3,000 men under his adjutant, Eduardo Hernández, to occupy the Guerrero district, which he considered the basis of Villismo, and destroy Villa's forces there. In addition, Villa could now employ all of the artillery that he had captured in Torreón.

Unfortunately for Villa, he now fell prey to the same overconfidence and lack of preparation that had led to his defeats in Celaya and León. As his adjutant put it, "the general, after every triumph, was so flushed by his victory that he underwent a complete transformation and instead of an offensive fighter became inoffensive. His great fighting abilities disappeared after a victory of the size of Torreón."[32]

On the eve of his decisive battle with Murguía, as both sides were preparing to meet on the next day at Estación Reforma near the town of Jiménez, Baudelio Uribe suggested that with 1,000 men, he should surreptitiously march by night to the rear of Murguía so that when the battle began he would be able to attack him from the rear. Villa liked the plan but felt that it was not necessary. "Why wake up the men and tire the horses? Murguía is already morally defeated," he said.[33]

Convinced that his enemy was as completely demoralized as Talamantes's troops had been in Torreón, Villa felt that a massive cavalry charge would be sufficient to defeat Murguía. Not only did he refuse to send Uribe to circle Murguía's line but he refused to set up a reserve and even sent out Nicolás Fernández with 2,000 men on another expedition. The battle of Estación Reforma turned into a complete rout for Villa. His cavalry charge was repelled by Murguía's men, who, far from being demoralized, were mainly veterans of a successful campaign against Villa in 1915, and when Murguía's men counterattacked, Villa vainly sought the reserves he did not have.[34]

With the remnants of his army, Villa retreated to Parral, where most of the goods that he had appropriated in Torreón were stored in railway cars that he had taken from the city. Villa was now too weak to hold on to Parral and these supplies, so he called on the people of Parral to take whatever they wanted for themselves. Thousands of men from the city and from its surroundings converged on the railway station, and many must have felt the way Cortez's soldiers did when, on the eve of his evacuation of Tenochtitlán, he allowed his soldiers to take whatever they wanted from the treasure that Moctezuma had offered to the Spaniards. Within a few hours, the trains had been completely cleaned out, and Villa had gained new adherents in Parral. This may be one reason why his popularity, as it waned in other parts of Chihuahua, continued to be significant in Parral.[35]

Villa's strength was further undermined when Murguía's deputy Eduardo Hernández, who had occupied parts of the Guerrero district, while failing to destroy Villa's detachments there, succeeded in capturing most of the supplies Villa had taken from Ciudad Chihuahua. In spite of these disasters, Villa was not ready to give up his hope of once more controlling most of northern Mexico. He now divided most of his army into small detachments, allowing many of the impressed men to go home. With a small contingent of troops, he set out for the states of Durango and Zacatecas in the hope of uniting the different rebel groups that were fighting there, many of them still loyal to him, and thus setting up a new army capable of facing Murguía once again.

Like a phoenix rising from the ashes, Villa at the beginning of March of 1917 had once again assembled an army of several thousand men and was awaiting Murguía near the town of Rosario in Chihuahua. Murguía was overjoyed when he heard that Villa had reappeared and was ready to meet him with his whole army on the battlefield. He was convinced that he now had the opportunity to destroy Villa once and for all.

This time the roles that the two men had played at Estación Reforma were reversed. It was Murguía who was overconfident and Villa who carefully prepared for battle. He had chosen the terrain, and this time he made sure he had ample reserves. He hid a large number of his men behind some hills and ordered his cavalry to charge the federal lines, where it was decimated by withering fire from

Murguía's infantry. Thinking that Villa had once again attempted one of the fruitless charges in which his forces had engaged at both Horcasitas and Estación Reforma, Murguía was sure that he had won when the Villista cavalry retreated in disorder.

Convinced that he had decisively defeated Villa, Murguía relaxed his guard and allowed his men to rest. He did not notice that Villa's men had surreptitiously encircled his position. When Villa's forces attacked from all sides, Murguía's forces were so surprised that they could offer no effective resistance. He lost more than 2,500 men and himself escaped only by a hair's breadth when one of Villa's officers, who did not recognize him, beat him on the back several times with his sword. It was only at the last moment that Murguía managed to escape. He was so humiliated by this incident that he swore to silence the few officers who witnessed it. Of the 2,500 men he lost, 600 were taken prisoner by the Villistas.[36]

Villa ordered all of them to be executed. "At the beginning of the campaign," Villa's adjutant explained, "in order to humanize the war as far as possible, we freed all prisoners and allowed them to go to the nearest town and they again entered the Carrancista army. We found men (and this is definitely proven), who were taken prisoner three or four times." The executions took a particularly grisly form. Villa's Dorados lined the men up in rows of five, and in order to save bullets they were killed with one shot in the head. Even Villa's adjutant remarked that "this parade of these groups of five was something horrible to see."[37]

Villa's Renewed Decline

After his stunning victory, Villa decided that the time had come to deal Murguía a final blow, but disaster struck from a completely unexpected quarter.

Most of Villa's reserves of arms and ammunition had been stockpiled by him in a secret hiding place in Chevarría in the waning months of 1915 as his División del Norte was dissolving. It contained several million cartridges, as well as large numbers of rifles, with which Villa intended to arm his troops for the coming attack on Chihuahua. He had been extremely careful about maintaining the secrecy of the location of this arms depot. Only a few men in his immediate entourage whom he trusted were allowed to accompany him when he took supplies out of Chevarría. One of these men was Rafael Mendoza, a major in Villa's personal guard, the Dorados. Mendoza had suffered a wound in his foot during Villa's campaign, and his chief had allowed him to return to his family, who lived near the Hacienda de Bustillos, in order to recover from his wound. There Mendoza got drunk, was discovered by the Carrancistas, and brought to Murguía, who immediately ordered his execution. When he faced the firing squad, Mendoza lost his nerve and told Murguía that he was ready to reveal the location of Villa's depot at Chevarría if the Carrancistas would spare his life. Murguía enthusiastically agreed, and within a few days he was in possession of this depot, which constituted Villa's main reserve of arms and ammunition. When Villa heard the news, he was so devastated that he broke into tears. He now decided on a desperate expedient. Although his troops were short of ammunition, he nevertheless went ahead with his planned attack on Ciudad Chihuahua, hoping that

Murguía's troops would have been so demoralized by their defeat at Rosario that they would be unable to put up an effective resistance, and that in Chihuahua he would be able to replenish his supplies.

On the evening of April 1, Villa's troops arrived at the southern outskirts of Ciudad Chihuahua. Villa set up large campfires there, hoping to delude Murguía into believing that the main Villista attack would come from the south and thus lead him to concentrate his troops there. In the dark of the night, the bulk of Villa's cavalry rode to the northern outskirts of Chihuahua and at daybreak began its attack on the city. Murguía did not fall into Villa's trap, however, and his troops had recovered from their demoralizing defeat at Rosario. After the battle had raged for several hours, the Villistas' munitions gave out. They suffered a crushing defeat. Murguía captured more than 200 prisoners, all of whom he hanged, leaving their bodies dangling on one of Chihuahua's main avenues, the Avenida Colón. As a special concession, "Murguía allowed one of Villa's generals whom he had captured, Miguel Saavedra, to choose the tree from which he would be hanged."[38]

Villa now became so enraged that he wanted revenge at all costs from those who had betrayed his munitions depots. He could not locate Mendoza, who in the meantime had joined the Carrancista army, but he did know that some of the inhabitants of Namiquipa had betrayed the secret of another arms depot to Pershing, and it was there that he decided to take his revenge. For a long time he had kept away from that part of Chihuahua, since it was too close to where Pershing's troops were stationed. But on February 5, the Americans had evacuated Chihuahua, and Villa felt that he now would have no problems in occupying that region. His aim was to execute the members of the *defensa social* (home guard) established in Namiquipa under Pershing's auspices, but when they heard that Villa was approaching, they fled into the mountains. Villa decided to take his revenge on them in a particularly gruesome and savage way. He forcibly assembled all their wives and allowed his soldiers to rape them.

Even some of Villa's commanders were repelled by this act of savagery. Nicolás Fernández took some of the women under his own protection and ordered his soldiers to shoot anyone who attempted to attack them. Many of the inhabitants of Namiquipa had been among Villa's most fervent supporters, but as a result of this act of savagery, "the feelings of the people had been hurt forever."[39] Meanwhile, in neighboring Bachíniva, one of Villa's commanders, General Geronimo Padilla, allowed his troops to loot part of the town.[40]

Soon Villa came to feel the results of his ferocious acts of reprisal, which had sent shock waves throughout the villages of Chihuahua. He had established his headquarters at the hacienda of Babicora and stationed the remnants of his army, about 2,000 men, around it. Through his agents, Murguía was informed of Villa's location and sent troops to make a surprise attack on him there. Time and time again, federal troops had hoped to surprise Villa, but they had never succeeded, since there were always villagers who warned the revolutionary leader of the approach of hostile forces. This time, no one warned Villa, and Murguía's attack on his headquarters came as a complete surprise. Hundreds of Villistas were killed, including one of his most loyal generals, Francisco Beltrán. Villa himself was nearly captured when at the head of 400 men he desperately fought his way out of the Carrancista encirclement. His forces had been decimated by this attack, and even some of his most loyal subordinates decided to turn against him. One of Villa's most trusted lieutenants, Colonel Pérez of the Dorado escort, invited Villa to his headquarters, stationed his troops on the roof, and ordered them to kill the general as soon as he appeared. Villa's innate caution and the sense of distrust that he had acquired in his years as an outlaw saved him. When he saw men stationed on the roof, he sent three of his adjutants to reconnoiter. When they were fired upon, Villa immediately retreated, and for a number of days, he refused to make contact with his troops.[41]

Villa suffered another grievous blow when he failed in a major effort to smuggle arms across the border from the United States. He sent his lieutenant, José María Jaurrieta, with several thousand dollars to buy arms there. The arms were to be sent to Presidio, Texas, which faced the Mexican town of Ojinaga. On April 17, after a long march to the eastern part of the state, where Ojinaga was located, Villa captured the border city, waiting for the arms. Practically none came. Jaurrieta had failed to persuade any of the arms dealers who had previously dealt with Villa to renew that relationship. Not only was the border heavily guarded by U.S. troops, the dealers were afraid of suffering reprisals if they sold arms to a man who was considered the avowed enemy of the United States.[42]

Villa now faced one of the most profound crises of his life. The drying up of all sources of arms and ammunition created a problem for him similar to the one he had faced in late 1915 after the dissolution of the División del Norte. He was no longer able to maintain a regular army and permanently control a large territory that would constitute his base of operations. The military and logistical crisis of Villismo was supplemented by two other crises: a drastic deterioration of Villa's relations with the people in Chihuahua's countryside and an ideological crisis as well. Popular support for Villa had begun to erode in part as a result of his tactic of forced impressment and the savagery of his reprisals at Camargo and above all at Namiquipa. In addition, since Villa was unable to control a territory and thus to grant them protection, many country people in Chihuahua now attempted to reach an accommodation with the government.

The ideological crisis of Villismo was a direct result of the evacuation of Mexico by Pershing's expedition at the beginning of February 1917. From the end of 1915 until his occupation of Torreón in late 1916, Villa's appeals to the Mexican people and his justification for continuing to fight against the Carrancistas were that they had sold out Mexico to the United States, and that when the Punitive Expedition invaded the country, they had failed to oppose the Americans. He wished to unite all Mexicans against the foreign invaders, he claimed, and was only fighting the Carrancistas because they refused to stand up to Pershing's army. Now, not only were the Americans gone, but relations between the Wilson administration and the Carranza government had reached an all-time low. After the United States entered World War I, the Carrancistas openly expressed support for Germany.

Villa was never able to overcome the crisis he now faced. He would never regain the popularity he had enjoyed prior to 1915 or even the more limited popular support he had secured in 1916. Nor would his army ever achieve the strength it had briefly regained in 1916. What Villa did accomplish was to survive, together with several hundred men, against all odds. In order to do so, he was forced to apply a fairly new strategy, which he had never used before, dividing his army for part of the year into small units, which carried out dozens of hit and run attacks on Carrancista garrisons and on small towns, thereby supplying themselves with food, arms, and ammunition. They would unite again under Villa's leadership at harvest time, when there was enough food to supply a large force.

It was a tactic that allowed Villa's army, which had now shrunk to about 1,000 men, to survive, but it held out no prospect of victory. It also weakened Villa's movement in several respects. Villa now exercised direct control over his men for only part of the year. As a result, Villa's restraint on his soldiers' mistreatment of the civilian population, despite the fact that he himself was guilty of atrocities, may now have been lifted for part of the year. The new tactic also probably weakened Villa's overall control over his men, although it is remarkable that every year they would still meet and again accept Villa's unquestioned authority. This was owing both to Villa's charisma and to the fact that he continued to hold the purse-strings of his movement, thanks to large-scale forced contributions from foreign enterprises.

After the departure of the Pershing expedition, Villa made no attempt to explain why he was still fighting Carranza and the aims he pursued in doing so. In part this was because in its later guerrilla phase, after 1915, with one exception, no intellectuals participated in the Villa movement. In this respect, the Villa movement was very different from its counterpart in the south headed by Emiliano Zapata, many of whose intellectual advisors stayed with him until the end. A few Villista intellectuals such as Miguel Díaz Lombardo and Ramón Puente continued to support Villa from exile, but no intellectual except for Angeles, during the brief months when he rejoined Villa in 1918, participated in his guerrilla campaigns.

This does not mean that there were no literate men in the Villa movement. Villa had two secretaries, Miguel Trillo, who would fulfill that function until Villa's death and be assassinated together with his chief in Parral in 1923, and José Maria Jaurrieta, who was perhaps the Villista closest to being what one might call an intellectual, in the sense that he later wrote the only significant account of Villa's later guerrilla life. However, Jaurrieta never attempted to formulate any ideological platform; nor, in contrast to Villa's earlier secretaries, did he ever give advice to Villa on either ideological or practical issues. A third literate man, Manuel Gómez Morentin, constituted Villa's link to his supporters in the United States. Gómez Morentin frequently crossed the border bringing messages from Villa to Villistas in the United States. Unlike Villa's earlier representatives in the United States, he seems to have been no more than a messenger. In one respect, he was eminently successful. He was never captured or imprisoned. The main reason for this was that the U.S. government tolerated his activities, not because it supported them, but because it was able to intercept all the letters he brought and thus keep a close check on Villistas activities in the United States.[43]

Villa's ideological disarray is best reflected in the first public pronouncement that he made after his defeat in Chihuahua in 1917. It came as a response to one of the few developments during this period that could be called "positive" from his point of view: an exchange of letters between Treviño and Murguía that helped to discredit both of them in the public eye. After Murguía's defeat at Rosario, Treviño, who in the meantime had entered politics as a state representative to the National Congress in Mexico City and who had been humiliated by Murguía's attacks on him, felt that the time had come to exact his revenge. After having been allowed to see the disparaging remarks that his successor had made about him, Treviño sarcastically wrote to Murguía, "You erroneously believed that your capacities were nearly superhuman and you allowed yourself to be overwhelmed by the flattery of a few fools around you, who, as far as I know, have publicly compared you with the great Napoleon, a comparison that has made you the laughing stock of those who heard it." Treviño added:

You have passed judgment on a man [Treviño himself] whom you do not know and who has never sullied his name with murder or with attacks on private property and who has remained poor and always maintained his dignity, in unfortunate contrast to many of your officers, of whom the whole country knows that they have become wealthy during the revolution. The whole country knows of the recent defeats that you and our army have suffered in different parts of the state of Chihuahua and does not believe in your bombastic reports of great successes.

Although Murguía had had more men, more money, and more ammunition than ever before at his disposal, Treviño observed, he had not been able to achieve a decisive victory. In conclusion, Treviño told Murguía:

you have now been convinced of the great truth that General González articulated, "that the victor of today could be the vanquished of tomorrow." Success depends on a large number of circumstances with chance playing an important role as well as what others would call the star of the one who leads. The star, compañero Murguía, which was shown in "Ebano" [Treviño's greatest victory] and twice in "Icamole" has not been eclipsed in Chihuahua.[44]

Murguía's answer was even sharper and more sarcastic than Treviño's letter. He repeated all the attacks he had made on Treviño in his reports to Carranza and Obregón. He enumerated the long list of defeats that Villa had inflicted on Treviño's forces, and that his predecessor had attempted to describe as victories. "Perhaps," he sarcastically wrote him, "you have no direct responsibility for this, since you have never taken part in any battle outside of the city of Chihuahua." Murguía again accused Treviño of cowardice for the sudden evacuation of Ciudad Chihuahua in November 1916. Since Treviño had accused him of corruption, Murguía responded in kind. He quoted details about Treviño's padding of the payroll. Officially, he had received funds to pay 21,300 men, but when Murguía arrived in Chihuahua, Treviño had told him that he only had 5,870 men, and that number was finally reduced to 2,100.[45]

Murguía decided to publish this exchange in the Chihuahuan press, and it helped to discredit both himself and Treviño. Treviño was so shaken by the publication of these letters, which he had not expected, that he had recourse to a desperate public relations ploy in order to convince the public of his honesty. He suggested that both he and Murguía should list, under oath before a notary, all the wealth and properties they had acquired in the course of the revolution and transfer all of it to public ownership.[46] Murguía agreed, and the Chihuahuan press rejoiced, but neither of the two men ever mentioned the proposal again or attempted to follow up on it.

Villa felt that the time had come for him to intervene in the debate. Since he had no access to the government-controlled Mexican press, he sent an open letter to Murguía, full of bravado and defiance, to *El Heraldo del Norte*, a U.S. newspaper, which immediately published it. Chihuahua's newspapers then felt under strong pressure to reproduce it. Its main purpose was to convince the people of Chihuahua, and of Mexico as a whole, that Villa was still a military presence to be reckoned with. He enumerated all of Murguía's defeats and the grievous losses suffered by his troops:

Do you realize the disaster suffered by you on March 4 of the current year at Rosario, Durango, has no precedent in the history of the state because of the bloody and heavy losses of your men? Don't you remember that at 10:00 on the morning of that day, you precipitously fled, abandoning your forces most shamefully, which even up to 3:00 in the afternoon were fighting, each defending himself, one battalion especially distinguishing itself, who wore blue uniforms and red bands, and who fought in retreat all the way from La Rueda, Durango, to Peinados, Chihuahua, where they were totally annihilated, my men having captured the last bunch of 60 infantrymen, who were immediately executed by my troops? I want to state that if I or any of my officers had arrived on time, the execution of those courageous men who protected your escape, would have been prevented.

Villa then "for your honor and glory" proceeded to analyze the losses suffered by himself and by Murguía in every battle they had fought and arrived at the conclusion that "according to the foregoing statistics, which may be very disagreeable to you but are true nevertheless, you have lost 4,449 men from December 1, 1916, to April 23, 1917."

Villa then proceeded to challenge Murguía to a duel, either between the two men or between their armies. "I want to tell you that in the field of honor you are nothing and in order to prove this to you, I solemnly invite you to a duel where the courage of both of us can be shown. Either the two of us personally or our two respective forces could meet at the day, hour, and place that you designate. You, Señor Murguía, have said that you are the man who will capture me, and to fulfill your promise, we can meet face to face, and there you can attempt to realize your golden dream."[47]

There was no mention at all in Villa's letter of what the two men were fighting for or against, no attempt to explain to the people of Chihuahua why, after the withdrawal of the U.S. Punitive Expedition, Villa was still continuing to fight. There was no mention of any social issue that might have been the basis for his campaign. The letter far more resembled a challenge to mortal combat from one medieval warlord to another than a polemic by a revolutionary leader.

The Low Point of Villa's Revolutionary Career

In spite of the bravado of his letter to Murguía, Villa knew he was in desperate straits after losing all access to reserves of arms and ammunition. Hitherto, when Villa had reached a low point in his career, he had never given up, but had always sought some unconventional means to redress his situation. In November 1913, after suffering a grievous reverse in his attack on Ciudad Chihuahua, he had done what no one expected him to do: by hiding his troops in a coal train, he had succeeded in capturing Ciudad Juárez. He never was satisfied to stay on the defensive but always took the offensive. In 1915, after his disastrous defeats in Celaya, León, and Aguascalientes, he again did the unexpected by marching into Sonora. And after the dissolution of the División del Norte, his attack on Columbus had once more snatched at least a temporary victory from the jaws of defeat.

Now, once again, Villa sought an expedient that would reverse the tide of his misfortune. This time, however, the elements of mirage and fantasy outweighed any realistic possibility of success. What Villa attempted to do in July and August of 1917 was to set out for Mexico City with 100 men in order to capture Carranza, bring him into territory controlled by Emiliano Zapata, and put him on trial there. Villa had learned that Carranza took a ride in Chapultepec Park every day, accompanied by only an aide, and it was there that he hoped to ambush him. He sent two of his literate supporters, José María Jaurrieta and Alfonso Gómez Morentín, to Mexico City to prepare the ground for the expedition, while he himself set out with a small armed force, disguised as a Carrancista detachment, to march from the north to Mexico City. Villa did not know about the enormous security forces that protected Carranza, and he completely underestimated the difficulties that such a march through most of Mexico would entail. Mao Tsetung once declared that a guerrilla, in order to operate, has to be able to submerge among the population. "The people are like water and the army is like fish," he said.[48] In Chihuahua, which he knew, and where he still enjoyed the sympathies of many, Villa had been able to move easily, but now when he left his home base, he was a fish out of water. He did not know the country or the people, and even if he had, he did not want to identify himself. He soon discovered that much of Mexico had become a kind of armed camp. In many villages, people had formed armed defensas sociales to keep intruders out of their communities. When Villa arrived at a village, its leaders rarely doubted his statement that he was in command of a federal unit. That was precisely what created fear among them, most villages having experienced the pillage and looting carried out by federal troops. When Villa's column arrived at Huejocuilla, El Alto, he found the roofs and surroundings of the village full of armed men pointing their rifles at him. They would only allow his men, ostensibly a federal detachment, to enter the village if they laid down their arms before doing so.

In order that their presence not be revealed, the expedition killed every guide they recruited in villages along the way. When, after a long and arduous trek, they met and captured 27 armed men pursuing bandits, Villa ordered all of them put to death. This triggered alarm in all the surrounding villages, and large groups of men now set out to capture the murderers of the 27 villagers. The expedition retreated to Aguascalientes, lost its way, and was plagued by hunger and increasing desertions. When Villa finally gave up, the way back turned out to be even more traumatic. Villa divided the remnants of his expedition into two small forces; one he personally commanded, and the other was headed by Colonel Bonifacio Torres. On the way, for reasons that are not clear, a mutiny broke out among Torres's troops, and they killed their leader. This led to a new wave of violence, reprisals, and desertions that further weakened Villa. The mutineers were relatives of the Murga brothers, who had followed Villa loyally from the beginning of the revolution. Two of the brothers, Ramón and Aurelio, had participated in Villa's expedition to Mexico City and had gone back north with him. When he learned of the killing of Torres, Villa decided to execute Aurelio and Ramón Murga because of their family relationship to the mutineers, although these men had had nothing to do with Torres's death. Aurelio was killed, but Ramón managed to flee and reached the camp of his brother Juan, who commanded one of Villa's detachments. Juan immediately decided to surrender to Murguía and join the latter's forces.[49]

From a logistical point of view, Villa's plan had been unrealistic. It was simply impossible for an armed body of men to make its way surreptitiously into the capital. Even if Villa had succeeded and brought Carranza to Morelos, it is questionable, once Villa's identity had been revealed, if it would have been possible for him to return north across thousands of miles of territory controlled by his enemies. Yet, viewed in political terms, the plan was not so unrealistic. What Villa obviously hoped was that Carranza's death would trigger a struggle for the succession among his generals, and that one or the other faction might be inclined either to make an alliance with him or at least to grant him an amnesty. To a certain degree, this is what happened after Carranza's death in 1920.

The failure of his expedition to Mexico City seems to have triggered a kind of despair in Villa that he had never known before. For the first time since joining the revolution in November 1910, Villa seriously contemplated laying down arms. In August 1917, he sent a letter to Murguía that was different in every respect from the open letter full of bravado and defiance that had been published two months before. "I send you this letter . . . with my head held high, as someone who has always demanded justice for his people," Villa wrote Murguía. The latter's successes he attributed chiefly to "good fortune, since you [meaning not only Murguía but the Carrancistas in general] have unfortunately been able to utilize for your own ends my labors and my sufferings. . . . You do not know who I am; all you want to do is to kill me." Villa called on Murguía to

listen to the voice of your conscience and to ask yourself what the tremendous influx of American money into our country means. Ask yourself if these large sums are being given to Carranza because the gringos love us.

I shall continue to suffer, and perhaps tomorrow you will kill me as you wish to do, but I shall die conscious that I have done my duty and that no one will ever be able to call me a traitor.

You should be conscious of the fact, my friend, that your country, which is also mine, will never be rich, great, or free as long as we do not interrupt all communications and transactions with the Yankees, who are the real enemies of our country, although you, blinded by personal hatred, do not understand this.

Villa warned Murguía "that you and your armies are incapable of capturing me, since I have been raised in the desert and am accustomed to facing the burdens of life. If in some battle you do succeed in killing me, when personal passions have calmed down or disappeared, and you are able to think in a sane and realistic way, you will understand that you have removed from our country one of its main defenders." Saying that he could have left Mexico at any time and led the good life anywhere he wanted to, Villa asked,

Why have I not left my country, sir? Because I love it, I love my race, and I want to prove this by my deeds. . . . If I were a traitor I would curse the hour in which I was born, but my conscience is clear, and I know that this is not so.

Neither you nor any Carrancista is capable of judging the feelings that are in my heart, because you do not know them, and your only aim is to kill me without thinking or looking to the future, considering the fact that I could be of use to my country, if not as a general, even as a soldier.

Let me repeat that you are spending the Yankee treasure and do not act in accordance with the dictates of your conscience and the dignity of a Mexican.

I do not write you more, since I am convinced that all you are interested in is your personal gain without thinking of your country that is so poor and so full of suffering.[50]

This letter seems to have been linked to an offer that Villa made to Murguía to lay down his arms and retire to a peaceful life. It is not clear what conditions Villa had asked for. In any case, according to Chihuahua's premier historian, Francisco Almada, Murguía refused "under the pretext that Villa had been declared an outlaw."[51] It is not clear whether the refusal to deal with Villa came from Murguía alone or was endorsed by Carranza. Such a decision was certainly in line with Carranza's general policy of refusing any reconciliation with members of the revolutionary factions that had opposed him, and was also in line with Murguía's plan to use the civil war in Chihuahua for his own personal enrichment. The Carrancistas now left Villa no choice but to fight on. Even if he had wanted to leave Mexico, which he never did, he had nowhere to go. After the massacre of Santa Isabel and his attack on Columbus, the Americans would never have granted him asylum but would have placed him on trial. Had he gone anywhere else, both the United States and Britain (because of the shooting of Benton) would have asked for his extradition. Villa felt he had no choice but to fight on in the hope that at some point Carranza would either resign or be deposed, and that his successors would finally make peace with him.

As Villa, after his failed attempt to make peace with the government, reluctantly took up arms again in what were to be his last campaigns, he found that his popular support had shrunk to its lowest point since the day that he first joined the revolution, although he could still count on the loyalty of many of his former soldiers. Their attitude might be compared with that of some of Napoleon's old soldiers on learning of their emperor's capture, so tellingly described in Heinrich Heine's famous poem "The Grenadiers":

> "What matters wife? What matters child?
>   With far greater cares I am shaken.
> Let them go and beg with hunger wild—
>   My Emperor, my Emperor is taken![52]

The Mexican equivalent of Heine's description might be Rafael Muñoz's famous, although probably apocryphal, account of how Villa brought one of his old soldiers into his forces. When he asked him to join him once again the soldier sadly refused, saying that he had to take care of his wife and his child. "If that is the reason you cannot join me, I shall free you of this worry," Villa said, and shot both the wife and the child. Instead of turning against the murderer of his family, Villa's old soldier saddled his horse, took his rifle, and rode into battle with his erstwhile leader.[53]

For obvious reasons—his army was far smaller than that of Napoleon—Villa's relationship with his soldiers had always been far more personal. He had been a godfather to their children, given them money in times of need, eaten at their campfires, personally led them into battle, and created a complex web of relationships that for many of his men superseded all other types of allegiance. In addition, the behavior of the Carrancista army constantly brought in new recruits to Villa's forces. That behavior was partly due to the cupidity of Carranza's generals and to his policy of garrisoning what had been Villista territory with men from other parts of the country who bore no relationship whatsoever to the people of Chihuahua and Durango. They operated as quasi-occupation forces. In addition, many government soldiers were underpaid or not paid at all. Carranza's generals sometimes appropriated the funds and food intended for the soldiers, and the Carrancista treasury did not in any case have the funds to supply the huge army it had raised. As a result, the soldiers frequently had to live off the land. What this meant was aptly, if melodramatically, described by Patrick O'Hea.

These hordes of locusts, these soldiers and their women, haggard, savage, starving, reeking of filth and disease, are consuming and wasting everything. They complain that they are not paid, that for weeks they have received not a cent. Whether their officers have pocketed their pay or not, I do not know, the result is the same.

"Villista!" is the cry and a blow or shot for the wretch that would save his family's sustenance from their clutches; I have seen it myself, seen a small town left like a city of the dead, the women hidden out trembling, the food all gone and the man too worn even sullenly to try to save his blanket and his bed from the invaders.[54]

This description is more than borne out by innumerable complaints and reports that reached Carrancista headquarters. On August 12, 1917, a Carrancista general, Favela, reported that a number of villages in Chihuahua were preparing to attack the troops of another of Carranza's generals, Sosa. The villages were vainly demanding "that they be paid for everything that has been taken from them by force, and that these troops have respected no one and nothing."[55]

Inhabitants of Santa Isabel protested to Murguía that soldiers commanded by one of his subordinates had used "the doors, windows, and roofs of their houses as firewood," and that they stole their cattle in order to sell them across the border in the United States.[56] Carranza's nephew wrote a letter to his uncle describing how four agricultural colonies in the vicinity of Ojinaga were being despoiled of their corn by Carrancista soldiers, who also confiscated their cattle and horses and sold them in the United States.[57] In this particular case, Murguía admonished his subordinate to cease robbing the peasants,[58] but he refused on the whole to restrain his troops.

Some of the victims of these depredations by Carranza's troops joined Villa. He could offer them revenge but not protect their properties, since he did not exercise permanent control over any part of northern Mexico, and there seemed no prospect of him ever achieving a decisive victory again. These were not the only reasons that restrained men who hated the Carrancistas from joining Villa. Many felt repelled by the atrocities his troops committed. The story of the rape of the women of Namiquipa had spread through the Chihuahuan countryside. Many felt betrayed, since Villa had impressed them into his army in order to fight the Americans, but instead forced them to fight the Carrancistas. Once the Americans left Mexico, Murguía appealed to the frustration of these soldiers and offered them amnesty. On February 17, 1917, Murguía issued a proclamation to the people of Chihuahua stating:

The American forces who formed the Punitive Expedition have withdrawn completely from our national territory and have crossed the American border on February 5. This event has put an end to the only pretext that the bandit [Villa] has utilized to enroll in his army a large number of working citizens who . . . believed it was their duty to reinforce the vandalic hordes of Villa. The reactionary hydra is now in its death throes under the leadership of the criminal Francisco Villa and the only cause it advocates is that of a disastrous vandalism. . . . I will give guarantees to any citizen who, disillusioned by [Villa's] anti-patriotic attitude, abandons the bandit and lays down his arms.[59]

The Defensas Sociales

Many of Villa's soldiers responded to Murguía's appeal. Villa had never attempted to explain to them why he still continued to fight after the withdrawal of the Americans. In the heyday of Villismo between 1913 and 1915, he had been seen by the country people of Chihuahua as the champion of land redistribution; and in fact the first steps toward agrarian reform had been taken during his administration, although in contrast to what occurred in Morelos, for reasons described above, no large-scale land divisions had taken place. From 1916 onward, Villa, in word and deed, seems to have lost any interest in land reform, and that apparently disillusioned many of his erstwhile supporters. Many were simply tired of fighting, and others saw no hope of victory. They had continued to fight in Villa's ranks because of their anti-American nationalism and their hatred of the Carrancistas and their exactions. Now that the Americans were gone, Carranza offered them a way out that would allow them to resist both the incursions of Villa's troops and the depredations of the Carrancista soldiers.

The Carranza administration not only allowed but encouraged Chihuahua's villagers to form local militias, which the government outfitted with arms and ammunition. They were required to fight the Villistas but in return would be able to defend their homes against Villa's soldiers and against bandits roaming the countryside, as well as against the depredations of Carranza's soldiers. These organizations, called defensas sociales, existed not only in Chihuahua but in many parts of Mexico. Their social composition varied enormously. One of the first defensas sociales, founded during the Huerta period in the city of Durango, was at one end of the social spectrum. Its membership was limited to the wealthiest families of the city, and it fought desperately to prevent the capture of Durango by the revolutionary forces led by Calixto Contreras and Tomás Urbina in 1913. At the other end of the social spectrum was the defensa social of San José de Gracia, located in the state of Michoacán. It included practically all the adult males of the village capable of bearing arms and resisted any armed force from outside attempting to penetrate the community.[60] Such defensas sociales did not develop in all of Mexico. Where the government was in firm control, as in Yucatán, or where the majority of the population supported the revolutionaries, as in Zapatista Morelos, such organizations scarcely developed.

Shortly after becoming governor of Chihuahua in early 1916, Ignacio Enríquez had attempted to form such organizations in Chihuahua. His success in early 1916 was very limited. His tenure in office was far too short, and Villa's popularity still too great. The only successful attempt to establish such an organization was the Pershing-organized defensa social of Namiquipa and surrounding villages. Treviño made no attempts to create such defensas and neither could he have done so, since Villa controlled all of Chihuahua's countryside in late 1916. It was from mid 1917 onward, when Villa lost control of the countryside and the sympathies of a large part of its population, that defensas sociales began to proliferate there.

Their social composition and leadership was varied. At Hearst's Hacienda de Babicora, the defensa social was led by one of Hearst's foremen, Maximiano Márquez, and reflected a clear hacendado influence. In some villages, all the inhabitants participated in the formation of the defensa social, but frequently it reflected divisions within the village that had existed long before the revolution broke out, divisions that had been papered over during the Villa period and now reemerged. In most cases the wealthier inhabitants took over control of the defensa social. Many members of the defensas sociales were former Villistas who felt, as one former soldier of the División del Norte put it, that "Villa was not fighting for justice any more or for any legal cause. It had become a personal struggle between Carranza and Villa . . . and since Carranza now constituted the government, it was better to unite with him or to retire to private life."[61]

"What we wanted to achieve," one member explained, "was to prevent strangers from entering our villages; they all did what they wanted here: they stole, they looted in the name of Villa, in the name of the government, in the name of anyone. . . . We did not even know whether they were coming from Villa or the government or simple bandits. Seeing this, we decided to organize ourselves."[62]

While the defensas sociales often fought against Villa, their relations with the federal army and the federal government were anything but harmonious. In extreme cases, they fought federal detachments that entered their villages and attempted to loot. More frequently, the federal army wanted them to join in expeditions against Villa far from their native villages, which they usually refused to do.

The history of the defensa social in one village in Chihuahua, Los Llanos de San Juan Bautista, shows the aims of these home guards and the problems that attended their formation. "Tired of suffering from endless aggravations caused by the horrors of war, we were unable to protect our interests, our food, and our security, and seeing no other way of protecting ourselves, we decided to form an armed defensa social," the villagers said. They had asked the government for its approval and for arms, and then met and elected a leader. At the meeting, they declared that their main purpose was to defend their own village and to come to the help of defensas sociales in surrounding communities. The first action the defensa took was not directed against Villa but against a colonel commanding the Carrancista garrison in an adjacent village, who had regularly confiscated cattle from the village in order to feed his troops. Hitherto, no one had resisted him, but the newly formed defensa social decided that the time had come for a change. When the colonel's men arrived in the village, they faced the rifles of 30 villagers. The colonel was told in no uncertain terms that unless he paid for what he took, he would get no more cattle.

This was the first episode in a long history of conflict between the defensa social of the Llanos de San Juan Bautista and the federal army. In October 1917, 82 men from the village's defensa social went to the aid of the neighboring village of San Francisco de Borja, which had been attacked by Villista guerrillas. They were joined by federal troops under the command of General Alfredo Rueda Quijano. Within a few hours the two forces were on the verge of an armed confrontation, since Rueda Quijano tried to take away their flag and incorporate them into his army. It was only when the defensa threatened to shoot at his troops that he desisted. A new confrontation ensued when he attempted to force the defensa to join his troops in a campaign against Villa far away from their village. Once again, they had to threaten him with armed resistance before he allowed them to go home.

Relations were even worse during the next campaign, in which the villagers again "cooperated" with Rueda Quijano and his troops. The villagers were incensed when the federal general allowed his men to loot the village of Santa Cruz de Mayo and became even angrier when the horses of Rueda Quijano's cavalry trampled corn planted by inhabitants of the Mesa de Chilicote. "All of these actions created a deep feeling of revulsion among us, since we had come to give guarantees and not to cause harm, but we could not prevent them since the military commanders fully agreed with these actions; we continued our march until we came to Santa María de Cuevas, where the federal troops continued to carry out their atrocities. At this point, our people mutinied, saying that they did not want to take part in such atrocities . . . and we returned home."[63]

The disillusionment of many in the defensas sociales with the federal army did not prompt them to join Villa. On the contrary, they continued to fight the Villista guerrillas, whom many of them considered the main impediment to the establishment of peace.

Carranza soon realized the potential that the defensas sociales represented for his regime. If his administration could mobilize sufficient support in the Chihuahuan countryside, Villa, even if he were not captured or killed, would cease to command an effective fighting force. Yet Carranza also understood by mid 1918 that in spite of increasing popular opposition to Villa, many in the Chihuahuan countryside would not fight for the government as long as it gave the military unlimited control over the affairs of Chihuahua. Ever since Enríquez had abandoned his governorship in mid 1916 and been replaced by Treviño's brother, the civilian administration of the state had been a creature of the military commanders. Treviño's brother had been succeeded by Arnulfo González, a military sub-ordinate of Murguía's, who blindly obeyed the orders of his commander. By reestablishing a civilian authority in the state not directly controlled by the military, Carranza hoped to increase popular mobilization against Villa. With this purpose in mind, he sent Enríquez back to Chihuahua to reassume the provisional governorship of the state. Unlike Murguía or Arnulfo González, both of whom were from Coahuila, and whom a large part of the state's population regarded as leaders of a foreign occupation force, Enríquez was a Chihuahuan, who during his provisional administration of the state in the early months of 1916 had begun to establish links to the country people of Chihuahua's mountain region. When he reassumed the governorship of Chihuahua, he soon realized that if he were to exercise any real power, he would have to command armed forces of his own. With this purpose in mind, he attempted to take control of the defensas sociales, most of whose members supported him as a counterweight to Murguía's federal army.

Murguía was not ready to give in to a man like Enríquez, whom he considered an upstart politician. In a sharply worded telegram to Carranza, he expressed his resentment at Enríquez's effort to assume control of the defensas sociales.[64] Carranza now found himself in a dilemma. He had sent Enríquez to Chihuahua in the hope that he would be able to mobilize the civilian population in his favor more effectively than Murguía could, and because in principle he wanted to weaken the role of the military and strengthen civilian authority in Mexico. Yet Murguía was one of his most loyal and effective generals.

Carranza finally decided on a compromise that satisfied no one. On the one hand, he clearly established that the defensas sociales would remain under Murguía's control; on the other, he allowed Enríquez to set up a rural police force of 600 men under his command. Enríquez was disappointed. He wired Carranza that if he were given control over sufficient military forces, above all of the defensas sociales, he would be able to carry out "the absolute pacification of Chihuahua with forces of this state, without any cost to the government. I implore you not to deny me your support and to give me the only opportunity I shall have in my life to do something great and to develop my faculties. You have taught me to fight, and I shall put my state in order or die attempting to do so."[65]

In November 1918, Enríquez nearly did die. His life was threatened not by Villa but by Murguía, who ordered his deputy Hernández to attack Enríquez and his forces and to destroy them. He was only saved by a desperate appeal for help to Carranza, who decided to recall both Murguía and Enríquez to Mexico City.[66] Murguía was permanently removed from command of Chihuahua; in order to retain his loyalty, Carranza sent him as commander in chief to Tamaulipas in eastern Mexico. After a few months, Enríquez was sent back to Chihuahua not as governor but as commander of all paramilitary forces in the state, including the defensas sociales, whose numbers then began to increase dramatically.

For Villa, the defensas sociales were a nightmare. In previous years, except for the Orozquista period, Villa had been welcomed with open arms by the population of every village in Chihuahua and had only had to fight federal garrisons that the villagers intensely disliked. Now he had to fight his way into most rural communities, and his main opponents were not federal troops but the inhabitants of the villages themselves. It was probably this situation that Villa had in mind when years later, after he had laid down his arms, he responded to a question Raúl Madero asked him: "General, what was the most difficult situation you ever faced?" "When the people turned against me," he answered.[67] Perhaps the worst blow to Villa occurred when communities that had always been at the center of his movement, from which some of his most loyal subordinates had been recruited, such as San Andrés, formed their own defensas sociales and fired on Villistas when they attempted to enter a village.

The anger that the actions of these defensas provoked in Villa, the frustration he felt, but also the uncertainty they engendered in him were clearly expressed in a long proclamation that he issued to the defensas sociales in late 1918. He both cajoled and threatened them, and for the first time since the end of the U.S. occupation of Mexico, he attempted to explain what he was fighting for.

As long as the Americans occupied parts of Mexico, Villa's appeals had attempted to kindle Mexican nationalism against the United States. Now that the Americans were gone, Villa appealed to Chihuahuan nationalism against outsiders. He accused Carranza and his commanders of stealing much of Chihuahua's wealth and taking it out of the state. He knew that he would strike a sympathetic chord among Chihuahua's population when he accused the Carrancistas of bringing soldiers "from outside, men who are pressed into the army or who have been recruited from the jails in order to steal our wealth officially and destroy our well-being."

Villa's appeal was strongly mixed with threats. He stressed that until 1918, he had always spared all prisoners captured from the defensas sociales, freeing them after their capture. Should the defensas sociales continue to fight him, he warned, he would be forced to take stronger measures than he had in the past. He would, he indicated, be forced to exterminate the local militias. Villa appealed to the defensas sociales to join him in the fight against Carranza, whom he called the most corrupt tyrant in the history of Mexico, in order to safeguard the sovereignty of Chihuahua.[68]

Villa's proclamation significantly lacked any mention of the land issue and any accusation against Carranza for not carrying out a massive land reform. Did he believe that raising the land issue might divide his potential support, or had he simply lost interest in it? The latter does not seem to have been the case, since in individual talks with captured members of the defensas sociales, he did emphasize the issue. On one occasion, Villa captured members of the defensa social of the Hacienda del Rubio. Instead of shooting these men, as he would have done with captives from the federal army, he practically entreated them to lay down their arms: "I know that you are defensas sociales, and that's all right, but don't come here, defend your homes; that's fine; but why are you here. . . . what harm have I done you?. . . . I have joined the revolution precisely so that the people of Mexico should be master of Mexico and that the great latifundia be divided among the poor."[69]

To a large degree, the defensas sociales were deaf to Villa's appeals. They continued to proliferate, and they continued to fight him. In his proclamation, Villa had called Murguía and Enríquez birds of a feather, but that was not how many of Chihuahua's peasants viewed them. Once Carranza removed Murguía from command and put Enríquez at the head of the defensas sociales, many Chihuahuans felt that for the first time one of their own was commanding them and they were not being made instruments of foreign control.

By the end of 1917, Villa seemed to have reached the low point of his career. When Villa had undertaken his last great campaign in 1916, he had faced a difficult situation but he still had significant resources. His financial support at that time had been the American estates, which he had spared while he held power in Chihuahua and the wealth of which he seized in 1916. His access to arms had been equally favorable. In 1916, thanks to the large amounts of arms and ammunition he had hidden before the dissolution of the División del Norte, he had managed to supply his men so well that they could repeatedly defeat the Carrancistas and arm and supply themselves at Carranza's expense. Not only in the 22 battles that he had won but through the occupation of both Chihuahua and Torreón, he had accumulated large stocks of arms. In addition, many villagers were still ready to fight for him and to supply him with food in 1916.

By the end of 1917, none of these resources were available to Villa. The large estates of Chihuahua's oligarchy had been depleted. Most Americans had left the country, and after the massacre of Santa Isabel, few had ventured to return. Villa had too few arms to attack the Carrancistas successfully and supply his troops with captured matériel. Moreover, thanks to the increased manpower that the U.S. government had at its disposal after conscription was instituted in the United States, the U.S. border was better patrolled than it had ever been before.

Villa did not want to resort to a survival strategy of living at the expense of the pueblos and feeding his men from their harvests. It would have transformed him into a bandit and exacerbated existing popular opposition to him. In this desperate situation, Villa once more showed his creativity and pragmatism. In spite of his hostility to Americans, he gave up his strategy of expelling them from the country and allowed them to return and to resume operations as long as they paid taxes to him. In view of the sharp rise of the price of minerals as a result of World War I, many U.S. companies resumed operations in Mexico. These companies now paid regular taxes to Villa, and there was never a repetition of the massacre of Santa Isabel.

One of the executives of the Mexican Northwestern Railroad reported to his chief "that he knows that practically every company operating in the Parral district are paying him [Villa] for protection and that in no other way can they operate. He told me of one concern that had been paying in 2,000 per month; a short time past they decided it was too much and when they sent in one of their amounts they made it for 1,000 only. Only a few days later about $20,000 of their property was destroyed. They very promptly sent the other 1,000 and since then have had no trouble."[70]

As a result of the money he got this way, Villa was able to pay his men in silver and to do the same when he acquired supplies from the pueblos. These resources allowed him and his movement to keep their heads above water. It may also have changed the character of his army. Some of the men who followed him were former soldiers of his who were still fascinated by his charismatic appeal. Others had been victims of Carrancista depredations or were opposed to defensas sociales. In a number of villages, the defensas represented not all of the village community but rather certain factions in it, who did not hesitate to persecute opposing factions or at times to plunder other villages. José María Salcido of San Buenaventura complained to Enríquez that the head of the defensa social of Cruces, Anastasio Tena, had captured his son and made off with some of his property because Salcido had been forced for a short time to join Villa's forces, although he had deserted as soon as he could.[71] Others—men who were unemployed, Carrancista deserters—joined Villa because, unlike the Carrancistas, he paid them not in paper money but in silver.

The Hacendados Return to Chihuahua

Without any fanfare, without meeting any strong opposition, almost surreptitiously, more and more of Chihuahua's hacendados returned to assume control of their estates.

The first group of Chihuahuan hacendados regained possession of their properties in early 1916 during the provisional governorship of Enríquez. That group included some members of the Terrazas family, such as Señora Creel de Lujan.[72] This first stage of the return of their properties to Chihuahua's traditional oligarchy ended in mid 1916, when Enríquez relinquished his post as governor and went to Mexico City. But Enríquez's departure was not the primary reason why this process was interrupted: of greater importance, Carranza had decided that it was to be the federal government, and not the state governors, that would have the ultimate decision on the fate of the confiscated properties. In most of Mexico, this decision slowed but did not end the process of return of haciendas. In Chihuahua, the possibility of war with the United States in 1916 and the resurgence of Villa in late 1916 and early 1917 contributed to interrupting this process. The increasing number of Carrancista soldiers stationed in Chihuahua needed the revenues from the confiscated estates, and there was political fear on the part of the Carrancista authorities that a massive return of the hacendados would play into Villa's hands. As a result, in January 1917, Carranza not only refused to return properties to the Terrazas clan but officially decreed their "intervention." This decision was triggered by Luis Terrazas Sr. himself, who in late 1916 applied to a Texas court to prevent the sale of cattle from his estates across the border. In his lawsuit, Terrazas stated that these cattle had been stolen from him, since the Mexican government had never officially confiscated his estates.[73] Terrazas thus left Carranza no choice. If he wanted to be able to sell Terrazas's cattle, he had to decree the intervention of all the properties of the Terrazas family, to which he added the properties of Villa and some of his leading commanders, including even those of men such as Fidel Avila who had made their peace with the Carrancistas.[74]

By late 1918, Carranza's policies toward the traditional Chihuahuan oligarchy underwent a change. He decided to make his peace with them and to allow them to regain control of the bulk of their properties. This decision was part of a general turn to the right with respect to land reform by the Carranza government.

Further prompting Carranza's decision, his generals had so plundered the confiscated estates that by 1918, they were bringing no revenues to the state.[75] In his report to Carranza, Governor Andrés Ortíz reported that although the confiscated estates made up one-third of the landed property in the state, they brought no benefit of any kind to the government.[76] Carranza now decided to return most of their properties first to hacendados closely linked to the Terrazas, then to junior members of the Terrazas family, and finally to Luis Terrazas himself.

In May 1916, Guillermo Muñoz, a wealthy hacendado from Chihuahua closely linked to the Terrazas, had asked for the return of properties that Pancho Villa had expropriated, insisting "that my humble personality is well known in the whole state of Chihuahua and the honorable persons in that same state can certainly give you any necessary information concerning my person and attest to the fact that I have never intervened in political affairs."[77] But in 1916 the state governor, Francisco Treviño, strongly objected, stating that "these properties should not be returned since Señor Muñoz can be considered an enemy of the constitutionalist cause since he helped the Orozco and Huertista movements and, besides, belongs to the Creel and Terrazas families, maintaining close links to them."[78] In 1919, in spite of the earlier objection by Chihuahua's governor, Carranza decided in favor of Muñoz.[79] In that same month, Juan Terrazas was allowed to resume control of his properties.[80]

These decisions were a prelude to a more important decision by Carranza that led for the first time to strong objections from his own officials in Chihuahua: the return of properties to the state's richest and most powerful hacendado, Luis Terrazas.

Ever since Carranza's victory over Villa, Luis Terrazas had indicated that he wished to make his peace with the constitutionalists and would be willing to support them if they returned his properties to him. In August 1918, he obviously felt that the time had come to make an open bid for Carranza's support. That month he wrote a long letter to the Mexican government in which he called for the return of his expropriated holdings and attempted to refute all the charges that, in the long course of the Mexican Revolution, revolutionaries of very different persuasions had leveled against him. His large holdings, he insisted, had not been obtained by despoiling peasants and poor people of their lands but by buying estates from wealthy landowners at a time when their value was minimal because of repeated Apache raids and lack of communications and railways in the state. His fortune, he wrote, was the result of the increase in value of these properties once the Apaches had been defeated, railways had been built, and economic conditions in general had improved. Terrazas gave a lengthy description of those aspects of his political activities in which he had cooperated with Benito Juárez in fighting the Conservatives and the French, and he noted that he had fought against Porfirio Díaz's attempts to seize power in 1872 and 1876.

Terrazas glossed over the periods during the Porfirian era when he had been governor of the state and insisted that after the revolution had broken out in 1910, he never took any active role in fighting against it, and that he had completely withdrawn from politics in that period. He claimed that he was essentially a victim of Pancho Villa, who had expropriated his properties and for two years imprisoned his son Luis, who, after coming to the United States, had died as a result of the hardships he endured during his imprisonment. The proceeds from his estates, Terrazas maintained, had contributed to the military victory of the División del Norte and later of the Carranza forces in the state. "From all I have shown, it can be clearly concluded that I have always fulfilled my duty as a citizen and as a public official by supporting the general constitution of the country as well as its autonomy and its legitimate government; in the last years of my life I have had nothing to do with politics and for that reason there is absolutely no justification for preventing me for so long from taking control of my legitimately acquired properties, and for that reason I ask and request that the confiscation of my properties in the state of Chihuahua be ended and that all of them be returned."[81]

Carranza submitted Luis Terrazas's letter to the state's governor, Andrés Ortíz, for consideration. In the reply he sent to Carranza, Ortíz refuted each of Terrazas's arguments. He challenged Terrazas's contention that his empire had been acquired solely by sales of rich landowners and not at anyone's expense. "In the majority of cases," Ortíz stated, Terrazas's haciendas had been acquired from a "surveying company that obtained these lands by surveying the lands of the state. The state then gave them great amounts of land, which in many cases had belonged to owners who through negligence or ignorance did not have their titles in order and many others [that] did have them in order but they were not recognized by the authorities." Ortíz stressed that during the Porfirian period, Terrazas's main aim was "the absolute control of the government of the state for the protection and broadening of his interests, for which purpose he never hesitated to use proceedings well known in the Porfirian period. He did not limit himself to this but declared that . . . the tax laws of the state were protectionist laws for the Terrazas interests." Ortíz stated that these properties were systematically undervalued so that their tax bracket would be extremely low.

Ortíz refuted Terrazas's contention that he had not intervened in politics since the beginning of the revolution. Ortíz insisted that the family had acted as a whole, and that the elder Luis Terrazas had remained in the background, letting his sons bear the brunt of political activities. Thus after the revolution broke out in 1910, Luis's son Alberto had organized a corps of 1,000 men to fight the revolutionaries, while his brother Juan had raised forces of similar size in other parts of the state.

After Orozco rebelled in 1912, when the Orozco movement had levied a "loan" of 1,200,000 pesos on wealthy Mexican individuals and businesses in the state of Chihuahua, "a large amount of the bonds were taken over by the Terrazas family to the amount of $500,000 (as well as by local banks, which the family controlled almost totally)." After Huerta's victory, he had enjoyed the full support of the Terrazas family. Luis's son Alberto had organized a new corps of volunteers, which until 1914 had fought for the Huerta government. In 1914, the Banco Minero, which was controlled by the Terrazas interests, issued special bonds to finance the Huerta government. "In the period between 1910 and 1915, Luis Terrazas the elder essentially worked through his sons, thus succeeding in apparently remaining aloof from public affairs."

Ortíz discussed the huge size of the holdings, stating that Terrazas controlled about a tenth of the lands in the state of Chihuahua, including its richest and most valuable agricultural land. He stressed that a return of these lands to their former owner would have a tremendous impact on the state. Perhaps because he knew the opinions of his chief, Governor Ortíz did not rule out the possible return of the Terrazas estates to their former owner, but he insisted that if this were done, the state should at least obtain some guarantees, such as the right to buy them any time at their tax-assessed price.[82]

The objections of the governor had no influence on Carranza. In March 1919, he decided to make a major overture to the Terrazas clan. In that month, he decreed the return of the properties of a number of Terrazas's sons and relatives and the return of all nonagricultural properties to Luis Terrazas Sr.[83] The haciendas were at first excluded from this settlement. Perhaps before returning all his properties to the northern caudillo, Carranza hoped for some tangible sign of his support. Carranza may even have hoped that Terrazas would persuade his American lawyer, Senator Albert B. Fall, to moderate his views regarding U.S. military intervention in Mexico. If so, he was mistaken, for Fall continued his interventionist campaign. Nevertheless, Carranza, in what was perhaps his last important social measure before he was forced out of office, completed what he had begun one year before. In May 1920, after a lengthy interview with Carlos Cuilty, another Terrazas lawyer, Carranza decreed the unconditional return of all of Terrazas's properties.[84] He had now come full circle and decided to make his final peace with Mexico's traditional oligarchy.

Carranza's decision to return Luis Terrazas's properties remained a secret and could not be implemented before Carranza fell from power. As a result, there was no public reaction to the measure. When Enríquez, sometime after the fall of Carranza, attempted to implement Carranza's directive, there was such a public outcry that the federal government forced him to desist.

The return of properties to many hacendados did not elicit a strong reaction either among Carranza's generals or among Chihuahua's villagers prior to 1920. The attitude of the generals is easy to understand, since they had plundered the haciendas and may have hoped that once the hacendados had come back and their estates were again prospering, they might extract further benefits from them. Also, some generals may have been bribed. As one of Chihuahua's hacendados put it in a letter to Carranza, "There are persons who offer to arrange the return of properties if they receive a certain sum of money."[85]

But the lack of protest against these measures by hacienda peons and free villagers is at first difficult to understand. The confiscation of the estates of the oligarchy by Villa had been a popular measure, from which many of the state's inhabitants had benefited. After the end of the revolution, they hoped to benefit even more. Villa had sold meat from the haciendas at cut-rate prices and utilized part of the proceeds to support widows, orphans, and unemployed workers in Chihuahua. While at first the conditions of tenantry on the confiscated estates had been identical to those in the Terrazas period, they improved dramatically, since Villa allowed sharecroppers and tenants to work the land without giving any part of the revenues to the government. Above all, the confiscation of the estates gave hope that once the revolution had come to fruition, they would be divided among the peasants. All this had changed once the Carrancistas took them over. On some estates, looting by generals such as Murguía went so far that seed was taken away from the peasants, so that they could not plant the next year's harvest.[86] The living standard of hacienda tenants drastically deteriorated. "On the Santiago Ranch near Pearson," an informant reported to U.S. intelligence authorities,

which was the property of Don Luis Terrazas, the same farmer tenants have been compelled by the confiscation agency of the state to fence their little places at their own expense, and the state government is demanding one-third of the crops as rent [the rent exacted by the Terrazas had been only one-fourth of the crop]; whereas the entire crop will not be enough for food. These are the lands which were to be divided up and given to the people. The people are forbidden to sell any of their corn or beans until the government third has been paid in, and even then they can only sell to the cuartel general. . . . Our informant states that he never has seen such dire poverty among the small farming class who have always before had enough to eat of plain foods and sufficient clothes to keep them warm in winter. He says that for the first time in his life he has seen the Chihuahua peons wearing sandals. Formerly they had the Mexican-made shoes or cheap shoes imported from the States. He mentioned one family living on a small ranch near Pearson whom he had known for a number of years, and has several times employed the man of the family; this time he wanted the man for a cook on his trip, and on going to the house found all the bedding that they had for the mother, father and seven children was one small badly worn blanket. Coffee and sugar, which formerly all peons considered necessities, are now more than luxuries—they are worth their weight in gold.[87]

Many peons felt that the traditional paternalism of the hacendados was preferable to the rapacity of Carranza's generals. Others, especially free villagers, may have hoped that it would be easier to force the hacendados to divide the land than to put pressure on Carranza's generals. Such hopes were dimmed by the fact that no land was granted to peasants prior to 1920, although an agrarian commission had existed intermittently (Enríquez had dissolved it when he became governor in 1918).

Country people who might have wanted to protest against these measures were easily intimidated by martial law, which had been imposed in Chihuahua, and by the ease with which any critic of government policy could be labeled a Villista.

It is more difficult to understand why Villa did not protest against measures that destroyed what many considered his most cherished project: the expulsion of the oligarchy from Chihuahua and the division of the lands among Chihuahua's peasants. This is what he had set out to do in December 1913, when he issued his famous confiscatory decree. Indeed, one of the main reasons for his conflict with Carranza in 1914 was Carranza's desire to return the confiscated estates to their former owners. Was Villa's attitude based on the hope that with the return of the hacendados, he would be able to do to them what he had done to the U.S. companies: force them to pay protection money to his movement? Or was Villa's attitude a reflection of his moral decline and his increasing isolation from rural Chihuahua's people? This may have been the case, but it must be emphasized that after 1920, when Villa had made his peace with the government and declared that he would not participate in politics, the only time he allowed himself to breach that rule was when he vehemently protested against a new plan by Governor Enríquez that in a limited way might have maintained the Terrazas empire under a new owner.

Villa's failure publicly to protest the hacendados' return may also be linked to his failure to issue manifestos or proclamations of any kind after June 1917, with the exception of his proclamation to the defensas sociales in 1918. This might reflect a moral decline, a lack of belief in the effectiveness of political manifestos and activities, or a decision to leave political activities in the hands of his exiled supporters in the United States, such as his most loyal adherent, the former head of his civilian administration in the north, the lawyer Miguel Díaz Lombardo. Villa's decision to quit issuing proclamations may have been motivated by the paradoxical situation that as his popular support decreased in Mexico, new support or at least interest in his movement was developing outside of Mexico, mainly in the United States. That interest came from heterogeneous sources. Arms dealers, smugglers, and shady entrepreneurs of all kinds took a renewed interest in Villa when they discovered that he once again had money to pay for arms and supplies. Villista and Conventionist exiles who had kept a low profile as long as Pershing's expedition was in Mexico and the possibility of a U.S.–Mexican war existed now attempted to establish new links with Villa. German intelligence and, to a lesser degree, British intelligence were interested in using Villa for their own ends, as were U.S. oil companies, which had even greater resources. While many of the machinations and intrigues of these groups never went beyond mere scheming, some of them did exercise an influence on Villa and his movement.

CHAPTER SEVENTEEN

Villa and the Outside World

After Villa's troops withdrew from Columbus, he seemed to have become a pariah, isolated from and shunned by the outside world. The same heterogeneous forces in the United States that had supported him in 1913–14 now turned against him. The U.S. media, which had praised him before, now savaged him. American radicals saw him as a provocateur in the pay of U.S. business interests, while American conservatives accused President Wilson of having supported a bandit. The Wilson administration dispatched the Punitive Expedition against him, and U.S. business withdrew from Mexico. The few supporters Villa still had in the United States were so intimidated that none of them dared to speak out in his favor. Moreover, his access to supplies and arms from the United States seemed to have entirely disappeared. And yet within a year after the Punitive Expedition left Mexico, Villa's relationship to the outside world changed once again; important forces both in and outside the United States once again attempted to play the Villa card, and his supporters again made their voices heard.

The Smugglers and Con Men

Smuggling arms and ammunition to Villa from 1916 onward was a more risky and difficult undertaking than it had been in 1913 and early 1914, during Wilson's arms embargo. In 1913, smuggling arms to Mexican revolutionaries had been a mass phenomenon and something of a popular sport. The U.S. side of the border was not closely watched, and the U.S. authorities were frequently reluctant to enforce the embargo strictly against Mexican revolutionaries. Villa enjoyed considerable sympathy north of the border among groups ranging from officials of the Wilson administration to segments of the American left and to Mexican-Americans. Even before he captured Ciudad Juárez in late 1913, most of the Mexican side of the border was controlled by revolutionaries, so that smugglers found a warm welcome once they reached Mexico.

From 1916 onward, especially after Villa's attack on Columbus, arms smugglers who attempted to supply him faced obstacles that had been practically nonexistent three years earlier. Many more U.S. troops and federal agents patrolled the border than ever before. U.S. officials were uniformly hostile to Villa, although he still continued to enjoy strong sympathies among Mexican-Americans. If the arms smugglers did succeed in eluding U.S. surveillance and reaching Mexico, the risks they faced were not over but, on the contrary, increased, for the Carrancistas controlled most of the border. With the exception of a few months from November 1916 to March 1917, the Villistas did not exercise permanent control over any region of Mexico. In order to deliver arms to Villa, smugglers had to cross Carrancista lines and make complex arrangements with Villa's troops to meet them at points designated by both sides, which might at times be revealed to the Carrancista authorities. Only a limited number of men were willing to engage in this kind of smuggling, and the cast of characters involved would doubtless provide material for dozens of films. The most important of the smugglers, the one Villa trusted most, and who by his very origins was closest to Villa's heart, was George Holmes. Born in Uvalde, Texas, Holmes, like Villa, came from a poor family; and, like Villa, he soon became a cattle rustler.[1]

There is no evidence that Holmes and Villa ever met prior to the outbreak of the revolution, since Holmes confined his rustling activities to south Texas. "George might have made a great cattle man if he had been on the level," a police chief who pursued him while he was alive commented sympathetically after his death. "There's big money in the cattle business if things go right, and you work hard, and don't mind the years that pile up while you're building. But George was impatient. He just couldn't help misreading brands on cattle. Lots of time when it came to calves, George's cows used to violate the laws of nature. When nature is that generous the law steps in."[2]

Officers of the U.S. military and federal agents who had to deal with Holmes in the years 1916 to 1919 had a less sympathetic view of him. Holmes "was an ardent Villista and made considerable money as a selling agent of Villa's stolen goods," Captain Grinstead of the U.S. Infantry in El Paso reported to his superior.

He gathered around him persons of all classes and characters, high and low, but all having a common interest, that is, profiting by the sale of other people's property. His associates in his enterprises scale from that of high officials of banking institutions in this city down to the lowest criminals and crooks. When Villa was forced to leave the border in 1915 the marketing of his stolen goods became more difficult and many of those who had thrived in that business with ease were forced to abandon it to more skilled management and only a few, like Holmes, were successful in eluding the cordons of the de facto government officials on the border and smuggling through this confiscated property.

But even Grinstead could not disguise a certain admiration for Holmes's talents when he attempted to use the Punitive Expedition to help Villa:

As an illustration of his [Holmes's] boldness I will recite that in June 1916, he conceived the idea of using the United States Army to assist him in getting cattle out of Mexico from a region so remote that without its assistance the task would be hopeless. To accomplish this he secured from a representative of one of the leading banks here a letter of recommendation to the commander of the Punitive Expedition in Mexico and also one from the commander of the state ranger force here vouching for his reliability and integrity. The whole plan was nothing but a cattle-stealing expedition and fortunately the military authorities were uninfluenced by his attempt at deceptions.[3]

The bases for Holmes's smuggling activities were a number of ranches he had acquired near the border, where he received stolen cattle and from which he exported whatever arms and ammunitions he had been able to gather. For three years, from 1916 to 1919, federal officials carefully watched Holmes but were unable to gather sufficient evidence to prosecute him.[4]

In between raiding Holmes's ranch and attempting to indict him, U.S. federal agents were not averse to using his services. In 1918, when Villa kidnapped Frank Knotts, a U.S. mining executive working in Mexico, and threatened to kill him unless a ransom of $15,000 was paid, the head of the El Paso office of the Bureau of Investigation, Gus Jones, went to see Holmes and asked him to go to Villa's camp in Mexico and attempt to persuade Villa to release Knotts without a ransom or to pay him the $15,000. "I am . . . convinced that the only living American that could in any way exercise any influence over Francisco Villa looking to the rescue of this man," Gus Jones wrote to the chief of the BI, "is George Holmes. I will also state that in my opinion Mr. Holmes has undertaken a very dangerous mission and is deserving of some kind of commendation in that he has undertaken this trip without any promise of pay and for the reason that an American's life is at stake."[5]

Holmes was able to obtain Knotts's release. Actually, during his captivity, Knotts had established some kind of friendship with Villa, who told him his life story and even embraced him when they parted, saying, "I talk very little with my men, with you I have been a regular parrot."[6]

Holmes's success in rescuing Knotts and the relatively friendly relations he had thus established with the BI may have made him reckless, for a few months later federal agents were finally able to gather sufficient evidence to convict him. With the help of two U.S. soldiers he had bribed, Holmes broke into a military supply depot and stole a machine gun and several other weapons, which he attempted to smuggle to Villa. Holmes was captured, tried, and sentenced to five years in a penitentiary.[7] The federal government was relentless in its pursuit of him. He was tried once again on a charge of perjury and sentenced to three more years. Holmes never went to prison, however, for Villa proved to be an extremely loyal friend. When Holmes appealed his sentence, the judge trying his case agreed to free him on a $15,000 bond, a huge sum. Holmes did not have it, but Villa sent the money, Holmes was freed, and he escaped to Mexico. He was murdered eight years later in Chihuahua, but not for political reasons. "The motive for his killing was revenge," a neighboring American rancher informed U.S. authorities; "the body was not robbed even of his pistol."

La Cumbre San Manuel is in the high mountains in a sparsely settled region, the population of which is mostly Indians. Having lived there for about two years I can state that the people are unusually friendly and are in no way hostile to Americans or to other foreigners. The direct cause of Holmes' death is said to be because he tried to buy a twelve year old girl from her mother and upon her refusal to sell the girl he put the family out of the house in which they were living, claiming that it belonged to him. Two uncles of the girl, Gonzalo and Raya Lugo, are in jail in Guadalupe Calvo, together with an accomplice. I understand that confessions have been obtained and it is practically certain that these three will be shot; apparently they are the guilty parties. The authorities were unusually prompt and active in hunting down the assassins in spite of the fact that Holmes bore such an unsavory reputation.[8]

Holmes had been able to avert effective federal prosecution until 1919 partly because of the abilities of his lawyer, Frank Miller. Unfortunately for Miller, his capacities as a lawyer were not matched by his ability as a smuggler. When he decided that representing Holmes in federal court did not bring him enough money and tried to go into the smuggling business himself, he was caught together with Holmes in the break-in at the federal arms depot and was also sentenced to five years in prison.[9]

Another of Villa's representatives in the United States, Luis Cedaño, was assigned not only to smuggle arms into Mexico but also to make U.S. companies pay protection money. When the U.S. authorities arrested him, intending to deport him to Mexico, where he faced execution, Cedaño obtained bail and fled across the border, hoping to rejoin Villa. "He was captured by a small scouting party near Santa Rosalia de Cuevas and taken to the garrison town of Satevo where he was identified by some of the Carranza soldiers, tried and ordered to be hanged, which hanging was accomplished the day following his capture."[10]

While Holmes and Cedaño were crooks by the standards of U.S. law, they were honest crooks, in the sense that they were genuinely devoted to Pancho Villa and to his cause. There were also con men, however, among those who attempted to smuggle arms to Villa or to establish other kinds of relationships with him, whom the U.S. Customs agent Zach Lamar Cobb, who was stationed at the border, called "an infernal stream of impostors and grafters who do no good for the government and who at best confuse the Mexican mind."[11]

These con men sought to extract money from all sides in the Mexican conflict, Mexican as well as North American, by misrepresenting themselves, their aims, and their power. The king of the con men, the man to whom Cobb was specifically referring when he spoke of grafters and impostors, was J. F. Keedy. He was a lawyer from Hagerstown, Maryland, who in 1914 set out to make a fortune at Villa's expense. Together with a business associate, Edward Linss, he went to Villa's headquarters in 1914. Contact with Villa had not been difficult to establish, since Linss had a son-in-law, Dario Silva, who was a colonel and general staff member in Villa's army. "Keedy represented to Villa that he was a close personal friend of a nephew of the president (Secretary [William G.] McAdoo) and that he came and went to the White House at will to see the president and that further, he came to talk with General Villa as he represented a set of men who were 'the watchdog of the American government.'" Keedy, Silva told agents of the U.S. Justice Department, "was constantly pressing Villa for money for his services or for a loan every time he came to see him."[12] In exchange, Keedy promised to exercise all of his allegedly considerable influence to gain U.S. recognition for Villa.

Villa finally agreed, although he did not trust Keedy enough to give the money to him but gave it instead to Keedy's partner, Linss, who, after all, was related to one of his senior officers. Linss was to monitor Keedy's activities carefully and pay him only when he achieved results. While there is no evidence that Keedy had ever spoken to Woodrow Wilson, let alone had a major influence on him, he did have some connections in Washington. He had been U.S. attorney in the Panama Canal Zone and in Puerto Rico and was a good friend of León Canova, the corrupt head of the State Department's Mexican desk. What Keedy brought back from Washington was not recognition but an invitation to Villa to participate in one of Canova's many schemes for a conservative restoration in Mexico. Canova sent Keedy back with a list of cabinet officials Villa was to appoint in return for recognition. Villa, convinced that such a plan would make him a satellite of the United States and threaten Mexico's independence, refused and broke off all relations with Keedy. There is little doubt that this plan of Canova's and Keedy's helped to convince Villa that the United States had a secret plan for controlling Mexico—a conviction that contributed to his decision to attack Columbus.

Keedy did not give up easily. Hoping to secure confidential information on events happening on the Mexican border, Keedy misrepresented himself as a BI agent, a serious offense, and the Department of Justice began to investigate him in 1915–16. His close connections to León Canova seem to have been one factor that prevented any indictment from being brought against him. A year later, Keedy was once again involved in a scheme to make money from the Villista movement, this time by smuggling arms to Villa. Keedy was no risk taker like Holmes, but he had connections that Holmes never had and so he attempted to find a legitimate reason for establishing contact with Villa. He came up with a fantastic scheme, once more sanctioned by his friend Canova. According to a Justice Department report:

Mr. Keedy has now made a proposition to Mr. Canova, and Mr. Canova has made it to the secretary that Villa will leave Mexico, instruct all of his soldiers not to molest any Americans or to stir up any trouble on the border, will show proof that he was not at Columbus at the time of the raid and will come to this country, probably to Maryland in the vicinity of Hagerstown and live a quiet and orderly life.

Mr. Canova tells me an agent of the Justice Department informed a high official of the State Department that the secretary thinks this might be a good idea from the standpoint of improving conditions in Mexico, contingent, as I understand it on Villa producing the proof that he was not at Columbus.

The Justice Department agents were by no means convinced of either Keedy's or Canova's project and came to the conclusion "that Keedy is probably a dangerous man to deal with."[13]

This apprehension was heightened when Keedy established contact with German intelligence in Mexico. Zach Lamar Cobb went so far as to call him a traitor. The fears of U.S. agents with respect to Keedy were misplaced. He was no German agent—he was just out to con the Germans in the same way that he had attempted to con Villa. In 1917, he promised the Germans to use his influence to free German citizens interned in the United States after the nation entered World War I. "Keedy has impressed the Germans with the idea that he speaks with real authority," Cobb noted, in an involuntary tribute to Keedy's capacities as a crook.[14]

In 1920, Keedy seemed on the point of carrying off one of the greatest scams of his life. He had succeeded in persuading the otherwise highly capable chief of German intelligence in Mexico, Kurt Jahnke, that he was a cousin of Secretary of State Robert Lansing's and thus had great influence on the U.S. government. At the same time, he claimed, he represented the Republican party and was in the position to propose a major deal to the Germans if they could get Carranza to abrogate the constitution of 1917 and adopt a policy more favorable to the Americans. In return, Keedy said, the Republicans and the U.S. government would support Germany in its efforts to stave off demands for reparations by Great Britain and France. German agents only narrowly realized that Keedy was a con man and prevented him from enlisting the German government in his scheme.[15]

If Keedy was the big fish, various little fish also attempted to make money out of schemes related to Villa. The most prominent of these was John J. Hawes, a businessman who seems to have established relations with Villa during the heyday of the División del Norte. Like Keedy, Hawes took on a prominent partner who both was corrupt and had close ties with the U.S. government as well as with Villa. This was George C. Carothers, the former U.S. envoy to Villa, whom the State Department had retained as a special agent even after it withdrew any recognition from Villa and recalled Carothers to the United States. Carothers now gave up his official position in order to attempt to make money in partnership with Hawes.[16] Hawes also enlisted the services of Antonio Castellanos, who had been one of Villa's defense lawyers in 1912. Castellanos wrote a letter to Villa recommending Hawes and advocating a fantastic plan in which Villa would enlist the support of both Pablo González and Murguía, and, with money given by American capitalists, topple Carranza and set up a new government in Mexico.[17]

There is no evidence that Murguía or González had agreed to such a plan or that the large number of senators to whom Castellanos referred were in any way involved in it, but there was genuine interest on the part of both U.S. high officials and business interests in using Villa for their own ends. Some U.S. officials were obsessed by the fear that Carranza might accept Germany's offer of an alliance, transmitted in the famous Zimmermann telegram, and attack the United States, and they considered giving some support to Villa if that occurred. Large business interests, particularly British and U.S. oil companies, were hoping to use Villa to topple the Carranza government and put an end to its nationalistic attempt to restrain the power of the foreign oil interests in Mexico. Hawes was not involved in these schemes. His main interest was simply to use his relations with Villa to get protection money from U.S. companies. Hawes, a BI agent reported, was "the financial agent of such large corporations as are contributing to the Villista cause" and

receives the collections, deducts his commission, and remits the balance to some agent of Villa. Hawes is more interested in his commissions than he is in the Villista cause and in order to continue a prosperous business he leads the Villistas to believe that he is enlisting the sympathy of high U.S. officials and financiers, and on the other hand he induces certain corporations interested in Mexico to believe that through him protection to their interest can be secured from Villa.[18]

Another con man loosely associated with Hawes was Frank Thomas, sometime postmaster in Topeka, Kansas, and state treasurer of the Democratic Committee. "It is stated though not verified that he was removed from office as postmaster because of summary dismissal by him of entire office force," a BI report noted.[19] Feeling that his own political position was not strong enough to influence the Villistas, Thomas told his friends to introduce him to Villista agents in the United States as "Senator Frank Thomas" (there was, in fact, a Senator Frank Thomas from Colorado).[20]

Thomas was anything but a Villista idealist. "As stated that in event Villa victorious he would get domain, sufficient graze 100,000 cattle," a BI agent wired his superiors.[21] Thomas did not rely on future gains alone. He attempted to extract as much as he could from Villista agents in return for wielding his influence as a "U.S. senator" in favor of Villa.

One great problem that all of these agents, would-be agents, and con men faced in their relations with Villa was that in 1916 and most of 1917, it was an extremely difficult undertaking to establish any kind of contact with Villa. He had no accredited representative in the United States, and neither could he have had one as long as U.S. troops were hunting him in Mexico. He himself was constantly on the move, had not set up an administration of his own, and did not firmly control any territory in Mexico. Only in late 1917 and from 1918 onward were there émigrés whom Villa recognized as his representatives, with whom he maintained regular contact through a courier system headed by one of his agents, Alfonso Gómez Morentín. That system was allowed to function by the BI, since it was able to decipher and copy all the messages that Gómez Morentín transmitted.[22] In 1916 and early 1917, however, those seeking to communicate with Villa did so through his brother Hipólito. That proved to be very difficult, for Hipólito had only sporadic contact with his brother and was under constant surveillance by U.S. government agents.

The Intelligence Services

Money was the main reason why American con men and smugglers (George Holmes aside) sought to establish links with Villa, but there were also forces in both Europe and the United States whose interest in Villa was based on very different considerations. The German intelligence service sought to use Villa to provoke an all-out war between Mexico and the United States, while its British counterpart made plans to involve him in a scheme to topple Carranza, whom the British considered too pro-German and too strongly opposed to British interests, above all, British oil companies. U.S. oil companies and other business interests, too, regarded Carranza as inimical and sought to make use of Villa to topple him.

It is not at all clear to what degree, if any, Germany's 1915 plot to provoke a war between Villa and the United States was responsible for the Columbus attack, but there is little doubt that the Germans were elated by it and by the entrance of the Punitive Expedition into Mexico. They did their best to strengthen Villa and to encourage him to carry out new attacks on the Americans. The German government's view was expressed in a dispatch sent by the German ambassador to the United States, Count Johann von Bernstorff, who wrote Chancellor Theobold von Bethmann-Hollweg on April 4, 1916, "As long as the Mexican question remains at this stage, we are, I believe, fairly safe from aggressive attack by the American government."[23]

Every ebb in the tensions between Mexico and the United States, every possibility that the situation would be settled without war, created uneasiness among the diplomats of the Central Powers. "Unfortunately," the Austrian ambassador in Washington wrote to his foreign minister, "the hope is disappearing that the United States will be forced actually to intervene militarily in Mexico and that the administration would therefore be prompted to drop its pretensions toward the Central Powers."[24]

U.S. intervention in Mexico was to have facilitated the launching of unlimited U-boat warfare, so much desired by the German High Command, which hoped to starve Britain and France into submission. "If intending reopening of U-boat war in old forms," Ambassador von Bernstorff wired his chief on June 24, 1916, "please delay beginning until America really tied up in Mexico. Otherwise to be expected that president will immediately settle with Mexico and will use war with Germany to win elections with help of Roosevelt people."[25]

The German government did not limit itself to applauding the U.S. intervention secretly but did everything it could to increase and prolong it. It undertook efforts to intensify the anti-Mexican mood in the United States and at the same time, with the help of German-controlled factories, provided Villa with arms and other equipment. As early as March 23, 1916, the head of the Mexican desk in the German Foreign Office wrote:

There is little point, in my opinion, in sending money to Mexico. To the extent that anything can be achieved there with money, the Americans will always be able to outbid us easily since they simply have more money and because, moreover, they have infinitely more channels at their disposal than we do, since the Americans have been working this way for a long time in Mexico. It would be something quite different if we could get arms and ammunition to Villa and his band surreptitiously. This is however complicated by the fact that communications with northern Mexico from Veracruz are currently very poor.[26]

However, it was not too difficult for the German secret service to get American weapons to Mexico. The German government had sought to prevent armaments from the neutral United States from reaching the Entente powers by buying U.S. arms factories, such as one in Bridgeport, Connecticut. It may also have hoped to ship the arms produced in such factories to Germany, but the British naval blockade prevented this, and as a result the Germans did not know what to do with their U.S.-produced arms. After Villa's attack on Columbus, however, they did. There is no reason to doubt the report of British secret agents that weapons from Bridgeport were smuggled out of the United States to Villa in Mexico in coffins and oil tankers. The German consulate in San Francisco appears to have been centrally involved in these arms shipments.[27]

When it became increasing clear that in spite of the U.S. intervention in Mexico, there would be no war between the two countries, the German authorities looked for new ways to provoke an armed conflict through Villa. What had not been achieved by border violations might perhaps be brought about by an attack on the Mexican oil fields. According to Juan Vargas, one of Villa's officers, the German consul in Torreón, with whom Villa was evidently already acquainted, suggested this to him at a victory banquet held in his honor after he occupied that city in December 1916. After eulogizing Villa's military achievements and capabilities, the consul proposed that he attack the oil fields, pointing out that there were no large garrisons between Torreón and Tampico. If Villa took Tampico, he promised, German ships would be waiting for him there with money and arms. The consul apparently even declared himself willing to accompany Villa as a hostage.[28]

Villa apparently liked the idea at first and prepared to march on Tampico, but he changed his mind at the last minute and moved instead in the direction of Chihuahua. Vargas assumed that Villa was afraid of provoking an international conflict that would have been costly for Mexico. Perhaps; but Villa must also have realized that an attack on Tampico might prove suicidal and would not necessarily bring him any substantial benefit. Not only would the Villistas have to contend with Carrancista garrisons on the way, but a large U.S. fleet was concentrated around Tampico. There is little doubt that had Villa invaded the oil region, the Americans would have intervened. Villa must also have asked himself how, in view of the large U.S. naval presence near Tampico, German ships laden with arms and ammunition would get through to him. The consul's readiness to accompany Villa as a hostage, if true, testified either to his stupidity—he may really have believed the German High Command's promise of arms shipments—or to his readiness to die for the Fatherland, since had the Germans not delivered, Villa might have had him shot.

As the German authorities became increasingly convinced that Villa was either not able or not disposed to provoke a full-scale war between the United States and Mexico, their interest began to shift to Carranza, whose relations with the United States had greatly deteriorated both as a result of the Punitive Expedition's presence in Mexico and of the nationalistic new Mexican constitution. The most dramatic expression of this shift in Germany's interest was the Zimmermann telegram, in which Germany proposed an alliance with Mexico against the United States, in return for which Germany would agree to Mexico's recovering Texas, Arizona, and New Mexico. Even after the telegram was deciphered by British intelligence and published in the American press, thus creating an enormous scandal, and even after Carranza had told the Germans that he would not start a war with the United States, the Germans did not give up. Hoping both for German help in case of a U.S. attack, which Carranza still believed possible, and that Germany might provide a counterweight to the United States in the postwar period should Germany win, Carranza, while officially remaining neutral, did everything he could to help the Germans. Important Carrancista newspapers were pro-German, and Carranza allowed German intelligence services to function in Mexico.[29]

As a result, both the German government and its representatives in Mexico became more and more enthusiastic about Carranza, although they did not completely break with Villa. The German foreign secretary, Arthur Zimmermann, developed a scheme as grandiose as it was fantastic. Villa and Zapata and científico forces under Félix Díaz were to join Carranza for a joint attack on the United States. Obregón was to lead this army. At the same time, uprisings in the southern United States in support of this attack were planned. In a statement to the German Reichstag, Zimmermann said:

Villa appears to be rallying to Carranza. The hostility between these two men appears to be diminishing in the face of the common American enemy. In Mexico what we have been expecting has thus come to pass. Mexico's attitude toward Germany is a thoroughly favorable one, and should America actually turn against us, I think it can be assumed that the Mexicans will not miss the opportunity to stir up trouble on the Mexican border and to launch an attack there.[30]

These German hopes for unity against the United States by all parties in the Mexican struggle proved to be illusory, as the German agents who actually attempted to bring about a reconciliation between Carranza and Villa soon found out. According to a report to the U.S. consul in Nogales from a German-American, Biermann, who had close ties to German operations in Mexico, German agents had attempted to bring about an agreement between Carranza and Villa; Carranza, however, had refused to go along. Several days later, Carothers reported that a German businessman had attempted in vain to bring about a meeting between Villa and Murguía in Chihuahua.[31]

Hopes for success in these efforts may have prompted the Germans to continue to deliver arms to Villa in March 1917. "The vice-consul in Mazatlán reports that Villa is supported by Germans, and is expecting to receive three shipments of ammunition, which are to be landed by sailboats between Mazatlán and Manzanillo," the German military attaché in Mexico reported.[32] When no agreement was worked out between Villa and Carranza, and it became necessary to choose between them, the Germans appear to have dropped Villa completely. After April–May 1917, there are no reports in either German or U.S. documents about German aid to Villa.

In addition to the German intelligence service in Mexico, its British counterpart also showed interest in Villa. The British government, and especially the British military, hoped to overthrow the Carranza administration because of its pro-German attitude and its anti-foreign nationalism, which they feared might affect the large British oil interests in Mexico. To this end, the British supported the conservative forces of both Félix Díaz and Manuel Peláez and supplied them with arms.[33] They soon realized, however, that the conservatives did not have the power to overthrow Carranza on their own. If at all, this could be done only with

Villa's help. Throwing their support to Villa, however, would be a risky proposition. Not only would it negatively affect relations between the British and the Americans, who had become allies after the United States entered World War I against Germany, but it might also outrage British public opinion, which had become extremely hostile to Villa after the killing of the British hacendado William Benton in 1914.

Three British agents presented three different plans for enlisting Villa's help in toppling Carranza. Each scheme was designed to circumvent these obstacles in different ways. The ranking British diplomat in Mexico, Cunard Cummins, suggested a plan to topple Carranza that "will save our properties, lives and prestige and will not cost one drop of our blood." Only Mexican blood was to be involved. Under Cummins's plan, the United States and its allies were to give their support to a coalition consisting of supporters of Villa, led by Felipe Angeles and Roque González Garza, conservatives led by Eduardo Iturbide, and Zapatistas led by Francisco Vázquez Gómez. While Villa would thus cooperate with the coalition, he would remain practically invisible. Angeles, who was far less controversial than Villa, would be the nominal and perhaps even the real head of the Villista element in the coalition. In return for support from the Allies, the new rulers would have to state their willingness to grant special privileges to foreigners. Cummins was convinced that they would be willing to do so:

The exiled Mexicans and those opposed to the Carrancistas are so reduced by hopelessness that they will accept any terms imposed upon them. The following conditions should be imposed:

Foreigners in the commission handling all government funds—to give confidence and protect lending banks.

The foreigners must enjoy the same rights as Mexicans abroad.

Foreign claims must be examined and acknowledged when just.

All foreigners and foreign corporations must have the right to appeal to their respective government's diplomatic representatives, notwithstanding that they may have waived such rights.[34]

John B. Body, the representative of the Mexican Eagle Oil Company, a huge British concern, had a somewhat different plan. Only conservatives representing Peláez and Félix Díaz should assume leadership functions in the coalition to overthrow Carranza; Villa should at best be marginally involved. Body at first had not wanted to involve Villa in the new movement at all but later arrived at the conclusion that Villa, who, he said, would "seek and listen to good advice," would eventually offer full support to the plan for Carranza's overthrow. In that case, there would be no problem in providing him with arms—while carefully preventing him from assembling a larger army—and then buying him off after the victory by making him a regional chief of the rurales. Villa would, of course, first have to apologize for the murder of Benton and "go through the formality of saluting the British flag."[35]

The idea that Villa would subordinate himself to Díaz and Peláez and humiliate himself by saluting the British flag was, of course, ludicrous. Another businessman, Bouchier, suggested a third plan: "infusing new blood into the reactionary party so that the latter could oust Carranza and his crowd." To this end, he recommended that help be obtained from the revolutionaries, albeit with caution. Villa, he wrote, "should be used for a specific purpose and if he abused the position that was given him it would be exceedingly easy for him to accidentally disappear." Zapata, Bouchier explained, "is a bad man and his troops unprincipled but would serve their purposes until they were either subsequently brought into line or practically wiped out through concentration methods, which is about the only manner in which to tackle these men owing to the extraordinary accidental nature of their territory."[36] The idea of using the services of Villa and the Zapatistas and then murdering Villa and exterminating Zapata's supporters in concentration camps was appealing to the British embassy in Washington, which found the plan "interesting" and felt that it ought to be considered carefully.[37]

Unlike the Germans' plans, those of British intelligence never went beyond the planning stage, and there is no evidence that British agents ever contacted Villa.

The Business Interests

In contrast to British intelligence agents, representatives of U.S. business interests intent on toppling Carranza, especially of the U.S. oil companies, made concrete attempts to enlist Villa's services.

When the Punitive Expedition first entered Mexico, U.S. oil companies as well as other U.S. business interests hoped that this was the beginning of a full-scale occupation of the country. When that did not happen, the U.S. politician most closely identified with the oil interests, Senator Albert Bacon Fall, sought to use the presidential campaign of 1916 to make U.S. intervention in Mexico a central issue of the election. He attempted to pressure Wilson into a full-scale intervention and at the same time to have his Republican opponent make a firm commitment to do so should he be elected. Fall berated Wilson for calling American businessmen who advocated intervention in Mexico selfish. "Why, Mr. President," Fall said addressing the U.S. Senate, "the selfish American capitalists and the self-seeking American mechanic, and the selfish American spike driver and track-layer have made civilization in Mexico. . . . They pay the taxes. They support the governments. They develop the mines. They build the factories. They build the railroads. They build the electric lines."[38] The interests of these businesses and Fall's assertion that the Mexicans by themselves would never be able to reestablish peace were the ideological foundations for his repeated calls for massive U.S. intervention and occupation of Mexico.

By late 1916, after Wilson's reelection, it had become abundantly clear to both Fall and to the oil companies that at least in the short run, there would be no such intervention. Not only was Wilson opposed to it, but the increasing possibility of war with Germany made the withdrawal of the Punitive Expedition from Mexico imperative. U.S. business interests at least as powerful as the interventionists, if not more so, backed Wilson in this. Powerful firms such as the Morgan banking interests were closely involved with Great Britain and France and would have suffered huge losses if the Allies had been vanquished.

This did not mean that either the oil companies or Fall had given up on their plans to topple Carranza, but the means they adopted to do so changed. They now armed and supplied Mexican opponents of Carranza's in the hope that these forces might be able to topple the Mexican president now that Wilson had embargoed the sale of arms to the Mexican government and prevented it from securing loans in the United States. The oil men at first limited themselves to arming and supplying conservative rebels in southern Mexico, Félix Díaz and Peláez, and to plotting with Iturbide and representatives of the Catholic church.[39] Like the British, they soon realized, however, that these conservative forces could not overthrow Carranza on their own. By late 1916, it seemed to them that Pancho Villa was the only man in Mexico who had the strength, the charisma, and the energy to wage genuine offensive warfare against the Mexican government. In January 1917, the U.S. military were reporting "that Villa sent word from Torrcón to Hipólito last week . . . that they have offers of financial assistance from Standard Oil Company."[40]

This interest was more than confirmed by a startling letter that one of Senator Fall's close associates, Charles Hunt, a cattle dealer with many interests in Mexico, sent Villa, offering to arrange a conference between Villa and the senator from New Mexico. "If you will meet me at a place designated by you on the border, I promise to bring to our conference one of the most eminent statesmen in the United States with powerful influence with both our political parties relative to questions pertaining to Mexico. I refer to U.S. Senator Albert B. Fall, who appreciates the Mexican people and no living American knows the conditions in Mexico better than he. Senator Fall as you are well informed, is bitterly against Carranza and all his methods, regarding him as a tyrant dragging down the Mexican nation and people into the depth of misery and ruin and disgracing them before the world."[41]

At a time when Pershing's Punitive Expedition was still stationed in Mexico with the ostensible aim of pursuing Villa and bringing him to justice in the United States, Hunt wrote the Mexican revolutionary:

Now General Villa, I have discussed this question thoroughly with Senator Fall and most of the prominent mining men of Chihuahua, and the press of this country is generally with you in forming a stable government especially in northern Mexico, and I firmly believe that if you will fix a time and place to meet Senator Fall in Chihuahua that he and some of his friends will visit you at the time and place fixed and I believe that you can organize the plan to forward your interests, there being only one condition which they will require of you, that is that you protect American lives and property within the country which you dominate. With a combination like this to assist you, you will soon have large revenues from mines of Chihuahua and from many other sources.[42]

In his letter, Hunt had been vague as to what Villa was supposed to do in return for the help that Fall and his associates were promising, except to protect American property and form "a stable government especially in northern Mexico." Seven years later, in an interview, Hunt spelled out what this phrase had meant in his opinion and that of Senator Fall. Villa was to divide Mexico and set up a separate northern republic made up of Baja California, Sonora, Chihuahua,

Coahuila, Nuevo León, Tamaulipas, and the northern portion of Veracruz.[43] This would encompass most of the oil region in Mexico.

A few days after sending off the letter, Hunt wrote a note to Fall making it clear that the two men had discussed the matter before Hunt had decided to write to Villa. "Soon after your departure I framed a letter to the party in Mexico, telling him that it was on my own motion which I wrote and reciting facts discussed. It took some time to discover a mode to transmit same, but I finally found two different sources through which I finally consigned my letter."[44]

Unfortunately for Hunt and for Fall, the man to whom Hunt gave the letter and whom he considered a loyal follower of Villa, Dario Silva, one of the original eight men who had entered Mexico with Villa in March of 1913, had no compunction about betraying his former chief. He sold one copy of the letter for 50 pesos to Andrés García, the Carrancista consul in El Paso and the head of the Mexican secret service there, and gave another copy to George Carothers, an enemy of Fall's.[45]

When Fall learned that both Carothers and the State Department had copies of the Hunt letter, he hastily attempted to dissociate himself from his friend and associate. In a long letter, ostensibly written to Hunt but in reality to Secretary of State Lansing, Fall stated that while he did speak to Hunt about Villa while visiting him at a hospital, he had never authorized him to write a letter to the Mexican revolutionary leader. Interestingly enough, this disclaimer came only after Fall found out that the State Department was in possession of the Hunt letter. At the same time, Fall implied that he was ready to talk to Villa and under certain circumstances would even be ready to support him. "I stated to you that in the event Villa came to the border or had his representatives come, that I would have no hesitancy in talking with them openly and discussing Mexican matters with them, but that I would not discuss with any representative of any faction anything touching Mexico, except that as preliminary thereto, there must be an absolute pledge of respect for American lives and property, a respect for treaty obligations, etc."

Fall then expressed grudging respect for Villa. "Murderer and outlaw as I have known Villa to be for many years, yet I believe that he endeavored to keep every promise made to the United States." He then made it clear that he by no means excluded the possibility of throwing his support to Villa:

If Mr. Villa could convince me that he was in a position where if not interfered with by this government, he could restore order and maintain peace and order in Mexico, and thus would be in a position to and would give me satisfactory assurances that he desired and would perform all international obligations, as well as the national obligation to protect foreign citizens and property investments in Mexico, I would without hesitation publicly in the Senate or elsewhere, lay before the people of the United States such assurance and frankly and impartially advise them from my knowledge of Mexican affairs, etc. as I have heretofore done.[46]

It was a clear statement that Fall and his associates, which no doubt included the oil companies, were now prepared to play the Villa card.

This attitude changed somewhat when a copy of the Hunt letter was leaked to the *New York Times*, and American newspapers began publishing editorials sharply critical of Fall. The oil companies also realized by mid 1917 that Villa had lost the power to control northern Mexico. Nevertheless, they had not given up on him. He could still be a powerful instrument to topple Carranza, not so much as a leader but as part of a broader coalition of anti-Carranza forces.

The oil men realized after the publication of the Hunt letter that Fall's usefulness as an intermediary with Villa had been compromised. They now chose a man highly experienced in Mexico and even more adept at intrigues than Fall: Sherbourne G. Hopkins, who after having briefly faded out of the Mexican picture was now back in play. Hopkins realized that the only way for Villa to gain renewed acceptance in the United States was to deny that he had been involved in the Columbus attack. In 1917, Hopkins drafted a statement for the press ostensibly signed by Villa but, as far as can be ascertained, written by Hopkins himself. "In response to many inquiries I have received I desire the following to be known to the American public," Villa was made to say:

First: I had nothing whatsoever to do with the so-called Columbus Raid, directly or indirectly, a fact of which there is ample proof, inasmuch as I was many miles from the border at that time.

Second: As every American in Chihuahua knows I had no responsibility for the murders of Santa Isabel. Had I had opportunity, I would have adequately and immediately punished those who committed the outrage, many of the victims being good friends of mine.

Third: Let the Americans who have been engaged in business in the states of the north speak out and say who always offered them protection and permitted them to freely go and come, Carranza or Villa.

Hopkins's Villa then accused Carranza of being an agent of the Germans, of being "controlled by the greatest of all criminals, the Kaiser." The statement concluded:

I am not ambitious of high office. I will accept none. But I propose to see that the executive power of this nation is delivered into the hands of some good strong just man, a real statesman who, surrounded by a cabinet composed of men of character, will be capable of guiding our destinies, with a safe and steady hand. Then I will retire but not until then.[47]

The last part of the "Villa statement" by Hopkins did in fact reflect the aims of the oil companies. They were looking among the Mexican exiles in the United States for a man who would be capable of uniting both the conservative and revolutionary opponents of Carranza and who would be far more favorable to their interests than the First Chief. There is no evidence that Villa ever responded positively to any of these schemes. He did receive Fall's letter, but he rejected it out of hand.[48]

The World of the Exiles

Since the end of the nineteenth century, revolutions against Mexican governments have largely been prepared north of the border. It was there that opposition newspapers and pamphlets were printed, revolts were planned, arms were bought, and raiding parties or full-fledged revolutionary groups prepared for action.

The first important opponents of a Mexican government to initiate such activities in the United States in the twentieth century were the Flores Magón brothers and their Partido Liberal. They were followed by Francisco Madero. It was again from the United States that Villa crossed into Mexico to begin the revolutionary odyssey that brought him to Mexico City.

The most important center of such revolutionary activity and preparations was El Paso, Texas, and it was in the rooms and lobbies of its Sheldon Hotel that countless revolutionaries met, planned, plotted, and prepared to fight one another or the federal government.

Mexican revolutionaries faced two major obstacles in the United States. Infiltration of their ranks by agents of the Mexican government was the first of these. Under Porfirio Díaz, the Mexican government engaged the services of a private American detective firm, the Furlong Agency, which did most of its spying and undercover work. In the Madero period, Félix Sommerfeld, the Mexican-American-German newspaperman who later joined Villa and then betrayed him in favor of German intelligence, carried out that function. From 1915 on, the Carrancistas organized their own secret service, headed by the Mexican consul at El Paso, Andrés García. The Carrancistas had much to offer would-be collaborators beyond cash incentives: amnesty and the return of expropriated properties frequently proved persuasive.

The efforts of the U.S. authorities to prevent infringement of U.S. neutrality laws were the second obstacle with which Mexican conspirators had to contend. While it was not illegal to make propaganda against the Mexican government, organizing and preparing revolts and setting up expeditions to cross into Mexico constituted an infringement of U.S. law. If such activities could be proven in a court of law, the would-be revolutionaries could be prosecuted and jailed. Selling arms across the border to revolutionaries was not illegal, however, unless the U.S. government had prohibited such sales, as was the case in 1916.

The enforcement of the neutrality laws largely depended on the attitude of the U.S. authorities toward the Mexican revolutionaries. While the Flores Magón brothers, whose anarcho-syndicalist ideas were anathema to U.S. officials, were relentlessly persecuted, Madero was treated more leniently and for several months was allowed to prepare his revolution without interference. Even when U.S. authorities wanted to act, the sheer length of the U.S.–Mexican border made control extremely difficult. From 1916 on, the U.S. government made greater efforts than ever before in its history to control the border and to exercise vigilance over Mexican exiles in the United States. Large concentrations of U.S. troops along the border, which began with the entrance of the Punitive Expedition into Mexico but did not end when Pershing's men were withdrawn, facilitated the Americans' efforts, as did the creation of a new, well-staffed military intelligence department, which, together with the reinforced Bureau of Investigation, exercised an unprecedented degree of surveillance over all Mexican exiles: expatriate organizations were infiltrated by U.S. agents, their mail was opened, and their movements were monitored.[49] The activities of these agents did not put an end to revolutionary plots and did not prevent plotters from slipping across the border, but they were effective in preventing the kind of massive smuggling of arms and ammunition that had taken place in 1913–14.

Most of the exiles who crossed over to the United States had no intention of engaging in Mexican revolutionary politics. Many were happy when they were able to find work in the United States, which was in the throes of a war-induced economic boom. Those exiles who did engage in politics and participated in plots (the two activities were not always identical or complementary) tended to be prominent political or military figures antagonistic toward each other. While divided into a large number of cliques, the exiles fell into two main categories: supporters of the defeated Conventionist faction, including Zapatistas, Villistas, and former Villistas who repudiated Villa but still considered themselves revolutionaries, and former supporters of Díaz and Huerta, who were basically and fundamentally opposed to the Mexican Revolution;

These conservatives included a broad spectrum of political forces ranging from científicos to former officials of the Huerta administration, supporters of Félix Díaz, and members of the Catholic party, whose spokesman was Eduardo Iturbide.

All conservative groups were frequently subdivided by personal rivalries, yet they did tend to have certain characteristics in common. They all sought military, political, and financial help from the British and U.S. governments and insisted on their opposition to Germany and to the pro-German policies of the Carranza administration. They all opposed the new Mexican constitution of 1917, and most of them, with the exception of the Catholic party, wanted a return to the 1857 constitution, which lacked the nationalistic planks of the 1917 document. Most of these groups maintained strong links to U.S. business interests, particularly oil companies. Some of them were spokesmen for the armed conservative revolutionaries operating mainly in southern Mexico. The hopes of many of these conservatives were centered on armed U.S. intervention in Mexico, but they realized that such an intervention could not take place as long as World War I was raging and U.S. troops were occupied in Europe.

Those conservatives and their American supporters who did not want to wait until the end of the European war to topple Carranza were faced with a difficult dilemma. Their own armed forces were too weak to overthrow the Mexican government, and their only chance of success lay in an alliance with those forces who had been their greatest enemies both in 1910 and 1914: the Zapatistas and Villistas and smaller groups of rural revolutionaries throughout Mexico who were fighting the Carranza administration. From 1916 on, Mexican conservatives in the United States concocted all kinds of schemes and plans to utilize the revolutionaries for their own ends. Some of the expatriate revolutionaries, although by no means all of them, were thinking along similar lines. They too did not have the power to overthrow Carranza, and they hoped that they could use the financial resources of the conservatives to do so and then assume power in Mexico. As a result, a series of informal and uneasy alliances of heterogeneous social forces emerged, although their practical consequences would be extremely limited.

To a certain degree, the conservatives, particularly the armed supporters of Félix Díaz and Peláez, succeeded in making some deals and temporary alliances with the Zapatistas, in spite of the ideological differences that separated them. While Zapata himself, who had a national perspective, was reluctant to enter into such agreements, many of his leaders felt no compunction about aligning themselves with the conservatives as long as the latter were willing to recognize Zapatista control of Morelos and its surroundings and to accept the land reform that the Zapatistas had carried out in the zone under their control. What happened in the rest of Mexico was of less interest to the men of Morelos.[50] In addition, since at times conservative military units operated in zones adjacent to those of the Zapatistas, military cooperation against Carranza's forces could be of strategic importance. The Zapatistas did not seem greatly concerned about the close links of the conservatives with foreign business interests. Nor were they disturbed by the fact that some of the leaders of Félix Díaz's movement, above all Díaz himself, had been implicated in the murder of Madero. The Zapatistas had, after all, themselves relentlessly fought the former Mexican president.

The conservatives had far greater difficulties in establishing links either to Villa or to the Conventionist exiles in the United States. The military advantages of such a deal were far smaller than in the case of the Zapatistas, since very few conservative rebels operated in the north. Both Villa and the Conventionist émigrés in the United States were more suspicious than the Zapatistas of the links between the conservatives and U.S. oil companies. For obvious reasons, the northern revolutionaries, practically all of them ex-Maderistas, were wary of making alliances with men who had been implicated in the overthrow and murder of Madero.

The main proponent among the conservative leaders of some kind of an agreement with Villa and the ex-Villista exiles in the United States was Manuel Calero, a politician who had played an important role during the latter years of the Díaz dictatorship, the Madero presidency, and the Huerta era. He felt that he had some "revolutionary credentials" that might appeal to the ex-Villista exiles. He had been a supporter of Reyes during the Díaz dictatorship, had been Mexican ambassador to the United States and foreign minister during the Madero presidency, and had broken with Huerta before the military strongman had finally been toppled. Unfortunately for him, the revolutionaries felt that he had also turned against Madero in the crucial days before his overthrow and had long been ready to support Huerta. "Calero," wrote one of the revolutionary exiles, Hurtado Espinosa, "betrayed the man who elevated him to high office [Madero] and then contributed as far as we know to his assassination." He accused Calero not only of "working against Madero and the revolution" but also of attempting to become president of Mexico with the support of Huerta. Calero was a political chameleon and had turned against every leader he had once supported: Reyes, Madero, and Huerta. In the eyes of many revolutionaries, there was only one cause to which Calero remained true throughout his political life: that of the oil companies, whom he had begun to represent long before the revolution began:

What are the reasons for the difficulties between Mexico and the American oil companies? They are due to the lawyers acting as consultants for the American oil companies, among whom Calero plays a decisive role. . . . Like men of his class, everything is subordinated to his egotism, to his limitless ambition, to the fact that he cares about no one and nothing. Nevertheless, when he talks . . . it is only in terms of everything for our country, including the sacrifice of his own life.[51]

In spite of the deep hostility that many revolutionaries manifested toward him, Calero felt that he had one card to play: the gratitude of Felipe Angeles. Calero had been Angeles's lawyer in the weeks that followed the overthrow of Madero and he also finally secured Angeles's freedom. It was through Angeles, who was deeply wary of Calero but who nevertheless felt that he could not be ungrateful to his former lawyer, that he would attempt to influence both Villa and the revolutionary exiles. This was a difficult undertaking, for the ex-Villista exiles were deeply divided. These splits were not clear-cut or homogeneous. A schism existed between the haves and the have-nots: those who had lined their pockets during the revolution and those who had remained poor. There were divisions between those who wanted to maintain links to Villa and those who had definitely broken with him. There were those who were willing to come to an agreement under certain terms with the Carrancistas and those who rejected any kind of deal with them. Finally, the attitude they should assume toward the Americans was a further point of controversy and division among the exiles.

The first of these divisions among the exiles, in this case between the wealthy and the less wealthy, was reflected in a bizarre trial that took place in a Los Angeles courtroom in 1918.

The main figure in this trial was Villa's corrupt former business representative Lázaro de la Garza, who had made a huge fortune by betraying Villa and selling ammunition destined for him to the French in World War I. "Señor de la Garza is admittedly one of the cleverest financiers which the Mexican troubles have produced," the *Los Angeles Examiner* observed.

De la Garza was at the head of the Torreón bank and remained such until the Villa boom went to smash and the Villa money fell from a value of sixteen cents gold on the dollar to a sum approximating nothing. Large sums of money are said to have been realized by the foresighted who borrowed largely of the Villista money, sold it for American gold even at a ruinous discount, and later repaid their debts to the Villa treasury in the same currency but after it had dropped to no value at all.[52]

De la Garza was resolved to hang on to every cent of that money whatever the cost. He refused all demands for even a small loan by impoverished Conventionist exiles such as Federico González Garza.[53] He rejected out of hand a demand by Villa's brother Hipólito that he return part of his profits from the arms deal he had made with France to Villa, since it was the División del Norte that had put up the money for the deal in the first place. "I sent Gonzalitos . . . to treat with Don Lázaro," Hipólito Villa wrote his brother, "in the matter of the $100,000 which we gave him for the ammunition contract but he refused to deliver it to us in the most boldfaced manner, not withstanding the transaction. I cannot begin to tell you of the inconsiderateness that he showed my envoy, showing himself completely out with you and me." Bitterly, Hipólito added, "They call us bandits . . . but they are the ones with the $100,000."[54] Hipólito Villa could do nothing to enforce his claim as long as de la Garza lived in the United States.

Unlike Hipólito Villa, there was another former partner of de la Garza's who could appeal to the U.S. courts and attempt to force Villa's former finance representative to repay money he claimed to have put up for the munitions deal. This was Salvador Madero, the brother of the late president, who had also represented Villa in the United States. In 1916, Salvador Madero sued de la Garza for $75,000, which he claimed was the sum he had loaned to the Villista administration and to de la Garza personally to buy the arms that were first destined for Villa and later sold to the French. Madero was unsuccessful in his efforts, and the suit aroused no great interest; the press simply described it as a conflict between two businessmen. Three years later, when Salvador Madero resumed his suit, it created a sensation and made the headlines of the Los Angeles press. The reason was that this time he did not claim to speak for himself but rather for Pancho Villa. The idea that Villa, who had attacked Columbus and whom U.S. troops had gone into Mexico to capture, was now attempting to enforce a claim to money from an arms deal through a U.S. court created a sensation. It is not clear whether Salvador Madero was really acting in Villa's name or whether he simply thought that doing so would help his lawsuit. If he did, he was deeply mistaken. De la Garza, claiming that Villa was an enemy of the United States, was easily able to have the court dismiss the suit.[55] In spite of his victory in court and the huge amounts of money he had amassed, de la Garza's troubles were by no means over. His ill-gotten gains followed him to his grave, since once he returned to Mexico, Hipólito Villa, the Maderos, as well as others relentlessly pursued him with lawsuits, which caused his temporary imprisonment and got him labeled in the Mexican press as one of the greatest scoundrels the Mexican Revolution had produced.[56]

A far more important issue than money that divided the former Villista exiles was whether to continue supporting Villa after his attack on the United States. Among the exiles who once had been close to him, Villa's strongest opponents were the brothers Federico and Roque González Garza, particularly the latter, who had been Villa's personal representative to the Convention of Aguascalientes. "A resurgence of Villa," he wrote a friend, "is not possible any more. His action in Columbus . . . today constitutes the greatest obstacle in the glorious career of this man and prevented the victory of the underdogs in Mexico, whom he represented and still represents." Roque González Garza was the only important political figure in Mexico who did not condemn Villa's attack on Columbus on moral grounds; on the contrary, in the same letter he told his friend that Villa's attack could "very well be justified in the light of history and political morals."[57]

Roque González Garza never explained his attitude in his letter, but a year earlier, when he had told Villa of Wilson's recognition of Carranza, he had implied that the price for that recognition had been some kind of secret pact between the United States and Mexico. His brother Federico, according to the Chihuahuan historian Francisco Almada, was the author of Villa's Naco manifesto, in which the secret pact was spelled out, and the González Garza brothers might very well thus have shared Villa's conviction that Carranza had sold out Mexico to the United States.[58] Nevertheless, while not morally condemning Villa's attack on Columbus, Roque González Garza did say that Villa's former intellectual adherents would no longer be able to support him on moral grounds.

Perhaps tomorrow and the day after, Villa will have a large army, but unfortunately he will not be able to count in any way on the moral support of the large number of honest men of good faith who followed him when he was fighting for principles and not for men. Villa has passed into history, and whatever he does, it will be completely impossible for him to regain the moral heights he once achieved. If I could, you can be sure that I would do everything in my power to convince my old companion that the best thing he could do would be to retire to private life and leave Mexico after issuing a long, clear manifesto to the nation. . . . The retirement of Villa would help his party and the nation and would take away from Washington a pretext for intervention.

In spite of their break with Villa, the González Garza brothers were not disposed to give up politics altogether or to make an unconditional peace with Carranza. Together with other exiles, the González Garza brothers in 1916 began organizing the former Villistas and ex-Maderistas into a political formation first called the Legalista party and later the Liberal Alliance. In the eyes of the González Garza brothers, this was to be a pressure group that, through propaganda and perhaps other means, would attempt to transform Carranza's policies in Mexico.

At the other end of the political spectrum among the Villista exiles was another leader of this political party whose loyalty to Villa was almost unconditional. This was Miguel Díaz Lombardo, who had been one of the three leaders of the government Villa had established for northern Mexico in 1915.

It is difficult to explain the loyalty of this lawyer, scion of one of Mexico's oldest and most conservative families, to Villa. He was a nephew of Miguel Miramón, one of Mexico's most important Conservative generals under Emperor Maximilian, who had been executed together with the emperor on the day that Miguel Díaz Lombardo was born. Miguel was named in honor of his uncle but turned out to have very different views. His distinguished career as a professor of law at the National University during the Díaz period did not prevent him from voicing both liberal ideas and strong opposition to the Porfirian dictatorship. He became an ardent supporter of Madero, who first appointed him minister of education in his government and later sent him as ambassador to Paris, where after Huerta's coup he rallied Maderista exiles against the dictator and did much to prevent a substantial French loan from being granted to Huerta. Díaz Lombardo's decision to side with Villa and not Carranza seems to have been based primarily on Villa's loyalty to Madero.[59]

Miguel Díaz Lombardo never shared the doubts of Roque González Garza as to the possibility of Villa once again regaining supremacy in Mexico or with respect to his moral qualifications for doing so. On February 4, 1917, the day before the last member of the Punitive Expedition pulled out of Mexico, in a letter transmitted through Alfonso Gómez Morentín (a somewhat mysterious emissary who in years to come would act as intermediary between Villa and his American supporters), Díaz Lombardo wrote Villa:

I wanted you to know that the best of us who were intimately associated with you, and the Convencionistas, we have remained faithful to the revolutionary spirit of 1910, and our convictions have not changed in spite of the sorrow and hardships of exile; and I can assure you that we are confident that you with your indefatigable energy, your true interest for the good of the Mexican people and your adherence to democratic ideas will contribute to establish peace in our country and with it equal rights for all Mexicans and better the conditions of the middle and working classes, upon whom will depend the future prosperity of the nation.

In the same letter, Díaz Lombardo proposed a concrete series of reforms to Villa. One of them was the holding of elections. "I believe, Señor General, that if you would establish civil government in the states that you dominate, after the enemy has been completely defeated and if you make an agreement between the rest of the chiefs who have revolted, principally with General Zapata, to establish a government originating with an election, it will be possible to obtain a definite triumph of the popular cause." Apart from the elections, the most important plank in Díaz Lombardo's program was agrarian reform. "The agrarian problem, indeed, should be solved in a definite manner if we do not want that in fifteen or twenty years we have another civil war, with causes identical to those of the present one, which will not happen if the authorities have the power to divide land when it is necessary and if the people of the country have a legal way to obtain lands to cultivate."

Díaz Lombardo concluded his letter by expressing his conviction not only that Villa could win but that he would establish a more humane and bloodless regime in Mexico. "I have the certainty, Señor General, that you will crown the brilliant victories that you have been having against those whom we may call the enemies of Mexico with a work of regeneration that would stop the effusion of blood, and when this has taken place, the people will certainly bless your name and will remain eternally grateful."[60]

Villa rewarded Díaz Lombardo's loyalty by appointing him as his main representative in the United States. He was in charge of mobilizing public opinion in favor of Villa, securing financial resources for him, establishing relations with exile factions, and screening out the con men from those Americans attempting to make legitimate deals with Villa. His devotion to Villa was total, and there is no evidence that he ever sought to use his relationship to his chief for personal gain. As far as he could trust anyone, Villa trusted him, and he never sought to replace him with any other intermediary. For a brief time, however, in 1916 and 1917, it seemed that Díaz Lombardo's preeminence might be challenged by the presence in the United States of another man who for obvious reasons was much closer to Villa than he was. This was Villa's younger brother, Hipólito. Hipólito had an intimate knowledge of all the American businessmen who had ever been associated with Villa or had approached him. In 1914 and 1915, he had been Villa's main financial representative along the U.S. border. While loyal to his brother, Hipólito shared neither Francisco's intelligence nor his commitment to the underprivileged. His lack of ideological commitment and his love of money and the good life were well known on both sides of the border.

After the defeat of the División del Norte, and once he had decided to attack the United States, Villa sent Hipólito Villa and those members of his family who had been living in Texas to Latin America. American newspapers reported that their aim was to go to Argentina and buy an estate there,[61] but they finally decided to remain much closer to Mexico and the United States and established themselves in Havana, Cuba. It is not clear why Villa sent Hipólito into exile along with the rest of the family. Was his main purpose to have his brother protect the rest of the family or did he in fact want to protect his brother, to whom he was extremely attached? If Hipólito had hoped to enjoy the same good life in Havana as he had in Ciudad Juárez and El Paso, he soon found out that he had made a serious mistake. Only four weeks after his arrival in Cuba, he was arrested and held for extradition to the United States, where he had been indicted on charges of attempting to blow up railroad tracks along the line on which Carranza's troops had traveled across U.S. territory to the border city of Agua Prieta. For Hipólito, imprisonment was a devastating experience, and he blamed his brother for his predicament. "You have no idea of the sufferings I have had to bear in this region of miserable gringos," he wrote Villa in July 1916,

even here in Cuba, for you and I both made a mistake when you sent me here with the family. Twenty days after my arrival, the American minister presented an order from the American government to extradite me and until the proofs arrived I had to spend two months in the public jail in this city. They accused me of having blown up some trains in the state of Texas, and they declared it a violation of order, as you will remember. I never had any such intentions. I consider it useless to enumerate to you all my hardships, for you know I owe all these misfortunes to you, since when I left you, I did so in obedience to your orders, as I have always done. I tell you this frankly because I really feel it. I would not have left my country if it had not been to obey your orders, and what a life I have had to lead.

You know that I do not mind the trials of the campaign with you, and I would have had none of the worries I have today, far from my country, thinking what anyone else would think, for you know that a man's pride never leaves him. Ask yourself if I am right. Why have you not done it [i.e., left Mexico]? Simply because you have dignity and pride, and I want to enjoy an equal right.

He pleaded with his brother to rescue him from Cuba, but it was also characteristic of Hipólito that he now concocted a scheme that in every sense would have run counter to Pancho Villa's beliefs and social commitment. He had been approached by representatives of Yucatán's hacendados, who resented the Carrancista general Salvador Alvarado's policy of forcing them to split the profits of the lucrative henequen export to the United States with the Carrancista administration and of mobilizing their own peons against them. They offered Hipólito $5 million to arrange for Villista troops to land in Yucatán and "protect all their properties, which Carranza is exploiting."[62]

There is no evidence that Pancho Villa showed any interest in Hipólito's Yucatán scheme, but he did rescue his brother from jail in Havana by sending George Holmes to Cuba. Holmes smuggled the unhappy exile out of the country and back to his ranch in the United States. There he was discovered by U.S. agents, who, although they did not arrest him, forced him to live under extremely restricted conditions and under constant surveillance in San Antonio. They could not arrest him, since he had not participated in the Columbus raid and they could not produce any convincing proof that he had in fact attempted to sabotage railway installations in the United States. The restrictions imposed on Hipólito were both stringent and humiliating. When U.S. agents allowed him to travel briefly to El Paso in order to secure some jewels that he had left in a safe deposit box, he was prohibited from using a car while in the city and had to transact whatever business he was engaged in on foot or by streetcar.[63]

Hipólito hoped to assume control of the pro-Villa Legalista party that Villista exiles had founded in the United States and to send an armed expedition into Mexico. But the vigilance of the U.S. authorities, as well as his own intellectual limitations and incompetence, scotched such plans. While he was being held in jail for having violated U.S. immigration laws (he had entered the United States in Florida under an assumed name), he described these plans to a cell mate, who immediately reported them to U.S. agents.[64] The only small bit of help Hipólito gave his brother in this period was through a newspaper interview in which he absolutely denied Pancho Villa's involvement in either the Santa Isabel massacre or in the Columbus raid, saying:

My information is that my brother was nowhere near Columbus, had nothing to do with instigating or directing the raid or in fact with anything directly bearing on the raid. My brother has been charged with many things but nobody has yet accused him of being either a fool or a coward. It is said that his anger toward Americans induced him to make the raid. If that had been his motive, why did he not yield to the temptations at Juárez where he had 22,000 men when he was urged to cross the border and attack an unprotected city? It has been said that influences outside of Mexico induced him to attack Columbus. That charge is untrue because more than once as I happen to know he turned down offers which if he had accepted would have greatly enriched him, providing he had been willing to compromise the sovereignty of Mexico.[65]

It soon became clear to Pancho Villa that his brother could do very little for him in the United States, and that he possibly ran a greater risk there than if he went back to Mexico. So in spite of the surveillance by U.S. authorities, Hipólito Villa returned to his native country, where he headed a band of guerrillas in Chihuahua, fighting alongside his brother.[66] There is no evidence that he showed any prowess as a military leader, although he was able to survive the harsh and difficult guerrilla war in which he was engaged.

With his only potential rival gone, Díaz Lombardo now became the unquestioned spokesman for Villa in the United States. It is nevertheless unclear how much real authority this gave him. He was not involved in Villa's most important negotiations with American companies at that time—namely, over the payment of protection money—and neither does he seem to have participated in arms smuggling across the border. While he may have been involved in some efforts to raise money, his main functions in Villa's eyes were to improve his image in the United States, to establish relations with other revolutionary factions, and to flush out con men. In 1916, the U.S. authorities had briefly imprisoned him, but from 1917 on, Díaz Lombardo was given relative freedom, probably because of the increasing tensions between the United States and Carranza; at least some U.S. politicians were again thinking of using Villa against the First Chief. Moreover, U.S. intelligence agencies intercepted most letters addressed and written by Díaz Lombardo and were thus able to exercise a certain degree of control over Villista operations in the United States.

Díaz Lombardo remained an uncompromising foe of any agreement with Carranza's conservative opponents. This attitude was shared by the González

Garza brothers and other former Conventionists, although, unlike Díaz Lombardo, they wanted no relations with Villa either. The attitude of these men would on the whole not be very relevant to developments in Mexico, where none of them had a genuine constituency or any real influence. None of them returned to their country during the revolution in order to influence its fate. Their attitude differed profoundly from that of the one revolutionary exile who still had support in Mexico, who still had a constituency there, and who would return and finally would lose his life in an attempt to shape his country's destiny. This was Felipe Angeles.

CHAPTER EIGHTEEN

The Attempt to Create Villismo with a Gentler Face

The Return of Felipe Angeles

Señores, con atención
les diré lo que ha pasado,
fusilaron en Chihuahua
a un general afamado.

—El reloj marca sus horas,
se acerca mi ejecución;
preparen muy bien sus armas,
apúntenme al corazón.

—Yo no soy de los cobardes
que le temen a la muerte,
la muerte no mata a nadie,
la matadora es la suerte.

—Aquí está mi corazón
para que lo hagan pedazos,
porque me sobra valor
pa' resistir los balazos.[1]

Gentlemen, give me your attention,
I will tell you what has happened;
A very famous general has been
executed in Chihuahua.

"The clock ticks off the hours,
my execution draws near;
prepare well your weapons,
and aim at my heart.

"I am not one of those cowards
who are afraid of death.
Death does not kill anyone;
it is our fortune that kills us.

"Here is my heart so you may
shoot it to pieces, for I have more
than enough courage to
bear the force of your bullets."

Angeles's Ideological Evolution

In the final days of 1915, when the División del Norte dissolved and Villa re-treated into the mountain fastnesses of Chihuahua, Felipe Angeles was oper-ating a small ranch on the U.S. side of the border, trying to make ends meet and support his wife and four children. In the course of the revolution, he had shown the same scruples and honesty in financial matters that had characterized him during the Díaz era, when he had refused to partake of the huge profits that his standing as an artillery expert could easily have garnered him. He had emerged from the revolution as poor as he had entered it, and the meager profits from raising horses and producing milk on his ranch were not sufficient to maintain himself and his family. In addition, Angeles was worried, since his ranch was lo-cated directly along the Mexican border, that Carranza's men might attempt to kidnap him. He also feared that Carrancista agents might attempt to involve him in some scheme and then denounce him for violating U.S. neutrality laws. When two men, calling themselves representatives of Zapata, came to offer him the military leadership of Zapata's campaign in the south, he was convinced that they were Carrancista spies attempting to compromise both him and Maytorena, whom they also went to see.[2]

He was equally suspicious when George Carothers, the former U.S. special agent with Villa, came to see him. He felt that Carothers might be looking out for his own interests, which he felt were threatened by Carranza, and might encourage an anti-Carrancista revolutionary movement "without caring whether that movement will be headed by liberals or conservatives." Suspecting, too, that Carothers might be under instructions from the U.S. government to watch out for violations of the neutrality laws, Angeles cautioned Maytorena to be careful when speaking to Carothers. He was also worried, even before Villa's attack on Columbus, about "the indignation that exists here [in El Paso] against all Villistas and the attempts to expel them from the city. Yesterday Díaz Lombardo was arrested as a vagrant simply in order to humiliate him." Angeles was deeply concerned about these potential dangers for him and his family. "What should I do now?" he asked Maytorena.

Should I continue to work until I am kidnapped? Should I give everything up, attempting to sell it when the buyer will probably give me so little that I cannot even pay for the land?

I am building a small house. Should I give up construction with the result that the contractor will claim damages?[3]

Angeles finally decided to leave El Paso and go north to find work. For a time he contemplated working as a miner, but he soon decided that he did not have the physical stamina to do so. He finally went to New York, where he apparently did some kind of manual work. He did not mind this, since it put him in contact with the lower classes of society. "I had no problems being understood by 'decent' people but I could not understand the common people and they could not understand me. Finally, I must say, while I loved the common people, I had very little contact with them." A few months later Angeles felt that this handicap had been overcome. "I have friends among the Indians here, among the poor, among the blacks," he wrote from New York.[4]

In the first month of his exile, while repeatedly expressing the hope that Carranza would fall, he did not intend actively to intervene in Mexican events, but this changed after Villa attacked Columbus and Pershing entered Mexico, when many Mexican exiles, including Maytorena, wrote Carranza offering him their services in the event of war.[5] Angeles could not bring himself to join Carranza, but his sense of military honor and his patriotism would not allow him to stand aside if there were a war. "It seems to me," he wrote Maytorena a few days after Villa's raid,

that the recent attack on Columbus will inevitably bring about an American intervention. . . . It seems that the only thing that we can do if an intervention against Mexico takes place is to unite with all our friends, enter Mexico, and defend ourselves against everyone: the Americans, the Carrancistas, the Villistas, the Felicistas. . . . We should be especially careful not to associate ourselves with the plebs and not to admit them into our group, since a painful experience has shown us that although we must fight and work for the progress of the lower classes, we should not admit them into our ranks, for in that case we would be responsible for their excesses.[6]

Angeles gave up this idea once it became clear that no U.S.–Mexican war would break out in the near future. Most exiles saw war as a remote possibility after Pershing's withdrawal from Mexico, but Angeles saw the situation in a different light. He was obsessed by the conviction that once World War I ended, the United States, now in possession of a huge army, would intervene in Mexico. In April 1917, about two months after Pershing left Mexico and war broke out between the United States and Germany, Angeles wrote Maytorena:

The war between the United States and Germany opens a new era of Mexican-American relations.

Up to now these relations have been influenced by the weakness of the American army and the goodness and good intentions of President Wilson. Under such circumstances the president could impose his will. As a result of the American-German war, within a very short time the American army will be strong and the wishes of the president will not be predominant and the seeds sown by Carranza with his characteristic rudeness and megalomania will bear fruit; and then perhaps President Wilson will become flexible and bend to the hurricane of special interests that will soon blow against our country.[7]

Angeles now became haunted by the fear of U.S. intervention in Mexico, and all his subsequent actions, which would finally lead to his death, were designed to prevent such an intervention.

A strange conversation between a mysterious Mr. X and Frank Polk, the State Department counselor largely responsible for intelligence and covert activities, who also oversaw Mexican affairs, may well have been linked to Angeles's increasing fears. On June 19, 1916, as tensions between the United States and the Carranza administration mounted (two days later they would result in an armed clash in the Mexican town of Carrizal that brought the two countries to the brink of war), Mr. X, having vainly attempted to see the secretary of state, was received by Polk, who noted in his diary:

He said that he felt that the Carranza government was on its last legs and he hated the thought of this government intervening or making war on Mexico, as the consequences were horrible to contemplate. He hoped that something could be done to prevent it, as Carranza could do nothing. He felt that Angeles was the one man who could inspire confidence, not only in the people of Mexico, but the desirable Mexicans now in exile.

He said he did not want any assistance from the American government, but all they wanted to know was whether this government would not oppose a movement of this kind by force. Nothing could be done, if this government would take such an attitude. He felt that as we had recognized Carranza, we could now state that we no longer recognized his government, as it was not a government, and that Angeles and his friends would at once secure the power and restore order.

He spoke very strongly on the subject and hoped that we would look with favor on the proposition.[8]

Polk's response was negative:

I did not argue the question with him and expressed no opinion beyond saying that I did not see how it would be possible for this government to tacitly permit a revolution against the existing government, that we could not undertake to plunge that country into another revolution. He stated that he was particularly anxious that there should not be a break, as it meant that all the factions would probably have to be against the United States. I told him I realized that fact, but that would make no difference in any of our plans. If the de facto government forced Mexico into a war the responsibility was not ours. He then said I knew where I could reach him, and while he had no authority to speak for General Angeles, he thought the general would be guided by his opinion.[9]

Polk underscored his rejection of X's proposal by delivering an oral message through a Mr. Patchin "that no consideration could be given to any suggestions in regard to Mexico at this time."

Polk's diary does not reveal the identity of Mr. X, but the only person in the United States who had close contact with both Angeles and the highest levels of the State Department was Manuel Calero. His insistence that he had no authority to speak for Angeles may indicate that Angeles knew nothing of this meeting, but that Calero hoped to sway him to lead a new revolutionary movement in Mexico should the United States withdraw its recognition from Carranza. Calero certainly knew about Angeles's overriding fear of U.S. intervention in Mexico and his readiness to do anything in his power, including risking his life, to prevent it. Calero himself probably had very different aims in mind, hoping to regain his lost influence in Mexico and put an end to Carranza's nationalistic policy.

Angeles might have been ready to lead an anti-Carrancista movement that had the tacit support of the United States, but he would never have joined in a war against Mexico. In this respect, his attitude stood in stark contrast to that of Eduardo Iturbide, who came to visit Frank Polk only three days after Mr. X. Iturbide was willing to cooperate with a U.S. occupation force in Mexico. "When we have taken the City of Mexico, if we should have to do so," Polk noted in his diary, "he felt sure that all the good Mexicans who are now exiles would be only too glad to come to Mexico with the idea of establishing a government."[10]

In spite of his fear of U.S. intervention, Angeles was the most optimistic of all the exiles. This optimism arose out of his analysis of what had gone wrong with the Mexican Revolution. Although at first glance extremely pessimistic, his analysis nonetheless led him to optimistic conclusions. In Angeles's eyes, the single most important cause of all the sufferings and disasters that Mexico had undergone was the assassination of Madero. Unlike other Maderistas, Angeles was not ready to concede that Madero had committed any mistakes. Had he lived, Mexico would have been spared all the problems and sufferings that the revolution had brought about. "Madero," he wrote, "had two great virtues. He was a democrat and he was a good man."[11]

The first tragic consequence of Madero's assassination was the assumption of leadership by Carranza, a man who was "intelligent and bad." While he protested against the murder of Madero and against the violation of the constitution of 1917, Carranza himself "was a supporter of dictatorship and a man ambitious for power. And we saw in 1913 the anti-ethical phenomenon of a democratic revolution headed by a man of clearly defined dictatorial tendencies."[12] Angeles bitterly contrasted the personalities and attitudes of Madero and Carranza:

Madero fought for freedom and gave us freedom. Carranza has said that freedom is an error.

Madero fought for our democratic institutions and Carranza thinks like Pineda [one of the leading científicos of the Díaz era] that democracy is a utopia and nonsense.

Madero had a heart of gold and Carranza has a heart of steel.

Angeles contrasted Madero's humanity with the fact that "Carranza like Porfirio Díaz kills his enemies in the name of the public good."[13] Angeles nevertheless was far too intelligent a man to put the blame for every negative development in Mexico since the outbreak of the constitutionalist revolution only on Carranza's shoulders. A more fundamental cause of what happened, in his opinion, was "a natural lack of culture of the lower classes of the people."[14]

The tragedy of February 1913 created such an indignation among the people against the reactionary dictatorship that it believed that it consisted . . . of all "the decent people," as we improperly call them in Mexico. This meant that to be cultivated, to be properly dressed, or to have material wealth were characteristics of all enemies of the revolution and in this way in the vague popular conscience the revolution of 1913 became a class war.[15]

Angeles was not only critical of the lower classes as such but also of the policies of their leaders. In a letter to Maytorena, he spoke of the "foolish idea of the Zapatistas to extend their rule to all of the country, since I believe that the Plan of Ayala is bad and should not even be applied in the region where Zapatismo holds sway. Don't tell anyone about this idea of mine."[16]

Angeles criticized not only Zapata's policies but Villa's as well, although he was extremely cautious in voicing his reservations. He stated that Villa "could not understand democracy for lack of culture" but linked this assertion to a statement in which he reiterated his profound admiration for Villa. "All Carrancistas and Huertistas should know that I do not feel humiliated by having served under Villa's orders but that on the contrary I am proud of it. I am proud of having felt for many months the affection and the regard of a man like Villa."[17] Nevertheless, without naming Villa, Angeles was sharply critical of one of the mainstays of his policy: the confiscation of the large estates and properties of the rich. "The natural leaders of the people, who had only had the benefit of primary schooling, had read the doctrines of socialism without understanding them. Their first impulse was to dispossess the enemy of their wealth." Angeles did not blame the popular leaders, including Villa, for this policy, but laid the blame squarely at Carranza's doorstep for having "supported this impulse, which was a confused mixture of just demands and instincts of robbery, with his authority as head of the revolution."[18]

Some exiles thought that sooner or later Carranza would be deposed by more liberal, progressive-minded members of his own faction, such as Obregón (which was in fact what happened), but Angeles did not share this optimistic view. He did not believe that Obregón would rise against Carranza, and if he did, he felt that he would not be able to hold on to power.[19]

Looking at Angeles's gloomy assessment of the situation in Mexico, it is at first difficult to find any reason for optimism: Mexico was ruled by a bloody dictator, Carranza, and there was no strong opposition to him in his own movement. His main opponents, Villa and Zapata, had no real understanding of democracy and had propounded programs that in many respects carried the seeds of disaster. After the end of the war with Germany, Wilson might very well be induced to intervene in Mexico. Yet in spite of this pessimistic assessment, Angeles retained a basically optimistic view of Mexico's future.

The primary reason for Angeles's optimism was his belief that Villa and Zapata and his leaders were basically honest, good men, whose errors were due to ignorance and to their lack of intellectual mentors to give them the right advice. He referred "to the admirable tenacity of the southern hero Emiliano Zapata, who has strengthened the conviction that an agrarian problem exists in our country that needs an urgent solution."[20]

Angeles also expressed profound admiration for one of Zapata's main lieutenants, against whom he had fought in 1913,[21] Genovevo de la O. He spoke of Villa as a "basically good man." He felt that if these lower-class leaders were given the right advice, they could play an extremely positive role in the revolution. Above all, he was convinced that they now understood how erroneous their policy of massive confiscation of the property of the rich had been. "There is a unanimous consensus that the confiscation of property and the dispossession of all kinds of goods was nothing more than violent revenge, which destroyed wealth and enormously harmed the prestige of the revolutionary cause."[22]

Having abandoned this erroneous attitude, the lower-class leaders now presented a much greater danger to Carranza. But not only the attitude of the lower classes had changed; that of Mexico's upper class had also undergone a profound transformation:

Today the revolution of 1910 has triumphed in the consciousness of nearly everyone; the famous statement "After General Díaz, the Law" . . . has become a desideratum for the whole republic. . . . [but] our political enemies refused to accept this idea. Today, they state in their most important organ, *La Revista* of San Antonio, Texas, "We also believe in the basic principles proclaimed by the revolution but we want to carry them out by proceedings in accordance with the supreme law of the nation." What else did the revolutionaries of 1910 want?[23]

Since the revolution had now taken hold of the consciousness of the vast majority of Mexicans, Angeles felt that the conservatives did not constitute a major threat to it. Since they had now accepted the revolution, and since the lower-class leaders of Mexico—Zapata and Villa—had moderated their views by rejecting wholesale confiscation of the property of the upper classes, Angeles believed that a unity of all these forces against Carranza could be established.

His optimism with respect to the situation in Mexico was strengthened by a belief that a kind of socialism in which he had come to believe would soon triumph all over the world. Although he had read the works of Marx and Engels and greatly respected them, he did not believe in revolutionary socialism but rather in a gradual evolution toward a socialist society. He credited Marx with two achievements: one was to show that "free competition creates a production without plan, without organization, which is thus chaotic and as a result anti-scientific and inefficient." He also credited Marx with showing that "private property of the means of production and generally the right to unlimited private property justifies our calling today's society unjust."[24] Angeles was convinced that socialism was advancing all over the world:

When the men of my generation sat in the universities, we listened with respectful silence to the economists predicating their eternal truth; we heard the metaphysical demonstrations of the right to property and we laughed at the mental lack of equilibrium of Proudhon, who in the passion of his struggle shouted, "Property is robbery!"

We did not imagine that in the field of science the triumph of the madman was a fact. From then on the truth is inundating the world more and more with a new light.

These madmen of yesterday who died of hunger while in exile . . . were slowly conquering the world.

The madmen and criminals of yore were filling the jails, were exiled from their country, and are now invading the governments and now make up half of the popular representation in the Reichstag, are practically ruling in France, are in power in some British colonies, and have a president in the United States who is guided by the spirit of the new freedom.[25]

Angeles's idea that the most important European countries were moving toward socialism, since many of their governments included social democrats, stood in sharp contradiction to the opinion of radical socialists such as Rosa Luxemburg, who on the contrary felt that the presence of social democrats in governing coalitions meant that they had betrayed the principles of socialism.

In spite of his attacks on the principles of private property, Angeles did not believe that its expropriation was justified, and he sharply criticized the revolutionaries for doing precisely that. He was convinced that socialism could only come gradually and only at a point where the people were sufficiently educated and the country sufficiently developed for socialism to become a realistic alternative. In the meantime, both the principle of the sanctity of private property and the rights of the rich and wealthy in Mexico should be respected.

The one who in his opinion seemed to be implementing the principles in which Angeles believed and creating the basis for a socialist society was Woodrow Wilson. Wilson's doctrine of the New Freedom, in Angeles's opinion, had nothing to do with classical liberalism, but on the contrary meant a new beginning, which was identical with a socialist tendency.[26] Since he had identified the Wilson administration as socialist and took Wilson's rhetorical commitment to the Mexican Revolution seriously, he had no compunction about hoping to secure U.S. help for his movement. U.S. help, however, was different from U.S. military intervention in Mexico. An intervention, he felt, constituted a mortal danger for his country, and from mid 1917 on, he was animated by an almost messianic zeal to return to Mexico to unite all factions and thus prevent such a catastrophe.

There is little doubt that Angeles's optimism was also based on his profound conviction that he was the one man in Mexico capable of establishing this kind of unity. He was not mistaken. He was in a unique position with respect both to the various factions fighting Carranza and to the United States. None of the leaders fighting in the field—Zapata, Villa, Félix Díaz, Peláez, the Cedillos— could have enjoyed the trust and support of all other leaders, led a national coalition, or hoped to enjoy support in the United States. The same was true of the politicians who lived in exile. Although the brothers Francisco and Emilio Vázquez Gómez (the first of whom enjoyed Zapata's support) had originally laid claim to the leadership of the Mexican Revolution, they had little support in the Mexican countryside and no authority among revolutionary leaders aside from Zapata, who was willing to recognize Francisco Vázquez Gómez as national leader of the revolution. For the conservative rebels in southern Mexico, Angeles would have been in many respects a very attractive leader. He was a former federal officer, pro-American, deeply opposed to Carranza's constitution of 1917, and in spite of his socialist convictions, he had repeatedly emphasized his deep respect for the principle of private property. In the eyes of the Villistas, he was the former artillery chief of the División del Norte, had been responsible for some of its most glorious victories, and had never openly turned against Villa. Even the Zapatistas, who had the most cause to oppose him, had accepted his mediation in 1914 during the Convention of Aguascalientes and knew that he had personally persuaded the Convention to accept the Plan of Ayala. He was held in high esteem by both Woodrow Wilson and U.S. military men. Significant U.S. business interests hoped that he would prove capable of revoking the constitution of 1917. Finally, at least in the north, he also seems to have inspired genuine popular support going beyond the ranks of the revolutionary army.

There may have been one other factor that in the case of Angeles, like that of most important revolutionaries, fueled both his optimism and his belief in himself: the profound conviction that history was on his side.

Angeles's Political Activities

Angeles's ambitious aims stood in sharp contrast to his absolute lack of any means to accomplish them. He had neither money, an independent body of loyal men waiting for him in Mexico, nor a political organization to help and sponsor him. In spite of these obstacles, he was not discouraged and sought to create both a political base for himself and to find support from various quarters.

In the United States, Angeles attempted to create a kind of prototype for the kind of unity he hoped to establish in Mexico. In the newly formed Liberal Alliance, he sought to unite both radical and conservative enemies of Carranza. To that end, he enlisted the help of former Villistas, including the González Garza brothers, and dissident radical supporters of Carranza's, such as socialist Antonio Villareal, who had broken with Carranza in 1917, as well as conservatives, headed by Manuel Calero, who since Carranza's victory had vainly attempted to create some kind of rapprochement with the former revolutionaries now in exile. Angeles's efforts created resentment among some former revolutionaries, and it is not clear to what degree he was successful in his endeavors to unite the different strands of the opposition to Carranza.

One of the most important sources of support that he hoped to gain was that of his closest friend and ideological brother-in-arms in the years after Madero's death: José María Maytorena, who still had connections in Sonora, as well as money and influence. Maytorena, whose original alliance with Villa had largely been engineered by Angeles, now made it clear to his friends, however, that he was only willing to support a revolutionary movement in Mexico and get involved in it if two preconditions existed: money and *disimulo* (feigning, pretense). Both Maytorena and Angeles used code words for fear that their letters might fall into the hands of U.S. authorities or of the Carrancistas. For example, the planned revolution was called *el negocio* (the business). *Disimulo*, as Maytorena himself (or his son) later wrote on the margin of one of his letters, meant "that no revolutionary movement that could not at least rely on the dissimulation of the American government and on money for buying arms and ammunitions could succeed."[27] What Maytorena was obviously referring to was covert support by the United States that would allow them to prepare their revolution north of the border, permit them to buy arms and ammunition there, and perhaps even give them diplomatic support. In a long correspondence between the two men, Angeles again and again insisted that such preconditions were unnecessary:

You and I only differ (perhaps not any more) in that you require two preconditions to act, "dissimulation" . . . and money.

I have argued from the beginning that these two conditions cannot be realized *a priori* but only *a posteriori*. And I am sure that if you do not yet agree with me, you will soon come to do so. . . .

It would be very good if one could count on the preconditions that you speak of, but since these can only come about *a posteriori*, one has to do without them. What one really needs to begin is personal energy and an understanding of what our country really needs. . . . Is this rashness? It certainly is.

The call for the independence of Mexico was also an act of rashness, and everything that is great and disinterested is rash.

If one fails, everyone says: this was stupid. If one is successful, all the friends who for flimsy reasons felt that such an *a priori* agreement was illogical suddenly unite.[28]

Neither Angeles's letter nor subsequent personal discussions and further letters persuaded the former Sonoran governor to change his view that without covert U.S. support, any revolutionary movement in Mexico was doomed to failure. In December 1917, Angeles made one last call to his friend, not only for support, but to join him in returning to Mexico to unite all the revolutionary factions against Carranza. "Roque [González Garza, who originally had agreed to join Angeles] has desisted, but I have been assured of another companion," Angeles wrote. "If you come to see me, you will feel inclined to unite with us."[29]

Maytorena disagreed. "Without the resources of which we spoke I continue to believe that nothing should be attempted and that everything that will be done without them will lead to failure, although the objective circumstances may seem favorable. . . . If the business cannot be carried out à la Yankee . . . the business will not be successful."[30]

Angeles's answer to Maytorena manifested both a certain disillusionment with the attitude of his friend and a resolve to proceed with his plans to return to Mexico under any circumstances. "When I sent you my telegram," he wrote Maytorena,

I thought that you had definitely given up your first point of view. I thought that you had become fully convinced that the preconditions that you demanded were impossible to comply with and that you had more or less explicitly agreed in this with me. I too had more or less explicitly agreed that your circumstances would not allow you to begin the business under very deficient conditions; but I thought that this did not imply that to begin, impossible conditions would have to be met, but only that you would not collaborate until the business was far more advanced. . . . All businesses of this kind are at the beginning uncertain, and this one, in my opinion, has a maximum of uncertainty. You know that I am not an optimist, that I do not look at things with rose-colored glasses, and that my decision rests not on illusions but on a sense of duty.

You are a man of good sense; you will understand that under the circumstances and knowing how people are, I shall not begin the business with the millions of Morgan or the thousands of Señor Hurtado or the hundreds of Rafael Hernández or the dozens of Llorente or the dollars of Señor Bonilla. Why? Because it is impossible to obtain anything. You will then say, to begin any business without capital necessarily leads to failure. I deny this, since I know of many who have prospered in spite of having begun in this way.[31]

Angeles expressed his disillusionment with the attitude of the former Sonoran governor in a letter to another friend, Emiliano Sarabia, a former general and Villista governor of the state of San Luis Potosí:

Our friend believes that in order to begin the work, conditions must be met that can never be met; that means abandoning any action. I believe that only three things are needed: (1) find out what the real national needs are; (2) gain confidence inside and outside our country; (3) act with full resolve and escape capture for several months in order not to be hanged on a telegraph pole. Then time, a good friend of good causes, will help to implement the work that we hoped for.

In what was perhaps the clearest indication of how he saw his own role in Mexico, Angeles wrote Sarabia: "The Sanchos [Angeles here refers to the character of Sancho Panza in the classic Spanish novel *Don Quijote*] have never done anything great; whenever anything of real importance is to be done, one needs madmen like Madero or Don Quijote."[32]

Maytorena's consistent refusal to support his planned return to Mexico led Angeles to seek support elsewhere. In spite of the friendship that united them, for several months, Angeles interrupted all communications with Maytorena and in that period seems to have fallen increasingly under the sway of a man whom many of Mexico's exiles considered as one of the country's most unscrupulous politicians, Manuel Calero.

Calero was one of the leaders of the Mexican conservatives exiled in the United States. He made a systematic effort to woo the most conservative revolutionaries. He attempted to convince Manuel Bonilla, Madero's former minister and the man in charge of elaborating agrarian reform for the Villistas, that they should form a common front against Carranza. In spite of Bonilla's rejection of these overtures, Calero became insistent, stressing that they had far more in common than Bonilla believed. With equal vigor, Calero tried and failed to gain the support of Maytorena, whom he had invited to a conference with Iturbide, the hero of both the conservatives and the oil men.[33] These rebuffs did not deter Calero, who now concentrated his efforts more and more on Angeles. Angeles reluctantly accepted Calero's suggestion for a meeting of the two men. "I could not refuse his call," Angeles had written Maytorena, "since I owe him a debt for having freed me from Huerta's clutches.

"I thought that the matter would be very important, but in my opinion it was utopian. . . . It is clear that he is desperate since he has witnessed the breakdown of his brilliant career."[34]

Calero had the hide of an elephant, and rebuffs did not count with him. He bombarded Angeles with publications in which he stated that some of the claims of the revolution were in fact legitimate, and Angeles slowly began to accept the idea that Calero was one of the vast majority of Mexicans who were ready to accept the basic demands of the revolution.[35]

For Calero, gaining Angeles's confidence was a triumph. At very least, it enabled him to convince the oil men, who had employed him for so long and with whom he still maintained relations, that he continued to be an important man with important connections whom they would have to reckon with. He probably hoped to play a primary role in Mexico's politics again if Angeles's mission succeeded, and he had no compunction about risking Angeles's life to achieve this. Calero now attempted to involve Angeles in the shady world of lobbyists, con men, and oil men. It is doubtful whether Angeles, who had never shown any interest in money and who had never had any relations with such men, really knew who he was dealing with. He looked at these men through the rose-colored glasses of Wilson's lofty rhetoric.

Calero's first attempt to secure money for Angeles's project seems to have involved Keedy and failed. A BI agent reported on March 26, 1918:

Last night in Washington, I had a long conference with General Felipe Angeles, Alfredo S. Farías [a well-known El Paso Villista] and with an American lawyer named Kidy [Keedy?]. I do not know how he spells his name but it is pronounced Kidy. This lawyer was *procurador* in Puerto Rico and in Panama and is also a great friend and sympathizer of Villa's. . . . They told me that they were arranging with some bankers and a well-known contractor of Washington for funds for a new movement to be headed by General Angeles but from which Villa is not excluded as Kidy told me they were arranging for a passport so that he could interview Villa accompanied by Alfredo S. Farías with a view to obtaining data which would prove Villa had not been in the Columbus Raid. This new movement as I understand it is nothing but a reorganization of the Villista party with General Angeles as a figurehead on account of the well-earned repulsion which the American government and people feel towards Villa on account of the cowardly occurrences at Columbus. General Angeles read his manifesto aloud to me. . . . From what I was told I understand that the "brain" of the movement is Mr. Manuel Calero. I think they have had some difficulty with the American bankers who are holding back on the money question until Kidy and Farías return from the interview with Villa.[36]

Angeles and the Oil Men

According to Ramón Puente, a fellow exile, who later wrote a biography of Villa, Calero played a major role in advising Angeles to return to Mexico and launch a new anti-Carrancista movement there.[37] Did Calero hold out a promise of aid from the oil companies? That is quite possible. He did have close connections to the companies and to Senator Fall, who had been interested in wooing Villa. Zapata's representative in the United States, Octavio Paz, was convinced that the oil companies were in fact ready to help both Villa and Angeles. An agent of the Mexican secret service reported that Paz, who maintained contact with representatives of Villa and of Angeles, had told him in confidence that he had seen letters from supporters and representatives of Villa and Angeles containing evidence that the oil men and their supporters were sending money and ammunition to Villa and Angeles, and that they also sent military matériel to General Aureliano Blanquet, Huerta's former war minister, who had returned to Mexico to head a conservative revolution. "He also told me that one of their aims in supporting the present movement of Villa and Angeles was to create in every possible sense as threatening a situation as possible for the present government in order to force it to dictate laws that would favor the oil companies in Mexico."

These accusations, though, are of a dubious nature. On previous occasions, Angeles had manifested a great aversion to intrigues by U.S. oil companies in Mexico. Early in 1917, Manuel Peláez, whose forces were financed by U.S. oil companies, sent an agent to the United States, who first contacted Calero, who put him in touch with high U.S. officials. Peláez's representative told the Americans that he would be willing to subordinate his troops to Angeles if the Americans supported him, and that in return he would abrogate all laws relating to oil that did not favor foreign oil companies. When Angeles heard of this proposal, he told Roque González Garza that he was indignant "and angry" at Calero for supporting such a project, and that the only reason he did not break with Calero was that he felt he owed him a debt of gratitude for having saved his life in 1914.[38]

There is no evidence that Angeles ever received money or supplies from the oil companies. He seems to have been practically penniless when he crossed the border into Mexico, and one of the first letters he wrote to Maytorena after having entered his native country was to ask his friend to send him a horse.[39] Obviously, he did not have the money to buy one, and he may have been too proud to accept it as a gift from Villa.

There is no evidence that Angeles made any promises to the oil companies. He did not have to do so to gain their sympathy. He was honestly convinced that Carranza's nationalistic policies with regard to American business interests were leading to a U.S. occupation of Mexico, and he felt that only through cooperation with the United States would Mexico be able to make significant progress. In addition, he believed that Carranza's new constitution of 1917, which the oil companies rejected, was undemocratic, and that Mexico should return to the liberal constitution of 1857.

Even if Villa and Angeles had accepted help from the oil companies, as Carranza had done in 1913–14, neither they nor Carranza could be characterized as agents or instruments of oil interests.

The Return of Sherbourne Hopkins to the Political Stage and the Release of Felíx Sommerfeld

The interest of the oil companies in a revived Villa movement was expressed by the activities of one of their most intelligent, knowledgeable, and unscrupulous representatives, Sherbourne G. Hopkins. He once again attempted to emerge as a central actor in Mexican affairs, this time as a spokesman for the oil lobby. Part of his activity was open and of a public relations nature. In 1919, he was one of the main witnesses at the Senate hearings staged by Senator Fall with the aim of pushing for U.S. intervention in Mexico. During those hearings, Hopkins acted as one of the main witnesses against his former employer, Carranza. His covert activities seem to have taken the form of encouraging an uprising by the Villistas, which the oil men hoped would lead either to U.S. intervention or to the fall of Carranza and the emergence of a government that would revoke the radical and nationalist constitution of 1917. In 1917, hoping to revive U.S. support for Villa, Hopkins circulated the ersatz declaration in which the latter purportedly denied all participation in and responsibility for the attack on Columbus.

The phony denial had aroused little interest and much disbelief, but that did not prevent Hopkins from continuing to support Villa and seeking to establish links between him and U.S. business interests. This seems to have been the basis for his energetic campaign to secure the release of Felíx Sommerfeld, Villa's former agent in the United States, whom the Americans had interned as a dangerous enemy alien after the United States entered World War I. Hopkins bombarded the Justice Department with letters in favor of Sommerfeld and finally went to the Justice Department himself to testify in Sommerfeld's favor. David Lawrence, a well-known newspaperman, special agent of Woodrow Wilson's in Mexico, and later founder of *U.S. News and World Report*, told the Justice Department that the aim of Hopkins's activities was "to arrange for Sommerfeld's release for the purpose of cooperating with the recent Villa uprising in Mexico."[40] Hopkins faced no easy task, since officials of the Justice Department had correctly become convinced that Sommerfeld was a German agent.

As long as Germany and the United States were at war, all of Hopkins's efforts proved futile. But after Germany's defeat, the Justice Department showed itself to be more flexible. Hopkins was called to the department, where agents had an extensive interview with him. Since Sommerfeld was repeatedly caught lying during the long hearings that Justice Department officials held—among other things he denied ever having written a letter to the German military attaché, Franz von Papen, in spite of the fact that the department had a copy of the letter—it is doubtful whether the U.S. officials were impressed by some of Hopkins's testimony: "I do not believe that Sommerfeld ever tried to deceive me in his life. . . . Sommerfeld is a man whose facial expression readily indicates his feelings. . . . I wish to add that it is impossible for Sommerfeld to conceal his feelings, as anyone can readily determine by talking with him."[41] They were more impressed when a Justice Department official asked Hopkins:

"Do you have any general reason in mind why it would be to the advantage of the United States to parole Sommerfeld at this time?"

"Most decidedly. Sommerfeld has a more intimate knowledge of Mexican conditions and men in Mexico than any person in America. I think that knowledge could later on perhaps turn to considerable advantage."

It is significant that Miguel Díaz Lombardo, Villa's quasi-official representative in the United States, cooperated so closely in this endeavor with Hopkins that, in the words of one Justice Department official, "Mr. Hopkins . . . has sent Miguel Díaz Lombardo . . . to intercede on behalf of Mr. Sommerfeld."[42]

One of the senior Justice Department officials responsible for the case, John Hanna, became more and more favorably disposed toward Sommerfeld. "In view of the connection of this man with Mexican affairs and especially with the anti-Carranza interests," he wrote, "I suspect that Mr. Sommerfeld's acquaintance with Mexican conditions is desired to assist Americans and Mexicans in some Mexican intrigue. As Sommerfeld is probably rather favorably inclined to Americans, it is not impossible that some entirely legitimate business interest wishes to enlist his cooperation." A few days later, Hanna recommended that Sommerfeld be freed, stating: "I do not believe we need fear he will do anything for Germany. He has too much concern for his own interest to have much sympathy for lost causes. . . . He doubtless will continue to be an intriguer in Mexican affairs though he will not dare to return to Mexico so long as Carranza is in power. The logic of events makes it likely that Sommerfeld will cooperate with a pro-American group in Mexico."[43]

It was not too difficult for the federal officials to understand what interests Hopkins was representing and whose interests Sommerfeld would defend if he were free, for when Hopkins was asked what his protégé would do once he was out of federal detention, he said that Sommerfeld would go into the oil business. (He also mentioned possible employment with a film company.) On August 25, 1919, the Justice Department agreed to free Sommerfeld upon condition that he "pledged himself to abstain from all connection with Mexican political intrigue."[44]

Three months later, the War Department received a report "that a man by the name of Sommerfeld is entertaining Mexicans and indulging in various intrigues at the Astor Hotel."[45] It is not clear how reliable this report was, since, according to the informant, a Mr. Ralph Hayes, "this report is supplied by the woman who sells cigars at the Astor and although Mr. Hayes does not give full credit to his informant, it appears that the matter is worthy of some consideration." It is not clear whether Sommerfeld played any further role in Mexican events. He was probably freed too late to do so, since after Villa's disastrous attack on Ciudad Juárez, the likelihood of any cooperation between the Americans and Villa had drastically declined.[46]

Villa and Angeles

While Calero's urgings and the possible support U.S. business interests may have promised certainly encouraged Angeles to return to Mexico, there was another more important factor that finally tipped the balance. This was a reply by Villa to a letter that Angeles had sent him in June asking how Villa would react if he were to join him. Villa's response was a letter full of warmth, of expressions of loyalty, and of readiness to listen to Angeles's advice. "I am your friend who will never turn his back on you," Villa wrote,

no matter what may be the condition I am in; the words you will find in the course of this letter are dictated by my honorable conscience, they are the thoughts of my heart.

I admire you as one of the honorable men of my country, and I have never left off thinking that the country needed you. Therefore I shall receive you with open arms, with the affection and respect with which I have always treated you.

Obviously referring to the tensions that had developed between the two men in 1915, Villa wrote: "If at any time I told you that you could not stay in the revolution because fatal times were going to come, they were sincere words given in good faith, because for you to have suffered the calamities that I had to stand in the past years, you would have needed to have a heart of iron." Knowing that Angeles's ideal as a Maderista was to have a civilian government in Mexico, Villa assured him:

I shall never stain you—a conscientious man—by wishing to impose my own will, because I solemnly invite you to assist me in establishing a civil government, emanating from the popular will, which will give guarantees to the nation, and we as military men shall obey it, and walk in the height of our duty in order not to stain ourselves as did the army that betrayed the government of the people, a stain of which you are free; for I have the satisfaction of assuring you that when I see the destiny of my country clearly, I shall ask for nothing for myself, and you will be proud of my deeds. I shall always consider and hear with prudence your advice, for I repeat I admire your honor and your culture, and although I might have obtained control of the army and have the fortune of a warrior who up till now has not found anyone who can overthrow me, I would not be ashamed to be a soldier under you.[47]

Together with this letter, brimming with affection and respect, Villa sent a second letter to Angeles, written in very different language and addressed to Maytorena. "In order to clear the stain that you have in the eyes of the nation," Villa wrote the former Sonoran governor,

I shall speak later to the people and tell them to accept you in the bosom of our friends, for without vanity I believe that the words that I may utter in different parts of the state of Sonora will be those that will clear you of the stain that you have; . . . I send you this sincere letter by General Angeles in order that you alone may know its contents and you entirely alone receive that shame, for I did not support you in the state of Sonora in order that you should exploit it, and I repeat that only I, by supplication, can revindicate you in the eyes of the people of that state, as you will clearly comprehend.

In order to clear Maytorena of "the stain" he had incurred, Villa asked him to give $10,000 to Angeles "in order that he may begin to organize the army that he may lead." Villa intimated that Maytorena had stolen large amounts of money from his native state. "I do not wish that you give me that sum of your own money, but I wish that you give to me of that which belongs to Sonora." Villa then charged that Maytorena bore the main responsibility for the civil war between Villa and Carranza:

Bear in mind that your suggestions greatly influenced our revolting against Carranza. I have never given this information to the press because, I repeat, I wish to clear you, I wish to return you to the bosom of our friends, and for that reason I speak to you with perfect clarity, for I am a man who cannot dissemble my sentiments, and for this reason I enter into these details and I open the door to you. Each day the Mexican people love me more, and on this occasion, you are going to sign your sentence of hatred forever from them or you will consent to what I tell you in this letter and enter the bosom of your friends, which are we and the people.[48]

Villa's letter to Maytorena, which Angeles never delivered, showed that Villa had a poor understanding of the character of his former artillery chieftain. Angeles would never have agreed to pressure his friend Maytorena into giving him money to finance his campaign. Villa's advisers may have realized this, which is why they were so worried about the tenor of the letter, or they may have feared that Maytorena might make a public statement against Villa.[49]

For seven months, until July 1918, Angeles severed all communications with Maytorena. It was only then that he again wrote to his old friend, intimating that his mind was finally made up:

As far as my silence is concerned, let me tell you something: I cannot spell it out clearly but I am sure that you will understand everything. You know, since I have told you, of the resolution I took some time ago. I wanted to carry it out, first in one way, then in another, finally in another. From one failure to the other, though, time passed, and in this way many months have gone by. Why did I fail on the first two occasions? I failed because I did not have the help that I firmly believed I could count on. And since then my action has been imminent, and it has been necessary to be silent. Now I find myself in a similar situation; nevertheless, my state of mind has greatly changed, and I now dare to do what I have not done before. If I were to tell you everything, you would certainly object to my intentions, as any good friend would do; but I am disposed to play one probability against 999.[50]

Angeles's letter was somewhat cryptic, but whatever doubts Maytorena may have had as to his friend's intentions were clarified by a desperate letter that Angeles's wife sent him asking him to dissuade her husband from returning to Mexico and joining Villa. "I have just received a letter from your wife," Maytorena wrote Angeles,

who explains to me "the things" that you do not tell me. She, poor woman, is greatly distressed and asks me to dissuade you from your last resolution, and in order to comply with her wishes, I am sending you a copy of the letter that I have sent her. I should not add one more word; nevertheless, I cannot fail to tell you that I do not understand how a man such as you, with your logical and mathematical thinking, can resolve to accept odds of 1 to 999, and I say the same about the pretension of returning to join a man whose contact can only be fatal [i.e., Villa]. I do not understand this, I repeat, however desperate you may be and however worried you are by our situation. We have waited for a long time; let us wait a little more, confident that our action can always be opportune, since there will not always have to be hatred and fighting amongst us.[51]

In his letter to Angeles's wife, Clara, Maytorena attempted to sound much more optimistic. He told her that he believed Angeles had desisted from his original intention, and that "I believe that if in a moment of impatience or hallucination he had such an idea, he has given it up as absurd, which would correspond to his intelligence and clear-mindedness, since as you say he has had a long experience of that man [i.e., Villa], who in days of political exaltation, and under the force of circumstances only, was joined by many of us, who finally suffered only the most bitter deception as a result of our errors."[52]

Maytorena may have felt that his optimism was justified, for in letters the next month, Angeles said nothing about returning to Mexico and joining Villa but limited himself to analyzing the political situation and speaking of articles that he intended to write. In December 1918, however, Maytorena received a farewell letter from Angeles, in which his friend sketched a blueprint for political action on the part of Maytorena and other Mexican exiles in the United States. Angeles wrote that he was now returning to Mexico with the aim "of making propaganda among the revolutionaries who are up in arms so that they should affiliate with the [Liberal] Alliance." He called on his friend and, through him, on other members of the Liberal Alliance, which until then had limited participation and membership to former revolutionaries, to admit conservatives into its ranks:

I hope that this organization will carry out its patriotic task and will save Mexico from intervention. I place great hopes in your cooperation. Since I shall be in Mexico, I shall not be able to take a hand when you sign a pact with the counterrevolutionaries to create the basis of the unity of all Mexicans. I have full confidence that you and all our friends will actively campaign to make sure that the Alliance elects an executive committee consisting of reputable, significant, and talented personalities who nevertheless are not intransigent and do not believe that it is up to the *pelados* [rabble] alone to determine the fate of Mexico. We have to examine our consciences and confess that all of us have made mistakes, and that even if we had not made them, all persons of value must participate and have the right to participate in determining the fate of our country. . . .

What will the future bring us? Whatever it is, we must maintain our hope until the last that something good will emerge, and if death rewards this attitude, our last thought will be that we have done well and that a reward will come, although it may come somewhat belatedly. . . . P.S. Keep my departure secret.[53]

Manuel Calero was the only other person to whom Angeles wrote on the same day that he wrote to Maytorena, in a more cordial and personal vein. "I would have liked not to be alone and I would have preferred to be accompanied by twenty patriots well known in our republic, but I did not find them; perhaps many of them wanted to come, but because of their education as refined and extremely sensitive men they were not able to do so."

In his letter to Calero, Angeles reiterated the justification he had given Maytorena for his decision to return to Mexico: his desire to prevent U.S. intervention. "It would be a shame for the Mexicans not to have done everything in their power to solve our problem in order to prevent an intervention from the United States." He appealed to Calero, as he had to Maytorena, to unite all political exiles, both revolutionaries and conservatives, in a common organization: "You are one of the most brilliant, best-known, most reputable and wealthy Mexicans. You must do everything you can. You should appeal to all the liberals, to all worthy Mexicans who may have been excluded from the Mexican Liberal Alliance by the intransigence of some revolutionaries. You should risk your own welfare and even that of your family. Do everything in your power to prevent me from being humiliated."

In his letter to Calero, in contrast to that which he sent to Maytorena, Angeles revealed some of the doubts and hesitations that had plagued him and some of the obstacles he knew he would face:

You know well that I am conscious of every problem to which I am exposing myself. I am already old, and I shall not easily be able to resist the difficulties of life in the open without food, without clothes, and plagued by dirt. I shall be joining men who through ignorance or savagery commit crimes without knowing that they are doing so, and naturally your good friend, the pious señor (. . . I omit the name since he is a friend of yours) will call me a bandit. Since Villa is one of the most important factors in the present struggle, I shall have to force myself to transform him from an element of anarchy into an element of order, and these endeavors of mine will certainly be used by my enemies to discredit me with both the American government and the American people.

In spite of everything, I leave with optimism, since I am going to fulfill a duty, and because I have full confidence that my good friends will help me either to be successful or will vindicate me if I fail.

Angeles told Calero that only one man, his own son Alberto, had been willing to follow him. But Angeles would not allow his son to accompany him, since he would be the main support of the family.[54]

Angeles's call for the unity of revolutionaries and counterrevolutionaries in the Liberal Alliance was not well received by some of the most prominent revolutionary exiles. One of the most radical of them, Federico González Garza, wrote his brother Roque González Garza, the former head of the Revolutionary Convention, "Angeles persisted in his opinion that the only way we could establish an organic peace in Mexico was to unite completely with our enemies without any distinctions or limitations." The reactionaries had at first wanted to eliminate Angeles from the board of the Liberal Alliance, but their attitude changed completely, Federico González Garza said,

when it became known here that in a private letter, General Angeles called for the help of Calero and Maytorena, and since it became known that he had published a manifesto, which he had sent us before, with some of whose clauses we never agreed.

Now under no circumstances are they willing to accept his resignation [prior to leaving the United States, Angeles had tendered his resignation as a member of the board of the Liberal Alliance in New York], since he changed from being their enemy to becoming their leader.

Federico González Garza felt that uniting the revolutionaries and reactionaries in a common organization would be a tragedy, since the revolutionaries only constituted 2 percent of the exiles. "I very much fear that the forces of reaction may gain the support of General Angeles and will lead him to his doom, since it seems that the Alliance will end by being a splendid means, which our enemies never thought they could employ, to assume a dominating position once again and forget everything except the interests of their class."[55]

The manifesto to which Federico González Garza referred had been written by Angeles shortly before his departure and in early 1919 was published in the newspaper *La Patria*, edited by Mexican exiles hostile to Carranza. In it, Angeles called for free elections, first at the local, then at the regional, then at the national level, and demanded the creation of a civilian government. None of the revolutionary leaders should be allowed to become a candidate for the presidency of Mexico (in this way Angeles also excluded himself).

Federico González Garza did not spell out what parts of the manifesto he objected to, but it was certainly Angeles's categorical demand that the new constitution of 1917 be abrogated, and that Mexico return to the liberal constitution of 1857. While the revolutionary exiles may have sympathized with Angeles's criticism that the 1917 constitution gave too much power to the president, they may not have wanted to abrogate its nationalistic articles or those that proclaimed land reform as one of the main aims of the revolution. Angeles stated that such reforms should not be implemented by any one caudillo, but only by a freely elected parliament. This was the old controversy that Angeles and González Garza had voiced in 1915 when Angeles had stated that one of the main differences between the Conventionists and the Carrancistas was that the Carrancistas wanted to implement reforms before elections, whereas the Conventionists wanted to do so afterward. Federico González Garza had at the time strongly objected to Angeles's position, and this may have been the basis for his criticism of Angeles's manifesto.[56]

It is doubtful whether Angeles ever heard of the controversy that his letter and manifesto provoked among the exiles in the United States. Once he crossed into Mexico, his communications with his friends north of the border largely ceased. The only time a letter of his reached Maytorena was shortly after Angeles's arrival in Mexico, when he asked his friend to send him a horse and a first-aid kit.

The Return of Angeles to Mexico and Villa's Last Great Campaign

Angeles's journey into Mexico began on George Holmes's ranch on December 11, 1918. There José María Jaurrieta, Villa's secretary and emissary, awaited him in order to escort him to Villa's camp. Angeles's prediction in his letter to Calero that conditions in Mexico would be harsh for him proved to be entirely true during the initial days of his journey. In order not to alert Carrancista troops, he had to sleep in an open field, without benefit of a campfire, in the freezing December climate of Chihuahua. It was only when they arrived in the small village of Cuchillo Parado that he could relax. This was Toribio Ortega's old home base, from which the first men to take up arms against Porfirio Díaz had set out on November 17, 1910. Ortega was long since dead, but the village remained a center of revolutionary activities deeply committed to Villa. The government had never been able to establish a defensa social there. Sympathies for Villa were so strong and open that a public dance was organized in honor of Angeles. A short time later, he finally arrived at Villa's camp, which was located on the hacienda of Tosesihua. The two men embraced, addressed each other as "mi General," and then reminisced about the glorious days of the División del Norte. It was at a somewhat later moment when Villa wanted to discuss the coming military campaign with Angeles that he suffered a surprising and disagreeable shock. Angeles told him that he had not come to Chihuahua to fight. "I come," he told Villa, "on a mission of love and peace. I have come here to find a way to put an end to this savage struggle that is consuming the Mexican people in order to unite all political factions in Mexico without discrimination, in one common front."[57]

He told Villa that he had come to Mexico in the name of the Liberal Alliance that had recently been founded in New York, and that his aim was to secure the support of both Villa and all other revolutionary leaders in Mexico for the program of the Alliance. Villa was taken aback by Angeles's statement, but he did not fly into one of his violent rages and did not turn against Angeles. Rather, Villa patiently explained to his old ally that his idea of joining one revolutionary group after the other was in fact utopian. Hundreds of miles separated Chihuahua from the nearest anti-Carranza revolutionary forces in central Mexico and in the south. Villa told Angeles how he himself had tried with a group of men to march to central Mexico but finally, because of Carrancista control of the intervening territory, had had to return to Chihuahua.[58]

It is doubtful whether Angeles maintained his stance of complete aloofness from the military side of the Villa movement. Soon after his arrival, and for the first time in the two years since the loss of his major reserves of arms and ammunition to Murguía in early 1917, Villa again undertook a regular military campaign and again attacked a large town, Parral.

So large a military campaign required the solution of three logistical problems: securing money; getting arms and ammunition; and recruiting additional men. It was money that Villa got most easily. Since late 1917, he had successfully raised funds by "taxing" foreign companies—that is, demanding protection money from them. On the eve of his offensive, these taxes were greatly increased. Villa's and Angeles's campaign involved "forced loans from everyone, both Mexican and American companies," the Chihuahuan manager of the Mexican Northwestern Railroad reported to his president in Canada, "as well as the forcible taking of merchandise and supplies for their army. Almost every foreign mining company in the state of Chihuahua was compelled to give them money at one time or another."[59]

It was also easier for Villa to secure arms in 1919 than it had been two years before when he had had to abandon his offensive against the Carrancistas. This was because Carranza had set up a series of ammunition factories in Mexico, thus decreasing his dependence on the United States and increasing the supply of arms and ammunition he was able to furnish his soldiers. The latter in turn sold arms and ammunition on the black market in Ciudad Chihuahua to the Villistas. In contrast to the heyday of the División del Norte, Villa's greatest difficulty lay in recruiting men. By 1919, he seems to have abandoned the tactic of forced impressment that he had so amply utilized in 1916 and 1917. This change was partly voluntary and partly involuntary. It was voluntary in the sense that Villa had realized how unpopular forced impressment was and how much hostility it generated among the common people in Chihuahua. It was involuntary in the sense that when Villa's troops approached a town, most young men, fearing impressment, fled into the mountains or desert or fought against him in the ranks of the defensas sociales.[60]

Villa's army was thus once again composed of volunteers. Its core consisted of his Dorados and those men who had remained loyal to him throughout the years. The new volunteers seem to have been a heterogeneous array. Many were local men chiefly motivated to join Villa by the persecutions and depredations they had suffered at the hands of Carrancista troops. Others were prisoners and de-

serters from the Carrancista army who felt that Villa provided better for his soldiers than the federal commanders did. A third group were cowboys who had
lost their occupation once the great herds of cattle and horses that had roamed
Chihuahua had largely disappeared as a result of the revolution. "Cowboys we
are, and cowboys we shall be," Villa told Angeles.[61]

His logistical measures and the added prestige that Angeles's arrival provided
enabled Villa to triple the number of his men and gave his movement a new quality. "Up until January 1st their [the Villistas'] combined forces numbered probably
four hundred to five hundred men," the manager of the Mexican Northwestern
Railroad reported to his chief.

Early in the present year Felipe Angeles, a former federal officer, and a very intelligent Mexican, crossed the border near El Paso and allied himself with Villa. Prior to
this time the movement had been practically nothing except a bandit affair, but with
the advent of Angeles the movement became a revolutionary one, and for a time it
seemed probable that it would be a considerable factor in the general situation. Apparently Angeles discussed with Villa and formulated definite plans which they attempted to follow out. Within few months they had gathered about 2,000 men who
were fairly well armed and equipped.[62]

Single-handedly, Angeles—it was no coincidence that he compared himself
to Don Quijote—attempted to impose his agenda on both Villa and his army.
That agenda was political, humanitarian, and military. The political dimensions
of his agenda were the least controversial but also least significant parts of it and
were easiest to implement.

With tremendous vigor, Angeles set about politicizing the Villa movement
and persuading American public opinion that its attitude to the United States
had radically changed. As long as U.S. troops were occupying parts of Mexico,
Villa's program had been one of radical nationalism. With the evacuation of Pershing's troops from Mexico and Carranza's increasingly nationalistic anti-American policies, Villa's accusations that Carranza was a U.S. agent lost all credibility.
He needed another program, but he was obviously incapable of formulating it.
Angeles hoped to fill this void.

Villa was quite willing to accommodate his old comrade in political terms.
Even before Angeles joined him, he had agreed to accept a program similar to
the one Angeles proclaimed in his manifesto. When Villa occupied the town of
Río Florido, one of his lieutenants, Miguel Trillo, read the manifesto of the Liberal Alliance. Villa then asked if anyone objected. No one did. Finally, he addressed one of his generals directly, asking him, "What do you think of the plan?
What do you think of the constitution of 1857?" The general perhaps best reflected the views of the army. "I know very little about constitutions, but since
Carranza abolished the constitution of 1857, it means that it must be good," he
replied.[63] It is doubtful whether allegiance to this constitution animated either
Villa or his followers. The time when a political manifesto could mobilize the
whole people, as Madero's Plan of San Luis Potosí had done in 1910 or Zapata's
Plan of Ayala had done in 1911, had long since passed. Plans and manifestos were
a dime a dozen in revolutionary Mexico.

Angeles, by contrast, took political activity very seriously. In every town occupied by the Villistas, he addressed the civilian population and described his program to them. That program focused more on peace and reconciliation than on social reform. It called for the restoration of the constitution of 1857, democratic reforms in Mexico, and the abolition of the power of the caudillos. Angeles appealed to the revolutionaries to respect the foreigners, who "bring us science and know how to exploit our natural resources and bring us the capital that is indispensable to carry out this exploitation." He condemned attacks on religion. "To oppose religion and not only the abuses of the clergy represents an attack on our most noble feelings and against all moral tendencies."[64]

The problem that Angeles faced in his political campaign was that only a fraction of the population in the villages Villa's troops occupied, consisting mainly of women and old men, came to listen to him. The young men had mostly fled into the mountains, since they either belonged to a defensa social or were afraid of being impressed into Villa's army. In one case, Angeles decided to risk his life in order to bring his message not only to the old men but to the young as well. After Villa's troops occupied the village of San Juan Bautista and the young men as usual had fled into the adjoining mountains, where their campfires could be seen from afar, Angeles decided to go there all alone and to speak to the villagers. He did so without Villa's knowledge, and the men listened to him for hours and allowed him to return unscathed. Villa was horrified at Angeles's rashness and at the same time impressed by his courage.[65]

It was nevertheless clear to Angeles that programs and speeches alone would not suffice to transform the attitude of Chihuahua's civilian population. He had to radically end the fear that Villa inspired, transform the bloody image of him that Villa's own actions and the Carrancistas' propaganda had combined to create.

What Angeles required of Villa was a fundamental change of tactics: he was to put an end to the execution of prisoners and abstain from any reprisals against foreign and Mexican civilians. Villa justified his executions by stating that the Carrancistas never took any prisoners but killed every Villista they captured. Another explanation for Villa's policy was that no guerrilla army could set up prisoner of war camps. His only choice was either to free the prisoners or to execute them. Early on, he had released his prisoners with the warning that if they joined the federal army again and were again captured, they would immediately be shot, and each of them had an ear cut off as identification. Villa told Angeles that this had been ineffective. Once freed, the soldiers had still rejoined their old federal units. Nonetheless, Villa largely complied with Angeles's wishes. After the battle of Moctezuma, a small engagement and the first to take place after Angeles joined him, Villa freed all the federal prisoners he had taken.[66] He did the same in Parral, although to a more limited degree.

The attack on Parral, the first and only large city he was able to completely occupy during his offensive, was a bloody affair. Both the federal garrison, commanded by a former high officer of Villa's División del Norte who had defected to the Carrancistas, Manuel Madinaveitia, and the defensa social of the town, which included the sons of its wealthiest inhabitants, put up a desperate resistance. The defensa social retreated to a hill known as the Cerro de la Cruz and continued to fight even after the federal garrison had either fled the town or had

surrendered to the Villistas. They only laid down their arms when they were assured either by Villa himself or by one of his officers (the matter is still in dispute) that their lives would be spared if they surrendered.[67]

With three significant exceptions, Villa kept his word: 85 out of 88 members of
the defensa social were freed, although not before they had spent a few very anxious moments listening to Villa. All of the prisoners had been led into the main
auditorium of a girls' school in Parral, where Villa addressed them. "As far as I
understand it villages organized defensas sociales to prevent bandits from entering their towns, bandits whose main aim is plunder and persecution of honest
families. . . . You constitute this defensa social. . . . I, the bandit who attacks your
town, am the bandit who has taken you prisoners. There is no need for you to
ask what your punishment will be."[68] After a few moments when the prisoners
were expecting the worst, Villa told them, "I shall set you free so that you can
take care of your families who have congregated at the door of the school weeping and wailing." The relief of these men was so great that some of them left the
school shouting, "Viva Villa!"[69]

In the cases of three leaders of the defensa social, however, Villa refused to
abide by the promise of safe conduct that had been given them, in spite of entreaties on their behalf by Angeles. These were the head of the defensa social,
José de la Luz Herrera, and two of his sons. Herrera was the father of two of
Villa's most prominent former commanders, Maclovio and Luis Herrera, who
had fought alongside him in the División del Norte and had then been the first
of his commanders to turn against him and join Carranza. Villa justified the execution of the elder Herrera by telling a subordinate that the latter had lied to
him and betrayed him. When his son Maclovio had joined Carranza, José de la
Luz Herrera, who was at the time in Villa-controlled territory, had requested a
special train from Villa in order to join his son and persuade him to change his
attitude. Instead, once he had joined Maclovio, he sent a message to Villa in
which he called him a bandit and declared that he would also turn against him.
Villa also reproached him for having forcibly opposed the anti-American demonstration that had taken place in Parral when U.S. troops had briefly entered the
city.[70]

There was more to it than that. If Herrera's actions had been the only reason
for his execution, Villa could have spared his two sons, who bore no responsibility for the action of their father. Instead, he decided that all three had to die. It
was a blood feud to the death, with Villa resolved to exterminate the Herreras.
His hatred of them had been so strong that after the capture of Torreón, when his
men found the lifeless body of Luis Herrera, he had ordered it hung from a tree
with a picture of Carranza in its hand.[71] Villa personally came to watch the execution of the Herreras, who died with great courage, manifesting their hatred and
contempt for Villa until the end.

In addition to the lives of the members of the defensa social of Parral Villa
spared those of the federal prisoners. He turned them over to Angeles, who harangued them and persuaded them to join Villa's forces.

The tactic of sparing prisoners paid off. When Villa's army approached the
neighboring town of Valle de Allende, the members of the defensa social told
him that they would not resist if he agreed to spare their lives. He promised to do

this provided they turned over all their weapons to him. They did so, and Villa was thus able to gather new arms and momentum.

Villa's more tolerant attitude toward Chihuahua's civilian population expressed itself once more when his troops entered San Isidro, the village where his enemy and rival Pascual Orozco had begun his uprising against Porfirio Díaz in 1910, and where Orozco still enjoyed much sympathy. When news reached the village that a train carrying Villa and his men was on its way to San Isidro, panic gripped the inhabitants. The men fled into the mountains for fear of being either shot or inducted into Villa's army, and the women and children hid trembling in their homes, fearful that Villa would orchestrate a repetition of the rapes his troops had committed in Namiquipa.

The one person who did not lose her head was San Isidro's schoolteacher, Julia Franco Domínguez. She gathered the village's schoolchildren, and carrying a large Mexican flag, they proceeded through the deserted streets of San Isidro to the railway station. As the train carrying Villa and his men steamed into the station, the children stood at attention and intoned the national anthem. Villa was so moved that he made a speech to the children telling them that they were the future of Mexico, and that he would do everything in his power to protect them. He then proceeded on his way without even entering the village.[72]

Villa's more conciliatory attitude also extended to Americans. In April 1919, Villa rode into the mining camp of Santa Eulalia mounted on a mule called President Wilson. The American managers of the camp feared for their lives. All Villa did, however, was to give the Americans a lecture, "in which he expressed his opinion on President Wilson." An American who witnessed this event recalled: "No one objected to the remarks, all felt as he did. No American in the camp was harmed."[73]

But Angeles had more difficulty implementing his military agenda. The issue of transforming Villa's guerrilla force into a regular army soon led to conflicts between the two generals. Villa had no objection when Angeles attempted to implement some of the practices of a regular army: constant practice with military equipment as well as constant exercises. He not only allowed these practices, but when Angeles set up running as an obligatory exercise, Villa participated despite his leg wound. Villa remained inflexible, however, when Angeles objected to Villa's tactic of periodically dispersing his men and then having them congregate again under his direct command. "Roaming through the mountains," Angeles told Villa, "may be adequate for a guerrilla leader but certainly not for the commander in chief of the National Army of Reconstruction."[74] As an alternative, Angeles suggested that Villa should occupy the city of Durango, establish a firm basis there, and from then on proceed to occupy more and more territory.

Villa was not convinced by Angeles's arguments. Although Angeles might have had a better military education, Villa felt that he had a better grasp of the economic situation in Chihuahua, as well as of the imperatives of guerrilla warfare. He explained that he simply did not have the supplies for a long-term offensive, and that the men and horses should periodically be allowed to rest, which they could only do if they were dispersed into the countryside, where it would be difficult for the Carrancistas to reach them, and where provisions might be found.

"The campaigns are hard, and since we don't have many men, we must let them as well as the horses rest. What could we do with tired men? And if the horses get worn out, where do we get new ones?" Villa asked Angeles. "The situation is very different now from what it was five years ago, when after hundreds of horses had been killed, we were able to replenish our supplies within hours from the haciendas. But now, General, you will see that there are no horses in all of Chihuahua, and that soon we will have to go into Coahuila or Nuevo León to obtain them, for the supplies in Chihuahua are not sufficient for a revolution."[75]

In spite of these differences of opinion, Villa had in fact come close to waging a regular military campaign once Angeles joined him. He told Angeles that once he took the offensive in 1919, he was willing to grant him a large degree of leeway in organizing the military campaign and the army.

At first glance, Villa's plan of going back to regular warfare and staging a major offensive against the Carrancistas in 1919 seemed reminiscent of his excessive optimism after every victory that he had secured in the past. According to one knowledgeable observer of the situation in Chihuahua, the federal forces in the state numbered 17,000 men, while Villa at the most led 3,000. Moreover, the federal troops were better supplied with ammunition, since Carranza had begun to set up his own ammunition plants.

Nevertheless, in spite of their numerical superiority, Carranza's forces in Chihuahua were beginning to reflect the same weaknesses that their Porfirian predecessors had shown in 1910–11. The Carrancista commanders in Chihuahua, Manuel Diéguez and Jesús Agustín Castro, were bitter rivals and could not agree on a joint plan for proceeding against Villa. Moreover, as one observer noted, the Carrancista forces in Chihuahua were also weakened by

the profiteering and wholly commercialized instincts and tendencies of their commanders who have no desire for fight . . . [and] the poor fighting quality of their men who, in many cases, are wretched Indians from the south as opposed to Villa's sturdy guerrillas, and whose pay so rarely reaches them in adequate quantity, [so] that they can have no desire to fight, must be vaguely discontented and certainly would be prepared to yield many recruits to the rebels from the very government ranks as an escape from the misery of their condition, if Villa can offer them anything better. The government cavalry in regard to the horses, is also in wretched shape and almost starved, presumably by the officers pocketing the funds destined for the forage with the result that this army is no longer a mobile force, and certainly not prepared to take up the pursuit of rebels who as their lives depend upon it, take care to have their horses in the best possible condition.[76]

An even greater advantage for Villa was that many of the defensas sociales were refusing to fight and laying down their arms. They had been an enormous help to the Carrancista authorities, but now, Patrick O'Hea, who reported on these events, noted,

On account of the cowardly desertion in moment of need by government troops of several "Defensas Sociales," notably at Parral where the armed townsfolk were left by the retreating government troops to conduct a gallant but unaided defense against Villa the other "Defensas Sociales" that were organized and existed as powerful allies in their own interest, and the government, have mostly laid down their arms and delivered them to the Villistas. The advantage accrued to the latter and against the government thereby cannot be exaggerated.[77]

Carranza's forces thus found themselves in a situation resembling that of their Porfirian predecessors, who similarly in 1910–11 had not been able to count on any significant help from the local population. O'Hea was pessimistic about the government's long-range prospects:

The day will arrive however when the government of necessity will have to withdraw from Chihuahua some considerable parts of the troops that it has amassed there, to Tampico, Veracruz, Puebla, Michoacan and the capital itself, on account of new trouble in some or more of these points and if by that time General Diéguez and Castro have not succeeded, as I fear they will not succeed, in crushing the Villa movement and reorganizing the state of Chihuahua, there will be the very great danger or rather the certainty that the Villa menace will increase and spread, the inability of the overwhelming forces to crush it being a victory for it.[78]

What further strengthened the Villista movement was the perception by many observers that the U.S. government was so disgusted with Carranza that it would be willing to support, not a Villa-led, but an Angeles-led movement, with Villa playing some kind of role in it. At very least, it was assumed that the United States would remain neutral in such a conflict.

Very real differences between Villa and Angeles emerged, however, with respect to two questions. One of these was completely unexpected for Angeles, while the other came as no surprise to him. Like many other former Maderistas, Angeles was convinced that Villa was as ardent a follower of the martyred president as he was. He was first surprised and then angered when during a conversation Villa was sharply critical of the dead president. Villa called Madero "dumb" for having signed the agreements of Ciudad Juárez and for not having shot Félix Díaz for having attempted his coup in Veracruz. Angeles sharply disagreed with this criticism of the man whom he considered the incarnation of the Mexican Revolution. "The first discussion," Angeles later related at his trial, "took place in Tosesihua when Villa called Madero an imbecile; I answered, our language got harsher and harsher until we shouted at each other. Villa's soldiers waited for him to order me to be hanged, which he did with all who contradicted him, but this did not take place. Once he had calmed down Villa told me, 'You are the first man who contradicts me and who has not died.'"[79]

The greatest point of contention between the two men was the attitude they should take to the United States. Villa was furious when he heard the speeches made by Angeles in the villages they captured praising the Americans. One evening when the two men were talking about the changes that were to take place in Mexico, Angeles described the new Mexico to Villa for an hour, stressing the need to reform the family and to return to the constitution of 1857, but also to establish better relations with the Americans. Villa answered, "Mi General, por lo que parece, usted se ha agringado. . . . Todo está bueno, menos que agringue usted a mi pueblo" ("General, as far as I can see, you have become gringoized. . . . Everything that you say is all right, except that you should not gringoize my people").[80]

These differences of opinion may partly explain Villa's decision to attack Ciudad Juárez, despite Angeles's urgent warning that if he did so, the Americans would cross the border and attack him (to which Villa flippantly replied that he had enough bullets to fight them off).[81] This fateful blunder would lead to a major defeat of Villa's forces, put an end to all his attempts to set up a regular army, force him back into the errant life of a guerrilla fighter, and lead to a final break with Angeles.

Villa's Defeat at Ciudad Juárez

It is not clear what motivated Villa to risk attacking Ciudad Juárez. Perhaps he wanted to put Angeles to the test. Since Angeles was constantly emphasizing the need for reconciliation with the Americans and implying that the United States might then change its attitude toward Villa, he perhaps wanted to see whether the Americans had indeed become less hostile to him than had been the case two years before, when Pershing entered Mexico in order to capture him. Logistical reasons may have contributed to Villa's decision. He explained to one of his subordinates that he urgently needed to feed his army, and that the only sources of food were located in large cities. Since Ciudad Chihuahua was too strongly garrisoned to be overrun, and Parral had already been captured by his troops, Ciudad Juárez, in view of the limited size of its garrison, was the best possible target. Perhaps, too, he became overconfident, as was usually the case with Villa after a victory. Not only had he captured Parral and destroyed a whole series of federal garrisons, he also had great contempt for the new commander in chief of the Carrancista forces in Chihuahua, Jesús Agustín Castro. Unlike his predecessor, Murguía, who had relentlessly taken the offensive against Villa, Castro was content to fortify himself in a few towns without ever taking offensive action. Villa thus felt relatively confident that if he attacked Ciudad Juárez, Castro would not send troops from Ciudad Chihuahua to strike at him from the rear.

The attack on Ciudad Juárez began on June 15, 1919. At first, it seemed to proceed as Villa hoped it would. He did not lead the attack, since he was feeling sick, but entrusted it to Martín López, his best lieutenant. With the same audacity and reckless courage with which he had stormed Santa Rosa hill during the siege of Ciudad Chihuahua, López stormed Ciudad Juárez from an angle that made it possible to shoot without hitting El Paso. His troops cut the barbed wire entanglements surrounding the town with pincers smuggled from the United States, and within a few hours, they were in control of the border city, the Carrancista garrison having retreated to nearby Fort Hidalgo.

López, however, was not Pancho Villa. He had neither the understanding nor the capacity that Villa always showed to maintain the rigid discipline of his troops. After the city was captured, the Villistas, unaccustomed after their long life as guerrilla warriors to the luxury that a city provided, dispersed into the streets of Ciudad Juárez looking to buy or plunder goods or simply attempting to enjoy a moment of respite. Due to a fluke, that respite would end in disaster.

In Fort Hidalgo, where the remnants of the Carrancista garrison had retreated, a scuffle broke out between two Carrancista units. One accused the other of cowardice for having left its flag in the city. Stung by this criticism, a small Carrancista unit decided to brave the Villistas, return to their headquarters, secure their flag, and thus show their courage. Instead of having to confront a huge Villista force as they had feared, they found that this force had dispersed, and when they began to fire on the individual soldiers they encountered, panic broke out among the Villistas, and they retreated in disorder from the city that they had attacked with such courage and for whose capture they had paid a high price in blood.

The retreat nearly cost Villa his life. Unaware of what was happening, he was proceeding to Ciudad Juárez in order to have a meal in a restaurant when he was suddenly confronted by a Carrancista unit, which until the last moment he had thought was one of his own. Emptying his pistols at the oncoming Carrancistas, Villa and the small group of men who were with him managed to flee and to return to their own lines.

But Villa was not about to give up. Once more he gave the orders to attack, and once more, after bloody fighting, his troops were able to occupy the city, and the Carrancistas once again retreated to Fort Hidalgo. Villa now prepared to storm the fort. At this point, Angeles's dire prophecies were fulfilled. The adjutant general had given permission to the commander of U.S. forces in El Paso to cross the border in case any Americans were wounded or killed in the fighting. On the morning of June 15, General James B. Erwin, the commander of the U.S. forces in El Paso, reported that

upon investigation by the district inspector . . . showing that shots undoubtedly coming from Villistas had been fired into El Paso; because of the wounding of several innocent persons residing in El Paso and of two American soldiers performing their duty on June 14th and 15th, under authority given me in your telegram . . . this date [I] ordered troops of my command to cross the border and disperse Villistas but on no account to undertake an invasion into Mexico. Troops of my command are now crossing the border to carry out this order. As soon as I have accomplished this and the safety of the citizens of El Paso is assured, troops will be withdrawn to this side of the border.[82]

Unable to face the superior firepower of the U.S. troops, Villa's men retreated from Ciudad Juárez.

For Angeles, the U.S. attack on Villa represented the collapse not only of his strategy but of all his dreams. "The situation is hopeless," he told Villa's secretary Jaurrieta, who had brought him over from the United States and was one of the few literate members of Villa's army. "The government in the White House will never accept Villa. Since my presence among you will have no effect whatsoever, I should return to American territory. But I shall never do that. Only death will put a period to my last revolutionary adventure. With all my heart I want to die."[83]

Angeles's despair increased even more when a last-ditch attempt at damage control with the Americans failed. Angeles sent Gómez Morentín, who had acted as Villa's unofficial and secret emissary to the United States, to see General Erwin in El Paso. Gómez Morentín's charge was to assure him that the Villistas were not anti-American and that they had done their best not to fire across the border—that in fact it was the Carrancistas who were responsible for the deaths of Americans. Erwin refused to have any dealings with Angeles's emissary, however, and turned him over to the U.S. immigration authorities, who immediately deported him back to Mexico.[84]

Whatever hesitation Angeles may have had about leaving Villa must have disappeared once he heard the threats that Villa was uttering against Americans. He may not have been overly impressed by Villa's often-repeated wish that God should grant him the occasion to "tickle" Wilson in his own way, but the threats issued against Americans in Chihuahua were much more concrete in nature. "After the Juárez fighting," the representative of the Mexican Northwestern Railroad reported to his chief, "Villa made every effort to capture the only American in the vicinity of Villa Ahumada, and told his men that they had his permission to kill any and all Americans encountered in future. He also told the Mexican people that if any of them were guilty of working for or doing business with Americans in future, he would return someday and kill them."[85]

It was the fear of being associated in people's minds and even being held responsible for Villa's anti-American actions that finally led Angeles to leave him. "One of the motives for my quarrel with Villa," Angeles later explained at his trial, "and that led to my separation from him was his hatred of the Americans."[86]

Villa never carried out his threats against Americans. There is no evidence of executions of Americans, and in an October 1919 proclamation to the American people, Villa stated that during the attack on Ciudad Juárez, he had done everything in his power to prevent any bullets from reaching the U.S. side. He said he wanted to prevent an international conflict with the United States, "a conflict that had no justification since the act [the attack of U.S. troops on Villa] was an expression of the policies of American military authorities but not that of the people of the United States."[87]

It was clear to Villa, after his initial fury had abated, that any massacre of Americans could only have disastrous consequences for him. At worst, it might provoke a renewed U.S. offensive larger than Pershing's expedition. Even if a renewed intervention did not occur, Villa's actions might drive American entrepreneurs out of Chihuahua and thus kill the goose that laid the golden eggs. Villa had become more and more dependent for his subsistence on forced loans and taxes imposed on the Americans.

The Villista offensive of 1918–19 had some traits in common with the Villista offensive of 1916–17, but there were also sharp differences between the two. Both in 1916–17 and in 1918–19, the corruption of and the atrocities committed by the Carrancista military created much support for Villa. In both cases the most formidable opposition that Villa had faced in his guerrilla struggle in Chihuahua, that of the defensas sociales, had been reduced to a minimum. In 1916–17, only a small number of such defensas existed, and in 1918–19, after the defensas sociales of Parral had been abandoned to their fate by the Carrancista garrison, many of the defensas had laid down their arms in return for promises of immunity from looting, reprisals, and forced conscription. By all accounts, Villa kept his promise. In both cases, Villa's campaign was financed by involuntary contributions by Americans. In 1916–17, Villa had occupied and looted American-owned properties in Chihuahua that had been spared until then. In 1918–19, his campaign was financed by forced loans from American investors and American mining companies. In both cases, attitudes toward the United States profoundly influenced the success of Villa's campaigns. In 1916–17, it was nationalism and anti-Americanism fueled by the presence of the punitive expedition in Mexico that greatly strengthened Villa's influence. In 1918–19, it was the perception by many Chihuahuans, fostered and strengthened by Angeles's pro-American speeches that, having won World War I, the United States would now turn on Carranza, and that possibly Angeles was the Wilson administration's candidate to replace the Mexican president. Thus Villa was seen as far stronger than he really was. That impression disappeared once the Americans crossed the border into Ciudad Juárez to attack Villa's forces, and from then on his campaign began to fizzle out.

The most significant difference between Villa's offensive in 1916–17 and his new offensive in 1918–19 was that his popular support in Chihuahua had shrunk significantly. In 1916–17, both Carrancista leaders and foreign observers believed that the vast majority of Chihuahuans still supported Villa. This was not the case in 1918–19. Increasing war-weariness and the atrocities committed by Villa had alienated important segments of the civilian population.

Angeles's Capture, Trial, and Execution

It is remarkable that although Villa tended to consider anyone who left his ranks as a deserter, traitor, and renegade and treated him accordingly, Villa and Angeles parted as friends. While it is not clear whether Angeles told Villa that this was a definite break—he left Villa's army at a time when Villa was carrying out one of the periodic dispersals of his troops into small bands in order to allow them to secure provisions and rest—Villa strongly suspected that Angeles would not return and warned him again and again that if he did not remain with him, the Carrancistas would capture and hang him. When Angeles insisted, Villa gave him a small escort to accompany him. The next seven months in Angeles's life, as he wandered with only a few men through the Mexican countryside, constantly hiding from the population and from Carrancista troops, remain a mystery. It is not clear why he so insistently refused to return to the United States, which offered comparative safety and even the possibility of renewed political activity. Was he afraid of being indicted for breaking the neutrality laws? There is no evidence that he entertained such fears, and the Americans would have had a hard time proving that he had plotted to organize a revolt in Mexico from U.S. soil. It is far more probable that it was due to his pride, to his refusal to acknowledge that his strategy had been a mistake. Was he looking for death, as he had implied to Jaurrieta, or, as he later stated to the court that tried him, was he attempting to make contact with revolutionary leaders in the south whom he hoped to join? There were a number of revolutionary leaders in southern and central Mexico who might very well have wanted Angeles's services and his prestige. In Morelos, Gildardo Magaña had taken the reins of the revolution after Zapata's death at the hand of the Carrancistas. An intellectual who lacked Zapata's prestige, Magaña might very well have thought of using Angeles to rally the remains of the demoralized Zapatistas. It is even more likely that other revolutionaries who had been closely allied to Villa—the Cedillo forces in San Luis Potosí or Tiburcio Fernández Ruiz, who had fought in the División del Norte and was leading the revolutionary anti-

Carrancista Mapache movement in the state of Chiapas—would have welcomed
Angeles with open arms. But it is not at all clear how Angeles could have traveled
south through hundreds of miles of Carrancista-controlled territory without being
recognized or captured. In fact, the best way for him to have gone south from
northern Mexico would have been to return to the United States and take a ship
from there to a rebel-controlled zone. Angeles did not do this. Perhaps, as he told
Jaurrieta, he really hoped to die and become a martyr. If that was the case, his
wishes were soon fulfilled.

In November 1919, Felíx Salas, one of Martín López's former commanders,
provided Angeles with what he told him was a secure hiding place, a cavern in a
remote part of Chihuahua. After Angeles had settled in there, Salas (whose primary loyalty had always been to Martín López, who had just died in battle) surrendered to the Carrancistas and for 6,000 pesos betrayed Angeles's whereabouts
to them.[88]

Gabino Sandoval, a former Villista who now headed the local defensa social,
set out with 40 men to capture Angeles. When they finally reached the Cerro de
los Moros, where Angeles and four other men were camped,

We first seized Nestor Arce and Antonio Trillo, who formed a kind of vanguard, and
since we surprised them, they could not resist. When Angeles and the other two saw
us, they fled, shooting at us, and after about a kilometer, we reached them. When I
approached Angeles, I holstered my gun and took out my lasso in order to stop Angeles's horse, whose description the prisoner we had taken in San Tome had given
me. When Angeles saw that I was right behind him, he turned to me with a pistol in
his hand, telling me that he was ready to give himself up if I did not kill him. Since I
told him I would not do so, he holstered his pistol and surrendered.[89]

By capturing Angeles instead of killing him, Sandoval had created a difficult
dilemma for the Carranza administration. They could not summarily execute him,
as they did with the three men of his escort, who were immediately shot after
their capture. Such an execution would have further discredited the Carranza administration in the eyes of Mexican and foreign public opinion. Its image had already suffered badly as a result of the assassination of Emiliano Zapata only a few
months before. That had been a particularly nasty affair. One of Carranza's local
commanders, Jesús Guajardo, had told Zapata that he and his forces wanted to
join him, and as a proof of his complete break with the Carrancistas, he had captured a town held by government troops and massacred all of the captured Carranza soldiers. Guajardo had then invited Zapata to meet him at the Hacienda
de Chinameca. When Zapata arrived, Guajardo's troops presented arms, ostensibly as a guard of honor to welcome the revolutionary leader, but at a sign from
their leader, they fired on the unsuspecting Zapata, killing him and his escort.

Angeles, Carranza decided, should be executed, but legally, after a public
court-martial. The trial would not only constitute proof that the Carranza government did not resort to assassinations but, its organizers obviously hoped,
would also help to discredit Angeles in the court of Chihuahuan public opinion.
The government hoped to gain a favorable audience for this trial by having it
take place in the state capital, where the majority of Chihuahua's middle classes,
who were hostile to Villa, were concentrated. In order to prevent any kind of

sympathy for Angeles from crystallizing inside Mexico or in the United States, he would not be subjected to a regular trial but to a court-martial, which was scheduled to last for only two days.

In many ways, Angeles's trial, the only major, public political trial to take place during the Mexican Revolution, was counterproductive for Carranza. The degree of sympathy that this former federal general, who was not even from Chihuahua, evoked among the Chihuahuan population was remarkable. To many, he was a symbol of the springtime of Villismo, with its message of hope and its brief period of both peace and prosperity in Chihuahua. He also seemed for many to be a symbol of humanity that both sides in the increasingly bloody civil war in Chihuahua had abandoned. The contrast between the behavior of the Villistas in Parral during Villa's latest occupation of the city, when Angeles was with him, and an earlier occupation by Villa was present in everyone's mind. His humanity and his relative poverty also stood in stark contrast to the behavior of all the Carrancista generals. In their sympathy and solidarity with Angeles, the lower and middle classes of Chihuahua fleetingly managed to recreate the unity that they had achieved briefly under Madero and González and for a somewhat longer time in the early days of Villismo.

Huge crowds, largely friendly, came to the railway stations of Parral and Ciudad Chihuahua to witness the arrival of Angeles and two fellow prisoners, Nestor Arce and Antonio Trillo. Committees of ladies (both the U.S. press and the Spanish-language press in El Paso strongly differentiated between *damas*, i.e., ladies, or middle- and upper-class women, and *mujeres*, or women of the lower classes) supplied Angeles with food, offered him clothing and even money, and interceded on his behalf with the Carrancista authorities.

The court-martial opened in Chihuahua's largest theater, the Teatro de los Héroes, on November 26, and its many seats were all filled, with thousands more waiting outside. It was presided over by one of Carranza's generals, significantly, not a northerner but a general from Veracruz, Gabriel Gavira.

Angeles was charged with insubordination and rebellion against the Mexican government and the Mexican constitution. He had designated a lawyer, Pascual del Avellano, to represent him, but Avellano (ostensibly for reasons of health) refused. Two court-appointed lawyers, Gómez Luna and López Hermosa, therefore assumed his defense. The lawyers' arguments were basically legal in nature. They questioned the jurisdiction of a court-martial, since Angeles had ceased to be a member of the military and thus was subject to civilian courts. They insisted that he had not fought actively against the government but only acted as an adviser to Villa, trying to restrain his excesses. They noted that when faced with capture, Angeles had surrendered voluntarily, thus he could not be accused of actively resisting his capture, which would have converted him into a rebel.

Angeles's real case was made by the accused himself, who, unlike his lawyers, did not limit himself to legal arguments. His defense was political in nature and can in fact be considered as a kind of ideological testament. "From the very outset of the trial," the U.S. consul in Chihuahua reported to the State Department,

Angeles' superiority to the generals who were trying him for his life was apparent to all. His strong personality and brilliant intellect soon won the sympathy and admiration of the crowd which immediately lost sight of the fact that he had been keeping company with Villa. Notwithstanding the formidable military display in the Theater of the Heroes, the audience once during Angeles' remarks burst out in applause and no doubt would have continued showing their approval had it not been for a warning from the presiding judge. In this connection it is rumored that General Diéguez had Angeles brought to the city for trial against his own best judgment and that when he realized the favorable impression he was making, and the grand opportunity that the public trial was affording a man with Angeles' talents to impress the multitude, he was sorry that he had taken the advice of others including it is rumored Governor Ortiz.[90]

Angeles's political defense made a strong impression on his listeners, because it struck some deep chords among Chihuahuans. Instead of denouncing Carranza and his government, Angeles called for peace and reconciliation. Again and again, he stressed that that had been the purpose of his return to Mexico. Among a people weary of years of war, turmoil, and revolution, this demand, not surprisingly, generated enthusiastic approval.

When his accusers sought to discredit him by asking how a man with his purported humanitarian ideals could join a leader who committed such "monstrosities" as Villa, he was able to turn their arguments around in a way that again responded to deep feelings among the Chihuahuans. "Villa is basically good," he stated. "It is circumstances that have made him bad."[91] Among these circumstances, Angeles cited the decision of the Carrancista administration not to allow those intellectuals who had supported Villa and who might have led him to moderate his conduct to return to Mexico. The idea that there was a good side to Villa was something that many Chihuahuans were inclined to believe. Many had witnessed the positive side of Villa when he had governed Chihuahua and commanded the División del Norte. Many of his former supporters, who for a time had included the majority of Chihuahua's population, did not want to reject their own past by believing that they had succumbed to a monster. The idea that the good side of Villa had predominated at the time when they supported him was a justification of their own conduct and sacrifices.

One of the two times that Angeles elicited a wave of applause, immediately quashed by the president of the court, was when he called for socialism and social justice. "When I went to the United States," he said,

I began to study socialism and I saw basically that this was a movement of fraternity and love between men of different parts of the world. Fraternity is a movement, as it has been, which for centuries has impelled society toward the welfare of the masses; those masses who are fighting, those masses who remain masses in all parts of the world. The poor are always downtrodden, and the rich care little or nothing about the needy; this is the reason why the masses are protesting. They are fighting because of the lack of equality with regard to the law. An Austrian communist has proven that if all men in the world would only work three hours per day, there would be much more wealth; the situation we have, though, is that there are those who work and those who eat well.

At this point, the transcript of the trial mentions strong applause. "This applause is not for me. It is for socialism, for the ideas of fraternity and love," Angeles said, "which are those that at the beginning inspired the members of the Convention of Aguascalientes, and even the constitutionalists."[92]

Angeles received most applause the only time he raised his voice in accusation, castigating those who had betrayed him, saying: "The ones who are now betraying me and have risen against me are the same men who attacked Columbus, who violated girls of thirteen or fourteen years, those who robbed and murdered; they are the same persons who were telling me, 'General, come to us in full confidence. We shall treat you with respect in the same way that you have always treated us. We shall give you all kinds of guarantees.'" The applause was so great that the president of the court threatened to expel all spectators from the room.[93]

Many of his listeners were convinced that Angeles was sincere when he condemned the atrocities committed by both Villistas and Carrancistas, since he could show that both during the period he fought in the ranks of the División del Norte and after he joined Villa in his last campaign, he had done everything he could to save the lives of prisoners. It is less clear what effect Angeles's strong pro-American declarations had on his listeners. Whatever negative effects these declarations may have had on Mexican nationalists were tempered, however, by Angeles's repeated assurance that the main reason he had returned to Mexico was to create the kind of unity that would prevent a U.S. intervention from taking place.

While Angeles was victorious in the political debate during the trial, there was another struggle going on beneath the surface, in which the Carrancistas prevailed. This was the fight for time. The Carrancistas were firmly determined to end the trial within two days, so as not to allow public opinion either in Mexico or in the United States to rally behind Angeles. It is significant that Diéguez, the military commander of Chihuahua, who officially had nothing to do with the trial, reported on every interruption, be it only for an hour, by telegram to headquarters in Mexico City. In a telegram marked "most urgent," he wired the *oficial mayor* of the War Department in Mexico City, Francisco Urquizo, that "at 1:45 in the afternoon the extraordinary court-martial was suspended . . . and resumed work one hour later so that during that time the participants could eat." One day later, in a telegram again marked "urgent," Diéguez announced to Urquizo that at 5:00 A.M. the court-martial had been suspended for five hours so that "the participants could rest."[94]

Interrupting a normal trial for an hour to allow the participants to eat or for four so that they could sleep would at best have been routine, scarcely worth reporting. In this case, these reports were wired to Mexico City in telegrams marked "most urgent" and "urgent," and Urquizo in the capital sent another telegram acknowledging the receipt of Diéguez's wire and giving his approval to the five hours(!!) that the judges as well as the accused had been allowed to rest.

Angeles, too, understood the importance of the time factor, and he spoke at length not only about his political program, his philosophical ideas, his appreciation of the international situation, but also about matters that could be considered trivial but that helped him to gain some valuable time. He insisted on the importance of dress for the population at large and described at length how he had been prevented from seeing a fellow general some years back because he was not properly dressed. Paradoxically, the greatest delay in the trial was not due to Angeles's efforts but to the case of one of the men who had been part of his escort and who was captured together with him: a common soldier, Antonio Trillo, brother of Villa's secretary. Trillo declared that he was a minor, only seventeen years old, and his defense lawyer called for the dismissal of all charges against him for that reason. The prosecution refused and attempted to prove that Trillo was eighteen. Since it was not ready to wait until a certificate of birth could be secured from Trillo's native town, doctors were summoned to examine Trillo in order to determine his age. Expert opinions by these doctors as to bone structure, growth factors, and so forth somewhat delayed the proceedings. The trial continued until 5:00 in the morning of November 25, and five hours later the court-martial met again, in a room once more filled with thousands of spectators, to pronounce sentence upon Felipe Angeles.

Few doubted what the sentence would be. Not only did Carranza want Angeles's death but the members of the court-martial had been carefully chosen for both their hostility to Villa and their readiness to order executions. According to one newspaper, Gabriel Gavira, the head of the court-martial, who had for a time been military commander of Ciudad Juárez, had carried out more executions there than any other of its military administrators, and he had the habit of doing so while a band played martial music. General Gonzalo Escobar had been wounded during Villa's attack on Ciudad Juárez; General Fernando Peraldi, Carranza's nephew, was so corrupt that by order of his uncle he had been removed from his native state of Coahuila and sent to Chihuahua; Pablo Quiroga, the last member of the court-martial, had been defeated by Villa in the battle of Villa Ahumada.[95]

The court-martial sentenced Angeles to death for having rebelled against the government and the constitution. It brushed aside all objections that it had no jurisdiction over the case, since Angeles was not a member of the federal army.

In legal terms, there was still a way out for Angeles. The Mexican constitution granted him the right to appeal to the Supreme Military Tribunal. This was fully understood by Diéguez, who, although he officially had nothing to do with the trial, wired Carranza's chief of staff, Urquizo, for instructions on how to proceed, saying: "It is nearly certain that the defenders of Angeles, based on section 5A of article 107 of the federal constitution will ask court-martial to suspend the execution of the sentence it will pronounce. I ask you to immediately send me the opinion of the Justice Department as to this matter." Urquizo, later one of Mexico's most successful writers, immediately wired Diéguez that in the opinion of the Justice Department, only the court-martial had jurisdiction over the matter, that it was not subject to revision by the Supreme Military Tribunal, and that regardless of any appeal, the sentence should be carried out immediately.[96]

It must have been clear to Urquizo that his instructions were an unmistakable violation of the Mexican constitution: when he did receive an appeal from the attorneys for Angeles's defense, he did not dare to use the argument that he had given Diéguez—namely, that the Supreme Military Court had no jurisdiction. Rather, he wired back to the defending attorneys that he could not act because he had not been officially notified of the sentence. Wires to the Supreme Court and to the Chamber of Deputies received the same bureaucratic replies. Neither the court nor the chamber could do anything, since both were in recess.

Although the supporters of Angeles had only had two days in order to mobilize public opinion, an unprecedented number of Chihuahuans as well as foreigners called on Diéguez and Carranza to suspend Angeles's execution. Diéguez at first attempted to blunt public opinion by telling a group of women who came to see him that he could not imagine that a man as cultivated and educated as Angeles would be executed.[97] And in spite of possible reprisals by the government, more than 1,000 Chihuahuans signed a petition to Carranza appealing for clemency.[98]

In the United States, Hopkins tried to intervene with U.S. authorities in favor of Angeles, while Arce, Trillo, and Angeles sent a wire to Carranza protesting their innocence and asking for a suspension of their sentence. "At this moment, at 11:30 of the morning, we are being judged by an extraordinary court-martial. We are accused of military rebellion, an offense we have not committed. We ask you, as an act of justice, should we be sentenced to the ultimate penalty, to order its suspension."[99]

In spite of his telegram to Carranza, Angeles expected no mercy from the Mexican president and he quietly prepared for his death. "My beloved Clarita," he wrote his wife,

I am now lying down sweetly resting. I hear the pious voice[s] of some friends who are sharing my last hours with me. . . . I am thinking with the greatest affection of you, of Chabela, of Alberto, Julio, and Felipe. I have had these same thoughts from the moment I became separated from you. I express my deepest wishes for your good health and for the happiness of Chabela. I have the great hope that my three sons will be full of love for you and for their country. . . . Tell them that I dedicate the last moments of life to the memory of all of you and that I send all of you an ardent kiss.[100]

It is significant that the only Mexican politician to whom he wrote during these last hours of his life was Manuel Calero, whom he thanked for having saved him from prison during the Huerta dictatorship.[101]

When a priest came to hear his confession, Angeles refused his offices, saying that although he was a Christian, he did not believe in confession. He elaborated on his philosophical opinions as to religion, and finally told him, "Rather than a confessor, a psychologist should have come here to study for the good of humanity the last moments of a man who loving life is not afraid to lose it."[102]

Angeles himself chose the spot for his execution. After embracing his lawyer Gómez Luna and calling for the reestablishment of peace in Mexico, he quietly faced the firing squad.

"The verdict of the court, condemning Angeles to death," the U.S. consul in Chihuahua reported, "was extremely unpopular in this district, so much so that it is probably not an exaggeration to say that from ninety to ninety-five percent of the people condemned its action and were firmly convinced that the court proceedings were a pretense as the military judges received their instructions from Mexico City through General Diéguez."[103] More than 5,000 Chihuahuans formed a huge funeral procession that accompanied Angeles's body to its grave. In an apparent gesture to appease public indignation at the trial, Arce and Trillo were not executed, and they were freed a short time later.

Villa's response to Angeles's execution was swift and bloody. Two days after the death of Angeles, Villa's troops fell upon the Carrancista garrison of Santa Rosalia and killed it to the last man.

PART FOUR

Reconciliation, Peace, and Death

CHAPTER NINETEEN

From Guerrilla Leader
to Hacendado

The Surrender

With the failure of the attack upon Ciudad Juárez and the departure of Angeles, a period of steep decline in Villa's military fortunes began. "At the present time Villa has not more than 350 men, who are badly demoralized, poorly clothed, with practically no ammunition," the manager of the Mexican Northwestern Railroad reported in July 1919, a few weeks after Villa's futile attack on Ciudad Juárez. This report may have been somewhat exaggerated, but José María Jaurrieta, Villa's secretary, also speaks of increasing demoralization among the Villistas. Desertions increased. One of Villa's lieutenants, Epifanio Holguin, left Villa to pursue a life of banditry at the expense of the Mexican Northwestern Railroad, threatening to destroy its bridges and tracks if it did not pay him protection money.[1]

A clearer manifestation of demoralization took place when Villa attacked the city of Durango, hoping to replenish his supplies there. In order to make sure that he would not be attacked from the rear while besieging Durango, he had instructed his commanders in the region, Ricardo Michel and José Galaviz, to destroy all railway tracks between Durango and Torreón, where a large contingent of federal troops was stationed. They did not obey his orders, and as his troops were making ready to storm Durango, troop trains laden with federal soldiers steamed into their rear.[2]

Villa's troops were now forced to a disastrous retreat, during which he suffered what he doubtless considered his greatest loss in all his years of guerrilla warfare: the death of the man who was practically his alter ego, Martín López. Villa openly wept when he heard the news. "What? What are you saying . . . ? Martín is dead . . . my loyal and courageous boy. . . . How can I have lost Martín, who was my favorite leader, in whom I had placed all my hopes as a warrior? He came to me when he was only eleven years old."[3] Villa lost not only López but most of his men, who deserted. It was one of López's lieutenants, Felíx Salas, who betrayed Angeles to the federal authorities.

The failure of Villa's last offensive, the increasing demoralization of his troops, led to a further alienation of Chihuahua's countrypeople from Villa and his movement. Villa now took steps he would never have contemplated in the heyday of his movement. In every village through which he passed, he now took several old men as hostages to ensure that the inhabitants would not denounce him to the authorities. Once he arrived at the next village, he would free the hostages but take new ones from among the inhabitants of the succeeding community .

The federal government felt that it was now finally in a position to destroy Villa. It sent one of its most experienced generals, Joaquín Amaro, with thousands of reinforcements to begin an offensive against him. Fortunately for Villa, the campaign against him was interrupted when large segments of the defensas sociales, as well as the federal troops in Chihuahua, instead of fighting Villa turned against his greatest enemy, Venustiano Carranza.

Carranza's term of office was set to expire in 1920. Since his regime had drafted and adopted the Mexican constitution of 1917, which specified that a president could not be reelected, Carranza could not and did not dare to become a presidential candidate for a second time. He did not want to relinquish power either, and so he persuaded his supporters to nominate Ignacio Bonillas, an obscure politician who had been Mexican ambassador to the United States, to succeed him. It was clear to everyone that Bonillas had no constituency of his own and would be entirely dependent on Carranza.

Bonillas's opponent in the forthcoming election, by contrast, had an enormous constituency. He was Alvaro Obregón, who had held his great ambition in check until Carranza's term of office expired, and who was by no means ready to be shunted aside. When it seemed that Carranza would arrest Obregón and carry out truncated elections, the state legislature of Obregón's home state of Sonora revolted in April 1920, declared Carranza deposed as president, named the Sonoran governor, Adolfo de la Huerta, as provisional president, and charged him with holding new elections within three months. The revolt found the support of the vast majority of Mexico's military leaders. Carranza attempted to flee to Veracruz in order to set up his government there, but he was murdered on the way in the town of Tlaxcalontongo.

When the armed conflict between Carranza and Obregón broke out, Villa's representative in the United States, Miguel Díaz Lombardo, and probably Villa himself, had some illusions about a long-drawn-out conflict between the two sides that would radically weaken them, thus relieving the pressure on Villa and even allowing the Villistas to take the offensive again. "It is my opinion that we should allow the Obregonistas and Carrancistas to fight and debilitate themselves," Díaz Lombardo wrote to another Villista representative, Ramón Puente, "and then take advantage of the opportunity thus afforded to finish them."[4]

It was this illusion that led Díaz Lombardo to advise Villa to reject an offer by two representatives of the Sonoran rebels, General Salvador Alvarado and Ramón Denegri. Díaz Lombardo wrote that the representatives "have come to see me and asked me to request the cooperation of General Villa . . . I have however addressed a letter to the general advising of their request, and then proceeded to caution him as to the inadvisability of such an alliance to even his political prestige, since one of our principal points of attack is the constitution of 1917, which is sustained by the Obregonistas and their Plan of Agua Prieta." Nevertheless, Díaz Lombardo did not reject their offer out of hand. He hoped that by holding out the promise of cooperation by Villa with their faction "to force them to confess that General Villa is not a bandit, but on the contrary that he is a valuable factor, by which admission from them our cause would gain much morally here and there."[5]

Whatever hopes Villa and his supporters may have had about a bloody, long-drawn-out civil war between his enemies soon proved to be an illusion. With a minimum of bloodshed, the Sonoran rebels took control of Mexico.

After the death of his most implacable enemy, Carranza, his forces plagued by desertions, and faced with increasing difficulties in securing money and arms, Villa was ready to make a deal with the new Mexican government. The government, however, seemed extremely reluctant to offer any deal that might be acceptable to Villa. On the contrary, it increased the price on Villa's head to 100,000 pesos and instructed Amaro to take the offensive against Villa.[6] Amaro was known for both his opposition to Villa and his ruthlessness.

Villa nevertheless twice made overtures to the government. First, he approached one of the most powerful generals in the new administration, the Sonoran Plutarco Elías Calles. Villa had clashed with Calles some years earlier, when he had supported Maytorena against him. Now Villa proposed that he and Calles should meet to discuss terms. Calles himself refused to attend such a conference, giving reasons of health, but he sent an emissary to negotiate with Villa. The conditions for surrender that Villa seems to have suggested were that his soldiers should be given a hacienda so that they could work land on their own, while he should be appointed either commander of rurales of the whole state of Chihuahua or at least of its southern region, which was closest to his heart. The troops with which he declared he was ready to maintain law and order in the region were his own men. Calles rejected these conditions, suggesting instead that Villa, with a small group of men, should settle somewhere in Sonora, far from his native haunts. Had he accepted, Villa would have been forced to go to a completely unfamiliar environment, where he had no supporters, and where he would have been at the mercy of his erstwhile enemies.[7]

Villa nevertheless did not give up his hope of coming to some kind of an arrangement with the government. Next he approached his old enemy Ignacio Enríquez, who had become an important political force in Chihuahua since he had mobilized the state's defensas sociales in favor of Obregón. The two men scheduled a meeting, which ended even more disastrously than Villa's negotiations with Calles. Not only did Enríquez reject Villa's conditions, after the negotiations, since Villa was on hand, he planned to attack him, destroy his forces, and if possible kill him. Villa, who had no confidence in Enríquez, had anticipated such a move. He had set up a dummy camp, lit by campfires, and hidden his men all around it. When Enríquez's defensas sociales charged into the empty camp, they were decimated by Villa's riflemen.[8]

In a bitter vein, Villa now wrote to Díaz Lombardo that he saw no difference between the new government and Carranza, and that he would continue to fight them:

I've seen the whole affair only as the idea of assassinating one master for the purpose of setting up another in his place by means of a dirty coup d'état [*cuartelazo*], which brings shame to every honest Mexican. In a word it is a case of "get out of the road so that I can get in it," because the gentlemen have enough bayonets to override law and justice.

I and all the persons who accompany me, who have never made common cause with coups, because we always uphold the dignity of honorable Mexicans, we ask your valued opinion and that of all our good friends who are known to you as to what road we should follow without staining the honor of our beloved country.[9]

Within a few weeks, Villa again changed his attitude to the new government and its provisional president, Adolfo de la Huerta, and made peace overtures to him. Villa had realized, and was attempting to utilize for his own ends, the fact that Mexico's new rulers were deeply divided as to the policy they should pursue toward him. Villa's most powerful opponent, who wanted no compromise with him, was his old nemesis, soon to be Mexico's president, Alvaro Obregón. He was in full agreement with the government military leaders in Chihuahua, Amaro and Enríquez.

The most important proponent of coming to an arrangement with Villa was Mexico's provisional president, Adolfo de la Huerta. Not only did he hope to gain the prestige that pacifying northern Mexico and an agreement with Villa would bring him, he probably also hoped that such a move might finally win the support of the U.S. government, which until then had refused officially to recognize his regime. In addition, unlike Obregón or Calles, de la Huerta had never directly clashed with Villa. On the contrary, in 1913, on the eve of Villa's return to Mexico, de la Huerta had helped him and thus never incurred Villa's enmity. Since de la Huerta had political ambitions of his own, he may very well have assumed that if they came to an agreement, Villa might repay him at some future date by granting him political and perhaps even military support.

It is not clear why de la Huerta did not choose an official representative, but entrusted the task of contacting Villa to a Mexican newspaperman, Elías Torres, who had gone to school with his secretary of state, Cutberto Hidalgo. Torres told de la Huerta that he knew men in El Paso who enjoyed Villa's confidence and could put him in touch with the revolutionary leader. De la Huerta seems to have appointed him as a kind of semi-official emissary. Torres had in fact established contact with Francisco Taboada, one of Villa's compadres. After many difficulties—Amaro was informed of his mission and was extremely unsympathetic— and a long and grueling journey, Torres finally met Villa on July 2, 1920, on the Terrazas' hacienda of Encinillas, which Villa had occupied. There Villa wrote an official letter to de la Huerta, spelling out in great detail his terms for making peace with the government. His first condition was that the government should grant him a hacienda, "which should not be destined for the sole use of General Villa but to be divided among the troops—that is, among the leaders, officers and soldiers under his command, and for the widows and orphans of those who have died in the state of Chihuahua during the revolution." Villa insisted "that the property of which he was thinking has not paid contributions to the state for 30 years, so that it will be very cheap for the government to acquire it."[10] For himself, Villa asked that he be granted command of a rural police force of 500 men, whose task it would be to put an end to banditry in the state of Chihuahua. His third condition was that free elections for governor were to be held in the state. Villa declared that he would be loyal to whatever national government emerged from the forthcoming elections; in other words, he asserted his loyalty to Obregón. He also declared that he "forgave all his enemies" and would punish no one who had turned against him.

As a precondition for making any deal with the government, Villa demanded that not only de la Huerta but his three most important generals—Obregón, Calles, and Hill—should sign such an agreement. These proposals clearly reveal Villa's thinking at the time. He had not asked for a hacienda for himself alone. He was still interested in the agrarian problem, but only insofar as it affected his men or their widows and orphans. Unlike the Zapatistas, who, when they made their peace with the government, demanded respect for land reform throughout the state of Morelos, Villa made no social demands and said nothing about the division of the lands of the large haciendas, which he had so strongly advocated some years before. Had he lost all interest in the land question? Had he become disillusioned with the Chihuahuan peasants who had turned against him, or did he feel too weak to demand such reforms?

Villa's second concern was both to ensure his own security by remaining in control of a large troop of armed men and to continue to exercise a decisive influence on the state of Chihuahua, thus largely rendering meaningless that part of his peace proposal where he stated that he would not interfere or participate in Chihuahuan politics.

De la Huerta was quite willing to grant land to Villa's soldiers, although he limited their number to 250 men, and to give them military pay for one year. He refused to accede to Villa's demand that he exercise some kind of military role in Mexico, but he acknowledged Villa's need for protection. To satisfy that need, he offered Villa the hacienda of Canutillo, which his old crony of bandit days, Urbina, had occupied. He also offered Villa the right to keep 50 men of his escort there, who would be allowed to retain their arms and who would be paid by the government. Villa, he insisted, would have to retire completely to private life.

Both Calles and Hill agreed to countersign whatever agreement de la Huerta reached with Villa, but the most important general of them all, Alvaro Obregón, did not. This created a delicate situation for the negotiations, which suffered an even greater blow from the publicity-seeking of Torres, who unilaterally revealed Villa's terms to the press,[11] thus giving the impression that de la Huerta had agreed to grant Villa military command in Chihuahua. A wave of indignation took hold of some of Mexico's generals—in an interview with an American newspaper, Amaro threatened to rise against the government if Villa's conditions were met. De la Huerta was forced at least temporarily to end his negotiations with Villa. In an official statement, the secretary of war declared that Villa's conditions would never be met and that Torres was not an official emissary of the government.[12] Within a few days, under the influence of Obregón, de la Huerta would revise his attitude even more drastically.

Villa had agreed to meet Torres again in the town of Saucillo, so that Torres could bring him de la Huerta's reply. The two had also agreed that as long as the negotiations lasted, Villa would not be attacked by government troops. Villa, in turn, had stated that he would refrain from any military action during this same period. On July 17, Amaro received instructions from Mexico City to suspend hostilities with Villa. On that same day de la Huerta received a scathing telegram from Obregón. "Please tell me," Obregón wired Mexico's provisional president,

if the government that you preside over has effectively entered into negotiations with the bandit Villa. In all sincerity I want to state that such negotiations would be the greatest moral defeat for the present administration since in order to be accepted by Villa, their basis would have to be his impunity for all the crimes that he has committed; both here and in our neighboring country, the news that the government wants to make a deal with Villa has caused an extremely bad impression. As the leader of a political party that is calling for morals and for justice, I would like to most respectfully protest against any pact with Villa, since it would be in conflict with the principles that our party has stated since the beginning of this struggle.

Obregón emphasized that Mexico's army would never again accept Villa in its ranks. Obregón warned de la Huerta of unpredictable events in Chihuahua owing "to the painful impression that this affair is making on the military leaders who are loyal to the government."[13]

The next day Obregón was even more emphatic in a second wire to de la Huerta. He told the provisional president that an agreement with Villa might precipitate a dangerous conflict with the United States. If the Americans were to demand Villa's extradition because of his attack on Columbus, de la Huerta's administration would be faced with an insoluble dilemma. It could either break its word to Villa or it would be "justly accused of complicity with him." Obregón raised the specter of a possible uprising by a number of generals against de la Huerta's government if an agreement with Villa were signed. He quoted an interview Amaro had given American newspapermen in which he had said that if there was a treaty with Villa, he would "resign rather than to continue to serve the government." Obregón continued: "As far as I know, the majority of the leaders who have been outstanding in their loyalty to the principles of our cause share Amaro's feelings."

Obregón had heard that de la Huerta had sent a letter to Villa in which he had outlined possible terms for a peace agreement. He warned de la Huerta "that Villa will obtain a great deal if he is in possession of a letter from you and soon it will be published and commented in the press of our neighboring country, giving him an importance that he should not have."[14] De la Huerta caved in. He ordered one of his generals, Gonzalo Escobar, to ask Torres to return a letter that de la Huerta had written to Villa, but that had not yet been delivered, and at the same time he ordered Amaro "to activate the persecution [of Villa] so as to secure his complete extermination."[15]

Torres now showed himself to be an honest negotiator. Fearing that an unsuspecting Villa, whom he had assured that the government would not proceed against him as long as negotiations lasted, might be killed by the treachery of federal troops, Torres sent him a warning. Villa retreated from Saucillo.[16]

Villa now realized that the Mexico City administration was divided about what to do with him. He felt that the only way to force the government's hand was to make it clear to the Sonoran leadership that if they continued the war against him, they would pay a higher price than they had imagined. Once again he showed his capacity to survive what was at first glance a situation that offered no way out. He decided to transfer his operations to the state of Coahuila. Unlike neighboring Chihuahua, from 1916 onward, Coahuila been spared the horrors of civil war and had managed an impressive economic recovery. He would thus be able to achieve what had become increasingly difficult in war-ruined Chihuahua: to replenish his supplies by taking whatever he wanted from the thriving Coahuilan haciendas. He would also threaten one of the wealthiest regions of Mexico with economic devastation. In the process, the new Mexican government might be seen in the United States as incapable of reestablishing order and controlling the whole country and thus considered unworthy of diplomatic recognition. By leaving Chihuahua, he would also be leaving the jurisdiction of the federal generals most hostile to him.

In logistical terms, a march from Chihuahua to Coahuila would put Villa's capacities as a leader and organizer to the test. The two states were separated by the Bolsón de Mapimi, a desert stretching over 700 miles, with practically no water. Villa's soldiers would remember the march to Coahuila as their most horrendous experience. Some died, others went mad for lack of water, and many of their horses died en route. Once they reached Coahuila, however, they felt as if they had come into the Garden of Eden. The state had been spared guerrilla fighting; it was prosperous, and its haciendas were full of horses, cattle, and food. The Villistas were able to replenish their supplies before falling on the city of Sabinas, which they occupied without great difficulty and from whence Villa wired de la Huerta that he was now again ready to resume negotiations. This time he asked for an official military representative, the one general in Chihuahua in whom he had confidence, Eugenio Martínez.[17] In the eyes of the British vice-consul in Torreón, Patrick O'Hea, Villa's occupation of Sabinas was the smartest thing that he could have done:

Their [the Villistas'] arrival in force at a point where they completely dominated one of the most important arteries of communication with the American border, and from which if so inclined they could commit depredations of a most important order through that district and particularly in regard to the coal fields which are completely at their mercy must have constituted a delicate and difficult problem for the government which may have understood that Villa was virtually confessed by his own actions to be a beaten man, yet could in his death struggle inflict untold material damage and vitally affect the prestige of the government itself in a most important and flourishing district that at last has begun to forget their losses that were caused there of old by the revolution.

In other words, Villa, by a clever stroke, placed himself in a position to virtually be able to dictate terms to the government, a circumstance which undoubtedly inclined the president to the acceptance of a truce, and to the making of peace with Villa in a way that will provoke much chagrin and disgust among the strictly military element of the ruling regime.[18]

O'Hea had clearly stated the dilemma in which de la Huerta now found himself. On one hand, if renewed civil war should engulf the prosperous state of Coahuila, located on the U.S. border, not only would the de la Huerta administration suffer great economic losses, but the new, interventionist Republican administration in Washington might be convinced that the only way to reestablish order in Mexico was once more to send U.S. troops against Villa. On the other hand, if de la Huerta signed an agreement with Villa, he would have to confront Obregón and the threat of a military uprising. Fortunately for de la Huerta, he managed to persuade two of the most important Sonoran generals, Plutarco Elías Calles and Benjamin Hill, to agree to make peace with Villa. The terms de la Huerta offered Villa were those that had already been contained in Torres's letter, although they were now somewhat broadened. In return for Villa's agreement to retire to private life, the government granted him for his own use the hacienda of Canutillo and an escort of 50 men, chosen by Villa and paid by the government. It agreed to give land and pay not just to 250 but to nearly 800 soldiers of Villa's army.

Villa's troops were to proceed to the Anglo-American hacienda of Tlahualilo (it is not clear why this place was chosen, and the British consul was incensed over this decision), where all Villa's soldiers except his escort were to lay down their arms, receive their first half year's pay, and secure title to lands. When he heard the news of the signing of this agreement, Obregón was furious. In a telegram to Hill and Serrano, Obregón unmistakably stated his opposition to any kind of treaty with Villa, calling such an agreement contrary "to the dignity of the government and of the nation." He offered to assume the leadership of a renewed campaign against Villa himself. Citing all the crimes that he felt Villa had committed, apart from his attack on Columbus, such as "the fate of the Herrera family . . . [and] the federal soldiers who lost their ears or who were castrated by Villa," he wrote ominously: "I am convinced that there is no authority in the country that has the right to come to an agreement with Villa that forgets his past and prevents present and future courts from demanding full accounting from him."[19]

Obregón refused to co-sign the agreement, which Villa had requested as a precondition for making peace with the government. Nevertheless, Villa went ahead and signed. It was now Obregón who faced a dilemma. If he publicly repudiated the treaty, as he had threatened in his wire to Hill and Serrano, not only might Villa take up arms again, but Obregón would find himself in the disagreeable posture of being the one man who refused to make peace. Furthermore, public disagreement between de la Huerta and him might precipitate a government crisis, destabilize the new regime, prevent U.S. recognition, and perhaps even provoke U.S. intervention. Thus, in spite of his misgivings, Obregón told de la Huerta that he would approve "the solution that the present government will give to this matter."[20] While he refused to co-sign the agreement or to write Villa personally, Obregón unofficially sent a message through Raúl Madero that he would not oppose the treaty.[21]

In spite of Obregón's refusal officially to ratify the peace agreement, Villa sent the man who had defeated him in battle and whom he had considered his greatest enemy a letter written in surprisingly obsequious language. "I want to tell you," he wrote on July 29,

that until a few days ago in my heart I believed that I was your personal enemy. But since a few days ago I learned that Raúl Madero had a message from you to me I have completely changed my opinion and I want to become your friend, although I do not know if you would not be ashamed of my friendship. My duty as a good patriot is to conciliate everyone in order to retire to private life without harming anyone, since I want to put the insignificant prestige that I still enjoy in our republic at your disposal, since a man who loves his country and his race must show this by concrete acts. . . . If you are ashamed of being my friend, since I am not worth anything, I hope that you will be so good as to tell me, "I do not want to be your friend." A brother of your race speaks to you with his heart.[22]

It took two months for Obregón to respond:

I had refused to respond to your two preceding letters since I doubted your sincerity in wishing to lay down your arms in order to dedicate yourself to a life of work and I even thought that the government acted ingenuously in this case; but now since facts have shown your firm resolution to withdraw completely from every military and political action without listening to the insidious advice of many men who in your shadow have attempted to obtain personal advantages, I want to write you in order to tell you very clearly that you can be sure that when the change of government takes place on December 1, you will continue to enjoy all the guarantees that the present provisional government has given you, and I want to congratulate you for your frank wish to carry out every sacrifice in order to restore peace to the country.[23]

The U.S. administration voiced its satisfaction with these agreements, since Mexico seemed finally to have been pacified. It did not demand that the Mexican government punish Villa for his attack on Columbus.

The only significant objection to the peace treaty between Villa and the government came from Great Britain, where the secretary of state for war, Winston Churchill, sharply protested. In a secret communication to the Foreign Office, he wrote:

I observe from the telegram from Mexico of the 29th of last month that the question of the British government demanding that proceedings should be taken against General Villa for the murder of Mr. Benton in 1914 is now raised. I hope this brutal murder of a British subject will not be allowed to drop out of sight. I took an interest in the case at the time and have never forgotten it during the war. I felt sure an opportunity would occur of bringing this murderer to justice. One of the true signs of a great nation is the care and patience with which it pursues just claims in regard to the lives and safety of its subjects. I earnestly trust that everything possible will be done.[24]

One of Churchill's failings had always been to overestimate the power of the British empire, and the Foreign Office officials dealing with Churchill's letter were very conscious of that fact. "If Villa is granted pardon, Britain can do nothing," one of the officials commented. "The Mexican government is more afraid of Villa than of Great Britain." "Yes," another official added, "but I should be disposed to add that His Majesty's government would deplore a free pardon for the murderer (unless our hobnobbing with a bunch of murderers in Moscow is held to preclude us from taking up this attitude)."[25]

The British chargé d'affaires in Mexico, Cunard Cummins, was now placed in the disagreeable position of having somehow to salvage the prestige of the British empire in the Benton case. On the one hand, he tried to defuse the anger of Churchill and other British officials by stating that Villa had not really murdered Benton in cold blood. There had been a violent altercation between the two men, and when Benton sought to take out his handkerchief, Fierro had thought he was reaching for his pistol and shot him. Villa, in conversations with Cummins, had regretted his action and even given some money to Benton's widow.[26]

Cummins proposed to de la Huerta that he should go and see Villa, so that the latter could apologize for the killing of Benton. "The president begged me with some agitation not to go and see Villa. He was more than distrustful. He would imagine that the government were merely getting him in their power with the object of treacherously making him pay for his crimes. He trusted that I would not take a step which might upset everything and set this man loose again, preying on innocent people." Cummins had no choice but to comply. The one concession the British were able to extract from the Mexican government was that compensation would be paid to Benton's widow.[27]

Villa's overland march from Sabinas to Tlahualilo had more the making of a triumphal parade than the retirement of a defeated leader. In most villages people came to greet Villa—the dark side of his character had not been manifested in Coahuila as it had in Chihuahua—and he went to visit his old friend Raúl Madero, with whom relations seem to have been excellent, even though Madero had left him in 1915 and called for his resignation. He refused to give any answers to the many newspapermen who had come to Tlahualilo asking him to explain why he had made his peace with the government. He did speak at length to an old acquaintance (although anything but a friend), the British consul in Torreón, Patrick O'Hea. "The man is slightly aged since last I met him in the early part of the year 1914," O'Hea described Villa, "but is still absolutely in his prime, stouter and heavier than of old."

He told O'Hea that "patriotism and the fear of probably provoking difficulties with the United States . . . had induced him at last to enter into terms with a government that could never have conquered him with force of arms." Villa was quite open with O'Hea when "he gave it clearly to be understood that he had no greater faith in the personality of the men constituting the present governing regime than in that of those against whom he had been fighting for many years and he was decidedly convinced that his country was not being best served by them." But he insisted that he would not rise against the new government. "On the other hand he repeated the danger of American intervention was such that he now saw it to be his patriotic duty not to overthrow any more Mexican governments no matter how poor their quality might be."

O'Hea's report on Villa was a mixture of sarcasm and reluctant admiration. After describing Villa's professions of love for his fellow man, O'Hea commented, "It is true that his profession of extreme humanitarianism suffered somewhat by his involuntary confession of having caused the death, in his estimation, of some 50,000 people, but this was explained away by the fact of the loss of so much human life having been necessary for the eternal welfare of his country." O'Hea was even more sarcastic when he reported that "there were some particularly wild flights of fantasy for he declared that he governed and controlled his officers and men by the theory and practice of love and forgiveness, so that whereas often they served him in a deficient way, he had always found that the supreme virtue in this world was forgiveness and by the exercise of it controlled his brave troops."

Having said all this, O'Hea could not disguise his admiration for Villa's intelligence and cunning. "[Villa's] raid into the state of Coahuila across arid wastes from the state of Chihuahua to which he could not return in safety in the face of an armed force that might contest his passage, represented as much a last desperate resource adopted by him when all other avenues of escape had been closed, as a move that, at the end of his outlaw career, proved once more the extreme astuteness and native intelligence of the man, in playing the one card that was left to him with such admirable skill and success." Yet O'Hea was extremely skeptical that Villa would refrain from armed actions against the government. "It is the universal opinion throughout the north that whatever the advantages obtained by the government by accepting the surrender, they are really outweighed by the consideration that Villa's surrender is equally or more potentially dangerous than Villa in the field."[28]

In fact, O'Hea was wrong. Throughout his last years, Villa refrained from participating in any of the many uprisings that the new Obregón administration faced. Whether he would have risen in the greatest revolt against Obregón, that of 1923, remains an open question.

Mexico Under Obregón

The administration of Alvaro Obregón was the last Mexican government in the twentieth century to take power through a violent coup and the first since the outbreak of the revolution that was able to consolidate its power and establish control over most of the country. The contradictions of this revolution are perhaps best illustrated by the disparity of opinions among foreign observers about the new Mexican government. For some American businessmen and politicians, obsessed by the Bolshevik revolution in Russia, the Mexican revolutionaries were nothing but hidden Bolsheviks, whose final aim was the establishment of a regime not much different from that which Lenin and his supporters were installing in Russia. For others, such as Spanish writer Blasco Ibáñez, the Mexican revolutionaries were not revolutionaries at all but a pack of thieves replacing another pack of thieves that had ruled the country prior to 1910.[29]

These contradictory views of the Mexican revolution reflected the contradiction between the radical program embodied in the constitution of 1917 and a much more conservative practice. Such contradictions are inherent in all revolutions. A major difference between the Mexican and Bolshevik revolutions and the classic Latin American coup was the fate of the traditional elite. In Russia, the traditional political, social, and economic elite was completely eliminated in economic and political terms and physically had been mostly killed or exiled. In a classic Latin American coup, the elite have tended to survive, with the exception of the outgoing political leadership. In Mexico, developments differed from both of these scenarios. Unlike in Russia, a great part of the prerevolutionary economic elite survived in Mexico, although it suffered a great transformation in the process. Among the foreign elite, European investors and entrepreneurs had been greatly weakened, while their American counterparts achieved a supremacy that they had never enjoyed before. Within the group of American investors and entrepreneurs, great changes had also taken place. Small and middle-level enterprises had not been able to survive the revolutionary storm and had largely sold their holdings to large American companies, which now dominated the economic scene in Mexico to a far greater degree than ever before.

The Mexican industrial and urban elite had not suffered much from the revolution, but the country's hacendado class had been greatly weakened. Although they seem to have regained control of most estates in the country, some had lost their properties to revolting peasants—especially in Morelos—while others had to share not only power but income with the new revolutionary elite. They had lost much of their traditional political power both to the new political and military elite and to militant peasants, who were organizing themselves in many parts of Mexico in the 1920s.

In contrast to the situation in Latin American countries after a typical military coup, not only Mexico's political elite but the whole of its political power structure, as well as the old army, had practically disappeared in the years of revolutionary turmoil. The judges, policemen, jefes políticos, and Porfirian army of the Díaz period were gone for good. They had been replaced by local authorities who often refused to submit to centralized control and by an enormous army frequently primarily loyal to regional warlords.

This new and complex reality led to constantly shifting positions, to a kind of zigzag policy by the new Obregón administration. On one hand, it feared U.S. military intervention and desperately wanted U.S. recognition and support, especially since the United States had refused to recognize the new Obregón administration. On the other hand, for political and ideological reasons, it could not afford to meet the main demand of the Americans, which was the abolition of the constitution of 1917. Nor was it possible for the Mexican government, in view of its desperate economic situation and the lack of new American investments, to refrain from increasing taxes on American property. This, of course, provoked howls of protest from Washington.

Obregón's attitude toward the army was equally contradictory. On one hand, it was the army that had brought him to power; Obregón was the greatest military leader the revolution had produced. On the other hand, not only did many other revolutionary generals envy him his power and reputation, Obregón simply did not have the means to maintain the huge army he had inherited from the revolution. Once he began to demobilize soldiers, however, they and their commanders became prone to revolt. With the shifting loyalty of many of its members, the revolutionary army was too weak a basis upon which to maintain his power and to support his efforts to create a strong new centralized Mexican state. Obregón felt that the only way to consolidate the state was to arm contingents of peasants and industrial workers whose loyalty he had secured, who would serve to counteract rebellious tendencies in the army. This necessity in turn forced him into a new set of contradictory policies. Both by conviction and by personal practice, Obregón and the group that supported him were avowed capitalists. Obregón had become a millionaire during the revolution by cornering the chickpea market in Sonora. He did not believe in socialism or in land reform. He seems to have shared the opinions of both Madero and Carranza that radical land reform might very well destroy the Mexican economy and lead to a return to subsistence agriculture. Yet in order to gain peasant support for his regime, he had no choice but to begin a limited program of land division. To gain the support of labor in his struggle with military uprisings, he gave increasing power to the unions but made sure that the government controlled them.

In view of the complex situation it faced, the constant shifts in the policies of the Obregón administration are not difficult to understand. One day Obregón would make nationalistic pronouncements against the United States, and a short time later he would make substantial concessions to American companies. In one region of Mexico, Obregón might arm peasants to counter a military coup and give them land to retain their allegiance, while in another part of the country, he might order his army to expel peasants occupying hacienda lands. While in some cases his administration supported strikes by industrial workers when they were led by unions loyal to him, in other cases he used the same energy to break strikes. Similar contradictions were characteristic of the policies of both governors and local officials. This was certainly the case with respect to the man who governed Chihuahua in the period that Villa resided in Canutillo: Villa's old enemy, Ignacio Enríquez. Even before Obregón assumed national power in 1920, Enríquez had reflected the contradictory nature of his leader's relationship to the lower classes of society. When he first became Carrancista governor of Chihuahua in 1916, Enríquez had immediately begun to return the confiscated estates to their former owners and had not even remotely considered setting up an agrarian commission in his native state. But paradoxically he had always been able to establish close relations with the lower classes of society, first when he commanded one of the Red Battalions and later when he became the organizer of the defensas sociales. These contradictions continued into his governorship after 1920. During his first two years in office, up to 1922, Enríquez not only refused to pass any agrarian law in his state but became involved in a complex scheme to sell off the huge Terrazas estates to an American operator, A. J. McQuatters. In his last two years in office, he made a radical turnabout and implemented the first agrarian law in the history of the state, which led to a widespread division of lands. This change of attitude by both Enríquez and Obregón toward the peasantry was no coincidence. It was a direct result of the revolution and the changes in mentality it had brought forth in the Mexican countryside. All over the country, militant peasant unions were emerging, demanding the implementation of the reforms that the constitution of 1917 had promised. In Chihuahua in 1922 and 1923, congresses of peasants met to organize and coordinate their demands for land reform in the state, and they exercised a strong influence on the policies of Governor Enríquez.

Villa in Canutillo

There is no evidence that in the first two years after making peace with the government and settling down in Canutillo, Villa showed any interest in participating in either national, regional, or local politics, or attempted to establish political contacts with former friends and associates. His main interests seem to have been to remain on good terms with the government, to develop his estate in Canutillo, to "put some order" into his complex family life, and to protect himself from assassination.

The transition from war to peace after ten years of revolutionary turmoil proved to be a difficult if not impossible undertaking for many of Mexico's revolutionary generals. Very few were either willing or able to return to civilian life, although many of them had accumulated large sums of money during the revolution. Most of them either retained their military functions as part of Obregón's governing coalition or rose in arms against him, as did Manuel Diéguez, Enrique Estrada, Francisco Murguía, Lucio Blanco, and Manuel Chao, to name but a few of the most prominent among them, and with the exception of Estrada ended up in front of a firing squad. Villa was one of the few exceptions who showed himself to be as successful in a civilian career as in a military one. He did not lie back, let others do the work, and enjoy life, as some traditional hacendados had tended to do. Nor were his days occupied with plotting a political or military comeback, although by 1922 he seems to have developed some political ambitions. He applied his talents as an organizer, which had allowed him to transform the División del Norte from a series of ragged guerrilla bands into a regular force and to efficiently administer the state of Chihuahua, into rebuilding and developing his hacienda at Canutillo. This proved no easy task.

Canutillo had indeed been a wealthy estate on the eve of the revolution, "situated at the headwaters of the Río Conchos in the state of Durango, and including rich valley land on both sides of the river and grazing lands extending many miles from the hacienda or ranch headquarters." It comprised 163,000 acres, 4,400 of which was extremely rich irrigated land. Before the revolution, 24,000 sheep, 4,000 goats, 3,000 head of cattle, and 4,000 horses had grazed on Canutillo's lands.[30] In the heyday of Villista rule in northern Mexico, the estate had been occupied by Urbina, who had ruled it with an iron fist and administered it like a medieval fiefdom. He had become so enamored of the estate that he was willing to betray Villa in order to keep it. In the years of revolutionary turmoil, most of the animals had disappeared from the estate: they had been either requisitioned, stolen, or sold across the border to the United States. Much of the land had been abandoned and most of the buildings destroyed. "The ranch house was in the form of a city square, about 500 feet on each side," wrote an American mining engineer, Ralph Parker, whom Villa had invited to Canutillo to survey some mining properties. Parker visited the estate in November 1920, only a few months after Villa had taken it over. The compound was "completely closed in by houses or rooms which only had doors opening into the inner court which held horses, wagons, et cetera. General Villa and myself and the chapel occupied the only rooms that held roofs. All the rest had only four walls and were open to skies and were used by his officers."[31]

Three years later, another American visiting Villa, Fred Dakin, had a completely different impression of Canutillo:

Upon my arrival at the hacienda I was impressed by the air of efficiency and accomplishment about the place. I learned that during the three years of occupation of the land the numerous buildings, stables, and warehouses had been rebuilt, twenty-five miles of telephone lines had been extended to all parts of the ranch, a post office and telegraph office had been established, a flour mill was under construction, and a school had been built providing for all the primary and grammar grades. The school was large enough for the attendance of 200 pupils and was the particular pride of the General.[32]

The school was indeed the object of Villa's "particular pride." Building it had been one of his top priorities once he took over Canutillo, and he named it after Felipe Angeles. In 1921, when American newspaperman Frazier Hunt visited, Villa waxed enthusiastic about his plans for building the school. "He [Villa] led me out of the church, down a filthy, narrow mud street, through a large door into a big patio surrounded by a line of rooms made of adobe brick. 'This is to be our school,' he said with tremendous pride. 'I am fixing it up as fast as I can. Everything has tumbled down and the roofs have fallen in but I am repairing them and in a few weeks we shall have a school here with four teachers. It's going to be the best school I know how to start and every child on this ranch is going to attend. Schools are what Mexico needs above everything else. If I was at the head of things I would put plenty of schools in the cities and towns and besides, I'd put a school on every hacienda and ranch.'"[33]

In 1922, Regino Hernández Llergo, editor of one of Mexico City's most important newspapers, visited Canutillo. Villa could not stop talking about the school. He insisted that he had paid for most of it and he led the newspaperman through every room of the school, including the toilets, tapped his feet on the floor to show how solid it was, praised the ventilation, and showed his respect for the teachers by only entering the school after having formally requested the permission of its director, Professor Cuello.

Hernández Llergo was impressed. He felt that the school that Villa had built could be compared to the best schools in Mexico. The 300 children who attended it came not only from Canutillo but from surrounding ranches and estates as well. The five teachers who had volunteered to go to Canutillo and were paid by the federal government were deeply impressed by Villa's commitment to and interest in education. He gave them free food and lodging, supplemented their salaries, which were already high by the standards of the time, and persuaded the government to increase them. He frequently took part in classes and at night sometimes asked the teachers to read to him from biographies of famous men and books on military tactics.[34]

During the years he spent in Canutillo, Villa attempted to educate himself as much as possible. Apart from attending classes at the school and from having the teachers read to him, he himself seems to have attempted to read a wide variety of books. When Hernández Llergo visited him, he was just reading the "Treasure of Youth," a kind of introductory book of knowledge for young people, and at the same time Hernández Llergo saw a book on geography and Dante's *Divine Comedy* among Villa's books.[35] Villa did not want to limit the benefits of education to himself and to the children on the estates and its surroundings either. He set up a night school for workers on the hacienda, who were thus able to learn to read and write.[36]

Villa was intensely involved in every aspect of Canutillo's economic life. On one occasion, Hernández Llergo found him personally repairing a machine, and for a long time he would describe to the journalists the respective advantages and problems of planting potatoes or peanuts. " 'I alone have done all this, working without any rest,' Villa told the visiting journalists from Mexico City. 'I have applied the tenacity that I showed during the war to the present work. I am at the same time a soldier, an engineer, a carpenter . . . yes, even a bricklayer. . . . If all the Mexicans were Francisco Villas, my country and my race would be different.' But then he sadly stated, 'What I lacked was culture. I am an intelligent man with a natural intelligence. Ah, friends, if my parents had only educated me.'"

Villa told Hernández Llergo that he had spent 300,000 pesos to renovate the hacienda, and that while the government had contributed some money, much of it had come out of his own pocket. While it is not clear where that money came from, there is some indication of its amount. On August 9, 1920, shortly after the peace agreements with the government had been signed, Villa wrote a letter to Elías Torres telling him:

I am giving you power of attorney so that in my name and as my representative you can collect from Señor Gabino Vizcarra three checks for the following amounts: one for 900,000 pesos, another one for 600,000 pesos, and another one for 400,000 pesos, emitted by the German bank, Torreón branch, in favor of the First National Bank of El Paso, Texas, and in the name of my wife, Luz Corral de Villa, and these checks should be endorsed by Señor Vizcarra so that they can be cashed.[37]

This letter raises far more questions than can be answered. Who was Gabino Vizcarra? I have not been able to discover his identity. Where did the money come from? Was it money that Villa had taken for himself? Was it government money? Were the checks ever cashed? It is remarkable that Elías Torres, a writer who put to use in his books even the most minute scrap of information that he obtained, never even mentions this letter. Did he in fact collect these checks? Why would Villa have chosen a man he scarcely knew for such a delicate task?

It was obvious to Villa that his ownership of Canutillo must have raised many questions among the people of Mexico. He had always insisted that he wanted nothing for himself and had repeatedly stated, as he did in an interview with John Reed, that he dreamed of being a simple soldier in a military colony to be established once the revolution triumphed, in which every one of his soldiers would have land of his own. In his conversation with Hernández Llergo, Villa insisted that he had not asked for this hacienda. "When I made arrangements with Fito [nickname of Adolfo de la Huerta], who was then president of the republic, he gave me this hacienda. . . . I did not ask for it. When I laid down my arms, I wanted to work on my small properties in Chihuahua, but the government told me that this was to be my residence and I did not want to resist. I had no other intention than to work so as to not further shed the blood of my brothers."

It was indeed true that Villa, when he began his negotiations with the government, had only asked for a hacienda for his soldiers and not for himself. It might also be noted that Villa indeed had very little choice in the matter. One of the main problems for both Villa and the government when he decided to lay down his arms was how his security could be guaranteed. After the many years of civil war and the many people Villa had executed, he had made a host of enemies, so that guaranteeing his personal security was an enormous problem. Villa's original suggestion as to how this problem could be solved was to allow him to retain command of 500 men, who would be charged with policing either the whole of the state of Chihuahua or that part of the state that Villa considered his home region: Parral and its surroundings. Since the government was under no circumstances ready to make this concession to Villa, the only way of guaranteeing his security was to put him and an escort of his chosen men on an estate sufficiently isolated from the rest of the country to allow him to maintain effective control there to shield him from attempts on his life.

Canutillo was nevertheless a far cry from the egalitarian military colony in which each one of his soldiers would receive a parcel of his own. One reason for this, but by no means the only one, was that the laborers on the estate were not his former soldiers but rather workers who had been at Canutillo before Villa took over the estate. His own soldiers were settled on two adjacent haciendas, and it is difficult to determine under what conditions they lived. On the estate of El Pueblito, the man in charge was one of Villa's former generals, Albino Aranda. It is not clear how much control he exercised. In February 1922, he thanked President Obregón "in the name of the colonists of Pueblito" for "having received lots of land through a commission of engineers sent by the Ministry of Finance."[38] One year later, however, the military commander of Chihuahua reported to Obregón that the estate had not yet been divided.[39] In fact, reports surfaced about violent clashes between Aranda and his former soldiers, who were dissatisfied because they were only allowed to work part of the lands on the estate. Villa is said to have supported Aranda in this controversy.[40]

On Canutillo itself, sharecropping seems to have been the predominant form of labor relations. After a detailed economic study, Villa seems to have reached the conclusion that this was the most profitable way to work his lands.

Shortly after he took possession of Canutillo, Villa "decided to try out three farming systems. On one piece . . . he would use only machines, paying the mechanics by day wages. On a second piece he would do the work with horses and oxen, paying wages to the farmers. And on the third . . . the workers used the old Mexican system of shares. He furnished the horses and seed, his farmers did the work, and paid him one-third of the crop when harvested."[41] Two years later, when Hernández Llergo visited Villa, he found that while very modern machinery was used, the majority of workers on the estates were sharecroppers.[42]

There are contradictory reports as to the living and working conditions on Canutillo. Some of the laborers who left the estate after Villa was assassinated reported that Villa was paying them too little for their wheat and threatened to shoot them if they protested.[43] By contrast, the former teachers on Villa's estate describe him as generous to his laborers. At the hacienda store, he sold those products that had to be bought outside of the estate at cost, while goods and food produced at Canutillo were given to the laborers free of charge.[44]

The one similarity that Canutillo had with a military colony was the quasi-military discipline that Villa maintained. For example, he implemented strict work rules—everyone had to begin to work at 4:00 in the morning, which he himself supervised, since his own work day began one hour earlier at 3:00 A.M. In general, Villa seems to have retained the life-and-death control over his men that he had exercised in wartime. There are reports, although unconfirmed, of executions taking place on the estate,[45] and Villa himself was by no means reticent in this respect. When the teachers arrived from Mexico City to take up their positions in Canutillo, Villa attempted to dispel any fears they might have of robbery, saying, "Look—here in Canutillo nothing is lost, for if anyone steals, I have him shot."[46]

His own security presented an ever-present problem for Villa. He was very conscious of the threat of assassination. Canutillo was located in a region where he had frequently roamed as an outlaw. He had also operated in that region not only in the glorious heyday of the Maderista uprising of 1910–11 but also in the long guerrilla years between 1915 and 1920, when so much blood had been shed. He still enjoyed much popularity among many inhabitants of the region, as his quasi-triumphal march through many villages after his surrender attested. But the many executions he had carried out in the bloody years of 1915 to 1920 and the depredations committed by some of his troops had also left a legacy of hatred there. Local enemies were only part of the problem he felt he had to face. Mexico's two most powerful political leaders, President Obregón and Secretary of the Interior Calles, were not only commanders whose armies he had faced on the field of battle but men with whom he had personally clashed. He had insulted and nearly executed Obregón and had imprisoned his brother. And he had threatened Calles with a most dire reprisal if he did not stop attacking Villa's ally, Governor Maytorena of Sonora. Villa's relations with the two governors of Chihuahua and Durango, Ignacio Enríquez and Jesús Agustín Castro, were even worse. Enríquez's hatred for Villa, against whom he had fought for many years and whom he had tried to ambush after peace negotiations, was almost pathological. Two of his political critics who were anything but friendly toward Villa wrote Obregón that "because of the grudge that Enríquez bore against the bandit Francisco Villa, he has constantly and covertly worked against him, and we would be the first to applaud him if his conduct had not seriously threatened the peace of half the Republic and the plans of the central government."[47] In fact, Enríquez was rebuked by Obregón when in 1921 he reported to Obregón that rumors had emerged that Villa's men had risen against him in Canutillo, that Villa was wounded, and that he was asking local officials to report on the matter.[48] On the day he received the telegram, Obregón sent a sharply worded reply to Enríquez:

My government has precise data to state that the information that has been given to you is absolutely mistaken, and I believe that the greatest discretion should be observed in the investigation that you have ordered the mayors of Parral and Allende to carry out, since this could create animosity among many of the leaders who are supporters of this general if they know that the government does not have any confidence in them and is watching them without any reason for doing so.[49]

The only government official Villa seems to have trusted was Eugenio Martínez, who commanded government forces in Coahuila, and to whom Villa had surrendered. For this very reason, Obregón named him military commander of federal armed forces in Chihuahua.

The two strategies that Villa used to ensure his own safety were to transform Canutillo and its surroundings into a kind of impregnable fortress, and, at least until 1922, to maintain cordial relations with the Obregón administration.

According to one of the teachers who resided at Canutillo when it was in Villa's possession, he had chosen it from a list of estates that the government had submitted to him "because it is a hacienda that is very difficult to attack, since it is located in such a manner that from all sides it can easily be defended even with a few men." Villa could count not only on his escort of 50 Dorados, who were paid and equipped by the government, but also on numerous retainers on his estate, and above all on former soldiers of his who had received land on haciendas surrounding Canutillo, and who were led by some of Villa's most loyal former generals, such as Nicolás Fernández.[50]

In the first year after settling down, Villa still maintained an absolute military discipline on his estate. "Everything there was run as a military camp," the American mining engineer Parker reported in 1920. "Bugles sounded at six A.M., an hour before daylight, and again in the evening, and at intervals during the day. Everyone including myself followed orders for meals, lights out, et cetera." Parker noted regular reviews of the troops. "The Dorados rode up, faced the building in single file, and then General Villa, followed by the colonel commanding the troops, rode very slowly from one side to the other, closely examining each man and his equipment."[51]

Two years later, when Hernández Llergo visited Canutillo, the military discipline seems to have been somewhat relaxed. There were no daily reviews of troops, and no bugle sounded throughout the day, but there was still a quasi-military discipline, and Hernández Llergo reported that practically everyone on the estate was armed and at least had a gun strapped to his side.[52] After Villa's death, the government found large numbers of weapons hidden on the estate, which could have been used for both defensive and offensive purposes.[53] Villa limited the number of visitors allowed on his estate and posted a colonel of his army, Nicolás Flores, at the nearest railway station to report on every arrival and departure.[54]

While strengthening his defensive potential at Canutillo, Villa made every effort, at least until 1922, to conciliate the Obregón administration. If one remembers that Villa not only had faced Obregón several times in battle but had nearly had him executed, the tone of his letters and telegrams to the Mexican president sounds almost unreal. On the occasion of New Year's and Obregón's saint's day, Villa wished him "every kind of happiness."[55] Once when he had omitted to send a telegram of greetings to Obregón on the occasion of the latter's saint's day, Villa wired him an apology, saying that "because of the grave illness of a sister of mine, who died yesterday in Chihuahua, I did not send you a message on time to congratulate you on your saint's day, but you know that I remember you with sincere esteem and in my deep pain I know how to appreciate such a friend as you."[56] On another occasion, Villa was even more effusive in a telegram to Obregón, saying: "Although we have been separated in space, we are united in our thoughts and in our sincere affection. I am with you today on this your saint's day and I am with you by sending you my respectful greetings and a sincere *abrazo*."[57]

In his efforts to impress the Mexican president, Villa did not limit himself to expressions of sympathy for Obregón. As he had agreed to at Sabinas, until 1922, Villa refrained from any political activity and any private or public criticism of government policy. In addition, he not only refused to participate in any of the military revolts that were breaking out against Obregón but at times actively intervened on the side of the administration.

In 1921, Villa made a symbolic gesture of support for Obregón. He wrote him that in case of a war with the United States, he would be ready to fight on his side. Obregón politely replied, telling him: "I fully appreciate the value of your spontaneous offer in the remote case that our difficulties cannot be solved, something I do not expect, since we are making great progress in the public opinion of our neighboring country."[58] A few months later, Villa's help for Obregón took on a much more concrete shape. When two men came to see Villa "who attempted to carry out a seditious propaganda with me, I handed them over to the military authorities in Parral."[59]

American newspapers reported that Villa had helped to put down a revolt in Durango against the Obregón administration by his former rivals the Arrieta brothers. This fact so impressed the *New York Times* that it commented that Villa would make a first-rate chief of rurales, and that he might be a useful citizen to his country and an instrument of its pacification.[60]

When a former supporter of Villa's who later turned against him, General Rosalio Hernández, attempted to rise against Obregón, Villa, according to American newspapers, asked for permission from the Mexican authorities to take the field against Hernández.[61] Another American newspaper, the *New York American*, reported that both during the Carranza administration as well as the presidency of Obregón, American oil men had offered Villa large sums of money if he would participate in an uprising against the Mexican government or at least remain neutral in such a case. Villa repeatedly refused, and one oil man came regretfully to the conclusion that although Villa was a bandit, he was "a very honest bandit."[62]

There was one rebellion during which the government was convinced that it could count on Villa's help. In 1922, Villa's most relentless enemy in the long and bloody guerrilla warfare in Chihuahua, Francisco Murguía, decided to revolt against Obregón. Murguía was one of the few generals who had remained loyal to Carranza until the end, and he had been imprisoned by de la Huerta for crimes committed during his military campaigns. He had fled to the United States, and in 1922, he crossed into Chihuahua with 30 men, convinced that he could repeat what Villa had done nine years before—that is, get thousands of men to rally to his side to defeat Obregón's army. Murguía counted both on his former soldiers and on the prestige he felt he had acquired in Chihuahua by fighting against Villa. He was mistaken. Not only did no one rally to his side, but one-third of his men defected, and soon Murguía, with only a few men, was fleeing across Chihuahua hotly pursued by Obregón's troops. When he arrived in the vicinity of Villa's hacienda, the commander of Obregón's troops, General José Gonzalo Escobar, suggested alerting Villa and obtaining his help in capturing Murguía.[63]

There is no evidence that the government ever told Villa that Murguía was in the vicinity of Canutillo or that it called on him for help. Villa, however, not only knew that Murguía was in the vicinity but knew precisely where he was hidden with only a few men. It would have been easy for him to capture his old enemy. Instead, he did nothing and allowed Murguía to flee to the town of Tepejuanes.[64] There the local priest hid the rebel general, but his adjutant betrayed him to the authorities. After his capture, Murguía was immediately court-martialed. At the trial, the public prosecutor accused him of rebellion and sedition and proceeded to denounce his corruption and the atrocities he had committed while commanding government troops: "You did not have a cent when you joined the revolution and today you have several million pesos, and this means that you did not go to battle with a patriotic purpose but you transformed rebellion into a lucrative business that brought the capital that you now possess." The most bitter accusation the public prosecutor leveled against Murguía was that he had put Calixto Contreras's home village of Cuencame to the torch. "In this village of Cuencame in this state, the orphans and widows still curse your name. You remember, General, when you ordered the village to be burned, expelling a huge number of families from their homes who are today living a life of misery; these are the marks of progress and pacification in the state of Durango that your activities as a revolutionary left when you were the military commander there." Murguía never answered the accusation of corruption, but he did justify his having burned down Cuencame by stating that the villages was "a refuge of Villistas and a center of bandits." Murguía was sentenced to be shot. There was a final irony to his death when his execution squad first presented their arms to him with all the marks of respect due to his rank, and then used the same rifles to kill him.[65]

Villa showed no satisfaction at the death of his old nemesis. On the contrary, he paid a kind of last tribute to Murguía that in his eyes was one of the greatest compliments he could pay to an enemy, saying, "He was a soldier of the revolution."[66] The respect that Villa showed this man, who had been responsible for more executions of his soldiers than anyone else in Mexico, is surprising. Had Murguía earned Villa's respect as one of the few northern commanders who had never been afraid of him? Did he see in him a replica of his own harshness, toughness, cruelty, and courage? None of his other former enemies ever inspired similar feelings in Villa.

The Obregón administration responded positively to Villa's overtures. Obregón showered Villa with expressions of cordiality. "General Eugenio Martínez is with me and both of us send the most affectionate greetings on your saint's day," Obregón wired Villa on one occasion.[67] Obregón made a point of personally answering every letter Villa sent him. Obregón's attempts to woo Villa went beyond simple expressions of cordiality. The government invested large sums of money in this process. The Obregón administration had not confiscated the hacienda of Canutillo, which it gave to Villa, but rather bought it from its owners at the considerable price of 575,000 pesos. In addition, it took care of $44,000 in tax arrears that the estate owed the local and central governments. It also spent large sums on the haciendas adjacent to Canutillo where Villa's soldiers were settled. The money the government allotted to Villa went considerably beyond these sums. The Mexican consul in the United States spent $60,000 in 1921–22 to buy agricultural implements for Canutillo.[68] When Villa asked the administration to pay him $40,000 to compensate for losses he had suffered when a packing plant that he had owned in Ciudad Juárez had been confiscated by the Carranza administration, Obregón promptly paid.[69] A year later the government paid an additional 25,000 pesos to Villa.

The Intimate Life of Villa in Canutillo

One of the most difficult decisions that Villa had to make when he settled down in Canutillo concerned the kind of family life he would now lead. It was time, he decided, to "regularize" his family affairs. This proved to be a complex undertaking. His first priority was to concentrate as many of his children as he could on his hacienda. Three of his sons, Agustín (the oldest), Octavio, and Samuel, and four of his daughters, Micaela, Celia, Juana María, and Sara (called "la Cubana" by her teachers), went to live with Villa in Canutillo. One was the daughter of Juana, one of Villa's former wives, who had died in the meantime; others were from wives who lived in the vicinity; others were taken from mothers who were not invited to live with Villa on his estate, although they may not have given up custody voluntarily. Villa's last wife, Austreberta, bore him two more children at Canutillo, Francisco and Hipólito (the latter was born after Villa's death). In addition, Villa had adopted Samuel, the son of Trinidad Rodríguez, one of his favorite generals, who had been killed in the course of the revolution.

Villa was an attentive father. He frequently took his sons along when he rode through the hacienda, explaining his ambitious economic projects to them. He followed their progress at school with great attention, frequently sitting in on their classes.[70] Every day his children sat down with him at the family meal, which was attended by about 30 persons. Apart from his official wife and his children, administrators and at times teachers were also invited.

Villa was ambitious for his children. When he introduced his eldest son to Hernández Llergo, he told him, "I want this one, Agustín, to be a doctor. The other, Octavio, will become a military man, while the smallest, Panchito, who is only seven months old, will become a lawyer. . . . I have great hopes for my children. Once they finish their secondary studies, I will send them to the best schools of France, Spain, or Germany." When one of the reporters interjected he might also send them to the United States, Villa became adamant. "No, Señorita," he protested. "Not to the United States. The first thing I am teaching my children is to hate the enemy of my race."[71] With children, Villa also showed a sense of humor that in other contexts he seems to have lacked. One evening Villa's nephew, Hipólito's son Frank, whom his father had forcibly taken from the boy's American mother and brought to Canutillo, was vainly clamoring for Villa's attention at the dinner table. "Little Frank was sitting beside Pancho at dinner," his mother (to whom Villa returned her son a short time later) recounted. "He wanted the sugar and when he kept asking for it, Pancho, busy talking, told Frank to be quiet. Little Frank got mad and said, loud as he could, 'When I be a big man, I'll bring the American army down to kill you.' That got attention. Pancho broke off talking, looked at Frank and roared with laughter. He was very pleased with my little son's spunk and said that Frank was just like him."[72]

Villa's relations with his wives were more contradictory. They were passionate but could also be brutal. Luz Corral had been living in exile in the United States, and Villa had occasionally sent her money and even love letters, one of which was intercepted (and badly translated) by U.S. intelligence agents. He wrote:

To my adored wife,

With how much pleasure do I write this little letter to convey to you my fond recollections of you and how happy shall I be when I have finished this work for my beloved country; and this profound suffering in my soul because of the separation from you shall be a thing of the past. It seems to me that when I am away from you I am an unfortunate for whom there is no perfume, no sunlight, nothing. I miss being able to confide my inmost thoughts to you with a certainty you will understand; but I trust in God that he will allow us to be together again; and I swear we shall never again be separated; for I come to appreciate your virtues and your wisdom gained by experience more and more every day and you are and ever will be the love of my heart, which heart is heavy when you are not with me.

A little money is sent you for expenses, and by the twentieth day of this month we hope to send more. . . . Kiss my children for me, Your husband, Francisco Villa.[73]

In spite of Villa's romantic letter, Luz Corral was by no means surprised when she returned to Canutillo and had to share Villa with another semi-official wife, Soledad Seañez. She had been engaged to a man with whom she was very much in love, whom Villa had either killed or had executed. Seañez's relationship to Villa seems to have been ambivalent. On one hand, in a letter written ten years after Villa's death to the then Mexican president Abelardo Rodríguez, she intimated that Villa had forced his attentions upon her and had betrayed her by carrying out a simulated marriage:

I have grown up in an atmosphere of honesty and work, that I can prove to anyone; during this period of our history, Francisco Villa exercised a reign of terror among the inhabitants of this part of the republic, which he dominated, and all of us, as is well known, depended on his will and whims. In this situation, destiny put me within reach of the claws of Villa, who utilized his control of civilian authorities to simulate a marriage with him in the presence of witnesses and the judge of the civilian registry of Valle de Allende. There are still witnesses alive who were present when the marriage document was signed, but this document can nowhere be found now that I have tried to obtain a copy, and I understand now that all this was just a simulated legal marriage in order to persuade me to live with him.[74]

In Soledad Seañez's later years, she remembered Villa far more fondly than in the letter she wrote in 1933 to President Rodríguez. In describing her first meeting with Villa 30 years later, she made no mention of his having forced his attentions upon her or of any kind of violence. When she was pregnant, he sent her to El Paso to get the best medical care, and he also sent her love letters, although they were couched in somewhat more prosaic terms than the letters he sent to Luz Corral. While she was in her native village, he wrote her from Canutillo: "I cannot go to town because I don't want to, and this deprives me of seeing you soon, but soon I shall come by auto for you. . . . If you are short of money, I shall send someone from Canutillo that you can trust with a note for you. Let me hear from you quickly if you want me to send money. You are my life."[75]

Soledad Seañez was installed in a separate house in Canutillo, where she cared for her own son and two of Villa's other children, Miguel and Micaela. She intimated that all the wives together took care of the children. "We all, Austreberta, Luz, and the others, took care of all the children. Everyone loved the children."[76]

Villa's most passionate relationship in the last years of his life seems to have been with Austreberta Rentería, but it was probably also his most brutal one. It did not begin on a romantic note: Villa raped her. Austreberta, a pretty young girl from a middle-class family in Jiménez in Chihuahua, was kidnapped by one of Villa's most brutal commanders, the "ear-cutter," Baudelio Uribe, who practically offered her to Villa to gain his goodwill. When Austreberta fearfully asked Villa to allow her to return to her family, Villa (according to an interview she granted to a Mexican newspaperman),

convinced that Austreberta would not accede to his wishes out of the love that he thought to inspire in her in a few minutes took her by force.

The final scene of this violence was terrible. Not only Austreberta was crying . . . but the General, sitting on the bed, was also crying. "I will marry you, Betita," General Villa said, stuttering, and added, "You are not like other women."[77]

Villa then practically imprisoned her for several months by ordering a family in Jiménez, under threat of death, to hide her from anyone when he evacuated the town. It was only after many months that he finally allowed her to return home, assuring her that she was his wife and that he would soon marry her. Her return to her family was marred by tragedy. She arrived just in time to witness the death of her brother, who in her words had died of grief because of her disappearance. Her father's main aim in life was now to protect his daughter from Villa's attentions. To that end, he gave up his business in Jiménez, fled from town to town, and finally crossed into the United States, where he lived a harsh and miserable existence, doing all kinds of manual work, with the sole aim of shielding his daughter from Villa. As she told a newspaperman, José Valadés, in what was apparently the only interview she ever gave, Astreberta at some point decided that she had fallen in love with Villa. After Villa had settled down at Canutillo, he asked her to rejoin him, and she surreptitiously fled from her father's house in Gómez Palacio, where he had moved on returning to Mexico after Villa's surrender. Villa now showered her with attentions and gifts and in her presence, in an extremely humiliating scene, forced Luz Corral to leave Canutillo. When she first entered Villa's bedroom, Austreberta told Valadés:

a tall, portly woman entered the room, smiling in a very friendly way at her.

When Villa saw her coming in, he jumped to his feet. "Didn't I tell you that I didn't want to see you anymore and that you should leave?" he shouted at her.

The woman lowered her head. "Didn't I tell you to leave since this house now has a mistress?" the General repeated with greater determination. "It concerns the children," the woman dared to answer.

Austreberta was aghast. Her whole body was trembling. She felt as if she was going to faint. This woman was Luz Corral, the first wife of Francisco Villa. "Leave the children alone. Betita will take care of them, for Betita is my wife, my real wife," Villa shouted again.

Luz Corral, who had come closer to Austreberta Rentería, wanted to answer once again, when she felt Pancho's hand on her shoulders. When he saw that Betita was crying, he shouted with great fury at Luz, "What have you done to her? What have you done to her?"

"Speak up, Señora, speak up," Luz implored Betita, fearful that Pancho would believe that these tears of the young girl were the result of Luz Corral having hurt her.

"The Señora has not done anything to me, and I only implore her to leave," Austreberta answered. "Get out of here," Villa ordered, and he added, "and if you do not leave the hacienda by tomorrow you will see what will happen to you. And remember this lady is my wife, and you should recognize her as such." Without saying a word of protest, Luz Corral left the room.[78]

Villa not only forced Luz Corral to leave Canutillo but he gave her very little money to subsist on, and she now depended on the charity of the not-very-charitable Hipólito Villa. Finally, left without any means of survival when Hipólito was either unable or unwilling to support her, Luz Corral made the one gesture that could most humiliate Villa. She wrote for help to the one man who had defeated Villa, his archrival, President Alvaro Obregón. "As you know," she wrote Obregón in March 1923, "I have been separated from my husband, General Francisco Villa, for two years and though he promised to give me a monthly allowance to be able to subsist, he has not done so until now."[79]

After some hesitation—it took him two months to answer—Obregón decided to help. "I have learned with great sorrow from your letter about the difficult conditions under which you are living. If, as you say in your letter, you come to this capital, if you advise me on time, I shall be happy to receive you so that you can tell me about your situation in detail and that we can see whether it is possible that my government can give you some help so that you can find the work that you are looking for."[80]

Until Villa's death, Austreberta, whom Villa affectionately called Betita, was the official mistress at Canutillo. She bore him two children. Villa lived to see one son, Francisco. Another, Hipólito, was born after Villa's death. When Hernández Llergo visited Canutillo, it was to Austreberta that Villa introduced him as his official wife. The newspaperman did not have the impression that she was a very happy woman.

[Villa] shouted: "Betita, Betita!" "I am coming, sir."

And a tall, white, good-looking lady with big, black, melancholical, sad, and opaque eyes, as if she had been weeping, appeared. The pale face of the señora showed intense suffering.[81]

Did this "suffering" reflect mistreatment by Villa or rather that Austreberta had more difficulties than Luz Corral with Villa's extramarital relationships? Apart from his semi-official second wife, Soledad Seañez, who lived near the estate, Villa had another mistress who also lived in the vicinity and who also bore him a child. This was Manuela Casas, for whom Villa had acquired a house and a hotel in Parral.[82]

Villa's family life was further complicated by a conflict with his sister Martina and his brother Hipólito. It is not clear how the conflict with Martina broke out. Luz Corral mentions people—she never said who—who turned him against his sister for "trivial reasons," so that he stopped supporting her.[83] The break with Hipólito may have had more substantial causes. In January 1921, Villa had written a strong letter of recommendation for his brother to Obregón asking him to help Hipólito in his business affairs. Obregón was quite willing to do so, but the deals that Hipólito proposed to him seem to have been so outrageous that in spite of his wish to conciliate Francisco Villa, Obregón could not accede to them. In one case, Hipólito proposed selling a locomotive to the Mexican National Railroads that, according to one expert, was in such terrible condition that buying it would have been "a ruinous operation for our company."[84] Villa may have felt that his brother's greed was undermining whatever credit he might have with the government, and on September 4, 1922, one and a half years after having recommended Hipólito, he wrote the president, "As a friend I firmly ask you not to make any loan to my brother Hipólito in the event that he should ask for one, since we should understand the needs of the government, and I feel above all, as I have told you before, that when it comes to money, friendship should play no role, and he [Hipólito] should be obligated to fulfill his obligations like everyone else."[85]

One of the reasons why Villa was angered by his brother's dubious business deals may have been that in 1922, he had once again begun to participate in political events in northern Mexico. He may have contemplated even greater involvement in years to come and feared that his brother's activities might bring discredit upon him.

Villa in Canutillo: Hacendado or Popular Leader?

When Hernández Llergo visited Canutillo for nearly a week in June 1922 to interview Villa, his report aroused great interest throughout Mexico. More than any other revolutionary leader, Villa had become a legend in his own lifetime. His every action provoked the most intense curiosity. Moreover, many Mexicans wondered about Villa's future intentions. Would he participate in politics again? Did he contemplate rising against the government? Now that he had become a hacendado, had he made a complete turnaround in his ideology and ideals, or was he still what he had always professed to be, and what, in the opinion of this author, he really was, at least for a time—a spokesman for the peasants and for the poor in general?

These questions were difficult for Hernández Llergo to answer, and even for present-day historians, with all the documents at their disposal, the answers can only be ambivalent. Above all, this is true of Villa's ideology. There are a number of indications that Villa was growing more conservative than he had been in the past, but this conservatism was less a product of his newfound status as a hacendado than of his increasing alienation from large parts of the population of Chihuahua in the last three years of his guerrilla campaign. Again and again in the bloody and desperate years from 1917 to 1920, he had called on the members of the defensas sociales in the villages of Chihuahua, many of whom had served under him in the División del Norte, to join him or at least not to fight against him. His words had fallen on deaf ears. His resulting sense of betrayal and rage increased his feeling of alienation and led him to commit terrible depredations against some of the defensas sociales and their families, which may explain why, when he stated his conditions for making peace with the government, Villa demanded land for his soldiers but said nothing about land for Chihuahua's peasants.

Villa was not much given to introspection or self-criticism. In the few times that he did reflect on his defeats, he blamed them on betrayals. In 1915, in his Naco manifesto, he attributed his defeat to the betrayals of Eulalio Gutiérrez and Woodrow Wilson. Seven years later, in an interview with Frazier Hunt, an American correspondent, he expressed the view that it was the people who had let him down, because they could not understand him. "And I know what it is to try to help people who can't understand what you are trying to do for them," he told Hunt. "I fought for ten years for them. I had a principle. I fought ten years so that the poor man could live as a human being should, have his land, send his children to school, and enjoy human freedom. But most of them were too ignorant to understand my ideas. That's the reason I quit fighting." Nevertheless, Villa did not feel that his revolution had been in vain: "he had tried to do something for the poor people of Mexico he explained. They had stopped him from doing much, but he had helped some. Peons were getting the land now. The great Spanish and foreign owned plantations and ranches were being broken up. Even soldiers were being put on the land and helped to get a new start." Villa felt, however, that this was only a beginning. Social reform could only progress further once the Mexican people had become educated. "Poor ignorant Mexico," he said slowly. "Until they have education nothing much can be done."[86]

In view of his belief that social change in Mexico could only be a gradual affair, it is not surprising that Villa should have expressed strong opposition to Bolshevism, which was making headway in Mexico at that time. That opposition was not only based on ideological reasons. Villa personally opposed Plutarco Elías Calles, the powerful minister of the interior. Public opinion considered Calles the most important advocate of Bolshevism in Mexico and he was presumed to be the heir to the presidency once Obregón's term of office expired. "Radicalism as our politicians understand it is not possible," Villa told Hernández Llergo.

The leaders of Bolshevism . . . in Mexico and outside of it advocate an equality of classes that cannot be attained. Equality does not exist and cannot exist. It is a lie that we can all be equal. . . . For me society is a big stair with some people at its lower end, some people in the middle, some rising, and some very high. . . . it is a stair clearly determined by nature. One cannot proceed against nature. What would happen to the world if all of us were generals or capitalists, or all of us were poor? There must be people of all kinds. The world, my friend, is like a big store where there are owners, employees, consumers, and manufacturers. . . . I would never fight for the equality of the social classes.[87]

It is probably this attitude that led some conservatives in the early 1920s to see Villa as their man. In May 1922, Monsignor Francis C. Kelley, who for many years had been the strongest lobbyist for Mexico's Catholic church in the United States and had advocated U.S. military intervention, paid a visit to one of the State Department's highest officials, Leland Harrison. Kelley told Harrison that he considered that Obregón "was well intentioned and a good man, but he was surrounded by traitors. He mentioned Calles and his Bolshevik tendencies." He then told Harrison that "he considered Villa as the most probable future leader of a conservative Catholic revolution. He happened to know that Villa had recently called in his followers and had told them that while he had taught them to kill and slay and steal, he had now built a church for them and he desired them to reform. He wished to be able to leave a bag of gold in the open field and have the certainty that he would be able to find it again upon returning to the spot where he had left it."[88]

The U.S. embassy in Mexico shared a similar impression of Villa's ideology. The U.S. chargé d'affaires in Mexico, George T. Summerlin, was convinced that Raúl Madero was the preferred candidate of the conservatives, and that

Villa and representatives of the conservative factions in Mexico had . . . formed plans of a general nature for a campaign in opposition to General Calles for the presidency of Mexico. Villa's staunch personal friend and one-time subordinate and life-saver, Raul Madero, was most spoken of as a presidential candidate which this Villista conservative group would support. Guillermo Pons, president of the Syndicate of Agriculturalists and prominent conservative leader, is reported to have joined with those who are working actively but quietly to effect the unification of the conservative factions behind a Villa-Madero movement. No general convention of conservatives has indeed been held but various informal conservative juntas, notably that in Puebla a fortnight ago, decided definitively in favor of the Villa-Madero combination.[89]

Vague indications that Villa sought a rapprochement with the United States are perhaps consistent with his possible newfound conservative orientation. In January 1923, a Texas newspaper reported that Villa was contemplating a trip to the United States in order to buy farm implements. "Mexican papers state," the Texas newspaper concluded, "that 'Pancho' has already corresponded with Governor Pat M. Neff on the subject and has been informed that he will not be molested or arrested while in the state of Texas."[90]

The impression that Villa had become a conservative landlord was not limited to the United States; it was shared by members of what had once been Villa's natural constituency: Chihuahua's radical peasants. This impression was largely because of events at the village of Villa Coronado.

In 1921, the agrarian commission of Chihuahua adjudicated lands adjacent to Villa's Canutillo hacienda to 242 peasants of the village of Villa Coronado. When, in December 1922, the peasants tried to take possession of their lands, they were met by armed men, headed by Villa's lieutenant Nicolás Fernández, who prevented them from doing so and stated that they were acting under Villa's orders.[91] When, one month later, from January 11 to January 13, 1923, an agrarian congress of Chihuahua's villages met for the first time in Ciudad Chihuahua to demand the application of land reform, its leaders bitterly denounced Villa's actions. In attendance was Castulo Herrera, Villa's chief in the heyday of the Maderista uprising, who had later joined Orozco and who had always maintained links to the state's revolutionary peasants. Like a voice out of the past, Herrera admonished Villa to remember "the blood that was shed on the battlefield in order to regain the sacred rights of the people, which includes the acquisition of land."[92] The head of the agrarian convention, Abelardo Amaya, sent a telegram to President Obregón asking him to intervene to force Villa to comply with the decision of the agrarian commission.

It is not clear what motivated Villa in this case, since no reaction from him has been found up to now in any archive. A statement made by Governor Ignacio Enríquez after Villa's death seems to indicate that Villa wanted to settle his former soldiers on these lands rather than to acquire them for himself. According to Enríquez, Villa wanted to help "a group mainly composed of outlaws who fought with him during his fighting days in Chihuahua."[93] Rather than being those of a ruthless hacendado, his actions in this case seem to correspond to those of a military chieftain who privileged the men who had fought on his side during the revolution over peasants who had not taken up arms, or who might even have fought against him. Apparently, Villa still sought land for his men, although the government had promised to expropriate the haciendas El Pueblito and San Salvador and deliver them to the Villistas. But the lands of San Salvador were never distributed to Villa's men,[94] and he thus felt that he was now free to seek alternative lands for them, disregarding any action by the state government.

It is also possible that Villa strongly suspected that the granting of lands to Villa Coronado was a provocation by his enemy Governor Enríquez. In 1921, when Enríquez granted their petition, there was as yet no agrarian law in Chihuahua, and practically no lands had been given to any peasants. Why this exception? Enríquez's actions are all the more suspicious in that immediately after Fernández's occupation of the lands of Villa Coronado, Enríquez sent a strongly worded telegram to President Obregón asking for troops to forcibly dislodge the Villistas from these lands. This might easily have triggered a new uprising by Villa, and Obregón refused to take any action, telling Enríquez that he would instead send one of his friends, Luis de León, to confer with Villa on the subject.[95]

Reinforcing the negative impression that his behavior made on many of Chihuahua's peasants, Villa never bothered to reply publicly to questions or accusations that they leveled at him. While the case of Villa Coronado does not necessarily show that Villa had become a conservative, other actions of his seem to point in that direction. Certainly, a letter that Villa sent to Obregón urgently asking him to pressure the governor of Durango, his old enemy Jesús Agustín Castro, to return lands to a hacendado friend of his tends to show conservative leanings.[96] Even a call by Villa to neighboring hacendados to meet in order to relieve unemployment among the region's peasants may have reflected more the thinking of an enlightened conservative hacendado than of a popular leader.[97]

And yet there was another side to Villa, which largely remained hidden, not only to many of Chihuahua's peasants but to popular opinion as well, since he did not publicly want to break his agreement with the Obregón government not to interfere in Mexico's politics. Nevertheless, the radical and populist side of Villa would have far more profound consequences for Chihuahua's peasants than his conservative tendencies. It was expressed in two cases, those of Bosque de Aldama and of the McQuatters contract, one of minor relevance, the other of major importance to Chihuahua.

It was as if time had stood still for the inhabitants of the agricultural colony of Bosque de Aldama. They were locked in a bitter fight with wealthy inhabitants of the neighboring town of Villa de Aldama to retain control of their water rights. The state governor, Enríquez, supported their enemies, and in a bitter complaint to President Obregón—a petition that could have been written when the Terrazas exercised their iron control over Chihuahua—the inhabitants of Bosque de Aldama stated that "ambitious men have attempted . . . to expel us from our lands, something that not even the dictatorial government of General Porfirio Díaz had dared to do, and it is the present governor, General Ignacio Enríquez, who declares himself to be a revolutionary and a democrat, who is carrying out one of the most detestable acts of his terrible administration, sending a force of rurales consisting of more than 40 men under the command of Captain Simón Armendariz and Manuel Arzate, who since the 20th of this month have been attacking our families as well as ourselves. They drove their horses into our houses, they aimed their weapons at us, they dispersed our cattle, they closed our water holes, they destroyed our machinery."[98]

This was the culmination of a long series of attacks by armed men backed by the governor against the peasants of Bosque de Aldama. When a newly formed, radical confederation of the workers and peasants of Chihuahua sent a wire to Obregón protesting the attacks on the peasants, Governor Enríquez dismissed the whole matter by telling Obregón that it was the work of a group of insignificant political agitators, and that "the agriculturalists know that I am the first agrarista in this state."[99]

There is no evidence that at this point Obregón was inclined to intervene on behalf of the peasants of Bosque de Aldama. All he did was to ask Enríquez for information, and when Enríquez assured him that this was the work a few ambitious politicians, Obregón did not even answer the peasants' petition. His attitude changed completely, however, once the peasants secured the support of Pancho Villa, who now decided to intervene in the matter. He called on Obregón to return the lands to the inhabitants of Bosque de Aldama and not only to send a commission there immediately to study the matter but also to station a detachment of federal troops in the community to protect its inhabitants from the governor's attacks. Villa warned that this conflict was "endangering the peace that your government has established with such great prestige." "I am sure," he added, "that you will find no difficulty in meeting my wishes and those of the peasant workers of the Bosque."[100]

This time Obregón reacted at once. He wrote Villa that the "secretary of agriculture immediately sent a commission to Bosque de Aldama to study the matter and take decisions as rapidly as possible."[101] Obregón's reply to Villa was no mere promise. Four days after he wrote his letter, he received a telegram from a commissioner sent to the region confirming the complaints of the inhabitants of Bosque de Aldama.[102]

Obregón was now resolved not only to recognize the rights of the inhabitants of Bosque de Aldama but also to carry out a major division of land in the region, including lands belonging to one of the wealthiest hacendados of Chihuahua who had been closely linked to Terrazas and Creel, Martín Falomir. But neither Enríquez nor Falomir were ready to give in. Enríquez ordered the arrest of the peasants' spokesman, E. Juare, for being a political agitator,[103] while Martín Falomir succeeded in persuading a federal judge to suspend the implementation of the government's decision.[104] It took another message from Villa to Obregón, calling on him to implement the government decision in favor of the peasants "without any change,"[105] for the Mexican president to act. Obregón unequivocally stated that after sending several commissions to the region, a decision had been taken to grant the peasants of Bosque de Aldama definite possession of their land, and that this decision could not be appealed.[106] After Villa's death, attacks on the village lands resumed again.[107]

On the whole, the conflict of Bosque de Aldama was a minor affair in political terms. It did not have significant repercussions on the politics of either Chihuahua or the nation. The same cannot be said of the one other matter in which Villa intervened, a problem that began to assume major dimensions. This was the fate of the huge Terrazas haciendas in Chihuahua.

Villa and the Terrazas Empire

The desire to break the stranglehold of the Terrazas-Creel family on Chihuahuan politics, and the hope that the Terrazas estates might be redistributed, had been the main thing that inspired many of the revolutionaries of 1910 to join Madero. With only one exception, however, none of the major leaders of the Mexican revolution had been willing to confront the Terrazas. Madero had quashed judicial proceedings against Enrique Creel in the Banco Minero affair and prevented Abraham González from proceeding against the family, even though the revolutionary Chihuahuan governor claimed to have evidence that the Terrazas had supported the Orozco uprising; furthermore, Madero had invited Luis Terrazas to return to Mexico and guaranteed his personal safety and that of his properties. Carranza, too, after some initial hesitation, had given in to the family. Although in 1916 he had ratified Villa's decree intervening the Terrazas haciendas shortly after his troops took over Chihuahua, both out of fear of how Chihuahua's peasants might react and because his generals wanted to utilize the resources of these estates for their own purposes, he had completely changed his attitude by 1919. In that year, he had returned the Terrazas' urban properties to the family. A year later, in early 1920, he had decreed that they would get their haciendas back. Only Villa had openly defied the Terrazas, and his expropriation of their properties and his promise to divide them after the victory of the revolution had been one of the main reasons for his popularity in Chihuahua.

Carranza had not been able to implement his decree with regard to the Terrazas before he was toppled by the rebellion of Agua Prieta. It was up to Obregón and Governor Enríquez to decide on the ultimate fate of the Terrazas properties. The problem had assumed new dimensions because of a series of clever maneuvers by the former Chihuahuan governor Alberto Terrazas, who had assumed the leadership of the family clan. He realized that in the climate of the 1920s, when Obregón was depending more and more on the support of radical peasant organizations, simply returning the properties to a family that had become the symbol of the prerevolutionary hacendado class was a political impossibility. Far more dependent on peasant support than Carranza ever was, Obregón could not boldly acquiesce to such a measure. Alberto Terrazas decided to make a deal with A. J. McQuatters, a wealthy mining entrepreneur who had operated in Chihuahua for many years, had struck deals with every revolutionary leader in the state, including Villa, and had, unlike many other American investors, managed to do very well economically in the process.

The deal was that McQuatters would buy all the Terrazas estates and sign a contract with the Mexican government under which he would sell the agricultural lands of the haciendas in installments to peasant farmers. In addition, McQuatters would obligate himself to build large irrigation installations, set up an agricultural bank in Chihuahua with a capital of $125,000, and bring 50,000 head of cattle into the state, which had lost most of its large herds during the turmoil of the revolution. McQuatters would also set up a series of schools and experimental agricultural stations. In return, the state government of Chihuahua would not only sell the Terrazas lands to McQuatters but would also exempt him from many taxes. Above all, it would sign the agreement before enacting an agrarian law that would sharply restrict McQuatters's ability to dispose of the Terrazas lands.

Apart from McQuatters and the Terrazas, the most enthusiastic supporter of the planned agreement was Governor Enríquez. It was rumored at the time that Enríquez had a personal stake in the matter, since he was allegedly related to the Terrazas and might profit from this agreement. No proof of such allegations has as yet been found, and neither are personal gain or personal relations the only logical explanations for Enríquez's attitude. He was a basically conservative man who did not believe in agrarian reform as envisaged in Mexico's constitution, especially those reform projects in which land would be turned over to village communities (*ejidos*).[108] In 1916, he had been one of the first Carrancista governors to return confiscated lands to their former owners, and he had refused to set up any agrarian commission in Chihuahua as long as he was governor. Selling the Terrazas' agricultural lands in parcels that were relatively small, but not too small, would allow them to be bought by entrepreneurially minded Chihuahuan farmers, who would form the kind of agrarian middle class Enríquez hoped would become a conservative agricultural backbone in the state. In addition, in a state devastated by years of savage revolutionary warfare, the project seemed to offer hope of rapid economic recovery. The irrigation works that McQuatters planned to build and the 50,000 head of cattle he proposed to import into Chihuahua, as well as the $125,000 he was ready to invest in a bank, might lead to rapid economic development. The governor portrayed McQuatters as a kind of philanthropist, an opinion definitely not shared by McQuatters, who anticipated enormous profits from this project, in which he was willing to invest $25 million.[109]

In the eyes of President Obregón, at least in 1921, the McQuatters plan seemed to present a solution to a difficult dilemma with respect to the Terrazas estates. He knew that he could not return the Terrazas lands to the hacendado's family without creating tremendous opposition in the country, especially among the peasants. Nor was he willing simply to expropriate these estates without, or with only minimal, compensation and divide them up among the peasants, which the constitution would have allowed. He had good legal grounds for not paying any compensation to the Terrazas family at all. As Abraham González had argued eleven years earlier, the Terrazas had undervalued their properties for many years and thus paid practically no taxes on them, and the family owed so much to the federal government that either all or a large segment of their properties could be expropriated in lieu of tax arrears. This was a measure that Obregón was not willing to resort to. He never gave an explanation for his attitude, but in all probability, while attempting to win peasant support, he did not want a radical break with Mexico's landowners, practically all of whom had understated the value of their properties for tax purposes and might fear a similar fate. In addition, since his government had not yet been recognized by the United States, he may have feared that such a radical decree of expropriation might so antagonize the U.S. government that it would consider him a Bolshevik and deny him recognition. The one way he could get the support of Chihuahua's peasants without antagonizing Mexico's landowners or the United States was to buy the Terrazas properties. That was a costly undertaking for a budget-strapped government that had committed most of its resources to paying an overblown army in order to prevent it from revolting, and Obregón considered it as a last resort.

Enríquez felt that the McQuatters plan had an additional advantage. For public consumption, the plan could be described as a kind of land reform, since McQuatters proposed to sell the agricultural parts of the estates in small lots to Chihuahuan peasants. To influence both the Mexican president and Mexican public opinion, the Terrazas mobilized many of their peons to write petitions to Obregón calling for the implementation of the McQuatters plan. The Terrazas had promised them that they would have the first option to buy, and that McQuatters would furnish them with credit to do so. The peons were tired of government control of the Terrazas estates and the difficult conditions it imposed upon them. They believed, not entirely without justification, that if the lands were simply divided up, it was not they but the peasants from surrounding villages who would be the main beneficiaries.[110]

The McQuatters plan would have cost the federal government nothing, would probably have brought in additional taxes, and might have encouraged economic recovery, which was one of the cornerstones of the policy of Obregón and the Sonora leadership. In addition, it might have improved relations with the United States and facilitated recognition of Obregon's administration by the U.S. government, which was one of his foremost aims. As long as no massive opposition against it emerged in Chihuahua, Obregón seems to have favored the plan. In December 1921, he wrote McQuatters that he welcomed "the noble efforts which you and your group . . . are putting forth" and told him that he would help him in every way.[111]

Once the project became known in Chihuahua, a tremendous wave of opposition, which neither Enríquez nor Obregón had anticipated, engulfed the state. Long-standing opposition to the Terrazas family and demands for land reform now became linked to revolutionary nationalism. Newly formed peasant unions in Chihuahua, peasant organizations outside the state, and labor unions, as well as many individuals, protested privately and publicly, making their voices heard in the newly elected state assembly. There was deep resentment that a foreign company would take over the estates and fear that Americans would now exercise more control over Chihuahua than ever before. There was anger that the Terrazas lands were to be exempted from any future laws on agrarian reform— laws that had, thanks to Enríquez, not yet been adopted in Chihuahua; there were demands for redistribution of these lands without any compensation and without peasants being charged for them. In spite of this opposition, both Enríquez and the overwhelming majority of the state legislature ratified the McQuatters contract.[112]

Obregón, however, hesitated. His enthusiasm was obviously fading, and on March 6, he wired Enríquez that no decision should be taken on the McQuatters contract before it had been studied in greater detail, saying:

As far as I know, this affair has provoked general discontent in your state and this is due to the fact that attempts have been made to implement it before an agrarian law has been adopted and this had led to great alarm among groups who are anxiously waiting for the implementation of such a law. My government believes that the matter is of such importance both internally and externally that it has to be studied with great discretion and in great detail and the pros and cons have to be weighed. When I have studied the contract, I shall deal with it with great interest and give you my opinion.[113]

On March 6, Obregón was still weighing the merits of the McQuatters contract. Eleven days later, however, he came down firmly against it. The most important factor that changed his mind was a letter from Villa, written on March 12, 1922, containing an unmistakable threat. Hitherto, except for his relatively mild advocacy of the demands of the peasants of Bosque de Aldama, Villa had practically never intervened in either regional or national politics since his surrender. His letter to Obregón thus constituted a radical change, and as such, it must have impressed the Mexican president all the more.

In Villa's eyes, the McQuatters contract was a conspiracy of his three greatest enemies—the Terrazas clan, the Americans, and Governor Enríquez. Obregón did not realize what the real situation in Chihuahua was, Villa said. McQuatters "was nothing but a loyal servant of the high officials of North America, and since the Mexican people understands this, this constitutes the first step in the decadence of the government that you represent, and I think that you must do something to immediately remedy the situation." Villa told Obregón that he was writing this letter in order "to save my country as well as the government that you presently represent, which I really support, as my behavior has shown and is still showing." Villa insisted that even though the governor and the state legislature had approved it, the people of Chihuahua had unanimously repudiated the Mc-Quatters contract. If nothing were done "after the unanimous protests of the Chihuahuan people, doubtless bullets will fly, and it is said that this will occur before three months have passed." Villa did not say that some of these bullets might be fired by him and his forces, but it could be inferred that he might support a rebellion should it occur in Chihuahua. Villa insisted that the McQuatters contract was part of a plan by American capitalists and oil men to overthrow Obregón, which was to be implemented within three months. He sent his letter to Obregón by special messenger and asked the Mexican president for an immediate reply.[114]

In Obregón's eyes, Villa's letter raised the possibility that Chihuahua's country people might rise up once more against the government, and that Villa might again lead them into battle. At the very least, this might play into the hands of Obregón's enemies and lead to massive loss of peasant support for his administration. It might have even more serious consequences if the rebels attacked American property. With Villa on the rampage, a U.S. military intervention might once again be a real possibility. Obregón therefore immediately replied to Villa's letter expressing his complete and unequivocal agreement with Villa's position. He wrote Villa that ever since learning about the McQuatters contract, "I have intervened with the greatest energy to prevent this plan from being implemented, since I believe that it contains a very serious danger for our country, and because many of the clauses in this contract are in absolute contradiction to our laws, which we are obligated to defend."[115]

Obregón's reply may also have been influenced by Calles, who also voiced opposition to the contract two days after Villa wrote his letter to the Mexican president. He expressed his opposition in the shape of a devastating memorandum written by a high official of the Ministry of the Interior (Secretaría de Gobernación), over which Calles presided. The memorandum criticized the McQuatters contract on three points, each of which by itself constituted a decisive obstacle to acceptance of the contract by the Mexican government. The first objection was that while McQuatters had promised all kinds of concessions to the Mexican and Chihuahuan governments, the contract in fact contained no clauses that would force him to carry out his promises. Even if the new company created by McQuatters did not do what had been promised, "it would still keep full property of the estates it had acquired, which would mean that we would allow a company to acquire a huge amount of land on the basis of a promise to divide it up, but in fact giving it the freedom not to do so." Instead of subdividing or selling lots, the company could simply cultivate the land itself, as hacendados had traditionally done. The second objection was that the state government of Chihuahua, which had signed a contract with McQuatters, was in fact usurping the prerogatives of the federal government in Mexico City. The memorandum implied that if the right of the Chihuahuan administration to take such a decision were recognized, other states would make deals both with local hacendados and with foreign enterprises, thereby completely undercutting the federal government. The main objection by the Ministry of the Interior was based on nationalism. How could the Mexican government, whose policies were based on the constitution of 1917 and on its article 27, which strongly limited the right of foreigners to acquire land, allow a foreign company to assume control of properties of two and a half million hectares? Although McQuatters had officially agreed to register his company as a Mexican undertaking operating under the laws of Mexico, it would in fact still be a foreign company, since all of its shareholders would be foreigners and the U.S. State Department would actively intervene in any conflict between the Mexican government and the company. The memorandum ended with an ominous warning, in which the author quoted the words of a Mexican deputy spoken 37 years earlier, during a meeting of the Mexican parliament in 1885, when the matter of extensive land concessions to foreigners was being debated. "Who will the buyers be?" Manuel Sánchez Facio had asked.

Reason and experience clearly indicate the answer, gentlemen. It is American capitalists who are looking for grazing land for their cattle. After the cattle, what will come?
Thus began the colonization of Texas and New Mexico![116]

A few days later, Obregón decreed the expropriation of the Terrazas estates in order to divide the land among Chihuahua's peasants.

Not surprisingly, howls of protest arose in the American press. The *Chicago Tribune* bitterly condemned the cancellation of the McQuatters project and ominously charged that "Obregón had to give way to the radicals in his camp."[117] Such accusations were not limited to the *Tribune*, and they worried the Obregón administration, which was desperately seeking to secure recognition by the conservative Republican Harding administration in Washington. McQuatters strongly objected, stating he had incurred great expense because he had been encouraged in his project by the initially favorable response to it by Obregón, and he cited a favorable letter that Obregón had sent him in 1921. The Terrazas clan recurred to the courts. The Mexican courts did not present a serious problem for Obregón, but the protests of the American press, implying that Obregón had become some kind of a Bolshevik, and McQuatters's implied threat to publicize Obregón's initially favorable attitude to his contract were serious problems for the Mexican president. He saw no other way out of his dilemma than to richly compensate both the Terrazas and McQuatters. McQuatters seems to have made $1 million on the deal,[118] while the Terrazas obtained nearly $13 million for their lands, although not all of it was paid at once.[119]

Enríquez now switched sides and said that the sale of the Terrazas land would be an undesirable precedent, since it would allow other landowners to sell their land to foreigners. "From now on," he stated, "everyone who pretends to sell his lands to foreigners can be very certain that he exposes himself to the same proceedings of expropriation."[120] He now became a strong supporter of a new agrarian law passed by the Chihuahuan legislature, and the division of the Terrazas estates among peasants began. Enríquez's "change of heart" was such that he now blamed Obregón for delays in the distribution of the Terrazas estates. This was too much for the Mexican president, who reminded Enríquez "how long the promulgation of an agrarian law was delayed in order not to affect these lands when it seemed that they would be controlled by an American trust and with what energy you now proceed against the government, which acted in order to resolve one of the most difficult problems of the present administration."[121]

Obregón's decision was a victory for Chihuahua's peasants and a defeat for the Terrazas, but neither the victory nor the defeat was of decisive proportions. By 1930, only 20 percent of the Terrazas estates had been given to peasants and the Terrazas themselves had bought back an equivalent amount of land, about 20 percent, over which they once again assumed control.[122]

Obregón's decision on the McQuatters contract was Villa's last great victory. It may also have foreshadowed his death. One of the factors that contributed to each of Villa's defeats was the overconfidence inspired by a prior victory. After the cancellation of the McQuatters contract and Obregón's apparent capitulation to Villa's threats, he seems to have undergone a change of attitude.

Villa and Politics

It was in the spring of 1922, a few weeks after Villa had sent his dramatic letter to Obregón, that *El Universal* sent Regino Hernández Llergo to interview Villa. The ostensible reason for the interview, as Hernández Llergo described it, was the intense curiosity of people all over Mexico about Villa, what he was doing at Canutillo, and what he thought of Mexico's future development. While there is little doubt about this curiosity, there is also little doubt that the government wanted Villa to give an interview to the press. Not only did *El Universal* have strong links to the Mexico City administration but the government's military leaders in northern Mexico encouraged Villa to receive Hernández Llergo. The commander of federal forces in the north, Gonzalo Escobar, gave the Mexico City reporter a letter of introduction to Villa and requested Felíx Lara, commander of the garrison in the city of Parral, which was adjacent to Villa's hacienda of Canutillo, to support Hernández Llergo in every possible way. Lara, who was later implicated in Villa's assassination, did so. He was on good terms with Villa and introduced him to Hernández Llergo. When Villa was reluctant to grant a press interview, Lara spoke with him for an hour and finally persuaded him to accede to the newspaperman's request.[123]

The reasons for the government's eagerness to have Villa give a press interview are not too difficult to understand. Although Obregón still had two years left in office—new presidential elections were not due until 1924—the struggle for his succession had already begun. Since one of the main demands and platforms of all revolutionary factions had been no reelection of the president, it was clear that Obregón could not run again in 1924. The two leading contenders to succeed him were Minister of the Interior Plutarco Elías Calles and Finance Minister Adolfo de la Huerta. Obregón clearly favored Calles, but de la Huerta enjoyed a relatively large measure of support within the country. To a certain degree, the differences between the two men were ideological. Radical labor leaders, most of the union movement, and most of the newly formed peasant organizations supported Calles. Landowners and more conservative Mexicans, as well as a substantial part of the army, were in favor of de la Huerta. The ideological differences should not be exaggerated, however, since a number of radical Mexican politicians such as Salvador Alvarado also supported de la Huerta. Rumors had been appearing in the press that Villa had political ambitions of his own, that he might not support the official candidate, that he might even rise up in arms against the administration. The government obviously hoped that Villa would repeat in his interview with Hernández Llergo what he had been constantly stating in his letters to Obregón: that his sole interests were his hacienda at Canutillo and his business and family affairs, and that he would refrain from participating in politics in any way.

These hopes were dashed by the interview that Villa gave Hernández Llergo. On the one hand, he did project the image of a man deeply involved in his estate and his business affairs. For hours, he took Hernández Llergo around Canutillo and described the estate's economy to him in detail. For hours, he elaborated on the technical side of his estate, proudly showed him the cocks he was raising for cockfights, and wandered through the school with him.

But another part of Villa's interview was bound to cause consternation within the Obregón administration, and especially among Calles and his supporters. Villa clearly stated that his pledge not to participate in politics would only extend until the end of Obregón's administration in 1924. He intimated that after that date he might become a candidate for the governorship of Durango:

From many parts of the republic, from many districts of Durango I have received letters and commissions proposing my candidacy and asking for my authorization to work in its favor, but I have told them that they should wait . . . that they should do nothing on this matter now. I have told them that according to the arrangements I made with the government I had given my word that I would not participate in politics during the administration of General Obregón . . . and I am ready to keep my word. . . . I have told the same to all of my friends: they should wait, and when they least expect it, an opportunity will arise . . . then things will be very different.

Villa evidently believed that he was enormously popular in Mexico:

The affair of my candidacy for the governorship of Durango is of little importance for me right now, but it will show you the enormous support I have. . . . I am enormously popular, sir. . . . my race loves me. I have friends in all social groups, among the rich, the poor, the educated, and the ignorant. . . . Sir, I do not believe that anyone has the support that Francisco Villa has. . . . For this reason the politicians are afraid of me. They are afraid of me because they know that on the day that I decide to fight, I shall destroy them.[124]

Villa did not clearly state what kind of a fight he had in mind, whether it would be political or military, but another remark he made no doubt deepened the fears his interview generated. "I am a real soldier, gentlemen," he told Hernández Llergo. "I can mobilize 40,000 men in 40 minutes."[125]

Even more disquieting for the government, and above all for Calles, was Villa's clearly indicated preference for de la Huerta. Calling de la Huerta by his nickname, Fito, Villa said: "Fito is a very good man, and the defects he has are due to his excessive goodness of heart. Fito is a politician who likes to conciliate the interests of all, and anyone who achieves this does great service to his country. . . . Fito is a good person, very intelligent, and he would not be bad as president of the republic."

"And General Calles?" Hernández Llergo asked him.

"General Calles has many good qualities, but like any other man he also has some defects. . . . his political point of view, as far as I can see, is to solve the problem of the working class on the basis of radicalism."

It is not clear what Villa intended when he gave this interview. On the one hand, he may simply have been talking off the cuff, as he frequently did, all the more so since there were no political advisors to restrain him. On the other hand, the interview could also be seen as an attempt to influence the coming presidential election. Since Villa was convinced of the popular support he enjoyed in Mexico, his advocacy of the candidacy of de la Huerta might be seen as an attempt to shift the balance de la Huerta's favor. His reference to the 40,000 men he could raise in 40 minutes might also be considered as a warning to the Obregón administration not to permit a fraudulent election and to respect an electoral victory by de la Huerta. Villa's failure to discount the possibility that he might become a candidate for governor of Durango in the future might be considered as an indication of the price he would exact from de la Huerta for his support. The two aims that Villa insinuated in his interview—a friendly president and his own control of one of the country's northern states—were similar to the demands he had made in 1914 and 1915. It is significant that he took aim at the governorship of Durango rather than Chihuahua. He had far more enemies in Chihuahua, where the bloodiest fighting had occurred between 1915 and 1920, than in Durango, which had been marginal to Villa's activities in this period. In Chihuahua, many of the popular organizations were strongly influenced by Enríquez, as well as by memories of the bloody civil war, and therefore opposed Villa. This seems to have been less true in Durango, where the defensas sociales, which fought with such persistence against Villa, were far smaller and less developed.

Villa's interview with *El Universal* led to an astonishing development. Eleven months after the interview was published, Adolfo de la Huerta met with Villa in a railway compartment on the way from Jiménez to Torreón and urged him to support the candidacy of Calles. In addition to Villa and de la Huerta, the commander of federal forces in northern Mexico, Eugenio Martínez, Villa's secretary Trillo, and the undersecretary of the Finance Ministry, Luis L. León (who was also a confidant of Calles's), were present at the meeting. In a highly optimistic vein, León reported to Calles on the results of that meeting. "General Villa insinuated once more," León reported, "that it would be convenient if de la Huerta were to become a presidential candidate, but the latter immediately objected. He reminded Villa that one year ago he had clearly told him that he would not be a candidate." De la Huerta insisted, according to León, that Calles was the right candidate for the revolutionary group:

He described the very difficult situation in which the revolution would find itself if conflict between the two of you [de la Huerta and Calles] would emerge due solely to petty personal resentment, and that this might lead to the triumph of reaction; he explained in what way you and he were united so that nothing and no one could separate you, so that if you were president of the republic, de la Huerta would consider himself as such. General Villa agreed that as long as the revolutionaries were united, the revolution would be guaranteed, and he was happy about this fraternal union between you and Señor de la Huerta, and of which we gave him innumerable proofs,

Señor de la Huerta as well as I. His final word was that it was not necessary once again to deal with the matter. . . . General Villa reminded us that in previous days he had been a good friend of yours, and that in spite of everything that had happened, you behave very well toward him. . . . Villa is a strong element.

León stated that "in my opinion General Villa has understood that his situation is linked to ours; for that reason his interest is to support the present administration. . . . In addition, I believe he is somewhat tired as a guerrilla fighter and wants to continue to enjoy the peaceful conditions in which he now lives." According to León, a strong indication of Villa's peaceful intent was Villa's constant urging of Finance Minister de la Huerta to build a railroad that would link central Mexico to Villa's hacienda and the surrounding Durango area. That area had been largely impenetrable to outsiders and had been a refuge for Villa in his guerrilla days. But building such a railroad, León reasoned, would make it far easier for the government to send troops to the area and would make it far more difficult for any guerrilla fighter to find refuge there. In León's opinion, this was a crucial proof that Villa had no intention of rising in arms against the government; in addition, Villa "has become something of a bourgeois and does not think of getting involved in rebel adventures." León concluded his report by suggesting to Calles that he meet with Villa and invite him on board his train on the way to Torreón.[126]

It is not clear whether such a meeting ever took place, although unconfirmed reports state that the two men met, that Calles asked for Villa's support, and that Villa's response was ambiguous. He answered Calles's direct question, "Can I count on you?" by saying, "This depends . . . you know, if you are with justice and the majority of the people, yes. If no, no."[127]

While this account may be apocryphal, there is little doubt that Villa remained strongly opposed to Calles's candidacy. But his interview with de la Huerta may have convinced Villa that the former president was not his man. Villa then appears to have switched allegiances to another candidate, one of the few of his former collaborators whom he continued to see at Canutillo, Raúl Madero. As early as 1921, contacts between Villa and Raúl Madero had aroused the suspicion of government agents. An agent had reported to Obregón that Raúl Madero and a brother of his had come to interview Villa in Canutillo. "What impressed those who knew about this trip was that the visitors did not go by train but went through the whole region through back alleys in their car."[128]

Were the Mexican conservatives, who seem to have rallied to Villa, correct in their assessment that he had made a 180° turn and was now a reliable ally? The conservatives had a long history of attempting to woo Villa and finding out that their hopes had been in vain. They had helped him to escape from prison in 1912, hoping that he would turn against Madero. Instead, he had effected a reconciliation with the Mexican president. They had entertained great hopes that in 1914 he would return the confiscated properties of Mexico's landowners. Instead, he had made an alliance with Zapata and continued to expropriate hacienda lands. In spite of his newfound status as a hacendado, it is doubtful whether he would have been a more reliable ally of the conservatives in 1923. He had rejected two basic tenets of conservative policy in his interview with Hernández Llergo—

support for the clergy and a pro-U.S. stance—had supported the peasants of Bosque de Aldama and prevented the implementation of the McQuatters project; and he seems to have maintained close links to popular organizations in Durango, although, significantly perhaps, not in Chihuahua.

There was nevertheless one aspect of his policy in 1914 that had encouraged conservatives and that seems to have continued to do so in 1923. His interest in social transformations had always centered on his own region. He had always been willing to allow regional and local leaders in other parts of Mexico to proceed as they saw fit. The conservatives may have hoped that with Adolfo de la Huerta or Raúl Madero as president, Villa would have allowed them to proceed as they saw fit in the rest of Mexico.

While, on the one hand, one cannot entirely disregard the possibility that Villa's increasing alienation from large segments of Mexico's peasants in the bloody guerrilla war of 1915–20 and his transformation into a hacendado may have altered both his attitudes and his social philosophy, on the other hand, that alienation seems to have taken place mainly in Chihuahua and far less in Durango, where, once he made peace with the government, Villa was welcomed as a returning hero in the villages through which he passed. Thus, had he in fact become governor of Durango, it is very possible that his old alliance with popular forces would have been revived. This makes the hypothesis of a complete turnaround in his social policies problematic.

Whatever Villa's political orientation in the last weeks of his life may have been, there is little doubt that both Obregón and Calles had reason to consider him a great potential danger. Not only had he intimated in his interview with Hernández Llergo that he was opposed to Calles but he had also indicated that once Obregón's term of office expired he would participate in politics again and possibly seek the governorship of Durango. The idea that Villa might once more control one of the volatile states of northern Mexico, where he still enjoyed great popularity, was anathema to both Obregón and Calles. Villa's veiled threat that he would take up arms if the McQuatters plan were adopted and his boast that he could mobilize 40,000 men in 40 minutes were not taken lightly. While the boast may have been exaggerated, there were several thousand men who would have followed Villa at his first call. The U.S. chargé d'affaires, George Summerlin, considered Villa a strong autonomous force in Mexico:

Villa's estates appeared moreover to be to a certain extent extraterritorial insofar as the present administration was concerned. They were under the control of Villa himself and his own heavily-armed escort. The advantages for political plotting which lay in such an arrangement are readily seen. Quite recently he is reported to have added to his properties the hacienda of "El Pueblito" near the town of Ojinaga on the Kansas City Railway, a significant strategical point.[129]

A poll of its readers as to their choice for president by *El Universal*, one of Mexico's largest newspapers, may have added to the government's fears. The results, published by *El Universal* on July 10, 1922, indicated that 142,872 of its readers would vote for Senator Carlos B. Zetina, a businessman; 139,965 for Adolfo de la Huerta; 84,129 for Calles; and 72,854 for Villa. In several respects the results of this poll must have been extremely worrisome to both Obregón and Calles. It showed that Calles might very well be defeated in a free general election and indicated that de la Huerta was more popular than Calles, while the strong vote for the relatively unknown Zetina, who was the only candidate not identified with the revolution, seemed to indicate a large-scale repudiation of any revolutionary leader. Moreover, Villa's strong showing among the newspaper's largely middle-class and even upper-class readership might indicate that his popularity transcended the lower classes of society.[130]

In view of Villa's increasing opposition to the government, foreign observers such as Summerlin were not surprised when he was assassinated on July 20, 1923.

CHAPTER TWENTY

The End and the Survival of Villa

The Assassination of Villa

Between 1910 and 1920, three of the major leaders of the Mexican Revolution—Madero, Zapata, and Carranza—were assassinated. As different as their cases were, the deaths of all three had one element in common: they had trusted the wrong person, and that trust had cost them their lives. Until the end, Madero had believed in Huerta's loyalty; Zapata had trusted Jesús Guajardo, a Carrancista officer promising to defect to Zapata's cause; and Carranza had believed in the professions of loyalty of Rodolfo Herrero, who killed him on his way to Veracruz, in the village of Tlaxcalontongo.

Villa, by contrast, was wary of everyone. When Raúl Madero came one day to visit him, both men slept outside of the main house while on a tour of Villa's estate. Madero, who had gone to sleep near Villa, found upon awaking that Villa had gone away to sleep by himself in a spot where he could not find him.[1] Villa's distrust of everyone manifested itself in small details. At one point during his interview with Hernández Llergo, the newspaperman wanted as a matter of courtesy to let Villa go ahead of him, but Villa told him that he never allowed anyone to walk behind him. Yet in the final account, the same overconfidence that had doomed Madero, Zapata, and Carranza would overtake Villa. In Villa's case, however, it was not overconfidence in another person but in himself, and perhaps in the government as well, that led to his death.

From the very first day that he settled down at Canutillo, the fear of assassination haunted Villa. He scarcely left the estate during his first year there, and when he did so he was always accompanied by an escort of 50 Dorados. As relations with the Obregón administration improved, Villa's fear that the government might be out to kill him gradually decreased. Obregón helped to dispel these fears, not only by giving in to all of Villa's demands and sending him constant cordial letters, but also by sending him two machine guns as a special gift, additional evidence that the government was interested in protecting Villa.[2]

As Villa's wariness of the government diminished, his fear concentrated on one individual who had every reason in the world, and perhaps even a large measure of justification, for killing Villa. This was Jesús Herrera, one of the last male members of the Herrera clan, whom Villa had with unequaled ferocity attempted to exterminate. As the last son of José de la Luz Herrera, Jesús Herrera determined to use his considerable wealth to seek revenge on Villa by any means. For more than a year, a secret war went on between the two. According to Villa, Herrera had bribed a number of men to kill him, but they had all died before being able to do so. According to Villa, one of them, Primitivo Escárcega, had been killed in a drunken brawl in a brothel, "probably at the hands of my sympathizers."[3]

It may then have been Villa's turn to take the offensive. Jesús Herrera bitterly denounced Villa for sending two of his former subordinates, General José García and Colonel Rosario Jiménez, to kill him. García and Jiménez did not succeed and were arrested, in spite of Villa's protests that the charges against them had no basis in fact.[4]

Villa decided to put pressure on the government to take action against his enemy, although he never specified the kind of action he expected the government to take. Hitherto, Villa had attempted to keep out of the public eye and to handle every problem he faced through discreet letters to the government. This time, he began with a press campaign. In March 1923, he wrote a long letter to *El Universal*, with which, since the interview he had granted the editors in Canutillo, he seems to have maintained privileged relations. In the letter, Villa said that for more than a year and a half, Jesús Herrera had been attempting to assassinate him. He had never formally protested or complained, since Herrera's actions "affected only my life, and the life of a man retired to private life has no importance in relation to the rest of society," but that he was now speaking out, since "recently a few men have died who had been seduced by the money of Jesús Herrera and had attempted to kill me. And I believe that it is important to prevent such losses of people, which should not occur."

The killers' deaths and the assassination attempt to which Villa was referring had occurred a short time before. During a visit to Ciudad Chihuahua, Villa's adopted son Francisco Gil Piñon, who was the administrator of Canutillo and Villa's part-time secretary, had received a warning from a politician friend, Alfredo Chávez, who said that a group of men were on their way to Canutillo to assassinate Villa. He could only identify two of them: one Primitivo Escárcega and Atenógenes López, brother of two of Villa's most loyal generals, Pablo and Martín López. Piñon immediately warned his chief, and Villa undertook a two-pronged counterattack in order to foil the attempt on his life. He set out with a number of men to find the would-be killers. And in case they escaped and made their way to Parral, he ordered a number of men of his escort to go into town to simulate drunkenness, to attempt to make friends with the killers, invite them into a brothel, and kill them there. Villa's strategy proved eminently successful.

Most of the killers fled and returned to Chihuahua when they heard Villa and his men were looking for them. Primitivo Escárcega, who was probably the most reckless, did, however, go into Parral, along with another man. There they were picked up by Villa's men playing the part of drunks, enticed into a brothel, and killed.[5]

Atenógenes López escaped. It is at first glance surprising that the brother of Villa's two best-known and most loyal lieutenants should have been involved in a plot to kill him. Atenógenes, the oldest of the brothers, had taken part in the Orozco revolt of 1912. He remained opposed to Villa but in order not to fight his brothers he migrated to the United States. The reason that after his return to Mexico he was set on killing Villa was his conviction that Martín López had not died at the hands of the Carrancistas but had been executed by Villa. There is no evidence to substantiate such an accusation.[6]

Villa was enraged by this attempt on his life, for which he blamed Herrera. The imprisonment of García and Jiménez further angered him. Villa's bile spilled over into his letter. Herrera, wrote Villa, was not only a would-be assassin but also a thief. He had become a millionaire, although he had never participated in the war. "All he did was to steal money from our country in the shadow of his brothers."

Villa concluded his letter with "open and frank words born from the bottom of my heart." These words constituted a clear warning. "I, a man of war at other times, who now is completely dedicated to active and quiet work in the country-side, I have no guarantees, and this state of affairs is due uniquely to the threats of Herrera, but I could obtain such guarantees if I had Herrera shot and he would be the only one responsible for what would happen."[7] Villa called on his *hermanos de raza* (his Mexican brothers) to prevent Herrera from continuing his attempts to assassinate him. He did not specify what concrete measures his brothers should take.

The fury that Villa expressed in his letter was nothing compared to that of Jesús Herrera, who publicly replied to Villa a few days later. In a letter *El Universal* refused to publish, but that was printed in *El Portavoz*, a Torreón newspaper run by enemies of Villa, he denied any intention of killing Villa and said that if Villa really wanted peace of mind, the only place he could find it would be in an insane asylum. He wrote that "this criminal had lost his mind . . . that the whole country is full of the blood that this infamous bandit has shed," and he compared Villa to "a savage beast shouting with pain and rage, anxiously looking for anyone whom he could sully with his filthy spittle."[8]

In his letter to *El Universal*, Villa had threatened to have Herrera shot, but after the publicity given to the affair and the arrest of the two men whom Villa may have sent to kill Herrera, he felt unable to do this. So he now directly appealed to Alvaro Obregón and Plutarco Elías Calles to rein in Herrera.

In a long letter that he sent to Obregón on April 18, 1923, Villa emphasized the appreciation "that those of us who are completely dedicated to agricultural labor in this small corner of the world" felt for Obregón, and said that "while in general I do not tend to display my affectionate feelings, you do know that when necessary here in the rear-guard I am at your disposal." He drew Obregón's attention to the constant attacks—he called them calumnies—that Herrera was spreading in the press of Torreón. Villa sent Obregón a copy of Herrera's letter and ominously wrote, "Knowing my character, Mr. President, you must know what sacrifice I have had to make in order to prudently tolerate the grave misdeeds of Herrera," and he insisted that he had only done so "because of the respect and esteem that I have for you and I hope that as a friend you find a means to put an end to this matter, which I place in your hands."[9]

Obregón's hands were not the only ones in which he placed the matter. On the same day that Villa wrote the president, he wrote another letter to Calles with similar content. The letter to Calles was similar to the letter to Obregón but for a few subtle differences. His letter contained the same professions of sympathy for Calles that he had expressed for Obregón. "Here in this far corner of the world where one only hears the noise of agricultural implements, we are thinking of your person as good friends do, and here in the extreme rear-guard we are at your disposal in case that should prove necessary."

In his letter to Calles, Villa insisted that "since the beginning of the revolutionary struggle of 1910 there has been perfect comprehension and affinity of ideas between us," something he could scarcely have written to Obregón in view of the battles of Celaya, León, and Aguascalientes, to mention but a few that had taken place between them. He complained about the press in Torreón having published Herrera's letters, "which contain very grave offenses and deeply hurt me and in which Herrera shows no respect for me or for society." As in his letter to Obregón, he insisted that the only reason he had tolerated Herrera's attacks was out of "the respect and esteem I have for you," and he called on him "as a friend to have the kindness to find a solution to this matter and put an end to it." He mentioned in his letter to Calles that he had also written Obregón, saying "as good revolutionaries you as well as I must have an affinity in our ideas, since we are a family, born out of the same ideals, and we should have mutual consideration for each other, since we have undergone similar sufferings."[10]

Obregón took an unusually long time to reply to Villa. Villa had written him on April 18 but it was only on May 9 that Obregón, citing "excessive obligations of his presidency," replied. He praised Villa's prudence in the matter and promised that he would look for a "discreet way" to prevent the repetition of such "painful incidents."[11]

One such discreet way had in fact been suggested a few weeks earlier by Jesús Herrera's sister, Dolores, who was deeply worried that Villa "wants to exterminate my whole family" and would kill her brother, "the only being who watches over all of us." She wrote Obregón that her brother, a high government official attached to the Customs Service, was too proud to ask for a transfer. But she was convinced that if Obregón were to transfer him, he would agree to go to Guadalajara or to another city located further south and thus be safer from any reprisal or attack that Villa might want to undertake against him.[12]

Obregón sent a noncommittal reply to Dolores Herrera, stating that he would take the matter into consideration.[13] There is no evidence that Herrera was ever transferred from Torreón, but his public attacks on Villa ceased. One reason for this may have been that Obregón envisaged a very different kind of solution to the problem involving Jesús Herrera: the assassination of Villa, three months after Villa sent his letters of complaint to Obregón and Calles.

In July, Villa decided to go to Río Florido, a village located at some distance from Canutillo. There he was to be made godfather of the child of a friend. Villa loved acting as godfather. In the heyday of the División del Norte, when he seemed the most powerful man in Mexico, hundreds of families had asked him to be the godfather of their children. Villa had frequently acceded to these requests and made gifts to the children. His trip to the baptism was to be combined with another trip to Parral, where he would visit one of his wives, Manuela Casas, who resided at a hotel that he owned and where he would arrange some business matters.

Rumors that some kind of plot against him was under way had reached him, but he did not take them too seriously. Such rumors were his daily fare. He was on good terms with both Obregón and Calles, and they even seemed to have reined in Jesús Herrera. When his secretary Trillo noted that taking his whole escort of 50 men along—something he had always done in the first year at Canutillo the few times he left the estate—was too expensive, Villa acceded. He decided to go by car. In any case, Villa had fallen in love with automobiles. Apart from his driver and Trillo, he took along four men from his escort, who could ride in his car. But he did not entirely disregard the warnings he had heard. He ordered Gil Piñon to send three heavily armed men of his escort to the outskirts of Parral to await him there and to make sure that nothing happened on the way to Canutillo. Driving through Parral on July 10 on his way to Río Florido, he did not notice several rifles were pointed at him and his car from behind the windows of an apartment at the intersection of Benito Juárez and Gabino Barreda Streets. They did not fire, for precisely at the moment when Villa reached the intersection, hundreds of children were leaving an adjacent school.

On the morning of July 20, after having spent some time in Parral and collected some money there, Villa decided to return to Canutillo. On the eve of his return, he sent a wire to Gil Piñon asking him to send him three cheeses.[14] This was code for three members of his escort who, as agreed upon when he left, were waiting for him on the outskirts of Parral. He felt completely secure in Parral. The city was garrisoned by hundreds of troops, and its commander, Félix Lara, was a good friend.

What Villa did not know was that Lara and his men had left Parral for the adjoining town of Maturana that very day, allegedly in order to practice for the military parade that was to take place on September 16, Mexico's national holiday. Had he known this, he might have become suspicious. Not only was September 16 still far away, but Maturana was the worst possible place to rehearse for a parade. The streets were narrow, irregular, and hilly; there was simply no reason why Maturana should have been chosen for such a purpose.

Villa was in a good mood. He was driving the car himself and joking with his escort and with Trillo. When his car approached the intersection of Benito Juárez and Gabino Barreda, a man standing there raised his hand in salute and shouted the old war cry of the División del Norte, "Viva Villa!" Villa did not know that this call, which had greeted him so frequently in battle, was this time a prelude to his death, for the man had been sent out by the killers to watch for Villa. The cry of "Viva Villa" and the raised hand signaled the men waiting in an apartment at the junction of the two streets to open fire when Villa's car reached the intersection and slowed down to turn.

Villa was hit by nine bullets and killed instantly; so were Trillo, the chauffeur, and Villa's assistant, Daniel Tamayo. Three members of the escort were wounded. Rafael Medrano, who was shot in the arm and in the leg, managed to get out of the car and laid down beneath it, playing dead. Two members of the escort, Ramón Contreras and Claro Hurtado, ran toward an adjacent bridge. Although badly wounded, Contreras pulled out his pistol and managed to kill one of the assassins before escaping. He proved to be the only survivor. Hurtado tried to flee down to the river embankment, but found the exit closed, and as he turned around, he was shot by one of the assassins. More than 40 shots had hit Villa's car, and the killers had used dumdum bullets. After making sure that Villa was dead, the killers leisurely rode away on horseback.

The first news that Obregón received of Villa's assassination was a wire by the head of the telegraph office in Parral stating that Villa had been killed by men of his own escort.[15] Obregón was highly skeptical about the identity of the killers. "The version that Villa was killed by members of his own escort seems very strange to me," he wrote to Eugenio Martínez, the commander of government forces in Chihuahua. "If members of the escort had accompanied Villa since he left Canutillo, it would be illogical for them to have waited until they arrived in the city to kill him, and if they had not been with him when he left Canutillo, it would have been very strange for members of the escort to have been in Parral or near that city when the general would have been in Canutillo."[16]

A few hours later Obregón got a much clearer idea of what had happened in Parral when he received a telegram from the head of the Parral garrison, Colonel Lara, saying that seven to nine very well armed men, "apparently all of them rancheros," had been the ones who assassinated Villa. "The pursuit of these individuals was not possible, as you wished and as I would have wished, since I had no horses that could be utilized for this purpose," Lara wired Obregón. This excuse was ludicrous. There were large numbers of horses in Parral, and all Lara would have had to do was to borrow or requisition them. That was the gist of Obregón's reply to Lara. Expressing his astonishment, Obregón observed that only ten to fifteen horses would have been needed, and that Lara would have been completely justified in requisitioning them from their owners.[17] Lara's conduct was highly suspicious, but no investigation of it was ever carried out, and no action taken against him.

While Obregón was notified of the assassination immediately after it occurred, telegraph service to Canutillo was interrupted for six hours. News of the murder of their chief thus only reached Villa's people at Canutillo six hours later. This interruption may have been intentional, since Obregón, once he heard of Villa's killing, immediately ordered the army to occupy Canutillo. The reason Obregón gave for his decision was that the troops should prevent any looting and at the same time should locate any evidence that might be found in Villa's correspondence that could help to identify Villa's killers.[18] News of Villa's assassination nonetheless reached Canutillo before Obregón's men, and a bloody confrontation between federal troops and Villistas seemed imminent. Nicolás Fernández, who was visiting his sick son on the hacienda, immediately ordered all residents to arm themselves and to fire on any strangers attempting to enter the estate.[19]

Once the inhabitants of Canutillo learned that federal troops were on their way to occupy the estate, one of their leaders, Alfredo Paz Gutiérrez, urgently wired Obregón asking him "to order that these troops should remain at Rosario, Durango." Paz Gutiérrez stated that Villa's escort could keep order on the estate and explained that he had gotten in touch with the Villista colonists on the adjoining haciendas and told them to take similar precautions.

By ordering the occupation of Canutillo, Obregón doubtless hoped to prevent a possible Villista uprising triggered by Villa's assassination. Alfredo Paz Gutiérrez's telegram showed him that the measures he had ordered might very well provoke such an uprising by the men and women of Canutillo and the Villistas from the adjoining haciendas, all of whom were heavily armed.[20] Obregón tried to quiet the fears of Canutillo's residents by announcing that the troops were only coming to maintain law and order, that all existing arrangements would be respected, and full guarantees given to all inhabitants of the estate.[21] Nevertheless, no federal troops entered Canutillo. A standoff now occurred between federal troops and Villistas, with the soldiers remaining at Rosario but still under orders to occupy Canutillo.

Three days later, on July 23, the standoff between the Villistas and government troops was relaxed when Hipólito Villa wired Obregón, "I have arrived yesterday afternoon at the hacienda in order to take control of the affairs and interests of my deceased brother, and naturally I am at your disposal." He also thanked Obregón for the expressions of condolence that he had sent him on the occasion of his brother's death. Hipólito's telegram reassured Obregón that someone was in effective control of the Villistas and Hipólito's protestations of loyalty may have quieted the president's fear of an imminent uprising. Nevertheless, Obregón waited ten more days, until August 2, before rescinding the order to his troops to occupy the estate. He then wired the commander of federal troops in the north, General Eugenio Martínez, that Hipólito's assumption of control seemed to guarantee law and order at Canutillo, and that an occupation of the estate might appear to the Villista leaders as a "lack of confidence of the government in them."[22]

Villa was buried one day after his death, on Saturday, July 21, 1923. It was not entirely the kind of funeral he would have wished for, although the spectacle of thousands of inhabitants of Parral following his coffin, which was carried to the cemetery in a carriage drawn by two black horses, would have gratified him. He would also have appreciated the military guard and the band that paid him the honors due to his rank as general in command of a division. He would also have agreed with the identity and the words of the man who paid him his final respects at the funeral ceremony. This was the head of the school in Canutillo, Professor Jesús Cuello, who spoke directly to General Martínez, telling him that his uniform as a soldier was "stained with the blood of this victim, whose assassination has clear political aspects, and you will not be doing your duty either as a man or as a soldier or as a compadre of General Villa if you do not clear this matter up without any consideration of who may be affected."[23]

Villa would, however, have been repelled by the scurrilous debate that developed between Martínez and the doctors who embalmed his body over their fee. In a wire to the president, Martínez stated that the 3,000 pesos they charged was "somewhat high, and they protested that they had to carry out an enormous amount of work because of the seventeen bullet holes that Villa's and Trillo's bodies showed."[24]

Villa would have deeply resented Governor Ignacio Enríquez's refusal to allow his body to be buried in the mausoleum he had erected for himself a few years before in Ciudad Chihuahua. The reason Enríquez gave Obregón was that the cemetery where Villa had wanted to be buried had been closed for years, and that the plot in which Villa had chosen to be buried belonged to another person.[25] He would also have been sad that none of his men or the people closest to him had been present at his funeral. They were holed up in Canutillo, their arms at the ready, waiting to repel an invasion by government troops.

The World Press and Villa

What he would have appreciated was the enormous echo that his death produced in the press all over the world. While British newspapers generally condemned him—the killing of William Benton in 1914 was still very much an issue in their editorials—comments in the American press were surprisingly mixed, in spite of Villa's attack on Columbus. "[Villa] has long carried the stigma of bandit," the *New York Times* wrote,

but he really was one of Mexico's strong men, although illiterate and undisciplined. In a way, Villa for all his excesses, lawlessness, crime and escapades, was a moving example of talents running to waste for want of common schooling. An educated Villa might have been president of the republic. . . .

Francisco Villa was never so black as he was painted nor did he receive credit for abilities of a higher order and for a dog-like fidelity to Madero in whose integrity he implicitly believed. For a long time he was loyal to Carranza. But when Villa found that Venustiano had feet of clay, there was a breach that nobody could mend. Even Obregón[,] who saw things more clearly than Villa, could not endure Carranza and overthrew him for the good of Mexico. . . . John Reed brought out the humanity and humor of the man, his sympathy with the peons, his simplicity, the struggles of his clouded intellect with economic and state problems. . . . He fed starving populations with an auxiliary supply train that kept pace with his army. . . . After the worst has been said of Francisco Villa, after his crimes have been proved and his vices passed in review, the reflection is provoked that in a progressive and enlightened Mexico he might have been a useful servant of the state.[26]

"The standards of civilized life cannot be applied to him," the *Newark and Evening News* wrote.

His environment was one of violence. He was guided by his instincts, which were often the instincts of passion although intermixed with the instincts of justice. He belonged in the picture of illiterate, undeveloped Mexico, groping to escape from the oligarchic rule of the *científicos* and the oppressions and exploitation of the powerful. What he might have been in a civilized country is a question—he might have been greater or nothing.

The *Louisville Courier-Journal* wrote, "the spirit of Pancho was by every credible system of pagan theology transported to the Valhalla that is surely reserved for the world's elect who live and die with their boots on." "He was not solely a plunderer," the *Lincoln Star* commented. "His sympathies were always with the peon class of Mexico, victims of an oppression more terrible than language describes."

Others were far less favorable to Villa. "We can at least say that he deserves admission to the Valhalla of the picturesque heroes who have made the world laugh while they made it suffer," according to the *Albany Knickerbocker Press.* "Villa, from an angle of strict practicability was never anything better than a horse thief and cattle stealer and semi-sentimental, semi-bloodthirsty squire of dames. He grinned most of the time and he was never so dangerous as when he grinned most broadly."

"He was not a statesman nor a man of any great intelligence," asserted the *Danville Bee*, "but he lived a reckless life and there was adventure and romance in it, and these three qualities combined to win him a lasting place in Mexico's history." Inasmuch as he was a "butcher" by trade and a gunman by choice, the *Pittsburgh Gazette Times* felt that Villa had met "a just fate," to which the *New York World* added, "born with extraordinary talents, he set himself purposefully for his goal of a true villain. It was no easy task, yet he succeeded magnificently. To cap his inconceivable villainy he did not love women, tobacco or wine. With Villa it was villainy for art's sake."[27]

The reactions of the Mexican press were more varied and extreme. Some papers opposed to Villa employed a kind of crude terminology that their U.S. counterparts would never have used. On the other hand, there was an admiration for Villa going far beyond any kind of favorable treatment for Villa north of the border. Finally, there was one element in the Mexican press that was completely lacking in the United States: admiration, by people who otherwise did not like Villa, because he had successfully attacked and defied the Colossus of the North.

For *Omega*, a newspaper opposed to all revolutionary movements, Villa was "a gorilla" and "a troglodyte." It compared him to Emiliano Zapata, "the southern bandit, who is as much a murderer, a thief, and as guilty as Francisco Villa." *Omega* spoke of this "wretch, whose generation is one more blot for the revolutionary leadership."[28] For *El Universal*, Villa's death "meant the disappearance of a danger for the peace that the government has ensured up to now with so little brilliance."[29]

And yet, in spite of these adjectives, most Mexican newspapers expressed some kind of admiration for Villa. Even *Omega*, which deeply abhorred the revolution and said that calling Villa a general was an insult to the title,[30] subsequently wrote that he "was worth more than the great political personalities in power today," and mentioned "the good side of this man," which consisted in "loyalty and gratitude."[31]

El Universal opined that "whatever value posterity will place on him, [Villa] was a man who at certain moments was able to mobilize a tremendous amount of forces and popular sympathies, a man who doubtless in a devious way, even in an accidental way, one can say, but in a very real way, was able to incarnate at least a part of the desires of our nation."[32] The editors came to the conclusion that "Mexico . . . has been known in the past ten years . . . thanks to General Villa. . . . Let us take an example: X is an ignorant man, a worker with little curiosity, who has spent his whole life living in Alaska. Do you think that X would have known about the existence of Mexico without General Villa? I am very much afraid that this is not the case."

After having spoken of Villa's horrible crimes and accused him "of killing for the pleasure of killing," *Excelsior* wrote: "No one except for him has defied our neighbor and no one has ever dared to do as much against them as he has."[33]

Others were clear and open admirers of Villa. *El Demócrata* praised the fact that Villa, "practically without knowing how to read, did more but much more than so many scholars and members of governments. In a decided and effective way, he protected public education, and this title alone would be sufficient to make his enemies hesitate in their attacks on him."[34]

El Demócrata's views of Villa stood in stark contrast to those of many other newspapers. "To the humble who groaned under the slave driver's lash, Villa was the avenger; to those who were despoiled by the master, Villa was justice; to those whose blood still boiled from the outrage of '47, Villa was the soul of Mexico confronting Pershing; to the speculators in land and blood, Villa was a bandit and a monster."[35]

Popular perceptions of Villa and his assassination were far less ambiguous than those of newspapers and clearly expressed in a number of *corridos* (ballads) that were written on the occasion of his assassination:

> Pobre Pancho Villa.
> Fue muy triste su destino.
> Morir en una embuscada.
> Ya la mitad del camino.
> Ay, Mexico está de luto.
> Tiene una gran pesadilla.
> Pues mataron en Parral al valiente Pancho Villa.

> Poor Pancho Villa.
> How sad is his fate
> to die in an ambush
> in the middle of the road.
> Poor Mexico is mourning.
> It is afflicted by a grave loss.
> They've killed brave Pancho Villa in Parral.

Another *corridista* wrote in similar vein:

> Despedida no les doy.
> La angustia es muy sencilla.
> La falta que hace a mi patria
> el señor Francisco Villa.

> Políticos traidores de instintos tan venales
> que a Villa le temian por su gran corazón
> y crearon en conjunto sus planes criminales
> que sirven de verguenza a toda la nación.

> Adiós General Villa.
> Gran héroe entre los héroes,
> el bardo que te quizó,
> no te olvidará jamás.
> Descansa entre los muertos,
> el mundo de otros seres.
> Y sea en gloria que goces por siempre eterna paz.

I do not bid you farewell.
Anguish is very simple.
Señor Francisco Villa,
what a loss to my country.

Corrupt and traitorous politicians
who feared Villa's nobility of heart
conceived their criminal plan.
They shame the whole nation.

Adiós, General Villa.
Great hero among the heroes,
this singer will never forget you.
Rest among the dead,
in the world of other beings,
and if there is glory, may you rest in eternal peace.[36]

The Assassins

"On the lips of everyone is the question: Who killed Villa?" declared the secretary of Mexico's Chamber of Deputies, Emilio Gandarilla. "'Calles!'" *El Universal* said, "was the spontaneous reply from the Chamber."

This conclusion was shared by foreign observers. "General Calles had, then, all of the traditional incentives for a Mexican political murder," the U.S. chargé d'affaires, George Summerlin, wrote. He added, "the representative of British interests in Mexico, having had long experience with Mexican politics and many personal associations with both Villa and Calles, is confidentially of the opinion that Calles is responsible for Villa's death. This view appears to be held more or less fixedly by many responsible men here not affiliated in some way with the Mexican administration." These same foreign observers did not believe that Obregón was in any way involved in the assassination. "There is moreover a strong belief among observers," Summerlin wrote to the secretary of state, "that to whatever extent Calles acted in causing the assassination he did so without the connivance of his chief. General Obregón's public attitude has been one of pained surprise at this violent breach of the public order."

Immediately after the assassination, Obregón declared to the press: "It is a degrading sign that personal hatreds and rancors of any kind are still vented in violence and treason. Villa relied upon the protection of the authorities of the country, and for that reason the government will make a thorough investigation of the events and endeavor to apprehend the culprits."[37]

In private letters to two of the men suspected by many of having been involved in Villa's murder, Obregón emphasized that his administration had had no reason to kill Villa, had not been involved in the assassination, and strongly condemned it. "The enemies of the government have tried to awaken suspicions," Obregón wrote to Calles, "that will meet with no response, since this administration has not carried out one act that would give anyone the right to assume that it is capable of such macabre acts, all the less so since in the past month General Villa has again and again emphasized his loyalty to the government and his satisfaction in the way this government was treating him."[38] In a similar letter to the governor of Durango, Obregón said that even at the time when he was secretary of war in Carranza's government, he had strongly opposed Carranza's decree placing a price on Villa's head.[39]

Obregón's protestations of innocence became less convincing when a committee of the Mexican Chamber of Deputies sent to investigate the assassination of Villa came out with its report. The committee stated that Villa's murder was of a political nature and that the local authorities were in some way involved. It noted that on the day of the assassination, the whole garrison of Parral had left the city for the neighboring town of Maturana. The committee felt that Maturana was less suited for a military rehearsal than Parral itself, since the streets were hilly and "not at all suited for a parade." It pointed out that in the first 45 minutes after the assassination, no pursuit of the killers was undertaken. Not only did the local authorities do nothing, but the telegraph connection to Canutillo had inexplicably been interrupted. Villa's bodyguard would immediately have undertaken the pursuit of their leader's killers, but it took six hours for the news of Villa's assassination to reach his men.

What impressed the committee above all was that the killers had seemed absolutely self-assured and relaxed and in no hurry to leave the scene of their crime:

They took a coat worn by Colonel Trillo; they then went to a corner called La Bajadita, about 50 meters from where the event had taken place; they proceeded without any hurry; they quietly lit some cigarettes; they laughed and rejoiced; they calmly took hold of their horses; and at a slow gait they left town. They were seen by a barber from the town who was going to work, and this barber told us that the killers were proceeding without any hurry and those that rode behind told the one who rode in front that there was no reason to be afraid, that he had no reason to run.[40]

The committee members also noted that both the local military authorities and the local judge had not been helpful at all, but had tried to undermine their investigation in every possible way.

The report did not directly implicate Obregón; in fact, Deputy Gandarilla, the secretary of the Chamber of Deputies, who was the head of the committee, wrote Obregón telling him that in his opinion the Mexican president was not involved.[41] Nevertheless, public opinion became more and more suspicious of the Obregón administration, since the local military officials were directly under the federal authorities. Suspicion of Obregón deepened when no action was ever taken against any of the local military or civilian authorities.

Relief for both the Obregón administration and Calles came two and a half weeks after Villa's assassination in the shape of a letter from a deputy to the state legislature of Durango, Jesús Salas Barraza, claiming that he had both organized and carried out Villa's murder, and that no government authority and no other politician had had any hand in it. Salas Barraza had never fought against Villa, and neither had he or his family been victimized by him. The reason he gave for assassinating this "bloody soul, born for evil," this "cowardly and cruel viper," was that countless people of the district he represented, El Oro, had been killed by Villa. He especially emphasized Villa's destruction of an electric plant at Magistral that put 1,000 families out of work, and his killing of one of the employees, Catarino Smith, "whom I loved like a brother." Salas Barraza described himself as the avenger of thousands of Villa's victims, as a man driven solely by his conscience to the point of disregarding "the consequences that this act could have for his poor children." The reason why he was confessing to the assassination was to "save the name of our present government, to put an end to suspicions voiced by the press that some public officials had been intellectual authors of this matter."[42]

Obregón and Calles were greatly relieved when this confession was published. "I have received with the greatest satisfaction your message of yesterday," Calles wrote Obregón, "identifying the author of the assassination of Villa and the men who were with him. This will be the greatest punishment for all those who with such bad faith have been trying to involve your government."[43]

For the parliamentary opposition in Mexico and large segments of Mexico's public opinion, the idea of Salas Barraza's having voluntarily confessed to Villa's assassination solely in order to save the prestige of the government seemed incredible. These suspicions were reinforced when, a few days after Salas Barraza's confession had been published, Deputy Gandarilla read an anonymous letter in parliament stating that after Villa had been assassinated, Salas Barraza had had meetings with both Jesús Agustín Castro, governor of Durango, and Villa's old enemy Plutarco Elías Calles. Once again, Salas Barraza issued a vigorous declaration stating that he and he alone was responsible for Villa's assassination.[44]

Obregón was slow to deal with Villa's killer. He sent a high official, General Paulino Navarro, with instructions to watch Salas Barraza but to take no other action. On August 8, Navarro suggested that Villa's killer be arrested, but Obregón vetoed the proposal. "We cannot carry out the arrest of Colonel Salas, since he is a deputy, and the Durango legislature would protest and the whole matter would escalate. You should constantly watch him and only should he intend to cross the border should you arrest him and advise me by telegram. If necessary, send me reports every six hours. I have ordered the immediate mobilization of a regiment and a battalion to Durango and it would be imprudent to proceed before these units have arrived."[45] A day later, Obregón surprisingly ordered Navarro to return immediately to Mexico City to await new instructions.[46] Then, within a few hours, Obregón canceled his earlier message to Navarro, asked him to arrest Salas Barraza immediately, and warned him "not to obey any order that does not come from this executive office."[47]

Obregón's sudden change of heart may partly have been due to the fear that Villa's assassin would cross the border into the United States, which would probably not have been willing to extradite him to Mexico. The Obregón administration would then be blamed for allowing Salas Barraza to escape. There may have been another reason as well, however. Obregón feared that the Villistas might take the matter into their own hands. A deputy close to the Villistas, Manuel Azueta, had been exerting pressure on Obregón. On August 10, not knowing that Salas Barraza had already been arrested, Azueta suggested that he might take matters in his own hands and arrest Salas Barraza.[48]

Within a few days, the self-confessed murderer was sent to Chihuahua, where on September 13, he was sentenced to 20 years in jail. Only three months later, in December, he was pardoned and set free by Governor Enríquez. No one else was ever accused, arrested, or detained for the murder of Villa.

In December 1923, Adolfo de la Huerta and his supporters rose against the Obregón administration. Soon they were joined by Hipólito Villa and some of Villa's supporters in Canutillo. After de la Huerta's defeat, the situation completely changed. The parliamentary opposition disappeared from the Chamber of Deputies, the remaining Villistas were discredited because of their participation in the rebellion, and Villa's assassination ceased to be a political issue. Villa himself became a nonperson for official Mexico.

It was only many years later, when both Obregón and Calles were no longer in power, that Mexican historians and investigative reporters began looking for and finding new clues as to the identity of Villa's murderers and their possible links to the government. The first result was the identification of Villa's actual murderers. While Salas Barraza had participated in the assassination, he was by no means its main organizer. Its intellectual author was Melitón Lozoya, who had strong motives for killing Villa. These motives went back to the postrevolutionary period rather than to the revolution itself. Lozoya had been an administrator of the Canutillo hacienda for the Jurado family, who had owned the hacienda before the government transferred it to Villa. During his tenure at the estate, Lozoya took large amounts of property away from Canutillo and sold it for his own profit, stating that he had done so with the full permission of the owners. When Villa heard of these transactions, he threatened Lozoya with unspecified reprisals unless he returned everything taken from Canutillo or paid the money equivalent to it. At this point, Lozoya decided that his only hope of staying alive and escaping Villa's reprisals was to kill him. At a small ranch called La Cochinera, he recruited eight other men, many of whom had personal grievances against Villa. They had rented the house from which the shots that killed Villa were fired. Salas Barraza, who had heard of the plot through a relative, later joined it. Until their deaths, both Lozoya and Salas Barraza maintained that they had acted alone, without any help, support, or connivance on the part of the Mexican government.[49]

Other evidence that Mexican researchers gathered contradicts these assertions and strongly implicates both Obregón and Calles in Villa's assassination.

The first piece of evidence uncovered by these researchers was that Salas Barraza maintained close relations with two officials of the Obregón administration, who helped him to draft his confession. These were Abraham Carmona, head of the artillery department of Mexico's Defense Ministry, and Juan Serrano, who headed the telegraph office in Torreón. Carmona himself submitted Salas Barraza's confession to Obregón, whose reaction was to say of Salas Barraza, "our friend has a great heart."[50]

These links between Salas Barraza and high officials of the Obregón administration do not by themselves implicate either Obregón or Calles. But a conversation that a Mexican reporter, Justino Palomares, had with Félix Lara, the former commander of the Parral garrison and the man who refused to pursue the murderers, does directly implicate Calles. "A few months before [Villa's assassination], I was called to Mexico by General Calles," Lara stated, "who told me that it was necessary to eliminate the new Cincinnatus of Canutillo, because he was a danger to the whole country, above all, since Calles knew that the latter owned a great amount of arms, which he could utilize at any moment." Lara recounted that after returning to Parral, he had sought out some of Villa's greatest enemies, to whom he added some officers of his garrison who were particularly good shots. After the assassination, he allowed some of them to stay in his own headquarters, while publicly stating that troops had been sent out to pursue the assassins.[51] From another source, Palomares heard that Lara had been paid 50,000 pesos for organizing Villa's murder and had also been promoted to the rank of general.[52]

Lara's interview placed the responsibility for Villa's killing squarely on the shoulders of Calles but did not implicate Obregón. Many years after he died, Obregón's complicity was hinted at in new interviews that his former undersecretary of the interior, Gilberto Valenzuela, gave to researchers. In the first, he stated that the agent of Obregón's who finally arrested Salas Barraza, Paulino Navarro, found documents during a search of Salas Barraza's hotel room in Monterrey that implicated both Jesús Herrera and Calles in the assassination. When Navarro presented these documents to the Mexican president, Obregón told him, "I do not want to see these documents. Do whatever you want with them." Completely confused, Navarro returned to his office with the documents. On that same day, an unnamed man came to see him and suggested that the documents be burned. Navarro agreed and turned them over to the man who was never identified, who presumably destroyed them.[53] This episode implicates Obregón in a cover-up, but not necessarily in the assassination. In other interviews, given to an American scholar years later, Valenzuela was more forthright. He stated that he had resigned from the government because of its involvement in the murder of Villa.[54]

The strongest accusation against Obregón came from his old enemy, Adolfo de la Huerta, in a conversation with Villa's adopted son and administrator of Canutillo, Francisco Gil Piñon. De la Huerta recounted that Gabriel Chávez, a rich merchant from Parral and a personal enemy of Villa's, had gone with Jesús Herrera to the government in Mexico City with an offer to kill Villa if they were granted immunity. Calles and Secretary of War Joaquín Amaro, a general who had unsuccessfully fought Villa in Chihuahua, were in full agreement, but Obregón hesitated. He insisted that Villa had complied with the agreement he had made with the government not to participate in politics, and that if action were to be taken against Villa, he would want it to take place in an open fight on the battlefield and not through murder. When Calles and Amaro insisted, Obregón finally acquiesced, but he told them that they should make all the preparations, and that his government should not be implicated in any way. Adolfo de la Huerta was not an impartial witness, however, since he had every reason to hate both Obregón and Calles.

While all the foregoing evidence is quite believable, it is all based on oral testimony. The "smoking gun," written evidence that actually implicates the government in the murder of Villa, has appeared only since the papers of Calles and Amaro in the Calles-Torreblanca archives have been made available to researchers and the files of both the BI and U.S. military intelligence have been declassified. A clear reconstruction of Villa's assassination and the role leading Mexican politicians played in it is now possible, although some questions remain.

Four weeks after Villa's assassination, a BI agent reported to the bureau, "Different sources, in close touch with Mexican affairs express the opinion that Villa

was assassinated by order of P. Elías Calles; that the Barraza confession was prepared for public consumption by Barraza and Calles; that Barraza will not be
punished by the government; may not even be tried; that he will be paid the rewards outstanding."[55] Both ensuing events and the papers of leading Mexican officials tend to confirm most of the BI's assessment. The BI erred only in believing
that Salas Barraza would not be tried, and it may not have known which Mexican
officials below the rank of Calles were implicated in the assassination. The official
most closely linked to the assassination of Villa was General Joaquín Amaro. He
had repeatedly fought against Villa both in 1914–15 and in 1920 when he had been
commander of government forces in Chihuahua. When news that de la Huerta
was negotiating with Villa reached him, he was so incensed that he threatened
to rise against the government. In July 1923, he was the head of government forces
in the northeastern state of Nuevo León. A second official who also seems to
have played an important role in these events was another general, who had also
fought against Villa in Chihuahua, and who was now governor of the state of
Durango, Jesús Agustín Castro.

On July 7, 1923, several weeks before the assassination of Villa, Salas Barraza
wrote a letter to Amaro, addressing him as "Highly Respected General and Dear
Friend," telling him of his plans to kill Villa. His justification was that Villa was
plotting another uprising, and as proof of this, he cited the fact that men such as
Antonio Villareal, Raúl Madero, Enrique Llorente, Miguel Díaz Lombardo, and
other enemies of the government were constantly visiting him. In addition, he
said that the government was wasting the huge amounts of money that it was
giving to Villa, mentioning a monthly payment of 10,000 pesos and 200,000 pesos compensation for the butcher shops that Villa had lost during the revolution.

Salas Barraza made a clear call for some kind of monetary compensation from
Amaro, saying that his financial situation was very bad, and that if anything happened to him, Amaro should help his family. The letter was written from Parral,
and Salas Barraza told Amaro: "I have found a group of friends all fully conscious
of their obligations who have entrusted me with the leadership of the enterprise
of putting an end to the bandit Francisco Villa." He called on Amaro, "Should
this be necessary to help with your important influence on the government, since
I do not want under any circumstances to be judged as an assassin since I am only
carrying out the duty of an honest citizen, putting an end to the life of this man
who could ruin our country."[56]

This letter was probably not the first communication between the two men
with regard to the assassination of Villa. Five days earlier, on July 2, Salas Barraza's brother had hand-delivered a confidential, anonymous letter to Amaro that
seems to have contained the same proposals. Obviously, before pledging officially
to kill Villa, Salas Barraza wanted some kind of assurance from Amaro that the
latter would protect him. At very least, Amaro made no effort to stop Salas Barraza. In fact, he seems to have informed Calles of these plans, since there is a
copy of the unsigned letter, minus the addressee, among the Calles Papers.[57]

Other documents reveal the clear complicity of Jesús Agustín Castro in Villa's
assassination. According to BI agents, Salas Barraza first reported to Governor
Castro immediately after the murder of Villa, and then to Calles at his estate of
Soledad de Mota.[58] This FBI report confirms an anonymous letter that Deputy

Gandarilla quoted in the Mexican Chamber of Deputies. The source of the BI report was Paulino Navarro, the secret service man sent by Obregón to arrest Salas Barraza. The fact that both Castro and Calles were implicated in the report may be the reason why Obregón refused to see it and sent one of his associates to persuade Navarro to burn it.

Two letters with an unreadable signature sent to Obregón on July 29 and kept under lock and key for many years among the papers of Calles's secretary, Fernando Torreblanca, also implicate Castro. The first letter, written on July 29, one week before Salas Barraza sent his confession to Obregón, named Salas Barraza, an assistant to Governor Castro, and Castro's driver as men whom witnesses had seen participating in Villa's murder. Since the letter had correctly identified the man who only a week later would publicly confess to Villa's assassination, had he really been interested in apprehending the killers, Obregón would at least have had to have had Castro's assistant and the chauffeur interrogated. He did not do so and never revealed the existence of the letter to anyone.[59]

Embittered by the government's unwillingness to follow up on their denunciation, the authors of the letter wrote to Obregón again on August 22, giving even more details of the assassination. They identified two more men who were working for Castro as participants in the assassination, a Colonel Soto and a man named Facdoa. The authors stated that these men, together with Salas Barraza, the driver, and the assistant to Castro, had felt so secure that on the evening after the assassination they had gone on a drinking spree in the bars of Parral, where they had openly boasted of their role in Villa's killing and proclaimed that they enjoyed full immunity and could not be touched.

Castro had paid a large sum of money to the murderers, charged the letter's authors, who may have been government employees, for they accused the governor of taking this money from the state payroll. They concluded bitterly, "people are beginning to say that Governor Castro has been clearly supported by the central government, and that is the reason why he could carry out the murders for which he is responsible, such as that of Villa, as well as robberies and many other crimes, and that nothing will happen either to him or his accomplices, since everyone is asking why these murderers are not being apprehended, beginning with the governor; he is a tyrant, ten times worse than Porfirio Díaz."[60] The Obregón administration was as indifferent to this letter as to its predecessor. No action was ever undertaken to investigate the matter.

Governor Castro had in fact strong reasons to both dislike and fear Villa. Not only had he fought against him during the guerrilla campaign in Chihuahua, but after Villa settled down, a conflict broke out between the two men. When Castro demanded that Villa pay back taxes for his Canutillo estate, Villa refused, declaring that the government had assumed all responsibilities for the hacienda.[61] The governor was also worried by Villa's published implication that at some point in the future he might become a candidate for the governorship of Durango.

Salas Barraza not only organized the assassination and acted as an intermediary between the government and the murderers, he also both covered up the roles of Amaro and of the government and acted as a scapegoat. The cover-up consisted not only in Salas Barraza's personally assuming responsibility for the assassination and stating that the government had nothing to do with it but also in making sure that his associates remained silent and were never interrogated by Mexican officials. Obviously, the other participants in the assassination had every reason to fear that once he was detained, Salas Barraza might reveal their names, either under duress or to reduce the charges against himself. In the letter sent to "All my compañeros," he explained why he felt it necessary to confess publicly to the murder and then stated: "I have assumed all responsibility, and you have nothing to fear, since I have maintained complete silence on everything related to you, and I shall do everything to safeguard your lives and interests. I shall be more explicit on another occasion."[62]

Salas Barraza was nevertheless worried about how some of his "compañeros" would react if they were arrested. In a letter to Amaro castigating the press for its speculations, he wrote, "I am sure that [the reporters] will find no concrete evidence, in spite of everything they are doing to find the author of these events." He expressed his worry nevertheless that the reporters might know the names of two or three "of the boys who worked with me; this does worry me since it could harm them." Although confident that even if faced with a threat of death, they would not speak, he was worried that a clever judge might get them to reveal information; in fact, one had already been arrested but had been freed because he had remained silent throughout the whole time of his arrest. "I would like to know your opinion and that of our friend from nearby [*nuestro amigo de las cercanías*] about how I should proceed." Since Calles was at this time at his hacienda, Soledad de la Mota, which was close by, there is little doubt that Salas Barraza was referring to him. This letter thus clearly involves not only Amaro but Calles as well in Villa's assassination. It is not clear whether Amaro took any measures in this respect.

An even more important part of the cover-up was to prevent Amaro's name from being in any way associated with Villa's assassination. This was a possibility, since Salas Barraza and Amaro seem to have been close friends. In order to achieve this aim, Salas Barraza attempted to establish links with other military men and to secure some kind of protection from them. He thus went to see General Gonzalo Escobar, who was stationed in Torreón, and told him how disappointed he was with Amaro, since the latter had refused to help or protect him at "one of the most critical moments in my life." "He absolutely believed me," Salas Barraza wrote Amaro, "[and] offered to help me in everything that I would need, but when I asked for a letter of introduction and recommendation to the president, he told me that without knowing what the opinion of the latter was on this matter, he could not give it to me, but he repeated that he would be willing to help me in every possible sense."[63] The letter in which Salas Barraza confessed publicly to the murder was addressed to another general, Abraham Carmona, whom he addressed as "distinguished and dear friend." Obviously, he thus hoped that if any suspicion of implication in Villa's murder were to fall on Mexican military men, it would be Escobar and Carmona, and not Amaro, who would be implicated.

Salas Barraza was no heroic and willing martyr. He firmly hoped that his status as a member of Durango's state legislature would protect him from arrest, and that if any demand for lifting his immunity were voiced in the legislature, Governor Castro would make sure it was not granted. Even Obregón seems to have

. assumed that this was the case, but Castro refused to go along, probably for fear of implicating himself. Salas Barraza had expected a public letter of support from Castro certifying that he was an honorable man, which Castro refused to write, "telling me that his well-being was more important than his duties as a public official." He had hoped that at the very least, Castro would keep the promise he had made to a number of friends of his that, as Salas Barraza was being transported by the federal authorities from Mexico City to be tried in Parral, on the way through Durango, a commission of the state legislature would demand his release, since he was entitled to immunity. Nothing of the kind happened, however, and Salas Barraza expressed his deep disappointment with Castro.[64]

It was at this moment that Salas Barraza lost his nerve and attempted to escape to the United States. After he had been sentenced to 20 years in prison, he wrote to Amaro urgently requesting his help. In the letter, he expressed his thanks to "all the authorities who directly or indirectly have intervened in my affairs, from the president of the republic to officials of the state," with the exception of the prosecutor and the judge who had sentenced him. He asked not only for help with regard to his release but also for financial help.[65]

Amaro immediately responded. He told Salas Barraza that he would intervene on his behalf with the governor of Chihuahua, Ignacio Enríquez, and give money to his brother.[66] Amaro kept his word. On the same day that he had responded to Salas Barraza's letter, he wrote to Enríquez asking him to free Villa's murderer and telling him that the assassination had been more than justified, since Villa had never had to account to any court for the many crimes that he had committed. He also thanked Enríquez for the kindness and attention he had shown to Salas Barranza.[67]

Enríquez was ready to oblige. On his last day in office, he officially granted an amnesty to Salas Barraza, who was thereupon released from jail. Shortly afterward, he became an officer in the federal army and saw action in the suppression of the de la Huerta rebellion. On May 17, 1924, ten months after the murder of Villa, he was granted a friendly interview by Obregón at the request of two of his generals.[68]

Obregón may have had closer links to the actual murderers than has previously been assumed. On January 2, 1923, seven and a half months before Villa was assassinated, one of Obregón's subordinates, General José Amarillas, wrote the Mexican president a letter recommending "Melitón Lozoya Jr., who wishes to discuss some matters with you." Amarillas did not say what these matters were, but strongly recommended Lozoya, saying that he had been the guide "of a column under my directions in the Canutillo area and enthusiastically supported the Plan of Agua Prieta."[69]

Unfortunately, the archives do not reveal whether Obregón in fact received Lozoya. The ambiguous tone of the letter is suspicious. Generally, if an audience with the president is requested, the matter on which he has to spend his valuable time is spelled out beforehand. The fact that this was not done, and that seven and a half months later, Lozoya played a key role in Villa's assassination, is significant. Three years later, Lozoya may have claimed his reward, which was of a substantial nature. He asked for nothing less from President Calles than the construction of a dam to irrigate the lands of a hacienda belonging to his father.[70]

Except for the matter of Salas Barraza's trial, which for a time Obregón seems to have attempted to avoid, every other hypothesis advanced by the BI seems to have been true: a draft of Salas Barraza's confession was found among the Calles Papers; he was released from prison after only a few weeks; he was received in a personal audience by Obregón; and, according to the anonymous letter writers who identified him as one of the killers, a week before his confession was published, he was given large sums of money for the assassination by Durango's Governor Castro.

There can, on the whole, be little doubt that the Mexican government was not only implicated in but probably organized the assassination of Villa. The foregoing revelations nevertheless still leave three questions open to doubt: Did the government have genuine grounds to fear a Villa uprising? Was the fear of a possible uprising by Villa the only reason that motivated the government to have him killed? Who was primarily responsible for Villa's assassination: Obregón, Calles, or both? The first two questions are easier to deal with than the third.

U.S. military intelligence agents obtained a copy of a report sent to Obregón by the commander of the federal troops in northern Mexico, Eugenio Martínez, which implied that the federal government may have had genuine reasons to fear an uprising by Villa. A few days after Villa's assassination, Martínez reported that a huge cache of arms was located in Canutillo, far beyond what the defense of the estate would have required. It mentioned 6,400 Winchester carbines, 250,000 cartridges for these carbines, 1,110 Mauser rifles, 800 Mauser carbines, and 300,000 cartridges for these rifles, as well as a large supply of hand grenades and bombs of various types, including bombs charged with dynamite. The existence of this depot seems to confirm the suspicions expressed to an agent of U.S. military intelligence by an informant that he had heard that de la Huerta had supplied large quantities of arms and ammunition to Villa,

that Raul Madero had been a mere smoke screen so far as the opposition to the administration was concerned and that, at the opportune movement, de la Huerta was to have declared his candidacy and have been supported actively by Villa.

Informant also stated that it was the current belief in Mexican military circles that both General Obregón and General Calles were informed of Villa's apparent preparations for active opposition and had agreed as to the necessity of eliminating him in some way.[71]

The assumption that in case of a civil war between the supporters of de la Huerta and of Calles, which indeed broke out a few months later, Villa would have supported de la Huerta is by no means unreasonable. Villa had expressed his support for de la Huerta and his opposition to Calles in his interview with *El Universal*, and it is conceivable that Villa would not have remained neutral in such a civil war. He had been engaged in bloody battles with both Obregón and Calles in the past, whereas he had never confronted de la Huerta, the selfsame leader who had granted him amnesty. This meant not only that his life would be safer under a de la Huerta administration, but that de la Huerta might object far less than Obregón and Calles to Villa's openly stated aim of resuming political activity after 1924.

Obregón and his colleagues had an even better reason to believe that Villa might take part in an uprising: they were in the process of achieving an agreement with the United States, which they knew would be viewed as a kind of capitulation by many Mexican nationalists. In the Bucareli agreements, which were signed between the U.S. and Mexican governments only a few weeks after Villa's assassination, the Obregón administration, in return for U.S. recognition, gave in to the demands of American oil companies that the nationalistic clauses of article 27 of the Mexican constitution should not be applied retroactively to foreign oil companies. De la Huerta strongly objected to this agreement, and it would have been one of the main reasons why he might have taken up arms against Obregón and Calles. In view of Villa's anti-Americanism, there was a distinct possibility that he might take part in a rising against the government out of feelings of nationalism.

The Mexican government had another reason for eliminating Villa that was closely linked to his nationalistic attitudes. According to American sources, pressure from officials of the Harding administration who entertained similar views as to the possibility of a Villa uprising may have played a significant role in the Obregón administration's involvement in Villa's assassination. BI and military intelligence agents reported that important Mexican officials were convinced that the assassination of Villa was a precondition for U.S. recognition of the Obregón administration. One theory that BI agents in Mexico reported to headquarters in Washington was

that the Mexican government itself had brought about the assassination because of alleged pressure from the American commissioners now in Mexico City, who as claimed had informed Obregón that one stumbling block to recognition was Pancho Villa and that the sooner they removed him, the sooner recognition would be extended; that Obregón and his advisors thereupon sanctioned the killing of Villa and would reward the slayers, who they predict will never be captured.[72]

While the BI agent who reported on this hypothesis had been noncommittal as to the validity of these accusations, neither denying nor confirming them, a military intelligence agent who heard similar rumors denied them. He reported "that a not inconsiderable element in the capital—of the less intelligent types—attributed Villa's assassination to intimations from the American members of the United States–Mexican Commission to the effect that Villa must be punished for the Columbus raid, etc. before any favorable recommendation would be made re recognition." To which the agent added, "Of course, not true."[73]

The BI was less dismissive of these reports and did not assume that only "less intelligent" Mexicans believed them. "A reliable source states," one of its agents, Manuel Sorola, reported, "that when Calles was notified of Villa's assassination, his only comment was 'The second of the fundamental conditions imposed by the United States as necessary to recognition has been complied with.'"[74] If this were true, as the BI believed it was, then Calles in all probability received some indications from important American personalities that they wanted Villa eliminated.

There is no definite proof that American representatives on the U.S.–Mexican negotiating commission made such a demand, or if they did, that they acted with the full accord of the Harding administration, since no corresponding written records are presently available. In any case, such demands would scarcely have been made in writing. Yet it is not illogical to assume that one precondition for recognition was that the Obregón administration should be able to guarantee stability in Mexico, and Villa was certainly an element whom the Americans perceived as a threat to such stability. Members of the Harding administration like Secretary of the Interior (formerly Senator) Albert B. Fall, who was subsequently convicted and sent to prison for taking bribes in return for the leasing of naval oil reserves in Wyoming (the so-called Teapot Dome scandal), are unlikely to have had moral scruples about prompting Villa's murder.

It will probably never be possible to establish definitely whether it was Obregón or Calles who bore ultimate responsibility for Villa's assassination. On the one hand, assassination was more Obregón's than Calles's style. Calles was minister of the interior and thus had authority over the police, but he had none over the army. The army was clearly implicated in the assassination, and it fell within Obregón's sphere of influence. On the other hand, Calles, who was the official candidate for president, may have had more to gain from the assassination, and most foreign observers tended to implicate both in the killing of Villa. At this point, this question must remain open.

The Last Villista Uprising

His time had finally come. For years, Hipólito had lived in the shadow of his big brother. The last months before Francisco's death had been particularly onerous for him. The multifarious financial undertakings in which he had engaged—attempting to sell a train and selling horses to the government, dabbling in oil prospecting—had all gone sour. He had ended up owing 126,000 pesos to the federal government. Obregón had canceled these debts,[75] but Hipólito's activities had infuriated his brother, who banished him from Canutillo.

His dreams shattered, Villa's younger brother was living a life of obscurity at his ranch of El Fresno when Villa's death offered him a new chance to reach the limelight. He immediately proceeded to Canutillo and took command of the estate and of the Villista colonists. Legally, he had no authority to do so, since his brother had not designated him as his heir. But in practice both the Villista colonists and the government favored his takeover. The Villista colonists hoped that Hipólito would be able to persuade the government to let them keep the rights and the possessions they had acquired. In the eyes of the government, Hipólito was considered the one man who might keep the Villista colonists in check and prevent them from spontaneous acts of vengeance for Villa's death, as well as from joining a possible de la Huerta revolt. The Obregón administration had some reason for hoping that Hipólito would not become involved in any armed adventure. Obregón may not have expected gratitude from Hipólito for the canceled 126,000 peso debt, but he did know how much Hipólito enjoyed the good life, and control of Canutillo and its great wealth gave him every opportunity to do so. In addition, Hipólito did not have the charismatic appeal of his older brother, and his incentive for rising against the government was thus smaller.

When he took control of Canutillo, Hipólito rode roughshod over the rights of both of Villa's main widows, Austreberta and Luz Corral. They bitterly complained about his behavior in letters to Obregón. After leaving Canutillo in order to be present at Villa's burial ceremony, Austreberta complained,

I left all our goods under the care of my brother-in-law, Don Hipólito, who at the beginning offered altruistically to take care of its administration since my situation [she was pregnant with Villa's child] did not allow me to personally assume those functions.

Later when my situation allowed me to do so, I could not return, since my own brother-in-law, once he had seized control of everything, had armed men at his command, and I was afraid to personally ask him to return what was due to me.[76]

With equal bitterness, Luz Corral complained that "my brother-in-law Hipólito does not consider my interests, why I do not know, and refuses either to see me or to correspond with me."[77] Neither the Villista colonists nor the government showed any great interest in protecting the rights of Villa's widows, although Obregón's attitude would change later on.

The Villista colonists were ready to recognize the legitimacy of Hipólito's control. Not only was he Villa's brother, but he had fought alongside Francisco in the hard and bitter days of guerrilla struggle. Above all, he had delivered what they expected him to deliver. On August 3, Obregón had written him to say that the government was ready to respect all rights that the colonists had acquired after Francisco Villa had made his peace with it, and that orders for federal troops to occupy Canutillo had been rescinded.[78] In return, Hipólito again and again reiterated in letters to Obregón his loyalty and his desire to live in peace.[79] In fact, shortly after de la Huerta revolted, on December 22, Hipólito congratulated Obregón on defeating one group of de la Huerta supporters.[80]

A few weeks later, in January 1924, Hipólito joined the de la Huerta uprising. It is not clear what induced him to do so: Did he simply want to jump on the bandwagon, believing that de la Huerta was winning? Did he fear assassination at the hands of Obregón and Calles? Did he want revenge for his brother? Nothing is known of Hipólito's motive.

The uprising bore the marks of Hipólito's usual ineptness. He could not even get all the colonists at Canutillo to join him. While 150 men participated in the uprising, the rest refused.[81] Of the Villista generals living on surrounding estates, Nicolás Fernández joined the uprising, but Albino Aranda did not. The villagers of Durango and Chihuahua did not join Hipólito either. He lacked the prestige his brother had enjoyed.

Hipólito's ineptness was shown not only by the limited number of men he managed to recruit but also by his first important political "activity." He kidnapped a British executive named Mackenzie and asked $400,000 for his ransom.[82] This was the last thing that the de la Huerta people wanted, since they hoped to secure both American and European recognition. It would definitely label them as bandits, and de la Huerta ordered Hipólito to free Mackenzie.[83]

A few weeks later, Hipólito's uprising petered out. On February 10, Obregón wired Calles that the campaign against Villa was no longer necessary, and that the troops should be moved elsewhere to fight the de la Huerta rebels further south.[84] In May 1924, the most experienced guerrilla commander among the Villista rebels, Villa's old companion Nicolás Fernández, surrendered. So did Hipólito a few months later, in October of that same year, but not before having botched another enterprise to which he had been committed.[85] On May 30, forty Villistas led by Hipólito attacked six government soldiers who were escorting Jesús Salas Barraza, Villa's murderer, who had been freed by Obregón in the meantime and was operating against the Villistas. In spite of their overwhelming superiority in numbers, they were repelled and were unable to avenge Francisco Villa's death.[86]

On the whole, Hipólito Villa was lucky. Unlike other revolutionary leaders, such as Manuel Chao, Villa's former companion from revolutionary days, who was captured and shot by government troops, Hipólito was granted amnesty and did not even have to go into exile. The one thing he did not get back was Canutillo, which was taken over by the government. "You can be sure," Obregón had affirmed to one of his subordinates, "that neither Canutillo nor any other property belonging to the Villistas will be returned to them."[87]

If there was one quality Hipólito never showed, it was shyness or reticence. Only two months after having fought the government, he asked the government-appointed administrator of Canutillo for the return of 66 mules and some other property that he stated belonged to him. This was too much for Obregón, who only two years before had showered money and benefits on Hipólito. "Give absolutely nothing to Hipólito Villa," he told his administrator, "and should Villa in fact prove that some of these mules belong to him, they should be confiscated and used to pay the debt that Villa still owes to the monetary commission."[88] Hipólito was not one to give up easily, especially when it came to money. He again petitioned the government to return his estate of El Fresno, which had belonged to him and had been confiscated once he began his uprising. Calles, who responded to this petition, showed himself as adamant as Obregón in refusing any of Hipólito's claims. He too stated that the hacienda should be confiscated to pay Hipólito's debts.[89]

From the moment he surrendered, Hipólito ceased to have any relevance for the history of Mexico. He retired to his ranch, seems to have been embroiled in endless lawsuits, and died a forgotten man in 1957.[90]

The War of the Widows

During his lifetime, Villa had never bothered with conventional arrangements in his family life. It is thus not surprising that he made no provisions for his succession in case of death and that he left behind a legal mess. It is ironic that the man who would have to sort out this mess was Alvaro Obregón, who had defeated Villa in 1915 and probably played a part in his assassination.

The stakes in the conflict over Villa's succession were substantial. The properties he left were valued at 630,000 pesos. They included the hacienda of Canutillo, six houses in Ciudad Chihuahua, two houses in Hidalgo del Parral, one hotel in the same city, and two small ranches.[91] After Villa's death, it was rumored that he had buried large amounts of money, and treasure hunters went through

Canutillo and other areas that Villa had frequented looking in vain for his treasure. Such a buried treasure seems to have existed, but it had been stolen years before Villa died. In 1921, a lawyer hired by Villa, Manuel Puentes, lodged a complaint against a man named Pedro Meraz accusing him of having stolen 500,000 pesos in gold coins, eighteen kilograms of gold, and three gold bars weighing six kilograms each that Villa had hidden on his ranch "La Boquilla." Although Puentes lodged his accusation in 1921, Meraz was never prosecuted during Villa's lifetime, and the matter was considered in court only in 1924–25, after Villa had died. Since Villa normally pursued cases where money was owed him or had been stolen from him with the greatest energy, he may been reluctant to broach this matter, since it would have been asked where the money had come from, a question he might not have wanted to answer. When the case was finally taken up in court, from October 1923 to mid 1925, Villa was dead, and two of his Dorados, José García and Baltazar Piñones, could only state that another associate of Villa's, Barnabe Sifuentes, had told Meraz where the money was hidden and the latter had stolen it. Since they could not say where the money had come from, had no proof that it had existed, and could not say under what circumstances Meraz had taken it, the suit was dismissed by the judge for lack of evidence.[92]

For all but one of his widows, and for Villa's children, his death would prove an unmitigated disaster in both personal and economic terms. In the short run, Hipólito was to blame for the financial imbroglio; in the longer run, it resulted from the policies of the Mexican government. At the time of his death, Villa had had more or less permanent relationships with three women: Austreberta was his official wife, the mistress at Canutillo; Soledad Seañez lived somewhere in the vicinity; while Manuela Casas, who had borne Villa a son, administered a hotel belonging to him in Parral and had been given a house of her own by Villa. Luz Corral had been banished from Canutillo, was receiving no support from Villa, and depended on the charity of the uncharitable Hipólito.[93]

Once Hipólito occupied Canutillo, he appropriated all of its revenues, and gave nothing to Villa's wives. Austreberta sent an appeal for help to Obregón, asking for protection for herself and her children in the name "of the man who was my husband, Francisco Villa, who felt great friendship for you, was loyal to you, and may have died because of his loyalty." She appealed to Obregón's "nobility of heart" and to his conscience, asking him to protect her sons, who had now become orphans.[94] Obregón's answer was to suggest a compromise between Villa's heirs. "I believe that from the legal point of view, your affairs are too complicated. If all of you could come to an agreement privately to obtain an equitable distribution of the properties of the general among his children, you would carry out a labor of peace, [and] you would save money and above all time."[95]

The spirit of compromise was not present among Villa's heirs. Austreberta seems to have made no effort to come to an agreement with any of her husband's other heirs. On the contrary, she wrote Obregón again requesting that the government should appoint someone to administer the estate and take it away from Hipólito.[96] This was the last thing Obregón wanted to do. His main aim with respect to the Villistas was to prevent them from rising against him, and any effort to expel Hipólito from Canutillo might have had such a result. Obregón replied to Austreberta saying that he had no authority to intervene in the matter; rather, a judge would have to decide who the legal heir of Villa's property was.[97]

Austreberta eagerly accepted this suggestion. With the help of Villa's former compadre Eugenio Martínez, who had negotiated Villa's surrender in 1920, she appealed to a judge in Inde, Durango, who pronounced her the legal executor of Villa's properties. This court order had no effect whatsoever, however, on Hipólito, who simply refused to meet with Austreberta's representatives. Once Hipólito had risen against the government and federal troops had occupied Canutillo, Austreberta thought that her day had finally come. Armed with the judge's decision naming her legal executor of Villa's properties, she called on the military authorities occupying Canutillo to give her control of the estate and its revenues. Her calls fell on deaf ears. Federal military commanders, as well as the governors of Chihuahua and Durango, told her that the decision in this matter was up to the government in Mexico City. Once again Austreberta wrote to Obregón. She told the Mexican president that she had now been named legal executor of Villa's estate and asked him to turn Canutillo over to her. She discovered that Obregón had very different ideas as to who was Villa's legal heir and successor at Canutillo.

Shortly after Villa's death, Luz Corral had also written Obregón, claiming Villa's inheritance. "I wish to tell you," she wrote Obregón, "that I have documents that clearly prove that I am the legal wife of the deceased General Villa. If, as I believe, my husband married Señora Rentería, I do not believe this marriage is valid, since no divorce was ever signed between General Villa and myself, so that this new marriage has no legality at all." She called on Obregón to help her secure her rights. She asked the president for an audience so that she could personally describe her claims to him.[98] Obregón's reply to Luz Corral was more cordial than the reply he had sent Austreberta. Obregón was not one to forget debts that he had incurred. During his visit to Chihuahua, Luz Corral had played an important role in saving his life in 1914, when she had helped prevent Villa from having him shot, and she seems to have played an equally important part in saving Obregón's brother, Francisco, from execution when he was imprisoned by Villa. Obregón replied to Luz Corral, telling her that he would be glad to grant her an audience in Mexico City, "for it is my wish to be of help to you, since I have always remembered with gratitude the attentions you showed me during my stay in Chihuahua and in a special way those you showed my brother Francisco when he was a prisoner in the capital of that state."[99] He ordered the government to pay for her railway transportation to Mexico City, where he received her, and he instructed the head of the monetary commission in Mexico to give her 5,000 pesos so that she could take steps to secure her inheritance.

Up to that point, Obregón had always claimed his neutrality, but when Austreberta officially laid claim to be Villa's heir, he felt that the time had come to make his opinion clear. "According to the information available to me, I was told that Francisco Villa legally married Luz Corral, who was his first wife; since she is alive and there is no information that that marriage was legally dissolved, I believe that I should cease intervening in a matter which is so complicated, especially from a moral point of view."[100] While thus denying Austreberta's claim, Obregón still kept up a semblance of neutrality by stating that he would not intervene in the matter of Villa's legacy.[101] In fact, a few weeks later, he did intervene in a very direct way. The government recognized Luz Corral as Villa's de facto heir by buying from her all her rights to Canutillo and then occupying the estate.[102]

In his letters to Austreberta, Obregón was always somewhat devious. He never told her the real meaning of his decision to buy Luz Corral's rights to Canutillo. It was only when she was denied any access to either the estate or its revenues, and when the government made no effort to buy any rights from her, that Austreberta realized that she had been completely excluded from Villa's inheritance. Her constant pleas to Obregón that Luz Corral be obliged to recur to the courts, that she was not authorized to sell any rights to Canutillo, fell on deaf ears. Obregón's patience with Austreberta began to wear thin. "I do not want to be involved in the controversies that will certainly emerge between the different ladies who married the deceased General Villa," he wrote her when she again asked for his help.[103]

Yet only a few weeks later, Obregón was once again forced to intervene, when a conflict concerning another of Villa's wives, Manuela Casas, erupted. Casas had been in charge of the Hotel Hidalgo, which had belonged to Villa (Manuela claimed, but offered no proof, that it belonged to her). Five days after Villa's assassination, Austreberta had taken it from her. Now she was greatly afraid that Austreberta would take her last possession, the house that Villa had given her. In her letter to Obregón, she told the Mexican president that she had a son by Villa and appealed to him as the "protector of widows and orphans" to prevent her house from being taken. She had no quarrel with Luz Corral, she wrote, but "the other señora" (she was obviously referring to Austreberta) "had taken from me possession of the hotel and she now wants to take from me the house in which I live, and I believe that I have as much right to it as she."[104]

Obregón now summoned Luz Corral to Mexico City. The president asked Luz Corral to give her opinion of a petition that Austreberta had sent him requesting the government to recognize her ownership of the Hotel Hidalgo. Luz Corral now took a final revenge on the woman who had displaced her in Villa's affection and contributed to her exile from Canutillo. With the support of Eugenio Martínez, Austreberta had requested from Obregón that he give her possession of the Hotel Hidalgo in order to care for the children that she had borne Villa. Now Luz Corral bluntly told him, "Mr. President: I know about ten children of Pancho Villa, and I know that there are at least as many others; some I have raised myself, and I love them as if they were my sons, and should you want to give the Hotel Hidalgo to the children of Austreberta, there should be at least as many other properties with the same value as the Hotel Hidalgo for each of Villa's children." Obregón agreed that they should receive nothing and sent her to speak with General Martínez, who had been Austreberta's protector. She told Martínez that Austreberta should receive nothing, since she had taken all the money that was in the hacienda and even appropriated the jewelry that Luz Corral had been forced to leave at Canutillo. "Do you think, General, that only Señora Rentería has a right to the inheritance that Pancho left for his children?" she asked. "And don't the other children have the same right? I would give them all the same or give nothing to anyone, and this is what I told General Obregón."[105] Martínez agreed, and Austreberta lost control of the hotel. What its fate finally was cannot be discerned from the existing documents.

Austreberta was now forced to plead for a pension for herself and financial help to allow her children to be educated. The archives of successive Mexican presidents are full of requests from her for help. In 1931, Chihuahuan Governor Andrés Ortiz granted stipends of 20 pesos a month apiece to her children, Francisco and Hipólito, for their education. His successor as governor canceled it, however, and Austreberta appealed to Calles to revoke that decision, telling him that her "innocent sons" were not responsible for the errors of their father, and that he should take into consideration "the great battles in which their father had fought and that will always be part of the history of the revolution."[106] Austreberta and Soledad Seañez, who had not intervened in the conflict in the 1920s, both continued to plead with successive Mexican governments in the 1930s, 1940s, and 1950s, until they were finally granted small pensions.

In contrast to all the other widows, Luz Corral was intent throughout her life to preserve her husband's memory. To that end, she wrote a book entitled *Pancho Villa en la intimidad*, which was both a personal description of her husband and a kind of history of many episodes of his political and social life that she had shared. She waited to publish the book until Obregón was dead and Calles was out of office. It was only during the presidency of Lázaro Cárdenas, who although he had fought against Villa had a much more favorable view of the former commander of the División del Norte, that she completed her book. One of her greatest successes in this respect was to persuade José Vasconcelos, who had broken with Villa in 1915 and had in fact described him as a kind of monster in his memoirs, to write a preface in which he expressed a much more favorable attitude to his former enemy. One of Mexico's most influential intellectuals, Vasconcelos wrote, "When General Villa assumed an office in the government he should never have assumed, I became his open but not irreconcilable enemy . . . and I once more became an admirer of Villa, defeated by the Carrancistas with the help of foreigners but who precisely for this reason became a symbol of a humiliated people. . . . Villa the caudillo was in error, but Villa the citizen was always a valuable man, and he would pay for his virtue with his martyrdom."[107]

Luz Corral presided at official meetings, gave interviews to newspapermen, and converted the home that she had shared with Villa, the Quinta Luz, into a museum, where she personally showed visitors the rooms they had shared, many of Villa's possessions, and the car in which he had been assassinated. The widows were never reconciled. On the rare occasions when they met, such as at the ceremonies all three attended each year in the cemetery in Parral honoring Villa's memory on the anniversary of his assassination, each would lay a wreath on his grave, and the woman coming last would at times remove the flowers the other had laid there.[108]

The Remains of Pancho Villa

Villa's body seems to have found as little rest in death as it had found in life. When he was at the height of his powers in Chihuahua, he had prepared a magnificent crypt in the cemetery of Ciudad Chihuahua, where he hoped that he would lie after his death. That hope was frustrated when Governor Enríquez prevented his remains from being buried there. But even in the cemetery of Parral, where his body was to remain for many years, it found no rest. On February 6, 1926, the administrator of cemetery found that Villa's grave had been opened, and that his head had disappeared. The perpetrators were never caught. Suspicion at first focused on Emil Holmdahl, a soldier of fortune who for a time had fought in Villa's ranks. He was in Parral at the time, ostensibly to do some mining work, and together with a Mexican companion, Alberto Corral, had been heard to inquire where Villa's grave was located. Suspicions about him became stronger when a bloody ax was found in his room. Nothing could be proven against Holmdahl—no head was found in his possession, and the blood on the ax could not have come from a body that had been buried for two and a half years.[109]

Many years later, a Mexican investigative reporter, Manuel Ceja Reyes, located a different culprit for the desecration of Villa's body. According to a Captain Garcilaso who had been stationed in Parral at the time, his commanding officer, a Colonel Durazo, had ordered him to take a squad of soldiers, excavate Villa's body, and cut off his head, since President Obregón wanted Villa's skull for himself. Garcilaso's squad complied with Durazo's instructions and gave him the head, but Garcilaso had no idea what finally happened to it. There is not the least evidence that Obregón ever entertained such macabre ambitions. Durazo himself denied all responsibility in this affair but did state that a well-known Carrancista general, Arnulfo Gómez, a great admirer of Villa's, wanted to have Villa's skull examined by scientists to determine why he was such a military genius. According to Durazo, one of Gómez's subordinates, a colonel known as El Chololo, had taken Villa's skull. In any case, it was never recovered.

All kinds of rumors surfaced as to the fate of Villa's head: it had been bought by an American scientific institute, it was in the possession of a Mexican general, and the latest story to surface was that it had been acquired by Skull and Bones, a secret society at Yale University (to which George Bush, subsequently president of the United States, once belonged).[110]

The remainder of Villa's body was reburied in Parral, but did not stay there either. In 1976, President Luis Echeverría decided that the proper place for Villa's remains was the monument of revolutionary heroes in Mexico City, and on November 18, his remains were solemnly dug up in Parral to be brought to the Monument of the Revolution in Mexico City. Thus, 53 years after his death, he received the kind of official recognition and official burial he did not obtain after he was assassinated. Representatives of the Defense Ministry of Mexico, of its Ministry of the Interior, of the governor of Chihuahua, and of garrisons throughout the north were present at the ceremony. So were Austreberta and Villa's children and grandchildren. The only important member of the family who refused to take part in the ceremony was Luz Corral, who continued to believe that Villa's place was not in Mexico City but at the crypt in Chihuahua.

A federal deputy praised Villa as a great revolutionary, a great military leader, and stated that his burial in the Monument of the Revolution would help to bring about "the unity of all Mexicans." The casket containing Villa's remains was then solemnly transported through the streets of Parral. It was preceded by both a cavalry and an infantry detachment, and behind the casket came a black horse without any rider, led by a civilian from the mountain region of Chihuahua from which most of Villa's soldiers had come. Behind the horse came a detachment dressed in the uniform of Villa's Dorados. As the casket was being led through Parral, a woman broke through the military guard, threw some flowers on the casket, and said, "Adiós, mi General."

When Villa's remains arrived in Mexico City, a further ceremony took place, in which President Echeverría took part. Villa's remains were buried alongside those of Madero, whom he had revered, and Carranza, his most bitter and hated enemy.[111]

Villa in Myth, Legend, Literature, History, and Film

"There is no doubt that history is written by the victors," one of the speakers at Villa's grave said before his remains were transported to the Monument of the Revolution in Mexico City. "But it is also true that legends are written by the people. . . . For that reason, the name of Francisco Villa has remained enshrined forever in the heart of the poor."[112] This opinion was accurate in regard both to official and to popular perceptions of Villa.

For many years after his death, Villa was excluded from official Mexican ideology. His name was scarcely mentioned during commemorations of the Mexican Revolution, no monument to him was set up for many years, and neither the date of his birth nor the date of his death was ever commemorated by official Mexico. In this respect Villa constituted the exception rather than the rule. Once the National Party of the Mexican Revolution was formed in the late 1920s to co-opt and conciliate all revolutionary factions, a conscious effort was made to include all revolutionary leaders in its pantheon: Madero, Carranza, Obregón, and Zapata, some of whom had fought bloody battles against each other while they were alive, were all now accepted as heroes by the official authorities. Villa remained a conspicuous outsider at least until 1934. This was no coincidence. The Sonoran leaders Obregón and Calles, who controlled the destinies of Mexico until 1934, had fought their main battles against Villa and his supporters and had acquired much of their revolutionary legitimacy by the victories they had thus achieved. An even partial rehabilitation of Villa would have downplayed their own achievements. Under the radical administration of Lázaro Cárdenas, the government assumed a much more favorable attitude toward Villa, in spite of the fact that Cárdenas himself had also fought against the Villistas during the revolution. This turnaround may have been linked to Cárdenas's effort to carry out a major agrarian reform in the Laguna area of Durango and Coahuila, for many of whose inhabitants Villa was a great revolutionary hero.

Villa's full rehabilitation in the eyes of official Mexico came only many years later, in 1966, when a new generation of Mexican presidents emerged who had not participated in the revolution, but who considered themselves as its heirs, and as such needed Villa's prestige to bolster their position. In this respect, it is no coincidence that the greatest mark of respect that official Mexico could give Villa occurred during the administration of one of Mexico's most repressive presidents, Gustavo Díaz Ordas. With his support constantly shrinking—two years later, Díaz Ordas would order a bloody massacre of students in Tlatelolco—his Institutional Revolutionary party (PRI) proposed putting Villa's name in letters of gold on the walls of the Chamber of Deputies alongside those of Madero, Carranza, and Zapata. The debate that thereupon ensued both showed how controversial a personality Villa still was in Mexico and also pointed out the profound divisions within Mexico's political class.[113]

In order to make the official proposal to honor Villa as uncontroversial as possible, its authors mentioned only those merits of Villa about which no revolutionary faction could express any doubt. The resolution praised Villa for his role in fighting Porfirio Díaz and above all for organizing the División del Norte, which had played such a decisive role in defeating the Huerta dictatorship. In an ironical twist, in order to bolster the case, the PRI nominated Deputy Juan Barragán, one of Mexico's leading Carrancista historians and supporters of Carranza, to explain why Villa should thus be honored. Barragán stated that he, as a Carrancista, felt that Villa's merits in the struggle against Madero and Huerta should definitely be recognized, and then went on to enumerate the long series of battles in which Villa had participated.

Opposition to the proposal ran deep in the Chamber of Deputies, even in the ranks of the PRI. One of the deputies of the PRI, Salgado Baz, refused to support the proposal, saying that Villa had opposed Mexico's revolutionary constitution of 1917 and implying that he had been responsible for the civil war that shook Mexico after the victory over Huerta. In a statement full of irony, he likened the Chamber of Deputies to the temple of the Aztec god Huitzilopochtli, in the sense that sacrificers and sacrificial victims were linked together. Baz pointed out that Carranza had ordered the execution of Zapata, that Obregón had been responsible for the killing of Carranza, and that all of them now had their names inscribed together in letters of gold in the Chamber of Deputies. If Villa's name were to be added, why not include those of his killers and those of Obregón's too? Deputies from the conservative Accion Nacional party also refused to support the proposal. Perhaps because it had so many supporters in the north, the party did not attack Villa outright, but one of its representatives simply stated that the Chamber of Deputies was not an academy of history and should not make historical decisions.

The debate was highly emotional. The galleries were packed with supporters of Villa, the opposition was booed, and shouts of "Viva Villa!" constantly echoed through the Chamber of Deputies. During the debate, the only serious attempt to analyze not only Villa but the movement that he represented was made by one of Mexico's greatest intellectuals, the head of the Popular Socialist party (PPS), Vicente Lombardo Toledano. Lombardo stated that three heterogeneous social forces had carried out the revolution, and that their conflicts had been inevitable, but that all three deserved credit for the successes of the revolution. The first faction was composed of progressive hacendados, who had established links to Mexico's scarcely emerging industrial bourgeoisie. The representatives of that group were Madero and Carranza. A second social force was constituted by free peasants from communal villages who wanted the return of their lands, their leader and representative being Emiliano Zapata. Villa, Lombardo said, represented a third force, the hacienda peons.

"Who was right?" Lombardo asked, speaking of the three factions in the revolution. "All three large sectors: but only partially so. . . . Together all three were right." And he concluded: "The revolutionary movement of Mexico owes a great debt to Francisco Villa. . . . today that debt is partially paid, but not totally, for the only way of totally paying [it] . . . is not to praise the personalities of the leaders but to carry out their historical mandate."

The resolution in favor of including Villa was adopted by 168 votes to 16. When the results were announced, shouts of "Viva Villa!" and a tremendous wave of applause shook the Chamber of Deputies.

In part at least, Villa's rehabilitation may also have been inspired by the rediscovery by Mexico of John Reed's famous book *Insurgent Mexico*, which exercised a tremendous influence on U.S. public opinion when it was published in 1914. Although the book was never entirely forgotten, it was largely ignored after Reed's more famous book about the Russian Revolution, *Ten Days That Shook the World*, was discarded by many leftists as a result of a conscious decision by Stalin, who deeply resented the fact that he was scarcely mentioned in it, whereas his rivals Trotsky, Kamenev, and Zinoviev figured in it prominently. After the 20th Congress of the Communist Party of the Soviet Union, which sharply condemned Stalin, *Ten Days That Shook the World* enjoyed a resurgence, and *Insurgent Mexico* was rescued from oblivion. It may have inspired many Mexicans to see Villa in a different light than their predecessors of the 1920s.

Revolutionary Mexico was never a totalitarian state, however, and outside of official Mexico, Villa was very much alive. He lived on in Mexican newspapers and popular ballads—the *corridos* of the revolution.

An index of articles published in newspapers and weekly publications registers nearly 2,000 articles dealing with Villa written in Mexico alone up to 1978. Frequently printed in the Sunday editions of Mexican newspapers, between comics and advertisements for cures of everything ranging from baldness to impotence, readers could find polemics between Villistas and anti-Villistas, interviews with participants in the revolution, articles by journalists, reports by witnesses, and stories about Villa's love life, including interviews with his widows. Nearly 100 books, ranging from memoirs to history and novels, have been written about Villa. Among the authors are some of Mexico's most prestigious writers, such as Martín Luis Guzmán, Rafael Muñoz, Nellie Campobello, Mariano Azuela, and Carlos Fuentes.

Hollywood, which had embraced Villa in 1913–14 and then discarded him, rediscovered him in 1934, when Wallace Beery and Fay Wray starred in a famous motion picture entitled *Viva Villa!* Ben Hecht's script grossly underestimated Villa's intelligence, invented episodes that had never happened, and oversimplified the complex Mexican Revolution, thus drawing sharp criticism from many Mexicans, including Villa's widow Luz Corral, but the film was sympathetic to both Villa and the revolution; it received a tremendous welcome in the United States and in Europe and helped to popularize the Mexican Revolution. Subsequently, a number of other Hollywood films and several Mexican films have been made about Villa.

Villa lived on in the mass media and in popular perceptions. This was clearly reflected in the popular myths of Villa that had developed during the revolution and that were expressed above all in corridos, which continue to be known all over Mexico, with new ballads even being added. It would require a book at least as long as this one to analyze, describe, and assess the enormous development of the Villa legend. The corridos emphasize a number of Villa's contradictory traits. There was the self-made man who rose from the lowest rungs of the social ladder to become one of Mexico's greatest military chieftains. While the image of an ever-victorious, irresistible army led by Villa suffered after his defeats by Obregón, it revived when 10,000 Americans under Pershing entered Mexico and were unable to capture Villa. There was also the image of Villa the avenger: the avenger of personal wrongs—the rape of his sister and his imprisonment by Huerta; the avenger of political wrongs—the assassination of Madero; the avenger of social wrongs—the man who punished brutal overseers and hacendados; and finally the avenger of Mexico's humiliated honor—the man who attacked Columbus, New Mexico, and eluded Pershing's pursuit. There was the image of Villa as the friend of the poor, helping widows and orphans. And then there was the image of Villa the macho. Here a remarkable development took place, as one analyst of the Villa legend perceptively remarked. "The revolutionary legend of Villa was never really concerned to deny the two principal elements of the black legend—Villa's rude way with women and his wanton and arbitrary destruction of life—but rather to glamorize them and incorporate them into the picture it presents of the he-man hero in the Mexican tradition of machismo—overpowering, dominant, and larger than life."[114]

Villa lived on in another shape that would probably have greatly surprised and perhaps even shocked him. He became the object and the subject of religious cults. Every year in Chihuahua when meetings take place on the anniversary of Villa's death, members of a religious cult for whom Villa has become a supernatural being also participate. This Villa cult is by no means limited to Chihuahua. The anthropologist Ruth Behar has described a ceremony in a small village on the road to San Luis Potosí, 800 miles from the U.S. border, where a medium assumed the personality of Pancho Villa and in front of a large audience blessed the food that they were eating and promised them: "You will not die of hunger, for it is not my wish." At the end of the ceremony, the participants were shouting, "Viva Villa!"[115]

The fact that official Mexico repudiated Villa for such a long time may paradoxically have helped to keep him very much alive among popular sectors wary of the government. What has also continued to spark interest in Villa is that he, like no other Mexican revolutionary leader, continues to generate a huge amount of controversy, in spite of the fact that both those who fought for him and those who fought against him are practically all dead. These controversies are fueled by the fact that Villa left no archive, fitted no convenient slot, and is claimed as their own by extremely heterogeneous factions, frequently at opposite ends of the political spectrum. The fascist movement that emerged in Mexico in the 1930s, the Camisas Doradas, was named after Villa's famous bodyguards and was led by an ex-Villista officer, Nicolás Rodríguez. For the left, in turn, Villa was one of Mexico's great peasant revolutionaries, and a Mexican unit fighting in the ranks of the International Brigades against Franco in Spain was named for Pancho Villa. Today, the leader of revolutionary Indian peasants in Chiapas, where Villa never fought, says that he has been profoundly inspired by Villa's tactics, and one of the revolutionary peasant groups in Chiapas has taken Villa's name. They constitute but one of many popular groups far beyond Villa's original zone of operation that call themselves Villistas and claim to be his heirs.

The Villistas fared worse that their leader. In contrast to their southern Zapatista allies, the Villistas were not recognized as bona fide agrarian revolutionaries, either by official Mexico or by the vast number of historians dealing with the Mexican Revolution. Many tended to agree with one prominent U.S. historian of Mexico, who described the Villistas as men

recruited from the mining camps and cattle ranches, and from the gambling and red light towns, filled with the rattle of slot machines and with the tinkling mechanical pianos of cheap dance halls, which lined the American border. The slogans of the men of the North might be "Freedom" and "Democracy," the overthrow of the hacendados and *científicos* and the *jefes políticos*; but for most of them as they rode southward on troop trains . . . the Revolution meant power and plunder, the looting of haciendas, and the sacking of cities.[116]

It is only in recent years that both Mexican historians, largely from Chihuahua and Durango, and non-Mexican historians have begun to unravel the enormous agrarian conflicts in Chihuahua and Durango and the agrarian basis of the popular revolution in these states, thus bringing about a new understanding and definition of the Villistas and of Villismo.

Conclusion

The Chihuahuan revolution was only one of the many movements that made up what is generally called the Mexican Revolution, but one of the most important: in 1910–11, and again in 1913–15, the Chihuahuan revolutionaries and their allies changed the course of the nation. The Chihuahuan movement's historical experience differed from that of the movements based in other regions in at least five respects. The first was its military strength. In 1910, the Chihuahuan revolution was the only large-scale movement to rise up against the Porfirian regime. It was only after the Chihuahuans showed the rest of Mexico how vulnerable Díaz was that mass revolts broke out in other parts of the country. In 1913–14, it was again the Chihuahuan revolutionaries and their allies from Durango and parts of Coahuila who bore the brunt of the fighting against Huerta and achieved the most significant victories against the federal army. Second, the revolutionary movement in Chihuahua was unique in its social composition. It was the only movement in the Mexican Revolution that included members of all social classes but excluded hacendados. In that respect, the Chihuahuan revolutionaries were different from their counterparts in Coahuila and Sonora, on the one hand, and in Morelos, on the other. Hacendados led the revolutionaries in both Coahuila and Sonora, and the Zapatista rebellion in Morelos basically consisted of peasants from free villages, largely excluding peons, workers, and (except for a handful of intellectuals) members of the middle classes. Third, no other revolutionary movement had such volatile relations with both the U.S. government and American business interests. For a time the Chihuahuans maintained closer links to the Americans than any other movement. Later they became the group most hostile to the United States. Fourth, the personal history of the Chihuahuan leader was unlike that of any other. Among the major revolutionary figures in Mexico, only Villa had been both a peon and an outlaw prior to the revolution. Finally, the Chihuahuan revolution was unique in the controversy and radically different interpretations it sparked. Ever since the revolutionary period, popular perceptions, official government attitudes, and scholarly interpretations alike have been unable to find common ground with regard to either the movement or its leader, Pancho Villa.

Why Chihuahua?

One of the major controversies deals with the social composition of the Chihuahuan revolution: was it essentially a peasant movement, did miners constitute its main component, or was it essentially made up of a coalition of marginals and the riffraff of the frontier? What role, if any, did Chihuahua's middle classes play in it?

It is by no means easy to explain the breadth of the 1910–11 Chihuahuan revolution. It constituted an upheaval of what might perhaps best be called the whole of civil society against an existing regime. In an unprecedented show of unity, rarely achieved in other parts of Mexico, it included both rural and urban sectors and all classes of society, with the exception of the ruling hacendado oligarchy. Its roots are all the more difficult to understand since ostensible causes that have led to revolutionary outbreaks in other parts of the world were absent in Chihuahua. There was certainly no similarity to the factors that triggered the Russian revolutions of 1905 and 1917: a lost war in 1905 against Japan, and a bloody and endless war that cost millions of lives from 1914 to 1917. There was no similarity either to the xenophobic characteristics of the Boxer Rebellion in China at the end of the nineteenth century. Some Spaniards and a relatively large number of Chinese were killed by Mexican revolutionaries in the initial and most spontaneous phase of the revolution, but the main group of foreigners in Chihuahua, the Americans, were left unscathed. In fact, many Americans, including entrepreneurs and mine owners, showed strong sympathies for the Mexican revolutionaries. Nor could the regime of Luis Terrazas and Enrique Creel, or that of Porfirio Díaz, for that matter, be compared to bloody, repressive Latin American dictatorships along the lines of those of Trujillo, Somoza, or Batista. In fact, Terrazas had for a long time been a highly popular leader and had enjoyed great prestige among large segments of Chihuahua's population as a result of the successful Indian wars waged during his administration. The transformation of Terrazas from a popular caudillo into a man who, together with his son-in-law Enrique Creel, was universally hated in Chihuahua was caused by his attempt to destroy what had until then been a highly autonomous frontier society. This process began toward the end of the nineteenth century when the Apaches were defeated. Foreign investors poured into the country, railroads were built, land values rose, and market production developed, thus creating incentives for both the expropriation of private lands and the closing of the open range. It reached a high point once Creel assumed the governorship of the state and enacted his land law of 1905 and his political reforms, which undermined the autonomy that frontier communities had enjoyed throughout the eighteenth and nineteenth centuries.

Yet these developments alone do not explain the outbreak of the revolution. They created profound dissatisfaction among the free village communities, the heirs of what had been military colonies in Chihuahua. But they also profoundly divided them. Not only hacendados but many villagers as well profited from Creel's land law and his restrictions on municipal autonomy, since he frequently tended to favor one clique in the villages, generally composed of outsiders, whom he felt he could better dominate and manipulate by granting them political offices. The problem for Creel was that what he gave with one hand, he took away with the other. When a deep recession originating in the United States hit Chihuahua in 1907–8, combined with extremely bad harvests, thus causing a dramatic rise in food prices, Creel reacted by imposing new taxes on the already strained and impoverished poorer and middle classes of the state. He could not tax foreign investors, who had received tax-exempt status when they brought their capital into Chihuahua, and he refused to increase the taxes on his own class, the hacendados. As a result, in many parts of Chihuahua's countryside heterogeneous forces deeply at odds with one another over Creel's land law would unite against the taxes that the governor had imposed on all of them. This was the case in San Andrés, where, after a contentious and divisive struggle between Indians and non-Indians over the rights to land, the whole village united in a small-scale revolt against the new taxes. Another measure that equally contributed to unifying contending factions in villages against the hacendados was the abrupt cancellation of grazing rights by hacendados both on their own lands and on the public lands they had acquired at extremely cheap prices. This measure was complemented by the arbitrary confiscation of cattle belonging to villagers that were found on hacienda lands. In the eyes of Díaz's generals, this was one of the main causes of the hatred that the regime of Terrazas and Creel had engendered among Chihuahua's villagers.

The economic crisis of 1907–8 had another devastating effect on Chihuahua's free villagers that also contributed to a rise in revolutionary consciousness. Many of them had been able to overcome at least partly the effects of losing their lands and losing traditional privileges by finding work in mines both in northern Mexico and across the border in the United States. In the economic crisis of 1907–8, Mexican workers were the first to be dismissed north of the border, while many mines closed in Mexico itself. Traditionally, in such a situation of crisis, the miners had been able to return to their villages and scratch out a living there. Now that they had lost a large part of their lands, this proved to be difficult or impossible for many of them.

The free villagers of Chihuahua did not make up the majority of the population, yet they peopled the columns of the armed revolution that broke out in the state. On former occasions when they had staged armed uprisings, such as in 1891–93, they had been practically alone. They had found little support either among hacienda peons, who still made up a large part of the rural population, or among the growing urban population of Chihuahua. This situation dramatically changed in 1910–11.

One significant aspect of the Chihuahuan revolution is that a majority of the heterogeneous group best referred to as the middle classes also sympathized with the revolutionary movement. The group that considered itself middle class in Chihuahua, which included economically very divergent groups—small ranchers and store owners in the countryside, better-paid employees, merchants, teachers, bureaucrats, small entrepreneurs, and local notables in villages and towns—was deeply divided. A significant part of this "middle class" consisted of clients and beneficiaries of Terrazas and Creel. They did not join the revolution, but they did not fight for the oligarchy either. Outside of this group, the vast majority of middle-class Chihuahuans were opposed to Terrazas and Creel.

The urban classes and above all the middle classes of Chihuahua repudiated the regime in part because of the new taxes imposed by Creel after the outbreak of the crisis of 1908. They were considered unfair and illegitimate. But middle-class resentment of the regime went much deeper than that. It was linked to Díaz's decision in 1903 to turn power over to Terrazas and Creel, thus abandoning a policy that had for a long time given his regime a degree of legitimacy and popularity and created an illusion of democracy in Chihuahua. When Díaz was consolidating his dictatorship after 1884, one of the main things he did was to remove traditional caudillos such as the Terrazas from power in their native states and impose his own men. Sometimes these were outsiders, and sometimes they were rivals of the traditional oligarchy, but they were generally weaker than the men they replaced. Díaz's aim was to prevent one faction from becoming too powerful and to play off the different groups against one another. By so doing, he hoped to maintain himself in power and to defuse local or regional revolts, so frequent in the early nineteenth century. Díaz's policy had given a certain amount of leeway to regional middle classes, who were wooed by both sides as each attempted either to consolidate or to regain power in their native states. At the beginning of the twentieth century, Díaz largely abandoned this policy. On the one hand, some local oligarchies, such as the Terrazas clan, had become so powerful that it was difficult to deny them political power. Moreover, Díaz realized that these local oligarchies, unlike their predecessors in the early nineteenth century, would never rise up in arms against the central government. They had too much to lose. Their interests were now inextricably linked to those of foreign investors, for whom stability was an absolute precondition for investing in Mexico. Foreign investors meant large profits to the local oligarchies who generally served as their intermediaries. Díaz's new policy meant that the middle classes now lost whatever leeway they had enjoyed as a result of splits in the local oligarchies. They were now helpless against the whims of the governor, the jefes políticos, and the appointed mayors. In this situation of profound political and economic crisis in the first decade of the twentieth century, events that under other circumstances might have elicited only a limited response now suddenly became major factors in shaping the consciousness of the people of Chihuahua. This was the case of the robbery of the Banco Minero, which largely undermined and perhaps even destroyed whatever legitimacy remained to the Creel administration.

In contrast to many other parts of Mexico, large segments of Chihuahua's middle classes were willing to fight alongside of the state's rural revolutionaries. In contrast to much of Mexico, where a deep cleavage existed between a Spanish-speaking and mestizo or white urban society and an Indian countryside, no such cleavage appeared in Chihuahua. The Tarahumara Indians who constituted the bulk of indigenous society in Chihuahua only marginally participated in the revolution. The urban classes had no fear that the mestizo or Indian villagers would wage a caste war against them. On the contrary, for a century, city dwellers had seen Chihuahua's villagers as their main defenders against the attacks of the "barbarians" from the north. Large segments of the middle classes in Chihuahua were thus very different from their counterparts in Morelos, who were desperately afraid of the state's peasants.

The germ of revolution in Chihuahua also spread to a social group that had hitherto been considered the most docile segment of society: the peons on the large estates. Terrazas had done his best to maintain the traditional paternalism that was characteristic of the relations on his haciendas. Whenever he visited an estate, he made it a point to recognize each peasant and each family, to make gifts to everyone, and to provide them with sustenance in periods of famine and bad harvests. Nevertheless, that paternalism had been deeply undermined. After Geronimo's defeat in 1884, Terrazas had lost one of the main bulwarks of legitimacy in the eyes of his peons, since they no longer needed the protection he provided from Apache raiders. As communications improved in Chihuahua, many hacienda peons contrasted their living conditions with those north of the border and even with those on foreign-owned estates. On the latter, the foreigners were forced to make concessions that were absent on traditional estates in order to attract laborers. They did not resort to debt peonage and tended to pay their employees in cash, thus making them independent of the company store.

On the whole, the concentration of political and economic power in the hands of one family and the tremendous arbitrariness it engendered centered all resentments in the state of Chihuahua on the ruling oligarchy of Terrazas and Creel.

But it would be a great error to see the causes of revolution only in economic terms. The men who constituted the core of the revolutionary army, the former military colonists on the Apache frontier, had lived according to a certain code of honor for nearly two centuries. They had fought to "preserve civilization against the barbarians," as the inhabitants of Namiquipa put it. In return, "civilized" society respected and honored them and allowed them to retain the large amounts of land that the Spanish colonial administration and later the government of Benito Juárez had granted them. In their eyes, that code of honor was broken when the rulers of Chihuahua, above all Creel, attempted to reduce them to the level of poor or landless peasants, which would have demoted them to the lowest social rung in the state and taken away the status and dignity they had earned in their long fight against the Apaches.

A major distinguishing feature of the Chihuahuan revolution was the absence of hacendados in its leadership. This was no coincidence. In other states of the north, both in Coahuila and in Sonora, the hacendados were deeply divided and only part of them were identified with the coalition in power. In Chihuahua, Terrazas and Creel had co-opted practically all of the hacendado class through intermarriage, absorption, or the destruction of rivals. This does not mean that Chihuahuan hacendados would blindly support Terrazas and Creel, but they certainly had no reason to revolt and never joined the revolution. No Chihuahuan equivalent to Maytorena in Sonora or the Maderos and Carranza in Coahuila emerged.

Villismo: Banditry or Revolution?

Another focus of controversy is the question of whether the revolutionary movement in Chihuahua was a premodern movement in which banditry played a major role, as the personality of Villa might suggest. Was it a backward-looking movement opposed to modernization?

The Chihuahuan revolutionary movement can certainly not be called premodern. Banditry always played a far smaller role in Chihuahua than it did in most other states of Mexico. As long as the Apaches raided in the state, banditry was far too dangerous an occupation, while the underdeveloped state of its economy and the difficulties of transportation made banditry an unprofitable enterprise. There was no tradition in Chihuahua of heroic social bandits prior to the revolution, as was the case further south, for instance, in Durango. In spite of the enormous echo of the Tomóchi rebellion, millenarianism was the exception rather than the rule. Religious opposition to the regime manifested itself either in conversions to Protestantism or in the emergence of social Catholicism, as exemplified by Silvestre Terrazas.

Neither were opposition movements that did emerge in the Porfirian era in some sense premodern. The revolutionary cells that the Partido Liberal Mexicano established in the countryside and the cities were very similar to those established by revolutionaries in Europe. Dissatisfied former military colonists by no means sought to isolate themselves from the rest of society but, on the contrary, through letters to newspapers and even demonstrations attempted to find support in the cities. Many villagers had traveled to other parts of the state or even across the border of the United States and had a knowledge of other societies that peasants in many other parts of Mexico never managed to acquire. Chihuahua had one of the highest literacy rates in Mexico, and it was one of the few states where newspapers played an important role in the outbreak of the revolution. The organ of the PLM, *Regeneración*, had one of its largest readerships in Chihuahua, and Luis Terrazas was convinced that the *Correo de Chihuahua* had played a decisive role in bringing about the revolution.

Chihuahua's free villagers did not oppose the trappings of the modern world. They were used to a market economy, and they strongly respected education. For them, a return to traditional society meant a return to the democratic institutions that had existed in the heyday of the Chihuahuan frontier. It was "modernization" at their expense to which they objected, a modernization that consisted of the expropriation of their land, the elimination of their autonomy, and the imposition of centralized control over their lives.

One of the main characteristics of the revolutionary movement in Chihuahua, as well as of the army that it produced, was that unlike its counterpart in Morelos, its social composition varied enormously in different periods of the revolution. During the Maderista revolution, an unprecedented unity emerged among the lower classes of society—that is, former military colonists, peons, industrial workers, miners, railwaymen, and large segments of the state's middle classes. That unity fell apart only a short time after the triumph of the revolution, when significant segments of Chihuahua's lower classes united with dissident elements of the middle classes, and even the state's powerful hacendados, in the Orozco uprising. The unity of these heterogeneous forces was even more tenuous than that of the revolutionaries a year earlier, and it soon fell apart. In 1913, Villa was able to reunite the social groups that had made up the Madero revolution, and he in fact created even greater unity among them on the basis of the enormous resources that he controlled, his charismatic personality, his victories, and the support that the movement enjoyed from the United States. After Villa's defeat, the coalition that he had so painfully set up in 1913–14 again fell apart. Segments of it were briefly reunited when U.S. troops occupied parts of Chihuahua and Carranza's troops treated the state as if it were an occupied territory. When the Americans left and Carranza agreed to arm significant parts of Chihuahua's population, the Villista coalition of middle and lower classes finally disintegrated. Not only the middle classes but significant groups of Chihuahua's free villagers and industrial workers turned against Villa, and from 1917 to 1920 his support seems to have dwindled more and more.

The División del Norte

The profound and rapid changes in the social basis of the revolutionary movement in Chihuahua were reflected in equally profound and rapid transformations of its armed forces. One of the most difficult tasks faced by any historian is to define the nature of the División del Norte. Was it a revolutionary army imbued with a profound sense of mission, with a vision of a new, different, and more just society? Was it a people in arms, as the Zapatistas were in southern Mexico, in which civilian thinking and civilian mentality were more important than militarism? Or was it in the final account a professional fighting force, primarily loyal to its leader, similar to the caudillo armies that had roamed throughout Latin America in the nineteenth century? The question is extremely difficult to answer, for in the final analysis, all three elements existed within the army, although in varying degrees at varying times.

The Maderista army that had risen in 1910–11 to topple both the Terrazas-Creel regime in Chihuahua and Porfirio Díaz's rule in Mexico was clearly a revolutionary army imbued above all with a sense of mission, of creating a different society. It had mainly been composed of men in their thirties, frequently owning some property and at times able to read and write. It was a strictly disciplined army that largely eschewed pillage and robbery, one made up of volunteers who had gone out to fight of their own free will. Much of the spirit, ideology, and organization of this Maderista army was present in the División del Norte as well. Many of its soldiers had already fought in 1910–11, and many of its leaders had also led their followers then. Like its predecessor, the División del Norte consisted mainly of volunteers, although it contained a number of federal prisoners who had chosen to rejoin Villa rather than be shot. Nevertheless, by early 1914, the División del Norte acquired characteristics that made it very different from the Maderista army that had preceded it. By controlling Chihuahua, and through their good relations with the United States, the revolutionaries now acquired resources that they had never possessed in 1910–11. As a result, the army tended more and more to combine very heterogeneous traits.

On the one hand, since the army was hugely popular and reflected the composition of the Chihuahuan population, and since many soldiers were accompanied by their wives or girlfriends, it still had many elements of a people in arms. On the other hand, it began to assume many of the structures of a professional army. While pillage and robbery continued to be banned—Villa was very strict in this respect—fighting became a way of life for many of these men. After each victory, Villa gave them substantial rewards. An increasing number of officers, instead of being elected by the men from their localities, were named by Villa and the army command. To a certain degree, the ideology of the División del Norte changed concurrently with its social composition. The heads of families, who had predominated in the Madero period, were now replaced by younger men, and even boys of between 12 and 15. For obvious reasons, they lacked the ideological conviction of the older Maderista soldiers, and this dilution of ideology was reinforced as more and more deserters from the federal army joined Villa's forces. This process accelerated as the army moved further and further from its native region, and esprit de corps increasingly tended to replace revolutionary ideology.

After the dissolution of the División del Norte, and especially after the departure of Pershing's expedition in 1917, the character of Villa's armed forces changed once again. It now consisted of a heterogeneous mix of veterans of the División del Norte (largely Dorados) whose loyalty to Villa transcended every other loyalty, of villagers taking up arms after having been despoiled of their belongings by Carrancista soldiers, of federal deserters who preferred the gold paid by Villa to Carranza's worthless paper money, and by an increasing number of out-of-work cowboys. "Cowboys we are, and cowboys we shall be," Villa told Angeles in 1918. Many preferred to join Villa rather than to migrate to the United States, where some feared being drafted into the U.S. Army once the United States entered World War I.

The reasons for the enormous successes of Chihuahua's revolutionary movement in 1910–11 and 1913–14 are easier to assess than the reasons for its final defeat in 1915. Chihuahuan revolutionaries could count on the unity of all of civil society against Terrazas and Creel, and later against Huerta. The fighting tradition of the Chihuahuan frontier played a major role in their determination to fight in the first place and in the victories they achieved in the course of the revolution. To this must be added the resources that the haciendas of the oligarchy offered the Chihuahuans and the relatively easy access to arms across the border in the United States. The presence of charismatic leaders—Madero and Orozco in 1910–11, and Villa in 1913–14—was also of decisive importance.

There is no single explanation for the defeat of the forces of the Revolutionary Convention, of which the Chihuahuan revolutionaries constituted the most important segment. The heterogeneity of its composition and the regional outlook of its leader played an important role. Furthermore, it was poorer in terms of money and resources than its Carrancista counterparts.

Villa's military defeats derived above all from his errors of strategy and tactics. Unlike any of the Carrancista generals, he possessed absolute authority over his army, so that frequently no real discussion of strategy and tactics was possible. Yet these defeats need not have led to the kind of debacle that Villa suffered had his social policies been different. As one of his most intelligent intellectual advisors, Federico González Garza, put it, "Since Huerta was ousted, we have to agree, that from a practical point of view, if we had known how to conduct an orderly confiscation subject to strict rules, and if we had had a distribution of land guided by an intelligent plan and without violence, we would by now have created new interests, which would have helped to sustain the new regime."[1] Such a land distribution might have created such a base for Villismo that it might have become invincible in spite of its military defeat. But such a program was not carried out because of Villismo's alliance with and partial dependence on the United States, an association that proved both a source of strength and a critical point of weakness.

Villa and the United States

On the one hand, the close links to the Americans and the possibility of securing arms and resources north of the border allowed Villa to transform his fighters from a guerrilla force into a regular army that was able to defeat the federal troops in large-scale pitched battles. But the other side of the coin was that the need to secure resources to buy arms and ammunition in the United States made it imperative for Villa to keep the large estates under his control. Unlike Zapata, he could not divide them among the peasantry, which might have undercut his support in the United States by making him seem a radical revolutionary unwilling to respect the sanctity of private property. In addition, Villa feared that any radical land distribution as long as the war wore on would significantly reduce the will of many villagers to fight outside of their native region.

In another respect, his close links to the Americans proved a double-edged sword. By printing huge amounts of paper money, which at first the Americans were willing to accept, he managed for a brief time to finance his military and social expenditures. This was nevertheless only a short-term gain. As soon as he suffered his first important defeat, the value of his currency plummeted and so did the economy of Chihuahua. In this context, Villista rule stood in profound contrast to Zapatista Morelos, where large-scale commercial estates had been replaced by subsistence farming. Zapata never printed any paper currency. Villa paid his soldiers in money and not in land, as Zapata did, making his support all the more precarious. Once his money lost its value, his support dwindled.

There is thus little doubt that Villa's links to the United States had profound indirect consequences both for his victories and for his defeats. A more difficult question is whether U.S. policy directly contributed to his defeat. This is one of the most controversial issues in the hotly debated historiography of the Mexican Revolution. The long-held idea that the United States unilaterally favored and supported Villa until his defeat at the hands of Obregón is an extremely dubious proposition. While there are indications that for a brief time both the Wilson administration and American business saw Villa as the coming man in Mexico and the best solution for U.S. interests, that attitude had waned long before Villa's defeat in Celaya.

This does not mean that the United States wholeheartedly switched allegiances to Carranza in this early period. The U.S. administration had lost faith that Villa's faction alone would carry out the kind of policies it wanted in Mexico, and it felt that playing Villa off against Carranza was the best means of securing U.S. interests in Mexico. For a brief time, in 1914, long before Carranza's victory in the civil war, only his forces and not those of Villa could acquire arms in the United States. At a time when the Carrancistas controlled ports and the Villistas did not, the Wilson administration decreed that only arms shipped by sea could be bought by the revolutionaries. When the U.S. military handed Veracruz over to Carranza and his supporters, it also delivered huge amounts of arms into the hands of the constitutionalist government. And while Villa's decisive defeats in the Bajío cannot be attributed to U.S. policy, his final defeat at Agua Prieta certainly can. By allowing Obregón's troops to cross U.S. territory in order to enter Sonora, the Wilson administration played a decisive role in bringing about the final defeat of Villa's División del Norte.

One of the most interesting questions is why the alliance between Villa and the United States, which for a brief time did exist, and which was favored on the one hand by the Wilson administration and American business and on the other by Villa, broke down. Some American and official Carrancista historians have a simple answer to this problem: even before Villa was defeated, the Wilson administration discovered that he was no more than a bandit. Assuming for the moment this had been the case (and in the opinion of this author it was not), U.S. authorities throughout history have allied themselves with Latin American rulers with extremely unsavory reputations. Even the Wilson administration had no compunction about doing so with some Central American and Caribbean rulers. What made the break between the Villa movement and the United States practically inevitable was the fact that the Wilson administration, in spite of its "idealism," was no different from its Republican predecessors when the traditional rights of U.S. companies were threatened. Villa appeared so attractive to the Americans because he had neither touched American property nor imposed new taxes on their holdings. That policy could only be carried out as long as the huge fortunes of the Mexican oligarchy, above all the Terrazas, were available to Villa, and as long as his currency still had value in the United States. When he could no longer finance his movement from the resources of the hacendados, and his currency plummeted, Villa had no choice but to turn on the one remaining wealthy group in northern Mexico, the Americans, and to begin taxing them or forcing the mining companies to resume work.

The resistance of the United States to Villa's measures was but one factor that undermined the northern revolutionary's confidence in the U.S. administration. The main factor was that he soon realized that in the eyes of the Americans, their alliance was not a relationship between allies but that of master and subordinate. This was certainly the relationship that León Canova and his clique in the State Department, along with businessmen and some members of the Wilson administration, envisaged when they proposed a pact to Villa that would have turned Mexico into a protectorate of the United States. Villa had no way of knowing that this was not the official policy of the Wilson administration. But the Wilson administration too had no compunction about treating Villa and his faction in a way that contravened the norms of relations between nations. As an important faction in Mexico, the Villistas were invited to participate in a conference in Washington, and through Hugh Scott, they were promised that there would be no unilateral recognition of Carranza, at a time when the administration in Washington was contemplating precisely that. Without giving any explanation to the Villa delegates in the United States, Washington recognized Carranza between one day and the next. Furthermore, the United States violated its neutrality by allowing Carranza's troops to cross U.S. territory in order to attack Villa.

While the alliance between Villa and the United States thus met an inglorious end, the symbiotic relationship between the two did not. It lasted until his death. Villa's attack on Columbus, New Mexico, and the ensuing Pershing expedition gave him a new lease on life in the years 1916–17, while the taxes he imposed on American companies attempting to do business in Chihuahua after 1917 enabled him to survive the long years of guerrilla warfare. In all probability, Villa's assassination was largely the result of the Mexican government's desire for recognition by the United States in 1923.

Villa the Man

The controversies that the Villa movement has sparked are nothing in comparison to those that the personality of its leader has provoked. Villa has been variously referred to as the Robin Hood of the frontier, a friend of the poor, the leader of Mexico's revolutionary peasantry, the Zapata of the North, the scourge of the frontier, the Attila of the North, a scarcely human bandit, and the Fifth Horseman of the Apocalypse. Significantly, the controversy about Villa is not about some of the main traits of his character. There is widespread agreement among friend and foe that Villa was capable both of great acts of generosity and of equally great acts of cruelty.

Some of the main points of controversy with respect to Villa concern the nature of his outlaw past, the reasons for his spectacular rise to prominence within the revolutionary movement in 1910–11 and above all in 1913–15, and questions surrounding Villa's ideology and the degree to which it influenced the policies he pursued.

We shall probably never know exactly why Villa became an outlaw. His story of the rape of a sister may have been true, but the facts surrounding it that he relates with such great detail in his memoirs—his shooting of a hacendado and his killing of rurales sent out to pursue him—do not fit well with contemporary records. The only motive for which the authorities in Durango arrested him in 1898 was for stealing two mules and a gun. It must also be said that if ever there was a system that forced men who might have had no criminal intent to become outlaws, it was the political and social structure of Porfirian Durango. Any peon who incurred the dislike of a hacendado could be sent into the army without a hearing, a fate that in many respects was akin to slavery. Unless exceptional circumstances obtained, he had no possibility of appeal. Faced with that choice, it is not surprising that many men, especially if they were strong-willed and courageous, chose the alternative of becoming outlaws.

Villa's move to Chihuahua, as well as his change of name, was in all probably due to his desertion from the army. In Chihuahua, Villa seems to have lived in a twilight zone between legal occupation for the most part and cattle rustling on the side. His above-board jobs consisted primarily of working for foreign enterprises, mainly railroads and mining companies, supervising men and bringing valuable goods through dangerous regions. The prestige Villa thus acquired with powerful foreign interests in Chihuahua may explain why the state's authorities for a long time treated him with great leniency, so that when in mid 1910 a Porfirian official arrested him for what was obviously a minor offense, he was immediately released, his gun and money were returned to him, and he even felt secure enough to lodge a complaint with a high Porfirian official. Villa's break with the Porfirian authorities seems to have occurred when he killed one of his former partners, Claro Reza, who had become a government agent. It is not clear whether this killing was a result of Villa's having joined the revolutionaries or, on the contrary, whether his joining the revolutionaries was at least in part the result of his killing of Reza and the proceedings against him that the government now undertook.

The three main legends about his activities as an outlaw prior to the outbreak of the Mexican revolution are largely flawed. He was not the mass murderer his enemies held him to be in the years prior to 1910; he was not a relentlessly pursued victim who killed dozens of rurales, as he described himself; nor was he the legendary "Robin Hood of the frontier," the scourge of the Terrazas-Creel oligarchy, although he sometimes distributed some of the proceeds of his robberies to the poor.

The reasons why he joined the revolutionary movement can only be inferred. He was in many respects very different from other popular leaders who rose against the Díaz regime in 1910. Unlike Zapata, Ortega, or Contreras, he had never been leader of a village community, representing it to the outside world. Unlike the great majority of the popular leaders who rose in 1910–11, he had not participated in an opposition political group prior to the revolution. He had no links to the PLM, and neither had he joined the anti-reelectionist party, or if he did so it was very shortly before the outbreak of the revolution. While it will never be known exactly why he joined the revolution, he had every reason to hate the oligarchy of Durango, which had forced him into the army and probably into a life as an outlaw in the first place. Likewise, the Chihuahuan oligarchy seems to have prevented him from starting a legitimate meat business. As was the case with many outlaws, the revolution presented him with the possibility of leading a legal life once again and an opportunity to improve his social status. But unlike the others, there is no evidence that he joined the Madero revolution for purposes of looting, pillage, and banditry. On the contrary, his troops were considered to be among the most disciplined in the revolutionary army, and there is no evidence that he acquired any significant wealth, aside from the 10,000 pesos that Madero gave him, during that period of his life.

Villa's spectacular rise to prominence during the Maderista revolution of 1910–11 seems at first glance surprising in view of his lack of a political or social constituency prior to 1910. It has frequently been assumed that what more than made up for this drawback was Villa's immense reputation among Chihuahua's country people, who, once he called on them, flocked to his banner. But as this book has tried to show, there was no such immense reputation prior to 1910. Villa's rise to prominence was based on other factors. There is little doubt that he was a charismatic leader, but saying so means both very much and very little. Several qualities seem to have helped him to become the unquestioned leader of his men, among them traditional caudillo characteristics such as audacity, courage, willingness to take personal risks, ability with a gun, and his magnificent ridership (ballads have been written about his horses), but perhaps more important was his genuine dedication to his men, for whose welfare he seems to have cared more than most other military leaders. The care he took of widows and orphans, the frequent gifts he gave his men, and the hospital train he set up in later years are clear proof of this attitude. The iron discipline Villa maintained from the moment he took command meant that no resources would be wasted in pillage and mindless destruction; instead, everything would be used to supply his army and his soldiers. An essential characteristic of Villa was his ability to identify personally, materially, and ideologically with his men. Not only did he partake of their food, sit at their campfires, and remember their faces, he also to a large degree was ready to assume their ideology. Paradoxically, the fear that he inspired enhanced his macho image and his popularity.

A second and very different factor that contributed to Villa's rise to prominence was that Madero for a time saw in him the most loyal of his Chihuahuan subordinates. Paradoxically, again, this fact may have been due not only to Villa's personal loyalty to Madero but to his lack of a political past. To a large degree, Madero's enthusiasm for Villa was sparked by the fact that he was the only leader willing to take on and disarm the members of the PLM. Villa was unique in this respect, because most other revolutionary leaders at one time or another had entertained connections with that party, which for a long time was the main opposition force in Chihuahua.

There was an enormous qualitative difference between the role Villa played during the Madero revolution of 1910–11 and during the constitutionalist revolution of 1913–14. During the Maderista revolution, the forces he personally led amounted to no more than 700 men, while the whole of the Maderista army in Chihuahua never included more than 5,000 to 7,000 men. In the Maderista period, Villa never exercised any political responsibility.

In 1914, at the height of his power, his army numbered between 40,000 and 100,000 men. Instead of guerrilla warfare, Villa fought regular campaigns and exercised political authority over vast parts of Mexico's north. In the years 1913–14, this semiliterate former peon showed himself to be a superb organizer, an extremely efficient manager of resources, and a surprisingly able creator of consensus. Millions flowed through his hands, and although he had no political organization and only a small number of technicians and intellectuals to help him, he managed at one and the same time to deal effectively with three problems, each of which by itself was enormously complicated. First, within a short span of time, he succeeded in transforming a motley array of guerrillas into an extremely efficient regular fighting force capable of laying siege to cities defended by Mexico's professional regular army. Second, he concurrently managed to maintain and even increase his popular support in Chihuahua, feeding the poor and the unemployed and reestablishing the precarious unity of the middle and lower classes that had been the basis of the Madero revolution in the state. Third, he was no less successful in gaining first the neutrality and then the support of decisive segments of both the population and the power elite in the United States, ranging from radicals such as John Reed and Mother Jones to Woodrow Wilson, important business interests, and, for a time, even William Randolph Hearst.

Did Villa have an ideology and, above all, did that ideology have a practical bearing on the policies he applied? He genuinely hated the oligarchies of Durango and Chihuahua, but he by no means included all hacendados in that category; nor does the destruction of the hacienda as an institution seem to have been one of his main priorities. He had admired and continued to admire Madero and allowed the Madero family and other hacendados he considered friendly to retain their properties. He had no compunction about aligning himself with Maytorena, one of Sonora's most conservative hacendados.

At least up to 1915, he sincerely and genuinely believed in redistribution of income from the rich to the poor. One part, but in his eyes not necessarily the most significant part, of that redistribution was the granting of land. Nevertheless, it never assumed the importance in his eyes that land reform held for Emiliano Zapata. One reason for this difference in attitude was that Chihuahua in relative terms had a larger nonagricultural population than Morelos. In addition, Villa was in many respects a warlord, his men constituting his main interest. Since these men for a time included the major part of Chihuahua's young male population, that interest was very broad and probably encompassed the majority of Chihuahua's inhabitants.

Villa's ideology always had concrete consequences. His hatred for the oligarchy manifested itself in the confiscation of their lands and properties. His conviction that the redistribution to the poor should take place expressed itself in massive distributions of food and other goods to the poorer segments of society. His commitment to his soldiers was reflected in the huge sums he dispensed to the wounded and the orphans and widows of his men.

In his plans for Chihuahua, Villa was both a traditionalist and a modernizer. He was a traditionalist in the sense that he wished to return to the main form of organization of Chihuahua's free villagers, both in the colonial period and in the nineteenth century: military colonies. He was a modernizer in his profound belief in the benefits of education. During his rule in Chihuahua, a tremendous boost was given to the construction of the schools and to help for teachers. While Villa manifested xenophobia toward Spaniards and Chinese, until the end of 1914, Villismo was far less nationalistic than other Mexican factions, above all that of Carranza. Villa treated Americans in the regions he controlled far better than his counterparts elsewhere in Mexico did.

Villa was far more a regionalist than a nationalist. When it presented itself, Villa never took the opportunity of becoming president of Mexico. While he formulated a coherent plan for Chihuahua, he was incapable of setting a national agenda for all of Mexico. His national plan for land reform came at a very late date and was never applied. His most coherent national program was decentralization, with every faction taking over the territories it controlled and implementing whatever policies it wanted in those regions. The plan envisioned a weak national government exercising practically no control over the regions. There is a tremendous contrast between Villa's remarkable legislative, ideological, and administrative activity as governor and his lack of any such activity when he officially assumed control over a regional government in the north that ruled over an area far larger than his bailiwick of Chihuahua and Durango.

To a very large degree, Villa's ideology reflected that of the former military colonists in Chihuahua. This was certainly the case with respect to his idea of founding military colonies all over Mexico, and it was also true of his conviction that land had to be earned by fighting. In their petitions to the Díaz regime, the military colonists had always insisted that they had earned their land by fighting against the Apaches, and they were thus quite ready to accept Villa's idea that the primary recipients of land should be the soldiers who had shed their blood for it.

Chihuahua's villagers had always been wary of the central government. Villa's emphasis on decentralization certainly corresponded to their desires. Except in those regions where foreigners were directly involved in the expropriation of their land, they tended to be less nationalistic than the population of the cities, and that fact too was reflected in Villa's ideology.

Villa's main shortcoming in the eyes of large segments of his rural constituency, as well as with Chihuahua's middle classes, was, as Felipe Angeles noted, that Villa "was no democrat." He tolerated no opposition; there were no elections, either at the local, regional, or national level, during his administration. Although the one newspaper his faction edited, *Vida Nueva*, frequently discussed agrarian and social issues, it never questioned the Villista administration's decisions and propagated a personality cult of Villa that made it at times sound like a newspaper from a Latin American dictatorship. With respect to democracy, Villa's ideology corresponded far more closely to that of northern Mexico's traditional caudillos than to that of its free villagers.

Was Villa, as his enemies made him out, nothing but a bandit intent on loot and power? Had he been such a bandit, he would have acted after his defeat in the same way that corrupt Latin American politicians such as Batista in Cuba or Somoza in Nicaragua acted once they were militarily defeated. They took hold of whatever parts of the state treasury they could get their hands on and attempted to lead the good life in exile. Villa had similar opportunities. For a long time he controlled the treasury of the División del Norte. Wilson had offered him asylum in the United States. Instead of leading the good life far from Mexico, he chose to return to the harsh, savage, and extremely dangerous life of a guerrilla warrior.

Did Villa bear the main responsibility for the bloody civil war that engulfed Mexico in the years 1914–15? In practically all revolutions, armed conflict between revolutionary factions with very different national agendas are the rule rather than the exception after the demise of the old regime. In Mexico, it was Villa who offered the one solution that might have assured peace in the short run, although probably not in the long run: decentralization, with its recognition of the military status quo, in which each faction would continue to govern the territory under its control, and commitment to land reform. It is significant that even after Villa faded from the national scene, civil war continued in much of Mexico throughout the Carranza presidency.

The motives for the civil war between the revolutionary factions that broke out in 1914–15 are still one of the major sources of disagreement in the historiography of the Mexican Revolution. One hypothesis sees the conflict as the result of personal rivalries among the leaders; another, as the product of different mentalities of the revolutionary elites (i.e., an urban-oriented Carrancista elite versus a much more rural-oriented Conventionist elite). According to a very different hypothesis, class warfare constitutes the essential explanation for the new civil war between the peasant-oriented Villistas and Zapatistas versus a new bourgeoisie, which headed the Carrancista alliance. In the final account, these hypotheses do not exclude each other. There was certainly a large degree of personal rivalry, as well as fear by the largely urban Carrancista elite that if the Villistas and Zapatistas took over, "barbarians" from the countryside would destroy civilization and the Mexican state. Conversely, the rural Zapatista and Villista elite feared that a Carrancista victory would once again undermine their autonomy and subordinate them to a state over which they would have little influence.

Yet the issue of land was of decisive importance. There is no doubt that it largely explains the conflict between the Zapatistas and the Carrancistas, but controversy has arisen as to whether this issue was of major relevance in the Villa-Carranza conflict. The notion that Carranza was a hacendado while Villa had been a peon (and thus was far more interested in the land issue) has rightly been dismissed as a simplistic explanation for the conflicts that broke out between their two factions. It was not primarily the social differences of the two leaders but the profound differences in the regions from which they came and that shaped their constituencies that explain their very different approaches to agrarian issues. As this book has tried to show, the expropriation of village lands had been a major issue prior to the revolution in the core areas of the Villa movement, Chihuahua and Durango. The same cannot be said of the core areas of Carrancismo, Coahuila outside of the Laguna area and Sonora (with the significant exception of the Yaqui Indians).

The differences between the Villistas and Carrancistas with respect to the land issue were not expressed in their programs, which were largely similar. Unlike the Zapatistas, neither the Carrancistas nor the Villistas envisioned the immediate division of haciendas.

It was the fate of the hacendados and the hacienda system that distinguished Villistas from Carrancistas. In the territories controlled by Villa and some of his allies (except for Sonora), the vast majority of hacendados fled, and their estates to a large degree were taken over and administered by the revolutionary government. The problem facing the constitutionalists was whether the estates should be returned to their former owners, as Carranza wished, or permanently confiscated as a prelude to their division, as Villa had advocated in his decree of December 1913. This profound difference in policy between Villa and Carranza was most clearly articulated by one of Villa's most important intellectual advisors, Silvestre Terrazas, who observed: "One of the leaders wants to act very radically, confiscating the properties of the enemy and expelling the corrupt elements; the other disapproves of his conduct, proposes the return of some of the confiscated properties and allows himself to be influenced by an infinite number of enemies, who day after day estrange him from the aims, principles, and goals of the revolution."[2]

Another issue that divided the two sides was the problem, going back all the way to the nineteenth century, of centralization versus decentralization. Neither the rural leadership nor the peasant component of the Conventionist movement wanted a strong centralized government. Such regimes had consistently attacked their culture, autonomy, and material well-being. For Carranza and many of his supporters, a weak central government might result in the disintegration of Mexico and in the possible absorption of part of its northern regions into the United States. In addition, large segments of Mexico's urban population desired a strong central government that could protect them from the rural population.

How bloodthirsty was Villa? Was his ferocity part of the Villa myth, or was it grounded in reality? There is little doubt that Villa was capable of the utmost brutality when he flew into one of his periodic rages. Overall, however, the Villa movement was no more ferocious than any other revolutionary movement in Mexico. For a time it was less so. The Huerta government routinely executed all prisoners, and it was Carranza who had ordered the revolutionary factions to execute their prisoners. In fact, Villa was reprimanded by the First Chief for decreeing a partial amnesty for some of the prisoners he had taken, and it was Carranza who publicly defended Villa's executions in a letter to the governor of Arizona. The difference between Villa and the other revolutionary leaders was that he felt that he had no reason to hide what he was doing and carried out the executions publicly, and at times personally. Until 1915, Villa tended to respect civilians, unless they belonged to the oligarchy or were Chinese. After his initial occupation of Ciudad Chihuahua, Villa resisted suggestions that he execute supporters of Huerta or Orozco; on the contrary, he decreed a general amnesty for these men if they agreed to lay down their arms.

In the years 1915 to 1920, Villa doubtless underwent a process of moral decline, forcing unwilling conscripts into his army and massacring groups of civilians as increasing parts of Chihuahua's population withdrew their support from his movement. After 1920, Villa was buffeted by extremely contradictory tendencies. On the one hand, he had become a wealthy and successful hacendado. On the other hand, when he proposed making peace to the government in 1920, he had not asked for an estate. "It is an infamy to state that Villa demanded a hacienda as a condition for surrendering." "It was I," Adolfo de la Huerta, who was provisional president of Mexico when Villa surrendered, later stated in an interview, "who decided that he should obtain it."[3] What he had wanted was to be a military commander in part of Chihuahua. Such a command was one way to protect himself against the numerous enemies he had made in his long revolutionary career. Once the government refused to grant him that request, the best means that he had of protecting himself against would-be assassins was to ensconce himself with a strong escort of men on a remote estate. Had he remained on the estate and not made trips outside it, his assassination would have been far more difficult. On the one hand, he administered his hacienda in an authoritarian way, no different than that of Terrazas or Creel; on the other hand, he did something no traditional hacendado would ever have allowed on his estate: he set up one of the best schools in Mexico both for his children and for the children of all the laborers on the hacienda. On the one hand, he established no links to the newly formed agrarian organizations in Chihuahua, which criticized his policies. On the other hand, he implemented demands that they never had the strength to impose on the state government: Villa prevented the sale of the Terrazas properties to McQuatters, thus making the division of a large part of this land to Chihuahua's villagers possible. It was not the protests of Chihuahua's agrarian organizations but Villa's threats that forced the state government to stop the expropriation and persecution of the inhabitants of Bosque de Aldama.

Villa supported Adolfo de la Huerta for Mexico's presidency against the wishes of Obregón, who wanted Plutarco Elías Calles to be his successor. Some historians consider de la Huerta to have been more conservative than Calles, but that fact is by no means clearly established, and for Villa personal allegiances were far more important in this case than political ideology. De la Huerta had helped him in 1913, never fought against him during the revolution, and granted him amnesty in 1920. Obregón and Calles had been his worst enemies.

In 1923, Villa made statements to the press against agrarianism that were far more conservative than the ideology he had publicly espoused in 1913, 1914, and 1915. Yet he maintained strong links to radical peasant organizations in Durango, although not in Chihuahua. Some conservatives in 1922 and 1923 claimed him as their own, but they had done so in 1912 and again in 1914, and Villa had dashed their hopes. In view of the enormous popularity Villa still enjoyed among large segments of the popular classes in the north, it is doubtful whether he would have turned against his natural constituency. Thus the question of whether Villa by 1923 had made a full turn and become an entrenched conservative or remained in his heart a popular leader committed to the poor will probably always remain open.

Like Villa, his closest ideological collaborator, Felipe Angeles, although far less well known than his leader, remains an enormously controversial figure. His enemies have painted him both as an opportunist and as a reactionary whose main aims were to become president of Mexico and to reestablish some kind of conservative order with the help of the remnants of the federal army. His opportunism, they believe, manifested itself in extremely contradictory policies. In 1912, he fought against Zapata, and in 1914, he became the architect of an alliance between Zapata and Villa. He called himself the strongest supporter of Madero, yet he never warned Madero about Huerta's suspicious policies during the Decena trágica. According to his enemies, he attempted to affect a reconciliation with the federal army, which constituted the greatest danger to the survival of the Mexican Revolution. Finally, in their view, he betrayed Mexican nationalism by persuading Villa not to endorse Carranza's warning to the Americans, after their invasion of Veracruz, to retreat from Mexico. Finally, they say, he betrayed Villa by abandoning him in 1915 and by trying to put him at the head of a reactionary alliance when he returned to Mexico in 1918. Yet I believe that Angeles's personality and his policy can also be seen in very different terms. He had a consistent ideology, which he attempted to implement in Mexico. He was a moderate social democrat in a country that had no social democratic party. Like all moderate social democrats, he believed in democracy, in profound social and economic reforms, which nevertheless would have to be implemented gradually. In spite of the fact that he was a military man, in the business of killing, he was a humanist and had greater respect for human life than any other leader the Mexican Revolution produced, with the possible exception of Madero. Implementing such a policy in a country that had no political party or no tradition of modern political organization was a task fit for Don Quijote, a literary figure with whom Angeles in fact strongly identified. He believed that he could achieve his aims through popular leaders such as Villa and Zapata. Partly, he may have overestimated his own influence on Villa, but he had made allowances for that. Angeles was the architect of Villa's alliances with Zapata, on the one hand, and with the conservative Maytorena, on the other, as well as with the United States. Such alliances, he hoped, would restrain Villa's dictatorial tendencies and force him to compromise. Above all, he was convinced that the closer Villa's relations were to the Wilson administration in Washington, which he considered a typically social democratic government, the more Villa would in fact become the kind of reformer who would at least allow democracy in Mexico and carry out the profound social reforms the country needed.

There is no evidence that Angeles betrayed either Madero, Villa, or the cause of Mexican nationalism. While he did not warn Madero of Huerta's contradictory policies, probably because of a long-imbued tradition of military discipline, there is little doubt that Huerta considered him the only federal officer who would back Madero and had him arrested and finally put on trial and exiled for that very reason. He did leave Villa in mid 1915, but in a later letter to Angeles, Villa himself assumed responsibility for the break and apologized to Angeles for the way he had treated him in 1915. Although he did not join Carranza's protest against the U.S. occupation of Veracruz in 1914, fearing that an armed conflict between the revolutionaries and the United States would doom the revolution, after Pershing's invasion of Mexico, he was ready to return to his native country to fight against the Americans should a full-scale war between the United States and Mexico break out.

Independently of these ideological controversies, three facts do stand out with regard to Angeles. He manifested a degree of humanity unique among Mexican revolutionary leaders, with the exception of Madero. His release of 3,000 prisoners after the battle of Monterrey was unprecedented in the annals of the Mexican Revolution. After returning to Mexico in 1918, he did everything in his power to restrain the violence that Villa was using against the civilian population. He left the revolution as he had entered it, a poor man unable to make ends meet, although he too had had ample opportunities to enrich himself. He returned to Mexico all alone in 1918, believing that the only way to prevent a U.S. intervention was to defeat Carranza. He paid for that belief with his life.

Would a victory of the Convention have altered the face of Mexico and changed the course of the Mexican Revolution? Few historians have been willing to speculate on this subject. One of the few who has is Alan Knight. In *The Mexican Revolution*, Knight paints a bleak picture of what Mexico would have looked like after a Conventionist triumph. "A hypothetical Villista regime, arising from a hypothetical Villista victory, would certainly have differed from that which emerged, but not by virtue of any greater social egalitarianism or revolutionary fervour," Knight writes. He sees the possibility of a far weaker Villista state,

a fainéant Mexico City regime weakly presiding over dozens of local, largely independent fiefs. Villa showed no personal appetite for the presidency. . . . National power would have been delegated to proxies—to Angeles, or effete civilians like Dr.

Silva—while Villa and his generals retired to their newly acquired northern estates, lording it over Chihuahua, living in the primitive seigneurial style anticipated by Urbina in 1913 and later emulated, with evident satisfaction, by Villa after 1920.

Knight believes that the Villista civilians would have been allowed to rule Mexico and would have tried to secure the same aims Obregón and Calles did in the 1920s, "rebuilding the shattered state, reducing the swollen armed forces, restoring the economy and currency, securing foreign recognition and investment, striving to legitimize the new regime on the basis of formal laws and parties." That government, though, would have been far weaker than the administrations of Obregón and Calles in the 1920s,

for the Villista caudillos, though they might not want to run the government themselves, did not want the government to infringe on their new parochial rights and properties. They would relinquish (formal) power to aspiring, nationalist civilians so long as the civilians left them alone; but this condition at once set tight limits on the reconstruction of the state and, in many respects, condemned the state to impotence. . . . A hypothetical Villista regime would have less resembled (real) post-revolutionary Mexico than post-revolutionary Bolivia, where weak civilian politicos, somewhat fortuitously installed in government, struggled, but failed, to establish a dependable power base, where the state abdicated control over large sections of political society, and where the outcome was eviction from power and a legacy of instability and praetorianism.[4]

In addition, Knight believes a Villista government would have meant a kind of governmental "banditry—rank, rowdy, criminal banditry—writ large."[5]

This gloomy image of a Villista Mexico does have a certain basis in fact. It is an extrapolation into the future of much that took place in 1915. Neither Villa nor Zapata was willing to allow a strong central government to emerge in Mexico. Executions and kidnappings by Villista officials and troops did take place during the Villista occupation of Mexico City. No substantial land divisions occurred in Villista-controlled territory during the time that Villa exercised power.

And yet I believe that Knight's projection suffers from two major flaws. The first is his underestimation of the influence of Zapata, and the other is constituted by his rejection of the agrarian component of Villismo. Had the Convention triumphed, there is little reason to doubt that the influence of Zapatismo would have rapidly spread beyond the confines of Morelos and its surroundings into large areas of central and southern Mexico. As a result, the same groundswell of peasant demands and land seizures that emerged in 1911 as a result of Madero's victory would have surfaced once again in much of Mexico.

From 1911 to 1913, Madero, with the help of his conservative supporters, the federal army, and the hacendados, managed to limit but not to destroy those peasant movements. By 1914, the federal army was gone, and most hacendados in north and central Mexico had fled.

Would land divisions have stopped at the borders of territories where Villa exercised direct control? This is highly improbable. Tens of thousands of Villista veterans would have demanded the land that Villa had promised to give them once the revolution was victorious. Those communities that had lost their lands to haciendas would have reclaimed them, and landless peasants would have clamored for land. Would Villa have resisted these demands, and could he have done so? This is extremely doubtful. Independently of whether Villa was committed to land reform—as I believe he was—he certainly knew that this was one of the main demands of his constituency. He had lived through the Orozco uprising and seen the price that the administration of Abraham González had paid for not carrying out the land reform for which so many Chihuahuans had fought when they joined the Maderista revolution. In addition, Villa clearly opposed returning the expropriated haciendas to their former owners as Carranza did. Nor is there any proof that Urbina, who set out to build a new agrarian empire on the model of the Terrazas' for himself, was characteristic of most of Villa's commanders. As this book has tried to show, most of the expropriated haciendas were not in the hands of Villa's generals, but were controlled by state-appointed managers, who had no power bases of their own, and thus could scarcely have appropriated these estates for themselves. It is by no means clear that a victorious Villa, at the height of his power and popularity in 1915, would have behaved like Villa the hacendado of 1920, who had become disillusioned and demoralized by his repeated defeats and by his increasing loss of popular support. Even in 1920, when he initially put out peace feelers to the de la Huerta administration, Villa did not ask for a hacienda. Even if, after achieving victory, Villa had wanted to become a hacendado and taken a hacienda for himself, he could still have acceded to massive distributions of land to his followers.

The political and economic consequences of so vast a redistribution of land and income in Mexico are not easy to define. In social terms, the country would have been far more egalitarian than it actually was after the victory of Carranza and Obregón. The economic consequences in the short run could have included an increase in subsistence agriculture at the expense of commercial production. Yet throughout Mexico's history, small rancheros and free village communities traditionally produced surpluses for the market. Northern rancheros had, insofar as they possessed sufficient resources, engaged in production for the market for as long as they had land. One of Villa's pet projects was to encourage them to expand production for the market by creating a bank to provide cheap credit to small landowners.

Would a Conventionist Mexico have been more democratic? In the long run, more egalitarian societies with more individual peasant proprietors certainly tend to be more democratic than societies in which wealthy landowners control large parts of the countryside. In addition, had a massive land division evolved from below and not from above, as was the case in Mexico in the 1920s and 1930s, the country's rancheros and peasants would have become far more independent from the state. In the short run, in the Zapatista area, democracy at the local level was far greater than in any other part of Mexico. This was not true of wartime Chihuahua, but that state had a long tradition of municipal autonomy and a degree of frontier democracy that Villa would not have been able to ignore.

This does not mean that Villa was a committed democrat. He was not, but his main rivals, Carranza and Obregón, were scarcely committed to open and honest elections either. None of them could aspire to absolute dictatorial power, because all of them headed regional alliances, whose leaders and followers they had to constantly conciliate. Carranza and Obregón tried to limit the power of regional caudillos by removing them from their places of origin and giving them military commands in states where they had no roots and thus were less likely to challenge them. Villa carried out no such policies and allowed his local supporters to remain in control of their native regions, thus defusing even more his potential for becoming a national dictator. This fact might tend, at least at first glance, to strengthen Knight's argument that the Convention would have been incapable of creating a strong and viable Mexican state, and that Mexico might have become another Bolivia. There is nevertheless one profound difference between Mexico and Bolivia that would have impeded the Bolivianization of Mexico—Mexico's common border with the United States. It is extremely doubtful whether either the Wilson administration or its Republican successors would have acquiesced to an anarchic Mexico on the southern border of the United States in which American properties were threatened and instability had become permanent. The U.S. threat would have been all the greater in that by 1918, the United States had the greatest and strongest army it had ever had since the country's creation. Mexico had a long tradition of rallying to a strong national government when faced with the threat of foreign invasion. Even in the 1860s, when the country was far more divided and far less integrated than in the early twentieth century, large numbers of Mexicans had rallied around Benito Juárez to defend the country against Napoleon III's empire. In 1920, the threat of U.S. intervention constituted a decisive factor in the peace that Obregón was able to make with many conservative and revolutionary leaders who had fought the Carranza administration until its demise. In the face of a threat from the United States, it is quite possible that in spite of the reluctance of both Villa and Zapata, as well as their supporters, to permit the creation of a strong central government, such a government might very well have emerged, possibly under the leadership of Angeles.

Summary

It is not easy to assess the overall impact of Villa and his movement on the Mexican Revolution and on Mexico's development. The most widely held perception of Villa is radically different from that of other revolutionary leaders. Zapata, Carranza, Obregón, and Calles are considered creators and builders. Zapata established one of the most egalitarian societies Mexico has ever known in Morelos. Carranza, Obregón, and Calles were the creators of the new nationalistic revolutionary Mexican state, which proved to be one of the most stable constructs in the history of Latin America.

Villa is perceived as a destroyer. In the eyes of his enemies, he destroyed law and order and civil society. In the eyes of his supporters, and finally in the eyes of a Mexican government in the 1950s, he was given credit for playing a decisive role in the destruction of the Huerta dictatorship. Indeed, Villa more than any other leader of the 1910–20 revolution contributed to the destruction of the old regime. In 1910–11, he played a decisive role in preventing Madero from carrying out a retreat from Ciudad Juárez that might have had effects as disastrous for Mexico's revolution as Hidalgo's retreat from Mexico City in 1811 was. In 1913–14, not only did Villa play a decisive role in putting an end to Huerta's military dictatorship, but his massive expulsions of hacendados from their properties contributed to weakening their power as a social class. Although many of them recovered their properties under Carranza or after 1920, their hold over their estates and their peons had been decisively weakened in economic, political, and social terms. When Cárdenas expropriated their holdings in the 1930s, they were incapable of waging an effective resistance.

One of the most decisive ways in which Villa contributed to the destruction of the old regime also constituted his most controversial undertaking: his attack on Columbus, New Mexico. On the one hand, it led to the killing of innocent American civilians, provoked a U.S. invasion of Mexico that seriously endangered the country's sovereignty, and created the threat of a major U.S.–Mexican war. On the other hand, it led to a result that Villa had hoped for. Relations between the United States and Carranza deteriorated to such a degree that the Wilson administration imposed an arms embargo on the Carranza administration and American banks did not grant him any loans. Carranza thus became too weak to carry out his agenda of destroying the still rebellious peasant movements in Mexico and returning all the confiscated estates to their former owners. As a result, the Zapatistas in Morelos, the Cedillo brothers in San Luis Potosí, and the movement led by Villa himself, as well as many local insurgencies, managed to survive into the Obregón era, when the new Sonoran rulers proved willing to make concessions to which Carranza would never have agreed. In short, the hacienda system and the old regime were decisively weakened.

It may even be hypothesized that nationalist reaction to the Pershing expedition's presence in Mexico radicalized the constitutional convention in Querétaro that finally adopted a much more radical constitution than the one Carranza had advocated.

There is also little doubt that the land reform carried out in Chihuahua in the 1920s, which was greater in scope in that period than in any other part of Mexico (with the exception of Morelos), was due to the revolutionary movement that Villa had headed and the new self-confidence that it had given to the rural population of Chihuahua. The fact that his army was defeated in 1915 because of Villa's strategic errors and a number of economic and political developments within and outside of Mexico does not detract from that achievement.

While the state that Villa set up in Chihuahua was less revolutionary and less democratic than Zapatista Morelos, it was still in many respects unique in Mexico. Villa expelled the old oligarchy from their economic and political power in Chihuahua. A large-scale redistribution of goods to the poorest segments of the people took place. Revolutionary Chihuahua presented unparalleled possibilities of social mobility for the lower classes of society. An unprecedented boost was given to education. Up to the end of 1914, crime and banditry reached a low point in the history of the state. In its heyday of 1913–14, revolutionary Chihuahua constituted one of the few societies where state administration of large parts of the economy proved to be of surprising effectiveness. In some ways, it might be called the first welfare state in Mexican history.

Finally, Villa produced a highly potent revolutionary myth, one that is still very much alive, and that spread from Mexico over large parts of the world. It has had an influence even in countries as far away from Mexico as my native

Austria. A few years ago, I had a long conversation with Dr. Bruno Kreisky, the former Austrian chancellor. When he asked me what I was working on, I replied that I was writing the biography of a man he probably did not know, the Mexican revolutionary Pancho Villa.

"You are more than mistaken," Kreisky told me, "when you think I do not know about Villa. I am a great fan of his, and so are most of my generation of Austrian socialists. In fact, he played an important role in our political activities."

To say that I was surprised is to put it mildly. The story that Dr. Kreisky told me was an astonishing one. In February 1934, after a bloody coup, in which thousands of workers who resisted were either shot or imprisoned, the Socialist party of Austria, along with all other opposition forces, was driven underground, and an authoritarian regime was established in Vienna. Dissent of every type was suppressed, and the press, radio, and books were censored. The Socialist party was forced to go underground, and so was its youth wing, headed by Dr. Kreisky. Its aim was to mobilize young Austrians against the regime, but to do so in a peaceful way.

Jack Conway's film *Viva Villa!* starring Wallace Beery reached Austria in 1935, at the high point of the Austrian fascist dictatorship under Kurt von Schuschnigg, a year after the coup. *Viva Villa!* extolled the Mexican Revolution, Villa himself, and the struggle of the underprivileged for justice. The Austrian authorities had not realized the potential of the film, treating it like any other American western. After Kreisky and the leadership of the Young Socialists saw the film, however, they decided to make it a focus of political activity and mobilization against Austria's authoritarian regime. Hundreds of Young Socialists filed into the Kreuzkino, in the center of Vienna, where *Viva Villa!* was playing. When Villa appeared on the screen calling on Mexico's peons to rise against their oppressors and shouting "Long live the revolution!" the Austrian audience rose from their seats too, shouting "Down with the dictatorship of Schuschnigg! Long live democracy! Long live the Socialist party!" Thanks to this film, Villa became a major hero to Austria's dissidents.

Some 80 years earlier, an Austrian, Maximilian of Habsburg, had gone to Mexico to set up an authoritarian empire. Now, in one of history's ironies, the image of a Mexican revolutionary, in the shape of Pancho Villa, had come to Austria and became an instrument of democratic struggle in that country.

Appendix

APPENDIX

On the Archival Trail
of Pancho Villa

When I began writing both the biography of Villa and the history of his move-ment, I faced four main obstacles in terms of sources. The first was the enor-mous discrepancy between the great quantity of memoirs and articles on Villa (more than 2,000 in Mexican newspapers alone) and the apparent paucity of contemporary archival records (with the significant exception of the years 1913–15).

The second significant discrepancy I found was between the huge number of man-uscript sources available for the period when Villa was a public personality and leader of one of the largest revolutionary movements in Mexico and the earlier and later pe-riods of his life. From December 1913 to the fall of 1915, Villa was in constant contact with foreign diplomats and gave many interviews to foreign correspondents, who for a time accompanied him on his major military campaigns. The richness of sources for this period stood in stark contrast to what appeared to be a complete lack of man-uscript sources on Villa's life prior to 1910 and the relative paucity of archival sources on Villa for the Maderista period and for Villa's life after his defeat in 1915.

The third discrepancy was the difference between the very extensive archival sources originating in the United States and the far fewer corresponding sources of European and South American origin.

The fourth discrepancy seemed even greater than that between foreign and Mex-ican documents. Among the Mexican sources, the most difficult problem I had to deal with was the paucity of documents of Villista origin, especially of letters or other documents written by Villa himself, in comparison to those originating from his opponents.

What I have attempted to do over many (perhaps too many) years of work on the subject has been either to resolve or at least to alleviate these discrepancies, with the significant help of the colleagues, friends, students, and research assistants whose names are mentioned at the beginning of this book, to whom I owe an enormous debt of gratitude. The results are described in the following evaluation and enumeration of the archival sources on which this book is based.

Mexican Primary Sources

Under this heading I include all sources originating in Mexico, although sometimes the relevant materials are now located in the United States.

The Papers of Villa and His Associates

Unlike Carranza and Zapata, Villa left no major archive. The only papers that might be called the Villa archive are the texts of letters Villa wrote to different personalities from his hacienda of Canutillo after his surrender in 1920, which are in the private archives of Dr. Rubén Osorio Zuñiga in Chihuahua. These letters mainly relate to Villa's business affairs, although some of them deal with Jesús Herrera and his alleged attempts to assassinate Villa.

For the earlier period of Villa's life, the papers of men who had been associated with him are far more revealing. The largest collection of such documents is contained in the papers of Silvestre Terrazas, which are located today in the Bancroft Library of the University of California at Berkeley. They contain extensive correspondence between Villa and Silvestre Terrazas, correspondence of Silvestre Terrazas with many of Villa's highest officials, reports by secret policemen to the Villista authorities on conditions in the state of Chihuahua, and a survey of social and economic conditions on the estates confiscated by Villa in early 1914. In addition, when he became secretary of state under Villa, Silvestre Terrazas came into possession of many of the papers of Enrique Creel, which contain valuable information on the Magonista movement in the early twentieth century, as well as some of Creel's correspondence with his subordinates.

The papers of Roque González Garza, Villa's representative at the Revolutionary Convention of Aguascalientes, who later became president of the Convention, are equally revealing. They contain much of Villa's correspondence with Roque González Garza and detailed reports on the activities of the Convention, as well as correspondence with his brother Federico describing the activities of Mexican exiles in the years between 1915 and 1920. When I consulted these papers, they were the property of Roque González Garza's family. Of equal interest are the papers of Federico González Garza. Federico had less contact with Villa than his brother, but his papers contain interesting information on internal conditions in Chihuahua. They also include some very valuable Villista documents: Villa's ultimatum to Madero in 1913 and the contract that Villa signed in early 1914 with the Mutual Film Company. The papers have been donated by his family to the archives of the Centro de Estudios de Historia de México (CONDUMEX) in Mexico City.

The papers of José María Maytorena, governor of Sonora, which are held by the library of Pomona College, Claremont, California, are an extremely important source of information about both Villa and, especially, Angeles. They contain Maytorena's partly unpublished memoirs and the correspondence of the Sonoran governor with Villa and, above all, with his agents in charge of relations with Villa and the Villistas. Even more important is Maytorena's correspondence with Angeles during their exile in the United States. While some of that correspondence has now been made public in a book edited by Alvaro Matute, *Documentos relativos al General Felipe Angeles* (1982), many of the letters by Angeles and to Angeles in the archive have never been published.

The papers of Lázaro de la Garza at the Nettie Lee Benson Library at the University of Texas at Austin are rich in information about the equipment of Villa's armies and the deals that Villa made to secure arms and ammunition in the United States. They contain many letters from Villa to Lázaro de la Garza and reports on Villa that reached the emissary in 1914 and 1915.

There is also correspondence with Villa—notably the papers of one of Villa's representatives in the United States, Enrique Llorente—at the New York Public Library, although it is less interesting than that found in the archives of other Villista personalities.

The papers of Eusebio Calzado, Villa's superintendent of railways, are located in the Museum of the Daughters of the American Revolution in San Antonio, Texas.

The Buckley Collection at the University of Texas at Austin contains the correspondence of the two Urquidi brothers, who first represented Carranza and later the Revolutionary Convention in the United States. The same collection also included testimony about Villa's efforts through intimidation to extract money from Jesuit priests.

The Private Papers of Non-Villista Mexican Personalities

The papers of Porfirio Díaz located at the Universidad Iberoamericana in Mexico City constitute an extremely valuable source for assessing conditions in Chihuahua during the Porfirian era and for understanding the activities of Terrazas and Creel. For the revolutionary period, the Díaz archives contain revealing reports by the Chihuahuan governors Alberto Terrazas and Miguel Ahumada, as well as confidential reports by Díaz's generals and subordinate officers on the Maderista uprising in Chihuahua. These reports not only deal with the military situation but assess the unpopularity of the Terrazas family, the social composition of the revolutionaries, and the general mood of Chihuahua's population.

Some papers of Luis Terrazas are located at the Centro de Investigaciónes y Documentación del Estado de Chihuhua (CIDECH) in Ciudad Chihuahua.

The papers of Miguel Cárdenas, governor of Coahuila, which are the property of Fernando Perez Correa, contain interesting data on the early career of Venustiano Carranza.

The huge collection of the papers of Venustiano Carranza is to be found in the CONDUMEX archives in Mexico City. It contains many reports and letters to Carranza, although Carranza's answers are frequently missing. The telegrams exchanged between Carranza and his commanders in Chihuahua in the period 1915–20 are perhaps the most important part of these archives with regard to Villa.

The papers of the federal general Rubio Navarrete, also located at CONDUMEX, include some interesting descriptions of Villa's near-execution on Huerta's orders, when Rubio Navarrete seems to have been primarily responsible for saving Villa's life. This archive also contains some important analyses from the federal side of the reasons for the defeats Villa inflicted on the federal army.

Among the papers of four Carrancistas generals—Amado Aguirre, Juan Barragón, Jacinto Treviño, and Francisco Urquizo, all housed in the archives of the National University of Mexico—those of Jacinto Treviño are the most interesting. Treviño was Carrancista military commander in Chihuahua until the end of 1916 and suffered resounding defeats at Villa's hands. His papers contain his correspondence with his superiors and his explanations of Villa's victories.

Among the papers of the Carrancista general Pablo González, microfilms of which are located at the University of Texas, Austin, there is some information on the battles against Villa, although on the whole they are of limited importance for the history of Villa and of Villismo.

The private papers of Elías Torres, who was one of the government's intermediaries in the surrender negotiations with Villa in 1920, shed some interesting light on Villa's surrender and are in the possession of his family in Mexico City.

The Gildardo Magaña papers, which include the Emiliano Zapata archives, are of great interest with regard to the relationship between Villa and Zapata. They are located at the library of the National University of Mexico. One of the most interesting letters that Zapata wrote Villa in early 1914, though, can be found in the papers of Reyes Aviles in the special collections of the University of Texas at El Paso.

The papers of the Martínez del Río family contain day-to-day reports from the administrator of the huge Santa Catalina hacienda in Durango, where a series of peasant uprisings took place, and where one of Villa's most important generals, Calixto Contreras, operated. They also include a private letter that sheds some information on the outlaw Francisco Villa from Coahuila, whose name, according to some authors, the revolutionary Pancho Villa assumed.

Many of the papers of Alvaro Obregón, Plutarco Elías Calles, and the latter's secretary, Fernando Torreblanca, are to be found in the Obregón-Calles-Torreblanca Archives in the Archivo General de la Nación, Mexico City. They provide very interesting information on the Villa campaigns of 1916–17, on Villa's surrender, and, above all, on his assassination in 1923.

A second set of archives relating to Calles and Obregón is the private archive called Fideicomiso Calles-Torreblanca, which is held by the Calles family. It is cited in this book as Fideicomiso.

The papers of Joaquín Amaro, located in the same archive, provide conclusive proof of the Mexican government's involvement in the assassination of Villa.

Thanks to the generosity of Marta Rocha Islas, I was able to consult some of the notes she took from the papers of Ignacio Enríquez, the Carrancista governor of Chihuahua, with large amounts of data on the formation and operation of the defensas sociales in that state.

Doctor Rubén Osorio Zuñiga allowed me to consult copies of unpublished papers of Abraham González, written during his governorship of Chihuahua. His archives also contain the highly interesting record of the defensa social of Los Llanos de San Juan Bautista.

Apart from very valuable information on Martín Luis Guzmán, the latter's papers contain the highly interesting questionnaires he sent out to many of Villa's collaborators, copies of the Angeles-Maytorena correspondence, and Villa's original memoirs.

Mexican Public Archives

The State Archives of Chihuahua unfortunately burned down in 1940. Nevertheless, some of the most important files of these archives relating to the Mexican Revolution were examined by the Chihuahuan historian Francisco Almada before the destruction of the archives, and copies of some of the most important of these documents were sent to the historian Manuel González Ramírez, who donated them to Mexico's National Archives.

The most valuable archival sources on both the prerevolutionary history of Chihuahua and the history of the revolution there can be found in the district archives of Guerrero in Ciudad Guerrero. They focus mainly, although not exclusively, on the prerevolutionary period and contain detailed correspondence between local, regional, and state authorities. Thanks to the generosity of Ana María Alonso and Daniel Nugent, I was also able to consult some of the material that they have collected from the archives of Namiquipa. Maria Teresa Koreck also allowed me to examine some sources from the village of Cuchillo Parado.

I also consulted the municipal records of Ciudad Juárez and Ciudad Chihuahua, which on the whole contain very little information on the revolutionary period. In the municipal archives of Parral, there is an indictment of Villa from 1910.

The archives of the Chihuahuan supreme court (Supremo Tribunal de Justicia del Estado de Chihuahua) contain the judicial records of the claims of Villa's widows and the court cases arising from them. The handwritten records of the day-to-day proceedings of the administration that Villa established in northern Mexico in 1915 can also be found there.

Some of the most important sources on Chihuahua's prerevolutionary history, as well as on the social history of the revolution in that state, are housed in the Archivo de la Reforma Agraria in Mexico City. In a part of that archive that for a long time was of difficult access to researchers, the Sección de Terrenos Nacionales, I found dozens of complaints and petitions by villagers in Chihuahua, Durango, and Coahuila on expropriation of their lands and abuses from which they suffered.

The Durango archives contain some highly interesting records of Villa's early life as an outlaw.

I found the papers of the Secretaría de la Defensa Nacional, to which I was given access, of immense value. The archive comprises two very different sections. The first, the Archivo Histórico, contains detailed reports by federal authorities under Díaz, Huerta, and Carranza on the campaigns in the north against Villa and his army. They also include a large number of complaints by civilians, as well as by military officers, on abuses committed by federal forces in the north.

I found the papers of a second section of the Defense Ministry, the Archivo de Cancelados, even more interesting. They contain files and dossiers of commanders and officers who participated in the revolutionary army. Villa's dossier contains the only available copy of the judicial proceedings against him in 1912. Angeles's file contains information on his trial in 1913 by Huerta's authorities and some hitherto unknown information about his court-martial in 1919. Equally revealing are the files of many officers who served with or against Villa.

The papers of Mexico's Foreign Ministry are extremely important not just for the external but also for the internal history of the revolution. Once the revolutionary forces had taken control of the north, it was the federal consuls along the border who organized an intelligence service to find out what went on in the territories occupied by the revolutionaries. Their reports are thus of decisive importance for the military, political, and social history of the revolution. After 1915, these consuls again concentrated their activities on intelligence-gathering among Mexican exiles, whose organizations they managed to penetrate, and thus these reports again give a unique history of the activities of exiles and their relationship to different U.S. interest groups and organizations. Recently, the Mexican Foreign Ministry acquired some hitherto inaccessible papers. The ones that proved to be most important for my research were the records of the Mexican embassy in Washington, D.C., and the diary of Adrián Aguirre Benavides.

The well-organized Mexican National Archives are also of decisive relevance to the history of Villa and Villismo. The Madero Papers in the National Archives contain Villa's correspondence with Madero in 1912, as well as correspondence dealing with Villa between Madero and Abraham González. They also contain letters sent to Madero by Angeles and Calixto Contreras.

Detailed reports on confiscated estates in Chihuahua can be found in the papers of Gobernación, also located in the National Archive. A small collection of Zapata papers includes correspondence between Villa and Zapata. One of the most important sources in the National Archives is the correspondence between Villa and Obregón, written after Villa's surrender in 1920, which can be found among Obregón's presidential papers. The files of the Comisión Monetaria largely deal with the fate of the Terrazas estates after the revolution.

U.S. Sources

Fortunately for historians, Villa operated near the border with the United States and aroused tremendous interest in that country. As a result, there is an enormous wealth of information concerning Villa and his movement in U.S. archives.

The records of the State Department are the most important American source and were for a long time unfortunately practically the only one accessible to researchers. They contain the files both of the U.S. embassy in Mexico City and of U.S. consulates throughout Mexico, which provide a huge amount of information on events and personalities linked to the revolution. Useful as these documents are, however, they also present a great number of problems. Most of the consuls who reported on local conditions were not professional diplomats but businessmen acting as honorary consuls. From the historian's perspective, this is both an advantage and a disadvantage. The advantage is that these men had lived for many years in the area where they exercised their consular responsibility and tended to know a lot about conditions and personalities in their respective regions. The disadvantage is that they were by no means disinterested observers of what was going on. Most of them had significant business interests linking them to groups in their areas, and this consciously or unconsciously prejudiced their reports. In addition, most of them tended to be profoundly racist. They subsumed most of the Mexican lower classes, whom they despised, under the general title of *pelados*, or, if they were somewhat more positively inclined, *peons*. Most of them were incapable of differentiating the very heterogeneous social groups among Mexico's lower classes.

Apart from the consuls, a host of intelligence agents kept a very close watch on events and personalities during the Mexican Revolution, and to a certain degree at times counterbalanced the reports of the consuls and diplomats. It was only a relatively short time ago that the papers of these intelligence agencies were declassified and made available to researchers. They comprise a variety of organizations and agencies, frequently at odds with one another. Unlike the consuls, who were extremely reticent about reporting on deals and secret links of U.S. businessmen or officials with different Mexican factions, the intelligence agencies of the U.S. government were far more forthcoming in this respect, knowing how restricted access to their reports would be.

The State Department had its own intelligence-gathering and intelligence-evaluating bureau, the Office of the Counselor, whose records contain extremely revealing information on links between U.S. officials, U.S. business interests, and different factions in the Mexican Revolution.

The records of U.S. military attachés in Mexico, reports of unofficial agents sent out by U.S. military officials in the early days of the revolution, and the papers of the Military Intelligence Department, which enormously expanded its activities once the United States entered World War I, are our most voluminous source of information on the Mexican Revolution. These papers include not only a host of confidential reports on Mexican revolutionary activities, and above all on Villa and his men, but also copies of intercepted letters between Villa and his agents in the United States, as well as copies of letters of any kind between Mexico and the United States, or Mexico and Europe, that were intercepted and copied by U.S. censors. In addition to sending agents to Mexico, U.S. military intelligence interviewed travelers returning from that country and tried systematically to organize their information.

Another highly relevant group of military records are those of the Punitive Expedition, above all its intelligence section, which interviewed hundreds of witnesses and tried to piece together, day by day, the activities of Villa's raiders before, during, and after the Columbus Raid. These files contain the detailed reports of the Japanese agents that U.S. military authorities sent to spy on Villa and to poison him. The intelligence department of the Punitive Expedition also wrote some highly interesting surveys of social conditions in the regions it occupied.

Although less voluminous than the military intelligence files, the papers of the Bureau of Investigation of the Justice Department (the predecessor of the FBI) also contain a wealth of information on revolutionary Mexico. The BI intercepted even more correspondence between Villa and his supporters than military intelligence had done, and BI agents managed to infiltrate most organizations of Mexican exiles in the United States. As a result, they were able to uncover practically every plot and intrigue between exiles on the one hand and U.S. interests on the other, as well as plots by the exiles themselves to act in Mexico.

The papers of the BI are unfortunately only available in the shape of badly photographed microfilms in the National Archives. All BI files after 1920 are still held by the FBI, but under the Freedom of Information Act much of the information they contain has been declassified. I have thus been able to obtain from the files of the BI confidential reports on the assassination of Villa.

In comparison to the papers of these three large U.S. intelligence services, I found the records of the U.S. Secret Service and the telegrams intercepted by the National Security Agency to be far less revealing and important.

Fortunately for historians, most prominent American political and military personalities who in one way or the other dealt with Villa have left papers. The most revealing are those of Woodrow Wilson, William Jennings Bryan, Robert Lansing, John J. Pershing, Leonard Wood, Tasker Howard Bliss, Edward M. House, and Frank L. Polk. These men shaped U.S. policy toward Villa, although none of them had any direct contact with him. There was only one major U.S. political figure who established a personal relationship with Villa, and his papers are perhaps the most interesting in this respect of all private documents left by American politicians. This was Hugh Lenox Scott.

With very few exceptions, the munitions dealers, shady lobbyists such as Sherbourne Hopkins, corrupt diplomats such as León Canova, and con men such as J. F. Keedy have left no papers. Fortunately, though, they have left traces of their activities and some kind of record. Hopkins testified twice before committees of the U.S. Senate, and both U.S. intelligence agencies, as well as Mexican politicians, have left vivid records of his activities. The author of his obituary in the *New York Times* also had access to information concerning Hopkins's life and dealings not only with Latin American but with eastern European governments. The papers of two lobbyists who were very prominent in Washington, and whose activities had important bearings on Villa, have been preserved. The first is Chandler Anderson, whose diary contains enormously valuable information on the dealings of American business interests with different revolutionary factions and on the way these business interests sought to influence U.S. policy. James Garfield, son of a former president, became a lobbyist for Villa in 1914–15, and his papers describe the somewhat clumsy activities he undertook in order to secure U.S. recognition for the northern revolutionary.

Very few of the U.S. companies who did business in Mexico and established contact with Villa and his faction have allowed researchers to examine their records. For obvious reasons, the most important exceptions are companies that have gone out of business or sold their Mexican holdings. The most revealing company records that I have found are those of the Mexican Northwestern Railroad, located in the manuscript divisions of the University of Texas at El Paso and at Austin, and the papers of the Corralitos Hacienda in the manuscript division of the Nettie Lee Benson Library at the University of Texas at Austin. The papers of the International Harvester Corporation, which I was also able to consult, are far less interesting.

This limited access to company records does not mean that their activities cannot be studied by researchers. Some of their records were sent to the Mexican-American Mixed Claims Commission, which was charged with representing all claims by U.S. companies for damages suffered during the Mexican Revolution. Some companies also wrote memoranda to different political figures or had conversations with politicians that were recorded in the diaries of the latter. In addition, many of them went to great lengths to expound their points of view to Senator Albert B. Fall, and these letters are preserved in his files.

I have found, though, that the most important way of assessing the activities of U.S. business interests in Mexico is to look at the papers of other powers, above all those contained in the British, French, German, and Spanish archives, since the diplomatic representatives of these countries did not have the inhibitions that American representatives frequently had when dealing with U.S. business interests.

The papers of Senator Fall, held by the University of New Mexico at Albuquerque and the Henry E. Huntington Library in San Marino, California, and preserved on microfilm at the University of Nebraska, are frequently biased but highly interesting. They contain many reports by Americans in Mexico strongly affected by the Mexican Revolution.

The courthouse in Deming, New Mexico, contains the proceedings of the trial of the Villista participants in the Columbus Raid who were captured by U.S. troops.

Reports by American missionaries in Chihuahua and in northern Mexico in general can be found in the papers of the Board of Missions in the Widener Library of Harvard University. They include both records concerning the many revolutionary leaders who were Protestant and some descriptions of daily life in Chihuahua during the revolution. The Widener Library also contains the papers of John Reed, which include some materials not mentioned in his publications.

British Sources

Unlike the United States, Britain has not yet declassified its intelligence records for the period of the Mexican Revolution. Fortunately, many of these records are located in the papers of the Foreign Office, which are now available to all researchers. Among the British consuls, the most interesting and most cultivated was Patrick O'Hea, who after attending Cambridge University came to Mexico for reasons of health, became administrator of one of the haciendas belonging to Pablo Martínez del Río, and during the revolution became British vice-consul in Torreón. O'Hea had constant dealings with all revolutionary leaders who passed through Torreón and met frequently with Pancho Villa. While he was not objective—he hated Villa—he seems to have had a better grasp of the social problems of the Mexican countryside and even of the inner workings of the revolutionary factions than most diplomatic representatives in Mexico.

The papers of Sir Weetman Pearson, later Lord Cowdray, the head of the Mexican Eagle Oil Company, contain very revealing appraisals of the political, social, and economic situation in Mexico during the revolution by Cowdray's representatives in Mexico. To a lesser degree, the same can be said of the papers of the officials of the British-American Tlahualilo Company.

French Sources

The most important sources on Villa in French archives can be found in the papers of the Ministère des Affaires étrangères at the Quai d'Orsay and the papers of French military intelligence at the Château de Vincennes. The Foreign Ministry papers contain some internal reports on the situation in Mexico and Villa's occupations of both Mexico City and Guadalajara. They also document the hopes of the French chargé d'affaires Victor Ayguesparse, who was closely linked to Mexico's traditional oligarchy, that Villa could be co-opted by it. The reports of the French military attaché in French intelligence files include some very revealing conversations about Villa that the French military attaché in Washington had with President Woodrow Wilson.

German Sources

The most important German sources on the Mexican Revolution are located at the Foreign Ministry Archives in Bonn and in what used to be the main archive of the former GDR at Potsdam, near Berlin. These archives reveal German plots to launch Villa into an attack on the United States but also include internal reports from Chihuahua concerning Villa and Villismo. The papers of the German consul in Ciudad Juárez, Máximo Weber, are located in the manuscript division of the library of the University of Texas at El Paso. Like their British and French counterparts, the German archives are especially important with regard to the activities of U.S. agents and business interests in Mexico during the revolution

Spanish Sources

Spanish merchants and hacienda owners were more persecuted until 1915 by Villa and the Villistas than any other group of foreigners, with the exception of the Chinese. As a result, the Spanish government showed very strong interest in Villa and his activities, and in 1915, it sent a special agent, Antonio Zapico, to obtain guarantees from Villa for Spanish citizens. Zapico witnessed the last months of the División del Norte and wrote detailed reports about his encounters with Villa and the disintegration of the Villista administration to the Foreign Ministry in Madrid.

Austrian Sources

The Austro-Hungarian monarchy showed little interest in Mexico before 1910—diplomatic relations between the Austro-Hungarian empire and Mexico had only been resumed at the beginning of the twentieth century, since Austria's emperor Franz Joseph felt that Porfirio Díaz shared in the responsibility for the execution of his brother Maximilian in 1867. The Austrians became very interested in Mexico after the outbreak of World War I. Like the Germans, they hoped that the United States would be embroiled in Mexico and thus become incapable of participating in World War I on the side of the Entente. For that reason, the Austrians were very interested in Villa's activities, and the files of the Austrian Foreign Ministry contain some interesting reports on relations between the United States and Mexican revolutionaries.

Oral History

Unfortunately, no attempt to interview veterans of the Mexican Revolution in any systematic way were made prior to the 1960s. The first systematic attempts to do so were by Pindaro Uriostegui Miranda in the 1960s. It was only in the 1970s that the oral history program of the National Institute of Anthropology, headed by Dr. Eugenia Meyer, for which I acted as a consultant, carried out interviews with more than 100 veterans of all ranks of the División del Norte. The historians Alicia Olivera de Bonfil and Laura Espejel mainly interviewed Zapatista veterans, but they also carried out valuable interviews with some veterans of the División del Norte. This constituted the largest and most systematic endeavor to salvage the memories of the participants in a revolution that official Mexico had ignored for a long time. In addition, some of the best interviews with Villista veterans that I have ever seen were carried out by Dr. Rubén Osorio Zuñiga of Ciudad Chihuahua, who managed to interview dozens of participants in the Chihuahuan revolution from all sides of the political spectrum. I also found interviews carried out by the Oral History Project of the University of Texas at El Paso very helpful. These interviews with veterans who were in their seventies and eighties obviously present some problems beyond the fact that so much time had elapsed since their participation in the revolution. Many had been influenced by what different media have written or said about the revolution. Some might have wanted to enhance their role in order to obtain a pension from the government. Yet these interviews offer unique subjective views of the revolution that written documents frequently cannot provide.

Memoirs

There are two books that call themselves memoirs of Pancho Villa. The first of these autobiographies was written by Ramón Puente, who at the time he wrote it was a Villista exile living in the United States. Puente does not claim that these memoirs were dictated verbatim by Villa but rather that they were the result of long conversations he had about his life with the Mexican revolutionary leader. While there is little doubt that Puente knew both Chihuahua and Villa, it should be pointed out that in 1919, when he wrote the book, Puente was an interested party. He was a Villista agent in the United States, one of whose main aims was to rehabilitate Villa in the eyes of Mexican and U.S. public opinion.

The most famous book of memoirs of Villa was written by one of Mexico's greatest literary figures, Martín Luis Guzmán. In his preface, Guzmán indicates that the early part of the memoirs is based on three original memoirs dictated by Villa. The first is a typewritten service record in autobiographical form that describes Villa's military activities during the Madero revolution. The second consists of handwritten notes, probably taken by Manuel Bauche Alcalde, a Villista intellectual and for a time editor in chief of the Villista newspaper *Vida Nueva*, with whom Villa had long conversations about his life. The third is a series of handwritten notebooks by Manuel Bauche Alcalde called "The Life of General Francisco Villa." Martín Luis Guzmán felt that the first two documents had been changed by stenographers or typists who did not accurately reflect Villa's language. The third, by Bauche Alcalde, was written in the style of a man from Mexico City in Guzmán's opinion. Since Guzmán knew Villa and knew how he spoke, he felt that he would make some minor changes in order to better reflect Villa's personality and style.

Since the original memoirs have never been published, questions have been raised about the authenticity of the Guzmán text. Did he take too many liberties with the original sources? Having been given access to the original memoirs by the Guzmán family, I can confirm that Martín Luis Guzmán was not only a great literary figure but an extremely serious scholar as well.

There are interesting discrepancies among the three documents, which go beyond language. While the service record and the handwritten notes, which can be attributed more directly to Villa, are straight narratives of events, Bauche Alcalde's text contains both ideological justifications and ideological appreciations. For instance, it includes a six page enumeration of all the negative policies and politics of Porfirio Díaz, including details that Villa, who was only semiliterate, would scarcely have known. In this respect, one can scarcely doubt that Guzmán was right in feeling that it did not reflect Villa's authentic memoirs. On the other hand, the text does include some ideological appreciations that conform to Villa's thoughts, such as a long passage where Villa dreams of the establishment of military colonies, thoughts that he would again and again develop at later dates in talks with John Reed and with Woodrow Wilson's emissary Duval West, and that I have quoted in this text (Villa's granddaughter Guadalupe, who had seen the memoirs, also felt that this quotation accurately reflected Villa's thinking). Bauche Alcalde's text, the only one for which a date is given, was completed on February 27, 1914. It seems to have been originally intended for publication. "I have no intention of even justifying myself nor defending myself," Villa told Bauche Alcalde. "People should know me as I am and as I was, so that they can appreciate what I am." Although it would have been easy for Bauche Alcalde to have published them in book form or to have sent them to a newspaper in the United States, the memoirs were never published. This may have been because Villa did not recognize himself in Bauche Alcalde's text or because of Villa's increasing distrust of Bauche Alcalde, who was soon dismissed as editor in chief of *Vida Nueva* and rejoined the Carrancistas, or because the memoirs were completed one week after the killing of Benton, and Villa may not have wanted to draw attention to his outlaw past in such a delicate situation.

When Bauche Alcalde left Chihuahua, he turned the memoirs over to Villa's personal physician, a Dr. Raschbaum, and when the latter left Villa's service in October 1914, he gave the memoirs to Luz Corral, Villa's wife.[1] For unknown reasons, she was not able to keep them, and they came into the possession of Villa's last wife, Austreberta Rentería. Through Nellie Campobello, a prominent literary figure, who had written admiring books about Villa, Austreberta provided Martín Luis Guzmán with the text of the memoirs. Recognizing his debt to the two women, Guzmán signed a contract with them giving each of them 30 percent of the 27.77 percent of his total royalties for the book that represented the part based on the original memoirs.[2] These royalties continued to be paid even after the death of Martín Luis Guzmán, and I found records in the Guzmán archives that they continued to be paid to Nellie Campobello up to 1978.

The latter part of Guzmán's book is not based on Villa's original memoirs, and neither does Martín Luis Guzmán state that this was the case. Unlike the earlier part of the memoirs, it is a reconstitution by Guzmán of the way Villa, in his opinion, would have written his memoirs. Some doubts have at times been expressed about its authenticity, since Guzmán never indicated what sources he based himself on, apart from his own knowledge of Villa. His papers show him to have been an extremely serious scholar. He sent dozens of questionnaires to former Villistas, who in the 1930s were still in their prime, and they furnished him with detailed information. In addition, according to one of Villa's former secretaries, Luis Aguirre Benavides, the latter had long conversations with Guzmán about Villa's decisions and activities.

Although Guzmán's book is perhaps the most important work written about Villa, it had two drawbacks. The first is that Guzmán did not have access to much of the archival material of either Mexican or foreign origin concerning Villa. The second is that the original memoirs on which the first part of the book are based were dictated to Manuel Bauche Alcalde, who in 1915 defected from the ranks of Villismo and became the secretary of one of Villa's greatest enemies, Pablo González. Did Bauche

Alcalde alter the manuscript before he left Villa? Even if this is not the case, Villa seems to have had a rather selective memory, which at times contradicts contemporary documents. During the judicial proceedings against him in 1912, Villa testified that he had worked for the Mexican Northwestern Railroad Company and transported large amounts of money for it. Nothing of this is said in his memoirs. Even more striking is the absence of any reference to the ultimatum that he presented to Madero after his escape from prison in early 1913. There are rumors that Villa dictated a set of memoirs at Canutillo that were taken down in shorthand and that are in the possession of one of his daughters. I have not been able to see these memoirs, and I am still not sure whether they exist.

Memoirs by Villa's Collaborators

Many of the intellectuals who worked with Villa, most of whom at one time or another became disillusioned with him, although to varying degrees, wrote memoirs. The first of these, *¿Quien es Francisco Villa?* whose author long remained anonymous, was published in 1916 under the pseudonym Juvenal. The most valuable parts of the book describe Villa's relations with the other leaders of his movement, and it attempts to assess Villa's character and the internal organization of the División del Norte. It was long not taken very seriously, since Juvenal was the pseudonym of a contemporary Spanish newspaperman, and historians doubted that a Spaniard could really have inside knowledge of the Villista movement. In 1945, however, the Mexican newspaper *El Nacional* revealed that the real author of these memoirs was one of Villa's secretaries, who had known him intimately, Enrique Pérez Rul. What makes Pérez Rul's memoirs particularly interesting is the early date at which they were written (1915–16), when events were still very fresh in the author's mind. In addition, Pérez Rul, although he broke with Villa, had not become a supporter of Carranza but lived in exile in the United States. He was not intent on proving that either side was right, and he wrote with surprising objectivity. The memoirs of another secretary of Villa's, Luis Aguirre Benavides, who left Villa before Pérez Rul, were published only in the 1960s and seem also to have been written far later than Pérez Rul's memoirs. They nevertheless also contain interesting information on Villa.

Parts of *El águila y la serpiente* (The Eagle and the Serpent), a novel that Martín Luis Guzmán wrote years before his *Memorias de Pancho Villa*, can also be considered as personal reminiscences of Villa and his movement. In this book, Martín Luis Guzmán paints a far more negative image of Villa than he does in his subsequent work.

It is perhaps symptomatic of the contradictory attitudes of official Mexico toward Villa that the extremely important reminiscences of Villa published by Silvestre Terrazas, his secretary of state, were only published in installments in a relatively obscure journal in Chihuahua in the 1930s. It was only in the 1970s that they were published in book form, first in Chihuahua and then in Mexico City. While the book contains some extremely important information on Villa, it should also be examined with caution, since Silvestre Terrazas, who by the 1930s had become far more conservative than he had been during the revolution, was attempting to justify his conduct with respect to Villa. Fortunately for historians, his published work can be compared to the voluminous papers and contemporary documents that he left in his archives, which are now located in the Bancroft Library of the University of California at Berkeley.

The reliability of José Vasconcelos's very hostile reminiscences of Villa has been questioned by other participants in the revolution. It is significant that some years after writing these memoirs, Vasconcelos wrote a much more laudatory preface about

Villa for the memoirs of Luz Corral, the only one of his wives who seems to have played a genuine role in his political life. Luz Corral's memoirs, *Pancho Villa en la intimidad,* give some unknown personal glimpses and shed much new light on Villa's meeting with Obregón in 1914. Nevertheless, they should also be looked on with great caution. Luz Corral was intent both on rehabilitating Villa's memory and on insisting on her own importance vis-à-vis the other women in his life. Austreberta Rentería and Soledad Seañez have not published any memoirs but both have been interviewed (I myself was able to speak to Soledad Seañez) and their feelings toward their husband seem to have been far more contradictory than those of Luz Corral, although Villa broke with the latter in the early 1920s.

Apart from these memoirs published in book form, there are innumerable letters, interviews, and brief memoirs by other supporters of Villa, generally published in the Sunday editions of Mexico's newspapers, which have been indexed by Stanley Ross and a team of researchers in a five-volume collection entitled *Fuentes de la historia contemporánea de México: Periódicos y revistas* (1965).

There are two unpublished memoirs that I also found highly interesting. The first are the brief reminiscences of Máximo Castillo, which Professor Jesús Vargas from Chihuahua allowed me to consult. In some respects, Castillo, who called himself a Zapatista, can be considered Villa's main Chihuahuan opponent on the left. Unlike Villa, Castillo saw no need to manage American properties or the susceptibilities of Americans and wanted to carry out an immediate land division. As a result, in spite of his attempts to make an alliance with Villa, it never materialized, and Castillo had to flee from Mexico and was long interned by the U.S. authorities.

The most important memoirs of the later guerrilla period of Villa's life were written by José Maria Jaurrieta, who only joined Villa in 1916. Jaurrieta, the only intellectual who fought alongside Villa and remained true to him until the end, is the best—and, in many cases, the only—Villista source for Villa's guerrilla activities from 1915 to 1920. Being highly literate, he became both Villa's secretary and his confidential agent for missions in the United States. Only parts of Jaurrieta's memoirs have been published, but through the intermediation of Richard Estrada, the González family, who possess the original text, graciously allowed me to consult it.

Some of the most interesting memoirs by participants in the revolution have been published either as articles or as interviews in Mexican and Mexican-American newspapers.

Newspapers

The most important newspaper sources for the Villista movement are the two papers edited by the Villista government: *Vida Nueva,* which was published from early 1913 until the end of 1915, and the *Periódico Oficial del Gobierno Constitucionalista del Estado de Chihuahua.*

The *Correo del Bravo* published in El Paso by agents of the Sonoran governor, Maytorena, sheds some interesting new light on the relationship between Villa and Carranza.

A number of first-rate American correspondents followed Villa in his campaigns in 1914, and they are the authors of some of the best work that has been written on Villa. The best-known and most influential of these reporters was John Reed, whose articles on Villa were collected in the book *Insurgent Mexico.* The work of other reporters such as John W. Roberts of the *New York American* and Edwin Emerson (who was also a secret agent of the U.S. military) of the *Philadelphia Inquirer* has undeservedly been forgotten.

From mid 1915 on, no newspaper reporters had any access to Villa. The best reports on his activities in those years came from eyewitnesses and were published by two newspapers in El Paso, the *El Paso Times* and the *El Paso Herald*, which followed events in nearby Chihuahua in the greatest detail. From 1919 onward, *La Patria*, a newspaper published in Spanish in the United States by Silvestre Terrazas, who was living there in exile, paid very great attention to the civil war in Chihuahua. Although anti-Carrancista, *La Patria* was not strongly pro-Villa.

Reference Matter

Abbreviations

AA Bonn	Archiv des Auswärtiges Amts, Bonn
ABCFMA	American Board of Commissioners for Foreign Missions Archive, Cambridge, Mass., Houghton Library
ADU	Archivo de Durango
AGN	Archivo General de la Nación, Mexico, D.F.
AHDN	Archivo de la Secretaría de la Defensa Nacional, Mexico D.F.
AJV	Archivo Jesús Vargas
AMAE	Archives du Ministère des Affaires Étrangères, Paris, Correspondance Politique
APD	Archivo Porfirio Díaz, Universidad Ibero-Americana, Mexico D.F.
ASARCO	American Smelting and Refining Company
ATJ	Archivo del Supremo Tribunal de Justicia de Chihuahua
BI	Bureau of Investigation (U.S.)
CIDECH	Centro de Investigaciónes y Documentación del Estado de Chihuhua
CONDUMEX	Centro de Estudios de Historia de México, Mexico, D.F.
CP	Archives du Ministère des Affaires Étrangères, Paris, Correspondance politique et commerciale, n.s., Mexique
DHRM	*Documentos historicos de la revolución mexicana*. See Fabela and de Fabela 1960–76.
DZA	Deutsches Zentralarchiv Potsdam, Auswärtiges Amt
exp.	*expediente* (dispatch)
FBI	Federal Bureau of Investigation (U.S.)
Fideicomiso	Fideicomiso Archivos Plutarco Elias Calles y Fernando Torreblanca
HHSTA	Haus, Hof und Staats Archiv, Vienna
IWW	Industrial Workers of the World (Wobblies)
leg.	*legajo* (dossier)

MID	Military Intelligence Department, National Archives, Washington, D.C.
MLG	Archivo Martín Luis Guzmán
MMR	Museum of the Mexican Revolution
MR Archives	Martínez del Río Archives
NA	National Archives, Washington, D.C.
PHO	Programa de Historia Oral files at the Instituto José Maria Mora, Mexico, D.F.
PLM	Partido Liberal Mexicano
PRI	Partido Revolucionario Institucional
PRO, FO	Public Record Office, London, Foreign Office Papers
RAT	Archivo de la Secretaría de la Reforma Agraria, Sección de Terreno Nacionales, Mexico, D.F.
RO	NA, "Report of Operations of 'General' Francisco Villa Since November 1915, Headquarters Punitive Expedition in the Field, Mexico, July 31, 1916"
SDF	U.S. Department of State Papers, National Archives, Washington, D.C.
SRE	Archivo de la Secretaría de Relaciones Exteriores, Mexico, D.F.
ST Papers	Silvestre Terrazas Papers
UNAM	Universidad Nacional Autonoma de Mexico
WWP	*The Papers of Woodrow Wilson*, edited by Arthur S. Link

Notes

Prologue

1. The transfer of Villa's remains to the Monument of the Revolution in Mexico City and the ceremonies and events that took place on that occasion are described in Ching Vega 1977.

2. Alonso Cortés 1972.

3. The discussion and controversy that the erection of a statue of Villa in Tucson provoked are best expressed in "Hero or Villain: Scholars, Witnesses Debate Ruthless Actions by Pancho Villa," *Arizona Republic*, Apr. 3, 1983. See also "Villa Gets Mixed Reviews in Tucson," *El Paso Times*, May 17, 1981, and "Critics Fire on Pancho Villa Statue," *Arizona Republic*, Nov. 17, 1982.

4. Thanks to the family of Martín Luis Guzmán, I was given access to the original memoirs of Villa from which these quotations are taken. For an analysis of the relationship of these memoirs to Guzmán's *Memorias de Pancho Villa*, see Appendix. These memoirs comprise three different texts. The first is written in pencil, and Guzmán assumes that it was probably based on notes taken by one of Villa's collaborators, Manuel Bauche Alcalde. I have labeled it "penciled memoirs." The second is a far longer text, entitled "El general Francisco Villa," by Manuel Bauche Alcalde, cited here as "Bauche Alcalde." The third is a service record, written in the first person, called "Hoja de servicios del general Francisco Villa," which is cited here as "Villa service record."

5. MLG, Bauche Alcalde, 6, 7.
6. Ibid., 9.
7. Ibid., 11.
8. Ibid., 12.
9. Ibid., 14.
10. Ibid., 22.
11. MLG, penciled memoirs, 52, 53.
12. MLG, Bauche Alcalde, 63.
13. MLG, penciled memoirs, 15.
14. Ibid., 13, 14.

15. MID, 8321-8, copy filed with 10460-847, John Biddle to chief of staff, June 12, 1914.

16. MID, 5761-1091-3, Carlos E. Husk to Hugh L. Scott, June 5, 1914.

17. Herrera 1981. Although Herrera offers no proof for these allegations, except in one case, this does not mean that Villa did not commit some of these crimes. Herrera does not say where she learned these facts or where they were published, if they were published at all, either by historians or by contemporary Porfirian authorities. The origins of such allegations come out more clearly in a memorandum that the Huerta administration forwarded to the British legation in Mexico, entitled "Criminal Record of Francisco Villa," which lists a long series of crimes, some of them identical to the ones described by Herrera, attributed to Villa. In no case does the memorandum offer any proof, except to state that these crimes were widely reported in the newspapers of the time, but without specifically asserting that Villa was named in those newspapers as the culprit. "It is noteworthy that for many of his crimes and robberies Villa managed to escape arrest due to his audacity and his tactics of operating by various aliases," the memorandum explains. What the Huerta government had done was to attribute crimes committed under aliases to Villa. (MFMP, SRE, archive of the Mexican embassy, Washington, D.C., leg. 442, exp. 23, Miguel Diebold, consul general of Mexico at large to British consul Charles Perceval, El Paso, Mar. 1, 1914.) Villa at times did operate under a pseudonym, but no proof of any kind (such as judicial records, etc.) is offered that the names of the criminals linked to these crimes were in fact aliases of his.

18. Reed [1914] 1969, 116.

19. *WWP*, 29: 229, Sir Cecil Arthur Spring Rice to Sir Edward Grey, Feb. 7, 1914.

20. Herrera 1981, 42–43.

Chapter One

1. MR Archives, Francisco Gómez Palacio to Barbarita, July 21, 1911.

2. Neumann 1969, 13.

3. For the history of Chihuahua in the colonial period, see Almada 1955; Jones 1988; Jordán 1981; Lister and Lister 1966. The following more general works on the Spanish frontier in New Spain are also important: Bannon 1963; Moorhead 1968; Spicer 1962; Weber 1979.

4. For the formation of these military colonies, see Alonso 1995 and Nugent 1993. For a more general history of Spanish settlements in northern New Spain in the eighteenth century, see Jones 1979 and Griffen 1958.

5. Jordán 1981, 213–16.

6. The best works on the role of these military colonists in the nineteenth century are Nugent 1993, Alonso 1995, and V. M. Orozco 1994 and 1995a.

7. RAT, 1: 29 (1906), L2X, exp. 178, letters of the inhabitants of Namiquipa to Porfirio Díaz, July 20, 1908.

8. See V. M. Orozco 1994, 55–78.

9. See Limerick 1987. For a discussion of these issues, see also Gressley 1994.

10. The history of the Terrazas family has aroused great interest among researchers. It is not surprising that both anti-Terrazas and pro-Terrazas schools of thought emerged. The most important works of the anti-Terrazas school, *Gobernadores del estado de Chihuahua* (1950) and *Juárez y Terrazas, Chihuahua* (n.d.), are by Chihuahua's most distinguished historian, Francisco Almada.

As a counterweight to Almada, the Terrazas hired another of Chihuahua's best-known historians, José Fuentes Mares, who wrote a book based on information supplied to him by the family, entitled . . . *y México se refugió en el desierto: Luis Terrazas, su historia y destino* (1954). A more recent work by Lulu Creel de Müller entitled *El conquistator del desierto* (1982) belongs to the same school of thought. The first substantive U.S. contribution to the history of the Terrazas was an essay by Harold Sims, "Espejo de caciques: Los Terrazas de Chihuahua" (1969). The best-documented and the most serious analysis of the Terrazas and their role in Chihuahua is Mark Wasserman's *Capitalists, Caciques, and Revolution* (1984). Wasserman has followed this up with another remarkable book, documenting the history of the family in both the revolutionary and postrevolutionary periods, *Persistent Oligarchs: Elites and Politics in Chihuahua, Mexico, 1910–1940* (1993).

11. RAT, exp. 178, letter of the inhabitants of Namiquipa to President Porfirio Díaz, July 20, 1908.

12. See Nugent 1993, 44–46. I have used several terms to designate those inhabitants of Mexico's north who possessed lands of their own. The term *free villagers* designates all of them. The term *rancheros* is limited to former military colonists or other settlers who received lands from the state under very different conditions from traditional Indian communities. These *rancheros* could be white, mestizo, or Indian, but the legal basis of their property was different from that of the Indian communities.

13. Over the past few years, an impressive amount of work has been done on the structure of land tenure in Chihuahua and the social groups that existed in the state's rural areas. Ana Alonso and Daniel Nugent, who spent more than a year living in one of the former military colonies, Namiquipa, both interviewed inhabitants and examined every possible archival source on this village and surrounding communities. See Alonso 1995 and Nugent 1993.

Maria Teresa Koreck has done similar research in a village in eastern Chihuahua, Cuchillo Parado, which also had a history of conflict with the authorities over land, and, like Namiquipa, played a major role in the Mexican Revolution. Although her work had not yet been completed at the time of going to press, she has published a number of essays documenting the history of Cuchillo Parado and the whole region around it, which seek to examine the mentality of the free peasants in eastern Chihuahua. See Koreck 1988 and 1995.

Jane-Dale Lloyd did extensive research in the Galeana district of northwestern Chihuahua. See Lloyd 1987 and 1988. Carlos González Herrera (1992 and 1993) has studied statistics for the number of small properties in Chihuahua. Orozco Orozco 1995a examines land-tenure patterns and their transformation in the Guerrero district of nineteenth-century Chihuahua, as well as the influence of the Apache wars on those patterns. On the influence of the hacendados, and particularly the Terrazas, on these landholding patterns, see Wasserman 1984.

14. One of the colonies that seems to have been granted land by Juárez was Cuchillo Parado (see Koreck 1995).

15. John Womack has rightly drawn my attention to the fact that one should not exaggerate the importance of the Homestead Act for the United States, noting that "it may not be quite fair to refer only to the Homestead Act in the United States without some modifying reference to the grants of land to the railroads also, which in effect drew farmers and ranchers back under the domination of great corporations" (Womack, letter to the author, Sept. 14, 1992).

16. Wasserman 1984; Nugent 1993.

17. The role of the surveying companies in land expropriation has provoked some of the most interesting controversies among historians. In 1891, during the Porfirian period, one of the earliest critics of the dictatorship, Wistano Luis Orozco, published a book, *Legislación y jurisprudencia sobre terrenos baldíos* (reprint 1985), charging that

it was above all the surveying companies that were responsible for a large amount of expropriation of lands belonging to communities, and that these companies tended to ride roughshod over the rights of traditional villages. Although long accepted by most historians of prerevolutionary Mexico, this thesis has been challenged by Robert Holden (1990, 1994), the first historian to have gained access to the papers of the surveying companies in the archives of the Departamento de la Reforma Agraria in Mexico. Holden believes that expropriation of lands occupied by villagers was the exception rather than the rule, and that judges and even the Mexican government frequently tended to side with the villagers when they protested against the activities of the surveying companies. On the basis of local archives in Chihuahua, Jane-Dale Lloyd concluded that, as far as three of the five original military colonies were concerned, the surveying companies simply refused to recognize the 112,359 hectares the Spanish colonial authorities had granted them and reduced them to 28,080 hectares apiece (Lloyd 1987, 74). I have nevertheless found, however, that most expropriations of village lands in Chihuahua were not the work of the surveying companies. There is no evidence, for example, that these companies were involved in the huge land grant to the Limantour brothers, which resulted in a series of peasant uprisings in the 1880s and 1890s. In the twentieth century, the vast majority of land expropriations were based on Enrique Creel's agrarian law of 1905.

18. See Almada 1965, 1: ch. 1. 19. Wasserman 1984, 108.

20. Nugent 1993, 56–58. 21. Johnson 1961.

22. RAT, exp. Cargill Lumber Co., Pablo Guerrero to Secretaría de Fomento, Feb. 8, 1889.

23. On Terrazas's support of revolts, see Almada 1955, 350–51.

24. Almada 1965, 1: 93–105.

25. The Tomóchi revolt has been the subject of a vast amount of literature and historical controversy. The controversy has centered above all on the importance of the religious factor in the revolt, as well as on the role that Luis Terrazas may have played in encouraging or even fomenting it. The first account, written in the shape of a novel by an eyewitness and participant in the government's campaign against Tomóchi, was Frías 1983. For another contemporary work, see Lauro Aguirre 1896. And see also Chávez 1955, Almada 1938, and Chávez Calderón 1964. In recent years, there has been a new surge of interest in the Tomóchi rebellion. See Illades Aguilar 1993 and Vanderwood 1992. One of the most recent and best-documented books on Tomóchi is Rubén Osorio Zuñiga's 1995 *Tomóchic en llamas* (Tomóchi in Flames). See also Vargas 1994, Saborit 1994, and Pozo Marrero 1991.

26. APD, José María Rangel to Porfirio Díaz and Díaz to Rangel, Dec. 9, 1891.

27. APD, Carrillo to Porfirio Díaz, Jan. 18, 1892; Díaz to Carrillo, Jan. 28, 1892.

28. On the rise of Protestantism in Porfirian Mexico, see Baldwin 1990 and Bastian 1989.

29. On the Saint of Cabora, see R. C. Holden 1978 and Osorio Zuñiga 1995.

30. Chávez Calderón 1964, 48–49.

31. Almada 1955, 350. Not all authors share this interpretation by Almada.

32. APD, Márques Rosendo to Porfirio Díaz, Oct. 17, 1892.

33. Jordán 1981, 295–97, writes that Santana Pérez's men opened fire on the federal troops. According to Osorio Zuñiga (1995, 127–31) Santana Pérez's troops did not participate in the battle and their leader strongly denied accusations by federal officials that his men had fired on federal troops.

34. Almada 1955, 351.

35. For an analysis of the wave of revolts that swept Mexico in 1891–95, see Katz and Lloyd 1986.

36. Frías 1946, 40.

37. APD, Rosendo Márquez to Porfirio Díaz, Nov. 6, 1892.

38. Osorio Zuñiga 1995.

39. For the best description and analysis of the influence of the Tomóchi uprising on subsequent social movements, see Osorio Zuñiga 1995.

40. Luis Terrazas's son Juan was a partner in one of the largest surveying companies in Chihuahua, Ignacio Gomez del Campo, Guerrero y Socios, and his son-in-law, Enrique Creel, was manager (Lloyd 1987, 71).

41. Arías Olea 1960.

42. RAT, 1: 29 (1906), L1. E83, inhabitants of Nonoava to Porfirio Díaz, Feb. 1, 1905.

43. On the effect of railroad construction on land expropriation on rural unrest in Mexico, see Coatsworth 1981. On the impact of railroad construction on Chihuahua, see Wasserman 1984, 76–77, 105–12.

44. Almada 1964, 1: 24–25.

45. For an analysis of Creel's land law, see Lloyd 1988.

46. The villagers' petitions are held in a section of the Secretaría de la Reforma Agraria en Terrenos Nacionales that was long closed to researchers. I was first given access to these files in 1978, and their discovery completely changed my attitude to the land problem in Chihuahua. Until then, I had believed that the agrarian problem in Chihuahua was essentially of a minor nature.

47. RAT, 1: 29 (1906), L1, exp. 74, Hilario Silva to Secretaría de Fomento, May 30, 1904; decision of Secretaría, June 7, 1904.

48. Ibid., exp. 88, inhabitants of Redondeados to Secretaría de Fomento, June 18, 1905.

49. Ibid., exp. 78, Feliciano Ochoa and inhabitants of Monterde y Aremoyo to Secretaría de Formento, Sept. 18, 1905.

50. J. Terrazas 1980.

51. RAT, 1: 29 (1906), L2, exp. 143, Macario Nieto to Secretaría de Fomento, Dec. 13, 1906.

52. Ibid.

53. RAT, 1: 29 (1906), L2, exp. 178, inhabitants of Namiquipa to Porfirio Díaz, July 20, 1908.

54. *El Correo de Chihuahua*, Nov. 7, 1907. For a history of the agrarian conflict in Namiquipa, see Alonso 1995 and Nugent 1993.

55. For a history of Cuchillo Parado, see Koreck 1988.

56. Ibid.

57. Ontiveros 1914, 4.

58. Koreck 1988, 127–49.

59. RAT 129 (1906), L3, inhabitants of Namiquipa to Secretaría de Fomento, Apr. 1892. See Nugent 1993, 60–75.

60. RAT, Namiquipa, mayor to Secretaría de Fomento, July 7, 1909.

61. RAT, exp. 75-1407, Porfirio Talamantes to Secretaría de Fomento, Feb. 22, 1908.

62. Ibid., Enrique Creel to Secretaría de Fomento, Oct. 23, and Porras to Creel, Oct. 13, 1908.

63. Ibid., petition of inhabitants of Janos to Secretaría de Fomento, 24 Dec. 1908.

64. Ibid., Aldasoro to Enrique Creel, Mar. 11, 1909.

65. Ibid., Enrique Creel to Aldasoro, Apr. 25, 1909.

66. Ibid., Aldasoro to Enrique Creel, Apr. 30, 1909.

67. RAT, Janos, López Moctezuma to Aldasoro, June 15, 1909.

68. Ibid., message of the villagers of Janos to Secretaría de Fomento of May 5, 1910.

69. Ibid., memorandum of Sección Primera of Fomento, May 3, 1909.

70. Ibid., Enrique Creel to minister of Fomento, July 9, 1909.

71. Ibid., memorandum of Secretaría de Fomento, Jan. 11, 1911.

72. RAT, 1.29 (1906), 64.E, 193, complaint of the inhabitants of San Antonio and San Carlos, Apr. 29, 1909.

73. Ibid., C. Reynaut to Loera, Dec. 6, 1909.

74. Ibid., Loera to Secretaría de Fomento, Aug. 17, 1909.

75. Ibid., memorandum, Secretaría de Fomento, Jan. 10, 1910.

76. Ibid., Secretaría de Fomento to governor of Chihuahua, Nov. 22, 1910.

77. Ibid., note of villagers of San Carlos complaining of reprisals by Creel.

78. APD, 003 062, anonymous report to Porfirio Díaz.

79. Estimates of the number of *rancheros* who still held land in Chihuahua in 1910, as well as estimates of the number who were deprived of their lands during the Porfirian era, are difficult to come by and contradictory. McCutchen McBride 1923 estimated that only 2,283 persons, i.e., 4 to 5 percent of heads of families in the state, owned land in 1910 (154). This seems far too low and is contradicted not only by the number of villagers whose petitions to the authorities indicate that by 1910 they still possessed land of their own but also by the censuses of Chihuahua, although the latter are not very reliable.

The census takers divided the rural population into three categories: *agricultores, peones,* and *hacendados.* According to a Villista journalist writing in 1915 in the Villista *Periódico Oficial,* agricultores were "individuals who worked their own lands" (in Gomez 1966, 221). The same author indicates that the census data were not all too reliable since they were frequently based, not on the reports of individual census takers, but on the estimates of local and regional Porfirian officials. The census of 1895 estimated that there were 33,819 agricultores and 29,913 peones. These numbers changed drastically five years later to 62,489 agricultores and only 15,973 peones. By 1910, the numbers had changed radically again. The number of agricultores had declined by about 40,000 from 62,489 to 22,529, while the number of peones had increased from 15,973 to 63,353. (Seminario de Historia Moderna de México, n.d.a, 40.)

The most difficult thing to explain is the increase in the number of agricultores in only five years, between 1895 and 1900, from about 33,000 to 62,000. There are no facts in the history of Chihuahua to warrant such a drastic increase, so there must be some other reason for the change in numbers. More reliable census takers and a better grasp by local and regional officials of the real situation in their districts might be one reason. While this may to a certain degree have been the case, another hypothesis seems more plausible: the number of reported landowners may have increased because local officials, deeply worried by the way rural uprisings had swept Chihuahua between 1891 and 1895, were now ready to recognize the validity of peasant properties they had not been willing to acknowledge before.

The reduction in the number of agricultores between 1900 and 1910, on the other hand, is borne out by a wide spate of historical data. In the Archives of the Sección de Terrenos Municipales of the Secretaría de la Reforma Agraria, I have found complaints of more than 60 villages about the despoiling of their lands. Some bore hundreds of signatures, while others were only signed by the villagers' spokesman, so that the exact number of petitioners cannot be ascertained. There is no doubt, though, that there were thousands of them. Another indication of the number of land expropriations is the number of adjudications of municipal land, which Mark Wasserman has estimated at 4,363 between 1905 and 1909 (Wasserman 1984, 110). In addition, as this book has tried to show, Creel's land law was not the only means by which hacendados appropriated village lands. These numbers certainly help to explain the powerful hold that the revolution had on Chihuahua's rural population and the preponderance of expropriated rancheros in the ranks of Chihuahua's revolutionary forces.

80. Wasserman 1984, 96.

81. Ibid.

82. Seminario de Historia Moderna de México, n.d.b, 47, 55.

83. ST Papers, letter from Heliodoro Arias Olea to Governor Luis Terrazas, n.d.

84. Arías Olea 1960, 6–9.   85. Ibid., 21–26.

86. Ibid.   87. Martínez del Río 1928, 15.

88. Wasserman 1984, 98.

89. SDF, 812.00/993, Leonard to secretary of state, Mar. 19, 1911.

90. Lloyd 1987, 86–91, 141.

91. For the history of the Partido Liberal Mexicano, see Guerra 1985, 2: 7–68; Cockroft 1968; Hart 1987b; Knight 1986, vol. 1. The role of the PLM in Chihuahua is assessed by Almada 1965, Lloyd 1987, Raat 1981, and Sandels 1967.

92. Raat 1981, 175–203.

93. Sandels 1967, 175.

94. On Silvestre Terrazas's role in the years preceding the Mexican Revolution, see Sandels 1967; Terrazas Perches 1985, 213; Almada 1981 [1951], 519–22.

95. See Sandels 1967, 70.   96. Baldwin 1990, 89–90.

97. Terrazas Perches 1985, 213   98. Fuentes Mares 1954, 240.

99. Wasserman 1984, 122–28; Lloyd 1987, 127–43.

100. DZA, AA II, no. 4491, consul in Chihuahua to Bülow, May 10, 1909.

101. Ibid.

102. APD, Evaristo Madero to Porfirio Díaz, July 8, 1908.

103. Ross 1955, 11–14.

104. APD, Enrique Creel to Porfirio Díaz, Nov. 8, 1908.

105. APD, 003707, Miguel Ahumada to Porfirio Díaz, Feb. 21, 1911.

106. Almada 1965, vol. 1; Terrazas Perches 1985, 218, 230, 231.

107. Bush 1939, 165.

108. For the Reyes movements, see Bryan 1970.

109. Beezley 1973, 27.

Chapter Two

1. Sanchez 1952, 54–57.   2. Ontiveros 1914; Koreck 1988.

3. Ontiveros 1914, 40.   4. Duarte Morales 1967, 6.

5. On the revolt in Namiquipa, see Nugent 1993, 75–77.

6. See Arías Olea 1960.

7. ABCFMA, James Eaton to Barton, Dec. 23, 1910.

8. For a biography of Pascual Orozco, see M. Meyer 1967. In a report to Porfirio Díaz's secretary, Rafael Chousal, the federal commander García Cuellar stated that Orozco earned around 1,000 pesos per month. UNAM, Rafael Chousal Papers, box 33, exp. 329 Fo 69–70, García Cuellar to Chousal, Jan. 13, 1911.

9. V. M. Orozco 1994, 87–90.

10. ABCFMA, James Eaton to Barton, Dec. 23, 1910.

11. Antonio Ruíz, in *El Correo de Chihuahua*, Nov. 20, 1912. These elections reflected the relationship of forces within the revolutionary contingent. Villa had brought 28 men to the meeting, and the elections ratified his command of them. See MLG, Antonio Ruíz, "El Maderismo en Chihuahua" (MS).

12. See Puente 1937.

13. ADU, Díaz Couder to governor, Nov. 1, 1899.

14. Octaviano Meraz, the head of the mounted police in Durango, had an unusual reputation for brutality, not only against presumed and real bandits but against peasants as well. In 1903, at the request of one of the region's hacendados, Joaquín Martos, who had long been in conflict over lands with peasants from the neighboring settlement of Yerba Buena, Meraz ordered these peasants to vacate their properties within four days. Those who did not do so were tied to the soldiers' horses and forced to leave their native village. Unsigned report on stationary of the Jefe Político, Mar. 13, 1903.

15. ADU, Duran to governor, Jan. 9, 1901.

16. In his memoirs, Villa calls Valenzuela "a good as well as a rich man" (Guzmán 1965, 11), to whom he sold dried meat and hides, which, though he does not say so, probably came from stolen cattle. Juan Gualberto Amaya, who was very well informed about these events in Villa's early life, writes that Valenzuela was the most important merchant in Canatlán and had "suspicious" business dealings with Villa (Amaya 1947, 483, 484).

17. ADU, Avelino Molina to governor, Mar. 4, 1901.

18. Ibid.

19. Ibid., Díaz Couder to governor Mar. 24, 1902. While to my knowledge no other author has as yet seen these records from the Durango archives, two authors have been able to glean part of the truth from oral testimony. Máximo García, one of Villa's former generals, told the historian Juan Gualberto Amaya that Villa once spoke to him of having been arrested by the jefe político Díaz Couder, and how he had been rescued by Pablo Valenzuela (Amaya 1947, 483, 484). García told Amaya that Villa himself had told him the story of his arrest. What Villa evidently did not mention, and Amaya did not know, was that Villa was forcibly inducted into the army and then deserted. This was discovered by the Chihuahuan historian Francisco Almada, who thought that Villa had been arrested on only minor charges (Almada 1981 [1951], 478–79).

20. John Reed says that a government official violated Villa's sister and Villa killed him (Reed 1969 [1914], 115). Colonel John Biddle (see Prologue, n. 15) thought that it was the sheriff who eloped with Villa's sister and fled to the mountains, where Villa killed him. Puente's account resembles Villa's, except in one respect: the victim is not Villa's younger sister, Martina, but the elder, Mariana (Puente 1937, 134).

21. ADU, Castillo to governor, Apr. 5, 1892.

22. Ibid., Marín to governor, Feb. 18, 1907.

23. Ibid., Díaz Couder to governor, Feb. 25, 1903.

24. PRO, FO 371-1147-17946, Vice-Consul Graham to Hohler, Apr. 19, 1911.

25. For charges against Soto, see ADU, Díaz Couder to governor, Nov. 20, 1893; Joaquín Camacho to governor, July 3, 1894; Díaz Couder to governor, Oct. 25, 1899.

26. Giron 1976, 86–87.

27. For a biography of Ignacio Parra, see Arreola Valenzuela et al. 1979–80.

28. Giron 1976, 65.

29. ADU, Díaz Couder to governor, June 17, 1903.

30. Ibid., Castillo to governor, Oct. 19, 1892.

31. Ibid., Castillo to governor, May 21, 1892.

32. Ibid., Florentino Soto to governor, Oct. 29, 1894, 77–78.

33. MLG, penciled memoirs, 17.   34. Ibid.

35. What seems to indicate that Arango changed his name to Villa in order to hide his desertion from the army is that prior to 1902, when he deserted, the authorities only referred to him by the name of Doroteo Arango. There is little doubt that there was a real bandit named Francisco Villa. In 1879, the authorities in Coahuila

briefly mentioned the existence of a dangerous bandit called Francisco Villa. In 1938, Miguel Soto, an old-timer from Durango, was asked by the historian Pablo Martínez del Río, the descendant of a family that had owned one of the largest haciendas in the state, Santa Catalina, to carry out research on the life of this first Francisco Villa for a book that Martínez del Río was planning to write on the history of banditry in Durango. Soto spoke to old-timers and reconstructed the life of the first Francisco Villa. He was born in the state of Zacatecas, the illegitimate son of a powerful local man. For a time he worked on a hacienda in a privileged position, as a cowboy in charge of taming wild horses. He roamed through the states of Zacatecas and Durango, and the greatest crime in which he was involved was an attack on the hacienda of La Estanzuela in Durango. During the attack, the owner of the estate, Guillermo Mueller, a German, was killed. This event took place in 1888, and Villa died soon afterward during a fight with the state police. He seems to have maintained contacts with Ignacio Parra, whose band Arango later joined. In the papers of the jefe político of San Juan del Río, where Parra is mentioned again and again, I have never found any reference to Francisco Villa. If he was indeed killed in 1889 or 1890, as Soto assumes, it is doubtful whether Arango might have known him, since he would only have been eleven or twelve years old at the time. Nevertheless, his reputation as an extremely courageous man and a superb rider may have been one of the factors that induced Arango to adopt his name. See Martínez del Río papers, Miguel Soto to Pablo Martínez del Río, Feb. 26, 1938.

36. Archivo de Ciudad Guerrero, Castillo to jefe político, Ciudad Guerrero, June 29, 1910.

37. AHDN, Cancelados, 343, deposition of Francisco Villa, June 25, 1912.

38. PRO, FO 371-2229-54830, Furber to Foreign Office, May 14, 1914.

39. Furber 1954, 109.

40. *Saturday Evening Post*, Feb. 4, 1928.

41. Peterson and Knoles 1977, 25.   42. Puente 1938, 57.

43. Hobsbawm 1965.   44. Torres 1975d, 13.

45. Parral Archive: Juzgado 1 de lo penal del Distrito de Hidalgo 53.

46. APD 001346, Alberto Terrazas to Díaz, Jan. 18, 1911.

47. Although it was doubtless also a matter of personal revenge, Reza's murder was definitely a political act, according to Villa's memoirs, where Reza is depicted as spying on a meeting that Villa had with Abraham González to discuss revolutionary strategy. See MLG, Bauche Alcalde, 65; Reed 1969 [1914], 116.

48. ST Papers, jefe político of the Jiménez district, Oct. 17, 1910, and jefe político of the Hidalgo district, Oct. 8, 1910, to governor of Chihuahua.

49. Villa does not give any exact date in his memoirs as to when he joined the revolution. More exact and reliable information is provided by the memoirs of Antonio Ruíz, one of the leaders of the anti-reelectionist party in Ciudad Chihuahua, who places Villa's participation in the revolutionary movement at a relatively early date. Ruíz states that as soon as it was clear that the results of the presidential election had been falsified, the Chihuahuan revolutionaries made plans for an armed uprising, and Abraham González contacted Villa, who agreed to participate if González sent him arms and ammunition. González agreed and did so through his brother Santiago González Casavantes. See MLG, Antonio Ruíz, "El Maderismo en Chihuahua" (MS).

50. S. Terrazas 1985, 14.

51. O'Hea 1966, 31–32.

52. MID, Carlos E. Husk to Hugh L. Scott, June 5, 1914, 5761-1091-3.

53. S. Terrazas 1985, 183.

54. Ibid., 185–86.

55. Almada 1955, 1: 171.

56. MLG, Bauche Alcalde, 72.

57. Villa's military activities during the first phases of the Maderista revolution have led to few controversies among historians. For the best account of Villa's activities in this period of his life, see MLG, "Villa service record"; Sanchez Lamego 1977, 1; and, above all, Portilla 1995. While there are no discrepancies concerning Villa's attempted attack on Ciudad Chihuahua, the use of the sombreros as a deceptive tactic has not been accepted by all authors, but is reported in Juvenal 1916, 51.

58. MLG, Bauche Alcalde, 77.

59. See Almada 1964, 1: 181–82; Sanchez Lamego 1977, 78–79.

60. APD, 019888, José Yves Limantour to Porfirio Díaz, Nov. 23, 1910.

61. Almada 1981 [1951], 451–54.

62. APD, 019790–019791, Alberto Terrazas to Porfirio Díaz, Dec. 14, 1910.

63. Ibid., Juan Terrazas to Porfirio Díaz, Jan. 7, 1911.

64. Ibid., 001317–001318, Alberto Terrazas to Porfirio Díaz, Jan. 8, 1911.

65. Ibid., 001302, Alberto Terrazas to Porfirio Díaz, Jan. 10, 1911.

66. Fuentes Mares 1954, 244.

67. Ibid., 245.

68. APD, 001308, Alberto Terrazas to Porfirio Díaz, Jan. 6, 1911.

69. ST Papers, letter of Enrique Creel, Dec. 22, 1910, quoted in Rocha 1979, 30–31.

70. See Vanderwood 1976.

71. UNAM, Rafael Chousal Papers, García Cuellar to Chousal Jan. 13, 1911.

72. APD, 006146–006147, governor of Campeche to Porfirio Díaz, Apr. 10, 1911.

73. Ibid., 005793, governor of Zacatecas to Porfirio Díaz, Mar. 30, 1911.

74. Ibid., 003569, governor of Durango to Porfirio Díaz, Feb. 22, 1911.

75. Ibid., 000486, governor of Tamaulipas to Porfirio Díaz, Jan. 28, 1911.

76. Ibid., 007171, governor of Queretaro to Porfirio Díaz, Apr. 17, 1911.

77. Ibid., 007157, governor of Puebla to Porfirio Díaz, Apr. 17, 1911.

78. Ibid., 006981, Luis Torres to Porfirio Díaz, Apr. 9, 1911.

79. Ibid., 007218, official from Tula, signature unreadable, to Porfirio Díaz, Apr. 26, 1911.

80. Ibid., governor of Campeche to Porfirio Díaz, Mar. 23, 1911.

81. Ibid.

82. Ibid., 005280, governor of Yucatán to Porfirio Díaz, Mar. 8, 1911.

83. Ibid., 006374, governor of Yucatán to Porfirio Díaz, Apr. 19, 1911.

84. Ibid., 006762–06763, José María de la Vega to Porfirio Díaz, Apr. 16, 1911.

85. Ibid., 020703, Juan Hernández to Porfirio Díaz, Dec. 7, 1910.

86. Ibid., 020642, Juan Hernández to Porfirio Díaz, Dec. 14, 1910.

87. Ibid., 020623, Juan Hernández to Porfirio Díaz, Dec. 25, 1910.

88. Ibid., 000074, Juan Hernández to Porfirio Díaz, Jan. 1, 1911.

89. Ibid., 017356–017365, anonymous, undated report transmitted by Juan Hernández to Porfirio Díaz.

90. Ibid., 000045, Juan Hernández to Porfirio Díaz, Jan. 19, 1911.

91. Ibid., 000029, Juan Hernández to Navarro, Jan. 10, 1911.

92. Almada 1964, 1: 184.

93. APD, 019806, Medina Barrón to Porfirio Díaz, Dec. 19, 1910.

94. M. Terrazas 1985, 220–21; Sandels 1967, 209–20.

95. Fuentes Mares 1954, 246.

96. M. Terrazas 1985, 224–25; Sandels 1967, 212.

97. PRO, FO 371, Hohler to Sir Edward Grey, Feb. 16, 1911.

98. APD, 003666, Juan Hernández to Porfirio Díaz, Feb. 12, 1911.

99. Ibid., 002646, Juan Hernández to Porfirio Díaz, Dec. 16, 1910.

100. Ibid., 003087, Juan Hernández to Porfirio Díaz, Jan. 30, 1911.

101. Ibid., 019313, Mauricio Cavazos to Porfirio Díaz, Dec. 22, 1910.

102. Ibid., 000942–000946, Andrés to "Papacito," Feb. 8, 1911.

103. Ibid., 002869, unnamed officer to Rafael Chousal, Feb. 23, 1911.

104. There is a substantial literature on the settlement of the Mormons in Chihuahua and their experiences during the revolution. See Young 1968; Hatch and Hardy 1985; and H. Taylor 1992.

105. See Lloyd 1987, 86–91.

106. Portilla 1995, 334–75.

107. UNAM, Rafael Chousal Papers, García Cuellar to Chousal, Jan. 13, 1911.

108. Garibaldi 1937, 225–26.

109. Ibid., 348.

110. AJV, unpublished memoirs of Castillo.

111. APD, 003800, Juan Hernández to Porfirio Díaz, Feb. 27, 1911.

112. APD, 005422, Juan Hernández to Porfirio Díaz, Mar. 25, 1911.

113. See J. G. Amaya 1947.

114. APD, 006757, Lauro Villar to Porfirio Díaz, Apr. 8, 1911.

115. This description of the Maderista army and its internal problems is based on Portilla 1995, 304–98.

116. MLG, "Villa service record," 22–23.

117. There are contradictory accounts of Villa's activities during this early phase of the revolution. In his memoirs, Villa claims he participated in the battle of Cerro Prieto along with Orozco and then withdrew to San Andrés in order to ambush a federal ammunition convoy (MLG, "Villa service record," 5, 6). He says nothing about a quarrel with Orozco but on the contrary states that he left Orozco's camp with the latter's full agreement in order to intercept the ammunition convoy (ibid., 6). Francisco Almada on the contrary says that Villa left Orozco after quarreling with the latter before the battle of Cerro Prieto (Almada 1965, 183, 184). Sanchez Lamego 1977 (1: 57, 58) does not mention Villa's participation in that battle, while Valadés in his *Historia general de la revolución mexicana* (1976, 1: 227, 228) mentions constant disputes between Villa and Orozco that led to the separation of their respective forces. In an interview given many years later, Roque González Garza said that Orozco had outlawed Villa (González Garza, PHO interview, 34).

118. MLG, "Villa service record," 7.

119. MR Archives, Gómez Palacio to Barbarita, Feb. 11, 1911.

120. MLG, "Villa service record," 14–15; Sanchez Lamego 1977, 1: 80.

121. APD, 001345, Alberto Terrazas to Porfirio Díaz, Jan. 18, 1911.

122. There is no evidence that Villa fought in Zacatecas during the Maderista revolution.

123. AJV, unpublished memoirs of Máximo Castillo, 13. It must be emphasized that Castillo was an enemy of Villa's and that I have found no other report corroborating this accusation.

124. *El Tiempo*, Apr. 1911.

125. Desiderio Madrid Carrasco, interview in Osorio Zuñiga 1991, 34–37.

126. Roque Gonzáles Garza, PHO interview, p. 36.

127. Guzmán 1965, 38.

128. Letter of Francisco Madero to the *El Paso Morning Times*, Apr. 25, 1911.

129. SDF, 812.00-1222, consul in Chihuahua to State Department, Mar. 29, 1911.

130. *El Tiempo*, Apr. 1911.

131. Terrazas Papers, Museum of the Mexican Revolution, Chihuahua, Luis Terrazas Jr. to Luis Terrazas Sr., Apr. 4, 1911.

132. Jorge Vera Estañol to Francisco de León de la Barra, Apr. 29, 1911, in Vera Estañol 1957, 148–52.

133. APD, 004076–006080, José Yves Limantour to Porfirio Díaz, Feb. 17, 1911.

134. Ibid., 004761, Ambassador Francisco de León de la Barra to Porfirio Díaz, Mar. 9, 1911.

135. Ibid., Gerónimo Treviño to Porfirio Díaz.

136. Ross 1955, 160.

137. Juan Sánchez Azcona to Vázquez Gómez, Apr. 25, 1911, in Vázquez Gómez 1933.

138. SDF, 812-00-1548.

139. Vázquez Gómez 1933, 138–43.

140. Ibid., 137.

141. Villa asserts in his memoirs that he and Orozco had decided to attack Ciudad Juárez against Madero's wishes, and most historians tend to accept this. See Ross 1955, 164–65; Valadés 1976, 1: 304; Sanchez Lamego 1977, 2: 106–8.

142. T. Turner 1935, 55.

143. Ibid., 58–59.

144. AHDN, X1/481.5/66, box 24, Chihuahua, 1911, testimony of Francisco Madero, Dec. 22, 1911.

145. Guzmán 1965, 50–51. This passage exactly reproduces MSG, "Villa service record," 36–37.

146. Ibid.

147. For the most detailed description, see Meyer 1967, 38–42, and Ross 1955, 167–69. More recent historiography has not substantially deviated from these interpretations.

148. Guzmán 1965, 52. This is taken verbatim from MSG, "Villa service record," 40.

149. Meyer 1967, 36.

150. These facts are based on the hitherto unknown and unpublished correspondence between Finance Minister José Yves Limantour, the Porfirian governor of Veracruz, Teodoro Dehesa, and a newspaperman who was one of the founders of Reyes's Democratic party, Francisco P. de Senties. They are contained in the papers of Heriberto Jara in UNAM, box 8, exp. 248, and I thank Anthony Goldner for locating these documents and copying them for me. The description of the conference in Porfirio Díaz's house is contained in a letter from de Senties to Dehesa of Mar. 24, 1912, based on a long conversation between de Senties and Victoriano Huerta (papers of Heriberto Jara, nos. 4801–11). Limantour's warnings about a possible U.S. intervention are also in the Heriberto Jara papers, nos. 4779–82, Dehesa to Limantour, Nov. 14, 1911.

151. Ross 1955, 171.

152. Osorio Zuñiga n.d., 152–53.

153. Guzmán 1965, 52. This is taken from MLG, "Villa service record," 40.

154. Taracena, 1992a, 117.   155. Garibaldi 1937, 293–94.

156. *New York Times*, May 18, 1911.   157. Ibid., May 19, 1911.

158. PRO, FO 371-1396-11269-3738, prefect of Etla to state government, Jan. 31, 1911; enclosed with message from Francis William Stronge, British minister to Mexico, of Feb. 20, 1912.

159. MR Archives, Gómez Palacio to Barbarita, June 27, 1911.

160. Ponce Alcocer 1981, 205.

161. AA Bonn, archives of the German legation in Mexico, letter of longtime American residents of Mexico to President Woodrow Wilson, n.d.

162. Doubtless expressing the opinion of the many Spanish hacendados and hacienda administrators in Mexico, the Spanish minister to that country reported that Madero had "initiated the so-called 'Zapatismo,' which is the uprising of the Indian agrarian plebeians, with their continuous killings, plunders, rapes, arson, and barbarism, and this movement was in a certain way perhaps encouraged by the central government (of that he was accused) as a political reserve. The landowners, merchants, industrialists, agriculturalists, and miners, including the foreigners, finally believed that he was incapable of restoring peace and lost all confidence in him." Spanish Foreign Ministry Archives, Madrid, Cologan to minister of foreign affairs, Mar. 2, 1913.

163. PRO, FO 371-1148-00479-30407, Cunard Cummins to Foreign Office, enclosed in Hohler's dispatch of July 17, 1911.

164. Buve 1988, 338–75.

165. Aguilar Camín 1977, 251–54.

166. After rebellious peasants from the village of Peñon Blanco had occupied lands belonging to the hacienda of Santa Catalina, the administrator of the estate, Gómez Palacio, wrote his boss, "I'm working so as to win the confidence of the chief [Contreras, commander of the Maderista garrison that had replaced the federal army near the hacienda as a result of the Treaty of Ciudad Juárez] and obtain his help through financial remuneration" (MR Archives, Gómez Palacio to Barbarita, July 21, 1911). Only a few months later, when peasants from Peñon Blanco joined in an attack on the hacienda, burning down some of its buildings, Gómez Palacio had to acknowledge (ibid., Gómez Palacio to Barbarita, Nov. 12, 1911) that his attempt to bribe Contreras had had no effect. The rebellious peasants had

> wanted to destroy all proofs of the debts of the sharecroppers and tenants and all proofs of the advances they had received, as well as all the old debts of the servants. Soto [the administrator of the estate] also told me that the tenants had been loudly stating that they will not surrender to the hacienda that part of the corn and bean harvest that they owed, since Contreras told them that everything belongs to them, and they believe that having destroyed the contracts, we shall not be able to prove that they use the land only as tenants, and they will say that they own the land on orders of Contreras and in compliance with the plan of San Luis.

Chapter Three

1. *El Paso Morning Times*, Feb. 19 and 20, 1914.

2. Beezley 1973: 109–10.

3. Ibid., 99–105. See also Almada 1967.

4. Dr. Rubén Osorio, Archivo Privado, microfilm, Abraham González to Juan Terrazas, Aug. 29, 1911.

5. SDF, 81200-3424, Marion Letcher to secretary of state, Mar. 20, 1912.

6. AGN, Madero Papers, 9546–47, Abraham González to Francisco Madero, Nov. 5, 1912.

7. Ibid., 9523, Abraham González to Francisco Madero, Aug. 2, 1912.

8. For an account of Senator Fall's relationship to Mexico, see Trow 1966. Relations with Orozco's rebellion are dealt with on p. 39, while Fall's business relations with Terrazas are described on pp. 92–95. See also Ulloa 1971, 46.

9. SDF, 81200-3424, Marion Letcher to secretary of state, Mar. 20, 1912.

10. APD, 009661, Enrique Creel to Porfirio Díaz, Sept. 15, 1911.

11. BI memo, Oct. 20, 1911. Only two months later, Creel sounded far more optimistic. *El Correo* in Chihuahua reported on Nov. 18, 1911, that Creel had stated that with two científicos in Madero's new cabinet, Mexico's evolution would be far more positive. In addition, the newspaper reported that Creel and Ernesto Madero, the president's uncle and minister of economics, had become partners in a series of joint ventures.

12. When a coup in Veracruz threatened his presidency shortly after he had assumed power, Porfirio Díaz had instructed his governor in Veracruz to kill a number of men suspected of planning a coup immediately and without trial; "Matalos en caliente [kill them immediately]," he had ordered the governor.

13. Library of Congress, Manuscript Division, Charles D. Rhodes, "Diary of a Special Mission to Mexico, Mexico, 1911."

14. BI, microfilm, reel 1085, no. 851, memo of Feb. 26, 1912.

15. AGN, Madero Papers, 9546–47, Abraham González to Francisco Madero, Nov. 5, 1912.

16. Almada 1964, 1: 91–92.　　　　17. Ibid.

18. Beezley 1973, 92–93.　　　　　19. Ibid., 99–103.

20. Nugent 1993, 80–81; Maria Teresa Koreck, oral communication.

21. *El Correo de Chihuahua*, Oct. 10, 1911.

22. Ibid., Nov. 20, 1911.

23. RAT, exp. 6114, 1.29 (1906), L2E122, Terrenos Nacionales, petition by Castulo Herrera and others, Jan. 3, 1912.

24. *El Correo de Chihuahua*, Feb. 19–20, 1912.

25. Ibid., Oct. 28, 1911.　　　　　26. Ibid., Sept. 1, 1911.

27. Ibid., Aug. 16, 1911.　　　　　28. Ibid., Feb. 5 and 6, 1912.

29. *El Paso Morning Times,* Feb. 19 and 20, 1914.

30. *El Correo de Chihuahua*, Feb. 19–20, 1912.

31. Almada 1981 [1951], 458.

32. RAT, exp. 5571, 1.29 (1906), L2E133, F. Lombardo to Abraham González, Aug. 24, 1912.

33. On Emilio Vázquez's role before and during the Orozco uprising, see M. Meyer 1967, 46–52, 59–61.

34. Ibid., 52.

35. For different appreciations of the Orozco revolt, see M. Meyer 1967 and Knight 1986, 1: 289–333. One of the most original contributions to the history of Orozquismo is Richard Estrada's study of the popular leaders who backed Orozco, "Liderazgo popular en la revolución mexicana" (MS).

36. Almada 1964, 267–315.

37. *El Correo de Chihuahua*, Mar. 9–10, 1912.

38. Ibid., Mar. 13–14, 1912.

39. AGN, Madero Papers, 9509, Abraham González to Francisco Madero, Feb. 16, 1912.

40. M. Meyer 1967, 75.

41. SDF, 81200-3424, Marion Letcher to secretary of state, Mar. 20, 1912.

42. *El Paso Morning Times*, Feb. 19–20, 1914.

43. BI, microfilm reel 1085, no. 851.

44. AGN, Madero Papers, Abraham González to Francisco Madero, Nov. 5, 1912.

45. BI, microfilm reel 1085, no. 851.

46. UNAM, Rafael Chousal Papers, García Cuellar to Chousal, Jan. 13, 1911.

47. SDF, 81200-3424, Marion Letcher to secretary of state, Mar. 20, 1912.

48. BI, microfilm reel 1085, no. 851.

49. Knight 1986, 1: 298.

50. AGN, Madero Papers, 9548–49, Abraham González to Francisco Madero, Nov 10, 1912.

51. AGN, Ramo Gobernación, box 88, exp. 32, Andrés Ortiz to Manuel Aguirre Berlanga, Feb. 24, 1919. Was Ortiz's report to Carranza based on reliable information, or did he hope by stating that the Terrazas had contributed such a large sum to the Orozco uprising to prevent the Mexican president from returning their properties to Chihuahua's richest families? The evidence concerning the financial involvement of Terrazas and Creel in the Orozco uprising is contradictory. Michael Meyer believes that the only known contribution of the family to the Orozco uprising was the sum of 45,000 pesos voluntarily donated by Juan Creel's son (M. Meyer 1967, 75). Alan Knight, while increasing the sum to 80,000 pesos, is of the same opinion (Knight 1986, 1: 298). At a hearing organized by a committee of the U.S. Senate to investigate U.S. participation in revolutions in Mexico, however, Terrazas himself stated that he had contributed 110,000 pesos to the Orozco movement but insisted that this was a forced contribution. He had had to pay 50,000 as ransom for his son, while a manager of his had had to pay 60,000 to the rebels (Trow 1966, 54–59). At the same hearing, the Orozquista governor of Chihuahua, Félix Gutiérrez, a man close to the oligarchy, testified that after Orozco occupied Chihuahua and the Chamber of Commerce had assigned a contribution to Orozco's war chest to each business in Chihuahua, Terrazas had paid his share, and Gutiérrez did not mention any objection on his part.

There is some evidence that Creel was for a time not in agreement with the junior members of the clan's support of the Orozco rebellion, and that in a letter to Creel, Terrazas protested his innocence, but contemporary observers who were far from being Maderistas were convinced that the clan was behind the Orozco uprising. They included such men as E. H. Houghton, the manager of one of the largest American-owned estates in Chihuahua, the Corralitos Company, who stated in hearings before the same Senate committee that it was Terrazas and Creel who were supporting, fomenting, and financing the Orozco uprising (Trow 1966, 54–59). Mexico's conservative ideologue Francisco Bulnes, who had been one of the stalwarts of the Díaz regime, made similar accusations (Fuentes Mares 1954, 250), as did the agrarian revolutionary Máximo Castillo, who was initially allied with Orozco. These judgments square with reports by a BI agent (BI, microfilm reel 1085, no. 851) and by the U.S. consul in Chihuahua (SDF, 81200-3424, Marion Letcher to secretary of state, Mar. 20, 1912), who believed that one of the main instigators and backers of the Orozco rebellion was Terrazas's son-in-law Federico Sisniega, who was Spanish consul in Chihuahua (SDF, 812.00/11043, Marion Letcher to secretary of state, Feb. 21, 1914).

52. AGN, Madero Papers, Francisco Madero to Abraham González, Dec. 8, 1912.

53. M. Meyer 1967, 57.

54. AGN, 9515, Madero Papers, Abraham González to Francisco Madero, July 12, 1912.

55. AJV, unpublished memoirs of Castillo.

Chapter Four

1. Corral de Villa 1976, 18–19.

2. Herrera 1981, 49–53.

3. Corral de Villa 1976, 18–19.

4. Ibid., 23.

5. Guadalupe Villa, letter to the author.

6. AGN, Madero Papers, 9510–12, Abraham González to Francisco Madero, July 12, 1912.

7. Ibid., Francisco Villa to Francisco Madero, 35605, Aug. 12, 1912.

8. AGN, Ramo Revolución, *carpeta* 2, folder 10, Francisco Villa to Francisco Madero, Nov. 6, 1911.

9. On the conference with González, see Calzadíaz Barrera 1967–82, 1: 82–83.

10. AGN, Gobernación, leg., relations with the state of Chihuahua, in exp. 1 (1911–12), Terrazas to minister of internal affairs, Aug. 11, 1911.

11. MSG, "Villa service record," 41.

12. AGN, Manuel González Ramírez Papers, vol. 60, *secretario de hacienda* to Abraham González, Aug. 7, 1911.

13. AGN, Madero Papers, 35605, Francisco Villa to Francisco Madero, Aug. 12, 1912.

14. *El Correo de Chihuahua*, Aug. 19, 1911.

15. AGN, Manuel González Ramírez Papers, vol. 66, archive of the supreme court of Chihuahua, private correspondence of former governor Abraham González, letter of Sept. 27, 1911.

16. AGN, Madero Papers, Abraham González to Francisco Madero, Oct. 10, 1911.

17. AGN, Manuel González Ramirez Papers, archive of the supreme court of Chihuahua, private correspondence of former governor Abraham González, José de Luz Soto to González, Aug. 13, 1911.

18. AGN, Madero Papers, Abraham González to Francisco Madero, Oct. 10, 1911.

19. Ibid., 9515–18, Abraham González to Francisco Madero, July 12, 1912.

20. I have not found the letter from Villa to Madero, but Madero's secretary, Juan Sánchez Azcona, quoted extensively from this letter in his reply to Villa on Feb. 14 (AGN, Sánchez Azcona, *libro copiador*, vol. 4, box 53, Sánchez Azcona to Francisco Villa, Feb. 14, 1912).

21. Ibid.

22. Ibid., Juan Sánchez Azcona to Abraham González, Feb. 14, 1912.

23. Francisco Villa to the people of Chihuahua, open letter, in *El Correo de Chihuahua*, Feb. 15–16, 1912.

24. Ibid.

25. BI, microfilm reel 1085, no. 851, report of L. E. Rocks for Aug. 4, 1911, written on Aug. 5, 1911.

26. CONDUMEX, Archivo Federico González Garza, p. 2809, Francisco Villa to Francisco Madero, Jan. 20, 1913, received by Madero on Jan. 25, 1913.

27. See Herrera 1981, 48–50, and Caraveo 1992, 28, 29.

28. AGN, Madero Papers, Abraham González to Francisco Madero, Feb. 16, 1912.

29. Ibid., Abraham González to Francisco Madero, Feb. 16, 1912.

30. Francisco Villa to Braulio Hernández, open letter, in *El Correo de Chihuahua*, Mar. 2–3, 1912.

31. *El Correo de Chihuahua*, Feb. 28–29, 1912.

32. M. Meyer 1967, 70–71.

33. A strong pro-Orozco lobby in the United States, including William Randolph Hearst and unnamed mining and railway interests, is reported in HHSTA, Pa Berichte Mexico, 1912, minister to Mexico to Berchtold, Oct. 22, 1912.

34. AA Bonn, archives of German legation in Mexico, Carlos Flohr to German minister in Mexico, Apr. 30, 1912.

35. These complaints are contained in the transcripts of Villa's cross-examination

by a judge after his imprisonment in June 1912, AHDN, Cancelados, exp. XI/481.5/343, file of Francisco Villa, June 18, 1912.

36. AA Bonn, archives of the German legation in Mexico, papers of consulate in Chihuahua, report of Carlos Roth to German consul in Mexico City.

37. Ibid.

38. AGN, Madero Papers, 9512, Abraham González to Francisco Madero, July 12, 1912.

39. Ibid., 35626, Francisco Madero to Francisco Villa, Apr. 10, 1912.

40. LaFrance 1989, 115–18.

41. In a letter to Enrique Creel, dated Aug. 7, 1912, quoted in Fuentes Mares 1954, 250, Terrazas stated that Huerta supported him in his efforts to remove González. See also M. Meyer 1972, 42–43.

42. Account of Felipe Angeles, quoted by Cervantes 1960, 36–37.

43. SDF, 312-115-T541-16, George C. Carothers to State Department, May 5, 1912.

44. Ibid., 312-115-T541-21, James Brown Potter to State Department, May 23, 1912.

45. Cervantes 1960, 39.

46. AHDN, Cancelados, exp. XI/481.5/343, file of Francisco Villa.

47. Portilla 1995, 424.

48. Cervantes 1960, 41. In a letter that he wrote in 1917, while in exile, Angeles expressed the conviction that "the real reason for Villa's arrest was that Huerta knew that Madero had a very firm supporter in Villa, and the apparent motive for the arrest was a vulgar episode that does not do honor to Huerta and that I do not want to write about" (Angeles to Manuel Marquez Sterling, Oct. 5, 1917, published in *Proceso*, no. 907 [Mar. 21, 1994]).

49. CONDUMEX, Rubio Navarrete Papers, undated account by Rubio Navarrete.

50. AHDN, exp. XI/481.5/343, examination of Villa by prosecuting military judge, June 12, 1912.

51. Papers of Rubio Navarrete, undated letter by Rubio Navarrete.

52. Rubio Navarrete at three different times gave an account of these events, once in conversation with Villa's biographer Federico Cervantes, who had been a lieutenant of Angeles's (see Cervantes 1960, 40–42), and in two documents that I found in his papers, the first an undated memorandum, the second a letter he sent to *El Universal* on Apr. 11, 1930.

53. Madero's role in saving Villa's life is by no means clear. Traditional accounts speak of Emilio Madero wiring his brother that Villa was about to be executed and coming back, literally at the last moment, with a telegram from the president ordering Huerta to spare Villa. I have found no proof of any such action. In the telegram he sent Madero announcing Villa's arrest, last-minute reprieve, and transportation to Mexico City, Huerta nowhere mentions any order Madero might have given him to spare Villa's life. In his memoirs, Villa makes no mention of Madero saving his life, and neither does Rubio Navarette do so, but what the latter does state is that somewhat later, after the execution had been interrupted, "the intervention of different military and civilian personalities prevented Villa's execution" (Rubio Navarrete Papers, Rubio Navarrete to Miguel Lanz Duret, Apr. 11, 1930). Madero was probably one of the personalities Rubio Navarrete refers to, although he never mentions him by name.

54. AHDN, exp. XI/481.5/343, Victoriano Huerta to Francisco Madero.

55. Ibid., Victoriano Huerta to Francisco Madero. Huerta's attempt to have the ley fuga applied to Villa is described in an unsigned statement in the Buckley Papers, University of Texas, Austin. In view of Huerta's character and policies, this account is very believable.

56. MSG, Bauche Alcalde, 176–77.

57. Wilson 1927, 293–94.

58. SDF, 81200-4169, Montgomery Schuyer to secretary of state, June 5, 1912.

59. Ibid., 312-115-T541-22, Henry Lane Wilson to State Department, June 3, 1912.

60. L. Aguirre Benavides 1966, 44.

61. AHDN, exp. XI/481.5-343, Villa trial transcripts.

62. See n. 49 above. Shortly after Villa was imprisoned, Madero sent two deputies of his party and his stenographer to interview him. Villa not only assured them of his innocence but also warned them about Huerta, saying that he was an alcoholic and was unwilling really to fight Orozco. Moreover, Villa charged, some of Huerta's officers were actually selling ammunition to the Orozquistas. The warning was relayed to Madero by his stenographer, but the president does not seem to have taken it seriously. See Ursua de Escobar 1964.

63. AHDN, exp. XI/481.5/343, statement of Villa to judge.

64. Ibid., declarations of Encarnación Márquez and Blas Flores, June 15, 1912.

65. AHDN, Cancelados, exp. XI/481.5/343, transcript of interrogation of Villa by military prosecutors, June 25, 1912.

66. Ibid.

67. AHDN, exp. XI/481.5/343, June 15, 1912.

68. Ibid.

69. AGN, Madero Papers, 35599, Francisco Villa to Francisco Madero, July 11, 1912.

70. See ch. 2, n. 102.

71. AGN, Madero Papers, 35609–35611, Francisco Villa to Francisco Madero, Dec. 6 and 21, 1912.

72. AGN, Madero Papers, Abraham González to Francisco Madero, 9515–9519, July 12, 1912.

73. AHDN, vol. 353, Abraham González to Francisco Villa, July 17, 1912.

74. Guadalupe Villa, private archive, Francisco Villa to Abraham González, July 17, 1912.

75. AHDN, exp. XI/481.5/343, Abraham González to Aguirre Benavides, Aug. 12, 1912.

76. AGN, Madero Papers, 35599, Francisco Villa to Francisco Madero, July 11, 1912.

77. Ibid., 35601, Francisco Villa to Francisco Madero, July 12, 1912.

78. Ibid., 35600, Francisco Villa to Francisco Madero, July 24, 1912.

79. Ibid., 35602, Francisco Villa to Francisco Madero, July 30, 1912.

80. Ibid., 35603, Juan Sánchez Azcona to Francisco Villa, Aug. 2, 1912.

81. Ibid., 35604, Francisco Villa to Francisco Madero, Aug. 10, 1912.

82. Ibid., 35605, Aug. 12, 1912.

83. Ibid., 35607–8, Sept. 7, 1912.

84. Ibid., Juan Sánchez Azcona to Francisco Villa, Sept. 12, 1912.

85. Ibid., 35609–11, Francisco Villa to Francisco Madero, Dec. 6 and Dec. 21, 1912.

86. AHDN, exp. XI/481.5/343, Villa trial transcripts

87. *DHRM*, 7: 494–95.

88. See Case 1917, 173–75.

89. *DHRM*, 8: 101–103, Rafael Hernández to Francisco Madero, Aug. 24, 1912.

90. AGN, Madero Papers, 9531, 9533–34, Abraham González to Francisco Madero, Oct. 3 and 5, 1912.

91. Beezley 1973, 150–51.

92. Ibid., 143–44.

93. Fabela 1977, 45–47.

94. Ibid.

95. *DHRM*, 3: 448, secretary of Francisco Madero to Walter Whiffen of the Associated Press, June 12, 1912.

96. M. Meyer, 1972, 42.

97. Ibid., 43.

98. See below.

99. AGN, Madero Papers, Francisco Villa to Francisco Madero, Oct. 4, 1912.

100. MSG, Bauche Alcalde, 187.

101. LaFrance 1989, 114–15, and Magaña 1985, 2: 211–36.

102. Magaña 1985, 225.

103. Once Huerta took power, Castellanos became a member of his secret police and an informer. He denounced several railwaymen who were sympathetic to the revolution, whom the Huerta authorities executed. Once the revolution triumphed, Castellanos may have attempted to trade on his defense of Villa in 1912. He called himself a revolutionary, but his only "military" action seems to have consisted in attacking a Spanish grocery store. His activities came to public attention when he asked the Revolutionary Convention to recognize him as a bona fide revolutionary general in 1914. At this point, the revolutionary leaders from Durango sharply protested, calling him a Huerta agent, and on their recommendation the Convention not only refused to recognize him as a revolutionary leader but ordered his arrest (see *DHRM*, vol. 22 [vol. 1 of the series "La Convención"]: 166–69). He seems to have escaped, for his name turns up in 1918, when he was living as an exile in the United States and once again attempted to capitalize on his defense of Villa by trying to introduce a con man to his erstwhile client.

104. AGN, Madero Papers, 35613, Francisco Villa to Juan Sánchez Azcona, Oct. 22, 1912.

105. Ibid., Villa-Madero correspondence, José Bonales Sandoval to Juan Sánchez Azcona, Nov. 6, 1912

106. Ibid., Francisco Villa to Francisco Madero, Oct. 7, 1912.

107. Ibid., 35614, Francisco Villa to Francisco Madero, Oct. 24, 1912.

108. Ibid., Francisco Villa to Francisco Madero, Nov. 4, 1912.

109. Ibid., 35615, Juan Sánchez Azcona to Francisco Villa, Nov. 5, 1912.

110. Ibid., 35617, Juan Sánchez Azcona to Francisco Villa, Nov. 7, 1912.

111. Aguirre Benavides 1966, 44.

112. *DHRM*, 8: 197–98, Emilio Madero to Juan Sánchez Azcona, Nov. 9, 1912.

113. *DHRM*, 4: 235, Francisco Madero to Abraham González, Dec. 8, 1912.

114. *DHRM*, 6: 151–52, Abraham González to Francisco Madero, Sept. 1911.

115. *El Correo de Chihuahua*, Dec. 11, 1912.

116. AGN, Madero Papers, Villa-Madero correspondence, 35622–24, Francisco Villa to Francisco Madero, Dec. 24, 1912.

117. MSG, Bauche Alcalde, 199–200.

118. *El Paso Herald*, Jan. 1913.

119. *El Correo de Chihuahua*, Jan. 10, 1913.

120. AGN, Madero Papers, 9573, Francisco Madero to Abraham González, June 18, 1913.

121. Ibid., Abraham González to Francisco Madero, Feb. 6, 1913.

122. Womack 1969, 158.

123. CONDUMEX, Archivo Federico González Garza, p. 2809, Francisco Villa to Francisco Madero, Jan. 20, 1913, received by Madero on Jan. 25, 1913. That such a letter existed was first revealed to me a number of years ago by the historian María

Teresa Franco, who mentioned having seen it in the Madero Papers. After going through all the Madero Papers, I was unable to find it, however, and it was finally located in the Archivo Federico González Garza, which had only recently been made available to researchers. This letter is a copy of Villa's original and lacks the spelling mistakes of Villa's other letters to Madero, either because González Garza transcribed it into correct Spanish or because Villa dictated it to a friend or a scribe in El Paso. Villa does not quote this letter in his memoirs, but on the contrary includes a letter to Abraham González, which I have not found in the archives, that omits any threat against Madero: "Don Abraham, I am safe and sound in El Paso, Texas where I am at your orders. I am the same Pancho Villa as ever. Give the president a report on my actions. If my presence is harmful to my country, I will remain in the United States, but I am ready to serve him" (Guzmán 1966, 90).

124. AGN, Madero Papers, 9568–9569, Madero correspondence, Francisco Villa to Abraham González, Jan. 6, 1913.

125. Ibid., 9566–9567, Aureliano González to Abraham González, Jan. 9, 1913.

126. AGN, Madero Papers, Abraham González to Francisco Madero, Jan 9, 1913.

127. *DHRM*, 4: 262–263, José Bonales Sandoval to Francisco Madero, Dec. 28, 1912.

128. AGN, Madero Papers, Aureliano González to Abraham González, Jan. 16, 1916.

129. Ibid., Francisco Madero to Abraham González, Jan. 18, 1913.

130. *DHRM*, 4: 371, Juan Sánchez Azcona to Carlos Patoni, governor of Durango, Jan. 23, 1913.

Chapter Five

1. Simmons 1957, 256.
2. For an account of the coup, see Katz 1981, 92–115.
3. Beezley 1973, 155.
4. Archivo de Ciudad Guerrero, Abraham González to mayor of Ciudad Guerrero et al., Feb. 11, 1913.
5. Ibid., Feb. 15, 1913.
6. Ibid., Feb. 18, 1913.
7. AA Bonn, von Hintze Diary, Feb. 18, 1913.
8. Cumberland 1972, 225.
9. Magaña 1985, 2: 363–64.
10. Fabela 1977, 144–45.
11. The one time Carranza seems to have challenged Porfirio Díaz was in 1893, when he rose in arms together with other Coahuilans against an extremely unpopular governor, Garza Galán. His revolt had the support of Reyes, however, so Díaz acquiesced to it. See Richmond 1983, 2–15.
12. Ibid., 36.
13. Fabela 1979, 45–49.
14. Knight 1986, 1: 478–80.
15. Gilderhus 1986, 299.
16. Aguilar Camín 1977, 279.
17. Breceda 1920, 73.
18. De la Huerta 1957, 55
19. For very contradictory interpretions of this issue, see Richmond 1983, 44–45, and Knight 1986, 2: 14–16.
20. AA Bonn, Mexico 1, vol. 34, Paul von Hintze to Theobald von Bethmann-Hollweg, Feb. 25, 1913.
21. Silva Herzog 1960, 2: 24.
22. Nugent 1993, 77–81.

23. Francisco Villa to Abraham González, Nov. 7, 1912, copy in Dr. Rubén Osorio, Archivo Privado. Villa never exhibited any resentment of the warden and guards of the prison. He took no reprisals against them when he later occupied Mexico City; in fact, he had a cordial reunion with them.

24. Peterson and Knoles 1977, 186.   25. Ibid., 187.

26. De la Huerta 1957, 56–57.   27. McCreary 1974, 87.

28. Puente 1937, 70. Villa's decision to leave the United States was hastened by accurate rumors that the Mexican government had asked for his extradition (MFMP, 9-9-49, de la Barra to Mexican consul in Douglas, Arizona, Mar. 5, 1913).

29. Sánchez Lamego 1956, 2: 134.   30. Ibid., 2: 195–221.

31. Valadés 1976, 178   32. Almada 1964, 2: 26–27

33. Ibid.   34. Puente 1937, 73.

35. Cervantes 1960: 50; Puente 1937, 72.   36. Guzmán 1965, 101.

37. Ontiveros 1914, 59.   38. Case 1917, 176.

39. SDF, 8128847, weekly report no. 22, Sept. 13, 1913.

40. H. Taylor 1992, 301–3.   41. *El Paso Times*, Feb. 5, 1914.

42. Almada 1964, 2: 40.   43. M. Meyer 1967, 104.

44. Almada 1964, 2: 36–37.   45. Puente 1937, 78.

46. Cruz 1980, 211.   47. Barragán Rodriguez 1985, 1: 207–9.

48. Mercado 1914, 29.   49. Sánchez Lamego 1956, 4: 105.

50. Gárfias 1981, 159.

51. SDF, 812-00-9658, George C. Carothers to State Department, Oct. 15th, 1913.

52. Ibid., Hamm to State Department, Oct. 15, 1913.

53. Ibid.

54. Clendenen 1972, 37.

55. AA Bonn, Mexico 1, vol. 37, Paul von Hintze to Theobald von Bethmann-Hollweg, Mar. 24, 1914.

56. *WWP*, 29: 15, John Lind to William Jennings Bryan, Dec. 5, 1913.

57. Martínez del Rio Papers, Patrick O'Hea to [Francisco Gómez Palacio], June 3, 1913.

58. Ontiveros 1914, 82.

59. Aguirre Benavides and Aguirre Benavides 1979, 33.

60. S. Terrazas 1985, 160.

61. *New York Times*, Dec. 10, 1913; *Periódico Oficial*, Jan. 14, 1914.

62. Guzmán 1987.

63. L. Aguirre Benavides 1966, 128–29.

64. Ibid., 129.

65. Aguirre Benavides and Aguirre Benavides 1979, 49–52.

66. *Sun* (El Paso), Nov. 16, 1913.

67. Mercado 1914, 37.

68. Guzmán 1966, 113–14. Villa states without going into details: "When Huerta attempted to shoot me in Jimenez, [Francisco Castro] befriended me."

69. Ivar Thord-Gray obviously mistook mestizos for Indians, since only a small part of Chihuahua's native Indian population, the Tarahumaras, participated in the revolution. In later years, some Yaqui Indians would join the División del Norte, but this was certainly not the case at the time of Villa's capture of Ciudad Juárez.

70. Thord-Gray 1960, 36–37.   71. Ibid., 38.

72. Ibid., 39.   73. *Sun* (El Paso), Sept. 28, 1913.

74. Thord-Gray 1960, 51.   75. Ibid., 40, 41.

76. Mercado 1914, 47–48.

Chapter Six

1. Simmons 1957, 257.
2. For González's reforms, see Beezley 1973, 89–94, and Almada 1967, 49–71. For Madero's policy of "Mexicanizing the railroad employees," see Cumberland 1952, 250.
3. S. Terrazas 1985, 90–91.
4. ST Papers, Silvestre Terrazas to Porfirio Díaz, Apr. 4, 1911. On Terrazas's attitude to Díaz, see also Sandels 1967, 213–21, and S. Terrazas 1985, 224.
5. Cervantes 1960, 79–81.   6. Ibid.
7. *El Paso Times*, Dec. 27, 1913.   8. Ibid., Jan. 17, 1914.
9. S. Terrazas 1985, 97. The original letter is in the ST Papers, "Lista de enemigos."
10. Ibid., 97–99.   11. Ibid., 91.
12. Ibid., 112.   13. Ibid., 115.
14. ST Papers, Terrazas-Villa correspondence, proclamation of Dec. 9, 1913.
15. Clendenen 1972, 52, 78.   16. S. Terrazas 1985, 93–96.
17. Ibid.   18. Reed 1969 [1914], 123.
19. Spanish Foreign Ministry Archives, Madrid, Bernardo Colgan y Cologan, the Spanish minister in Mexico, to the Spanish minister of state, Mar. 16, 1913.
20. ST Papers, "Lista de enemigos."
21. S. Terrazas 1985, 91–92.
22. AGN, Comisión Monetaria, folder 231-10, report of the director of the Banco Minero, Oct. 4, 1917.
23. AGN Comisión Monetaria, folder 231-10, memorandum of Luis Terrazas Jr., written on Feb. 9, 1916, in Los Angeles.
24. L. Aguirre Benavides 1966, 106.
25. Clendenen 1972, 52, 78.
26. ST Papers, unsigned memorandum, Dec. 1913.
27. CONDUMEX, Carranza Papers, commercial representative of constitutionalist government to Venustiano Carranza, July 27, 1914.
28. Trow 1966, 96, 97.
29. ST Papers, Villa correspondence, Francisco Villa to Fidel Avila, Nov. 27, 1914.
30. S. Terrazas 1985, 92.
31. AGN, Ramo Gobernación, box 88, exp. 32, Luis Terrazas to secretario de gobernación, Aug. 10, 1918.
32. S. Terrazas 1985, 110.
33. Ibid., 109–12.
34. ST Papers, Francisco Villa to Venustiano Carranza, Jan. 11, 1914.
35. Reed 1969 [1914], 119.
36. Ibid., 133–34.

Chapter Seven

1. "An idea of Villa's character may be formed by the following advice which Villa gave to Mr. Grey [a constitutionalist agent who evidently also worked for the U.S. military], given half in jest, 'Drink, but never get drunk; love without passion; steal, but only from the rich,'" Colonel Griffith, commanding the U.S. 17th Infantry, reported to the commanding general, Southern Department, from Camp Eagle Pass, Texas, on June 19, 1914 (MID 8529-6).
2. See Juvenal 1916.
3. Lázaro de la Garza Papers, telegram from Lázaro de la Garza to Francisco Villa, Aug. 14, 1914.

4. *El Paso Herald*, Nov. 1915.   5. Corral de Villa 1976, 74.

6. Ibid., 73.   7. Ibid., 82.

8. Ibid.   9. Ibid., 73.

10. L. Aguirre Benavides 1966, 107–8.   11. Corral de Villa 1976, 82–84.

12. L. Aguirre Benavides 1966, 133.   13. S. Terrazas 1985, 88.

14. AGN, Ramo Presidente Abelardo Rodríguez, Soledad Seañez to Abelardo Rodríguez, May 23, 1933.

15. See introduction by José Vasconcelos to Corral de Villa 1976.

16. Peterson and Knoles 1977, 247–50.

17. Reed 1969 [1914], 158.

18. MR Archives, Gómez Palacio to Barbarita, Nov. 12, 1911.

19. RAT, 124 [07-E34], petition of the inhabitants of Peñon Blanco to the governor of Durango, Aug. 6, 1912, Antonio Castellanos to governor of Durango.

20. O'Hea 1966, 50–51.

21. Reed 1969 [1914], 200.

22. A straightforward and convincing assessment of Contreras came from a long-term American resident of Coahuila who was interviewed by U.S. military intelligence in 1916. The man, who had labored for years in Mexico, had lost all his savings and all his properties as a result of the revolution. His bitterness against Mexican revolutionary leaders was enormous, yet there was one figure among the revolutionaries for whom he expressed respect: Calixto Contreras, who had just been shot by a Carrancista firing squad. "The people liked him," he said. See MID, 8534-127, report from A. G. Reese, Sept. 18, 1916.

23. Juvenal 1916, 34.   24. W. Meyers 1988, 448–87.

25. Urquizo 1985, 387.   26. W. Meyers 1988, 448–87.

27. Puente 1937, 77.   28. Almada 1981 [1951], 514.

29. Ibid.   30. Carranza Castro 1977, 194.

31. See Grimaldo 1916.   32. L. Aguirre Benavides 1966, 15.

33. Caraveo 1992, 38–39.

34. AHDN, Cancelados, exp. José Isabel Robles, XY-III-3-144, Raúl Madero to Ramón Iturbe, June 2, 1943.

35. Reed 1969 [1914], 37.   36. Ibid., 57.

37. Juvenal 1916, 44.   38. Reed 1969 [1914], 194.

39. Urquizo 1985, 200–202.   40. Almada 1981 [1951], 520.

41. See AHDN, Cancelados, exp. Juan Medina.

42. Juvenal 1916, 8.

43. Mabel Silva, quoted in Peterson and Knoles, 1977, 193.

44. Peterson and Knoles 1977, 230.   45. O'Hea 1966, 70–71.

46. Marvin 1914, 270.   47. S. Terrazas 1985, 125.

48. Corral de Villa 1976, 86–88   49. Uriostegui Miranda 1970, 83–87.

50. Almada 1981 [1951], 522–23.

51. See Calzadíaz Barrera n.d., and interview with Jesús María López Aguirre in Osorio Zuñiga 1991, 157–77.

52. Apart from Villa, no other leader of his movement has sparked as much interest as Felipe Angeles. See, e.g., Cervantes 1964, 412; Mena Brito 1936, 303; and Mena Brito 1938, 455. These two authors are at opposite extremes concerning Angeles. Federico Cervantes was his subordinate and remained loyal to him until his death, whereas Bernardino Mena Brito was very hostile to Angeles. For more objective accounts than either of these writers provide, see Guilpain Peuliard 1991 and Gilly 1991.

53. AHDN, XI/111.1/17, Cancelados, Hoja Servicios Angeles, Dec. 1902.

54. Katz 1964, 135.

55. Cervantes 1964, 28.

56. AHDN, XI/III.1/17, vol. 2, Hoja Servicios Angeles, letter of jefe de departamento to Justicia, Apr. 23, 1908.

57. Cervantes 1964, 30–31.

58. AHDN, XI/III.1/17, vol. 1, Hoja Servicios Angeles, memorandum, Sept. 24, 1910.

59. John Womack describes this relatively mild policy of Angeles but states that at the end of his campaign, "Angeles too resorted to bombarding and burning suspect villages and executing captives en masse" (Womack 1969, 151–58).

60. King 1940, 99.

61. Cervantes 1964, 58–59.

62. King 1940, 118.

63. The strongest attack on Angeles and the most virulent accusation ever brought to bear against him was formulated in 1914 by Alvaro Obregón in a public manifesto to the Mexican people, in which he accused Angeles of having stopped bombarding the Ciudadela, where Félix Díaz's men had entrenched themselves, because Francisco de Léon de la Barra, the former provisional president, had told him that there were plans afoot to depose Madero and to replace him by Angeles (Mena Brito 1936, 49). The one thing that is correct about these accusations is that de la Barra indirectly suggested to Angeles that he might be the best candidate to replace Madero. In an interview given to the Villista newspaper *Vida Nueva* in April 1914, Angeles said that during a conference with the British minister to Mexico in the British legation, who had protested against the emplacement of Angeles's artillery near the legation, he did have a talk with de la Barra, who had taken refuge in the British compound. De la Barra told Angeles that the only way to bring peace to Mexico was for Madero to resign and be replaced by a general. Angeles objected that no general was fit to be president of Mexico, and that the one who had the most power, Huerta, was not only an alcoholic but had very bad character. De la Barra agreed and said that the military successor to Madero would have to be a friend of the latter's and would have to be chosen by Madero. The clear implication, as Angeles understood it, was that he himself would be the best candidate. De la Barra made no concrete proposal to Angeles, however, so Angeles did not follow up on this (*Vida Nueva*, Apr. 16, 1914). It seems that Madero did in fact briefly contemplate something of the sort. On February 17, 1913, the German minister to Mexico went to see Madero's secretary of foreign affairs, Pedro Paredes Lascurain, and proposed "installation of General Huerta as governor general of Mexico with full powers to end the revolution according to his own judgment." Lascurain told Huerta that he had relayed his suggestion to Madero, and that "returning after a considerable amount of time he implies that suggestion is centrally accepted. Whether it will be Huerta or someone else not yet decided" (Katz 1981, 104). That someone else might very well have been Angeles.

What is highly improbable is that Angeles suspended the bombardment of the Ciudadela because of de la Barra's suggestion. Angeles insisted that he had been given faulty shells, which were not capable of destroying the Ciudadela. Above all, had he indeed, as Obregón claimed, entered into a secret compact with Huerta, the latter would certainly not have had him arrested on the day that he overthrew Madero. A second assumption, that his hopes of becoming president prevented him from warning Madero, is equally illogical. On the contrary, if he had hoped that Madero would resign and name him as his successor, gaining Madero's confidence by denouncing Huerta would have been his best strategy.

64. AGN, Madero-Angeles correspondence, Felipe Angeles to Francisco Madero, Oct. 31, 1912.

65. AHDN, Cancelados, 8, Angeles, testimony of Garciá de la Cadena and others.

66. See Cervantes 1964, 39–57.   67. Márquez Sterling 1958 [1917], 269.

68. Ibid.   69. Cervantes 1964, 49–50.

70. AHDN, XI/III.1/12, Hoja Servicios Angeles, Cancelados.

71. SDF, 812-00-7011, H. L. Wilson to secretary of state, Apr. 4, 1913.

72. Cervantes 1964, 63–67.

73. Buckley Papers, Urquidi to Juan Urquidi, Sept. 23, 1913.

74. Guilpain Peuliard 1991, 73; Fabela 1977, 160.

75. Juvenal 1916, 33–37.   76. See Cosío Villegas 1966.

77. See Garciadiego Dantan 1988.   78. Knight 1981, 143.

79. The Zapatistas' role is best documented in Womack 1969.

80. Juvenal 1916, 33–37.

81. *Diccionario histórico y biográfico de la revolución mexicana*, 6: 281–82.

82. See Puente 1938, biography of Díaz Lombardo.

83. Federico González Garza's book *La revolución mexicana: Mi contribución político-literaria* (1936) describes his role in the Madero revolution and contains some biographical data, but it supplies no information about his activities in Chihuahua in the Villista period. His attitude to Carranza is dealt with in a series of newspaper articles entitled "Don Venustiano, el unico responsable," which he published in the newspaper *El Universal* (Mexico, D.F.), June 9, 10, and 11, and July 5, 15, 19, and 22, 1930. The most detailed information on his activity in Chihuahua is to be found in his papers in the CONDUMEX archives and in those of his brother Roque González Garza.

84. CONDUMEX, Carranza Papers, Federico González Garza to Carranza, Aug. 11, 1913.

85. On Azuela, see Robe 1979, and on Martín Luis Guzmán, Perea and Guzmán Uribiola 1987. The attitudes of these two men to Villa seem to have evolved in opposite directions. In the first edition of his famous novel *Los de abajo*, Azuela has parts favorable to Villa that were deleted from later editions of the book (Robe 1979, 19). On the other hand, Guzmán's autobiographical novel *El águila y la serpiente* (The Eagle and the Serpent) is far more critical of Villa than his presumably later *Memorias de Pancho Villa*.

86. Juvenal 1916, 21.

87. Ibid., 8.

88. Ibid., 9.

89. MFMP, subsecretario encargado del despacho to Ramon Lara, Mexican consul general, Dec. 31, 1919. See also letter from the Swiss Foreign Ministry to the Mexican minister of foreign affairs, Nov. 23, 1919.

90. Luis Alberto Sánchez 1960, 302–3; Hinojosa 1991.

91. Luis Alberto Sánchez 1960, 302.   92. Ibid., 338–39.

93. *Periódico Oficial*, June 7, 1914.   94. Juvenal 1916, 8.

95. See Hinojosa 1991.

96. In spite of his professed sympathy for Mexico, Santos Chocano supported the Guatemalan president when the latter tried to bribe a Mexican revolutionary general from southern Mexico, Carrascosa, by offering him $20,000, arms, ammunition, and other support if he would agree to create an independent republic of southern Mexico in the territories that Guatemala claimed as its own. Carrascosa, a patriot, refused, and the Guatemalan president imprisoned him. Estrada Cabrera did not give up his hope that in some way Carrascosa might still be persuaded to become head of a se-

cessionist movement in southern Mexico, however, and he sent Santos Chocano to see Carrascosa, who again refused. Santos Chocano obviously did not feel that there was a contradiction between his professed sympathy for the Mexican Revolution and his support for Guatemalan territorial encroachment on southern Mexico. See Luis Alberto Sánchez 1960, 283–84.

97. L. Aguirre Benavides 1966, 44, 94, 95.

98. See ibid., 235.

99. Shortly after Villa's defeat, Pérez Rul published a pamphlet entitled *¿Quien es Francisco Villa?* (1916) under the pseudonym Juvenal, in which he attacked both Villa and Carranza, but also insisted that Villa was not a common bandit and said that many of Villa's followers were men of honor (see also Appendix). Since Juvenal was also the pseudonym of a Spanish newspaperman who had scarcely had access to Villa, Pérez Rul's pamphlet was not taken seriously by historians and was practically forgotten. On Pérez Rul's life, see his answer to a questionnaire that Martín Luis Guzmán sent him in the Martín Luis Guzmán Papers.

Chapter Eight

1. Enrique Sánchez 1952, 12.

2. PRO, FO 371 2026 XC-A-60639, Cunard Cummins to Foreign Office, Dec. 30, 1913.

3. MID, 5761-1091-31, box 2348, Edwin Emerson to Leonard Wood, May 14, 1914.

4. *El Paso Morning Times*, July 24, 1914.

5. Gregory Mason, "Campaigning in Coahuila," *The Outlook*, June 20, 1914.

6. PHO-146.

7. Reed 1969 [1914]: 198. Edwin Emerson was more skeptical about Villa's care for the wounded. While he lauded the quality of the doctors on Villa's sanitary train and the fact that it could take care of 1,800 wounded, he also felt "that the means at their disposal were shockingly inadequate, the cars were mostly rough, ill-ventilated dirty freight cars without cots or field beds and the sufferings of the wounded in them were horribly aggravated by the ruthless conduct of the train crews, who shunted and bumped their trains back and forth with violent stops and starts, without any regard to the terrible consequences to patients lying on hard springless floors with bullet holes causing internal hemorrhages." He felt that only when the fighting took place near the railway was it possible to care for the wounded. MID, 5761-1091-31, box 2348, Emerson to Leonard Wood, May 14, 1914.

8. Urquizo 1985, 211–12.

9. Reed 1969 [1914], 64.

10. Ibid., 64–67.

11. Dr. Rubén Osorio, Archivo Privado, interview with Jesús Maria Lopez Aguirre.

12. Osorio Zuñiga 1991, 34–38, interview with Desiderio Madrid Carrasco.

13. Ibid., 113–20, interview with Pedro Romero.

14. Ibid., 186–94, interview, with Laura Trevizo Delgado.

15. Ibid., 194–208, interview Ramon Murga.

16. PHO 1-137.

17. PHO 1-148.

18. PHO 1-146.

19. PHO 146.

20. PHO 1-140.

21. PHO 1-140.

22. PHO 196.

23. PHO 1-46.

24. Osorio Zuñiga 1991, 113–20, interview with Pedro Romero.

25. Dr. Rubén Osorio, Archivo Privado, interview with Lucio Alvarado Portillo, July 21, 1988.

26. PHO 1-137.

27. PHO 1-97.

28. PHO 1-91.

29. PHO 1 97.

30. Urquizo 1985, 204–5.

31. Ibid.

32. Vargas-Arreola 1988, 27–28, 36–37, 68–69.

33. Ibid., 28.

34. Lázaro de la Garza Papers, letter of Félix Sommerfeld to Lázaro de la Garza, Aug. 6, 1914.

35. Ibid., letter of Máximo García to Lázaro de la Garza, Dec. 1, 1913.

36. Reed 1969 [1914], 142–43.

37. Thord-Gray 1960, 29.

38. Ibid.

39. Goltz 1917, 125.

40. Ibid., 132–33.

41. MID, 5761-1091-31, box 2348, Edwin Emerson to Leonard Wood, May 14, 1914.

42. For the most complete history of mercenaries during the Mexican Revolution, see L. Taylor 1993.

43. O'Hea 1966, 153–54.

44. Fatout 1951, 314.

45. The notion that Villa shot Bierce was taken up by one of Mexico's most brilliant writers, Carlos Fuentes, in his remarkable novel *The Old Gringo* (1985). Roy Morris Jr., one of Bierce's biographers, is skeptical of this account, arguing that had Bierce really spent a longer time with Villa, the numerous American correspondents who went along on Villa's campaigns would certainly have seen him and reported on his presence. Morris believes that Bierce never went to Mexico, and that his trip there was a hoax; in reality, Morris thinks, he went back to the Grand Canyon and killed himself there. No trace of his body has ever been found there, however, and there is no reason to doubt his secretary's accounts of his letters from Mexico, although one of Morris's arguments is that the originals of Bierce's letters were destroyed by his secretary, and that all that remains are the notes that she made of those letters. See Morris 1995, 254.

During and after the Mexican Revolution, U.S. consular officials and men who had been with Villa were questioned about Bierce's fate, and the responses were contradictory. Marion Letcher, who was U.S. consul in Chihuahua at the time, said that he had never heard of Bierce crossing into Mexico. Villa's representative in the United States, Félix Sommerfeld, after receiving a letter of inquiry from the U.S. chief of staff, Hugh Scott, went to Chihuahua to investigate and reported that Bierce had been sighted in Ciudad Chihuahua in January but had left there for a destination unknown. See McWilliams 1931.

46. Reed 1969 [1914], 130.

47. MID, 5761-1091-31, box 2348, Edwin Emerson to Leonard Wood, May 14, 1914.

48. Ibid.

49. MID, 5761-975, RG 165, entry 65, box 2347, report by William Mitchell, "Notes on Mexican Constitutionalists or the Northern Mexican Insurgents, July 1914."

50. MID, 5761-1091-31, box 2348, Edwin Emerson to Leonard Wood, May 14, 1914.

51. Ibid.

52. Urquizo 1985, 211–12.

53. MID, 5761-1091-31, box 2348, Edwin Emerson to Leonard Wood, May 14, 1914.

54. MID, 5761-975, RG 165, entry 65, box 2347, report by William Mitchell, "Notes on Mexican Constitutionalists or the Northern Mexican Insurgents, July 1914."

Chapter Nine

1. There is a huge literature on Woodrow Wilson's Mexican policy. The most important books on the subject are Link 1947–65 and 1963, and R. F. Smith 1972. I have also relied heavily on my own research, for which see also Katz 1981.

2. Katz 1981, 156–200.

3. Link 1963, 120.

4. Clendenen 1972, 49.

5. *WWP*, 30: 408–20, memorandum of Paul Fuller to Wilson, Aug. 20, 1914.

6. *El Paso Morning Times*, "Uncle Sam Is Alert," Feb. 16, 1914.

7. Archives du Ministère de la Guerre, Vincennes, France, 7, in 1716, Bertrand, French military attaché in the United States, to Deuxième Bureau, Dec. 30, 1914.

8. CP, vol. 9, Jean-Jules Jusserand to Gaston Doumergues, Jan. 27, 1914. Wilson's favorable attitude toward Villa seems to have been largely inspired by the report of John Reed as well as by those of his emissary John Lind (see ch. 5). The State Department representatives in Chihuahua seem to have been sharply divided over assessments of Villa. Thomas D. Edwards, the U.S. representative in Ciudad Juárez, reported: "General Villa's policy, notwithstanding the seeming harshness and cruelty in some cases, is carrying out the only promising solution for restoring peace." He applauded Villa's actions against the Spaniards, stating that "their sympathies are quite unanimous with the Huertistas and in favor of restoring the old regime and were liberal contributors to the Huerta cause." He said that they had received "lucrative concessions from the government and which they in turn used to pauperize the natives" (SDF, 812.00/10336, Edwards to secretary of state, Dec. 23, 1913).

Marion Letcher, the U.S. consul in Chihuahua, harbored an almost pathological hatred for Villa, but he conceded that "public order has been and is excellent. Drinking saloons have been closed since Villa entered Chihuahua. Military movements are conducted almost noiselessly and soldiers are rather conspicuous by their absence on the streets. The discipline of the troops appears to be excellent and the morale among officers and men is exceptional." He considered Villa as nothing more than a common bandit, while the Spaniards whose property Villa had expropriated were with few exceptions harmless merchants who had not intervened in Mexican politics (ibid., 812-0011043, Letcher to secretary of state, Feb. 21, 1914). Letcher's attacks on Villa in a later report exhibit his own profoundly racist attitude: "Villa has at least but shown himself faithful to the bloody laws of his race which has never at any period of his history shown any regard for human life," he wrote, and described Villa's "loutish, half domineering leer; his bulging eyeballs, with glittering starry pupils surrounded by half right whites, which give the impression of being bloodshot; his unkempt, eerily standing hair; his coarse thick lipped mouth, suggesting a mixture of Negro blood; his rather delicate hands giving the lie to the claim sometimes made that he has ever done an honest day's work." Letcher insisted that "the diabolical love of torture which is common to Indian blood everywhere can not be understood by a white man," and he called Villa "a very devil incarnate" (ibid., 812-00-13232, Letcher to secretary of state, Aug. 25, 1914).

9. Katz 1981, 156–200.

10. H. O'Connor 1937, 336–37.

11. Mora 1991, 624.

12. AA Bonn, Mexiko 1, Paul von Hintze to Theobald von Bethmann-Hollweg, Sept. 24, 1913.

13. Yale University Library, Diary of Col. House, Oct. 24, 1913.

14. Hill 1973, 134–37.

15. AMAE, CP, Politique intérieure, vol. 9, Ayguesparse to foreign minister, Dec. 26, 1914.

16. Hill 1973, 133, 227, 196.

17. HHSTA, Pa Berichte, USA, 1914, ambassador in Washington to Count Leopold Berchtold, May 5, 1914.

18. Hill 1973, 227–28.

19. *New York Times*, Hopkins Obituary, June 23, 1932.

20. Grieb 1971.

21. Katz 1991, 135.

22. Fabela and de Fabela 1960–76, 8: 246–49.

23. Grieb 1971, 66.

24. *New York Herald*, July 1, 2, 3, 4, 1914. Sometime in 1914, probably after these revelations by the *Herald* about the links between Hopkins, Pierce, and Carranza, the latter broke off relations with Hopkins, who by mid 1915 seems to have switched sides radically and was now opposed to the recognition of Carranza by the United States. In September 1915, Felíx Sommerfeld expressed the conviction that Hopkins could be very helpful in a campaign of public relations in favor of Villa and of opposition to the recognition of Carranza (Garfield Papers, Scott to Garfield, Sept. 10, 1915). At the beginning of 1915, Hopkins was replaced by another lobbyist, Charles A. Douglas, a former judge, who was also a personal friend of Secretary of State Bryan's and had a history of working as a lobbyist for Latin American countries. He was offered the huge sum of $50,000, plus an additional premium if the Carranza administration were recognized by the United States before the end of 1915 (SRE, Aw leg. 480-X7, Zubaran Capmany to Arredondo, June 1, 1915; Douglas to Arredondo, Jan. 21, 1915). He was, in fact, paid an extra $20,000 in December 1915 after the United States recognized the Carranza government (ibid., Douglas to Arredondo, Dec. 9, 1915).

25. Department of Justice, file nos. 9-16-12-5305, summary sheet for disposal of interned alien enemy, Felíx Sommerfeld, n.d.; SDF, 812.00/13232, Marion Letcher to William Jennings Bryan, Aug. 25, 1914.

26. Katz 1981, 335.

27. Department of Justice, Sommerfeld file, undated statement by S. G. Hopkins, Hibbs Building, Washington, D.C., Department of Justice, continuation of hearing of Felíx A. Sommerfeld, held at the New York Port Alien Enemy Bureau, June 24, 1918.

28. Katz 1981, 335–36.

29. Harper 1968, 129.

30. Scott Papers, letter to his wife, Sept. 26, 1914.

31. Harper 1968, 1–33, 48, 63–93.

32. The best general biographies of Reed are Hicks 1936, Rosenstone 1982, and Hovey 1982. For Reed's activities in Mexico, see Ruffinelli 1983, 11–107.

33. O'Hea 1966, 157.

34. Hicks 1936, 134.

35. Rosenstone 1982, 166–67.

36. *WWP*, 30: 231–38, John Reed, June 30, 1914.

37. Clendenen 1972, 200–201.   38. E. Meyer 1970.

39. Foner 1983.   40. *Appeal to Reason*, Mar. 21, 1914.

41. Foner 1983, 243.

42. SDF, 812.00/13232, Marion Letcher to secretary of state, Aug. 25, 1914.

43. *Charleston News and Courier*, quoted in *Literary Digest*, May 16, 1914.

44. *Sunset* 32 (1914): 408–9.

45. *World Herald*, quoted in *Literary Digest*, May 16, 1914.

46. Alexander Powell quoted in *Literary Digest*, Apr. 11, 1914.

47. *Birmingham Herald* quoted in *Literary Digest*, July 25, 1914.

48. For an excellent description and analysis of the complex relationship between Villa and Hollywood, see de los Reyes 1985 and 1986, 98–132; and de Orellana 1991.

49. De los Reyes, 1986, 103.

50. The original contracts, between "Francisco Villa acting by and through General E. Aguirre-Benavides, the duly authorized and empowered agent and attorney in fact of the said Francisco Villa and Gunther R. Lessing . . . Mutual Film Company . . . acting by and through Frank N. Thayer," can be found in CONDUMEX, Archivo Federico González Garza, folio 3057.

51. See de los Reyes 1986, 125.

52. *New York Times*, Feb. 11, 1914.

53. De Orellana 1991, 119–21.

54. PRO, FO 371 2035, C-A-60539, affidavit of Mr. Frances Michael Tone regarding the death of Mr. William S. Benton.

55. *El Correo de Chihuahua*, June 7, 10, 11, 1910; see also Wasserman 1984, 111–12.

56. CONDUMEX, Federico González Garza Papers, proceedings of the Commission of Inquiry into the Benton Affair, doc. 3135, *comprobante* 57, testimony of Luis Hernández on Mar. 24, 1914.

57. Mexican Northwestern Railroad Papers, University of Texas at Austin, H. C. Ferris to H. I. Miller, Feb. 22, 1912.

58. This account is based on two contemporary investigations into the Benton affair carried out independently of each other by British authorities and by the Carranza administration.

59. Proceedings of the Commission of Inquiry (cited n. 56 above), p. 17, Mar. 17, 1914.

60. PRO, FO 371-4496-3228, Cunard Cummins to Foreign Office, Aug. 13, 1920.

61. PRO, FO 371 2035, C-A-60539, affidavit of Mr. Frances Michael Tone regarding the death of Mr. William S. Benton.

62. The Commission of Inquiry that Carranza appointed received the proceedings of the phony court-martial, one of whose participants was supposed to have been Adrián Aguirre Benavides. When the commission requested more details from him, he told them that the court-martial was a fake, that Benton had in fact been executed by Fierro, and that he had told this to Carranza. Proceedings of Commission of Inquiry, pp. 17–18.

63. Ibid.

64. For detailed analysis, including Carranza's reaction to the Benton episode, see Fabela 1985, Grieb 1969, and Cumberland 1972, 281–87. The record of the investigation carried out by the British consul, John Percival, without the help of the Mexican authorities can be found in PRO, FO 371-2035-XC-A-60539, Sir Cecil Spring-Rice to Sir Edward Grey, Apr. 7, 1914, containing both the results of Percival's inquiries and various affidavits and documents. For the papers of the commission that Carranza named to examine the Benton case, whose findings have never been published, see CONDUMEX, Archivo Federico González Garza, document 3135. The American documents on the case, which are widely known, have been published in *Foreign Relations of the United States*, while the unpublished parts are contained in the 812-00 files of the State Department.

65. S. Terrazas 1985, 117–18, 119.

66. Ibid., 131.

67. De la Huerta 1957, 68–69.

68. Cervantes 1960, 55.

69. Gómez 1966, 32; and Magaña 1985, 3: 287.

70. Buckley Papers, University of Texas at Austin, Manuel Urquidi to Roberto Pesqueira, Dec. 18, 1913.

71. *DHRM*, Revolución constitucionalista, 1: 201, Venustiano Carranza to Silvestre Terrazas, Dec. 18, 1913.

72. Ibid.

73. L. Aguirre Benavides 1966, 74–75.

74. *DIIRM*, Revolución constitucionalista, 2, no. 1: 409–10, Meza Gutiérrez to Venustiano Carranza, Dec. 18, 1913.

75. Ibid., 1: 206–8, Francisco Villa to Venustiano Carranza, Dec. 23, 1913.

76. "Carranza has wired . . . Villa in Chihuahua that further confiscation of property by the constitutionalists in the state of Chihuahua must cease . . . even in the case of the vast Terrazas property which had been confiscated by General Villa if the Terrazas family can show that they acquired their land in a legal manner it will be restored to them" (*El Paso Morning Times*, Mar. 12, 1914).

77. *DHRM*, Rev. Const., 1: 180, Jesús Acuña to Venustiano Carranza, Nov. 18, 1913.

78. S. Terrazas 1985, 130–31; L. Aguirre Benavides 1966, 119–20.

79. S. Terrazas 1985, 133.

80. Barragán Rodriguez 1985, 1: 443–45.

81. For somewhat differing assessments of the U.S. landing in Veracruz, see Quirk 1964 [1962] and Ulloa 1971, 162–87.

82. *WWP*, 29: 484–85.

83. *WWP*, 29: 494–95, George C. Carothers to William Jennings Bryan, Apr. 23, 1914.

84. Ibid., 504–5, Francisco Villa to Woodrow Wilson, Apr. 25, 1914.

85. L. Aguirre Benavides 1966, 124–25.

86. Barragán Rodriguez 1985, 1: 456. While Barragán is not an objective observer—he was a high Carrancista official—there is no reason to doubt his statement. Angeles was probably the most pro-American of all the revolutionary leaders and a great admirer of Woodrow Wilson. In addition, he was deeply opposed to Carranza, so that it is quite logical that he should have encouraged Villa not to join Carranza in his protest against the U.S. invasion of Veracruz.

87. Since Zapata's answer to it exists, it is possible to reconstruct some of the main contents of Villa's letter, although I have not been able to find it. For Zapata's reply, see n. 88 below.

88. Archive of Carlos Reyes Aviles, owned by Salvador Reyes, Ensenada, Baja California, Emiliano Zapata to Francisco Villa, Jan. 19, 1914.

89. Magaña 1985, 2: 274–86.

90. *El Correo del Bravo*, Apr. 30, 1914.

91. For the best description and analysis of the origins and ideology of the men from Sonora, see Aguilar Camín 1977.

92. Ibid., 180, 186, 222–28.

93. Ibid., 366–68.

94. Maytorena Papers, letters from Alberto Piña to José María Maytorena, Apr. 4, 1914 and July 13, 1914.

95. Ibid., Alberto Piña to José María Maytorena, Apr. 11, 1914.

96. Ibid., Alberto Piña to José María Maytorena, Apr. 30, 1914.

97. *El Correo del Bravo*, Apr. 15, 1914.

98. Archivo Roque González Garza, undated memorandum.

99. Guzmán 1965, 193.

100. S. Terrazas 1985, 191–92.

101. Ibid.

102. Ibid., 145–46.

103. Ibid., 147.
104. Archivo Roque González Garza.
105. Guzmán 1966, 214.
106. Cervantes 1960, 161.
107. Ibid., 162.
108. Guzmán 1965, 270.
109. Barragán Rodriguez 1985, 1: 446–47.
110. Guzmán 1965, 220.
111. Almada 1981 [1951], 516.
112. Barragán Rodriguez 1985, 1: 542.
113. Muñoz 1961, 2: 185. The most complete description and analysis of the siege of Zacatecas can be found in Candelas Villalba 1989.
114. PRO, FO 204 444 136852, James Caldwell to Lionel Carden, Mexico City, June 29, 1914
115. There are widely differing estimates as to the number of federal troops in Zacatecas. The revolutionaries estimated the number to be 12,000, but some historians, relying on scattered federal sources, have estimated it at no more than 5,000 men. The different estimates are best summarized in Candelas Villalba 1989, 158 n. 53. For the British estimates, see PRO, FO 204 444 136852, James Caldwell to Lionel Carden, Mexico City, June 29, 1914. I believe the estimates by the revolutionaries to be correct, since the number of 12,000 is corroborated by a report from the British consul in Zacatecas, who maintained close relations with the federal commanders in the city.
116. CONDUMEX, Rubio Navarrete Papers, undated memorandum on government plans, "Situacion especial el 21 de Abril de 1914."
117. Felipe Angeles, "La Batalla de Zacatecas," in Cervantes 1960, 165.
118. Ibid.
119. PRO, FO 204 444 136852, James Caldwell to Lionel Carden, June 29, 1914.
120. Felipe Angeles, in Cervantes 1960, 177–78.
121. PRO FO 204 444 136852, James Caldwell to Lionel Carden, June 19, 1916.
122. Felipe Angeles, in Cervantes 1960, 179.
123. PRO FO 204 444 136852, James Caldwell to Lionel Carden, June 19, 1916.
124. Muñoz 1965, 2.
125. PRO FO 204 444 136852, James Caldwell to Lionel Carden, June 19, 1916.
126. Muñoz 1965, 2: 215.
127. Ibid., 260.
128. Ibid., 217.
129. Ibid., 222–23.
130. Cumberland 1972, 137.
131. PRO, FO 204 444 136852, James Caldwell to Lionel Carden, June 29, 1914.

Chapter Ten

1. Hill 1973, 148
2. SDF, 81200-11654, secretary of state to George C. Carothers, Apr. 24, 1914.
3. *WWP*, 30: 220–21, Francisco Villa to Woodrow Wilson, in Lázaro de la Garza to Felíx A. Sommerfeld, June 27, 1914.
4. Ibid.
5. From the behavior of the U.S. authorities, it was clear that they neither wanted Villa to have sufficient ammunition to attack Mexico City nor wanted him to be so short of weapons that he would be decisively weakened. This was probably the reason why smuggling regulations were relaxed along the U.S.–Mexican border. While smuggled arms could be confiscated, the smugglers themselves were not subjected either to arrest or to penalties. This was clear encouragement to smuggling. See Holcombe 1968, 89, 90.

6. Fabela and de Fabela 1960–76, 114: 10–11; Link 1947–65, 2: 41; Haley 1970, 83–107; Ulloa 1971, 203–60.

7. L. F. Amaya 1975, 35.

8. Ibid.

9. Maytorena Papers, undated statement by José María Maytorena; statement by Alberto Piña, written on Aug. 28, 1918.

10. L. Aguirre Benavides 1966, 160–61.

11. Maytorena Papers, undated statement by José María Maytorena; statement by Alberto Piña, written on Aug. 28, 1918.

12. *WWP*, 30: 411, Paul Fuller to Woodrow Wilson, Aug. 20, 1914.

13. Ibid., 411–15.   14. Cervantes 1960, 196.

15. Ibid., 200–201.   16. Quirk 1960, 42–43.

17. Maytorena Papers, Alberto Piña to José María Maytorena, July 13, 1914.

18. Ibid.

19. Ibid., Francisco Villa to José María Maytorena, Aug. 19 and 24.

20. Obregón 1970, 171.   21. Ibid., 172.

22. Ibid.   23. Ibid., 174.

24. Aguilar Camín 1977, 371–72.   25. Obregón 1970, 169.

26. Ibid., 186–87.

27. Maytorena Papers, José María Maytorena to Felipe Angeles, Sept. 17, 1914.

28. Obregón 1970, 199–200.   29. Ibid., 202–3.

30. Osorio Zuñiga 1991, 50.   31. Obregón 1970, 203.

32. Corral de Villa 1976, 107–8. There is no disagreement between Obregón's own memoirs and those of Villistas who were present during this event that Obregón was on the point of being executed by Villa. Obregón leaves open the question as to who, if anyone, persuaded Villa to change his opinion and to rescind the order of execution. He indicates that both Fierro and Raúl Madero were in the room to which Villa proceeded when he left Obregón and seems to intimate that Raúl Madero interceded in his favor. Though he says nothing about the role of Luz Corral, Obregón was in later years very favorably disposed toward her, and in a letter written to her in 1923, he thanked her for the *atenciónes* (attentions) she had shown him during his stay in Chihuahua. This reference is ambivalent; it could simply refer to her hospitality, since he lived at Villa's house when he went to Chihuahua, but it could also refer to attempts to save his life. It is not entirely surprising that some of Villa's former supporters who survived the revolution attempted to take credit for saving Obregón's life. Luis Aguirre Benavides, Villa's former secretary, states that as soon as he heard about the violent Villa-Obregón altercation and Villa's threats to kill Obregón, he called Raúl Madero, and believes that it was the latter who pacified Villa (L. Aguirre Benavides 1966, 168). Silvestre Terrazas claims to have been one of the first to try to talk Villa out of executing Obregón, telling him that he had no bad intentions toward Villa and was ready for a compromise, and that the real villain was Carranza; in addition, Terrazas says, Angeles, Raúl Madero, and Federico Gonzáles Garza all tried to persuade Villa to rescind the order of execution (S. Terrazas 1985, 168).

33. Obregón 1970, 204.   34. Osorio Zuñiga 1991, 50.

35. See Obregon 1970.   36. Cervantes 1960, 263.

37. Ibid., 262.   38. V. Alessio Robles 1979, 91.

39. Two of Villa's former supporters give different accounts of these events. According to Silvestre Terrazas (1985, 168, 169), it was not Villa but someone else—Terrazas does not say who—who gave the orders to have Obregón shot; Terrazas concurs, however, with Obregón's assertion that Robles and Roque González Garza

saved Obregón's life. Enrique Pérez Rul, one of Villa's secretaries, says (Juvenal 1916, 21) that the head of the telegraph office in Chihuahua, a man named Orozco, came to see Luis Aguirre Benavides, another secretary of Villa's, asking whether a telegram he had been instructed to send ordering General Almanza to have Obregón shot was genuine and had indeed been signed by Villa. Aguirre Benavides consulted Pérez Rul, who went to see Villa and asked him to confirm the authenticity of the telegram. When Villa did so, Pérez Rul objected, telling him that Obregón's life should be sacred to all members of the División del Norte, and Villa finally relented and rescinded the execution order. Pérez Rul's account seems somewhat improbable. Why should a secretary have been able in a short conversation to persuade Villa to spare Obregón's life when some of his most powerful generals had failed to do so? See also V. Alessio Robles 1979, 91.

40. Obregón 1970, 209.

41. L. F. Amaya 1966, 60. For a history of these negotiations, see also Quirk 1960, 81–86.

42. Quirk 1960, 40–45, 84.

43. L. F. Amaya 1966, 95.

44. The two standard works on the history of the Revolutionary Convention are Quirk 1960 and L. F. Amaya 1966. A new and interesting analysis can be found in Avila Espinosa 1988, and Aguascalientes 1990 contains essays and panel deliberations on the history of the Convention. Some of the most outstanding work on the Convention can be found in *Asi fué la revolución mexicana*, vol. 5 (1985).

45. *WWP*, 30: 339–40, William Jennings Bryan to Woodrow Wilson, Aug. 3, 1914.

46. L. F. Amaya 1966, 123.

47. The most exhaustive biographical data on Roque González Garza can be found in his interviews with Daniel Cazes (Cazes 1973, 75–127).

48. Angeles expressed this view in a letter to José Maria Maytorena, saying, "I believe that their [the Zapatistas] Plan of Ayala is bad even if it is only applied locally in the region controlled by Zapatismo" (Angeles 1982, 230–31).

49. Barrera Fuentes 1965, 1: 228. 50. Ibid., 1: 230.
51. Ibid., 1: 228. 52. Ibid., 1: 230–31.
53. Cumberland 1972, 178. 54. Barrera Fuentes 1965, 1: 254–55.
55. Magaña 1985, 5: 198. 56. Ibid., 199.
57. Barrera Fuentes 1965, 1: 506. 58. Aguilar Camin 1977, 371, 372.
59. Vasconcelos 1983: 616. 60. V. Alessio Robles 1979, 316.

61. *Diccionario histórico y biográfico de la revolución mexicana* (1991), 4: 89. This was not a clever move on Obregón's part, since he and Diéguez had never been close. Several years later, when Obregón was president, Diéguez revolted. When Diéguez was captured, Obregón had him shot.

62. Silva Herzog 1960.

63. Cumberland 1972, 164. Like Cumberland, Ramón Ruíz feels that there were no "major ideological barriers standing between Villa and the Constitutionalists," and that what drove Villa and his generals to fight was to a large extent possession of the haciendas they had taken over from the traditional oligarchy in Chihuahua (Ruíz 1980, 188, 196–99).

64. Gilly 1994. John Hart, too, sees class as a main element of the Villa-Carranza conflict, a "struggle that surfaced in mid-1914 between the victorious provincial elite and pequeña burguesa-led forces arrayed with Carranza and the populist northern cohorts of Villa with their initially ranchero artisans and rural lower-class leaders" (Hart 1987, 14).

65. Knight 1986, 2: 263–74.

66. Womack 1991, 154.
67. Guerra 1981, 785–814.
68. *Appeal to Reason*, Apr. 3, 17, and May 1, 1915.
69. Aguilar Camín 1977, 432–33.
70. Mora Torres, 1991.
71. I derive this from my own research in the Archivo de la Reforma Agraria in Mexico City, where the complaints from Coahuila outside of the Laguna area are far fewer than those emanating from Chihuahua, Durango, or the Laguna.
72. ST Papers, Silvestre Terrazas to Luis Caballero, July 2, 1914.
73. Aguilar Camín 1977, 416.

Chapter Eleven

1. ST Papers, Manuel Chao, memorandum, n.d., 2.
2. Beezley 1973, 89–114; Almada 1964, 242–44.
3. Archivo de Ciudad Guerrero, Piedad Pérez de Olveda to municipal president, c/o Julio Acosta, Mar. 22, 1915.
4. ST Papers, pt. 1, box 14, Chihuahua (state) Cuerpo Especial del Supremo Gobierno folder, 1915.
5. *El Paso Morning Times*, Feb. 5, 1914.
6. ST Papers, draft electoral law, Oct. 1914.
7. ST Papers, undated memorandum.
8. ST Papers, draft of report by Fidel Avila, Apr. 1, 1915.
9. Barrera Fuentes 1965, 2: 258–59.
10. Barrera Fuentes, 2: 254, intervention of Quevedo at the meeting of the Revolutionary Convention in Cuernavaca on Feb. 4, 1915.
11. ST Papers, MB-18, box 110, pp. 1–89, report of the Administración General de Confiscaciones.
12. Ibid., report from Hacienda San Miguel de Bavicora.
13. Reed 1969 [1914], 53.
14. See Schulze 1990 and 1993, with whose estimates my own largely correlate.
15. Silvestre Terrazas mentions and rejects these accusations in his memoirs. See S. Terrazas 1985, 183–84, 203.
16. SDF, 812-00-15595, David Barrows to Benjamin Ide Wheeler, president of the University of California, July 25, 1915.
17. ST Papers, report from San Isidro.
18. Ibid., report from the Rancho de San Vicente y Palma.
19. Ibid., report from the Rancho de San José and Hacienda de San Carmen.
20. Ibid., report from the Hacienda de Orientales.
21. Ibid., report from the Mancomunidad Ciénaga de Mata.
22. Ibid., report from the Rancho de San Vicente y Palma
23. Ibid., report from the Hacienda de Sombreretillo.
24. Ibid., reports from the properties confiscated from Miguel Guerra.
25. ST Papers, undated memorandum, "Asuntos que tratar con el General Villa."
26. S. Terrazas 1985, 181.
27. SDF, 812-00-14365, Zach Lamar Cobb to William Jennings Bryan, Feb. 1, 1915.
28. Koreck 1988; Alonso 1995; Nugent 1993, ch. 3.
29. Lloyd 1988.
30. *Periódico Oficial*, Mar. 8, 1914.
31. MLG, Francisco Villa to Colonel Gabino Duran, Nov. 12, 1914.

32. Ibid., Oct. 18, 1914.

33. For biographical data on Manuel Bonilla, see M. Gómez 1966, 102–5.

34. CONDUMEX, Archivo Federico González Garza, letter of Federico González Garza to Manuel Bonilla, Apr. 7, 1914.

35. See M. Gómez 1966, 155–216.

36. Ibid., 101–23.

37. *Periódico Oficial*, Jan. 24 and 31, 1915.

38. Almada 1964, 2: 212.

39. Cervantes 1960, 773–74.

40. Archivo de Ciudad Guerrero, Comisión Agraria del Estado de Chihuahua al Presidente Municipal de Ciudad Guerrero, Feb. 11, 1915.

41. Nugent 1993, 100–105.   42. Hart 1987, 274–75.

43. See Castillo n.d.   44. Young 1968, 157–60.

45. Weekly report #46, Feb. 1914.

46. Corral de Villa 1976, 58. In an interview with the *El Paso Morning Times*, Feb. 17, 1914, Villa said that he had not pursued Castillo for some time because he owed him "a debt of gratitude, because, when I was struggling to obtain mastery in Chihuahua and sent my wife to the border Castillo permitted her to pass through his lines unmolested. I was grateful to him for that act of kindness and always had a liking for him because of the great service he rendered to our chief, Madero, in the early days of the first revolution." Villa's attitude to Castillo changed entirely after the Cumbre Tunnel attack, when he said that Castillo had "forfeited all claims upon me by the savagery he displayed in causing the great sacrifice of the lives of innocent in the burning of the Cumbre Tunnel" (*El Paso Morning Times*, Feb. 17, 1914).

47. Almada 1968, 129.   48. Castillo n.d.

49. H. O'Connor 1937: 336–37.   50. *El Paso Times*, Jan. 3, 1914.

51. Ibid., June 23, 1914.

52. *Engineering and Mining Journal*, vol. 101, Jan. 1 and 8, 1916.

53. Clendenen 1972, 160–63.

54. Meyers 1991.

55. Osorio Zuñiga 1991, 123–24, interview with Dr. Francisco Uranga Vallarta.

56. Ibid., 60–61, interview with Francisco Gil Piñon.

57. Guzmán 1984 [193?], 393–94.

58. S. Terrazas 1985, 151–59.

59. ST Papers, draft report by Silvestre Terrazas, p. 8.

60. S. Terrazas 1985, 179.

61. Herman Whitaker, "Villa Bandit-Patriot," *The Independent*, May 6, 1914.

62. *Periódico Oficial*, Feb. 15, 1914.

63. *El Paso Morning Times*, July 17, 1914.

64. Herman Whitaker, "Villa-Bandit Patriot," *The Independent*, June 8, 1914.

65. Case 1917, 134–35.

66. Mexican Northwestern Papers, J. O. Crockett to James Morgan, Feb. 8, 1913.

67. *Periódico Oficial*, Sept. 6, 1914.   68. Ibid.

69. W. Meyers 1991, 339.   70. *Vida Nueva*, Apr. 2, 1914.

71. ST Papers, "Velada musical y literaria."

72. Reed 1969 [1914], 113–15.

73. *Vida Nueva*, Apr. 13, 1914.

74. ST Papers, memorandum to all *jefes de oficina*, Mar. 13, 1914.

75. Ibid., Cuerpo Especial del Supremo Gobierno folder, 1915.

76. ST Papers, draft of report of Fidel Avila, Apr. 1, 1915.

77. SDF 81200-15595, David Barrows to Benjamin Ide Wheeler, July 25, 1915.

78. Knight 1986, 2: 125.

79. ST Papers, report from San Ignacio.

80. Hall 1981, 200–202.

81. SDF, Record Group 59, file 812.00/14622, undated report by Duval West to secretary of state.

82. *Vida Nueva*, Apr. 11, 1914.

83. SDF, 812-00-15595, David Barrows to Benjamin Ide Wheeler, July 25, 1915.

84. PRO, FO 204:445:822, Patrick O'Hea to W. B. Hohler, Gómez Palacio, Durango, Dec. 8, 1914.

Chapter Twelve

1. SDF, 81200-14061, George C. Carothers to secretary of state, December 18, 1914.

2. Ibid., 81200-14048, León Canova to secretary of state, December 8, 1914.

3. Ibid.

4. Cervantes 1960: 362–66.

5. Ibid.

6. Quirk 1960, 136–40.

7. Quoted in Ankerson 1984, 66.

8. See Ankerson 1984, 73–75, and Falcón 1984, 84–85.

9. See Buve 1988, 338–75.

10. *Diccionario histórico y biográfico de la revolución mexicana*, 4: 123–24.

11. On Maytorena's conservative policies, see Aguilar Camín 1977, 364–67.

12. Knight 1986, 2: 18.

13. Valadés 1984, 77.

14. Barrera Fuentes 1965, 2: 152–67, meeting of Feb. 2, 1915.

15. These activities of some members of the Madero family were revealed at a trial in Los Angeles in 1919, in which Alberto Madero sued Lázaro de la Garza for the return of a large sum of money that Madero claimed he had advanced to de la Garza to buy ammunition for Villa. See *Los Angeles Express*, Mar. 27, 1919.

16. Katz 1976, 259–73.

17. Ruiz 1980, 189–91.

18. CONDUMEX, Archivo Roque González Garza, Federico González Garza to Roque González Garza, Sept. 1915.

19. Quirk 1960, 118.

20. For the best description and assessment of Lucio Blanco, see Aguilar Mora 1990, 158–63.

21. Antonio Agacio, Chilean chargé d'affaires in Mexico to Chilean ambassador in the United States, Jan. 9, 1915, in Serrano 1986, 204.

22. *Vida Nueva*, Feb. 16, 1915.

23. Alvaro Obregón to Venustiano Carranza, Nov. 16, 1916, quoted in Ulloa 1981, 4: 36.

24. *Vida Nueva*, Nov. 21, 1915.

25. Garciadiego Dantan 1981.

26. *New York American*, July 19, 1914, interview with Villa by John Roberts.

27. Corral 1976, 92.

28. Buckley Papers, University of Texas at Austin, papers of Eber C. Byam, Nov. 15, 1915, Archives of Catholic Church Extension Society; Quirk 1973, 54.

29. Cuzin 1973, 65.

30. *Vida Nueva*, Feb. 5, 1915.

31. See Quirk 1973, 68–69.

32. Aguilar Camín 1977, 364–67.

33. Villa never mentioned in his memoirs or in interviews that he had any deal-

ings with the Zuloagas prior to 1910. It is far more probable that his leniency toward them was owing to their family ties to Madero.

34. AMAE, CP, 12: 99.

35. Ibid., Ayguesparse to Ministère des Affaires étrangères, Aug. 22, 1914.

36. Ibid., Oct. 6, 1914.

37. AMAE, CP, vol. 9, Ayguesparse to Ministère des Affaires étrangères, Dec. 31, 1914.

38. PRO, FO 371 2961 3167, Harrison to Cunard Cummins, May 12, 1917.

39. Carranza's southern strategy is described and analyzed for Yucatán in Joseph 1980, 93–150. For Chiapas, see Benjamin 1989, 99–143, and Garcia de Léon 1985, 2: 14–155. For Tabasco, see María y Campos 1939.

40. In addition to the sources cited in n. 39, see also Hernández Chávez 1993 on the rebellion in Chiapas.

41. On the Peláez movement, see Brown 1993, 253–307, and Garciadiego Dantan 1981, 95–153. See also L. Meyer 1991a, 201–34. On Britain's relations with Peláez, see L. Meyer 1991a, 201–34, and Katz 1981, 461–71.

42. On Carranza's attitude to Limantour, Terrazas, and Creel, see Katz 1981, 293, 534–38.

43. Valadés 1976, 2: 541.

44. SDF, 812.00/14061, León Canova to secretary of state, Dec. 16, 1914.

45. Quirk 1960, 139.   46. Ibid., 144; Womack 1969: 222.

47. L. Aguirre Benavides 1966, 231.   48. Guzman 1930, 290–92.

49. L. Aguirre Benavides 1966, 231.

50. Pearson Papers, Frederick Adams to Lord Cowdray, Jan. 11, 1915.

51. Ibid.

52. *El Paso Morning Times*, Dec. 14, 1914.

53. Ibid.

54. Pearson Papers, Frederick Adams to Lord Cowdray, Jan. 11, 1915.

55. SDF, 812.00/14061, Canova to secretary of state, Dec. 16, 1914.

56. L. Aguirre Benavides 1966, 214–15.   57. Quirk 1960, 148.

58. Ibid. 150–79.   59. Ibid.

60. SRE, Mexican embassy, Washington, D.C., intercepted telegram, Eugenio Aguirre Benavides to Felipe Angeles, Jan. 24, 1915.

61. Ibid., Angeles to Eugenio Aguirre Benavides, Jan. 24, 1915.

62. Luis Aguirre Benavides 1966, 214–15.

63. Obregón 1970, 236–38.   64. *New York Times*, Apr. 30, 1915.

65. Ibid.   66. Ibid., May 1, 1915.

67. Ibid. This was by no means the only attempt by the Carrancista propaganda machine to discredit Angeles by forging letters attributed to him. Another letter that also has all the earmarks of a forgery seems to have been transmitted by Carrancistas in the United States to the State Department. It was a letter, allegedly, addressed by Felipe Angeles to one of the main representatives of Mexico's conservatives in the United States, Jorge Vera Estañol, stating that he and Villa were willing to enter into an alliance with Huerta, who had just returned to the United States from exile in Spain: "I am sending you copies of the message sent to me by General Villa relative to Huerta's propositions as contained in his letter of the 16th ultimo. I must say to you that General Villa as well as myself and other chiefs are disposed to entering into the agreement, so long as the result of it will be the peace of Mexico and pleasing to the members of the Convention, all of whom are the friends of Villa and of our cause. In the meantime, inform General Huerta that his presence on the frontier at the present time would be entirely inopportune and dangerous and serve to compli-

cate a situation already lamentable. It is better to wait than to act precipitately." The letter is dated May 8, 1915, and according to the Mexican consul in Los Angeles, he had obtained the document from a man named Solano and his wife, "who in exchange for remuneration are being very useful in our cause." The archives of the Mexican embassy in Washington contain no copy of the original and no signature that can be claimed to be that of Angeles. Solano also sold another letter to the Mexican consulate, allegedly written by Vera Estañol to Huerta, and dated May 10, 1915, stating: "Villa is the representative of large groups of armed forces tending to the creation of a savage military system with no other laws than those of violence and robbery. If we could direct all these energies into one single current of order, the victory of our cause would be infallible. But Villa is enriching his friends and creating a military caste that will constitute the nucleus of restoration. If we could eliminate the Maderos from Villa's ranks, General Angeles could take care of the rest: but the latter is an ambitious character and we must keep him on our side" (Mexican embassy, Washington, D.C., leg. 461-XF.XP 3). Not only is the authenticity such a letter highly unlikely, in view of Villa's and Angeles's profound hatred of Huerta, but such an alliance would also have been counterproductive. This was a time when Villa was seeking by all means to obtain, if not recognition by, at least the goodwill of, the United States, and aligning himself with Huerta, Woodrow Wilson's bête noire, would have been suicidal. In addition, Huerta had very little to offer. He had no troops and practically no supporters in Mexico. In the final analysis, the Carrancista authorities themselves must have been convinced that the letter was a forgery, since unlike other forgeries, such as Díaz's alleged letter to Angeles, they never attempted to use it in their propaganda.

68. AHDN XI/481.5/294, Tamaulipas, folio 40, Antonio Villareal to Venustiano Carranza, Jan. 22, 1915.

69. J. Turner 1915.

70. On the Red Battalions, see Carr 1976, 1: 77–120; J. Meyer 1970, 30–55.

71. Quirk 1960, 66.

72. *Vida Nueva*, Nov. 18, 1914.

73. Ibid., Nov. 21, 1914. Félix Palavicini, a newspaper editor, was secretary of education under Carranza and was considered one of Carranza's most influential advisors.

74. Ibid.

75. *Vida Nueva*, Jan. 30, 1915.

76. Ibid., Mar. 19, 1915.

77. Ibid., Mar. 20, 1915.

78. Barrera Fuentes 1965, 2: 248.

79. Ibid., 2: 237.

80. Ibid., 2: 229, 240.

81. Ibid., 3: 150, meeting of the Revolutionary Convention on Mar. 8, 1915.

82. Amaya 1966, 264–65.

83. Barrera Fuentes 1965, 3: 364–68.

84. Ibid. 364–65.

85. Amaya 1966, 271.

86. Barrera Fuentes 1965, 3: 548.

87. This was clearly expressed by the fact that when miners in Chihuahua demanded to be paid in gold, and not in worthless Villista paper, Villa agreed, although his financial adviser, Lázaro de la Garza, strongly urged him to reject the workers' demands (Lázaro de la Garza Papers, de la Garza to Villa, May 9, 1915, 1–148).

88. Katz 1981, 283. See also Díaz Soto y Gama 1976.

89. María y Campos 1939, 101–3.

90. Aguilar Camín 1977, 416.

91. Almada 1964, 2: 212.

92. Ibid.

93. V. Alessio Robles 1979, 408–9.

94. Cervantes 1964, 194–95.

95. Hall 1981, 102–4.

96. Cuzin 1983, 37.

97. Ibid., 38–39.

98. Ibid., 42.

99. Ibid., 50.
101. Ibid., 60.
103. Ibid.
105. Ibid., 77.
107. Cuzin 1983, 66.

100. Ibid., 57.
102. Ibid., 76.
104. Ibid., 68.
106. Davis 1920, 71–72.

108. Sanchez Lamego 1983, 91–92; Barragán Rodriguez 1985, 2: 177–79.

109. Cervantes 1964, 206.

110. Mora 1991, 542–48.

111. Spanish Foreign Ministry Archives, vice-consul of Spain in Monterrey, J. P. Laguera, to ambassador in Washington, D.C., May 31, 1915.

112. *Vida Nueva*, Nov. 5, 1915.

113. Such acts might account for the fact that when Fierro was being sucked in by quicksand, none of his men, according to some reports, went to his aid.

114. Juvenal 1916.

Chapter Thirteen

1. Sanchez 1952, 12.
3. Cervantes 1960, 407–10.
5. Holcombe 1968, 103.

2. Valadés 1976, 2: 691–93.
4. Ibid., 421–22.

6. See Lázaro de la Garza Papers, de la Garza to Francisco Villa, Mar. 31, 1914.

7. SDF, Department of Justice, Felíx A. Sommerfeld, file no. 5305-9, statement of Sommerfeld.

8. Lázaro de la Garza Papers, 1–15, Francisco Villa to Lázaro de la Garza, n.d.

9. Ibid., 8–48, Alberto Madero to Lázaro de la Garza, Nov. 4, 1933.

10. Ibid., deposition of Lázaro de la Garza on June 26, 1916, in superior court of California.

11. *Vida Nueva*, Apr. 9, 1915.

12. Obregón 1970, 324.

13. For one of the best military analyses of the battle of Celaya, see Gárfias 1981, 2.

14. Archivo Roque Gonzalez Garza, *carpeta* 12, undated memorandum.

15. Ibid.
17. Cervantes 1960, 432.
19. Ibid., 437.
21. *Vida Nueva*, Apr. 21, 1915.
23. Cervantes 1960, 458.
25. Barragán Rodriguez 1985, 2: 335.

16. *Vida Nueva*, Apr. 10, 12, 1915.
18. Ibid., 439.
20. Ibid., 436.
22. Ibid.
24. *Vida Nueva*, May 7, 1915.
26. Cervantes 1960, 460.

27. *Todo*, Dec. 19, 1933. These remarks were not part of a public pronouncement by Villa but rather are based on the memories of one of Villa's subordinates, Alfonso Gómez Morentin, who was Villa's emissary to the United States in the years 1916 to 1920. According to Gómez Morentin, Villa made these remarks to him in 1918 when the liberal junta in New York suggested to Villa that Angeles should come to rejoin his ranks. In the remarks that Gómez Morentin attributed to Villa, the latter was far less enthusiastic about Angeles's return to Mexico than he was in the letter he wrote Angeles.

28. *WWP*, 29: 498, William Jennings Bryan to George C. Carothers, Apr. 24, 1914.

29. Clendenen 1972, 89.

30. *WWP*, 30: 463, diary of Colonel Edward House, entry of Aug. 30, 1914.

31. Clendenen 1972, 131.

32. Haley 1970, 150.

33. *San Francisco Examiner*, Sept. 26, 1914. Mange 1989 analyzes Hearst's attitude to the Mexican Revolution.

34. Lázaro de la Garza Papers, de la Garza to Francisco Villa, Sept. 14, 1914.

35. John Hart 1987b, 294, 423–24.

36. Ulloa 1971, 198; Holcombe 1968, 78–79.

37. *WWP*, 30: 220–21, Francisco Villa to Woodrow Wilson, in Lázaro de la Garza to Felíx A. Sommerfeld, June 27, 1914.

38. Quirk 1964 [1962], 157–71.

39. Link 1947–65, 4: 261.

40. Quirk 1960, 279–81.

41. Joseph and Nugent 1994, 152–60.

42. Katz 1981, 329–30.

43. *WWP*, 33: 188.

44. Ibid.

45. The files of the Ministère des Affaires étrangères do not reveal any intention by the French government to intervene militarily in Mexico. On the whole, the French were far more restrained than the British in opposing U.S. policy in Mexico. See Katz 1981, 489–93.

46. Quirk 1960, 256–57.

47. Cervantes 1960, 504.

48. Quirk 1960, 279–81.

49. Serrano 1986, 204, report by the Chilean chargé d'affaires in Mexico to the Chilean ambassador in the United States, Jan. 9, 1915.

50. *WWP*, 32: 388, interview with Villa by Duval West, Mar. 6, 1915, report by Duval West to President Woodrow Wilson.

51. Albert B. Fall Papers, University of Nebraska, group R, p. 6.

52. SDF, John R. Silliman to State Dept. 812.00/14010, Dec. 14, 1914. In a letter to Zapata, one of Zapata's highest officials, Manuel Palafox, described Eduardo Iturbide as a millionaire who owned large haciendas in Colima and Michoacán and who as governor of the federal district under Huerta and Corral was responsible for "many assassinations" (Magaña Papers, Palafox to Zapata, Dec. 29, 1914).

53. Magaña Papers. Palafox wrote Zapata that Iturbide had bribed two of Wilson's special agents with hundreds of thousands of dollars so that they would smuggle him out of Mexico. An American sympathizer of Senator Fall's stated that Iturbide had bought Canova's service for $5,000. See source cited in n. 56 below.

54. Hill 1973, 294–98.

55. Teitelbaum 1967, 222–23.

56. Albert B. Fall Papers, University of Nebraska, group R, Roberts to Scrugham, Aug. 29, 1916.

57. AMAE, CP, Pol. Int., vol. 9, Ayguesparse to foreign minister, Dec. 26, 1914.

58. SDF, Record Group 59, file 812.00 1-55311/2, León Canova to secretary of state, May 29, 1915.

59. Diary of Chandler Anderson, May 28, 1915, Library of Congress. The State Department files contain only the barest outline of Canova's plot. Most of the available information is contained in Anderson's diary, especially the entries for Apr. 23, May 14, May 19, May 28, June 1, June 29, July 23, and July 31, 1915. Very apparent is the conservatives' desire to apply a strategy in 1915 similar to that which they had employed in 1911. They were willing to agree to some "compromises" as far as the composition of the government was concerned. Iturbide was quite willing, for example, to include Manuel Bonilla as a representative of the pro-Villa forces and Alvaro Obregón as a representative of the pro-Carranza forces. To ensure conservative control of the Mexican Army similar to that in 1911, "Iturbide himself would have no

part in the new Government, but would act as the leader of the military forces supporting it, which he regarded as essential, in order that he might be in a position to compel the new government to carry out the pledges which it would have to make in order to secure the support of the United States" (diary of Chandler Anderson, July 22, 1915).

60. For Anderson's role as lobbyist for American mining, oil, and other interests, see R. F. Smith 1972, 95.

61. See Katz 1978, 119–23.   62. R. F. Smith 1972, 95.

63. As quoted in Houston 1926, 1: 133.   64. Link 1947–65, 3: 475–76.

65. SDF, Group 59, file 812-00-15531-2, León Canova to secretary of state, July 17, 1915.

66. Teitelbaum 1967, 270–76.

67. Justice Department File 180178, Zach Lamar Cobb to Attorney General Gregory, Mar. 7, 1916.

68. SDF, Office of the Counselor, E. B. Stone to Justice Dept., Mar. 14, 1916.

69. Throughout his career in the State Department, Canova was dogged by accusations of corruption. See Teitelbaum 1967, 398.

70. See Meyers 1991.

71. R. F. Smith 1972, 28n. Garfield's activities in favor of Villa are amply documented in the James A. Garfield Papers, Library of Congress.

72. *WWP*, 33: 533.

73. *WWP*, 33: 305, William Jennings Bryan to Woodrow Wilson, June 2, 1915.

74. Clendenen 1972, 179.

75. *WWP*, 33: 488, Woodrow Wilson to Robert Lansing, July 8, 1915.

76. Clendenen 1972, 179.

77. *WWP*, 33: 463–64, Franklin Lane to Woodrow Wilson, July 1, 1915.

78. Teitelbaum 1967, 260–61.

79. Spanish Foreign Ministry archives, Madrid, Emilio Zapico to minister of state.

80. SDF, 812-00-15656, Francisco Villa to secretary of state, Aug. 5, 1915.

81. Spanish Foreign Ministry archives, Madrid, Emilio Zapico to minister of state, Aug. 15, 1915.

82. Ibid.

83. Spanish Foreign Ministry archives, Madrid, Emilio Zapico to minister of state, Aug. 23, 1915.

84. PRO, FO 204-462-136857, Patrick O'Hea to Cecil Spring-Rice, June 4, 1915.

85. Ibid., O'Hea to Spring-Rice, Oct. 7, 1915.

86. Villa's relations with Juan F. Brittingham are another example of the kind of compromises he had to make with the Terrazas family. Brittingham was an American entrepreneur who had become friends with Luis Terrazas's son Juan while both were students at the Christian Brothers College in St. Louis, Missouri. That friendship played a major role in Brittingham's migration to Mexico and in the fact that the two men became partners in a series of enterprises. One of the most important of these was the Compania Jabonera de la Laguna, which had established a monopoly in buying up cottonseed and processing it into soap and cottonseed oil. When Villa occupied the Laguna area, Brittingham fled to El Paso, Texas, but appointed an Englishman, Patrick O'Hea, who was soon to become British vice-consul in Torreón, as his general manager. Brittingham's U.S. citizenship and O'Hea's diplomatic status probably played a major role in persuading Villa after his arrival in the Laguna not to confiscate the company, but rather to make a deal with it. The cotton plantations confiscated by Villa and administered by Villista officials continued to sell their cottonseed

to Brittingham, who also sold their cotton to his foreign customers. Villa received more than $350,000 in taxes from the Compañía Jabonera, but Brittingham nevertheless seems to have been one of the few businessmen who outwitted him, which he did by buying cotton well under the market price and selling it at inflated prices in Great Britian. Brittingham's influence with the U.S. authorities was so great that the return of his factory to him was one of the main points on General Scott's agenda when he met with Villa to try to get him to rescind his anti-American measures (see Haber 1989, 89–90, 133). For an exhaustive and highly illuminating biography of Brittingham, see Barragán and Cerrutti 1993. Detailed descriptions of Brittingham's dealings with Villa can be found in the Brittingham archives in the possession of Juan Ignacio Barragán in Monterrey, Mexico.

87. Clendenen 1972, 183–84.

88. Ibid., 185, 186.

89. Haley 1970, 175.

90. See chapter 14, n. 15.

91. Almada 1964, 2: 276.

92. *El Paso Herald*, Sept. 10, 1915.

93. Hinojosa 1991.

94. Maytorena Archive, Raúl Madero to José María Maytorena, Sept. 2, 1915.

95. Maytorena Archives, Raúl Madero to Francisco Villa, Sept. 9, 1915.

96. Ibid., 9, 29.

97. Fabela 1970, 1: 366.

98. Archivo Federico González Garza, Manuel Bonilla to Federico González Garza, Oct. 19, 1915.

99. SDF, 812-00-23133, memorandum of Canova.

100. Teitelbaum 1967, 303.

101. SDF, 812-00-16083, George C. Carothers to secretary of state, Sept. 8, 1915.

102. Ibid., 812-00-16142, Zach Lamar Cobb to secretary of state, Sept. 13, 1915.

103. Ibid., 812-00-16209, Zach Lamar Cobb to secretary of state, Sept. 17, 1915.

104. *El Paso Morning Times*, Sept. 24, 1915.

105. One reason why Angeles left Villa may have been that the latter suspected him of plotting with Maytorena to depose him. This was the gist of an anonymous letter sent to Maytorena from Ciudad Juárez on June 23, 1915 (Martin Luis Guzmán Papers, letter of an unnamed captain of the Brigada Morelos to José María Maytorena, June 23, 1915). There is little doubt that Maytorena informed Angeles of the contents of this letter. Since Maytorena's close friend Aureliano González had been shot by Villa, Angeles may have felt that a similar fate awaited him if he remained with the División del Norte.

106. Aguilar Camín 1977, 416.

107. Maytorena Archives, Roque González Garza to José María Maytorena, Sept. 23, 1915.

108. Ibid., undated memorandum by José María Maytorena entitled "Reasons for My Estrangement from General Villa."

109. Ibid., José María Maytorena to José María Acosta and Francisco Urbalejo, Oct. 18, 1915.

110. Almada 1981 [1951], 464; S. Terrazas 1985, 185–88.

111. Valades 1984, 84.

112. Ibid., 92.

113. Ibid.

114. Ibid.

115. Ibid.

116. See Juvenal 1916, 47.

117. Ibid.

118. *Vida Nueva*, Sept. 14, 1915.

119. AHDN, XI-481-5-121, box 7, Guanajuato, Ramírez to secretary of defense, memorandum of 1917, no exact date.

120. *El Paso Morning Times*, Oct. 8, 1915.

121. Calzadíaz Barrera 1967–82, 3: 87–88.

122. John W. Roberts, *Villa's Own Story of His Life*, McClure Newspaper Syndicate publication no. 35 (August 1916).

123. Sonnichsen 1979.

124. Albert B. Fall Papers, University of Nebraska, statement by Dr. R. H. Thigpen. Nov. 7, 1915.

125. *Vida Nueva*, Nov. 21, 1915.

126. Katz 1981, 302; Link 1963, 134.

127. Further proof that these proposals were not a figment of Villa's imagination is provided by a secret pact that Canova signed two and a half years later with a number of U.S. businessmen to bring the head of the conservative Mexican émigré faction, Eduardo Iturbide, to power with the help of the United States. The pact contains provisions strikingly similar to those mentioned by Villa in his accusations against Carranza. Point 10 of this secret agreement stated:

> In recognition of the services which you and your principals obligate themselves to perform I do, for myself, my principals, and associates, obligate myself and them to the end that I and they and the political party which sustains us will use all our influence and the means at our disposal to bring about the following: (a) That the appointments of the secretaries of Foreign Relations and of the Treasury of the Mexican government will be given to men especially fitted to re-establish and maintain complete harmony between the governments of Mexico and the United States and inspire confidence in you and your principals with reference to the carrying out of the obligations herein contained. (b) That the Mexican government will appoint your principals, with the character of financial adviser or fiscal agent, for the negotiation of all financial questions which are to be negotiated in the United States. . . . Such appointment as fiscal agent will also carry with it the designation of the bank recommended by your principals as depository of the Mexican government upon qualification as such in a proper way.

Point 10 (g) specified that a mission be nominated by the new government to negotiate with the United States about "the bases which are to serve for the following matters: Chamizal of the Colorado River, naval stations in the Pacific, the strategic military railroads of the Republic of Mexico; and to agree upon the appropriate measures that are to be taken so that your principals may supervise in Mexico the expenditure of the Funds secured by loans placed by them."

In Point 10 (i), it was stated that "To bring about the utmost harmony and cooperation between the government of Mexico and the United States . . . we are in favor of and will work to bring about the voluntary creation by the government of Mexico of military zones to cover and include the lines of all north and south trunk railways, now existing or to be hereafter constructed under a stipulation that will provide for a mutual offensive and defensive alliance and require both parties to protect the said zones in all cases of threatened danger." Point 10 (j) had as its purpose "the termination to a compromise satisfactory to them of the concession under which Sir Weetman Pearson, now Lord Cowdray, and his associates operate the railway line between Puerto Mexico and Salina Cruz, across the Isthmus of Tehuantepec, and the return of the said railway and the control and complete operation of the same to the government of Mexico." It did, moreover, grant to the parties involved, "the conditions being equal, the profits from the sale of the bonds to provide the necessary funds to enable the government of Mexico to bring about the termination of such concessions, to place the said railway in first-class operating condition, and to double-track the same for its entire length, with all the necessary equipment, terminals, etc." It was "understood," under the terms of the agreement, that "in all cases the Mexican government" would "retain control or majority of the stock of the railway company, granting to your principals, together with such compensation as may be agreed upon, such portion of said stock as may be proper but not exceed 49% of the same." Also included was a clause to the effect that this railway would be made part of military zone, which the United States would have the right to protect if it felt the railway was threatened. SDF, bilingual, unsigned agreement, Nov. 1917, Leland Harrison File, box 208 (Mexican intrigue).

128. Archivo Roque González Garza, Roque González Garza to Francisco Villa, Oct. 26, 1915.

129. Calzadíaz Barrera 1967–82, 3: 141–43.

130. See Naylor 1977.

131. See S. Terrazas 1985, 194–200.

132. BI, microfilm reel 863, undated statement to unnamed newspaper by Hipólito Villa.

133. The best description and reconstruction of Villa's last days in Ciudad Chihuahua can be found in Aguilar Mora 1990, 116–20. See also Terrazas 1985: 194–200.

134. See SDF, Edwards to secretary of state, Dec. 17, 1915.

135. SDF, 81200-16964.

136. *El Paso Herald*, Oct. 24, 1915.

137. Katz 1978, 112.

138. S. Terrazas 1985, 209.

139. Ibid., 203.

140. Ibid.

141. BI, microfilm reel 856, interview by Agent F. O. Pendleton with Manuel Medinabeitia.

142. Almada 1964, 2: 300.

143. *El Paso Herald*, Nov. 1915.

144. *El Paso Times*, Oct. 8, 1915.

145. Cervantes 1960, 431, 463–64.

146. Angeles 1982, 163.

147. Ibid., 164.

148. Juvenal 1916, 91.

149. Archivo Roque González Garza, Federico González Garza to Roque González Garza, Sept. 1915.

150. Gilly 1994, 216–18.

Chapter Fourteen

1. On Enrique Creel's intrigues in the United States, see reports by Carrancista agents in CONDUMEX, Carranza Papers, 5048, 5102, 7471.

2. Luis Herrera had always been overshadowed by his brother Maclovio. Although he inherited the troops his brother had commanded, he never achieved the latter's prestige.

3. For biographical data on Enríquez, see AHDN XI/III/2/876, Enríquez 371–37, 7 Hoja de Servicios, Archivo de Cancelados; Rocha Islas 1988, 130; Almada 1981 [1951], 525–32.

4. Goldner 1993.

5. Altamirano and Villa 1988 277–78.

6. Ibid.

7. The best work on these militias is Rocha Islas 1988.

8. See ch. 15 nn. 1 and 2.

9. E. Meyer et al. 1961, 122.

10. STF, Office of the Counselor, intercepted letter from Acosta to Francisco Villa, Jan. 12, 1916.

11. For different viewpoints on the motives for Villa's Columbus attack, see Katz

1978; also Harris and Sadler 1975, 335–47; L. Harris 1949; Katz 1962; Munch 1969; Sandos 1970; Tuchman 1966; and White 1975.

12. Almada 1964, 2: 298, 299. Almada says that the British consul in El Paso, Homan C. Hyles, had told newspapermen that should Villa cross the border into the United States, Hyles would request his apprehension and trial for the murder of Benton. This news was published in different Mexico City newspapers, including *El Demócrata*, and Almada believes that this made Villa change his mind and decide to stay in Mexico.

13. Calzadíaz Barrera 1972; 1977, 11–17. It is extremely doubtful whether taking revenge on Sam Ravel was Villa's primary aim when he decided to launch an attack on the United States. Had this been the case, Columbus would have been his primary target. Villa's original target was Presidio, Texas, however, and not Columbus, New Mexico. One of Villa's soldiers, Juan Caballero, who participated in both the failed attack on Presidio and in the Columbus raid doubted, for the same reason, that Ravel was the primary target of Villa's expedition (testimony of Juan Caballero written on Dec. 7, 1971 and submitted to the "Confederacion de Veteranos Revolucionarios de la División del Norte," typescript, p. 3). In its thorough investigation of all aspects of the Columbus raid, the U.S. intelligence commission makes no mention of Sam Ravel.

In a conversation with his lawyer, one of the captured Columbus raiders nonetheless said that he had orders from his Villista commander, Candelario Cervantes, to capture Ravel dead or alive (statement of Santos Torres, in Calzadíaz Barrera 1972, 188). The history of the relationship between Ravel and Villa is murky. Sam Ravel's younger brother Arthur subsequently noted: "We did do business with practically all the other revolutionary groups that came to the Columbus border but never with Villa" (Bloom Southwest Jewish Archives, University of Arizona, Tucson, Arizona, Arthur Ravel, letter to Rabbi Floyd Fierman, Nov. 16, 1961). Nevertheless, the papers of Senator Albert Bacon Fall contain a letter from Sam Ravel dated July 26, 1914, stating that he was "held by a bunch of Villa men at Palomas across the border from Columbus, New Mexico" (Fall to Secretary of State William Jennings Bryan, July 27, 1914). In the same file there is an unsigned letter, probably written by Ravel, since it is contained in the Ravel file, stating that in January 1914, he had delivered merchandise to a Lieutenant Colonel Puentes of Villa's army (Albert B. Fall Papers, Huntington Library, San Marino, Calif., Ravel file). It is quite possible that once Villa decided to attack Columbus, Ravel became a secondary target. Luckily for him, he was not in Columbus at the time of the raid. His younger brother Arthur was captured by Villistas, who forced him to lead them to the Ravel warehouse. On the way there, however, the guards were killed by U.S. soldiers, and Arthur Ravel managed to escape.

14. This letter was part of a collection of documents found on a dead Villista after the Columbus attack. They never reached the State Department files but are contained in NA, Papers of the Adjutant General's Office, Record Group 94, file 2384e662, along with file 2377632. The complete text of this letter was first published in White 1975. A complete list of the documents and an attempt to analyze them was published at the same time in Harris and Sadler 1975, 345–47.

15. *El Paso Herald*, May 25, 1916.

16. Reed 1916, 11.

17. Bill McGaw quoted in Rakoczy 1981, 148–50.

18. Katz 1981, 330–31.

19. AA Bonn, Mexico 1, secr., vol. 1, Dernburg to Holtzendorff, May 1915.

20. Katz 1981, 338.

21. Ibid., 547–48.

22. Ibid., 337–38. In 1917, the new German foreign secretary, Arthur Zimmermann, who had replaced von Jagow, sent a dispatch that proposed an alliance with Mexico if the United States entered the Great War and suggested the return to Mexico of Arizona, New Mexico, and Texas as quid pro quo. Zimmermann's telegram was intercepted and deciphered by the British, however, who turned it over to the U.S. government.

23. Or Villa may have been planning to recruit a larger force (with Zapatistas) over six months and, finding that impossible, and his resources still diminishing, moved up his timetable.

24. Calzadíaz Barrera 1967–82, 3: 198–99.

25. NA, "Report of Operations of 'General' Francisco Villa Since November 1915, Headquarters Punitive Expedition in the Field, Mexico, July 31, 1916" (hereafter cited as RO), 6–7.

26. Jaurrieta n.d.

27. SDF, 312-115 C96, affidavit of Thomas B. Holmes, included in evidence submitted to the State Department in the matter of the killing of C. R. Watson, manager of the Cusi Mining Company and others, near Santa Ysabel in the state of Chihuahua, Mexico, January 10th, 1916, submitted by the Cusi Mining Company, Winston, Payne, Strawn, and Shaw, Attorneys, First National Bank Building, Chicago, Illinois.

28. SDF, 312-115 C96, affidavit of Cesar Sala.

29. SDF, 312-115 C96, affidavit of Manuel Silveyra.

30. SDF, 312-115 C96, affidavit of R. Calderon, Jr.

31. SDF, 312-115 C96, affidavit of B. M. Freudenstein.

32. SDF, 312-115 C96, W. D. Pierce to S. L. Pierce, Jan. 9, 1916.

33. Clendenen 1972, 224.   34. RO, 8.

35. *El Paso Herald*, May 25, 1916.   36. RO, 11.

37. Ibid., 11, 12.

38. These reports from American sources are confirmed by an independent Mexican source. Juan Caballero, who was Nicolás Fernández's secretary, also said that Villa's initial aim was to attack Presido, Texas, and that the expedition had to return after Colonel Pérez deserted with his men. See María Guadalupe Santa Cruz, "Por que Villa invadio Columbus?" *El Sol*, Nov. 25, 1971.

39. RO, 19.   40. Osorio Zuñiga 1991, 189.

41. Ibid.   42. RO, 21–23.

43. Mason 1970, 7–9.   44. Rakoczy 1982, 27.

45. Calzadíaz Barrera 1967–82, 6: 15–17.

46. Pablo López did not mention Ravel either in the final interview he gave before his death, when he dealt with the motives for the Columbus attack. Nevertheless, it is not impossible that hostility to Ravel may have been a supplementary reason for the attack, although in a letter written in 1961 (cited in n. 13 above), Sam Ravel's brother Arthur said "to the best of his knowledge" his brother had never had any dealings with Villa, although he did have dealings with other revolutionary leaders. The Ravel file in the Albert B. Fall Papers at the Huntington Library, San Marino, Calif., does indicate that in 1914, Sam Ravel had business relations with one of Villa's officers, Lieutenant Colonel C. Puentes. In addition, in an affidavit written shortly after the Columbus attack in 1916, Arthur Ravel specifically mentions that the Villista raiders were looking for his brother.

47. RO, 28.

48. Ibid., 28.

49. Ibid., 28, 29.

50. Mahoney 1932. The "Report of Operations" in the National Archives (elsewhere cited as RO), carefully assembled by intelligence officers of the Punitive Expedition and based on statements by captured Villista prisoners, does not mention the speech. Many of the captured Villistas who were hauled before American judges said that they had not known that they were on American territory attacking U.S. troops. If Villa did indeed mention the burning alive of Mexican-Americans in an El Paso jail, it would be one of the few times, if not the only time, that he expressed any interest in the plight of Mexican-Americans. In this respect, his attitude was quite different from that of Carranza, who attempted to use dissident and revolutionary Mexican-American movements for his own purposes (see Sandos 1992). When Villa was approached by members of the Plan of San Diego movement to support a possible Mexican-American rebellion, he not only opposed such a movement but threatened to execute the men who had sought his help (Albert B. Fall Papers, Huntington Library, San Marino, Calif., undated, unsigned statement attached to memorandum for Dan M. Jackson, signed Gus T. Jones, written on Dec. 28, 1919).

51. Sandos 1992, 98.
52. RO, 32.
53. Clendenen 1972, 239.
54. Ibid., 236, 246.
55. Link 1947–65, 4: 202.
56. Tumulty 1921, 159.
57. Haley 1970, 194.
58. Ibid., 189.

59. Ulloa 1983, 6: 64. There is a very large body of literature on the Punitive Expedition. For some of the main works written by Americans, see Braddy 1966; Clendenen 1972; Link 1947–65, vols. 12 and 13; Mason 1970; Smythe 1973; Tate 1975; and Tompkins 1939. For two Mexican works, one a monograph and the other a collection of documents by authors sympathetic to Carranza, see Salinas Carranza 1936 and Fabela and de Fabela 1967–68, vol. 4. For works by Mexican authors sympathetic to Villa, see Calzadíaz Barrera 1972, Campobello 1940, and Cervantes 1960.

60. Clendenen 1972, 251–52.

61. Haley 1970, 190.

62. See Karnow 1989, 139–96.

63. NA, Record Group 165, Records of the War Department, General and Special Staffs, General Correspondence, 1920–42, Green File on Mexican Affairs, Office of the Chief of Staff, War Department, Mar. 25, 1916 and July 14, 1919.

64. Haley 1970, 195.

65. Ibid., 197.

66. E. Meyer et al. 1961, 1: 71–72.

67. NA, Papers of the Adjutant General's Office, Record Group 94, HEO Document file 2379210, filed with 2377632, John J. Pershing to adjutant general, Apr. 18, 1916.

68. RO, 33–34.
69. Calzadíaz Barrera 1967–82, 6: 54.
70. RO, 38.
71. Ibid.
72. Ibid., 41.
73. Ibid.
74. Ibid.
75. *WWP*, 36: 586.
76. Calzadíaz Barrera 1967–82, 6: 71.
77. Uriostegui Miranda 1970, 120.
78. RO, 52; see proclamation of Cervantes.
79. Ibid.

80. Calzadíaz Barrera 1967–82, 6: 72; Nugent 1993, 83.

81. Alonso 1988, 217. This letter was found on Cervantes's body by the Americans who killed him.

82. RO, 61. Acosta obviously meant "Hidalgo y Costilla" and "Allende," but this was the way the names were spelled in the translation contained in RO. Whether the error was that of the Americans or of Acosta is not clear.

83. Calzadíaz Barrera 1965, 1: 95–96; RO, 62.

84. RO, 63.

85. Alonso 1988, 216.

86. Calzadíaz Barrera 1967–82, 6: 54; Alonso 1988, 216.

87. Alonso 1988.

88. Calzadíaz Barrera 1965, 1: 92.

89. *El Paso Herald*, May 25, 1916; NA, MID, Record Group 395, E1210.

90. Dr. Rubén Osorio, Archivo Privado.

91. RO, 59, attached newspaper report.

92. Calzadíaz Barrera 1967–82, 6: 72.

93. *WWP*, 36: 424, House diary, Apr. 6, 1916.

94. Link 1947–65, 4: 282.

95. Ibid., 280–81.

96. *WWP*, 36: 424, House diary, Apr. 6, 1916.

97. Ibid., 36: 434.   98. Katz 1981, 312; Haley 1970, 235.

99. Haley 1970, 197.   100. Ibid., 199.

101. Ibid., 199.   102. Ibid., 200.

103. Holcombe 1968, 127; Rosenberg 1975.

104. Almada 1981 [1951], 526.

105. CONDUMEX, Carranza Papers, Sección Telegramas Chihuahua, Jacinto Treviño to Alvaro Obregón, with copy to Venustiano Carranza, June 10, 1916.

106. AHDN, Chihuahua, Dec. 31, 1916.

107. MID, U.S. intelligence report, Nov. 11, 1916.

108. Ibid., Dec. 17, 1916.

109. NA, Papers of the Adjutant General's Office, Record Group 395, MRE 1187, box 29, DF3337, James B. Ord to camp commander, El Valle, Mexico, Dec. 12, 1916.

110. MID, U.S. intelligence report, Nov. 24, 1916.

Chapter Fifteen

1. SDF, 81200-19083. Charles Montague to Sec. of State, Aug. 30, 1916.

2. MID 8529-60, intelligence officer to commanding general, Southern Department, July 26, 1916.

3. RO, 71.   4. Ibid., 75.

5. Ibid.   6. Ibid., 74.

7. Ibid., 78.   8. Ibid., 79.

9. Ibid.   10. Ibid., 76.

11. MID, 8529-60, intelligence officer to commanding general, Southern Department, July 26, 1916.

12. PRO, FO 371-2702-PO6322, Patrick O'Hea to E. W. P. Thurstan, May 26, 1916, 133407.

13. Ibid.

14. Ibid., Patrick O'Hea to E. W. P. Thurstan, Jan. 2, 1916 (1917?).

15. Almada 1964, 2: 322.   16. See Jaurrieta n.d.

17. Hernández y Lazo 1984.   18. Jaurrieta n.d., 31.

19. Marcelo Caraveo was, in fact, not a prisoner in Chihuahua, and he never joined Villa.

20. Jaurrieta n.d., 35.

21. NA, Record Group 393, World War I, Organization Records, Punitive Expedition to Mexico, Chief of Staff, File 1191220, 1916, interview with Luis J. Comaduran.

22. Jaurrieta n.d., 39.

23. Hernández y Lazo 1984, 38–39, Jacinto Treviño to Alvaro Obregón, Sept. 20th, 1916.

24. SDF, 812-00-19439, "Chronology of Villa Movement."

25. NA, Record Group 185, Records of the War Department, General and Special Staffs, Military Intelligence Division, memorandum, Nov. 9, 1916. This account is based on that given by Rafael Grejala of Pedernales, who, according to U.S. intelligence agents, had influential relations in Chihuahua.

26. SDF, 812-00-19529, U.S. Consul William P. Blocker to State Department, Oct. 14, 1916.

27. Ibid., 812-00-19295, Zach Lamar Cobb to secretary of state, Sept. 25, 1916.

28. Ibid., 812-00-19288, Zach Lamar Cobb to State Department, Sept. 25, 1916.

29. Jaurrieta n.d., 44.

30. Ibid., 48.

31. Hernández y Lazo 1984, 49, Francisco Villa to Jacinto Treviño, Santa Isabel, Oct. 23, 1916.

32. This manifesto can be found in SDF, Record Group 76, entry 145, as well as in Almada 1964, 382–86.

33. SDF, 812-00-19719, George C. Carothers to State Department, Nov. 1, 1916.

34. AHDN, Chihuahua, 1916, XI/481-5-72, box 28, Alvaro Obregón to Fortunato Maycotte, Oct. 28, 1916.

35. AHDN, Chihuahua, 1916, XI/481-5-72, box 28 Alvaro Obregón to Fortunato Maycotte, Oct. 29, 1916.

36. AHDN, XI/481-5-72, box 28, Alvaro Obregón to Francisco Murguía, telegram, n.d.

37. AHDN, XI/481-5-72, box 28, Francisco Murguía to Venustiano Carranza, Nov. 22, 1916.

38. SDF, 812-00-20067.

39. PRO, FO 371-2958 PO 6322, Patrick O'Hea to E. W. P. Thurstan, Dec. 11, 1916, enclosure in Thurstan's dispatch no. 499 of Dec. 19, 1916, pp. 326–32.

40. SDF, 81200-19972, W. M. Stell to Lieutenant H. O. Flipper, Oct. 30, 1916.

41. Ibid.

42. Ibid.

43. Ibid., 81200-19403, Zach Lamar Cobb to State Department, Oct. 3, 1916.

44. Ibid., 81200-19867, John J. Pershing to adjutant general.

45. Jaurrieta n.d., 67–68.

46. AHDN, XI/481.5/72, box 28, Luis Herrera to Alvaro Obregón, Oct. 29, 1916.

47. Ibid., Jacinto Treviño to Alvaro Obregón, Oct. 31, 1916.

48. Ibid., Alvaro Obregón to Jacinto Treviño, Nov. 3, 1916.

49. Ibid., Alvaro Obregón to Jacinto Treviño, Nov. 1916.

50. AHDN XI/481.5/72, box 28, Francisco Murguía to Venustiano Carranza, Nov. 22, 1916. See also ibid., Murguía to Carranza, Dec. 25 and 31, 1916.

51. SDF, 812-00-19395, Zach Lamar Cobb to State Department, reporting on opinion of Hunter McKay, Associated Press correspondent in Chihuahua, Oct. 3, 1916.

52. NA, Record Group 393, World War I, Organization records, Punitive Expedition to Mexico, nos. 120–23, "The Reign of Terror in Chihuahua," Nov. 27, 1916, unnamed informant to Captain Reed.

53. Jaurrieta n.d., 83.

54. Ibid., 85.

55. MID, statement on the defense and attack of Ciudad Chihuahua, Captain Reed to Captain Campanole, Nov. 11, 1916.

56. UNAM, Treviño Papers, box 19, exp. 73, report of commander, 9th Battalion, 1st Division, to commander in chief, Northeastern Army, n.d. Villa made one exception. He refused to spare an old rival who had fought against him on the side of the Orozquistas, Luis Comaduran, who told U.S. agents that Villa hated him so much that he had decided to burn him alive in a public ceremony, but that he had managed to escape at the last moment (MID, interview with Luis J. Comaduran, Dec. 20, 1916). There is no evidence to indicate whether Comaduran was exaggerating or whether Villa really intended to do this.

57. UNAM, Treviño Papers, box 19, exp. 73: 24, Jacinto Treviño to Alvaro Obregón, Jan. 23, 1917.

58. AHDN, exp. XI/481.5/72, vol. 3, undated report of Alvaro Obregón to Venustiano Carranza.

59. Ibid., Alvaro Obregón to Venustiano Carranza, Nov. 29, 1916.

60. See AHDN, exp. XI/481.5/76, box 30, Francisco Murguía to Jacinto Treviño, Mar. to May, 1917, and Murguía to Treviño, May 9, 1917; UNAM, Treviño Papers, Murguía to Treviño, July 18, 1917.

61. SDF, 81200-19846, George C. Carothers to State Department, Nov. 7, 1916.

62. NA, Record Group 120, World War I, Organization records, Punitive Expedition to Mexico, headquarters, 1916–17, doc. file 775-908-876 B, telegram, Farnsworth to John J. Pershing, Dec. 16, 1916.

63. MFMP, 725-1-435, Andrés García to Foreign Ministry.

64. UNAM, Treviño Papers, box 19, exp. 73, Jacinto Treviño to Alvaro Obregón, secret annex to his report of Jan. 23, 1917.

65. Haley 1970: 206.

66. Ibid., 217.

67. *WWP*, 38: 547, Frederick Funston to War Department, Oct. 25, 1916.

68. Ibid., 40: 202–3, John J. Pershing to Frederick Funston, Dec. 9, 1916.

69. NA, Record Group 120, World War I, Organization records, Punitive Expedition to Mexico, Document File 5254-5274, confidential documents, John J. Pershing to Frederick Funston, June 6, 1916.

70. Blumenson 1972–74, 1: 373–74.

71. Ibid., 351, George S. Patton to his father, Sept. 28, 1916.

72. NA, Record Group 94, AGO document file 2379210, additional 8203, May 31, 1916, added to 2377632, Frederick Funston to adjutant general, quoting message from John J. Pershing, May 29, 1916.

73. Calzadíaz Barrera 1965, 2: 89.

74. Albert B. Fall Papers, Huntington Library, San Marino, Calif., Edward L. Medler to Fall, Dec. 13, 1918.

75. Transcript of proceedings in the District Court of the 6th Judicial District of the State of New Mexico within and for the County of Luna, State of New Mexico, Plaintiff vs. Eusevia Rentéria, Taurino García, José Rodríguez, Francisco Alvares, José Rangel, and Juan Castillo, no. 664, p. 177.

76. Unpublished essay on the Deming, N.Mex., trial, p. 7. This article was sent to me by courtesy of the Deming courthouse, but I have unfortunately misplaced it and cannot find the name of the author. See Zontea 1993.

77. Albert B. Fall Papers, Huntington Libary, San Marino, Calif., report of operative of the Ben Williams Agency, May 18, 1916, included with Edward L. Medler's letter to Fall.

78. See essay cited in n. 76 above, p. 7. 　79. See Calzadíaz Barrera 1972.

80. Ibid., 290–91. 　81. See essay cited in n. 76 above, p. 9.

82. Calzadíaz Barrera 1972, 245, 265. 　83. Harris and Sadler 1988a, 7–23.

84. "All of these men claimed that in the event of the United States intervening in Mexico, that Japan will make war on the United States. This was told them by Pancho Villa," the undercover agent who had interviewed the convicted Villistas reported (Albert B. Fall Papers, Huntington Library, San Marino, Calif., Medler-Fall correspondence, report of operative of Ben Williams Detective Agency, May 16, 1916).

85. BI, microfilm reel 14, E. B. Stone, report, Aug. 9, 1916, quoted by Harris and Sadler 1988a, 11.

86. NA, Records of the Punitive Expedition, Record Group 395, Dyo and Fusita report, Sept. 23, 1916; Harris and Sadler 1988, 16.

87. Harris and Sadler 1988a, 15.

88. Ibid., 18.

89. Ibid., 22, Baker to Thomas W. Gregory, Feb. 29, 1917.

90. Ibid., 21.

91. Ibid., 22, Baker to Thomas W. Gregory, Feb. 29, 1917.

92. CONDUMEX, Carranza Papers, Andrés García to Venustiano Carranza, Aug. 23, 1916, telegram reading: "The Japanese Tsuto Mudio has informed me from San Geronimo, Chihuahua, in a letter of July 25, which I received today, that on July 9 he poisoned Francisco Villa in Talamantes, near Parral. I believe that this is the same individual who five months ago proposed to me that he do so, but we did not come to any arrangement, because the First Chief refused the offer. I am attempting to obtain confirmation." Obviously, Mudio was the Dyo to whom the Americans were referring, and who told them that he had administered the poison to Villa.

93. See Katz 1981, 311–12.

94. Koopmann 1990, 297.

95. Hill 1973, 370.

96. Christopulos 1980, 247.

97. Ibid., 248.

98. Ibid., 249.

99. Reed 1916.

100. Mexican Northwestern Files, University of Texas at Austin, Secret File 1-201, manager of Mexican Northwestern to R. Holme Smith, Toronto, Mar. 15, 1916.

101. Not all U.S. business interests were in favor of intervention. This was especially the case with mining interests. James W. Malcolmson, who had for a long time been employed by ASARCO and now worked as a consulting engineer for the El Tigre Mining Company, told U.S. agents:

> I can see no special advantage that the mines which I have been connected with would receive from intervention by the United States government. Our operations have been free from labor troubles and from the costly interference of the Western Federation of Labor and other unions. We have been entirely free also from all kinds of personal damage suits, which I believe in the United States take up more than three-fourths of the time of all the courts but which never affected the mining business to any degree in Mexico.
>
> We have produced our ore with silver labor and have marketed our products on a gold basis during the whole of the time and in fact the only serious inconvenience which we have suffered is that of the past few years, due entirely to the lack of orderly government and the chaotic conditions of disputed leadership.

Malcolmson felt that labor costs in Mexico were from 20 to 50 percent lower than U.S. costs and that this might change if the United States occupied Mexico: "I can only repeat that from a professional mining standpoint, we will gain nothing by intervention beyond the simple fact that orderly conditions such as existed until five years ago, always mean more economic work. Beyond this we would gain nothing from American intervention on account of the fact that labor is paid in Mexico in silver, personal and other damage suits are unknown, and our products are sold on a gold basis." National Archives, War College Division, 8534-114. intelligence officer to commanding general, Arizona district, Douglas, Ariz., Aug. 3, 1916.

Chapter Sixteen

1. Paredes 1976, 89–91.

2. Roque and Federico González Garza to Venustiano Carranza and the civilian and military members of his de facto government, Feb. 22, 1916, quoted in Fabela and de Fabela 1960–76, 17: 33–46.

3. María y Campos 1939, 101–3.

4. Pearson Papers, A. E. Worswick to John B. Body, June 29, 1917.

5. See Benjamin 1990, Hernández Chavez 1979, García de León 1985, Garner 1988, and Garciadiego Dantan 1981.

6. Hernández Chavez 1979, 208.

7. Salazar 1962, 216.

8. Carranza 1917, 2–3.

9. PRO, FO 371 2961, Leland Harrison to Cunard Cummins, May 12, 1917.

10. Goldner 1993, ch. 2.

11. PRO, FO 371 2964, Patrick O'Hea to Foreign Office, Nov. 12, 1917.

12. AHDN XI/481.5/72, box 28, Francisco Murguía to Venustiano Carranza, Dec. 16, 1916.

13. MID, 8532-345, District Intelligence Office, El Paso, Texas, Nov. 10, 1917.

14. Womack 1969, 260.

15. Osorio Zuñiga 1991, 189.

16. The preceding quotations in this section are from NA, Record Group 393, World War I, Organization Records, Punitive Expedition to Mexico, nos. 120–23, "The Reign of Terror in Chihuahua," report sent to Captain Reed, Nov. 27, 1916.

17. Vigil 1978, 147.

18. UNAM, Treviño Papers, Jacinto Treviño to Francisco Murguía.

19. Jaurrieta n.d., 106; Calzadíaz Barrera 1965, 2: 104, 105. The latter source gives a somewhat different reason for Villa's killing of the Carrancista soldaderas, saying that one of them had tried to assassinate Villa. The account by Jaurrieta is far more believable.

The massacre of these soldaderas and the rape of the women in Namiquipa were the greatest atrocities against civilians that Villa carried out during his years as a revolutionary. They constituted a basic change from Villa's policy prior to his defeat in 1915. Until that time, practically all observers were impressed by the discipline Villa maintained and by the efforts he made to protect civilians, and especially members of the lower classes.

Not surprisingly, the Carrancista press not only reported on these atrocities but invented others that Villa never committed. Thus, in 1920, the Carrancista press in Mexico reported that Villa had detained a train with Carrancista soldiers and their women. After the soldiers fled and one of the women had tried to kill Villa, the latter ordered the 300 of them, together with their children, to be killed. When these news reports reached the Carrancista provisional governor of Chihuahua, Abel S. Rodriguez, he wrote to the Ministry of Defense that in his opinion, "This news is not only exaggerated but wrong" (AHDN: XI/481.5/79, box 71, Abel Rodriguez to Defense Ministry, June 18, 1920). The Carrancista press reported that Villa burned many of his prisoners alive. I have found no corroboration of these accusations, although Calzadíaz Barrera, an author favorable to Villa, does mention that Santos

Merino, an inhabitant of the village of Bachiniva who had served as a guide for Pershing's expedition, was burned alive after Villa captured him (Calzadíaz Barrera 1965, 2: 95).

Another atrocity attributed by the Carrancista press to Villa was the murder of the González family, consisting of four women and a child, in the town of Jiménez. According to these accounts, Villa and a few of his men stormed into the house of the González family and tried to rape Señora González and her three daughters. When the latter resisted, Villa shot all of them, including a small baby that one of them was carrying in her arms.

Jaurrieta strongly disputes this account, although Villa does not come out very well from his description either. According to Jaurrieta, Villa had entrusted $50,000 to Señora González, whom he had long known as a friend, and also given her a safe conduct through his lines. She had used the safe conduct to help the Carrancistas, however, and when Villa upon capturing Jiménez asked her to return part of the $50,000, she refused. At that point, Villa sent three men to intimidate her by appearing to want to burn her, but under no circumstance were they to do so if the women resisted. The women were armed and shot at Villa's soldiers, however, and the latter returned the fire, killing all of the women. Jaurrieta emphatically states that Villa could never have harmed a child. Since Jaurrieta never attempts to hide or mitigate Villa's atrocities, his account is believable (Jaurrieta n.d., 223–25).

20. AHDN, X1 481-5-72, box 28, Francisco Murguía to Alvaro Obregón, Dec. 11, 1916. Barragán archives, UNAM, 373–60, iv–9, folio 1–134, Obregón to Venustiano Carranza, Dec. 19, 1916, reporting on the messages he had sent to Murguía.

21. Ibid., Francisco Murguía to Alvaro Obregón, Dec. 16, 1916.

22. Ibid., Francisco Murguía to Severiano Talamantes, Dec. 19, 1916.

23. UNAM, Barragán Papers, 373-60, IV-9, folio 1-134, Alvaro Obregón to Venustiano Carranza, Dec. 19, 1916, reporting on the messages he repeatedly had sent Murguía.

24. AHDN, X1/481.5/72, box 28, Venustiano Carranza to Francisco Murguía, Dec. 24, 1916.

25. Ibid., Francisco Murguía to Venustiano Carranza, Dec. 25, 1916.

26. SDF, 81200-20271, unsigned report from Torreón, written on Jan. 3, 1917, included in U.S. consular report.

27. PRO, FO 371-2959-126937, Patrick O'Hea to E. W. P. Thurstan.

28. AMAE, CP, 14, Bernadini to French minister in Mexico, Jan. 2, 1917.

29. PRO, FO 371-2959-126937, Patrick O'Hea to E. W. P. Thurstan.

30. PRO, FO 371-2939-126937-41521, E. W. P. Thurstan to Foreign Office, Jan. 19, 1917.

31. SDF, 81200-20271, unsigned report from Torreón, written on Jan. 3, 1917, included in consular report on Torreón, Jan. 12, 1917.

32. Jaurrieta n.d., 117.

33. Ibid., 116.

34. Ibid. A description of the battle of Estación Reforma from Murguía's point of view is contained in an essay by José Valadés based on oral testimony by a number of Murguía's lieutenants and published in *La Prensa* in San Antonio, Texas, Mar. 19, 1935.

35. Jaurrieta n.d., 116.

36. José Valadés, *La Prensa*, San Antonio Texas, Mar. 19, 1935.

37. Jaurrieta n.d., 116.   38. Cervantes 1960, 570.

39. Jaurrieta n.d., 144.   40. Ibid., 147.

41. Ibid., 147–48.   42. Ibid., 149–50.

43. Charles Hunt, interview, *El Universal Gráfico*, Mar. 17, 1924.

44. AHDN, X1/481.5/76, box 30, Jacinto Treviño to Francisco Murguía, Mar. 23, 1917.

45. Ibid., Francisco Murguía to Jacinto Treviño, May 9, 1917.

46. *El Universal*, June 20, 1917.

47. Part of Villa's letter is reproduced in SDF, 812oo-21096.

48. Mao Tse-tung, "Aspects of China's Anti-Japanese Struggle" (1948).

49. Jaurrieta n.d.; *Todo*, Dec. 19, 1933, interview with Alfonso Gómez Morentín; Osorio Zuñiga,"General Pancho Villa's Expedition to Capture Venustiano Carranza" (MS), n.d.

50. UNAM, Urquizo Papers, Aug. 10, 1917, Francisco Villa to Francisco Murguía.

51. Almada 1964, 2: 332. Almada unfortunately neither provides source notes for his statements nor explains on what he bases them. Yet I have found him to be an extremely serious historian who has worked through a huge quantity of primary sources and archives in Chihuahua. In the talks I had with him, he was able to document every statement that he had made in his books. Another historian, José Valadés, basing his work on unpublished sources among former Villistas, also came to the conclusion that in mid 1917, Villa had intended to withdraw from politics and active resistance although he does not say whether Villa made any concrete effort to enter into negotiations with Murguía (Valadés 1976, 3: 520).

52. "The Grenadiers," in *Poems of Heinrich Heine*, trans. Louis Untermeyer (New York: Harcourt, Brace, 1923), 36.

53. Muñoz 1978, 92.

54. PRO, FO, 371-2959-126937-41521, Patrick O'Hea to E. W. P. Thurstan, Jan. 11, 1917.

55. AHDN, X1/481-5, Favela to Joaquín Amaro, Aug. 12, 1917.

56. AHDN, X1/481-5-76, box 30, Francisco Murguía to Chávez, May 30, 1917.

57. Ibid., José Riojas to Venustiano Carranza, Aug. 24, 1917.

58. Ibid., Francisco Murguía to Chávez, May 30, 1915.

59. *Periódico Oficial*, no. 7 (Feb. 17, 1917).

60. González y González 1968.

61. Rocha Islas 1988, 67.

62. Ibid., 68.

63. Dr. Rubén Osorio, Archivo Privado, "Reseña de los acontecimientos más notables de la defensa social de los Llanos de San Juan Bautista desde su organización a la fecha."

64. CONDUMEX, Carranza Papers, telegram section, Francisco Murguía to Venustiano Carranza, July 17, 1918.

65. Ibid., Enríquez to Carranza, July 22, 1918.

66. Almalda 1964, 2: 333.

67. Raúl Madero, interview by the author.

68. Katz 1981, 324.

69. Rocha Islas 1988, 95.

70. Papers of the Mexican Northwestern Railroad, University of Texas at Austin, report to A. R. Home Smith, president, El Paso, Tex., Apr. 24, 1919.

71. Enríquez Archive, Salcido to Enríquez, Aug. 25, 1919.

72. RAT, Venustiano Carranza to Manuel Aguirre Berlanga, Jan. 9, 1917.

73. RAT, subsecretario de hacienda to Venustiano Carranza, Dec. 26, 1916.

74. Goldner 1993, ch. 2.

75. For the looting of the confiscated properties by Murguía, see UNAM, Treviño Papers, Domínguez, administrator of confiscated estates, to Venustiano Carranza,

Jan. 30, 1917. The report has been erroneously dated Jan. 30, 1916, but since it mentions events that took place in late 1916, such as the assumption of command of the federal forces in Chihuahua by Murguía, it is obvious that the date has to be corrected to 1917.

76. RAT, Andrés Ortíz to Venustiano Carranza, Nov. 15, 1918.

77. Katz 1981, 290; AGN, Gobernación, box 5, exp. 19, Guillermo Muñoz to Venustiano Carranza, May 10, 1916.

78. AGN, Gobernación, provisional governor to Venustiano Carranza, July 1, 1916.

79. Ibid., Caja Chica 5, exp. 19, subsecretario de hacienda to Secretaría de Gobernación, Mar. 31, 1919.

80. AGN, Gobernación, provisional governor of Chihuahua to Venustiano Carranza, July 1, 1916.

81. Ibid., box 88, exp. 32, Luis Terrazas to Secretario de Gobernación, Aug. 10, 1918.

82. Ibid., Andrés Ortíz to Manuel Aguirre Berlanga, Feb. 24, 1919.

83. Ibid., subsecretario de hacienda to Luis Terrazas, Mar. 18, 1919.

84. Ibid., Carlos Cuilty to Venustiano Carranza, Feb. 6, 1920; Manuel Aguirre Berlanga to Cuilty, Mar. 17, 1920.

85. AGN, Gobernación, box 211, exp. 57, Rodolfo Cruz to Carranza, Feb. 8, 1917.

86. UNAM, Treviño Papers, Domínguez, administrator of confiscated estates, to Venustiano Carranza, Jan. 30, 1916.

87. MID, 8532-345, report of Lieutenant Colonel of Cavalry Harry C. Williard to District Intelligence Office, Nov. 10, 1917.

Chapter Seventeen

1. BI, report of John Wren, El Paso office, Texas, Feb. 9–14, 1917.

2. Stevens 1930, 243.

3. MID, 8532-49, Grinstead to district commander, El Paso, Oct. 27, 1916.

4. BI, report of John Wren, El Paso office, Texas, Feb. 9–14, 1917.

5. BI, Gus T. Jones to Bielaski, Nov. 6, 1918.

6. Peterson and Knoles 1977, 67.

7. BI, report of Gus T. Jones, May 6, 1919.

8. U.S. Consul Blocker to Department of Justice, quoting letter from Harry B. Bradley, contained in BI, 184162, J. Edgar Hoover to Assistant Attorney General Luhring, May 16, 1927.

9. BI files, report of Gus T. Jones, May 5, 1919.

10. BI, 1085-867, report of Gus T. Jones, Oct. 10, 1918.

11. NA, Justice Department file 180178, Zach Lamar Cobb to Attorney General Gregory, Mar. 7, 1916.

12. BI, microfilm reel 864, report of E. B. Stone on a discussion with Colonel [Dario] Silva, Mar. 18, 1916.

13. BI, memorandum of Justice Department to Harrison at State Department, June 7, 1917.

14. SDF, 862.202 12/1759, microfilm 336, roll 56, Zach Lamar Cobb to secretary of state, Oct. 26, 1917.

15. See Katz 1981, 543–49.

16. See MID, 8532-262, report of Gus T. Jones, Oct. 6, 1917.

17. Ibid. Jones's report contains a copy of the letter written by Antonio Castellanos to Villa, dated Sept. 12, 1917.

18. Justice Department report, Jan. 21, 1917, BI, microfilm reel 857.

19. Frank Thomas was also "proprietor of a 'burial association,' i.e., an association in which a large number of poor persons make weekly or monthly payments in return for which he guarantees them a burial to cost so much, varying as to their contract. . . . He is known principally as a ten per cent a month loan shark, and bears just such a reputation as a man in that line of business would be expected to in a town of 40,000 inhabitants" (BI, 1085-869, Dec. 23, 1916).

20. BI microfilm 1085-869, report of E. B. Stone, Jan. 22, 1917.

21. Ibid., report of Arthur T. Bailey, Dec. 19, 1916.

22. BI interceptions of Gómez Morentín messages.

23. AA Bonn, Mexico 1, vol. 56, Bernstorff to Bethmann-Hollweg, Apr. 4, 1916.

24. HHSTA, PA, Mexico Reports, 1916, ambassador in Washington, D.C., to foreign minister, Apr. 17, 1916.

25. AA Bonn, Mexico, vol. 56, Bernstorff to Bethmann-Hollweg, June 24, 1916.

26. Ibid., Montgelas memorandum, Mar. 23, 1916.

27. Voska and Irvin 1940, 917.

28. J. B. Vargas 1939. I have found no reference to such a proposal in any German document, but this does not mean very much, since most German intelligence files from World War I were destroyed, and not all German sabotage projects were reported to the Foreign Ministry, the only major German agency whose records are still intact.

29. Katz 1981, 387–459.

30. DZA, Reichstag, no. 1307, minutes of the Budget Committee, Apr. 28, 1917. See also SDF, 862.202 12, microfilm 336 R. 56, Secretary of State Robert Lansing to U.S. embassy, Mexico, D.F., Oct. 30, 1917.

31. SDF, 862.202 12/270 MC 336 R. 55, consul in Nogales to secretary of state, Apr. 9, 1917.

32. Hendrick 1923–25, 2: 175, telegram from a German intelligence agency intercepted by the British.

33. PRO, FO, 371 3961, Foreign Office minutes, June 29, 1917.

34. Ibid., 371 2961 3167, undated memorandum by Cunard Cummins.

35. Ibid., undated memorandum by Body, and letter by Body, Apr. 29, 1917.

36. Ibid., 371 2964 3204, memorandum from Bouchier, Oct. 29, 1917.

37. Ibid., Barclay to Balfour, Nov. 1917.

38. Quoted by Trow 1966, 151.

39. Katz 1981, 500–503.

40. SDF, Office of the Counselor, report from War Department to State Department, Jan. 17, 1917.

41. Albert B. Fall Papers, University of Nebraska, microfilm E9330, Charles Hunt to Francisco Villa, Jan. 17, 1917. In the Fideicomiso Archive there is a photocopy of a follow-up letter that Hunt sent to Villa, which refers to previous communications that Hunt had sent to Villa but like the original letter is dated Jan. 17. Does this mean that the original letter was written at an earlier date or that the subsequent one was a falsification? That is not impossible, since the second letter contains glaring errors in spelling and in the English grammar. It states that soon the United States would withdraw its troops from Mexico, and that public opinion might now turn against Carranza since he "is only a lower tyrant and a complete failure, unable of established [*sic*] a firm and honest government in Mexico." The letter then proposes that Villa meet at the border with Senators Fall and Frank B. Brandegee "who are very interested in meeting you and to offer their valuable influence to your orders, for the establishment of a firm and stable government in the Northern part of Mexico, where given its abounding natural resources of strong financially support can be secured

from a certain group of American capitalists that hold large maining [*sic*] and oil interests in Mexico which groups is already greatly influenced by Senator Fall in your favor; and only is specting [*sic*] that a stable and honest government be established in Mexico, that could give amply guarinties [*sic*] to all foreign investments which are the only means of bring fore [*sic*] the true peace and posterity that most of the Mexican people is eager of it [*sic*]." Fideicomiso, Plutarco Elías Calles Papers, 2398 86, leg. 5–7, Fojas 221–24, "Gomez Arnulfo." This letter may be a falsification by Mexican propagandists in the United States intending to capitalize on Fall's first letter. It may also just be a bad transcription.

42. There was a bizarre twist to the Hunt letter. Although it was signed in his name and in fact written by him, the signature was not his. He had asked his wife to sign his name, probably as a measure of protection so that in case it was intercepted, he could claim it was a forgery. Albert B. Fall Papers, University of Nebraska, microfilm E9330, Charles Hunt to Francisco Villa, Jan. 17, 1917.

43. L. Meyer 1991a, 101.

44. Albert B. Fall Papers, University of Nebraska, E9330, Hunt to Fall, Feb. 5, 1917.

45. *El Universal Gráfico*, Mar. 17, 1924.

46. Albert B. Fall Papers, Huntington Library, San Marino, Calif., E9330, Fall to Hunt, Feb. 1, 1917.

47. MID, 9700-840, statement by Villa given to an officer of MID by Hopkins, n.d.

48. Jaurrieta n.d., 246.

49. For historians of the Mexican Revolution, the activities of the Carrancista agents recorded in the archives of the Mexican Foreign Ministry and of U.S. agents available in the files of the U.S. Bureau of Investigation, military intelligence, the State Department, and other U.S. agencies provide a bonanza of information.

50. See Womack 1969, 301–4, 356–58.

51. Maytorena Papers, Hurtado Espinosa to José María Maytorena, July 31, 1922.

52. *Los Angeles Examiner*, Mar. 27, 1919.

53. Lázaro de la Garza Papers, Lázaro de la Garza to Federico González Garza, May 20, 1916.

54. BI, microfilm reel 863, intercepted letter, Hipólito Villa to Francisco Villa, July 10, 1916.

55. *Los Angeles Examiner*, Mar. 27, 1919.

56. Lázaro de la Garza Papers, Adrian Aguirre Benavides to Lázaro de la Garza, Oct. 27, 1933.

57. CONDUMEX, Archivo Roque González Garza, Roque González Garza to Nieto, Aug. 15, 1916. In his letter, Roque González Garza does not explain the moral reasons for rejecting Villa. Since the attack on Columbus was not one of them, he most probably meant the atrocities and executions that Villa was committing by 1916, which now affected not only the upper class but the lower and middle classes of society as well.

58. Almada 1981 [1951], 505.

59. For a biography of Díaz Lombardo, see Puente 1938, 205–9. See CONDUMEX, Archivo Federico González Garza, manifesto of Díaz Lombardo as corrected by González Garza.

60. SDF, 81200-20987, Miguel Díaz Lombardo to Francisco Villa, Feb. 4, 1917, letter intercepted by U.S. authorities.

61. *El Paso Herald*, Dec. 22, 1915.

62. BI, microfilm reel 863, Hipólito Villa to Francisco Villa, July 10, 1916.

63. BI, microfilm reel 863, E. B. Stone, report, Apr. 29, 1917.

64. BI, microfilm reel 863, BI agent's report, Sept. 10, 1916.

65. BI, microfilm reel 863, interview of Hipólito Villa with unnamed, undated newspaper.

66. Jaurrieta 1935, 15, says that by 1918, Hipólito had returned to Mexico and was fighting alongside his brother.

Chapter Eighteen

1. Paredes 1976, 94–96.

2. Maytorena Papers, Pomona College Library, Claremont, Calif., Felipe Angeles to José María Maytorena, Jan. 11, 1916.

3. Ibid., Feb. 13, 1916.

4. Guilpain Peuliard 1991, 14 (introduction by Adolfo Gilly).

5. Angeles 1982, 189.

6. Maytorena Papers, Pomona College Library, Claremont, Calif., Felipe Angeles to José María Maytorena, Mar. 13, 1916.

7. Angeles 1982, 215, Felipe Angeles to José María Maytorena, Apr. 10, 1917.

8. Yale University Library, diary of Frank Polk, entry of June 22, 1916.

9. Ibid., entry of June 19, 20, 1916.

10. Ibid.

11. Angeles 1981, 143.

12. Ibid.

13. Ibid., 145.

14. Ibid., 163.

15. Ibid, 144.

16. Gilly 1991, 25.

17. Cervantes 1964, 238.

18. Angeles, 1981, 144.

19. Ibid., 180.

20. Ibid., 164.

21. Ibid., 25–49.

22. Ibid., 164.

23. Ibid., 163–64.

24. Ibid., 157.

25. Ibid., 158–59.

26. Ibid., 156.

27. Maytorena Papers, Pomona College Library, Claremont, Calif., José María Maytorena to Felipe Angeles, Dec. 11, 1917.

28. Angeles 1982, 211–12, Felipe Angeles to José María Maytorena, Mar. 21, 1917.

29. Ibid., 224, Felipe Angeles to José María Maytorena, Dec. 6, 1917.

30. Maytorena Papers, Pomona College Library, Claremont, Calif., José María Maytorena to Felipe Angeles, Dec. 11, 1917.

31. Angeles 1982, 226–27, Felipe Angeles to José María Maytorena, Dec. 19, 1917.

32. Maytorena Papers, Pomona College Library, Claremont, Calif., Felipe Angeles to Emiliano Sarabia, Dec. 28, 1917.

33. For both of these overtures, see Maytorena Papers, Calero to Bonilla, July 8, 1916; Calero to José María Maytorena, Jan. 30, 1917.

34. Angeles 1981, 178–79, Felipe Angeles to José María Maytorena, June 8, 1916.

35. See Angeles 1981, 189; 197–99, Felipe Angeles to José María Maytorena, Aug. 20, 1916 and Oct. 10, 1916.

36. MID, 8532-262, report of A-R, Mar. 26, 1918.

37. Puente 1986, 188.

38. SRE, exp., Angeles. Angeles had no liking for either American oil companies or Manuel Peláez, whose forces in Mexico were financed by the oil companies.

39. Angeles 1981, 233.

40. Justice Department, unsigned memorandum from David Lawrence about A. Félix Sommerfeld, June 4, 1919.

41. Department of Justice, Sommerfeld file, undated statement by S. G. Hopkins. In 1915, Sommerfeld had been publicly accused (although never indicted or convicted) of funneling German money to Villa and of participating in a ring that forged passports to allow German reservists in the United States to rejoin their units in Germany. Far more incriminating for Sommerfeld were two letters intercepted by the Justice Department, one from the German naval attaché in the United States to the German ambassador relaying information on military contracts for Italy given to him by Félix Sommerfeld and an even more incriminating letter by Sommerfeld to the German military attaché in the United States, Franz von Papen, describing Allied munitions contracts with American firms. The final straw that convinced U.S. authorities that Sommerfeld was a German agent was a canceled wedding invitation. When the sister of an American oil executive in Mexico who knew Sommerfeld well married a German diplomat, a great wedding reception was held in the German embassy in Washington under the auspices of the Ambassador Bernstorff. Sommerfeld was on the list of invited guests, but at the last moment the ambassador himself canceled the invitation, stating "that it would not do to have him appear at any function in connection with the German embassy, as it was important that his association with the embassy should be kept secret" (Justice Department, Félix Sommerfeld file, Boy Edd to Bernstorff, Dec. 18, 1914; Sommerfeld to von Papen, May 4, 1915; statement by Mrs. Walker to Justice Department contained in memorandum by John Hanna of Apr. 26, 1919). U.S. intelligence agents never uncovered Sommerfeld's plot with the German Secret Service to provoke Villa into attacking the United States.

42. Justice Department, Félix Sommerfeld file, statement of S. G. Hopkins, n.d.

43. Justice Department, Félix Sommerfeld file, statement by John Hanna, May 8, 1919.

44. Justice Department, Félix Sommerfeld file, memorandum of John Hanna to Mr. O'Brian, May 27, 1919.

45. Justice Department, Félix Sommerfeld file, Creighton to Hopkins, Aug. 25, 1919.

46. NA, report by R. E. MacKenney to War Department, 9140-1754-46, June 12, 1919.

47. BI, microfilm reel 867, Francisco Villa to Felipe Angeles, written in Jimenez, Chihuahua, on Sept. 14, 1918, intercepted by BI, translated by BI agent.

48. Ibid., microfilm reel 867, Villa to José María Maytorena, Sept. 14, 1918, intercepted letter, translation of text by BI agent.

49. Villa wrote this letter against the strong objections of two of his advisers, one of whom was his brother Hipólito, who for once seemed to have a more objective point of view than his brother. "The chief wrote a letter to Don Pepe," one of Villa's advisers, codenamed Benjamín, wrote to Ramón Puente, one of Villa's closest supporters in the United States,

> to be sent on to its destination or delivered in person, requesting him to furnish the same A [Angeles] with a certain sum of money in order that he might join under the most advantageous conditions. . . . Neither Polo [Hipólito's

nickname, according to the BI] nor myself approved of the letter, and so expressed ourselves, even emphatically; but the chief had his mind made up to
do the thing and he did, of course. For heaven's sake, keep this as a sacred secret; it may be that the matter will turn out well, and the course of events will
move on as an unruffled and untroubled stream; but I am telling you that you
may not be surprised at any sort of happening, and that you may be prepared to
take the proper action to halt the course of events should the circumstances
and the good of the cause demand it, with the tact and diplomacy which are
your natural gift. [MID, file 10541-842, Benjamín to Ramon Puente, Oct. 20,
1918]

50. Maytorena Papers, Pomona College Library, Claremont, Calif., Felipe Angeles to José María Maytorena, July 9, 1918.
51. Ibid., José María Maytorena to Felipe Angeles, July 16, 1918.
52. Ibid., José María Maytorena to Clara Angeles, July 12, 1918.
53. Ibid., Felipe Angeles to José María Maytorena, Dec. 11, 1918.
54. Cervantes 1964, 384–85, Felipe Angeles to Manuel Calero, Dec. 11, 1918.
55. Archivo Roque González Garza, Federico González Garza to Roque González Garza, Feb. 17, 1919.
56. For Angeles's manifesto, see Cervantes 1964, 271–75.
57. Jaurrieta 1935, 24, 25.
58. Ibid.
59. Mexican Northwestern Papers, University of Texas at El Paso, manager of
Mexican Northwestern Railroad to Home Smith, president, July 3, 1919. According to
Alfonso Gómez Morentin, an aide to Villa during his guerrilla years, Villa received
about $1 million a year from U.S. mining companies. See Luis F. Bustamante, "Los
Americanos contra Villa," *Todo*, Dec. 26, 1933.
60. Jaurrieta 1935, 26.
61. Cervantes 1964, 330.
62. Papers of Mexican Northwestern Railroad, University of Texas at El Paso,
manager of Mexican Northwestern Railroad to Home Smith, July 3, 1919.
63. Cervantes 1960, 585.   64. Cervantes 1964, 296–99.
65. Jaurrieta 1935, 26.   66. Ibid., 25.
67. According to Jaurrieta (1935, 34), one of Villa's lieutenants, Colonel Silverio
Tavares, had promised the Herreras to spare their lives, but had not been authorized
by Villa to do so.
68. Jaurrieta 1935, 36.   69. Ibid., 37.
70. Ibid., 34, 35.   71. Ibid., 37.
72. The events of San Isidro are described in Orozco Orozco 1990b.
73. Albert B. Fall Papers, Huntington Library, San Marino, Calif., H. H. Taft to
Fall, July 22, 1919.
74. Cervantes 1964, 294.
75. Ibid.
76. Brittingham Papers, 370065, Monterrey, undated communication from Patrick
O'Hea.
77. Ibid.   78. Ibid.
79. Cervantes 1960, 601–2.   80. Ibid., 290.
81. Villa's decision to disregard Angeles's warning may have been an expression
of his increasing distrust of Angeles's views.
82. SDF 81200-22827, Erwin to adjutant general, June 15, 1919.
83. Jaurrieta 1935, 70.

84. Cervantes 1960, 601–2.

85. Papers of Mexican Northwestern Railroad, University of Texas at El Paso, manager in Chihuahua to Home Smith, president, July 3, 1919.

86. Cervantes 1964, 333.

87. BI, 10640-1186.

88. Cervantes 1964, 300–301.

89. AHDN, XI/481.5/79, box 31, Gabino Sandoval to the chief of military operations in the north, Sept. 20, 1919.

90. SDF, 812-00-23259, U.S. consul in Chihuahua to State Department, Dec. 1, 1919.

91. Cervantes 1964, 324. For an excellent description and analysis of Angeles's trial, see Osorio Zuñiga n.d., "La muerte de dos generales."

92. Cervantes 1964, 329.

93. Ibid., 326–27.

94. AHDN, Cancelados, exp. Angeles, XI/171.1/17, vol. 2, Diéguez to Urquizo, Nov. 24, 1919.

95. *La Patria* (El Paso, Tex.), Nov. 27, 1919.

96. AHDN, Cancelados, exp. Angeles, XI/171.1/17, vol. 2, Urquizo to Diéguez, Nov. 24, 1919.

97. Calzadíaz Barrera 1967–82, 8: 127. This statement was probably an expression of Diéguez's strategy to publicly dissociate himself from the trial. Diéguez always stressed that he had nothing to do with the trial and that all decisions were up to the court martial. In fact, it was Diéguez who directed the trial, was responsible for it to the central government, and informed Carrancista headquarters of every detail of what was taking place.

98. AHDN, XI/481.5/79, box 31, petition of Nov. 24, 1919.

99. Ibid.   100. Cervantes 1964, 360.

101. Ibid.   102. Ibid., 359.

103. SDF, 812-00-23259, U.S. consul to State Department, Dec. 1, 1919.

Chapter Nineteen

1. Mexican Northwestern Papers, University of Texas at El Paso, manager of Mexican Northwestern Railroad to Home Smith, July 3, 1919.

2. Jaurrieta 1935, 91.

3. Ibid., 81.

4. BI, intercepted letter, Miguel Díaz Lombardo to Ramón Puente, May 2, 1920, reported by E. Kosterlitzky, May 13, 1920.

5. Ibid.   6. Cervantes 1960, 606.

7. Ibid., 618.   8. Ibid., 620; Jaurrieta 1935, 90–92.

9. MID, 10541-842-18, intercepted letter, Francisco Villa to Miguel Díaz Lombardo, June 6, 1920.

10. Torres Papers, conditions published on June 3, 1920.

11. Ibid.

12. Cervantes 1960, 624.

13. Fideicomiso, Fondo Alvaro Obregón, ser. 030400, inventario 2403, exp. 387, de la Huerta, Adolfo, fojas 34–35, Obregón to de la Huerta, July 17, 1920.

14. Ibid., Obregón to de la Huerta, July 8, 1920, 38–39.

15. Cervantes 1960, 624.

16. Ibid.; Vilanova 1966, 63.

17. Cervantes 1960, 627.

18. PRO, FO, 371, 4496, A6267, Patrick O'Hea to Norman King, consul general of Great Britain in Mexico, Aug. 3, 1920, annexed to report by Cunard Cummins to Foreign Office, Aug. 9, 1920.

19. Fideicomiso, Fondo Alvaro Obregón, ser. 030400, Inventario 2391, exp. 375, Hill, Benjamín, Obregón to Hill and Serrano, July 26, 1920, p. 13.

20. See Altamirano and Villa 1991, 12.

21. Fideicomiso, ser. 10201, exp. Francisco Villa, Secretaria particular de la presidencia.

22. Ibid.

23. Ibid., Fondo Alvaro Obregón, ser. correspondence 1920 [030400], exp., Villa, Francisco, General [2849], Obregón to Villa, Sept. 29, 1920.

24. PRO, FO, 371, 4495, 1920, Secret CP 1742, Winston Churchill to Foreign Office, Aug. 5, 1920.

25. Ibid., 4495, A5426, FO comments made on Aug. 9, 1920.

26. Ibid., 4496, A6271, Cunard Cummins to Foreign Office, Aug. 13, 1920.

27. Ibid., 371, 4496, A6277, Cunard Cummins to Foreign Office, Aug. 14, 1920.

28. Ibid., 371-4496, Patrick O'Hea to Norman King, British consul general in Mexico, Aug. 13, 1920.

29. Blasco Ibañez 1920, 124–43.

30. Albert B. Fall Papers, University of Nebraska, microfilm, M-N 1734, Fred H. Dakin, "Some Notes on Francisco Villa."

31. Ralph Parker, "A Visit to General Pancho Villa," MS, "dedicated to my grand-nephew Ralph Materna." My thanks to Eva Zeisel for allowing me to consult this.

32. Albert B. Fall Papers, University of Nebraska, microfilm, M-N 1734, Fred H. Dakin, "Some Notes on Francisco Villa."

33. Hunt 1922, 726.

34. E. Meyer et al. 1986, 170–83.

35. Interview with Regino Hernandez Llergo, *El Universal*, June 15, 1922.

36. E. Meyer et al. 1986.

37. Elías Torres Papers, Francisco Villa to Elías Torres, Aug. 9, 1920.

38. AGN, Presidentes, Obregón-Calles, exp. 818 B 13, Albino Aranda to Alvaro Obregón, Feb. 14, 1922.

39. Ibid., Martínez to Alvaro Obregón, Mar. 23, 1923.

40. Ruíz 1980, 198.

41. Parker, "A Visit to General Pancho Villa" (MS cited in n. 31 above).

42. *El Universal*, June 15, 1922.

43. *El Diario* (Chihuahua), July 26, 1923.

44. E. Meyer et al. 1986, 174.

45. *El Diario* (Chihuahua), July 26, 1923.

46. E. Meyer et al. 1986, 178.

47. AGN, Obregón-Calles Papers, 307-E-10, Juan Rivas and Jay Romero to Alvaro Obregón, Mar. 4, 1923.

48. AGN, Obregón-Calles, telegrams, box 400, exp. 23, VIII, 1921, Enríquez to Alvaro Obregón, Aug. 23, 1921.

49. Ibid., Alvaro Obregón to Enríquez, Aug. 21, 1921.

50. E. Meyer et al. 1986, 170–71, 172.

51. Parker, "A Visit to General Pancho Villa" (MS cited in n. 31 above).

52. Regino Hernández Llergo, *El Universal*, June 15, 1922.

53. MID, Military Intelligence Reports on Mexico, 1919–41, no. 4065, microfilm reel 1, report dated July 28, 1923.

54. E. Meyer et al. 1986, 173.

55. AGN, telegrams, Obregón-Calles, exp. 223-5-3, Francisco Villa to Alvaro Obregón, Jan. 3, 1921.
56. Ibid., Villa to Alvaro Obregón, n.d.
57. AGN, telegrams, Obregón-Calles, box 403, 19, II, Feb. 19, 1922.
58. AGN, Obregón-Calles Papers, Alvaro Obregón to Francisco Villa, Aug. 22, 1921.
59. Ibid., Francisco Villa to Alvaro Obregón, Feb. 20, 1922.
60. AGN, telegrams, Obregón-Calles, box 397, Mexican legation in Washington, D.C., to Alvaro Obregón, Feb. 6, 1921.
61. AGN, telegrams, Obregón-Calles, box 403, legation in Washington to Alvaro Obregón, Feb. 20, 1922.
62. Ibid., Mexican legation to Alvaro Obregón, Feb. 13, 1922.
63. Ibid., Escobar to Alvaro Obregón, Oct. 13, 1922.
64. Jaurrieta n.d., 92.
65. Calzadíaz Barrera 1967–82, 7: 266.
66. Jaurrieta n.d., 92.
67. AGN, telegrams, Obregón-Calles, box 401, Oct. 5, 1921.
68. *Novedades*, Apr. 4 and 11, 1973.
69. AGN, Obregón-Calles, box 237, decision by Alvaro Obregón, Apr. 25, 1921.
70. E. Meyer et al. 1986.
71. Regino Hernández Llergo, interview with Villa, *El Universal*, June 15, 1922.
72. Peterson and Knowles 1977, 205, interview with Mabel Silva.
73. MID 69-756-0, Francisco Villa to Luz Corral, n.d.
74. AGN, Ramo Presidente Abelardo Rodríguez, Soledad Seañez to Abelardo Rodríguez, May 23, 1933.
75. Peterson and Knoles 1977, 251.
76. Ibid., 253.
77. Valadés 1935. This description is based on an interview that Valadés had with Austreberta.
78. Ibid. In an interview that she gave to Silvestre Terrazas's newspaper *La Patria*, published in El Paso, Luz Corral did not attribute the break between her and Villa to Villa's newfound love for Austreberta, but rather to letters sent by Matías García, a former tutor of one of Villa's sons, Agustín, to Villa, in which Matías accused Luz Corral of "leading the life of a queen, who was on good terms with the politicians constantly taking part in fiestas while he (Pancho) was making sacrifices enduring terrible hardships and being pursued by the Carrancistas and by American troops" (*La Patria*, Aug. 9, 1923).
79. Corral de Villa 1976, 240. The letter can also be found in Mexico's National Archives.
80. Corral de Villa 1976, 241.
81. Regino Hernández Llergo, *El Universal*, June 15, 1922.
82. AGN, Obregón-Calles Papers, folder 04958, Manuela Casas, viuda de Villa, to Alvaro Obregón, May 28, 1924.
83. Corral de Villa 1976, 239.
84. General director of Mexican National Railroads to Alvaro Obregón, Oct. 11, 1922.
85. AGN, Obregón-Calles Papers, Francisco Villa to Alvaro Obregón, Sept. 4, 1922. Another manifestation of Villa's increasing hostility to his brother was his decision to return the two children Hipólito had kidnapped from his American wife, Mabel Silva. See Peterson and Knoles 1977, 200–201.
86. See Hunt 1922.

87. *El Universal,* June 15, 1992.

88. Library of Congress, Leland Harrison Papers, General correspondence, 1915–17, container 8, Mexico, memorandum of Leland Harrison of May 3, 1922.

89. MID, 2657-91410, Summerlin to secretary of state, July 27, 1923.

90. The U.S. government had a long memory, however, and Villa's attack on Columbus had not been forgotten. "I want you to give this matter attention, particularly in view of the fact that he is under indictment," J. Edgar Hoover wrote to his most important agents in Texas. The BI agent who had the longest experience in dealing with Mexican revolutionaries, Gus T. Jones, answered Hoover by stating that while he would give great personal attention to the matter, "there is little chance of Francisco Villa coming to the United States as he is fully aware that he is at the present time under indictment in the state of New Mexico under a charge of murder incident to the Columbus Raid." The BI nevertheless took no chances. "Immediately upon receipt of such instruction," another agent reported to Hoover:

> Agent conferred with the heads of the following departments: U.S. Customs, U.S. Immigration Service, U.S. Public Health Service, U.S. quarantine officials, Galveston Pilots' Association, boarding officers of both Customs and Immigration, Galveston Maritime Association, Galveston County Sheriff, and Galveston City Police.
>
> Agent informed all of such officials regarding instructions upon hearing reports first referred to and requested their cooperation towards the utmost vigilance and surveillance of the ports of Galveston and Texas City, Texas with the view of apprehending subject should he endeavor to enter at either of these ports.

Villa's visit to Texas never took place. His secretary, Miguel Trillo, had written one of the few former associates and confidants whom Villa still had in the United States, Ramón Puente, and asked for his advice. Puente told Trillo "that in his opinion Villa should desist from his intention to enter the United States, notwithstanding the Texas governor's assurance of protection, Villa would be exposed to arrest, if not assassination, not only in Texas but in every part of this country that Villa would visit." See BI, WWG-AB 64-125-5, Gus Jones to J. Edgar Hoover, Feb. 23, 1923; Agent Sullivan to J. Edgar Hoover, Feb. 23, 1923; interview of BI agent with Puente, report of E. Kosterlitzky to BI, Feb. 6, 1923.

91. AGN, Obregón-Calles Papers, Enríquez to Alvaro Obregón, Dec. 9, 1922.

92. Acta de la convención agrarista, Chihuahua, 1923.

93. AGN, Obregón-Calles Papers, Ignacio Enríquez to Alvaro Obregón, Feb. 12, 1924.

94. AGN, Gobernación, box 6/48 (C.2.34–48).

95. AGN, Obregón-Calles-Torreblanca Papers, exp. 818-C-77, Ignacio Enríquez to Alvaro Obregón, Dec. 9, 1922; Obregón to Enríquez, Dec. 19, 1922.

96. AGN, Obregón-Calles Papers, 219-B-8, Francisco Villa to Alvaro Obregón seeking return of hacienda to Señores Bayan, Feb. 4, 1922.

97. On the other hand, such an appeal by Villa could be considered pressure on the hacendados to help the poor.

98. AGN, Obregón-Calles Papers, petition of the inhabitants of Bosque de Aldama, Aug. 27, 1922.

99. Ibid., Ignacio Enríquez to Alvaro Obregón, May 24, 1922.

100. Ibid., Francisco Villa to Alvaro Obregón, Aug. 31, 1922.

101. Ibid., Alvaro Obregón to Francisco Villa, Sept. 11, 1922.

102. Ibid., Undersecretary of Agriculture R. P. Denegri to Alvaro Obregón, Sept. 15, 1922.

103. Ibid, Ignacio Enríquez to Alvaro Obregón, Dec. 21, 1922.

104. Ibid., Dec. 27, 1922, report to Alvaro Obregón on decision of judge of the second civil court.

105. Ibid., Francisco Villa to Alvaro Obregón, Jan. 17, 1923.

106. Ibid., Alvaro Obregón to Ramón Molinar, Mar. 7, 1923.

107. Ibid., Governor Almeida to Alvaro Obregón, Nov. 22, 1924.

108. Ignacio Enríquez's conservative views are clearly expressed in his book *Ni capitalismo, ni comunismo* (1950).

109. See Machado 1981, 41–47. The most comprehensive and recent analysis of the McQuatters plan is to be found in Wasserman 1987. See also Aboites Aguilar 1988, 119–33, and Ruíz 1980, 336–39.

110. AGN, Obregón-Calles Papers, leg. 3 T/V Y Z 86, labradores Hacienda Torreón, Mar. 13, 1922.

111. Wasserman 1987, 97–99.

112. Ibid., 98.

113. AGN, Obregón-Calles Papers, exp. 806-T1, Alvaro Obregón to Ignacio Enríquez, Mar. 6, 1922.

114. Ibid., Francisco Villa to Alvaro Obregón, Mar. 12, 1922.

115. Ibid., Alvaro Obregón to Francisco Villa, Mar. 17, 1922.

116. Ibid., memorandum by Secretaría de Gobernación, undecipherable signature, Mar. 28, 1922.

117. *Chicago Tribune*, Apr. 4, 1922.

118. Machado 1981, 41–47.

119. For a closer examination of the McQuatters-Terrazas contract, see Machado 1981, 41–47; Ruíz 1980, 336–39; and Wasserman 1993, 87–107. See also Wasserman 1993.

120. Machado 1981, 44.

121. AGN, Obregón-Calles Papers, Alvaro Obregón to Ignacio Enríquez, Jan. 23, 1923.

122. Wasserman 1993, 75–83.

123. Regino Hernández Llergo, *El Universal*, June 15, 1922.

124. Ibid., June 14, 1922.

125. Ibid., June 16, 1922.

126. Fideicomiso, Luis León to Calles, May 21, 1923, exp. León, sec. 39, exp. 121, leg. 2/11, fojas 59–61. It is not clear why de la Huerta, who only a few months later in September would break with Obregón and Calles and in December would head a revolution against the Mexican government, acted as he did. Did he still hope for a genuine reconciliation with Calles and Obregón? If so, it is not clear what he wanted from the government in return for his placating Villa. Or was he afraid that Villa might stage a premature uprising that would only discredit him?

127. Blanco Moheno 1969, 236.

128. AGN, Obregón-Calles Papers, box 127, 307-4-14, report by anonymous agent on Nov. 1, 1921.

129. MID, 2657410, Summerlin to State Department, July 27, 1923.

130. Vilanova 1966.

Chapter Twenty

1. Interview with Raúl Madero.

2. This was a clever measure by Obregón, which aimed to demonstrate to Villa that the federal government harbored no hostile intentions toward him, since its

own soldiers would have been the victims of these machine guns had they attacked Canutillo.

3. Francisco Villa, letter to *El Universal*, Mar. 17, 1923.

4. Ibid., and response of Jesús Herrera, *El Portavoz* (Torreón), Mar. 31, 1923.

5. Osorio Zuñiga 1991, 86–87.

6. Ibid., 174, 175. Osorio Zuñiga interviewed the youngest surviving brother of the family, Jesús López, who told him that his brother Martín had clashed with Villa because he had not taken the time to bury one of Martín's subordinates, Anaya, who had died in a battle in which Villa had been defeated. According to Jesús, Martín López went to see Villa and there was a violent quarrel between them. Atenógenes López came to believe that Villa subsequently had Martín López shot because of this.

7. Francisco Villa, letter to *El Universal*, Mar. 17, 1923.

8. *El Portavoz* (Torreón), Mar. 31, 1923.

9. AGN, Obregón-Calles Papers, Francisco Villa to Alvaro Obregón, Apr. 18, 1923.

10. Dr. Rubén Osorio, Archivo Privado, correspondence of Villa from Canutillo, Francisco Villa to Calles, Apr. 18, 1923.

11. AGN, Obregón-Calles Papers, Alvaro Obregón to Francisco Villa, May 9, 1923.

12. Ibid., Dolores Herrera to Alvaro Obregón, Mar. 2, 1923.

13. Ibid., Alvaro Obregón to Dolores Herrera, Mar. 24, 1923.

14. Osorio Zuñiga 1991, 89.

15. AGN, Obregón-Calles Papers, box 414, Alvaro Obregón to Eugenio Martínez, July 20, 1923.

16. Ibid.

17. Ibid.

18. Ibid.

19. Dr. Rubén Osorio, Archivo Privado, interview with Francisco Gil Piñon, 92–93.

20. AGN, Obregón-Calles Papers, Alfredo Paz Gutiérrez to Alvaro Obregón, July 20, 1923.

21. Alvaro Obregón to Alfredo Paz Gutiérrez, July 20, 1923.

22. Ibid., Alvaro Obregón to Eugenio Martínez, Aug. 2, 1923.

23. Villanova 1966, 93.

24. AGN, Obregón-Calles, telegrams, Eugenio Martínez to Alvaro Obregón, July 22, 1923.

25. Ibid., Ignacio Enríquez to Alvaro Obregón, July 21, 1923.

26. *New York Times*, July 24, 1923.

27. *Washington Post*, Editorial Digest, July 24, 1923.

28. *Omega*, July 24, Aug. 2 and 10, 1923.

29. *Excelsior*, July 23, 1923.

30. *Omega*, July 2, 1923.

31. Ibid., July 27, 1923.

32. *El Universal*, July 24, 1923.

33. *Excelsior*, July 21, 1923.

34. *El Demócrata*, July 21, 1923.

35. Ibid., July 23, 1923.

36. Simmons 1957, 268–77; Mendoza 1976, 67–69; Moreno 1978, 160–61.

37. MID, 2657-4110, Summerlin to secretary of state, July 27, 1923.

38. AGN, Alvaro Obregón-Calles Papers, exp. 101-V-29, Alvaro Obregón to Calles, July 23, 1923.

39. AGN, Alvaro Obregón-Calles Papers, telegrams 1923, folio 5, Alvaro Obregón to Castro, July 23, 1923.

40. Quoted by Ceja Reyes 1979, 51–54.

41. AGN, Obregón-Calles Papers, Gandarilla to Obregón, Aug. 8, 1923; Fideicomiso, Archive Fernando Torreblanca, Fondo secretaría particular de la presidencia, subser. 10201, original no. 1, exp. Villa, Francisco (65).

42. AGN, Alvaro Obregón-Calles Papers, exp. 101-V-29, Jesús Salas Barraza to Abraham Carmona, Aug. 5, 1923.

43. Ibid., exp 101-V-8, Plutarco Elías Calles, telegram to Alvaro Obregón, Aug. 10, 1923.

44. Villanova 1966, 99–100.

45. AGN, Obregón-Calles telegrams, Alvaro Obregón to Navarro, Aug. 8, 1923.

46. Ibid., Alvaro Obregón to chief of garrison at Monterrey, Aug. 9, 1923.

47. Ibid., Alvaro Obregón to chief of garrison in Tampico, Lorenzo Muñoz, and to the head of the garrison in Monterrey, asking both to contact Navarro, Aug. 9, 1923.

48. AGN, Obregón-Calles Papers, Azueta to Obregón, Aug. 9, 10, 1923.

49. Vilanova 1966, 101.

50. Torres 1975b, 224–25, Abraham Carmona to Juan Serrano, Aug. 9, 1923.

51. Cervantes 1960, 641–42.

52. Ceja Reyes 1979, 196.

53. Villanova 1966, 98–99.

54. Personal communication from David C. Bailey.

55. BI, 64-125-16, report by Luis D. Nette, July 24, 1923.

56. Fideicomiso, Amaro Papers, Salas Barraza to Joaquín Amaro, July 7, 1923.

57. Fideicomiso, exp. Obregón, Alvaro Gaveta 48, exp 5, leg 3.

58. BI, 78149, report by Manuel Sorola, Aug. 20, 1923.

59. Fideicomiso, Fondo secretaría particular de la presidencia, subser. 10201, documents in box, exp. Villa, Francisco, no. 61.

60. Ibid., anonymous letter to Alvaro Obregón, Aug. 22, 1923.

61. AGN Obregón-Calles Papers, Castro to Obregón, July 7, 1921. See also Torres 1975b, 196.

62. Ibid., Jesús Salas Barraza to "All my compañeros," Aug. 6, 1923.

63. Ibid., Jesús Salas Barraza to Joaquín Amaro, n.d.

64. Ibid.

65. Ibid., Jesús Salas Barraza to Joaquín Amaro, Oct. 3, 1923.

66. Ibid., Joaquín Amaro to Jesús Salas Barraza, Oct. 11, 1923.

67. Ibid., Joaquín Amaro to Enriquez, Oct. 11 1923.

68. Ibid., Manuel Aguirre Berlanga to Alvaro Obregón, May 8, 1924; Obregón to Berlanga, May 17, 1924.

69. AGN, Obregón-Calles Papers, box 76, exp. 219-L-6, José Amarillas to Alvaro Obregón, Jan. 2, 1923.

70. Ibid., box 259, exp. H05-1-188, undersecretary of agriculture to Calles, Jan. 22, 1926.

71. Military Intelligence Reports on Mexico, 1919–41, no. 4065, microfilm reel 1, report dated July 28, 1923. Many years after the revolution, in 1951, de la Huerta said in an interview: "Villa promised me his help for a new campaign for the presidency. 'I still have support,' he told me. 'I am not finished as many believe'" (*Mundo*, May 3, 1951).

72. BI, 64-125-16, report of Louis D. Nette, July 28, 1923.

73. MID, military intelligence reports on Mexico, 1919–41, no. 4065, microfilm reel 1, report dated July 28, 1923.

74. BI Files, Manuel Sorola to BI, Aug. 20, 1923, no. 78149.

75. AGN, Comisión Monetaria, exp. 389 Hipólito Villa, Hipólito to Fernando Torreblanca, Feb. 18, 1925.

76. AGN, Obregón-Calles Papers, Austreberta Rentería Villa to Alvaro Obregón, Aug. 28, 1924.

77. Ibid., Luz Corral to Alvaro Obregón, Nov. 10, 1923.

78. Ibid., Alvaro Obregón to Hipólito Villa, Aug. 3, 1923.

79. Ibid., Hipólito Villa to Alvaro Obregón, Aug. 20, 1923.

80. Ibid., Hipólito Villa to Alvaro Obregón, Dec. 22, 1923.

81. Ibid., telegrams, Obregón-Calles, Ignacio Enríquez to Alvaro Obregón, Feb. 12, 1924.

82. AGN, Obregón-Calles Papers, intercepted letter from Hipólito Villa to Gómez Morentin, Feb. 23, 1924.

83. Ibid., J. M. Alvarez del Castillo to Hipólito Villa, n.d.

84. AGN, Obregón-Calles telegrams, Alvaro Obregón to Plutarco Elías Calles, Feb. 10, 1924.

85. For the surrenders of Nicolás Fernández and Hipólito Villa, see AGN, Alvaro Obregón-Calles telegrams, Gonzalo Escobar to Alvaro Obregón, May 11, 1924 (Arnulfo Gómez to General Michel, Sept. 30, 1924, and secretary of agriculture to president, Oct. 25, 1924, ibid.).

86. AGN, Alvaro Obregón-Plutarco Elías Calles Papers, Gonzalo Escobar to Alvaro Obregón, May 30, 1924.

87. Ibid., Alvaro Obregón to Francisco Rodríguez Leon, Oct. 22, 1924.

88. AGN, Alvaro Obregón-Calles telegrams, Garduño to Alvaro Obregón, Nov. 11, 1924; Obregón to Garduño, Nov. 12, 1924.

89. Ibid., Arnulfo Gómez to Plutarco Elías Calles, Dec. 14, 1924; Calles to Gómez, Dec. 15, 1924.

90. Peterson and Knoles 1977, interview with Mabel Silva, 193–204.

91. AJT Juzgado 2° De lo Civil, Feb. 19, 1924, Intestado Francisco Villa.

92. AJT Archivo No 31 Toca a la Apelación interpuesta en el Juicio Civil que sigue el Lic Manuel Puente, Como Apoderado del Gral Franciso Villa, en contra del Sr. Pedro Meraz, Feb. 1925.

93. In July 1923, the newspaper *La Patria* gave the following list of Villa's wives and children: "Esther Cardona de Villa, with two children, Francisco Villa Cardona and Esther; Luz Corral de Villa; Soledad R. de Villa, who has one son; Paula Alamillo de Villa, who lived in Torreón and bore him no children; a girl Maria, whose mother is unknown, who is now in Canutillo; a son of Juana Torres, whose mother has died in Guadalajara; a son by Guadalupe Coss, who is also living in Canutillo; another son of Petra Espinosa from Santa Barbara, who is also in Canutillo; a son, Agustin, from Asuncion R. de Villa, who is also living in Canutillo; a son by Austreberta Rentería, who lives together with his mother in Canutillo" (*La Patria*, July 28, 1923).

94. AGN, Alvaro Obregón-Calles Papers, Austreberta Rentería Villa to Alvaro Obregón, Aug. 8, 1923. It is not clear what Austreberta meant by saying that Villa might have been killed because of his loyalty to Alvaro Obregón. Did she imply that Villa had been killed by Alvaro Obregón's enemies, who either wanted to discredit Mexico's president or believed that Villa would fight on the side of the goverment should de la Huerta rise in arms? Or did she mean that because of his loyalty and belief in Obregón, Villa had neglected to take more stringent precautions to ensure his safety? In later correspondence with Obregón, Austreberta never repeated this argument.

95. Ibid., Alvaro Obregón to Austreberta Rentería Villa.

96. Ibid., Austreberta Rentería Villa to Alvaro Obregón, Aug. 21, 1923.

97. Ibid., Alvaro Obregón to Austreberta Rentería Villa, Oct. 11, 1923.

98. AGN, Obregón-Calles Papers, Luz Corral to Alvaro Obregón, July 30, 1923.

99. Ibid., Aug. 20, 1923.

100. Ibid., Alvaro Obregón to Austreberta Rentería Villa, Apr. 14, 1924.

101. AGN, Obregón-Calles Papers, Alvaro Obregón to Austreberta Rentería Villa, Sept. 12, 1924.

102. There is little doubt that Alvaro Obregón's decision was strongly influenced by his personal sympathy for Luz Corral and the debt that he felt he owed her. Had he based his decision purely on objective reasons, however, he would probably have reached the same conclusion.

The legality of Luz Corral's marriage to Villa was twice challenged in and twice upheld by the courts. In 1925, Austreberta challenged the validity of Luz Corral's marriage to Villa, stating that since the marriage certificate between Luz Corral and Villa was dated Dec. 16, 1915, it was invalid, because Chihuahua had then still been under Conventionist administration and the subsequent Carrancista administration had declared all the decisions of the Conventionist government to be illegal. Apart from the fact that neither the Carranza administration nor its successors ever revoked marriage licenses or other civil measures taken during the Conventionist period, it was at the very least very strange for the widow of Pancho Villa to base her claims on the theory that her husband's administration of Chihuahua had been illegal (Archivo del Supremo Tribunal de Justicia de Chihuahua).

The more serious challenge to the legality of Luz Corral's marriage to Villa was submitted to the Mexican courts nine years later in 1934 by a lawyer representing Villa's daughter by Juana Torres. The accusation stated that the marriage license between Villa and Luz Corral was dated Dec. 16, 1915, but that Villa had married Juana Torres on Oct. 7, 1913, and since the latter died only in 1916, Villa had committed bigamy by marrying Luz Corral while his legal wife was still alive, and that his marriage to Luz Corral was thus invalid. The lawyer demanded that Juana Torres's daughter be declared Villa's sole legal heir. Somewhat strangely, this petition was supported by another widow of Villa's, Soledad Seañez, who declared that since Luz Corral's marriage to Villa was invalid and Juana Torres had died in 1916, her marriage to Villa, which had taken place on May 1, 1919, established her as Villa's sole legal widow. She was nevertheless ready to recognize Juana Torres's daughter as the only legal heir to Villa's properties.

Luz Corral rejected these claims by stating she had married Villa in 1911, but that the original marriage license had been lost, and the certificate of 1915 did not constitute a new marriage license but simply a ratification of a wedding that had already taken place in 1911. This was in fact stated in the marriage license of 1915, and the judge decided in favor of Luz Corral. Ibid.

103. Ibid., Alvaro Obregón to Austreberta Rentería Villa, Sept. 12, 1924.

104. Ibid., Manuela Casas to Alvaro Obregón, May 28, 1924.

105. Corral de Villa 1976, 265–66.

106. Fideicomiso, exp. Francisco Villa, gaveta 69, exp. 136, Austreberta Rentería Villa to Plutarco Elías Calles, Jan. 7, 1932.

107. Corral de Villa 1976, preface.

108. Ching Vega 1977, 50.

109. On Emil Holmdahl's role in Villa's decapitation, see *Novedades*, Oct. 18, 1954, interview with the Mexican deputy Pedrero.

110. On the decapitation of Villa's corpse, see Torres 1975c, Ceja Reyes 1971, Braddy 1960, and Singer 1989.

111. On the transport of Villa's remains to Mexico City and the ceremony at Parral, see Ching Vega 1977.

112. Ching Vega 1977, 140.

113. The minutes of the debate can be found in the Mexico City newspaper *El Día*, Nov. 11, 1966.

114. Rutherford 1971, 152–53.

115. Behar 1993, 211–13.

116. Parkes, 339.

Conclusion

1. Archivo Roque González Garza, Federico González Garza to Roque González Garza, Sept. 1915.

2. Silvestre Terrazas Papers, Bancroft Library, Berkeley, Calif., Silvestre Terrazas to Luis Caballero, July 2, 1914.

3. *Mundo*, May 3, 1951, interview with Adolfo de la Huerta.

4. Knight 1986, 2: 291, 301.

5. Ibid., 288.

Appendix: On the Archival Trail of Pancho Villa

1. MLG, questionnaire of Dr. Raschbaum.

2. MLG, Martín Luis Guzmán, contract with Austreberta Rentería Villa and Nellie Campobello.

Archival Sources

Mexico

Mexico City

Archivo General de la Nación
    Ramo Presidentes
        Francisco Madero
        Alvaro Obregón–Plutarco Elías Calles
        Lázaro Cárdenas
        Adolfo Ruíz Cortines
        Adolfo López Mateos
        Avila Camacho
            Hipólito Villa and El Fresno estate
            Babicora (former William Randolph Hearst estate)
            Canutillo residents
            Villa memorial
    Ramo Gobernación
        Subramo Bienes Intervenidos
    Ramo Revolución
    Serie Manuel González Ramirez
    Serie Emiliano Zapata
    Documentos donados por José López Portillo y Rojas
        Melitón Lozoya
        "Pancho Villa" film controversy
    Comisión Nacional Agraria
    Dirección General de Gobierno
        Correspondencia Villa-Zapata

Serie Fernando Iglesias Calderón
Comisión Monetaria
Archivo Histórico de Hacienda
Serie Convención de Aguascalientes
Archivo Genovevo de la O.
Archivo del Instituto de Estudios Históricos de la Revolución Mexicana
Instituto Mora
Programa de Historia Oral: Entrevistas con Villistas
Hemeroteca Nacional
Newspaper Articles
Archivo de la Secretaría de Relaciones Exteriores
Archivo de la Secretaría de la Defensa Nacional
Archivo Histórico
Archivo de Cancelados
Archivo de la Secretaría de la Reforma Agraria
Sección de Terrenos Nacionales
Archivo Porfirio Diaz: Universidad Iberoamericana
Archivo de la Embajada de la República Española en Mexico: Colegio de Mexico
Archivo de la Universidad Nacional Autónoma de Mexico
Archivo Amado Aguirre
Rafael Chousal
Heriberto Jara
Gildardo Magaña
Manuel Barragán
Francisco Urquizo
Archivo del Instituto Nacional de la Revolución Mexicana
Biblioteca Nacional
Archivo de Francisco Madero
Biblioteca del Instituto Nacional de Antropología e Historia—Microfilm Archive
Madero Microfilms Archivo del Patronato de Historia de Sonora
Private Archives: Mexico City
Papers of Miguel Cárdenas
Fideicomiso Archivos Plutarco Elías Calles y Fernando Torreblanca
Archivo Joaquin Amaro
Archivo Roque González Garza
Archivo Martin Luis Guzmán
Archivo Martinez del Rio
Papers of Elías Torres
Fundación CONDUMEX
Archivo Venustiano Carranza
Archivo Bernardo Reyes
Archivo Guillermo Rubio Navarrete
Archivo Federico González Garza
Private Archive: Fernando Perez Correa
Archivo Miguel Cárdenas

Chihuahua

Archivo de Ciudad Guerrero
Archivo Municipal de Ciudad Juárez
Archivo de Namiquipa

Dr. Rubén Osorio Zuñiga, Archivo Privado
    Correspondencia de Francisco Villa en Canutillo
    Correspondencia de Abraham González
    Oral interviews with revolutionaries

Durango

Archivo Histórico del Estado de Durango
Archivo de San Juan del Rio

Nuevo León

Monterrey: Archivo Privado de Juan F. Brittingham
CIDECH, Ciudad Chihuahua
    Papers of Luis Terrazas
Private Archive of Jesús Vargas Valdés
    Memoirs of Máximo Castillo
Papers of Marta Rocha Islas
    Copias del Archivo de Ignacio Enríquez
Archivo del Supremo Tribunal de Justicia de Chihuahua

United States

Arizona

University of Arizona at Tucson, microfilm of the Alberto Piña Collection

California

Bancroft Library, University of California at Berkeley
    Silvestre Terrazas Collection
    Holmdahl Papers
    Flores Magón Papers
Library of Pomona College, Claremont, Calif., Papers of José María Maytorena
Henry E. Huntington Library, San Marino, Calif., Papers of Albert Bacon Fall

Connecticut

Sterling Library of Yale University New Haven
    Diary of Frank Polk
    Diary of Colonel House

Illinois

University of Illinois at Carbondale
    Papers of Francisco Vázquez Gomez
International Harvester, Chicago, Archives

Indiana

Lilly Library University of Indiana at Bloomington
    Miscellaneous Papers on the Mexican Revolution

Massachusetts

Harvard University
    Widener Library, Papers of John Reed

Houghton Library, Papers of the American Board of Commissioners for
Foreign Missions
Papers of Walter H. Page

Minnesota

Minnesota Historical Society
Microfilm Papers of John Lind

Nebraska

University of Nebraska
Microfilm of the Papers of Senator Albert B. Fall

New Mexico

University of New Mexico at Albuquerque
Papers of Senator Albert B. Fall
Historical Museum, Columbus
Letter of Arthur Ravel
Deming Courthouse: Transcript of proceedings in the District Court of the 6th
Judicial District of the State of New Mexico within and for the County of
Luna, State of New Mexico, Plaintiff vs. Eusevia Rentéria, Taurino García,
José Rodríguez, Francisco Alvares, José Rangel, and Juan Castillo, number 664

New York

New York Public Library, Papers of Enrique Llorente

Texas

University of Texas at Austin
Lázaro de la Garza Papers
Buckley Papers
Papers of the Mexican Northwestern Railroad
University of Texas at El Paso
Papers of the Mexican Northwestern Railroad
Máximo Weber Papers
McNeely Collection
Reyes Aviles Papers
Interviews with former Villistas
San Antonio
Museum of the Daughters of the American Revolution
Eusebio Calzado Papers

Washington, D.C.

National Archives
Records of the Department of State
1. Foreign Affairs Branch, State Department Decimal File, 1910–29, File
812.00, Political Affairs, Mexico. Record Group 59
2. File 862.202 12, German Military Activities in Mexico, Microcopy 336,
Rolls 55–59
3. Files of the Office of the Counselor
Records of the Department of Justice, Felíx Sommerfeld File

Records of the Adjutant General's Office
Records of the Punitive Expedition
Records of Military Intelligence
Records of the Bureau of Investigation
 Papers of the Mexican-American Mixed Claims Commission
 National Security Agency, Intercepted Telegrams
Library of Congress, Manuscript Division
 Papers of Chandler Anderson
 Papers of Tasker Howard Bliss
 Papers of William Jennings Bryan
 Papers of Henry F. Fletcher
 Papers of James R. Garfield
 Papers of Robert Lansing
 Papers of John J. Pershing
 Papers of Hugh Scott
 Papers of Woodrow Wilson (microfilm)
 Papers of Leonard Wood
Federal Bureau of Investigation
 Records Pertaining to Villa's Assassination

Germany

Archive of the Foreign Ministry, Bonn
 Mexico
  Mexico 1 Written exchanges with the German ambassador to Mexico, as well as with other missions and foreign cabinets concerning the internal affairs and relations of Mexico. Subsequent to January 8, 1882, the heading reads "General Affairs of Mexico, 58 volumes (1879–1920)"
  1 sccr. General Affairs of Mexico, vol. 1 (1915)
  1 add "Information about Private Persons and Protection of Their Interests in Case of Unrest," 8 vols. (1913–19)
  7 Relations with North America, 5 vols. (1889–1920)
  15 Press, 1 vol. (1914–16)
  16 Germany's Relations with Mexico, 3 vols. (1917–20)
  16 secr. Private Documents of Privy Councillor Dr. Goeppert, 1 vol. (1917)
 Germany
  2n Parliamentary Addresses (1916–17)
  127, No. 21 The Mexican Mission in Berlin (1888–1918)
    Legation Archive, Mexico, Bundle 1-20
German Federal Archives, Section of Military History, Freiburg im Breisgau,
Archives of the German Navy
German Central Archive, Potsdam
 Foreign Ministry, Trade Policy Division
  Nos. 1724–26 Mexico's Economic Situation (1887–1920)
  4491 Chihuahua (1907–14)
  4493 Durango (1907–15)
  52734 Durango (1871–87)
  54044 Durango (1887–1906)
  54064 Chihuahua (1900–1906)

Department of the Interior
    6113   Secret Matter (1917)
Reichsbank
    H II B 41   Mexico's Economic Situation: Trade, Industry, Business
Reichstag, Protocol of the Reich's Budget Committee
    1314–15   July–August 1917
Legacies
    Legacy of Herwarth von Bittenfeld
German Central Archive, Merseburg
    Rep. 92, E I, no. 13   Legacy of Kapp
        CXIII, 17

Austria

Haus, Hof und Staats Archiv, Vienna
Political Archives
    Mexican Reports (1904–18)
    Washington Reports (1904–17)
    Embassy Archive, Mexico (1904–18)
    War 7, Mexico, Mexico's position regarding the World War
Administration Archives
    Trade Relations with Mexico
War Archives, Vienna
    Files of the Evidence Bureau of the General Staff

Cuba

Archivo Nacional de Cuba, Havana
    Comisión de Estado
        Informes diplomáticós y consulares de México, leg. 38 (1904), 266 (1907), 313 (1903), 324 (1904), 341 (1905), 335, 375 (1907), 377 (1903), 378 (1903), 843 (1911)
        Guerra Mundial, leg. 1148–55 (1914–18)

France

Archives du Ministère des Affaires Étrangères, Paris
    Correspondance politique et commerciale, n.s., Mexique
        1. Politique intérieure. Révolution. Attitude de Puissances, vols. 1–15 (1897–1918)
        2. Armée. Marine, vols. 16–17 (1897–1917)
        3. Politique Étrangère. Dossier général, vols. 18–20 (1896–1913)
        4. Relations avec la France, 2 vols. (1891–1917)
        5. Finances, vols. 23–32 (1895–1918)
        6. Travaux Publics–Mines, vols. 33–40 (1902-18)
        7. Guerre 1914–1918, 2 vols. (1914–18)
Archives du Ministère de la Guerre, Vincennes
    Reports by French military attachés in Mexico and the United States

Great Britain

Public Record Office, London
    Foreign Office Papers
    Balfour Papers
British Science Museum, London
    Papers of Sir Weetman Pearson (later Lord Cowdray)
Archives of the Tlahualilo Company

Spain

Archivo del Ministerio de Relaciones Exteriores, Madrid

Bibliography

Aboites Aguilar, Luis. 1988. *La irrigación revolucionaria: Historia del sistema nacional de riego del Rio Conchos, Chihuahua, 1927–1938.* Mexico, D.F.: Secretaria de Educacion Publica; CIESAS.

Actas del Segundo Congreso de Historia Comparada, 1990. 1990. Ciudad Juárez: Universidad Autónoma de Ciudad Juárez.

Actas del Tercer Congreso de Historia Comparada, 1991. 1992. Ciudad Juárez: Universidad Autónoma de Ciudad Juárez.

Actas del Cuarto Congreso de Historia Comparada, 1993. 1995. Ciudad Juárez: Universidad Autónoma de Ciudad Juárez.

Adame Goddard, Jorge. 1990. *El pensamiento político y social de los Católicos Mexicanos, 1867–1914.* Mexico, D.F.: Universidad Nacional Autónoma de Mexico.

Aguascalientes, gobierno del estado. *La soberana convencion revolucionaria en aguascalientes, 1914–1989.* Aguascalientes: Instituto Cultural de Aguascalientes, 1990.

Aguilar, José Angel, ed. 1978. *En el centenario del nacimiento de Francisco Villa.* Mexico, D.F.: Biblioteca del Instituto Nacional de Estudios Históricos de la Revolución Mexicana.

Aguilar, Rafael. 1911. *Madero sin máscara.* Mexico, D.F.: Imprenta Popular.

Aguilar Camín, Héctor. 1977. *La frontera nómada: Sonora y la revolución mexicana.* Mexico, D.F.: Siglo Veintiuno.

Aguilar Camín, Héctor, and Lorenzo Meyer. 1993. *In the Shadow of the Mexican Revolution: Contemporary Mexican History, 1910–1989.* Austin: University of Texas Press.

Aguilar Mora, Jorge. 1990. *Una muerte sencilla, justa, y eterna: Cultura y guerra durante la revolución mexicana.* Mexico, D.F.: Ediciones Era.

Aguirre, Lauro, and Teresa Urrea. 1896. "Tomóchic." *El Independiente* (El Paso, Tex.), Aug. 7.

Aguirre Benavides, Adrian. 1980. *Errores de Madero*. Mexico, D.F.: Editorial Jus.
———. N.d. "Diario." MS diary in the archives of the Mexican Foreign Ministry.
Aguirre Benavides, Luis. 1966. *De Francisco I. Madero a Francisco Villa: Memorias de un revolucionario*. Mexico, D.F.: A. del Bosque Impresor.
Aguirre Benavides, Luis, and Adrian Aguirre Benavides. 1979. *Las grandes batallas de la División del Norte*. Mexico, D.F.: Editorial Diana.
Alessio Robles, Miguel. 1935. *Obregón como militar*. Mexico, D.F.: Editorial Cultura.
———. 1949. *Mi generación y mi época*. Mexico, D.F.: Stylo.
———. 1985. *Historia política de la revolución*. Mexico, D.F.: Instituto Nacional de Estudios Históricos de la Revolución Mexicana.
Alessio Robles, Vito. 1979. *La convención en Aguascalientes*. Mexico, D.F.: Instituto Nacional de Estudios Históricos de la Revolución Mexicana.
Almada, Francisco R. 1938. *La rebelión de Tomochic en Chihuahua*. Sociedad Chihuahuense de Estudios Históricos.
———. 1955. *Resumen de la historia de Chihuahua*. Mexico, D.F.: Libros Mexicanos.
———. 1965. *La revolución en el estado de Chihuahua*. 2 vols. Mexico, D.F.: Talleres Gráficos de la Nación.
———. 1967. *Vida, proceso y muerte de Abraham González*. Mexico, D.F.: Talleres Gráficos de la Nación.
———. 1968. *Diccionario de história, geografía, y biografía Chihuahuenses*. Ciudad Juárez: Impresora de Juárez.
———. 1971. *La revolución en el estado de Sonora*. Mexico, D.F.: Talleres Gráficos de la Nación.
———. 1981. *Gobernadores del estado de Chihuahua*. 1951. Reprint. Ciudad Chihuahua: Centro Librero La Prensa.
———. N.d. *El presidente Madero y los problemas populares*. Ciudad Chihuahua: Editorial el Labrador.
———. N.d.a. *Juárez y Terrazas: Aclaraciones históricas*. Mexico, D.F.: Libros Mexicanos.
Alonso, Ana María. 1988. "U.S. Military Intervention, Revolutionary Mobilization, and Popular Ideology in the Chihuahuan Sierra, 1916–1917." In *Rural Revolt in Mexico and U.S. Intervention*. Tucson: University of Arizona Press.
———. 1995. *Thread of Blood: Colonialism, Revolution, and Gender on Mexico's Northern Frontier*. Tucson: University of Arizona Press.
Alonso Cortés, Rodrigo. 1972. *Francisco Villa: El quinto jinete del apocalipses*. Mexico, D.F.: Editorial Diana.
Alperovich, Moisei S., and Boris T. Rudenko. 1976. *La revolución mexicana de 1910–17: La política de los Estados Unidos*. Mexico, D.F.: Ediciones de Cultura Popular.
Alperovich, Moisei S., Boris T. Rudenko, and Nikolai M. Lavrov. 1955. *La revolución mexicana: Cuatro estudios Soviéticos*. Mexico, D.F.: Ediciones de los Insurgentes.
Altamirano, Graziella, and Guadalupe Villa. 1988. *Chihuahua: Una historia compartida, 1824–1921*. Chihuahua: Gobierno del estado de Chihuahua; Mexico, D.F.: Instituto de Investigaciónes Dr. José María Luis Mora.
———. 1991. "Los sonorenses y sus alianzas: La capitalizacion del poder." *Boletín Fideicomiso Archivos Plutarco Elías Calles y Fernando Torreblanca*, 7, 12 (September).
Altamirano, Graziella, Cesar Navarro, and Guadalupe Villa. 1992. *Durango: Bibliografía comentada*. Mexico, D.F.: Instituto de Investigaciónes Dr. José María Luis Mora.
Alvarez Salinas, Gilberto. 1969. *Pancho Villa en Monterrey*. Monterrey: Ediciones Continentes.
Amaya, Juan Gualberto. 1947. *Venustiano Carranza, caudillo constitucionalista: 2a Etapa—febrero de 1913 a mayo de 1920*. Mexico, D.F.

Amaya C., Luis Fernando. 1966. *La soberana convención revolucionaria, 1914–1916*. Mexico, D.F.: Editorial F. Trillas.

Anderson, C. N.d. Diary. MS.

Anderson, Rodney. 1976. *Outcasts in Their Own Land: Mexican Industrial Workers, 1906–1911*. De Kalb, Ill.: Northern Illinois University Press.

Angeles, Felipe. 1982. *Documentos relativos al general Felipe Angeles*. Edited by Alvaro Matute. Mexico, D.F.: Editorial Domés.

——. N.d. *La toma de Zacatecas*. Mexico, D.F.: Secretaría de Educación Pública.

Ankerson, Dudley. 1984. *Agrarian Warlord: Saturnino Cedillo and the Mexican Revolution in San Luis Potosí*. De Kalb: Northern Illinois University Press.

Anon. 1915. *Cartilla revolucionaria para los agentes de propaganda de la causa constitucionalista*. Yucatan.

Anon. 1975. *Romance historico villista: Diário en verso de un soldado de Villa*. Ciudad Chihuahua: Talleres de Litográfica Regma.

Anon. N.d. "Pancho Villa and Germany: A Preliminary Report." MS.

——. N.d.a. "Social Elements of the Orozco Revolt: The Mexican North, 1912." MS.

——. N.d.b. "Soviet Historians and the Mexican Revolution." MS.

Araquistain, Luis. 1927. *La revolución mejicana*. Madríd: Biblioteca del Hombre Moderno.

Archivo de la Palabra del Instituto José Luis Mora. 1986. *Tres revolucionarios, tres testimonios. Tomo I: Madero (Juan Sánchez Azcona), Villa (Ramón Puente)*. Mexico, D.F.: Editorial Offset.

Archivo General de la Nación. 1979. *Documentos inéditos sobre Emiliano Zapata y el Cuartel General*. Mexico, D.F.: Comisión para la Comemoración del Centenario del Natalicio del General Emiliano Zapata.

Archivo Histórico Diplomático Mexicana. 1986. *La diplomacia chilena y la revolución mexicana*. Compilación e Introducción de Sol Serrano. Mexico, D.F.: Secretaria de Relaciones Exteriores.

Arenas Guzmán, Diego. 1971. *Proceso democrático de la revolución mexicana*. Mexico, D.F.: Instituto Nacional de Estudios Históricos de la Revolución Mexicana.

Arías Olea, Heliodoro. 1960. *Apuntes históricos de la revolución de 1910–1911*. Bachiniva, Chihuahua: n.p.

Arnold, Oren. 1979. *The Mexican Centaur: An Intimate Biography of Pancho Villa*. Tuscaloosa, Ala.: Portals Press.

Arreola Valenzuela, Antonio, Máximo N. Gámiz, and José Ramón Hernández. 1979–80. *Summa Duranguense*. Durango: Gobierno del Estado.

Arriaga, Guillermo. 1991. *Relato de los esplendores y miserias del Escuadron Guillotina, y de cómo participó en la leyenda de Pancho Villa*. Mexico, D.F.: Editorial Planeta.

Arroyo Irigoyen, Luz Elena, and María del Carmen Barreneche. 1985. *El cambio social en sureste de México: Dos estudios*. Mexico, D.F.: Centro de Investigaciones y Estudios Superiores en Antropología Social.

Asi fué la revolución mexicana. Mexico, D.F.: Consejo Nacional de Fomento Educativo, Comision Nacional para las Celebraciones del 175 Aniversario de la Independencia Nacional y 75 Aniversario de la Revolución Mexicana, 1985– . 8 vols.

Avila Espinosa, Felipe Arturo. 1988. "El pensamiento económico, político y social de la convención de Aguascalientes." Ph.D. diss. Universidad Nacional Autónoma de México.

Avita Hernández, Antonio. 1989. *Corridos de Durango*. Mexico, D.F.: Instituto Nacional de Antropología e Historia.

Azcárate, Juan F. 1975. *Esencia de la revolución (lo que todo mexicano debe saber)*. Mexico, D.F.: B. Costa-Amic.

Azuela, Mariano. *Los de abajo: Novela, cuadros y ecenas de la revolucion mexicana*. El Paso, Tex.: El paso del norte, 1916.

Badillo Soto, Carlos. *¡A sus ordenes mi general!* Durango: Talleres Gráficos del Gobierno del Estado de Durango, 1993.

Baecker, Thomas. 1971. *Die Deutsche Mexikopolitik 1913/14*. Berlin: Colloquium Verlag.

Baerlein, Henry. 1914. *Mexico, the Land of Unrest: Being Chiefly an Account of What Produced the Outbreak in 1910*. 1913. 2d ed. London: Simpkin, Marshall, Hamilton, Kent & Co.

Baldwin, Deborah. 1983. "Broken Traditions: Mexican Revolutionaries of Protestant Allegiances." *The Americas* 40, no. 2 (Oct.): 229–58.

––––––. 1990. *Protestants and the Mexican Revolution: Missionaries, Ministers, and Social Change*. Urbana: University of Illinois Press.

Bannon, John Francis. 1963. *The Spanish Borderlands Frontier, 1513–1821*. Albuquerque: University of New Mexico Press. Reprint, 1974.

Barragán, Juan Ignacio, and Mario Cerutti. 1993. *Juan F. Brittingham y la industria en Mexico, 1859–1940*. Monterrey: Urbis Internacional.

Barragán Rodriguez, Juan. 1985. *Historia del ejército y de la revolución constitucionalista*. 2 vols. Mexico, D.F.: Instituto de Estudios Históricos de la Revolución Mexicana.

Barrera Fuentes, Florencio. 1965. *Crónicas y debates de las sesiones de la soberana convención revolucionaria*. 3 vols. Mexico, D.F.: Talleres Gráficos de la Nación.

Barrientos, Herlinda, Ma. Dolores Cárdenas, and Guillermo González Cedillo. 1991. *Con Zapata y Villa, tres relatos testimoniales*. Mexico, D.F.: Instituto Nacional de Estudios Históricos de la Revolución Mexicana.

Bastian, Jean-Pierre. 1966. "Protestantismo y política en México." *Revista Mexicana de Sociología* 43, special no. (E): 1947–66.

––––––. 1983. *Protestantismo y sociedad en México*. Mexico, D.F.: Casa Unida de Publicaciones.

––––––. 1989. *Los disidentes: Sociedades protestantes y revolución en México, 1872–1991*. Mexico, D.F.: Fondo de la Cultura Económica.

Beezley, William H. 1970. "State Reform During the Provisional Presidency: Chihuahua 1911." *Hispanic American Historical Review* 50, no. 3 (Aug.): 524–37.

––––––. 1973. *Insurgent Governor: Abraham González and the Mexican Revolution in Chihuahua*. Lincoln: University of Nebraska Press.

––––––. 1983. "In Search of Everyday Mexicans in the Revolution." *Revista Interamericana de Bibliografía* 33, no. 3: 366–82.

Behar, Ruth. 1993. *Translated Woman: Crossing the Border with Esperanza's Story*. Boston: Beacon Press.

Bell, Edward I. 1914. *The Political Shame of Mexico*. New York: McBride, Nast & Co.

Bellingeri, M. 1988. "Formación y circulación de la mercancía tierra-hombre en Yucatán (1880–1914)." *Historias* 19: 109–18.

Benavides, Adán. 1971. "In Search of the Elusive Ally: Pancho Villa and the Mexican American." MS.

Benítez, Fernando. 1977. *Lázaro Cárdenas y la revolución mexicana: II. El Caudillismo*. Mexico, D.F.: Fondo de la Cultura Económica.

Benjamin, Thomas. 1989. *A Rich Land, a Poor People: Politics and Society in Modern Chiapas*. Albuquerque: University of New Mexico Press.

––––––. 1990. "Regionalizing the Revolution: The Many Mexicos in Revolutionary Historiography." In *Provinces of the Revolution: Essays on Regional Mexican His-*

tory, 1910–1929, ed. Thomas Benjamin and Mark Wasserman. Albuquerque: University of New Mexico Press

Benjamin, Thomas, and William McNellie, eds. 1984. *Other Mexicos: Essays on Regional Mexican History, 1876–1911*. Albuquerque: University of New Mexico Press.

Benjamin, Thomas, and Mark Wasserman, eds. 1990. *Provinces of the Revolution: Essays on Regional Mexican History, 1910–1929*. Albuquerque: University of New Mexico Press.

Betanzos, Oscar, et al. 1988. *Historia de la cuestión agraria mexicana: 3: Campesinos, terratenientes y revolucionarios, 1910–1920*. Mexico, D.F.: Siglo Veintiuno Editores.

Bethell, Leslie, ed. 1991. *Mexico Since Independence*. Cambridge: Cambridge University Press.

Blaisdell, Lowell L. 1962. *The Desert Revolution: Baja California, 1911*. Madison: University of Wisconsin Press.

Blanco Moheno, Roberto. 1969. *¡Pancho Villa, que es su padre!* Mexico, D.F.: Editorial Diana.

Blasco, Wenceslao. 1921. *Las indiscreciones de un periodista*. Mexico, D.F.: Librería Editorial de Manuel Mañón.

Blasco Ibañez, Vicente. 1920. *Mexico in Revolution*. New York: Dutton.

Blumenson, Martin. 1972–74. *The Patton Papers*. 2 vols. Boston: Houghton Mifflin.

Bonilla, Manuel. 1976. *Diez años de guerra*. Mexico, D.F.: Fondo para la Historia de las Ideas Revolucionarias en México.

Braddy, Haldeen. 1955. *Cock of the Walk: Qui-qui-ri-quí! The Legend of Pancho Villa*. Albuquerque: University of New Mexico Press.

———. 1960. "The Head of Pancho Villa." *Western Folklore* 19, no. 1 (Jan.).

———. 1962. "The Loves of Pancho Villa." *Western Folklore* 19, no. 3 (July).

———. 1965. *Pancho Villa at Columbus: The Raid of 1916*. El Paso: Texas Western College Press.

———. 1966. *Pershing's Mission in Mexico*. El Paso: Texas Western College Press.

———. 1978. *The Paradox of Pancho Villa*. El Paso: Texas Western College Press.

Brading, D. A., ed. 1980. *Caudillo and Peasant in the Mexican Revolution*. Cambridge: Cambridge University Press.

Breceda, Alfredo. 1920. *México revolucionario, 1913–1917*. Vol. 1. Madrid: Tipografía artística.

Brenner, Anita. 1971. *The Wind That Swept Mexico: The History of the Mexican Revolution*. Austin: University of Texas Press.

Brown, Jonathan C. 1993. *Oil and Revolution in Mexico*. Berkeley and Los Angeles: University of California Press.

Bryan, Anthony T. 1970. "Mexican Politics in Transition, 1900–1913: The Role of General Bernardo Reyes." Ph.D. diss., University of Nebraska.

Bullock, Marion Dorothy. 1982. "Pancho Villa and Emiliano Zapata in the Literature of the Mexican Revolution." Ph.D. diss., University of Georgia.

Bulnes, F. 1920. *El verdadero Díaz y la revolución*. Mexico, D.F.

Burdick, Charles. 1966. "A House on Navidad Street: The Celebrated Zimmerman Note on the Texas Border." *Arizona and the West* 8, no. 1 (Spring).

Bush, I. J., M.D. 1939. *Gringo Doctor*. Caldwell, Idaho.

Buve, Raymond Th. J. 1975. "Peasant Movements, Caudillos, and Land Reform During the Revolution (1910–1917), in Tlaxcala, Mexico." *Boletín de Estudios Latinoamericanos y del Caribe* 18 (June): 112–52.

———. 1979. "Movilización campesina y reforma agraria en los valles de Nativitas,

Tlaxcala (1919–1923)." In *El trabajo y los trabajadores en la historia de México: Ponencias y comentarios presentados en la V Reunión de Historiadores Mexicanos y Norteamericanos, Pátzcuaro, 12 al 15 de Octubre de 1977*, ed. Elsa Celia Frost, Michael C. Meyer, and Josefina Zoraida Vázquez. Mexico, D.F.: Colegio de Mexico.

———. 1984. "Agricultores, dominación política, y estructura agraria en la revolución: El caso de Tlaxcala (1910–1918)." In *Haciendas in Central Mexico from Late Colonial Times to the Revolution: Labour Conditions, Hacienda Management, and Its Relation to the State*, ed. Raymond Th. J. Buve, pp. 199–271. Amsterdam: Centre for Latin American Research and Documentation.

———. 1984a. "El movimiento revolucionario de Tlaxcala (1910–1914): Sus orígenes y desarollo antes de la gran crisis del año 1914 (la rebelion arenista)." *Anuario de Humanidades* 8: 141–83.

———, ed. 1984b. *Haciendas in Central Mexico from Late Colonial Times to the Revolution: Labour Conditions, Hacienda Management, and Its Relation to the State*. Amsterdam: Centre for Latin American Research and Documentation.

———. 1988. "'Neither Carranza nor Zapata!': The Rise and Fall of a Peasant Movement That Tried to Challenge Both, Tlaxcala, 1910–1919." In *Riot, Rebellion, and Revolution*, ed. Friedrich Katz. Princeton: Princeton University Press.

———. 1994. *El movimiento revolucionario de Tlaxcala*. Tlaxcala: Universidad Autonoma de Tlaxcala.

Caeser, Dorothy. 1973. "The United States and Carranza Before the Split with Pancho Villa." MS.

Calhoun, Fredrick. 1977. "The Military, Woodrow Wilson and the Mexican Revolution: A Study in Lost Opportunites and American Frustration." MS.

Calvert, Peter. 1968. *The Mexican Revolution, 1910–1914: The Diplomacy of the Anglo-American Conflict*. Cambridge: Cambridge University Press.

———. 1969. "The Mexican Revolution: Theory or Fact?" *Journal of Latin American Studies* 1, no. 1 (May): 51–68.

Calzadíaz Barrera, Alberto. 1965. *Villa contra todo y contra todos*. 2 vols. Mexico, D.F.: Editores Mexicanos Unidos.

———. 1967–82. *Hechos reales de la revolución*. Mexico, D.F.: Editorial Patria. Vol. 1: 1967. Vol. 2: 1967. Vol. 3: 1972. Vol. 4: 1973. Vol. 5: 1975. Vol. 6: 1977. Vol. 7: 1980. Vol. 8: 1982.

———. 1969. *Víspera de la revolución: El abuelo Cisneros*. Mexico, D.F.: Editorial Patria.

———. 1972. *Porque Villa atacó Columbus: Intriga internacional*. Mexico, D.F.: Editores Mexicanos Unidos.

———. 1975. *El general Martín Lopez*. Mexico, D.F.: Editorial Patria.

Camp, Roderic A., Charles A. Hale, and Josefina Vásquez, eds. 1991. *Los intelectuales y el poder en Mexico*. Mexico, D.F.: El Colegio de Mexico.

Campobello, Nellie. 1940. *Apuntes sobre la vida militar de Francisco Villa*. Mexico, D.F.: Edición y Distribuición Ibero-Americana de Publicaciones.

———. 1988. *Cartucho*. Austin: University of Texas Press.

Candelas Villalba, Sergio. 1989. *La batalla de Zacatecas*. Zacatecas: Gobierno del Estado de Zacatecas.

Canto y Canto, Carlos H. 1969. *Los halcones dorados de Villa*. Mexico, D.F.: Editorial Diana.

Caraveo, Marcelo. 1992. *Crónica de la revolución (1910–1929)*. Mexico, D.F.: Editorial Trillas.

Cárdenas, Leonard, Jr. 1963. "The Municipality in Northern Mexico." *Southwestern Studies* 1, no. 1 (Spring).

Cárdenas Noriega, Joaquín. 1982. *José Vasconcelos, 1882–1982, Educador, Politico, y Profeta*. Mexico, D.F.: Ediciones Oceano.

Cardoso, Ciro F. S., Francisco G. Hermosillo, and Salvador Hernández. 1980. *La clase obrera en la historia de Mexico, de la dictadura porfirista u los tiempos libertarios*. Mexico, D.F.

Carr, Barry. 1972. *Organized Labor and the Mexican Revolution 1915–1928*. Oxford: Occasional Papers, Latin American Studies Center, St. Anthony's College.

———. 1972–73. "Las Peculiaridades del Norte Mexicano, 1880–1927: Ensayo de Interpretación." *Historia Mexicana* 22, no. 3 (Jan.–Mar.): 320–46.

———. 1976. *El Movimiento Obrero y la Política en México, 1910–1929*. 2 vols. Mexico, D.F.: Secretería de Educación Pública.

Carranza, Venustiano. 1917. *Informe del C. Venustiano Carranza, primer jefe del ejército constitucionalista encargado del poder ejecutivo de la república, leído ante el congreso de la unión en la sesión del 15 de abril de 1917*. Mexico City, D.F.

———. 1986. *Antología*. Edited by Josefina Moguel. Mexico, D.F.: Instituto Nacional de Estudios Históricos de la Revolución Mexicana.

Carranza Castro, Jesús. 1977. *Orígen, destino y legado de Carranza*. Mexico, D.F.: B. Costa-Amic.

Carry, James C. 1977. "Felipe Carrillo Puerto and the Ligas de Resistance: Upheaval in Yucatan 1915–1923." In *Latin America: Rural Life and Agrarian Problemas*, ed. Steffen W. Schmidt and Helen Hogt Schmidt. Ames: Iowa State University.

Casasola, Gustavo, ed. 1973. *Historia gráfica de la revolución mexicana, 1900–1970*. 10 vols. Mexico, D.F.: Editorial Trillas.

Case, Alden Buell. 1917. *Thirty Years with the Mexicans: In Peace and Revolution*. New York: Fleming H. Revell Co.

Caserini, Aldo. 1972. *Le battaglie di Pancho Villa: L'epopea della rivoluzione messicana*. Azzate, Italy: Varesina Grafica Editrice.

Castañeda Jiménez, Héctor F., et al. 1988. *Jalisco en la revolución*. Guadalajara: Gobierno de Jalisco.

Castillo, Herberto. 1977. *Historia de la revolución mexicana*. Mexico, D.F.: Editorial Posada.

Castillo, Máximo. N.d. "Diario del General Máximo Castillo." MS.

Cazes, Daniel. 1973. *Los revolucionarios*. Mexico, D.F.: Editorial Grijalbo.

Ceballos Ramirez, Manuel. 1986. "El manifesto revolucionario de Braulio Hernández." *Estudios (ITAM)* 5 (Summer): 115–21.

Ceja Reyes, Victor. 1971. *Yo decapité a Pancho Villa*. Mexico, D.F.: B. Costa-Amic.

———. 1979. *Yo maté a Francicso Villa*. Ciudad Chihuahua: Centro Librero de la Prensa.

———. 1979a. *Francisco Villa, el hombre*. Ciudad Chihuahua: Centro Librero de la Prensa.

———. 1987. *Yo, Francisco Villa y Columbus*. Ciudad Chihuahua: Centro Librero de la Prensa.

———. 1987a. *Cabalgando con Villa*. Ciudad Chihuahua: Centro Librero de la Prensa.

Cerda, Luis. N.d. "Causas económicas de la revolución mexicana." *Revista Mexicana de Sociología* 53, no. 1 (Jan.–Mar.): 307–47.

Cervantes, Federico. 1960. *Francisco Villa y la revolución*. Mexico, D.F.: Ediciones Alonso.

———. 1964. *Felipe Angeles en la revolución (biografía, 1869–1919)*. Mexico, D.F.

Chávez, José Carlos. 1955. *Peleando en Tomochic*. Ciudad Juárez: Imprenta Moderna.

Chávez, José. 1960. "Francisco Villa, the Mexican Revolutionary Leader." MS. United States Naval Academy, Anapolis, Md.

Chávez Calderón, Plácido. 1964. *La defensa de Tomochí*. Mexico, D.F.: Editorial Jus.

Chávez Chávez, Jorge. 1995. "Recuento indigenista en el estado de Chihuahua (1880–1950)." In *Actas del Cuarto Congreso de Historia Comparada, 1993*, pp. 421–34. Ciudad Juárez: Universidad Autónoma de Ciudad Juárez.

Chevalier, François. 1961. "Un Facteur décisif de la révolution agraire au Mexique: Le Soulèvement de Zapata, 1911–1919." *Annales: Economies, sociétés, civilisations* 16, no. 1 (Jan.–Feb.): 66–82.

Ching Vega, Oscar W. 1977. *La última cabalgata de Pancho Villa*. Ciudad Chihuahua: Centro Librero La Prensa.

Christopulos, Diana K. 1980. "American Radicals and the Mexican Revolution, 1900–1925." Ph.D. diss., State University of New York at Stony Brook.

Clendenen, Clarence C. 1969. *Blood on the Border: The United States and the Mexican Irregulars*. New York: Macmillan.

———. 1972. *The United States and Pancho Villa: A Study in Unconventional Diplomacy*. Port Washington, N.Y.: Kennikat Press.

Cline, Howard F. 1968. *The United States and Mexico*. New York: Athenaeum.

Coatsworth, John H. 1981. *Growth Against Development: The Economic Impact of Railroads in Porfirian Mexico*. De Kalb: Northern Illinois University Press.

———. 1987. "Patterns of Rural Rebellion in Latin America: Mexico in Comparative Perspective." In *Riot, Rebellion, and Revolution*, ed. Friedrich Katz, pp. 21–64. Princeton: Princeton University Press.

———. 1988. "La historiografía económica de México." *Revista de Historia Económica* [Madrid] 6, no. 2 (Spring/Summer): 277–91.

———. 1989. *Images of Mexico in the United States*. San Diego: Center for U.S.– Mexican Studies.

———. 1990. *Los orígenes del atraso: Nueve ensayos de historia económica de México en los siglos XVIII y XIX*. Mexico, D.F.: Alianza Editorial Mexicana.

Cockcroft, James D. 1968. *Intellectual Precursors of the Mexican Revolution*. Austin.

———. 1983. *Mexico: Class Formation, Capital Accumulation, and the State*. New York.

Coello Avedaño, Jesús. 1974. "Pancho Villa, Pacífico, Leal, y Patriótico." In *Memórias del Congreso Nacional de Historia de la revolución mexicana, Nov. 19–21*. Mexico, D.F.: SCHEH.

Coerver, Don M., and Linda B. Hall. 1984. *Texas and the Mexican Revolution: A Study in State and National Border Policy, 1910–1920*. San Antonio: Trinity University Press.

Coker, William S. 1968. "Mediación Britanica en el conflicto Wilson-Huerta." *Historia Mexicana* 18, no. 2 (Oct.–Dec.): 224–57.

Contreras, Mario, and Jesús Tamayo. 1983. *Mexico en el siglo XX: 1900–1913*. Vol. 1. Mexico, D.F.: Universidad Nacional Autónoma Mexicana.

Córdova, Arnaldo. 1973. *La ideología de la revolución mexicana: Formación del nuevo régimen*. Mexico, D.F.: Ediciones Era.

Corral de Villa, Luz. 1976. *Pancho Villa en la intimidad*. Ciudad Chihuahua: Centro Librero de la Prensa.

Correa, Eduardo J. 1991. *El Partido Católico Nacional y sus directores*. Mexico, D.F.: Fondo de Cultura Económica.

Corzo Ramírez, Ricardo, José G. González Sierra, and David A. Skerritt; con la colaboración de Ana Laura Romero López. 1986. *. . . Nunca un desleal: Cándido Aguilar, 1889–1960*. Mexico, D.F.: El Colegio de México.

Cosío Villegas, Daniel, ed. 1956. *Historia moderna de México*. 11 vols. Mexico, D.F.: Editorial Hermes.

————. 1966. "Politics and the Mexican Intellectual." In *The Intellectual in Politics*, ed. H. Malcolm McDonald. Austin: University of Texas Press.

Cosío Villegas, Daniel, et al., eds. 1981. *Historia general de México.* Vol. 1. Mexico, D.F.: El Colegio de México.

Creel de Müller, Lulú. 1981. *El conquistador del desierto (biografía de un soldado de la república).* Ciudad Chihuahua: Lourdes Creel de Müller.

Crónicas y debates de las sesiones de la soberana convención revolucionaria. 1964. Intro. and notes by Florencio Barrera Fuentes. Mexico, D.F.: Instituto Nacional de Estudios Históricos de la Revolución Mexicana.

Cruz, Salvador. 1980. *Vida y obra de Pastor Rouaix.* Mexico, D.F.: Instituto Nacional de Antropología e Historia.

Cumberland, Charles C. 1952. *Mexican Revolution: Genesis Under Madero.* Austin: University of Texas Press. Reprint, 1974.

————. 1972. *Mexican Revolution: The Constitutionalist Years.* Austin: University of Texas Press.

Curiel, Fernando. 1987. *La querella de Martín Luis Guzmán.* Mexico, D.F.: Editorial Oasis.

Cuzin, M. 1983. *Journal d'un Français au Mexique, Guadalajara: 16 Novembre–6 Julliet 1915.* Paris: Editions J.-L. Lesfargues.

Davis, Will B. 1920. *Experiences and Observations of an American Consular Officer During the Recent Mexican Revolutions.* Chula Vista, Calif.

De Arellano, Luz. 1966. *Palomas, Torreon, y Pancho Villa.* Mexico, D.F.: Imprenta Venecia.

De Becker, J. L. 1914. *De cómo se vino Huerta y cómo se fue: Apuntes para la historia de un régimen militar.* Mexico, D.F.

De la Garza Treviño, Ciro R. 1973. *La revolución mexicana en el Estado de Tamaulipas, 1885–1913.* Mexico, D.F.: Librería de Manuel Porrúa.

De la Huerta, Adolfo. 1957. *Memorias de don Adolfo de la Huerta según su propio dictado.* Transcripción y comentarios del Lic. Roberto Guzmán Esparza. Mexico, D.F.

De los Reyes, Aurelio. 1981. *Cine y sociedad en México.* Mexico, D.F.

————. 1985. *Con Villa en México: Testimonios de camarógrafos norteamericanos en la revolución.* Mexico, D.F.: Universidad Nacional Autónoma de Mexico.

————. 1986. *With Villa in Mexico on Location.* Washington D.C.: Performing Arts Annual, Library of Congress.

De Orellana, Margarita. 1982. "Quand Pancho Villa était vedette de cinema." *Positif: Revue de Cinema* 251 (Feb. 1): 43–46.

————. 1988. *Villa y Zapata: La revolución mexicana.* Madrid: Ediciones Anaya.

————. 1991. *La mirada circular: El cine norteamericano de la revolución mexicana, 1911–1917.* Mexico, D.F.: Editorial Joaquín Mortiz.

————. N.d. "Pancho Villa: Primer actor del cine de la revolución." MS.

Del Castillo, José R. 1985. *Historia de la revolución social de México.* Mexico, D.F.: Instituto Nacional de Antropología e Historia.

Díaz Soto y Gama, Antonio. 1976. *La cuestion agraria en México.* Mexico, D.F.: Ediciones El Caballito.

Diccionario histórico y biográfico de la revolución mexicana. 1991. 7 vols. Mexico, D.F.: Instituto Nacional de Estudios Históricos de la Revolución Mexicana.

Diccionario Porrúa de historia, biografía y geografía de México. 1986. 3 vols. Mexico, D.F.: Editorial Porrúa.

Doerries, Reinhard R. 1989. *Imperial Challenge: Ambassador Count Bernstorff and*

German-American Relations, 1908–1917. Translated by Christal Shannon. Chapel Hill: University of North Carolina Press.

Dromundo, Baltasar. 1936. *Villa y la "Adelita".* Durango: Victoria de Durango.

Duarte Morales, Teodosio. 1967. *El rugir del cañon.* Ciudad Juárez: n.p.

———. N.d. *Villa y Pershing: Memorias de la revolución (20 de noviembre de 1910 a 1913).* Ciudad Juárez, Chihuahua: Ediciones El Labrador.

Durán, Esperanza. 1985. *Guerra y revolución: Las grandes potencias y México, 1914–1918.* Mexico, D.F.: El Colegio de Mexico.

Eisenhower, John S. D. 1993. *Intervention! The United States and the Mexican Revolution, 1913–1917.* New York: Norton.

Eiser-Viafora, Paul. 1974. "Durango and the Mexican Revolution." *New Mexico Historical Review* 49, no. 3 (July): 219–40.

Emiliano Zapata y el movimiento zapatista: Cinco ensayos. 1980. Mexico, D.F.: Secretaria de Educación Pública.

En el centenario del nacimiento de Francisco Villa. 1978. Mexico, D.F.: Instituto Nacional de Estudios Históricos de la Revolución Mexicana.

Enciso, Xavier. 1919. *El ataque a Ciudad Juárez y los acontecimientos del 14 al 18 de Junio.* El Paso, Tex.

Enríquez, Ignacio C. 1950. *Ni capitalismo ni comunismo, una democracia económica.* Mexico, D.F.: Editorial Porrúa.

Escárcega, Alfonso. 1975. "Giner: Sub-Jefe de la División del Norte." Trabajo presentado en el Sexto Congreso Nacional de Historia de la Revolución Mexicana, celebrado en la Ciudad de Chihuahua, Chih., durante los días 20 y 21 de Noviembre de 1975 convocado por la Sociedad Chihuahuense de Estudios Históricos.

Estrada, Richard. 1979. "The Mexican Revolution in the Ciudad Juárez–El Paso Area, 1910–1920." *Password* (quarterly review of the El Paso County Historical Society) 24, no. 2 (Summer): 55–69.

———. 1981–82. *Zapata to Villa, Revolutionary Camp in Morelos, January 19, 1914.* Proceedings of the Pacific Coast Council on Latin American Studies, vol. 8. San Diego, Calif.: San Diego State University Press.

———. N.d. "Liderazgo popular en la revolución mexicana." MS.

Fabela, Isidro. 1977. *Mis memorias de la revolución.* Mexico, D.F.: Editorial Jus.

———. 1979. *La política interior y exterior de Carranza.* Mexico, D.F.: Editorial Jus.

———. 1985. *Historia diplomática de la revolución mexicana.* 2 vols. Mexico, D.F.: Instituto Nacional de Estudios Históricos de la Revolución Mexicana.

Fabela, Isidro, and J. E. de Fabela, eds. 1960–76. *Documentos históricos de la revolución mexicana.* 27 vols. and index. Mexico, D.F.: Fondo de la Cultura Económica. Cited as *DHRM.*

Falcón, Romana. 1979. "¿Los orígenes populares de la revolución de 1910? El caso de San Luis Potosí." *Historia Mexicana* 29, no. 2 (Oct.–Dec.): 197–240.

———. 1984. *Revolución y caciquismo en San Luis Potosí, 1910–1938.* Mexico, D.F.: El Colegio de México.

———. 1988. "Charisma, Tradition, and Caciquismo: Revolution in San Luis Potosí." In *Riot, Rebellion, and Revolution,* ed. Friedrich Katz. Princeton: Princeton University Press.

Falcón, Romana, and Soledad García. 1986. *La semilla en el Surco: Adalberto Tejeda y el radicalismo en Veracruz, 1883–1960.* Mexico, D.F.: El Colegio de Mexico.

Fatout, Paul. 1951. *Ambrose Bierce, the Devil's Lexicographer.* Norman: University of Oklahoma Press.

Fischer Wood, Eric. 1920. *Leonard Wood: Conservator of Americanism.* New York: George H. Doran Co.

Flores Caballero, R. R. 1981. *Administración y política en la historia de México*. Mexico, D.F.

Flores Vizcarra, Jorge, and Otto Granados Roldán. 1980. *Salvador Alvarado y la revolución mexicana*. Culiacán: Universidad Autónoma de Sinaloa.

Florescano, Enrique, ed. 1980. *Bibliografía general del desarrollo económico de Mexico, 1500–1976*. Mexico, D.F.: SEP, Instituto Nacional de Antropología e Historia, Departamento de Investigaciones Historicas.

————. 1992. *El nuevo pasado Mexicano*. 1991. Reprint. Mexico, D.F.: Cal & Arena.

Florescano, Enrique, and Javier Garciadiego, eds. 1985. *Así fue la revolución mexicana*. 8 vols. Mexico, D. F.: Consejo Nacional de Fomento Educativo.

Foix, Pere. 1976. *Pancho Villa*. Mexico, D.F.: Editorial Trillas.

Foner, Phillip S. 1983. *Mother Jones Speaks: Collected Writings and Speeches*. New York: Monad Press.

French, William E. 1989. "Business as Usual: Mexico North Western Railway Managers Confront the Mexican Revolution." *Mexican Studies* 5, no. 2 (Summer): 221–38.

————. 1990. "A Peaceful and Working People: The Inculcation of the Capitalist Work Ethic in a Mexican Mining District (Hidalgo District, Chihuahua, 1880–1920)." Ph.D. diss., University of Texas at Austin.

————. 1992. "Trabajadores mineros y la transformación del trabajo minero durante el porfiriato." In *Actas del Tercer Congreso de Historia Comparada, 1991*, pp. 297–306. Ciudad Juárez: Universidad Autónoma de Ciudad Juárez.

Frías, Heriberto. 1983. *Tomóchic*. Mexico, D.F.: Editorial Porrúa.

Friedrich, Paul. 1970. *Agrarian Revolt in a Mexican Village*. Englewood Cliffs, N.J.: Prentice-Hall.

Frost, Elsa Celia, Michael C. Meyer, and Josefina Zoraida Vázquez, eds. 1979. *El trabajo y los trabajadores en la historia de México: Ponencias y comentarios presentados en la V Reunión de Historiadores Mexicanos y Norteamericanos, Pátzcuaro, 12 al 15 de Octubre de 1977*. Mexico, D.F.: Colegio de Mexico.

Fuentes, Carlos. 1962. *La Muerte de Artemio Cruz*. Mexico, D.F.: Fondo de Cultura Económica.

————. 1985. *The Old Gringo*. New York: Farrar, Straus & Giroux.

————. 1992. *The Buried Mirror: Reflections on Spain and the New World*. Boston, Houghton Mifflin.

Fuentes Mares, José. 1954. *. . . y México se refugió en el desierto: Luis Terrazas, historia y destino*. Mexico, D.F.: Editorial Jus.

————. 1986. *La revolución mexicana: Memorias de un espectador*. Mexico, D.F.: Grijalbo.

Furber, Percy N. 1954. *I Took Chances: From Windjammers to Jets*. Leicester: Edgar Backus.

Furman, Necah S. 1978. "Vida Nueva: A Reflection of Villista Diplomacy, 1914–1915." *New Mexico Historical Review* 53, no. 3 (Apr.): 171–92.

García de León, Antonio. 1985. *Resistencia y utopia: Memorial de agravios y crónicas de revueltas y profecias en la provincia de Chiapas durante los últimos quinientos años de su historia*. Vol. 2. Mexico, D.F.: Ediciones Era.

García Naranjo, Nemesio. N.d. *Memorias de Nemesio García Naranjo*, vol. 7: *Mis andanzas con el general Huerta*. Monterrey: Talleres de "El Porvenir."

García Riera, Emilio. 1990. *Mexico visto en el cine extranjero, 1970–1988*. Mexico, D.F.: Ediciones Era.

Garciadiego Dantan, Javier. 1981. "Revolución constitucionalista y contrarevolución (movimientos reaccionarios en Mexico, 1914–1920)." Ph.D. diss., El Colegio de México.

———. 1988. "The Universidad Nacional and the Mexican Revolution, 1910–1920." Ph.D. diss., University of Chicago.

———. 1990. "Movimientos estudiantiles durante la revolución mexicana." In *The Revolutionary Process in Mexico: Essays on Political and Social Change*, ed. Jaime E. Rodriguez O., pp. 115–60. Los Angeles: UCLA Latin American Center.

———. 1991. "Salutacion a un paradojico historiador." *Casa del Tiempo* 10, no. 100 (Mar.–Apr.).

———. 1996. *Rudos contra cientificos: La Universidad Nacional durante la revolución mexicana*. Mexico, D.F.: El Colegio de Mexico.

Gárfias M., Luis. 1981. *Breve historia militar de la revolución mexicana*, vol. 1. Mexico, D.F.: Secretaria de la Defensa Nacional.

———. 1981a. *Truth and Legend on Pancho Villa: Life and Deeds of the Famous Leader of the Mexican Revolution*. Mexico, D.F.: Panorama Editorial.

Garibaldi, Giuseppe. 1937. *A Toast to Rebellion*. Garden City, N.Y.: Garden City Publishing Co.

Garner, Paul H. 1988. *La revolución en la provincia: Soberanía estatal y caudillismo en las montañas de Oaxaca (1910–1920)*. Mexico, D.F.: Fondo de Cultura Económica.

Gerdes, Claudia. 1987. *Mexikanisches Banditentum (1827–76) als Sozial-Geschichtliches Phänomän*. Saarbrucken: Verlag Breitenbach.

Gilderhus, Mark T. 1977. *Diplomacy and Revolution: U.S.–Mexican Relations Under Wilson and Carranza*. Tucson, Ariz.: University of Arizona Press.

Gilly, Adolfo. 1983. *The Mexican Revolution*. London: Verso, NLB.

———. 1991. "Felipe Angeles camina hacia la muerte." In Odile Guilpain, *Felipe Angeles y los destinos de la revolución mexicana*. Mexico, D.F.: Fondo de Cultura Económica.

———. 1994. *La revolución interrumpida*. Mexico, D.F.: Ediciones Era.

Giner Durán, Práxedis. N.d. "Como y cuando conoci a Francisco Villa, el Maderista." MS.

Girón, Nicole. 1976. *Heraclio Bernal: Bandolero, cacique, o percursor de la revolución*. Mexico, D.F.

Goldner, Anthony. 1987. "Nobody but Venustiano: The Utility of 'Bourgeois Mediocrity Incarnate.'" MS.

———. 1993. "The Demise of the Landed Elite in Revolutionary Mexico, 1913–1920." Ph.D. diss., University of Chicago.

Goltz, Horst von der. 1917. *My Adventures as a German Secret Agent*. New York: Robert M. McBride & Co.

Gómez, Marte R. 1966. *La reforma agraria en las filas Villistas, años 1913 a 1915 y 1920*. Mexico, D.F.: Talleres de la Nación.

———. 1972. *Pancho Villa: Un intento de semblanza*. Mexico, D.F.: Fondo de la Cultura Económica

———. 1975. *Historia de la Comisión Nacional Agraria*. Mexico, D.F.

Gómez Quiñones, Juan. 1977. *Sembradores: Ricardo Flores Magón y el Partido Liberal Mexicano: A Eulogy and Critique*. Los Angeles: Chicano Studies Center Publications.

———. 1992. *Mexican Nationalist Formation: Political Discourse, Policy and Dissidence*. Encino, Calif.: Floricanto Press.

González, Carlos. 1992. *Miguel Ahumada: El gobernador porfirista*. Ciudad Juárez: Meridano 107 Editores.

González, Manuel W. 1985. *Con Carranza: Episodios de la revolución constitucionalista, 1913–1914. 1933.* Reprint. Mexico, D.F.: Instituto Nacional de Estudios Históricos de la Revolución Mexicana.

———. 1935. *Contra Villa: Relato de la campaña, 1914–1915.* Mexico, D.F.: Ediciones Botas.

González, Pablo, Jr., ed. 1971. *El centinela fiel del constitucionalismo.* Saltillo, Coah.: Textos de cultura historiografica.

González Calzada, Manuel. 1972. *Historia de la revolución mexicana en Tabasco.* Mexico, D.F.: Instituto Nacional de Estudios Históricos de la Revolución Mexicana.

———. 1980. *El agrarismo en Tabasco.* Mexico, D.F.: Consejo Editorial del Gobierno del Estado de Tabasco.

González Flores, Enrique. 1949. *Chihuahua de la independencia a la revolución.* Mexico, D.F.: Ediciones Botas.

González Garza, Federico. 1936. *La revolución mexicana: Mi contribución político-literaria.* Mexico, D.F.

———. 1982. *La revolución mexicana.* Mexico, D.F.: Partido Revolucionario Institucional.

González Herrera, Carlos. 1992. "Los terrenos nacionales durante el porfiriato." In *Actas del Tercer Congreso de Historia Comparada, 1991,* pp. 243–54. Ciudad Juárez: Universidad Autónoma de Ciudad Juárez.

———. 1993. "La agricultura en el proyecto económico de Chihuahua durante el porfiriato." *Siglo XIX: Cuadernos de Historia* 2, no. 5 (Feb.): 9–38.

González Navarro, Moisés. 1985. *La pobreza en México.* Mexico, D.F.: El Colegio de México.

———. 1987. "El Maderismo y la revolución agraria." *Historia Mexicana* 37, no. 1 (July–Sept.): 5–27.

González Pacheco, Cuauhtémoc. 1983. *Capital extranjero en la selva de Chiapas, 1863–1982.* Mexico, D.F.: Universidad Nacional Autónoma de México.

González Ramírez, Manuel, ed. 1954–57. *Fuentes para la historia de la revolución mexicana.* 4 vols. Mexico, D.F.: Fondo de la Cultura Económica.

———. 1966. *La revolución social de México.* 3 vols. Mexico, D.F.: Fondo de la Cultura Económica.

González Roa, Fernando. N.d. *Aspecto agrario de la revolución mexicana.* Mexico, D.F.: Secretaría de la Reforma Agraria.

González y González, Luis, ed. 1962–63. *Fuentes de la historia contemporánea en Mexico: Libros y folletos.* 3 vols. Mexico, D.F.

———. 1968. *Pueblo en vilo.* Mexico, D.F.: El Colegio de Mexico.

———. 1985. "La revolución mexicana desde el punto de vista de los revolucionados." *Historias* 8–9: 5–14.

Gordillo y Ortiz, Octavio. 1986. *La revolución en el estado de Chiapas.* Mexico, D.F.: Instituto Nacional de Estudios Históricos de la Revolución Mexicana.

Gracia García, Guadalupe. 1982. *El servicio médico durante la revolución mexicana.* Mexico, D.F.: Editores Mexicanos Unidos.

Gressley, Gene M., ed. 1994. *Old West / New West: Quo Vadis?* Worland, Wyo.: High Plains Publishing Co.

Grieb, Kenneth J. 1969. *The United States and Huerta.* Lincoln: University of Nebraska Press.

———. 1971. "Standard Oil and the Financing of the Mexican Revolution." *California Historical Society Quarterly* 50, no. 1 (Mar.): 59–71.

Griffen, William B. 1988. *Apaches at War and Peace: The Janos Presidio, 1750–1858.* Albuquerque: University of New Mexico Press.

Grimaldo, Isaac. 1916. *Apuntes para la historia. Contiene la vida, muerte y funerales del general Maclovio Herrera y ligeros apuntes biográficos de sus principales compañeros de armas. Precedidos de un juicioso proemio del modesto escritor Rafael S. Lechón.* San Luis

Potosí, Mexico, D.F.: Edición del Gobierno Potosino. Imprenta de la Escuela Industrial Militar.

Gruening, Ernest. 1928. *Mexico and Its Heritage.* New York: Century Co.

Guerra, François-Xavier. 1981. "La Révolution mexicaine: D'abord une révolution minière?" *Annales: Economies, sociétés, civilisations* 35, no. 5 (Sept.–Oct.): 785–814.

———. 1983. "Réponse de François-Xavier Guerra." *Annales: Economies, sociétés, civilisations* 38, no. 2 (Mar.–Apr.): 460–69.

———. 1985. *Le Mexique, de l'ancien régime à la révolution.* 2 vols. Paris: L'Harmattan.

———. 1989. "Teoría y método en el análisis de la revolución mexicana." *Revista Mexicana de Sociología* 51, no. 2 (Apr.–June): 3–24.

Guerrero, Praxedis G. 1991. *Praxedis G. Guerrero, artículos literarios y de combate; pensmientos crónicas revolucionarias, etc. . . . .* Mexico, D.F.: Centro de Estudios Históricos de Movimiento Obero Mexicano, 1977.

Gugliotta, Tom. 1986. "True Grit." *Tropic* [Sunday Magazine of the Miami Herald], Nov. 9.

Guilane, Jacques. 1985. *Pancho Villa, l'aventurier de la révolution.* Paris: La Pensée Universelle, 1985.

Guilderhus, Mark T. 1986. *Pan-American Visions: Woodrow Wilson in the Western Hemisphere, 1913–1921.* Tucson: University of Arizona Press.

Guilpain Peuliard, Odile. 1991. *Felipe Angeles y los destinos de la revolución mexicana.* Mexico, D.F.: Fondo de Cultura Economica.

Gutelman, Michel. 1971. *Réforme et mystification agraires en Amérique latine: La cas du Mexique.* Paris: François Maspero.

Guzmán, Martín Luis. 1938. *Memorias de Pancho Villa.* Mexico, D.F.: Botas.

———. 1966. *Memoirs of Pancho Villa.* Translated by Virginia H. Taylor. Austin: University of Texas Press.

———. 1987 [1930]. *El águila y la serpiente.* Mexico, D.F.: Editorial Porrúa.

———. 1990. *The Border and the Revolution.* Silver City, N.Mex.: High-Lonesome Books

———. 1990. *Muertes históricas.* Mexico, D.F.: Consejo Nacional para la Cultura y las Artes.

Guzmán Esparza, Roberto. 1957. *Memorias de don Adolfo de la Huerta.* Mexico, D.F.: Ediciones Guzmán.

Gwin, J. B. 1920. "Mexico After Ten Years of Revolution." *The Survey,* Nov. 13: 248–49.

Haber, Stephen. 1989. *Industry and Underdevelopment: The Industrialization of Mexico, 1890–1940.* Stanford, California: Stanford University Press.

Haley, J. Edward. 1970. *Revolution and Intervention: The Diplomacy of Taft and Wilson with Mexico.* Cambridge, Mass.: MIT Press.

Hall, Linda B. 1981. *Alvaro Obregón: Power and Revolution in Mexico, 1911–1920.* College Station: Texas A&M University Press.

Hall, Linda B., and Don M. Coerver. 1988. *Revolution on the Border: The United States and Mexico, 1910–1920.* Albuquerque: University of New Mexico Press.

Harper, James William. 1968. "Hugh Lenox Scott: Soldier Diplomat, 1876–1917." Ph.D. diss., University of Virginia.

Harrer, Hans Jürgen. 1973. *Die Revolution in Mexico.* Cologne: Paul Rugenstein Verlag.

Harris, Charles H., III, and Louis R. Sadler. 1975. "Pancho Villa and the Columbus Raid: The Missing Documents." *New Mexico Historical Review* 50, no. 4 (Oct.): 335–46.

———. 1978. "The Plan of San Diego and the Mexican–United States War Crisis of 1916: A Reexamination." *Hispanic American Historical Review* 58, no. 3 (Aug.): 381–408.

———. 1982. "The 'Underside' of the Mexican Revolution: El Paso, 1912." *The Americas* 39, no. 1 (July). 69–83.

———. 1988. *The Border and the Revolution: Clandestine Activities of the Mexican Revolution, 1910–1920.* Silver City, N.Mex.: High-Lonesome Books.

Harris, Larry A. 1949. *Pancho Villa and the Columbus Raid.* El Paso, Tex.: McMath Co.

———. 1989. *Pancho Villa: Strong Man of the Revolution.* Silver City, N.Mex.: High-Lonesome Books.

Hart, John M. 1972. "Agrarian Precursors of the Mexican Revolution: The Development of an Ideology." *The Americas* 29, no. 2 (Oct.): 131–50.

———. 1978. *Anarchism and the Mexican Working Class, 1860–1931.* Austin: University of Texas Press.

———. 1984. "The Dynamics of the Mexican Revolution: Historiographic Perspectives." *Latin American Research Review* 19, no. 3: 223–331.

———. 1987. *Revolutionary Mexico: The Coming and Process of the Mexican Revolution.* Berkeley and Los Angeles: University of California Press.

Hatch, Nelle Spilsbury, and B. Carmon Hardy. 1985. *Stalwarts South of the Border.* El Paso, Tex.: M. Knudsen.

Henderson, Paul V. N. 1979. *Mexican Exiles in the Borderlands, 1919–1913.* El Paso, Tex.: Texas Western College Press.

———. 1981. *Felix Diaz, the Porfirians, and the Mexican Revolution.* Lincoln: University of Nebraska Press.

———. 1984. "Woodrow Wilson, Victoriano Huerta, and the Recognition Issue in Mexico." *The Americas* 41, no. 2 (Oct.): 151–76.

Hendrick, Burton J. 1923–25. *The Life of Walter H. Page.* 3 vols. New York: Doubleday, Page & Co.

Hernández Chávez, Alicia. 1979. "La defensa de los finqueros en Chiapas, 1914–1920." *Historia Mexicana* 28, no. 3 (Jan.–Mar.): 335–69.

———. 1984. "Militares y negocios en la revolución mexicana." *Historia Mexicana* 34, no. 2 (Oct.–Dec.): 181–212.

———. 1989. "Origen y ocaso del ejército porfiriano." *Historia Mexicana* 39, no. 1 (July–Sept.): 257–96.

———. 1993. *La tradición republicana del buen gobierno.* Mexico, D.F.: Fondo de la Cultura Económica.

Hernández y Lazo, Begoña. 1984. *Las batallas de la Plaza de Chihuahua 1915–1916: Cuaderno.* Ciudad Universitaria, Mexico, D.F.: Coordinacion de Humanidades, Universidad Nacional Autonoma de Mexico, 1984.

Hernández y Lazo, Begoña, et al., eds. 1992. *Las mujeres en la revolución mexicana, 1884–1920: Biografias de mujeres revolucionarias.* Mexico, D.F.: Instituto Nacional de Estudios Históricos de la Revolución Mexicana.

Herrera, Celia. 1981. *Francisco Villa: Ante la historia.* Mexico, D.F.: B. Costa-Amic.

Herrera-Sobek, María. 1990. *The Mexican Corrido: A Feminist Analysis.* Bloomington: University of Indiana Press.

Herrera-Vargas, Benjamin. N.d. *La revolución en Chihuahua, 1910–1911.* Mexico, D.F.

Hicks, Granville. 1936. *John Reed: The Making of a Revolutionary.* New York: Macmillan.

Hill, Larry D. 1973. *Emissaries to a Revolution: Woodrow Wilson's Executive Agents in Mexico.* Baton Rouge: Louisiana State University Press.

Hinojosa, Ivan. 1991. "José Santos Chocano: A Poet in the Mexican Revolution." MS.

Hobsbawm, Eric. 1965. *Primitive Rebels: Studies in Archaic Forms of Social Movements in the Nineteenth and Twentieth Centuries*. New York: Norton.

———. 1969. *Bandits*. New York: Delacorte Press.

Holcombe, Harold Eugene. 1968. "United States Arms Control and the Mexican Revolution, 1910–1924." Ph.D. diss., University of Alabama.

Holden, Robert. 1990. "Priorities of the State in the Survey of Public Land in Mexico." *Hispanic American Historical Review* 70, no. 4 (Nov.): 579–608.

———. 1994. *Mexico and the Survey of Public Lands: The Management of Modernization, 1876–1911*. De Kalb: Northern Illinois University Press.

Holden, Robert Curry. 1978. *Teresita*. Owings Mills, Md.: Stemmer House.

Houston, David F. 1926. *Eight Years with Wilson's Cabinet, 1913–1920*. Garden City, N.Y.: Doubleday, Page & Co.

Hovey, Tamara. 1982. *John Reed: Witness to Revolution*. New York: George Sand Books.

Hu DeHart, Evelyn. 1971. "The Villista Bureaucracy: Men and Organization." MS.

Huerta, Victoriano. 1957. *Memorias*. Mexico, D.F.: Ediciones "Vertica."

Hunt, Frazier. 1922. "New Peons for Old: A Decade of Revolution in Mexico." *New Century Magazine*, Mar. 22.

Hurtado y Olin, Juan. 1978. *Estudios y relatos sobre la revolución mexicana*. Mexico, D.F.: B. Costa-Amic.

Illades Aguilar, Lillian. 1993. *La rebelión de Tomochic*. Mexico, D.F.

Illiades, Carlos. 1985. *México y España durante la revolución mexicana*. Mexico, D.F.

Instituto Cultural de Aguascalientes. 1990. *La soberana convención revolucionaria en Aguascalientes: 1914–1989*. Aguascalientes, Mexico, D.F.: Instituto Cultural de Aguascalientes.

Instituto Nacional de Estudios Históricos de la Revolución Mexicana. 1985. *Abraham González*. Mexico, D.F.: Instituto Nacional de Estudios Históricos de la Revolución Mexicana.

———. 1985. *Alvaro Obregón*. Mexico, D.F.

———. 1985. *Batalla de Celaya*. Mexico, D.F.

———. 1985. *Felipe Angeles*. Mexico, D.F.

———. 1985. *Francisco Villa*. Mexico, D.F.

———. 1985. *Periodismo en la revolución*. Mexico, D.F.

———. 1985. *Salvador Alvarado*. Mexico, D.F.

———. 1985. *Toma de Torreón*. Mexico, D.F.

———. 1985. *Tratados de Teoluyucan*. Mexico, D.F.

———. 1985. *Ultimos meses de Porfirio Díaz en el poder: Antología documental*. Mexico, D.F.

———. 1985. *Venustiano Carranza*. Mexico, D.F.

Irving, Clifford. 1982. *Tom Mix and Pancho Villa*. New York: St. Martin's Press.

Iturriaga de la Fuente, José. 1987. *La revolución hacendaria*. Mexico, D.F.: Secretaría de Educación Pública.

Jackson, Byron C. 1976. "The Political and Military Role of General Felipe Angeles in the Mexican Revolution, 1914–1915." Ph.D. diss., Georgetown University.

Jacobs, Ian. 1983. *Ranchero Revolt: The Mexican Revolution in Guerrero*. Austin: University of Texas Press.

Jauffret, Eric. 1986. *Révolutions et sacrifice au Mexique*. Paris: Les Editions du Cerf.

Jaurrieta, José Maria. N.d. "Seis años con el General Villa." MS.

———. 1935. *Seis años con el General Francisco Villa*. Vol. 2. Mexico, D.F.: Ediciones de "El Instante," Artes Gráficas Mexicanas, S.C.L.

Johnson, Annie R. 1972. *Heartbeats of Colonia Díaz*. Mesa, Ariz.

Johnson, Kenneth M. 1961. *José Yves Limantour v. United States.* Los Angeles.

Johnson, Robert Bruce. 1964. "The Punitive Expedition: A Military, Diplomatic, and Political History of Pershing's Chase After Pancho Villa, 1916–1917." 2 vols. Ph.D. diss., University of Southern California.

Johnson, William W. 1984. *Heroic Mexico: The Narrative History of a Twentieth-Century Revolution.* San Diego: Harcourt Brace Jovanovich, Publishers.

Jones, Oakah L., Jr. 1979. *Los Paisanos: Spanish Settlers on the Northern Frontier of New Spain.* Norman: University of Oklahoma Press.

———. 1988. *Nueva Vizcaya: Heartland of the Spanish Frontier.* Albuquerque: University of New Mexico Press.

Jordán, Fernando. 1975. *Crónica de un país bárbaro.* Ciudad Chihuahua: Centro Librero de la Prensa.

Joseph, Gilbert M. 1980. *Revolution from Without: Yucatán, Mexico, and the United States, 1880–1824.* Durham, N.C.: Duke University Press.

Joseph, Gilbert M., and Daniel Nugent, eds. 1994. *Everyday Forms of State Formation: Revolution and the Negotiation of Rule in Modern Mexico.* Durham, N.C.: Duke University Press.

Joseph, Gilbert M., and A. Wells. 1990. "Yucatán: Elite Politics and Rural Insurgency." In *Provinces of the Revolution: Essays on Regional Mexican History, 1910–1929,* ed. Thomas Benjamin and Mark Wasserman, pp. 93–131. Albuquerque: University of New Mexico Press.

———. 1990a. "Seasons of Upheaval: The Crisis of Oligarchical Rule in Yucatán, 1909–1915." In *The Revolutionary Process in Mexico: Essays on Political and Social Change,* ed. Jaime E. Rodriguez O., pp. 161–85. Los Angeles: UCLA Latin American Center.

Juvenal [Enrique Pérez Rul]. 1916. *¿Quien es Francisco Villa?* Dallas, Tex.: Gran Imprenta Poliglota.

Karnow, Stanley. 1989. *In Our Image: America's Empire in the Philippines.* New York: Foreign Policy Association.

Katz, Friedrich. 1962. "Alemania y Francisco Villa." *Historia Mexicana* 12, no. 1 (July–Sept.): 88–102.

———. 1964. *Deutschland, Díaz und die Mexikanische Revolution.* Berlin: Deutscher Verlag der Wissenschaften.

———. 1969. "Zu den Spezifischen Ursachen der Mexikanischen Revolution von 1910." In *Studien über die Revolution,* ed. Manfred Kossok. Berlin: Akademie Verlag.

———. 1974. "Labor Conditions on Haciendas in Porfirian Mexico: Some Trends and Tendencies." *Hispanic American Historical Review* 54, no. 1 (Feb.): 1–47.

———. 1976. "Peasants in the Mexican Revolution of 1910." In *Forging Nations: A Comparative View of Rural Ferment and Revolt,* ed. Joseph Spielberg and Scott Whiteford. East Lansing: Michigan State University Press.

———. 1976a. "Einige Besonderheiten der Mexikanischen Revolution: Kommentar." *Geschichte und Gesellschaft* 2, no. 2: 241–43.

———. 1976b. "Agrarian Changes in Northern Mexico in the Period of Villista Rule, 1913–1915." In *Contemporary Mexico: Papers of the IV International Congress of Mexican History,* ed. James W. Wilkie, Michael C. Meyer, and Edna Monzón de Wilkie. Berkeley and Los Angeles: University of California Press.

———. 1978. "Pancho Villa and the Attack on Columbus, New Mexico." *The American Historical Review* 83, no. 1 (Feb.): 101–30.

———. 1979. *Pancho Villa y el ataque a Columbus, Nuevo México.* Chihuahua: Sociedad Chihuahuense de Estudios Históricos.

————. 1979a. "Pancho Villa as Revolutionary Governor of Chihuahua." In *Essays on the Mexican Revolution: Revisionist Views of the Leaders*, ed. George Wolfskill and Douglas W. Richmond. Austin: University of Texas Press.

————. 1980. "Pancho Villa's Agrarian Roots and Policies." In *Caudillo and Peasant in the Mexican Revolution*, ed. D. A. Brading. Cambridge: Cambridge University Press.

————. 1981. *The Secret War in Mexico*. Chicago: University of Chicago Press.

————. 1984. *Villa: El gobernador revolucionario de Chihuahua*. Translated by Rubén Osorio, with intro. Mexico, D.F.: Talleres Gráficos del Estado de Chihuahua.

————. 1986. "Mexico: Restored Republic and Porfiriato, 1867–1910." In *Cambridge History of Latin America*, vol. 5, ed. Alan Knight. Cambridge Cambridge University Press.

————. 1988. "From Alliance to Dependency: The Formation and Deformation of an Alliance Between Francisco Villa and the United States." In *Rural Revolt in Mexico and U.S. Intervention*. San Diego: Center for U.S.–Mexican Studies, University of California, San Diego, Monograph series, 27.

————. ed. 1988a. *Riot, Rebellion, and Revolution*. Princeton: Princeton University Press.

————. 1988b. "Rural Rebellions After 1810." In *Riot, Rebellion, and Revolution*, ed. Friedrich Katz, pp. 277–91 Princeton: Princeton University Press.

————. 1989. "Pancho Villa y la revolución mexicana." *Revista Mexicana de Sociología* 2, no. 89 (Apr.–June): 87–113.

————. 1991. "La ultima gran campaña de Francisco Villa." Fideicomiso Archivos Plutarco Elías Calles y Fernando Torreblanca, Mexico, D.F., *Boletín*, no. 5.

————. 1991a. "Debt Peonage in Tulancingo." In *Circumpacifica: Festschrift für Thomas S. Barthel*, pp. 239–48. Frankfurt a.M.: Peter Lang.

————. 1992. "Los motivos agrarios de la revolución en Chihuahua." In *Las formas y las políticas del dominio agrario: Homenage a François Chevalier*, coord. Ricardo Avila Palafox, Carlos Martínez Assad, and Jean Meyer, pp. 276–83. Guadalajara, Jal.: Editorial Universidad de Guadalajara.

————. 1993. "Zum Werdegang der Nachkommen von Azteken, Inka und Maya seit der spanischen Eroberung." In *Zeitschrift für Latein-Amerika* (Vienna), no. 44–45: 91–101.

————. 1994. "The Demise of the Old Order on Mexico's Haciendas, 1911–1913." In *Ibero-amerikanisches Archiv* (Berlin) 20, no. 3–4: 399–435.

————. 1995. "Los hacendados y la revolución mexicana." In *Actas del Cuarto Congreso de Historia Comparada, 1993*, pp. 396–408. Ciudad Juárez: Universidad Autónoma de Ciudad Juárez.

Katz, Friedrich, and Jane-Dale Lloyd, eds. 1986. *Porfirio Diaz frente al descontento regional*. Mexico, D.F.: Universidad Iberoamericana.

Kemmerer, Edwin. N.d. "The Mexican Problem." MS. The Edwin Kemmerer Papers, Princeton University Library, Princeton, N.J.

King, Rosa E. 1940. *Tempest over Mexico: A Personal Chronicle*. Boston: Little, Brown.

Knight, Alan. 1981. "Intellectuals in the Mexican Revolution." In *Los intelectuales y el poder en Mexico*, ed. Roderic A. Camp, Charles A. Hale, and Josefina Vásquez. Mexico, D.F.: El Colegio de Mexico.

————. 1983. "La Révolution mexicaine: Révolution minière ou révolution serrano." *Annales: Economies, sociétés, civilisations* 38, no. 2 (Mar.–Apr.): 449–59.

————. 1985. "The Mexican Revolution: Bourgeois? Nationalist? Or Just a 'Great Rebellion?'" *Bulletin of Latin American Research* 4, no. 2: 1–37.

————. 1986. *The Mexican Revolution*. 2 vols. Cambridge: Cambridge University Press.

———. 1987. *U.S.–Mexican Relations, 1910–1940: An Interpretation.* La Jolla, Calif.: Center for U.S.–Mexican Studies, University of San Diego.

———. 1989. "Los intelectuales en la revolución mexicana." *Revista Mexicana de Sociología* 51, no. 2: 25–65.

———. 1990. "Revolutionary Project, Recalcitrant People: Mexico, 1910–1940." In *The Revolutionary Process in Mexico: Essays on Political and Social Change,* ed. Jaime E. Rodriguez O., pp. 227–64. Los Angeles: UCLA Latin American Center.

Koopmann, Friedhelm. 1990. *Diplomatie und Reichsinteresse das Geheimdienstkalkül in der deutschen Amerikapolitik 1914 bis 1917.* Frankfurt a.M.: Peter Lang.

Koreck, Maria Teresa. 1988. "Space and Revolution in Northwestern Chihuahua." In *Rural Revolt in Mexico and U.S. Intervention,* ed. Daniel Nugent. San Diego: Center for U.S.–Mexican Studies at the University of San Diego, Monograph Series 27.

———. 1995. "Social Organization and Land Tenure in a Revolutionary Community in Northern Mexico, Cuchillo Parado, 1865–1910." Paper delivered at the Septima Reunion de Historiadores Mexicanos y Norteamericanos. Oaxaca, Mexico, Oct. 25–26.

Krauze, Enrique. 1987. *El vértigo de la victoria: Alvaro Obregón.* Mexico, D.F.: Fondo de Cultura Económica.

———. 1987a. *Francisco Villa: Entre el ángel y el fierro.* Mexico, D.F.: Fondo de Cultura Económica.

———. 1987b. *Francisco Madero: Místico de la libertad.* Mexico, D.F.: Fondo de Cultura Económica.

———. 1987c. *Plutarco E. Calles: Reformar desde el origen.* Mexico, D.F.: Fondo de Cultura Económica.

———. 1987d. *Venustiano Carranza, puente entre siglos.* Mexico, D.F.: Fondo de Cultura Económica.

———. 1994. *Siglo de Caudillos: Biografía política de Mexico (1810–1910).* Mexico, D.F.: Tusquets Editores.

LaFrance, David G. 1989. *The Mexican Revolution in Puebla, 1908–1913.* Wilmington, Del.: Scholarly Resources.

———. 1990. "Many Causes, Movements, and Failures, 1910–1913: The Regional Nature of Maderismo." In *Provinces of the Revolution: Essays on Regional Mexican History, 1910–1929,* ed. Thomas Benjamin and Mark Wasserman. Albuquerque: University of New Mexico Press.

LaMond Tullis, F. 1987. *Mormons in Mexico: The Dynamics of Faith and Culture.* Logan: Utah State University Press.

Langle Ramírez, Arturo. 1961. *El ejército Villista.* Mexico, D.F.: Institutio Nacional de Antropología e Historia.

———. 1973. *Crónica de la cobija de Pancho Villa.* Mexico, D.F.: Instituto Nacional de Estudios Históricos de la revolución Mexicana.

———. 1980. *Los primeros cien años de Pancho Villa.* Mexico, D.F.: B. Costa-Amic.

Lansford, William Douglas. 1965. *Pancho Villa.* Los Angeles: Shelbourne Press.

Lara Pardo, Luis. 1938. *Madero: Esbozo político.* Mexico, D.F.: Ediciones Botas.

Lau, Ana, and Carmen Ramos. 1993. *Mujeres y revolución, 1900–1917.* Mexico, D.F.: Instituto Nacional de Estudios Históricos de la Revolución Mexicana.

Lavretski, I., and Adolfo Gilly. 1978. *Pancho Villa: Dos ensayos.* Mexico, D.F.: Editorial Macehual.

Lavrov, Nikolai M. 1972. "Verkhouni revoliutsionnyi konvert (iz istorii mekiskanskoi revoliutsil 1910–1977gg." *Vop. Ist.* 3 (Mar.): 94–106.

———. 1978. *La revolución mexicana de 1910–1917.* Mexico, D.F.: Ediciones de Cultura Popular.

Leal, Juan Felipe. 1972. *La burguesía y el estado Mexicano*. Mexico, D.F.: Ediciones El Caballito.

Leal, Juan Felipe, and José Woldenberg. 1980. *La clase obrera en la historia de Mexico: Del estado liberal a los inicios de la dictadura porfirista*. Mexico, D.F.: Siglo Veintiuno.

León, Luis L. 1987. *Crónica del poder: En los recuerdos de un político en el México revolucionario*. Mexico, D.F.: Fondo de Cultura Económica.

León G., Ricardo. 1992. "Comerciantes y mercado crediticio en el Chihuahua porfiriano; el caso del Banco Minero de Chihuahua." In *Actas del Tercer Congreso de Historia Comparada, 1991*, pp. 255–64. Ciudad Juárez: Universidad Autónoma de Ciudad Juárez.

Lerner, Victoria. 1995. "Rebelión y disidencia en la frontera norte de Mexico, 1914–1920 (Estados Unidos tierra de conspiraciones mexicanas)." In *Actas del Cuarto Congreso de Historia Comparada, 1993*, pp. 533–42. Ciudad Juárez: Universidad Autónoma de Ciudad Juárez.

———. N.d. "Historia de la reforma educativa." MS.

———. N.d.a. "Los fundamentos socioeconómicos del cacicazgo en Mexico postrevolucionario: El caso de Saturnino Cedillo." MS.

Liceaga, Luis. 1958. *Felix Díaz*. Mexico, D.F.: Editorial Jus.

Lida, Clara E., ed. 1981. *Tres aspectos de la presencia española en México durante el porfiriato*. Mexico, D.F.: El Colegio de Mexico.

Limantour, José Yves. 1965. *Apuntes sobre mi vida pública, 1892–1911*. Mexico, D.F.: Editorial Porrúa.

Limerick, Patricia Nelson. 1987. *The Legacy of Conquest: The Unbroken Past of the American West*. New York: Norton.

Link, Arthur S. 1947–65. *Wilson*. 5 vols. Princeton: Princeton University Press.

———. 1963. *Woodrow Wilson and the Progressive Era, 1910–1917*. New York: Harper Torchbooks.

Lister, Florence C., and Robert Lister. 1966. *Chihuahua: Storehouse of Storms*. Albuquerque: University of New Mexico Press.

Lloyd, Jane-Dale. 1987. *El proceso de modernización capitalista en el noroeste de Chihuahua (1880–1910)*. Mexico, D.F.: Universidad Iberoamericana, Departamento de Historia.

———. 1988. "Rancheros and Rebellion. " In *Rural Revolt in Mexico and U.S. Intervention*, ed. Daniel Nugent. San Diego: Center for U.S.–Mexican Studies at the University of San Diego, Monograph Series 27.

———. 1995. "Cultura ranchera en el noroeste de Chihuahua." Ph.D. diss., Universidad Iberoamericana, Mexico, D.F.

López, Angel Rivas. N.d. *El verdadero Pancho Villa*. Mexico, D.F.: B.Costa-Amic.

López de Lara, Laura, ed. 1982. *El agrarismo en Villa*. Mexico, D.F.: Centro de Estudios Históricos del Agrarismo en Mexico.

Løtveit, Morten. 1984. "The Rise of Pancho Villa." MS.

Lou, Dennis Wingsou. 1963. "Fall Committee: An Investigation of Mexican Affairs." Ph.D. diss., Indiana University.

Lowery, S. 1988. "The Complexity of a Revolutionary: Pancho Villa." *Twin Plant News* (Nibbe, Hernández and Associates, El Paso), Nov.

Lozoya Cigarroa, Manuel. 1988. *Francisco Villa, el grande*. Durango: Impresiones Gráficas México.

Mac Gregor, Josefina. 1986. "La XXVI legislatura frente a Victoriano Huerta: ¿Un caso de parlamentarismo?" *Secuencia* 4 (Jan.–Apr.): 10–23.

———. 1992. *Mexico y España del porfiriato a la revolución*. Mexico, D.F.: Instituto Nacional de Estudios Históricos de la Revolución Mexicana.

Machado, Manuel A., Jr. 1981. *The North American Cattle Industry, 1910–1975: Ideology, Conflict, and Change.* College Station: Texas A&M University Press.

————. 1988. *Centaur of the North: Francisco Villa, the Mexican Revolution, and Northern Mexico.* Austin, Tex.: Eakin Press.

Machuca Macías, Pablo. 1977. *Mil novecientos diez: La revolución en una Ciudad del Norte.* Mexico, D.F.: B. Costa-Amic.

MacLachlan, Colin M. 1991. *Anarchism and the Mexican Revolution: The Political Trials of Ricardo Flores Magón in the United States.* Berkeley and Los Angeles: University of California Press.

Madero, Francisco I. 1908. *La sucesión presidencial en 1910.* San Pedro, Coahuila. Facsimile edition, Mexico City: Ediciones de la Secretaria de Hacienda, 1960.

————. 1987. *Antología.* Edited by María de los Angeles Suárez del Solar. Mexico, D.F.: Instituto Nacional de Estudios Históricos de la Revolución Mexicana.

Madero, Gustavo A. 1991. *Epistolario.* Mexico, D.F.: Editorial Diana.

Magaña, Gildardo. 1985. *Emiliano Zapata y el agrarismo en México.* 5 vols. Mexico, D.F.: Instituto Nacional de Estudios Históricos de la Revolución Mexicana.

Mahoncy, Tom. 1932. "The Columbus Raid." *Southwest Review* 17 (Winter): 161–71.

Mange, Steven A. 1989. "William Randolph Hearst and the Mexican Revolution." MS

Mantecón, Pérez, Adán. 1967. *Recuerdos de un Villista: Mi campaña en la revolución.* Mexico, D.F.

Margo, Dr. A. N.d. *Who, Where, and Why is Villa?.* New York: Latin American News Association.

María y Campos, Armando de. 1939. *Múgica: Cronica biografica aportación a la historia de la revolución mexicana.* Mexico, D.F: Ediciones Populares.

Márquez Sterling, Manuel. 1958 [1917]. *Los ultimos dias del presidente Madero: Mi gestión diplomática en Mexico.* 2d ed. Mexico, D.F.: Porrúa.

Martin, Louis A. M. 1965. *Viva Villa.* Amsterstam: H. Meulenhoff.

Martínez, Oscar J. 1971. *Border Boom Town: Ciudad Juárez Since 1848.* Austin: University of Texas Press.

————. 1983. *Fragments of the Mexican Revolution: Personal Accounts from the Border.* Albequerque: University of New Mexico Press.

Martínez del Rio, Pablo. 1928. *El suplicio del hacendado.* Mexico, D.F.

Martínez Fernández del Campo, Luis, ed. 1975. *De cómo vino Huerta y cómo se fue: Apuntes para la historia de un régimen militar.* Mexico, D.F.: Ediciones El Caballito.

Marvin, George. 1914. "Villa: The Bandit Chieftain Who Has Risen to Become the Most Powerful Man in Mexico." *World's Work* 28 (July): 269–84.

Mason, Herbert Molloy, Jr. 1970. *The Great Pursuit: General John J. Pershing's Punitive Expedition Across the Rio Grande to Destroy the Mexican Bandit Pancho Villa.* New York: Random House.

Matute, Alvaro. 1980. *Historia de la revolución mexicana, periodo 1917–1924,* vol. 8: *La Carrera del Caudillo.* Mexico, D.F.: El Colegio de Mexico.

McCreary, Guy Weddington. 1974. *From Glory to Oblivion.* New York: Vantage Press.

McCutchen McBride, George. 1923. *The Land Systems of Mexico.* New York: American Geographical Society.

McLeroy, James David. 1976. "The Minds of Pancho Villa: A Study in Insurgent Leadership." M.A. thesis, University of Texas at Austin.

McWilliams, Carey. 1931. *The Mysteries of Ambrose Bierce.* Camden, N.J.: American Mercury.

Mcdillín M., José de Jesús. 1986. *Las ideas agrarias en la convención de Aguascalientes.* Mexico, D.F.: Centro de Estudios Históricos del Agrarismo en México.

Medina Ruiz, Fernando. 1972. *Francisco Villa: Cuando el rencor estalla.* . . . Mexico, D.F.: Editorial Jus.

Mejía Prieto, Jorge. 1990. *Las dos almas de Pancho Villa.* Mexico, D.F.: Editorial Diana.

———. 1992. *Yo, Pancho Villa.* Mexico, D.F.: Editorial Planeta Mexicana.

Memoria del Congreso Internacional sobre la revolución mexicana. 1991. Vol. 5. Mexico, D.F.: Instituto de Estudios Históricos sobre la Revolución Mexicana.

Mena Brito, Bernardino. 1936. *Felipe Angeles, federal.* Mexico, D.F.: Ediciones Herrerias.

———. 1938. *El lugarteniente gris de Pancho Villa.* Mexico.

Mena, Mario. 1983. *Alvaro Obregon: Historia militar y politica, 1912–1929.* Mexico, D.F.: Editorial Jus.

Mendoza, Vicente T. 1976. *El corrido Mexicano.* Mexico, D.F.: Fondo de Cultura Económica.

Mercado, Salvador R. 1914. *Revelaciones históricas, 1913–1914.* Las Cruces, N.Mex.: author.

Metz, Leon C. 1989. *Border: The U.S.–Mexico Line.* El Paso: Mangan Books.

Mexico y los Estados Unidos: Opiniones de intelectuales y de los periodicos mas serios acerca de los últimos acontecimientos. 1916. Mexico, D.F.: Talleres Linotropicos de "Revista de Revistas."

Meyer, Eugenia. 1970. *Conciencia histórica norteamericana sobre la revolución de 1910.* Mexico, D.F.: Instituto Nacional de Antropologia e Historia.

———. 1973. *La vida con Villa en la hacienda de Canutillo.* Mexico: INAH.

———. 1978. *El Archivo de la Palabra: Hacia una historia de masas y Hablan los villistas.* Mexico: Boletín del INAH, INAH, Epoca III, no. 23 (July–Sept.).

Meyer, Eugenia, Graciela Altamirano, Mónica Cuevas, Laura Herrera, Gema Lozano, and Guadalupe Villa. 1961. *Museo histórico de la revolución en el estado de Chihuahua.* Mexico, D.F.: Instituto Nacional de Antropología e Historia.

Meyer, Eugenia, Ma. Alba Pastor, Ximena Sepúlveda, and María Isabel Souza. 1986. "La vida con Villa en la Hacienda de Canutillo." *Secuencia* 5 (May–Aug.): 170–83.

Meyer, Jean. 1970. "Les Ouvriers dans la révolution mexicaine: Les Bataillons rouges." *Annales: Economies, sociétés, civilisations* 25, no. 1 (Jan.–Feb.): 30–35.

———. 1973. *La Révolution mexicaine, 1910–1940.* Paris: Calmann-Levy.

———. 1974. "Grandes campañas, ejércitos populares y ejército estatal en la revolución mexicana (1910–1930)." *Anuario de Estudios Americanos* 31: 1005–30.

———. 1976. "Periodización e ideología." In *Contemporary Mexico: Papers of the IV International Congress of Mexican History*, ed. James W. Wilkie, Michael C. Meyer, and Edna Monzón de Wilkie, pp. 711–22. Berkeley and Los Angeles: University of California Press.

———. 1978. "Le Catholicisme social au Mexique jusqu'en 1913." *Revue Historique* 260: 143–59.

Meyer, Lorenzo. 1984. "La revolución mexicana y las potencias anglosajones." *Historia Mexicana* 34, no. 2: 300–352.

———. 1991. *México y Estados Unidos en el conflicto petrolero (1917–1942).* Mexico, D.F.: El Colegio de Mexico.

———. 1991a. *Su Majestad Británica contra la revolución mexicana, 1900–1950: El fin de un imperio informal.* Mexico, D.F.: El Colegio de Mexico.

———. 1992. *La segunda muerte de la revolución mexicana.* Mexico, D.F.: Cal & Arena.

Meyer, Lorenzo, and Isidro Morales. 1990. *Petróleo y nación (1900–1987).* Mexico, D.F.: Fondo de Cultura Económica.

Meyer, Michael C. 1967. *Mexican Rebel: Pascual Orozco and the Mexican Revolution, 1910–1915*. Lincoln: University of Nebraska Press.

———. 1972. *Huerta: A Political Portrait*. Lincoln: University of Nebraska Press.

Meyers, William K. 1984. "La Comarca Lagunera: Work, Protest, and Popular Mobilization in North Central Mexico." In *Other Mexicos: Essays on Regional Mexican History, 1876–1911*, ed. Thomas Benjamin and William McNellie. Albuquerque: University of New Mexico Press.

———. 1988. "Second Division of the North: Formation and Fragmentation of the Laguna's Popular Movement, 1910–1911." In *Riot, Rebellion, and Revolution*, ed. Friedrich Katz. Princeton: Princeton University Press.

———. 1991. "Pancho Villa and the Multinationals: United States Mining Interests in Villista Mexico, 1913–1915." *Journal of Latin American Studies* 23, no. 2 (May): 339–63.

———. 1994. *Forge of Progress, Crucible of Revolt: Origins of the Mexican Revolution in the Comarca Lagunera, 1880 1911*. Albuquerque: University of New Mexico Press.

Miller, Simon. 1991. "Lands and Labour in Mexican Rural Insurrections." *Bull. Latin Am. Res.* 10, no. 1: 55–79.

Mistron, Deborah, 1983. "The Role of Pancho Villa in the Mexican and the American Cinema." *Studies in Latin American Popular Culture* 2: 1–13.

Moheno, Querido. 1939. *Mi actuación política después de la decena trágica*. Mexico, D.F.: Ediciones Botas.

Molina, Silvia. 1993. *La familia vino del norte*. Mexico, D.F.: Cal & Arena.

Monsivais, C., 1985. "La aparición del subsuelo: Sobre la cultura de la revolución mexicana." *Historias* 8–9: 159–78.

Monticone, Joseph Raymond. 1981. "Revolutionary Mexico and the U.S. Southwest: The Columbus Raid." M.A. thesis, California State University, Fullerton.

Moorehead, Max L. 1968. *The Apache Frontier*. Norman: University of Oklahoma Press.

Mora Torres, Juan. 1991. "The Transformation of a Peripheral Society: A Social History of Nuevo León, 1848–1920." Ph.D. diss., University of Chicago.

Moreno, Daniel, ed. 1978. *Batallas de la revolución y sus corridos*. Mexico, D.F.: Editorial Porrúa.

Morris, Roy, Jr. 1995. *Ambrose Bierce: Alone in Bad Company*. New York: Crown.

Munch, Francis J. 1969. "Villa's Columbus Raid: Practical Politics or German Design?" *New Mexico Historical Review* 44, no. 3 (July): 189–214.

Muñoz, Ignacio. 1965. *Verdad y mito de la revolución mexicana (relatada por un protagonista)*, vols. 1–4. Mexico, D.F.: Ediciones Populares.

Muñoz, Rafael F. 1971. *Pancho Villa: Rayo y azote*. Mexico, D.F.: Populibros La Prensa.

———. 1985. *Relatos de la revolución*. Mexico, D.F.: Grijalbo.

———. 1978. *¡Vámonos con Pancho Villa!* Mexico, D.F.: Espasa-Calpe Mexicana.

Natividad Rosales, José. 1955. "Pancho Villa, el hombre y la fiera." *¡Siempre! Presencia de Mexico* 9, no. 84 (Feb. 2): 33–34, 70.

Naylor, Thomas H. 1977. "Massacre at San Pedro de la Cueva: The Significance of Pancho Villa's Disastrous Sonora Campaign." *Western Historical Quarterly* 8, no. 2 (Apr.).

Neumann, Joseph. 1969. *Revoltes des Indiens Tarahumars (1626–1724)*. Paris: Université de Paris.

Niemeyer, Eberhardt Victor, Jr. 1966. *El general Bernardo Reyes*. Biblioteca Nueva León. Monterrey: Universidad de Nueva León.

————. 1974. *Revolution at Querétaro: The Mexican Constitutional Convention of 1916–1917.* Austin: University of Texas Press.

Nugent, Daniel, ed. 1988. *Rural Revolt in Mexico and U.S. Intervention.* San Diego: Center for U.S.–Mexican Studies at the University of San Diego, Monograph Series 27.

————. 1993. *Spent Cartridges of Revolution: An Anthropological History of Namiquipa, Chihuahua.* Chicago: University of Chicago Press.

Nuñez, Ricardo E. 1973. *La revolución en el estado de Colima.* Mexico, D.F.: Instituto Nacional de Estudios Históricos de la Revolución Mexicana.

Obregón, Alvaro. 1970. *Ocho mil kilómetros en campaña.* Mexico, D.F.: Fondo de Cultura Económica.

O'Brien, Dennis J. 1977. "Petroleo e intervencion: Relaciones entre Estados Unidos y Mexico, 1917–1918." *Journal of Interamerican Studies and World Affairs* 17, no. 2: 123–52.

O'Brien, Steven. 1991. *Pancho Villa.* New York: Chelsea House.

O'Connor, Harvey. 1937. *The Guggenheims: The Making of an American Dynasty.* New York: Covici, Friede. Reprint, New York: Arno Press, 1976.

O'Connor, Richard. 1961. *Black Jack Pershing.* Garden City, N.Y.: Doubleday.

O'Hea, Patrick. 1966. *Reminiscences of the Mexican Revolution.* Mexico, D.F.: Editorial Founier.

Oikión Solano, Verónica. 1992. *El constitucionalismo en Michoacán: El período de los gobiernos militares (1914–1917).* Mexico, D.F.: Consejo Nacional para la Cultura y las Artes.

Olea, Hector R. 1964. *Breve historia de la revolución en Sinaloa (1910–1917).* Mexico, D.F.: Instituto Nacional de Estudios Históricos de la Revolución Mexicana.

O'Malley, Ilene V. 1986. *The Myth of the Revolution: Hero Cults and the Institutionalization of the Mexican State, 1920–1940.* New York: Greenwood Press.

Ontiveros, Francisco de P. 1914. *Toribio Ortega y la Brigada González Ortega.* El Paso, Tex.: Familia Martínez Ortega.

Orozco, Serafina. 1980. "My Recollections of the Orozco Family and the Mexican Revolution of 1910." *Password* (Spring).

Orozco, Wistano Luis. 1985. *Legislación y jurisprudencia sobre terrenos baldíos.* 1891. Reprints, Mexico, D.F: Ediciones El Caballito, 1975; Imprenta de El Tiempo, 1985.

Orozco Orozco, Victor Manuel. 1990. "Notas sobre las relaciones de clase en Chihuahua durante la primera fase de las guerras indias." In *Actas del Segundo Congreso de Historia Comparada, 1990,* pp. 369–84. Ciudad Juárez: Universidad Autónoma de Ciudad Juárez.

————. 1990b. "Una maestra, un pueblo." *Cuadernos del Norte: Sociedad, Politica, Cultura* 12 (Nov.–Dec.): 17–23.

————. 1994. "Política y sociedad en una región del norte de México: Los pueblos libres del distrito Guerrero, Chihuahua en el siglo XIX." Ph.D. diss., Facultad de ciencias políticas y sociales, Universidad Nacional Autónoma de México.

————. 1995. "Revolución y restauración: La lucha por la tierra en San Isidro y Namiquipa." In *Actas del Cuarto Congreso de Historia Comparada, 1993,* pp. 495–514. Ciudad Juárez: Universidad Autónoma de Ciudad Juárez.

————. 1995a. *Historia General de Chihuahua,* vol. 3: *Tierra de libres: Los pueblos del distrito Guerrero en el siglo XIX.* Ciudad Juárez: Universidad Autónoma de Ciudad Juárez–Gobierno del Estado de Chihuahua.

Ortoll, S., and A. Bloch. 1985. "Xenofobia y nacionalismo revolucionario: Los tumultos de Guadalajara, Mexico, en 1910." *Cristianismo y Sociedad* 86.

Osorio Zuñiga, Rubén. 1985. "Francisco Villa y la guerilla en Chihuahua (1916–1920)." *Boletin del Cemos, Memoria* 1, no. 10 (May–June).

———. 1991. *Pancho Villa, ese desconocido.* Ciudad Chihuahua: Ediciones del Gobierno del Estado de Chihuahua.

———. 1995. *Tomóchic en llamas.* México, D.F.: Consejo Nacional para la Cultura y las Artes.

———. N.d. "General Pancho Villa's Expedition to Capture Venustiano Carranza." MS.

———. N.d. "La muerte de dos generales." MS.

———. N.d. "Francisco Villa, la guerilla en Chihuahua y la paz con el gobierno de Mexico." MS.

Palavicini, Félix F. 1915. *Los diputados.* Reprint. Mexico, D.F.: Fondo para la historia de las ideas revolucionarias, 1976.

———. 1937. *Mi vida revolucionaria.* Mexico, D.F.: Ediciones Botas.

———. 1938. *Historia de la constitución de 1917.* 2 vols. Reprint. Mexico, D.F.: Consejo Editorial del Gobierno del Estado de Tabasco, 1980.

Palomares, Justino N. 1954. *Anecdotario de la revolución.* Mexico, D.F.: Ediciones del Autor.

Palomares, Noé. 1992. "Minería y metalurgia chihuahuense: Batopilas y Santa Eulalia entre 1880 y 1920." In *Actas del Tercer Congreso de Historia Comparada, 1991.* Ciudad Juárez: Universidad Autónoma de Ciudad Juárez.

———. 1992a. *Proprietarios norteamericanos y reforma agraria en Chihuahua, 1917–1942.* Ciudad Juárez: Universidad Autónoma de Ciudad Juárez.

Pani, Alberto J. 1936. *Mi contribución al nuevo régimen, 1910–1933: A proposito del "Ulises criollo," autobiografia del licenciado don José Vasconcelos.* Mexico, D.F.: Cultura.

———. 1945. *Apuntes autobiográficos.* Reprint. Mexico, D.F.: Libreria de Manuel Porrúa, 1951.

Paredes, Américo. 1976. *A Texas-Mexican Cancionero: Folksongs of the Lower Border.* Urbana: University of Illinois Press.

Parker, George. 1951. *Guaracha Trail.* New York: Dutton.

Parker, Ralph. N.d. "A Visit to General Pancho Villa." MS.

Parkes, Henry B. 1938. *A History of Mexico.* Boston: Houghton Mifflin.

Pasquel, Leonardo. 1972. *La Revolución en el Estado de Veracruz.* 2 vols. Mexico, D.F.: Instituto Nacional de Estudios Históricos de la Revolución Mexicana.

Paulsen, G. E. 1981. "The Legal Battle for the Candelaria Mine in Durango, Mexico, 1890–1917." *Arizona and the West* 23, no. 3: 243–66.

———. 1983. "Reaping the Whirlwind in Chihuahua: The Destruction of the Minas de Corralitos, 1911–1917." *New Mexico Historical Review* 58, no. 3: 253–70.

Paz, Octavio. 1985. *The Labyrinth of Solitude.* New York: Grove Press.

Pazuengo, Gral. Matias. 1915. *Historia de la revolución en Durango.* Cuernavaca: Tip. Gobierno del Estado.

Perea, Hector, and Xavier Guzmán Uribiola. 1987. *Martín Luís Guzmán: Iconografía.* Mexico, D.F.

Peterson, Jessica, and Thelma Cox Knoles, eds. 1977. *Pancho Villa: Intimate Recollections by People Who Knew Him.* New York: Hastings House.

Pierri, Ettore. 1978. *Pancho Villa: La verdadera historia.* Mexico, D.F.: Editores mexicanos unidos.

Pierson Kerig, Dorothy. 1975. *Luther T. Ellsworth, U.S. Consul on the Border During the Mexican Revolution.* El Paso: Texas Western College Press.

Pinchon, Edgcumb. 1933. *Viva Villa! A Recovery of the Real Pancho Villa, Peon . . . Bandit . . . Soldier . . . Patriot.* New York: Grosset & Dunlap.

Pittman, Kenneth D. N.d. "The Agrarian Roots of Rebellion: The Plantation Economy of Mexico (1860–1910)." MS.

Plana, Manuel. 1991. *El reino del algodón en México: La estructura agraria en la Laguna (1855–1910)*. Mexico, D.F.: Patronato del Teatro Isauro Martínez.

———. 1993. *Pancho Villa et la révolution mexicaine*. Florence: Casterman, Giunti Gruppo Editoriale.

Ponce Alcocer, Maria Eugenia. 1981. *Las haciendas de Mazaquiahuac, El Rosario, El Moral, 1912–1913*. Mexico, D.F.: Universidad Iberoamericana, Centro de Información Académica, Departamento de Historia.

Portal, Marta. 1977. *Proceso narrativo de la revolución mexicana*. Madrid: Ediciones Cultura Hispanica,

Portilla, Santiago. 1995. *Una sociedad en armas: Insurrección antireeleccionista en Mexico, 1910–1911*. Mexico, D.F.: El Colegio de Mexico.

Pozo Marrero, Acalia. 1991. "Dos movimientos populares en el noroeste de Chihuahua." Master's thesis, Universidad Iberoamericana. Mexico, D.F.

Prida, Ramon. 1958. *De la dictadura a la anarquía*. Mexico, D.F.: Ediciones Botas.

Prieto Reyes, Luis, et al. 1993. *VII jornadas de historia de occidente: Francisco J. Múgica*. Jiquilpan de Juárez, Michoacán: Centro de Estudios de la Revolución Mexicana "Lázaro Cárdenas."

Puente, Ramón. 1912. *Pascual Orozco y la revuelta de Chihuahua*. Mexico, D.F.: Gómez de la Puente.

———. 1937. *Villa en pie*. Mexico, D.F.: Editorial Mexico Nuevo.

———. 1938. *La dictadura, la revolución, y sus hombres*. Facsimile ed. Mexico, D.F.: Instituto Nacional de Estudios Historicos de la Revolución Mexicana, 1985.

Py, Pierre. 1991. *Francia y la revolución mexicana, 1910–1920, o, la desaparición de una potencia mediana*. Translated from "La France et la révolution mexicaine, 1910–1920" (Ph.D. diss., Université de Perpignan), by Ismael Pizarro Suárez and Mercedes Pizarro Suárez. Mexico, D.F.: Fondo de Cultura Económica, Centro de Estudios Mexicanos y Centroamericanos.

Quintero Corral, Lucio. 1990. *Pancho Villa derrotado en Tepehuanes, Durango al intentar tomar la ciudad de Durango*. Ciudad Juárez.

Quirk, Robert E. 1960. *The Mexican Revolution, 1914–1915: The Convention of Aguascalientes*. Bloomington: Indiana University Press.

———. 1964. *An Affair of Honor: Woodrow Wilson and the Occupation of Veracruz*. 1962. Paperback reprint, New York: McGraw-Hill.

———. 1973. *The Mexican Revolution and the Catholic Church, 1910–1929*. Bloomington: University of Indiana Press.

Quiroga, Alfonso. N.d. *Vida y hazañas de Francisco Villa*. San Antonio: Tip. La Epoca.

Raat, W. Dirk. 1981. *Revoltosos: Mexico's Rebels in the United States, 1903–1923*. College Station: Texas A&M University Press.

———. 1982. *The Mexican Revolution: An Annotated Guide to Recent Scholarship*. Boston: G. K. Hall.

———. 1992. *Mexico and the United States: Ambivalent Vistas*. Athens: University of Georgia Press.

Rakoczy, Bill. 1981. *Villa Raids Columbus NM*. El Paso, Tex.: Bravo Press.

———. 1983. *How Did Villa Live, Love, and Die?* El Paso, Tex.: Bravo Press.

Ramirez, Guillermo H. N.d. *Melitón Lozoya, único director intelectual en la muerte de Villa*. Durango.

Ramírez Rancaño, Mario. 1986. "Los hacendados y el huertismo." *Revista Mexicana de Sociología* 48, no. 1: 167–200.

————. 1990. *El sistema de haciendas en Tlaxcala*. Mexico, D.F.: Consejo Nacional para la Cultura y las Artes.

Rascoe, Jesse, ed. 1962. *The Treasure Album of Pancho Villa*. Toyahuala, Tex.: Fontier Book Co.

Razo Oliva, Juan Diego. 1983. *Rebeldes populares del Bajío (hazañas, tragedias y corridos 1910–1927)*. Mexico, D.F.: Editorial Katun.

Reed, John. 1916. "The Mexican Tangle." In *John Reed for "The Masses,"* ed. James C. Wilson, pp. 104–6. Jefferson, N.C.: McFarland & Co., 1987.

————. 1969. *Insurgent Mexico*. 1914. Reprint, New York: Simon & Schuster, Clarion Books.

————. 1983. *Villa y la revolución mexicana*. Mexico, D.F. Editorial Nueva Imagen.

Reed, Raymond J. 1938. "The Mormons in Chihuahua, Their Relations with Villa and the Pershing Punitive Expedition 1910–1917." M.A. thesis, University of New Mexico.

La revolución en las regiones: Memorias. 1986. 2 vols. Guadalajara, Jal.: Universidad de Guadalajara, Instituto de Estudios Sociales.

Richmond, Douglas W. 1982. "Mexican Immigration and Border Policy During the Revolution." *New Mexico Historical Review* 57, no. 3: 269–88.

————. 1983. *Venustiano Carranza's Nationalist Struggle, 1893–1920*. Lincoln: University of Nebraska Press.

Riding, Alan. 1989. *Distant Neighbors: A Portrait of the Mexicans*. New York: Random House.

Rivas López, Angel. 1970. *El verdadero Pancho Villa*. Mexico, D.F.: B. Costa-Amic.

Rivera, Librado. 1980. *¡Viva tierra y libertad!* Mexico, D.F.: Ediciones Antorcha.

Rivero, Gonzalo G. 1911. *Hacia la verdad: Episodios de la revolución*. Mexico, D.F.: Compania Editora Nacional S.A.

Robe, Stanley S. 1979. *Azuela and the Mexican Underdogs*. Berkeley and Los Angeles: University of California Press. Includes the original Spanish text of Mariano Azuela's novel *Los de abajo* and an English translation.

Roberts, Donald Frank. 1974. "Mining and Modernization: The Mexican Border States During the Porfiriato, 1876–1911." Ph.D. diss., University of Pittsburgh.

Roberts, John W. 1916. "Villa's Own Story of His Life." *McClure Newspaper Syndicate*, no. 35: 8.

Robinson, Carlos T. 1933. *Hombres y cosas de la revolución*. Tijuana: Imprenta Cruz Galvez.

Robles Linares, Manuel. 1976. *Pastor Rouaix: Su vida y su obra*. Mexico, D.F.: Avelar Hermanos Impresores.

Robleto, Hernán. 1960. *La mascota de Pancho Villa: Episodios de la revolución mexicana*. Mexico, D.F.: LibroMex.

Rocha, Rodolfo. 1981. "The Influence of the Mexican Revolution on the Mexico-Texas Border, 1910–1916." Ph.D. diss., Texas Tech University.

Rocha Islas, Martha Eva. 1979. "Del villismo y las defensas sociales en Chihauhua (1915–1920)." Ph.D. diss., Universidad Nacional Autonoma de México.

————. 1988. *Las defensas sociales en Chihuahua*. Mexico, D.F.: Instituto Nacional de Antropología e Historia.

————. 1991. "Nuestras proprias voces: Las mujeres en la revolución mexicana." *Historias* 25 (Oct. 1990–Mar. 1991).

Rodriguez, Maria Guadalupe, Antonio Arreola, Gloria Estela Cano, Miguel Vallebueno, Mauricio Yen, Guadalupe Villa, and Graziella Altamirano. 1995. *Durango (1840–1915): Banca, transportes, tierra e industria*. Monterrey: Universidad Autónoma de Nuevo León, Facultad de Filosofía y Letras–Universidad Juárez del Estado de Durango, Instituto de Investigaciones Históricas.

Rodriguez O., Jaime E., ed. 1990. *The Revolutionary Process in Mexico: Essays on Political and Social Change.* Los Angeles: UCLA Latin American Center.

———, ed. 1992. *Patterns of Contention in Mexican History.* Wilmington, Del.: Scholarly Resources.

Rojas, Beatriz. 1983. *La pequeña guerra: Los Carrera Torres y los Cedillo.* Zamora: El Colegio de Michoacán.

Rojas González, Francisco. 1952. *El Diosero.* Reprint. Mexico, D.F.: Fondo de Cultura Económica, 1974.

Roman, Richard. 1976. *Ideología y clase en la revolución mexicana: La convención y el congreso constituyente.* Mexico, D.F.: Secretaría de Educación Pública.

Romero Flores, Jesús. 1963. *La revolución como nosotros la vimos.* Mexico, D.F.: Instituto Nacional de Estudios Históricos de la Revolución Mexicana.

Rosenberg, Emily S. 1975. "Economic Pressures in Anglo-American Diplomacy in Mexico, 1917–1918." *Journal of Interamerican Studies and World Affairs* 17 (May): 123–52.

———. 1982. *Spreading the American Dream: American Economic and Cultural Expansion, 1895–1945.* New York: Hill & Wang.

———. 1987. *World War I and the Growth of United States Predominance in Latin America.* New York: Garland.

Rosenstone, Robert. 1982. *Romantic Revolutionary: A Biography of John Reed.* New York: Penguin Books.

Ross, Stanley R. 1955. *Francisco I. Madero: Apostle of Mexican Democracy.* New York: Columbia University Press.

———, ed. 1965. *Fuentes de la historia contemporánea de México: Periódicos y revistas.* Mexico, D.F.: El Colegio de México.

Rouaix, Pastor. 1927. *Consideraciones generales sobre el estado social de la nación mexicana.* Durango: Imprenta del Gobierno del Estado.

———. 1927. *Regimen político del estado de Durango durante administracion porfirista.* Durango: Imprenta del Gobierno del Estado.

———. 1932. *La revolución maderista y constitucionalista en Durango.* Durango: Imprenta de Gobierno del Estado.

Rouverol, Jean. 1972. *Pancho Villa.* New York: Doubleday.

Rubluo, Luis. 1983. *Historia de la revolución mexicana en el estado de Hidalgo.* 2 vols. Mexico, D.F.: Instituto de Estudios Históricos de la Revolución Mexicana.

Ruffinelli, Jorge. 1983. *Reed en México.* Mexico, D.F.: Nueva Imagen.

Ruis Facius, Antonio. 1963. *La juventud católica y la revolución mejicana, 1910–1925.* Mexico, D.F.

Ruiz Cervantes, Francisco José. 1986. *La revolución en Oaxaca: El movimiento de la soberanía, 1915–1920.* Mexico, D.F.: Fondo de Cultura Económica.

Ruíz, Ramón Eduardo. 1976. *Labor and the Ambivalent Revolutionaries: Mexico, 1911–1923.* Baltimore: Johns Hopkins University Press.

———. 1980. *The Great Rebellion: Mexico, 1905–1929.* New York: Norton.

———. 1988. *The People of Sonora and Yankee Capitalists.* Tucson: University of Arizona Press.

Rutherford, John. 1971. *Mexican Society During the Revolution: A Literary Approach.* Oxford: Clarendon Press.

———. 1972. *An Annotated Bibliography of the Novels of the Mexican Revolution of 1910–1917.* Troy, N.Y.: Whitson.

Saborit, Antonio. 1994. *Los doblados de Tomóchic: Un episodio de historia y literatura.* Mexico, D.F.: Cal & Arena.

Salas, Elizabeth. 1990. *Soldaderas in the Mexican Military: Myth and History.* Austin: University of Texas Press.

Salazar, Rosendo. 1962. *La casa del obrero mundial.* Mexico, D.F.: B. Costa-Amic

Salgado, Eva. 1985. "Fragmentos de historia popular II: Las mujeres en la Revolución." *Secuencia* 3 (Dec.): 206–14.

Salinas Carranza, Alberto. 1936. *La expedición punitiva.* Mexico, D.F.: Ediciones Botas.

Salomon, Doris. 1986. "John Reed, Frank Tannenbaum, and the Mexican Revolution." MS, University of Chicago.

Sámaro Rentería, Miguel Angel. 1993. *Un estudio de la historia agraria de México de 1760 a 1910: Del colonialismo feudal al capitalismo dependiente y subdesarrollado.* Mexico, D.F.: Universidad Autonoma Chapingo.

Sánchez, Enrique. 1952. *Corridos de Pancho Villa.* Mexico, D.F.: Editorial del Magisterio.

Sánchez, Luis Alberto. 1960. *Aladino, o, Vida y obra de José Santos Chocano.* Mexico, D.F.: Libro Mex.

Sánchez Azcona, Juan. 1961. *Apuntes para la historia de la revolución mexicana.* Mexico, D.F.

Sánchez Lamego, Miguel A. 1956–60. *Historia militar de la revolución constitucionalista.* 5 vols. Mexico, D.F.: Talleres Gráficos de la Nación. Vols. 1–2: 1956; vols. 3–4: 1957; vol. 5: 1960.

——. 1977. *Historia militar de la revolución mexicana en la época maderista.* 2 vols. Mexico, D.F.: Talleres Gráficos de la Nación.

——. 1983. *Historia militar de la revolución en la época de la convención.* Mexico, D.F.: Instituto Nacional de Estudios Históricos de la Revolución Mexicana.

Sandels, Robert Lynn. 1967. "Silvestre Terrazas, the Press, and the Origins of the Mexican Revolution in Chihuahua." Ph.D. diss., University of Oregon.

Sandos, James A. 1970. "German Involvement in Northern Mexico, 1915–1916: A New Look at the Columbus Raid." *Hispanic American Historical Review* 50, no. 1 (Feb.): 70–89.

——. 1984. "Northern Separatism During the Mexican Revolution: An Inquiry into the Role of Drug Trafficking, 1919–1920." *The Americas* 41, no. 2 (Oct.): 191–214.

——. 1992. *Rebellion in the Borderlands: Anarchism and the Plan of San Diego, 1904–1923.* Norman: University of Oklahoma Press.

Santos Chocano, José. N.d. *Los fines de la revolución mexicana considerados dentro del problema internacional.* Ciudad Chihuahua: Imprenta del Gobierno.

——. 1954. *Obras completas.* Mexico, D.F.: Aguilar.

Santos, G. N. 1984. *Memorias.* Mexico, D.F.

Santos Santos, Pedro Antonio. 1990. *Memorias.* San Luis Potosí: Consejo Estatal para la Cultura y las Artes, Archivo Histórico del Estado de San Luis Potosí.

Sapia-Bosch, Alfonso Franco. 1977. "The Role of General Lucio Blanco in the Mexican Revolution, 1913–1922." Ph.D. diss., Georgetown University.

Sariego, J. L. 1985. "Anarquismo e historia social minera en el norte de México, 1906–1918." *Historias* 8–9: 111–24.

Schmidt, Henry C. 1978. *The Roots of Lo Mexicano: Self and Society in Mexican Thought, 1900–1934.* College Station: Texas A&M University Press.

Schmidt, Steffen W., and Helen Hogt Schmidt, eds. 1977. *Latin America: Rural Life and Agrarian Problemas.* Ames: Iowa State University Press.

Schulze, Karl Wilhelm. 1990. "Las leyes agrarias del villismo." In *Actas del Segundo*

Congreso de Historia Comparada. Ciudad Juárez: Universidad Autónoma de Ciudad Juárez.

―――. 1993. "Konzept und Realität der Agrarpolitik Pancho Villas auf dem Hintergrund der Sozial- und Landverhältnisse in Chihuahua während des Porfiriats und der Revolution." *Jahrbuch für Geschichte von Staat, Wirtschaft und Gesellschaft Lateinamerikas* 30: 279–328.

Schuster, Ernest Otto. 1947. *Pancho Villa's Shadow: The True Story of Mexico's Robin Hood as Told by His Interpreter*. New York: Exposition Press.

Seminario de Historia Moderna de México. N.d. *Comercio exterior de México, 1877–1911*. Mexico, D.F.: El Colegio de México.

―――. N.d.a. *Estadísticas sociales del porfiriato, 1877–1910*. Mexico, D.F.: El Colegio de México.

―――. N.d.b. *Fuerza de trabajo y actividad económica por sectores: Estadísticas económicas del porfiriato*. Mexico, D.F.: El Colegio de México.

Semo, Enrique. 1988–89. "La cuestión agraria y la revolución mexicana: Nuevos enfoques." *Historias* 21 (Oct. 1988–Mar. 1989).

Séptimo Congreso Nacional de Historia de la Revolución mexicana. 1977. Ciudad Chihuahua: Sociedad Chihuahuense de Estudios Históricos.

Serralde, Francisco. 1921. *Los sucesos de Tlaxcalantongo y la muerte del ex-presidente de la república C. Venustiano Carranza*. Mexico, D.F.

Serrano, Sol, ed. 1986. *La diplomacia chilena y la revolución mexicana*. Mexico, D.F.: Secretaría de Relaciones Exteriores.

Sessions, Tommie Gene. 1974. "American Reformers and the Mexican Revolution: Progressives and Woodrow Wilson's Policy in Mexico, 1913–1917." Ph.D. diss., The American University.

Shorris, Earl. 1980. *Under the Fifth Sun: A Novel of Pancho Villa*. New York: Delacorte Press.

Silva Herzog, Jesús. 1960. *Breve história de la revolución mexicana*. 2 vols. Mexico, D.F.: Fondo de Cultura Económica.

―――. 1964. *El agrarismo mexicano y la reforma agraria*. Mexico, D.F.: Fondo de Cultura Económica.

Simmons, Mearle E. 1957. *The Mexican Corrido as the Source for Interpretive Study of Modern Mexico (1870–1950)*. Bloomington: University of Indiana Press.

Sims, Harold. 1968. "Espejo de caciques: Los Terrazas de Chihuahua." *Historia Mexicana* 18, no. 3 (Jan.–Mar.): 379–99.

Singer, M. 1989. "La cabeza de Villa." *New Yorker*, Nov. 27, 1989.

Slatta, Richard W., ed. 1987. *Bandidos: The Varieties of Latin American Banditry*. New York: Greenwood Press.

Slattery, Matthew T. N.d. *Felipe Angeles and the Mexican Revolution*. Parma Heights, Ohio: Greenbriar Books, Prinit Press.

Slotkin, Richard. 1992. *Gunfighter Nation: The Myth of the Frontier in Twentieth-Century America*. New York: Athenaeum.

Smith, John Dunn. 1986. "Literary Treatments of the Mexican Revolution." MS, University of Chicago.

Smith, Michael M. N.d. "Carrancista Propaganda in the United States, 1913–1917: An Overview of Institutions." MS.

Smith, Robert Freeman. 1972. *The United States and Revolutionary Nationalism in Mexico, 1916–1932*. Chicago: University of Chicago Press.

Smythe, Donald. 1973. *Guerrilla Warrior: The Early Life of John J. Pershing*. New York: Scribner.

Solares, Ignacio. 1991. *La noche de Angeles*. Mexico, D.F.: Editorial Diana.

Sonnichsen, C. L. 1974. *Colonel Greene and the Copper Skyrocket: The Spectacular Rise and Fall of William Cornell Greene, Copper King, Cattle Baron, and Promoter Extraordinary in Mexico, the American Southwest, and the New York Financial District.* Tuscon: University of Arizona Press.

———. 1979. *Pancho Villa and the Cananea Copper Company. Journal of Arizona History* 20.1 (Spring).

Sotelo Inclán, Jesús. 1970. *Raíz y razón de Zapata.* Mexico, D.F.

Spenser, Daniela. 1988. *El Partido Socialista Chiapaneco: Rescate y reconstrucción de su historia.* Mexico, D.F.: Centro de Investigaciones y Estudios en Antropología Social.

Spicer, Edward H. 1962. *Cycles of Conquest: The Impact of Spain, Mexico, and the United States on the Indians of the Southwest, 1533–1960.* Tucson: University of Arizona Press.

Spielberg, Joseph, and Scott Whiteford, eds. 1976. *Forging Nations: A Comparative View of Rural Ferment and Revolt.* East Lansing: Michigan State University Press.

Spikes, Paul. 1971. "Francisco Villa and San Agrarismo." MS.

Stein, Max. 1916. *General Francisco Villa, Peon Chief, Terror of Mexico.* Chicago: Max Stein.

Stevens, Louis. 1930. *Here Comes Pancho Villa: An Anecdotal History of a Genial Killer.* New York: Fredrick A. Stokes Co.

Stillwell, Arthur. 1928. "I Had a Hunch." *Saturday Evening Post*, Feb. 4.

Tablada, José Juan. 1913. *La defensa social: Historia de la campaña de la División del Norte.* Mexico, D.F.: Imprenta del Gobierno Federal.

Tannenbaum, Frank. 1930. *The Mexican Agrarian Revolution.* Washington, D.C.: Brookings Institution.

———. 1933. *Peace by Revolution: An Interpretation of Mexico.* New York: Columbia University Press.

Taracena, Alfonso. 1967. *La verdadera revolución mexicana (1913–1914).* Mexico, D.F.: B. Costa-Amic.

———. 1973. *Madero, víctima del imperialismo yanqui.* Mexico, D.F.: Talleres de la Editorial.

———. 1987. *Historia extraoficial de la revolución mexicana.* Mexico, D.F.: Editorial Jus.

———. 1991. *La verdadera revolución mexicana (1901–1911).* Mexico, D.F.: Editorial Porrúa.

———. 1992. *La verdadera revolución mexicana (1915–1917).* Mexico, D.F.: Editorial Porrúa.

———. 1992a. *La verdadera revolución mexicana (1918–1921).* Mexico, D.F.: Editorial Porrúa.

Tardanico, R. 1982. "State, Dependency, and Nationalism: Revolutionary Mexico, 1924–1928." *Comparative Studies in Society and History* 24, no. 3 (July): 400–424.

Tate, Michael L. 1975. "Pershing's Punitive Expedition: Pursuer of Bandits or Presidential Panacea?" *The Americas* 32: 46–72.

Taylor, Harold. 1992. *Memories of Militants and Mormon Colonists in Mexico.* Yorba Linda, Calif.: Shumway Family History Services.

Taylor, Lawrence D. 1986. "The Great Adventure: Mercenaries in the Mexican Revolution. 1910–1915." *The Americas* 43, no. 1 (July): 25–45.

———. 1993. *La gran aventura en México: El papel de los voluntarios extranjeros en los ejércitos revolucionarios mexicanos, 1910–1915.* 2 vols. Mexico, D.F.: Consejo Nacional para la Cultura y las Artes.

Teitelbaum, Louis M. 1967. *Woodrow Wilson and the Mexican Revolution, 1913–16: A History of United States–Mexican Relations from the Murder of Madero Until Villa's Provocation Across the Border.* New York: Exposition Press.

Tello Díaz, Carlos. 1993. *El exilio: Un relato de familia.* Mexico, D.F.: Cal & Arena.

Terrazas, Filiberto. 1989. *El tesoro de Villa.* Mexico, D.F.: Editorial Universo.

Terrazas, Joaquin. 1980. *Memorias de sr. coronel D. Joaquin Terrazas.* Ciudad Chihuahua: Centro Librero de la Prensa.

Terrazas, Silvestre. 1985. *El verdadero Pancho Villa.* Mexico, D.F.: Ediciones Era.

Terrazas Perches, Margarita. 1985. "Biografía de Silvestre Terrazas." In *El verdadero Pancho Villa,* by Silvestre Terrazas. Mexico, D.F.: Ediciones Era.

Testimonios de la revolución mexicana. 1989. Ciudad Chihuahua: Talleres Gráficos del Gobierno del Estado de Chihuahua.

Thord-Gray, Ivar [Ivar Thord Hallström]. 1960. *Gringo Rebel: Mexico, 1913–1914.* Coral Gables, Fla.: University of Miami Press.

Tinker, Edward Larocque. 1970. *New Yorker Unlimited: The Memoirs of Edward Larocque Tinker.* Austin and Encino: University of Texas at Austin / Encino Press.

Tobler, Hans Werner. 1971. "Alvaro Obregón und die Anfänge der Mexikanischen Agrarreform: Agrarpolitik und Agrarkonflikt, 1921–1924." In *Jahrbuch für Geschichte von Staat, Wirtschaft und Gesellschaft Lateinamerikas* 8: 310–65.

———. 1971a. "Las paradojas del ejército revolucionario: Su papel social en la reforma agraria mexicana, 1920–1935." *Historia Mexicana* 21, no. 1: 38–79.

———. 1975. "Zur Historiographie der Mexikanischen Revolution, 1910–1940." In *Jahrbuch für Geschichte von Staat, Wirtschaft und Gesellschaft Lateinamerikas* 12: 286–331.

———. 1984. "La burguesía revolucionaria en México: Su origen y su papel." *Historia Mexicana* 34, no. 2: 213–37.

———. 1988. "Die Mexikanische Revolution in vergleichender Perspektive: Einige Faktoren Revolutionären Wandels in Mexiko, Russland, und China im 20. Jahrhundert." *Ibero-Amerikanisches Archiv* 14, no. 4: 453–71.

———. 1992. *Die Mexikanische Revolution: Gesellschaftlicher Wandel und Politischer Umbruch, 1876–1940.* Frankfurt a.M.: Suhrkamp Verlag.

———. N.d. "Bauernerhebungen und Agrarreform in der Mexikanischen Revolution." MS.

———. N.d. "Die Mexikanische Revolution Zwischen Beharrung und Veränderung." MS.

———. N.d. "Einige Aspekte der Gewalt in der Mexikanischen Revolution." MS.

———. N.d. "Kontinuität und Wandel der Auslandsabhängigkeit im Revolutionären und Nachrevolutionären Mexiko." MS.

Tomás, Fray. 1932. *Fulgores siniestros.* Guadalajara: Talleres linotipográficos de "Las Noticias."

Tompkins, Frank. 1939. *Chasing Villa.* Harriburg, Pa.: Service Publishing Co.

Torales, Cristina. N.d. "Los industriales y la revolución mexicana." MS.

Torres, Elias L. 1934. *20 vibrantes episodios de la vida de Villa.* Mexico, D.F.: Editorial Sayrols.

———. 1975a. *Como murió Pancho Villa.* Mexico, D.F.: Editoria y Distribuidora Mexicana, Apartado Postal.

———. 1975b. *Hazañas y muerte de Francisco Villa.* Mexico, D.F.: Editorial Epoca.

———. 1975c. *La cabeza Pancho Villa.* Mexico, D.F.: Editora y Distribuidora Mexicana, Apartado Postal.

———. 1975d. *Vida y hazañas de Pancho Villa.* Mexico, D.F.: Editora y Distribuidora Mexicana, Apartado Postal.

———. 1975e. *Vida y hechos de Francisco Villa.* Mexico, D.F.: Editorial Epoca.

Toussant Aragón, Eugenio. 1979. *Quién y cómo fue Pancho Villa.* Mexico, D.F.: Editorial Universo.

Treviño, Jacinto B. 1984. *Memorias tomadas del original manuscrito del autor*. Mexico, D.F.

Treviño Villareal, Mario. 1990. "Fases previas al constitucionalismo en Nuevo Leon." Paper presented at Congreso Internacional Sobre la Revolución Mexicana, San Luis Potosí, Oct. 1–5, 1990.

Trow, Clifford Wayne. 1966. "Senator Albert B. Fall and Mexican Affairs: 1912–1921." Ph.D. diss., University of Colorado.

Trowbridge, Edward D. 1919. *Mexico To-day and To-morrow*. New York: Macmillan.

Trujillo Herrera, Rafael. 1973. *Cuando Villa entró en Columbus*. México, D.F.: Librería de Manuel Porrúa.

Tuchman, Barbara Wertheim. 1966. *The Zimmermann Telegram*. New York: Macmillan.

Tuck, Jim. 1984. *Pancho Villa and John Reed: Two Faces of Romantic Revolution*. Tucson: University of Arizona Press.

Tudela, Mariano. 1971. *Pancho Villa: Vida, leyenda, aventura*. Barcelona: Plaza & Janes.

Tumulty, Joseph P. 1921. *Woodrow Wilson as I Knew Him*. New York: Garden City, N.Y.: Doubleday, Page & Co.

Turner, Ethel Duffy. 1984. *Ricardo Flores Magón y el Partido Liberal Mexicano*. Mexico, D.F.: Partido Revolucionario Institucional.

Turner, John Kenneth. 1911. *Barbarous Mexico*. Chicago: Charles H. Kerr.

———. 1915. *¿Quién es Francisco Villa?* El Paso, Tex.: El Paso del Norte.

———. 1915a. *La Intervencion en Mexico y sus nefandas factores: Diplomacia del dollar y prensa mercenaria*. Laredo, Tex.: Laredo Publishing Co.

Turner, Timothy G. 1935. *Bullets, Bottles, and Gardenias*. Dallas, Tex., South-West Press.

Tutino, John. 1986. *From Insurrection to Revolution in Mexico: Social Bases of Agrarian Violence, 1750–1940*. Princeton: Princeton University Press.

———. 1990. "Revolutionary Confrontation, 1913–1917: Regional Factions, Class Conflicts, and the New National State." In *Provinces of the Revolution: Essays on Regional Mexican History, 1910–1929*, ed. Thomas Benjamin and Mark Wasserman. Albuquerque: University of New Mexico Press.

Ulloa, Berta. 1963. *Revolución mexicana, 1910–1920*. Archivo Histórico Diplomático Mexicano, Guías para la História Diplomática de Mexico, no. 3. Mexico, D.F.: Secretaría de Relaciones Exteriores.

———. 1971. *La revolución intervenida: Relaciones diplomáticas entre México y los Estados Unidos, 1910–1914*. Mexico, D.F.: El Colegio de Mexico.

———. 1979. *La revolución escindida*. Historia de la revolución mexicana, 1914–1917, vol. 4. Mexico, D.F.: El Colegio de Mexico.

———. 1979a. *La encrucijada de 1915*. Historia de la revolución mexicana, 1914–1917, vol. 5. Mexico, D.F.: El Colegio de México.

———. 1983. *La constitución de 1917*. Historia de la revolución mexicana, 1914–1917, vol. 6. Mexico, D.F.: El Colegio de México.

———. 1986. *Veracruz, capital de la nación (1914–1915)*. Mexico, D.F.: Centro de Estudios Historicos, Colegio de Mexico; Gobierno del Estado de Veracruz, 1986.

Uriostegui Miranda, Pindaro. 1970. *Testimonios del proceso revolucionario de México*. Mexico, D.F.: Talleres de Argrin.

Uroz, Antonio. 1957. "La injusta leyenda de Pancho Villa." *America*, Jan.–Mar.: 18–20.

Urquizo, Francisco L. 1969. *¡Viva Madero!* Mexico, D.F.: Populibros La Prensa.

———. 1971. *Memorias de campaña, de subteniente a general*. Mexico, D.F.: Fondo de Cultura Económica.

———. 1976. *Venustiano Carranza*. Mexico, D.F.: Editorial Libros de México.

———. 1981. *Paginas de la revolución*. Mexico, D.F.: Biblioteca del Oficial Mexicano.

———. 1985. *Recuerdo que . . .* Mexico, D.F.: Instituto Nacional de Estudios Históricos de la Revolución Mexicana.

Ursua de Escobar, Aurora. 1964. "Mis recuerdos del general Francisco Villa." *Novedades*, July 12.

Vagts, Alfred. 1928. *Mexico, Europa und Amerika und der besonderer Berücksichtigung der Petroleumpolitik.* Berlin: Dr. Walter Rothschild.

Valadés, José C. 1976. *Historia general de la revolución mexicana.* 5 vols. Mexico, D.F.: Editores Mexicanos Unidos.

———. 1984. *Rafael Buelna: Las caballerias de la revolución.* Mexico, D.F.: Ediciones Leega-Jucar.

Valdiosera, Ramón. 1982. *Zapata: 3000 años de lucha.* Mexico, D.F.: Editorial Universo.

Valenzuela, Clodoveo, and A. Chaverri Matamoros. 1921. *Sonora y Carranza.* Mexico, D.F.

Vanderwood, Paul J. 1976. "Response to Revolt: The Counter-Guerrilla Strategy of Porfirio Diaz." *Hispanic American Historical Review* 56, no. 4 (Nov.): 551–79.

———. 1981. *Disorder and Progress: Bandits, Police, and Mexican Development.* Lincoln: University of Nebraska Press.

———. 1987. "Building Blocks but Yet No Building." *Mexican Studies* 3, no. 2: 421–32.

———. 1990. "Explaining the Mexican Revolution." In *The Revolutionary Process in Mexico: Essays on Political and Social Change*, ed. Jaime E. Rodriguez O., pp. 97–114. Los Ángeles: UCLA Latin American Center.

———. 1992. "'None but the Justice of God': Tomochic, 1891–1892." In *Patterns of Contention in Mexican History*, ed. Jaime E. Rodriguez O., pp. 227–41. Wilmington, Del.: Scholarly Resources.

Vanderwood, Paul J., and Frank N. Samponaro. 1988. *Border Fury: A Picture Postcard Record of Mexico's Revolution and U.S. War Preparedness, 1910–1917.* Albuquerque: University of New Mexico Press.

Vargas Arreola, Juan Bautista. 1988. *A sangre y fuego con Pancho Villa.* Mexico, D.F.: Fondo de Cultura Económica.

Vargas Valdes, Jesús. 1990. "Máximo Castillo y la revolución en Chihuahua." Paper presented at Congreso de Historiadores, San Diego, Calif., Oct. 17–19, 1990.

———. 1991. "Una flor para Francisco Villa." Paper presented at Congreso de Historia Comparada. MS.

———, ed. 1994. *Tomochic: La revolución adelantada.* Ciudad Juárez.

———. N.d. "Los obreros de Chihuahua: Algunas experiencias de organización (1880–1940)." MS.

Vasconcelos, José. 1983. *Memorias: Ulises Criollo La Tormenta.* Mexico: Fondo de Cultura Económica.

Vaughan, Mary Kay. 1982. *The State, Education, and Social Class in Mexico, 1880–1928.* De Kalb: Northern Illinois University Press.

Vázquez Gómez, Francisco. 1933. *Memorias políticas, 1909–1913.* Mexico, D.F.: Imprenta Mundial.

Vera Estañol, Jorge. 1957. *Historia de la revolución mexicana, orígenes y resultados.* Mexico, D.F.: Editorial Porrúa.

Vigil, R. H. 1978. "Revolution and Confusion: The Peculiar Case of José Inés Salazar." *New Mexico Historical Review* 53, no. 2: 145–69.

Vilanova, Antonio. 1966. *Muerte de Villa.* Mexico, D.F.: Editores Mexicanos Unidos.

Villa, Francisco. N.d. *Contestación que el sr. general Villa dio a la nota Americana.* Ciudad Chihuahua: CIDECH.

———. 1923. *Memorias de Pancho Villa.* Mexico, D.F.: El Universal Gráfico.

Villa Guerrero, Guadalupe. 1976. "Francisco Villa: Historia, leyenda, y mito." Thesis, Universidad Autonoma de Mexico, Facultad de Filosofía y Letras, Colegio de Historia, Mexico D.F.

———. 1992. "Durango y Chihuahua: Los lazos financieros de una élite." In *Actas del Tercer Congreso de Historia Comparada, 1991*, pp. 265–74. Ciudad Juárez: Universidad Autónoma de Ciudad Juárez.

Villarello Vélez, Ildefonso. 1970. *Historia de la revolución mexicana en Coahuila.* Mexico, D.F.

Vives, Pedro A. 1987. *Pancho Villa.* Madrid: Historia 16, Ediciones Quorum: Sociedad Estatal para la Ejecución Programas del Quinto Centenario.

Voska, Emmanuel, and Will Irvin. 1940. *Spy and Counterspy.* New York: Doubleday Doran.

Voss, S. F. 1990. "Nationalizing the Revolution: Culmination and Circumstance." In *Provinces of the Revolution: Essays on Regional Mexican History, 1910–1929*, ed. Thomas Benjamin and Mark Wasserman. Albuquerque: University of New Mexico Press.

Walker, David. 1981. "Porfirian Labor Politics: Working-Class Organizations in Mexico City and Porfirio Díaz, 1876–1902." *The Americas* 37, no. 3 (Jan.): 257–89.

———. 1995. "'Y hay que quedar conforme porque a nadie se le puede exigir nada': The Villista Legacy and Agrarian Radicalism in Eastern Durango, Mexico, 1913–1930." Paper presented at the First Joint Conference of the Rocky Mountain Council for Latin American Studies and the Pacific Coast Council for Latin American Studies, Las Vegas, Nev., Mar. 5–9.

Wasserman, Mark. 1984. *Capitalists, Caciques, and Revolution: The Native Elite and Foreign Enterprise in Chihuahua, Mexico, 1854–1911.* Chapel Hill: University of North Carolina Press.

———. 1987. "Strategies for Survival of the Porfirian Elite in Revolutionary Mexico: Chihuahua During the 1920's." *Hispanic American Historical Review* 67, no. 1 (Feb.): 87–107.

———. 1990. "Provinces of the Revolution." In *Provinces of the Revolution: Essays on Regional Mexican History, 1910–1929*, ed. Thomas Benjamin and Mark Wasserman. Albuquerque: University of New Mexico Press.

———. 1992. "Home-Grown Revolution: The Hacienda Santa Catalina del Alamo y Anexas and Agrarian Protest in Easter Durango Mexico 1897–1913." *The Hispanic American Historical Review* 71.2.

———. 1993. *Persistent Oligarchs: Elites and Politics in Chihuahua, Mexico, 1910–1940.* Durham, N.C.: Duke University Press.

———. 1995. "La reforma agraria en Chihuahua, 1920–1940: Algunas notas preliminaras y ejemplos." In *Actas del Cuarto Congreso de Historia Comparada, 1993*, pp. 461–80. Ciudad Juárez: Universidad Autónoma de Ciudad Juárez.

Wasserstrom, Robert. 1983. *Class and Society in Central Chiapas.* Berkeley and Los Angeles: University of California Press.

Waterbury, Ronald. 1975. "Non-Revolutionary Peasants: Oaxaca Compared to Morelos in the Mexican Revolution." *Comparative Studies in Society and History* 17, no. 4: 410–42.

Weber, David J. 1979. *New Spain's Northern Frontier.* Dallas: Sexton Methodist University Press.

Wells, Allen. 1985. *Yucatán's Guilded Age: Haciendas, Henequen, and International Harvester, 1860–1915.* Albuquerque: University of New Mexico Press.

Wessel, Harald. 1979. *John Reed: Roter Reporter aus dem Wilden Westen: Biografische Reisebriefe.* Berlin: Verlag Neues Leben.

Westphall, Victor. 1973. *Thomas Benton Catron and His Era.* Tucson: University of Arizona Press.

White, E. Bruce. 1975. "The Muddied Waters of Columbus, New Mexico." *The Americas* 32, no. 1 (July): 72–98.

Wickham-Crowley, Timothy P. 1992. *Guerrillas and Revolution in Latin America: A Comparative Study of Insurgents and Regimes Since 1956.* Princeton: Princeton University Press.

Wiemers, E. N.d. "Interest and Intervention: Business Groups and Intervention in the Mexican Revolution." MS.

Wilkie, James W. 1967. *The Mexican Revolution: Federal Expenditure and Social Change Since 1910.* Berkeley and Los Angeles: University of California Press. 2d ed. rev. 1970.

———. 1985. "Changes in Mexico Since 1895: Central Government Revenue, Public Sector Expenditure, and National Economic Growth." In *Statistical Abstract of Latin America,* ed. James W. Wilkie and Adam Perkal, 24: 861–80.

Wilkie, James W., Michael C. Meyer, and Edna Monzón de Wilkie, eds. 1976. *Contemporary Mexico: Papers of the IV International Congress of Mexican History.* Berkeley and Los Angeles: University of California Press.

Willis, Standish E. N.d. "Pancho Villa's Army." MS.

Wilson, Henry Lane. 1923. *Diplomatic Episodes in Mexico, Belgium and Chile.* Garden City, N.Y.: Doubleday, Page & Co.

Wilson, Woodrow. *The Papers of Woodrow Wilson.* Edited by Arthur S. Link. Princeton: Princeton University Press, 1966–94. 69 vols.

Wolf, Eric R. 1969. *Peasant Wars of the Twentieth Century.* New York: Harper & Row.

Wolfskill, George, and Douglas W. Richmond, eds. 1979. *Essays on the Mexican Revolution: Revisionist Views of the Leaders.* Austin: University of Texas Press.

Womack, John, Jr. 1969. *Zapata and the Mexican Revolution.* New York: Knopf.

———. 1970. "Spoils of the Mexican Revolution." *Foreign Affairs* 48, no. 4. (July): 674–87.

———. 1978. "The Mexican Economy During the Revolution; 1910–1920: Historiography and Analysis." *Marxist Perspectives* 1, 4 (Winter): 80–123.

———. 1991. "The Mexican Revolution." In *Mexico Since Independence,* ed. Leslie Bethell. Cambridge: Cambridge University Press.

Wulff, J. 1982. "The Mexican Herald: An American Newspaper in the Mexican Revolution." MS.

Young, Karl E. 1968. *Ordeal in Mexico: Tales of Danger and Hardship Collected from Mormon Colonists.* Salt Lake City: Deseret Book Co.

Ysunza Uzeta, Salvador. 1968. "Francisco Villa, el centauro del norte." *Magisterio,* July.

Zapata, Emiliano. 1988. *Antología.* Edited by Laura Espejel. Mexico, D.F.: Instituto Nacional de Estudios Históricos de la Revolución Mexicana.

Zimmerman, R. 1986. "Wirtschaftlich-Gesellschaftliche Aspekte der Mexikanischen Eisenbahnen vor und in der Revolution (1888–1920): Das Beispiel des 'Mexicano del Sur' (Puebla-Oaxaca)." MS.

Zontek, Kenneth S. 1993. "'Damned if They Did, Damned if They Didn't': The Trial of Six Villistas Following the Columbus Raid, 1916." Master's thesis, New Mexico State University.

Zuno, José G. 1971. *Historia de la Revolución en el Estado de Jalisco.* Mexico, D.F.: Instituto Nacional de Estudios Históricos de la Revolución Mexicana.

Index

In this index an "f" after a number indicates a separate reference on the next page, and an "ff" indicates separate references on the next two pages. A continuous discussion over two or more pages is indicated by a span of page numbers, e.g., "57–59." *Passim* is used for a cluster of references in close but not consecutive sequence.

Library of Congress Cataloging-in-Publication Data

Katz, Friedrich.
   The life and times of PanchoVilla / Friedrich Katz.
      p.   cm.
   Includes bibliographical references and index.
   ISBN 0-8047-3045-8 (alk. paper)
   ISBN 0-8047-3046-6 (pbk. : alk. paper)
    1. Villa, Pancho, 1878–1923. 2. Mexico—History—
Revolution, 1910–1920. 3. Chihuahua (Mexico : State)—
History. 4. Social movements—Mexico—History.
I. Title.
F1234.V63K38   1998
972.08'16—dc21   97-47271
                                     CIP

∞ This book is printed on acid-free, recycled paper.

Original printing 1998

Last figure below indicates year of this printing:
07   06   05   04   03   02   01   00   99   98